Peter O. Müller, Susan Olsen and Franz Rainer (eds.)
Word-Formation – European Languages

This volume is part of a larger set of handbooks to Word-Formation

1   **Word-Formation: History, Theories, Units and Processes**
    Peter O. Müller, Susan Olsen and Franz Rainer (eds.)

2   **Word-Formation: Special Patterns and Restrictions**
    Peter O. Müller, Susan Olsen and Franz Rainer (eds.)

3   **Word-Formation: Semantics and Pragmatics**
    Peter O. Müller, Susan Olsen and Franz Rainer (eds.)

4   **Word-Formation: Language Contact and Diachrony**
    Peter O. Müller, Susan Olsen and Franz Rainer (eds.)

5   **Word-Formation: European Languages**
    Peter O. Müller, Susan Olsen and Franz Rainer (eds.)

Word-Formation
European Languages

Edited by
Peter O. Müller, Susan Olsen and Franz Rainer

DE GRUYTER
MOUTON

ISBN 978-3-11-141431-7
e-ISBN (PDF) 978-3-11-142052-3
e-ISBN (EPUB) 978-3-11-142098-1

Library of Congress Control Number: 2025934177

Bibliographic information published by the Deutsche Nationalbibliothek
The Deutsche Nationalbibliothek lists this publication in the Deutsche Nationalbibliografie;
detailed bibliographic data are available on the Internet at http://dnb.dnb.de.

© 2025 Walter de Gruyter GmbH, Berlin/Boston, Genthiner Straße 13, 10785 Berlin
Cover image: nadtytok / iStock / Getty Images Plus
Typesetting: Meta Systems Publishing & Printservices GmbH, Wustermark

www.degruyterbrill.com
Questions about General Product Safety Regulation:
productsafety@degruyterbrill.com

Contents

Irmhild Barz
1 **German** —— 1

Ingo Plag
2 **English** —— 29

Kristina Kotcheva
3 **Swedish** —— 49

Þorsteinn G. Indriðason
4 **Icelandic** —— 79

Franz Rainer
5 **Spanish** —— 105

Maria Grossmann
6 **Romanian** —— 131

Brian Ó Curnáin
7 **Irish** —— 157

Alicja Nagórko
8 **Polish** —— 193

Igor' S. Uluhanov
9 **Russian** —— 221

Cvetanka Avramova and Julia Baltova
10 **Bulgarian** —— 251

Bonifacas Stundžia
11 **Lithuanian** —— 277

Monica Genesin and Joachim Matzinger
12 **Albanian** —— 299

Angela Ralli
13 **Greek** —— 317

David Erschler
14 **Ossetic** —— 341

Kaarina Pitkänen-Heikkilä
15 **Finnish** —— 369

Ferenc Kiefer
16 **Hungarian** —— 393

Xabier Artiagoitia, José Ignacio Hualde and Jon Ortiz de Urbina
17 **Basque** —— 417

Joseph Brincat and Manwel Mifsud
18 **Maltese** —— 445

Jens Wilkens
19 **Turkish** —— 467

Gulnara Iskandarova
20 **Bashkir** —— 491

Galina N. Semenova and Alena M. Ivanova
21 **Chuvash** —— 507

Danara Suseeva
22 **Kalmyk** —— 527

Viacheslav A. Chirikba
23 **Abkhaz** —— 553

Timur Maisak and Dmitry Ganenkov
24 **Aghul** —— 577

Wolfgang Schulze
25 **Lak** —— 597

Madzhid Khalilov and Zaira Khalilova
26 **Avar** —— 617

Map of languages —— 633

Index —— 637

Irmhild Barz
1 German

1 Introduction
2 General overview
3 Composition
4 Derivation
5 Conversion
6 Backformation
7 Reduplication
8 Blending
9 Clipping
10 Word-creation
11 References

Abstract: This article gives a brief overview of important characteristics of word-formation in German and then describes the central models of compounding, derivation and conversion according to their morphosyntactic and semantic properties, specifically differentiated for the word classes noun, adjective, verb and adverb. Since the remaining kinds of word-formation only play a secondary role in vocabulary growth, they will be given a less detailed treatment.

1 Introduction

Word-formation in contemporary German is regarded as relatively thoroughly investigated, both from a diachronic and a synchronic structural-morphological perspective. Synchronic descriptions of different degrees of detail are provided by DWb 1–5 (1973–1992), Olsen (1986), Eichinger (2000), Motsch (2004), Donalies (2005), Erben (2006), Barz (2009), Elsen (2011), Fleischer and Barz (2012), Müller and Olsen (2022). Topical questions in research on the contemporary language include the relation between word-formation and inflectional morphology on the one hand and syntax on the other, as well as systematic variety-specific, pragmatic and text-oriented analyses. For historical word-formation in German, cf. Müller (2025b).

Irmhild Barz, Leipzig, Germany

https://doi.org/10.1515/9783111420523-001

2 General overview

2.1 Structural and morphosyntactic aspects

Word-formation in German (also lexeme or stem formation) is characterized by the following characteristics. It has at its disposal a great wealth of productive models of formation, the quantitative and qualitative use of which are specifically regulated depending on the meaning and the word class of the output (nouns, adjectives, verbs and adverbs).

The largest number of models can be found for the formation of nouns, using compounding and derivation as well as conversion. Also the number of suffixes is largest for nouns in comparison to adjectives and verbs. Nominal conversion is distinguished by its diversity of models as well as by the fact that, for almost all kinds, unrestricted productivity can be ascertained.

Adjectives use compounding and derivation in a manner similar to nouns, although fewer models are available and these are subject to stronger restrictions. Conversion constitutes a peripheral phenomenon in the formation of adjectives.

The word-formation of verbs is organized in a completely different manner. In this case, compounding and suffixal derivation only play a subordinate role. Leftward expansion of verbs through prefixes and particles dominates, along with conversion.

Finally, relatively few suffix models are productive in the formation of adverbs.

Just as the models of word-formation, the means of word-formation are extraordinarily multiform, especially with regard to their morphological status, their meaning and their origins.

Beside uncontroversial affixes (*be-, -lich, -ung*) there are affixes with homonymous stems (*-los* vs. *los* 'rid of') and also bound elements which have both affix and stem properties (*Riesenapplaus* 'giant applause', *blitzschnell* 'lightning fast', *fettarm* 'low fat; lit. fat poor', *umweltfreundlich* 'environment(ally) friendly'). The latter are conceived diachronically as a sort of transitional category, as affixoids, without it being possible to determine clear boundaries to unambiguous affixes on the one hand and to stems on the other. Their status must still be clarified from a synchronic perspective.

The inventory of means of word-formation is also multiform because, in addition to the native affixes, a large number of non-native affixes exist which primarily combine with non-native bases (*re|vitalisieren* 'to re|vitalize', *affekt|iv* 'affect|ive', *Abstrakt|ion* 'abstract|ion') and in this way constitute a complementary system alongside the native constituents.

Word-formation in German is also distinguished by close links to syntax. An identical sequence of words in syntactic structures and complex lexemes and a lack of morphological marking of the constituents in particular syntactic structures lead to overlap. This is apparent in adjective-verb constructions, which exhibit both properties of lexemes and syntactic structures. In the case of semantic equivalence such as in *die Suppe warm stellen/warm stellen* 'to warm the soup; lit. the soup warm put', both interpretations are acceptable. In the case of prosodic and semantic differences, on the other hand, syntactic structures and lexemes must be differentiated: *frei sprechen* 'to speak without a manuscript; lit. free(ly) speak' vs. *freisprechen* 'to acquit; lit. free-speak'.

In the case of noun-verb constructions, the interpretation of the structure depends on whether the noun can be assigned complement status – then the construction is considered a syntactic structure (*Rad fahren* 'to cycle; lit. bicycle drive') – or whether the noun is syntactically and semantically dependent, then we have a product of word-formation (*eislaufen* 'to skate; lit. ice-run'; Pittner 1998: 106–109). Double interpretations are also possible with these structures (*Brust schwimmen* vs. *brustschwimmen* 'to swim the breast stroke; lit. breast-swim'). This is the case when the initial elements do not unambiguously behave as free nouns (Fuhrhop 2007: 52–55).

Word-formation and syntax interact additionally inasmuch as word-formation models can furnish their output with specific syntactic properties. For example, the valency of the verb in so-called government or rectional compounds with deverbal second elements provides the base for their semantic interpretation: *Kinder erziehen* 'to raise children; lit. children raise' → *Erziehung der Kinder* 'raising (of) the children' → *Kindererziehung* 'raising children; lit. children-raising'.

Further models involving specific syntactic properties of input or output are adjectival government compounds (*dem Gold ähnliches Material* 'material similar to gold; lit. the-DAT gold similar material' → *goldähnliches Material* 'material similar to gold; lit. gold-similar material'), phrase-based derivatives (*in Anspruch nehmen* 'to claim (something for someone); lit. in claim take' → *Inanspruchnahme* 'claims, demands') and participial compounds (*gegen Grippe geimpft* 'vaccinated against flu; lit. against flu vaccinated' → *grippegeimpft* 'vaccinated against flu; lit. flu-vaccinated'). And finally in verbal word-formation, especially derivation with prefixes and the formation of particle verbs often lead to syntactic restructuring with respect to the base verbs, cf. *jmdm. dienen* 'to serve somebody; lit. somebody-DAT serve' → *jmdn. bedienen* 'to serve somebody; lit. somebody-ACC serve', *sich jmdm. andienen* 'to offer somebody one's services; lit. REFL somebody-DAT serve'.

In German word-formation, a native and a non-native system of formation stand side by side as two relatively autonomous subsystems (Bergmann 2005: 168). A basic parallelism between the native and the non-native subsystems makes their complementary interaction possible (Seiffert 2008: 373) as, for instance, in the combination of native and non-native means of formation; the autonomy, on the other hand, provides for specific models of formation for each. On foreign word-formation in German, cf. Müller (2025a).

2.2 Semantic-functional aspects

From a semantic-functional perspective, products of word-formation can be classified into modifications and transpositions. This classification captures the semantic changes the original elements undergo during the process of formation. In modification, the lexical meaning of the input is nuanced within the same semantic category and word class (*Brot* 'bread' → *Roggenbrot* 'rye bread', *Ernte* 'harvest' → *Missernte* 'bad harvest', *klug* 'smart' → *unklug* 'not smart', *krank* 'sick' → *kränklich* 'sickly'). In transposition, formations result which belong to another semantic category and usually also another word class (*lesen* 'to read' → *Leser* 'reader', *lesbar* 'readable'; *binden* 'to bind' → *Band* '(bound) volume', *Stadt* 'city' → *Städter* 'city dweller'). Should the fact be taken into account that affixes can contribute to very different degrees to the semantic characteristics of the products of word-formation, then transposition is defined more narrowly – as morphosyntactic transformation (*klug* 'smart' → *Klugheit* 'smartness', *heute* 'today' → *heutig* 'of today') – and a third functional-semantic class, mutation, is assumed (Dokulil 1968: 209). This comprises derivatives with a clearer semantic accretion with respect to the semantics of the base: *malen* 'to paint' → *Maler* 'painter'. The boundaries between the classes are fluid (Ohnheiser 1987: 131).

3 Composition

3.1 Nominal compounds

3.1.1 Morphosyntactic characteristics

Almost 80 % of all German nominal compounds consist of two nominal constituents (DWb 4: 37). The constituents are simplex or complex stems (*Haus|wand* 'house wall', *Schönheits|kult* 'beauty cult', *Frühjahrs|müdigkeit* 'spring tiredness', *Haustür|schloss* 'front door lock'). There are no structural restrictions with respect to the possible degree of complexity of a compound, as highly complex designations from technical vocabulary show (*Lebensmittelfarbstoffzulassungs|verordnung* 'food coloring approval regulation; lit. life-means-color-stuff-approval|regulation). Though for pragmatic reasons, especially due to a universal need of speakers for brevity and clarity of designations, compounds consisting of two or three simple or derived stems dominate in non-technical communication. Usually the first element is more complex (*Berufsunfähigkeits|versicherung* 'insurance against disability; lit. profession-un-able-ness|insurance', *Schadenersatz|summe* 'amount of compensation for damages; lit. damage-compensation|sum', *Hintergrund|artikel* 'background article'); right branching occurs less frequently (*Teppich|fachgeschäft* 'carpet shop; lit. carpet|specialization-shop').

The first position can be occupied by stems of all word classes, by confixes, short forms, bound short forms and also by phrases: *Speise|saal* 'dining hall', *Ess|besteck* 'cutlery; lit. eat-instruments', *Fein|staub* 'fine dust', *Beinahe|zusammenstoß* 'near miss; lit. almost-collision', *Rundum|schlag* 'sweeping blow; lit. round-about blow', *Auf|wind* 'up|draft', *Stief|sohn* 'step|son', *AKW-|Debatte* 'nuclear power station debate', *US-|Marine* 'US Navy', *Vor-Ort-|Termin* 'on-site appointment', *Klarsicht|folie* 'transparent film; lit. clear-view film'. Morphological restrictions limit nominal compounding inasmuch as stems with particular structures are not allowed in the first position in communicatively unmarked formations, e.g., adjective stems ending with *-abel* (**Komfortabelhotel* 'comfortable hotel'), *-ant, -bar, -ent, -isch, -lich, -los, -mäßig*, neither are verbs ending with *-ig(en)*.

German compounds are right-headed, that is, the second element determines the morphosyntactic properties of the compound. The first element is morphosyntactically dependent and is not inflected (except for the special case of phrasal compounds). It occurs either in the basic stem form (*Tag|falter* 'butterfly; lit. day lepidopter') or in stem variants (*Schul|buch* 'school book' vs. *Schule*, *Tage|geld* 'daily benefits', *Tages|reise* 'day trip' vs. *Tag*). Adjectival first elements occasionally occur in the superlative (*Schwerst|arbeit* 'hard labor; lit. hardest labor').

The semantically empty elements which are added to the basic stem form are referred to as linking elements. These are, for nominal first elements, *-e-, -en-, -es-, -ens-, -er-, -s-*; for verbal first elements *-e-*; adjectival and uninflectable first elements don't have linking elements. There are no strict rules for the placement of linking elements (Heringer 2011: 111), at best strong tendencies. Accordingly, properties of the constituents and the linking elements relating both to phonetics and syllabic phonology as well as paradigmatic-analogical aspects can be determining factors for the form of the linking elements. The syllabic linking elements *-e-*, *-en-*, *-er-*, *-ens-* ensure, for example, the trochaic disyllabicity which is preferred for monosyllabic first elements in German (*Tage|lohn* 'daily wage', *Helden|stadt* 'city of heroes', *Häuser|meer* 'sea of houses'). The non-syllabic linking element *-s-* on the other hand highlights the boundary between first and second elements (*Gehalts|liste* 'payroll', *Arbeits|zeit* 'work hours'; Wegener 2003: 446–456).

Polysemous first elements occasionally exhibit linking elements which are specific to a particular reading: (*Herz|chirurg* 'heart surgeon' – *Herz* 'heart' in the reading 'organ'; *Herzens|angelegenheit* 'topic close to one's heart; lit. heart matter' – *Herz* 'heart' in a metaphorical reading). Their use, which partially overrides phonotactic principles, can be explained with the help of analogy. Lexicalized compounds function as models for further formations, such as *Herzdiagnose* 'heart diagnosis', *-zentrum* '-center'; *Herzensbildung* 'nobleness of the heart; lit. heart education', *-wunsch* '-wish' (Becker 1992: 14–16). For further discussions see Fuhrhop and Kürschner (2025) on linking elements in Germanic.

3.1.2 Semantic characteristics

In the typical nominal compounds of German, the determinative compounds, the first element is semantically subordinate to the second element. The determined second element represents as a hyperonym the complex word, the determining first element restricts the extension of the second element, e.g., *Tagesreise* 'day trip' (i.e. 'trip which takes a day'). Compounds with a coordinative relation between the elements, i.e. coordinative compounds, are rare (*Hörerleser* 'listener-reader', *Spielertrainer* 'player-coach'); most of them can also be interpreted as determinative, depending on the context (Motsch 2004: 377).

The word-formation meaning of the nominal determinative compounds, that is, the semantic relation between first and second element, results from morphosyntactic and semantic properties of the immediate constituents.

In the case of nominal first elements, three groups can be distinguished:

In the first group, there are basic semantic relations between the constituents (Fandrych and Thurmair 1994: 39), e.g., local: *Straßenbelag* 'road surface', temporal: *Monatsplan* 'monthly plan', causal: *Schmerzensschrei* 'cry of pain', instrumental: *Handbremse* 'handbrake'. To this group belong as well metaphorical compounds, in which the first or second member is used figuratively: *Marathonsitzung* 'marathon session', *Kostenlawine* 'explosion of costs; lit. cost avalanche'.

In the second group the word-formation meaning is determined by properties resulting from the valency of the second element. The first element is the 'patient' of the indicated action, as in *Kinder erziehen* 'to raise children; lit. children raise' → *Kindererziehung* 'raising children; lit. children-raising' or 'agent', as in *Direktoren tagen* 'directors meet' → *Direktorentagung* 'meeting of directors; lit. directors-meeting'.

In the case of occasional compounds, not only the meaning of the constituents but also the context ultimately characterize the word-formation meaning: *der Streit um die Elefanten* 'the argument about the elephants' or *der Streit der Elefanten* 'the argument of_the elephants' → *Elefantenstreit* 'elephant argument'.

In compounds with an adjectival first element, this first element characterizes either an outstanding property of the designated object (*Steilküste* 'cliff; lit. steep coast', *Süßkirsche* 'sweet cherry') or it expresses an intensification or a diminution (*Großbrand* 'large fire', *Schwachstrom* 'weak current').

Important word-formation meanings for compounds with a verbal first element are 'purpose' (*Rasierapparat* 'electric razor; lit. shave-apparatus'), 'active' (*Putzfrau* 'cleaning lady'), 'passive' (*Räucheraal* 'smoked eel'); cf. Fleischer and Barz (2012: 162–164).

3.2 Adjectival compounds

3.2.1 Morphosyntactic characteristics

As is the case for nominal compounds, compounding involving constituents of the same word class also dominates in adjectives (*dunkel|blau* 'dark blue'). Other first elements before adjectival second elements are nominal stems (*herz|krank* 'suffering from a heart condition; lit. heart-sick', *EU-|weit* 'EU-wide') and verb stems (*bügel|arm* 'iron-free'); very rarely uninflectable words (*vor|schnell* 'hastily; lit. pre-fast') and confixes (*thermo|elektrisch* 'thermoelectric').

Usually, compounds with a participle as second element are also counted among the adjectival compounds. These are then either isolated participle forms, which clearly have the status of adjectives (*hoch|begabt* 'highly gifted', *alt|bekannt* 'well-known; lit. old-known'), or which are also common as verb forms (*hände|ringend* 'imploring; lit. hand-wringing' – *um Fassung ringend* 'struggling to keep one's composure; lit. around composure struggling'). When the participles are not opaque, a phrase with identical or similar phonological form can be used (*besorgnis|erregende Zustände* 'alarming situation; lit. concern-raising states' – *Besorgnis erregende Zustände* 'alarming situation; lit. concern raising states', *ein fernseh|bekannter Moderator* 'a moderator known through television; lit. a television-known moderator' – *ein durch das Fernsehen bekannter Moderator* 'a moderator known through television; lit. a through the television known moderator').

While the phrase designates a temporary property, the compound tends to be conceptually fixed. If this difference is lacking, the combination can alternatively be used as a word or a phrase.

The adjectival compounds are, as are the nominal compounds, right-headed and not inflectable word-internally; superlative forms, though, can occur in first position: *schnellst|mögliche Entscheidung* 'fastest possible decision'. Compounds rarely consist of more than two stems, they are then usually left branching (*kornblumen|blau* 'cornflower blue').

Adjectival compounds can contain linking elements. As in the case of nouns, the form of the linking element usually depends on the phonological form and the morphology of the first element (DWb 5: 25–27); for the most part, the same linking elements occur. Nominal first elements have the linking elements *-s-* (*bildungsfern* 'less educated; lit. education-far'), *-es-* (*tagesaktuell* 'on a daily basis; lit. day-current'), *-n-* (*taubenblau* 'pigeon blue'), *-ens-* (*herzensgut* 'kindhearted; lit. heart-good'). In the case of verbal first elements with stem final *b, d, g*, the linking element *-e-* can be inserted (*badewarm* 'warm enough to swim; lit. bathe-warm', *gebefreudig* 'generous; lit. give-joyful'; cf. also nouns such as *Badeschuh* 'bathe slippers', *Lebemann* 'playboy; lit. live-man', *Zeigefinger* 'index finger; lit. point-finger').

A special characteristic of adjectival word-formation is the strong tendency to form series with particular simplex and complex adjectives in second position. This concerns, among others, *-arm* 'poor', (*abgas-* 'exhaust', *alkohol-* 'alcohol', *antriebs-* 'propulsion', *arten-* 'species', *baum-* 'tree', *blut-* 'blood', *ehrgeiz-* 'ambition', *energie-* 'energy', *erlebnisarm* 'uneventful; lit. experience-poor', etc.), *-fertig* 'finished', *-fest* 'solid', *-frei* 'free', *-gerecht* 'appropriate', *-intensiv* 'intensive', *-leer* 'empty', *-reich* 'rich', *-sicher* 'certain, safe', *-tüchtig* 'capable', *-weit* 'far', *-wert* 'worth', *-würdig* 'worthy'. Usually, independent lexemes occur along with these second elements (*arm* 'poor' – *-arm*), but some also develop through reanalysis of denominal derivatives (*Birnenform* 'pear shape' → *birnenförmig* 'pear-shaped' → *-förmig* 'shaped'). They differ from phonologically identical free lexemes by a more general meaning, occurrence in series, a characteristic distribution, a lack of ability to function as a base, as well as through a complementary distribution with affixes (Erben 2006: 144; Motsch 2004: 11), whereby not all of these properties are developed for each element. In comparison to affixes, these bound elements are mostly semantically more definite and precise, cf. *biegsam* 'flexible' vs. *biegefähig* 'able to be bent', *glockig* 'bell-like' vs. *glockenförmig* 'bell-shaped'. They establish – in contrast to suffixes – a clear semantic relation between the first member and referential noun and permit among other things the expression of relations, for which in German no suffixes are available (*baumarme Landschaft* 'landscape with few trees; lit. tree-poor landscape', *krisenfeste Stelle* 'crisis-proof position'). Because of their specific properties and their importance for adjectival word-formation, these formations should be treated as a special kind of word-formation, as lexematic nexus formations (Ger. "lexematische Junktionsbildungen", Fandrych 2011: 142). A pending task of synchronic research consists of working out their communicative functions more clearly than has been done until now.

3.2.2 Semantic characteristics

As in the case of nouns, one differentiates with adjectives between determinative and coordinative compounds (*blutrot* 'blood-red' vs. *süßsauer* 'sweet-sour'). The quantitatively dominating word-formation meanings of determinative compounds are 'similative' and 'intensive' (*aalglatt* 'slippery as an eel; lit. eel-smooth', *zitronengelb* 'lemon yellow', *hellblau* 'light blue', *hochexplosiv* 'highly explosive').

3.3 Verbal compounds

If one chooses stability as the central feature of compounding, only a few verbal products of word-formation can be called compounds, namely complex verbs consisting of two verb stems (*sprechsingen* 'to sing in a recitative style; lit. speak-sing', *grinskeuchen* 'to gasp with a grin; lit. grin-gasp'). They are morphologically and syntactically inseparable. More than two verb stems are not combined. One can interpret them as determinative or coordinative depending on the meaning of the constituents and the context: 'to sing in a speaking style' or 'to speak and sing'.

If, on the other hand, the word status of the constituents counts as a classifying feature, separable complex verbs with adjectival, adverbial and nominal first element also belong to compounding (*hochklappen* 'to fold up', *wegfahren* 'to drive away', *teilnehmen* 'to take part'; Eichinger 2000: 106–110).

3.4 Adverbial compounds

Compounding is limited in adverbs inasmuch as hardly any new formations occur.

To the adverbial compounds belong right-headed compounds such as *woher* 'wherefrom', *dahin* 'thither; lit. here-towards', *dorthin* 'thither; lit. there-towards' as well as compounds with prepositional second elements. These are the closed classes of prepositional adverbs with the first elements *da(r)-* 'there', *wo(r)-*

'where', *hier-* 'here' (*damit* 'therewith', *daran* 'thereon', *wogegen* 'against what; lit. where-against', *woran* 'whereon', *hieran* 'hereon') and prepositional second elements as well as others with adverbs, prepositions, adjectives and nouns as first elements and prepositions as second elements (*heran* '(come) close', *nebenan* 'next door; lit. besides-at', *kurzum* 'in short; lit. short-around', *bergauf* 'uphill; lit. hill-up').

Adverbial compounding deviates from nominal compounding in various ways. The degree of complexity of the formations is limited; adverbs consisting of two or three elements are common: *daher* 'therefrom', *überallhin* 'everywhere; lit. over-all-towards'. Adverbs consisting of three elements, combined in the same order as in phrases, can be separated, and then have phrasal accent: *sie gehen dorthinauf/dort hinauf* 'they go up-there/up there'.

A systematic semantic description is hardly possible, due to the frequent lack of motivation of the compounds. Only the expression of directional meanings of adverbs with *her* and *hin* as first or second element is relatively systematically developed; *her* designates a movement towards the speaker, *hin* away from the speaker: *herüber* 'over here', *dorther* 'from there'; *hinüber* 'across', *dorthin* 'thither'. But here as well there are many opaque formations, which are only formally segmentable: *immerhin* 'after all', *mithin* 'therefore', *nachher* 'afterwards', *vorher* 'before', *vorhin* 'earlier on'.

Adverbs with nominal first elements are on the other hand usually fully motivated. They correspond semantically to lexically identical phrases: *flussabwärts paddeln* 'to paddle downstream; lit. to stream-downwards paddle' – *den Fluss abwärts paddeln* lit. 'the stream downwards paddle'; *tagsüber nichts essen* 'to not eat anything during the day; lit. day-over nothing eat' – *den Tag über nichts essen* lit. 'the day over nothing eat'.

4 Derivation

Depending on the affixes which are involved, one differentiates between prefix derivation (*Glück* 'luck' → *Unglück* 'bad luck', *alt* 'old' → *uralt* 'very old', *grüßen* 'to greet' → *begrüßen* 'to welcome'), suffix derivation (*schön* 'pretty' → *Schönheit* 'prettiness', *erklären* 'to explain' → *erklärbar* 'explainable', *Krise* 'crisis' → *kriseln* 'to go through a crisis') and – rather a peripheral phenomena in German – circumfix derivation (*reden* 'speak' → *Ge|red|e* 'gossip', *aufhalten* 'to stop' → *un|aufhalt|sam* 'unstoppable', *Erde* 'earth' → *be|erd|igen* 'to bury'). Prefixes combine exclusively with bases in the form of words; in the case of suffixes, lexemes are derived from stems, confixes and phrases.

The most important productive derivational models of the contemporary language are collected in the following tables (cf. Barz 2009: 727–732).

4.1 Nominal derivation

Significantly more affixes are available for the derivation of nouns than for the derivation of adjectives, verbs and adverbs. The number of models is still greater due to the fact that most affixes are polyfunctional. The suffix -er, e.g., forms agent nouns, action nouns and instrument nouns from verbs (*Maler* 'painter', *Jauchzer* 'jubilant cheer', *Schalter* 'switch').

4.1.1 Denominal nouns

The bases of the denominal derivational models are nominal stems and noun phrases. Models of transposition and modification must be differentiated.

Tab. 1.1: Denominal nouns derived by transposition.

Kind of transposition	Affix	Example
Status nouns	-(er)ei	*Tyrannei* 'tyranny' ← *Tyrann* 'tyrant'
		Paktiererei 'deal making' ← *paktieren* 'to strike a deal'
	-(i)at	*Patriarchat* 'patriarchy' ← *Patriarch* 'patriarch'
	-schaft	*Feindschaft* 'enmity' ← *Feind* 'enemy'
	-tum	*Abenteurertum* 'adventurousness' ← *Abenteurer* 'adventurer'
	-ismus	*Despotismus* 'despotism' ← *Despot* 'despot'
Personal nouns	-ant	*Asylant* 'asylum seeker' ← *Asyl* 'asylum'
	-er	*Musiker* 'musician' ← *Musik* 'music'
	-ler	*Künstler* 'artist' ← *Kunst* 'art'
	-iker	*Alkoholiker* 'alcoholic' ← *Alkohol* 'alcohol'
	-ist	*Gitarrist* 'guitarist' ← *Gitarre* 'guitar'
Place nouns	-(er)ei	*Ziegelei* 'brickworks' ← *Ziegel* 'brick'
		Käserei 'cheesery' ← *Käse* 'cheese'

Tab. 1.2: Denominal nouns derived by modification.

Kind of modification	Affix	Example
Diminution	-chen	Kindchen 'little child' ← Kind 'child'
		Mäuschen 'little mouse' ← Maus 'mouse'
	-lein	Kindlein 'little child' ← Kind 'child'
		Mäuslein 'little mouse' ← Maus 'mouse'
Augmentation	un-	Unsumme 'enormous sum' ← Summe 'sum'
	erz-	Erzfeind 'archenemy' ← Feind 'enemy'
Gender marking	-in	Malerin 'female painter' ← Maler 'painter'
		Ärztin 'female physician' ← Arzt 'physician'
	-euse	Masseuse 'female masseur' ← Masseur 'masseur'
Collectives	-schaft	Schülerschaft 'student body' ← Schüler 'pupils'
	-heit	Christenheit 'Christendom' ← Christ 'Christian'
Negation	un-	Unvermögen 'inability' ← Vermögen 'ability'
Valuation	miss-	Missernte 'bad harvest' ← Ernte 'harvest'
	un-	Untat 'misdeed' ← Tat 'deed'
	ur-	Urform 'original form' ← form 'Form'

4.1.2 Deadjectival nouns

Tab. 1.3: Deadjectival nouns.

Kind of transposition	Affix	Example
Quality nouns	-heit/-keit/	Dunkelheit 'darkness' ← dunkel 'dark'
		Sauberkeit 'cleanliness' ← sauber 'clean'
	-igkeit	Trostlosigkeit 'hopelessness' ← trostlos 'hopeless'
	-ismus	Radikalismus 'radicalism' ← radikal 'radical'
	-ität	Naivität 'naiveté' ← naiv 'naive'
	-e	Größe 'greatness' ← groß 'great'
	-nis	Düsternis 'somberness' ← düster 'somber'
	-schaft	Bereitschaft 'readiness' ← bereit 'ready'
Personal nouns	-ling	Fremdling 'stranger' ← fremd 'strange'
		Schwächling 'weakling' ← schwach 'weak'
	-chen	Frühchen 'preemie' ← früh 'early'
	-i	Dummi 'dummy' ← dumm 'dumb'

4.1.3 Deverbal nouns

Tab. 1.4: Deverbal nouns.

Kind of transposition	Affix	Example
Action nouns	-e	*Absage* 'cancellation' ← *absagen* 'to cancel'
	-(er)ei	*Hüstelei* '(repeated) coughing' ← *hüsteln* 'to cough'
		Schufterei 'drudgery' ← *schuften* 'to toil'
	-er	*Seufzer* 'sigh' ← *seufzen* 'to sigh'
	ge-...-e/ge-	*Gesinge* '(constant, annoying) singing' ← *singen* 'to sing'
		Angebelle '(constant, annoying) barking at' ← *anbellen* 'to bark at'
		Gewimmel 'bustling activity' ← *wimmeln* 'to swarm'
	-ion/-ation	*Diskussion* 'discussion' ← *diskutieren* 'to discuss'
		Manipulation 'manipulation' ← *manipulieren* 'to manipulate'
	-ung	*Deutung* 'interpretation' ← *deuten* 'to interpret'
		Verlangsamung 'slowing down' ← *verlangsamen* 'to slow down'
Agent nouns	-er	*Maler* 'painter' ← *malen* 'to paint'
	-eur	*Kontrolleur* 'controller' ← *kontrollieren* 'to control'
	-i	*Knacki* 'convict' ← *knacken* 'to crack'
Instrument nouns	-e	*Bremse* 'brake' ← *bremsen* 'to brake'
	-el	*Deckel* 'cover' ← *decken* 'to cover'
	-er	*Schalter* 'switch' ← *schalten* 'to switch'
Place nouns	-e	*Umkleide* 'dressing room' ← *umkleiden* 'to change clothes'
	-(er)ei	*Bügelei* 'ironing shop' ← *bügeln* 'to iron'
		Druckerei 'printing shop' ← *drucken* 'to print'
Patient nouns	-e	*Spende* 'donation' ← *spenden* 'to donate'
	-er	*Aufkleber* 'sticker' ← *aufkleben* 'to stick on'
	(ge-)...-sel	*Anhängsel* 'appendage' ← *anhängen* 'to hang on'
		Geschreibsel 'scribblings' ← *schreiben* 'to write'
	-ling	*Impfling* 'vaccine recipient' ← *impfen* 'to vaccinate'
	-ung	*Sammlung* 'collection' ← *sammeln* 'to collect'

4.2 Adjectival derivation

The most important kind of derivation of adjectives is suffix derivation. Verbal and nominal stems are turned into adjectives with the help of the suffixes *-bar*, *-ig*, *-isch*, *-lich*, *-mäßig*. Only weakly productive are *-sam* (*heilen* 'to heal' → *heilsam* 'healing') and *-haft* (*Frühling* 'spring' → *frühlingshaft* 'spring-like'). Prefix derivatives are produced mainly via the negating prefix *un-*.

The following tables contain a selection of construction models. The adjectives are used in attribute position with a typical referential word.

4.2.1 Denominal adjectives

Bases are nominal stems and noun phrases.

Tab. 1.5: Denominal adjectives.

Kind of transposition	Affix	Example
Adjectives of resemblance	-haft -ig -isch -lich -mäßig	traumhaft(e Reise) 'wonderful (trip)' ← Traum 'dream' mehlig(e Birne) 'mealy (pear)' ← Mehl 'flour' träumerisch(e Augen) 'dreamy (eyes)' ← Träumer 'dreamer' kindlich(es Verhalten) 'childlike (behavior)' ← Kind 'child' geschäftsmäßig(es Vorgehen) 'businesslike (approach)' ← Geschäft 'business'
Possessive (ornative) adjectives	-haft -ig -isch -lich be-/ge-....-t	fehlerhaft(es Diktat) 'flawed (dictation)' ← Fehler 'mistake' ölig(e Substanz) 'oily (substance)' ← Öl 'oil' blauäugig(es Kind) 'blue-eyed (child)' ← blaue Augen 'blue eyes' neidisch(er Nachbar) 'envious (neighbor)' ← Neid 'envy' widersprüchlich(es Urteil) 'contradictory (verdict)' ← Widerspruch 'contradiction' bemoost(er Stein) 'mossy (stone)' ← Moos 'moss' genarbt(es Leder) 'grained (leather)' ← Narbe 'grain'
Privative adjectives	-los	humorlos(er Text) 'humorless (text)' ← Humor 'humor'

4.2.2 Deadjectival adjectives

Tab. 1.6: Deadjectival adjectives.

Kind of modification	Affix	Example
Negation	un- a(n)-	unklug(e Entscheidung) 'unwise (decision)' ← klug 'smart' atypisch(e Form) 'atypical (form)' ← typisch 'typical' anorganisch(e Chemie) 'inorganic (chemistry)' ← organisch 'organic'
Intensification	erz- ur- -lich	erzreaktionär(er Politiker) 'ultra-reactionary (politician)' ← reaktionär 'reactionary' urkomisch(e Situation) 'hilarious (situation)' ← komisch 'comical' grünlich(es Sekret) 'greenish (secretion)' ← grün 'greenish'
Quantification	bi-	binational(e Konferenz) 'bi-national (conference)' ← national 'national'

4.2.3 Deverbal adjectives

Bases are verbal stems and verb phrases.

Tab. 1.7: Deverbal adjectives.

Kind of transposition	Affix	Example
Active-modal adjectives 'that can V'	-abel	rentabl(e Firma) 'profitable (company)' ← sich rentieren 'to be profitable'
	-bar	brennbar(e Flüssigkeit) 'flammable (liquid)' ← brennen 'to burn'
	-(er)isch	zänkisch(e Nachbarin) 'quarrelsome (neighbor)' ← zanken 'to quarrel'
Dispositional adjectives 'that tends to V'	-(er)lich	weinerlich(es Kind) 'whining (child)' ← weinen 'to cry'
	-haft	schwatzhaft(e Schülerin) 'chatty (pupil)' ← schwatzen 'to chat'
		rührig(er Chef) 'active (boss)' ← rühren 'to stir'
	-ig	leichtgläubig(e Partnerin) 'gullible (partner)' ← leicht glauben 'to believe'
	-iv	informativ(e Veranstaltung) 'informative (event)' ← informieren 'to inform'
	-sam	bedeutsam(e Entdeckung) 'significant (discovery)' ← bedeuten 'to mean'
Active adjectives	un-...-lich	unermüdlich(er Helfer) 'tireless (helper)' ← ermüden 'to become tired'
Passive-modal adjectives 'that can be Ved'	-abel	akzeptabl(e Lösung) 'acceptable (solution)' ← akzeptieren 'to accept'
	-bar	lieferbar(e Ware) 'deliverable (goods)' ← liefern 'to deliver'
	-lich	erblich(e Krankheit) 'hereditary disease' ← erben 'to inherit'
	-sam	biegsam(er Stab) 'flexible (staff)' ← biegen 'to bend'
	un-...-lich/	unglaublich(e Geschichte) 'unbelievable (story)' ← glauben 'to believe'
	-bar/-sam	unverkennbar(e Handschrift) 'unmistakable (handwriting)' ← verkennen 'to misjudge'
		unaufhaltsam(e Entwicklung) 'unstoppable (development)' ← aufhalten 'to stop'

4.3 Verbal derivation and particle-verb formation

Verbal prefix derivatives are morphologically and syntactically inseparable, the prefix is unstressed: *verbrauchen* 'to consume' – *verbrauchte* 'consumed' – *hat verbraucht* 'has consumed', *umrunden* 'to go around' – *umrundete* 'went around' – *hat umrundet* 'has gone around'. They are formed with prefixes without homonymous particles (*be-, ent-, er-, ver-, zer-*) and prefixes with homonymous particles (*durch-, über-, um-, unter-*). In the case of particle verbs, the verb particle carries word stress, the verbs are morphologically and syntactically separable: *anrechnen* 'to credit' – *rechnete an* 'credited' – *hat angerechnet* 'has credited'. Suffix derivatives are formed with *-(e)l(n)* and *-ier/-isier/-ifizier(en)*: *lächeln* 'to smile', *amtieren* 'to hold office', *computerisieren* 'to computerize', *personifizieren* 'to personify'. The suffix *-ig(en)* (*festigen* 'to consolidate') is unproductive. In order to clarify each intended verbal reading, a context noun is added in the following summary.

4.3.1 Denominal verbs

a) Prefix and suffix derivation

Tab. 1.8: Denominal verbs derived with prefixes and suffixes.

Word-formation meaning	Affix	Example
Ornative 'to provide with N'	be-	(*den Umschlag*) *beschriften* 'to write on (the envelope)' ← *Schrift* 'writing'
	über-	(*den Vorbau*) *überdachen* 'to roof (the front building)' ← *Dach* 'roof'
	um-	(*das Rohr*) *ummanteln* 'to sheathe (the pipe)' ← *Mantel* 'sheath'
	unter-	(*das Haus*) *unterkellern* 'to build (the house) with a cellar' ← *Keller* 'cellar'
	ver-	(*den Ring*) *vergolden* 'to gild (the ring)' ← *Gold* 'gold'
	-isier(en)	(*den Fluss*) *kanalisieren* 'to canalize (the river)' ← *Kanal* 'canal'
Agentive 'to act as/in the manner of N'	be-	(*den Sohn*) *bemuttern* 'to mother (the son)' ← *Mutter* 'mother'
	ver-	(*die Patientin*) *verarzten* 'to doctor (the patient)' ← *Arzt* 'doctor'
	-ier(en)	*spionieren* 'to spy' ← *Spion* 'spy'
Privative 'to remove N'	ent-	(*den Fisch*) *entgräten* 'to bone (the fish)' ← *Gräte* 'fish-bone'
Causative 'to make into N'	ver-	(*den Text*) *vertonen* 'to set (the text) to music' ← *Ton* 'tone'
	zer-	(*den Fels*) *zertrümmern* 'to smash (the rock)' ← *Trümmer* 'debris, rubble'
	-(e)l(n)	(*die Erde*) *häufeln* 'to pile up (the dirt)' ← *Haufen* 'pile'
	-isier(en)	(*das Material*) *pulverisieren* 'to pulverize (the material)' ← *Pulver* 'powder'
Inchoative 'to become N'	ver-	*versumpfen* (*Land*) 'to turn (land) into swamp' ← *Sumpf* 'swamp'
Instrumental 'to act with N'	über-	(*das Tier*) *überlisten* 'to trick (the animal)' ← *List* 'guile'
	ver-	(*die Tür*) *verriegeln* 'to bolt (the door)' ← *Riegel* 'bolt'
	zer-	(*das Gebäude*) *zerbomben* 'to bomb (the building)' ← *Bombe* 'bomb'

b) Particle-verb formation

Only prepositional verb particles combine with nominal bases. Adverbial and adjectival verb particles (*her* 'movement towards speaker', *hinauf* 'up there', *fest* 'firm', *frei* 'free', etc.) cannot on the other hand trigger a change in word class with respect to the base.

Tab. 1.9: Denominal particle verbs.

Word-formation meaning	Verb particle	Example
Instrumental 'to act with N'	an- auf- ein- zu-	(*den Kletterer*) *anseilen* 'to rope up (the climber)' ← *Seil* 'rope' (*die Ausgaben*) *aufschlüsseln* 'to break down (the expenses)' ← *Schlüssel* 'key' (*die Initialen*) *einmeißeln* 'to engrave (the initials)' ← *Meißel* 'chisel' (*die Flasche*) *zukorken* 'to cork up (the wine)' ← *Korken* 'cork'
Locative 'to put into N'	ein-	(*die Ware*) *eintüten* 'to bag the goods' ← *Tüte* 'bag'
Privative 'to remove N'	ab- aus-	(*Johannisbeeren*) *abbeeren* 'to destalk the currants' ← *Beere* 'berry' (*den Stall*) *ausmisten* 'to muck out the stall' ← *Mist* 'manure'

4.3.2 Deadjectival verbs

a) Prefix and suffix derivation

Tab. 1.10: Deadjectival verbs derived with prefixes and suffixes.

Word-formation meaning	Affix	Example
Inchoative 'to become A'	er- ver-	*erbleichen* (*Person*) 'to blanch (person)' ← *bleich* 'pale' *vereinsamen* (*Person*) 'to become lonely (person)' ← *einsam* 'lonely'
Causative 'to make A'	be- durch- ent- er- ver- -ier -isier(en)	(*das Kind*) *befähigen* 'to enable (the child)' ← *fähig* 'able' (*das Tragwerk*) *durchfeuchten* 'to soak (the supporting structure)' ← *feucht* 'damp' (*Fördergeld*) *entfremden* 'to misappropriate (aid money)' ← *fremd* 'strange' (*die Spieler*) *erfrischen* 'to refresh (the players)' ← *frisch* 'fresh' (*das Unglück*) *verharmlosen* 'to play down (the accident)' ← *harmlos* 'harmless' (*das Team*) *komplettieren* 'to complete (the team)' ← *komplett* 'complete' (*den Text*) *aktualisieren* 'to update (the text)' ← *aktuell* 'current'
Agentive 'to behave A'	-el(n)	*fremdeln* 'to be shy with strangers' ← *fremd* 'strange'

b) Particle-verb formation

Tab. 1.11: Deadjectival particle verbs.

Word-formation meaning	Verb particle	Example
Inchoative 'to become A'	ab-	*abflauen* (*Sturm*) 'to wane (storm)' ← *flau* 'weak'
Causative 'to make A'	ab-	(*die Kante*) *abschrägen* 'to bevel (the edge)' ← *schräg* 'slanting'
	an-	(*die Oberfläche*) *anrauen* 'to rough up (the surface)' ← *rau* 'rough'
	auf-	(*den Kranken*) *aufmuntern* 'to cheer up (the sick)' ← *munter* 'cheerful'
	aus-	(*den Betrunkenen*) *ausnüchtern* 'to sober up (the drunk)' ← *nüchtern* 'sober'
	ein-	(*den Schüler*) *einschüchtern* 'to intimidate (the pupil)' ← *schüchtern* 'shy'

4.3.3 Deverbal verbs

a) Prefix and suffix derivation

Tab. 1.12: Deverbal verbs derived with prefixes and suffixes.

Word-formation meaning	Affix	Example
Ingressive 'to begin to V'	ent- er-	*entbrennen* (*Machtkampf*) 'to erupt (power struggle)' ← *brennen* 'to burn' (*den Vogel*) *erblicken* 'to catch sight of (the bird)' ← *blicken* 'to glance'
Egressive 'to stop Ving'	ver-	*verblühen* (*Blume*) 'to wither (flower)' ← *blühen* 'to bloom'
Intensive 'to V intensely'	be- ver- zer-	(*das Kind*) *beschützen* 'to protect (the child)' ← *schützen* 'to protect' (*im Betrieb*) *verbleiben* 'to remain (in the plant)' ← *bleiben* 'to stay' (*das Kabel*) *zertrennen* 'to sever (the cable)' ← *trennen* 'to separate'
Destructive 'to V into pieces'	zer-	(*Porzellan*) *zerschlagen* 'to smash (the porcelain)' ← *schlagen* 'to hit'
Negative 'not to V'	über- ver-	(*die Kritik*) *überhören* 'to not hear (the criticism)' ← *hören* 'to hear' (*die Kunst*) *verachten* 'to despise (the art)' ← *achten* 'to respect'
Diminutive-iterative 'to V a little, repeatedly'	-(e)l(n)	*hüsteln* 'to cough a bit' ← *husten* 'to cough'

The prefixation of verbs is often accompanied by a restructuring of the valency frame of the base. The prefixes *be-*, *er-* and *ver-*, e.g., can make the base transitive: *auf der Straße fahren* 'to drive on the street' → *die Straße befahren* 'to drive on the street; lit. to drive the street', *um den Pokal kämpfen* 'to fight for the cup' → *den Pokal erkämpfen* 'to win the cup; lit. to fight the cup', *über jmdn. lachen* 'to laugh about someone' → *jmdn. verlachen* 'to ridicule someone'. Incorporation is present when the prefix shifts the meaning of a prepositional argument into the meaning of the verb: *Folie über das Loch kleben* 'to stick film over the hole' → *das Loch mit Folie be-/überkleben* 'to seal up the hole with film'.

b) Particle-verb formation

Prepositional, adverbial, adjectival and – in a very limited manner – nominal verb particles combine with verbal bases. The complex verbs designate particular phases or manners of progression of the occurrences expressed in the base verb. The valency of the verb can thereby change.

In view of the semantic and grammatical diversity of particle-verb formation in German only exemplary, important models of formation with prepositional verb particles are listed here.

Tab. 1.13: Deverbal particle verbs.

Word-formation meaning	Verb particle	Example
Locative 'to V upwards or downwards';	*ab-/auf-*	*ab-/aufsteigen (vom Fahrrad/auf das Fahrrad)* 'to get off/on (the bicycle)' ← *steigen* 'to climb'
'to be brought in contact with';	*an-*	*(den Hund) anbinden* 'to leash up (the dog)' ← *binden* 'to tie'
'to be placed in/ taken out of'	*aus-/ein-*	*(das Geschenk) ein-/auspacken* 'to wrap/unwrap (the gift)' ← *packen* 'to pack'
Locative and temporal 'to V through N';	*durch-*	*durchkriechen (durch die Öffnung)* 'to crawl through (the opening)' ← *kriechen* 'to crawl'
'to V before/after N'	*vor-/nach-*	*(eine Szene) vor-/nachspielen* 'to act out, imitate (a scene)' ← *spielen* 'to play'
Egressive 'to stop Ving'	*ab-*	*abblühen (Rose)* 'to wilt (rose)' ← *blühen* 'to bloom'
	aus-	*(die Aufgabe) ausrechnen* 'to work out (the assignment)' ← *rechnen* 'to calculate'
Ingressive 'to begin to V'	*an-*	*(am Berg) anfahren* 'to start driving (on an incline)' ← *fahren* 'to drive'
	auf-	*(vor Schreck) aufschreien* 'to let out a shriek' ← *schreien* 'to shout'

Tab. 1.13 (continued)

Word-formation meaning	Verb particle	Example
Intensive	ab-	(*den Text*) *abändern* 'to revise (the text)' ← *ändern* 'to change'
	auf-	(*Fehler*) *aufzeigen* 'to point out (the mistake)' ← *zeigen* 'to point'

Especially *her* and *hin* as well as corresponding complex forms (*heran, hinauf*) are productive as adverbial verb particles, and specifically preferred with verbs of locomotion and verbs of transportation (*hinaufsteigen* 'to climb up', *herüberreichen* 'to hand over'), but also with verbs with other meanings. In each case, they add a directional component: *seinen Ärger herausschreien* 'to scream out in (his) anger', *Hilfe herbeirufen* 'to call for help (to come)'. Primarily adjectives occur as adverbial verb particles: *festfahren* 'to get stuck; lit. fixed-drive', *freisprechen* 'to acquit; lit. free-speak', *hochheben* 'to lift up; lit. high-lift'.

4.4 Adverbial derivation

A systematic differentiation between adjective and adverb in terms of derivational morphology as in English or French does not exist in German. Only a few suffix models are used for the formation of adverbs. Prefix and circumfix derivation do not occur.

The suffixes -*s* (*anfangs* 'initially' ← *Anfang* 'beginning'), -*halber* (*umzugshalber* 'due to the move' ← *Umzug* 'move'), -*wärts* (*himmelwärts* 'towards heaven' ← *Himmel* 'heaven'), -*weise* (*andeutungsweise* 'allusively' ← *Andeutung* 'allusion') combine with nouns. Adverbs with -*ermaßen* (*konsequentermaßen* 'consistently' ← *konsequent* 'consistent'), preferred bases are departicipial adjectives (*bekanntermaßen* 'as is generally known' ← *bekannt* 'known'), and -*(er)weise* (*angenehmerweise* 'pleasantly' ← *angenehm* 'pleasant', *berechtigterweise* 'in an authorized manner' ← *berechtigt* 'authorized') are derived from adjectives. Adverbs ending in -*(er)weise* are inflected like adjectives in attributive position before verbal nouns: *blattweises Scannen* 'scanning sheet by sheet' ← *Blatt* 'sheet'.

5 Conversion

In conversion, lexemes are shifted into another word class. In the case of morphological conversion, this occurs without morphological alteration of the input (*hoch* 'high' → *das Hoch* 'the high'); in the case of syntactic conversion, the output retains an inflectional feature of the input (*lesen* 'to read' → *das Lesen* 'the reading', *alt* 'old' → *der/die Alte* 'the old person', *ein Alter/eine Alte* 'an old person').

5.1 Nominal conversion

Words of all word classes can generally be the input to nominal conversion; most often verbs, adjectives and particles are converted. Also phrases occur as bases (*sich den Kopf zerbrechen* 'to rack one's brain' → *das Kopfzerbrechen* 'headache, worry').

Verbal base forms are the infinitive as well as also the present, preterite or participial stem (*benehmen* 'to behave' → *das Benehmen* 'the manners', *rufen* 'to call' → *der Ruf* 'the call', *binden* 'to bind' → *das Band* 'string, cord', *trinken* 'to drink' → *der Trunk* 'the drink', *Trank* 'drink'). In the case of adjectival or participial bases, inflected forms are the input (*der/ein fremde/r Gast* 'the unfamiliar guest' → *der/ein Fremde/r* 'the stranger', *angestellt* 'employed' → *der/ein Angestellte/r* 'the employee'). Only in the case of a few adjectives are uninflected base forms converted (*nass* 'wet' → *das Nass* 'the wetness').

Since syntactic conversion shares certain contexts with its input (*irren/Irren ist menschlich* 'to err is human', *der kranke Schüler* 'the sick pupil'/*der Kranke* 'the invalid'), its interpretation as a phenomenon of word-formation is controversial (Eichinger 2000: 39–40). The closeness to syntax is indicated in particular by a peripheral position in the secondary word class, as the forms don't have all inflectional properties: deverbal nouns don't generally have a plural (counterexample: *die Schreiben* 'the letters; lit. the write'), deadjectival or departicipial nouns retain adjectival inflection.

5.2 Adjectival conversion

Bases of adjectival conversion are mainly participles. Nouns are preferred for conversion to adjectives in the fashion industry for the production of color terms such as (*eine Handtasche in*) *creme/cognac/türkis* '(a handbag in) cream/cognac/turquoise', which is rare in other areas. Verbs don't occur as bases for conversion in the contemporary language.

The adjective status of the converted participles is developed to differing degrees. Prefixation with *un-*, the ability to form a comparative, predicative usage, gradability with *sehr* 'very' as well as the loss of semantic bonds to the corresponding verb count as typical features of adjectives. Not processuality, but quality is designated (Motsch 2004: 304), cf. *ein angemessenes Urteil* 'an appropriate, correct verdict', *ein bedeutender Autor* 'an important, eminent author'.

Denominal converted adjectives are neither morphologically nor syntactically full representatives of their word class. They do not form comparatives, are not declinable and usually cannot be used attributively (*der Film ist klasse, hammer* 'the film is classy, unbelievable'; Pittner and Berman 2006). For this reason, the model is relatively rarely used in the standard language. The conversion of designations for inhabitants ending in *-er* to indeclinable adjectives is on the other hand almost unrestrictively productive: *Prager Burg* 'Prague Castle', *Berliner Bär* 'Berlin bear'. For the classification of these forms as derivation, cf. Fuhrhop (2003).

5.3 Verbal conversion

Bases for verbal conversion are nouns and adjectives; words from other word classes are rarely, and adverbs never converted (*Traum* 'dream' → *träumen* 'to dream', *weit* 'far' → *weiten* 'to widen', *miau* 'meow' → *miauen* 'to meow').

The word-formation meanings of converted verbs correspond for the most part with those of prefix and particle-verb formation. Denominal verbs are ornative (*ölen* 'to oil'), agentive (*kellnern* 'to wait (tables)'), privative (*köpfen* 'to behead'), causative (*schroten* 'to grind coarsely'), instrumentative (*hämmern* 'to hammer'), locative (*wassern* 'to land on water'). Weather verbs such as *tagen* 'to become day', *stürmen* 'to be stormy', *donnern* 'to thunder' represent a special class.

Deadjectival verbs are stative (*gleichen* 'to be the same as'), ingressive (*faulen* 'to rot'), causative (*kürzen* 'to shorten'). In a few cases, not the adjectival base form, but rather the comparative serves as input (*mildern* 'to alleviate; lit. to make milder').

5.4 Adverbial conversion

Adverbial conversion does not occur in contemporary German. Only a few opaque individual cases such as *Morgen* 'morning' → *morgen* 'tomorrow', *Heim* 'home' → *heim* 'home' are found.

6 Backformation

Almost only verbs develop via backformation in German, and specifically from complex nouns. These are nominal compounds with deverbal, suffixed second elements, the suffix of which is deleted: *Zwangsernährung* 'force-feeding' → *zwangsernähren* 'to force-feed'. Backformations differ from derivatives of compounds (*schriftstellern* 'to write' ← *Schriftsteller* 'author; lit. writing putter') and particle verbs with nominal initial elements (*teilnehmen* 'to take part') in that their form paradigm is usually incomplete. Usually, backformed verbs are only used in the infinitive and in the past participle, and the finite forms are completely lacking. If finite forms do develop, they usually remain syntactically inseparable: *notlanden* 'to make an emergency landing; lit. to need-land' – *er notlandete* 'he made an emergency landing'.

Only occasionally do backformed participles arise from complex nouns: *Allgemeinbildung* 'general education' → *allgemeinbildend* 'providing general education'. Backformed nouns do not occur, with the exception of a few individual cases such as *hämisch* 'malicious' → *Häme* 'malice'. If one doesn't count the change in complexity of words or the change in word class as an obligatory feature of the word-formation process, then substitutional formations such as *Territorialverteidigung* 'territorial defense' → *Territorialverteidiger* 'territorial defender' could be dealt with here as well (Becker 1993: 192).

7 Reduplication

Products of reduplication typically belong to the vocabulary of spoken language; many words of child language are also reduplicating. Nouns, verbs, adjectives, adverbs and interjections are produced. They can hardly be dealt with systematically. It is necessary to distinguish simple doublings (*Pinkepinke* 'money', *plemplem sein* 'to be nuts'), rhyme doubling (*Techtelmechtel* 'affair') as well as ablaut doubling (*Tingeltangel* pejorative 'honky-tonk music').

8 Blending

A blend is an interleaving of two lexemes, mostly combined with a shortening of one or both lexemes. Either an initial or a final segment of the source lexemes are thereby combined (*Europa* 'Europe', *Asien* 'Asia' → *Eurasien* 'Eurasia'; *ja* 'yes', *nein* 'no' → *jein* 'yes and no') or a segment which is identical in both lexemes is used only once in the new lexeme (*Computer* 'computer', *kompetent* 'competent' → *computent* 'computent'; Schmid 2003: 266).

Between the source lexemes one can find either paradigmatic semantic relations (*Demokratie* 'democracy', *Diktatur* 'dictatorship' → *Demokratur* 'democrature'), a factual connection (*Kur* 'course of treatment', *Urlaub* 'holiday' → *Kurlaub* 'holiday cure') or the amalgamation is facilitated by assonance and homophony (*Literatur* 'literature', *Tour* 'tour' → *Literatour* 'literatour').

Blends are often only understandable through contextual or factual knowledge. The discovery of their semantics can cause a pleasant surprise effect. As a result, they are particularly popular in the language of advertising.

For a sophisticated corpus-based formal and semantic modeling of blends, cf. Müller and Friedrich (2011).

9 Clipping

The creation of short forms is a special kind of word-formation, inasmuch as the output of most kinds does not allow the unequivocal reconstruction of the initial form. As there are no obligatory structural-morphological rules for shortening, it takes place on the basis of principles such as euphony and pronounceability. Above all, phrases and nouns are shortened (*größter anzunehmender Unfall* 'maximum credible accident' → *GAU* 'MCA', *Ultrakurzwelle* 'ultra-short wave' → *UKW* 'USW'), but increasingly adjectives are as well, especially in more colloquial registers (*asozial* 'asocial' → *aso*; Balnat 2011: 121). Shortened verbs rarely occur, they are mostly marked as technical or sociolectal (*schiedsrichtern* 'to umpire' → *schiedsen* 'to ump').

The dominating need for shortening is a striving for economical and playful forms of expression.

Short forms consist of segments of the full form. Different types of short forms result, depending on the kind and the number of segments used as well as on their position in the full form. Depending on the number of segments, one differentiates between unisegmental (*Universität* 'university' → *Uni* 'uni') and multisegmental short forms (*Schiedsrichter* 'umpire' → *Schiri* 'ump'). Multisegmental short forms are generally subdivided in abbreviations (*Allgemeine Ortskrankenkasse* 'general local health insurance company' → *AOK*), syllabic short forms (*Kriminalpolizei* 'Criminal Investigation Department' → *Kripo* 'CID') and mixed short forms (*Auszubildender* 'trainee' → *Azubi*). They can be spelled out (*NOK* 'National Olympic Committee') or read phonetically (*TÜV* 'Technical Inspection Agency', 'MOT' in the UK).

Short forms are often used in compounds, especially as first elements. When the full form is a phrase, as in *TÜV*, only the short form of the phrase is a possible first constituent: *TÜV-Plakette* 'MOT sticker', *TÜV-geprüft* 'MOT tested'. Short forms also occur as the bases for derivatives and conversions (*SPDler* 'member of the SPD', *SMS* 'SMS' → *simsen* 'to text').

Short forms differ from their full form at the time of coinage if not semantically, then at least usually in terms of connotation. Both, accordingly, present clear differences in usage (cf. Michel 2011). Unisegmental forms occur in verbal language and especially in intimate communication. The multisegmental abbreviations and syllabic short forms are rather bound to written formal language and occur, above all, in specialized contexts.

10 Word-creation

The assignment of word-creation (also: word invention, word manufacturing) to word-formation is controversial. Admittedly new words come into existence through word manufacture, but their formation does not take place in a rule-based manner on the basis of existing language material, as is the case in word-formation, but rather a content is assigned an arbitrary sequence of sounds, so that it acquires the character of a sign. Word-creation hardly plays a role in the expansion of the class of common nouns, as most formations remain occasional. Only a few, especially onomatopoetic nouns of child language as well as interjections are lexicalized (*Wauwau* 'bow-wow', *tatütata* 'nee-naw, nee-naw', *igitt* 'eww'). Recently, manufactured words are gaining increasing importance as company and product names: *Elmex* (brand of toothpaste), *Fa* (personal hygiene products), *Tchibo* (brand of coffee), *Cif* (scouring agent).

So-called pass words or code words, which are either customary lexemes or are constructed from numbers and/or letters, are not to be seen as word-creations. They do not have lexical meaning, but rather serve exclusively as a key for the identification of a person.

11 References

Balnat, Vincent (2011): *Kurzwortbildung im Gegenwartsdeutschen*. Hildesheim: Olms.
Barz, Irmhild (2009): Die Wortbildung. In: Duden. *Die Grammatik. Unentbehrlich für richtiges Deutsch*, 634–762. 8th ed. Mannheim/Zürich: Dudenverlag.
Becker, Thomas (1992): Compounding in German. *Rivista di linguistica* 4: 5–36.
Becker, Thomas (1993): Morphologische Ersetzungsbildungen. *Zeitschrift für Sprachwissenschaft* 12: 185–217.

Bergmann, Rolf (2005): Autonomie und Isonomie der beiden Wortbildungssysteme im Deutschen. In: Peter O. Müller (ed.), *Fremdwortbildung. Theorie und Praxis in Geschichte und Gegenwart*, 161–177. Frankfurt/M.: Lang.

Dokulil, Miloš (1968): Zur Theorie der Wortbildung. *Wissenschaftliche Zeitschrift der Karl-Marx-Universität Leipzig. Gesellschafts- und sprachwissenschaftliche Reihe* 17: 203–211.

Donalies, Elke (2005): *Die Wortbildung des Deutschen. Ein Überblick.* 2nd ed. Tübingen: Narr.

Donalies, Elke (2018): Wetterbeobachter, Zeitlang, wahrsagen, zartfühlend, kurzerhand, dergestalt. *Handbuch zur Univerbierung.* Heidelberg: Winter.

Donalies, Elke (2021): *Wortbildung – Prinzipien und Problematik. Ein Handbuch.* Heidelberg: Winter.

DWb 1 = Wellmann, Hans and Ingeburg Kühnhold (1973): *Deutsche Wortbildung. Typen und Tendenzen in der Gegenwartssprache. Eine Bestandsaufnahme des Instituts für deutsche Sprache. Forschungsstelle Innsbruck. Erster Hauptteil. Das Verb.* Mit einer Einführung von Johannes Erben. Düsseldorf: Schwann.

DWb 2 = Wellmann, Hans (1975): *Deutsche Wortbildung. Typen und Tendenzen in der Gegenwartssprache. Eine Bestandsaufnahme des Instituts für deutsche Sprache. Forschungsstelle Innsbruck. Zweiter Hauptteil. Das Substantiv.* Düsseldorf: Schwann.

DWb 3 = Kühnhold, Ingeburg, Oskar Putzer and Hans Wellmann (1978): *Deutsche Wortbildung. Typen und Tendenzen in der Gegenwartssprache. Eine Bestandsaufnahme des Instituts für deutsche Sprache. Forschungsstelle Innsbruck. Dritter Hauptteil. Das Adjektiv.* Düsseldorf: Schwann.

DWb 4 = Ortner, Lorelies, Elgin Müller-Bollhagen, Hanspeter Ortner, Hans Wellmann, Maria Pümpel-Mader and Hildegard Gärtner (1991): *Deutsche Wortbildung. Typen und Tendenzen in der Gegenwartssprache. Eine Bestandsaufnahme des Instituts für deutsche Sprache. Forschungsstelle Innsbruck. Vierter Hauptteil. Substantivkomposita.* Berlin/New York: de Gruyter.

DWb 5 = Pümpel-Mader, Maria, Elsbeth Gassner-Koch and Hans Wellmann (1992): *Deutsche Wortbildung. Typen und Tendenzen in der Gegenwartssprache. Eine Bestandsaufnahme des Instituts für deutsche Sprache. Forschungsstelle Innsbruck. Fünfter Hauptteil. Adjektivkomposita und Partizipialbildungen.* Unter Mitarbeit von Lorelies Ortner. Berlin/New York: de Gruyter.

Eichinger, Ludwig M. (2000): *Deutsche Wortbildung. Eine Einführung.* Tübingen: Narr.

Elsen, Hilke (2011): *Grundzüge der Morphologie des Deutschen.* Berlin/Boston: de Gruyter.

Elsen, Hilke and Sascha Michel (eds.) (2011): *Wortbildung im Deutschen zwischen Sprachsystem und Sprachgebrauch. Perspektiven – Analysen – Anwendungen.* Stuttgart: ibidem.

Erben, Johannes (2006): *Einführung in die deutsche Wortbildungslehre.* 5th ed. Berlin: Schmidt.

Fandrych, Christian (2011): Wie geht es eigentlich den "Affixoiden"? *Deutsche Sprache* 39: 137–153.

Fandrych, Christian and Maria Thurmair (1994): Ein Interpretationsmodell für Nominalkomposita: Linguistische und didaktische Überlegungen. *Deutsch als Fremdsprache* 31: 34–45.

Fleischer, Wolfgang and Irmhild Barz (2012): *Wortbildung der deutschen Gegenwartssprache.* 4th ed. Berlin/Boston: de Gruyter.

Fuhrhop, Nanna (2003): "Berliner" Luft und "Potsdamer" Bürgermeister: Zur Grammatik der Stadtadjektive. *Linguistische Berichte* 193: 91–108.

Fuhrhop, Nanna (2007): Verbale Komposition: Sind *brustschwimmen* und *radfahren* Komposita? In: Maurice Kauffer and René Métrich (eds.), *Verbale Wortbildung im Spannungsfeld zwischen Wortsemantik, Syntax und Rechtschreibung*, 49–58. Tübingen: Stauffenburg.

Fuhrhop, Nanna and Sebastian Kürschner (2025): Linking elements in Germanic. In: Peter O. Müller, Susan Olsen and Franz Rainer (eds.), *Word-Formation – Special Patterns and Restrictions*, 55–70. Berlin/Boston: De Gruyter Mouton.

Gaeta, Livio and Barbara Schlücker (eds.) (2012): *Das Deutsche als kompositionsfreudige Sprache. Strukturelle Eigenschaften und systembezogene Aspekte.* Berlin/Boston: De Gruyter.

Heringer, Hans Jürgen (2011): Neue Bildungen, der Gemeinschaft vorgeschlagen. In: Hilke Elsen and Sascha Michel (eds.), *Wortbildung im Deutschen zwischen Sprachsystem und Sprachgebrauch. Perspektiven – Analysen – Anwendungen*, 109–132. Stuttgart: ibidem.

Kopf, Kristin (2018): *Fugenelemente diachron. Eine Korpusuntersuchung zu Entstehung und Ausbreitung der verfugenden N+N-Komposita*. Berlin/Boston: De Gruyter.

Michel, Sascha (2011): Das Kurzwort zwischen 'Langue' und 'Parole' – Analysen zum Postulat der Synonymie zwischen Kurzwort und Vollform. In: Hilke Elsen and Sascha Michel (eds.), *Wortbildung im Deutschen zwischen Sprachsystem und Sprachgebrauch. Perspektiven – Analysen – Anwendungen*, 135–163. Stuttgart: ibidem.

Motsch, Wolfgang (2004): *Deutsche Wortbildung in Grundzügen*. 2nd ed. Berlin/New York: de Gruyter.

Müller, Peter O. (ed.) (2005): *Fremdwortbildung. Theorie und Praxis in Geschichte und Gegenwart*. Frankfurt/M.: Lang.

Müller, Peter O. (2025a): Foreign word-formation in German. In: Peter O. Müller, Susan Olsen and Franz Rainer (eds.), *Word-Formation – Language Contact and Diachrony*, 69–95. Berlin/Boston: De Gruyter Mouton.

Müller, Peter O. (2025b): Historical word-formation in German. In: Peter O. Müller, Susan Olsen and Franz Rainer (eds.), *Word-Formation – Language Contact and Diachrony*, 295–352. Berlin/Boston: De Gruyter Mouton.

Müller, Peter O. and Cornelia Friedrich (2011): Kontamination. In: Hilke Elsen and Sascha Michel (eds.), *Wortbildung im Deutschen zwischen Sprachsystem und Sprachgebrauch. Perspektiven – Analysen – Anwendungen*, 73–107. Stuttgart: ibidem.

Müller, Peter O. and Susan Olsen (2022): Systematische Einführung in die Wortbildung. In: Peter O. Müller and Susan Olsen (eds.), *Wortbildung. Ein Lern- und Konsultationswörterbuch. Mit einer Systematischen Einführung und englischen Übersetzungen*, 37–115. Berlin/Boston: De Gruyter.

Neef, Martin and Aişe Yurdakul (2020): Derivational networks in German. In: Lívia Körtvélyessi, Alexandra Bagasheva and Pavol Štekauer (eds.), *Derivational Networks Across Languages*, 167–177. Berlin/Boston: De Gruyter Mouton.

Ohnheiser, Ingeborg (1987): *Wortbildung im Sprachvergleich. Russisch-Deutsch*. Leipzig: VEB Verlag Enzyklopädie.

Olsen, Susan (1986): *Wortbildung im Deutschen. Eine Einführung in die Theorie der Wortstruktur*. Stuttgart: Kröner.

Pittner, Karin (1998): *Radfahren* vs. *mit dem Rad fahren*: Trennbare Verben und parallele syntaktische Strukturen. In: Irmhild Barz and Günther Öhlschläger (eds.), *Zwischen Grammatik und Lexikon*, 103–112. Tübingen: Niemeyer.

Pittner, Karin and Judith Berman (2006): video ist echt schrott aber single ist hammer. Jugendsprachliche Nomen-Adjektiv-Konversion in der Prädikativposition. *Deutsche Sprache* 34: 233–250.

Schlücker, Barbara (2019): Compounds and multi-word expressions in German. In: Barbara Schlücker (ed.), *Complex Lexical Units – Compounds and Multi-Word Expressions*, 69–94. Berlin/Boston: De Gruyter.

Schmid, Hans Ulrich (2003): Zölibazis Lustballon: Wortverschmelzungen in der deutschen Gegenwartssprache. *Muttersprache* 113: 265–278.

Seiffert, Anja (2008): *Autonomie und Isonomie fremder und indigener Wortbildung am Beispiel ausgewählter numerativer Wortbildungseinheiten*. Berlin: Frank & Timme.

Wegener, Heide (2003): Entstehung und Funktion der Fugenelemente im Deutschen, oder: Warum wir keine *Autobahn haben. *Linguistische Berichte* 196: 425–457.

Ingo Plag
2 English

1   Introduction
2   General overview
3   Composition
4   Derivation
5   Conversion
6   Paradigmatic processes: backformation and local analogy
7   Prosodic morphology: clipping, blending, infixation
8   Conclusion
9   References

Abstract: This article gives an overview of English word-formation. It is shown that, in spite of being a language with hardly any inflection, there is a rich inventory of word-formation devices, including compounding, affixation, conversion, and prosodic morphology. The formal and semantic characteristics of these devices are discussed, and examples are given to illustrate the intricate patterns that English complex words present.

1 Introduction

English is a language with very little inflectional morphology, but with a large inventory of word-formation devices that have attracted the interest of many researchers for a long time. Hence, there is a rich literature on most aspects of English word-formation, ranging from numerous monographs and research articles on individual phenomena to textbooks such as Adams (1973), Bauer (1983), Carstairs-McCarthy (2002), Plag (2003), Schmid (2011), and handbook-style overviews such as Jespersen (1942), Marchand (1969), Adams (2001), Bauer and Huddleston (2002) and Bauer, Lieber and Plag (2013).

In recent years, studies in English word-formation have profited from the availability of electronic corpora, databases and dictionaries such as *Cobuild* (Sinclair 1987), *The British National Corpus* (e.g., Davies 2004), *The Corpus of Contemporary American English* (Davies 2008–), *CELEX* (Baayen, Piepenbrock and Gulikers 1995), the *Oxford English Dictionary* or general internet search engines. In

Ingo Plag, Düsseldorf, Germany

particular, these resources have been employed to systematically search for newly created words, which is crucial for any attempt at describing the present-day speakers' word-formation knowledge. Most of the examples to be given below are taken from such sources.

2 General overview

Word-formation in English makes use of composition (also known as compounding), of prefixation, suffixation and (only marginally) infixation, and of non-affixational processes such as conversion, blending, and clipping. In addition, one can find paradigmatic processes such as backformation and analogy. We will discuss each of these in the subsequent sections. Before we do so, however, we need to clarify some more general theoretical and empirical problems involved in the study of word-formation in English.

One such problem is the demarcation of compounding and syntax, which is especially intricate because English has so little inflection that, unlike in other Germanic languages like German, this criterion is not very helpful in defining the boundary between phrases on the one hand, and words on the other. The literature on this problem is vast, but in spite of the many efforts to clarify this particular boundary area, success has been very limited.

The problem is particularly evident in discussions of compounding. Unlike in many other languages, none of the criteria (nor all criteria applied together) proposed in the literature for English (e.g., stress assignment, pronominalization, lexicalization, spelling) is able to neatly differentiate between constructions that are clearly syntactic (i.e. phrases) and others that are clearly morphological (i.e. compound words) in nature (see Bauer, Lieber and Plag 2013 for an overview discussion). The search for a clear boundary for the language under discussion is therefore futile, and I will be inclusive rather than exclusive in my discussion of pertinent forms in section 3.

Another subproblem of the syntax-morphology divide is the issue of lexicalized multi-word expressions like *forget-me-not*, *jack-in-the-box*, verb-particle constructions or phrasal verbs such as *get along*, *put up with*, *give up* or idiomatic expressions like *tongue in cheek*. In accordance with the literature I consider these lexicalized phrases, which are outside the realm of word-formation.

A study of word-formation as against inflection also raises the question of which morphological processes belong to which of the two domains. For English this is generally not an issue apart from one suffix, adverbial *-ly*. In spite of some good arguments for treating it as inflectional, it will be included in our discussion of adverbial derivation in section 4.4.

The problem of productivity and lexicalization looms large in the study of word-formation, since many complex words have meanings or phonological properties that cannot be compositionally derived on the basis of the constituent elements. Such cases of semantic or phonological opacity (as in *butterfly* or *government* [gʌvmənt] 'the body of persons governing') are numerous in English, especially due the to extensive borrowing of foreign complex words. In this article we will mainly focus on transparent and productive morphologial processes in order to describe the present-day speaker's word-formation system. The reader is referred to Plag (1999), Bauer (2001) and Plag (2006) for discussions of the role and nature of productivity in English word-formation.

3 Composition

3.1 General remarks

Composition or compounding, especially noun-noun compounding, is generally regarded as the most productive word-formation process in English, but studies systematically comparing the productivity of compounding with that of other processes are lacking.

Compounds can be defined as words that consist of two or more bases. Bases in turn can be defined as elements that can serve as input to further word-formation, i.e. to compounding and suffixation. Bases can be words (as in *breath test*), bound roots (*astro-physics*), or even phrases (*strawberries-in-July talk*). There is, however, the restriction that the right-hand base cannot be a phrase, but must be a bound root or a word. According to this definition, neoclassical formations are also compounds (to be discussed in section 3.3).

One can distinguish between determinative and coordinative compounds. In the former the left-hand element is either a modifier of the head (as in *opera glass, hothouse, razor-sharp, knee-deep*), or serves as an argument of the head (*opera singer, club member, sugar-free*). Determinative compounds are right-headed, which means that the righthand base determines the grammatical properties of the compound as a whole (e.g., syntactic category, count vs. mass, etc.), as well as the semantic category of the compound. Thus an opera glass is a kind of glass, not a kind of opera. Determinative compounds are binary structures, even if they contain more than two bases. Thus, multi-word compounds such as *street soccer day* or *child care center administration staff* can be analyzed as consisting of two immediate constituents, one or both of which may be a compound itself: [[street soccer] day], or [[[child care] center] [administration staff]].

Coordinative compounds, on the other hand, are compounds which consist of elements of the same syntactic category and in which the elements are in an equal semantic relationship, i.e. none of the two concepts denoted is subordinate to the other. These compounds are therefore not clearly right-headed, at least semantically. Coordinative compounds may be appositional, additive or compromise (Bauer 2008). Appositional compounds refer to single entities that represent the intersection of two sets. A *nerd-genius* is both a nerd and a genius, a *scholar-activist* is both a scholar and an activist. Additive compounds refer to entities that represent the sum of two sets, as in many territory names (*Bosnia-Herzegovina, Austria-Hungary*). Adjectival additive compounds combine two properties (*deaf-mute* refers to a state of being both deaf and mute). Compromise compounds refer to intermediate or blended properties, as in *blue-green, southwest*. Coordinative compounds may contain more than two elements (as in *AOL-Time Warner, artist-singer-songwriter*), in which case it is hard to argue for hierarchically structured binary structures, instead of flat ternary structures.

An important issue in the discussion of English compounds is their stress behavior. While traditional accounts hold that two-member compounds are stressed on the first element (*ópera singer*, e.g., Bloomfield 1935: 180, 228), it is often acknowledged (e.g., even by Chomsky and Halle 1968: 15–18, the inventors of the so-called "compound (stress) rule") that compounds can also be right-stressed (e.g., *home phóne*). In natural speech, about one third of the noun-noun compounds are in fact right-stressed (cf. Sproat 1994; Plag 2010; Bell and Plag 2012), which shows that stress variability is not a marginal phenomenon. Which of the two constituents will be more prominent in a given compound is an intricate question. First, there is variability across and within speakers (Kunter 2011, ch. 8), second, there is variability across different varieties of English (cf. Giegerich 2004: 15–16), and, third, there is variability across contexts when contrastive stress comes into play. Abstracting away from these three sources of variability, a number of factors have been successfully shown to determine compound stress assignment in noun-noun compounds, namely semantics, lexicalization, constituent family and informativity (cf. Plag et al. 2008; Arndt-Lappe 2011; Bell and Plag 2012). These factors work in the following way: compounds that express certain semantic relations (e.g., 'N2 is located at N1', 'N2 is made of N1', coordinative compounds) tend to prefer a certain stress pattern, more lexicalized compounds tend to be left-stressed, compounds that share a left or right member tend to be stressed in the same way, and less informative second constituents tend not to be stressed. Compounds with more than two constituents seem to follow the same principles as compounds with only two constituents (Kösling and Plag 2009; Giegerich 2009), contra theoretical claims that branching direction is the decisive influence (cf. Liberman and Prince 1977).

Let us now turn to the kinds of combinations we find in English compounds. Table 2.1 gives an overview, grouped by the four major syntactic categories nouns, adjectives, verbs and prepositions.

Tab. 2.1: Compound types by syntactic category.

	noun	adjective	verb	preposition
noun	house speaker	ankle-deep	babysit	year-in
adjective	loudspeaker	light-green	blackmail	tuned-in
verb	spoilsport	go-slow	stir-fry	push-up
preposition	afterthought	incoming	downgrade	into

Perhaps surprisingly, all combinations are attested. However, as will become clear as we go along, not all of these combinations are productive, and not all of the combinations arose through a process in which a speaker combined two bases to form a new word exhibiting the properties of compounds as described above. Following Bauer, Lieber and Plag (2013) I will use the term *canonical compound* for compounds productively formed by combining two or more bases, and *non-canonical compound* for forms that arose in a different way.

For example, complex prepositions like *into, onto, throughout, whereafter, therefore, notwithstanding, hereby* arose through the univerbation of frequently adjacent forms. Other non-canonical compounds seem to be the product of a process of inversion, as in the case of preposition-verb or preposition-adjective compounds like *download, outsource* and *inbuilt, upcoming* (Berg 1998). There are also non-canonical compounds resulting from conversion and stress shift (as in, for example, *break dówn → bréakdown, push úp → púsh-up*), or from backformation. Backformation is especially prevalent with compound verbs that are backderived from synthetic compounds, as evidenced in *babysit ← babysitter, chainsmoke ← chain-smoker*.

3.2 Nominal composition

The least productive of the four patterns in Table 2.1 is the combination of verb and noun. In this pattern the noun frequently functions as the object of the verb in first position (e.g., *spoilsport, pickpocket, cut-throat*). Compounds of this type are semantically exocentric. There are, however, also endocentric verb-noun compounds in which the noun is not the object of the verb, as in *cry-baby, think-tank*. Nominal compounds with prepositions or adjectives as first elements are rather frequent (*afterbirth, backseat, downside, upland, hothouse, whitewater, clean-living*).

The largest group consists of noun-noun compounds, which are semantically extremely diverse, ranging from determinative compounds through argument-head compounds to various types of coordinative compounds. In general, noun-noun compounds are ambiguous and any compound may in principle receive different interpretations according to context. This may even affect lexicalized compounds, where the institutionalized meaning may be overridden by a contextual interpretation. Thus, given the right situation, a speaker may refer to a fly sitting on the butter as a *butterfly*. Out of context, compounds tend to be interpreted in such a way that a reasonable or typical relation between the two constituents is established. For compounds with a deverbal head, this may often lead to an argumental interpretation of the first element, as in *car sale* 'the selling of cars', but not necessarily so, as evidenced in *garage sale* 'selling from one's garage'.

3.3 Adjectival composition

Adjectival compounds can be productively formed with nouns or other adjectives as non-heads. The interpretation of adjectival compounds follows principles similar to those of nominal compounds. There are determinative, argumental and coordinative adjectival compounds (e.g., *dog-lean, structure-dependent, brown-grey*, respectively). A common type of interpretation of determinative adjectival compounds involves a comparison (*dog-lean* 'lean as a dog', *blood-red* 'red like blood'). Argumental adjectival compounds often have a deverbal head, as in (object-oriented) *confidence-inspiring* or (subject-oriented) *state-controlled*.

3.4 Verbal composition

Most compounds that are verbs seem to be non-canonical, i.e. derived by processes other than the combination of two bases (Erdmann 1999). We find conversions from nominal or adjectival compounds (*breath test, carbon-copy, cold-shoulder, head-shake*), inverted phrasal constructions (e.g., *upgrade* ← *grade up*), backformations from nominal or adjectival compounds (de-nominal: *crash-land* ← *crash-landing*, deadjectival: *tailor-make* ← *tailor-made*). There are, however, also canonical verbal compounds, which can be determinative (*window-shop*) or coordinative (e.g., *blow-dry, stir-fry, trickle-irrigate*). Perhaps as a consequence of the wide variety of derivational histories just outlined, nouns, adjectives, verbs and prepositions can all occur as first elements.

3.5 Neoclassical composition

Neoclassical formations are (mostly nominal) compounds in which bases of Latin or Greek origin are combined to form new combinations that are not attested in the original languages.

The list of forms that can be argued to belong to the class of neoclassical forms is long, and it is not entirely clear which elements should belong to this class (cf. Bauer 1998; Baeskow 2004 for discussion). Some examples are *astro-* 'space', *bio-* 'life', *biblio-* 'book', *electro-* 'electricity', *-cracy* 'rule', *-graphy* 'write', *-itis* 'inflammation, disease', *-logy* 'science of'. Most neoclassical bases do not occur as a free form, which is the reason that they are called "combining forms". Some bases (like *morph-/-morph* and *phil-/-phile*), can occur both in initial and final position, while most forms occur either initially or finally. Combining forms can attach to other bound forms (*glaciology, scientology*) or to words (*hydro-electric, lazyitis, morpho-syntax*).

Neoclassical elements can show different segmental and prosodic structures depending on the kinds of element that combine. Initial combining forms that take a word as second element regularly have their main stress on the right constituent (e.g., *astro-phýsics*), while numerous final combining forms impose antepenultimate stress on the compound (e.g., *astrólogy*), accompanied by a different vowel quality (e.g., [oʊ] in *astro-physics* vs. [ɒ] *astrólogy*). Combining forms such as *-graphy*, *-cracy*, and *-logy* thus behave phonologically like certain stress-influencing suffixes (such as *-ity*, see section 4).

Characteristically, we find a vowel at the boundary between the two elements. This vowel is orthographically represented mostly as either <o> or <i>. The nature and morphological status of this vowel are not quite clear. Thus, there are compounds where the vowel is independent, as it occurs with initial elements that have no stem allomorph with that vowel, e.g., *film-o-graphy* or *steroid-o-genesis*. In other formations the vowel is part of the first element and cannot be omitted (e.g., *geo-physics/*ge-physics, telephone/*tel-phone*). Finally, there are cases with phonologically governed alternations. For instance, consonant-final variants of initial combining forms such as *gastr-* 'stomach' or *morph-* 'form' combine with vowel-initial final combining forms (such as *-itis, -osis*) without the addition of a thematic vowel, whereas the combination with a consonant-initial final combining form leads to the occurrence of a vowel (*gastr-o-graphy, morph-o-metry*). This alternation is restricted to combining forms, since vowel-final non-combining forms as initial elements preserve their final vowel (cf. *potato-itis, big company-itis*).

4 Derivation

Partly due to the history of the language with contact playing a major role, we find a large inventory of native and non-native prefixes and suffixes. English also possesses infixation, but due to its nature as prosodic morphology the reader is referred to section 7 for the discussion of infixation. Suffixes generally determine the syntactic category of the derived word, while the vast majority of prefixes do not. The discussion given below of the numerous suffixes is organized according to the syntactic category of the derivatives. As shown in Plag (2003), most suffixes attach to more than one base category, with affix-particular phonological, morphological, semantic and syntactic restrictions determining the combination of affixes and bases.

Derivation is largely constrained to the three major syntactic categories noun, adjective and verb. These three categories can quite freely derive new words from each other. The formation of adverbs is highly constrained: at best, only two suffixes exist that derive adverbs and these are very selective concerning the kinds of base they can attach to (see the discussion in section 4.4).

In the literature one can often find a distinction between native and non-native affixes, with the two classes being distinguishable through their combinatorial properties and phonological behavior. Recent studies have shown, however, that such a distinction is gradient at best, if not totally misguided (cf. Plag 1999; Plag and Baayen 2009; Zirkel 2010; Bauer, Lieber and Plag 2013).

Unlike prefixes, many suffixes trigger stem allomorphy, resyllabification or stress shift. For example, verbal derivatives in *-ize* involve the deletion of base-final segments under specific circumstances (cf. *summary → summarize, feminine → feminize*, see Plag 1999), and nominal derivatives in *-ity* are all stressed on the antepenultimate syllable, inducing resyllabification when possible, and imposing a stress shift when necessary to achieve antepenultimate stress (*prodúctive → productívity*). In spite of attempts to systematize the different patterns of morpho-phonological alternations found in English derivation, there is good empirical evidence that each morphological category comes with its own very particular morpho-phonology (cf. Plag 1999; Raffelsiefen 1999; Lappe 2007).

4.1 Nominal derivation

Semantically, one can distinguish between several large groups of suffixes, i.e. person noun-forming suffixes, event nominalizations (including those denoting results, states, products and means), and nominalizations denoting qualities, collectives and other abstract noun categories. Quite often, the same suffix can cover a wide range of meanings, even transgressing the major groups just outlined.

4.1.1 Event nominalizations

In this section we discuss nominalizations with the suffixes *-ing, -ion, -ment, -al, -ure, -ance/-ence* and *-ancy/-ency*. All non-auxiliary verbs have at least a nominalization in *-ing*, and many verbs have one or more additional nominalizations. Apart from *-ing*, the only other suffix that is fully productive in its domain is *-ion* (with its variants *-ation, -cation, -ion, -ition, -tion, -ution*), which obligatorily attaches to the verbal suffixes *-ize, -ate* and *-ify*. The other suffixes mentioned show only few new formations (e.g., *revisal, fluctuance*), with *-ment* yielding the highest number of neologisms among them (e.g., *ceasement, financement*).

All event nominalizations can give rise to different readings, with the event reading being perhaps the most prevalent. Other readings, also with suffixes whose function is primarily a different one, include results (*acceptance, compression*), products (*drawing, sculpture*), instruments (*trimming, refreshment*), locations (*enclosure, residence*), agents (*administration, government*), measure terms (*abundance*), paths (*ascendence, continuation*), patients (*payment, substitution*), and states (*annoyance, boredom*). Conversion of verbs into nouns show similar ranges of meanings, but these will be discussed in section 5.

While *-ing* and *-al* seem to attach only to verbs, the other suffixes are more versatile. We find *-ure* on verbs (*erasure*), nouns (*architecture*) and bound bases (*juncture*), *-ment* on verbs (*assessment*), nouns (*illusionment*), adjectives (*scarcement*) and bound bases (*segment*). With the suffixes *-ance/-ence* and *-ancy/-ency* there is no clear evidence whether the base of the nominal is a verb in *-ate* or the corresponding adjective in *-ant* (cf., for example, *hesitate* ↔ *hesitant* ↔ *hesitancy*). Phonologically, *-ion, -al,* and *-ure* are quite interesting. The derivatives with the suffix *-ion* are stressed on the penult with pertinent stress shifts if necessary, with the consequence that its productive allomorph *-(c)átion* is often referred to as auto-stressed (*personalizátion*). Deverbal nominal *-al* only attaches to iambic bases (*deníal, refúsal*), and *-ure* can trigger palatalization and base allomorphies (*disclo[z]e → disclo[ʒ]ure, join → juncture*).

4.1.2 Person nouns

This section deals with derived nouns denoting agents, patients, themes, instruments, inhabitants, locations, and gendered forms. The pertinent suffixes are *-er, -or, -ee, -ant/-ent, -ist, -an, -eer, -ster, -meister, -arian, -ite, -ese, -ess, -ette,* and *-trix*. Most of the suffixes attach to many kinds of bases, including phrases. Consider, for example, the probably most versatile suffix *-er,* which attaches to verbs (*attacker*), nouns (*islander*), proper nouns (*Montrealer*), compounds (*freestyler*), and phrases (*no-hoper*).

Some of the suffixes are polysemous and can express more than one of the above-mentioned meanings, and many of the above-mentioned meanings can be expressed by more than one of suffixes. For example, agent can be encoded by *-er* (*reader*), *-or* (*investor*), *-ee* (*escapee*), *-ant/-ent* (*student*), *-ist* (*journalist*), *-an* (*guardian*), and (adding an evaluative component) also by *-eer* (*summiteer*), *-ster* (*fraudster*), *-meister* (*ragemeister*), *-arian* (*fruitarian*). Viewed from the formal side, the suffix *-er* can express, for example, agent (*shrugger*), patient (*shooter*), experiencer (*smeller*), instrument (*whaler*), inhabitant (*Londoner*), location (*diner*), and measure (*fiver*).

4.1.3 Quality nouns, collectives and other abstracts

There are many suffixes that create various kinds of abstract and collective nouns, such as *-ness* (*remoteness*), *-ity* (*curiosity*), *-dom* (*heathendom*), *-ship* (*courtship*), *-hood* (*manhood*), *-ery* (*slavery*), *-ana* (*Victoriana*), *-age* (*voltage*) and *-ism* (*careerism*). The suffixes *-ness* and *-ity* prefer adjectival bases (but are not restricted to those), and the respective derivatives denote the quality or state denoted by the base adjective (*blueness* 'the qualtiy or state of being blue', *profunditiy* 'the quality or state of being profound').

The other suffixes mentioned in the previous paragraph are mostly (but not exclusively) found with nominal bases. The suffixes *-dom, -ship, -hood* express a similar meaning, which, due to the composition with mainly nominal bases, can be paraphrased as 'the state or condition of being X' (*stakeholderdom, advisorship, buddyhood*). Meaning extensions to territory, collective or other meanings are not infrequent (*kingdom, membership, brotherhood*), neither are triplets or doublets with the same base, for example *studenthood, studentdom, studentship,* and with no apparent difference in meaning.

The suffixes *-ery, -age,* and *-ana* primarily derive collective nouns or locations (*fernery, nunnery, cuttage, leakage, Africana, Nixoniana*). Nouns denoting fields of study or forms of doctrine are derived by -*ism*. Again, suffix polysemy is the rule, and meaning extensions are common (e.g., to 'behavior' with -*ery*, as in *clownery*).

4.1.4 Diminutives

English also has a number of productive suffixes that can be categorized as diminutive, as they usually express small size and a specific attitude of the speaker towards a referent (Schneider 2003). The suffixes include -*ie* (*thingy, Josie, howdy*), -*ette* (*kitchenette, sleeperette*), -*let* (*piglet, baylet, flamelet, trendlet*), -*o* (*kiddo*), -*s* (*Babs*), -*er* (*rugger*), and -*poo* (*huggypoo*). The majority of bases and derivatives are nominal, but other categories can be found (e.g., *howdy*).

Of these, -*ie* (with its spelling variants <y> and <ey>) is the most productive one. Due to its nature as a prosodic morphological category it will be discussed (together with -*o*) in section 7. The others attach primarily, if not exclusively, to nouns, with moderate productivity.

4.2 Adjectival derivation

There are at least 19 productive adjectival suffixes in English (-*able*, -*al*, -*ant*, -*ary*, -*ed*, -*esque*, -*ful*, -*an*, -*ible*, -*ic*, -*ical*, -*ine*, -*ing*, -*ish*, -*ive*, -*ly*, -*ory*, -*ous*, -*some*, -*y*), plus the formation of verbal present and past participles, which are readily used as adjectives. Most adjectival suffixes are non-native, and it is with this set that we find intriguing patterns of morphophonological alternations, including stress shifts as well as stem and suffix allomorphy. Let us briefly examine one example, derivatives in -*able*. Apart from some exceptional lexicalized forms (such as *ád.mirable, préferable*), derivatives with monosyllabic and disyllabic bases do not show stress shifts (e.g., *áskable, abúsable, chállengeable*). Derivatives with longer base words behave in a peculiar fashion, however. They show no stress shift if their antepenult is light (e.g., *jét.ti.so.na.ble, mó.ni.to.ra.ble*), but show optionally stress shift to the antepenult if it is heavy (e.g., *al.lo.cá.ta.ble, a.ro.ma.tí.za.ble, á.na.ly.za.ble/a.na.lý.za.ble, cér.ti.fy.a.ble/cer.ti.fý.a.ble*).

Quite often semantically empty formatives are involved in adjectival suffixation, such as <n> in *Plato-n-ic*, <t> in *aroma-t-ic* or <i> in *baron-i-an* (vs. *republican*), or one finds particular stem allomorphs (as in *assume* → *assumpt-ive*, *induce* → *induct-ive*).

Semantically, it is useful to distinguish between qualitative and relational adjectives. Relational adjectives are usually denominal, and they relate the noun which is modified by the adjective to the base word of the derived adjective. Thus an *algebraic mind* is 'a mind having to do with algebra'. Qualitative adjectives, in contrast, encode more specific meanings and show different syntactic properties (e.g., gradability, modification by *very*, predicative use). Of the suffixes mentioned, *-al, -ary, -ic* are relational in nature, although their dervatives may also be coerced into qualitative readings. For example, *grammatical* has a relational sense 'having to do with grammar' (as in *she is a grammatical genius*), and a qualitative sense 'conforming to the rules of grammar' (as in *this is a grammatical sentence*).

The qualitative adjectival meanings include potentiality (*-able*), ornative (*-ed*, as in *leather-soled*), similative (as in *hipsterish, Kafkaesque, Barbie-like*), possessive ('have X', *respectful*), eventive (*avoidant, explorative, explanatory*). Meaning extensions for these suffixes are common and depend on the kind of base a particular suffix attaches to and the context the form occurs in. For example, existing attestations in COCA of *brothy* suggest an affix interpreted as 'containing X' ("a hot, brothy bowl of vegetarian pho"), 'tasting like X' ("a well-seasoned filling with brothy undertones"), or 'smelling like X' ("... letting her smell the brothy steam").

4.3 Verbal derivation

Apart from conversion (see section 5) there are three productive suffixes that can derive verbs, mainly from nouns and adjectives. These are *-ize, -ify,* and *-ate*. The two suffixes *-ize* and *-ify* show roughly the same range of meanings: locative (*hospitalize, tubify*), ornative (*patinize, youthify*), causative (*randomize, aridify*), resultative (*peasantize, trustify*), inchoative (*aerosolize, mucify*), performative (*anthropologize*), and similative (*powellize*). Their distribution is governed by prosodic restrictions, with *-ize* attaching to polysyllabic bases, and *-ify* (productively) to monosyllables and to disyllables ending in /ɪ/. The suffix *-ate* is more restricted, productively deriving ornative and resultative verbs, mainly in the domain of the sciences (*mercurate, iodinate*).

4.4 Adverbial derivation

Adverbs are formed with the help of two suffixes, *-ly* (*expectedly, internationally*) and *-wise*. The status of deadjectival, adverbial-forming *-ly* as derivational is disputed (see, for example, Payne, Huddleston and Pullum 2010 and Giegerich 2012 for discussion) since it displays characteristics of inflection that suggest that *-ly* adverbs are in fact positional variants of adjectives.

The suffix -*wise* derives two kinds of adverbs from nouns. Manner and dimension adverbs (such as *lengthwise, sarong-wise*) can be paraphrased as 'in the manner of X, like X, along the dimension of X', while the meaning of the more productive viewpoint adverbs (such as *food-wise, language-wise*) can be rendered as 'with respect to, concerning X'.

4.5 Prefixation

There is an abundance of prefixes in English, which modify their bases in various ways. We find quantificational (*bi-, demi-, di-, hyper-, hypo-, mega-, micro-, mini-, mono-, poly-, semi-, super-, tri-, ultra-, uni-*), negative (*a-, anti-, counter-, de-, dis-, in-, mis-, non-, un-*), and spatial/temporal prefixes (*ante-, circum-, cross-, ex-, extra-, inter-, intra-, meta-, mid-, out-, pan-, post-, pre-, retro-, sub-, supra-, trans-*), often with pertinent meaning extensions, as well as many prefixes with various other meanings (*arch-* 'principal', *auto-* 'self', *pseudo-* 'false', *re-* 'again', *step-* 'taken over from a previous relationship', *vice-* 'acting in place of'). As mentioned above, most prefixes attach to many different kinds of base and do not determine the syntactic category of their bases. Exceptions to this generalization are the unproductive verbal prefixes *en-* (e.g., *enshrine*) and *be-* (e.g., *befriend*).

5 Conversion

Conversion, the change from one syntactic category to another with no change in form, is a highly productive process in English word-formation. Its theoretical status as lexical or syntactic is debated, as is the treatment of specific kinds of conversion as zero-suffixation, multifunctionality or underspecification. Furthermore, there is the problem of directionality, i.e. of determining which of a given pair of forms is the base and which is the derivative. I will be agnostic as to these theoretical and methodological issues and describe observable patterns of lexical relatedness that are considered as word-formation by most analysts.

5.1 Nominal conversion

Conversion into nouns is especially frequent with verbal bases (*cry*), but can also be based on adjectives (*intellectual, subconscious, sweet*), adverbs (*forward*), interjections (*oh*), conjunctions (*buts, ands*), and phrases (*no-go*). Semantically, the outcome of deverbal conversion into noun is largely determined by the semantics of the base, and can, preferably but not exclusively, denote an instance (*call, guess, jump*), a location (*dump*), or a person (*cook, cheat, spy*).

5.2 Adjectival conversion

The analysis of conversion into adjectives is quite problematic as the criteria for determining what an adjective is in English are not uncontroversial. Given that nouns can freely occur in attributive position with other nouns, it is very hard to find examples of nouns that have acquired adjective-like properties that go beyond their occurrence as nominal modifiers, such as modification with *very*, or comparative formation. Clear cases are *fun* and *key*, as in *this is a very fun read* or *ethnicity is a very key factor* (both examples from COCA). Many potential examples are of questionable status (e.g., *abstract, moderate, perfect* as presumably converted from verbs).

5.3 Verbal conversion

The most productive conversion process is conversion into verbs, with practically no restriction concerning the kinds of bases. We find, for example, nouns (e.g., *bottle, file, skin, blockhouse, bootstrap*), adjectives (*cruel, young*), phrases (*blindside, cold-call*), interjections (*oh-oh*) and conjunctions (*if*). Semantically, converted verbs are indeterminate, with the only restriction being that the derivative denotes an event, state or process that has to do with the denotation of the base.

6 Paradigmatic processes: backformation and local analogy

Many morphological formations in English can be easily analyzed as the concatenation of morphemes and are therefore often used as examples for a morpheme-based, syntagmatic view of morphology. However, there are also numerous complex words in English that do not lend themselves to such an approach and cannot be straightforwardly described without recourse to paradigmatic relationships between words in the mental lexicon.

The perhaps most prominent mechanism in this respect is backformation, which is usually defined as the deletion of a suffix or prefix in analogy to pairs of base and derivative that feature the affix in question. A textbook example is *edit* ← *editor* on the basis of many such pairs of words (*credit/creditor, exhibit/ exhibitor*), but other examples can be easily found (*to transcript* ← *transcription, self-destruct* ← *self-destruction*). Backformation is sometimes described as the deletion of a suffix, but crucially such a deletion necessarily involves analogical pairings of forms with and without the suffix, and is therefore paradigmatic in nature.

As shown in Plag (1999: 206–210), many derivatives in *-ate* are backformations, either from nouns in *-or*, or, more commonly, from nouns in *-ation* (e.g., *escalate, formate, cavitate*). As already mentioned above, verbal compounds are in their majority backformations (denominal: *houseclean* ← *house-cleaning*, deadjectival: *tailor-make* ← *tailor-made*).

Another source of new lexemes is the coinage of individual words on the basis of an analogy to single existing complex words or sets of existing words, as in *house husband* 'a husband responsible for the household work', on the basis of *housewife*, or as in *beefburger, cheeseburger, shrimpburger* on the basis of (mis-analyzed) *hamburger*. Consider also *seaquake* 'an earthquake originating under the sea' or *hangunder* 'the funny feeling you get when you wake up after a night of not drinking and you're not hungover like usual'.

7 Prosodic morphology: clipping, blending, infixation

The term *prosodic morphology* refers to those morphological processes where the relevant category is expressed predominantly or exclusively through prosodic means, i.e. by manipulating the prosodic make-up of the base. In some cases this may involve an additional affix (as in *-y* and *-o* formations or expletive infixation). We will distinguish three major categories: clipping (involving one base and the deletion of phonological material), blending (involving two or more bases) and infixation (the insertion of a morpheme into a base at a prosodically determined position). The first two categories have often been described as being highly irregular, but recent studies (e.g., Bat-El 2006; Lappe 2007) have shown that this characterization is false, once an output-oriented approach is taken.

7.1 Clipping

This category comprises mainly the clipping of common nouns (e.g., *lab* ← *laboratory, pro* ← *professional, celeb* ← *celebrity*), *-y*-suffixed common nouns (*daffy* ←

daffodil, veggie ← vegetable), *-o*-suffixed common nouns (*evo ← evening, delo ← delegate*), clipped proper nouns (*Pat ← Patricia, Kye ← Hezekiah*), *-y*-hypocoristics (*Pety ← Peter, Trishy ← Patricia*). Less common are formations in *-s* (*Gabs ← Gabrielle*) or *-a* (*Gazza ← Gascoigne*).

Semantically, clipped forms are often in-group markers and express familiarity with the concept or referent of the base. Sometimes a clipping may find its way into the speech community at large, in which case the form loses its in-group flavor, as can be observed for *ad* (← *advertisement*). Hypocoristics such as *sweety* or *Frannie* express not only familiarity, but also a (usually positive) attitude towards the person or thing referred to.

There are many similarities between the different processes, but as shown in Lappe (2007), each of them comes with its own set of prosodic and segmental restrictions that regulate the phonological structure of the derivative and the relationship between derivative and base. For illustration, let us take a look at the differences between clipped proper nouns and clipped common nouns. Clipped proper nouns systematically anchor to the first or to the main-stressed syllable (cf. *Patricia → Pat ~ Trish, Octavia → Oc ~ Tave*), while clipped common nouns can only anchor to the first syllable (cf. *fraternity → frat/*tern, mechanic → mech/*chan*). Proper noun clippings do not preserve certain consonant clusters that are preserved in common noun clippings (e.g., /kt/ or /pt/). Finally, dental fricatives may be optionally substituted in proper noun clippings (cf. *Bartholomew → Bart*), but not in common noun clippings, which always preserve the dental fricative (cf. *catheder → cath/*cat*).

7.2 Blending

Blends can be analyzed as compounds with at least one constituent having lost some of its phonological material. Semantically, they can be determinative or coordinative, and stress-wise they behave like a single word, normally adopting the stress pattern of one of the two source words. There are two basic patterns observable. In the first, shown in (1a), the first part of the left base word and the last part of the right base word form the blend. This type is most often discussed in the literature and seems much more frequent than the second type, given in (1b), where the respective first parts of the two bases are combined.

(1)   a. AB + CD → AD (*breakfast + lunch → brunch*)
     b. AB + CD → AC (*modulator + demodulator → modem*)

In terms of syntactic category, many different combinations are possible, e.g., noun + noun (*beer + nirvana → beervana*), adjective + noun (*British + sitcom →*

Britcom), adjective + adjective (*rural* + *urban* → *rurban*), verb + verb (*correct* + *rectify* → *correctify*).

The formal relationship between the bases and the blend is regulated by a compromise of two competing forces. One is the deletion of material to form a single word, the other the necessity to preserve as much material as possible to relate the blend to its bases. Let us look at some restrictions for illustration. The vast majority of blends have as many syllables as one of the bases, usually the second base (as in *boatel, brunch, guesstimate*). Counterexamples exist (e.g., *correctify*), but they often involve a considerable overlap of phonological or orthographic material, which facilitates the recoverability of both base words. If there is no overlap between the two bases because they do not share the same segments the location of the cut-off point between the two bases is largely determined by syllable structure. For example, with monosyllabic blends there is a strong tendency to combine the onset of the first word with rhyme of the second (as in *spoon* + *fork* → *sp#ork*, see also *br#unch*). Polysyllabic blends combine syllable constituents or whole syllables in various ways (as shown in Table 2.2, taken from Plag 2003: 124), and quite often the segmental overlap allows for more than one analysis (as exemplified by *boatel*).

Tab. 2.2: Combinations of syllabic constituents in polysyllabic blends.

A	D	A + D, examples
onset	penultimate rime and ultimate syllable	b + oatel ch + unnel
onset and nucleus	ultimate syllable	boa + tel
onset and nucleus	coda and ultimate syllable	Spa + nglish
onset	syllables	g + estimate
syllable	ultimate rime	boat + el
syllable	syllables	com + pander guess + timate stag + flation

7.3 Infixation

In English, there is the possibility of inserting expletives in the middle of words to create new words expressing the strongly negative attitude of the speaker (e.g., *kanga-bloody-roo, abso-blooming-lutely*). The insertion of the expletive is governed by a prosodic constraint: it must be inserted between two feet. Hence, it is not allowed to interrupt a foot, as shown, for example, by *(ám-EXPLETIVE-per)(sànd) vs. (ámper)-EXPLETIVE-(sànd) (parentheses are used to indicate foot boundaries). Nor may it appear between a foot and an unstressed syllable not belonging to a foot, as shown in *ba-EXPLETIVE-(nána) vs. (bàn)-EXPLETIVE-(dánna) (see Hammond 1999: 161–164 for more detailed discussion).

8 Conclusion

The present overview of English word-formation has shown that, although inflectionally impoverished, this language's word-formation resources are plentiful and lead to patterns of complex words that are quite intricate in form and meaning. These patterns are also a good testing ground for morphological theories, with English word-formation data presenting interesting challenges for concepts such as the morpheme, lexical integrity, lexical strata, or the lexicon-syntax divide.

9 References

Ackema, Peter, Sabrina Bendjaballah, Eulalia Bonet and Antonia Fábregas (2023): *The Wiley-Blackwell Companion to Morphology*. Oxford: Wiley-Blackwell.
Adams, Valerie (1973): *An Introduction to English Word-Formation*. London: Longman.
Adams, Valerie (2001): *Complex Words in English*. Harlow: Longman.
Arndt-Lappe, Sabine (2011): Towards an exemplar-based model of stress in English noun-noun compounds. *Journal of Linguistics* 47(11): 549–585. DOI: 10.1017 / S0022226711000028.
Arndt-Lappe, Sabine (2023): Different lexicons make different rivals. *Word Structure* 16(1): 24–48.
Baayen, R. Harald, Richard Piepenbrock and Leon Gulikers (1995): The CELEX Lexical Database (CD-ROM). Philadelphia, PA: Linguistic Data Consortium, University of Pennsylvania.
Baeskow, Heike (2004): *Lexical Properties of Selected Non-Native Morphemes of English*. Tübingen: Narr.
Bat-El, Outi (2006): Blends. In: Keith Brown (ed.), *Encyclopedia of Language and Linguistics*, 66–70. 2nd ed. Amsterdam: Elsevier.
Bauer, Laurie (1983): *English Word-Formation*. Cambridge: Cambridge University Press.
Bauer, Laurie (1998): Is there a class of neoclassical compounds, and if so is it productive? *Linguistics* 36(3): 403–422.
Bauer, Laurie (2001): *Morphological Productivity*. Cambridge: Cambridge University Press.
Bauer, Laurie (2008): Dvandva. *Word Structure* 1: 1–20.
Bauer, Laurie (2017): *Compounds and Compounding*. Cambridge: Cambridge University Press.
Bauer, Laurie and Rodney Huddleston (2002): Lexical word formation. In: Rodney Huddleston and Geoffrey K. Pullum (eds.), *The Cambridge Grammar of the English Language*, 621–722. Cambridge: Cambridge University Press.

Bauer, Laurie, Rochelle Lieber and Ingo Plag (2013): *A Reference Guide to English Morphology*. Oxford: Oxford University Press.

Bauer, Laurie (1998): When is a sequence of two nouns a compound in English? *English Language and Linguistics* 2(1): 65–86.

Bell, Melanie and Ingo Plag (2012): Informativeness is a determinant of compound stress in English. *Journal of Linguistics* 48: 485–520.

Berg, Thomas (1998): The (in)compatibility of morpheme orders and lexical categories and its historical implications. *English Language and Linguistics* 2: 245–262.

Bloomfield, Leonard (1935): *Language*. London: Allen & Unwin.

Carstairs-McCarthy, Andrew (2002): *An Introduction to English Morphology. Words and their Structure*. Edinburgh: Edinburgh University Press.

Chomsky, Noam and Morris Halle (1968): *The Sound Pattern of English*. New York: Harper & Row.

Davies, Mark (2004): BYU-BNC. (Based on the British National Corpus from Oxford University Press). Available online at http://corpus.byu.edu/bnc/ [last access 20 Oct 2015].

Davies, Mark (2008–): The Corpus of Contemporary American English: 450 million words, 1990–present. Available online at http://corpus.byu.edu/coca/ [last access 20 Oct 2015].

Erdmann, Peter (1999): Compound verbs in English: Are they pseudo? In: Guy A. J. Tops, Betty Devriendt and Steven Geukens (eds.), *Thinking English Grammar. To Honour Xavier Dekeyser, Professor Emeritus*, 239–252. Leuven: Peeters.

Giegerich, Heinz J. (2004): Compound or phrase? English noun-plus-noun constructions and the stress criterion. *English Language and Linguistics* 8: 1–24.

Giegerich, Heinz J. (2009): The compound stress myth. *Word Structure* 2: 1–17.

Giegerich, Heinz J. (2012): The morphology of -*ly* and the categorial status of 'adverbs' in English. *English Language and Linguistics* 16(3): 341–359.

Günther, Fritz and Marco Marelli (2023): CAOSS and transcendence: Modeling role-dependent constituent meanings in compounds. *Morphology* 33: 409–432.

Hammond, Michael (1999): *The Phonology of English*. Oxford: Oxford University Press.

Kösling, Kristina and Ingo Plag (2009): Does branching direction determine prominence assignment? An empirical investigation of triconstituent compounds in English. *Corpus Linguistics and Linguistic Theory* 5: 201–239.

Kotowski, Sven and Ingo Plag (eds.) (2023): *The Semantics of Derivational Morphology: Theory, Methods, Evidence*. Berlin/Boston: De Gruyter.

Kunter, Gero (2011): *Compound Stress in English. The Phonetics and Phonology of Prosodic Prominence*. Berlin/New York: de Gruyter.

Jespersen, Otto (1942): *A Modern English Grammar. On Historical Principles. Part VI Morphology*. London: Allen & Unwin.

Lappe, Sabine (2007): *English Prosodic Morphology*. Dordrecht: Springer.

Liberman, Marc and Alan Prince (1977): On stress and linguistic rhythm. *Linguistic Inquiry* 8: 249–336.

Lieber, Rochelle (2016). *English Nouns: The Ecology of Nominalization*. Cambridge: Cambridge University Press.

Lieber, Rochelle, Sabine Arndt-Lappe, Antonio Fábregas, Christina Gagné and Francesca Masini (eds.) (2021): *The Oxford Encyclopedia of Morphology*. Oxford: Oxford University Press.

Marchand, Hans (1969): *The Categories and Types of Present-day English Word-formation. A Synchronic-Diachronic Approach*. 2nd ed. München: Beck.

Marelli, Marco and Marco Baroni (2015): Affixation in semantic space: Modeling morpheme meanings with compositional distributional semantics. *Psychological Review* 122(3): 485–515.

Payne, John, Rodney Huddleston and Geoffrey K. Pullum (2010): The distribution and category status of adjectives and adverbs. *Word Structure* 3: 31–81.

Plag, Ingo (1999): *Morphological Productivity. Structural Constraints in English Derivation*. Berlin/New York: Mouton de Gruyter.

Plag, Ingo (2003): *Word-Formation in English*. Cambridge: Cambridge University Press.

Plag, Ingo (2004): Syntactic category information and the semantics of derivational morphological rules. *Folia Linguistica* 38: 193–225.

Plag, Ingo (2006): Productivity. In: Baas Aarts and April McMahon (eds.), *Handbook of English Linguistics*, 537–556. Oxford: Blackwell.

Plag, Ingo (2010): Compound stress assignment by analogy: The constituent family bias. *Zeitschrift für Sprachwissenschaft* 29(2): 243–282.

Plag, Ingo (2018): *Word-Formation in English. 2nd revised edition*. Cambridge: Cambridge University Press.

Plag, Ingo, Gero Kunter, Sabine Lappe and Maria Braun (2008): The role of semantics, argument structure, and lexicalization in compound stress assignment in English. *Language* 84(4): 760–794.

Plag, Ingo and Harald Baayen (2009): Suffix ordering and morphological processing. *Language* 85: 109–152.

Raffelsiefen, Renate (1999): Phonological constraints on English word formation. In: Geert Booij and Jaap van Marle (eds.), *Yearbook of Morphology 1998*, 225–288. Dordrecht: Kluwer.

Schmid, Hans-Jörg (2011): *English Morphology and Word-formation. An Introduction*. Berlin: Schmidt.

Schneider, Klaus P. (2003): *Diminutives in English*. Tübingen: Niemeyer.

Sinclair, John M. (ed.) (1987): *Looking up. An Account of the Cobuild Project in Lexical Computing*. London: Collins.

Sproat, Richard (1994): English noun-phrase accent prediction for text-to-speech. *Computer Speech and Language* 8: 79–94.

Stein, Simon David (2022): *The Phonetics of Derived Words in English: Tracing Morphology in Speech Production*. Berlin/Boston: De Gruyter.

Zirkel, Linda (2010): Prefix combinations in English: Structural and processing factors. *Morphology* 20: 239–266.

Kristina Kotcheva
3 Swedish

1 Introduction
2 General overview
3 Composition
4 Derivation
5 Conversion
6 Borrowed word-formation and neoclassical word-formation
7 Blending and clipping
8 References

Abstract: The main word-formation processes in Swedish are compounding and derivation. Nominal and adjectival compounding are productive processes, unlike verbal or adverbial compounding. Most compound lexemes are right-headed. Linking elements occur. Derivation is achieved by prefixation and suffixation. Nominal leftmost as well as adjectival rightmost constituents are sometimes reanalysed as affixes. Many affixes are borrowed from (Low) German or from classic languages (via French). Conversion, blending, and clipping are other methods used for enlarging the lexicon.

1 Introduction

Swedish is an East North Germanic language typologically grouped together with Danish and Norwegian as Mainland Scandinavian vs. the Insular Scandinavian languages Faroese and Icelandic. During the late Middle Ages, the Mainland Scandinavian languages were under the strong influence of (Middle) Low German. The intense language contacts affected both the lexicon and the grammar of Danish, Norwegian and Swedish and even resulted in the adoption of Low German word-formation patterns. Other sources of influence on Swedish word-formation are the classic languages Greek and Latin, as well as French.

Today, Swedish is the official language in Sweden, where it is spoken by 90 % of its ca. 9,500,000 inhabitants (census of 2012), as well as the second official language in Finland where it is mother tongue of ca. 300,000 Finland Swedes

Kristina Kotcheva, Freiburg/Br., Germany

living mostly in the southern and western parts of the country. The autonomous Finish province of Åland islands is a monolingual Swedish region (Braunmüller 2007).

Word-formation in Swedish has been the subject of numerous surveys in the research history of Swedish grammar. Generally, one can identify three periods focusing on different aspects of word-formation: mainly diachronically oriented (1880s–mid-twentieth century), mainly synchronically oriented (1960s–1980s) and corpus-based surveys of word-formation (mid-1980s and onward).

Representative for the diachronically oriented period in the study of word-formation in Swedish are Hellquist (1922) and Wessén (1943). Noreen (1906) offers a comprehensive survey of the history of word-formation principles in Swedish and provides lists of derivational affixes.

Several synchronic overviews of principles of Swedish word-formation exist, such as Söderbergh (1968), Teleman (1970), Liljestrand (1974), Thorell (1981, 1984). *Svenska Akademiens Grammatik* (Teleman, Hellberg and Andersson 1999, henceforth SAG 2) includes word-formation in its description of word classes in Swedish. Hinchliffe and Holmes (1994) (in English) deal with composition (though not with derivation) in Swedish. Recent publications addressing general issues in Swedish word-formation are Liljestrand (1993) (a revised edition of Liljestrand 1974) and Josefsson (2005). Josefsson places word-formation in Swedish in a broader context and includes aspects of word-formation patterns in language acquisition as well.

In recent decades, large corpora such as Språkbanken at Gothenburg University (http://spraakbanken.gu.se/), or the English-Swedish Parallel Corpus at Lund University (http://www.sol.lu.se/engelska/corpus/corpus/espc.html) are used for describing tendencies in the word-formation of Swedish, cf. Allén, Gellerstam and Malmgren (1989), Malmgren (1994) and Josefsson (2002). The comprehensive reference grammar of Swedish, *Svenska Akademiens Grammatik* (SAG2) is also based on data from Språkbanken.

Different aspects of word-formation in Swedish have been addressed within the ORDAT project (*Det svenska ordförrådets utveckling från artonhundra till tjugohundra* [The development of the Swedish lexicon from year 1800 to year 2000]), cf. the anthology of Malmgren and Olofsson (2003) and further publications such as Malmgren (2002a, 2002b) or Lundbladh (2002).

Josefsson (1998) offers a minimalist account of word-formation in Swedish. The study originated within the joint Scandinavian lexicon project NORDLEX (Herslund and Sørensen 1993), and deals with the basic principles of word-formation with Germanic morphemes, and with derivations of the Germanic type. Josefsson (1998) focuses on open word classes, primarily verbs and nouns.

2 General overview

The major word-formation processes in Swedish are composition and derivation. Blending and clipping also form new lexemes.

Two types of compounds exist in Swedish: determinative and copulative. The predominant compound type is determinative and right-headed. The first constituent in a compound can comprise a root, cf. *hus-vagn* house car 'caravan', a derived word as in *arbet-ar(e)-parti* 'worker's party', or a compound as in *husvagn-s-hjul* 'caravan tyre'. A univerbated phrase as the left constituent in a compound is less common, like the quantifier phrase *två man* 'two man' in *tvåman-s-bob* 'two-person bob sleigh'. Determinative compounds can comprise a linking element, historically a genitive case marking, cf. the linking element -*s*- in *husvagn-s-hjul* or *tvåman-s-bob* above. Coordinate compounds are formed by joining two (seldom more) heads, cf. *svart-vitt* 'black and white'. The order of the heads is conventionalised.

Derived lexemes are formed by suffixation and prefixation. Derivational suffixes alter the meaning of the base and can also change the word class of the derivate, as for example the suffix -*else*, which renders abstract nouns from a verbal base, cf. *röra* 'to move' → *rör-else* 'movement', or -*are* which yields agent nouns as in *arbeta* 'to work' → *arbet-are* 'worker'. Prefixes do not change the word class of the base but alter its meaning, like *gen*- in *gåva* 'gift' → *gen-gåva* 'gift in return', which adds a reciprocal meaning, or the negating prefix *mis*-, like in *gynna* 'to support' → *miss-gynna* 'to disadvantage'.

Lexemes can be formed by adding an affixoid (a prefixoid or a suffixoid) to a base. Affixoids are semantically bleached free lexemes, which resemble word-formation affixes in being used to generate series of lexemes, cf. the prefixoid *jätte*-, originally 'giant' in *jätte-liten* giant-small 'very small', *jätte-dyr* giant-expensive 'very expensive' or the suffixiod -*vänlig* 'friendly' in *miljö-vänlig* 'eco-friendly' or *bil-vänlig* 'car-friendly'.

The word-formation processes blending and clipping form shorter lexemes. An example for blending is *blomma* 'flower' + *telegram* → *blommogram* 'flower arrangement sent as a gift', *automobil* → *bil* 'car' for the latter.

Delimiting the boundary between word-formation, i.e. morphology, and syntax can pose a challenge in dealing with nominal compounds vs. (possessive) noun phrases as well as phrasal vs. prefix verbs.

Possession in Swedish is marked by adding the formant -*s*, a fossilized genitive case ending, to the rightmost element of the modifier in a possessive noun phrase: *Anna och Stinas mamma* 'Anna and Stina's mom'. In nominal compounds, the cognate morpheme -*s*- can occur as a linking element. However, possessive noun phrases and compounds differ with regard to stress pattern. The head of a possessive noun phrase bears primary stress (word accent) while the head of the compound receives secondary stress (and lacks word accent) (cf. Bruce 1977: 12–13). Possessive noun phrases and nominal compounds with the linking element -s- are also differentiated in writing: they are written separately like in *en skogs historia* 'history of a forest' (possessive noun phrase marker) vs. *en skogshistoria* 'forest story' (linking element in a compound) written as one word (cf. Delsing 2002 on the linking element -s-). Linking elements in Swedish have also been the subject of comparative surveys dealing with Danish, Dutch and German (Kürschner 2007, 2010; Fuhrhop and Kürschner 2025).

Particle verbs (phrasal verbs) i.e. verb phrases of the type *gå upp* 'to go up, rise', *ta(ga) med* 'to take along' on the one hand and prefixed verbs like *uppgå* 'to go up, rise', *medta(ga)* 'to take along' on the other are semantically close (or even equivalent) and thus often considered forms of the same verb (Thorell 1981: 53; see also Dehé 2025 on particle verbs in Germanic).

On word-formation in other North Germanic languages, cf. Petersen (2016) on Faroese, Götzsche (2016) on Danish, Askedal (2016) on Norwegian and article 4 in this volume on Icelandic.

3 Composition

Composition is the process of combining two constituents into a new lexical item. Most common in Swedish are determinative right-headed compounds, i.e. the left constituent modifies the right constituent (head), cf. *personbil* person-car 'car', *lastbil* load-car 'lorry' as different types of *bil* 'car'. All major word classes, i.e. nouns, verbs and adjectives occur as right constituents in determinative compounds. Coordinative compounds on the other hand contain two or more heads, while lacking modifying constituents, cf. the adjectival compounds *sötsur* sweet-sour 'sweet-and-sour' or *blå-vit-röd (flagga)* 'blue-white-red (flag)'.

3.1 Nominal compounds

The right constituent in a nominal compound is a noun. The first constituent can belong to any of the following word classes: nouns (N), adjectives (Adj), verbs (V), pronouns (Pro), quantifiers (Q), or adverbs (Adv). It can be a root *hus-vagn* house car 'caravan', a derived or a compound noun, or even a univerbated phrase (cf. Booij 2007: 19 on univerbation). The compounding process is recursive, thus the newly-formed lexeme can be subjected to subsequent composition, cf. (1). Compounds can serve as input to derivation processes as well (2).

(1) N → [[N]s[N]]ₙ → [[[N]s[N]]s[N]]
    skepp → skepp-s-kapten → skepp-s-kapten-s-mössa
    'ship'   'ship captain'   'ship captain's cap'

(2) N → [[N][V]]ᵥ → [[N][V]]ᵥ-areₙ
    tåg → tåg-luffa → tåg-luff-are
    'train' train-hitchhike   train-hitchhik-er
           'to travel with an 'person travelling
            InterRail pass'   with an InterRail pass'

Table 3.1 offers an overview of the leftmost constituents used in nominal composition in Swedish:

Tab. 3.1: Nominal compounds in Swedish.

	[[hus]ₙ[vagn]ₙ]ₙ	house car 'caravan'
NN		
PropNN	[[Zorn]ₙ[tavla]ₙ]ₙ	Zorn painting 'painting by Zorn'
AdjN	[[mjuk]_Adj[vara]ₙ]ₙ	soft ware 'software'
VN	[[kör]ᵥ[egenskap]ₙ]ₙ	drive characteristic 'quality of driving'
ProN	[[vi]_Pro[känsla]ₙ]ₙ	we feeling 'we-feeling'
QN	[tre]_Q[steg]ₙ]ₙ	three step 'triple jump'
PN	[[på]_P[annons]ₙ]ₙ	on announcement 'announcement'
AdvN	[[då]_Adv[tid]ₙ]ₙ	then time 'past tense'
[Adj+N]_NPN	[[[Svarta]_Adj[hav]ₙ]_NPs[flotta]ₙ]ₙ	'Black Sea fleet'
[Q+N]_NPN	[[[en]_Q[gång]ₙ]_NPs[flaska]ₙ]ₙ	one time bottle 'disposable bottle'
[P+N]_PPN	[[[under]_P[vatten]ₙ]_PPs[kamera]ₙ]ₙ	'under water camera'
[N+P]_PPN	[[[året]ₙ[runt]_P]_PP[bostad]ₙ]ₙ	year round flat 'flat where one lives all year long'

The grammatical gender and class of nominal compounds are usually determined by the rightmost constituent, cf. (3). However, the compound may also manifest gender and/or nominal class different from the original gender and/or nominal class of its head, cf. (4). The compound *smör-gås* butter goose 'sandwich' (cf. Hellquist 1980) yields a regular plural which differs from the plural of the original right constituent *gås* 'goose' presumably due to its being opaque to present-day speakers of Swedish.

(3) *skrivning* (common gender) → *biologi-skrivning* (common gender)
'test paper' → 'biology test paper'

(4) a. *blick* (common gender) → *ögon-blick* (neuter gender)
'glance' → eyes-glance 'moment'
b. *gås*.$_{SG}$ → *gäss*.$_{PL}$ but *smör-gås*.$_{SG}$ → *smör-gås-ar*.$_{PL}$
'goose' 'geese' 'sandwich' 'sandwiches'

Coordinative nominal compounds in Swedish are less frequent than determinative ones. Determinative compounds like [[*prins*]$_N$[*gemål*]$_N$]$_N$ 'prince consort' receive single definiteness marking on the rightmost constituent: *prinsgemål-en* 'the prince consort', while coordinative compounds such as [[*prins*]$_N$[*regent*]$_N$]$_N$ 'prince regent' allow for definiteness marking on both heads: *prins-en-regent-en* 'the prince regent' (SAG 2: 44).

Personal names like *Karl-Gustav* or *Anna-Lisa* can be characterized as coordinative compounds where the order of the constituents is constrained only by convention (SAG 2: 129–130; Thorell 1981: 29), others such as *Stor-Sven* 'Big Sven', *Lill-Babs* 'Little Babs', *Västgöta-Pelle* 'Pelle the Westrogoth (i.e. from West Gothland, a region in Sweden)', *Svält-Feldt* 'Starving Feldt' have to be analysed as determinative compounds with an adjectival or nominal first constituent (SAG 2: 130).

Swedish family names are often compounds. Besides the most common right constituent *-son* 'son (of)', family names frequently comprise a second constituent referring to a concept from the semantic field related to nature: *-berg* 'hill/mountain top', *-blad* 'leaf', *-blom* 'blossom', *-dal* 'valley', *-fors* 'waterfall/rapid', *-gren* 'branch', *-gård* '(farm)yard', *-holm* 'small island', *-hult* 'grove', *-kvist/-qvist/-quist* 'twig', *-löv* 'foliage', *-man* 'man', *-rot* 'root', *-skog* 'forest', *-strand* 'shore', *-ström* 'stream', *-vall* 'mound'. Typical left constituents in such names are *Al-* 'all', *Berg-* 'top', *Björk-* 'birch', *Blom-* 'flower', *Bäck-* 'stream', *Dal-* 'valley', *Ek-* 'oak', *Fors-* 'water fall/rapid', *Hag-* 'meadow', *Hall-* 'cliff', *Holm-* 'small island', *Karl-* 'man', *Kron-* 'crown', *Käll-* 'spring', *Lind-* 'lime tree', *Lund-* 'grove', *Malm-* 'ore', *Strand-* 'shore', *Val-/Vall-* 'mound', cf. *Holm-berg*, *Björk-lund*, *Fors-lund*, etc. (SAG 2: 130). Compound family names originated among the Swedish noble houses and were related to the symbols on the family's coat of arms, e.g., *Gylden-stierna* 'Golden Star' or *Leijonhufvud* 'Lion Head' referring to the golden star or the lion heads on the heraldic shield, respectively. In the 18th century, middle class families started adopting family names coined in the style of the names used by the nobility, employing terms referring to entities of the local nature.

In nominal compounds, a linking element can occur after the left constituent: [[*skog*]$_N$-s-[*historia*]$_N$]$_N$ 'forest story'. Linking elements are usually inserted after every other constituent in recursive composition: [[*mor*]$_N$[*mor*]$_N$]$_N$ 'grandmother (on the mother's side)' → [[[mor]_N[mor]_N]_N-s-[mor]_N]_N 'great-grandmother (on the mother's side)' → [[[mor]_N[mor]_N]_N-s-[[mor]_N[mor]_N]_N]_N 'great-great-grandmother (on the mother's side)' → [[[[mor]_N[mor]_N]_N-s-[[mor]_N[mor]_N]_N-s-[mor]_N]_N]_N 'great-great-great-grandmother (on the mother's side)', etc. The most frequent linking element in Swedish is -s-, less frequent elements are -o-/-u-, -e- and -er-, cf. (5). For an early account on linking elements, cf. Tamm (1900). Delsing (2002) is a survey on the linking element -s-.

(5) a. *man-s-röst*   'man's voice'
     b. *gat-u-kök*   street-u-kitchen   'food cart'
     c. *veck-o-penning*   week-o-coin   'pocket-money'
     d. *högskol-e-byggnad*   high school-e-building   'high school building'
     e. *rätt-ar-ting*   court-ar-thing   'law assembly'

Linking elements can affect compound segmentation, cf. [[barn]_N[[bok]_N[klubb]_N]_N]_N 'book club for children' vs. [[[barn]_N[bok]_N]_N-s-[klubb]_N]_N 'club for children's books' (Josefsson 1997: 60).

Historically, linking elements in Swedish are genitive case markings. With the exception of the linking morpheme -s- these formants are opaque to speakers of Modern Swedish.

3.2 Adjectival compounds

Adjective compounds have an adjectival right constituent. The most common pattern of adjectival composition in Swedish has a noun as its left constituent, other possible left constituents are adjectives, verbs, pronouns, adverbs, and prepositions (cf. Table 3.2).

Tab. 3.2: Adjectival compounds in Swedish.

NAdj	[[mord]_N[lysten]_Adj]_Adj	murder greedy	'murderous'
AdjAdj	[[mjörk]_Adj[blå]_Adj]_Adj	dark blue	'dark blue'
VAdj	[[kör]_V[klar]_Adj]_Adj	drive ready	'ready to run'
ProAdj	[[jag]_Pro[svag]_Adj]_Adj	I weak	'having an inferiority complex'
QAdj	[[mång]_Q[etnisk]_Adj]	many ethnic	'multiethnic'
PAdj	[[mellan]_P[stor]_Adj]_Adj	between big	'medium sized'
AdvAdj	[[ut]_Adv[fattig]_Adj]_Adj	out poor	'impoverished'

Coordinative adjectival compounds like *svartvitt* 'black and white' or (hyphenated) *norsk-engelsk* 'Norwegian-English' are less frequent than determinative ones (SAG 2: 188). Coordinative adjective-adjective compounds tend to be hyphenated in writing as long as they are not yet lexicalised, while lexicalised compounds are univerbated (cf. univerbation in Booij 2007: 19).

(6) lexicalised
blågul (*flagga*)   blue yellow   'blue-and-yellow, i.e. Swedish (flag)'

(7) not (yet) lexicalised
tysk-svensk (*ordbok*)   'German-Swedish (dictionary)'

Hyphenated compound adjectives used as attributes show agreement marking on both constituents if the head of the noun phrase is of neuter gender and in singular, cf. (8). If the head is marked for plural, and/or for definiteness, agreement is marked only on the last element of the adjectival compound (SAG 2: 188), cf. (9).

(8) agreement with head noun of neuter gender in singular
ett engelskt-svenskt lexikon
'an English-Swedish lexicon'

(9) a. no agreement with head noun (neuter or common gender) in plural
engelsk-svenska (*lexikon/ordböck-er*)
'English-Swedish lexicons/dictionaries'
b. no agreement with definite head noun (neuter or common gender)
det engelsk-svenska leksikon-et – denengelsk-svenskaordbok-en
'the English-Swedish lexicon' – 'the English-Swedish dictionary'

3.3 Verbal compounds

Verbal compounds comprise a verb as the rightmost constituent. The left constituent can belong to different word classes: nouns, adjectives, verbs, adverbs, prepositions, or can be a univerbated phrase (cf. Table 3.3).

Some verbal compounds with a preposition or an adverb as their first constituent and particle verbs are semantically, though not stylistically identical, while others differ both semantically and stylistically. Examples for the former are *insätta/sättain* 'to insert', *tillbakavisa/visa tillbaka* 'to reject', and for the latter *påpeka* 'to note'/*peka på* 'to point at' or *avbryta* 'to interrupt'/*bryta av* 'to break'. The verbal compounds often have a higher stylistic value than the particle verbs.

Tab. 3.3: Verbal composition in Swedish.

NV	[[tjuv]_N[lyssna]_V]_V	thief-listen 'to eavesdrop'
AdjV	[[kal]_Adj[hugga]_V]_V	bold-chop 'to deforest'
	[[ren]_Adj[göra]_V]_V	clean-do 'to clean'
VV	[[bränn]_V[märka]_V]_V	brand-mark 'to brand'
	[[kryp]_V[köra]_V]_V	crawl-drive 'to crawl along'
AdvV	[[ut]_Adv[sätta]_V]_V	out-set 'to expose'
PV	[[till]_P[foga]_V]_V	towards-join 'to add'
[P+Pro]_PPV	[[[för]_P[sig]_Pro]_PP[gå]_V]_V	for-oneself-go 'to proceed'
[P+N]_PPV	[[[i]_P[gång]_N]_PP[sätta]_V]_V	to in-motion-set 'to start'

However, exceptions exist: *fastslå/slå fast* 'to establish' share the same stylistic value (SAG 2: 528).

Forming compound verbs with a nominal first constituent (NV) is not productive in modern Swedish except for compounds which comprise *jul-* 'Christmas-', *vinter-* 'winter-', *chock-* 'shock-', *tjuv-* 'thief-', *hem-* 'home' as their left constituent: *jul-pryda* Christmas-decorate 'to decorate for Christmas', *vinter-förvara* winter-store 'to store during the winter', *chock-behandla* shock-treat 'to treat with a shock', *tjuv-lyssna* thief-listen 'to eavesdrop', *hem-köra* home-drive 'to drive home' (Mellenius 1996: 146–147). Similar verb-noun compounds are attested in other North Germanic languages as well, cf. Petersen (2016) on Faroese and article 4 on Icelandic in this volume.

3.4 Adverbial and prepositional compounds

Neither adverbial nor prepositional composition is a productive word-formation process in Swedish. However, a small group of compound adverbs/prepositions exists, consisting of directional adverbs as a left constituent and a directional adverb or preposition as a right constituent. The directional adverbs *hit* 'hither' and *dit* 'thither', or the interrogative directional adverb *vart* 'whereto' can occur as the left constituent, and the directional adverbs *åt* and *tills*, both '(in direction) to' as the right constituent. Other possible constituents in adverbial compounds are adverbs denoting a goal as the first constituent and a directional adverb denoting general movement meaning '(in direction) to/from' as the second constituent like in [[upp]_Adv[åt]_Adv]_Adv 'upwards' and [[ned]_Adv[till]_Adv]_Adv, [[ned]_Adv[åt]_Adv]_Adv, both down-to 'downwards'. Since most of the elements occurring as a second constituent in such compounds have homonymous adverbial or prepositional forms, even the compounds can be homonymous, cf. adverbial use of *uppåt* 'upwards' in (10) vs. prepositional use in (11):

(10) adverb *uppåt*
Kurserna på börsen klättrar uppåt.
market values.the on stock market.the climb upwards
'The market values on the stock market climb upwards.'

(11) preposition *uppåt*
Ödlan klättar uppåt väggen.
lizard.the climbs up wall.the
'The lizard climbs up the wall.'

Some prepositional compounds are synonymous with the non-compound form, but differ in style: *i* 'in' is neutral while [[ut]$_{Adv}$[i]$_P$]$_P$ out in 'in' is marked as archaic.

3.5 Affixoids

A lexical item used as a first or a second constituent in a series of compounds tends to be reanalysed as a prefix or a suffix, respectively (cf. Table 3.4). The adjective *vänlig* 'friendly' occurs as a second constituent in *miljö-vänlig* 'eco-friendly', *barn-vänlig* 'child-friendly', *läs-vänlig* read-friendly 'readable'. At the same time, it is still used as an independent lexical item Hon är en vänlig person 'She is a friendly person'. The noun *jätte* 'giant' has acquired an additional recurring and productive meaning as an intensifier in derived nouns and adjectives: *jätte-stad* giant-city 'very big city', *jätte-glad* giant-happy 'very happy'. Words like *jätte-* and *-vänlig* are referred to as affixoids, or as prefixoids and suffixoids, respectively (cf. Ascoop 2005; Lundbladh 2002; Malmgren 2002a; Andersson 2003 on affixoids in Swedish).

In colloquial Swedish, the swear words *(d)jävel, fan*, both 'devil' and *helvete* 'hell' can function as suffixoids, adding a pejorative meaning to the nominal base they are attached to: *dörrjävel* door devil 'door (pej.)', *jobbfan* job devil 'job (pej.)', *flickhelvete* girl hell 'girl (pej.)'. *Svenska Akademiens Grammatik* (SAG 2: 47) categorises pejorative words rendered by *-jävel, -fan* and *-helvete* as noun-noun compounds. However, compounds in Swedish are right-headed, thus *hus-dörr* house door 'front door' is a type of door and *dörr-handtak* 'door handle' is

Tab. 3.4: Affixoids in Swedish.

Affixoid	Base category	Base word		Derived word	
jätte-	Adj N	liten project	'small' 'project'	jätteliten jätteproject	giant-small 'very small' giant-project 'very big project'
skit-	Adj N	bra stämning	'good' 'mood'	skitbra skitstämning	shit-good 'very good' 'very bad mood'
-(d)jävel	N	bil	'car'	biljävel	'car (pej.)'
-fan	N	bil	'car'	bilfan	'car (pej.)'
-fri	N	drog mangel recept	'drug' 'defect' 'prescription'	drogfri mangelfri receptfri	'drug-free' defect-free 'free of defects' prescription-free 'over-the-counter (medicine)'
-helvete	N	bil	'car'	bilhelvete	'car (pej.)'
-lös	N	steg bostad kontakt	'step' 'dwelling place' 'contact'	steglös bostadslös kontaktlös	'step-less' 'homeless' 'contactless'
-vänlig	N	familj hud hund	'family' 'skin' 'dog'	familjvänlig hudvänlig hundvänlig	'family-friendly' 'skin-friendly' 'dog friendly'

a type of handle. *Dörr-jävel*, on the other hand, is not a subclass of *jävel* 'devil' but of *dörr* 'door', and thus should be analysed as a derived noun and not as compound.

4 Derivation

Derivation is the second relevant process in Swedish word-formation. In derivation, an affix is added to a base belonging to one of the major word classes (nouns, adjectives, verbs), to an adverb or to a univerbated phrase, yielding a new lexical item.

While suffixes may or may not alter the word class of the derivate, prefixes in Swedish solely modify the meaning of the base they are attached to. Etymologically, one can distinguish native North Germanic prefixes (e.g., *o-*, *van-*, both 'un-'), borrowings from classical languages (of Greek or Latin origin, e.g., *pre-*, *hyper-*) and prefixes borrowed from (Middle Low) German (e.g., *an-* or *för-*). Prefixes in Swedish can be divided in stress-bearing and non-stress-bearing. The group of non-stress bearing prefixes in Swedish comprises only two elements: *be-* and *för-*, both borrowed from Low German and used exclusively in verbal derivation. Stress-bearing prefixes can be added to nouns, adjectives or verbs (Teleman 1981: 69).

4.1 Nominal derivation

Nouns in Swedish can be derived by adding a nominal suffix to a nominal, adjectival, or verbal base: *land* 'land' → *landskap* 'landscape', *kär* 'loved/in love' → *kärlek* 'love', *arbeta* 'to work' → *arbetare* 'worker', or to an univerbated phrase *tre hjul* 'three wheels' → *trehjuling* 'tricycle'. The suffixes *-are*, *-är*, *-er*, *-ist*, *-(at)or* and *-ör* yield agent nouns. Adding the suffix *-essa* (from French), *-inna*, or *-ska* (both from Low German) to nouns denoting a male referent renders nouns denoting a female referent: *lärare* '(male) teacher' → *lärarinna* 'female teacher'. This word-formation pattern is not productive in present-day Swedish. The suffixes *-d*, *-else*, *-ande/-ende*, *-eri*, *-het*, *-nad*, *-skap*, and *-t* yield abstract nouns. The endearing suffix *-is* is highly productive: *bäst* 'best' → *bästis* 'best friend', *daghem* → *dagis* both 'day-care centre' (SAG 2: 40). Another colloquial suffix is the pejorative *-o*, which renders agent nouns: *pretentiös* 'pretentious' → *pretto* 'a pretentious person' (cf. Adelswärd 2001).

4.1.1 Suffixation

Productive suffixes in nominal derivation comprise *-het*, *-skap*, *-lek*, *-d*, *-ska*, *-ling/-ing*, *-(n)ing*, *-is* (on the productive colloquial suffix *-is*, cf. Inghult 1968; Josefsson 2002). Nouns derived by adding one of the following productive suffixes *-het*, *-dom*, *-lek*, *-skap*, *-(n)ing* receive accent 2 (a two-peaked pitch rise) in standard Swedish: *kär* (accent 1) 'loved/in love' → *kär-lek* (accent 2) 'love'. Accent 2 is characteristic of polysyllabic lexemes in Swedish, and can be assigned by a derivational suffix or even by an inflectional one. Loanwords like *mobbing* are realised with accent 1 (single-peaked pitch rise) as long as speakers consider them to be loanwords, but receive accent 2 once speakers reanalyse them as native words comprised of a stem, e.g., *mobb-* to which the native accent 2-inducing suffix *-ning* is added, thus *mobbing* (accent 1) but *mobb-ning* (accent 2) (SAG 2; Söderström 2012: 8). Other productive derivational suffixes like *-is* do not induce accent 2. Derivational suffixes

Tab. 3.5: Suffixes in nominal derivation.

Suffixid	Base category	Base word		Derived word	
-are	N	apotek	'pharmacy'	apotekare	'pharmacist'
	V	beundra	'to admire'	beundrare	'admirer'
	[Q+N]$_{NP}$	tre master	'three masts'	tremastare	'three-master'
	[V+N]$_{VP}$	ha vårdnad	'to have custody'	vårdnadshavare	'guardian'
-är	N	motion	'exercise'	motionär	'amateur athlete'
-d	Adj	bred	'wide'	bredd	'width'
-else	V	baka	'to bake'	bakelse	'pastry'
-er	Adj	dum	'stupid'	dummer	'silly'
-eri	N	pedant		pedanteri	'pedantry'
	V	krypa	'to crawl'	kryperi	'servility'
-essa	N	prins	'prince'	prinsessa	'princess'
-het	Adj	jämn	'equal'	jämhet	'equality'
-(i)an	PropN	Wagner		Wagnerian	'Wagnerian'
-inna	N	lejon	'lion'	lejoninna	'female lion'
-is	Adj	god	'good'	godis	'sweets'
		mjuk	'soft'	mjukis	'softie'
	N	lekskola	'day-care centre'	lekis	'day-care'
-ist	N	flöjt	'flute'	flöjtist	'flutist'
-lek	Adj	stor	'big'	storlek	'size'
-(l)ing	Adj	vek	'soft'	vekling	'softie'
		ful	'ugly'	fuling	'ugly person'
	V	segla	'to sail'	segling	'sailing'
		lära	'to learn'	lärling	'apprentice'
-nad	V	överleva	'to survive'	överlevnad	'survival'
-(n)ing	V	skriva	'to write'	skrivning	'test paper'
	[Adj+N]$_{NP}$	höga hjul	'high wheels'	höghjuling	'high wheel bicycle'
	[Q+N]$_{NP}$	fyra hjul	'four wheels'	fyrhjuling	'ATV'
-ska	N	sjukskötare	'male nurse'	sjuksköterska	'nurse'
		sångare	'singer'	sångerska	'female singer'
	Adj	grön	'green'	grönska	'verdure'
-o	Adj	full	'drunk'	fyllo	'drunkard'
		aggressiv	'aggressive'	aggro	'aggressive person'
		fet	'fat'	fetto	'fat person'
	N	alkoholist	'alcohol addict'	alko	'alcohol addict'
-skap	Adj	bered	'ready'	beredskap	'readiness'
	N	vän	'friend'	vänskap	'friendship'
-t	V	skriva	'to write'	skrift	'writing'

of Greek or Latin origin always bear the primary stress in a word, thus *DOKtor* 'doctor' but *doktorAND* 'PhD student' (capital letters indicate primary stress).

Nouns like *doktorand, dividend; leverans, konferens, debutant, konsument* can be analysed as derived by adding a suffix *-and/end, -ans/ens* and *-ant/-ent* to a verbal base. However, all these words are borrowings from Latin (via French or German) and the distribution of the suffixes arises from their use in the source language. Alternatively, the distribution of these suffixes in Swedish can be described as lexically determined (SAG 2).

The distribution of the homophonous suffixes *-tion, -sion* occurring only in loanwords is lexically determined by the form of the loanword in the source language. Thus we find *-tion* in *operation, konsumtion* 'consumption', *edition* vs. *-sion* in, e.g., *revision*. Other seemingly productive suffixes like *-ator, -ör, -tor, -ent* are either analogous formations (thus *kopiator* 'copier' is based on *plagiator* 'plagiarist'; *akupunktör* 'acupuncturist' based on *instructör* 'instructor'), or borrowed along with the whole lexeme: *dissident, reaktor* 'reactor'.

Adding a diminutive suffix to the altered stressed syllable of the given name can form hypocorisms in Swedish. Derived hypocorisms usually only allow short stem vowels, followed by a long consonant. In accordance with this rule, the length of any long vowel in the stressed syllable must be reduced while any single consonant following the stressed stem vowel has to be lengthened. Final consonant clusters are reduced to the final element in the cluster that is subsequently lengthened. The stem of a hypocorism may include an initial consonant or a consonant cluster, yielding a structure (C_{0-3})VCC (SAG 2: 127). A diminutive suffix is attached to the altered stem: typically *-e/-an* for male given names, and *-(s)a(n)/-i* for female ones. The suffix *-an* can occur with both male (*Stig* → *Stick-an*) and female given names (*Betty* → *Bett-an*).

(12) hypocoristic forms of male given names
    Knut → Knut-te
    Olof → Ol-le
    Manfred → Mann-e
    Lars → Lass-e
    Robert → Robb-an

(13) hypocoristic forms of female given names
    Gun → Gun-san
    Birgitta → Bigg-an, Margareta → Magg-an
    Ann-Kristin/Ann-Katrin/Annika → Ank-i
    Susanne → Suss-i, Katarina → Katt-i

Surnames can be used as hypocorisms as well: here, the suffix -*is* attaches to the unaltered first syllable of the name: *Lövgren* → *Löv-is*, *Eklund* → *Ek-is*.

Nouns derived by the suffix -*o* are bisyllabic and allow only for short stem vowels. Thus the base word may need to be shortened beforehand, as in *neggo* 'negative person' with a short vowel vs. a long vowel in its (clipped) base *negativ* 'negative'.

4.1.2 Prefixation

Native prefixes used in nominal derivation in Swedish are shown in Table 3.6 (for borrowed prefixes and prefixes used in neoclassical word-formation cf. section 6). The prefixes *icke-*, *miss-* and *van-* negate the meaning of the base. The prefix *gen-* 're-/against' adds a reciprocal or a contrastive meaning, the prefix *sam-* 'co-' an associative meaning, and the prefix *sär-* 'special/apart' a deliminative meaning.

Tab. 3.6: Prefixes in nominal derivation.

Prefix	Base word		Prefixed noun	
gen-	gåva	'gift'	gengåva	against-gift 'gift in return'
	bo	'inhabitant'	genbo	against-inhabitant 'inhabitant of the flat/room across the hall'
icke-	rökare	'smoker'	ickerökare	'non-smoker'
miss-	förhållande	'ratio'	missförhållande	'disproportion'
o-	tur	'luck'	otur	unluck 'bad luck'
	gräs	'grass'	ogräs	ungrass 'weed'
sam-	liv	'life'	samliv	'cohabitation'
sär-	klass	'class'	särklass	'special class' or 'class of it's own'
van-	heder	'honour'	vanheder	'disgrace'
	makt	'power'	vanmakt	'powerlessness'

4.2 Adjectival derivation

4.2.1 Suffixation

Adjectival derivation is achieved by suffixation and prefixation. Suffixes used for yielding deverbal adjectives comprise -*lig*, -*sam*, -*bar*, -*abel* such as *skad-lig* 'deleterious', *prat-sam* 'talkative', *vrid-bar* 'turnable', *diskut-abel* 'debatable'. De-

Tab. 3.7: Suffixes in adjectival derivation in Swedish.

Suffix	Base category	Base word		Derived adjective	
-aktig	N	mardröm	'nightmare'	mardrömaktig	'nightmarish'
-artad	N	pekpinne	'pointer'	pekpinneartad	'shaped like a pointer'
-bar	V	bära	'to bear'	bärbar	'portable'
-enlig	N	norm	'norm'	normenlig	'in accordance to the norm'
-ig	N	pop	'pop (music)'	poppig	'trendy'
	V	huttra	'to shiver'	huttrig	'shivering'
	[Adj+N]$_{NP}$	blek nos	'pale nose'	bleknosig	'having a pale nose'
	[Q+N]$_{NP}$	tre spalter	'three columns'	trespaltig	'having three columns'
	[V+N]$_{VP}$	frukta Gud	'to fear God'	gud(s)fruktig	'god-fearing'
		tåla stryk	'to endure beating'	stryktålig	'tough'
	[V+Adv]$_{VP}$	hitta på	'to excogitate, invent'	påhittig	'inventive'
-isk	N	film	'film'	filmisk	'cinematic'
-lig	N	landskap	'scenery'	landskaplig	'scenic'
-mässig	N	affär	'shop, business'	affärsmässig	'businesslike'
-s	[Q+N]$_{NP}$	tre veckor	'three weeks'	treveckors	'three week's (vacation)'
-sk	PropN	Mendel		mendelsk	'Mendelian'
-t/-(a)d/ -dd	V	larma	'to alarm'	larmad	'wired (to an alarm system)'
	[Adj+N]$_{NP}$	röd näsa	'red nose'	rödnäst	'red-nosed'
		lång hals	'long neck'	långhalsad	'long-necked'
		brun öga	'brown eye'	brunögd	'brown-eyed'
		torr sko	'dry shoe'	torrskodd	'having dry shoes'

nominal adjectives are derived by the suffixes -lig, -s, -isk, -sk: man-lig 'manly', flik-ad 'patched', geograf-isk 'geographical', tegnér-sk 'Tegnerian', göteborg-sk 'from Gothenburg'. Adjectives can be derived from an adjectival base as well, using the suffixes -lig, -aktig: sjuklig 'ailing', sötaktig 'sweetish'.

Adjectives like *stryktålig* 'tough, ruggedized', *gud(s)fruktig* 'god-fearing', *påhittig* 'inventive' can be analysed as derived by adding the suffix *-ig* to an univerbated phrase with the structure [V+N]$_{VP}$ or [V+Adv]$_{VP}$ (SAG 2: 184). However, in all these examples, an alternative analysis is possible: *Stryktålig* can be analysed as a compound comprising of *stryk* 'stroke' as a nominal left constituent, and the adjective *tålig* 'resistant' as right constituent: [[stryk]$_N$[tålig]$_{Adj}$]$_{Adj}$. *Svenska Akademiens ordlista* (SAOL 2006) lists several adjectives with a noun as first and *tålig* as second constituent: *slagtålig* 'impact resistant', *stresstålig* 'stress resistant', *tvättålig* 'detergent resistant'. The adjective *tålig* 'resistant' for its part is derived from the verb *tåla* 'to endure' by the productive adjectival suffix *-ig*. *Påhittig* 'inventive' is more probably derived from the verb *påhitta* 'to invent' to which the suffix *-ig* is added, thus [[påhitt]$_V$-ig$_{Adj}$]$_{Adj}$. *Gud(s)fruktig* 'god-fearing' can be analysed as derived from the compound noun *gudsfruktan* 'fear of God' a compound noun [[gud]$_N$[s][fruktan]$_N$]$_N$ to which again the suffix *-ig* is added. The proposed analyses differ from the ones in *Svenska Akademiens Grammatik* (SAG 2 1999) but are consistent with the use of the productive adjectival suffix *-ig* in denominal and deverbal adjectives, and conform to the morpheme boundaries as marked in *Svenska Akademiens Ordbok* (SAOB 1893–) and in SAOL (2006).

4.2.2 Prefixation

The prefixes used with an adjectival base (cf. Table 3.8) can be divided into two groups: negating and intensifying. The native prefixes *o-*, *miss-*, *icke-* yield adjectives with meanings complementary or contrary to the meaning of the base. Other prefixes with complementary semantics are *in-/il-/im-/ir-*, which are only used with bases of Latin origin, and *a-*, which occurs with bases of Greek or Latin origin (cf. section 6). Further neoclassical prefixes in adjectival derivation comprise the intensifying *extra-*, *hyper-*, *super-*, *ultra-*, *ärke-*, which however are only occasionally added to an adjectival base and are more common in noun derivation.

The prefixes *stört-* 'absolutely' and *döds-* 'death's' were originally used as a first constituent in compounds of the type AdvAdj and [N+Adj]$_{NP}$, respectively, but have acquired an additional prefix-like intensifying meaning. In present-day Swedish, however, they are not as frequent in this function as the intensifying affixoids *jätte-* or *skit-*. The diminutive prefix *pytte-* 'tiny' (from *pytte* 'small boy') is only used with the adjective *liten* (pl. *små*) 'small'. The use of the prefixes *ill-* 'ill' and *knall-* 'bang' is restricted to colour adjectives as bases.

Tab. 3.8: Prefixed adjectives in Swedish.

Prefix	Base word		Prefixed adjective	
döds-	skön	'beautiful'	dödsskön	'very beautiful'
icke-	kyrklig	'ecclesiastical'	ickekyrklig	'non-ecclesiastical'
ill-	grön	'green' (only colour adj)	illgrön	'poisonous green'
knall-	gul	'yellow' (only colour adj)	knallgul	'bright yellow'
miss-	klädsam	'becoming' (clothes)	missklädsam	'unbecoming'
o-	tålig	'patient'	otålig	'impatient'
pytte-	liten	'small'	pytteliten	'tiny'
sär-	svensk	'Swedish'	särsvensk	'typical only for Sweden'
stört-	skön	'beautiful'	störtskön	absolutely beautiful 'very beautiful'

4.3 Verbal derivation

Derived verbs can be formed by adding a verb-yielding suffix to a base which belongs to one of the following word classes: nouns, adjectives, pronouns, or quantifier. The most productive verbal suffix is -*a*, which creates regular verbs of the verbal class 1: *mejl* 'e-mail' → *mejla* 'to e-mail'. Most prefixes used in verbal derivation are loans from (Middle) Low German or from classical languages, but the prefixes *gen-* 're-/against' and the negating *miss-*, and *van-* are native.

4.3.1 Suffixation

Productive suffixes in verbal derivation comprise -*a*, -*na*, -*era*, -*isera*, -*(i)fiera* of which -*a* is the most frequently used and renders denominal and deadjectival verbs. The suffixes -*a* and -*na* are of native origin while -*era*, -*isera*, -*(i)fiera* are loans from Latin (via Low German or French).

Denominal and deadjectival verbs in Swedish become weak verbs of the sole productive conjugation 1. While verbs of the other conjugations show the suffix -*a* only in infinitives (cf. the conjugation 2 verb *köpa* (infinitive) 'to buy' – *köper* (present tense), *köpte* (past tense), *köpt* (supine)), conjugation 1 verbs retain the suffix -*a* in all their inflected forms: *mejla* (infinitive) 'to e-mail', *mejlar* (present tense), *mejlade* (past tense), *mejlat* (supine). The suffix -*a* in conjugation 1 verbs

Tab. 3.9: Productive suffixes in verbal derivation.

Suffix	Base category	Base word		Derived verb	
-a	N	bil	'car'	bila	'to travel by car'
		tejp	'tape'	tejpa	'to tape'
		idrott	'sports'	idrotta	'to go in for sports'
	Adj	lugn	'calm'	lugna	'to calm'
		snål	'scrimpy'	snåla	'to scrimp'
	Pro	du	'you.sg'	dua	'to address informally'
	Q	en	'one'	ena	'to unite'
-era	Adj	intensiv	'intensive'	intensivera	'to intensify'
	N	motiv	'motive'	motivera	'to motivate'
-ifiera	N	exempel	'example'	exemplifiera	'to exemplify'
	Adj	intensiv	'intensive'	intensifiera	'to intensify'
-isera	N	pulver	'powder'	pulv(e)risera	'to pulverise'
	Adj	popular	'popular'	popularisera	'to popularise'
-na	Adj	kall	'cold'	kall-na	'to become cold'

is notoriously difficult to analyse and has been classified either as an inflectional (e.g., Josefsson 1997) or as a derivational morpheme (e.g., Söderbergh 1968; Thorell 1981 and 1984; SAG 2: 36–37, 518–519). Teleman, Hellberg and Andersson (SAG 2: 519) consider verbs such as *majla* 'to e-mail' (← *mejl* 'e-mail'), *bila* 'to drive a car' (← *bil* 'car') or *lugna* 'to calm' (← *lugn* 'calm') as derivatives.

The suffixes *-era* and *-a* can attach to a nominal base to render a derived verb: *charma/charmera* 'to charm', *chocka/chockera* 'to shock', *skissa/skissera* 'to sketch', *bomba/bombardera* 'to bomb', *funka/fungera/funktionera* 'to function'. The shorter verbal derivates rendered by the suffix *-a* belong to a more colloquial style compared to the longer variants. In the case of *funka/fungera/funktionera* 'to function' there are even three levels of formality, *fungera* being the neutral term while *funka* is marked as colloquial and *funktionera* is only used as a technical term (SAOL 2006: 244). The suffix *-era* is used in higher registers due to its being attached mostly to bases of Latin origin, which in turn were associated with academic discourse.

A productive suffix rendering deadjectival verbs with inchoative semantics *-na* include: *svartna* 'to blacken', *kallna* 'to get cold', *mjukna* 'to soften' *hårdna* 'to harden', *(in)sjukna* 'to become ill', *(till)friskna* 'to convalesce'. Unproductive derivational suffixes in verbs with an inchoative or resultative meaning derived form adjectives comprise *-ga, -ka, -ska, -ra, -sa, -ta* as in *vidga* 'to broaden', *svalka* 'to begin to cool', *torka* 'to dry', *minska* 'to reduce', *mildra* 'to soften', *snävra* 'to narrow', *rensa* 'to clean', *hetsa* 'to bait', *fetta* 'to grease', *hetta* 'to heat'.

Swedish verbs can be derived from adjectives ending in *-iv* by adding either the suffix *-era* or *-isera*: *effektivera/effektivisera* 'to make more efficient', *relativera/relativisera* 'to relativise'. Again, the longer form belongs to a higher register. The suffix *-isera* yields deadjectival (*brutalisera* 'to brutalise') or denominal verbs (*pulverisera* 'to pulverise', *finlandisera* 'to finlandise'). Other adjectival and nominal bases require the suffix *-ifiera*, cf. *personifiera* 'to impersonate', *russifiera* 'to russify'. The distribution of *-isera* and *-ifiera* is lexically determined.

4.3.2 Prefixation

Prefixes can be added to a simplex verb *skriva* 'to write' → *beskriva* 'to describe', *söka* 'to seek' → *ansöka* 'to apply for', to a prefixed verb *fördela* 'to distribute' → *omfördela* 'to redistribute', or to a verb derived by suffixation *finansiera* 'to finance' → *refinansiera* 'to refinance', *vård* 'to care' → *vårda* 'to take care of' → *vanvårda* 'to neglect'. The prefixes *be-* and *för-* are unstressed, while the others listed in Table 3.10 bear word stress.

Tab. 3.10: Prefixes in verbal derivation in Swedish.

Prefix	Base word		Prefixed verb	
an-	ropa	'to shout'	anropa	'to call'
be-	skriva	'to write'	beskriva	'to describe'
bi-	stå	'to stand'	bistå	'to support'
er-	nå	'to reach'	ernå	'to achieve'
för-	dela	'to divide'	fördela	'to distribute'
gen-	gälda	'to pay'	gengälda	'to repay'
hop-	skriva	'to write'	hopskriva	'to write as one word'
miss-	tolka	'to interpret'	misstolka	'to misinterpret'
sär-	skriva	'to write'	särskriva	'to write apart'
und-	vika	'to give way'	undvika	'to avoid'
van-	tolka	'to interpret'	vantolka	'to misinterpret'
veder-	lägga	'to lay'	vederlägga	'to refute'

The prefix *be-* renders transitive verbs from an intransitive verbal base: *svara* + PP → *besvara* + N 'to answer'. The prefix *för-* alters the aktionsart (lexical aspect) of the verbal base it is added to: *bränna* 'to burn' → *förbränna* 'to burn up'. The meaning of the derived verb can even be identical to the meaning of its base, cf. *bestraffa=straffa* 'to punish', but again, the derived verb is often associated with higher registers. Thus the prefixed verbs *befläcka* 'to stain' and *förhjälpa* 'to help' are marked for higher style than *fläcka* 'to stain' and *hjälpa* 'to help', which lack a prefix.

Only the prefixes *gen-* 're-/against', *hop-* 'together', *miss-* 'wrong', and *sär-* 'special/apart' are native, *an-*, *be-*, *bi-*, *er-*, *för-*, *sär-*, *van-*, and *veder-* originally occurred in (Low) German loanwords but became common with native bases as well (cf. also section 6).

4.4 Adverbial derivation

4.4.1 Suffixation

Adverbs in Swedish can be derived by adding an adverbial-forming suffix to a base belonging to one of the following word classes: nouns, adjectives, verbs, quantifier, pronouns, adverbs, or univerbated phrases. Suffixes used in adverbial derivation comprise *-vis*, *-ligen*, *-en*, *-falt*, *-tals*, *-ledes*, *-lunda*, *-stans*, *-e*, *-s*, *-a* of which only *-vis*, and to some extent *-ledes* are productive (cf. Table 3.11).

Tab. 3.11: Suffixes in adverbial derivation in Swedish.

Suffix	Base category	Base word		Derived adverb	
-a	Adv	bort	'away (movement)'	borta	'away (state)'
	Adj	lik	'similar'	lika	'equally'
	[Adj+N]_{NP}	bar fot	'bare foot'	barfota	'barefoot'
-e	Adv	ner	'down (movement)'	nere	'down (state)'
		ut	'out (movement)'	ute	'outside (state)'
-en	Adj –ig	tydlig	'clear'	tydligen	'clearly'
		laglig	'legal'	lagligen	'legally'
-falt	N	hundra	'100'	hundrafalt	'hundredfold'
	Q	många	'many'	mångfalt	'many times'

Tab. 3.11 (continued)

Suffix	Base category	Base word		Derived adverb	
-ledes	N	telefon	'telephone'	telefonledes	'over the phone'
		land		landledes	'overland'
	Adv	så	'so'	således	'thus'
		lika	'alike'	likaledes	'likewise'
-ligen	Adj	säker	'certain'	säkerligen	'certainly'
		ny	'new, recent'	nyligen	'recently'
-lunda	Adv	så	'so'	sålunda	'thus'
	Pro	några	'some.pl'	någorlunda	'fairly'
		inga	'none.pl'	ingalunda	'by no means'
-s	PP	ut om land	'out of country'	utomlands	'abroad'
-stans	Pro	någon	'some'	någonstans	'somewhere'
		ingen	'none'	ingenstans	'nowhere'
-t	Adj	snabb	'quick'	snabbt	'quickly'
		snar	'quick'	snart	'soon'
	Adv	var	'where'	vart	'whereto'
-tals	N	hundra	'100'	hundratals	'by hundreds'
-vis	N	nation	'nation'	nationsvis	'by country'
	N	hundra	'100'	hundravis	'by hundreds'
	Adv	möjligt	'possibly'	möjligtvis	'possibly'
		lyckligt	'happily'	lyckligtvis	'luckily'

Deadjectival adverbs derived by *-t* are formally identical with the neuter form of the adjective. The *-t* derivation is a productive pattern, and even if the original adjective and the derived adverb are usually close in meaning (cf. *snabb* 'quick' → *snabbt* 'quickly'), there are a few exceptions. Thus the adjective *snar* 'quick' is semantically only remotely related to the derived adverb *snart* 'soon' (cf. Thorell 1981: 154).

4.4.2 Prefixation

In adverbial prefixation, the native prefixes *mis-* and *o-* are productive, yielding a negation of the base they are attached to.

Tab. 3.12: Native prefixes in adverbial derivation in Swedish.

Prefix	Base word		Prefixed adverb	
miss-	nöjt	'contentedly'	missnöjt	'discontentedly'
o-	lika	'same'	olika	'differently'
	gärna	'willingly'	ogärna	'unwillingly'

5 Conversion

Word-formation through conversion is usually regarded a special case of derivation (Booij 2007: 5). In conversion, the word class of a lexeme is altered without this being overtly marked on the lexeme itself. In Swedish, conversion renders nouns, adjectives and prepositions. Converted nouns derived from adjectives denoting a quality become neuter in gender. Converted nouns derived from adjectives denoting other properties are of common gender. Adjectives converted from nouns can only be used in predicative position: *Kaffet är slut* 'The coffee is used up'. When adjectives derived from adverbs are used as attributes in a noun phrase they do not usually show agreement in gender and number with the head noun: *Det är ett avsides hus/en avsides stad* 'It is a remote house/city' where *hus* 'house' is a neuter and *stad* 'city' a noun of common gender. An exception to this rule is the adjective (< adverb) *lagom* 'just right' which can show agreement with the head of the nominal phrase: *Det är ett lagomt hus, Det är lagoma hus* 'It is a just-right house / They are just-right houses' where the adjective hosts the neuter agreement suffix *-t* and the plural agreement suffix *-a*, respectively.

Nouns can be derived from verbs in a process sometimes characterised as conversion (cf. SAG 2). The resulting nouns differ from the verb in lacking the verbal ending *-a*. If conversion is defined as a change of word class only (cf. Booij 2007: 5; Haspelmath and Sims 2010: 39, 324), such a difference can serve as an argument for analysing word-formation processes such as *skrika* 'to shout' → *skrik* 'a shout' or *torka* 'to dry' → *tork* 'dryer', not as instances of conversion but rather of derivation (cf. Thorell 1981: 85 and Thorell 1984: 76; cf. also Söderbergh 1968: 182–183 who only lists V → N conversions which fall under the definition of conversion cited above, e.g., *röka* 'to smoke' → *ett röka* 'a smoke/a cigarette').

Present participles in Swedish are formed by adding the suffix *-ande/-ende* to a verbal base: *skriva* 'to write' → *skrivande* 'writing', *le* 'to smile' → *leende* 'smiling'. Some present participles function as nouns as well and should thus be classified as instances of Adj → N conversion.

Tab. 3.13: Conversion in Swedish.

Adj → N	ljus	'light, pale'	ljus	'a light'
	hög	'high'	hög	'height'
	svensk	'Swedish'	svensk	'a Swede'
	liberal	'liberal'	liberal	'a liberal'
	leende	'smiling'	leende	'smile'
	studerande	'studying'	studerande	'student'
Adv → Adj	avsides	'aside'	avsides	'remote'
N → Adj	slut	'end'	slut	'used up/at an end'
	synd	'sin'	sin	'pity'

6 Borrowed word-formation and neoclassical word-formation

During the Middle Ages, Swedish borrowed lexemes extensively from Low German. Frequent prefixes and suffixes in the borrowed contact language lexemes even became productive in Swedish. Some examples are the prefixes *an-*, *be-*, *för-*, *und-*, used in nominal and verbal derivation, cf. *anropa* 'to call', *beundra* 'to admire', *förlust* 'loss', *undvika* 'to avoid', and the suffixes *-else*, *-eri*, *-ska* used in nominal derivation, cf. *födelse* 'birth', *bedrageri* 'fraud', *sjuksköterska* 'nurse'. The suffixes *-else/-eri* and *-het* yield abstract nouns, and the suffix *-ska* nouns denoting female human referents.

Tab. 3.14: Low German affixes in Swedish.

Affix	Base category	Base word		Derived word	
an-	V	ropa	'to shout'	anropa	'to call'
be-	V	kämpa	'to struggle'	bekämpa	'to struggle with'
		röra	'to move'	beröra	'to touch'
för-	V	driva	'to drive'	fördriva	'to drive away'
und-	V	vika	'to back off'	undvika	'to avoid'
ur-	N	bild	'picture'	urbild	'archetype'
-else	V	baka	'to bake'	bakelse	'bisquit/cookie'

Tab. 3.14 (continued)

Affix	Base category	Base word		Derived word	
-eri	N	förräddare	'traitor'	förräderi	'treachery'
	Adj	pikant	'spicy'	pikanteri	'piquancy'
	V	brygga	'to brew'	bryggeri	'brewery'
-het	Adj	stolt	'proud'	stolthet	'pride'
-ska	N-are	sångare	'singer'	sångerska	'female singer'
		sjukskötare	'hospital nurse'	sjuksköterska	'female hospital nurse'

Some neoclassical elements are productive in Swedish word-formation, e.g., the negating *in-/il-/im-/ir-*, the intensifying *hyper-*, *super-*, *ultra-*, or the multiplying *multi-*, *poly-*, *bi-* (on neoclassical word-formation, cf. Wollin 2009). Most of the prefixed neoclassical elements can be added not only to stems of Greek or Latin origin but to native ones as well, cf. *ljud* 'sound' → *ultraljud* 'ultra sound'. Suffixed neoclassical elements on the other hand are usually only found in borrowed lexemes: *an-arki* 'anarchy', *tele-fon* 'telephone', *holo-gram*, *tele-graf* 'telegraph', *euro-krat* 'Eurocrat', *bio-log* 'biologist', *auto-mat*, *astro-naut*, *ergo-nom* 'ergonomist'. The neoclassical element *-tek* can be combined with native stems. Table 3.15 provides a (non-exhaustive) list of combining forms in neoclassical word-formation in Swedish.

Tab. 3.15: Neoclassical elements in Swedish word-formation.

a-	asocial	'anti-social'
	asymmetri	'asymmetry'
anti-	antirojalist	'antiroyalist'
bi-	bipolaritet	'bipolarity'
	bikonkav	'biconcave'
ärke-	ärkefiende	'arch enemy'
ex-	expresident	'ex-president'
extra-	extraföreställning	'extra show'
	extralång	'extra long'
il-/im-/in-/ir-	illegal	
	impopulär	'unpopular'
	inaktiv	'inactive'
	irrational	

Tab. 3.15 (continued)

hyper-	hyperinflation	'hyperinflation'
	hyperortodox	'hyperorthodox'
hypo-	hypostas	'hypostasis'
kontra-	kontraspionage	'counterespionage'
	kontraproduktiv	'counterproductive'
krypto-	kryptofascist	'crypto-fascist'
kvasi-	kvasifilosof	'quasi philosopher'
makro-	makrokosmos	'macrocosm'
maxi(mi)-	maxikjol	'maxi-skirt'
	maximistorlek	'maximal size'
mikro-	mikrokosmos	'microcosm'
mini(mi)-	minikjol	'miniskirt'
	minimistorlek	'minimal size'
mono-	monocentrism	
multi-	mulitmiljonär	'multimillionaire'
	multietnisk	'multiethnic'
poly-	polytheism	
	polycyklisk	'polycyclic'
pro-	prodemokrat	'supporter of democracy'
pseudo-	pseudoproblem	'pseudo-problem'
super-	supermakt	'super-power'
	supermodern	'ultramodern'
ultra-	ultraljud	'ultra sound'
	ultralätt	'ultra-light (adj.)'
-tek	lekotek (← *lek* 'play')	'play library'
	klippotek (← *klippa* 'to cut')	'hairdresser's shop'

7 Blending and clipping

Compounding and derivation are word-formation processes, which yield longer lexemes. The word-formation processes blending and clipping on the other hand reduce the length of a lexeme. Clipping usually preserves the meaning of the original word while blending alters it. Shortening of lexemes often originates in colloquial speech or in the creation of brand names. Blending and clipping do not induce word-class change.

The fusion of two separate lexemes into one yields lexical blends. Examples for blending in Swedish are *svenska* 'Swedish' + *engelska* 'English' → *svengelska* 'Swenglish', or *kälta* + *gnata*, both 'to nag' → *tjata* 'to nag' (<tj-> and <k-> before front vowels are pronounced alike in Swedish).

Clipping is a word-formation method applied to form a shorter version of a word by omitting one or more syllables of it. Clippings can comprise the initial part (usually a syllable) of the original lexeme: *biograf* → *bio* 'cinema', the final part of the original word *automobil* → *bil* 'car', or both the initial and final part: *livförsäkringsbolag* → *livsbolag* 'life insurance company'. The left constituent of a nominal compound can be reduced to its initial letter *tunnelbana* → *t-bana* 'underground', *parkeringsplats* → *p-plats* 'car park'.

Lexemes in Swedish can be abbreviated by reducing them to their initial letters which then can be read as an ordinary word (acronyms), e.g., <u>S</u>venska <u>A</u>eroplan <u>A</u>kti<u>e</u>bolaget 'Swedish Airplane Inc.' → *Saab* [sa:b]. Alphabetisms on the other hand are abbreviated words formed by selecting the initial letters of a compound word or a phrase. The letters are pronounced with their value in the alphabet: <u>A</u>llmänna <u>I</u>drotts<u>k</u>lubben 'The general sports club' → *AIK* [a: i: ko:]. The alphabet value of the letters in some acronyms can even be spelled out: *bh=behå* 'bra', *TV=tv=teve* 'television'. The name of the publishing house *Esselte* also belongs to this group: the original form *Sveriges LitografiskaTryckerier* 'Sweden's Lithographic Printing houses' was abbreviated *SLT*, pronounced [es: el: te:] which subsequently was spelled *Esselte* (Thorell 1981: 162).

For an analysis of clipping in Swedish compared to other North Germanic languages, cf. Nübling and Duke (2007).

8 References

Adelswärd, Viveka (2001): *Ord på glid*. Stockholm: Bromberg.
Allén, Sture, Martin Gellerstam and Sven-Göran Malmgren (1989): *Orden speglar samhället*. Stockholm: Allmänna Forlaget.
Andersson, Peter (2003): Ordbildningselementet *-vänlig*: Om produktivitet, suffixstatus och grammatikalisering. In: Sven-Göran Malmgren and Arne Olofsson (eds.), *Åtta ordbildningsstudier*, 1–10. Göteborg: Göteborgs universitet.
Ascoop, Kristin (2005): Affixoidhungrig? Skitbra! Status und Gebrauch von Affixoiden im Deutschen und Schwedischen. *Germanische Mitteilungen* 62: 17–28.
Askedal, John Ole (2016): Norwegian. In: Peter O. Müller, Ingeborg Ohnheiser, Susan Olsen and Franz Rainer (eds.), *Word-Formation. An International Handbook of the Languages of Europe*. Vol. 4, 2525–2554. Berlin/Boston: De Gruyter Mouton.

Booij, Geert (2007): *The Grammar of Words. An Introduction to Morphology.* Oxford: Oxford University Press.

Braunmüller, Kurt (2007): *Die skandinavischen Sprachen im Überblick.* Tübingen: Francke.

Bruce, Gösta (1977): *Swedish Word Accents in Sentence Perspective.* Malmö: Gleerup.

Dehé, Nicole (2025): Particle verbs in Germanic. In: Peter O. Müller, Susan Olsen and Franz Rainer (eds.), *Word-Formation – Special Patterns and Restrictions*, 85–102. Berlin/Boston: De Gruyter Mouton.

Delsing, Lars Olof (2002): Svenskt foge-s. *Folkmålsstudier* 41: 67–78.

Fuhrhop, Nanna and Sebastian Kürschner (2025): Linking elements in Germanic. In: Peter O. Müller, Susan Olsen and Franz Rainer (eds.), *Word-Formation – Special Patterns and Restrictions*, 55–70. Berlin/Boston: De Gruyter Mouton.

Götzsche, Hans (2016): Danish. In: Peter O. Müller, Ingeborg Ohnheiser, Susan Olsen and Franz Rainer (eds.), *Word-Formation. An International Handbook of the Languages of Europe.* Vol. 4, 2505–2524. Berlin/Boston: De Gruyter Mouton.

Haspelmath, Martin and Andrea D. Sims (2010): *Understanding Morphology.* London: Hodder.

Hellquist, Elof (1922): *Svensk ordbildningslära från historisk synpunkt.* Lund: Gleerup.

Hellquist, Elof (1980): *Svensk etymologisk ordbok.* Lund: Liber Läromedel.

Herslund, Michael and Finn Sørensen (eds.) (1993): *The Nordex Project. Lexical Studies in the Scandinavian Languages.* København: Institut for Datalingvistik, Handelshøjskolen i København.

Hinchliffe, Philip and Ian Holmes (1994): *Swedish. A Comprehensive Grammar.* London/New York: Routledge.

Inghult, Göran (1968): Ord med suffixed -is i svenskan. *Språkvård* 4: 9–15.

Josefsson, Gunlög (1997): *On the Principles of Word Formation in Swedish.* Lund: Lund University Press.

Josefsson, Gunlög (1998): *Minimal Words in a Minimal Syntax. Word Formation in Swedish.* Amsterdam/Philadelphia: Benjamins.

Josefsson, Gunlög (2002): *Tjänis, knäppis* och *brallis* – om suffixet -is i modern svenska. URL http://person2.sol.lu.se/GunlogJosefsson/is.okt02.pdf [last access 11 May 2012].

Josefsson, Gunlög (2005): *Ord.* Lund: Studentlitteratur.

Kürschner, Sebastian (2007): Grenzgänger zwischen Flexion und Wortbildung: Zur Geschichte des dänischen Fugen-s. In: Wolfgang Behschnitt and Elisabeth Herrmann (eds.), *Über Grenzen. Grenzgänge der Skandinavistik. Festschrift zum 65. Geburtstag von Heinrich Anz*, 349–367. Würzburg: Ergon.

Kürschner, Sebastian (2010): *Fuge-n-kitt, voeg-en-mes, fuge-masse* und *fog-e-ord*: Fugenelemente im Deutschen, Niederländischen, Schwedischen und Dänischen. Ein Grenzfall der Morphologie im Sprachkontrast. In: Antje Dammel, Sebastian Kürschner and Damaris Nübling (eds.), *Kontrastive Germanistische Linguistik.* Vol. 2, 827–862. Hildesheim: Olms.

Liljestrand, Birger (1974): *Om svenska ord.* Lund: Studentlitteratur.

Liljestrand, Birger (1993): *Så bildas orden. Handbok i ordbildning.* Lund: Studentlitteratur.

Lundbladh, Carl-Erik (2002): *Prefixlika förleder.Det svenska ordförrådets utveckling 1800–2000* (= ORDAT). Göteborg: Göteborgs universitet.

Malmgren, Sven-Göran (1994): *Svensk lexikologi. Ord, ordbildning, ordböcker och orddatabaser.* Lund: Studentlitteratur.

Malmgren, Sven-Göran (2002a): (Pseudo)suffixen -enlig, -stridig och -vidrig i svenskan 1750–2000. *Folkmålsstudier* 41: 167–176.

Malmgren, Sven-Göran (2002b): Tendenser i svensk ordbildning 1750–2000. In: Svante Lagman, Stig Örjan Ohlsson and Viivika Voodla (eds.), *Svenska språkets historia i Östersöområdet*, 241–252. Tartu: Tartu Ülikool.

Malmgren, Sven-Göran and Arne Olofsson (eds.) (2003): Åtta ordbildningsstudier. Göteborg: Göteborgs universitet.
Mellenius, Ingmarie (1996): On noun-verb compounding in Swedish. *Working Papers* 45: 133–149. Lund: Dept of Linguistics, Lund University.
Noreen, Adolf (1906): *Vårt språk. Nysvensk grammatik i utförlig framställning*. Vol. 7. Lund: Gleerup.
Nübling, Damaris and Janet Duke (2007): Kürze im Wortschatz skandinavischer Sprachen: Kurzwörter im Schwedischen, Dänischen, Norwegischen und Isländischen. In: Jochen A. Bär, Thorsten Roelcke and Anja Steinhauer (eds.), *Sprachliche Kürze. Konzeptuelle, strukturelle und pragmatische Aspekte*, 227–263. Berlin/New York: de Guyter.
Petersen, Hjalmar P. (2016): Faroese. In: Peter O. Müller, Ingeborg Ohnheiser, Susan Olsen and Franz Rainer (eds.), *Word-Formation. An International Handbook of the Languages of Europe*. Vol. 4, 2487–2524. Berlin/Boston: De Gruyter Mouton.
Rosenberg, Maria (2012): NV compounds in Swedish. In: Maria Bloch-Trojnar and Anna Bloch-Rozmej (eds.), *Modules and Interfaces*, 203–220. Lublin: Wydawnictwo KUL.
Rosenberg, Maria (2013): Semantic and formal structure: a corpus-based study of Swedish NN compounds and their French counterparts. In: Claire Thomas and Pius ten Hacken (eds.), *The semantics of word formation and lexicalization*, 102–120. Edinburgh: Edinburgh University Press.
Rosenberg, Maria (2020): Derivational networks in Swedish. In: Lívia Körtvélyessi, Alexandra Bagasheva and Pavol Štekauer (eds.), *Derivational Networks Across Languages*, 203–212. Berlin/Boston: De Gruyter Mouton.
Rosenberg, Maria (2024): The Swedish suffix -is and its place within evaluative morphology. In: Stela Manova, Laura Grestenberger and Katharina Korecky-Kröll (eds.), *Diminutives across Languages, Theoretical Frameworks and Linguistic Domains*, 153–178. Berlin/Boston: De Gruyter Mouton.
SAG 2 = Teleman, Ulf, Staffan Hellberg and Erik Andersson (1999): *Svenska Akademiens Grammatik*. Vol. 2. Stockholm: Norstedts Ordbok.
SAOB (1893–): *Ordbok öfver svenska språket*. Stockholm: Svenska Akademien.
SAOL (2006): *Svenska Akademiens ordlista över svenska språket*. Stockholm: Norstedts Akademiska Förlag.
Söderbergh, Ragnhild (1968): *Svensk ordbildning*. Stockholm: Liber Läromedel.
Söderström, Pelle (2012): Processing Swedish word accents. Evidence from response and reaction times. MA thesis, Centre for languages and literature, Lund University.
Tamm, Fredrik (1900): *Sammansatta ord i nutida svenska*. Uppsala: Almqvist & Wiksell.
Teleman, Ulf (1970): *Om svenska ord*. Lund: Gleerup.
Thorell, Olof (1981): *Svensk ordbildningslära*. Stockholm: Esselte Studium.
Thorell, Olof (1984): *Att bilda ord*. Stockholm: Scriptor.
Wessén, Elias (1943): *Svensk språkhistoria*. Vol. 2: *Ordbildningslära*. Stockholm: Almqvist & Wiksell.
Wollin, Lars (2009): *Inlåning och användning av latinska ord under (yngre) nysvensk tid. Det svenska ordförrådets utveckling 1800–2000* (= ORDAT). Göteborg: Göteborgs universitet.

Þorsteinn G. Indriðason
4 Icelandic

1 Introduction
2 General overview
3 Composition
4 Derivation
5 Conversion
6 Borrowed word-formation and neoclassical word-formation
7 Blending and clipping
8 References

Abstract: Icelandic is a settler's language that has preserved many morphological features of Old Norse. Two main word-formation processes exist in Icelandic: derivation and compounding. In addition one finds several other less productive processes. Icelandic has a rich morphological system in nominals, with four productive cases – nominative, accusative, dative and genitive – and person, number and mood conjugation in verbs.

1 Introduction

Icelandic is originally the language of settlers that immigrated to Iceland in the period of 870–930 AD. The majority of the settlers came from the districts of Hordaland and Sogn og Fjordane in Norway. Among the settlers were also immigrants from Sweden and from Irish-speaking areas. Old Norse was the main language of this era; it had various dialects and is commonly divided into West and East Nordic. Icelandic is a West Nordic language, together with Faroese and Norwegian whereas Danish and Swedish are East Nordic languages. From around 1400 AD Old Norse developed into separate languages with individual distinctive features. In Norwegian, Danish and Swedish the distinction among case forms disappeared. In addition, several other inflectional changes took place. In Icelandic the case system has remained intact until the present day, and this holds to a certain degree for Faroese as well (see Petersen 2016).

Going back to the 19th century, there is a fair amount of literature on Icelandic word-formation of different periods. A comprehensive picture of the development

---
Þorsteinn G. Indriðason, Bergen, Norway

https://doi.org/10.1515/9783111420523-004

is provided in Kvaran (2005: 28–49). According to her, word-formation is mentioned in various textbooks, from the earliest writings in the 19th century and through most of the 20th century. Few of those publications are theoretical but a comprehensive discussion of derivation and compounding can be found in Jóhannesson (1927, 1929). Around 1980, there was a growing interest in word-formation in parallel with similar developments in other countries. The number of books and articles on Icelandic increased. Rögnvaldsson (1990) was a popular textbook in morphology at the University of Iceland. Other major publications were the multimediadisk *Alfræði íslenskrar tungu* (2001), with several chapters on Icelandic morphology, among other things one on word-formation by Bjarnadóttir (2001) and Kvaran (2005), a handbook of Icelandic morphology.

Among other works and compilations on Icelandic morphology are Halldórsson (1969, 1976) on the productivity of foreign derivational suffixes and on the grammaticalization of words to derivational suffixes, Ingólfsson (1979) on the derivational suffix *-ug* and the productivity of the foreign suffix *-heit*, J. H. Jónsson (1980) on the semantics and function of the prefixoid *hálf-*, B. Jónsson (1984, 1987) on various types of compound words and on Icelandic word-formation in general, S. Jónsson (1984) on the difference between productive and "learned" word-formation, Konráðsson (1989) on possible types of compounds and derivations, Rögnvaldsson (1987) on various derivational suffixes and their frequency, Snædal (1992) on the possible length of words, Kvaran (1991–92) on adverbs ending in *-is*, Indriðason (1999, 2000a, 2000b, 2005, 2007, 2008, 2011) on compounds and their relation to syntax, on the relation between morphology and phonology, on the productivity of various derivational suffixes from both a diachronic and a synchronic point of view and on linking compounds in Norwegian, Faroese and Icelandic, Óskarsson (2006, 2009a, 2009b) on the nativization of foreign words and derivational suffixes, Bjarnadóttir (2000, 2002) on various types of compounds and derivations and Jónsdóttir (2005, 2006, 2009, 2010) on the role of the derivational suffixes *-væða*, *-sl(i)*, *-ing* and *-ung*.

Finally, a number of MA theses have been written on word-formation and related issues, both published and unpublished: Thorgeirsdóttir (1986) on prefixes, Svavarsdóttir (1993) on noun inflection, Indriðason (1994) on the lexical phonology of Icelandic, Theódórsdóttir (1996) on the genitive of weak feminine nouns, Gíslason (1996) on the classification of weak verbs, Halldórsson (2002) on the inflection of verbs in Icelandic, and Bjarnadóttir (2005) on compounding and derivation in the generative framework.

2 General overview

In Icelandic, derivation and compounding are the two main processes used to expand the vocabulary. Traditionally, derivation is divided into prefixation and suffixation. Prefixation is used for various purposes, for example, to stress the meaning of the base word, like in *bestur* 'best' → *lang-bestur* 'by far the best', or to express the opposite meaning of the base word, like in *þægur* 'obedient' → *ó-þægur* 'disobedient'.

Derivational suffixes add meaning to the base word in a multitude of ways. In Icelandic, there are suffixes like *-ari* which forms agent nouns from verbs, as in *baka* 'to bake' → *bak-ari* 'baker', *-ing* which forms action nouns as in *birta* 'to publish' → *birt-ing* 'publication', and *-ling* which adds a diminutive meaning to the base word, as in *diskur* 'disk' → *disk-lingur* 'diskette'.

In Icelandic, there is also word-formation with affixoids (prefixoids and suffixoids). An affixoid is an intermediate stage between word and either a prefix or a suffix. It is not an independent word but has a somewhat richer meaning than ordinary affixes. Suffixoids get their full meaning only when they occur with the base word. Examples of word-formation with suffixoids are *skóg-lendi* wooden land 'forest' and *ill-gresi* bad grass 'weed' where the suffixoids are derived from respectively *land* 'land' and *gras* 'grass'.

Also, there are instances of word-formation which are neither prefixation nor suffixation. The change occurs in the base word itself. The base word can be shortened or clipped as in *kalla* 'to call', and *kall* 'shout', or the word-formation can be expressed by sound change as in *brjóta* 'to break' and *brot* 'fracture'. Also, the word can be unchanged (conversion) like in *koma* 'to come' and *koma* 'arrival'.

Some derived words in Icelandic are the result of learned word-formation. Over the years, several attempts have been made to revive suffixes from earlier stages of Icelandic but most of them have failed. The suffix *-ald* is an example of such an attempt. The derived word *mót-ald* 'modem' was formed and presented as a neologism for a modern and widely used instrument.

Several types of compounds exist in Icelandic. In the first place, there are stem compounds where two stems are joined as in *hest-hús* horse house 'stable'. In the second place, there are so-called genitive compounds where the first part (the non-head, or modifier) has the genitive form independently of the case of the second part (the head). The genitival first part can either have the singular form, as in *land-s-lög* land laws 'national laws', or the plural form, as in *orð-a-bók* words book 'dictionary'. This type of compound is interesting in that a non-head seems to be inflected. This has been seen as rather unusual from a linguistic point of view (see, e.g., Perlmutter 1988; Booij 1994 and 1996). Genitive compounding is very productive in Icelandic, compared to similar processes in the neighbouring language of Faroese (see Petersen 2016, section 3.8). This could have something to do with the fact that the genitive in Icelandic is still actively used while the genitive in Faroese has for the most part disappeared (see Thráinsson et al. 2004: 248 and Indriðason 2011). In the third place, there are compounds where the elements *a*, *u* and *i* occur between the stems, but these elements are clearly distinct from the genitive endings. Examples are compounds like *ráð-u-nautur* (gen.sg. *ráð-s*, gen.pl. *ráð-a*) advice giver 'advisor', *tóm-a-hljóð* (gen.sg. *tóms-s*, gen.pl. *tóm-ra*) 'hollow sound', *eld-i-viður* (gen.sg. *eld-s*, gen.pl. *eld-a*) 'fire wood', *rusl-a-fata* (gen.sg. *rusl-s*) garbage bucket 'rubbish bin' and *skell-i-hlátur* (gen.sg. *skell-s*, gen.pl. *skell-a*) clapping laughter 'good laugh'. The linking element can also be *s-* as in the compounds *áhrif-s-breyting* (gen.pl. *áhrif-a*) influence change 'analogi' and *hræsni-s-fullur* (gen.sg. *hræsni*) hypocrisy full 'hypocritic'. Finally, so-called dative compounds can be mentioned (see Bjarnadóttir 2000). This is a small group of compounds where the non-head has the dative form and the head is a past participle, for instance *fánum-prýddur* flags decorated 'decorated with flags', *gulli-blandaður* gold blended 'blended with gold' and *hugsjónum-borinn* ideals filled 'idealistic'. These compounds resemble in many ways so-called incorporation, that is, the movement from verb (which is a participle form) + object to object + verb, as in [[*prýddur*]$_V$[*fánum*]$_{Obj}$]$_{VP}$ → NV compound: [[*fánum*]$_N$-*prýddur*]$_V$].

In the recent literature, there are also discussions about the boundary between word-formation and syntax in Icelandic. There is considerable resemblance between certain genitive compounds and syntactic structures and Indriðason (1999) has argued that these structures are related in certain ways. An example of this is the relation between the genitive compound [[*vél-ar*]$_N$-*hljóð*]$_N$]$_N$ 'machine sound' and the syntactic structure with a nominal head and genitival complement, *hljóð vél-ar* 'sound of a machine'. The former is a word-formation but the latter is a noun phrase with genitival attribute. One way of describing this is to say that the word-formation is the result of applying various operations to the syntactic structure (see Indriðason 1999: 137).

Fairly recently, various examples of phrasal compounds have been documented. The non-head is often a syntactic phrase as in *klippa-líma*$_{VP}$-*verkefni* 'copy-paste project' or an even more complex structure like in *Maðurinn spilaði út bannað-að-gera-grín-að-fötluðum-spilinu* 'The man played his it's-not-allowed-to-make-fun-of-the-handicapped-card' (see Bjarnadóttir 2005: 121–125 for more examples and analysis). Some of these phrases have existed in Icelandic for a long time, like the genitival phrase *sjö vikna* in *sjö-vikna-fasta* 'seven weeks fast'. Phrasal compounds are well documented in languages like English, Dutch and German (see Booij 2007, Meibauer 2007 and Sato 2010). They are interesting and challenge the ideas of those who believe that word-formation and syntax are two independent modules of grammar with their own rules and principles (see Bresnan and Mchombo 1995). And there are those who maintain that phrasal compounds show that word-formation must have at least a limited access to syntactic structures (see Sato 2010).

In Icelandic, a common method to expand the vocabulary is by puristic word-formation. Its goal is to replace all foreign words in the language with freshly created Icelandic words. Over the years many such words, both simple words, derivations and compounds, have been formed and used. Here are some of them (the morphological structure is shown):

Tab. 4.1: Puristic word-formation in Icelandic.

Word-formation	Category	Glossary
sam-úð	N	common-ness 'sympathy'
dæmi-gerð-ur	A	example-made 'typical'
rót-tæk-ur	A	root-admissible 'radical'
tölv-a	N	'computer'
þot-a	N	'jet'
fjöl-miðil-l	N	multi-medium 'mass medium'
van-þróað-ur	A	'undeveloped'
tog-ar-i	N	'trawler'
líf-rœn-n	A	'organic'
fúka-lyf	N	mould-medicine 'antibiotica'
smá-sjá	N	'microscope'

Another common method is to nativise imported compounds. Each part of the compound is then translated to Icelandic. Examples are *aðgangs-orð* 'pass-word', *heila-þvottur* 'brain-wash', *örbylgju-ofn* 'microwave-oven' and *peninga-þvætti* 'money laundring'.

3 Composition

Compounding is a productive type of word-formation in Icelandic. Two types are most common, stem compounds and genitive compounds. The third type, linking compounds, is not as productive as the others. The compounds are mostly right-headed and they can be nouns, adjectives, verbs, numerals, adverbs and prepositions.

3.1 Nominal compounds

It is possible to form the following types of nominal compounds in Icelandic: noun + noun (NN), adjective + noun (AN), verb + noun (VN), pronoun + noun (PronN), quantifier + noun (QN), adverb + noun (AdvN) and preposition + noun (PN). As mentioned in section 2, there also exist phrasal compounds with phrases in non-head position and a noun as a head.

Tab. 4.2: Nominal compounds in Icelandic.

NN	[[hesta]$_N$[maður]$_N$]$_N$	horses man 'rider'
AN	[[háa]$_A$[loft]$_N$]$_N$	high ceiling 'attic'
VN	[[sendi]$_V$[bréf]$_N$]$_N$	send letter 'letter'
PronN	[[sér]$_{Pron}$[viska]$_N$]$_N$	himself wisdom 'eccentricity'
AdvN	[[heim]$_{Adv}$[sókn]$_N$]$_N$	home fetch 'visit'
QN	[[þrí]$_Q$[fótur]$_N$]$_N$	three foot 'tripod'
PN	[[á]$_P$[veita]$_N$]$_N$	on distribution 'irrigation'

The inflection (gender, number and case) is expressed on the last part of the compound. In addition to genitive compounds of the type NN, there are also genitive compounds of the type AN like *sjúkra-skýli* (*sjúk-ur* 'sick') patients shelter 'shelter' and *holdsveikra-nýlenda* (*holdsveik-ur* 'leprous') 'leprouses colony'. Compounds where the first part co-inflects with the latter part as in *lang-a* (nom.) *-töng* (nom.) long-pliers 'middle finger', in the accusative *löng-u-töng*, the genitive *löng-u-tang-ar*, are the result of univerbation, that is: [[langa]$_A$ [töng]$_N$]$_{NP}$ → compound: [[langa]$_A$[töng]$_N$]$_N$.

In some compounds, individual word parts have coalesced into one in the course of time. As a result of that, language users do not have any knowledge of how the word was previously composed. Only historical grammarians or etymologists can figure out the original motivation. Examples of words which are simple words today but are historically compounds are *fjós* 'cowshed' < *fé-hús* 'livestock house', *frjáls* 'free' < *frí-háls* 'free neck' and *Noregur* 'Norway' < *Norð-vegur* 'North road'.

3.2 Adjectival compounds

It is possible to form the following types of adjectival compounds in Icelandic: noun + adjective (NA), adjective + adjective (AA), verb + adjective (VA), pronoun + adjective (PronA), adverb + adjective (AdvA), quantifier + adjective (QA) and preposition + adjective (PA). As in nominal compounds, the last part is marked for the inflection of the whole compound:

Tab. 4.3: Adjectival compounds in Icelandic.

NA	[[höfuð]_N[lítill]_A]_A	head-small 'small headed'
AA	[[hvít]_A[skeggjaður]_A]_A	'white-bearded'
VA	[[hreyfi]_V[hamlaður]_A]_A	movement-restrained 'handicapped'
PronA	[[sér]_{Pron}[vitur]_A]_A	himself-wise 'eccentric'
AdvA	[[nær]_{Adv}[göngull]_A]_A	near-walked 'importunate'
QA	[[ein]_Q[fættur]_A]_A	'one-legged'
PA	[[eftir]_P[lýstur]_A]_A	after announced 'wanted'

Adjectival compounds inflect like simple adjectives, for example, by degree as in *sérvitur* (positive) 'eccentric' – *sérvitr-ari* (comparative) 'more eccentric' – *sérvitr-astur* (superlative) 'most eccentric'.

3.3 Verbal compounds

It is possible to form the following types of verbal compounds in Icelandic: noun + verb (NV), adjective + verb (AV), verb + verb (VV), pronoun + verb (PronV), adverb + verb (AdvV), quantifier + verb (QV) and preposition + verb (PV) (see Table 4.4).

Tab. 4.4: Verbal compounds in Icelandic.

NV	[[tilrauna]_N[kenna]_V]_V	experiments-teach 'to teach in an experimental way'
AV	[[fljót]_A[afgreiða]_V]_V	fast-expedite 'to expedite fast'
VV	[[bull]_V[sjóða]_V]_V	bubble up-boil 'to boil over'
PronV	[[sér]_{Pron}[merkja]_V]_V	himself-label 'to label specially'
AdvV	[[endur]_{Adv}[greiða]_V]_V	re-pay 'to refund'
QV	[[tví]_Q[panta]_V]_V	'to double-order'
PV	[[til]_P[kynna]_V]_V	to-present 'to announce'

In general, this process is not very productive in Icelandic. Other examples of this type are: *teppa-leggja* (NV) carpet-lay 'to lay a carpet (on)', *jóla-skreyta* (NV) Christmas decorate 'to decorate for Christmas', *kross-festa* (NV) cross-fasten 'to crucify', *áfram-senda* (AdvV) forward send 'to forward', *sundur-greina* (AdvV) apart analyse 'to analyse', *heim-sækja* (AdvV) home fetch 'to visit', *fjór-falda* (QV) 'to quadruple' and *til-færa* (PV) to-bring 'to state'.

3.4 Numerals

Numerals from 1 to 4 inflect for gender and case as in *einn* 'one' (m.) – *ein* (f.) – *eitt* (n.) and *þrír* 'three' (m.) – *þrjár* (f.) – *þrjú* (n.). Numerals from 20 and above are formed as coordinated phrases. The numeral 22 is read *tuttugu og tveir* 'twenty and two', 34 is read *þrjátíu og fjórir* 'thirty and four', 903 is read *níuhundruð og þrír* 'ninehundred and three', i.e. with a compound word *níuhundruð* and coordination with the conjunction *og*. The following are the compound types possible in numerals with *og*:

Tab. 4.5: Compound types in Icelandic numerals.

Compounding	*sex-hundruð* '600', *átta-hundruð* '800', *eitt-þúsund* '1000'
Coordination	*tuttugu og tveir* '22', *þrjátíu og þrír* '33', *fjörutíu og fjórir* '44'
Univerbation	*tuttuguogtveir* '22', *þrjátíuogþrír* '33', *fjörutíuogfjórir* '44'
Coord. + comp.	*sexhundruð og níutíu* '690'

3.5 Adverbial compounds

Adverbial compounds are not frequent in Icelandic, but examples include the following types: noun + adverb (NAdv), adjective + adverb (AAdv), adverb + adverb (AdvAdv), quantifier + adverb (QAdv) and preposition + adverb (PAdv). No examples of verb + adverb (VAdv) or pronoun + adverb (PronAdv) can be found.

Tab. 4.6: Adverbial compounds in Icelandic.

NAdv	[[flug]$_N$[leiðis]$_{Adv}$]$_{Adv}$	flight-ways 'by air'
AAdv	[[rétt]$_A$[hendis]$_{Adv}$]$_{Adv}$	right-hands 'with the right hand'
AdvAdv	[[fram]$_{Adv}$[vegis]$_{Adv}$]$_{Adv}$	forward-road 'from now on'
QAdv	[[ein]$_Q$[hestis]$_{Adv}$]$_{Adv}$	one-horse 'travelling with one horse'
PAdv	[[um]$_P$[fram]$_{Adv}$]$_{Adv}$	about-forward 'extra'

3.6 Prepositional compounds

There are not many compound words with a preposition in head position in Icelandic. Only one type seems to be dominant, i.e. with an adverb in non-head position (see Bjarnadóttir 2005: 120–121):

Tab. 4.7: Prepositional compounds in Icelandic.

Preposition	Compounds	Examples
hjá	fram-hjá	Þau óku framhjá bílnum
'by'	'past'	'They drove past the car'
á	ofan-á	Jón lagðist ofaná manninn
'on'	'on top of'	'Jón lay down on top of the man'
yfir	út-yfir	Þau sigldu útyfir fjörðinn
'over'	'along'	'They sailed along the fjord'

3.7 Affixoids

As mentioned in section 2, affixoids (prefixoids and suffixoids) are a kind of intermediary stage between independent words and affixes. Bjarnadóttir (2005: 227) lists a number of examples of suffixoids, divided into one type that forms nouns and another one that forms adjectives often with *i*-umlaut between the base forms and the suffixoid (base forms in parantheses):

Tab. 4.8: Nominal and adjectival suffixoids.

Nouns		
-viðri (veður 'weather')	of-viðri	too much weather 'tempest'
-ræði (ráð 'advice')	til-ræði	to attack 'assault'
-hafi (hafa 'to have')	hand-hafi	hand keeper 'holder'
-fari (fara 'to go')	geim-fari	space goer 'astronaut'
-lífi (líf 'life')	harð-lífi	hard living 'constipation'
-hýsi (hús 'house')	hjól-hýsi	wheels house 'caravan'
-nefni (nafn 'name')	upp-nefni	up name 'nickname'
-nætti (nótt 'night')	lág-nætti	low night 'midnight'
Adjectives		
-gengur (ganga 'to walk')	hæg-gengur	slow going 'slow'
-vana (vanur 'deprived of something')	and-vana	without breath 'lifeless'
-lægur (liggja 'position')	land-lægur	land stuck 'endemic'
-sýnn (sjón 'vision')	ein-sýnn	one visioned 'narrow minded'
-rækinn (rækja 'pursue')	skyldu-rækinn	duty fulfilling 'conscientious'
-þættur (þáttur 'part')	marg-þættur	many featured 'complicated'
-sær (sjá 'see')	gegn-sær	through seeable 'transparent'
-róma (rómur 'voice')	ein-róma	one voiced 'unanimous'

Indriðason (2007) has argued for the grammaticalization of *líki* 'as something else', that is, its development from being an independent word to being a suffixoid or suffix.

It's not always easy to differentiate between prefixoids and prefixes but the following are probably prefixoids with nouns, adjectives and verbs as base words:

Tab. 4.9: Prefixoids with nouns, adjectives and verbs.

Prefixoids		Base word		Nouns with prefixoids	
aðal-	'main'	atriði	'thing'	aðalatriði	'main thing'
bak-	'behind'	hlið	'side'	bakhlið	'reverse side'
fram-	'forward'	fótur	'foot'	framfótur	'frontal foot'
gagn-	'opposite'	árás	'attack'	gagnárás	'retaliatory strike'
hálf-	'half'	bróðir	'brother'	hálfbróðir	'half brother'

Prefixoids		Base word		Adjectives with prefixoids	
afar-	'very'	feitur	'fat'	afarfeitur	'very fat'
eftir-	'after'	lifandi	'living'	eftirlifandi	'surviving'
frum-	'original'	ortur	'composed'	frumortur	'original'
gjör-	'totally'	ólíkur	'different'	gjörólíkur	'totally different'
hálf-	'half'	íslenskur	'Icelandic'	hálfíslenskur	'half Icelandic'
lang-	'very'	þreyttur	'tired'	langþreyttur	'sick and tired (of something)'
meðal-	'medium'	stór	'big'	meðalstór	'medium size'
ofur-	'super'	ölvi	'drunk'	ofurölvi	'dead drunk'

Prefixoids		Base word		Verbs with prefixoids	
blóð-	'blood'	langa	'to want'	blóðlanga	'to want something badly'
endur-	're'	óma	'to sound'	enduróma	'to echo'
fjar-	'distance'	stýra	'to control'	fjarstýra	'to operate by remote control'
frum-	'original'	semja	'to compose'	frumsemja	'to write an original composition'
gjör-	'totally'	eyða	'to destroy'	gjöreyða	'to destroy completely'
harð-	'hard'	neita	'to deny'	harðneita	'to deny vehemently'
hálf-	'half'	sjóða	'to boil'	hálfsjóða	'to half boil'
hríð-	'rapidly'	versna	'to worsen'	hríðversna	'to worsen rapidly'
kol-	'totally'	falla	'to fall'	kolfalla	'to totally collapse'
nauð-	'thoroughly'	þekkja	'to know'	nauðþekkja	'to know thoroughly'
snar-	'suddenly'	dýpka	'to deepen'	snardýpka	'to deepen suddenly'
þrá-	'repeatedly'	biðja	'to ask'	þrábiðja	'to ask repeatedly'

3.8 Linking elements

Several types of linking compounds exist in Icelandic. By *linking element* I mean all elements between stems in a composition. As mentioned before, there are genitive compounds where the non-head has the genitive form with diverse genitive endings, either singular or plural, and linking compounds with the linking elements *a, i, u* and *s*.

In genitive compounds one finds the genitive endings existing in Icelandic:

Tab. 4.10: Types of genitive compounds in Icelandic.

Gen. endings	Nouns with gen. endings			Genitive compounds		
-ar	vél-ar	(gen.sg.f.)	'machine'	vél-ar-hljóð	(nom.sg.n.)	'machine sound'
-a	bók-a	(gen.pl.f.)	'books'	bók-a-hilla	(nom.sg.f.)	'book shelf'
-s	land-s	(gen.sg.n.)	'land'	land-s-lög	(nom.pl.n.)	'national laws'
-na	nýr-na	(gen.pl.n.)	'kidneys'	nýr-na-aðgerð	(nom.sg.f.)	'kidney operation'
-u	tölv-u	(gen.sg.f.)	'computer'	tölv-u-útskrift	(nom.sg.f.)	'printout'
-ur	næt-ur	(gen.sg.f.)	'night'	næt-ur-gisting	(nom.sg.f.)	'sleepover'

As can be seen above, genitive forms in non-head positions in compounds are identical to the genitive forms found in the inflectional paradigms of individual words.

The linking compounds (see Kvaran 2005: 155) are often archaic as in the examples of *för-u-neyti* 'entourage', from the 19th century, *eld-i-brandur* 'flaming tree', from the 16th century or earlier, and *tóm-a-hljóð* 'hollow sound' from the 18th century. But there are also newer compounds like *drekk-u-tími* drinking time 'pause', *fell-i-hýsi* 'tent trailer' and *dót-a-kassi* 'toy-box', all from the 20th century.

Finally, the linking element of *s*-compounds occurs where one could expect an inflectional ending (*-a(r)*) like in *kúpling-s-diskur* 'clutch disk' (?*kúpling-ar*(gen.sg.)*-diskur*). In other cases, an *-s-* is inserted after feminine nouns which have no genitive ending at all in the paradigm, like *leikfimi* (gen.sg.) – *leikfimi-s-hús* 'gymnastics hall' and *keppni* (gen.sg.) – *keppni-s-skap* 'fighting spirit' (see Indriðason 1999: 116–117). The *s*-compounds have become more frequent in recent years.

4 Derivation

Derivation occurs in various forms in Icelandic. It can be prefixation as in *bíll* 'car' → *einka-bíll* 'private car' or *dæma* 'to judge' → *for-dæma* 'to condemn' or suffixation as in *baka* 'to bake' → *bak-ari* 'baker' and *senda* 'to send' → *send-ing* 'shipment'. Derivation can also be expressed by means of a stem-internal vowel change of Indo-European origin but this type is not productive, *bíða* 'to wait' → *bið* 'waiting' and *ljúka* 'to finish' → *lok* 'end' or with *i*-umlaut and a suffix as in *langur* 'long' → *leng-d* 'length' or *þungur* 'heavy' → *þyng-d* 'weight'.

A prefixal formation is in the same word class as the base word, but prefixation changes the meaning in most cases. Konráðsson (1989: 11–14) divides prefixes in Icelandic into several semantic categories (but as mentioned before some of these can be defined as prefixoids). Prefixes are used to emphasize the meaning of the base as in *afar-* 'very', they can express negative meaning (*van-* 'too little of something' or *ó-* 'dis-'), they can denote position (*ná-* 'near'), time (*ný-* 'newly'), quantity (*marg-* 'poly-'), numbers (*fjór-* 'four-'), the importance of something (*höfuð-* 'main'), or detail (*auka-* 'aside'). Prefixes can also express the dimension (*risa-* 'gigantic') and degree of something (*hálf-* 'half'). They are also used to place strong emphasis on the meaning of the base word, as in *óður* 'mad' → *band-óður* 'raving mad', *skamma* 'to scold' → *hund-skamma* 'to scold forcefully', *fullur* 'drunk' → *blind-fullur* 'dead drunk' and *illur* 'furious' → *ösku-illur* 'absolutely furious'. Prefixes can vary in productivity (see, e.g., Thorgeirsdóttir 1986 and Konráðsson 1989: 17). Prefixes or prefixoids which seem productive are *aðal-*, *einka-*, *grunn-* and *megin-*, those which are most probably productive are *lausa-*, *mis-*, *of-* and *vand-*, those which are probably unproductive are *auð-*, *dverg-*, *inn-* and *síð-*. Prefixes which are clearly unproductive are *að-*, *á-*, *eftir-*, *ger-*, *ná-*, *nær-*, *til-*, *tor-* and *van-*.

Suffixation can form a word of a different word class than the base word. It can, for example, derive a noun from a verb, but sometimes the word class does not change. Suffixes, like prefixes, can also derive a different meaning from that of the base word, for example, when a word denoting an agent or an action is derived from verbs, as in *lækna* 'to heal' → *lækn-ir* 'doctor' and *skipa* 'to order' → *skip-un* 'order', or an instrument, as in *hreyfa* 'to move' → *hreyf-ill* 'motor'. Derivational suffixes, like prefixes, can vary in productivity. The suffix *-leg-* is probably the most productive one. Suffixes like *-ari-*, *-ing-*, *-un-* and *-ug-* are quite productive as well but their productivity is limited in many ways. The suffixes *-ling-* and *-ul-* are semi-productive and *-ald-*, *-erni-*, *-indi-* and *-nað-* have little or no productivity, i.e. they do not form new words in the language today (see, e.g., Indriðason 2008).

4.1 Nominal derivation

4.1.1 Prefixation

Table 4.11 displays a list of common Icelandic prefixes that attach to nouns (see Konráðsson 1989: 15–16):

Tab. 4.11: Prefixes with nouns.

Prefix		Base word		Prefixed noun	
fá	'few'	bjáni	'fool'	fábjáni	'idiot'
inn	'in'	bær	'town'	innbær	'centre'
ofur	'super'	afl	'force'	ofurafl	'superforce'
til	'to'	vist	'stay'	tilvist	'existence'
út	'out'	hverfi	'district'	úthverfi	'suburb'
yfir	'over'	maður	'man'	yfirmaður	'boss'

4.1.2 Suffixation

There are numerous ways to derive nouns by suffixation. I will discuss four groups here: action nouns, agent nouns and instrument nouns derived from verbs; a group of suffixes that are grammaticalized words (see, e.g., Halldórsson 1976); suffixes that diminish the meaning of the base word; and suffixes that are not productive in modern Icelandic.

Action nouns are formed with the suffixes -un, -ing and -ning:

Tab. 4.12: Action nouns.

Suffix	Base word		Derived noun	
-un	hlusta	'to listen'	hlustun	'listening'
	stækka	'to grow'	stækkun	'enlargement, expansion'
-ing	senda	'to send'	sending	'shipment'
	binda	'to bind'	binding	'binding'
-ning	lesa	'to read'	lesning	'reading'
	auka	'to increase'	aukning	'increase'

Several suffixes can form a g e n t nouns. These nouns are in most cases derived from verbs with the suffixes *-ari*, *-andi* and *-i*, but also *-il*, *-uð* and *-ul*, where word-final *-i*, *-r*, *-ur* and *-l* are inflectional endings (see Jónsson 1987: 93–94):

Tab. 4.13: Agent nouns.

Suffix	Base word		Derived noun	
-ari	*rita*	'to write'	*ritari*	'secretary'
	kenna	'to teach'	*kennari*	'teacher'
	telja	'to count'	*teljari*	'counter'
-andi	*stofna*	'to found'	*stofnandi*	'founder'
	selja	'to sell'	*seljandi*	'seller'
	kaupa	'to buy'	*kaupandi*	'buyer'
-i	*lækna*	'to heal'	*lækni-r*	'doctor'
-il	*aka*	'to drive'	*ekil-l*	'driver' (with *i*-umlaut)
-uð	*hugsa*	'to think'	*hugsuð-ur*	'thinker'
	kanna	'to explore'	*könnuð-ur*	'explorer' (with *u*-umlaut)
-ul	*kveða*	'to assert oneself'	*frumkvöðul-l*	'originator'

The suffix *-ari* can also derive an agentive noun from a noun, as in *svik* 'betrayal' → *svik-ari* 'traitor' and *dómur* 'sentence, judgment' → *dóm-ari* 'judge'. It is also possible to derive agent nouns with the suffixoid *-maður* '-man', cf. *flug-maður* 'pilot' and *öku-maður* 'driver'. Additionally, one can derive agent nouns from compound nouns like *geimfar* 'spaceship' → *geimfar-i* 'astronaut', *landnám* 'settlement' → *landnem-i* 'settler' and *farandsala* 'peddle' → *farandsal-i* 'peddler'.

I n s t r u m e n t nouns are formed with the suffixes *-i* and *-il*:

Tab. 4.14: Instrument nouns.

Suffix	Base word		Derived noun	
-i	*kæla*	'to cool'	*kæli-r*	'cooler'
	geyma	'to store'	*geymi-r*	'tank'
-il	*hreyfa*	'to move'	*hreyfil-l*	'motor'

Examples of suffixes which are former words are: *-dóm*, *-skap*, *-leik* and *-átt*. These suffixes derive nouns from nouns and adjectives and they often yield s t a t u s nouns and q u a l i t y nouns:

Tab. 4.15: Word-formation with derivational suffixes which were former nouns.

Suffix	Base category	Base word		Derived noun	
-dóm	A	sjúkur	'sick'	sjúkdóm-ur	'disease'
-átt	N	vinur	'friend'	vinátt-a	'friendship'
-skap	N	drengur	'boy'	drengskap-ur	'honour'
-leik	A	sannur	'true'	sannleik-ur	'truth'

Various suffixes and suffixoids have diminutive meaning. The suffix *-ling* is mainly used as a diminutive suffix, e.g., as in *diskur* 'disk' → *disk-lingur* 'diskette' and *bók* 'book' → *bæk-lingur* (with *i*-umlaut) 'booklet'. But one can also use suffixoids like *-korn*, *-nefna*, *-líki* and *-mynd*, especially if one wants to express the diminutive feature in an ironic way, *piltur* 'boy' → *pilt-korn* 'tiny boy', *tímarit* 'journal' → *tímarits-nefna* 'journal, only by name', *skáldsaga* 'novel' → *skáldsögulíki* 'novel, only by name' and *móðir* 'mother' → *móður-mynd* 'mother, only by name' (see Kvaran 2005: 133).

Several suffixes are probably no longer productive in Icelandic:

Table 4.16: Some non-productive suffixes in Icelandic.

Suffix	Base category	Base word		Derived noun	
-erni	N	faðir	'father'	faðerni	'paternity'
-indi	A	veikur	'sick'	veikindi	'illness'
-nað	N	dugur	'vigor'	dugnað-ur	'drive'

Nouns are also formed by adding suffixes to compound words (see Bjarnadóttir 2005: 170–172). The following categories can be found: nominal compound + suffix, e.g., *búfræði* 'agronomy' → *búfræð-ingur* 'agronomist', *flugumaður* 'infiltrator' → *flugumenn-ska* 'infiltration'; adjectival compound + suffix, e.g., *arfgengur* 'hereditary' → *arfgeng-i* 'heredity', *einlægur* 'sincere' → *einlæg-ni* 'sincerity' and *einstakur* 'unique' → *einstak-lingur* 'individual'. Also, there are nouns derived from verbal compounds: *bólusetja* 'to vaccinate' → *bóluset-ning* 'vaccination', *fjármagna* 'to finance' → *fjármögn-un* 'financing' and *dáleiða* 'to hypnotise' → *dáleið-ari* 'hypnotist'.

4.2 Adjectival derivation

4.2.1 Prefixation

Prefixes with adjectives are, amongst others, the following (see Konráðsson 1989: 15–16 and Kvaran 2005: 125–130):

Tab. 4.17: Prefixes with adjectives.

Prefix		Base word		Prefixed adjective	
af	'very'	gamall	'old'	afgamall	'very old'
all	'very'	góður	'good'	allgóður	'very good'
for	'pre'	spár	'prophetic'	forspár	'predictive'
sí	'always'	grœnn	'green'	sígrœnn	'evergreen'
tor	'not'	læs	'literate'	torlæs	'illiterate'
út	'out'	dauður	'dead'	útdauður	'extinct'
ör	'very'	lítill	'small'	örlítill	'tiny'

4.2.2 Suffixation

The suffix *-leg* forms adjectives and is the most productive suffix in Icelandic, both historically and in the modern language (see Indriðason 2005, 2008). One of the main reasons for this high productivity is that the suffix derives adjectives from base words structured in various ways, as simple words or compounds, either stem compounds or genitive compounds. The suffix also derives adjectives from base words of different word classes, viz. nouns, adjectives, pronouns, adverbs and prepositions and possibly with verbs although such examples are not yet verified (*-ur* is an inflectional ending):

Tab. 4.18: Variety of base words with the suffix *-leg-*.

Base category	Base Word		Derived adjective	
N	aldur	'age'	aldursleg-ur	'old'
A	djarfur	'brave'	djarfleg-ur	'daring, bold'
V	hugsa	'to think'	hugsaleg-ur	'thinking'
Pron	ég	'I'	égleg-ur	'like myself'
Adv	heima	'home'	heimaleg-ur	'domestic'
P	yfir	'above'	yfirleg-ur	'superior'

Adjectives with *-leg* from verbs and prepositions are rare. Other suffixes that derive adjectives are as shown in Table 4.19, *-ur* and *-l* are inflectional endings (see Kvaran 2005: 139–142):

Tab. 4.19: Derivational suffixes which form adjectives.

Suffix	Base category	Base word		Derived adjective	
-(a)ð	V	*bila*	'to break down'	*bilað-ur*	'out of order'
-ótt	N	*skalli*	'baldness'	*sköllótt-ur*	'bold' (with *u*-umlaut)
	N	*flekkur*	'spot'	*flekkótt-ur*	'spotted'
-sk	N	*Ísland*	'Iceland'	*íslensk-ur*	'Icelandic'
	N	*Grænland*	'Greenland'	*grænlensk-ur*	'Greenlandic'
-ug	N	*snjór*	'snow'	*snjóug-ur*	'snowy'
	N	*máttur*	'power'	*máttug-ur*	'mighty'
-ul	V	*athuga*	'to check'	*athugul-l*	'attentive'
	N	*svik*	'betrayal'	*svikul-l*	'deceitful'
	V	*fara*	'to go'	*förul-l*	'someone who travels a lot' (with *u*-umlaut)

The suffixes *-látur*, *-rænn* and *-samur* are all derivational suffixes grammaticalized from independent words in Old Norse (see, e.g., Halldórsson 1976 and Indriðason 2007). They derive adjectives from nouns and adjectives for the most part: *blíður* 'tender' → *blíð-látur* 'tender', *geð* 'mind' → *geð-rænn* 'mental' and *góður* 'kind' → *góð-samur* 'kind'.

4.3 Verbal derivation

4.3.1 Prefixation

There are quite a few prefixes used with verbs (see Konráðsson 1989: 15–16):

Tab. 4.20: Prefixes with verbs.

Prefix	Base word		Prefixed verbs	
af 'off'	*stýra*	'to direct'	*afstýra*	'to prevent'
and 'opposite'	*mæla*	'to speak'	*andmæla*	'to protest'
auð 'empty'	*virða*	'to respect'	*auðvirða*	'to humiliate'

Tab. 4.20 (continued)

Prefix	Base word		Prefixed verbs	
inn 'in'	*leiða*	'to lead'	*innleiða*	'to implement'
mis 'mis'	*stíga*	'to step'	*misstíga*	'to miss one's footing'
tví 'double'	*borga*	'to pay'	*tvíborga*	'to pay the double'
upp 'up'	*skera*	'to cut'	*uppskera*	'to harvest'

4.3.2 Suffixation

In Icelandic, there are not many ways to derive verbs from base words. One can form verbs from a noun with conversion as in *leir* 'clay' → *leir-a* 'to clay'. This is a common process in Icelandic, compare examples like *borð* 'table' → *borð-a* 'to eat', *spil* 'cards' → *spila* 'to play cards', *útvarp* 'radio' → *útvarp-a* 'to broadcast' and *skíði* 'ski' → *skíða* 'to ski'. This type of word-formation is limited to nouns as base words. Another way is to derive verbs from adjectives with *-na* (see Kvaran 2005: 142). The adjectives are mostly colour words as in *blár* 'blue' → *blá-na* 'to become blue' and *gulur* 'yellow' → *gul-na* 'to become yellow', but they can also be of other types: *fölur* 'pale' → *föl-na* 'to become pale', *kaldur* 'cold' → *kól-na* 'to become cold'. Recently, Jónsdóttir (2005) has discussed verbs derived from nouns with *-væða* '-ise'. This seems to be an innovation in Icelandic. *-væða* should probably be regarded as a suffixoid since it cannot occur as an independent word:

Tab. 4.21: Word-formation with *-væða*.

Suffix	Base word		Derived verb	
-væða '-ise'	*raf*	'amber'	*rafvæða*	'to install electricity'
	aumingja	'weakling'	*aumingjavæða*	lit. 'to weakling-ise'
	sjónvarps	'television'	*sjónvarpsvæða*	lit. 'to television-ise'
	ESB	'EU'	*ESBvæða*	lit. 'to EU-ise'
	Laugavegs (street name)		*Laugavegsvæða*	lit. 'to Laugavegur-ise'
	nútíma	'the present'	*nútímavæða*	'to modern-ise'

4.4 Adverbial derivation

4.4.1 Prefixation

Bjarnadóttir (2005: 150–151) lists a number of prefixes that attach to adverbs:

Tab. 4.22: Prefixes with adverbs.

Prefix		Base word		Prefixed adverb	
and	'opposite'	fœtis	'foot'	andfœtis	'positioned head to toe'
		spœnis	'unclear direction'	andspœnis	'opposite, facing'
fjar	'distance'	lendis	'land'	fjar-lendis	'abroad'
fjöl	'multi'	víða	'far and wide'	fjölvíða	'in many places'
for	'pre'	dyris	'door'	fordyris	'in front of the door'
mis	'varying'	lengi	'long time'	mislengi	'various amounts of time'
ó	'not'	keypis	'buy'	ókeypis	'free of charge'
sam	'same'	aldra	'age'	samaldra	'of the same age'
		hliða	'side'	samhliða	'parallel'

4.4.2 Suffixation

Few suffixes form adverbs in Icelandic. From most if not all adjectives in -*leg* one can form adverbs by adding the suffix -*a*. Suffixation with -*is* is also quite common (see Kvaran 1990–91) but not as productive as with *a*. Their base words are for the most parts adjectives:

Tab. 4.23: Suffixes that form adverbs.

Suffix	Base category	Base word		Derived adverb	
-a	A	hrœðilegur	'terrible'	hrœðilega	'terribly'
	A	vinalegur	'friendly'	vinalega	'in a friendly manner'
	A	djarflegur	'bold'	djarflega	'boldly'
-is	N	flugleið	'flight route'	flugleiðis	'by plane'
	A	erlendur	'foreign'	erlendis	'abroad'

In addition to these suffixes, there exist some adverbial compounds where the nature of the adverbial part is unclear. Bjarnadóttir (2005: 123) argues that these parts are fixed or semi-fixed oblique case forms used as adverbs, but they can also be considered as suffixoids:

Tab. 4.24: Adverbs formed with fixed case forms or suffixoids.

Suffixoids		Base category	Base word		Derived adverb	
-konar	'kind of'	Pron	margur	'many'	margskonar	'various'
-skips	'ship'	A	miður	'middle'	miðskips	'in the middle of the ship'
-staðar	'place'	Pron	neinn	'nobody'	neinsstaðar	'nowhere'
-sumars	'summer'	Adv	snemma	'early'	snemmsumars	'early summer'
-tíma	'time'	Pron	einhver	'someone'	einhverntíma	'one day'
-vega	'road'	P	af	'off'	afvega	'lost (one's way)'
-vegar	'road'	Pron	hinn	'other'	hinsvegar	'on the other side'

5 Conversion

In Icelandic, one can find various examples of conversion, i.e. derivations where no material is added to the base word (see, e.g., Booij 2007: 5, 311). Conversion is for the most part a derivation between verb and noun but the direction isn't always clear. Here are some examples that most likely show the direction from verb to noun:

Tab. 4.25: Conversion from verb to noun.

Verb		Noun	
koma	'to come'	koma	'arrival'
þvæla	'to talk nonsense'	þvæla	'nonsense'
ríma	'to rhyme'	ríma	'Icelandic ballad'
sturta (niður)	'to flush (down)'	sturta	'shower'
sýsla	'to work'	sýsla	'administrative district'

And the following are most likely examples of conversion from noun to verb:

Tab. 4.26: Conversion from noun to verb.

Noun		Verb	
perla	'pearl'	*perla*	'to put pearls together'
leira	'clayey ground'	*leira*	'to build something from clay'
pípa	'pipe'	*pípa*	'to bluster'
messa	'mass'	*messa*	'to say mass'
glósa	'comment'	*glósa*	'to write down comments'

6 Borrowed word-formation and neoclassical word-formation

The following types of combination of native and non-native base words and derivational suffixes are found (from Indridason 2005: 59–61, 2008: 109–111; see also Halldórsson 1969):

Tab. 4.27: Types of native and non-native base words and derivational suffixes in Icelandic.

Types of combination	Word-formation		Base word	
Native base word + non-native suffix:	*dugleg-heit*	'effectiveness'	*duglegur*	'effective'
Non-native base word + non-native suffix:	*skikk-elsi*	'figure'	*skikka*	'to give an order'
Non-native base word + native suffix:	*dubb-un*	'dubbing'	*dubba*	'to dubb'

Despite a strict purist language policy in Iceland, there are a considerable number of non-native or borrowed derivational suffixes in the language. Most of them only occur with their non-native base words, like *-sjón* '-tion' and *-elsi* (Danish *-else*) in *spekúlasjón* 'speculation' from the 19th century, *inspírasjón* 'inspiration' from the 20th century, *skrífelsi* 'written text' from the 16th century and *sinnelsi* 'anger' from the 17th century (all datings of examples in this section are approximations). Some derivational suffixes have had a different development. Although, to begin with, they form derived words from non-native base words, they have also over time started to form derived words from native base words. A typical example is the suffix *-heit*, originally from German, but with Danish as an intermediary language. In the period from the 16th to the 20th century we find the following examples of *-heit* with non-native base words: *frí-heit* 'freedom' (16th c.), *hög-heit* 'highness' (17th c.), *besverlig-heit* 'difficulties' (18th c.), *viktug-heit* 'importance' (19th c.), and *pliktug-heit* 'duties' (20th c.). Relatively early in Icelandic, *-heit* became productive with native base words (see Ingólfsson 1979: 50) and we find the following examples: *heimska* 'stupid' → *heimsku-heit* 'stupidity' (16th c.), *föðurlegur* 'fatherly' → *föðurleg-heit* 'a sense of fatherhood' (17th c.), *bágur* 'miserable' → *bág-heit* 'miserability' (18th c.), *duglegur* 'efficient' → *dugleg-heit* 'effectiveness' (19th c.), and *sérkennilegur* 'peculiar' → *sérkennileg-heit* 'peculiarity' (20th c.). Halldórsson (1969: 93–98 and 100–102) also discusses the status of non-native suffixes like *-erí* and *-ía* and presents examples where they attach to native bases: *lóða* 'to skirt chase' → *lóð-erí* 'skirt-chasing', *kenndur* 'mildly drunk' → *kend-erí* 'binge', *bila* 'to fail' → *bil-erí* 'breakdown' and *gott* 'candy' → *gott-erí* 'candy'. Derivations with *-ía* are: *óráð* 'delirium' → *óráðs-ía* 'disorder' and *slen* 'sluggishness' → *slens-ía* 'under the weather'. An interesting example from modern Icelandic is the use of the borrowed suffix *-isti* with native base words as in *jafnrétti* 'equality' → *jafnréttis-isti* 'equal rightist' or *sjónvarp* 'TV' → *sjónvarps-isti* 'TV-addict'. These formations are relatively new indicating an ongoing change from non-native to native base words.

In Icelandic there are also quite a lot of examples of hybrid compounds where the first part is non-native and the second part is native (see Bjarnadóttir 2005: 148): *astral-heimur* 'astralworld', *glaxó-mjólk* 'Glaxomilk', *medister-pylsa* 'medister sausage' and *tsetse-fluga* 'tsetse-fly'.

Non-native prefixes occur for the most part in the areas of chemistry and physics, in words like: *desí-meter* 'decimeter', *infra-rauður* 'infrared', *mega-tonn* 'megaton' and *últra-fjólublár* 'ultra violet'.

7 Blending and clipping

Blending is a way to increase the vocabulary as in *breakfast* + *lunch* → *brunch* in English. This process is not common in Icelandic; an example like *skaffall* 'salad-fork' occurs, though, formed from *skeið* 'spoon' and *gaffall* 'fork'.

Kvaran (2005: 119) lists examples of various clippings. In the first place there exist clippings or shortenings where neither word class nor meaning changes (*-i* and *-a* are inflectional endings):

Tab. 4.28: Clipping without any change in word class.

Noun		Noun
alkóhólisti	'alcoholic'	alk-i
Trabant	'car type'	Trabb-i
prófessor	'professor'	proff-i
fáviti	'imbecile'	fáv-i
hjúkrunarkona	'nurse'	hjúkk-a
keisaraskurður	'caeserian section'	keisar-i (can also mean 'emperor')
inflúensa	'flu'	flens-a

In the second place, the suffix -ó is used to shorten the word and forms nouns and adjectives (see Jones 1964). The suffix does not stand for any fixed part of a word as shown below:

Tab. 4.29: Clippings where -ó replaces various parts of words.

Noun		Noun	-ó replaces
menntaskóli	'high school'	mennt-ó	-askóli
strætisvagn	'bus'	stræt-ó	-isvagn
Adjective		**Adjective**	**-ó replaces**
sveitalegur	'provincial'	sveit-ó	-alegur
hallærislegur	'lousy'	hall-ó	-ærislegur

In the third place, it is common to shorten names of individuals to use as hypocoristic or nicknames. If the names are disyllabic then the nick name is derived from either the first part or the second part of the name, usually with a weak inflectional ending (-a and -i), as in *Kristín* → *Stína*, *Þorsteinn* → *Steini*, *Kristján* → *Stjáni*, *Hafþór* → *Haffi* and *Hrafnhildur* → *Habba*.

8 References

Alfræði íslenskrar tungu [multimedia disc] (2001): Ed. by Heimir Pálsson and Þórunn Blöndal. Reykjavík: Lýðveldissjóður.

Bjarnadóttir, Kristín (2000): *Þágufallssamsetningar í ritmálssafni Orðabókar Háskólans*. www.lexis.hi.is/kristinb/datsams.html [last access 10 July 2015].

Bjarnadóttir, Kristín (2001): Orðmyndun. In: Heimir Pálsson and Þórunn Blöndal (eds.), *Alfræði íslenskrar tungu*. Reykjavík: Lýðveldissjóður [multimedia disc without page markings].

Bjarnadóttir, Kristín (2002): *A Short Description of Icelandic Compounds*. http://lexis.hi.is/kristinb/comp-short.pdf [last access 10 July 2015].

Bjarnadóttir, Kristín (2005): *Afleiðsla og samsetning í generatífri málfræði og greining á íslenskum gögnum*. Reykjavík: Orðabók Háskólans.

Bjarnadóttir, Kristín (2017): Phrasal Compounds in Modern Icelandic with reference to Icelandic word formation in general. In: Carola Trips and Jaklin Kornfilt (eds.), *Further investigations into the nature of phrasal compounding*, 13–48. Berlin: Language Science Press.

Booij, Geert (1994): Against split morphology. In: Geert Booij and Jaap van Marle (eds.), *Yearbook of Morphology 1993*, 27–50. Dordrecht: Kluwer.

Booij, Geert (1996): Inherent versus contextual inflection and the split morphology hypothesis. In: Geert Booij and Jaap van Marle (eds.), *Yearbook of Morphology 1995*, 1–16. Dordrecht: Kluwer.

Booij, Geert (2007): *The Grammar of Words*. 2nd ed. Oxford: Oxford University Press.

Bresnan, Joan and Sam Mchombo (1995): The lexical integrity principle: Evidence from Bantu. *Natural Language and Linguistic Theory* 13: 181–254.

Gíslason, Jón (1996): Beygingarflokkun veikra sagna. MA thesis, Department of Icelandic language and literature, University of Iceland, Reykjavík.

Halldórsson, Gunnar Þorsteinn (2002): Sagnagrunnur. 1888. Um sagnbeygingu í íslensku. MA thesis, Department of Icelandic language and literature, University of Iceland, Reykjavík.

Halldórsson, Halldór (1969): Nokkur erlend viðskeyti í íslenzku og frjósemi þeirra. In: Bjarni Guðnason, Halldór Halldórsson and Jónas Kristjánsson (eds.), *Einarsbók. Afmæliskveðja til Einars Ól. Sveinssonar 12. desember 1969*, 71–106. Reykjavík: Nokkrir vinir.

Halldórsson, Halldór (1976): Falling down to a suffix status: A morphosemantic study. In: Lars Svenson (ed.), *Nordiska studier i filologi och lingvistik. Festskrift tillägnad Gösta Holm på 60-årsdagen den 8. juli 1976*, 162–172. Lund: Bloms Boktryker.

Harðarson, Gísli Rúnar (2017): Cycling Through Grammar. On Compounds, Noun Phrases and Domains. Doctoral Dissertation, University of Connecticut.

Indriðason, Þorsteinn G. (1994): *Regluvirkni í orðasafni og utan þess. Um lexíkalska hljóðkerfisfræði íslensku*. Reykjavík: Málvísindastofnun Háskóla Íslands.

Indriðason, Þorsteinn G. (1999): Um eignarfallssamsetningar og aðrar samsetningar í íslensku. *Íslenskt mál* 21: 107–150.

Indriðason, Þorsteinn G. (2000a): Derivational suffixes in Icelandic: Changes and clines. In: Guðrún Þórhallsdóttir (ed.), *The Nordic Languages and Modern Linguistics. Proceedings of the Tenth International Conference of Nordic and General Linguistics*, 275–285. Reykjavik: University of Iceland.

Indriðason, Þorsteinn G. (2000b): Fonologi møter morfologi: Om blokkering av fonologiske regler i islandsk. *Nordica Bergensia* 23: 165–187.

Indriðason, Þorsteinn G. (2005): Historisk produktivitet. *Nordica Bergensia* 32: 39–65.

Indriðason, Þorsteinn G. (2007): Um líki í íslensku í ýmiss konar líki. *Íslenskt mál* 28: 95–111.

Indriðason, Þorsteinn G. (2008): Um virkar og frjósamar orðmyndunarreglur í íslensku. *Íslenskt mál* 30: 93–120.

Indriðason, Þorsteinn G. (2011): Om fugesammensetninger i vestnordisk. In: Gunnstein Akselberg and Edit Bugge (eds.), *Vestnordisk språkkontakt gjennom 1200 år*, 257–275. Tórshavn: Fróðskapur, Faroe University Press.

Indriðason, Þorsteinn G. (2016): Á mörkum afleiðslu og samsetningar. Um orðlíka seinni liði í íslensku. *Orð og tunga* 18: 1–41.

Indriðason, Þorsteinn G. (2017): Setningarlegar samsetningar í íslensku. *Íslenskt mál* 38: 125–145.

Indriðason, Þorsteinn G. (2018): On Bound Intensifiers in Icelandic. In: Hans Götzsche (ed.), *The Meaning of Language*, 148–170. Newcastle: Cambridge Sholars Publishing.

Indriðason, Þorsteinn G. (2019): Af hverju ‚góðlátlegur' og ekki ‚góðleglátur'? Um leyfilegar og óleyfilegar viðskeytaraðir í íslensku. *Orð og tunga* 23: 69–109.

Indriðason, Þorsteinn G. (2020): Derivational networks in Icelandic. In: Lívia Körtvélyessi, Alexandra Bagasheva and Pavol Štekauer (eds.), *Derivational Networks Across Languages*, 179–188. Berlin/Boston: De Gruyter Mouton.

Indriðason, Þorsteinn G. (2022): Leitin að stofninum. Um stofnsamsetningar og samanburð við eignarfallssamsetningar. *Íslenskt mál* 43: 71–99.

Ingólfsson, Gunnlaugur (1979): Lítið eitt um lýsingarorð sem enda á *-ugur*. *Íslenskt mál* 1: 43–55.

Jóhannesson, Alexander (1927): *Die Suffixe im Isländischen*. Reykjavík: Árbók Háskóla Íslands.

Jóhannesson, Alexander (1929): *Die Komposita im Isländischen*. Reykjavík: Rit Vísindafélags Íslendinga IV.

Jones, Oscar (1964): Icelandic Neologisms in *-ó*. *Scandinavian Studies* 20: 18–27.

Jónsdóttir, Margrét (2005): Um *væða* og *væðingu* og hlutverk þeirra í samsetningum. *Orð og tunga* 7: 95–120.

Jónsdóttir, Margrét (2006): Viðskeytið *-rænn* í íslensku nútímamáli. In: Malan Marnersdóttir, Leyvoy Joensen, Dagný Kristjánsdóttir and Anfinnur Johansen (eds.), *Bókmenntaljós. Heiðursrit til Turið Sigurðardóttur*, 285–299. Tórshavn: Felagið Fróðskapur. Faroe University Press.

Jónsdóttir, Margrét (2009): Um hvorugkynsorð með viðskeytinu *-sl(i)* í nútímamáli. *Íslenskt mál* 31: 149–166.

Jónsdóttir, Margrét (2010): Beyging orða með viðskeytunum *-ing* og *-ung*: Söguleg þróun. *Orð og tunga* 12: 83–108.

Jónsdóttir, Margrét, Veturliði Óskarsson and Þorsteinn G. Indriðason (2024): *-an* á undan viðskeytinu *-legur* í íslensku: Tilraun til túlkunar. *Orð og tunga* 26: 95–124.

Jónsson, Baldur (1984): Samsett nafnorð með samsetta liði: Fáeinar athuganir. In: Bernt Fossestøl, Kjell Ivar Vannebo, Kjell Venås and Finn-Erik Vinje (eds.), *Festskrift til Einar Lundeby, 3. október 1984*, 158–174. Oslo: Novus.

Jónsson, Baldur (1987): Íslensk orðmyndun. *Andvari: Nýr flokkur* 29: 88–103.

Jónsson, Jón Hilmar (1980): Um merkingu og hlutverk forliðarins *hálf-*. *Íslenskt mál* 2: 119–149.

Jónsson, Sigurður (1984): Af hassistum og kontóristum. *Íslenskt mál* 6: 155–166.

Konráðsson, Sigurður (1989): Um orðmyndun í íslensku. Ms., Kennaraháskóla Íslands, Reykjavík.

Kvaran, Guðrún (1990–91): Um atviksorð sem enda á *-is*. *Íslenskt mál* 12–13: 7–29.

Kvaran, Guðrún (2005): *Orð. Handbók um beygingar- og orðmyndunarfræði*. Reykjavík: Almenna bókafélagið.

Meibauer, Jörg (2007): How marginal are phrasal compounds? Generalized insertion, expressivity, and I/Q-interaction. *Morphology* 17: 233–259.

Óskarsson, Veturliði G. (2006): Af tveim tökuviðskeytum. *Íslenskt mál* 28: 79–93.

Óskarsson, Veturliði G. (2009a): Annarleg sprek á ókunnri strönd. *Orð og tunga* 11: 17–44.

Óskarsson, Veturliði G. (2009b): Um sögnina blífa, vöxt hennar og viðgang í íslensku. *Íslenskt mál* 31: 189–224.

Óskarsson, Veturliði and Þorsteinn G. Indriðason (2022): Eignarfallssamsetningar með sterkum lýsingarorðum í fyrri lið. Söguleg og samtímaleg úttekt. *Íslenskt mál* 43: 99–129.

Óskarsson, Veturliði and Þorsteinn G. Indridason (2024): Að snarbatna, steingleyma og dauðleiðast. Samtímaleg og söguleg athugun á áhersluforliðum með sögnum í íslensku. *Orð og tunga* 26: 57–94.

Perlmutter, David M. (1988): The split morphology hypothesis: Evidence from Yiddish. In: Michael Hammond and Michael Noonan (eds.), *Theoretical Morphology*, 79–99. San Diego: Academic Press.

Petersen, Hjalmar P. (2016): Faroese. In: Peter O. Müller, Ingeborg Ohnheiser, Susan Olsen and Franz Rainer (eds.), *Word-Formation. An International Handbook of the Languages of Europe.* Vol. 4, 2487–2524. Berlin/Boston: De Gruyter Mouton.

Rögnvaldsson, Eiríkur (1987): Nokkur viðskeyti og tíðni þeirra. *Morgunblaðið* May 15th.

Rögnvaldsson, Eiríkur (1990): *Íslensk orðhlutafræði.* Reykjavík: Málvísindastofnun Háskóla Íslands.

Sato, Yosuke (2010): Complex phrase structures within morphological words: Evidence from English and Indonesian. *Lingua* 120: 379–407.

Snædal, Magnús (1992): Hve langt má orðið vera? *Íslenskt mál* 14: 173–207.

Svavarsdóttir, Ásta (1993): *Beygingakerfi nafnorða í nútímaíslensku.* Reykjavík: Málvísindastofnun Háskóla Íslands.

Theódórsdóttir, Guðrún (1996): Hosnasterta. Um -*a* og -*na* endingar eignarfalls fleirtölu veikra kvenkynsorða. MA thesis, Department of Icelandic language and literature, University of Iceland, Reykjavík.

Thorgeirsdóttir, Sigrún (1986): Um forskeyti í íslensku. MA thesis, Department of Icelandic language and literature, University of Iceland, Reykjavík.

Thráinsson, Höskuldur, Hjálmar P. Petersen, Jógvan í Lon Jacobsen and Zakaris Svabo Hansen (2004): *Faroese. An overview and reference grammar.* Tórshavn: Føroya Fróðskaparfelag.

Franz Rainer
5 Spanish

1 Introduction
2 General overview
3 Composition
4 Derivation
5 Conversion
6 Backformation
7 Reduplication
8 Blending
9 Clipping
10 Word-creation
11 References

Abstract: The present article provides a short overview of processes of word-formation in Spanish from a largely synchronic point of view.

1 Introduction

Among the Romance languages, Spanish can boast today the most complete descriptions of word-formation. A first overview in book-form was published in 1920 by Alemany Bolufer who, in the spirit of his time, did not distinguish systematically between synchrony and diachrony. We then have to wait some 70 years to see more up-to-date full-scale descriptions of Spanish word-formation appear. For readers unfamiliar with Spanish or German, the only accessible manual is still Lang's (1990) short, didactically oriented overview of present-day Spanish derivation. The most complete synchronic treatment is Rainer (1993a), written in German. Those who read Spanish can consult the third volume of Bosque and Demonte (1999) as well as the new academy grammar (*NGLE* 2010), which both contain substantial chapters covering the whole range of present-day Spanish word-formation. As far as diachrony is concerned, Pharies (2002) and Pharies and Fischer-Dorantes (2024) provide a synthesis of the state of the art concerning affixation. For composition, one can consult Moyna (2011).

Franz Rainer, Vienna, Austria

For bibliographic information, the reader should turn to the bibliographies included in the works cited, as well as to Rainer (1993b), Pharies (1994), García-Medall (1995) and Pena (2003). It must not be forgotten, however, that Spanish word-formation is a burgeoning field in which dozens of monographs and articles are published every year. In this overview, bibliographic references must be limited to a small selection of recent works not retrievable from the standard handbooks and bibliographies mentioned.

2 General overview

With almost 400 million speakers, most of whom live in Latin America, Spanish is the most important of the Western Romance languages. Its great geographical extension is reflected in word-formation by the existence of many regionally confined patters. Due to space limitations, this aspect cannot be described in detail here. Geographical variation in word-formation, by the way, is a field where much research remains to be done (Tejera 2007; *NGLE* 2010). Overall, Spanish word-formation essentially presents the same general characteristics as that of the other standard Romance languages: affixation, especially suffixation, is by far the most important device.

As in other Romance languages (cf. Amiot 2015 on the grammaticalization of prepositions in French word-formation), the dividing line between prefixation and compounding is not neat. Many prefixes originate from adverbs or prepositions. The first constituent *sobre-* of *sobrevolar* 'to fly over', for example, is still formally and semantically identical to the preposition *sobre* 'over', while the meaning 'excessive' in *sobrepesca* 'over-fishing' is the result of a process of grammaticalization which has shifted *sobre-* towards the affixal pole. Another area where we observe a gradient transition between affixation and compounding are the combining forms of Greek and Latin origin, which raise the same problems of delimitation as in other European languages (cf. Eins 2025 on types of foreign word-formation as well as Rainer 2025 and Scherer 2025).

Since compounding was prevalently of literary usage in Latin, only very few patterns were passed down directly to Spanish and other Romance languages. (Whether V-N compounds of the type *sacacorchos* 'corkscrew; lit. remove-corks' were among these, as forcefully argued by Bork 1990, continues to be a moot question.) Most patterns of compounding, anyway, have arisen during the history of Spanish, and constitute so-called "syntagmatic compounds", i.e. formations on the basis of lexical patterns with a syntactic structure (cf. Booij 2025 on construction grammar, section 4).

Of the remaining techniques, conversion is by far the most important. Backformation, blending, clipping, reduplication and word-creation are also used to a certain extent.

3 Composition

3.1 Nominal compounds

Among nominal compounds, the most productive pattern is constituted by left-headed determinative N-N compounds of the type *hombre rana* (Czerwenka 2009; García-Page 2011), which are situated half-way between syntagmatic compounding and compounding proper. Semantically, these compounds are much less flexible than the right-headed determinative compounds in the Germanic languages, or even the French equivalents (cf. Arnaud 2025 on noun-noun compounds in French). Most of the time, only the first constituent is inflected for plural: *hombres rana* 'frogmen'. In that respect, such compounds differ from copulative N-N compounds, where both constituents must be inflected: *compositor-director* 'composer-director', pl. *compositores-directores*. A further difference between determinative and copulative compounds is that the former overwhelmingly consist of two nouns only, while the number of constituents of the latter is unlimited in principle: *marxismo-leninismo-fascismo-castrismo*, etc.

Right-headed nominal compounds also exist, but in productive use they are restricted to a small set of second constituents such as *terapia* 'therapy': *musicoterapia* 'music therapy' (← *música* 'music' + linking vowel -*o*-), jocular *dineroterapia* 'money therapy' (← *dinero* 'money'), etc. Most of these compounds or mini-patterns betray a foreign origin: *castrocomunismo*, *cóctel-bar*, *vasodilatación*, etc.

Equally marginal, as well as semantically heterogeneous, is the N-i-N pattern with a linking vowel -*i*-. Some are right-headed (e.g., jocular *puticlub* 'hostess club' ← *puta* 'whore'), others dvandvas (e.g., *ajiaceite* [also *ajoaceite*, without a linking vowel], the name of a dish containing *ajo* 'garlic' and *aceite* 'oil'). Even rarer are exocentric V-V compounds, where the V formally coincides with the third person singular or the informal imperative (which are largely identical): *pillapilla* (a children's game; ← *pillar* 'to catch'), *correcorre* 'unordered flight' (← *correr* 'to run'), *duermevela* 'light sleep' (← *dormir* 'to sleep', *velar* 'to be awake'), etc.

The second most frequent pattern is constituted by V-N compounds. This pattern has always been a favourite of students of Romance word-formation (see

Ricca 2025 on verb-noun compounds in Romance). On most interpretations, compounds of this type are considered to be exocentric, since their referent is not identical to that of the N, but designates a person, instrument or, more rarely, an event not formally expressed in the compound itself: *limpiabotas* 'shoe-shine boy; lit. shine-boots', *abrecartas* 'letter opener; lit. open-letters', *besamanos* 'kiss on the hand; lit. kiss-hands', etc.

The N of a V-N compound normally corresponds to the theme argument of the transitive verb V, as in the examples given, but there are also some exceptions. For example, with the first element *guarda* 'to protect', beside the regular pattern *guardabosque(s)* 'ranger; lit. protect-forest(s)', we also find compounds of the type *guardabarros* 'wing (of a car); lit. protect-muds', where the N does not refer to the thing protected but rather to the thing against which sb. or sth. is protected. This pattern obviously must have arisen by a metonymical reanalysis of the original, regular *guarda*-pattern.

Our examples also illustrate another notable feature of at least peninsular Spanish V-N compounds, viz. the tendency to pluralize the N even where this does not make sense semantically. In a *besamanos*, for example, one hand (*mano*) is kissed, not several (*manos*), and a *guardabarros* protects against mud (*barro*), which is a mass noun normally resisting pluralization. This anomalous behaviour bears witness to the fact that V-N compounds form a *lexical* pattern which cannot be derived from the corresponding syntactic phrases, at least synchronically. Another fact which points in the same direction are heavy restrictions which do not obtain for the corresponding verb phrases: a strong preference of the pattern for certain verbs (15 verbs account for half of all established formations), for bisyllabic verbs and for agentive verbs.

Due to the exocentricity of the pattern, gender-assignment in V-N compounds is not determined by the noun in second position. The syntactic category of the output is also independent from that of the two constituents. It can be a noun even in the few cases where the second constituent is not a noun (cf. *matasiete* 'braggart; lit. kill-seven', *mandamás* 'boss; lit. order-more'), and an adjective when it is a noun (cf. *monstruo tragaestrellas* 'star-devouring monster; lit. monster devour-stars'). This adjectival usage seems to be relatively recent and must have arisen through the reanalysis of V-N compounds as adjectives in appositional sequences of the type N V-N.

3.2 Adjectival compounds

Spanish has five patterns of adjectival compounds, A-A, A-i-A, N-A, N-i-A and A-N.

Due to their Neo-Latin origin, A-A compounds of the type *ético-moral* 'ethico-moral' are still by and large confined to written or at least formal language where, however, they are very productive. The constituents are mostly relational adjectives, the semantic relationship being determined by the modified noun: *sociedad helvético-panameña* 'Swiss and Panamanian company', *guerra palestino-israelí* 'war between Palestine and Israel, or Palestinians and Israelis', etc. With colour adjectives, the compound can also refer to an intermediate shade: *cielo amarillo-verdoso* 'yellow-greenish sky', etc. In some cases, furthermore, the meaning is not computed on the basis of the two adjectives, but by referring to a complex nominal base: *análisis semántico-generativo* 'an analysis in the style of generative semantics [*semántica generativa*], not: *semantic and generative analysis', etc. The first constituent in A-A compounds normally remains invariable (cf. *helvético* in the example above, which ends in *-o*, not feminine *-a*, though the modified noun *sociedad* is feminine), and very often it is a shortened form, as in *afro-asiático* 'Afro-Asiatic', where *afro-* represents *africano*, or a suppletive form, as in *greco-turco* 'Greek-Turkish', where *greco-* represents *griego*. There is, however, an increasing tendency to also inflect the first constituent; so we find *clase media alta* 'upper middle class' beside *clase medio-alta*, *cuestión matemática-estadística* 'mathematical-statistical question' beside *cuestión matemático-estadística*, etc. The closeness of these compounds to phrases is also underlined by the fact that normally all constituents are stressed, except for short(ened) first constituents, especially in established combinations. As a consequence of the coordinative semantics, compounds of this kind can contain an, in principle, unlimited number of constituents: *estudio antropológico-sociológico-lingüístico* 'a study which is anthropological, sociological and linguistic', etc.

Iteration, on the contrary, is excluded in A-i-A compounds, even though their meaning is also coordinative. This fact must therefore be encoded as a pattern-specific restriction. The constituents are linked with the vowel *-i-*: *rojiblanco* 'red and white' (← *rojo* 'red', *blanco* 'white'), *negriazul* 'black and blue' (← *negro* 'black', *azul* 'blue'), *verdigrís* 'green and grey' (← *verde* 'green', *gris* 'grey'), *agridulce* 'sour-sweet' (← *agrio* 'sour', *dulce* 'sweet'), etc. This pattern is modestly productive, especially with colour adjectives. The first constituent must be bisyllabic and end in a vowel (cf. **azulinegro*, **grisiverde*).

N-A compounds do not constitute a uniform set, but a heterogeneous collection of a relatively small number of patterns of rather limited productivity. These compounds are right-headed, which is due to their foreign origin via loan translations: *drogadicto* 'addicted to drugs; lit. drug-addict', *cristocéntrico* 'Christ-centered', *sur-americano* 'South-American', *mayahablante* 'Maya-speaking', etc.

The fourth type, possessive N-i-A compounds (Sánchez López 2003), on the contrary, is very homogeneous. Its first constituent always designates a part of the body and the adjective attributes some property to it: *pelirrojo* 'red-haired; lit. hair-red' (← *pelo* 'hair', *rojo* 'red'), etc. The first constituent, furthermore, is generally bisyllabic and ends in a vowel. Within these strict limits, the pattern is modestly productive.

Combinations such as *rubio platino* 'platinum blonde' are mostly considered to be N-N compounds used as appositions, since they used to remain invariable; cf. *chicas rubio platino* 'platinum blonde girls', where *rubio* 'blonde' has masculine singular inflection though *chicas* 'girls' is feminine plural. Such sequences, however, have been reanalysed as left-headed A-N compounds, which is why we now also commonly find examples where the adjectival head shows agreement in gender and number: *chicas rubias platino*.

3.3 Verbal compounds

Spanish has no really productive pattern of verbal compounds. The few N-i-V compounds are probably backformations from N-i-A compounds: *perniquebrar* 'to break the leg(s); lit. leg-break' < *perniquebrado* 'with a broken leg' (← *pierna* 'leg', *quebrado* 'broken'), etc. Compounds of the type Adverb + Verb are productive to a certain extent, but only with the first constituent *mal* 'badly': *maltratar* 'to treat badly', *maldormir* 'to sleep badly', etc.

3.4 Syntagmatic compounds

Syntagmatic compounding cannot be treated here in detail (cf. Buenafuentes de la Mata 2010 for an overview). In the nominal domain, the most frequent patterns are N de N, e.g., *hombre de negocio* 'businessman; lit. man of business', and N-A, e.g., *sociedad anónima* 'stock company; lit. company anonymous'. Formations of this kind are not, as often stated erroneously, the result of the lexicalization of regular syntactic sequences, but constitute very productive lexical patterns, which normally continue to obey the rules of Spanish syntax (for example, agreement rules), but may occasionally also deviate from them. Such is the case in A-N compounds of the type *nacionalcatolicismo* (← *nacional* 'national', *catolicismo* 'Catholicism'), the name for the ideology of Francoism, where the relational adjective precedes the noun, contrary to normal Spanish syntax. This unorthodox word order was introduced into the Spanish language via loan translations such as *nacionalsocialismo* (< German *Nationalsozialismus*) but has since become part of a small niche of similar formations.

3.5 Neoclassical compounds

Loanwords taken from (Neo-)Latin (directly or via other European languages) have been assimilated into Spanish to different degrees. The result of these processes of assimilation is that the native and the learned layer of vocabulary are much more difficult to distinguish for the speaker than, for example, in Germanic languages, or even in French. The difficulties that one faces are reflected by the important differences that exist among morphologists when it comes to compiling lists of affixes vs. combining forms. The most widely used criterion, concrete (lexeme-like) vs. abstract (affix-like) meaning, yields a cline, not a sharp division. Phonological criteria do not fare better.

Most of the Spanish combining forms are internationalisms: *aero-* 'air', *bio-*^{1} 'life', *crono-* 'time', *electro-* 'electric(ity)', *fito-* 'plant', *hidro-* 'water', etc. Only occasionally may one of these elements be considered to be a native creation. One such candidate could be *diplo-* in the Cuban-Spanish expression *diplotienda* 'shop reserved for diplomats' (← *diplomático* 'diplomat', *tienda* 'shop'). *Narco-*, first attested in *narcotráfico* 'drug trafficking' and *narcotraficante* 'drug dealer', also seems to have been a Latin-American innovation, later on adopted in other languages. In Peru, during the presidency of Fujimori, *fuji-* 'of Fujimori' became a productive combining form (*fujigolpe* ← *golpe* 'coup'). A fourth case in point could be *lumpen-*, which has been extracted from Marx' *lumpenproletariado* but is now occasionally also used in other combinations such as *lumpenburguesía* (← *burguesía* 'bourgoisie') or *lumpen-expresionismo*. Combining forms generally occur both before nouns and adjectives, sometimes even before verbs: *aeropuerto* 'airport' (← *puerto* 'port'), *aeronaval* 'air-sea, adj.', *aerotransportar* 'to transport through the air'. As in other languages, we also observe in Spanish that initial combining forms occasionally acquire the meaning of a prominent word of which they form part: so beside *bio-*^{1} 'life' we find *bio-*^{2} 'biology/biological' (*biocarburante* 'bio-fuel' ← *carburante* 'fuel'), and beside *lipo-*^{1} 'fat', *lipo-*^{2} 'liposuction' (*lipoescultura* 'sculpture/body-shape attained by liposuction; not: *fat sculpture').

4 Derivation

As already mentioned, affixation is by far the most important technique of word-formation in Spanish. In the following discussion, affixes will be arranged according to part-of-speech and meaning.

4.1 Nominal derivation

Nominal derivation is extremely rich in Spanish (Amador Rodríguez 2009).

4.1.1 Denominal nouns

Spanish has a wealth of **prefixes** which derive nouns from nouns. Most of these are of Neo-Latin origin (cf. Lindner and Rainer 2025 on word-formation in Neo-Latin) and therefore shared by other European standard languages. Table 5.1 displays the main functions fulfilled by these prefixes and provides one example of the most common prefixes.

Suffixes may be divided into the following semantic categories.

The category of **personal nouns** is dominated by the two highly productive suffixes *-ero* and *-ista*. Of these, the first one, which continues Latin *-arius*, is used for more traditional roles, while *-ista* is preferred for more modern or prestigious roles: *periodiquero* 'newspaper seller' vs. *periodista* 'journalist' (← *periódico* 'newspaper'), etc. Other suffixes remain rare: *bibliotecario* 'librarian' (← *biblioteca* 'library'), *cabrerizo* 'goatherd' (← *cabra* 'goat'), etc.

Spanish has over a dozen suffixes for forming **status nouns**, i.e. nouns expressing status or rank, but most of them are unproductive: *diaconado* (← *diácono* 'deacon'), *vasallaje* (← *vasallo* 'vassal'), *cardinalato* (← *cardinal* 'cardinal'), *almirantazgo* (← *almirante* 'admiral'), etc. Metonymically, some of these formations can also denote the corresponding collective, seat, territory, term of office or activity.

The number of suffixes deriving denominal **place nouns** is even greater, but again most of them are unproductive. Among the more productive ones, *-al/-ar* derive names of fields (*sandial* 'field of watermelons' ← *sandía* 'watermelon', *melonar* 'field of muskmelons' ← *melón* 'muskmelon'), *-eda* names of woods (*olmeda* 'elm wood' ← *olmo* 'elm'), *-era/-ero* names of containers (*azucarera* 'sugar bowl' ← *azúcar* 'sugar', *florero* 'flower vase' ← *flor* 'flower'), *-ería* names of points of sale (*hamburguesería* 'hamburger stand' ← *hamburguesa* 'hamburger').

The largest group of denominal nouns are **collective nouns**, which often acquire pejorative overtones. Most of the more than 40 suffixes only occur in one or a few formations, and many are probably better viewed as metonymic extensions of abstract nouns (*noviciado* 'noviciate', but also 'collective of novices'). Some of the more productive collective suffixes specialize in deriving human beings: *campesinado* (← *campesino* 'farmer'), *clerigalla* (← *clérigo* 'cleric'), *clientela* (← *cliente* 'client'), *rojerío* (← *rojo* 'communist'), etc.

Tab. 5.1: The main conceptual categories of prefixed nouns.

function	derivatives		bases	
locative	antealtar	'place in front of the altar'	altar	'altar'
	recocina	'room behind the kitchen'	cocina	'kitchen'
	subsuelo	'subsoil'	suelo	'soil'
	ultramar	'territories beyond the sea'	mar	'sea'
hierarchical	archiduque	'archduke'	duque	'duke'
	subcomandante	'deputy commander'	comandante	'commander'
	vicepresidente	'vice-president'	presidente	'president'
	bisabuelo	'great-grandfather'	abuelo	'grandfather'
	tatarabuelo	'great-great-grandfather'	abuelo	'grandfather'
temporal	precastrismo	'pre-Castro period'	castrismo	'Castroism'
	posguerra	'postwar period'	guerra	'war'
	entreacto	'intermission'	acto	'act'
	ex presidente	'ex president'	presidente	'president'
	neo-secretario	'newly appointed s.'	secretario	'secretary'
	neoliberalismo	'neoliberalism'	liberalismo	'liberalism'
	paleocapitalismo	'early capitalism'	capitalismo	'capitalism'
	protofrancés	'proto-French'	francés	'French'
	tardorrenacentismo	'late Renaissance'	renacentismo	'Renaissance'
comitative	co-editor	'co-editor'	editor	'editor'
quantitative	minifalda	'miniskirt'	falda	'skirt'
	microorganismo	'microorganism'	organismo	'organism'
	macroconcierto	'huge concert'	concierto	'concert'
	megabanco	'big bank'	banco	'bank'
intensive	supermujer	'superwoman'	mujer	'woman'
	hipersudoración	'excessive sweating'	sudoración	'sweating'
	hipofunción	'hypofunction'	función	'function'
	subdesarrollo	'underdevelopment'	desarrollo	'development'
	semifracaso	'half a failure'	fracaso	'failure'
negative	desamor	'aversion'	amor	'love'
	impudor	'shamelessness'	pudor	'shame'
	anti-héroe	'anti-hero'	héroe	'hero'
	pseudoprofeta	'false prophet'	profeta	'prophet'
	no discriminación	'non discrimination'	discriminación	'discrimination'
antagonistic	contracultura	'counter-culture'	cultura	'culture'

Names of trees are derived in Spanish by one of three suffixes: *almendral* ← *almendra* 'almond', *higuera* ← *higo* 'fig', *albaricoquero* ← *albaricoque* 'apricot'. Only rarely is the fruit derived from the tree: *hayuco* 'beechnut' ← *haya* 'beech'.

Names of – generally negatively valued – actions can be derived with the two suffixes *-ada* and *-ería*: *cochinada* 'filthy behaviour' (← *cochino* 'pig'), *cretinería* 'foolish action' (← *cretino* 'fool'). Some derivatives in *-ería* can also be interpreted as metonymic extensions of quality nouns in *-ería*. We could also mention here the recent jocular use of the English suffix *-ing* for designating activities: *puenting* 'bungee jumping' (← *puente* 'bridge'), etc.

The suffix *-ada* is highly polysemous. Apart from actions and the concept of contents (*palada* 'shovelful' ← *pala* 'shovel'), it can also denote blows, shots and related concepts, a derivational category which seems to be rather rare cross-linguistically, but is also represented in Spanish by the highly productive suffix *-azo*: *cuchillada/cuchillazo* 'knife thrust' (← *cuchillo* 'knife'), *fusilazo* 'gunshot' (← *fusil* 'gun'), etc. Metonymically, these formations can also refer to the ensuing wounds. The suffix *-azo*, furthermore, has been extended metaphorically to designate all kinds of spectacular events, such as coups (e.g., *pinochetazo* ← A. Pinochet).

Names of sciences can be productively derived by *-ística* (*balcanística* 'Balkan studies' ← *Balcanes* 'Balkans') and *-ología* (*sexología* 'sexology' ← *sexo* 'sex'), more rarely *-ografía* (*cristalografía*) or *-ometría* (*dialectometría*). Most morphologists would prefer to consider the last three as neoclassical combining forms (*-logía*, *-grafía*, *-metría*) preceded by the linking vowel *-o-*.

Suffixes for designating taxes or fees also exist, but are no longer productive: *pontaje/pontazgo* 'bridge tax' (← *puente* 'bridge'). More often, names for taxes and other fees are metonymic extensions of abstract nouns.

Other categories are represented by only one suffix, but not therefore less important. Names of doctrines, for example, take *-ismo* (*catolicismo* ← *católico* 'Catholic'), which also expresses other concepts.

Spanish is well-known for its exuberance of evaluative suffixes (over 70, if unproductive ones are included!). These may be divided into three broad groups: diminutives (including hypocoristics), augmentatives, and pejoratives. The quantitatively most conspicuous group is that of pejorative suffixes, with some 50 members, but most of these are unproductive or of very low productivity. In the augmentative group, three suffixes are productive, *-azo*, *-ón* and *-ote*: *cochazo* 'big car' (← *coche* 'car'), *memorión* 'prodigious memory' (← *memoria* 'memory'), *librote* 'big book' (← *libro* 'book'). Augmentatives often have meliorative or pejorative overtones, depending on the suffix, the base and the wider context. Among the diminutive suffixes, *-ito* is highly productive throughout the Spanish-speaking world, while suffixes like *-illo* or *-ico* are geographically restricted. In the Caribbean region, the latter is tied to bases ending in /t/, a context where *-ito* is avoided: *casita* (← *casa* 'house') vs. *galletica* (← *galleta* 'cookie'). In standard Peninsular Spanish the suffix *-illo* tends to convey a pejorative note as compared to *-ito*: a *musiquilla* (← *música* 'music') is always annoying, while the judgement attached to *musiquita* will entirely depend on contextual factors. For details about the semantics and pragmatics of diminutives, which is extremely complex in Spanish, the reader is referred to Hummel (2025) on the semantics and pragmatics of Romance evaluative suffixes, and for an example of subtle regional differences in the pragmatics of *-ito*, to Curcó (1998). As to the formal side, which is no less complex, let us mention that *-ito* appears as *-cito* after polysyllabic bases ending in *-n* and *-r* (*bastoncito* ← *bastón* 'stick', *pastorcito* ← *pastor* 'sheperd') and as *-ecito* after monosyllabic words (*florecita* ← *flor* 'flower'), as well as after disyllabic words ending in *-e* (*madrecita* ← *madre* 'mother' vs. *comadrita* ← *comadre* 'godmother') or containing a diphthong (*puertecita* ← *puerta* 'door' vs. *compuertita* ← *compuerta* 'gate'). But there is a lot of geographic, social and even individual variation concerning the exact conditions of use of these allomorphs (in Spanish word-formation it is customary to call elements such as the *-c-* of *-cito* or the *-ec-* of *-ecito* "interfixes"; Martín Camacho 2002). This variation is difficult to describe by rules of any generality, but can be successfully handled in analogical models (Eddington 2002). A fact worth mentioning is that *-ito* shows signs of becoming an **infix**: not only is the inflectional ending conserved in masculine words ending in *-a* like *di-it-a* (← *dí-a* 'day'), the diminutive suffix is even inserted into the body of some mono-morphemic words like *Carlos* (dim.: *Carl-it-os*) or *azúcar* 'sugar' (dim.: *azuqu ít ar*, beside regular *azucarcito*), whose last syllables vaguely resemble inflectional endings.

4.1.2 Deadjectival nouns

The only quantitatively important category of deadjectival nouns in Spanish are **quality nouns** (Pena 2004). There are some 30, mostly unproductive, suffixes in this category, but no default suffix. The productive suffixes are all subject to heavy restrictions. The suffixes *-ia* and *-ía*, for example, are tied to bases with certain second constituents of Greek origin, such as *-céfalo*, *-gamo*, etc. for *-ia* and *-fono*, *-latra*, etc. for *-ía*. With native bases, the latter suffix is slightly productive with adjectives in *-ero* (*patriotería* ← *patriotero* 'patriotic') and *-ano* (*cubanía* ← *cubano* 'Cuban', which however could also be analysed as a denominal status noun). The etymologically related suffix *-ería* only attaches productively to bases denoting negative qualities (*bobaliconería* ← *bobalicón* 'silly'). The suffix *-idad* (Martín Vegas 2005) is intimately tied to certain adjectival endings like '*-ico*, *-il*,

-ivo, -oso (sistematicidad ← sistemático 'sistematic', etc.). Of -eza and -ez, only the latter continues to be productive, especially with words ending in a dental and/or denoting negative qualities (absolutez ← absoluto 'absolute', plebeyez ← plebeyo 'plebeian'). Last but not least, the versatile suffix -ismo can also form quality nouns under certain conditions (conformismo ← conformista 'conformist', casticismo ← castizo 'genuine'). As in other languages, quality nouns also show metonymic extensions of the type una tontería 'a stupidity', una belleza 'a beauty', etc.

Apart from quality nouns, only two relatively marginal attributive suffixes deserve being mentioned: frescales 'cheeky monkey' ← fresco 'cheeky', guaperas 'handsome guy' ← guapo 'handsome'.

4.1.3 Deverbal nouns

Deverbal nouns are the most conspicuous part of Spanish word-formation, comprising large categories such as action nouns, agent nouns, instrument nouns and place nouns.

Spanish has some 60 suffixes forming action nouns, of which however only half a dozen can be considered as really productive, notably -ción, -miento, -da, -do, and -ón. There is no default suffix, each of the suffixes being subject to heavy restrictions concerning potential verbal bases. Action-noun suffixes are not all perfectly synonymous, but may imply aspectual differences: while most of them nominalize the verbal base in a neutral way, some imply features like semelfactivity or repetition (cf. Gaeta 2015 on action nouns in Romance). The suffix -ón, for example, apart from semelfactivity, also implies the features suddenness and intensity: empujón 'sudden push' (← empujar 'to push'), parón 'sudden stop' (← parar 'to stop'), etc. The suffix -dera, on the contrary, implies tedious repetition or long duration: lloradera 'crying for no reason' (← llorar 'to cry'), sudadera 'heavy sweating' (← sudar 'to sweat'), etc. This suffix is particularly productive in the Caribbean region. On semantic differences between -ción and -miento, cf. Lliteras (2003). As in other languages, Spanish action nouns also show frequent metonymic extensions towards the resultant state (agotamiento 'exhaustion' ← agotar 'to exhaust'), the product of the action (serraduras 'wood shavings' ← serrar 'to saw'), and other concepts closely associated with the action (agent, instrument, place, time, etc.). Action nouns require nominal syntax in Spanish (Monjour 2003), only nominalized infinitives allow maintaining the verbal syntax of the base.

The category of agent nouns is dominated by the suffixes -dor and -nte. The distribution of these two suffixes is a complicated matter, but one can say that the former requires the base verbs to be clearly agentive while this is not a necessary requirement for the latter, which goes back to the Latin present participle (*amante* 'lover' ← *amar* 'to love', *descendiente* 'descendant' ← *descender* 'to descend'). There are half a dozen of other agentive suffixes, but they are not productive. What is worth mentioning is a special series of agentive suffixes specialized in the designation of negative characters: *cagaza* 'coward' (← *cagar* 'to shit'), *acusica* 'telltale' (← *acusar* 'to accuse'), Mex. Sp. *metiche* 'nosy person' (← *meterse* 'to meddle'), etc.

Instrument nouns (Herwartz 2002) are derived either by adding *-dor* (*elevador* 'elevator' ← *elevar* 'to elevate') or its feminine counterpart *-dora* (*licuadora* 'blender' ← *licuar* 'to blend'), which is preferred for machines (in fact, it originated through the ellipsis of *máquina* 'machine'; Rainer 2009). The suffix *-dera* is no longer productive but occurs in many traditional names of tools (*podadera* 'shears' ← *podar* 'to prune'). The other ten instrumental suffixes are also non-productive.

For deriving deverbal place nouns Spanish has a dozen suffixes, of which however only *-dero* is slightly productive (*abrevadero* 'watering place' ← *abrevar* 'to water'). The presence of the agentive/instrumental suffix *-dor* in some place nouns (*comedor* 'dining room' ← *comer* 'to eat') is due to loan translations from Old Catalan (or Old Provençal), where the Latin instrumental-locative suffix *-torium* had been conflated with the Latin agentive suffix *-tor* by the action of the sound laws (Rainer 2011).

4.2 Adjectival derivation

Spanish has a rich set of derived adjectives. They can productively be formed on the bases of nouns, adjectives and verbs. Deadverbial/deprepositional adjectives are rare (*delantero* 'front, adj.' ← *delante* 'in front (of)', *trasero* 'rear' ← *tras* 'behind, prep.').

4.2.1 Denominal adjectives

The most important denominal group is that of relational adjectives (Holzer 1996). Relatively rare in older stages of the language, they witnessed a spectacular growth in the standard language beginning with the 18th century under the influence of Neo-Latin, French and English. Again we find a wealth of suffixes (over 60), each of which obeys strict restrictions concerning potential bases. There is no default suffix, which is why many nouns remain without a relational adjective despite the great number of suffixes (e.g., *precio* 'price'). Both with respect to the inventory of suffixes and the conditions of use, it is necessary to distinguish several subgroups: adjectives derived from common nouns and adjectives derived from proper nouns, which in turn have to be subdivided into those derived from names of persons and those derived from place names. In a complete analysis one would have to introduce even finer distinctions, since for example names of artists and politicians are not treated in exactly the same way: the first group prefers the suffix *-iano* (*celiano* ← C. J. Cela), the latter *-ista* (*chavista* ← H. Chávez), though we find both of them also in the opposite group. In the geographical series, place names from non-Spanish-speaking countries prefer *-iano* (cf. *sahariano*, *washingtoniano*), while this suffix is almost absent from adjectives relating to the Spanish-speaking world, where furthermore strong regional preferences can be observed, even within Spain. As García Sánchez (2005) has shown, the choice is made in analogy to the dominant suffix in the region: *-ano* is particularly frequent in the region around Toledo since its adjective is *toledano*. The effective distribution of relational adjectives is very complex, especially if compared to alternative ways of expressing the same concept: so *mercado petrolero* 'oil market' (← *petróleo* 'oil') or *industria petrolera* 'oil industry' are common expressions, but you could hardly say *precio petrolero* 'oil price', a concept most commonly expressed by the "syntagmatic compound" *precio del petróleo* (lit. 'price of the oil'). As in other languages, the semantic relationship expressed by combinations of noun + relational adjective is extremely flexible and essentially determined by our encyclopaedic knowledge about the two concepts involved, but the interpretation of relational adjectives is not completely free: the relation 'made of', for example, is almost always expressed by a combination of *de* 'of' + noun, even when a corresponding relational adjective exists (*industria lanera* 'wool industry' ← *lana* 'wool', but: *calcetín lanero 'wool sock' vs. *calcetín de lana*).

As in other languages, relational adjectives easily turn into qualitative adjectives: *la obra picassiana* 'Picasso's paintings' vs. *un estilo picassiano* 'a style resembling that of Picasso', etc. But Spanish also has some patterns which have the specific function of expressing r e s e m b l a n c e: *anaranjado* 'orange, adj.' (← *naranja* 'orange, n.'), a pattern containing the circumfix *a-...-ado*, *sanchopancesco* ← Sancho Panza, *ceniciento* 'ashen' (← *ceniza* 'ash'), *pajizo* 'straw-coloured' (← *paja* 'straw'), *draculoide* 'resembling Dracula', *sedoso* 'silky' (← *seda* 'silk'), *campanudo* 'bell-shaped' (← *campana* 'bell').

Some patterns expressing resemblance also have at the same time a p o s s e s s i v e function: *adinerado* 'wealthy' (← *dinero* 'money'), *mugriento* 'filthy' (← *mugre* 'filth'), *calizo* 'chalky' (← *cal* 'chalk'), *roñoso* 'mangy' (← *roña* 'mange'), *ventrudo* 'pot-bellied' (← *vientre* 'belly'), etc. All in all, some 25 suffixes express possession. Despite this partial overlapping in function between relational, possessive and similative adjectives, the three categories should be kept apart, since for several patterns one of the functions can clearly be regarded as the dominant one.

Other derivational categories also exist, but are of minor importance. I will only mention here the category of what one might call **appetitive** adjectives: *wagneriano*, or stronger: *wagnerómano/wagnerólatra* 'admiring Wagner' (← R. Wagner), *librecambista* 'in favour of free trade' (← *librecambio* 'free trade'), *chocolatero* 'chocoholic', *mujeriego* 'womanizing' (← *mujer* 'woman').

4.2.2 Deadjectival adjectives

A first group of patterns that could be mentioned here are combinations of prefixes and relational adjectives, where the prefix however has scope over the nominal base of the adjective. Table 5.2 lists the most important prefixes involved, most of which have equivalents in other European languages. To these one can add the series constituted by a **numeral prefix** and a relational adjective, of the type *mono-, bi-, tri-, cuatri-,* etc. *-lingüe*. For some prefixes, it is also possible to use the noun alone instead of the relational adjective: *(vehículo) bi-plaza* 'two-seated; lit. two-seat (vehicle)', *(servicio) post-venta* 'after-sales (service)', etc. According to Martín García (2005), however, such formations should be viewed as nouns in apposition, not adjectives.

Qualitative adjectives form the bases of a long series of intensive and diminutive prefixes, of which some are pan-European (*archi-, extra-, hiper-, super-, ultra-*), while others are specifically Spanish (*re-, requete-, rete-*); cf. Rodríguez Ponce (2002), García Jiménez (2009).

Spanish also has a rich set of deadjectival adjectival suffixes.

One important category is constituted by **intensive** affixes. The **high degree** is expressed by the suffix *-ísimo* (*guapísimo* 'very handsome' ← *guapo* 'handsome') or lexically governed *-érrimo*, in some Latin-American countries also by augmentative *-azo* and *-ote* (*grandote* 'very big' ← *grande* 'big'). In hyperbolic contexts, intensive prefixes and suffixes are sometimes combined (*archiviejísimo* ← *viejo* 'old', *requeteguapísimo*, etc.). The suffix *-ísimo* can also be subject to partial reduplication (*guapisísimo*), *-ote* can be iterated theoretically indefinitely in Mexico (*grandotototote*).

The second most important group is constituted by **approximative** suffixes. There are only a few unproductive prefixes expressing approximation, while the list of approximative suffixes is quite long. In part these are diminutive suffixes (*azulito* 'blueish' ← *azul* 'blue', *tontillo* 'a bit silly' ← *tonto* 'silly'), but most of them are specialized in this function. They are generally unproductive, however, and only occur in one or a few colour terms: *grisáceo* (← *gris* 'grey'), *amarillento*

Tab. 5.2: Patterns of prefix + relational adjective in Spanish.

prefix		example	nominal base	
inter-	'between'	intercontinental	continente	'continent'
intra-	'inside'	intramuscular	músculo	'muscle'
extra-	'outside of'	extramatrimonial	matrimonio	'marriage'
circum-	'around'	circumpolar	polo	'pole'
infra-	'below'	infrasónico	sonido	'sound'
sub-	'under'	submarino	mar	'sea'
super-	'over'	superindividual	individuo	'individual'
supra-	'over'	supranacional	nación	'nation'
cis-	'on this side of'	cisalpino	Alpes	'Alps'
hiper-	'beyond'	hipersónico	sonido	'sound'
trans-	'through, beyond'	transatlántico	Atlántico	'Atlantic Ocean'
ultra-	'beyond'	ultrapirenaico	Pirineos	'Pyrenees'
ante-	'before'	antediluviano	diluvio	'Flood'
pre-	'before'	precolombino	Colón	'Columbus'
pos(t)-	'after'	posconciliar	concilio	'council'
anti-	'anti-'	antichino	China	'id.'
filo-	'pro-'	filochino	China	'id.'
pro-	'pro'	prochino	China	'id.'
equi-	'same'	equicategorial	categoría	'category'
homo-	'same'	homocategorial	categoría	'category'
iso-	'same'	isosílabo	sílaba	'syllable'
hetero-	'other'	heterocategorial	categoría	'category'
pan-	'all'	panamericano	América	'id.'

(← *amarillo* 'yellow'), *blanquecino* (← *blanco* 'white'), *rojizo* (← *rojo* 'red'), *negruzco* (← *negro* 'black'), etc. The suffix *-ón* is productively used in this function, but only in some Latin-American countries (*gordón* 'somewhat fat' ← *gordo* 'fat').

Apart from these affixes expressing the high or approximative degree, there are also prefixes expressing e x c e s s or i n s u f f i c i e n c y: *hipercrítico* 'overly critical' (← *crítico* 'critical'), *infrapagado* 'underpayed' (← *pagado* 'payed'), *subempleado* 'underemployed' (← *empleado* 'emplyed').

Other degrees expressed derivationally are 'almost' (*cuasi-congelado* 'almost frozen' ← *congelado* 'frozen') and 'half' (*semiseco* 'half-dry' ← *seco* 'dry').

Last but not least, Spanish has a series of n e g a t i v e prefixes (Montero Curiel 1999). *a-* (*aconfesional* 'non confessional') and *no* (*no confesional* 'non confessional') express complementary negation, while *des-* (*desfavorable* 'unfavorable'), *dis-* (*disconforme* 'who disagrees' ← *conforme* 'who agrees') and *in-* (*incompetente* 'incompetent') express contradictory negation.

4.2.3 Deverbal adjectives

Deverbal adjectives fall into three categories: active, passive, and passive-potential.

A c t i v e adjectives are of two types: "pure" ones which may be glossed simply as 'that Vs', and others which have an additional dispositional feature ('prone to V'). Some suffixes can express both meanings at the same time, especially the most productive suffix *-dor*: *conmovedor* 'moving' (← *conmover* 'to move') vs. *ahorrador* 'thrifty' (← *ahorrar* 'to save'). But most of them express only one meaning. There are more than a dozen suffixes of the pure type: *deprimente* 'depressing' (← *deprimir* 'to depress'), *decorativo* 'decorative' (← *decorar* 'to decorate'), *difamatorio* 'defamatory' (← *difamar* 'to vilify'), etc. Half a dozen suffixes are of the dispositional type: *atrevido* 'daring' (← *atreverse* 'to dare'), *adulón* 'flattering' (← *adular* 'to flatter'), etc.

P a s s i v e adjectives are past participles and should probably be considered as cases of conversion (*asfaltado* 'asphalted' ← *asfaltar* 'to asphalt'). As we have just seen in the last paragraph (cf. *atrevido*), this same suffix is also used in Spanish in an active, mostly dispositional meaning, depending on the meaning of the verbal base.

P a s s i v e - p o t e n t i a l adjectives, i.e. those with the meaning 'that can be Ved', are formed productively by *-ble* (*inflable* 'inflatable' ← *inflar* 'to inflate'). In some contexts, *-ble* can also express a deontic meaning ('that should/must be Ved'): *condenable* 'reprehensible' (← *condenar* 'to condemn'), etc. Marginal suffixes of this type are *-dero*, *-dizo* and *-ntío*.

4.3 Verbal derivation

Spanish has a wealth of suffixes for deriving verbs (Rifón 1997; Beniers 2004).

4.3.1 Denominal verbs

Apart from conversion, Spanish has 14 denominal verb-forming patterns. Each of these patterns has a different degree of productivity, different preferences concerning the base nouns and to some extent also a different semantics, which cannot be described in detail here. Intransitive verbs with the meaning 'to behave like an N', for example, are almost exclusively formed by the suffix *-ear* (*gandulear* 'to laze about' ← *gandul* 'lazybones'), while at least four patterns can form transitive verbs with the meaning 'to act as an N (with respect to the object of the verb)' (*pilotar* 'to pilot' [conversion] ← *piloto* 'pilot'; *pastorear* 'to pasture' ← *pastor* 'herdsman'; *tiranizar* 'to tyrannize' ← *tirano* 'tyrant'; *apadriñar* 'to act as godfather of' ← *padrino* 'godfather'). There are a dozen further well-represented semantic niches of this kind (ornative, privative, ablative, causative, instrumental, resultative, locative, etc.), and in each niche the distribution of the patterns is different. Instrumental verbs, for example, are formed by conversion, by the suffix *-ear*, as well as by the parasynthetic patterns *aNar* and *aNear*, while the most productive suffix, *-izar*, is conspicuously absent. Such distributional facts, which await a detailed description, are hardly compatible with the popular view according to which denominal verbs are endowed with a minimal semantics, the concrete meanings being determined only by our encyclopaedic knowledge.

4.3.2 Deadjectival verbs

Deadjectival verbs are either factitive or inchoative. There are no less than 14 patterns expressing the first of these categories, of which however only parasynthetic verbs of the form *aAar* (*acortar* 'to shorten' ← *corto* 'short') and verbs in *-izar* (*rigidizar* 'to make more rigid' ← *rígido* 'rigid') are productive. Of the seven patterns forming inchoative verbs, none seems to be productive. Inchoativity is normally expressed by using the reflexive form of the corresponding transitive verb (*borracho* 'drunk' → *emborrachar* 'to make drunk' → *emborracharse* 'to get drunk').

4.3.3 Deverbal verbs

Spanish has about 50 deverbal verb-forming p r e f i x e s, of which however only a dozen are really productive (Martín García 1998; Felíu Arquiola 2003). *Auto-* stresses that the action is performed by the subject itself and not by somebody else (*autodestruirse* 'to destroy oneself' ← *destruirse* 'to destroy oneself'), *co-* expresses that it is performed together with somebody else (*cofabricar* 'to co-produce' ← *fabricar* 'to produce'), *des-* denotes reversal (*desmaquillar* 'to remove make-up' ← *maquillar* 'to put make-up'), *infra-* and *sub-* add a feature of insufficiency (*infra-/subvalorar* 'to undervalue' ← *valorar* 'to value'), *sobre-* one of excess (*sobrevalorar* 'to overvalue'), *medio* – which can be construed both as an adverb and as a prefix – and *semi-* indicate that only half of the action has been carried out (*medio desnudarse, semidesnudarse* 'to undress half way' ← *desnudarse* 'to undress'), *pre-* that it is carried out before some point in time (*precocinar* 'to precook' ← *cocinar* 'to cook'), and *re-* expresses repetition (*reescribir* 'to rewrite' ← *escribir* 'to write').

The approximately twenty s u f f i x e s which fall into this section invariably express a k t i o n s a r t (iteration, diminution), intermingled with evaluative – mostly pejorative – overtones (cf. Grandi 2015 for the corresponding Italian verbs). None of them is really productive (*besuquear* 'to cover with kisses' ← *besar* 'to kiss', etc.).

4.4 Adverbial derivation

Adverbs are productively derived from adjectives by adding *-mente* to the feminine form of the base (*rápidamente* 'swiftly' ← *rápido*, fem. *rápida* 'swift'); cf. Detges (2015) on the Romance adverbs in *-mente*. The meaning varies a lot, the most frequent readings being 'in an A manner' and 'from an A point of view' (with relational adjectives: *políticamente* 'politically' ← *político* 'political').

5 Conversion

Conversion exists in all parts of speech. Most of the time, the result is adapted to the inflectional morphology of the part of speech in question. On conversions on the basis of discourse elements, such as *pagaré* 'promissory note; lit. I shall pay', cf. Casado Velarde (2010).

5.1 Nominal conversion

The bases of nominal conversions can be nouns, adjectives or verbs. Nouns referring to males can be feminized by simple conversion or by adding the feminine inflectional suffix -*a* where required: *líder* f. ← *líder* m., *profesora* ← *profesor*, *chica* 'girl' ← *chico* 'boy', etc. The effective use of feminization, encouraged by gender-mainstreamers, is currently subject to great uncertainty and regional variation (Roca 2009; Haase 2010). Another type of denominal conversion transforms a fruit name into the corresponding tree name (*castaño* ← *castaña* 'chestnut'). Adjectives can be turned into abstract nouns ([*el*] *ancho* '[the] breadth' ← *ancho* 'broad'), and more productively into personal nouns ([*un*] *pobre* '[a] poor man' ← *pobre* 'poor'; [*un*] *físico* '[a] physicist' ← *físico* 'physical'). These are real conversions, while formations like *zoológico* 'zoo' (← *zoológico* 'zoological') are better viewed as elliptical (the noun *parque* 'park' is still retrievable). As we have already mentioned in section 4.1.3, the infinitive can freely be nominalised in Spanish, a process which is probably better viewed as syntactic (cf. *el haber bebido Juan tanta cerveza* 'John's having drunk so much beer; lit. the to-have drunk John so-much beer'), though some nominalized infinitives are now simple nouns which can even be pluralized (*cantar* 'poem', pl. *cantares* ← *cantar* 'to sing'). Real cases of conversion are action nouns such as *pesca* 'fishing' (← *pescar* 'to fish'), *cese* 'firing' (← *cesar* 'to fire'), *tapeo* 'tapas-eating' (← *tapear* 'to eat tapas'), which show the class markers -*a*, -*e* and -*o*, as well as *control* 'control' (← *controlar* 'to control').

5.2 Adjectival conversion

Nouns can be converted into adjectives in several ways. The most productive bases are nouns associated with a characteristic colour (*violeta* 'purple' ← *violeta* 'violet') and nouns associated with a characteristic behaviour (*cochino* 'filthy' ← *cochino* 'pig'). Nouns ending in a suffix-like sequence are often turned into relational adjectives by conversion (*matemático* 'mathematical' ← *matemática* 'mathematics'; *gomero* 'from La Gomera', cf. Rainer 2008). Some adverbs can be used in an adjectival position without formal adaptation, but this process is possibly better viewed as syntactic (*el entonces presidente* 'the then president').

5.3 Verbal conversion

Both nouns and adjectives are commonly turned into verbs by conversion, as we have already mentioned in sections 4.3.1 and 4.3.2.

5.4 Adverbial conversion

Besides those in *-mente*, there is also a sizeable number of adverbs which remain formally identical to the adjectives which they derive from: *hablar alto* 'to speak loud', *respirar hondo* 'to breathe deep', etc. In the standard language this kind of conversion is essentially restricted to a small set of adjectives in combination with a small set of verbs, while in informal varieties the process is more extensively used (Hummel 2000).

6 Backformation

Backformations have occurred throughout the history of Spanish word-formation (e.g., *legislar* 'to legislate', from *legislación* 'legislation' or *legislador* 'legislator'), but there is no synchronically productive pattern.

7 Reduplication

Reduplication is a relatively marginal phenomenon in Spanish. As we have seen in section 4.2.2, intensive affixes can be iterated, which is not a prototypical case of reduplication, however. Nominal V-V compounds (cf. section 3.1) are relatively rare. Felíu Arquiola (2011) argues that full reduplication of nouns (*mujer mujer* 'real woman' ← *mujer* 'woman'), which implies that the noun should be taken in its prototypical meaning, should be viewed as a "construction" and envisages a similar treatment for the intensifying reduplication of adjectives (*tonto tonto* 'very stupid') and adverbs (*muy muy grande* 'very very big'). As in all languages, there is some repetition of phonological material in onomatopoeia (*cucú* 'cry of the cuckoo', etc.), and Pharies (1986) has described a series of prosodic templates which can be granted the status of phonaestemes, especially in substandard varieties (cf. *ringorrangos* 'frills', *tiquismiquis* 'petty quibbling', etc.).

8 Blending

Blending was already practiced in jocular language in the Spanish of the Golden Age (cf. *ramería* 'wild pilgrimage' ← *romería* 'pilgrimage' x *ramera* 'whore'), but has gained great popularity over the last decades, probably under Anglo-American influence. Its general strategies are very much the same as in other languages (Piñeros 2004). The splinter *-gate* 'scandal', originally detached from *Watergate*, has become productive also in Spanish journalistic usage: *Zapaterogate*, *espía-gate* ← *espía* 'spy', etc. (Méndez Santos 2011).

9 Clipping

Clipping is a very popular process in colloquial Spanish. The output, in the normal case, corresponds to the unmarked foot in Spanish prosody (two syllables, stress on the first syllable; cf. Piñeros 2000): *progre* (← *progresista* 'progressive'), *cumple* (← *cumpleaños* 'birthday'), etc. In slang words, we also find trisyllabic outputs, occasionally with a "parasitic" ending: *Atleti* (← Atlético de Madrid, a football team), *masoca* (← *masoquista* 'masochist'), etc. This latter example comes close to colloquial formations in *-ata*, a suffix which truncates its base in order to produce a tri-, more rarely quadrisyllabic output: *bocata* (← *bocadillo* 'sandwich'), *ordenata* (← *ordenador* 'computer'), etc.

Furthermore, the use of acronyms (e.g., *OTAN* /otan/ 'NATO') and abbreviations (e.g., *S.A.R.* 'Her Majesty', from *Su Alteza Real*) has grown in Spanish as in other languages, especially since the second half of the 20th century.

10 Word-creation

There are two phenomena which might be classified as word-creation in the sense of this handbook. On one hand, brand names can be created in Spanish in a manner which is just as artificial as in other languages (cf. *Telmex*, name of a Mexican telephone company). More interesting are word games, practiced in some Latin-American countries, which consist in the playful deformation of words, often with the help of suffixes used in a fanciful way: *¡clarífico!*, *¡clarín!*, *¡clarinete!* (← *¡claro!* 'Of course!'), *cafesiano* (← *café* 'coffee'), etc.

11 References

Alemany Bolufer, José (1920): *Tratado de la formación de palabras en la lengua castellana*. Madrid: Suárez.
Amador Rodríguez, Luis Alexis (2009): *La derivación nominal en español. Nombres de agente, instrumento, lugar y acción*. Frankfurt/M.: Lang.

Amiot, Dany (2015): The grammaticalization of prepositions in French word-formation. In: Peter O. Müller, Ingeborg Ohnheiser, Susan Olsen and Franz Rainer (eds.), *Word-Formation. An International Handbook of the Languages of Europe*. Vol. 3, 1811–1824. Berlin/Boston: De Gruyter Mouton.

Arnaud, Pierre J. L. (2025): Noun-noun compounds in French. In: Peter O. Müller, Susan Olsen and Franz Rainer (eds.), *Word-Formation – Special Patterns and Restrictions*, 103–120. Berlin/Boston: De Gruyter Mouton.

Beniers, Elisabeth (2004): *La formación de verbos en el español de México*. México: El Colegio de México.

Bork, Hans Dieter (1990): *Die lateinisch-romanischen Zusammensetzungen Nomen + Verb und der Ursprung der romanischen Verb-Ergänzung-Komposita*. Bonn: Romanistischer Verlag.

Bosque, Ignacio and Violeta Demonte (eds.) (1999): *Gramática descriptiva de la lengua española*. Vol. 3: *Entre la oración y el discurso. Morfología*. Madrid: Espasa Calpe.

Booij, Geert (2025): Word-formation in construction grammar. In: Peter O. Müller, Susan Olsen and Franz Rainer (eds.), *Word-Formation – History, Theories, Units and Processes*, 99–117. Berlin/Boston: De Gruyter Mouton.

Buenafuentes de la Mata, Cristina (2010): *La composición sintagmática en español*. San Millán de la Cogolla: cilengua.

Casado Velarde, Manuel (2010): Discurso y creación léxica: Delocutivos y decitativos en español. *Revista de Investigación Lingüística* 13: 65–85.

Curcó, Carmen (1998): ¿*No me harías un favorcito?*: Reflexiones en torno a la expresión de la cortesía verbal en el español de México y el español peninsular. *Diálogos Hispánicos* 22: 129–171.

Czerwenka, Christine (2009): *Substantiv + Substantiv im Spanischen. Wortbildung und Grammatik*. Frankfurt/M.: Lang.

Detges, Ulrich (2015): The Romance adverbs in -mente: a case study in grammaticalization. In: Peter O. Müller, Ingeborg Ohnheiser, Susan Olsen and Franz Rainer (eds.), *Word-Formation. An International Handbook of the Languages of Europe*. Vol. 3, 1824–1842. Berlin/Boston: De Gruyter Mouton.

Eddington, David (2002): Spanish diminutive formation without rules or constraints. *Linguistics* 40: 395–419.

Eins, Wieland (2025): Types of foreign word-formation. In: Peter O. Müller, Susan Olsen and Franz Rainer (eds.), *Word-Formation – Language Contact and Diachrony*, 1–23. Berlin/Boston: De Gruyter Mouton.

Fábregas, Antonio (2016): *Las nominalizaciones*. Madrid: Visor.

Fábregas, Antonio (2020): *Morphologically derived adjectives in Spanish*. Amsterdam/Philadelphia: Benjamins.

Fábregas, Antonio (2023): *Spanish verbalisations and the internal structure of lexical predicates*. London: Routledge.

Fábregas, Antonio (2024a): *Diccionario de afijos del español contemporáneo*. London: Routledge.

Fábregas, Antonio (2024b): *The fine-grained structure of the lexical área*. Amsterdam/Philadelphia: Benjamins.

Fábregas, Antonio, Víctor Acedo-Matellán, Grant Armstrong, María Cristina Cuervo and Isabel Pujol-Payet (eds.) (2020): *The Routledge handbook of Spanish morphology*. London: Routledge.

Felíu Arquiola, Elena (2003): *Morfología derivativa y semántica léxica. La prefijación de auto-, co- e inter-*. Madrid: Ediciones de la Universidad Autónoma de Madrid.

Felíu Arquiola, Elena (2011): Las reduplicaciones léxicas nominales en español actual. *Verba* 38: 95–126.

Gaeta, Livio (2015): Action nouns in Romance. In: Peter O. Müller, Ingeborg Ohnheiser, Susan Olsen and Franz Rainer (eds.), *Word-Formation. An International Handbook of the Languages of Europe.* Vol. 2, 1209–1229. Berlin/Boston: De Gruyter Mouton.

García Jiménez, Inmaculada (2009): Apuntaciones sobre dos prefijos tan populares como desconocidos: *rete-* y *requete-. Romanistisches Jahrbuch* 60: 239–275.

García-Medall, Joaquín (1995): *Casi un siglo de formación de palabras del español (1900–1994). Guía bibliográfica.* València: Facultad de filología, Universitat de València.

García-Page, Mario (2011): *Hombre clave, hombre rana, ¿un mismo fenómeno? Verba* 38: 127–170.

García Sánchez, Jairo Javier (2005): Irradiación analógica en la formación de gentilicios. *Vox Romanica* 64: 160–170.

Grandi, Nicola (2015): Word-formation and lexical aspect: deverbal verbs in Italian. In: Peter O. Müller, Ingeborg Ohnheiser, Susan Olsen and Franz Rainer (eds.), *Word-Formation. An International Handbook of the Languages of Europe.* Vol. 2, 1467–1482. Berlin/Boston: De Gruyter Mouton.

Haase, Peter (2010): *Feminisierung im spanischen Sprachraum.* Hamburg: Kovač.

Herwartz, Rachel (2002): Lavadora, cafetera, sacacorchos – *Spanische Gerätebezeichnungen in Technik, Werbung und Alltag.* Frankfurt/M.: Lang.

Holzer, Peter (1996): *Das Relationsadjektiv in der spanischen und deutschen Gegenwartssprache.* Wilhelmsfeld: Egert.

Hummel, Martin (2000): *Adverbale und adverbialisierte Adjektive im Spanischen. Konstruktionen des Typs* Los niños duermen tranquilos *und* María corre rápido. Tübingen: Narr.

Hummel, Martin (2025): The semantics and pragmatics of Romance evaluative suffixes. In: Peter O. Müller, Susan Olsen and Franz Rainer (eds.), *Word-Formation – Semantics and Pragmatics*, 355–374. Berlin/Boston: De Gruyter Mouton.

Iglesias Cancela, Yolanda (2021): *Los temas cultos en la formación de palabras complejas del español.* Strasbourg: ELiPhi.

Lang, Mervyn F. (1990): *Spanish Word Formation. Productive derivational morphology in the modern lexis.* London/New York: Routledge.

Lindner, Thomas and Franz Rainer (2025): Word-formation in Neo-Latin. In: Peter O. Müller, Susan Olsen and Franz Rainer (eds.), *Word-Formation – Language Contact and Diachrony*, 47–68. Berlin/Boston: De Gruyter Mouton.

Lliteras, Margarita (2003): Concurrencia histórica de los derivados en *-ción* y *-miento.* In: Fernando Sánchez Miret (ed.), *Actas del XXIII Congreso Internacional de Lingüística y Filología Románica (Salamanca, 24–30 septiembre 2001).* Vol. 1, 377–384. Tübingen: Niemeyer.

Martín Camacho, José Carlos (2002): *El problema lingüístico de los interfijos españoles.* Cáceres: Universidad de Extremadura.

Martín García, Josefa (1998): *La morfología léxico-conceptual. Las palabras derivadas con RE-.* Madrid: Ediciones de la Universidad Autónoma de Madrid.

Martín García, Josefa (2005): Los nombres prefijados en aposición. *Verba* 32: 25–57.

Martín Vegas, Rosa Ana (2005): ¿Segmentación morfemática o reanálisis? Formaciones con el sufijo *-idad* o **-abilidad, *-icidad, *-eidad* ... . *Moenia* 11: 269–281.

Méndez Santos, María del Carmen (2011): Sobre *-gate*: Origen, significado y comportamiento morfológico. *Cuadernos del Instituto Historia de la lengua* 6: 23–43.

Monjour, Alf (2003): La valencia nominal en español: Observaciones y sugerencias. In: Fernando Sánchez Miret (ed.), *Actas del XXIII Congreso Internacional de Lingüística y Filología Románica (Salamanca, 24–30 septiembre 2001).* Vol. 1, 89–101. Tübingen: Niemeyer.

Montero Curiel, María Luisa (1999): *La prefijación negativa en español.* Cáceres: Universidad de Extremadura.

Moyna, María Irene (2011): *Compound Words in Spanish. Theory and history*. Amsterdam/Philadelphia: Benjamins.
NGLE = Real Academia Española and Asociación de Academias de la Lengua Española (2010): *Nueva gramática de la lengua española*. Madrid: Espasa.
Pena, Jesús (2003): Los estudios de morfología del español en España durante los últimos 25 años (1979–2003). *Lingüística Española Actual* 25: 7–38.
Pena, Jesús (2004): Morfología de los nombres de cualidad derivados. *Verba* 31: 7–42.
Pharies, David (1986): *Structure and Analogy in the Playful Lexicon of Spanish*. Tübingen: Niemeyer.
Pharies, David (1994): *Bibliography of Latin and Ibero-Romance Suffixation*. Madison: Hispanic Seminary of Medieval Studies.
Pharies, David (2002): *Diccionario etimológico de los sufijos españoles*. Madrid: Gredos.
Piñeros, Carlos-Eduardo (2000): Prosodic and segmental unmarkedness in Spanish truncation. *Linguistics* 38: 63–98.
Pharies, David and Erica Fischer-Dorantes (2024): *Diccionario etimológico e histórico de los prefijos de la lengua española*. Berlin/Boston: De Gruyter.
Piñeros, Carlos-Eduardo (2004): The creation of portmanteaus in the extragrammatical morphology of Spanish. *Probus* 16: 203–240.
Rainer, Franz (1993a): *Spanische Wortbildungslehre*. Tübingen: Niemeyer.
Rainer, Franz (1993b): Setenta años (1921–1990) de investigación en la formación de palabras del español moderno: Bibliografía crítica selectiva. In: Soledad Varela (ed.), *La formación de palabras*, 30–70. Madrid: Taurus.
Rainer, Franz (2008): Inhibition of suffixation by suffix-like final strings in Spanish. In: Bernard Fradin (ed.), *La raison morphologique. Hommage à la mémoire de Danielle Corbin*, 175–195. Amsterdam/Philadelphia: Benjamins.
Rainer, Franz (2009): El origen de los nombres de instrumento en -*dora* del español. *Vox Romanica* 68: 199–217.
Rainer, Franz (2011): The agent-instrument-place "polysemy" of the suffix -TOR in Romance. *STUF – Language Typology and Universals* 64: 8–32.
Rainer, Franz (2024a): El desarrollo de los sufijos -*īcius* e -*ĭcius* en la Iberorromania. *Lletres Asturianes* 130: 6–37.
Rainer, Franz (2024b): La proliferación del sufijo -*INA* en las lenguas románicas. *Revue de Linguistique Romane* 88(2): 381–432.
Rainer, Franz (2025): Mechanisms and motives of change in word-formation. In: Peter O. Müller, Susan Olsen and Franz Rainer (eds.), *Word-Formation – Language Contact and Diachrony*, 203–227. Berlin/Boston: De Gruyter Mouton.
Ricca, Davide (2025): Verb-noun compounds in Romance. In: Peter O. Müller, Susan Olsen and Franz Rainer (eds.), *Word-Formation – Special Patterns and Restrictions*, 121–143. Berlin/Boston: De Gruyter Mouton.
Rifón, Antonio (1997): *Pautas semánticas para la formación de verbos en español mediante sufijación*. Santiago de Compostela: Universidade de Santiago de Compostela.
Roca, Ignacio M. (2009): Todas las vascas son vascos, y muchos vascos también vascas: Género y sexo en el castellano. *Boletín de la Real Academia Española* 89: 77–117.
Rodríguez Ponce, María Isabel (2002): *La prefijación apreciativa en español*. Cáceres: Universidad de Extremadura.
Sánchez López, Cristina (2003): La relación de posesión inalienable en los compuestos. In: José Luis Girón Alconchel, F. Javier Herrero Ruiz de Loizaga, Silvia Iglesias Recuero and Antonio Narbona Jiménez (eds.), *Estudios ofrecidos al profesor José Jesús de Bustos Tovar*. Vol. 1, 157–169. Madrid: Editorial Complutense.

Scherer, Carmen (2025): Change in productivity. In: Peter O. Müller, Susan Olsen and Franz Rainer (eds.), *Word-Formation – Language Contact and Diachrony*, 229–242. Berlin/Boston: De Gruyter Mouton.

Tejera, María Josefina (2007): *La derivación mixta en el español de Venezuela*. Caracas: Universidad Central de Venezuela.

Maria Grossmann
6 Romanian

1 Introduction
2 General overview
3 Composition
4 Derivation
5 Conversion
6 Backformation
7 Reduplication
8 Blending
9 Clipping and acronymy
10 References

Abstract: This article offers a brief survey of the main word-formation patterns in present-day Romanian. Special attention will be paid to more productive processes, though patterns which are less or no longer productive will not be neglected.

1 Introduction

Word-formation in Romanian has not received much attention in recent literature on morphology. Even today the main reference texts remain the extensive monographs by Ciobanu and Hasan (1970), Graur and Avram (1978), Vasiliu (1989), which provide descriptive overviews of compounding, prefixation and verbal derivation, and the numerous contributions on individual word-formation patterns in SMFC (1959–72). Fischer (1989) and Vasiliu (2009) provide both synchronic and diachronic surveys of word-formation in Romanian, together with bibliographies of the most important studies. Very useful are the entries in Sala (2001), which cover all aspects of word-formation in Romanian. Recently two further works of reference have been published which also include chapters on word-formation (Dobrovie-Sorin and Giurgea 2013; Pană Dindelegan 2013). A number of studies published over the last fifteen years, such as Stoichițoiu Ichim (2001, 2006), Trifan (2010), Vârlan (2012), focus on the lexical creativity of contemporary Romanian and constitute important starting-points for the study of the productivi-

Maria Grossmann, L'Aquila, Italy

ty of certain patterns. Several examples of newly-coined lexemes cited in this article are taken from these sources. For studies on the history of Romanian word-formation, the reader is referred to Rădulescu Sala (2015a). In this survey bibliographic references will be strictly limited.

2 General overview

The differences between Romanian and other Romance languages can be attributed to independent evolution and different linguistic contacts. Up until the early decades of the 19th century loans and calques based on Slavic, Hungarian, Turkish and Greek models conferred specific characteristics on Romanian, also regarding word-formation patterns. Subsequent pattern-enrichment by numerous loans and calques from French, Italian and Latin has constituted one of the essential factors in the re-Romanization and modernization of Romanian. In recent decades English models have also exercised a strong influence. The wide range of etymological sources and their historical stratification have meant that Romanian has a much richer inventory of affixes and allomorphs than other Romance languages. The possibility of combining bases and affixes from different sources, entering at different historical epochs or belonging to different registers, is often exploited to create nonce-formations with ironic connotations and greater expressivity. The radical political transformation of Romania post 1989 and massive spread of mass communications, in particular the Internet, have also had important linguistic consequences. The disappearance of the need to use a kind of "wooden language" in all forms of public communication and the growth in the numbers of people with access to the media, has led to an explosion of lexical creativity, and to wider use of patterns which had been specific to colloquial registers and slang.

As in other Romance languages, the most important word-formation device in Romanian is affixation, in particular suffixation. Compared to other Romance languages, conversion plays a greater role due to the productivity of certain patterns, such as supine nominalization and adjective adverbialization. The most important distinguishing characteristic of Romanian suffixation consists of the presence – as in inflection – of a complex system of allomorphs due to the numerous vowel and consonant alternations which interact with stress assignment (for a more recent descriptive analysis of the phonological system of Romanian see Chitoran 2002; Pană Dindelegan 2013: 607–611 also provides an inventory of inflectional and derivational morphophonological alternations). Unlike suffixation, prefixation lacks alternations and stress-shift. Compound words are formed by concatenating two or more free forms, two combining forms, or a free form and a combining form; in some patterns constituents are joined by a linking element. As for the delimitation of compounds with respect to phrases, the various criteria proposed can be assimilated to two criteria often used in the literature: for a construction to exhibit compoundhood it should: a) denote a unitary concept; b) represent a syntactic atom. Stress assignment is not considered relevant since compounds behave differently as regards stress properties depending on the degree of lexicalization and frequency of usage. The most problematic issue appears to be the dividing line between phrases and certain types of nominal compounds (appositive N-N, N-A, N-N$_{GEN}$, N-Prep-N).

3 Composition

Among the various means by which Romanian and other Romance languages form new words from existing ones, compounding is by no means the one preferred (Ciobanu and Hasan 1970; Giurescu 1975; Grossmann 2012, which forms the basis of this overview). Although there are several patterns for forming compounds, in present-day Romanian only nominal and adjectival compounding are fully productive. Verbal compounds are rare and the process is no longer productive. Constructions made up of several free forms belonging to other syntactic categories are generally the result of univerbation of phrases or sentences. For numeral compounding with patterns that partially differ from those of other Romance languages, see the works cited above.

3.1 Nominal compounds

In Romanian, as in other Romance languages, most compounds are nouns. Compound nouns are formed according to various patterns, but only N-N compounding is fully productive. Established compounds formed according to other patterns usually belong to folk taxonomies and have a metaphoric or metonymic origin. The prototypical native compound is left-headed.

N-N compounds are typical of learned registers, and today are used in the language of the mass-media, in technical-scientific terminology, etc. In the recent spread of this type an important role has undoubtedly been played by French and English models. Compounds usually involve two juxtaposed N; the rare instances of constructions with more than two elements are formed recursively ([*sud*-[*sud-est*]] 'South-Southeast'). Unlike A-A compounds and constructions that involve combining forms, N-N compounds are usually formed without a linking element. Coordinate N-N compounds are made up of two constituents, semantically at the same taxonomic level, which simultaneously identify/classify the entity denoted by the compound. This type of construction can refer to: professions and roles (*finisor-asamblator* 'finisher-assembler'), instruments (*secerătoare-legătoare* harvester-binder 'combine harvester'), means of transport (*taxi-furgonetă* 'taxi-van'), ideologies (*centru-stânga* 'centre-left'), periods of time (*toamnă-iarnă* 'fall-winter'), cardinal points (*sud-est* 'south-east'), etc. Some are endocentric and have two semantic heads, whereas compounds that identify an entity not corresponding to any of the individual constituents, but rather to intersections of the two, are exocentric. As for gender assignment, in case of conflict coordinate compounds appear to inherit gender from the left-hand constituent. Plural marking usually occurs on both constituents. Case and definiteness markers are added to the left-hand member or, in compounds with a high degree of integration, word-finally. The order of constituents is in principle free, but not every ordering has the same probability of occurrence. Another group of N-N constructions which encompasses most of the new coinages is made up of appositive compounds. The head constituent, which occurs on the left, classifies/identifies the entity designated by the compound, whereas the non-head, whose function is appositive, characterizes/qualifies it. This group includes established compounds, such as *pasăre-muscă* bird-fly 'hummingbird', but is mostly made up of constructions systematically displaying as non-head elements a few specific N (some of them calques); examples are *cheie* 'key', *fluviu* 'river', *fulger* 'lightning', *şablon* 'pattern, template'. Such N carry in the construction meanings – often metaphoric – which only partially overlap with the meanings they carry when used autonomously (*femeie bombă* woman bomb 'gorgeous woman'). The left-hand constituent determines the gender of the compound and is usually also the locus of inflection. However, given that the non-head elements in this type of compound bear qualifying meanings of an adjectival nature, some tend to inherit also other properties of adjectives, such as number agreement, predicative use and modifiability. The third, a much smaller group of N-N compounds, is made up of constructions of the subordinate type. This kind of compound displays object-, subject-, or adjunct-oriented argumental relations between the constituents. Generally they are left-headed forms (*coborâre(-)femei* downhill run(-)women 'women's downhill'); right-headed compounds are calqued on non-native models, and some are obsolete (*argint-tăietoriu* silver-cutter 'silversmith'). This type of compound inherits gender from the head-constituent; inflectional and definiteness markers invariably appear on the head.

Many established subordinate nominal compounds belong to two rather similar patterns having very low productivity: N-N$_{GEN}$ and N-Prep-N. In the first of these, the genitive-marked constituent follows the head N (*cerul-gurii* sky:DEF-mouth:DEF.GEN 'palate'), whereas in the second, the two N are linked by a preposition (*lapte-de-pasăre* milk-of-bird 'snow eggs'). In both patterns the compound as a whole inherits the gender of its head and the head receives inflectional markers. Only constructions which are no longer transparent have external inflection. These constructions have a head as far as grammatical properties are concerned, but are exocentric from a semantic point of view. Many endocentric N-Prep-N compound-like constructions (*maşină de spălat* 'washing machine'; cf. Giurescu 1975) with similar characteristics require further analysis.

As for headedness, attributive nominal compounds involving an adjective can be divided into three groups: left-headed N-A c o m p o u n d s (*iarbă-mare* grass-big 'elecampane'), right-headed A-N c o m p o u n d s (*rea-voinţă* ill-will 'malevolence'), and exocentric constructions (*cap-sec* head-atrophied 'blockhead'). While in compounds formed in Romanian the N is on the left, in constructions calqued on non-native models both A-N and N-A orders can be found. Although compounds exhibit internal agreement based on syntactic rules, these constructions are quite different from the corresponding noun phrases: the A cannot be modified by an adverb, nor can it be coordinated with another adjective. Gender is determined by the N constituent, except in exocentric formations denoting humans, whose gender depends on the biological gender. As for inflection, some compounds exhibit a high degree of integration and take inflectional markers on the right-hand constituent. In other constructions both members are marked according to syntactic rules, while others are invariable. These patterns show low productivity.

The e x o c e n t r i c V-N p a t t e r n, quite common in other Romance languages, has very limited productivity in Romanian. Most compounds of this kind are made up of metaphorical derogatory epithets (*zgârie-brânză* scratch-cheese 'skinflint'); there are a limited number of plant and animal names (*suge-pin* suck-pine 'pinesap', *mulge-capre* milk-goat:PL 'nightjar'); even the few new coinages that do exist pertain to the domain of colloquialisms (*fură-becuri* steal-lightbulb:PL 'beanpole, tall person'). Another group of similar formations is made up of calques (*zgârie-nori* scrape-cloud:PL 'sky-scraper'). The combining form *port-* 'carry', productively used to form semantically similar constructions (*portochelari* 'glasses case'), is taken from the many compounds loaned from French containing this verbal element. The left-hand member is a transitive V that formally coincides with both the third-person singular of the present indicative and the singular imperative form, whereas the right-hand constituent is usually an indefinite N that is the object argument of the V. The second member can be either a singular or a plural N, but the compound as a whole is, with few exceptions, invariable.

3.2 Adjectival compounds

Compound adjectives are formed according to a number of patterns, but only A-A and N-A/A-N are fully productive. As well as two-item compounds, there also exist nonce-formations made up of more than two A that cannot be broken down into binary structures (*globalizare politico-economico-militară* 'political-economic-military globalisation'). As in other Romance languages, the vast majority of compound adjectives are made up of constructions involving adjectives only. The constituents can occur either in the form of a free word (*dulce-acru* 'sweet-sour') or with an internal readjustment consisting in the addition of the linking element *-o-* (*burghezo-democratic* 'bourgeois-democratic') as in compounds involving combining forms. Many constructions, with or without a linking element, are variants, but do not appear to have the same frequency. Constructions with a linking *-o-* have a single morphological locus for agreement at the end of the sequence and are characterized by a higher degree of integration. When they do not include a linking element, compounds that allow the double pattern show some wavering between agreement on the second A only, and agreement on both A. As regards the relationship between the constituents, adjectival compounds can be divided into two groups: coordinate and subordinate. Most belong to the first group. In coordinate compounding we have two or more A, semantically at the same taxonomic level, which modify the head N both independently and simultaneously (*spectacol comico-dramatic* 'comic-dramatic show', *steag roșu-galben* 'red-yellow flag'). However, most constituents of coordinate compounds are derived relational adjectives. Compounds of this kind represent adjectival transposition of the merging of two or more nouns, and classify/identify the *designata* of the head nouns (*dialog creștino-islamic* 'dialogue between Christians and Muslims', *expediție româno-italiană* 'Romanian-Italian expedition'). Constructions with a subordinate relationship between constituents are less frequent. These are mostly compound colour terms that refer to a given shade of the colour denoted by the left-hand constituent (*verde-aprins* 'bright green', *galben-verzui* 'greenish yellow', *verde-măsliniu* 'olive green'). As for inflectional properties, this type of compound exhibits fluctuation between agreement only on the first A, only on the second A, on both A and on neither A.

Among compounds involving an N and an A, the most productive patterns are: a) the left-headed type formed by a colour adjective and a N specifying shade (*alb-colilie* 'feather grass white') and b) the right-headed type formed by the name of a cardinal point and an ethnic adjective (*est-european* 'East European'). The adjectival head is the locus of inflection in both cases; compounds of the first type are sometimes invariable.

Right-headed Adv-A compounds, mostly calques, are made up of an adverb and a deverbal adjectival head that is the morphological locus for agreement (*nou-înfiinţat* 'newly set up', *prost-crescut* 'ill-bred'). This pattern exhibits low productivity.

3.3 Verbal compounds

As in other Romance languages, Romanian verbal compounds are rare and the process is no longer productive. Most established instances have the adverb *bine* 'well' as first element, followed by the verbal head (*binecuvânta* 'to bless'). Other examples are some slang V-V compounds inflected on the second constituent (*furlua* 'to steal, embezzle').

3.4 Compounds involving combining forms

Nominal, adjectival and verbal compounds involving combining forms differ from the above-mentioned types in that at least one of their constituents is not attested as a free form in Romanian. Such constituents may be neoclassical elements taken from Ancient Greek or Latin, directly or via other European languages, free forms borrowed from other languages that in Romanian become combining forms, or bound elements whose final segments are formally similar to those of a Romanian word but are attested only in compounding. Compounds involving combining forms, whether loans, calques or Romanian formations for the most part belong only to learned registers, but some have also entered common usage. As in other Romance languages, the pattern is highly productive. In compounds made up of a combining form and a Romanian word, the latter is usually final (*electrocasnic* 'home appliance'), seldom initial (*pomicol* 'relating to fruit-growing'). Combining forms may be members of endocentric and exocentric compounds. Most nominal compounds are endocentric but, unlike compounds not involving combining forms, they have a modifier-head structure (*lactometru* 'lactometer'). Left-headed (*filantropie* 'philanthropy'), coordinate (*gastroenterită* 'gastroenteritis') and exocentric (*portavion* 'aircraft carrier') compound nouns are less common. These same structures are displayed by adjectival compounds made up of two combining forms or of a combining form and a Romanian adjective: these are generally right-headed (*aurifer* 'auriferous'), more rarely left-headed (*filoenglez* 'anglophile') or coordinate ((*atac*) *angloamerican* 'Anglo-American (attack)'). The structure of verbal compounds is invariably modifier-head (*teleghida* 'to operate by remote control').

Many compounds made up of a Romanian word and a combining form are formed with a linking element in accordance with the neoclassical model. If the Romanian element ends in a consonant, the linking element is added (*cioboteca* 'collection of potsherds'), whereas in vowel-final forms the vowel is modified into *-i-* or *-o-* depending on whether the final combining form is of Latin or Greek origin (*legumicol* 'relating to vegetable-growing'). Many new terms coined according to this model are playful and often bear a negative connotation (*bârfologie* 'gossipology').

4 Derivation

In Romanian, as in other Romance languages, derivation is the most important device for forming new words. The subsections that follow offer an overview of the patterns classified according to output, input and semantic category.

4.1 Nominal derivation

4.1.1 Denominal nouns

The meanings of prefixed nominal lexemes formed in accordance with productive rules can be grouped into various categories, the most important being localization, intensification and oppositeness (Graur and Avram 1978). The category with the largest number of semantic values and prefixes is localization. It includes prefixes such as *ante-*, *ex-*, *extra-*, *inter-*, *neo-*, *post-*, *pre-*, *sub-*, *supra-*, with equivalents in other European languages, which express spatial, temporal and abstract localization (*extrasezon* 'off-season', *interstație* 'transit corridor between subway stations', *subprimar* 'deputy-mayor'). Several prefixes with originally locative meanings, such as *extra-*, *super-*, *supra-*, *ultra-*, are productive mainly with intensifying function (*extra(-)premiu* 'extra-prize', *super(-)gospodină* 'super-housewife'). Greater or lesser quantities/qualities are denoted also by other prefixes, these too internationalisms, such as *hiper-*, *maxi-*, *mega-*, *micro-*, *mini-*, *semi-* (*mega(-)reducere* 'mega-discount', *mini(-)oraș* 'mini-town'). A semantic niche consists of folk-names of certain ascending/descending degrees of kinship formed by the intensifying prefix *stră-* and/or the reiterative one *răs-* (*răz-*), sometimes applied recursively (*strănepot* 'great-grandson', *răs(-)străbunic* 'great-great-grandfather', *stră(-)strănepot* 'great-great-grandson'). All oppositive prefixes, namely *a-* (*an-*), *anti-*, *contra-*, *des-* (*dez-*, *de-*), *in-* (*im-*, *i-*), *ne-*, *non-*, select nominal and adjectival bases (cf. section 4.2.2), *contra-* and *des-* (*dez-*, *de-*) are added also to verbs (cf. section 4.3), while the domain of *ne-* includes also adverbs (cf. section 4.4), as well as pronouns and conjunctions. The most productive is *ne-*, which attaches mainly to abstract nouns (*plăcere* → *neplăcere* 'displeasure'), including established phrases (*în regulă* → *neînregulă* 'not all right'), and which forms contraries and contradictories of the base words. *Ne-*, rather than the negative particle *nu* 'not', is employed in the negation of some non-finite verbal forms, namely the gerund (*auzind* → *neauzind* 'not hearing'), the participle (*auzit* → *neauzit* 'unheard') and the supine (*de auzit* → *de neauzit* 'inaudible'). A characteristic of these types of forms is that they allow the intercalation of the adverbs *mai* 'yet' and *prea* 'quite' (*neauzit* → *nemaiauzit* 'not yet heard', *neavând* → *nepreaavând* 'not quite having'). Lexemes with *in-* (*im-*, *i-*) are mostly loans or calques; the numerous synonyms in *ne-* and *in-* sharing the same base are due to the tendency to substitute *in-* with *ne-* in these lexemes too. As for nominal *des-* (*dez-*, *de-*) derivatives, those formed in Romanian are few in number and refer to a lack of what is denoted by the base (*nădejde* 'hope' → *deznădejde* 'hopelessness'). Formations in *anti-*, *contra-*, *non-*, and especially *a-* (*an-*), belong to learned registers and are mostly loans or calques.

The numerous s u f f i x e s deriving denominal nouns in Romanian can be grouped in the following semantic categories.

P e r s o n a l n o u n s are derived, in decreasing order of productivity, with *-ist*, *-ar* (*-er*), *-giu* (*-agiu*, *-angiu*) and *-aș* (*-eș*). Among the bases of *-ist* we also find proper nouns, acronyms and established phrases (*habar n-am* 'I have no idea' → *habarnamist* 'ignorant, illiterate'), while the domains of *-ar*, *-giu* and *-aș* seem to be more restricted, but comprise some verbs too (*ospăta* 'to entertain sb. as a guest' → *ospătar* 'waiter'; *rata* 'to miss, fail' → *ratangiu* 'mistake-prone player'; *cerceta* 'to explore' → *cercetaș* 'scout'). To judge by newly-coined lexemes, a number of professional sectors, such as computing (*soft* → *softist* 'software technician'), mass-media (*știre* → *știrist* 'news presenter') and sport (*craul* → *craulist* 'crawl swimmer'), continue to make substantial use of *-ist* suffixation. As for derivatives in *-ar*, among both more recent coinages (*pizza* → *pizzar* 'pizza maker') and less recent ones (*ceasornic* 'clock' → *ceasornicar* 'watchmaker'), there prevail nouns denoting more or less manual and traditional trades. Also numerous are derivatives in *-ist* and in *-ar* denoting a person with a certain characteristic or habit (*ochelari* → *ochelarist* 'glasses wearer'; *fleac* 'babble' → *flecar* 'babbler'). The small number of newly-coined personal nouns in *-aș* are of this type too (*U[nitate] S[pecială de] L[uptă] A[ntiteroristă]* → *uslaș* 'member of the Special Unit for the Fight against Terrorism'). With few exceptions, such as *camion* → *camionagiu* 'trucker', derivatives in *-giu* denote extinct trades, or kinds of behaviour considered negatively (*scandal* → *scandalagiu* 'brawler').

Gender-marking is realized by inflectional class change, suffixation, compounding or backformation. As for derivation of nouns denoting female humans from nouns denoting males, inflectional class change (*student* → *studentă*) and compounding with the lexeme *femeie* 'woman' are characteristic above all of formal registers, whereas derivations with *-că*, *-easă*, *-iță* and *-oaică* (*țăran* 'peasant' → *țărancă*; *mire* 'bridegroom' → *mireasă*; *călugăr* 'monk' → *călugăriță*; *drac* 'devil' → *drăcoaică*) also occur in the colloquial register and often bear a playful and negative connotation. Some of these suffixes are also used to create diminutives. As for the opposite type, that is formation of nouns denoting males from nouns denoting females, Romanian makes recourse to inflectional class change (*prostituat* ← *prostituată* 'prostitute') or to backformation (*lenjer* 'garment worker' ← *lenjereasă* 'seamstress'). Nouns denoting female animals are derived from nouns denoting males by means of the above-mentioned suffixes (*catâr* 'mule' → *catârcă*; *păun* 'peacock' → *păuniță*; *vulpe* 'fox' → *vulpoaică*), but in the case of *-easă*, which is restricted to bases denoting human beings, only in playful nonce-formations. The inverse process, that is male ← female, is realized with the augmentative suffixes *-oi* and *-an* (*rățoi* ← *rață* 'duck'; *gâscan* ← *gâscă* 'goose'), by inflectional class change (*pisic* ← *pisică* 'cat') or by substituting the feminine form of a suffix or of a homophonous segment with the corresponding masculine form (*privighetor* ← *privighetoare* 'nightingale'; *turturel* ← *turturea* 'turtle dove').

Suffixation with *-ar* and *-aș* allows the formation not only of personal nouns but also of instrument nouns, though with differing inflectional properties: *-ar/-aș*$_{MSG}$ – *-ară/-așă*$_{FSG}$ – *-ari/-ași*$_{MPL}$ – *-are/-așe*$_{FPL}$ in the case of personal nouns, *-ar/-aș*$_{NSG}$ – *-are/-așe*$_{NPL}$ in the case of instrument nouns. These patterns, nowadays almost unproductive, have given birth to names of simple objects and tools (*deget* 'finger' → *degetar* 'thimble'; *umăr* 'shoulder' → *umeraș* 'coat hanger'). The suffix *-ieră*, on the other hand, has a certain vitality, forming, on the model of loans and calques from French, names of articles of clothing made to protect parts of the body (*genunchi* → *genunchieră* 'knee support'), pieces of furniture (*noapte* → *noptieră* 'night table'), containers (*unt* → *untieră* 'butter dish'), etc. The suffix *-niță*, which ocurrs in widely-used derivatives with similar meaning, seems to be no longer productive (*piper* → *piperniță* 'pepperpot').

Suffixation with *-ar* produced also place nouns, but as in the case of instrument nouns, the pattern is no longer productive. The most productive suffixes with locative meaning are *-ie* (*croitor* → *croitorie* 'tailor's'), which also forms status and quality nouns, and above all *-ărie* (*-erie*), result of reanalysis of the final sequence of place nouns in *-ie* derived from personal nouns formed with *-ar* (*blană* 'fur' or *blănar* 'furrier' → *blănărie* 'furrier's'; *clătită* → *clătitărie* 'pancakery'). Several derivatives also denote collective entities and/or exhibit meaning extensions relating to the profession exercized by the person working in the location referred to. A subgroup, half-way between place nouns and collectives, consists of derivatives from plant names with -*ărie*, -*et*, -*iş* and -*işte* (*brad* → *brădet*, *brădiş* 'fir wood'; *cânepă* → *cânepărie*, *cânepişte* 'hemp field').

The suffix -*ie* plays a key role in formation of s t a t u s   n o u n s (*preot* → *preoţie* 'priesthood', *şomer* → *şomerie* 'unemployedness', *văduv* → *văduvie* 'widowhood'). These denote a position or a condition and their meaning can include locative and temporal extensions as well as those referring to the activity performed by the referent of the base noun. Formations in -*at*, similar in meaning to derivatives in -*ie*, are in part loans or calques, in part created in Romanian (*voievod* → *voievodat* 'dignity of voievod, voievodship').

The derivational category of c o l l e c t i v e   n o u n s is realized by means of a large number of different suffixes. However only a few have as their primary function the formation of collectives; the others derive nouns denoting quality, status, place, etc. with collective meaning extensions. In contemporary Romanian the most productive suffix is -*ime* (-*ărime*) (*student* 'student' → *studenţime*), which also forms quality nouns (cf. section 4.1.2) and fractional nouns derived from cardinals (*zece* 'ten' → *zecime* 'one-tenth'). This suffix prefers bases which denote persons, and the resulting collective nouns often imply negative evaluation (*director* 'director' → *directorime*). Collective nouns in -*ăraie*, a suffix productive in the colloquial register, also have negative connotation (*vorbă* 'word' → *vorbăraie* 'chatter').

There remains a group of somewhat heterogeneous derivatives which do not fall into any of the categories mentioned so far. This is the case with the numerous lexemes in -*ism*, -*iadă* and -*ită*, in part loans or calques, but for the most part formed in Romanian in recent decades. The suffix -*ism* attaches mainly to nouns ([*Ion*] *Iliescu* → *iliescism* 'I. I.'s political ideology', *ureche* 'ear' → *urechism* 'hearsay'); adjectives may also fall within its domain (*ardelean* 'Transylvanian' → *ardelenism* 'Transylvanian word/phrase'), as may established phrases or sentences (*mi se rupe* 'I don't care' → *miserupism* 'indifference'). Many of the numerous nonce-formations in -*iadă* and -*ită* are created with jocular intentions and are used with negative connotation (*profesor* → *profesoriadă* 'teachers' protest'; *chiulangiu* → *chiulangită* 'slackeritis').

Derivatives with the e v a l u a t i v e suffixes -*ache*, -*an*, -*andru*, -*aş*, -*ău*, -*el* (-*icel*), -*eţ* (-*uleţ*), -*ic* (-*ulică*), -*ior* (-*işor*), -*iţă* (-*uliţă*), -*oi*, -*uc*, -*ui*, -*uş*, -*uţ*, almost all of which are productive in contemporary Romanian, belong to various categories identifiable as diminutives, augmentatives, melioratives, pejoratives, attenuatives, but can only be roughly assigned to one or other of these categories. Which value or values the derivative carries depends also on the base, context and speaker intention. Evaluative suffixes are added to nouns, but the domain of some includes adjectives too (cf. section 4.2.2) and, less frequently, adverbs (cf. section 4.4) and pronouns (*matale* 'you [informal]' → *mătăluță*). Certain suffixes are characterized by a rich allomorphy, sometimes also of a suppletive type (Maiden 1999, 2001). Most have forms for masculine and neuter bases which differ from those for feminine ones, but some show a certain preference for bases of a specific gender. They do not change the syntactic category of the base, but may lead to gender shift (*cuțit*$_N$ 'knife' → *cuțitoaie*$_F$, *piatră*$_F$ 'stone' → *pietroi*$_N$). Quite frequent is the cumulation of more than one suffix with the same base (*miel* 'lamb' → *mieluș* → *mielușel*), whereas recursive use of the same suffix is rarer (*carte* 'book' → *cărtică* → *cărticică*). Some evaluative suffixes also perform a gender-marking function and occur in the derivation of denominal agent and instrument nouns.

4.1.2 Deadjectival nouns

Quality nouns are derived by means of various suffixes. For some (*-eață*, *-enie* (*-anie*), *-eţe*, *-itate* (*-ătate*/*-etate*/*-utate*), *-itudine*), the formation of quality nouns is their primary function. Some derivatives show collective and locative meaning extensions and can also denote concrete or abstract entities manifesting the quality in question. Several widely-used quality nouns are derived with *-enie* (*curat* → *curățenie* 'cleanliness'), which continues to be productive in the colloquial register. Many new coinages are employed with playful intentions (*kitschos* → *kitschoșenie* 'kitschiness'). When *-enie* attaches to verbs it forms result nouns (*prăpădi* → *prăpădenie* 'destruction'). The suffixes *-eţe* and *-itate* (*-ătate*/*-etate*/*-utate*) occur not only in lexemes created on the patterns of other languages, but also in various commonly-used quality nouns formed in Romanian (*bătrân* → *bătrânețe* 'old age'; *singur* → *singurătate* 'loneliness'); more recently-coined derivatives bear witness to a certain productivity of *-itate* (*cretin* → *cretinitate* 'stupidity'). The suffix *-eață* attaches mainly to adjectives of colour (*roşu* → *roşeață* 'redness'). Derivatives in *-itudine*, on the other hand, are for the most part loans and calques, and the productivity of the pattern is limited to learned registers (*sterp* → *sterpitudine* 'barrenness'). The function of quality noun can also be performed by nouns not formed with one of the aforementioned primary suffixes. This is the case of lexemes derived with suffixes which chiefly form nouns denoting collectivity, status, state, etc. (cf. sections 4.1.1, 4.1.3).

4.1.3 Deverbal nouns

Action nouns are formed by suffixation or conversion (cf. section 5.1). Among the various rules, the most productive are *-re* suffixation and supine conversion

(Cornilescu 2001; Hill 2002; Stan 2003; Iordăchioaia and Soare 2008; Dobrovie-Sorin and Giurgea 2013: 663–717). Prevalent and systematic recourse to these two types of nominalization is a characteristic which distinguishes Romanian from other Romance languages. In Old Romanian action nouns in *-re* too were the output of conversion, that is of nominalization of the so-called "long infinitive" forms. With verbal value, "long infinitive" forms co-existed with "short" ones lacking the *-re* ending until the 18th century; since then they have assumed only nominal value, and borne the characteristics of feminine nouns. With few exceptions, the bases of *-re* are themes ending in: *-a* (*intra* → *intrare* 'entering, entrance'), '*-e* (*alege* → *alegere* 'choosing, choice'), *-e* (*vedea* → *vedere* 'seeing'), *-i* (*iubi* → *iubire* 'love'), *-î* (*coborî* → *coborâre* 'descent'). Bases of new coinages belong to the most productive inflectional classes, namely those with themes in *-a* and in *-i*. The domain of the suffix also includes nouns, but resulting forms can be interpreted as deriving from subsequently attested or not attested but possible verbs. Selection of verbs to which *-re* attaches is determined by their actional properties. The suffix prefers bases that denote a telic and punctual state-of-affairs, and therefore usually attaches to transitive and intransitive unaccusative verbs (*îmbătrâni* → *îmbătrânire* 'ageing', *pregăti* → *pregătire* 'preparation') and not to unergative verbs which denote an atelic state-of-affairs (*râde* 'to laugh' → **râdere*, *sforăi* 'to snore' → **sforăire*). Nominalization of the latter is realized by supine conversion (*râs* 'laugh', *sforăit* 'snore') which is not subjected to these restrictions. As for syntactic differences, it has been observed that while the behaviour of the two kinds of nominalization is similar in N-Object constructions, it diverges in N-Subject constructions, which are acceptable only with converted forms of the supine (*cititul cărţii* 'the reading of the book', *cititul lui Ion* 'Ion's reading' vs. *citirea cărţii* 'the reading of the book', **citirea lui Ion* 'Ion's reading'). The behaviour of the two kinds of nominalization also diverges with respect to pluralization, which is possible only in the case of *-re* derivatives. The main function of action nouns in *-re* is transpositional, but they can undergo various types of meaning extension. For example, they can denote the result of an action (*clădi* → *clădire* 'building'), the means used to carry it out (*cere* → *cerere* 'request'), the place where it occurs (*ieşi* → *ieşire* 'exit'), the agents who perform it (*conduce* → *conducere* 'management'), the entity affected (*mânca* → *mâncare* 'food'). As for the many cases of rivalry among action nouns derived from the same base by *-re* suffixation and supine conversion, most of the differences regard presence/absence of meaning extensions, which are much more frequent in the case of suffixed forms. They also differ according to register and frequency of use: forms in *-re* are preferred in more learned and formal varieties, while supine conversions are more widespread in popular and colloquial ones. Other suffixes which compete in forming action nouns are less productive, and extend their domains more easily also to other syntactic categories, especially to adjectives. Furthermore, derivatives are on average more exposed to meaning extensions and lexicalizations. The suffix *-ciune* exhibits a rich allomorphy due to the diachronic stratification of its various forms: *-ciune* is the inherited form, while '*-ţie*, '*-sie*, '*-zie* and their variants, *-ţiune*, *-siune*, *-ziune*, less common in contemporary Romanian, occur in Latin-Romance loanwords or are created according to these models. Some derivatives in *-ciune* have eventive and resultative meanings ((*se*) *strica* → *stricăciune* 'deterioration, damage'), others are only result nouns (*înşela* → *înşelăciune* 'cheat'), or state nouns ((*se*) *usca* → *uscăciune* 'dryness'). Derivatives in *-tură* (*-ură*) with only eventive meaning are few, and the majority denote, for example, results of actions (*tipări* → *tipăritură* 'printing'), resulting states ((*se*) *speria* → *sperietură* 'fright'), linguistic acts (*înjura* → *înjurătură* 'curse'), entities affected (*încărca* → *încărcătură* 'load'). The suffixes *-eală* (*-ială*) and *-nţă* attach above all to psychological verbs of the 4th conjugation and derive nouns which denote a resulting state ((*se*) *obosi* → *oboseală* 'tiredness'; *dori* → *dorinţă* 'wish'); derivatives from other types of bases have resultative ((*se*) *înghesui* → *înghesuială* 'crowd'), locative (*locui* → *locuinţă* 'dwelling') and instrumental (*căptuşi* → *căptuşeală* 'lining') meaning. New coinages testify to a certain productivity of *-eală*, especially in informal registers (*întâlni* → *întâlneală* 'meeting'). A semantically homogenous group is that constituted by nouns which denote sounds and noises derived with '*-et* ('*-ăt*) (*striga* → *strigăt* 'shout'). No longer productive are *-toare* (*-oare*), *-iş* (*-âş*) and *-uş*. With the exception of a limited number of lexemes inherited or formed in Romanian, result nouns in *-mânt* (*-ment*) are loans or calques, as are nouns in *-aj* denoting technical or professional activities.

The main suffix for the derivation of agent nouns is *-tor* (*-toare*$_F$). The rule gives rise to forms for the most part utilisable with either nominal or adjectival function, but also to derivatives with only one of the two functions. The suffix attaches above all to divalent and monovalent verbs which assign an agent role to the subject. As we shall see in section 4.2.3, lexemes derived from verbs whose subject is assigned a theme or experiencer role have adjectival function, but may sometimes undergo conversion into nouns (*convieţui* → *convieţuitor* 'cohabitant'). Derivatives in *-tor* denote a person who by trade habitually performs an action (*învăţa* → *învăţător* 'teacher') or habitually behaves in a certain way (*fuma* → *fumător* 'smoker'), or identify someone who performs a specific action (*prezenta* → *prezentatorul* [*este un medic*] 'the presenter [is a doctor]'). The suffixes *-ac* and *-ău*, which create negatively-connotated nouns (*aplauda* 'to applaud' → *aplaudac* 'yes-man'; *mânca* 'to eat' → *mâncău* 'glutton'), are almost unproductive. Except for a few lexemes used with nominal function (*cânta* → *cântăreţ* 'singer'), agent nouns in *-ăreţ*, *-cios* and *-uş* are the result of conversion of adjectives formed with these suffixes.

The most productive pattern for forming instrument nouns is deverbal derivation with -*tor* and -*toare*. The verbal bases may coincide with those of agent nouns, but the two patterns differ as to inflectional properties: -*tor*~MSG~ – -*toare*~FSG~ – -*tori*~MPL~ – -*toare*~FPL~ in the case of agent nouns, -*tor*~NSG~ – -*toare*~NPL~ and -*toare*~FSG~ – -*tori*~FPL~ in the case of instrument nouns. Derivatives refer to a wide range of objects including machines (*treiera* → *treierătoare* 'thresher'), simpler instruments (*felia* → *feliator* 'slicer'), substances (*fertiliza* → *fertilizator* 'fertilizer'), etc. Forms in -*tor* and in -*toare* derived from the same base can denote different instruments (*şterge* → *ştergător* 'wiper' vs. *ştergătoare* 'doormat'), or may be synonyms (*urzi* → *urzitor, urzitoare* 'warper'). To judge from new coinages derivation in -*tor* is more productive.

Suffixation with -*tor* and -*toare* has also produced place nouns (*spăla* → *spălător* 'washroom, washbasin'; *trece* → *trecătoare* 'passage'), but these patterns are no longer productive, and neither is derivation of place nouns with -*iş* and -*uş* ((*se*) *ascunde* → *ascunziş* 'hiding place'; (*se*) *culca* 'to put/go to bed' → *culcuş* 'bed (for an animal)'), which occur also in action nouns with locative meaning extensions.

4.2 Adjectival derivation

4.2.1 Denominal adjectives

A number of suffixes have the function of forming relational and qualifying adjectives from nouns (Ernst 1986). As far as relational adjectives are concerned, derivatives in -*al*, -*ar*, -*ic*, -*ier*, -*in*, -*istic* are for the most part loans and calques. The suffix -*icesc*, frequent in 19th-century technical terms, is nowadays found only in a few widely-used adjectives (*spital* 'hospital' → *spitalicesc*) and in some newly-coined colloquialisms (*internet* → *interneticesc*). Among suffixes forming both relational and qualifying adjectives, -*esc* is very frequent, and its productivity has been further reinforced by the presence of a homonymous suffix found in loanwords of French and Italian origin. This suffix attaches above all to bases denoting persons. Among its numerous derivatives, besides relational adjectives (*judecător* 'judge' → *judecătoresc*), two important groups are constituted on the one hand by ethnic adjectives, discussed below, and on the other by adjectives which are exclusively or mainly qualifying (*prieten* → *prietenesc* 'friendly'). No longer productive are -*nic* (-*elnic*) and -*atic*, occurring in relational and qualifying adjectives in common use (*casă* → *casnic* 'household', *putere* → *puternic* 'powerful'; *muiere* → *muieratic* 'effeminate'). As for derivation of possessive and resemblance adjectives, the most productive suffix, especially in colloquial varieties, is *-os* (*frică* → *fricos* 'fearful', *ulei* → *uleios* 'oily'); where bases denote inalienable properties, derivatives denote that an entity is endowed with N to an above average degree (*păr* → *păros* 'hairy'). A similar semantic function can also be performed by the less productive suffix *-at* (*sprânceană* → *sprâncenat* 'thick-browed'), which also forms resemblance adjectives (*borcan* → *borcănat* 'jar-like'). Other suffixes denoting resemblance are: *-iu* (*-uliu, -uriu*), which occurs mainly in colour adjectives (*portocală* → *portocaliu* 'orange'), *-ard* (*şablon* → *şablonard* 'clichéd') and *-oid*, found in loans and calques belonging to technical and scientific terminologies, but also in certain adjectives used in the mass-media and formed in Romanian (*legionar* 'iron-guardist' → *legionaroid*).

Among the numerous suffixes that form e t h n i c nouns and adjectives, the main one, which is found in the largest number of lexemes derived from Romanian toponyms, is *-ean* (*-an*). Two other suffixes, *-ez* and *-an* (*-ian*), have quite a rich inventory of derivatives. The rules for forming ethnic nouns and ethnic adjectives coincide only in part. The two forms are identical in the masculine, but in the feminine, besides the forms common to the two syntactic categories in *-ă* (*bucureştean*$_{N,A}$ 'from Bucharest' → *bucureşteană*$_{N,A}$; *chinez*$_{N,A}$ 'Chinese' → *chineză*$_{N,A}$), the ethnic nouns in *-ean* (*-an*) and *-an* (*-ian*) can also add the gender-marking suffix *-că* (*bucureşteancă*$_{N}$), and those in *-ez* the suffix *-oaică* (*chinezoaică*$_{N}$). Feminine-marking with *-că* and *-oaică*, which is also found in some unsuffixed inhabitant names (*ungur* 'Hungarian' → *unguroaică*), prevails in colloquial Romanian, and is typical of the oldest and most widely-used names. Alongside certain derivatives in *-ean* (*-an*), *-ez* and unsuffixed forms, used with both adjectival and nominal function, there coexist some exclusively adjectival derivatives formed by adding *-esc* (*moldovean*$_{N,A}$ 'Moldavian' → *moldovenesc*$_A$; *chinez*$_{N,A}$ → *chinezesc*$_A$; *grec*$_{N,A}$ 'Greek' → *grecesc*$_A$).

As for adjectival derivation from proper nouns (from a name or a surname or a compound base made up of name and surname), the suffixes *-ian, -esc* (*Charlie Chaplin* → *charliechaplinian*; [*Mircea*] *Eliade* → *eliadesc*) and, to a lesser degree, *-an, -ic, -ist* and *-istic* are productive, especially in the mass-media.

4.2.2 Deadjectival adjectives

The semantic values of prefixed adjectives can be grouped in two large categories: intensification and oppositeness (Graur and Avram 1978). The bases are qualifying adjectives and most prefixes used with these functions can also be found in other European languages. Productive prefixes with i n t e n s i f y i n g function, such as *arhi-, extra-, hiper-, super-, supra-, ultra-*, indicate that the quality denoted by the base is present to the highest degree (*arhi(-)folosit* 'widely used', *ultra(-)plicticos* 'ultra-boring'). Only marginally productive, if at all, are *răs-* (*răz-*), *stră-* (*răscunoscut* 'well known', *străvechi* 'very old') and *prea-*, which is found in religious terminology (*preaînalt* 'most high'). Intensifying prefixes can attach to the same base forming synonymous series, and in informal registers can also be used recursively. Among oppositive prefixes, the most productive is *ne-*, which is added mainly to deverbal adjectives (*asemănător* 'similar' → *neasemănător*), but also to denominals (*prietenos* 'friendly' → *neprietenos*) and, more rarely, to simplex bases (*clar* 'clear' → *neclar*). In cases of cumulation, *ne-* precedes other prefixes. As with nouns, *in-* (*im-*, *i-*), occurs in borrowed adjectives or calques, often synonyms of derivatives from the same base formed with *ne-*. Adjectives in *non-* and *a-* (*an-*) belong only to learned registers and are loans or calques. Several prefixes with localization and oppositeness functions can also attach to denominal relational adjectives. In these cases adjectives are prefixed only as far as the form is concerned, since the prefix has scope over the nominal base of the adjective (*extraşcolar* 'after-school'). This pattern is quite productive, also in analogy with numerous loans and calques. Similar meanings are expressed by certain adjectives with non-suffixed nominal bases also formed on foreign models ([*competiţie*] *inter(-)cluburi* 'inter-club [competition]').

Many evaluative suffixes which attach to nouns (cf. section 4.1.1) extend their domain also to qualifying adjectives to form derivatives with approximative/attenuative and/or evaluative meaning. Depending on the context, the positive or negative value judgement of the speaker may regard either the quality denoted by the adjectival base or the referent of the noun modified. Among most frequently occurring suffixes (*-aş* (*-ălaş*), *-el* (*-icel*), *-eţ* (*-uleţ*), *-ior* (*-cior*, *-şor*, *-işor*, *-uşor*), *-iu* (*-uliu*), *-oid*, *-os*, *-uc*, *-ui*, *-uş*, *-uţ*), the most productive seem to be *-el* and *-uţ* (*subţire* 'thin' → *subţirel*; *mic* 'little' → *micuţ*). Many derivatives are characterized by their availability for nominal conversion. Colour adjectives share a set of suffixes (*-atic*, *-icios*, *-ior*, *-iu* (*-uliu*, *-uriu*), *-ui*) expressing approximation to the focal point of a colour (*verde* 'green' → *verzui*). In combination with adjectives, augmentative suffixes with intensifying function have low productivity. For example *-an* occurs in derivatives which are often nominalized (*gras* 'fat' → *grăsan*); *-oi* occurs in some lexicalized forms (*viu* 'living' → *vioi* 'lively').

4.2.3 Deverbal adjectives

Suffixes forming adjectives from verbs are *-ant* (*-ent*), *-ăreţ*, *-bil*, *-cios*, *-os*, *-tiv* (*-iv*), *-tor*, *-uş*. As we have seen in sections 4.1.3, 4.2.1 and 4.2.2, some of these also derive nouns, and their domain can include nouns and/or adjectives too. From a semantic point of view, except for adjectives in *-bil* with potential-passive meaning, derivatives with other suffixes are active adjectives. Formations in *-ant* (*-ent*), *-tiv* (*-iv*) belong to learned varieties and are for the most part loans or calques. As for deverbal adjectives formed with other suffixes, those in *-ăreț* and *-cios*, which are negatively connotated, consistently convey an additional meaning, such as 'excessively', 'often', 'easily', and refer to reiterative events (*vorbi* → *vorbăreț* 'talkative'; *supăra* → *supărăcios* 'touchy'). A similar semantic matrix, but without negative connotation, can be found with deverbal adjectives in *-os* and *-uș* ((*se*) *luneca* → *lunecos* 'slippery'; *juca* → *jucăuș* 'playful'). The deverbal suffix *-tor* forms large numbers of derivatives, some of which are primarily nouns and only secondarily adjectives. Formations with exclusively adjectival function are derived from verbs which assign a theme or experiencer role to their subjects (*cădea* → *căzător* 'falling', *iubi* → *iubitor* 'loving'). Adjectives in *-bil* include both numerous loans and several formations derived in Romanian (some recently, e.g., *se vacanta* → *vacantabil* 'vacatable') from transitive passivizable verbs. Denominal derivatives are rare, and for these possible verbal bases may also be hypothesized (*pușcăriabil* 'imprisonable' ← *pușcărie* 'prison').

4.2.4 Deadverbial adjectives

Adverbs or established adverbial phrases can also be bases for adjectival derivation (*lesnicios* 'easy' ← *lesne* 'easily').

4.3 Verbal derivation

The main semantic values of prefixed deverbal verbs consist of designation of reiteration or reversal of an event (Graur and Avram 1978). Of the two reiterative prefixes, *răs-* (*răz-*, *ră-*) and *re-*, only *re-* is productive in contemporary Romanian. It is found both in loans and calques, and in lexemes formed in Romanian (*clădi* → *reclădi* 'to rebuild'). As well as reiteration of an event, verbs in *re-* can also denote movement in a contrary sense (*trimite* 'to send' → *retrimite* 'to return'). The prefix *răs-* (*răz-*, *ră-*) (cf. sections 4.1.1, 4.2.2) occurs in verbs which denote return to a previous state (*popi* → *răspopi* 'to defrock') or intensification of an action (*coace* → *răscoace* 'to overcook'). Reversal of an event is expressed by verbs prefixed in *des-* (*dez-*, *de-*), whose inventory comprises both verbs formed in Romanian and loans and calques. If the base is telic the verb in *des-* is reversative ((*se*) *lipi* → (*se*) *dezlipi* 'to unstick'); if the base is atelic, the prefixed verb denotes a contrary state (*nădăjdui* → *deznădăjdui* 'to despair'). The number of deverbal verbs formed with other prefixes is more limited. As for oppositive prefixes, we find derivatives in *contra-* (*pune* → *contrapune* 'to set against') and, more rarely, in *ne-* (*socoti* → *nesocoti* 'to disregard'), the latter mostly in verbs backformed from adjectives (*nedumeri* ← *nedumerit* 'perplex'). Other prefixed verbs denote, for example, spatial, temporal or abstract localization (*arenda* → *subarenda* 'to sublease', *fierbe* → *prefierbe* 'to preboil') or intensification (*luci* → *străluci* 'to shine'), or have comitative value (*regiza* → *co(-)regiza* 'to codirect').

Prefixes *în-* (*îm-*), *des-* (*dez-*, *de-*) and, to a lesser extent *a-*, which is no longer productive, occur in numerous p a r a s y n t h e t i c v e r b s (Reinheimer-Rîpeanu 1974). Suffixes are only rarely present in parasynthetic verbs; in most cases we find simultaneous prefixation and conversion of a nominal or adjectival base with assignment to the 1st or the 4th conjugation. Unlike *des-*, the prefixes *în-* and *a-* occur almost exclusively in parasynthetic derivatives and do not convey a specific meaning differentiating the semantic structure of this type of verb from those formed by conversion or suffixation. Interpretation of denominal verbs depends on the role of the referent of the base in the state-of-affairs represented. Referents of the base can, for example, represent instruments (*puşcă* 'gun' → *împuşca* 'to shoot down'), located entities (*cunună* → *încununa* 'to crown'), locations (*temniţă* → *întemniţa* 'to jail'). Deadjectival verbs are causative and/or inchoative and refer to a change of state (*bătrân* 'old' → *îmbătrâni* 'to age', *bolnav* → (*se*) *îmbolnăvi* 'to sicken'). In some cases the base is an adverb (*târziu* → *întârzia* 'to be late, delay') or a numeral (*zece* → *înzeci* 'to decuple'). The prefix *des-* (*dez-*, *de-*) also derives verbs for which no corresponding denominal or deadjectival base is attested. The formation of verbs such as *dezgropa* 'to unbury', (*se*) *descreţi* 'to uncurl' involve substitution of the prefix *în-* (*îm-*) of the corresponding denominal or deadjectival verbs, in this case *groapă* 'grave, pit' → *îngropa* 'to bury' and *creţ* 'curly' → (*se*) *încreţi* 'to curl'. Constitution of opposites by prefix substitution is also quite frequent in cases of homophonous segments of *în-* (*îm-*) and *a-* in the absence of a nominal or adjectival base (*destupa* 'to uncork' – *astupa* 'to cork', *dezvăţa* 'to unlearn' – *învăţa* 'to learn').

Romanian also has a fair number of s u f f i x e s for verb formation (Vasiliu 1989), but nowadays the only productive ones seem to be *-iza*, *-ona*, *-ui* and *-ăi* (*-âi*) with nominal and/or adjectival bases. Verb formation by suffixation of verbal bases is no longer productive. Whereas many verbs in *-iza*, and especially in *-ona*, are typical of more learned registers and are often analyzable loanwords, derivatives in *-ui* and *-ăi* (*-âi*) belong to the colloquial register. The suffix *-iza* attaches both to adjectives (*orăşean* → (*se*) *orăşeniza* 'to urbanize') and nouns (*muşama* 'oil cloth' → *muşamaliza* 'to cover up'), including proper nouns and acronyms. Compared to verbs in *-iza*, those in *-ona* formed in Romanian are much fewer in number. They stand in relationship to nouns in '-*ţie* ('-*zie*), or with their now less widely used synonymic variants in -*ţiune* (-*ziune*) (*incluzie* or *incluziune* 'inclusion' → *incluziona* 'to include'). The numerous derivatives in *-ui* are mainly denominal (*chin* → *chinui* 'to torment', *gazdă* → *găzdui* 'to host'). This suffix often occurs also in informal adaptations of English verbs or in verbs derived in Romanian from nouns of English origin (*blog(-)ui* 'to blog'). Adaptation of English loanwords can also come about with *-ăi* (*-âi*) (*bipăi* 'to beep'), which occurs mainly in delocutive verbs derived from onomatopoeic bases (*bâz* → *bâzâi* 'to buzz'). The semantic structure of suffixed verbs is by and large analogous to that of verbs formed by conversion (cf. section 5.3) or parasynthesis.

4.4 Adverbial derivation

Adverbs are mainly formed by conversion (cf. section 5.4), but also can be derived with *-eşte* (*-iceşte*) and, to a much lesser extent, with *-mente* (*-amente*). On the other hand, the suffix *-iş* (*-âş*) is no longer productive. The suffix *-eşte* (*-iceşte*) attaches to adjectives and nouns; its most important semantic restriction regards colour adjectives, which cannot be bases for adverb derivation. The correspondence between several *-eşte* (*-iceşte*) derivatives and denominal adjectives in *-esc* (*-icesc*), often allows both deadjectival and denominal readings (*prieteneşte* 'like a friend, in a friendly way' ← *prieten* 'friend' or *prietenesc* 'friendly'). The latter is favoured where the corresponding adjective in *-esc* (*-icesc*) is archaic or rare. To judge from newly-coined adverbs and nonce-formations cited by Mîrzea Vasile (2012), both *-eşte* and, to a much lesser extent, and sometimes with ironic connotation, *-iceşte*, continue to be productive (*bişniţar* 'racketeer' or *bişniţăresc* 'racketeerish' → *bişniţăreşte*; *liberal* 'liberal' → *liberaliceşte*). A numerically significant subgroup of adverbs in *-eşte* has glottonyms as bases ([*vorbeşte*] *româneşte* '[he/she speaks] Romanian'). The suffix *-mente* (*-amente*) occurs in loanwords or calques but, with very few exceptions, only in juridical-administrative terminology and highbrow journalism.

Prefixed adverbs are limited to a small group of forms (*nelesne* 'uneasily' ← *lesne*, *răspoimâine* 'two days hence' ← *poimâine* 'the day after tomorrow').

Some adverbs can be bases for evaluative suffixes with endearing and attenuative function (*acăsică* ← *acasă* 'at home', *binişor* ← *bine* 'well').

5 Conversion

In Romanian there are many productive patterns for the formation of new lexemes by conversion (Stoichiţoiu-Ichim 2006). In the following subsections we will illustrate various patterns classified by output and input category.

5.1 Nominal conversion

As in other Romance languages, there is in Romanian more than one type of adjective nominalization by conversion (Pană Dindelegan 2003). A number of nouns are the result of transcategorization due to ellipsis. The omitted head nouns belong to several semantic categories and can be reconstructed (*accelerat* accelerated 'fast train'). Other nominalizable adjectives include some denoting qualities considered relevant for animate entities (*bătrână* old:F 'old woman'), as well as adjectivizable past participles (cf. section 5.2). In learned registers we also find abstract nouns resulting from conversion of adjectives in their singular masculine form (*adânc* deep 'depth'). For derivatives which can be used with either nominal or adjectival functions, or primarily with one of the two, cf. sections 4.1.1, 4.1.3, 4.2.1, 4.2.3.

As for deverbal nouns formed by conversion, there are various types. The most productive, and the one which, along with suffixation in *-re*, constitutes the main source for a c t i o n n o u n formation, consists of conversion of the supine, homonym of the past participle in *-t/-s*, into a neuter noun (*dormi* → *dormit* 'sleeping', *mânca* → *mâncat* 'eating', *scrie* → *scris* 'writing'). For the characteristics of this pattern compared with those of suffixation in *-re*, and for references, see section 4.1.3. Almost unproductive is the formation of action and result nouns by conversion of the verbal root: one group is made up of neuter nouns (*îngheța* → *îngheț* 'frost', *omorî* → *omor* 'murder'), while another smaller group consists of feminine nouns in *-ă* (*certa* → *ceartă* 'quarrel', *pândi* → *pândă* 'watch'). No longer productive is the formation of action and result nouns by conversion of the feminine form of the past participle (*agonisită* 'earnings', *băută* 'drinking, booze-up'). The few examples of nominalized gerunds, such as *intrând* 'recess', are calques from French.

Frequently found in the colloquial register is nominal use of adverbs in *-ește* denoting linguistic varieties ([*în*] *nemțește* '[in] German').

5.2 Adjectival conversion

The most productive pattern consists of past participle adjectivization (Pană Dindelegan 2003). The rule is subject to restrictions: it can be applied only to participles of transitive verbs ([*persoană*] *iubită* 'beloved [person]'), intransitive unaccusative verbs representing a telic state-of-affairs ([*tren*] *sosit* '[train] which has arrived'), psychological verbs ([*fată*] *necăjită* 'worried [girl]'), and intransitive symmetrical verbs ([*prietenă*] *înrudită* '[girlfriend] who is related'). Participles of unergative and atelic unaccusative verbs cannot be adjectivized (*înota* 'to swim' –

*înotat, tremura 'to tremble' – *tremurat). Gerund conversion on the French model is found only in the literary language and is not productive ([femei] suferinde 'ailing [women]'). For derivatives which can be used with either nominal or adjectival function, or primarily with one of the two, cf. sections 4.1.1, 4.1.3, 4.2.1, 4.2.3. Certain simplex nouns (marfă ware 'excellent'), adverbs (bine well 'handsome, polite') and interjections (tralala tol-de-rol 'foolish') can sporadically function as invariable noun modifiers.

5.3 Verbal conversion

Like suffixed and parasynthetic verbs (cf. section 4.3), those formed by conversion are assigned to the 1st or 4th conjugation (Vasiliu 1989). Verbs distinguished only by inflectional class are usually synonyms (curat → (se) curăța, (se) curăți 'to clean'). Bases are nouns (mătură 'broom' → mătura 'to sweep'), adjectives (slab → slăbi 'to slim') or, more rarely, adverbs (alături 'beside' → (se) alătura 'to lay by, come near'), interjections (sictir → sictiri 'to swear') and onomatopoeia (cotcodac → cotcodăci 'to cluck, chatter'). Verbs derived from the same base by conversion or parasynthesis are in general (partial) synonyms distinguished by frequency of use (burghez → se burghezi, se îmburghezi 'to become bourgeois'; fărâmă → (se) fărâma, (se) sfărâma 'to shatter'); sometimes they are derived from different meanings of the base (gol 'empty' → (se) goli 'to empty' vs. gol 'naked' → (se) dezgoli 'to undress'). As with parasynthetic and suffixed verbs, interpretation of converted denominal verbs depends on the role of the referent of the base in the state-of-affairs represented: agent, instrument, located entity, etc. Deadjectival causative and/or inchoative verbs denote a change of state, and their semantic characteristics depend on the properties of the bases.

5.4 Adverbial conversion

The most productive pattern of adverb formation is conversion of the singular masculine form of a qualifying or relational adjective, simplex or derived, in its literal and/or metaphorical meaning (Mîrzea Vasile 2012). Outputs of the conversion process occur as modifiers of a predicate (se îmbracă ciudat 'he/she dresses oddly'), of an adjective (îmbrăcat ciudat 'oddly dressed') or of a sentence (sincer, nu mi place [...] 'honestly, I don't like [...]'). As for semantic restrictions, it has been observed that neither colour adjectives (unless used metaphorically), nor ethnic adjectives, can be converted into adverbs.

In informal registers a restricted number of nouns, with their metaphorical meanings and in combination with certain verbs and adjectives, can be converted into adverbs with intensifying function (*doarme tun* sleeps cannon 'sleeps soundly', *frumos foc* beautiful fire 'very beautiful'). Some of these can perform both adjectival and adverbial functions, modifying both nouns and verbs.

6 Backformation

Backformation is more or less sporadic. As we have seen in section 4.1.1, this device can be used for gender-marking. As for backformed verbs, in section 4.3 we mentioned verbs derived from adjectives in *ne-*; other verbs are backformed from action, agent or instrument nouns borrowed from other languages (*audia* 'to interrogate, hear' ← *audienţă* 'audience', *audiţie* 'hearing, audition', *auditor* 'auditor'; *picta* 'to paint' ← *pictor* 'painter', *pictură* 'painting').

7 Reduplication

Most reduplicative constructions are adjectives and adverbs. They consist of sequences with the same word (*merge încet-încet* goes slowly-slowly 'he/she goes very slowly', *ureche roşie roşie* ear red-red 'very red ear') or a derivative of that same word (*ajunge câine-câineşte* arrives dog-dog:ADV 'he/she arrives struggling', *telefon nou-nouţ* telephone new-new:DIM 'brand new telephone') as a reduplicant.

8 Blending

Most blends are created with jocular intentions and belong to informal registers or slang. Some are the result of combining the first part of the first lexeme with the second part of the second one (*intelectocan* ← *intelectual* 'intellectual' + *mitocan* 'boor', *jenibil* ← *jenant* 'unpleasant' + *penibil* 'painful', *loviluţie* ← *lovitură* 'coup' + *revoluţie* 'revolution', *scârbici(u)* ← *scârbă* 'disgust' + *servici(u)* 'job'). Others, which border on acronyms, are combinations of the initial parts of two lexemes (*aprozar* 'greengrocer's' ← *apro*[*vizionare cu*] *zar*[*zavat*] 'vegetable supply').

9 Clipping and acronymy

Among lexemes formed by clipping, besides various internationalisms, we find truncated forms of loanwords (*lebăr* ← *lebărvurst* 'liver sausage'), nouns and adjectives typical of the language of young people (*dirig/-ă* ← *diriginte* 'class teacher', *facultă* ← *facultate* 'faculty'), colloquial registers and slang (*naşpa* ← *naşparliu* 'foolish, bad, ugly', *obo* ← *obosit* 'tired', *plicti* ← *plictisit* 'bored' or *plictiseală* 'boredom', *prăji* ← *prăjitură* 'cake'). To judge from the examples available, we can hypothesize a certain preference for two-syllable outputs.

Acronyms (Ciobanu and Hasan 1970; Stoichiţoiu-Ichim 2006) are names of institutions, companies, geographical-political entities and, in informal registers, people. Their formation has at various times in history been subject to the influence of French, Russian and, more recently, English models; many acronyms in use in Romanian today are loans or calques. Acronyms can be formed by extracting the initial letters of the words which constitute the base phrase (*BCU* ← *B[iblioteca] C[entrală] U[niversitară]* 'Central University Library'), or by combining letters with syllables or portions of the base words larger or smaller than a syllable (*AGERPRES* ← *Age[nţia] R[omână] de] Pres[ă]* 'Romanian Press Agency'), or by combining fragments of words with each other or sometimes with whole words (*Oltcit* ← *Olt[enia]* + *Cit[roën]*, *Prodexport* ← *[Intreprindere de] Prod[use pentru] Export* 'Enterprise for Export Products'). In most cases constituents of acronyms are nouns or adjectives and only rarely prepositions or conjunctions (*ApR* ← *A[lianţa] p[entru] R[omânia]* 'Alliance for Romania').

10 References

Chitoran, Ioana (2002): *The Phonology of Romanian. A Constraint-Based Approach*. Berlin/New York: Mouton de Gruyter.

Ciobanu, Fulvia and Finuţa Hasan (1970): *Formarea cuvintelor în limba română*. Vol. 1: *Compunerea*. Bucureşti: Editura Academiei.

Cornilescu, Alexandra (2001): Romanian nominalizations: Case and aspectual structure. *Journal of Linguistics* 37: 467–501.

Croitor, Blanca (2021): *Sufixele în limba română actuală. Formaţii recente*. Bucureşti: Editura Universităţii din Bucureşti.

Croitor, Blanca (ed.) (2024): *Formarea cuvintelor în limba română*. Vol. IV: *Sufixele. 2. Derivarea nominală şi adverbială. Partea II*. Bucureşti: Editura Academiei Române.

Dobrovie-Sorin, Carmen and Ion Giurgea (eds.) (2013): *A Reference Grammar of Romanian*. Vol. 1: *The noun phrase*. Amsterdam/Philadelphia: John Benjamins.

Ernst, Gerhard (1986): Morphologie und Syntax der Relationsadjektive (RA) im Rumänischen: Spezifisches und Gemeinromanisches. In: Günter Holtus and Edgar Radtke (eds.), *Rumänistik in der Diskussion. Sprache, Literatur und Geschichte*, 317–338. Tübingen: Narr.

Fischer, Iancu (1989): Rumänisch: Wortbildungslehre / Formation des mots. In: Günter Holtus, Michael Metzeltin and Christian Schmitt (eds.), *Lexikon der Romanistischen Linguistik (LRL)*. Vol. 3, 33–55. Berlin/New York: de Gruyter.

Giurescu, Anca (1975): *Les mots composés dans les langues romanes*. The Hague/Paris: Mouton.

Graur, Alexandru and Mioara Avram (eds.) (1978): *Formarea cuvintelor în limba română*. Vol. 2: *Prefixele*. București: Editura Academiei.

Grossmann, Maria (2012): Romanian compounds. *Probus* 24(1): 147–173.

Grossmann, Maria (2022): The Peculiarities of Romanian Word Formation. In: Mark Aronoff (ed.), *Oxford Research Encyclopedia of Linguistics*. Oxford: Oxford University Press [Online available at: https://doi.org/10.1093/acrefore/9780199384655.013.686].

Hill, Virginia (2002): The gray area of supine clauses. *Linguistics* 40: 495–517.

Iordachioaia, Gianina and Elena Soare (2008): Two kinds of event plurals: Evidence from Romanian nominalizations. In: Olivier Bonami and Patricia Cabredo Hofherr (eds.), *Empirical Issues in Syntax and Semantics 7*, 193–216 (http://www.cssp.cnrs.fr/eiss7/iordachioaia-soare-eiss7.pdf) [last access 10 Sept 2012].

Leu Hanganu, Violeta (2021): *Diminutivele în limba română actuală vorbită. Aspecte lexicale, pragmatice și sociolingvistice*. București: Editura Universității din București.

Maiden, Martin (1999): Il ruolo dell'"idoneità" in morfologia diacronica: I suffissi romeni *-ea, -ică* ed *-oi*. *Revue de Linguistique Romane* 63: 321–345.

Maiden, Martin (2001): What sort of thing is a derivational affix? Diachronic evidence from Romanian and Spanish suffixes. In: Geert Booij and Jaap van Marle (eds.), *Yearbook of Morphology 1999*, 25–52. Dordrecht: Kluwer.

Maiden, Martin, Adina Dragomirescu, Gabriela Pană Dindelegan, Oana Uță Bărbulescu and Rodica Zafiu (2021): *The Oxford History of Romanian Morphology*. Oxford: Oxford University Press.

Mîrzea Vasile, Carmen (2012): *Eterogeneitatea adverbului românesc. Tipologie și descriere*. București: Editura Universității.

Mîrzea Vasile, Carmen (2020): Derivational networks in Romanian. In: Lívia Körtvélyessy, Alexandra Bagasheva and Pavol Štekauer (eds.), *Derivational Networks Across Languages*, 273–284. Berlin/Boston: De Gruyter Mouton.

Pană Dindelegan, Gabriela (2003): Aspecte ale substantivizării în limba română actuală: Forme de manifestare a substantivizării adjectivelor. In: Gabriela Pană Dindelegan (ed.), *Aspecte ale dinamicii limbii române actuale*. Vol. 2, 23–41. București: Editura Universității.

Pană Dindelegan, Gabriela (ed.) (2013): *The Grammar of Romanian*. Oxford: Oxford University Press.

Rădulescu Sala, Marina (2015a): From Latin to Romanian. In: Peter O. Müller, Ingeborg Ohnheiser, Susan Olsen and Franz Rainer (eds.), *Word-Formation. An International Handbook of the Languages of Europe*. Vol. 3, 1957–1975. Berlin/Boston: De Gruyter Mouton.

Rădulescu Sala, Marina (ed.) (2015b): *Formarea cuvintelor în limba română*. Vol. IV: *Sufixele. 2. Derivarea nominală și adverbială. Partea I*. București: Editura Academiei Române.

Reinheimer-Rîpeanu, Sanda (1974): *Les dérivés parasynthétiques dans les langues romanes. Roumain, italien, français, espagnol*. The Hague/București: Mouton/Editura Academiei.

Sala, Marius (ed.) (2001): *Enciclopedia limbii române*. București: Univers Enciclopedic.

SMFC (1959–72): *Studii și materiale privitoare la formarea cuvintelor în limba română*. 6 Vol. București: Editura Academiei.

Stan, Camelia (2003): *Gramatica numelor de acțiune din limba română*. București: Editura Universității.

Stoichițoiu-Ichim, Adriana (2001): *Vocabularul limbii române actuale. Dinamică, influențe, creativitate*. București: Editura All Educational.

Stoichiţoiu-Ichim, Adriana (2006): *Creativitate lexicală în româna actuală*. Bucureşti: Editura Universităţii.
Terţea, Andreea-Teodora (2022): *Conversiunea în limba română contemporană. Direcţii vechi şi noi*. Cluj-Napoca: Casa Cărţii de Ştiinţă.
Trifan, Elena (2010): *Formarea cuvintelor în publicistica actuală – Derivarea – Perioada 1990–2001*. Cluj Napoca: Editura Digital Data.
Vasileanu, Monica, Anabella-Gloria Niculescu-Gorpin and Cristina-Andreea Radu-Bejenaru (2024): Keep calm and carry on blending: Experimental insights into Romanian lexical blending. *Word Structure* 17(1–2): 56–90.
Vasiliu, Laura (1989): *Formarea cuvintelor în limba română*. Vol. 3: *Sufixele*. Part 1: *Derivare verbală*. Bucureşti: Editura Academiei.
Vasiliu, Laura (2009): Formation des mots. In: Gerhard Ernst, Martin-Dietrich Gleßgen, Christian Schmitt and Wolfgang Schweickard (eds.), *Romanische Sprachgeschichte. Ein internationales Handbuch zur Geschichte der romanischen Sprachen*. Vol. 3, 2710–2721. Berlin/New York: de Gruyter.
Vârlan, Mariana (2012): *Derivarea sufixală nominală în româna actuală*. Craiova: Universitaria.

Brian Ó Curnáin

7 Irish

1 Introduction
2 General overview
3 Composition
4 Derivation
5 Conversion
6 Backformation
7 Reduplication
8 Blending
9 Clipping
10 Word-creation
11 References

Abstract: The three most productive word-formation mechanisms in Irish (called Gaeilge in standard Irish) are a) prefixation, b) composition (with a small set of deadjectival and denominal premodifiers) and c) suffixation. Prefixation and composition are common only with nouns and adjectives as bases. The highly productive diminutive suffix *-ín* does not change the class of (mostly noun) bases. The category of the abstract comparative contains an intersection of the suffixes of both the inflectional comparative adjective and the derivational abstract noun. Many lexicalised phrases are important lexical items but are not considered as word-formation unless they show morphological signs of univerbation. Conversion is restricted, and blending and clipping are rare.

1 Introduction

Irish is the variety of Celtic spoken in Ireland. It is closely related to Scottish Gaelic. Both constitute the main members of the Goidelic subgroup which is the western sister of Brythonic (Welsh, Breton) within the Celtic language family. Accounts of Irish word-formation are found mostly in descriptive monographs. For Irish in general: Ó hAnluain (1999 [1960]: 136–137, 243–245, 266–267, 303–320). For particular dialects: County Kerry in Munster, Ó Sé (2000: 312–316, 385–386, 466–484); County Galway in Connacht, de Bhaldraithe (1953a: 130–132, 239–256)

Brian Ó Curnáin, Dublin, Ireland

and Ó Curnáin (2007: 124–129, 564–569, 582–656, 685–690, 892–898, 1075–1103, 1226, 1235–1249, 1254–1256, 1721–1724, 1803, 1875–1876, 2002–2013). These references include verbal-noun derivation. Indications of stress and phonetics in this article are from Ó Curnáin (2007) unless otherwise stated. Discussions of certain aspects of word-formation are: Armstrong (1981: 640–641, 653–706) and McManus (1994: 389–392) concerning the at times profligate prefixing and compounding in Classical Early Modern syllabic verse; de Bhaldraithe (1990) on diminutives (cf. de Bhaldraithe 1953b, a dialect list containing a thousand terms for types of people); County Waterford in Munster, Breatnach (1947: 79–82) regarding compound stress, County Cork in Munster, Ó Cuív (1944: 67–68) regarding compound stress, Ó hÚrdail (1995) on the preference for agentive *-éir* in South-West Co. Cork; Ní Dhomhnaill (1988) contains a list of alliterative doublets. Doyle (1992) is the only book-length analysis of Irish word-formation I know of, its subject is noun derivation (26–134) – abstract and activity nouns, agentives and diminutives – but it requires revision and improvement, in view, for example, of the data available in the valuable reverse dictionary of Doyle and Gussmann (1996).

Full traditional native speaker competence in Irish is only found among dialect speakers. These speakers have not acquired standard Irish in initial early language acquisition. This survey article, written by a non-native speaker to whom many of the words cited here are known only from dictionaries, will concentrate on the commonest productive use in dialects. The vitality-status of Irish as a threatened language is "semi-moribund" (Ó Curnáin 2012: 286) since c. 1990 because it is generally being incompletely acquired by native speakers born after c. 1990 who, through subtractive bilingualism, acquire greater proficiency in their second language, English (Ó Giollagáin et al. 2007: 303–320; Ó Giollagáin and Mac Donncha 2008: 114–117; Péterváry et al. 2014). Productivity of word-formation refers in this article to the knowledge of traditional speakers, the most competent of whom were generally born before 1940. Post-traditional speech can be situated on a cline of reduction regarding phonology, morphology, lexicon and word-formation; for instance, the absence of the traditionally obligatory verbalising suffix *-áil* with current borrowings (Lenoach 2012; Ó Curnáin 2012). Thus, although this description is cast in the present tense, much is currently being lost and can, or soon will be, generally by c. 2050, more accurately described in the past tense. From the point of view of word-formation in standardised Irish, given state support of the neological enterprise (applied primarily in official documentation and education), Irish is one of, if not *the* best provided-for (semi-)moribund language in the world, exemplified in many praiseworthy lexicographical endeavours, for instance, Uí Bhraonáin and Nic Pháidín (2004) and the ongoing terminological project available on the website www.focal.ie (Nic Pháidín 2008: 105) and English-Irish dictionary at www.focloir.ie as well as the valuable corpus at corpas.focloir.ie.

Irish is dying, so to speak, with its standardised terminological boots on, enabling some of its speakers and writers to deal with, deny, ignore or avoid the process of its death with greater sophistication than most speakers of dying languages (cf. Fishman 1991: 143).

2 General overview

David Greene (1966: 24–25, 30–31) provides an overview of many features of Irish relevant to word-formation:

> [...] Irish resembles French more than English in that words cannot, in general, be transferred from one category to another; [...]. The word has a structure which is common enough in other European languages; it can have one syllable (*bean*), two (*bata*), or three (*airgead* 'money', where a vowel is pronounced, but not written, between the middle consonants). Root words have seldom more than two syllables; when there are three or more syllables it usually means that we have a complex of some kind – an inflected form (*bus-anna* 'buses', *chuireadar* 'they put'), a derivative (*sagart-óireacht* 'practising as a priest', from *sagart* 'priest'), or a compound (*srac-fhéachaint* 'a glance'). This is very much the situation with the native (Germanic) vocabulary of English too; a language like Norwegian, which has fewer loanwords than English, would be even closer to Irish. [...] Irish differs from English and German, though it agrees with French, in avoiding prepositional prefixes (*input, output*, etc.) and compound nouns (*sparking-plug*); in the first case the natural thing is to say *putting in, putting out*, and in the second to use a noun followed by another in the genitive case, as in *inneall buailte* 'threshing machine', literally 'machine of threshing', like French *machine à coudre* 'sewing machine'. [...] Irish may be said to be a noun-centred language, [...]

Notes: *sracfhéachaint* ← *srac-* 'cursory' + *féachaint* 'look(ing)' (see section 3); in contemporary French compounding is used quite freely, see Arnaud (2025) for a discussion of noun-noun compounds in French.

From the evidence of monographs, the (West) Galway dialect (de Bhaldraithe 1953a; Ó Curnáin 2007), evinces the highest degree of productive prefixing and composition; whereas the Donegal dialect, with its possibly related high degree of verbal analyticity, may well evince the least amount of productive word-formation apparatus. Although recent (19th and 20th centuries) borrowing from English has been substantial, there has been no clear recent vernacular borrowing of English derivational affixes.

2.1 Literary and dialect (or vernacular) use

In comparison to dialect use, literary or standard Irish has a far greater range in productive use of most methods of word-formation, particularly of prefixation and composition. For well over a century, since the beginning of language revitalisation, literary Irish has undergone a process of (re)sophistication beyond dialectal resources, which has included much word coinage and major corpus planning initiatives, often, and increasingly so, by non-native speakers, based to a degree on folk literary use but also on historical linguistic resources of Irish as well as borrowing European and particularly neoclassical formations modeled on and responding to predominantly English word-formation. Modern lexical neologisms are often straight transliterations of neoclassical formations, including combining forms: *speictreascóp* 'spectroscope'. They frequently combine neoclassical with Irish constituents or affixes and are thus hybrid in character: *speictreascópach* (adjectival suffix *-ach*) 'spectroscopic'; *fonítrít* (← native *fo-* 'under, lower' + borrowed *nítrít* 'nitrite') 'hyponitrite'; *feithid* 'insect' → fully native *feithideolaíocht* 'entomology' ('-ology' corresponding to the neologism *eolaíocht* 'science' ← *eolaí* 'guide', *eol* and *eolas* 'knowledge'), but hybrid *feithidicíd* 'insecticide' alongside synonymous fully native *feithidnimh* (← *nimh* 'poison'). Cf. de Bhaldraithe (1959: v).

As in the example of *fonítrít* 'hyponitrite' an important modern neologistic feature is premodification with words, but also with prefixes and combining forms that were historically productive in word-formation but that are not generally productive in the vernacular. As well as numerical premodifiers, especially noteworthy are premodifiers of (relative) orientation, status and time, many of which have native prepositional equivalents and reflect important neoclassical or English usage: *ais-* 're-, back', *ban-* 'female', *dé-* 'bi-, di-', *eas- ~ eis-* 'ex-, out', *fear-* 'male', *fo-* 'under', *for-* 'over, super-', *frith-* 'against', *iar-* 'post-', *idir-* 'inter-', *i(o)m-* 'about, peri-, mutual', *il-* 'multi-, poly-', *i(o)n-* 'in-', *íos-* 'least, down', *neas-* 'near', *oll-* 'great, super-', *príomh-* 'prime', *ré-* 'even (number)', *réamh-* 'pre-', *sain-* 'special', *sár-* 'super-, per-', *seach-* 'by-', *tob-* 'quick', *tras-* 'cross-, trans-', *uas-* 'top, up', *ur-* 'formal'. An important concept in modernity is realised with *uath-* 'auto-' (< literary *uatha* 'singular') and *féin-* 'self-, auto-', the latter, *féin* 'self', a rare instance of a constituent which was impermissible in combination in the earlier language, *féin-* 'self-, auto-' thus illustrating, by the rarity of ahistorical formation, the relative ease of modernising composition and prefixation from an historical point of view. Innovative second constituents as combining forms are less numerous: *-eolaíocht* '-ology' (< *eolaíocht* 'science'); *-lathas* '-cracy' (< *flaitheas* 'rule' (via *fhlaitheas* with *f-* lenited and thus silent; see section 2.2) based on *flaith* 'ruler') as in *daonlathas* 'democracy' (literary *daon* 'human being'); *-lann* (< *lann* 'site') as in *leabharlann* 'library' (*leabhar* 'book'), *bialann* 'restaurant' (*bia* 'food') and with *-lann* in the base: *leabhar+lann+aí* 'librarian', *íoc+lann+óir* '(medical) dispenser; lit. healing+site+er'; collective *-ra* as in *daonra* 'population' (*daon* 'human being'). These illustrations also instantiate the modern corpus-planned combining form *daon-*: *daon+eolas* 'social studies; lit. human+knowledge', *daon+áireamh* 'census of population; lit. human+counting', *daon+chara* 'philanthropist; lit. human+friend', *daon+chairdeas* 'philanthropy; lit. human+friendship'. With regard to derivation, standard usage unhistorically differentiates agentive *-í* (native) and *-óir* (old borrowing from Latin) based on the useful contrast between English *-ee* (adapted from Anglo-Norman) and *-er*, thus *fostaí, fostóir* (← *fostaigh* 'to employ') correspond to *employee, employer* (whereas vernacular *siúlaí* and *siúlóir* 'walker, wanderer' ← *siúl* 'walk', *siúil* 'to walk', for instance, are synonymous); adjectival *-ach* can contrast with *-úil* similar to English *-ic* vs. *-ous* as in *nítreach* vs. *nítriúil* as English neoclassical *nitric* vs. *nitrous*; and processual *-ú+chán* (containing the *-ú* verbal-noun suffix of verbal 2 conjugation) corresponds to English *-ification* and *-isation* as in *nítriúchán* '(process or result of) nitrification' (← *nítriú* '(action of) nitrification'); and abstract *-achas* can contrast with abstract *-acht*, etc., as English *-ism* can contrast with *-ity*, etc. Standard verbalisation adopts the older verbal suffix *-igh* in contrast to dialectal *-áil: cnámh* 'bone' → *cnámhaigh* 'to ossify' vs. *cnámháil* 'to bone (fish)' (Uí Bheirn 1989 s. v.). Compounding is more preferred in standard formation than in vernacular (see section 2): *ban+dochtúir* 'woman doctor' for vernacular phrasal use *dochtúir mná* 'woman doctor; lit. doctor (of) woman' (appositional genitive); *leathan+bhanda* 'broadband' for vernacular formation *banda leathan* 'broadband; lit. band broad'.

An instance from Hussey (1999: 206) can illustrate scientific technical discourse built on native and borrowed word-formation resources of prefixing and composition:

(1) *An raon ultraivialait, an raon infheicthe, agus an raon infridhearg*
The range ultra+violet, the range capable-of+seen, and the range infra+red
formhéadaithe; agus fúthu sin thíos, an speictream leictreamaighnéadach de
over+enlarged; and under-3PL that below, the spectrum electro+magnetic of
réir tonnfhad.
accordance wave+lengths-GENPL
'The ultraviolet range, the visible range, and the infrared range magnified; and beneath them, the electromagnetic spectrum by wavelengths.'

This example contains the semantic specialisation of *raon* 'path, track, range', extension of *tonn* '(water) wave' to light or electromagnetic waves and six or seven neologisms:
a) neoclassical: *ultrai+vialait, speictream*;
b) hybrid: *infri+dhearg, leictrea+maighnéadach* (for *leictrea+mhaighnéad-ach*);
c) native: *in+fheicthe* (also non-terminological dialectal use; corresponding to older *so+fheicse(ana(ch))*, etc., 'visible'), *for+mhéadaithe, tonn+fhad.*

2.2 Phonology and initial mutations

Phonological changes occur mainly at juncture between elements and typically involve sandhi phenomena also found between words at phrase level, for instance, consonantal quality (palatal – diacritic´ – or non-palatal): *an-* /an/ 'very' and *deas* /dʹas/ 'nice' → *an-deas* /ˈanʹˈdʹas/ 'very nice' with palatalised *d* causing palatalisation of preceding *n* (as happens to *aon* /eːn/ 'any' in *aon deise* /ˈeːnʹ ˈdʹeʃə/ 'any niceness'), and similarly *an-fhear* /ˈanʹˈar/ 'great man' with lenited palatalised *f* causing palatalisation of preceding *n* (as occurs in *aon fhear* /ˈeːnʹ ˈar/ 'any man'). A distinctive feature in Munster is the lexicalisation of an original epenthetic vowel between a sonorant and a following consonant. Thus premodifiers such as *an-* 'very', *bun-* 'base', *corr-* 'odd', *fionn-* 'white, light', *feill-* 'foul, exceedingly', *gearr-* 'short', *sean-* 'old' have by-forms *ana-*, *buna-*, *corra-*, *feille-*, *fionna-*, *gearra-*, *seana-*. Thus southern *seana+bhean* 'old woman' doubly marks juncture, with the linking vowel and lenition, for northern *sean+bhean*. Otherwise premodifying nouns and adjectives typically have the same form as the nominative base.

Initial mutations are pervasive in the Celtic languages. The main initial mutations in Irish are lenition (< spirantisation) and eclipsis (< prenasalisation), which involve a reduction in the degree of consonantal occlusion and an increase in sonority respectively. In Irish word-formation, elements, be they words or prefixes, placed before a base regularly cause lenition of the initial consonant or consonants of the base. Lenition, when indicated in the orthography, is shown by placing *h* after the effected consonant. Thus *mórthír* /ˈmoːrhiːrʹ/ 'mainland' (← *mór* /moːr/ 'big' + *tír* /tʹiːrʹ/ 'country') with *t* /tʹ/ lenited to *th* /h/, *an-cham* /ˈanˈxaːm/ 'very crooked' (← *an-* 'very' + *cam* 'crooked') with *c* /k/ lenited to *ch* /x/, and *drochshlí* /ˈdroxˈhlʹiː/ 'bad way' (← *droch-* /drox/ 'bad' + *slí* /ʃLʹiː/ 'way') with *sl* → *shl* where both *s* and *l* undergo phonological lenition primarily in spirantisation and change of place of articulation respectively: /ʃLʹ/ > /hlʹ/. Absence or blocking of lenition is common in homorganic clusters, particularly coronals: *ceanndána* /ˈkʹaːndaːnə/ 'headstrong' (← *ceann* 'head' + *dána* 'bold') with retention of plosive dental *d* following homorganic *nn*.

Eclipsis of the initial of the base is mostly limited to dialectal *seacht-* 'sevenfold, very' (< independent numeral *seacht* 'seven' which eclipses; Ó Curnáin 2007: 609): *seachtmbearrtha* /ˈʃaxtʹmˈaːrhə/ 'shaven more than enough' (← *seacht* 'seven' + *bearrtha* /ˈbˈaːrhə/ 'shaven') in contrast to standard lenition: *seachtbhliantúil* 'septennial' (← *seacht* 'seven' + *bliantúil* 'yearly'). Diachronic eclipsis is evidenced: ˈ*iargúil* 'remote place' (← *iar-* 'after, remote' + *cúil* 'corner' with *c* > *g* through eclipsis) and ˈ*éadrom* 'light' (← *é-* 'not' + *trom* 'heavy').

The spelling *leictrea+maighnéadach* without lenition, example (1), is current but not standard. Standard lenition, *leictrea+mhaighnéad* (de Bhaldraithe 1959 s. v. *electro-magnet*), follows the rule whereby native elements are both targets and triggers of lenition, i.e. no lenition of premodified element in type a. (neoclassical+neoclassical) but lenition of premodified element in b. (neoclassical+native) and lenition of premodified element in c. (native+neoclassical) (An Caighdeán Oifigiúil 1958: 122). The native premodified constituent here is *maighnéad* 'magnet', an old borrowing from Latin, now revived in place of later-surviving *maighnéis* 'magnet'. A further instance is a. *cili+méadar* 'kilometre' without lenition because of the type (neoclassical+neoclassical) but c. *trí+mhéadar* 'trimeter' and *trasna+mhéadar* 'interferometer' with lenition because of the type (native+neoclassical) (An Coiste Téarmaíochta 2010: § 7.6) and b.+c. in *rada-thrasna+mhéadar* 'radio interferometer' with two instances of lenition because (neoclassical+native+neoclassical). This rule, effecting lenition of the native but not neoclassical element when premodified by a neoclassical constituent, can be rather demanding, requiring knowledge of etymology, as is evidenced by the presentation in McKenna-Lawlor and Ó Muirí (2010: 30) where the variable application of lenition is insufficiently described in terms of the preposed element only.

2.3 Stress

Default stress in Irish is on the initial syllable of words. In words containing more than one constituent, primary stress is typically placed on the initial constituent (and, most regularly in Connacht, secondary stress on the second constituent) in the structure ˈelement₁-element₂, typically a) ˈqualifier-head (or, regularly in Connacht, ˈqualifier-ˌhead – except North County Mayo, following Mhac an Fhailigh (1968: 61–63)) but double primary stress b) ˈqualifier-ˈhead is also common and a few prefixes do not take stress: c) qualifier-ˈhead. The tendency is for the more lexicalised complex items to take one single primary stress placed initially. The pattern of double primary stress ˈqualifier-ˈhead is common with intensifiers; thus contrasts occur such as ˈdubh-ˌhead 'black ...' with lexical meaning but ˈdubh-ˈhead 'utter / very ...' with figurative intensifier meaning. A similar distinction occurs in numeral adjectives, which, unlike canonical adjectives, are placed before the noun, but which also can occur initially in composition (an important complicating distinction – not clearly drawn in Ó Siadhail 1989: 118). Thus, *in* ˈaon(ˌ)teach 'cohabiting; lit. in one-house' but typically ˈaon ˈteach aˈmháin 'one (single) house' or ˈaon ˈteach 'any house'. And ˈan-ˈmhéid ~ ˈan-ˌmhéid 'great size' can generally contrast with ˈanmhéid 'hugeness' in Connacht (Ó Curnáin 2007: 587–588). In Ulster, in line with the overall Ulster tendency toward vowel reduction in weakly stressed position, distinctive secondary stress seems absent in words; so that, corresponding to Connacht stress type 'qualifier-ˌhead, Ulster typically has one distinctive stress 'qualifier-head. Phonetic realisation 'qualifier-ˌhead when found in Ulster corresponds to unreduced vowel quality in the head (thus resembling the rule in simple words where non-initial clear vowels take secondary – or tertiary – stress), which, when the vowel of the head is reduced, becomes 'qualifier-head (Quiggin 1906: 153–154; Ó Searcaigh 1923: 153; Ulster 'qualifier-'head ~ 'qualifier-ˌhead reported in Sommerfelt 1922: 120–124, 1965: 303). Emphasising through stress and de-emphasising through decreasing prosodic salience is, however, common: typical Connacht ro-'mhór 'too big' (since ro- is one of the typically unstressed prefixes) can become, with overall emphasis, 'ro-'mhór or, with emphasis of 'too', 'ro-ˌmhór or even 'ro-'mhór. Neologisms can be influenced by English stress of corresponding words: Connacht and Ulster speakers adopt idir'náisiúnta 'international' primarily due to English inter'national.

In Munster there is a general tendency to shift stress to phonologically heavy syllables in all words, including, although far from exceptionlessly, complex words formed through prefixation, composition or suffixation. Thus, as an example of prefixation, míshásta 'displeased' (← prefix mí- 'un-' + sásta 'satisfied'): a) Ulster 'mí'shásta ~ 'míshásta and b) Connacht 'míˌshásta but c) Munster mí'shásta with primary stress placement on a syllable containing a long vowel. Munster mí'shásta presumably can be transcribed as ˌmí'shásta but Munster monographs do not find this nescessary which can lead to some analytic ambiguities. Between two works of Ó Cuív (1947 and 1944) for the same Co. Cork dialect, stress pattern '_'_ often equates with '_ˌ_, and pattern _'_ with ˌ_'_, e.g., comhfhaid 'equal length' (← prefix comh- 'co-, equal' + faid 'length') transcribed as /'ko:'əd´/ in Ó Cuív (1947: 65) would presumably be */'ko:ˌad´/ following Ó Cuív's analysis (1944: 68 § 244), but comhchliamhain 'brother-in-law' /ko:x'l´iən´/ (← comh- 'co-' + cliamhain 'in-law') in Ó Cuív (1947: 65) would be */ˌko:x'l´iən´/ following Ó Cuív (1944: 68 § 246). But there are complications: 'bior'shrónach 'sharp-nosed' (← bior 'point' + srón+ach 'nose+d') in Ó Cuív (1947: 30) would be *ˌbior'shrónach according to Ó Cuív's analysis (1944: 68 § 246) and thus one would have expected rather *bior'shrónach in the system of Ó Cuív (1947) and, contrariwise, binnbha'rraíocht 'command' (← binn 'portion' + barraíocht 'excess, mastry'; Ó Cuív 1947: 30 s. v. binn-bhoraíocht) would be *'binnbha'rraíocht according to Ó Cuív's rule (1944: 68 § 248), and exceptional barr'fhalla 'upper part of internal wall' (← barr 'top' + falla 'wall'; Ó Cuív 1947: 25) is clearly counter to Ó Cuív's rule (1944: 68 § 244) and similar ambiguities occur with the prefix an- (Ó Cuív 1947: 10–12). Stress shift to heavy syllable is particularly common at the initial syllable of the second element, thus, lexicalised compound leath+ch(o)róin 'half-crown (coin)' (Wagner 1958–69 Vol. 1: 96):

(2) a. 'leathch(o)róin, Ulster and Connacht;
b. 'leath'chróin ~ 'leath₁chróin, North Munster (dialectally intermediate);
c. leath'chróin, general Munster (stressed long vowel).

And, as an example of derivation, *siopadóir* 'shopkeeper' (← '*siopa* 'shop' + agentive -*adóir*): Connacht and Ulster '*siopadóir* but Munster *siopa*'*dóir*. Distinctions can be made in Munster, when combining *sean(a)-* 'old', for example, with *tig* (corresponding to standard *teach*) 'house', between '*seanathig* '(the) 'old-house' (lexicalised unit) and *seana*'*thig* '(an) old 'house' (productive combination) similar to English '*black₁bird* vs. ₁*black* '*bird* respectively (Breatnach 1947: 79–82; cf. Ó Curnáin 2007: 610). Furthermore, with the secondary meaning 'bad', *sean(a)-* eschews primary stress: *seana*'*chos* 'bad leg/foot' (Ó Sé 2000: 468). There are interesting instances of conditioning of stress placement by syllable count; for *fo-* 'occasional': '*fo*-polysyllable but *fo-*'monosyllable (Ó Sé 2000: 472; implying *fo-*'*bhád* 'odd boat', cf. various instances of '*fo-*'*bhád* and '*fo-bhád* in Wagner 1958–69 Vol. 2: question 1155); an opposite tendency of a second element with high syllable count attracting stress: element₁'trisyllable (containing short syllables) (Breatnach 1947: 80). One can also mention the interesting condition of verbal adjectives attracting stress in the structure noun'verbal-adjective: *cos*'*nochtaithe* (also *cos*'*nochtaí* East Connacht) 'barefooted; lit. foot+bared', *cois*'*ligthithe* 'free; lit. foot+released' (Ó Sé 2000: 469; Wagner 1958-69 Vol. 1: 135; Breatnach 1961: 106).

Set nominal phrases generally show little or no phonological indication of lexicalisation or entrenchment, with typical phrasal stress ('noun + "dependent noun (genitive)) or (noun + 'dependent noun (genitive)). But in Ulster (see section 5.1 and section 10 on word-creation), where vowel reduction is common in unstressed syllables and in the stressed syllable of polysyllabic words, vowel-reduction can indicate singular stress on the phrase as a unit: *carn-*'*aoiligh* 'dunghill; lit. heap (of) manure' (with short *a* in destressed *carn*) in contrast to expected *cárn* '*aoiligh* as found in Connacht and Munster; '*deireadh-oiche* (shortened destressed -*oí-*) < *deireadh* '*oíche* 'late at night; lit. end (of) night'; '*dó-dheag* < *dó* '*dhéag* 'twelve; lit. two teen'; similarly in compounds: '*lin-eadach* 'linen-cloth' (*í* shortened due to polysyllabic context, *éa* shortened due to lack of stress) < *lín-éadach* (Wagner 1959: 92–93); also '*corr-*'*uair* ~ '*corr-uair* 'odd time' → '*corrbha(i)r* in Co. Donegal (Wagner 1958–69 Vol. 3: question 1156). Such lexicalised reduction through stress distinctions are important in Scottish Gaelic, contiguous dialectally with Ulster. At the opposite end of the dialectal prosodic continuum, in Munster, univerbation, for instance, of *tine* '*aoil* 'lime-kiln; lit. fire of lime' > *ti*'*níl* (plural *ti*'*níleacha*) can be related to the placement of stress on long vowels in non-initial position, including in monomorphemic words.

2.4 Prefixes

Prefixes are bound morphemes which function to semantically modify a base constituent. Prefixes which are clearly productive in (certain) dialects can be summarily classified based on semantic functions:

Positive: *dea- ~ ˈdeá-ˌ* 'good, well', *in-ˈ* 'capable of, fit to, possible to', ˈ*so-*ˌ 'easy to, possible to, good', ˈ*sár-*ˈ 'excellent';
Negative: ˈ*dí-*ˌ 'de-, in-, un-', ˈ*do-*ˌ 'difficult to, impossible to, un-, in-, ill-', ˈ*droch-*ˈ 'bad', ˈ*mí-*ˌ 'ill-, un-', ˈ*neamh-*ˌ 'in-, un-';
Degree, intensive: ˈ*an-*ˈ 'very', ˈ*comh-*ˈ 'equal', *fia-* 'large', *fri- ~ ˈfiod-*ˌ 'slight', ˈ*leas-*ˌ 'step-, by-', ˈ*rí-*ˈ 'very', *ró- ~ ro-*ˈ 'too'; cf. positive *sár-*;
Time, number: ˈ*ath-*ˌ 'again, re-', ˈ*fo- ~ fo-*ˈ 'occasional' (Ó Sé 2000: 472).

General Munster *fo-* 'odd' (prefix < preposition) corresponds to Connacht and Ulster *corr-* 'odd' (based on adjective *corr* 'odd'); one finds both in interstitial Co. Clare, and *corr- > corra-* in Co. Clare and South-East Co. Galway (Wagner 1958–69 Vol. 2 and 3: question 1155; O'Rahilly 1972: 242).

3 Composition

There was diachronically much compositional word-formation, particularly of nouns and adjectives. Productive composition in the dialects is limited to a small set of nominal premodifiers and a slightly larger set of adjectival premodifiers as well as a marginal deverbal premodifier. Examples of premodifiers are:

Nominal: *barr-* 'top, excellent', *bun-* 'base, quite', *cúl-* 'back', *feill-* 'foul, exceedingly', *leath-* 'half, one of two, medium', *meán-* 'middle, medium', *meath-* 'failing, middling', *sruth-* 'slight', *scoth-* 'excellent, medium';
Adjectival: *aon-* 'single', *ard-* 'high, excellent', *binn-* 'very' (← *go binn* 'splendidly' ← *binn* 'melodious'), *corr-* 'occasional' (also noun), *crua-* 'hard', *dearg-* 'utmost' (← 'red'), *fad-* (← *fada*) 'long', *fíor-* 'true, very', *fuar-* 'cold', *géar-* 'sharp', *gearr-* 'short', *glan-* 'clear, absolute' (← 'clean'), *lag-* 'weak', *lán-* 'full, too', *luath-* 'quick', *mion-* 'small', *mór-* 'big', *óg-* 'young', *ré-* 'moderate' (← *réidh* 'smooth'), *seacht-* 'sevenfold, very', *sean-* 'old' (← *sean* 'old') also *sain- ~ sean-* 'utmost', *síor-* (← *síoraí* 'continual', *tréan-* 'intense', *trom-* 'heavy, deep';
Verbal: *srac-* 'cursory, slight' (← *srac* 'to pull' or perhaps verbal noun *sracadh* 'pulling').

Only colour adjectives are synchronically common as a category: *bán-* 'white', *breac-* 'speckled, fair', *buí-* 'yellow', *dubh-* 'black, very', *fionn-* 'fair', *geal-* 'bright', *glas-* 'green', *liath-* 'grey'. Place function is noteworthy in nominal premodifiers and is also apparent in *iar-* ~ *giar-* 'distant' related to the adverb *thiar* 'west, back'. The semantic functions of the other premodifiers are similar to those of the productive prefixes. Note, for example, the number function of *leath-*: *leathsholas* 'one light (of two on car)' (Ó Sé 2000: 469), the degree function of *bun-*, *breac-*, *sruth-*, *srac-*, *leath-* and *meath-* as well as the intensifier function of *barr-*, *dearg-*, *dubh-*, *fíor-*, *glan-*, *seacht-* and *sean-*, not to mention *síor-* and *tréan-* whose premodifier function and independent lexical semantics coincide. Prefix *droch-* and preposed adjective *sean-* are the default attributive forms of adjectives *dona* and *sean* respectively. For instance, *tá an teach sean* 'the house is old; lit. is the house old' but *is seanteach é* 'it is an old house; lit. is old+house it'.

As for the bases they modify, premodifiers occur before nouns, ˈath˳obair 'repetition of work', before adjectives, ˈfíorˈbhreá 'very fine', and, least freely, before verbs, ˈath˳ghróig 'to refoot (peat)'. Verbal composition in dialects is limited to a few inflected verbs with common premodifiers: *comh+líon* 'to compensate; lit. co-fill' (Breatnach 1961: 104), *ath+ghróig* 'to refoot', *rua+dhóigh* 'to scorch; lit. russet+burn', *mór+chónaigh* 'to stay greatly; lit. big-stay'. Only the head is inflected: nominative *sean+bhean* 'old woman' → *teach na sean+mhná* 'the house of the old woman' (base *bean*, genitive singular *mná*); although there is a general tendency not to inflect qualified nouns whether with normal adjectival or nominal qualification or premodification or phrasal qualification (Ó Curnáin 2007: 508). Very exceptionally inflection of a premodifier is found: regular *ina dheas+láimh* 'in-his right+hand' but also synonymous *ina dheisláimh* where *deis-* is (historically) dative singular adjective as well as (synchronically) a nominal common case (Ó Curnáin 2007: 586).

Nominal and adjectival premodifiers can combine in sequence with each other or with prefixes, and prefixes can combine with other prefixes: ˈcorrˈfíorˈmháthair 'occasional truly good mother' (adjective+adjective+noun), ˈfíorˈdheáˈdhéanta 'truly well made' (adjective+prefix+verbal adjective), ˈanˈdeá˳dhéanta 'of very good physique' (prefix+prefix+verbal adjective). The preposed element can modify the immediately following element or, especially where the following combination is institutionalised, the following combination of element(s) plus base can be modified as a unit, and the difference can, at least optionally, be indicated by stress pattern: [[ˈanˈdeáˈ]dhéanta] '[[very well] made]' vs. [ˈanˈ[ˈdeá˳dhéanta]] '[very [well made]]'. Emphatic repetition of a preposed element is also found: ˈanˈanˈdeas 'very very nice', ˈfíorˈfíorˈmhaith 'truly truly good', and even ˈríˈríˈríˈfíorˈchorrˈdhuine 'very very very truly rare person' is permitted.

Copulative compounds are no longer common: *crua+chaol* 'hard and thin', *caol+dearg* 'thin and red' or in set phrases: *bun-barr* 'entirely; bottom (and) top'; inclusivity: *ó thús deireadh* 'from beginning (to) end'. Exocentric use is typically phrasal ('noun + "dependent noun (genitive))": *béal bráthair* 'person with a big mouth; lit. mouth (of) monkfish'; phrases based on *ceann* 'head': *ceann cipín* '... twig' ~ *ceann maide* '... stick' ~ *ceann máilléid* '... mallet', all three meaning 'blockhead' and *ceann leitean* '... porridge' ~ *ceann práisce* '... mess' both meaning 'pudding-head'. That the head noun of the phrase has figurative meaning is indicated by it not being inflected in the vocative: *a cheann cipín* '(oh) blockhead' (not *a *chinn ...* in vocative case) as with simplex items with figurative force: *a stór* 'my dear; lit. oh store or treasure'.

4 Derivation

Derivation primarily involves suffixation. Nonetheless, the three prefixes of ability *in-* 'capable of' as well *do-* 'difficult to' and its opposite *so-* 'easy to', effect a denominal transposition. Before nouns, which (optionally) take the genitive singular (the historical use), or, in the case of verbal stems, before the verbal adjective, these prefixes can occur in units with predicative and, less productively, with attributive function similar to adjectives: *tá tú inpheasála* 'you are passable' (← *in-* + *peasáil* (genitive singular) verbal noun < English *pass*), *áiteanna do-eolais* 'unknown places' (← genitive of *eolas* 'knowledge'). Abstracts of the shape *in-* + verbal base + *-acht* are also productive: *inchloisteacht* 'audibility' (← *in-* + *cloiste* 'heard' + *-acht* (abstract noun suffix), containing root *clois* 'to hear'). Denominal transposition to adjectival function can occur with other prefixes: *táimid comhairde* (← *comh-* 'co-' + *airde* 'height') 'we-are (of) equal height'. Although the three ability prefixes are by default passive in meaning, they can have active meaning: *inchúnta* 'able to help' (← *in-* + *cúnamh* 'helping' (verbal noun *cúnamh* → genitive of verbal noun *cúnta*, generally similar or identical to verbal adjective)), *dothuisceanach* 'lacking in understanding' (← *do-* + *tuiscint* 'understanding' (verbal noun) + *-ach* (adjectival suffix)), *do-mhaite* 'unforgivable' (passive) and 'unforgiving' (active) (← *do-* + *maith* 'to forgive'), *solabhartha* 'fluent' (← *so-* + *labhairt* 'speaking' (verbal noun)) (contrast the passive meaning of *dolabhartha* 'unutterable').

There are instances where a prefix is added to a derived base which is not found independent of prefixation: *droch+labhartha* 'evil-tongued' (← *droch-* 'bad' + *labhair* (verb) 'to speak') which has no corresponding base adjective **labhartha* (in contrast to synonymous variant *droch+labharthach* related to base *labharthach* 'talkative'; cf. regular verbal adjective *labhartha* 'spoken'). Similarly, *trom+chroí* 'heavy heart' and *dea+chroí* 'good heart' form adjectives *trom+chroí+och* and *dea+chroí+och* but the independent adjective from *croí* 'heart' is *croí+úil* 'hearty', thus resembling English dependent *-hearted* and independent *hearty*. Similarly, only the compound adjective *fannchroíoch* 'faint-hearted' is listed in Ó Dónaill (1978), corresponding to historical *fannchr(a)idech*. Historically, independent *cridech* (> *-croíoch*) and *cridemail* (> *croíúil*) are attested but the latter more frequently. And *amadán* 'fool' gives two independently derived forms in Co. Kerry: adjective *amadántúil* 'foolish' but abstract *amadántaíocht* 'foolishness' (Ó hÓgáin 1984: 103; Ó Sé 2000: 480, 475); as Co. Waterford *bleaigeard* 'blackguard' → adjective *bleaigeardúil* 'blackguardly' and activity *bleaigeardaíocht* 'blackguardism'.

Denominal adjectival suffixes *-úil* and *-ach* can be added to phrasal bases: *féar-pléúil* 'fair' (← *féar-plé* < English *fair play*); *trí chúinne* 'three corners' related to *tríchúinneach* 'having three corners' (Ó Sé 2000: 480).

The morphophonological processes of derivational suffixes are similar to those of inflection, effecting stress shift to heavy syllables (largely in Munster), both palatalisation and depalatalisation, delenition, syncope, coalescence, vowel alternation (lengthening, shortening, fronting, backing, raising), final changes such as *-ach* → *-í* (corresponding to palatalisation plus *-e* added to other consonants), consonantal extensions or interfixes (such as *th, r, n, s, l* but particularly *t* following *n, l, r* or a vowel), variable stems and irregular formations as well as suffixal allomorphy; *colg* /koləg/ 'anger' → *colgach* /koləgəx/ ~ *coilgneach* /kelʲəgʲnʲəx/ 'irascible'; adjectival suffix *-mhar* /vər/ ~ /uːr/ ~ /fər/ ~ /ər/. The stem of a given base to which a derivational suffix is added often resembles the genitive and/or plural stem of the same base. It can be analytically ambiguous whether, for instance, a given derivation should be taken to be formed either from a plural stem or from a general stem (on which both the plural and the derived form can be built).

Apart from widely suffixed diminutive *-ín*, the derivational suffix most commonly suffixed to other derivational suffixes is the abstract suffix *-acht* (see Table 7.1).

This can be contrasted with non-suffixation of, for instance, activity and abstract *-áil* in similar sequences: *+án(t)+áil, *+óg+áil, *+ín(t)+eáil (all five absent in Doyle and Gussmann 1996); although negative affect is indicated in sequenced activity and abstract *+arn+áil, +am+áil* and marginal *+amas+áil*. Abstract and activity *-acht* is also suffixed by activity *-áil*: *+acht+áil* and adjectival *-úil* and *-ach*: *+acht+úil* and *+acht+ach*. Instances of derivative sequences are: *fán* 'wandering' → *fánaí* 'wanderer' (agentive *-í*) also 'wandering' (abstract and activity *-í*) → *fánaíocht* 'wandering'; *maith* 'good' (adjective) → *maitheas* 'good' (noun) → *maitheasaí*

Tab. 7.1: Abstract and activity *-acht* in derivative sequences.

Noun	Adjective	Agentive	Abstract and Activity *-acht*
		-óir, -éir, -í	-óireacht, -éireacht, -íocht
	-úil		-úlacht
	-mhar		-mhaireacht
-ach	-ach		-acht
-áil	-áilte	-álaí	-áilteacht, -álaíocht
-án	-ánach, -ánta	-ánaí, -ánach	-ánaíocht, -ántacht, -ántaíocht
-óg	-ógach		-ógacht
-ín	-ín(t)each	-íneach, (-íneadóir)	-ín(t)eacht

'good worker'; cf. *suaimhneas* 'tranquility' related to *suaimhneach* 'tranquil' and derived *suaimhneasach* 'soothing'. Double occurrences of abstract *-acht* in sequence are very rare and involve *-acht+úl+acht* around adjectival *-úil*: (*daon* 'human being' >) adjective *daonna* 'human' → *daonnacht* 'humanity' → *daonnachtúil* 'humane' → *daonnachtúlacht* 'humaneness' (cf. also *duine* 'person' → *duineata* (adjective) 'human' → *duineatacht* 'kindliness' and similar *duiniúil* (adjective) 'human' → *duiniúlacht* 'kindliness'); *oidhre* 'heir' → *oidhreacht* 'inheritance' → modern biological terminology *oidhreachtúil* 'hereditary' → modern biology *oidhreachtúlacht* 'heredity; lit. hereditariness'; also *aer+ach+t+úl+acht* 'eeriness' (← base *aer* 'air'). Cf. also dialectal (diachronic) double agentive +*éar+aí* (section 4.1.1).

Regarding the interaction of composition and derivation, an instance of the typical idiosyncracies of word-formation is seen, for West Co. Galway, in compound adjective *bánlíoch* 'pallid' (← *bán* 'white', *lí* 'complexion') whose base compound noun *bánlí* 'pale complexion' and corresponding simple adjective *líoch* or *líogh(dh)ach* 'colourful' are not current in West Co. Galway (Ó Curnáin 2007: 2395, 2528). Also idiosyncratic: *margadh* 'market, bargain' (with dialectal plural *margáintí* in the meaning 'bargains') → *margáintíocht* (irregular) ~ *margáil* (regular) 'bargaining'; and *spág* 'broad foot' → *spág+áil* (regular) ~ *spáigirl+íneacht* (idiosyncratic with inserted *-irl-*) 'walking clumsily'.

4.1 Nominal derivation

Denominal suffixes have the largest set of endings; deadjectival or deverbal suffixes are generally a subset of denominal suffixes. The adjectival suffix *-ach* can regularly function as a nominaliser, for example with surnames: *Ó Súilleabháin*

'O'Sullivan' → *Súilleabhánach* 'an O'Sullivan' (noun) or 'belonging to O'Sullivan' (adjective), and with place names: *an Fhrainc* 'France' → *Francach* 'French person' or 'French'. In Ó Sé (2000: 477) *-ánach* is noteworthy in this function: *an Rúis* 'Russia' → *Rúiseánach* 'Russian person'; cf. *Meirice(á)* 'America' → adjective and noun *Meiriceánach* 'American'. Similarly, *Gaillimh* 'Galway' → *Gaillimheach* 'Galway person' but exceptional *-íneach* in *Condae an Chláir* 'County Clare' → *Cláiríneach* 'person from Clare'.

4.1.1 Denominal nouns

L a n g u a g e n a m e s are formed with *-is: an Ghearmáin* 'Germany' → *Gearmáinis* 'German (language)', non-vernacular formation *Gaelscoil* 'Irish-language (emersion) school; lit. Gaelschool' → *Gaelscoilis* 'emersion Irish'.

P e r s o n a l s u f f i x e s include *-í, -éir, -óir, -ire* (all of which are generally agentive; with borrowings all four are found but *-éir* is most frequent), and the typically non-agentive *-ach, -án* and *-óg*. Diminutive *-ín* is occasionally personal: *gruaim* 'gloom' → *gruaimín* 'gloomy little fellow', *fuaidrín* 'flighty woman' (← *fuaidreamh* 'wandering, fuss').

a) *-í: scéal* 'story' → *scéalaí* 'story-teller'; often following morphologically complex bases containing, for instance, *-án, -ún, -óid: amhrán* 'song' → *amhránaí* 'singer'; borrowing *comrádaí* 'comrade'; similarly, often added to bases in nominal and verbal suffix *-áil: útamáil* 'fumbling' → *útamálaí* 'fumbler', *crágáil* 'to plod' (← *cráig* 'large foot') → *crágálaí* '(strong) walker', thus common with English borrowings: English *box* → *bacsáil* (verb and verbal noun) → *bacsálaí* 'boxer'. Note *seanchas* 'lore' → *seanchaí* ~ *seanchasaí* 'traditional story-teller'.

b) *-éir* (also *-éar* (~ *-aer*), *-éara, -éaraí*): *siúinéir* 'carpenter' (cf. *siúnta* 'joint'), *bácáil* 'to bake (verb), baking (verbal noun)' → *báicéir* 'baker' (from which *báicéireacht* 'baking', see abstract *-acht* in this section).

c) *-óir* (also *-tóir, -teoir, -adóir*): *bád* 'boat' → *bádóir* 'boatman', noun *moill* 'delay' and verb *moilligh* 'to delay' → *moilleadóir* 'lingerer', *crú* '(horse)shoe' → *crúdóir* 'farrier', note *muirín* 'scallop' → *muiríneadóir* 'scallop gatherer' containing four syllables (the only word ending in *-íneadóir* given in Doyle and Gussmann 1996), in contradiction of the proposed maximum of three syllables in Doyle's "Rule 2" (1992: 88–89) as is *seomradóir* 'chamberlain' (← *seomra* 'room') when pronounced *seomaradóir* cited in Doyle (1992: 90). Non-compound words of five syllables are very rare: *corach+adóir+eacht* 'rowing a currach' (Ó Curnáin 2007: 2228, corresponding to standard tetrasyllabic *curachóireacht*), or *dealbh+adóir+eacht*, pronounced *dealabhadóireacht*

(~ *dealbh*+*óir*) 'sculptor' (← *dealbh* 'statue'), cf. *cailimhineog*+*ach* 'covered with green scum'. Interestingly, the activity noun corresponding to *muiríneadóir* is *muirínteacht* 'gathering scallops' and expected pentasyllabic **muiríneadóireacht* is not given in Ó Dónaill (1978). Final -*ach* of a base noun is absent in, for example, *criathrach* 'bog' → *criathróir* 'bog-worker', *gliomach* 'lobster' → *gliomadóir* 'lobster-fisher', as is -*ín* in the English borrowing *lóistín* 'lodging' → *lóisteoir* 'lodger' (also synonymous *lóist*+*éir* and, with retention of base -*ín*, *lóistín*+*each*).

d) -*ire*: *iasc* 'fish' → *iascaire* 'fisherman', cf. borrowing *ministir ~ ministéir* 'minister'. Non-agentive in *slat* 'rod' → *slataire* 'tall youth'.

e) -*ach* (also -*ánach*, -*íoch*, -*íneach*): *bréag* 'lie' → *bréagach* 'liar', *féar* 'grass' → *féaránach* 'grazing animal', *Corcaigh* 'Cork' → *Corcaíoch* 'Corkonian'; -*íneach*, which contains diminutive -*ín*, is typically disparaging: *meirg* 'rust, crustiness' → *meirgíneach* 'crabbed woman', also adjective and noun *meirgeach* 'crusty (person)'. Cf. borrowing *chaplain* > *séiplíneach* 'curate' (rare *séiplín* Wagner 1958–69: question 786).

f) -*án* (also -*achán*): *bocht* 'poor' → *bochtán* 'pauper'; -*achán* has disparaging meaning: *smaois* 'snot' (→ *smaoiseach* 'snotty') → *smaoiseachán* 'sniveller'.

g) -*óg*: feminine ending common with female reference: *planda* 'plant' → *plandóg* 'shapely woman', *pit* 'vulva' → *piteog* (~ *piteán* ~ *piteachán*) 'effeminate man', cf. *ciotóg* 'left hand, left-handed person' (cf. *ciotach* 'left-handed').

Variation between agentive suffixes is common both intra- and interdialectally, often with little or no semantic differentiation: *saothar* 'labour' → *saothraí ~ saothraíoch* 'toiler'; *gnotha* 'business' → *gnothaí ~ gnothach* 'industrious worker'; *reilig* 'graveyard' → *reiligire ~ reiligeadóir ~ reiligeoir* 'sexton'. Most of Connacht, as well as South-West Donegal, has suffixed agentive -*í* to agentive -*éir*/-*éar* to form -*éaraí* (except for two areas, one in the east and one in the south-west, the latter having interstitial -*éara*, an historical genitive form, interpretable as an interdialectal compromise or "fudge"). Cf. -*án* ~ -*ánaí*: *ceolán ~ ceolánaí* 'incessant talker' (Breatnach 1961 s. v.) ← *ceol* 'music'. Reduction of vocalic length can lead to -*éir* and -*óir* fusing in Ulster. An indication of some of the morphological, lexical and phrasal variation can be gained from a trawl through Wagner's questionnaire returns of his dialect survey (1958–69: questions 593, 681, 959, 525, 3, 678, 216, 746, 937, 786, 312, 624); ten of which are summarised here:

1. Two agentives, 'scythe-man' *spealadóir* (← noun (and verb) *speal* 'scythe, to scythe') and 'weaver' *fíodóir* (← verb '*figh*' 'to weave'), show no morphological variation but there is one instance of lexical variance: South-East Munster *spólaer* /spoːleːr/ 'weaver' ← noun *spól* 'shuttle'. The former also has instances

of the phrasal agentive alternant (person + genitive): *fear speile* 'man (of) scythe'.

2. 'Farmer' *feirmeoir ~ feirméir* ← noun *feirm* 'farm' with *-eoir* in Munster (also *-úir* through nasalised vowel-raising in Munster, thus homophonous with *-úir* in borrowings such as *saighdiúir* 'soldier') and *-eoir* as a variant in Ulster (also plural *fármarz*, cf. *farmóir* Ó Baoill 1996: 136; pronounced *feilmir* Wagner 1959: 221), and *-éir* (*-éar*, *-éara*, *-éaraí*) in Connacht and South-West Cork in Munster. Ulster also has the phrasal alternant *fear talamh* 'man (of) land'.

3. 'Thatcher' *díonadóir* (← *díon* 'shelter, covering, roof') is found only in Munster where it is the main lexeme, but Munster also returns *tuíodóir* (← *tuí* 'thatch, straw') which is the main word in Connacht and Ulster. Minor variants are: a. *díonóir* (disyllabic, thus interdialectal, form found in North Munster where disyllabic *tuíodóir* is also returned); b. North Connacht *clúdachóir* 'coverer' (← *clúdach* 'cover') and neighbouring c. phrasal *fear cumhdaigh* 'man (of) covering/roof'.

4. '(Cattle) buyer' *ceannaitheoir* (← verb *ceannaithe* (verbal adjective, genitive), *ceannaigh* 'to buy') is the main variant in Ireland based on the native verb. Three other related variants are: a. *ceannachóir* (← verbal noun *ceannach* 'buying') dominant in Connacht; North Ulster b. *ceannaí* and c. *ceannaíoch*; as well as phrasal West Connacht *fear ceannach beithígh* 'man (of) buying (of) cattle'. A later borrowed alternative from English *jobber* > *jab-* (also *job-*) is common in Munster and Connacht: *jaibéir ~ jabaer* in Munster with the main agentive suffix for borrowings but *jabaire* in Connacht with *-ire* which is, however, most frequent with native (non-verbal) bases (Doyle 1992: 104), although there are several semantically relatable words in *-baire* such as *cabaire* 'babbler', *sciobaire* 'snatcher', *bobaire* 'trickster'.

5. 'Miller' *muilleoir* varies with *muillteoir* (~ *muilltheoir* in Munster) (through syncope and coalescence ← *muileann* 'mill') in all three provinces. Minor variants: a. *muilléar* East Galway; b. *muileannóir* West Galway; c. *muilleadóir* North-West Mayo; as well as phrasal *fear (an) m(h)uilinn* 'man (of) (the) mill' and *fear meilte* 'man (of) grinding'.

6. 'Knitter' *cniotálaí* (← verb and verbal noun *cniotáil* 'to knit, knitting') found in all three provinces, but one instance of *cniotadóir* (West Mayo, cf. *muilleadóir*); phrasal variants *bean c(h)niotála* 'woman (of) knitting' are just as commonly returned as derived *cniotálaí*.

7. 'Beggar' *bacach* is the main lexeme (← adjective *bacach* 'lame'); commonest in Munster, but also found in Connacht and Ulster; literal *fear bocht* 'poor man' is also common (with variants *duine bocht* 'poor person', *bean bhocht* 'poor woman'). Noun phrases are *fear siúil* 'itinerant, tramp; lit. man (of) walking' and *fear déirce* 'man (of) alms'; as well as instances of the three-

constituent agentive phrases (agent + verbal noun (genitive) + object (genitive)): *fear iarraidh na déirce* 'man (of) asking (of) the alms' and *fear cruinniú déirce* 'man (of) gathering (of) alms'. Minor variants are derived *bocht+án* 'poor person' (← *bocht* 'poor') and *puicéaraí* 'packman' (standard *pacaire*) (← *paca* 'pack').

8. 'Herdsman' a. *aoire* main word in Munster, b. *maor* also in Munster but especially in Connacht, c. *sípéar(aí)* (borrowing 'shepherd; lit. sheep+er') in South-East Connacht; also commonly qualified by 'of (the) cow(s)': *aoire bó/ba/na mba*, and regularly qualified *buachaill* 'boy', d. *buachaill bó/ba/na bó/na mbó* in Munster, North-East Connacht and almost exclusive form in Ulster; rare e. *stíobhard* 'steward' (Co. Galway), f. *sréadaí* (Co. Donegal) < *tréad+aí* 'herd+er'.
9. 'Stranger' borrowing *stra(i)nséar, stróinséar* with variants of the suffix as described in this section, also *coimhthíoch* (noun) ~ *duine/fear coimhthíoch* (adjective) 'strange person/man' in Ulster, following the pattern of older and phrasal items found in Ulster agentives ((2) *fear talamh*, (8) *buachaill bó*) in contrast to innovations and borrowings to the south.

Suffixes *-ach, -án* and *-óg* are often, and the latter two predominantly, n o n - p e r s o n a l: *cnoc* 'hill' → *cnocán* 'hillock', *bréag* 'lie' → *bréagán* 'toy', *maoil* 'bare top, contents above rim of receptacle' → *maológ* 'part of contents placed above rim of receptacle'. Variation between personal and non-personal functions is common: *ailp* 'chunk' (also figuratively 'chunky person') and *alp* 'gulp' → *alp+aire* 'voracious eater, chunky object' (cf. variant *ailp+éir* 'voracious eater'), *alp+achán* 'voracious eater, chunky object or person', *alp+án* ~ *alp+óg* 'chunky object or person'. Suffixes *-ach, -án* and *-óg* are often found in synonymous or semantically close variants: feminine *brídeach* ~ *brídeog* 'bride'; *dona* 'bad' → *donán* 'wretch (person)' and *donóg* 'wretch (woman)'; *broc(ach)* 'dirt(y)' → *brocachán* 'dirty-faced person' and *brocóg* 'dirty-faced girl'; *briotachán* ~ *briotaire* 'lisping person' and *briotóg* 'lisping woman' (← adjective *briotach* 'lisping'). Given such pairs of male *-án* and female *-óg*, one might have expected a productive sex differentiation similar to English agent+*ess* (cf. borrowings *máistir* < *master* and *máistreás* 'mistress'); this *-án* vs. *-óg* contrast, however, is not productive and terminological premodifier *ban-* 'female' is used instead (as well as rarer *fear-* 'man' in compounds). Diachronic (*-án, -óg*) and synchronic (*-ín*) diminutive force is seen in variants such as *fearbán* ~ *fearbóg* ~ *feirbín* '(small) welt' ← *fearb* 'welt'. Compare (earlier) borrowings *cábán* < English *cabin*, *gairdín* < English *garden*.

Feminine suffix *-óg* is found most frequently in Northern dialects, particularly in Ulster, corresponding to southern *-án* (masculine) or *-ín* (masculine > both genders) in certain lexemes or to no suffix (O'Rahilly 1972: 186): Ulster and North Connacht *crumhóg* 'maggot' and *faoileog* 'seagull' (and even *faoileogán*) but Southern *cruimh, faoileán* (Wagner 1958–69 Vol. 1: 210, 217); including an instance counter to natural gender in the borrowing of English *bullock* > Ulster *bológ* but Southern (also South Donegal) *bullán* (Wagner 1958–69 Vol. 1: 7). (Other examples from Wagner 1958–69 Vol. 1: *eireog* 'chickens' 35, *bogóg* 'shell-less egg' 46, *tonnóg* 'duck' 48, *beachóg* 'bee' 49, *(s)corróg* 'hip' 133, *sopóg* 'sheaf' 185, *bachlóg* 'sprout' 186, *luchóg* 'mouse' 211, *bodóg* 'searod' 269, *faochóg* 'periwinkle' 271, *crannóg* 'winding frame (for fishing-line)' 275, *gobóg* 'dogfish' 287, cf. *tornóg* 'kiln' 263, *pardóg ~ feadhnóg* 'pannier-basket' 58.) Compare English *spoon* > *spúnóg* generally, except in farthest north and south: North Ulster *spáin* and South Munster *sp(i)ún* (Wagner 1958–69 Vol. 1: 165). The opposite dialectal distribution occurs in Ulster *scamhán* 'lung' but Southern (including South Donegal) *scamhóg* (Wagner 1958–69 Vol. 1: 140), and Northern *buil(bh)ín* 'loaf' but Munster *bulóg* (Wagner 1958–69 Vol. 1: 76) in contrast with Ulster *bológ* 'bullock', cf. Southern *neantóg* 'nettle' (Wagner 1958–69 Vol. 1: 249), also Connacht *bodóg* 'heifer' (Wagner 1958–69 Vol. 1: 9) in contrast with North Donegal *bodóg* 'searod'.

Denominal abstract suffixes also function in aggregate nouns of status and very commonly in nouns of activity which often enter into verbal use preceded by the progressive particle *ag* similar to verbal nouns: *Gaeilgeoir* 'Irish speaker' → *Gaeilgeoireacht* 'speaking Irish', *tá sí ag Gaeilgeoireacht* 'she is speaking Irish'. Similarly, *áibhirseoir* 'devil, rascal' → *ag áibhirseoireacht* '(engaged in) mischief-making' (Ó hÓgáin 1984 s. v., in contradiction of Doyle 1992: 59). The suffixes *-áil* and *-íl*, which are generally verbal-noun endings, are also found in abstract function: *bradach* 'thieving' (adjective) → *bradaíl* 'thieving' (noun). A subset of those suffixes found in denominal function are found in deadjectival abstract use. The analytic choice of actual base from an adjective, a related noun or even a verb, might be arbitrary: adjective *sásta* 'satisfied' and noun *sásamh* 'satisfaction' and verb *sásaigh* 'to satisfy' → *sástacht ~ sástaíocht ~ sásaíocht* 'satisfaction' (also adjectives *sásúil* and *sásmhar* 'satisfactory' → respectively *sásúlacht* and *sásmhaireacht* 'satisfactoriness').

a) -e: *bréag* 'lie' → *bréige* 'falseness';
b) -ach (also -úch), -acht (also -íocht): *béic* 'yell' → *béiceach ~ béiciúch* 'yelling', *cladhaire* 'coward' → *claidhreacht ~ claidhríocht* 'cowardice';
c) -as (also -achas, -amas, -anas): *muintir* 'kinsfolk' → *muintearas* 'kinship', *leanúint* 'following' → *leanúnachas* 'attachment';
d) -an, -án (also -achan, -achán): *maidin* 'morning' → *maidneachan* 'dawn(ing)'.

Although *-acht* and *-íocht* are often synonymous (e.g., *ainnis* 'wretched' → *ainnise ~ ainnisí ~ ainniseacht ~ ainnisíocht* 'wretchedness'), more common *-acht* can have more abstract meaning than *-íocht* which often has meaning of activity or behaviour. Thus *-acht* often retains a link with adjectival *-ach*, similar to adjective+*ness* evident in -*úl*+*acht* and -*mhair*+*eacht*, whereas -*íocht* retains a link with verbs and agentive -*í*, thus verb/noun+*ing*, and is similar to -*óireacht*, -*éireacht* which are clearly linked to agentive -*óir* and -*éir*. For instance, *aer* 'air, gaiety' → *aerach* 'light-hearted' → *aeracht* 'light-heartedness, gaiety' but *aeraíocht* 'open-air entertainment' including progressive *ag aeraíocht* 'taking the air', cf. activity *aermaíocht* ~ *aermáil* 'pleasure-seeking'. A similar distinction of abstract -*acht* (-*e*, etc.) vs. activity -*íocht* (-*áil*, etc.) can be found with greater variation in: *righin* 'tough, slow' (→ *righnigh* 'to toughen, linger') → abstract *righn*+*e* ~ *righn*+*eas* ~ *righn*+*eachas* ~ *righn*+*eadas* ~ *righn*+*eacht* 'toughness, slowness' but activity *righn*+*eáil* ~ *righn*+*eacáil* ~ *righn*+*eadóir*+*eacht* ~ *righn*+*ealtaíocht* ~ *righn*+*íocht* 'lingering' (related to agentive *righn*+*eál*+*aí* ~ *righn*+*eál*+*ach* ~ *righn*+*eacál*+*aí* ~ *righn*+*eadóir* ~ *righn*+*eartál*+*aí* 'lingerer'). Activity nominals are common from deverbal agentives, thus producing common related activity doublets: *coill* 'to geld' → *coillteoir* 'gelder' → *coillteoireacht* 'castration' functioning similar to verbal noun *coilleadh* 'gelding'. In some instances the agentive noun is not attested: *guí* 'prayer' → *guíodóireacht* 'constant praying' (Ó Curnáin 2007: 632), adverbial *istoíche* 'at night' (< *oíche* 'night') → *istoícheadóireacht* 'night-visiting' (Ó hAirt 1988 s.v.); *sagart* 'priest' → *sagartóireacht* 'priesthood' cited in section 2.

As well as considerable variation among synonymous suffixes added to the same or similar base, e.g., *bréan* 'putrid' → *bréin*+*e* ~ *bréan*+*adas* ~ *bréin*+*eadas* ~ *bréan*+*tas* ~ *bréan*+*tamas* ~ *bréan*+*tanas* 'putrefication', there is a tendency to combine abstract suffixes together, e.g., the creative effervescence in *cac* 'excrement' → *cacamas* 'filth', *cacamáil* 'smutty behaviour', *cacamasáil* 'working in filth' (such a combinational tendency, similar to synaffixes, is far more developed in nominal plural allomorphy). Compare further analysability in -*an*+*as* and -*ach*+*as* (cf. -*n*+*ach*+*as* in *maith*+*ún*+*ach*+*as* in section 4.1.2).

Some common denominal abstract nouns can also be count nouns: *maith* 'good' → *maitheas* 'goodness', plural *maitheasaí* 'gifts'; *fearas* 'equipment', plural *fearais(tí)* 'tools'; *eolas* 'knowledge', plural *eolais(t)í* 'items of knowledge' (Ó hAirt 1988 s.v.; Ó Sé 2000: 96); *nua* 'new' → *nuacht* 'news', plural *nuachta(í)* 'items of news' (Ó Curnáin 2007: 2304 s.v. *nuaíocht*; Dinneen 1911 s.v. *nuadhacht*).

D e n o m i n a l   d i m i n u t i v e s are derived by suffixation of -*ín* which is highly productive (except in most of Ulster; O'Rahilly 1972: 186): *pionta* 'pint' → *pintín* 'small pint', *bacach* 'tramp' → *baicín* 'small tramp', *cnocán* 'hillock' (< -*án* historical diminutive) → *cnoc*+*áin*+*ín* 'small hillock', *bád*+*óir* 'boatman' → *bád*+*óir*+*ín* 'small boatman' (Doyle 1992: 121 casts doubt on the productivity of -*ín* suffixed to complex agentives, but these are not uncommon: *táilliúir*+*ín* 'small tailor', and note *jabaeir*+*ín* 'small cattle-buyer' cited, in a different context, by Doyle 1992: 125), *sram*+*ach*+*án* → *sram*+*ach*+*áin*+*ín* 'little blear-eyed person'; current borrowings: *package* → *peaicijín* 'small package'; including, to a lesser extent, non-count and abstract nouns: *féar* 'grass' → *féirín* 'small or short (growth of) grass', *dochar* 'harm' → *dochairín* 'small (amount of) harm', *uaigneas* 'lonesomeness' → *uaignisín* 'small (degree of) lonesomeness', current borrowing *speed* → *spídín deas* 'nice bit of speed'. Infantile context allows for informal suffixation to inflected preposition in *chugaitín* (to-2SG-DIMINUTIVE) 'look out (to child)' (← *chugat* (to-2SG) 'to you; also: look out!' ← *chun* or *chuig* 'to'). Evaluative force is common, either affectionate or pejorative: affectionate *ainsín* 'darling' (← *ansa* 'dearest'), *stóirín* 'darling' (← *stór* 'darling, store'), *úillín* 'darling' (← *úll* 'apple') also *úillín óir* 'pampered child; lit. small apple/darling (of) gold', *leoinín* 'pet, darling' (← *leon* 'lion' or *leamhan* 'moth'); pejorative *dailtín* 'brat, cad' (← *dalta* 'foster-child, pupil'), *éigsín* 'poetaster' (← *éigeas* 'poet' also *éigse* 'poets'); pejorative with agentive force *déircín* 'beggarly person' (← *déirc* 'alms'). Incorporated in interjections: *seabhain ~ seabhainín ~ seabhain ~ seibhín ~ saidheoir*, etc., 'call to sheep' (de Bhaldraithe 1985 s. v.); *seoithín seó* 'lullaby'; cf. English *Hello+een* (Ó Curnáin 2007: 2005) with *-een < -ín*. Some word pairs contrast in lexicalised derivation vs. productive formation: *paidir* 'prayer' > *paidrín* 'rosary' but *paidir* → *paidirín* 'small prayer'. Although productive *-ín* can be suffixed to lexicalised *-ín* (*cúil+ín+ín* 'small beautiful(-haired) maid') productive *-ín* is avoided in **diúilicín+ín* 'small mussel'. In plant names, *-ín* is common: *duáinín an tseanchais* 'self-heal; lit. small kidney of the lore' also called *duán donn* 'brown kidney'.

In West Co. Galway (Ó Curnáin 2007: 652–653), one finds predominantly optional suffixation of *-ín* (in plural *-íní*) to nominal plural inflection of a small group of nouns with irregular or rarer plural allomorphs: *faocha* 'periwinkle' → plural *faochain* → plural with diminutive *faochainíní*; *teach* 'house' → diminutive *teachaín*, plural *teachaíní*, but also *titheabhaíní* ← plural *titheabhaí* 'houses'. The suffix *-ín* can act as a base for further derivational suffixation: *-íneach* noun and adjective, *-ínteacht* abstract noun, which can have repetitive meaning (short (repeated) events): *méar* 'finger' (→ *méirín*) → *méiríntéacht* 'fingering, meddling'; adjective *mín* 'smooth' (→ *mínigh* 'to smooth, explain') → *mínín(t)eacht* 'daintiness, niggling'; cf. *-ínteacht* as verbal noun suffix: *reith* 'to rut' → *reithínteacht* 'rutting' also *reithíocht*.

4.1.2 Deadjectival nouns

Diachronically, *-án* and *-óg* are important nominalising suffixes.
a) *-án* (also *-achán*): *bocht* 'poor' → *bochtán* 'poor person'; series analysable as *caill* 'to lose' → *caillte* (verbal adjective) 'lost' and adjective *caillteach* 'losing' → *caillteachán* 'wretch';
b) *-óg*: *bréan* 'putrid' → *bréanóg* 'refuse heap'.

	Comparative	Abstract Comparative			
Base					
garbh		goirbhe		goirfe	
misniúil		misniúla		misniúlacht	
uasal			uaisle	uaisleacht	
meirbh		meirbhe		meirbheadas	meirfean
breá			breácha	breáchadas	
te		teocha	teoichte	teoichteacht	teos teas
maith	fearr	maitheas		feabhas	maith
				Abstract	

Tab. 7.2: Intersection of comparative and abstract in abstract comparative.

Main deadjectival abstract suffixes are -*e*; -*adas* (-*as*, -*antas*). Suffixes which commonly both effect denominal and deadjectival functions are: -*as*, -*achas*, -*amas*; -*acht*, -*íocht*; -*an*, -*án*.

a) -*e* (also -*chte*), -*í*: *uasal* 'noble' → *uaisle* 'nobility', -*chte* follows vowels: *breá* 'fine' → *breáichte* 'beauty'; *déanach* 'late' → *déanaí* 'lateness';

b) -*ach*, -*acht* (also -*íocht*, -*ineacht*): *tirim* 'dry' → *triomach* 'drought', *glan* 'clean' → *glaineacht* 'cleanliness', *plánáilte* 'plain' → *plánáilteacht* 'plainness', *aimlithe* 'wretched' → *aimlitheacht* ~ *aimlíocht* 'wretchedness', added to adverbial *gan+fhios* (← *gan* 'without' + *fios* 'knowledge') 'without knowledge' or 'secretly' → *ganfhiosaíocht* 'secrecy', therefore *ag ganfhiosaíocht* 'acting secretively' (Ó hAirt 1988 s. v.), *bocht* 'poor' → *bochtaineacht* 'poverty';

c) -*as* (also -*adas*, -*achas*, -*amas*, -*anas*, -*antas*): *ciúin* 'silent' → *ciúineas* 'silence', *bocht* 'poor' → *bochtanas* 'poverty'; -*adas* is taken as productive (in contradiction of Doyle 1992: 26 n. 4; cf. Doyle and Gussman 1996: 317 who list over 40 lexemes in -*adas*), in variation with -*antas* and -*acht* ~ -*íocht* in *bodhar* 'deaf' → *bodhaireadas* ~ *bodhaireantas* ~ *bodhaireacht* ~ *bodhraíocht* 'deafness'; -*amas* indicates loathsomeness: *goirt* 'saline' → *goirteamas* 'saltiness';

d) -*an*, -*án* (also -*achan*, -*achán*): *gann* 'scarce' → *ganntan* 'scarcity'; *crua* 'hard' → *cruatan* ~ *cruaitean* 'hardship'.

An abstract comparative (of degree) is formed from adjectives using morphology of both comparative adjective (inflectional) and abstract noun (derivational) (cf. Table 7.2): *misniúil* 'courageous' → 'how courageous' or 'given the courageousness' *a mhisniúla* (= *níos misniúla* 'more courageous' comparative in final schwa) ~ *a mhisniúlacht* (= *an mhisniúlacht* 'courageousness' abstract in -*acht*) where *a* is (bleached from an original) proleptic 3 masculine possessive pronoun 'its'; one cannot say comparative *níos *misniúlacht* nor nominal *an *mhisniúla*. The morphological intersection of abstract comparative with comparative and abstract systems can be illustrated from Ó Curnáin (2007: 564–569, 642–647) by a selection of some of the alternants of *garbh* 'rough', *misniúil* 'courageous', *uasal* 'noble', *meirbh* 'sultry', *breá* 'fine', *te* 'warm', and irregular *maith* 'good'.

This indicates, for instance, that *uaisle* belongs to all three types: comparative *níos uaisle* 'more noble', abstract comparative *a uaisle* 'how noble', abstract *an uaisle* 'the nobility'; but that irregular *fearr* is comparative only: *níos fearr* 'better'; and that *maitheas* and *goirfe* were attested in abstract comparative only: *a mhaitheas* 'how good', *a ghoirfe* 'how rough'; and *meirfean* is abstract only: *an meirfean* 'the faintness, sultriness'.

Diminutive *-ín* is more limitedly found (Ó Curnáin 2007: 648–650) with adjectives, in contexts of familiarity, particularly in interactions with young children: *álainn* 'beautiful' → *álainnín*, *beag* 'small' → *beigín*, *beag bídeach* '(small and) tiny' → *beag bídeachaín*; *buidéil+íní beaga bídeach+aíne* 'small little tiny bottles'; cf. nominalised *láchaín* 'fondling' (← adjective *lách* 'kind') which corresponds to more common derivation of the diminutivised abstract noun *láinteacht* 'fondling' (← *lách* + *-ín* + *teacht*).

4.1.3 Deverbal nouns

Personal suffixes are instanced here.
a) *-í*: see examples of verbal *-áil* → *-álaí* (section 4.1.1);
b) *-óir* (also *-tóir*, *-teoir*, *-adóir*) largely with verbs of the 1st conjugation, and *-itheoir*, *-adóir* largely with verbs of the 2nd conjugation: *múin* 'to teach' → *múinteoir* 'teacher', *ceannaigh* 'to buy' → *ceannaitheoir* 'buyer' also *ceannach(t)* 'buying' → *ceannachóir* 'buyer' (cf. section 4.1.1 (4)), *dathaigh* 'to colour, dye' → *dathadóir* 'dyer, exaggerator', *mallaigh* 'to curse' → *mallaitheoir* ~ *mallaíodóir* 'curser', cf. *seol* 'sail, to sail' (noun and verb) → *seoltóir* 'sailor'. The *d* in *-adóir* can function similar to an interfix between vowels: *figh* 'to weave' → *fíodóir*; in South Connacht it often replaces *-itheoir*: *slánaigh* 'to redeem' → *slánaitheoir* ~ *slánaíodóir* 'saviour'.

The abstract noun derived from the verb *maith* 'to forgive' (converted from adjective *maith* 'good') can serve as a simple illustration of intra- and interdialectal variation of synonymous suffixes *-únas*, *-únachas*, *-anas* 'forgiveness, pardon' (mostly from Wagner 1958–69: question 785), set out from north to south:

(3) a. *maith+iúnas* most widespread; Ulster (where also metathesised *maúthnas*, and mixed *maúthúnas*), North-West Connacht, East and North Munster;

b. *mai+tiúnas* interstitial; North Connacht, between *maithiúnas* to north and *maiteanas* to south;
c. *mai+teanas* general in Connacht (for ahistorical *t* cf. verbal adjective *maite* 'forgiven') also for by-form *mai+teachas* (Ó Curnáin 2007: 631, 638) cf. *-únachas* to the south;
d. *maith+iúnachas* general in South-West Munster.

4.2 Adjectival derivation

The main adjectival suffix with native bases is *-ach*; most productive with modern borrowings is *-áilte* (identical to verbal adjective of verbs in *-áil*). Others are *-mhar*, *-úil* and, related to the verbal adjective, *-tha(í)* and *-ta(í)* and *-íthe* as well as *-í*, *-da* and *-a*.

4.2.1 Denominal adjectives

Denominal adjectives have the widest range of suffixes. Variation is common: *féar* 'grass' → *féarach* ~ *féarmhar* ~ *féarúil* 'grassy'.
a) *-ach*: *scéalach* 'news-bearing' (← *scéal* 'story, news'), *uachtarach* 'upper' (← *uachtar* 'top');
b) *-mhar*: *greannmhar* 'funny' (← *greann* 'fun'), *solasmhar* 'bright' (← *solas* 'light');
c) *-úil*: *nimhiúil* 'poisonous' (← *nimh* 'poison'), *dul-chun-cinniúil* 'progressive' (← *dul chun cinn* 'progress; lit. going a+head');
d) *-áilte* ~ *-álta* mostly with English borrowings: *geatáilte* 'affected' (← *geata* 'affected manner' < English *gait*), *prionsabálta* 'high-principled' (← *prionsabal* 'principle');
e) *-tha(í)* (also *-ta(í)*, *-íthe*, *-í*, *-da*, *-a*, *-ga*): *muineartha* 'friendly' (← *muintir* 'kinsfolk'), *diabhalta(í)* 'devilish' (← *diabhal* 'devil'); *sclutaíthe* 'starving' (← *gluta* 'maw'); *teasaí* 'hot' (← *teas* 'heat'); *gallda* 'foreign' (← *gall* 'foreigner'); *gruama* 'gloomy' (← *gruaim* 'gloom'); *fearga* 'manly' (← *fear* 'man').

4.2.2 Deadjectival adjectives

Deadjectival adjectives with semantic modification take suffixed *-mhar*, *-úil*, *-ga*: *beo* 'alive' → *beomhar* ~ *beodhúil* ~ *beoga* 'lively'; suffixed *-í*: *trom* 'heavy' → *tromaí* 'weighty'. Deadjectival adjectives with little or no semantic modification take suffixed a. *-ach: iargúil* 'remote' → *iargúlach* 'remote'; *cúthal* 'shy' → *cúthaileach* 'shy'; *duairc* 'morose' → *duairceach* 'morose'; *sí* 'fairy' → *siúil* 'fairy-like, haunted' → *siúlach* 'fairy-like, haunted'; *diabhaltach* 'devilish' can be derived from *diabhalta* 'devilish'; suffixed b. *-ta: cúthail* 'shy' → *cúthalta* 'shy', *fiáin* 'wild' → *fiánta* 'wild'. *-áilte* can be suffixed to most English adjectives: *cute* → *ciúiteáilte* 'cute'; *tough* → *tiufáilte* 'tough'. Many English adjectives in *-y* remain as such, thus resembling native *-í: busy* → *biusaí*; but English *tricky* (← *trick*) → *truicí* ~ *truiceáilte*.

4.2.3 Deverbal adjectives

The suffix *-ach* is attached to verbal stems (similar to verbal adjective and to genitive of verbal noun): *caillteach* 'short of' (← *caill* 'to lose', verbal adjective *caillte* 'lost'), *fiafraitheach* ~ *fiafraíoch* 'inquisitive' (← *fiafraigh* 'to inquire', verbal adjective *fiafraithe* 'inquired'), *deimhnitheach* 'certain' (← *deimhnigh* 'to assure', verbal adjective *deimhnithe* 'assured').

4.3 Verbal derivation

Verbalisation of native roots in the vernacular is quite restricted. The main verbalising suffixes are *-igh* and *-áil*, the latter being productive in speech, in particular in its largely obligatory function to nativise current verbal borrowings from English verbs, nouns and adjectives. For instance, *-igh: dath* 'colour' → *dathaigh* 'to colour'; *-áil: gualainn* 'shoulder' → *guailleáil* 'to shoulder'. Productive *-áil* is found with borrowed nouns which are also converted verbs in English: English *clock* → *clacáil* ('clock' *-áil*). Deadjectival verb in *-igh: íseal* 'low' → *ísligh* 'to lower'. Productive *-áil* is found with borrowed adjectives which are also converted verbs in English: English *tidy* → *teidhdíáil* ('tidy' *-áil*).

Deverbal verbs are arguably found along with converted bases which can have derived alternates: *cúl* 'back' → *cúl* ~ *cúlaigh* 'to back'. The two suffixes, as well as conversion, are found in variants of *snaidhm* 'knot' (noun) → *snaidhm* ~ *snadhmnaigh* ~ *snadhmáil* 'to knot', the latter being the most recent formation. Less commonly, verbal bases can acquire suffix *-áil: fuaigh* ~ *fuáil* 'to sew', the finite *fuáil* having extended from verbal noun *fuáil* 'sewing'.

4.4 Adverbial derivation

There is no productive adverbial derivation. Adjectives in adverbial position can be preceded by adverbial particle *go: go trom* 'heavily' (← *trom* 'heavy'). Diminutive *-ín* is lexicalised with diminutivised variants of the lexical adverbs *go fóill* 'yet' → *go fóillín* 'yet (a small while)' and *ar ball* 'later' → *ar baillín* 'a small while later'.

5 Conversion

Conversion is generally quite restricted. An alternative syntactic means is provided by the particle "verb" *is* 'is', known as the copula, which is noteworthy in its function to support constructions, based mainly on adjectives, which correspond to verbal predicates in other languages: *is maith le* 'likes; lit. is good with (experiencer)'.

5.1 Nominal conversion

Deadjectival nouns can be formed via conversion from simple adjectives and are typically masculine, the default gender: *trom* 'heavy' → 'weight, importance', *cothrom* 'level' → 'level, equal, equity' (*éagothrom* 'uneven, inequitable' → 'unevenness, inequality'), *caol* 'thin, narrow' → 'slender part', *marbh* 'dead' → 'dead person', *ceart* 'right' → 'right' (*éigeart* 'wrong' → 'wrong'); but some are feminine: *domhain* 'deep' → 'depth', *tanaí* 'thin, shallow' → 'shallow water', *cóir* 'just' → 'justice' (*éagóir ~ éagórach* 'unjust' → *éagóir* 'injustice'); abstract: *beag* 'small' → 'little', *mór* 'big' → 'great, friendliness', cf. deadjectival nouns *éadrom* 'lightness', *olc* 'evil', *maith* 'good' and derived abstracts *éadroime* 'lightness', *olcas* 'badness, evil', *maitheas* 'good'. Semantic restrictions are common, such as: a. person or creature: *bodhar* 'deaf' → 'deaf person', *caoch* 'blind' → 'blind person', cf. *breac* 'speckled' > 'trout, fish' (Ó Cearúil 1996: 389–392); b. plant-names: *buí* 'yellow' > *buí mór* 'dyer's rocket; lit. yellow big'; c. colour adjectives (although common colours have extended usage): *dubh* 'black' → 'black, black substance, black ink, smut, evil deed, darkness' (*geal* 'white, bright' → 'bright(ness)'), *bán* 'white' → 'white, lea', *gorm* 'blue' → 'blue, dyeing-blue', *dearg* 'red' → 'red, undersoil', *glas* 'green, grey' → 'green, grey material', *buí* 'yellow, brown' → 'yellow, yellow blight'; feminine nouns from colour adjectives refer to (names for) cows: *buí* 'yellow cow', *dubh* 'black cow', *glas* 'grey cow', *dearg* 'red cow'; d. ordinal numerals used as fractions: *ceithre* 'four' → *ceathrú* (adjective and feminine noun) 'fourth, quarter'. Syntagmatic or collocational restrictions are common: e. definite or plural: *íseal* 'low' → 'lowly person, low place' with preposition *os íseal* 'in a low voice', *uasal* 'noble' → 'nobleman', *caomh* 'gentle' → 'companion', *beo* 'alive'

→ 'living being, life, livelihood', *bocht* 'poor' → 'poor (person)', *nocht* 'bare' → 'naked person'; f. qualified: *ramhar* 'fat' → 'thick part', *leathan* 'broad' → 'broad part', *cúng* 'narrow' → 'narrow (part)'. The highest restriction is found in adjectives functioning syntactically as a noun (not strictly an instance of conversion): g. idiomatic *crua* 'hard' → '(being) hard (pressed)', *breá* 'fine' → 'beauty', *gránna* 'ugly' → 'plain person', *fiáin* 'wild' → with preposition *i bhfiáin* '(being) wild; lit. in wild', *daibhir* 'poor' → 'poor person' in collocation with *saibhir* 'rich person' (← adjective *saibhir* 'rich'); idiomatic definite *mion* 'small, tiny' → '(the) small' (s. v. *mór*² Ó Dónaill 1978); h. idiomatic definite or qualified: *bog* 'soft' → '(the) soft, lobe'; or combinations of these conditions a.–h. In this treatment, deadjectival nominalisation via conversion is thus presented as a cline, none of which (apart from colours) is productive, however, as most adjectives do not convert to nouns nor function syntactically as nouns: *fairsing* 'wide', *álainn* 'beautiful', *deas* 'nice' vs. idiomatic in noun syntax *deas deas* (section 7). Derived adjectives are not converted except the important class in *-ach*: *moing* 'mane, fen' → *mongach* adjective 'maned, marshy' and noun 'bush' (cf. *bacach* 'lame, beggar' section 4.1.1 (7)). Similarly, lexical adverbs can be used nominally, generally in quite a limited fashion: *faraor* 'alas', *arís* 'again', *amach* 'out', *amárach* 'tomorrow' (Ó Curnáin 2007 s. v. *aríst, amach*; 1701).

Set phrases often contain (noun + noun (genitive) qualifier), (noun + preposition + noun) or (noun + adjective qualifier), less often (noun + adverb), (preposition + noun), (verb + complement), (adjective + preposition + noun), (adjective + relative copula), etc. Certain of these can also be presented in an often variable cline of univerbation, indicated morphosyntactically by their functioning as a unit with the article, adjectives, premodifiers and plural morphology. Examples: *uisce faoi thalamh* 'water under ground', figuratively 'intrigue' → *droch-uisce-faoi-thalamh* 'bad intrigue'; *cac ar aithris* 'mimickry, mimick; lit. excrement on imitation' (de Bhaldraithe 1985: 38; Ó Curnáin 2007: 2210) → *ag cac-ar-athris ar* 'mimicking' (Uí Bheirn 1989 s. v. *cac*); *cur i gcéill* 'pretence; lit. putting in sense'; *líon tí* (*tí* genitive singular ← *teach* 'house') 'household; lit. (full-)number (of) house' → plural *líon-tíocha* 'households' in contrast to *tig/teach* → plural *tithe* (cf. phrasal *líon lán* used adjectivally 'full to the brim; lit. amount full'); *dul i bhfolach* 'going in hiding' → 'hiding place' (Nic Pháidín 1987: 56); *beag de mhaith* 'useless object, hardship; lit. little of good' (i.e. noun *beag* ← adjective, *de* 'of', noun *maith* ← adjective) → plural *beag-de-mhaitheanna* 'hardships' (Uí Bheirn 1989 s. v. *beag*¹); *mór le rá* 'significant; lit. big with/to say' → *daoine mór-le-rá* (without inflection for plural (*móra*)) and *mór is fiú* 'grandeur; lit. great which-is worth' → *an mór-is-fiú* 'the grandeur' and *éirí in airde* 'uppishness; lit. rising in-above'. First element with links to finite verb: 2nd singular imperative *ardaigh orm* 'free; lit. raise-2SG.IMP on-me' (Ó Curnáin 2007: 2187); (historical) 1st plural imperative *buail-*

eam sciath 'braggadoccio; lit. (let us) strike shield', 2nd singular imperative *druid abhaile* 'move home' → *ar dhruid-abhaile* 'close at hand' (Ó Curnáin 2007: 656, cf. s. v. *gort* 2275). Nominals with plurals: *i bhfastú* 'stuck' (originally 'in entanglement') → *vastú* 'entangling area' → plural *vastaíochaí*; *síneadh fada* 'length accent; lit. extension long' → plural *sínte fada* 'length accents' (with regular noun plural followed by adjective, of type of adjective which does not inflect for plural) but also *síneadh-fadachaí* (with plural nominal suffix following adjective, indicating univerbation). The variant plurals of phrasal *súil ribe* 'snare; lit. eye (of) hair', can be analysed to evince three positions on the univerbation cline, from a. least to c. most unitary item:

(4) a. *súilí ribe* (plural suffix -*í* normal plural found with independent *súil* 'eye');
 b. *súilte ribe* (plural suffix -*te* not found with independent *súil* 'eye');
 c. *súil-ribeachaí* (pluralised as unitary phrase with -*achaí* suffix common with polysyllabic stems; note that there is no variant *súil-ribí in Ó Curnáin 2007: 689, 878 in contrast to independent plural variant *ribí* 'hairs' ← *ribe*).

There are also lexical phrasal items with unanalysable parts: ˈ*damhán* ˈˈ*alla* 'spider' neither part of which is synchronically transparent; plural: historical (plural noun + adjective) ˈ*damháin* ˈˈ*alla* and innovative ˈ*damhán* ˈˈ*allaí* ~ ˈ*damhán* ˈˈ*allachaí*.

Noun *suc* 'pet calf' (de Bhaldraithe 1985 s. v.) can be interpreted as a conversion from interjection *suc* (call to calf), cf. derived *sucaí* '(child's name for) calf'. Interjection *leo-leoín* 'hushaby' can be used nominally meaning 'sleep' (Dinneen s. v. *leo-leo-ín*). In West Co. Galway, English adjectives *sorry* and *happy* can be used as nouns in the important construction *tá* noun *ar* X "is noun on X" (where X is experiencer), i.e. X is/feels + adjective: *tá sorry orm* 'I am sorry; lit. is sorry on-me' along the lines of synonymous native *tá aiféala orm* with *aiféala* 'regret, sorrow'.

5.2 Adjectival conversion

Conversion from attributive genitive to adjectival use is rare: *rud caca* 'worthless thing; lit. thing (of) excrement' (← *cac*), thus adverbial *go cac* 'badly' and predicative *is cac an scéal é* 'it is a wretched affair' (de Bhaldraithe 1985 s. v. *cac* 7); *seó* 'show, sport, profusion' → (attributive) genitive *seoigh*, thus adverbial *go seoigh* 'wonderfully'. Closed-class adverbs can function attributively: *an fear amach* 'the man who goes, has gone, etc., out; lit. the man out'.

5.3 Verbal conversion

Conversion typically involves placement of a stem in the 1st conjugation (monosyllabic stem) verbs: noun *speal* 'scythe' → *speal* 'to mow'. 2nd conjugation verbs typically have polysyllabic stems, including the suffix *-igh*, thus adjective *lag* 'weak' → *lag* (1st conjugation) ~ *lagaigh* (2nd conjugation) 'to weaken'; or adjective *crua* 'hard' → *cruaigh* 'to harden', present *cruann* (1st conjugation) ~ *cruaíonn* (2nd conjugation) 'hardens'; but disyllabic *éadrom* 'light' → 2nd conjugation only: *éadromaigh* 'to lighten'.

In idiomatic or informal use, the closed class of locative adverbs of direction undergo conversion to quasi-verbs in reflexive conjunction with inflected preposition *le* 'with' (Ó Curnáin 2007: 1176–1178; de Bhaldraithe 1953a: 69): *siar* 'to the west' (goal), *siar libh* 'go west!; lit. west with-you (plural)' but also → *siaraigí libh* (2nd plural imperative) 'go west!' and *aniar* 'from the west' (source) → *aniaraidís leo* (3rd plural imperative) 'let them come from the west!'.

As noted in section 4.1.1 regarding abstract derived nouns, the progressive particle *ag* can be placed before suitable nouns which thus function similar to (generally intransitive) verbal nouns but without a corresponding finite verb: *magadh* 'ridicule' → *ag magadh* 'mocking'; *amhrán* 'song' → *ag amhrán* 'singing'; *báisteach* 'rain' → *ag báisteach* 'raining'; *cantal* 'peevishness' → *ag cantal* 'complaining' (de Bhaldraithe 1985 s. v.); *braon* 'drop' → plural *braonachaí* 'drops' → rarer *ag braonachaí* (*báistí*) 'raining drops (of rain)' (de Bhaldraithe 1985 s. v.); *obair* 'work' → *ag obair* 'working' (intransitive) corresponding to morphological verbal noun *ag oibriú* 'working' transitive and intransitive (← *oibrigh* 'to work'); *caint* 'speech' → *ag caint* 'speaking' (including transitive *ag caint Gaeilge* 'speaking Irish'), also verb *caintigh* (*le*) 'to speak (to)'.

5.4 Adverbial conversion

Adjectives can function relatively freely as adverbs without adverbial particle *go: duine réasúnta* 'reasonable person', *labhair go réasúnta* or *labhair réasúnta* 'speak reasonably', *réasúnta deas* 'reasonably nice'. Adverbial use of temporal nouns and phrases is regular: *thiteas lá* 'I fell one day; lit. I-fell (a) day'; cf. *thiteas i-ndáil-le* 'I nearly fell; lit. I-fell close-to'.

6 Backformation

Instances of backformation are non-systematic or sporadic occurrences of metanalysis; the process of deadjectival backformation producing a noun: *ámharach* 'lucky' and *ámharaí(ocht)* 'good fortune' (< *ámhar* 'lucky' < *ádh* 'luck') → *ámhar* 'luck' (in South-West Munster: Ó hÓgáin 1984: 107; Ó Buachalla 2003: 99; Wagner 1958–69 Vol. 2: 88, 107, 117); borrowing *patraisc* 'partridge' > dialectal *pat(a)r uisce* containing two lexemes, the latter being *uisce* 'water' as qualifier, similar to *cearc uisce* 'waterhen; lit. hen of water'. In Ó Curnáin (2007: 636) a type of derivational metanalysis is found in abstract suffix *-amas* > action suffix *-amáil*: *brocach* 'filthy' → *brocamas* 'filth' → *brocamáil* 'filthy activity', besides rarer agglutinative *-amasáil*: *brocamasáil* 'filthy activity'. Mention can also be made of variation in suffix order in *-ach+án ~ -án+ach*: *sraoill ~ sraoilleachán ~ sraoilleánach* (*~ sraoilleamán*) 'ragged person'.

7 Reduplication

Reduplicative nominal compounds and phrases are common, generally informal and often disparaging: a. actual words *deas deas* 'finishing touch' (de Bhaldraithe 1985 s. v.), *breá breá* 'toy, finery'; b. non-words *neaim neaim* 'tasty portion' (← interjection *neaim* 'yum'), *hulach halach* 'commotion', *húirte háirte* (plural noun) 'hubbub', *hibile haibile* 'slovenly person', *niúide neáide* 'namby-pamby', *súm sám* 'listless person', *tromach tramach* (noun) 'pell-mell'; c. combination of words and non-words, conjunctions, etc., *driúilíní driongal* 'formication' (Ó Curnáin 2007: 2248); *scéal, duan ná duainicín* '(no) news of any kind; lit. story, poem or little poem'; *hob ná hé* '(no) move', *smig ná smeaig* '(no) strength'; (*thit*) *an drioll ar an dreall* (*aige*) 'he lost courage; lit. (fell) ... on the ... (at-him)'. A rare instance of verbal adjective derivation is *steig meig* '(no) strength' → *steig-meigeáilte* 'exhausted' (Ó Curnáin 2007: 2344).

8 Blending

Although systematic blending, on a par with English culturally innovative coinages such as *breakfast + lunch → brunch*, is not found in traditional Irish, formal and semantic analogy can produce words similar to the more systematic combinations encountered in blending. Forms such as standard *ceirín* 'poultice', *ciméar* 'chimera' and *cithréim* 'deformity' show mutual influence producing dialectal by-forms, basically meaning 'deformity': *ceirthín ~ ceirthím ~ ceirthéim ~ cirthéim ~ crithéim ~ cimir ~ cimear ~ ciméar ~ cimthéar* (e.g., *ceirthím* with *-ei-í-* < *ceirín* but *-th-m* < *cithréim*; Ó Curnáin 2007: 279–280). Similarly, interdialectalisms from synonymous by-forms: *ramharc* 'sight' < synonyms *radharc* and *amharc* 'sight'

(Wagner 1958–69 Vol. 1: 127); or *brúigh* 'win' < synonyms *buach* and *gnóthaigh* 'win' (Ó Curnáin 2007: 62, 255, 1170–1171). The borrowing *bagún* 'bacon' is commonly *magún* (Wagner 1958–69: question 109) influenced by *m-* of native *muic+fheoil* 'pork' ← *muic* 'pig' + *feoil* 'meat'. In post-traditional Irish, functional semantic reduction, common in reduced or attrited acquisition, is evidenced by amalgamation of *iarr* 'to request' and *fiafraigh* 'to enquire' → *fiar* 'to ask' (Ó Curnáin 2007: 1169). A recent coinage *Gaerla* 'mixed Irish and English' ← *Gaeilge* 'Irish' and *Béarla* 'English' is based on the model of such terms as *franglais* ← *français* 'French' and *anglais* 'English'. In fact, blends and dvandva compounds, quite common in English, are notoriously challenging to render in Irish.

9 Clipping

Clipping is not a productive process; a rather sporadic instance is *ribe róibéis* 'shrimp' → *bróibéis* 'shrimps' (Ó Curnáin 2007: 275, 2206). Abbreviation or phonological reduction of functors, including conjunctions, is common (Ó Curnáin 2007: 1558) and often involves pretonic elision (Ó Siadhail 1989: 23–24): *i riocht is go* 'so that; lit. in state and that' → *ros go* 'so that'; thus actually involving coalescence of words and word-creation. Initial abbreviation often involves pretonic reduction or elision as in native syllable loss through stress shift typical in Munster: ˈ*corrán* 'sickle' > *coˈrrán* > ˈ*crán*. This is common in English borrowings: *America* > *Meirice* ~ *Meiriceá*; *asylum* > *saighleam* 'madness', *dispensary* > *spionsaraí* (de Bhaldraithe 1985 s. v.); *sacristy* > *croistí* (Uí Bheirn 1989 s. v.); cf. *sanatorium* ~ *san* > *sain* (de Bhaldraithe 1985 s. v.). Acronyms are mostly borrowed from English in dialect use: *an t-IRA* 'the I.R.A.'; *an tRUC* 'the R.U.C'. *Raidió na Gaeltachta* 'Radio of-the Gaeltacht' (radio station of Irish-speaking areas) is abbreviated as *R na G* in recent usage, with letter names, pronounced following English pronunciation, joined by retention of the definite article. The plural of an organisation can stand for members of that organisation, including acronyms: *IRA's* 'I.R.A-men'.

10 Word-creation

Not all phenomena discussed briefly in this section, e.g., semantic splits, are word-creations, i.e. artificial formations outside the system of word-formation, as defined in this handbook. They are, nevertheless, noteworthy in this context. Preposing of *s-*, with disparaging associations, is common: *liobar* 'limp object' > *sliobar* 'limp object', *maiste* 'spill, twist' > *smaiste* 'spill, twist, straggling object', *meach* 'bee' > synonym *smeach*, compare adjective *cromán+ach* '(large-)hipped' (← *cromán* 'hip') with *scrom+ánach* 'tall stooped person' (< *crom* 'stooped') (de Bhaldraithe 1953b s. v.), *sclutaíthe* 'starving' (< *gluta* 'maw') (Ó Curnáin 2007: 258; cf. *l-* > *pl-* in "expressive clusters", Ó Siadhail 1989: 104, *leota* 'strip, sluggish person', *pleota* 'strip, fool', *sleota* 'strip', de Bhaldraithe 1985 s. v.). There is also a use of *s*, often prolonged, as an interjection of incitement or expulsion (de Bhaldraithe 1985 s. v. *s-*; Ó Curnáin 2007: 2320). Univerbation of original phrases, such as *beag-de-mhaitheanna* 'hardships', is discussed in section 5.1; a further instance is verbal *gabh i 'leith* 'come hither; lit. come in hither' which has a univerbised by-form in West Co. Galway *'goille* 'come here', with 2nd plural imperative *gabhaigí i 'leith* ~ *'goilligí* 'come here'. Similarly, phrasal *go 'leith* 'and a half; lit. with half' yields the adjective *'guile* 'and a half' in much of Munster (optionally in Co. Waterford and not at all in Co. Clare: question 118 in Wagner 1958–69 Vol. 2). Divergence of diachronic (morpho)phonological developments can bring about dialectal semantic splits: *adhbhar* 'matter, cause' > *abhar* 'cause' and *ábhar* 'amount' (Ó Cuív 1944: 113; Ó hÓgáin 1984: 10–11; Breatnach 1961: 2; also Ua Súilleabháin 1994: 491); noteworthy in Ulster (see section 2.3) *aon* 'one' > *aon* 'only' vs. *an* 'any'; *corr* 'point', 'pointed' > *corr* (higher vowel) 'edge' vs. *corr* (lower vowel) 'odd'; *fo* ~ *fa* ~ *fá* 'under, about' > *faoi* 'under' vs. *fá* 'round, about'; *ro-* 'most' > *ró-* 'too' vs. *ro-* 'much'; *deichniúr* 'ten persons' > *deichniúr* 'decade' vs. *deichear* 'ten'; borrowing *cupla* 'few' vs. *cúpla* 'twins'; including variation of coalescence in compounds: *seanduine* 'old person' > *'sean‚duine* 'old person' vs. *'seannaine* 'old man' (Ó Searcaigh 1923: 153; Wagner 1959: 26; Sommerfelt 1965: 303, 305–306; Ó Baoill 1996: 124–148; *cupla* vs. *cúpla* also in Connacht: Ó Curnáin 2007: 88).

Metanalysis is important diachronically and synchronically in a process of degrammaticalising certain suffixes which thus develop towards more independent word status. This occurs with regards to suffixes in demonstrative and pronominal categories, analysable in a cline from the emphatic stressing (see section 2.3) of normally unstressed suffixes through conjunct words to independent words: *mo 'thigse* ~ *mo 'thig'se* ~ *mo 'thig'seo* all three meaning emphasised 'my house', the latter resembling demonstrative adjective structure *an 'tig seo* 'this house' (Ó Sé 2000: 381–386, 376–377). Because of canonical verb-subject word order, synthetic 3rd plural past *bhío+dar* 'they were; lit. were+3PL' can be metanalysed as analytic *bhí dur* 'they were' thus developing innovative 3rd plural conjunct pronoun *dur*: *bheadh dur* 'they would' for historical synthetic *bheidís* 'they would' or established analytic *bheadh siad* 'they would' (Ó Curnáin 2007: 899–901, 1235–1249).

Acknowledgement

I would like to thank Gareth O'Neill and Roibeard Ó Maolalaigh for their helpful corrections and suggestions.

11 References

An Caighdeán Oifigiúil (1958): *Gramadach na Gaeilge agus Litriú na Gaeilge. An Caighdeán Oifigiúil.* Dublin: Oifig an tSoláthair.

An Coiste Téarmaíochta (2010): http://www.gaeilge.ie/Tearmai_&_Aistruchain/Treoirlinte.asp [Last access 10 June 2012].

Armstrong, John (1981): Vowel equivalences in Classical Modern Irish rime: Modern and medieval analyses compared. In: Calvin Watkins (ed.), *Indo-European Studies 4*, 613–724. Cambridge, MA: Department of Linguistics, Harvard University.

Arnaud, Pierre J. L. (2025): Noun-noun compounds in French. In: Peter O. Müller, Susan Olsen and Franz Rainer (eds.), *Word-Formation – Special Patterns and Restrictions*, 103–120. Berlin/Boston: De Gruyter Mouton.

Bloch-Trojnar, Maria (2020): Derivational networks in Irish. In: Lívia Körtvélyessi, Alexandra Bagasheva and Pavol Štekauer (eds.), *Derivational Networks Across Languages*, 299–308. Berlin/Boston: De Gruyter Mouton.

Breatnach, Risteard B. (1947): *The Irish of Ring, Co. Waterford*. Dublin: Dublin Institute for Advanced Studies.

Breatnach, Risteard B. (ed.) (1961): *Seana-Chaint na nDéise II*. Dublin: Dublin Institute for Advanced Studies.

de Bhaldraithe, Tomás (1953a): *Gaeilge Chois Fhairrge. An Deilbhíocht*. Dublin: Dublin Institute for Advanced Studies.

de Bhaldraithe, Tomás (1953b): Ainmneacha ar Chineálacha Daoine. *Béaloideas* 22: 120–153.

de Bhaldraithe, Tomás (1959): *English-Irish Dictionary*. Dublin: An Gúm.

de Bhaldraithe, Tomás (1985): *Foirisiún focal as Gaillimh*. Dublin: Royal Irish Academy.

de Bhaldraithe, Tomás (1990): Notes on the diminutive suffix *-ín* in Modern Irish. In: Ann T. E. Matonis and Daniel F. Melia (eds.), *Celtic Language, Celtic Culture. A Festschrift for Eric P. Hamp*, 85–95. California: Ford & Bailie.

Dinneen, Patrick S. (1911): *Foclóir Gaedhilge agus Béarla*. Dublin: Irish Texts Society.

Doyle, Aidan (1992): *Noun Derivation in Modern Irish. Selected Categories, Rules and Suffixes*. Lublin: Redakcja Wydawnictw Katolickiego Uniwersytetu Lubelskiego.

Doyle, Aidan and Edmund Gussmann (1996): *A Reverse Dictionary of Modern Irish*. Lublin: Wydawnictwo Folium.

Fishman, Joshua A. (1991): *Reversing Language Shift*. Clevedon: Multilingual Matters.

Greene, David (1966): *The Irish Language. An Ghaeilge*. Dublin: The Three Candles.

Hussey, Matt (1999): *Nod don Eolach. Gasaitéar Eolaíochta*. Dublin: An Gúm.

Lenoach, Ciarán, Conchúr Ó Giollagáin and Brian Ó Curnáin (eds.) (2012): *An Chonair Chaoch. An Mionteangachas sa Dátheangachas*. Indreabhán, Co. na Gaillimhe: Leabhar Breac.

McCone, Kim, Damian McManus, Cathal Ó Háinle, Nicholas Williams and Liam Breatnach (eds.) (1994): *Stair na Gaeilge*. Maynooth: Department of Old Irish, Saint Patrick's College, Maynooth.

McKenna-Lawlor, Susan and Damien Ó Muirí (2010): *An English-Irish Lexicon of Scientific and Technical Space-related Terminology*. Dublin: Four Courts Press.

McManus, Damian (1994): An Nua-Ghaeilge Chlasaiceach. In: Kim McCone, Damian McManus, Cathal Ó Háinle, Nicholas Williams and Liam Breatnach (eds.), *Stair na Gaeilge*, 335–445. Maynooth: Department of Old Irish, Saint Patrick's College, Maynooth.

Mhac an Fhailigh, Éamonn (1968): *The Irish of Erris, Co. Mayo*. Dublin: Dublin Institute for Advanced Studies.

Ní Dhomhnaill, Cáit (1988): Dúblóga uamacha Gaeilge. *Béaloideas* 56: 141–152.

Nic Pháidín, Caoilfhionn (1987): *Cnuasach Focal ó Uíbh Ráthach*. Dublin: Royal Irish Academy.

Nic Pháidín, Caoilfhionn (2008): Corpus planning for Irish. In: Caoilfhionn Nic Pháidín and Seán Ó Cearnaigh (eds.), *A New View of the Irish Language*, 93–107. Dublin: Cois Life.

Ó Baoill, Dónall (1996): *An Teanga Bheo. Gaeilge Uladh*. Dublin: Institiúid Teangeolaíochta Éireann.

Ó Cearúil, Micheál (1996): Sa teanga atá tábhacht na teanga. In: Micheál Ó Cearúil (ed.), *Gníomhartha na mBráithre. Aistí Comórtha ar Ghaelachas na mBráithre Críostaí*, 389–460. Dublin: Coiscéim.

Ó Cuív, Brian (1944): *The Irish of West Muskerry, Co. Cork*. Dublin: Dublin Institute for Advanced Studies.

Ó Cuív, Brian (ed.) (1947): *Cnósach Focal ó Bhaile Bhúirne*. Dublin: Dublin Institute for Advanced Studies.

Ó Curnáin, Brian (2007): *The Irish of Iorras Aithneach, County Galway*. 4 Vol. Dublin: Dublin Institute for Advanced Studies.

Ó Curnáin, Brian (2012): An Ghaeilge iarthraidisiúnta agus an phragmataic chódmheasctha thiar agus theas. In: Ciarán Lenoach, Conchúr Ó Giollagáin and Brian Ó Curnáin (eds.), *An Chonair Chaoch. An Mionteangachas sa Dátheangachas*, 284–364. Indreabhán, Co. na Gaillimhe: Leabhar Breac.

Ó Curnáin, Brian (2016): Cróineolaíocht na Gaeilge Iarthraidisiúnta i gConamara, 1950–2004. *Éigse* 39: 1–43.

Ó Curnáin, Brian (forthc. [2025a]): Modern Irish Morphology. In: Joseph F. Eska, Silvio Nurmio, Peadar Ó Muircheartaigh and Paul Russell (eds.), *The Palgrave Handbook of Celtic Languages and Linguistics*. London: Palgrave Macmillan.

Ó Curnáin, Brian (forthc. [2025b]): Modern Irish Initial Mutations. In: Joseph F. Eska, Silvio Nurmio, Peadar Ó Muircheartaigh and Paul Russell (eds.), *The Palgrave Handbook of Celtic Languages and Linguistics*. London: Palgrave Macmillan.

Ó Curnáin, Brian and Roibeard Ó Maolalaigh (forthc. [2025]): Scottish Gaelic Morphology. In: Joseph F. Eska, Silvio Nurmio, Peadar Ó Muircheartaigh and Paul Russell (eds.), *The Palgrave Handbook of Celtic Languages and Linguistics*. London: Palgrave Macmillan.

Ó Dónaill, Niall (1978 [1977]): *Foclóir Gaeilge-Béarla*. Dublin: Oifig an tSoláthair.

Ó Giollagáin, Conchúr, Seosamh Mac Donnacha, Fiona Ní Chualáin, Aoife Ní Shéaghdha and Mary O'Brien (2007): *Staidéar Cuimsitheach Teangeolaíoch ar Úsáid na Gaeilge sa Ghaeltacht. Tuarascáil Chríochnaitheach*. Dublin: Oifig an tSoláthair.

Ó Giollagáin, Conchúr and Seosamh Mac Donncha (2008): The Gaeltacht today. In: Caoilfhionn Nic Pháidín and Seán Ó Cearnaigh (eds.), *A New View of the Irish Language*, 108–120. Dublin: Cois Life.

Ó hAirt, Diarmaid (1988): *Díolaim Dhéiseach*. Dublin: Royal Irish Academy.

Ó hAnluain, L. A. (1999): *Graiméar Gaeilge na mBráithre Críostaí*. 3rd ed. Dublin: An Gúm.

Ó hÓgáin, Éamonn (1984): *Díolaim Focal (A) ó Chorca Dhuibhne*. Dublin: Royal Irish Academy.

Ó hÚrdail, Roibeárd (1995): A native bound-morpheme combines with fully nativised borrowed morphemes: A highly productive language-contact feature in the Irish of Cape Clear. *Teanga* 15: 71–80.

O'Rahilly, Thomas F. (1972 [1932]): *Irish Dialects Past and Present. With Chapters on Scottish and Manx.* Dublin: Dublin Institute for Advanced Studies.

Ó Sé, Diarmuid (2000): *Gaeilge Chorca Dhuibhne.* Dublin: Institiúid Teangeolaíochta Éireann.

Ó Searcaigh, Séamus (1925): *Foghraidheacht Ghaedhilge an Tuaiscirt.* Belfast: Brún agus Ó Nualláin, Teor.

Ó Siadhail, Mícheál (1989): *Modern Irish. Grammatical Structure and Dialectal Variation.* Cambridge: Cambridge University Press.

Péterváry, Tamás, Brian Ó Curnáin, Conchúr Ó Giollagáin and Jerome Sheahan (2014): *Iniúchadh ar an gCumas Dátheangach. An sealbhú teanga i measc ghlúin óg na Gaeltachta. Analysis of Bilingual Competence. Language acquisition among young people in the Gaeltacht.* Dublin: An Chomhairle um Oideachas Gaeltachta agus Gaelscolaíochta.

Quiggin, E. C. (1906): *A Dialect of Donegal. Being the Speech of Mweenawania in the Parish of Glenties.* Cambridge: Cambridge University Press.

Sommerfelt, Alf (1922): *The Dialect of Torr, Co. Donegal.* Vol. 1: *Phonology.* Christiana: Dybwad.

Sommerfelt, Alf (1965): Word limits in Modern Irish (dialect of Torr, Co. Donegal). *Lochlann* 3: 298–314.

Stifter, David (2025): From Old Irish to Modern Irish. In: Peter O. Müller, Susan Olsen and Franz Rainer (eds.), Word-Formation – Language Contact and Diachrony, 457–482. Berlin/Boston: De Gruyter Mouton.

Ua Súilleabháin, Seán (1994): Gaeilge na Mumhan. In: Kim McCone, Damian McManus, Cathal Ó Háinle, Nicholas Williams and Liam Breatnach (eds.), *Stair na Gaeilge*, 479–538. Maynooth: Department of Old Irish, Saint Patrick's College, Maynooth.

Uí Bheirn, Úna M. (1989): *Cnuasach Focal as Teileann.* Dublin: Royal Irish Academy.

Uí Bhraonáin, Donla and Caoilfhionn Nic Pháidín (eds.) (2004): *Foclóir Fiontar / Dictionary of Terminology. Gaeilge-Béarla / English-Irish.* Dublin: Fiontar, Dublin City University.

Wagner, Heinrich (1958–69): *Linguistic Atlas and Survey of Irish Dialects.* Vol. 1: *Introduction, 300 maps.* 1958. Vol. 2: *The dialects of Munster.* 1964. Vol. 3: *The dialects of Connaught.* 1966. Vol. 4: *The dialects of Ulster and the Isle of Man; specimens of Scottish Gaelic dialects; phonetic texts of East Ulster Irish.* 1969. Dublin: Dublin Institute for Advanced Studies.

Wagner, Heinrich (1959): *Gaeilge Theilinn.* Dublin: Dublin Institute for Advanced Studies.

Alicja Nagórko
8 Polish

1 Introduction
2 General overview
3 Composition
4 Derivation
5 Conversion
6 Backformation
7 Reduplication
8 Blending
9 Clipping
10 Word-creation
11 References

Abstract: The article presents an outline of contemporary Polish word-formation. Affixal derivation and conversion are identified as the most productive Polish word-formation processes. During the last decades, there has also been an increase in compounding. The different word-formation processes are analysed from a formal grammatical as well as from a semantic and pragmatic point of view.

1 Introduction

The first works in Polish that discussed word-formation were textbooks for national schools modeled on Latin and Greek. An academic approach to word-formation appeared first in the second half of the 19th century and the beginning of the 20th century. The first grammar of Polish based on the historical-comparative method by Małecki (1863) contained an overview of word-formation in a section under the heading "Etymology" (as in other Slavic grammars of the 19th century). The 19th-century approach to word-formation, in keeping with the spirit of the times, was characterised by biologism (research into the "genealogy", "word families", and vocabulary "bastardisation") and evolutionism (changes in language as part of "natural history", interest in "linguistic paleography"). The beginning of the 20th century brought about a turn towards historism and psychologism. An

---

Alicja Nagórko, Berlin, Germany

https://doi.org/10.1515/9783111420523-008

attempt at a complete description of historical word-formation was made by Łoś (1922–27), who analysed Polish lexis from Old Polish to contemporary neologisms. Baudouin de Courtenay (1974) noted the psychological mechanisms of word motivation and association leading to the creation of a secondary "folk etymology". Rozwadowski (1904) introduced the theory of the binary structure of words, based on the psychological law of apperception. Word-formation was the third branch of grammar, after syntax and phonetics, which formed an independent area of study; this was reflected in the publications by Benni (1905), Łoś (1914) and others.

The early postwar period was dominated by Doroszewski and his school. He introduced word-formation categories (1946) and the logico-syntactic division of derivatives into the subject-oriented "to, co" ('that, which') and the predicative "to, że" ('the fact that') (1952). However, he rejected synchronic word-formation, which was further developed by his students. The 1960s and 1970s introduced theories concerning the differences between synchronically transparent derivatives and derivatives inherited from earlier stages of the language, word segmentation and the degree of its synchronic motivation, the function of formatives and their types, and the classification of derivatives (Laskowski and Wróbel 1964; Brodowska-Honowska 1967; Puzynina 1969; Grzegorczykowa 1972). The above served as a basis for data-based synthetic studies of the Polish derivation system, cf. Grzegorczykowa and Puzynina (1979) as well as the word-formation section of the *Gramatyka współczesnego języka polskiego* (GWJP) [Contemporary Polish Grammar] (1984, 1998). Empirical examinations have also lead to the publication of series of derivational dictionaries of Polish (Jadacka 2001b; Skarżyński 2004).

2 General overview

2.1 Word-formation in the language system

According to the Polish linguistic tradition word-formation is a branch of morphology, and thus a branch of grammar. Within its limits the basic question is the boundary between derivation and inflection. For example, the status of verbal aspect is open to debate (aspectual pairs differentiated by suffixes are considered to be part of inflection, e.g., *chwytać* (ipf.) – *chwycić* (pf.) 'to grab', while pairs differentiated by a prefix are considered a part of word-formation, e.g., *łapać* (ipf.) – *złapać* (pf.) 'to catch'), as well as that of participles declined like adjectives, including forms ending with *-(a)ł(y)*, such as *osiwiały* 'whose hair turned gray', degree of adjectives (in GWJP recognised as a word-formation category). Due to their serial and productive character, verbal nouns, such as *malowanie* '(the action of) painting' (from *malować*), as well as nominal formations with the prefix *nie-* (*niezdrowy* 'unhealthy') also trigger doubts regarding their status. The status of feminine nouns such as *doktor* 'female doctor' is also not clear. They are regarded either as new epicenes equal to the traditional type illustrated by *beksa* 'crybaby' (referring to males and females, inspite of the female ending), or they are treated as examples of "paradigmatic derivation" (conversion accompanied by an inflectional ending marking the change of paradigm), in which, exceptionally, the inflection is blocked. Designations such as *szczoteczka do zębów* 'toothbrush; lit. small brush for teeth', *kobieta-demon* 'female demon; lit. woman-demon', and *zupa krem* 'cream soup; lit. soup cream' occupy the borderline between syntax and morphology. Also formal procedures in which a nominal modifier is replaced by an adjective derived from that noun tend to be located within the scope of syntax rather than word-formation, cf. *brzeg morza* 'the shore of the sea' → *brzeg morski* 'sea shore' (nevertheless dictionaries feature both nouns and adjectives as separate lexemes: *morze* 'sea', *morski* 'sea (adj.), marine'). Analytical adverbs such as *po polsku* 'in Polish' and derivatives of prepositional phrases, such as the adjective *przeciwbólowy* 'pain-killing' (← *przeciw bólowi* 'against pain') also stand at the borderline between derivation and composition.

2.2 Overall picture

Word-formation remains the major means of enriching the Polish lexicon and outnumbers in productivity other possibilities, such as lexical borrowings or neosemantisation (mostly metaphorisation, e.g., *rękaw* 'sleeve' > 'corridor to the plane'). The formation of nouns is the most productive type, including derivation proper as the most common procedure, derivation from prepositional phrases or composition. The word-formation structures vary in function and style, especially in case of the difference between the expressive colloquial language on the one hand, and the written formal register on the other. In colloquial Polish univerbation – in the Slavic literature on word-formation understood as the replacing of long official names with shorter synthetic forms (e.g., by combining ellipsis and suffixation) – is very common, cf. *jagiellonka* (← *biblioteka Uniwersytetu Jagiellońskiego* 'Jagiellonian University Library'). Some often used affixes get stigmatised as colloquial, e.g., agentive *-acz*, *-ak*, *-arz*, and *-nik*. The colloquial register tends to accept more readily feminine titles derived from masculine ones, cf. *profesorka* 'woman professor'. Non-morpheme-based word-formation, i.e. disintegrated structures with morphonological alternations, is widespread, such as *kałach* (informal) (← *karabin Kałasznikowa* 'Kalashnikov rifle'). Familiar language is also known for its hypocorisms, diminutives of names and their augmentative forms. Unofficial communication features also quasi-diminutives as a sign of polite familiarity, e.g., *kawusia* (← *kawa* 'coffee').

In written Polish there is a marked tendency for internationalisation, terminologisation and specialisation of word-formation means. Internationalisation leads to an increase of compounds, including serial analogical structures, e.g., those based on English *workaholic*, cf. *zakupoholik* 'shopping addict; lit. shoppingaholic' (*zakupy* 'shopping'), as well as to the mechanical linking of foreign and native stems, e.g., *telezakupy* 'teleshopping'. An increase in the productivity of foreign affixes has also been noted, especially *-acj(a), -ator, -ist(a), -izm, -er.* Terminologisation is visible in deverbal "paradigmatic derivation" (conversion), e.g., *zgniot* '(cold) squeeze' (← *zgniatać* 'to squeeze'). Specialisation leads to a narrowing of the semantic function of suffixes, e.g., *-ark(a)* to denote machines and appliances derived from verbs, cf. *niszczarka (dokumentów)* 'paper shredder; lit. destroyer' (← *niszczyć* 'to destroy'); the suffix *-owiec* is gradually narrowing down to form only denominal nouns, cf. *deskorolkowiec* 'skateboarder' (← *deskorolka* 'skateboard'); the suffix *-stw(o)* forms mainly status nouns, cf. *przeciętniactwo* 'mediocrity' (← *przeciętniak* 'the man in the street'), etc.

3 Composition

3.1 The degree of structural integration

Compounds comprise quite a heterogeneous group, with the only common feature being the presence of two (or less often three or more) lexical morphemes within a single word structure. Their formal coalescence and the manner in which they are connected may vary. Juxtapositions, such as *centrum handlowe* (N + relational adjective) 'shopping centre', *samochód pułapka* ($N_{NOM} + N_{NOM}$) 'car bomb; lit. car ambush', have the least tight structure. Some scholars question whether they are actually a part of word-formation, because they are located at the borderline of composition, phraseology and syntax. They meet the criteria established for words: the order of constituents cannot be reversed, the constituents cannot be replaced by other words.

Among the synthetic forms the simplest type is formed by "solid compounds" (Polish *zrosty*), i.e. the merger of syntactic structures without any linking material, cf. *czcigodny* 'esteemed; lit. esteem-GEN-worthy', *Ojczenasz* 'Our Father; lit. father-VOC-our' from the opening lines of the Lord's Prayer. These compounds are motivated by a syntactic group the coalescence of which occurs without an interfix (linking vowel). Among the numerous neologisms coined in the last twenty years it is the compounds without an interfix, i.e. a mechanic combination of two stems, that seem to prevail (cf. Jadacka 2001a: 93).

Compounds proper concern, for the most part, only two grammatical classes of Polish lexemes: nouns and adjectives. Base stems may be connected with the interfix -o-, like in *zleceni-o-biorca* 'contractor; lit. contract-taker', or in fewer examples with the interfix -i-/-y- or -u-, cf. *łam-i-główka* 'jigsaw, puzzle, brainteaser; lit. breakhead' (from *łamać* 'to break' and *główka* 'head-DIM') and *dw-u-ślad* 'four-wheeled vehicle; lit. two-track' (from *dwa-* 'two' and *ślad* 'track'). Suffixes may also function as co-formatives, cf. *wiel-o-ród-ka* 'multipara' (from *wiele* 'many' and *rodzić* 'to give birth'), in the same way as a paradigm change might, cf. *ciśnieni-o-mierz-Ø* 'manometer' (from *ciśnienie* 'pressure' and *mierzyć* 'to measure'). A strictly interfix or mixed (forms with both an interfix and a suffix) interpretation depends mostly on what is considered as the input base, cf. *bajkopisarz* lit. 'fablewriter', interpreted as either derived from *bajka* 'fable' and *pisarz* 'writer' with just the interfix or from the whole phrase *ktoś, kto pisze bajki* 'someone who writes fables', with a complex formative.

Another subclass of compounds proper (in works on Polish word-formation also called "quasi-compounds") corresponds to English neoclassical word-formations. They feature Greek or Latin stems that usually cannot appear independently, but form numerous series of terms usually from scholarly or scientific fields. Data from postwar dictionaries corroborate that the most numerous are the ones with combining forms such as *pseudo-*, *eks-*, *neo-*, *mono-*, *poli-*, *makro-*, *mikro-*, *izo-*, and the final combining forms *-logia*, *-metr*, *-grafia*, *-graf*, *-skop*, *-metria*, *-fon*, *-skopia*, *-fit*, *-fil*. In the 1990s a surge of international borrowings and structural calques appeared, which popularised combining forms such as *euro-* 'Euro-', *eko-* 'eco-', *narko-* 'drug related', *porno-* 'porn', *seks-* 'sex', *super-*, *tele-*, *wideo-* 'video', etc. In contrast to the previously mentioned formations, these are not erudite terms and are not restricted to written Polish (see also Waszakowa 2025 on foreign word-formation in Polish).

3.2 Nominal compounds (proper)

3.2.1 Determinative compounds

In determinative compounds the constituent being modified, i.e. the head, may appear as the right or the left constituent. According to the description of compounds in GWJP (1998: 455 ff.), the nominal determinative compounds proper are based on two types of phrases: verb phrases (VP) and noun phrases (NP). Their diversity depends on the type of the modifying, i.e. subordinate or dependent, constituent. A VP may contain a dependent noun or pronoun as its complement, cf. *cud-o-twórca* 'miracle worker; lit. miracle maker' (← *tworzy cuda* lit. 'makes miracles'), *sam-o-obrona* 'self-defense' (← *(ktoś) broni się sam* '(sb.) defends himself'), an adverb, cf. *skryt-o-bójca* 'assassin; lit. stealthy killer' (← *skrycie zabił* 'killed stealthily'), or a numeral, cf. *wiel-o-bój* 'a generic name for multisport competitions, such as biathlon, triathlon, etc.' (← *(ktoś) bije się wiele razy* '(sb.) competes many times'). The noun phrases that constitute the base of compounds may be divided into coordinate and non-coordinate. The subordinate word in the latter case may be a second noun: *gwiazd-o-zbiór* 'constellation; lit. starset'; an adjective: *płask-o-stopie* 'flat-footedness', or a numeral: *trój-dźwięk* 'triad; lit. three-sound', and *pierwsz-o-klas-ista* 'first grader'. An observation of the inner structure of the compounds reveals interesting regularities. Thus structures motivated by a noun phrase are always right-headed according to the location of the modified constituent. Compounds motivated by a verb phrase may be both right- and left-headed. Those in the latter group, with the verbal constituent at the end, are much more productive in contemporary Polish, cf. *bałw-o-chwal-ca* 'idolater; lit. idol-worshipper', *drog-o-wskaz* 'road sign; lit. road-indicator', *kąt-o-mierz* 'protractor; lit. angle measurer'. Left-headed structures (V+S), albeit with some exceptions, are considered dated or humorous, cf. *gol-i-broda* 'barber; lit. shave-beard', *łam-i-strajk* 'strikebreaker; lit. break-strike', *najm-i-morda* 'legal counsel; lit. hire-mug'. Therefore the Polish language is drifting, undoubtedly because of the foreign influence, towards the right-headed type of compounding.

In principle the word order in a compound is free, i.e. the agent noun *list-o-nosz* lit. 'letter carrier' could have taken the form of *nosilist lit. 'carry-letter', while the compound *tłucz-y-bruk* 'stone-breaker; lit. break-stone' could assume a more contemporary form in the shape of *brukotłuk 'stone-breaker'. It is believed that this free ordering is possible only in compounds in which the nominal constituent describes the object of the activity named by the verbal constituent and performed by somebody. Thus *ręk-o-pis* 'manuscript; lit. handwrit', for example, does not allow a transformation into *piszyręka lit. 'writehand' because *ręka* 'hand' is not the object, but the instrument, and the entire structure does not refer to 'somebody who ...', but to 'something that ...'.

Interfixed "paradigmatic compounds" (i.e. compounds whose second component is the result of verb-to-noun conversion) are ambivalent and allow both the interpretation 'person' or 'thing', cf. the personal noun *szczuro-łap* 'ratcatcher' vs. *wiatro-łap* 'storm doors; lit. wind-catcher'; similarly *dziejo-pis* 'annalist; lit. history-writer' vs. *ręko-pis* 'manuscript'. One of the ways of making the structure less ambiguous is by adding agentive suffixes, such as -*c(a)*, -*arz*, cf. -*bior-ca* 'taker' (*kredytobiorca* lit. 'credit taker'), -*bój-ca* 'killer' (*matkobójca* 'matricide; lit. mother-killer'), *-daw-ca* 'giver' (*reklamodawca* 'advertiser; lit. advertisement giver'), *-pisarz* 'writer' (*powieściopisarz* lit. 'novel-writer'), *-wier-ca* 'believer' (*innowierca* 'infidel; lit. else-believer'). Not all of them are however productive. The most frequently used are *biorca* and *dawca*, which are also used as independent elements in an equivalent phrase, especially in medical language, cf. *krwiodawca* 'blood donor', but *dawca organów* 'organ donor; lit. donor of organs'.

The description of compounds proper sometimes relies on a semantic distinction of two types: the exocentric and endocentric combinations. In the first type the center is as if outside of the compound, as opposed to the endocentric constructions. Kurzowa (1976: 39 ff.) applies this distinction only to nominal phrases, e.g., *prost-o-kąt* 'rectangle; lit. straight-angle' (it is not a 'right angle', but a shape with four right angles). These structures are also called "possessive", because they express a characteristic feature of the subject described, e.g., *goł-o-wąs* 'stripling' (from *goły* 'naked' and *wąs* 'moustache', i.e. 'somebody, whose face is yet not covered with facial hair, has no moustache'); *krzyw-o-nos* 'somebody, whose nose is crooked' (from *krzywy* 'crooked' and *nos* 'nose'). However, today these compounds are not very productive, often idiomatic, and their motivation is often related to a metaphor or metonymy that is now obscure. Endocentric structures may be assigned a metaphoric reading, cf. *zęb-o-dół* 'tooth socket; lit. tooth-hole', *żyw-o-płot* 'hedge; lit. live-fence', etc.

3.2.2 Copulative compounds

Copulative compounds, such as *barak-o-wóz* 'a wooden or tin caravan' (from *barak* 'shed' and *wóz* 'cart'), *komedi-o-dramat* 'comedy-drama', *kuchni-o-salon* 'open kitchen; lit. kitchen-living room' and *światł-o-cień* 'chiaroscuro; lit. light-shadow' may only be based on elements that are grammatically homogenous, thus combinations of a nominal stem with any other stem are impossible. They are always N-type structures (N_1+o+N_2). The question all cognitive researchers ask is what conceptualisations correspond to these amalgams. Even without referring to psycholinguistic tests it is apparent that the noun *barakowóz*, for example, is not a simple sum of the two meanings of the words *barak* + *wóz*, but a term describing a new concept: 'something that has the features of a shed (temporary shelter) and a cart (on wheels)'. The relationship between the elements is symmetrical.

Apart from an interfix, exocentric compounds contain also suffix co-formatives, cf. *rud-o-węglowi-ec* 'ore and coal carrier', i.e. 'a ship for transporting ore and coal'. In written form a hyphen may be used instead of an interfix, cf. *inżynier-lotnik* 'aeronautical engineer; lit. engineer-pilot'. These structures are relatively free and require inflection on both constituents. This structure is most common in two-element names of places, e.g., *Bielsko-Biała* (*w Bielsku-Białej* 'in Bielsko-Biała'), *Szlezwik-Holsztyn* 'Schleswig-Holstein'.

3.3 Adjectival compounds

3.3.1 Determinative compounds

The formative is usually complex, i.e. an interfix plus a suffix, cf. *prawd-o-mówny* 'truthful; lit. truth-speaking', or a "paradigmatic formative" (conversion + adjective inflection) and an interfix, cf. *tward-o-głow-y* 'hardliner; lit. hard-headed' (← *twarda głowa*). Compounds in which the government of the adjective is conserved are less common, cf. *wiary-godny* 'reliable; lit. faith-GEN worthy' (← *godny wiary*). The base of the compound is a syntactic determinative phrase, whose head may be a nominal constituent, cf. *historia literatury* 'literary history; lit. history literature-GEN' → *historyczn-o-literacki* 'literary-historical' or a verbal constituent, cf. (*co*) *niesie śmierć* '(which) brings death' → *śmierci-o-nośny* 'deadly; lit. death-bringing', (*co*) *daleko sięga* '(which) reaches far' → *daleko-siężny* 'far-reaching'.

Determinative compounds with two adjectival constituents are always head-final, cf. (*kościół*) *rzymsk-o-katolicki* 'Roman Catholic (Church)' means a Catholic Church of the Roman rite as opposed to *grek-o-katolicki* 'Greek Catholic (Church)', for example. The modifying adjective usually defines the time frame or the scope of the phenomenon, cf. *późn-o-romański* 'late Roman', or the intensity of a feature, cf. *ciemn-o-niebieski* 'dark-blue'. The verbal element, which can only be placed at the end of the compound, combines most often with a nominal stem in the object function (cf. *życi-o-daj-ny* 'life-giving'), a numeral stem (*trój-dzielny* 'three-part', *ob-o-sieczny* 'double-edged'), and an adverbial stem (*krótko-trwały* 'short, short-lived; lit. short-perduring', *wszystko-wiedzący* 'omniscient; lit. all-knowing'). Nominal heads appear in combination with adjectival stems (*mał-o-miasteczkowy* 'small-town', *cał-o-nocny* 'all-night'), numeral stems (*trzy-dniowy* 'three-day') and others. The N+N scheme underlies possessive adjectives, cf. *jaj-o-głowy* lit. 'egg-headed', *lask-o-nogi* lit. 'stick-legged', *błonk-o-skrzydły* '(singular for) Hymenoptera; lit. membrane-winged'. The latter group is used also as nouns, especially in the plural form.

3.3.2 Copulative compounds

The only possible structures must follow the A+A scheme, and their length, at least theoretically, is infinite, though practically the two-element compounds prevail, cf. (*brygada*) *remontowo-budowlana* 'renovation and construction (team)' and (*placówka*) *kulturalno-oświatowa* 'cultural and educational (centre)'. They are usually written with a hyphen and the order of the elements reflects iconically the state of affairs that has nothing to do with syntactic hierarchy, cf. (*flaga*) *biało-czerwona* 'white and red flag' referring to the Polish national flag, but *czerwono-biała* 'red and white' to the flag of Monaco. In rare cases copulative compounds are written without hyphen, among these are the adjectives *głuchoniemy* 'deaf and dumb', *cichociemny* lit. 'silent [and] dark (undercover soldiers in WW2 who were trained in Western Europe and dropped secretly on Polish territory)'. The interfix -*o*- is usually added to the first element. Terminological compounds may feature an abbreviation of the first constituent, either written together or hyphenated, cf. *anglo-amerykański* 'Anglo-American', *bałtosłowiański* 'Balto-Slavic', *psychofizyczny* 'psychophysical'. This process usually applies to Greek and Latin roots.

3.4 Other compounds

Within other word classes composition is a very rare phenomenon. A few existing compound verbs have vague motivation, cf. *cudz-o-łożyć* 'to commit adultery' (from *cudzy* 'someone else's' and *łoże* 'bed') and *zł-o-rzeczyć* 'to curse' (from *zły* 'evil' and *rzec* 'to say'). Genetically these are calques, as shown in the example of *lekceważyć* 'to disrespect' (cf. German *gering schätzen*), *równoważyć* 'to balance' from *równowaga* 'balance', and *zmartwychwstać* 'to rise from the dead; lit. from the dead rise'. Sometimes such forms can be deconstructed, cf. *lekceważyć* – *ważyć lekce* 'to weight lightly', *zmartwychwstać* – *wstać z martwych* 'to rise from the dead'.

Isolated examples may be found in invariable parts of speech, cf. interjections *dobranoc!* from the phrase *dobra noc* 'good night', *dzieńdoberek!* from the phrase *dzień dobry* + diminutive suffix -*ek* 'good morning; lit. good day-DIM', or onomatopoeic *stuk-puk* 'knock-knock' (cf. section 7).

4 Derivation

Derivation proper is morphological word-formation that involves the addition of specialised affixes, i.e. prefixes, suffixes, circumfixes, or infixes. In this section, the material is arranged according to the four basic parts of speech.

4.1 Denominal nouns

4.1.1 Prefixation

Prefix derivatives, among other things, express antagonism with *anty-* 'anti-' (*antypowieść* 'antinovel', *antyfeminizm* 'antifeminism'), *kontr-* 'counter-' (*kontrpochód* 'countermarch', *kontrpropozycja* 'counterproposition'), *przeciw-* 'anti-/counter-' (*przeciwciało* 'antibody'); antecedent events, formed with *pra-* (*prawykonanie* 'first performance'), *pre-* (*preromantyzm* 'pre-Romanticism', *preselekcja* 'preselection'), *proto-* (*protogwiazda* 'protostar'), *przed-* 'pre-' (*przedmecz* 'prematch', *przedbiegi* 'qualifying round'); words meaning 'outcome or reaction', such as *post-* (*postkomuna* 'post-Communism'), *po-* 'post-/after-' (*ponowoczesność* – a calque of *postmodernism*), *neo-* (*neopogaństwo* 'neopaganism'), *de-/dez-* (*destalinizacja* 'de-Stalinisation', *dezintegracja* 'disintegration'), *re-* (*reedycja* 'new edition'); forms denoting taxonomic hierarchies: *nad-* 'super-' (*nadburmistrz* 'Lord Mayor; lit. overmayor', *nadczłowiek* 'Nietzschean superhuman; lit. overman'), *pod-* 'sub-' (*podklasa* 'subclass', *podsekretarz* 'vice secretary; lit. subsecretary'), *sub-* (*subkultura* 'subculture'); quantitative: *nad-* 'over-/hyper-' (*nadprodukcja* 'overproduction', *nadczynność* 'overactivity, hyperactivity'), *hiper-* 'hyper-' (*hiperinflacja* 'hyperinflation'); and evaluative or intensifying derivatives with *arcy-* 'arch-' (*arcydzieło* 'masterpiece; lit. archwork', *arcymistrz* 'champion; lit. archmaster'), *hiper-* 'hyper-' (*hiperpoprawność* 'hypercorrectness'), *super-* (*superfilm*, *superniania* 'Supernanny').

The use of prefixes in nominal derivation is increasing mostly due to foreign prefixes. Morphemes borrowed from foreign languages sometimes cause problems of interpretation. Thus elements such as *auto-*, *hiper-*, *makro-*, *mega-*, *mikro-*, *mini-*, *multi-*, *pseudo-*, *super-* are considered to be so-called prefixoids, elements between derivational formatives and stems (in composition). The GWJP (1998: 430) applies the translation test: prefix derivatives are those whose foreign elements have the same meaning as an existing Polish preposition (and corresponding prefix), cf. *hiperprodukcja* – *nadprodukcja* 'hyperproduction – overproduction'. This criterion is not met by *auto* 'self' or *neo* 'again', though prefixes that express the same meaning do exist, cf. *neo-* and *re-*.

4.1.2 Suffixation

The suffixes listed below are related to various derivational categories:
  Personal nouns, e.g., names of professions with an implicit predicate: *blach-arz* 'auto-body mechanic' (← *blacha* 'sheet metal'), *port-owiec* 'docker'

(← *port* 'harbor'), *ogrod-nik* 'gardener' (← *ogród* 'garden'), and *ryb-ak* 'fisherman; lit. fisher' (← *ryba* 'fish'); names of followers/supporters of concepts, leaders, members of organisations, are often derived from proper names, e.g., *franciszk-anin* 'Franciscan' (← *Franciszek*), *hitler-owiec* 'Hitlerite, referring to Nazis during WW2', *marks-ista* 'Marxist', *piłsud-czyk* 'Pilsudski-ite', including acronyms, cf. *ak-owiec* 'AK soldier' (soldiers of the *Armia Krajowa* 'Home Army', Polish resistance organisation during WW2); names of inhabitants, e.g., *wyspi-arz* 'islander' (← *wys-pa* 'island'), *warszawi-ak* 'resident of Warsaw' (← *Warszawa*), *południowiec* 'southerner' (← *Południe* 'the South'), *Rosj-anin* 'Russian' (← *Rosja*), *Wietnam-czyk* 'Vietnamese' (← *Wietnam*); names of persons, motivated by special attributes or predilections, e.g., *brod-acz* 'bearded man' (← *broda* 'beard'), *herbaci-arz* 'tea-vendor' (← *herbata* 'tea'), and *szalik-owiec* 'football hooligan' (← *szalik* 'scarf (as attribute of a group of fans)').

Within the non-personal nouns, serial derivatives can be observed, i.e. names of soups, vodkas, meals, cakes, hats, fabrics, types of woods, buildings, ships and taxes. They are often formed through univerbation (ellipsis + suffixation) and have double, i.e. nominal and adjectival motivation, cf. *czapka do baseballa* lit. 'cap for baseball' → *czapka baseballowa* (adj.) 'baseball cap' → *baseball-ówka* 'id.'.

Instrument nouns are rarely derived from nominal bases, cf. -*ak* in *rowi-ak* 'chisel for making grooves' (← *rowek* 'groove') and -*ownic(a)* in *frytkownica* 'deep frier' (← *frytka* 'French fry'). A new means of forming derivatives is the suffixoid -*(o)mat*, cf. *tempomat* 'cruise control', *alkomat* 'breathalyzer'.

Place nouns are represented by derivatives such as *kawi-arnia* 'coffee house, café' (← *kawa* 'coffee'), *kwiaci-arnia* 'florist's' (← *kwiat* 'flower'), new *sush-arnia* 'sushi bar', *maszyn-ownia* 'engine room' (← *maszyna*), *kartofl-isko* 'potato field' (← *kartofel* 'potato'), and *dziec-iniec* 'nursery' (← *dcieci* 'children').

Nouns expressing similarity, comprise, e.g., names of buildings: *mrowisk-owiec* 'huge apartment block similar to an anthill (Pol. *mrowisko*)'; botanical names, such as *słonecznik* 'sunflower' (← *słońce* 'sun'), and *tasiemi-ec* 'tapeworm' (← *taśma* 'tape'). Structures based on metaphor and metonomy also appear in special languages, cf. biological terms such as *pałeczkowce* 'bacteria of an elongated shape, similar to a stick' (← *pałeczka* 'stick').

Abstract nouns, i.e. names of qualities, doctrines, positions, and events, are exemplified by *bohater-stwo* 'heroism' (← *bohater* 'hero'), *dziwac-two* 'weirdness' (← *dziwak* 'weird'), *sobk-ostwo* 'selfishness' (← *sobek* 'egoist'), *pszczelar-stwo* 'bee-keeping' (← *pszczelarz* 'beekeeper'), *marks-izm* 'Marxism', and humorous *wałęs-izm* 'Wałęsa-ism', *profes-ura* 'professorship', *telewizj-ada* (← *telewizja*), *para-fi-ada* (← *parafia*) – both names of events, referring to a TV fete and a parochial fete, modeled upon *olimpiada*.

Collective nouns: canonical collective names are motivated by nouns naming an element of a set, cf. *nauczyciel-stwo* 'teachers' (← *nauczyciel*), *dzieci-arnia* 'kids' (← *dcieci* 'children'), *zwierz-yna* 'game' (← *zwierzę* 'animal'), *list-owie* 'foliage' (← *liść* 'leaf'), *chuligan-eria* 'hooligans', *aksjomat-yka* 'axiom system'. Names of pairs based on the masculine form are also possible, cf. *wuj-ostwo* 'uncle and aunt' (← *wuj(ek)*) 'uncle', *dziadk-owie* 'grandfather and grandmother' (← *dziadek* 'grandfather'), and *Nowak-owie* 'the Nowaks', meaning 'Nowak and his wife'.

Singulative nouns are derived from substance nouns by means of the suffix -k-, cf. *blasz-ka* 'plaque' (← *blacha* 'sheet metal'), *szkieł-ko* 'a piece of glass' (← *szkło* 'glass').

Diminutives and melioratives: there are two semantic types that should be clearly distinguished – those that mean 'small' and quasi-diminutives that express the speaker's attitude. From the semantic point of view one can "downsize" physical parameters, hence names of things are good bases for diminutives: *dom-ek* 'little house' (← *dom*), *szabel-ka* 'small saber' (← *szabla*), as well as names of body parts as *nos-ek* 'small nose' (← *nos*), animals or plants: *ryb-ka* 'small fish' (← *ryba*), *kwiat-ek* 'small flower' (← *kwiat*), places: *poko-ik* 'tiny room' (← *pokój*), etc., but abstract ideas and individual names may not be "downsized" in this way, cf. *zdrów-ko* 'health' (← *zdrowie*), *idej-ka* 'little idea' (← *idea*). The attitudes thus expressed range from familiarity, tenderness and empathy on the one side and irony and sarcasm on the other (see Nagórko 2025 on morphopragmatics in Slavic).

Augmentatives and pejoratives: the semantic feature of these derivatives is the indication of large size that may imply a certain distancing or even dislike towards what is denoted by the base words. The suffixes available are -(*i*)*sk(o)*, cf. *gmasz-ysko* 'huge building' (← *gmach* 'edifice'), -*iszcz(e)*, e.g., *tom-iszcze* 'big volume', -*idł(o)*, and -*uch*. This category also contains purely expressive nouns indicating a negative attitude, yet sometimes expressing pity, or even sympathy, cf. *ps-ina* 'a sad-looking dog' (← *pes* 'dog'), and *piśm-idło* 'rag (about a newspaper or magazine)' (← *pismo* 'magazine'), see also sections 6 and 9.

Female personal nouns are derived from common and proper nouns referring to men. Regular types contain the formants -*k(a)*, e.g., *lekar-ka* 'woman doctor' (← *lekarz* 'doctor'); also -*in(i)/-yn(i)*, e.g., *zdrajcz-yni* 'traitoress' (← *zdrajca* m.), and -*ow(a)*, e.g., *szef-owa* 'lady boss' (← *szef*). The Panslavic affix -*ow(a)* forms feminine surnames, yet unlike in other Slavic languages it also conveys the woman's marital status: -*ow(a)* for wives, -*ówn(a)* for daughters. A second pair of suffixes -*ina/-anka*, which may be added to masculine surnames ending with -*a* is no longer productive.

Nouns referring to f e m a l e a n i m a l s are formed with the suffix -ic(a), cf. *lw-ica* 'lioness' (← *lew*), *wilcz-yca* 'she-wolf' (← *wilk*), which gives it a pragmatic marking when used for women (*biolog-ica* 'female biology teacher, pej.').

4.1.3 Circumfixation

Circumfixation is rarely used in nouns. Among the few post-1989 examples are *anty-aborcj-onista* 'person who is against abortion (Pol. *aborcja*)' and *anty-samo-chodz-izm* 'movement against the use of cars (Pol. *samochód*)'.

4.2 Deadjectival nouns

4.2.1 Suffixation

A b s t r a c t n o u n s: Most prominent in this case are the deadjectival abstract nouns ending with -*ość*, formed both from simple bases, cf. *blad-ość* 'paleness' (← *blady* 'pale'), *polsk-ość* 'Polish-ness' (← *polski* 'Polish'), and complex ones, cf. *ściągaln-ość* 'collectibility' (← *ściągalny* 'collectible, recoverable'). This category also includes names of illnesses, such as *krzyw-ica* 'rickets' (← *krzywy* 'askew, crooked'), *żółt-aczka* 'hepatitis' (← *żółty* 'yellow'). The formant -*stw(o)* appears in nouns denoting people's activities, such as *zawodow-stwo* 'professionalism' (← *zawodowy* 'professional'), and psychological qualities, such as *zuchwal-stwo* 'audacity' (← *zuchwały* 'audacious').

N o n - a b s t r a c t n o u n s constitute an open set, cf. *prost-ak* 'simpleton' (← *prosty* 'simple'), *grub-as* 'fatso' (← *gruby* 'fat'), *zielen-ina* 'greens; lit. greenery' (← *zielony* 'green'), *szar-ak* 'nonentity (about a person)' (← *szary* 'grey'), and *nów-ka* 'something new, e.g., a new car' (← *nowy* 'new'). It is important to distinguish personal from non-personal nouns, despite the fact that both classes share the same formants, cf. *wyczynowi-ec* 'somebody who specializes in sport competitions' (← *wyczynowy* 'professional') and *komórkowi-ec* 'cell phone, mobile' (← *telefon komórkowy* 'cellular phone'), more often replaced with the univerbation *komórka*.

4.2.2 Circumfixation

The few examples from recent data are: *anty-seksual-ista* lit. 'antisexualist' (← *seksualny* 'sexual'), *de-solidar-yzacja* (← *solidarny* 'loyal', but referring to *Solidarność*, the political and labor movement), and *pro-federal-ista* 'advocate/supporter of federalism' (← *federalny* 'federal').

4.3 Deverbal nouns

A c t i o n n o u n s with the suffixes -*ni(e)*, -*ci(e)* can be derived from simple verbs, such as *czytanie* 'reading' (← *czytać*), *klikni-ęcie* 'click' (← *kliknąć*), or from derived ones, such as *programowa-nie* 'programming' (← *programować*). Other productive suffixes are -*(iz)-acj(a)*, as in *prywatyz-acja* 'privatisation' (← *prywatyzować*); -*(s/z/c)tw(o)*, as in *dowód-ztwo* 'command, headquarters' (← *dowodzić* 'to command'), *budownictwo* 'construction' (← *budować* 'to build'). In many cases the action noun is motivated directly by the agent noun, cf. *krytykanc-two* 'nit-picking' (← *krytykant* 'caviller'), *lizusostwo* 'bootlicking' (← *lizus* 'bootlicker'), and *chodziar-stwo* 'race walking' (← *chodziarz* 'race-walker'), -*k(a)*, as in *zbiórka* (*pieniędzy*) 'collection (of money)' (← *zbierać* 'to collect'), etc.

A g e n t n o u n s: traditional affixes like -*c(a)*, cf. *odkryw-ca* 'discoverer' (← *otkrywać* 'to open, discover') and -*ciel*, cf. *oswobodzi-ciel* 'liberator' (← *oswobodzić* 'to liberate') are losing productivity. New derivatives ending with -*acz* are close in meaning to denominal nouns motivated by a characteristic feature, cf. *potakiwacz* 'a yes-man; lit. one who nods in agreement' (← *potakiwać* ← *tak* 'yes'), *wymyślacz* 'somebody who invents things (mainly due to overactive imagination)' (← *wymyślać* 'to invent'). The same suffix forms, though with decreasing frequency, instrument nouns, names of appliances and machines *odkurz-acz* 'vacuum cleaner' (← *odkurzać* 'to vacuum').

P a t i e n t n o u n s: one-place predicates or subjects of the semantic passive voice may become the base for personal nouns referring to patients: *zesłaniec* lit. 'exilee' (← *X został zesłany* 'X was exiled'), or to non-personal nouns, cf. *lat-awiec* 'kite; lit. flyer', *wisi-or* 'pendant', *stoj-ak* 'stand', derived from (*to, co*) *lata, wisi, stoi* '(that which) flies, hangs, stands respectively'.

O b j e c t n o u n s a n d r e s u l t n o u n s: the exponents of this category are the suffixes -*k(a)* and its variants -*anka*, -*onka*, cf. *nakręt-ka* 'nut' (← *nakręcać* 'to torque, twist on'), *czyt-anka* 'reader (a text or a schoolbook for children)' (← *czytać* 'to read'), *mroż-onka* 'frozen food' (← *mrozić* 'to freeze'); -*(t)ek*, as in *doda-tek* 'addition, add-on' (← *dodać* 'to add'); -*in(a)* as in *wydziel-ina* 'secretion' (← *wydzielić* 'to secrete'), *dzian-ina* 'knitted fabric' (← *dziać* 'to knit'). Nouns denoting by-products of activities, grammatical pluralia tantum, are formed by the suffixes -*iny*, e.g., *popłucz-yny* 'residue, dregs' (← *popłukać* 'to rinse'), and -*ki*, e.g., *obier-ki* 'peelings' (← *obierać* 'to peel').

Instrument nouns: apart from the suffixes already mentioned (*-arka* and *-acz*), this category takes the formatives *-ak*, as in *czerp-ak* 'scoop' (← *czerpać* 'to scoop'), *-nik*, as in *nadaj-nik* 'transmitter' (← *nadać* 'to transmit'), *-nica*, as in *chłod-nica* 'radiator; lit. cooler' (← *chłodzić* 'to cool'), *-aczka*, as in *wycier-aczka* 'door-mat' (← *wycierać* 'to wipe').

Deverbal place nouns are formed with the suffix *-ni(a)* and its variants *-alnia* and *-arnia*, cf. *pracow-nia* 'work room, atelier' (← *pracować* 'to work'), *sypi-alnia* 'bedroom' (← *sypiać* 'to sleep'), *susz-arnia* 'drying room' (← *suszyć* 'to dry'), etc.

4.4 Denominal adjectives

4.4.1 Suffixation

Relational adjectives such as *chłop-ski* (← *chłop* 'peasant'), *mlecz-ny* (← *mleko* 'milk'), *płaszcz-owy* (← *płaszcz* 'coat') indicate the features of one item as opposed to others, e.g., *chłopska rodzina* 'peasant family', *mleczny napój* 'milk drink', *płaszczowa wełna* 'wool for coats; lit. coat-REL.ADJ wool'. The function of the formative is to transpose a noun into an adjective. The meaning of the derivative depends on the noun modified by the derivative. Depending on the context, i.e. the head noun, the meaning of the same lexeme may correspond to either a relational or a qualitative adjective, cf. *marcowe zebranie* 'March meeting' = *zebranie w marcu* 'the meeting in March' and *marcowa pogoda* 'weather typical for March'. The relations with the head thus determines the type of meaning, which GWJP (1998: 482ff.) describes as contextual. The list given in this grammar is problematic, since relational adjectives constitute an open category that increases constantly. The most productive suffix *-ow(y)* can be applied to loanwords (foreign bases), cf. *biznes-owy* 'business', *kolagen-owy* 'collagen', *kompakt-owy* 'compact'. The nouns ending with *-cja* give rise to adjectives bearing the suffix *-n(y)* and its variants, cf. *prywatyzacyj-ny* (← *prywatyzacja* 'privatization'), *eurokrat-yczny* 'Eurocratic', and *komunij-ny* (← *komunia* '(Holy) Communion, particularly with reference to First Holy Communion)'.

In derived qualitative adjectives suffixes express similarity: *-owat(y)*, e.g., *beczułkowaty* 'barrel-like' (← *beczułka* 'barrel'), *-asty*, e.g., *gąbczasty* 'spongy' (← *gąbka* 'sponge'), and possessive meaning (with a quantitative nuance): *-ist(y)*, e.g., *gwiaździsty* 'full of stars, starry' (← *gwiazda* 'star'), *soczysty* 'juicy' (← *sok* 'juice').

4.4.2 Circumfixation

The few examples are *anty-depresyj-ny* 'anti-depressive' (← *depresja* 'depression'), *o-włosi-ony* 'hirsute' (← *włos* 'hair'), *za-kompleksi-ony* lit. 'complexed, suffering from inferiority complex' (← *kompleks* 'complex'), *wy-biedz-ony* 'emaciated, gaunt' (← *bieda* 'poverty'). The prefixes *o-* and *za-* express possessive (ornative) meaning (cf. German *behaart* 'hirsute', *bemoost* 'mossy' – see article 1 in this volume), *wy-* expresses intensity, exhaustiveness.

4.5 Deadjectival adjectives

Their meaning is independent of the noun they modify, i.e. in their derivational paraphrase the modified noun need not figure: *malutki* 'very small' (← *mały* 'small'). Three types of formatives occur in this class – prefixes, suffixes, and infixes.

4.5.1 Prefixation

Adjectives with a n e g a t i v e element, including the prefix *nie-* (*nie-brzydki* 'not ugly', *nie-głupi* 'not stupid') are used as a litotes instead of *ładny* 'pretty', *mądry* 'smart', respectively; other prefixes: *bez-partyjny* 'non-partisan, independent', *a-moralny* 'immoral', *ir-racjonalny* 'irrational'. Prefixes expressing the i n t e n s i t y of the quality named by the base are: *prze-piękny* 'very beautiful', *arcy-ciekawy* 'very, most interesting', *super-szybki* 'superfast', *nad-gorliwy* 'over-zealous'. Adjectives with an a p p r o x i m a t i v e meaning are derived with the prefixes *niedo-* and *przy-*: *niedo-rozwinięty* 'retarded; lit. under-developed', *przy-ciasny* 'a little tight'.

Other types: *pra-słowiański* 'Proto-Slavonic', *para-militarny* 'paramilitary', *za-przeszły* 'pluperfect; lit. plupast' (← *przeszły* 'past (tense)').

4.5.2 Suffixation

Adjectives expressing the i n t e n s i t y of the quality named by the base are derived with the suffix *-utk(i)*: *malutki* 'really small' (← *mały* 'small'), *mięciutki* 'really soft' (← *miękki* 'soft'). Adjectives with an a p p r o x i m a t i v e meaning are usually derived with the suffixes *-aw(y)* and *-it(y)*: *grubawy* 'a bit fat' (← *gruby* 'fat'), *zielonkawy* 'greenish' (← *zielony* 'green'), *słabowity* 'enfeebled, frail' (← *słaby* 'weak'). E x p r e s s i v e formations, in which the emotional component is the most prominent, are, for instance, *mal-uśki, mal-uchny, mal-uni, mal-usi* 'tiny, itsy-bitsy, minuscule' (← *mały* 'small').

4.5.3 Infixation

Markers of an emotionally intensified meaning of adjectives are the infixes -*eń*- and -*ecz*- placed within the suffixes -*utki*: *króci-uteńki* 'very short' (← *krótki*), *równi-uteńki* 'very straight/even' (← *równy*), and -*uśki*: *mal-usieńki* 'very small' (← *mały*). Longer chains of such elements are also possible, cf. *mal-usi-eniecz-ki* 'really very small'. They are used in baby talk, folk literature, fairy and folk tales.

4.6 Deverbal adjectives

In studies on Polish word-formation (cf. GWJP 1998: 471) it is customary to distinguish two types of deverbal adjectives, called "dispositional" and "non-dispositional". Within these two groups, active (i.e. subject-oriented) and passive (i.e. object-oriented) formations may be distinguished.

The dispositional derivatives include adjectives expressing the possibility of an action being carried out (e.g. *ulecz-alny* 'curable' ← *uleczyć* 'to cure') as well as formations expressing a habitual behavior (e.g. *ustęp-liwy* 'pliant, acquiescent' ← *ustępować* 'to make concessions to sb.') or proneness (e.g. *chor-owity* 'sickness-prone' ← *chorować* 'to be sick').

In the non-dispositional group the base verb is simply transposed into an adjective without adding further semantic features: *ostrzeg-awczy* 'warning, which warns' (← *ostrzegać* 'to warn'), *słyn-ny* 'famous' (← *słynąć* 'to be famous'), or object-oriented *upraw-ne pole* 'farm land; lit. cultivated land' (← *uprawiać* 'to cultivate').

4.7 Denominal verbs

4.7.1 Suffixation

The separation of this derivation technique is arbitrary, since the available suffixes have at the same time an inflectional character. Thus the derivatives quoted below are more often listed as examples of conversion ("paradigmatic word-formation" according to GWJP, i.e. conversion accompanied by an inflectional ending marking the change of paradigm).

The base noun may be
a) the subject of the state or activity named by the derivative, cf. *pan-ować* 'to rule; lit. to lord' (← *pan* 'lord'), *kucharz-yć* 'to cook' (← *kucharz* 'cook, chef'), sometimes used metaphorically, e.g., *matk-ować* 'to mother' (← *matka* 'mother'), *chomik-ować* 'to squirrel away, hoard' (← *chomik* 'hamster');
b) a tool, cf. *pedał-ować* 'to pedal' (← *pedał*), or an object, cf. *kartkować* 'to leaf through' (← *kartka* 'sheet of paper');
c) an effected object, cf. *dziurk-ować* 'to punch holes' (← *dziurka* 'hole'), *filet-ować* 'to fillet, cut into fillets' (← *filet*).

In addition there is a series of denominal intransitive verbs, e.g., *idioci-eć* 'to become stupid' (← *idiota* 'idiot'), *kamieni-eć* 'to freeze, turn to stone' (← *kamień* 'stone'), *owoc-ować* 'to bear fruit' (← *owoce* 'fruit').

Among the few purely derivational suffixes are *-ol-*: *bieda* 'poverty' → *biedol-ić* 'to complain about one's poor situation', *urząd* 'office' → *urzęd-ol-ić* 'to work (usually incompetently) as an official (pej.)', and the borrowed *-iz-/-yz-*: *biurokrata* → *biurokrat-yz-ować* 'to bureaucratise', etc.

4.7.2 Circumfixation

Causative verbs may be derived directly from nouns with a discontinuous formative, consisting of a prefix and a suffix, cf. *u-pup-ić* '1. to ridicule; 2. to kibosh' (← *pupa* 'bottom, buttocks'), *za-les-ić* 'to replant a forest; lit. to forest' (← *les* 'forest'), *od-grzyb-ić* 'to make mould-free' (← *grzyb* 'fungus, mould'), *pod-piwnicz-yć* 'to build with a cellar; lit. under-cellar-SUFF' (← *piwnica* 'cellar'), and with a prefix and the postfix *się*: *na-indycz-yć się* 'to get angry, get the hump' (← *indyk* 'turkey'). (In word-formation processes, *się* is not considered as reflexive pronoun, but as derivational morpheme – postfix – following the inflectional ending.)

4.8 Deadjectival verbs

4.8.1 Suffixation

The following verbs can be regarded as cases of "paradigmatic derivation" (conversion), cf. *gorzk-nieć* 'to become bitter' (← *gorzki* 'bitter'), *słab-nąć* 'to weaken (itr.)' (← *słaby* 'weak'), *słodz-ić* 'to sweeten' (← *słodki* 'sweet'). Deadjectival verbs denote a process that can be defined as 'to become (be) something' or 'to make something be in a certain way', e.g., *banal-iz-ować* 'to make banal' (← *banalny*).

4.8.2 Circumfixation

The combination of prefixation and paradigmatic derivation serves the purpose of forming causative verbs, such as *u-nowocześn-ić* 'to modernize' (← *nowoczesny* 'modern'), *u-tajn-ić* 'to make secret' (← *tajny* 'secret'), *u-widoczn-ić* 'to make visible' (← *widoczny* 'visible'), *od-realn-ić* 'to make unreal' (← *realny* 'real').

4.9 Deverbal verbs

4.9.1 Prefixation

The majority of Polish prefixes are homonymous with prepositions, from which they genetically originate – the only exceptions to this are *ob-*, *prze-*, *roz-*, *wy-*. The prefixes express the basic spatial categories (directional and locative formations from verbs of movement, cf. *po-biec* 'to run (to)', *wy-biec* 'to run out', *o-płynąć* 'to circumnavigate, swim around', *ob-jechać* 'to drive round') and temporal delimitation, cf. *po-czytać* 'to read for a short while'; some derivatives acquire secondary metaphorical meanings (*pod-kupić* 'to gazump; lit. underbuy', *o-płakać* 'to mourn; lit. cry after'). More complex meanings related to changes to the object are possible when the base is a transitive verb, cf. distributive *po-spłacać długi* 'to pay off one's debts (successively)', cumulative *na-kupić książek* 'to buy a lot of books' and others.

Aspect plays a crucial role in the formation of verbs. All prefix-bearing verbs are perfective. Prefixes usually convey amalgams of meaning, i.e. apart from the perfective aspect they bring an additional, more or less prominent, meaning (also known as aktionsart). It is however possible to distinguish in a set of derivatives coming from the same base, a verb that is the closest in meaning to that base and differs only in aspect. This is called an aspectual pair, such as *pisać* (ipf.)/ *napisać* (pf.) 'to write'.

4.9.2 Suffixation

The only possibility in suffix derivation is the substitution or exchange of stem suffixes that are part of the inflectional stem, thus this type of derivation is considered an instance of "paradigmatic word-formation" (conversion), cf. *kop-a-ć* 'to kick' and *kop-ną-ć* 'to kick once'. The *-ną-* element introduces the meaning of the instantaneity of the activity (semelfactivity). Suffixes are also used to backform imperfective forms from perfective verbs, cf. *przepisać* (pf.) → *przepis-ywa-ć* (ipf.) 'to copy', *zapisać* → *zapis-ywa-ć* 'to write down'.

4.9.3 Postfixation

Among the different types there are the postfixal derivatives with the postfix *się* added, such as the pseudo-transitive *spakować się* 'to pack; lit. to pack oneself', *uderzyć się* 'to hit oneself', intensive verbs such as *prosić się* 'to keep asking for something', as well as instances of backformation through subtraction of the *się* element, such as *cieszyć* 'to please, make happy' (← *cieszyć się* 'to be glad'), *martwić* 'to worry somebody' (← *martwić się* 'to worry about') (cf. section 6).

4.9.4 Circumfixation

Discontinuous formatives added to verbal bases are characteristic of diminutive derivatives with the combination *po-* + *-iwa/-ewa*, cf. *po-płak-iwa-ć* 'to cry a bit, whimper' (← *płakać* 'to cry'), *po-bol-ewa-ć* 'to ache of and on' (← *boleć* 'to ache'). A combination of a prefix and a postfix is considered a type of a circumfix, cf. saturative formations with *na-* + *się*, such as *najeść się* 'to eat one's fill' (← *jeść* 'to eat'), *naczytać się* 'to read to one's heart's content; to have read too much with sorry results' (← *czytać* 'to read'), evaluative with *roz-* + *się*, such as *roz-chorować się* 'to get sick' (← *chorować* 'to be sick'). What they share is the information about the intensity of a given process.

4.10 Derivation of adverbs

4.10.1 Suffixation

Grammars of Polish (e.g., GWJP 1998: 524) distinguish adverbs from homonymous "predicatives" on the basis of the fact that the latter are used with the copula *być* 'to be', cf. *pisze ładnie* (adv.) '(s/he) writes well' vs. *jest ładnie* (predicative) '(it) is nice outside'. (Predicatives are uninflectable predicates of impersonal (subject-less) sentences, designating, among others, the (mental or physical) state of living beings and natural/environmental phenomena.) In both cases we are dealing with deadjectival derivatives with the suffixes -e/-o, e.g., *wczesny* (adj.) 'early' → *wcześnie* 'early', *dobry* 'good' → *dobrze* 'well'; *suchy* 'dry' → *sucho* 'dry, drily', *głupi* 'stupid' → *głupio* 'stupid, stupidly'. Doublets, which are possible mainly with adjectives ending in *-isty*, may be differentiated functionally (between adverbs and predicatives) provided a copula construction is licensed, cf. *mgliście/mglisto* 'foggy' – *wyrażał się mgliście* (adverb) 'he expressed himself vaguely; lit. foggily' and *było mglisto* (predicative) 'it was foggy'.

4.10.2 Circumfixation

Structures with a prefix written separately and a suffix that is a genetic ending of the dative case may be interpreted as examples of circumfix derivation. The most common types are *po* + *-u*, formed on the basis of adjectives ending with *-sk(i)*, cf. *po angielsku* 'in English', *po pańsku* 'in a lordly fashion'; *po* + *-emu*, cf. *po staremu* 'in the old way' (← *stary* 'old'), *po kobiecemu* 'in a feminine way' (← *kobiecy* 'feminine'). Less common are those with *z* + *-a*, cf. *z francuska* 'after French fashion', *z rzadka* 'rarely'; *na* + *-o*, cf. *na miękko* 'soft (boiled)'; *do* + *-a*, cf. *do czysta* '(till) clean'.

5 Conversion

5.1 Nominal conversion

5.1.1 Denominal nouns

Conversion within the same part of speech implies a paradigm shift which involves a difference in lexical meaning, e.g., singulare tantum noun → plurale tantum (*brud* 'dirt' → *brudy* 'dirty laundry', *dobro* 'goodness' → *dobra* 'goods, possessions'); personal masculine name → feminine name (*pan* 'mister' → *pani* 'mistress, Ms.', also invariable titles such as *doktor* 'woman doctor', *minister* 'woman Minister'); branch of science → name of the specialist (*fizyka* 'physics' → *fizyk* 'physicist'); name of a living creature → name of the offspring (*kot* 'cat' → *kocię* 'kitten', *wilk* 'wolf' → *wilczę* 'pup').

5.1.2 Deadjectival nouns

The operation of transforming a syntactically dependent adjective into a noun may be seen as univerbation (ellipsis) of a complex phrase of the A+N type. Formally it is related to the selective category of grammatical gender. Masculine gender may be illustrated by *ślepy* '(the) blind' from *ślepy człowiek* 'blind man', *karny (rzut)* 'penalty (kick)'. Examples of feminine gender are *pomidorowa (zupa)* 'tomato (soup)', *żytnia (wódka)* 'rye (vodka)'. Neutral gender cases include, for example, *nieznane* '(the) unknown', *wolne* 'free (time)'. The pluralia tantum form a different group, cf. *bliscy* 'one's close (relatives)', *drobne (pieniądze)* 'coins, change; lit. small (money)'. These nouns retain adjectival inflection, but are reduced to one grammatical gender, which distinguishes them from adjectives. (From the substantivised masculine personal nouns it is possible to form feminine nouns that are separate lexemes, e.g., *uczony* 'scholar m.' → *uczona* 'scholar f.', *zmarły* 'deceased m.' → *zmarła* 'deceased f.'. However, this is an example of denominal conversion.)

Among the deadjectival nouns there are some abstract nouns that have nominal inflection, such as *dobro* n. 'goodness' (← *dobry* 'good'), *zdrowie* n. 'health' (← *zdrowy* 'healthy'), and *zieleń* f. 'green (colour)' (← *zielony* 'green').

5.1.3 Deverbal nouns

In this type not only the set of endings changes, but also the verbal stem suffix. Nevertheless, its inflectional character is rarely questioned (cf. the interpretation of suffix verbs in section 4.7.1): *dźwig-ać* 'to lift, carry' → *dźwig* 'crane', *walcz-yć* 'to fight' → *walka* 'fight', *nos-ić* 'to carry' → *nosze* pl. tantum 'stretcher'.

5.2 Adjectival conversion

Denominal adjectives are regularly formed from nouns denoting animals, e.g., *kot* 'cat' → *koci* 'cat (adj.)', *owca* 'sheep' → *owczy* 'sheep (adj.)'. Further structures include, for example, *martwica* 'necrosis' → *martwiczy* 'necrotic', *sprawozdawca* 'reporter' → *sprawozdawczy* 'reporting (adj.)'.

The issue of participles is deliberately ignored here due to its liminal status between verbal and adjectival forms, as the possible adjectivisation of participles does not trigger changes in their inflectional paradigms.

5.3 Verbal conversion

5.3.1 Denominal verbs

In section 4.7.1 we discussed suffixations, which may as well be considered an instance of conversion, cf. *sędzia* 'judge' → *sędziować* 'to judge', *król* 'king' → *królować* 'to reign'.

5.3.2 Deadjectival verbs

Conversion is used to form inchoative verbs, such as *blady* 'pale' → *blednąć* 'to (turn) pale', *stary* 'old' → *starzeć się* 'to grow old', and causative verbs, cf. *biały* 'white' → *bielić* 'to whiten'.

5.3.3 Deverbal verbs

Aspectual pairs, in which the difference is based on stem suffixes, cf. *kopać* (ipf.) – *kopnąć* (pf.) 'to kick', *przepisać* (pf.) – *przepisywać* (ipf.) '1. to copy (a written text); 2. to prescribe', belong to different conjugation classes; moreover, perfective verbs do not have a present tense. Hence, it is possible to perceive this as an instance of conversion, if aspect is considered a word-formation and not a grammatical category.

5.4 Adverbial conversion

Numerous adverbs are formed on the basis of syntactic phrases. They are either nouns in the instrumental case, e.g., *siłą* 'by force' (nom. *siła*), *wieczorem* 'in the evening' (nom. *wieczór*), *czasami* (instr. pl. of *czas* 'time') 'from time to time', or primary prepositional phrases, such as *na krzyż* 'crosswise, crossed; lit. on cross', *o czasie* 'on time'.

6 Backformation

This word-formation strategy is generally recognised as non-canonical, as it defies the rule of parallelism between form and content: while the derivative is semantically more complex, formally it is not. Thus words such as *ławka* 'bench' or *słoik* 'jar' name typical items from a given set, while *ława* and *słój* denote items that are bigger, hence semantically they are more complex. This results in a backformation, the products of which are augmentative forms: *ławka* → *ława*, *słoik* → *słój*. Genetically the words *ławka* and *słoik* are diminutives, but contemporary speakers do not consider them to signify 'something small', although the -*k*- and -*ik*- fragments are correctly identified with appropriate suffixes. Thus considering examples like *ława* and *słoj* a case of backformation is not out of place here.

Similar problems arise from a discrepancy between genetic and functional criteria in pairs of words such as *niedołęga* 'oaf' (← *niedołężny* 'clumsy, oafish'), *beż* 'beige' (← *beżowy* 'beige').

Common, especially in spoken language, is the continuous suppression of the -*k*- element, cf. *stówa* (← *stówka* 'a hundred'), or -*ek*, cf. *małolat* 'a youth' (← *małolatek* 'underage'). The multifunctional -*k*-affixes may be associated with diminutives. The shortened forms sound harsher and fit better the ambience of a youth culture.

7 Reduplication

Reduplication is common in baby-talk (*tata* 'dad', *am-am* 'to eat') and is also prominent in children's literature. Bańko (2008: 89–90) distinguishes exact reduplications: *bum-cyk-cyk* 'repeated quick rhythmic movement, also percussion music', *dylu-dylu* 'fiddle folk music', *gadu-gadu* 'prolonged, idle talk' and non-exact reduplications: *rach-ciach* 'quick movement, usually when insisting that something is done quickly'. Onomatopoeic exclamations are also used to mimic sounds: *chi-chi* (laughter), *gul-gul* (gulping), *chrum-chrum* (oinking of pigs), *tra-ta-ta* (trumpet). Despite their iconicity the linguistic form is completely conventionalised.

Bańko's model can also be applied to other parts of speech; cf. exact reduplications in adjectives like *tyci-tyci* 'very small', and adverbs like *ledwo ledwo* 'barely', *jako tako* 'so-so', whereas non-exact repetitions use rhyme as a means of expression, cf. the nominal reduplication *elegancja-francja* 'posh elegance; lit. elegance-France'.

8 Blending

Blends in Polish are rare and primarily nominal, such as *(urlop) tacierzyński* 'paternal leave' (← *tata* 'dad' + *macierzyński* 'maternal'), *chłopela* (← *chłopcy* 'boys'

+ *kapela* 'band') as an attempt to replace the English *boys band*. Numerous examples are ascribed to authors, such as Przyboś's *terroretyk* (*terror* + *teoretyk* 'theoretician'). Blending is also common in the daily press, cf. *Ubekistan* (*Urząd Bezpieczeństwa (UB)* 'Polish secret police during communism' + *Uzbekistan*). The merger is based on similarity in sound: the two words share a segment which is recognised in the derivative as the so-called contamination node (or blending locus), cf. *reżymieszek* (← *reżym* 'regime' + *rzezimieszek* 'criminal, thug'). This gives rise to problems in identifying some formations as instances of blending, cf. *gimbus* 'middle school coach' (← *gimnazjum* 'middle school' + *autobus* 'bus, coach'). Despite the lack of a shared segment, I would consider words such as *gimbus* an example of blending.

9 Clipping

Another form of backward derivation is clipping (subtraction). The deletion of elements occurs without any regularity and is therefore unpredictable. It is a realisation of the tendency, particularly in the spoken language, for briefness and expressive value, cf. in adolescent slang *impra* instead of *impreza* 'party', *promo* (← *promocja* 'promotion'), *dyr* (← *dyrektor* 'headmaster').

Clipping is often accompanied by alternations, among which depalatalisation, i.e. the replacement of *s*, *sz*, *ś*, *ż* with the velar *ch* is the most common, cf. *artysta* → *artycha* 'artist', *cias-tko* → *ciacho* 'cake', *poraż-ka* → *poracha* 'failure'. A reverse type of alternations involving palatalisation is present in clippings, such as *fac-et* → *facio* 'guy', *rącz-ka* 'hand-DIM' (← *ręka* 'hand') → *rąsia* 'hand', expressing tenderness, but also irony or sarcasm.

10 Word-creation

In Polish one can find only few examples, mainly among chrematonyms, such as *bistor* (a type of polyester fabric), *ixi* (a brand name for a washing powder), *melex* (a small electric car produced in a factory in the town of Mielec, also to be exported, which explains the *-ex* element, the *mel-* element also does not seem accidental), the name of the oil company *Orlen*, and the colloquial *miglanc* 'a lazy person'.

11 References

Bańko, Mirosław (2008): *Współczesny polski onomatopeikon. Ikoniczność w języku*. Warszawa: WN PWN.
Baudouin de Courtenay, Jan (1974): *Dzieła wybrane*. Vol. 1. Warszawa: PWN.
Benni, Tytus (1905): *Beiträge zur polnischen Wortbildung*. Vol. 1: *Einführung. Produktive Personalsuffixe*. Leipzig: Stauffer.
Brodowska-Honowska, Maria (1967): *Zarys klasyfikacji polskich derywatów*. Wrocław: Ossolineum.
Burkacka, Iwona (2015): Suffix Sets in Polish De-Nominal Derivatives. In: Stela Manova (ed.), *Affix Ordering Across Languages and Frameworks*, 233–258. New York: Oxford University Press.
Burkacka, Iwona (2024): Challenges in analyzing Polish diminutives. In: Stela Manova, Laura Grestenberger and Katharina Korecky-Kröll (eds.), *Diminutives across Languages, Theoretical Frameworks and Linguistic Domains*, 231–252. Berlin/Boston: De Gruyter Mouton.
Doroszewski, Witold (1946): Kategorie słowotwórcze. *Sprawozdania TNW*. Section 1, 39: 20–42.
Doroszewski, Witold (1952): *Podstawy gramatyki polskiej*. Warszawa: PWN.
Grzegorczykowa, Renata (1972): *Zarys słowotwórstwa polskiego. Słowotwórstwo opisowe*. Warszawa: Wyd. UW.
Grzegorczykowa, Renata and Jadwiga Puzynina (1979): *Słowotwórstwo współczesnego języka polskiego. Rzeczowniki sufiksalne rodzime*. Warszawa: PWN.
GWJP = Grzegorczykowa, Renata, Roman Laskowski and Henryk Wróbel (eds.) (1998 [1984]): *Gramatyka współczesnego języka polskiego. Morfologia*. Warszawa: WN PWN.
Jadacka, Hanna (2001a): *System słowotwórczy polszczyzny (1945–2000)*. Warszawa: WN PWN.
Jadacka, Hanna (ed.) (2001b): *Słownik gniazd słowotwórczych współczesnego języka ogólnopolskiego*. Vol. 2: *Gniazda odrzeczownikowe*. Kraków: Universitas.
Kolbusz-Buda, Joanna (2012): The Morpho-Semantics of Exocentric Synthetic Compound Nouns in Polish. In: Waldemar Skrzypczak, Tomas Fojt and Slawomir Wacewicz (eds.), *Exploring Language through Contrast*, 82–103. Newcastle upon Tyne: Cambridge Scholars Publishing.
Kolbusz-Buda, Joanna (2014a): *Compounding in Polish and English: A Morpho-Semantic Analysis of Synthetic Deverbal Compound Nouns in Polish in the Light of Parallel Constructions in English*. Lublin: Wydawnictwo KUL.
Kolbusz-Buda, Joanna (2014b): Peripheral Categories in Polish Compounding. In: Katarzyna Kozak and Joanna Kolbusz-Buda (eds.), *Novel approaches in language, literature and culturel studies*, 189–213. Siedlce: Wydawnictwo IKRBL.
Kolbusz-Buda, Joanna (2019a): Dephrasal adjectives in Polish – A case of syntax-inside-morphology. *Linguistics Beyond and Within* 5: 75–89.
Kolbusz-Buda, Joanna (2019b): Synthetic Compound Adjectives in Polish – A Case of the Morphology-Syntax Interface. In: Anna Malicka-Kleparska and Maria Bloch-Trojnar (eds.), *Valency in Verbs and Verb-Related Structures*, 141–154. Berlin: Lang.
Kolbusz-Buda, Joanna (2024a): Between compounding and phrasal derivation: Polish complex nouns in *sam(o)-*. *Word Structure* 17(3): 112–133.
Kolbusz-Buda, Joanna (2024b): A Morphological Analysis of Polish Complex Nie-Nouns: A Case of a Morphosyntactic Hybrid. *Roczniki Humanistyczne* 72(7): 157–174.
Konieczna, Ewa (2012): Lexical blending in Polish: the result of the internationalisation of Slavic languages. In: Vincent Renner, François Maniez and Pierre J. L. Arnaud (eds.), *Cross-Disciplinary Perspectives on Lexical Blending*, 51–73. Berlin/Boston: De Gruyter Mouton.

Konieczna, Ewa (2020): Derivational networks in Polish. In: Lívia Körtvélyessi, Alexandra Bagasheva and Pavol Štekauer (eds.), *Derivational Networks Across Languages*, 65–74. Berlin/Boston: De Gruyter Mouton.

Kurzowa, Zofia (1976): *Złożenia imienne we współczesnym języku polskim*. Warszawa: PWN.

Laskowski, Roman and Henryk Wróbel (1964): Użycie paradygmatu w funkcji formantu słowotwórczego we współczesnej polszczyźnie. *Język Polski* 44: 214–220.

Łoś, Jan (1914): *Složnyja slova v pol'skom jazyke*. Sankt-Peterburg: Trenke i Fjusno.

Łoś, Jan (1922–27): *Gramatyka polska*. Part 2: *Słowotwórstwo*. Lwów: Ossolineum.

Małecki, Antoni (1863): *Gramatyka języka polskiego większa*. Lwów: Nakł. Autora.

Nagórko, Alicja (2025): Morphopragmatics in Slavic. In: Peter O. Müller, Susan Olsen and Franz Rainer (eds.), *Word-Formation – Semantics and Pragmatics*, 375–393. Berlin/Boston: De Gruyter Mouton.

Puzynina, Jadwiga (1969): *Nazwy czynności we współczesnym języku polskim. Słowotwórstwo, semantyka, składnia*. Warszawa: Wyd. UW.

Rozwadowski, Jan (1904): *Wortbildung und Wortbedeutung*. Heidelberg: Winter.

Skarżyński, Mirosław (ed.) (2004): *Słownik gniazd słowotwórczych współczesnego języka ogólnopolskiego*. Vol. 3: *Gniazda odczasownikowe*. Kraków: Universitas.

Szymanek, Bogdan (2010): *A Panorama of Polish Word-Formation*. Lublin: Wydawnictwo KUL.

Szymanek, Bogdan (2014): Polish singulative derivation in a cross-linguistic perspective. In: Alicja Witalisz (ed.), *From Sound to Meaning in Context: Studies in Honour of Piotr Ruszkiewicz*, 95–110. Frankfurt/M.: Lang.

Szymanek, Bogdan (2017): Compounding in Polish and the absence of phrasal compounding. In: Carola Trips and Jaklin Kornfilt (eds.), *Further investigations into the nature of phrasal compounding*, 49–79. Berlin: Language Science Press.

Waszakowa, Krystyna (2025): Foreign word-formation in Polish. In: Peter O. Müller, Susan Olsen and Franz Rainer (eds.), *Word-Formation – Language Contact and Diachrony*, 149–169. Berlin/Boston: De Gruyter Mouton.

Igor' S. Uluhanov
9 Russian

1 Introduction
2 General overview
3 Composition
4 Derivation
5 Conversion
6 Backformation
7 Reduplication
8 Blending
9 Clipping
10 Word-creation
11 References

Abstract: This article presents an outline of Russian word-formation along with the history of studies on this topic. It contains data on essential meanings conveyed by models of Russian word-formation. Word-formation is one of the most frequent means of enriching the vocabulary, even more so than lexical borrowing. The main mechanism is affixation. The type and frequency of affixes may vary with word class: while nouns tend to add suffixes, verbs are more prone to prefixation. Composition is relatively common, though characteristic only of nominal word-formation.

1 Introduction

The dawn of theoretical studies of Russian word-formation was the last quarter of the 19th century. The most eminent of these being works by J. Baudouin de Courtenay (I. A. Boduèn de Kurtenè) and his disciples. According to their conception, a distinction must be made between derivational relations in the contemporary language, on the one hand, and the actual manner in which word-formation was carried out in the past, on the other; furthermore, it is necessary to study the means of word-formation in the contemporary language from the perspective of their productivity. The necessity of discerning between synchronic and diachronic approaches to word-formation was explicitly stated by F. F. Fortunatov.

Igor' S. Uluhanov, Moscow, Russia

https://doi.org/10.1515/9783111420523-009

J. Baudouin de Courtenay and other linguists of the Kazan School developed principles for dividing words and tokens into smaller meaningful parts such as the idea of degrees of analyzability (Boduèn de Kurtenè 1912: 232). The first scholar to pose the question of the systemic character of word-formation was M. Habdank Kruszewski (N. V. Kruševskij), who argued, "[E]verything which is known in grammars under the general name of word formation, represents a mass of systems. In the huge mass of words which constitute language, these systems are not distinct enough to be noticed under superficial observation" (Kruševskij 1883: 109; English translation cited after Radwańska Williams 1993: 104). The understanding of word-formation as a system was correlated with a desire to study material and semantic relations between words sharing the same morphemes, as well as relations between morphemes inside words. The determination of such relations would contribute to the "segmentation of morphological elements of the word". Besides, Kruszewski raised an issue of classifying "varieties" of those elements, and analyzed phonetic varieties of roots, suffixes and prefixes.

Prior to the 1940s, Russian word-formation was not treated as an object of study in its own right; grammars would have little to no data on word-formation, but what there was could be found in sections on morphology. The first description of affixal types of Russian nominal word-formation was presented by V. V. Vinogradov in his *Sovremennyj russkij âzyk* [Modern Russian] (Vinogradov 1938). They were analyzed in connection with the morphological categories (gender and declension) of affixed words. Vinogradov retained this approach to word-formation in his later treatise *Russkij âzyk. Grammatičeskoe učenie o slove* [The Russian Language. The Grammatical Theory of the Word].

Studying deverbal nouns, G. O. Vinokur demonstrated several techniques of analysis: contrastive analyses of constructions conveying similar meanings and of semantic and formal restrictions on the base words, along with extralinguistic stimuli that facilitate word-formation; these methods became recurrent in papers written afterwards.

A new approach towards Russian word-formation was proposed by Vinokur (1946) in *Zametki po russkomu slovoobrazovaniû* [Notes on Russian Word-Formation]. There he formulated basic principles of synchronic word-formation analysis based on the formal and semantic correlation of a compound or derivative with a "corresponding primary stem".

In 1951 and 1952, Vinogradov published articles on connections between word-formation, grammar, and lexicology, in which he revealed peculiarities of word-formation as a specific field of study. Vinogradov (1975a [1951], 1975b [1952]) was a pioneer in presenting a systematized classification of "varieties" and "types" (in his own terms) of word-formation, his works having been sources for sections on word-formation in Volume 1 of the scholarly Russian grammar

(*Grammatika russkogo âzyka* 1952) and in *Sovremennyj russkij âzyk. Morfologiâ* [Modern Russian. Morphology] (1952), which contained a more profound description of the word-formation of nouns and adjectives (included in the corresponding sections on morphology). Yet, in these works, there was little distinction drawn between the morphology and word-formation of Russian verbs.

From the mid-1950s to present, owing to the subsequent surge of interest in word-formation, numerous studies have appeared dealing with various types of nominal and verbal word-formation as well as research into various aspects of derivational relations. These include works by Šanskij (1959), Ânko-Trinickaâ (1962), Lopatin (1977, 2007), Uluhanov (1977, 2005, 2012), Miloslavskij (1980), Manučarân (1981), Ermakova (1984), Tihonov (1985), Grigor'ev (1986), Vinogradova (1992), Zemskaâ (1992), Krongauz (1998), Kubrâkova (1999, 2004), Blinova (2010), etc.

The most explicit description of word-formation as a system of types interacting with each other can be found in *Grammatika sovremennogo russkogo literaturnogo âzyka* [A Grammar of Modern Standard Russian] (1970) and the scholarly edition of *Russkaâ grammatika* [Russian Grammar], vol. 1 (1980), which include hierarchic relations of types and classes, general and specific meanings, and morphological differences between the motivating and motivated words.

The papers published in the period from the 1960s to the 1980s posed new questions essential for the theory of word-formation as well as for the adjacent field of morphemics, including the contemporary development of Russian word-formation (in particular, the increase of analytism and agglutination in the structure of derived and compound lexemes) with its linguistic and extralinguistic origins; the correlation between derivational and morphemic analyses, problems of discerning meaningful units within words ("degrees of analyzability"); debates over non-morphemic word elements having no semantic meaning, known as "interfixes", as well as identification of morphs and morphemes; the role of morphonology in word-formation; paradigmatic and syntagmatic relations between units; and the peculiarities of word-formation in the vernacular (see Panov 1968; Zemskaâ 1973; Lopatin 1977; Uluhanov 1977; Zemskaâ, Kitajgorodskaâ and Širâev 1981; Šmelev 1982).

Intensive studies on word-formation went on throughout the following years. The investigations include, e.g., relations between synchrony and diachrony, types of motivation, functions of motivated words in texts, general rules of morphemic compatibility (Ermakova and Zemskaâ 1991; Uluhanov 2005), and stylistic resources of word-formation (Vinogradova 1992).

Lately, there has been an increasing interest in neologisms and occasional words, not only for the purpose of illustrating how productive or widespread word-formation strategies are, but also in order to find certain patterns undetectable in the regular vocabulary. These studies are concerned with the dynamic aspect of word-formation, which is seen as an activity (cf. Zemskaâ 1992). Other investigations include the understanding of motivated words, their memorization and activation.

There is also a tendency to apply cognitive approaches to theoretical problems of word-formation, found, among others, in Kubrâkova (1999, 2004), as well as to study how aspects of word-formation might reflect the Russian mentality.

Intensive research on active processes in word-formation is ongoing, aided by dictionaries of new words, such as *Novye slova i značeniâ* [New Words and Meanings] (Levašov 1997) and recent advances in neology. A wealth of new data on the tendencies of Russian word-formation typical of the late 20th and the early 21st centuries has been gathered and analyzed, covering a period of dramatic changes in society, such as democratization (active use of informal and colloquial words and means of word-formation), internationalization (a wider use of foreign morphemes, new derivatives based on loanwords), deideologization (elimination of attitude in the semantics of many motivated words), the burst of neologisms and occasional words in everyday speech and mass media; cf. Zemskaâ (1996).

New dictionaries of word-formation have appeared (cf. Tihonov 1985; Širšov 2004; Belentschikow 2015).

2 General overview

The system of Russian word-formation is essentially similar to that of other Slavic languages.

Word-formation is one of the most frequent means of enriching the vocabulary, even more so than lexical borrowing. The main mechanism is affixation, comprising prefixation, suffixation, postfixation, as well as combined techniques (prefixation + suffixation, prefixation + postfixation as well as the less active suffixation + postfixation). The type and frequency of affixes may vary with word class: while nouns tend to add suffixes, verbs are more prone to prefixation. Composition is relatively common, though characteristic only of nominal word-formation.

Most morphemes are Slavic in origin, cf. the suffixes *-nik, -čik/šik, -tel'* (personal/agent/instrument nouns), *-nij-(e), -stv-(o)* (abstract nouns); *-n(yj), -ov(yj), -sk(ij)* (relational adjectives), *pere-* 'over-, trans-; again' and others, the prefix *po-* (perfective aspect and delimitative aktionsart), and the verbal suffix *-i(t)*, etc. Yet, borrowed morphemes, including classical and neoclassical ones (of Latin and Greek origin) are also widely present, e.g., *-acij-(a)* '-ation', *-izm* '-ism', *-(t)or, de-, avia-, avto-* 'auto-', *agro-, anti-, bio-, evro-* 'euro-', *kvazi-* 'quasi-', *neo-, post-, tele-, tehno-*

'techno-', *èko-* 'eco-', *èks-* 'ex-', etc. Neoclassical elements are regularly used in forming new terminology, e.g., *avia-kompleks* 'air hub', *bio-blok* 'filter media', *bio-komp'ûter* 'biocomputer', *tele-faks* 'fax', *èko-tehnika* 'recycling equipment' (Levašov 1997). They can also be found in informal speech, cf. informal nonce words *tele-klûkva* 'ridiculous television gossip; lit. TV cranberry', *bio-trëp* 'biology-related rant' (Zemskaâ 1996: 190), *èks-muž* 'ex-husband'.

Derivation and composition differ in respect of the number of words used: in derivation, a basic unit consists of one word, whereas compounds comprise two or more. This makes composition somewhat similar to word combinations, a syntactical phenomenon. The difference between the two is that a compound, like any other word, is an inseparable unit. Many compounds may be correlated with synonymous word combinations, cf. *samolëtostroenie* 'aircraft manufacturing' – *stroenie samolëtov* 'aircraft building; lit. building aircraft-GEN.PL'; yet, there are a lot of compounds that have no such correlation, cf. *vert-o-lët* 'helicopter; lit. whirl + linking vowel (interfix) -o- + flyer', *životn-o-vod* 'stock farmer; lit. animal-o-breeder', etc.

3 Composition

3.1 Composition proper

An inherent feature of a compound is two or more radical morphemes or stems (a head and its modifier) found in one inseparable lexeme. The head is represented by a stem with grammatical affixes, effectively a lexeme, while a modifier consists of only a stem.

The radical components have a linking element (interfix) between them. Russian interfixes include *-o-* (*les-o-zagotovki* 'logging; lit. timber-storing', *angl-o-russkij* 'English-Russian', *sam-o-ustranit'sâ* 'to keep aloof; lit. self-remove'); *-u-* (*pol-u-krug* 'semi-circle', *pol-u-šerstânoj* 'half-woolen', *pol-u-zakryt'* lit. 'to half-close'); *-i-* (*doz-i-metr* 'radiation detector', *gaz-i-ficirovat'* 'to gasify, provide gas supply'), *sorv-i-golova* 'daredevil; lit. tear-off-head' (an exocentric compound); *-â-* (*seb-â-lûbie* 'selfishness; lit. self-love', *seb-â-lûbivyj* 'selfish; lit. self-loving'); *-uh-* (*dv-uh-letie* 'second anniversary; lit. two-year-ABSTR', *dv-uh-tomnyj* 'in two volumes; lit. two-volumed'); *-ëh-* (*četyr-ëh-stenok* 'four-walled cabin', *tr-ëh-ètažnyj* 'three-storied'); zero interfix (*Nov-gorod*, *agit-massovyj* 'dealing with mass propaganda'). Of these, *-o-* is the most productive interfix.

3.1.1 Nominal compounds

Determinative nominal compounds have a nominal head and a modifying component (two or more are rare) that specifies the meaning of the head. Modifiers go first, featuring nominal (*hleb-o-zavod* 'plant bakery; lit. bread-factory'), adjectival (*suh-o-frukty* 'dried fruit; lit. dry-fruit') and numeric (*dv-u-okis'* 'dioxide') stems, as well as international borrowings (*ge-o-himiâ* 'geochemistry', *mikr-o-fil'm* 'microfilm', *mon-o-rel's* 'monorail'). The modifiers' final vowel *o* is considered an interfix here (see *Russkaâ grammatika* 1980: 252).

Nominal compounds with bound heads include words such as *tekst-o-log* 'textual critic', *slavân-o-fil* 'Slavophile', *fil'm-o-teka* 'film archives, film collection'.

Copulative nominal compounds combine semantic features denoted by their components, e.g., *sever-o-zapad* 'North-West', *les-o-park* 'recreational forest; lit. forest-park'.

3.1.2 Adjectival compounds

Heads of determinative adjectival compounds are adjectives or participles, both active and passive. Modifiers, which specify the meaning of heads, are usually represented by stems of nouns (*moroz-o-stojkij* 'frostproof'), adjectives (*star-o-moskovskij* 'typical of the old Moscow; lit. old-Moscow-REL.ADJ'), numerals (*odn-o-komnatnyj* 'studio [apartment] (adj.); lit. one-room-REL.ADJ'), as well as bound components (*psevd-o-narodnyj* 'faux folk, faux vernacular; lit. pseudo-folk', *mikr-o-poristyj* 'microporous').

Copulative adjectival compounds combine the semantic features of their components, e.g., *mâso-moločnyj* 'meat and dairy [products, etc.]; lit. meat-milk-REL.ADJ', *belo-rozovyj* 'pale pink; lit. white-pink'.

3.1.3 Verbal compounds

A compound verb is always subordinative, with its head being either a notional verb (*pol-u-obnât'* 'to give a little hug; lit. half-hug, half-embrace') or a bound component *-ficirovat'* (cf. English *-(i)fy*), e.g., *radi-o-ficirovat'* 'to equip with a radio, install a radio system'. Modifying components are usually stems of nouns (*gaz-i-ficirovat'* 'to gasify, provide gas supply') or adjectives (*intens-i-ficirovat'* 'to intensify'). Two more components are *polu-* 'half' (*pol-u-ležat'* 'to recline; lit. half-lie') and *samo-* 'self' (*sam-o-vosplamenât'sâ* 'to self-ignite').

3.1.4 Adverbial compounds

The heads of adverbial compounds are adverbs or adverbial participles modified by *polu-* 'half', cf. *pol-u-temno* 'dim, scantily; lit. half-dark', *pol-u-lëža* 'in a reclining posture; lit. half-lying'.

3.2 Composition combined with suffixation

This procedure of word-formation, where neither the combination of the first two stems nor of the second stem + suffix exist as independent words, is rather productive in Russian (see also Neef 2025 on synthetic compounds in German).

3.2.1 Nominal compounds combined with suffixation

Compounds of this type consist of a modifier, a head, and a suffix. The head contains a verbal or nominal stem, e.g., *basn-o-pis-ec* 'fable writer', *starš-e-klass-nik* 'senior high school student; lit. elder-grader', respectively. The modifier of a suffixal nominal compound may be a stem of a noun (*kon'k-o-bež-ec* 'ice-skater; lit. skates-runner', *narod-o-vlast-ie* 'grass-roots democracy; lit. people-reign'), adjective (*dolg-o-ži-tel'* 'long-liver', *pust-o-slov-ie* 'battology; lit. empty-word-ABSTR', *vtor-o-kurs-nik* 'second-year college student; lit. second-courser'), pronoun (*sam-o-podava-tel'* 'self-feeder', *sam-o-vlast-'e* 'autocracy, absolute rule; lit. self-power-ABSTR'), numeral (*desât-i-bor-ec* 'decathlete; lit. ten-fight-er'), and verb (*vert-i-hvost-ka* 'flirtatious girl; lit. whirl-tail-er').

3.2.2 Adjectival compounds combined with suffixation

The heads of these compounds have either nominal stems (*prav-o-berež-nyj* 'standing at the right bank; lit. right-bank-ADJ') or verbal stems (*ogn-e-strel-nyj* lit. 'fire-shoot-ing', a component of the collocations *ognestrel'noe oružie* 'firearms', *ognestrel'naâ rana* 'gunshot wound'). The stems of the modifiers are nominal (*piŝ-e-vari-tel'-nyj* 'digestive; lit. food-digest-ing'), adjectival (*skor-o-teč-nyj* 'transient, fleeting; lit. quick-flow-ing'), numerical (*pât-i-let-nij* 'five-year-long; lit. five-year-ADJ'), and, albeit rarely, pronominal (*seb-â-lûb-ivyj* 'selfish; lit. self-lov-ing') and adverbial (*mim-o-let-nyj* 'fleeting; lit. by-fly-ing').

3.2.3 Adverbial compounds combined with suffixation

The heads of these compounds have verbal stems. Two kinds of modifiers are possible, namely the adverb *mimo* 'by, passing by' or the pronominal component *samo* 'self', e.g., *mim-o-ezd-om* 'casually driving by; lit. by by-driving', *sam-o-hod-om* 'on foot; lit. by self-walking'.

3.3 Juxtaposition

Two or more words are amalgamated without interfixes and without any alterations of their morphemic structure, e.g., *dolgo igraûŝij* 'long playing' → *dolgoigraûŝij* 'long-playing'.

Adjectival juxtapositions have adjectives and participles serving as heads, with nouns in oblique cases (*uma-lišënnyj* 'insane; lit. mind-GEN-deprived') and adverbs as modifiers (*dorogo-stoâŝij* 'expensive; lit. expensively costing', *trudnodostupnyj* 'hard-to-reach; lit. hard-accessible').

Verbal juxtapositions have verbal heads and nominal (sometimes prepositional) modifiers, e.g., *zlo-umyšlât'* 'to harbor malicious thoughts; lit. evil-intend', *za-blago-rassuditsâ* 'to think, see fit, like, come into one's head; lit. for-good-decide'.

Juxtaposition combined with suffixation can be found in nouns (*ničegonedelanie* 'idleness; lit. nothing-doing' ← *ničego ne delat'* 'to do nothing'), adjectives (*potustoronnij* 'otherworldly, weird; lit. beyond that side-ADJ' ← *po tu storonu* 'beyond; lit. on that side'), and verbs (*hristaradničat'* 'to ask alms' ← *Hrista radi* 'for Christ's sake').

4 Derivation

4.1 Denominal nouns

4.1.1 Prefixation

Denominal prefixal derivatives convey the following meanings:
a) Locative: *za-granica* 'overseas; lit. behind-border'; *pod-zagolovok* 'subheading'; *Pred-al'py* 'Prealps';
b) Temporal: *do-istoriâ* 'prehistory'; *pere-sledstvie* 'reinitialized criminal investigation'; *re-èvakuaciâ* 're-evacuation'; *posle-dejstvie* 'aftereffect'; *èks-prezident* 'ex-president';

c) Intensive: *ras-krasavec* 'very handsome man'; *sverh-čelovek* 'Nietzschean superhuman; lit. over-man'; *èkstra-klass* 'extra-class';
d) Similarity: *pod-karakul'* 'cloth similar to Astrakhan wool; lit. under-Astrakhan';
e) Supplementary: *prizvuk* 'side tone; lit. by-tone';
f) Hierarchical: *vice-prezident* 'vice-president'; *pro-rektor* 'pro-rector'; *pod-gruppa* 'subgroup'; *arhi-episkop* 'archbishop'; *nad-semejstvo* 'superfamily'; *ober-master* 'general foreman of a blast-furnace plant';
g) Comitative: *so-avtor* 'co-author';
h) Privative/negative: *bes-porâdok* 'mess, turmoil; lit. without-order'; *ne-porâdok* 'mess, minor malfunction; lit. not-order'; *dis-garmoniâ* 'disharmony'; *anti-tezis* 'antithesis'; *de-montaž* 'disassembly, dismantlement'.

4.1.2 Suffixation

Suffixal denominal nouns are subdivided into those that convey specifying or mutational meanings, and those with modifying meaning (cf. Dokulil 1962: 129–149; *Russkaâ grammatika* 1980: 183, 257). The former ones are found in lexemes as *čajnik* 'kettle, teapot' (← *čaj* 'tea'). As for the latter, the meaning of the derivative is effectively identical to that denoted by its template, differing only in one modifying feature, cf. *čajnik* 'teapot' vs. *čajnič-ek* 'little teapot; lit. teapot-DIM'.

a) Denominal nouns of specifying (mutational) meanings include:

Abstract nouns denoting status, actions, and properties, cf. *kloun-ada* 'clownery, travesty' (← *kloun* 'clown'); *gero-izm* 'heroism' (← *geroj* 'hero'); *diktatura* 'dictatorship';

Personal nouns, e.g., *mor-âk* 'sailor' (← *more* 'sea'); *desant-nik* 'paratrooper' (← *desant* 'landing, landing operation'); *vodoprovod-čik* 'plumber' (← *vodoprovod* 'water-pipe');

Inanimate nouns denoting instruments, objects, substances, e.g., *gradus-nik* 'thermometer' (← *gradus* 'degree'); *topor-iše* 'axe handle' (← *topor* 'axe'); *svin-ina* 'pork' (← *svin'â* 'pig'); *kofe-in* 'caffeine' (← *kofe* 'coffee');

Place nouns, e.g., *pepel-iše* 'site of the fire, hearth and home; lit. ash-site' (← *pepel'* 'ashes'); *korov-nik* 'cowshed' (← *korova* 'cow'); *pekar-nâ* 'bakery' (← *pekar'* 'baker').

b) Modificational meanings include:

Diminutives, e.g., *kartin-ka* 'little picture' (← *kartina*); *statu-ètka* 'statuette, figurine' (← *statuja*);

Hypocoristics, e.g., *berëz-on'ka* 'little slender birch' (← *berëza* 'birch'); *pap-ulâ* 'daddy' (← *papa*);

Diminutives/hypocoristics, cf. *hleb-ec* 'nice little loaf' (← *hleb* 'bread'); *gorod-ok* 'small town (may have a degree of approval)' (← *gorod* 'town'); *ruč-onka* 'little hand, arm (usually that of a small child)' (← *ruka*);

Diminutives with pejorative shades, e.g., *zavod-iško* 'petty factory' (← *zavod*); *komnat-ënka* 'doghole; lit. room-DIM+PEJ' (← *komnata*). Depending on the context, pejorative connotations expressed by means of diminutive and hypocoristic suffixes may vary, cf. *vremečko* (← *vremâ* 'time') in *Skaži, pridët li vremečko* … 'Tell me if that sweet time will ever come' (N. A. Nekrasov) and *Nu i vremečko nastalo, užas* 'Oh, the times we live in, they are horrible' (conversation);

Augmentatives, often with pejorative shades, e.g., *holod-ina* 'extremely cold weather' (← *holod* 'cold, chill'); *žar-iŝa* 'blazing and annoying heat' (← *žara*); *vetr-ilo* 'very strong wind' (← *vetr*);

Female persons or animals, e.g., *gero-inâ* 'heroine' (← *geroj*); *pisateľ-nica* 'lady writer' (← *pisateľ*); *medved-ica* 'female bear' (← *medved*);

Similarity, e.g., *mač-eha* 'stepmother' (← *mat'* 'mother'); *meteor-it* 'meteorite' (← *meteor*);

Non-adult beings, e.g., *volč-onok* 'wolf cub' (← *volk* 'wolf'); *zver-ënyš* 'youngling, young animal' (← *zver'* 'wild animal');

Collective nouns, e.g., *metr-až* 'footage' (← *metr* 'meter'); *rebât-nâ* 'bunch of kids' (← *rebâta* pl. of *rebenok* 'child, kid'); *berez-nâk* 'birch grove' (← *bereza* 'birch');

Singulatives, e.g., *kartofel-ina* 'single, one potato' (← *kartofeľ* 'potato(es)'); *pyl-inka* 'speck of dust' (← *pyľ* 'dust');

Stylistic modification, cf. *staruš-enciâ* 'old woman (informal, ironic), old hag' (← *staruha* 'old woman'); *Nast-ëha* (an informal and somewhat offensive derivative of *Nastâ*, a diminutive form of the female name *Anastasiâ*); *vor-ûga* 'thief (informal, offensive)' (← *vor* 'thief').

4.1.3 Circumfixation

Circumfixal denominal nouns (prefixation combined with suffixation) consist of the following classes:

Abstract nouns denoting status, actions, and properties, e.g., *a-ritm-iâ* 'arrhythmia'; *bez-vetr-ie* 'calm; lit. without-wind-ABSTR'; *bez-rabot-ica* 'unemployment; lit. without-work-ABSTR'; here also belong nouns with temporal meanings, e.g., *pere-mir-ie* 'truce; inter-peace-ABSTR'; *pred-čuvstv-ie* 'presentiment';

Nouns denoting **human beings or animals**, cf. *bes-pridan-nica* 'fortuneless young girl; lit. without-dowry-FEM.PERS'; *so-kurs-nik* 'fellow student; lit. with-course-PERS';

Inanimate nouns, e.g., *bez-rukav-ka* 'sleeveless shirt, jerkin; lit. without-sleeve-SUFF'; *pod-snež-nik* 'snowdrop; lit. under-snow-SUFF'; *anti-gripp-in* 'popular antiinfluenzal medicine; lit. anti-flu-SUFF';

Place nouns, e.g., *za-les-'e* 'lands beyond the wooded area; lit. behind-wood-SUFF'; *pod-okon-nik* 'window-sill; lit. under-window-SUFF'; *pri-gor-ok* 'hill with gentle slopes; lit. by-/near-mountain-SUFF'; *pere-les-ok* 'field woodland, grove; lit. between-forest-SUFF';

Similarity, e.g., *pa-syn-ok* 'stepson; lit. by-son-SUFF'; *po-brat-im* 'sworn brother; lit. by-brother-SUFF'; *su-glin-ok* 'clay loam, loamy soil; lit. with-clay-SUFF';

Lower degrees in hierarchies, e.g., *pod-pas-ok* 'herdboy; lit. under-pasture-AGENT';

Names of **non-adult beings**, e.g., *pod-svin-ok* 'young pig; lit. under-pig-SUFF'.

4.2 Deadjectival nouns

4.2.1 Suffixation

Suffixal deadjectival nouns are subdivided into two groups:

Abstract nouns (often combined with other meanings), e.g., *nov-izna* 'novelty' (← *novyj* 'new'); *zl-oba* 'malice' (← *zloj* 'wicked, evil'); *bystr-ota* 'quickness, swiftness' (← *bystryj* 'quick, swift'); *udal'-stvo* 'daredevilry' (← *udaloj* 'daring, bold') and **bearer of the property** expressed by the base adjective, some of them specifying this meaning. These fall into two classes: animate, e.g., *hrabr-ec* 'brave man, valiant' (← *hrabryj* 'brave'); *umn-ic-a* 'clever person' (← *umnyj* 'clever, smart, wise'); *star-uha* 'old woman' (← *staryj* 'old'); *âder-ŝik* 'nuclear physicist' (← *âdernyj* 'nuclear'), and inanimate; the latter denote physical objects or phenomena, e.g., *kupal'n-ik* 'swimsuit' (← *kupal'nyj* 'bathing'); *lečebn-ica* 'clinic, nursing home' (← *lečebnyj* 'curing, healing').

4.2.2 Circumfixation

Circumfixal deadjectival nouns are divided into those which denote qualities (*pra-zelen'* 'green paint in icon painting, blue-green colour; lit. near to-green-Ø' ← *zelënyj* 'green'; the prefix expresses an approximative meaning), and those that denote animate (*pere-star-ok* 'sb. too old for sth.; lit. too-old-SUFF' ← *staryj* 'old') and inanimate objects (*pod-berëzov-ik* 'birch boletus; lit. under-birch-SUFF' ← *berezovyj* 'birch-REL.ADJ').

4.3 Deverbal nouns

4.3.1 Suffixation

Suffixal deverbal nouns are subdivided into the following categories:

Abstract nouns (transpositions), e.g., *instrukt-až* 'instructing' (← *instruktirovať*); *risova-nie* 'drawing, sketching' (← *risovať* 'to draw'); *bor'-ba* 'struggle, strife' (← *borotsja* 'to struggle'); abstract nouns, denoting properties, abilities, e.g., *soprotivlâ-emosť* 'resistibility' (← *soprotivlâtsâ* 'to resist').

Result nouns, e.g., *carap-ina* 'scratch, abrasion' (← *carapatsâ* 'to scratch'); *obrub-ok* 'stump, stub' (← *obrubiť* 'to chop off'); *vyžim-ki* 'squeezings' (← *vyžimať* 'to squeeze');

Agent nouns, e.g., *vož-ak* 'guide, leader' (← *vodiť* 'to lead, conduct'); *tk-ač* 'weaver' (← *tkať* 'to weave'); *pobir-uška* 'beggar' (← *pobirať* 'to collect'); *klevet-nik* 'slanderer' (← *klevetať* 'to slander'); *pisa-teľ* 'writer' (← *pisať* 'to write');

Instrument nouns, e.g., *čerp-ak* 'scoop' (← *čerpať* 'to scoop'); *nosil-ki* 'stretcher' (← *nosiť* 'to bear, carry'); *predohrani-teľ* 'safety catch, fuse box; lit. preserver' (← *predohraniť* 'to preserve'); *vis-ûľka* 'pendant, hanger' (← *viseť* 'to hang');

Object/patient nouns, e.g., *paš-nâ* 'ploughland' (← *pahať* 'to plough');

Place nouns, e.g., *hrani-liŝe* 'depository' (← *hraniť* 'to keep, save'); *kuril-ka* 'smoking room' (← *kuriť* 'to smoke'); *spa-ľnâ* 'bedroom' (← *spať* 'to sleep').

4.3.2 Circumfixation

Circumfixal nouns include the following categories:

Abstract nouns, e.g., *ne-hvat-ka* 'shortage, lack; lit. not-suffice-ABSTR' (← *hvatiť* 'to suffice');

Result nouns, e.g., *o-kur-ok* 'cigarette end; lit. by-smoke-SUFF' (← *kurit* 'to smoke');

Agent nouns, e.g., *po-pryg-un* 'jumper, hopper (informal)' (← *prygať* 'to jump'); *so-ži-teľ* 'cohabitant' (← *žiť* 'to live');

Patient or experiencer, e.g., *po-smeš-iŝe* 'butt of the joke' (← *smeâtsâ* 'to laugh');

Inanimate objects/instruments, e.g., *po-grem-uška* 'rattle' (← *gremet'* 'to rattle');

Place nouns, e.g., *na-kova-l'nâ* 'anvil; lit. on-forge-PLACE'.

4.4 Denominal adjectives

4.4.1 Suffixation

Suffixal denominal adjectives consist of three classes depending on their meaning.

a) Relational adjectives express various kinds of attributes of or relations with the entities denoted by the base nouns. These relations are diverse and cannot be covered completely, for they vary with the noun the adjective modifies, as well as with the context. Cf. *moločnyj* (← *moloko* 'milk') *sup* 'milk soup, soup made of milk', *moločnoe kafe* 'milk bar; lit. milk café', *moločnyj telënok* 'vealer; lit. milk calf', etc.; *lesnoj* (← *les* 'forest, wood') *domik* 'little house in a forest', *lesnye zveri* 'forest animals', *lesnoj rajon* 'wooded area', *lesnoj plug* 'plough for woodland', *lesnye problemy* 'problems concerning the forest', etc.

The most frequently occurring meanings are material: *kož-anyj* 'leather' (adj.) (← *koža*), *kirpič-nyj* 'brick, made of bricks' (← *kirpič*), *bajk-ovyj* 'made of baize' (← *bajka*); place: *ulič-nyj* 'street' (adj.) (← *ulica*), e.g., *uličnaâ palatka* 'street booth'; *gorod-skoj* 'town, city' (adj.) (← *gorod*), cf. *gorodskie vorota* 'city gates'; purpose: *tennis-nyj* 'tennis' (adj.), e.g., *tennisnaâ raketka* 'tennis-racket'; *gruz-ovoj* 'freight' (adj.) (← *gruz*), cf. *gruzovoj avtomobil'* 'lorry, truck'; possession: *us-atyj* 'mustached' (← *usy*), *dupl-istyj* 'hollow, hollowed-out' (← *duplo*), *âd-ovityj* 'poisonous' (← *âd*); similarity: *zme-ist-yj* 'winding; lit. snake-like' (← *zmeâ*), e.g., *zmeistaâ doroga* 'winding road', *moloč-nyj* 'milky, milk-like' (← *moloko*), cf. *moločnyj tuman* 'milky fog'. In works on Russian word-formation, the latter are not traditionally regarded as qualitative adjectives, because they do not express an evaluation.

b) Qualitative adjectives, apart from the relational meaning, are used to describe or specify something, for instance, large quantity/good quality, e.g., *žir-nyj* 'fat, greasy' (← *žir*), *vkus-nyj* 'tasty' (← *vkus*); possessing the features of that which is denoted by the base noun (e.g., *intelligent-nyj* 'cultured, educated' (← *intelligent* 'intellectual' (n.)).

c) Possessive adjectives ('belonging to sb.'), e.g., *otc-ov* 'father's' (← *otec*), *dâd-in* 'uncle's' (← *dâdâ*), *lis-ij* 'of a fox' (← *lisa*).

4.4.2 Circumfixation

Adjectives of this type convey s p a t i a l (*za-les-nyj* 'located beyond the forest; lit. behind/beyond-forest-ADJ'; *pri-gorod-nyj* 'suburban; lit. by-town-ADJ'), t e m p o r a l (*pred-polët-nyj* 'preflight' (adj.)), and p r i v a t i v e / n e g a t i v e meanings (*bez-lošad-nyj* 'horseless, carless; lit. without-horse-ADJ' ← *lošad́*; *ne-vin-nyj* 'chaste, innocent; lit. not-guilt-ADJ' ← *vina*).

4.5 Deadjectival adjectives

4.5.1 Prefixation

Prefixed adjectives denote:
a) Degrees of an attribute: high (*arhi-složnyj* 'extremely difficult'; *nai-lučšij* 'the best of the best'; *super-sovremennyj* 'ultramodern'), moderate (*nebez-opasnyj* 'not entirely safe') or low degree (*nedo-razvityj* 'underdeveloped');
b) Negation: *ne-vesëlyj* 'quite sad; lit. not-joyful'; *anti-gumannyj* 'inhuman';
c) Spatial meanings: *vne-zavodskoj* 'outplant' (adj.); *za-polârnyj* 'transpolar';
d) Temporal meanings: *poza-prošlyj* 'before last; lit. beyond-past';
e) Miscellaneous, e.g., *po-dohodnyj* 'income [tax]; lit. according to-income-ADJ'; *pro-amerikanskij* 'pro-American'; *so-vinovnyj* 'correal; lit. co-guilty'.

4.5.2 Suffixation

Suffixal deadjectival adjectives may express:
a) Degree of an attribute, which may be high (*bolš-uŝ-ij* 'extremely large, huge, monstrous' ← *bol'šoj*; *gluboč-ajš-ij* 'deepest' ← *glubokij*; *poln-ëhon'k-ij* 'quite full' ← *polnyj*), moderately high (*slab-enek* 'quite weak' ← *slabyj*; *molož-av-yj* 'young-looking, youngish' ← *molodoj*), or low or subdued (*grub-ovat-yj* 'a little rude, rough' ← *grubyj*);
b) Hypocoristic meaning: *molod-en'k-ij* (← *molodoj* 'young');
c) Possession of or similarity with sth. denoted by the base (relational) adjective: *sern-istyj* 'sulphurous, containing sulphur' (← *sernyj* 'sulphur' (adj.)), *mučn-istyj* 'containing flour, flour-like' (← *mučnoj* 'flour' (adj.));
d) Stylistic shades: *prostoj* 'simple, simplistic' and its suffixed substandard counterpart *prost-eck-ij* 'simplistic'.

Sometimes suffixation serves the formal adaptation of an indeclinable borrowed adjective, e.g., *bež-ev-yj* 'beige' (← *bež* 'id.').

4.6 Deverbal adjectives

4.6.1 Suffixation

Suffixal deverbal adjectives belong to the following categories:
a) Active adjectives are represented by examples like *dežur-nyj* 'on duty' (← *dežuriť* 'to be on duty'). Adjectives in *-l-* express the meaning 'being in a state resulted from the action', e.g., *spe-l-yj* 'ripe' (← *speť* 'to ripe'). Active-modal meanings can be differentiated as follows: 'favorable for the action', e.g., *lët-nyj* 'flyable, flying' (← *leteť*), cf. *lëtnaâ pogoda* 'flyable, flying weather'; 'serving for the action', e.g., *priceľ-nyj* 'aiming, sighting' (← *priceliťsja* 'to aim'), cf. *priceľnyj teleskop* 'sighting telescope'; 'capable of (or willing to perform) the action': *gor-ûč-ij* 'combustible, inflammable' (← *goreť* 'to burn'); *rabot-âŝ-ij* 'industrious, hard-working' (← *rabotať* 'to work');
b) Passive adjectives comprise formations such as *ssyľ-nyj* 'exiled, banished' (← *ssylať* 'to exile, banish'); *var-ënyj* 'boiled, cooked' (← *variť* 'to boil'); *kry-tyj* 'tiled, covered, roofed' (← *kryť* 'to cover'). Passive-modal meaning is expressed by adjectives like *zavid-nyj* 'enviable' (← *zavideť* 'to envy'); *izmenâ-em-yj* 'changeable, variable' (← *izmenâť* 'to change'); *čit-abeľn-yj* 'readable, easy, interesting to be read' (← *čitať* 'to read'); *lom-k-ij* 'fragile, beakable, easy to break' (← *lomať* 'to break').

4.6.2 Circumfixation

These adjectives may denote qualities, characterized by the result of the action, e.g., *za-sp-ann-yj* 'sleepy, cloudy with sleep' (← *spať* 'to sleep'), the lack of the action or the lack of an affinity or ability to perform the action, e.g., *bez-vylaz-n-yj* 'never leaving the place' (← *vylezať* 'to crawl out'); *ne-smolka-em-yj* 'ceaseless' (← *smolkať* 'to grow silent'). A passive-modal meaning (in connection with negation) is expressed by adjectives like *ne-pobed-im-yj* 'invincible' (← *pobediť* 'to defeat').

4.7 Denominal verbs

4.7.1 Suffixation

The following categories can be distinguished:
a) 'to be N/behave like N': *stolâr-ničať* 'to work as a carpenter' (← *stolâr* 'carpenter');

b) 'to become N': *sirot-eť* 'to get orphaned' (← *sirota* 'orphan');
c) 'to do N': *analiz-irovať* 'to analize' (← *analiz* 'analysis');
d) 'to do sth. in a manner typical of N (e.g., a place)': *bazar-iť* 'to chat or make noise in a vulgar manner, similar to sounds of a bazaar' (← *bazar*);
e) 'to have/exhibit N': *maloduš-estvovať* 'to be faint-hearted' (← *malodušie* 'faint-heartedness');
f) 'to get/achieve N': *baryš-ničať* 'to profiteer' (← *baryšnik* 'profiteer');
g) 'to produce N/turn sth. into N': *kopn-iť* 'to stack up' (← *kopna* 'stook');
h) 'to turn into N': *kaleč-iť* 'to cripple, maim' (← *kaleka* 'cripple');
i) 'to provide with N': *masl-iť* 'to cover with oil or butter' (← *maslo* 'oil, butter');
j) 'to act with N': *boron-iť* 'to harrow' (← *borona* 'harrow');
k) 'to place/put into N': *plen-iť* 'to capture, captivate' (← *plen* 'captivity');
l) 'to remove or separate N': *potroš-iť* 'to eviscerate' (← *potroha* 'giblets');
m) 'to spend N': *noč-evať* 'to stay overnight' (← *noč* 'night').

4.7.2 Circumfixation

Circumfixal verbs (prefixation combined with suffixation) express the following meanings:
a) 'to provide sb./sth. with N/the attributes of N': *za-dym-iť* 'to blacken with smoke' (← *dym* 'smoke'), *za-bolot-iť* 'to turn into a swamp' (← *boloto* 'swamp'); *raz-zador-iť* 'to enthuse, excite, stir up' (← *zador* 'fervour, ardour');
b) 'to deprive sb./sth. of N': *obez-žir-iť* 'to degrease' (← *žir* 'grease');
c) 'to make N': *s-grud-i-ť* 'to make a heap, pile' (← *gruda* 'heap');
d) 'to act with N': *s-bolt-iť* 'to bolt';
e) 'to approach N': *pri-gub-iť* 'to take a little sip; lit. by(near)-lip-SUFF' (← *guba* 'lip');
f) 'to get covered with N': *za-mš-eť* 'to get covered with moss' (← *moh* 'moss');
g) 'to be deprived of N': *obes-pamât-eť* 'to lose memory' (← *pamât* 'memory').

Suffixation combined with postfixation:
a) 'to be/behave like N': *nevest-iť-sâ* 'to behave like a bride' (← *nevesta* 'bride');
b) 'to become N/become similar to N': *kust-iť-sâ* 'to grow like a bush' (← *kust* 'bush');
c) 'to get covered with N': *ros-iť-sâ* 'to get covered with dew' (← *rosa* 'dew');
d) 'to make N': *luč-iť-sâ* 'to radiate, emanate rays of energy (also figuratively)' (← *luč* 'ray'), and others.

4.8 Deadjectival verbs

4.8.1 Suffixation

These verbs may express the following meanings:
a) 'to be A/to be like A': *bel-eť* 'to show (up) white' (← *belyj* 'white'); *važn-ičať* 'to show off demonstrating one's (real or fictitious) importance or status' (← *važnyj* 'important');
b) 'to become A': *pročn-eť* 'to harden, become hard, firm (or harder, firmer)' (← *pročnyj* 'hard, firm');
c) 'to provide with/to make A': *raznoobraz-iť* 'to make sth. (more) diverse' (← *raznoobraznyj* 'diverse');
d) 'to perform actions characterized by A': *čast-iť* 'to do, say sth. hurriedly' (← *častyj* 'quick, rapid').

4.8.2 Circumfixation

Circumfixal verbs which combine prefixation with suffixation have the following meanings:
a) 'to become A': *o-poloum-eť* 'to go mad' (← *poloumnyj* 'mad');
b) 'to provide with/make A': *o-složn-iť* 'to complicate' (← *složnyj* 'complicated');
c) 'to deprive of A': *ras-sekret-iť* 'to reveal, disclose; lit. de-secret' (← *sekretnyj* 'secret' (adj.));
d) 'to surpass sb./sth. in manifesting A': *pere-uprâm-iť* 'to prove to be more stubborn than sb. else' (← *uprâmyj* 'stubborn').

Suffixal-postfixal verbs are represented by the following categories:
a) 'to be A': *skup-iť-sâ* 'to be stingy' (← *skupoj* 'avaricious, stingy');
b) 'to become A': *truhlâv-iť-sâ* 'to rot' (← *truhlâvyj* 'rotten').

Prefixal-suffixal-postfixal verbs, such as *o-smel-iť-sâ* 'to dare' (← *smelyj* 'courageous, bold'), *ras-šedr-iť-sâ* 'to have a fit of generosity' (← *šedryj* 'generous'), are scarce.

4.9 Deverbal verbs

4.9.1 Prefixation

Verbal prefixes express the following meanings:
a) Space/direction: *podo-jti* 'to walk towards sb./sth.' (← *idti*); *ot-bežať* 'to run away on a short distance'; *razo-slať* 'to send out';
b) Time: *za-peť* 'to begin singing'; *po-stoât'* 'to stand for a while'; *do-sideť* 'to sit out, till the end of sth.';
c) Different degrees of intensity: *vy-beliť* 'to whitewash completely'; *iz-zâbnuť* 'to get totally frozen'; *pere-sporiť kogo-l.* 'to outargue sb.'; *pere-greť* 'to overheat'; *pod-bodriť* 'to cheer up, encourage';
d) Cumulative meaning, including multiple objects or subjects of the action, e.g., *o-begať* 'to run about sth. in order to find information or remuneration; lit. to about-run'; *iz"-ezdiť* 'to travel all over, move through many places'; *pere-hvatať* 'to seize or capture everyone around (one after the other)', *pere-boleť* 'to suffer through the illness' (*vse pereboleli grippom* 'everyone had flu once'; *pereboleli mnogimi boleznâmi* '(they) suffered through many illnesses');
e) Acquisition of the object, with subsequent destruction or rendering it useless, e.g., *za-voevať* 'to conquer'; *is-pisať* 'to use sth. for writing, thereby expending it'; *za-vodiť* 'to render sb. winded or exhausted while leading them';
f) Completion or adequacy of the action, e.g., *vy-lečiť* pf. 'to cure'; *na-pisať* pf. 'to write'; *s-delať* pf. 'to do'.

Most of the base verbs are imperfective; perfective or biaspectual ones occurring rarely. On the contrary, prefixal verbs derived from them are mostly perfective, with prefixes conveying both a derivational meaning and a grammatical one, e.g., *delať* ipf. 'to do' → *pere-delať* pf. 'to do again, this time differently; lit. redo'.

4.9.2 Suffixation

Suffixal deverbal verbs contain suffixes such as *-nu-*, *-anu-*, *-iva- (-va-)*, *-a-*, *-i-*. Verbs with the suffixes *-nu-* and *-anu-* belong to the perfective aspect, while the rest are imperfective (with an exception of a small number of verbs with *-i-*, which may be perfective as well).

The suffixes *-nu-* and *-anu-* mark the s i n g l e   o c c u r r e n c e of the event or process, e.g., *du-nu-t'* 'to blow once', *maz-anu-t'* 'to daub or smear sth. with one vigorous stroke'. The suffix *-anu-* conveys additional shades of meanings such as expressiveness, intensity and abruptness, all verbs in *-anu-* being substandard and informal.

The suffix *-iva-* marks i t e r a t i v i t y, with both the base verb and the resulting verb belonging to the imperfective aspect, e.g., *vidět* 'to see' → *vidyvať* 'to see repeatedly'. They are informal or substandard, usually appearing in the past tense, i.e. *vidyval* '(he) repeatedly saw'. By adding this suffix to perfective verbs they are transformed into imperfective ones, e.g., *perepisať* pf. 'to rewrite' → *perepis-yva-ť* ipf. 'id.'. Such verbs form aspectual pairs.

The suffixes *-i-* and *-a-* are c a u s a t i v e, cf. *voskresnuť* 'to rise from the dead, resurrect' → *voskres-i-ť* 'to resurrect sb., make sb. rise from the dead'; *sesť* pf., *siděť* ipf. 'to sit' → *saž-a-ť* 'to seat, plant'.

The suffixes *-i-* and *-a-* express the meaning 'to do sth. repeatedly or in more than one direction', e.g., *bresti* 'to plod' → *brod-iť* 'to ramble'; *bežať* 'to run' → *beg-ať* 'to run up and down'.

4.9.3 Postfixation

In works on Slavic word-formation, postfixation is defined as the addition of a derivational morpheme that follows the inflectional ending. Russian postfixal verbs are derived with the reciprocal postfix *-sâ*, mostly from transitive verbs, cf. *myť* 'to wash' → *myť-sâ* 'to wash oneself'. They may denote:
a) Reciprocity proper: *umyvať-sâ* 'to wash one's hands and face, wash up';
b) Mutual reciprocity: *celovať-sâ* 'to kiss each other';
c) Absence of a patient; the action or state of being a potential agent or patient is an inherent characteristic of sb./sth.: *sobaka kusaet-sâ* 'the dog bites' (agent), *nitki plohie, rvut-sâ* 'the threads are bad, they get ripped' (patient);
d) General reciprocity; the action takes place "within" the experiencer, i.e. verbs of this kind denote physical conditions or mental states: *serdiť-sâ* 'to be angry' (← *serdiť* 'to make angry');
e) Impersonality, e.g., *hočet-sâ* 'one feels a vague desire; lit. [it] wants itself'.

Postfixation by *-sâ* is also one of the ways to denote an action similar to the passive voice, cf. *dom stroitsâ rabočimi* 'the house is being constructed by workers'.

4.9.4 Circumfixation

Circumfixal (prefixal-suffixal) deverbal verbs may be both perfective and imperfective and express s p a t i a l (*ot-blesk-ivať* 'to reflect the light') and t e m p o r a l meanings (*pri-govar-ivať* 'to accompany sth. by talking' ← *govoriť* 'to speak, talk') and different degrees of i n t e n s i t y (*pod-pah-ivať* 'to emit a slight smell' ← *pahnuť* 'to smell').

Perfective verbs of this kind contain various prefixes along with the suffixes *-nu-*, *-i-*. They express the meanings of s p a c e, e.g., *ot-kus-iť* 'to bite off', and t i m e, e.g., *vs-plak-nuť* 'to sob, weep for a little while', and serve the formation of a s p e c t u a l p a i r s, e.g., *vešať* ipf. 'to hang (tr.)' → *po-ves-iť* pf. 'id.'.

Prefixal-postfixal verbs are derived primarily from imperfective ones, although there are a few examples derived from perfective verbs, e.g., *stupiť* pf. 'to step' → *ras-stupiť-sâ* pf. 'to make room'. Such verbs are perfective and intransitive, having the following meanings:

a) Spatial: *s-bežať-sâ* 'to run to one point from different places, gather';
b) Temporal: *ot-voevať-sâ* 'to stop fighting a war, cease fighting';
c) High degree of intensity: *u-begať-sâ* 'to be exhausted by running'; reaching a high degree of intensity, e.g., *raz-goreť-sâ* 'to flare up, start burning high or steadily'; *ob"-esť-sâ* 'to feel bloated after a heavy meal' (← *esť* 'to eat');
d) Abrupt or sudden start of the action: *vz-ahať-sâ* 'to start gasping and saying "Aah"';
e) Reaching a result: *do-stučať-sâ* 'to elicit a response by knocking (at the door, etc.) for a long time';
f) Low intensity of an action aimed at relaxation or pleasure: *pro-gulâť-sâ* 'to take a walk'.

Some other meanings may be illustrated by the verbs *pri-slušať-sâ* 'to listen carefully, to strain one's ears in order to hear sb./sth.'; *pri-nûhať-sâ* 'to get used to a certain scent while smelling it'; *ot-šutiť-sâ* 'to evade a serious answer to a question by telling a joke'; *s-rabotať-sâ* 'to reach accord and understanding while cooperating with sb.'; *v-dumať-sâ* 'to think about sth. carefully, to go into the question'; *o-govoriť-sâ* 'to make a slip of the tongue' (← *govoriť* 'to speak, talk'), etc.

There is only one type of prefixal-suffixal-postfixal verbs in Russian, meaning 'to do sth. denoted by the base verb in turn', e.g., *šutiť* 'to joke' → *pere-šuč-ivať-sâ* 'to banter, chaff with each other'.

4.10 Derivation of adverbs

4.10.1 Prefixation

Prefixal adverbs express the following meanings:
a) Negation: *ne-nadolgo* 'not for long';
b) Intensification: *nai-bolee* 'most'; *pre-bol'no* 'painful indeed'; *na-strogo* 'very strictly';
c) Time: *za-svetlo* 'while it is still daytime; lit. while light', *do-nyne* 'up to this day', *po-nyne* 'id.'; *ot-nyne* 'from now on';

d) Space: *do-tuda* 'up to there, thus far', *na-skvoz* 'through (and through), throughly', *ot-tuda* 'from there', *po-vsûdu* 'everywhere';
e) Stylistic shades, e.g., *vrâd li* 'hardly ever' and its substandard variant *na-vrâd li*.

4.10.2 Suffixation

Denominal adverbs with suffixes that are homonyms of instrumental case markers (inflections) denote t i m e (*let-om* 'in summer') and m a n n e r (*šag-om* 'on foot'; *petušk-om* '(to walk) like a cockerel').

Deadjectival and deverbal adverbs denote m a n n e r, e.g., *bystr-o* 'quickly'; *tvorčesk-i* 'in a creative way'; *šut-â* 'easily, without turning a hair; lit. joking' (← *šutiť* 'to joke'); *toč-mâ* 'in a grinding way' (← *točiť* 'to grind'); *polz-kom* 'in a crouching manner, on all fours' (← *polzti* 'to creep, crawl').

Deadverbial adverbs denote a d e g r e e of an attribute (*slab-ovato* 'rather badly', *čast-en'ko* 'quite often') or additional e x p r e s s i v e n e s s / e v a l u a t i o n (*râd-kom* '(lining up) in a little row').

4.10.3 Circumfixation

Denominal adverbs express:
a) Manner: *v-pravd-u* 'indeed; lit. in truth'; *na-iznank-u* 'inside out'; *po-istin-e* 'truly; lit. by the truth';
b) Space: *na-vstreč-u* 'heading towards sth.; lit. on meeting'; *s-verh-u* 'from above', *s-pered-i* 'in front of';
c) Time: *v-načal-e* 'in the beginning'; *po-utr-u* 'in the morning'.

Deadjectival adverbs denote:
a) Manner: *po-nov-omu* 'anew'; manner + intensity: *do-bel-a* '(wiping, washing sth.) till it turns white'; *na-suh-o* '(to wipe sth.) dry';
b) Space/direction: *v-prav-o* 'rightwards';
c) Time/duration: *iz-davn-a* 'from time immemorial, at all times'; *s-molod-u* 'from one's youth; lit. since-young'.

Deverbal adverbs designate attributes somehow related to the actions denoted by the base verbs, e.g., *v-dogon-ku* 'in pursuit of' (← *dognať/dogoniť* 'to catch up (with)'); *na-raspaš-ku* 'wide open, frank' (← *raspahnuť* 'to open wide').

5 Conversion

In the grammatical tradition of Russian, certain phenomenona which are referred to as *conversion* in, for instance, the Germanic languages are considered *zero affixation* and *zero nominalization*, i.e. a transition of lexical units between word classes or word-formation types with no formally expressed derivational affixes involved. (Though sometimes seen as a class of conversion, the formation of denominal and deadjectival verbs is regarded as suffixation, see sections 4.7, 4.8.)

5.1 Nouns

5.1.1 Zero suffixation

Denominal nouns with zero suffixes convey the following meanings:

Female person (formally, gender is expressed by the inflection *-a*), e.g., *rab* 'slave' → *rab-a* 'female slave', *Aleksandr* → *Aleksandr-a*;

Human being or animal (reference to habitat or work), e.g., *riznica* 'sacristy, vestry' → *riznič-ij* 'sacristan' (with adjectival inflection);

Collectiveness, e.g., *cifra* 'figure' → *cifir'* 'figures (obsolete, ironical)'.

Deadjectival nouns with zero suffixes convey the meanings of:

Abstract nouns (*udaloj* 'valorous, reckless' → *udal'* 'reckless valor', *intimnyj* 'intimate' → *intim* 'intimate or casual relationships', *dobryj* 'good, kind-hearted' → *dobro* 'good (n.)');

Bearer of an attribute (personal and non-personal), e.g., *intellektual'nyj* 'intellectual, intelligent' → *intellektual* '(an) intellectual, person of keen intellect', *suhoj* 'dry' → *suša* 'dry land, firm ground'; this type includes place names, e.g., *komsomol'skij* 'belonging to the Young Communist League (Komsomol)' → *Komsomol'sk* (toponym).

Deverbal nouns with zero suffixes belong to the following categories:

Action nouns: *zamenât'* 'to replace' → *zamena* 'replacement', *drožať* 'to tremble, shake, quake' → *drož'* 'tremor, shake, quake', *vybirať* 'to choose, elect' → *vybory* 'elections';

Agent nouns, result nouns, and others: *balaguriť* 'to jest, crack jokes' → *balagur* 'jokester', *obžiratsâ* 'to overeat' → *obžora* 'glutton', *poslať* 'to send' → *posol* 'ambassador'; *okovať* 'to enchain, enfetter' → *okovy* 'fetters, shackles', *tesať* 'to chip (wood)' → *tës* 'thin planks', *ryť* 'to dig' → *rov* 'ditch, trench, moat', etc.

5.1.2 Zero suffixation combined with prefixation

There are few nouns of this type (prefix + stem + zero suffix) whose unprefixed part does not exist as independent noun, cf. the following examples:
  Denominal nouns: *tolk* 'sense, use' → *bes-toloč* 'mess, confusion, dimwit; lit. without-sense-Ø' (+ alternation *k/č*), *lëd* 'ice' → *na-led'* 'ice blister; lit. on-ice-Ø' (+ alternation *d/d'*).
  Deadjectival nouns denote a not completely manifested attribute, e.g., *sedoj* 'grey-haired' → *pro-sed'* 'greyish hair, pepper-and-salt hair; lit. through-grey-Ø' (+ alternation *d/d'*).
  Deverbal nouns may denote a person (*ne-dotrog-a* 'touch-me-not; lit. no-touch-INFL'), a result of an action (*doit'* 'to milk' → *u-doj* 'milk yield'), a single act (*zabegat'* 'to run' → *zabeg* 'race, round').

5.1.3 Zero suffixation combined with composition

Compounds with a verbal head + zero suffix denote a b s t r a c t n o u n s: *sen-o-kos* 'haymaking', *krug-o-vert'* 'whirl, constant flow (of events); lit. round-whirl'; p e r s o n a l n o u n s: *knig-o-lûb* 'avid reader; lit. book-lover', *odn-o-lûb* 'constant lover; lit. one-lover', *gor-e-myka* 'no-hoper' (← *gore mykat'* (idiom.) 'to lead a dog's life'); i n s t r u m e n t n o u n s: *sam-o-kat* 'kick scooter; lit. self-roller'.
  In some works on Russian word-formation, complex nouns such as *tâžel-o-ves* 'heavyweight', *os'm-i-nog/vos'm-i-nog* 'octopus; lit. eight-leg', are not regarded as exocentric compounds, but as the result of zero suffixation combined with composition (cf. analogous words containing a formally expressed suffix, as, e.g., *mnog-o-nož-k-a* 'multiped; lit. much-leg-SUFF-INFL').

5.1.4 Nominalization of adjectives

Nominalized adjectives, i.e. nouns of adjectival declension, convey the following meanings:
a) Abstract noun: *novoe* 'novelty; lit. [the] new';
b) Person: *bol'noj* 'patient; lit. ill';
c) Place: *priëmnaâ* 'waiting room, reception';
d) Part of the whole: *pâtaâ* 'a fifth';
e) Type of clothes: *štatskoe* 'plain clothes; lit. civil';
f) Collective nouns: *s"estnoe* 'eatables';

g) Units of biological taxonomy, e.g., *bobovye* 'Fabaceae; lit. fabaceous, leguminous', *sumčatye* 'marsupials; lit. pouched';
h) Names of settlements, e.g., *Otradnoe* lit. 'pleasant, gratifying';
i) Remuneration, tolls and fees, e.g., *otstupnoe* 'compensation for termination of contract' (N ← A ← N *otstup* 'withdrawal'), *sutočnye* 'payment per diem' (N ← A ← N *sutki* 'day (and night), 24 hours').

Nominalized participles have the following meanings:
a) Abstract noun: *proishodâŝee* 'current events; lit. occurring, ongoing';
b) Person: *upravlâûŝij* 'manager, adminstrator; lit. managing'.

5.2 Adjectives

Denominal adjectives with a zero suffix convey the meanings 'made of, consisting of' (e.g., *zoloto* 'gold' → *zolot-oj* 'golden'), and 'belonging to' (*otec* 'father' → *otč-ij* 'paternal, father's'), cf. section 4.4.1.

Adjectives with a zero suffix can be also derived from the comparative degree of adverbs, retaining the meaning of comparison, e.g., *men'še* 'smaller, fewer, less (adv.)' → *men'š-ij* 'smaller, lesser (adj.)'.

Deverbal adjectives express the meaning 'sb./sth. characterized by the action', e.g., *priezžať* 'to arrive (by train, air, car)' → *priezž-ij* 'newcomer, visitor'.

If motivated by cardinal numerals, the adjectives express the meaning of ordinal adjectives (often regarded as numerals), e.g., *pâť* 'five' → *pât-yj* 'fifth'.

Zero suffixation of adjectives can be combined with prefixation (*noga* 'foot, leg' → *bez-nog-ij* 'legless') or with composition (cf. *bel-o-zub-yj* 'white-toothed', *pât-i-pal-yj* 'five-fingered, five-toed', *gorb-o-nos-yj* 'hawk-nosed; lit. hump-nosed').

Adjectival compounds whose heads are ordinal adjectives denote the degree of increase or iteration, e.g., *drugoj* 'other, second' → *sam-drug* 'twice, both'. As an example of deverbal adjectival compounds with zero suffix may serve *mal-o-ezž-ij* 'little-used (path); lit. little-driven'.

5.3 Adverbs and predicative adverbs

Zero suffixation is found in the predicative adverb *žaľ* 'it's a pity' (← *žaleť* 'to feel pity').

Zero suffixation combined with prefixation is found in denominal adverbs with the meanings a) direction toward sth., e.g., *niz* 'downward direction' → *v-niz* 'down, downwards', *verh* 'upward direction' → *na-verh* 'up, upwards'; b) action accompanied by pushing or hitting sb.'s part of the body specified by the stem, e.g., *šeâ* 'neck' → *v-za-šej* 'rudely driving sb. away while hitting his neck'; c) manner, e.g., *konec* 'end' → *v-konec* 'totally, completely; lit. in-end'; in d e a d j e c - t i v a l adverbs of manner, e.g., *kosoj* 'slant' → *v-kos* 'aslant'; and in d e v e r b a l adverbs, e.g., *skakať* 'to gallop' → *v-skač* 'at a gallop', *rashvatať* 'to snap sth. up' → *na-rashvat* 'greedily; (to buy, sell, take) like hot cakes', *provernuť* 'to hustle through sth.' → *ne-v-provorot* '(to have) a full plate of work; lit. not-in-hustling through'.

6 Backformation

This strategy is based on omitting morphemes (suffixes, prefixes or the reciprocal postfix) and clipping stems (including heads of compounds). A resulting lexeme looks like a missing link that did not appear in the process of regular word-formation, its stem lacking a number of phonemes in the initial or final position. In Russian, backformation is common in occasional words.

One of the means of backformation is desuffixation, found only in denominal nouns. The most frequently clipped suffix is *-k(a)*. This may be found in oral communication and in characters' speech patterns in works of fiction, e.g., *puha* 'large cannon' (← *puška* 'cannon'), *syroega* 'huge russule' (← *syroežka* 'russule'), *lâguš* 'male frog' and *lâguha* 'big frog' (← *lâguška* 'frog'), *pivnuha* 'beerhouse' (← *pivnuška* ← *pivnaâ* 'beerhouse, bar').

Words such as *puha* and *syroega* are perceived as derivatives of *puška* and *syroežka* because of their novelty, occasional character, and stylistic markedness. Should they lose these properties, they would become original lexemes, while *puška* and *syroežka* would be widely regarded as derivatives. In fact, this is exactly what happened to the word *zont* 'umbrella, parasol'. *Zontik* 'little umbrella' was initially a generic term borrowed from (obsolete) Dutch *zonnedeck* 'sun-deck' (cf. obsolete R. *zonnedek*).

New (occasional) words may be formed by means of deprefixation and de-postfixation, i.e. by clipping the reciprocal postfix *-sâ*. The former results in occasional lexemes derived from words of the same word classes, namely verbs, nouns, adjectives, and adverbs. This kind of clipping is used to coin antonyms, e.g., *uklûžij* 'not awkward' (← *neuklûžij* 'clumsy, awkward'). Besides, it may lead to the formation of imperfective verbs from perfective ones, e.g., coll. *šlâpiť* (← *prošlâpiť* 'to miss the opportunity'). Depostfixation results in deriving transitive verbs from intransitive ones. Those verbs are generally causative, cf. *razgovoriťsâ* 'to fall into talk' and *razgovoriť* (*kogo-l.*) 'to get sb. to talk'.

7 Reduplication

Reduplication is common in Russian informal speech where it serves expressive purposes, as well as in baby-talk. It may be radical or affixal. The kind of reduplication, in which the entire word is iterated, is known as word repetition. Reduplication may be identical, nearly identical, and non-identical.

Identical radical reduplication includes:
a) Interjections and onomatopoeic expressions; many of those are extensively used in informal talk (*hi-hi!* 'tee-hee', *ha-ha!*, *ku-ku!* 'cuckoo, peek-a-boo', *bi-bi!* 'honk honk', *gav-gav!* 'bow-wow', *nâm-nâm!* 'yum yum');
b) Notional words with reduplicated radical components and diverse affixes, e.g., adverbs: *davnym-davno* 'once upon a time', *krepko-nakrepko* 'very firmly'; adjectives: *gustoj-pregustoj* 'very dense', *malo-mal'ski* 'somewhat, in the slightest degree'.

Examples of nearly identical radical reduplication are: *fokus-pokus* 'hocus-pocus', *štučki-drûčki* 'stunts, shady dealings', *figli-migli* 'tricks, shticks', *bim-bam* 'bang-bang'.

Non-identical affixal reduplication stands for synonymous, though formally different affixes appearing one after another, e.g., the diminutive/hypocoristic suffixes -*oč*-, -*k*- in *vedëročko* 'nice little bucket, pail' (← *vedro*) and *polânočka* 'lovely little glade' (← *polâna*) and thereby expressing intensification as other types of reduplication, cf. the examples to follow.

Identical word repetition, e.g., *belyj-belyj* 'very white', *tiho-tiho* 'very quietly', *šël-šël* 'was walking by (for a long while)' may be included into word-formation only if the quoted examples are seen as a peculiar kind of compounds.

Non-identical word repetition, i.e. iteration of formally different synonyms, for instance, *put'-doroga* 'way, pathway, track; lit. way-road', *druz'â-tovariŝi* 'cronies; lit. friends-comrades', does not belong to the field of word-formation, but is regarded as a topic of the syntax of word-combinations.

8 Blending

A blend has a cluster of phonemes shared by the original lexemes from which it was formed. In Russian, blending may refer to two occasional types of word-formation:

a) Pure, or interlexical, blending:
The two lexemes that are blended share a certain segment of phonemes, cf. *kamazonki* 'women working at the Kama Automobile plant' ← *Kamaz* ('automobile plant and a brand of heavy trucks') + *amazonki* 'Amazons' sharing *-amaz-*, *èruditâtko* ← *èrudit* 'erudite' + *ditâtko* 'child, kid' (often used ironically) sharing *-dit-*, *katastrojka* 'the catastrophe of Perestroika' (← *katastrofa* + *perestrojka*), *beruši* 'ear plugs' (← *beregi uši* 'keep (your) ears safe').

b) Mixed blending, or interlexical blending combined with clipping (see section 9): In this type, the stem of one, or sometimes both, of the blended lexemes is omitted (clipped); nevertheless, a string of phonemes is shared by both of the original parts. For instance, the word *steklovica* is a blend of *Steklov* (a surname) and *peredovica* 'editorial'. The latter is clipped, leaving only *-ovica*; the suffix *-ov-* is shared with the proper noun, cf. *Tak postupal Ûrij Mihajlovič Steklov […] On predpočital vmesto podobnyh nikčëmnyh peredovic stavit' neskol'ko konkretnyh zametok. Oni tak i nazyvalis' – 'steklovicy'*. [That is what Ûrij Mihajlovič Steklov did […] He preferred placing several concrete articles instead of such useless editorials. That's why they have been named 'steklovicy'.] (A. Adžubej). Cf. also *lgavda* 'lies (apparently trying to pass for the truth)' ← *lgat'* 'to tell lies' + *pravda* 'truth') (ascribed to the poet Velimir Khlebnikov).

9 Clipping

Clipping, also known as non-morphemic clipping or abbreviation-based clipping in the linguistic tradition of Russian differs from backformation in that it is not a morpheme but a semantically insignificant element that gets clipped. Clipping disregards the morphemic structure of a given word. A missing link of the derivational chain is not reconstructed.

It is final elements of stems that tend to be clipped (*spec* ← *specialist* 'specialist', *foks* ← *fokstrot* 'foxtrot'), although sometimes initial phonemes may be omitted, too (*lâsy*, a unique component of the idiom *lâsy točit'* 'to chat light-heartedly; lit. to sharpen *lâsy*' ← *balâsy* 'rail-posts, balusters'); proper names such as *Rita* ← *Margarita*, *Tina* ← *Valentina*, *Riška* ← *Iriška* (← *Irina*), or mid position (*fiziâ* ← *fizionomiâ* 'mug, physiognomy', *tubik* ← *tuberkulëznik* 'person suffering from tuberculosis', *alik* ← *alkogolik* 'alcoholic'; all colloquial or occasional).

10 Word-creation

Apart from terminology, word-creation, i.e. artificial words deliberately (not spontaneously) coined by certain authors is scarce in Russian (cf. Grigor'ev 1986 and others on word-creation in Russian poetry). Traditionally, the term *word-creation* is not restricted to nonce-words, but also includes the formation and introduction of motivated words by famous writers who have contributed to the enrichment of the Russian vocabulary.

Some widespread words were presumably coined by writers; the plausibility of such presumptions may vary. For instance, *budušnosť* (← *budušij* 'future, to come (adj.)') as an attempt to replace the Old Church Slavonic borrowing *grâdušee* 'future, things to come', *promyšlennosť* 'industry' (← *promysel* 'craft, trade, line of work, e.g., of a fisherman or artisan'), *vlûblënnosť* 'infatuation' (← *vlûblënnyj* (past particple) 'in love'), *čelovečnosť* 'humanness' (← *čelovečnyj* 'humane'), and *obŝepoleznyj* 'suitable for everyone; lit. general(ly)-useful, suitable', *dostižimyj* 'achievable' were created (although on the basis of existing words) by Nikolaj M. Karamzin and his school of thought (Vinogradov 1940: 49 f., Vinogradov 1999: 574 f.); *nigilist* 'nihilist' by Ivan S. Turgenev (Vinogradov 1999: 23), *intelligenciâ* 'intelligentsia' by Petr D. Boborykin (Vinogradov 1999: 229), *stuševaťsâ* 'to melt into the background, to turn shy; lit. to ink out' (← *tuš'*) by Fedor M. Dostoevskij, *oblomovŝina* 'stagnation, apathy similar to that of Oblomov's (the hero of the eponymous novel)' by Ivan A. Goncharov, etc.

Cases of word-creation can be found in various domains of the language and may belong to various procedures and types of word-formation described above, cf.: *zapadnizm* 'Westernism' (← *zapadnyj* 'Western'), *ziâûŝie vysoty* 'gaping heights' (← *ziâûŝaâ dyra* 'gaping hole' + the Soviet cliché *siâûŝie vysoty* 'shining heights') coined by Aleksandr A. Zinov'ev; *nofelet* (*telefon* 'telephone' in reverse; from the catchphrase in the title of *Gde nahoditsâ nofelet?* [Could you tell me where the *nofelet* is?], a Soviet comedy film). They also include medical terms or names of remedies, such as *Antihrap* 'a brand of snoring remedies; lit. antisnore', *Negrustin* 'a brand of antidepressants' (← *ne grusti* 'do not feel sad, cheer up') (Zemskaâ 2007: 190), *Dlânos* 'a brand of nose sprays' (← *dlâ nosa* 'for the nose'), etc. as well as IT terminology and slang, e.g., *proapgrejdiť* 'to upgrade', *naguglit'* 'to google', *infa* 'info', *homâk* 'home page; lit. hamster' (a pun) (Kokorina 2010: 280, 284, 286).

11 References

Ânko-Trinickaâ, Nadiâ A. (1962): *Vozvratnye glagoly v sovremennom russkom âzyke.* Moskva: Nauka.
Belentschikow, Renate (2015): Dictionaries. In: Peter O. Müller, Ingeborg Ohnheiser, Susan Olsen and Franz Rainer (eds.), *Word-Formation. An International Handbook of the Languages of Europe.* Vol. 3, 2333–2354. Berlin/Boston: De Gruyter Mouton.
Blinova, Ol'ga I. (2010): *Âvlenie motivacii slov. Leksikologičeskij aspekt.* Moskva: Librokom.
Boduèn de Kurtenè, Ivan A. [Baudouin de Courtenay, Jan] (1963 [1912]): Ob otnošenii russkogo pis'ma k russkomu âzyku. In: Ivan A. Boduèn de Kurtenè, *Izbrannye trudy po obšemu âzykoznaniû.* Vol. 2, 209–235. Moskva: Izdatel'stvo AN SSSR.
Dokulil, Miloš (1962): *Tvoření slov v češtině.* Vol. 1: *Teorie odvozování slov.* Praha: Nakladatelství Československé akademie věd.
Ermakova, Ol'ga P. (1984): *Leksičeskie značeniâ proizvodnyh slov v russkov âzyke.* Moskva: Russkij âzyk.
Ermakova, Ol'ga P. and Elena A. Zemskaâ (1991): K utočneniû otnošenij slovoobrazovatel'noj proizvodnosti. *Russian Linguistics* 15(2): 105–116.
Grammatika russkogo âzyka. Vol. 1. (1952): Moskva: Izdatel'stvo AN SSSR.
Grammatika sovremennogo russkogo literaturnogo âzyka (1970): Moskva: Nauka.
Grigor'ev, Viktor P. (1986): *Slovotvorčestvo i smežnye problemy âzyka poèta.* Moskva: Nauka.
Kagan, Olga and Silva Nurmio (2024): Diminutive or singulative? The suffixes -in and -k in Russian. In: Stela Manova, Laura Grestenberger and Katharina Korecky-Kröll (eds.), *Diminutives across Languages, Theoretical Frameworks and Linguistic Domains,* 65–88. Berlin/Boston: De Gruyter Mouton.
Kakorina, Elena V. (2010): Âzyk internet-kommunikacii. In: Leonid P. Krysin (ed.), *Sovremennyj russkij âzyk. Sistema – norma – uzus,* 273–340. Moskva: Âzyki slavânskoj kul'tury.
Krongauz, Maksim A. (1998): *Pristavki i glagoly v russkom âzyke. Semantičeskaâ grammatika.* Moskva: Âzyki russkoj kul'tury.
Kruševskij, Nikolaj V. [Kruszewski, Mikołaj] (1883): Očerk nauki o âzyke. In: *Izvestiâ i učënye zapiski Imperatorskogo Kazanskogo universiteta* 19. (Appendix 148 pp.).
Kubrâkova, Elena S. (1999): Kognitivnye aspekty slovoobrazovaniâ i svâzannye s nimi pravila inferencii (semantičeskogo vyvoda). In: Reinhard Ibler and Renate Belentschikow (eds.), *Novye puti izučeniâ slovoobrazovaniâ slavânskih âzykov,* 23–36. Frankfurt/M.: Lang.
Kubrâkova, Elena S. (2004): *Âzyk i znanie.* Moskva: Âzyki slavânskoj kul'tury.
Levašov, Evgenij A. (ed.) (1997): *Novye slova i značeniâ. Slovar'-spravočnik po materialam pressy i literatury 80-h godov.* Sankt Peterburg: Dmitrij Bulanin.
Lopatin, Vladimir V. (1977): *Russkaâ slovoobrazovatel'naâ morfemika.* Moskva: Nauka.
Lopatin, Vladimir V. (2007): *Mnogogrannoe russkoe slovo.* Moskva: Azbukovnik.
Miloslavskij, Igor' G. (1980): *Voprosy slovoobrazovatel'nogo sinteza.* Moskva: MGU.
Manučarân, Ruben S. (1981): *Slovoobrazovatel'nye značeniâ i formy v russkom i armânskom âzykah.* Erevan: Lujs.
Neef, Martin (2025): Synthetic compounds in German. In: Peter O. Müller, Susan Olsen and Franz Rainer (eds.), *Word-Formation – Special Patterns and Restrictions,* 71–84. Berlin/Boston: De Gruyter Mouton.
Panov, Mihail V. (1968): *Slovoobrazovanie sovremennogo russkogo literaturnogo âzyka.* Moskva: Nauka.
Radwańska Williams, Joanna (1993): *A Paradigm Lost. The Linguistic Theory of Mikołaj Kruszewski.* Amsterdam/Philadelphia: Benjamins.
Russkaâ grammatika. Vol. 1. (1980): Moskva: Nauka.

Šanskij, Nikolaj M. (1959): *Očerki po russkomu slovoobrazovaniû i leksikologii*. Moskva: Učpedgiz.
Shevchenko, Viacheslav and Slávka Tomaščíková (2020): Derivational networks in Russian. In: Lívia Körtvélyessi, Alexandra Bagasheva and Pavol Štekauer (eds.), *Derivational Networks Across Languages*, 75–84. Berlin/Boston: De Gruyter Mouton.
Širšov, Ivan A. (2004): *Tolkovyj slovoobrazovateľnyj slovar' russkogo âzyka*. Moskva: AST; Astreľ; Russkie slovari; Ermak.
Sitchinava, Dmitri (2015): Closing suffix patterns in Russian. In: Peter O. Müller, Ingeborg Ohnheiser, Susan Olsen and Franz Rainer (eds.), *Word-Formation. An International Handbook of the Languages of Europe*. Vol. 2, 972–983. Berlin/Boston: De Gruyter Mouton.
Šmelev, Dmitrij N. (ed.) (1981): *Sposoby nominacii v sovremennom russkom âzyke*. Moskva: Nauka.
Tihonov, Aleksej N. (1985): *Slovoobrazovateľnyj slovar' russkogo âzyka*. Moskva: Russkij âzyk.
Uluhanov, Igor' S. (1977): *Slovoobrazovateľnaâ semantika v russkom âzyke i principy ee opisaniâ*. Moskva: Nauka.
Uluhanov, Igor' S. (2005): *Motivaciâ v slovoobrazovateľnoj sisteme russkogo âzyka*. Moskva: Azbukovnik.
Uluhanov, Igor' S. (2012): *Slovoobrazovanie. Morfonologiâ. Leksikologiâ*. Moskva: Logos.
Vinogradov, Viktor V. (1938): *Sovremennyj russkij âzyk*. Moskva: Učpedgiz.
Vinogradov, Viktor V. (1947): *Russkij âzyk. Grammatičeskoe učenie o slove*. Moskva: Učpedgiz.
Vinogradov, Viktor V. (1952): *Sovremennyj russkij âzyk. Morfologiâ*. Moskva: Izdateľstvo MGU.
Vinogradov, Viktor V. (1975a [1951]): Voprosy sovremennogo russkogo slovoobrazovaniâ. In: Viktor V. Vinogradov, *Izbrannye trudy. Issledovaniâ po russkoj grammatike*, 155–165. Moskva: Nauka.
Vinogradov, Viktor V. (1975b [1952]): Slovoobrazovanie v ego otnošenii k grammatike i leksikologii (Na materiale russkogo i rodstvennyh âzykov). In: Viktor V. Vinogradov, *Izbrannye trudy. Issledovaniâ po russkoj grammatike*, 166–220. Moskva: Nauka.
Vinogradov, Viktor V. (1978 [1940]): Osnovnye ètapy istorii russkogo âzyka. In: Vikor V. Vinogradov, *Izbrannye trudy. Istoriâ russkogo literaturnogo âzyka*, 10–64. Moskva: Nauka.
Vinogradov, Viktor V. (1999): *Istoriâ slov*. Moskva: IRÂ im. V. V. Vinogradova.
Vinogradova, Valentina N. (1992): *Stilistika russkogo slovoobrazovaniâ*. Frankfurt/M.: Lang.
Vinokur, Grigorij O. (1959 [1946]): Zametki po russkomu slovoobrazovaniû. In: Grigorij O. Vinokur, *Izbrannye raboty po russkomu âzyku*, 419–442. Moskva: Učpedgiz.
Zemskaâ, Elena A. (1973): *Sovremennyj russkij âzyk. Slovoobrazovanie*. Moskva: Prosvešenie.
Zemskaâ, Elena A. (1992): *Slovoobrazovanie kak deâteľnosť*. Moskva: Nauka.
Zemskaâ, Elena A. (ed.) (1996): *Russkij âzyk konca XX stoletiâ (1985–1995)*. Moskva: Âzyki russkoj kuľtury.
Zemskaâ, Elena A. (2007): Igrovoe slovoobrazovanie. In: Elena A. Zemskaâ and Mariâ L. Kalenčuk (eds.), *Âzyk v dviženii. K 70-letiû L. P. Krysina*, 186–193. Moskva: Âzyki slavânskoj kuľtury.
Zemskaâ, Elena A., Margarita V. Kitajgorodskaâ and Evgenij N. Širâev (1981): *Russkaâ razgovornaâ reč'. Obšie voprosy. Slovoobrazovanie. Sintaksis*. Moskva: Nauka.

Cvetanka Avramova and Julia Baltova
10 Bulgarian

1   Introduction
2   General overview
3   Composition
4   Derivation
5   Conversion
6   Minor processes of word-formation
7   Conclusion
8   References

Abstract: The present article gives an overview of word-formation in present-day standard Bulgarian. It describes the main means and patterns of producing new words laying the emphasis on derivation (affixation in the first place) and composition, which are central in the word-formation system of Bulgarian.

1 Introduction

Bulgarian belongs to the Southern branch of the Slavic language family. Old Bulgarian (Old Church Slavonic) has been documented historically since the 9th/10th century, as it served as basis for translations of Greek sacred texts during the Christianization of the Slavs. Especially in the Middle Bulgarian period, the language underwent significant changes, e.g., the elimination of case declension, the development of a suffixed definite article, and the demise of the infinitive, but it preserved the rich verb system and the characteristic features of an inflectional language in word-formation. Contemporary Bulgarian is the official language of Bulgaria (7.3 million inhabitants), one of the official languages of the EU and an acknowledged minority language in Serbia, Romania, and the Ukraine.

The earliest information on the main ways of forming new words in Bulgarian can be found in Petăr Beron (1824). Later grammars, up to the end of the 19th century, offer no separate treatment of the problems of word-formation. Nevertheless, fragments of word-formation analysis can be discovered in paragraphs characterizing the formal structure of words which are divided into "pri-

Cvetanka Avramova, Sofia, Bulgaria
Julia Baltova, Sofia, Bulgaria

mary" and "derivative" words. Derivatives are further subdivided into "simple" (i.e. words formed by affixation) and "compound" words. The latter can be formed out of "primary" or "simple" words (for historical linguistic terminology see also Kaltz and Leclercq 2025 on word-formation research from its beginnings to the 19th century).

The grammars appearing in the 19th and early 20th century, mainly pedagogical works, register and describe complex words with a view to their structure and constituent parts (roots, affixes, linking morphemes), which is the practice of European and Russian linguistic scholarship of the time.

The 1930's and 1940's saw the first attempts at a scientific explanation of word-formation phenomena and a characterization of the means of forming new words in Bulgarian. Word-formation is beginning to attract special attention and is given more space in linguistic publications. Relying on the achievements of comparative historical linguistics, Bulgarian scholars treat word-formation either diachronically or synchronically, but always as part of the morphology of one or another part of speech (Mladenov 1929; Conev 1934; Teodorov-Balan 1940; Andrejčin 1944).

Interest in word-formation grew stronger among Bulgarian linguists in the second half of the 20th century, which was characteristic of Slavic linguistics in general during that period. The first Slavic linguistic studies that were aimed at a theoretical interpretation of the meaning and form of complex words and offered models for their description were published in the 1940's and they had their impact on Bulgarian linguistics as well. The 1950's were a crucial period for the development of a new attitude towards word-formation in Slavic and Bulgarian linguistics.

During this time Ivan Lekov's monograph *Slovoobrazovatelni sklonnosti na slavjanskite ezici* [Word-Formation Propensities of the Slavic Languages] (Lekov 1958) was published. Its contribution to Bulgarian and Slavic word-formation studies is twofold:

a) t h e o r e t i c a l, mainly concerned with the place of word-formation among the other levels of language, the function of word-formation formants, the criteria and models for the comprehensive description and classification of complex words in the Slavic languages. Lekov regards word-formation as a specific area, which should be attributed its own independent status, without at the same time denying its connections with lexicology and grammar (Lekov 1958: 3). In his opinion, the semantic function of the formant is a criterion of paramount importance for the classification of derivatives, hence his idea of a model allowing the simultaneous description of word-formation in all the Slavic languages;

b) a p p l i e d, connected with the description of the distribution of formants in the Slavic languages, their origin and spread and their word-formational activity.

In his monograph, Lekov follows the main principles of structuralism, which had already become dominant in European linguistics. The monograph lays the foundations for the contrastive study of Bulgarian word-formation and other languages, thus establishing a tradition which persists to this day (cf. Igov 1967; Dejanova et al. 1980; Molhova 1986: 115–182; Avramova 2003; Maldjieva 2009; Kolarova 2010 and others).

The 1960's are characterized by intensive all-round research into Bulgarian word-formation. This includes the various means and patterns of word-formation in the standard language and dialects, the analysis of complex words in Old Bulgarian (Old Slavonic), the development of the word-formation system during the National Revival period (19th century), etc. Researchers make use of a number of approaches: Dokulil's onomasiological theory as well as that of the Russian word-formation school, Doroszewski's logico-syntactic theory, the principles of generative grammar and of case grammar, the predicate-argument structure of semantic syntax, etc. The direction of the analysis is from form to meaning or (more and more often in recent decades) from meaning to form. What unites the majority of these studies is the acceptance of the relative independence of word-formation as a linguistic level. At the same time some authors continue to treat word-formation as part of morphology (e.g., Stojanov 1964, 1983; Georgieva 1967). An attempt to give an overview of Bulgarian word-formation with respect to the word-formation structure and meaning of complex words is Radeva's monograph (Radeva 2007).

Bulgarian word-formation has also been approached from the viewpoint of the theory of naming. The main tendencies in the word-formation system of the standard language from that perspective are presented in Murdarov (1983). Murdarov believes that word-formation, which in his opinion includes phrasal naming units, serves the lexicon of the language, making possible its enrichment especially in periods of dynamic political, economic and social change. In a functional perspective the author shows that word-formation processes follow the schema "genus – species – subspecies", which determines the activity of each of the means of word-formation in the production of new words. On the basis of mainly terminological data Murdarov reaches the conclusion that in the investigated period phrasal word-formation is the most active means of word-formation in the standard language.

In the 1970's and 1980's a synchronic lexicographic description is carried out with the help of so-called word-formation nests, i.e. word families, cf. Ilieva et al. (1999: 6–8). See also Belentschikow (2015) on dictionaries.

Bulgarian linguists have been continually observing and interpreting trends in the development of Slavic word-formation at the end of the 20th and the beginning of the 21st century. Central among such innovations is internationalization (Selimski 2003; Avramova 2003; Georgieva 2007). Such investigations focus on the enrichment of the means of word-formation, the expansion and activation of composition, the establishment of new types and patterns, the changing attitude towards foreign affixes, etc.

Historical studies by Bulgarian and foreign authors reveal, from a synchronic or diachronic point of view, the development of the word-formation system from the 9th to the 19th century (Szymański 1968; Baltova 1978; Selimski 1983, 1984; Cejtlin 1986; Mostrova 2005). Word-formation in the Bulgarian dialects has also been the object of diachronic and synchronic analysis (Holiolčev 1965; Kočev 1971; Troeva 1988).

An important contribution to the study of Bulgarian word-formation has been made by a number of outstanding foreign Bulgarianists (T. Szymański 1977; Herej-Szymańska 1978; Maslov 1982; Scatton 1984: 245–310, etc.).

2 General overview

The specific historical development of Bulgarian from a synthetic to an analytical nominal structure, which (together with Macedonian) is unique within the Slavic language family, has not affected the stability of the Bulgarian word-formation system. During both periods in the development of the literary language – Old Bulgarian and Modern Bulgarian – there has been no conflict between the inherited Old Slavonic means of word-formation and the innovations resulting from the influence of foreign (Balkan, Slavic and West European) systems with which Bulgarian has been in direct or indirect contact. Enriched throughout its thousand-year-old history, the word-formation system of Bulgarian, especially in its literary form, has preserved its characteristic features: well-developed affixation and expanding composition (see sections 3 and 4). Changes during the various sub-periods of development are mainly connected with the intensification of some of the processes, the activation and increased productivity of individual means, models and patterns. This results in shifts of some entities (e.g., individual formants or some patterns of composition) from the centre to the periphery and the other way round, without affecting the basic features of the centre.

The main means of producing new words in Bulgarian is affixation (see section 4), which forms lexical items with the help of native and borrowed formants. Prefixation is most common in verbal derivation (see section 4.8). During the recent decades, however, prefixation has been expanding and is becoming more active in the nominal system as well, a process characteristic of all Slavic and European languages. The inventory is mainly enriched with foreign formants labelled as "neoclassical" in European linguistics (*a-, anti-, de-, eks-* 'ex-', *kontra-, re-*, etc.). The foreign formants make their way into Bulgarian through ready-made lexical borrowings. Suffixation is more typical of nominal word-formation (see sections 4.1 and 4.2) and less prominent in the formation of verbs. The use of borrowed formants often leads to shifts in the distribution of word-formation means. There is a group of formants which are labelled "affixoids" in Bulgarian works on word-formation. Their status is not yet well-defined theoretically and we include them here under affixation. Some affixoids (*eko-* 'eco-', *avto-* 'auto-', *geo-, vice-*, etc.) are sometimes treated as constituents of compounds. This blurs the boundaries between affixation and composition. According to a common definition of a compound, however, its components correlate in form and meaning with items which function freely as lexical units. Since there is no such correlation here, the products of "affixoidization" should be treated as affixal formations and the respective formants as affixoids, i.e. as belonging to affixation. (Some examples of "suffixoids" are *-log, -fil* '-phile', *-fen* '-fan', *-gejt* '-gate'.)

Another central means of word-formation, characteristic mainly of the literary language already in Old Bulgarian, is composition (see section 3). In the translation of liturgical texts from Greek, whole patterns have been borrowed which are today considered classical in the Slavic languages (see also Mengel 2025 on historical word-formation in Slavic). Composition is established as an active means of word-formation (Cejtlin 1986). Bulgarian compounds follow the classical patterns with a linking vowel (mostly -*o*-) between the components of determinative compounds (*ključodăržatel* 'key-holder', *pătevoditel* 'guide book; lit. way-guide'), coordinative compounds (*pokupko-prodažba* 'buying and selling', *železo-beton* 'reinforced concrete') or "synthetic compounds" (*vodonosec* 'water-carrier', *prahosmukačka* 'vacuum cleaner; lit. dust-sucker', *vlastoljubiv* 'power-loving', *rus-okos* 'fair-haired', etc.). The number of compounds containing two nominal units without a linking vowel (*stažant-advokat* 'trainee lawyer', *biznessrešta* 'business meeting', *skipista* 'ski piste', etc.; see section 3) has been constantly growing during the past decades, mainly under the influence of English (earlier also under the influence of German). We can also include under composition the so-called clipped compounds, albeit with reservation. Here the clipped component coincides with the root of the respective adjective (*specakcija* 'special action', *socsistema* 'socialist system'), or both components are clipped (*detmag* 'children's store' ← *detski magazin*). This model is relatively new for the Bulgarian word-formation system.

Other means of word-formation are poorly represented or else have completely lost their productivity. Some of the most recent patterns are limited to slang and various jargons and therefore remain outside the system of the Bulgarian standard language.

3 Composition

3.1 Introductory notes

After affixation, composition is the second most important means of Bulgarian word-formation (Andrejčin 1944; Radewa 1955; Stojanov 1964, 1983; Georgieva 1967). It is mainly characteristic of the literary language. The establishment and expansion of composition goes back to the Old Bulgarian period and is connected with the direct translation from the Greek of the liturgical texts for the needs of the Christian religion in Bulgaria. According to Cejtlin (1986: 207), every sixteenth complex word in the Old Bulgarian manuscripts of the 10th–11th century is a compound. The functions of composition subsided during the five-century long Ottoman domination: Bulgarian was not the official language and divine service was carried out in Greek. It was only in the 19th century that composition resumed its place once again to meet the needs of denomination as part of the establishment of the Modern Bulgarian literary language and the restructuring of the lexical and word-formation system. This secured the continuity in the historical development of the Bulgarian word-formation system (Baltova 1978). In the end of the 19th and the first half of the 20th century composition reduced its activity at the expense of affixation. Today the activity of composition is again on the increase, and new patterns of composition are becoming established mainly under the influence of English. In this way composition in present-day literary Bulgarian combines traditional (classical) Slavonic-Bulgarian models with innovative ones, typical of West European languages.

Slavic linguistics recognizes two types of compounds: compounds proper and "mergers" (Bulg. *srastvanija*), a term that corresponds to "univerbation" in the terminology of West European linguistics.

Compounds proper contain two bases or roots of full lexical items. They are formed after a pattern and are the result of a synchronic word-formation process (*komin-o-čistač* 'chimney sweep', *čušk-o-pek* 'pepper-roaster', *hleb-o-proizvodstvo* 'bread production', *dăžd-o-nosen* 'rain-bringing', *bingozala* 'bingo hall', etc.). The two components are connected by the linking vowels (interfixes) *o* or *e* (*beton-o-bărkačka* 'concrete mixer', *sin-e-ok* 'blue-eyed'), rarely *u* or *i* (*dv-u-kolka* 'two-wheeler', *pet-i-letka* 'five-year period') or else directly (*ofis-mebeli* 'office furniture', *fitnes-zala* 'fitness centre', *băndži-skok* 'bungee jump').

"Mergers", according to the interpretation accepted in Slavic linguistics, are formations resulting from the merging of the components of a phrase without any formal change or change of the word order. They are very rare in Bulgarian. The problem of the status of the lexemes containing a "quasi interfix" remains unresolved (*visoko-produktiven* 'highly productive', *večno-živ* 'forever living', *četi-ri-krak* 'four-legged', *stărči-opaška* 'wagtail', etc.). According to some linguists these formations are mergers of two independent units (adverb in *-o* + adjective, numeral in *-i* + noun, 3rd pers. sg. in *-i* in the verbal component of the exocentric compound). In our opinion, the establishment of patterns for their formation and the reproduction of their formal structure is sufficient reason to treat them as true compounds.

3.2 Nominal composition

3.2.1 Determinative compounds

In Bulgarian linguistics, the description of determinative compounds is based on the distinction between verb-centered and noun-centered compounds.

The components of verb-centered compounds are connected by a linking vowel (an interfix or a "quasi interfix", cf. section 3.1). The part of speech categorization of the compound is marked by a suffix added to the second component (*kart-o-igr-ač* 'card-player') or by a change of paradigm (*sneg-o-rin-Ø* 'snowplough' ← *rine snjag* 'to shovel snow'). (As Bulgarian has no infinitive, the motivating verb is given in the 3rd pers. sg. pres., where the present stem is obvious; otherwise, the citation form is the 1st pers. sg. pres.; the English equivalent is given in the infinitive.) The most common suffixes are: *-ec, -tel, -ač, -ačk-, -lk-, -ij-*, etc. The resulting compounds belong to the categories of agent nouns (*kominočistač* 'chimney sweep'), instrument nouns (*tărnokop* 'pickaxe; lit. thorn-dig'), place nouns (*korabostroitelnica* 'shipyard'), and action nouns (*počvonapojavane* 'soil irrigation').

The formations can be regarded as synthetic compounds where neither the combination of the first two nor of the last two elements exists as free word (cf. Neef 2025 on synthetic compounds in German). The compounds may be of the following structure:

N+V+SUFF: *orden-o-nos-ec* 'medal-holder; lit. medal-*o*-wear-AGENT', *păt-e-voditel* 'guide book; lit. way-*o*-guide-INSTR', *prah-o-smuk-ačka* 'vacuum cleaner; lit. dust-*o*-suck-INSTR';

Adv+V+SUFF: *visok-o-govori-tel* 'loudspeaker', *bărz-o-hod* 'fast-walker' (in this case, the linking vowel is a "quasi interfix");

Pron+V+SUFF: *vs-e-dărži-tel* 'the Omnipotent; lit. all-hold-AGENT', *sam-o-nastanjava-ne* 'squatting; lit. self-accomodation'.

The following V+N compounds are exocentric: *lapni-šaran* 'ninny; lit. gobble-carp', *razvej-prah* 'spendthrift; lit. scatter-dust'. This model, also occurring in other Slavic languages, is not productive in present-day Bulgarian. The first component is homonymous with the imperative form of the motivating verb. These compounds are more common in dialects and occasionally occur as place names (*Čujpetlovo* lit. 'listen to the cock'). In the literary language, they are stylistically marked and have a pejorative connotation.

Noun-centered compounds have the following structures:
a) Root compounds (N+N)
Here belong formations like *gost-režis'or* 'guest producer', *biznesdama* 'business lady', *fitnesklub* 'fitness club', *golfigrište* 'golf course', *duš-baterija* 'shower faucet', *kafemašina* 'coffee machine'. The compounds denoting places and instruments, mostly reveal a purposive connection between the components. This pattern whose components are identical in form with freely functioning nouns and linked without an interfix, is comparatively new to Bulgarian and other Slavic languages; it is influenced by English, and partially by German borrowings. At present this is the most active way of producing compounds in Bulgarian. The main stress usually falls on the first component (*fitneszăla* 'fitness centre'). The paraphrases revealing the semantics of the complex item provide a necessary objective criterion for clarifying the status of the first component, which is by some linguists regarded as a non-inflected (so-called analytical) adjective (see also Ohnheiser 2025 on compounds and multi-word expressions in Slavic, section 4.3). – Some compounds are exocentric, e.g., *pticečovka* 'duck-billed platypus; lit. bird-beak'.

b) Synthetic compounds
The components can be connected with a linking vowel or a "quasi interfix". The part of speech of the compound is marked by a suffix (*părv-o-klas-nik* 'first-grader'). The most frequently used suffixes are *-nik*, *-ec*, *-ij-*, *-k-*, etc. deriving personal, non-personal, and abstract nouns, e.g.,

A+N+SUFF: *drug-o-sel-ec* 'person from another village' (← *drugo selo* 'other village'), *prav-o-ăgăl-nik* 'rectangle' (← *prav ăgăl* 'right angle'), *păln-o-lun-ie* 'full moon' (← *pălna luna*); exocentric: *červen-o-šij-ka* 'redbreast' (← *červena šija* 'red front neck');

Num+N+SUFF: *părv-o-klas-nik* 'first-grader' (← *părvi klas* 'first grade'), *dv-u-ezič-ie* 'bilingualism' (← *dva ezika* 'two languages').

c) Appositive compounds
Nouns in which the determining component is in second position also show a subordinative relationship between the components (Baltova 1985). This is a relatively new type in Bulgarian word-formation and has a low productivity. It is typical of the literary language. The inflection of the second component only and the hyphenated spelling are an indication of its single-word character (*vagon-restorantăt* 'the dining car; lit. car-INDEF.SG-restaurant-DEF.SG'), *kandidat-studenti* 'university applicants; lit. applicant-INDEF.SG-student-INDEF.PL', *stažant-advokatite* 'the trainee lawyers; lit. trainee-INDEF.SG-lawyer-DEF.PL').

3.2.2 Coordinative compounds

The components of coordinative compounds can be united by a linking vowel and/or by hyphenated spelling, e.g., *želez-o-beton* 'reinforced concrete; lit. iron-concrete', *pokupk-o-prodažba* 'buying and selling' (← *pokupk-a + prodažba*), *Avstro-Ungarija* 'Austria-Hungary', *kasier-domakin* 'treasurer and stewart'). Formations with suffixes like *den-o-nošt-ie* 'twenty four hours' (← *den* 'day' + *nošt* 'night' + suffix -*ie*) are also regarded as coordinative compounds.

3.3 Adjectival composition

The formation of compound adjectives is an active process in present-day Bulgarian (Perniška 1980; Dejanova et al. 1980). The components are linked with or without an interfix (*igl-o-list-en* 'coniferous; lit. needle-*o*-leaf-SUFF', *sedem-strun-en* 'seven-string') or with a "quasi interfix" (*vsek-i-dnev-en* 'everyday'). The second component is shaped by a suffix (*pet-o-ăgal-en* 'pentagonal', *rus-o-kos-Ø* 'fair-haired'). The most common suffixes are -*en*- and -*iv*-.

Adjectives of the type *bjalo-zeleno-červen* 'white-green-red' are rare and not typical of Bulgarian.

3.3.1 Determinative adjectival compounds

Compounds with an adjectival head are of the following types.

Compounds whose second component is identical with an autonomous adjective:
N+A: *pravd-o-podoben* 'plausible; lit: truth-similar';
A+A: *svetl-o-zelen* 'light green', *tămn-o-červen* 'dark red';
A[<N]+A: *nebesn-o-sin* 'sky-blue', *snežn-o-bjal* 'snow-white';
Adv+A: *dălg-o-tărpeliv* 'long-enduring';
Pron+A: *vs-e-mogăšt* 'omnipotent'.

Synthetic compound adjectives:
A+N+SUFF: *širok-o-list-en* 'broad-leaved', *bel-o-snež-en* 'snow-white; lit. white-*o*-snow-SUFF', *drebn-o-zărn-est* 'fine-grained';
Num+N+SUFF: *edn-o-răk* 'one-armed; lit. one-*o*-arm-Ø', *tri-ăgăl-en* 'triangular', *trista-god-išen* 'three-hundred-year-old; lit. three-hundred-year-SUFF';
Pron+N+SUFF: *onzi-den-šen* 'of the day before yesterday; lit. before yesterday-SUFF';
N+N+SUFF: *igl-o-list-en* 'coniferous; lit. needle-*o*-leaf-SUFF', *konus-o-vid-en* 'cone-shaped', *kozl-o-nog* 'goat-legged; lit. goat-*o*-leg-Ø';
V+N+SUFF: *vărt-o-glav* 'muddle-headed; lit. turn-*o*-head-Ø'. These are exocentric adjectives. The model is not productive in present-day Bulgarian;
N+V+SUFF: *mes-o-jad-en* 'meat-eating', *tovar-o-podem-en* 'hoisting; lit. load-hoist-SUFF', *ogn-e-diš-ašt* 'fire-spitting', *stud-o-ustoj-čiv* 'cold-resistant';
Pron+V+SUFF: *samo-hval-en* 'boasting; lit. self-praise-SUFF', *sebe-ljub-iv* 'self-loving';
Adv+V+SUFF: *gore-spomen-at* 'above-mentioned', *dolu-podpis-an* 'undersigned'.

3.3.2 Coordinative adjectival compounds

The components of the corresponding compounds are combined with a linking vowel, e.g., *gluh-o-njam* 'deaf-and-dumb', *zemn-o-voden* 'amphibian; lit. earth-ADJ-*o*-water-ADJ', *agrarn-o-promišlen* 'agro-industrial; lit. agrarian-*o*-industrial', *anglijsk-o-bălgarski* 'English-Bulgarian'. The accumulation of more than three components is very rare in Bulgarian (as for instance in the name of a multilingual dictionary: *Bălgarsko-frensko-nemsko-anglijsko-ruski (politehničeski rečnik)* 'Bulgarian-French-German-English-Russian (polytechnical dictionary)').

3.4 Verbal composition

The formation of compound verbs is not common in present-day Bulgarian. Verbs like *blagodari* 'to thank', *blagoslavja* 'to bless' are no longer perceived as motivated due to the semantic bleaching of the component *blago-* 'kind, good, sweet'. Isolated examples occur in the literary language such as *vod-o-snabdjava* 'to supply water', *glas-o-podava* 'to cast one's vote', *răk-o-maha* 'to wave one's arms', which are synchronically motivated (N+V). Some of them have appeared in the literary language after the cognate nominal compounds (*vodosnabdjavane* 'water supply', *glasopodavane* 'voting; lit. vote-giving').

A specific type of verbal composition in Modern Bulgarian produces reflexive verbs with the initial component *samo-* 'self-', which correlates with the pronoun *sam* in its meaning 'acting on one's own, unassisted' (*samoubiva se* 'to commit suicide', *samouspokojava se* 'to console oneself', *samokreditira se* 'to finance oneself'). The verbs follow the rules of pure composition (see above) or combine composition and postfixation (*se* is regarded as a word-formation element, i.e. a postfix). This model is observed in the East Slavic languages and in some Balkan languages (Greek and Romanian). In Bulgarian it is more productive (Ivančev 1978: 250–270).

3.5 Quasi compounds (clipped compounds)

Quasi compounds are formations whose first, second, or both components are clipped forms of full lexical items, namely relational adjectives (*elektro-* ← *električeski* 'electrical', cf. *elektrocentrala* 'power station' besides *električeska centrala*; *moto-* ← *motoren* adj. 'motor', cf. *motosport* 'motorsports' and *motoren sport*, and only as compounds: *motociklet* 'motorcycle', *motokros* 'motocross'; *balkan-* ← *balkanski* 'Balkan' + *fest* ← *festival* 'festival', cf. *balkanfest* 'Balkanfest', besides nonproprial meaning: *balkanski festival*, etc.). The model is relatively new in Bulgarian word-formation. It goes back to the second half of the 20th century when it was established under Russian influence. It is very active and highly productive. The most frequently used components are: *avto-*, *video-*, *elektro-*, *narko-*, *rok-*, *tele-*, *folk-*, *foto-*, *-fest*, etc.

3.6 Neoclassical composition

The classification of some complex words as "neoclassical compounds" in West European linguistic literature, with a view to the origin (Greek or Latin) of one or both components, raises, in our opinion, the following question of what "neoclasssical" is – the origin of the components, the word-formation pattern with the interfixes <o>, <e>, <i> or the resulting lexical unit? In Bulgarian linguistics as well as in studies on word-formation of other Slavic languages, the term "neoclassical compounds" is not common for several reasons. The interfix is an obligatory formant in the traditional models, which have always been active in composition. The frequently repeated components of Greek or Latin origin (*elektro-* 'electro-', *morfo-* 'morpho-', *hidro-* 'hydro-', *socio-*, *-fil* '-phile', *-krat* '-crat', etc.) are not a "novelty" either from the point of view of present-day word-formation: they appear in a large number of lexemes or participate in their formation. The novelty for Bulgarian word-formation (and other Slavic languages) is the activation of these elements and the high productivity of the models in which they participate. In the literature on word-formation some of them are defined as affixoids and are subsumed under affixation (*eks-* 'ex-', *bio-*, *-fil* '-phile', etc.). Others are regarded as clipped adjectives (*elektro-*, *evro-* 'euro-', etc.), taking part in the formation of "quasi compounds" (see section 3.5).

4 Derivation

4.1 Denominal nouns

Nominal derivatives in Modern Bulgarian are formed by means of prefixation, suffixation, circumfixation and so-called paradigmatic derivation, i.e. the word-formation process that consists in the change of the paradigmatic characteristics with or without the participation of an inflectional ending. The results of paradigmatic derivation can correspond to word-formation categories (e.g., deverbal abstract nouns, denominal or deadjectival personal nouns, etc.).

4.1.1 Prefixation

Bulgarian prefixal noun derivatives are formed with the help of both well-established formants of predominantly foreign (Greek and Latin) origin, such as *anti-*, *arhi-* 'arch-', *vice-*, *eks-* 'ex-', *kvazi-* 'quasi-', *kontra-* 'counter-', *mega-*, *multi-*, *neo-*, *post-*, *psevdo-* 'pseudo-', *super-*, *ultra-*, etc., and new formants dating from the late 20th century, whose productivity is however rapidly increasing, such as *top-* (from English *top*). Because of their similar meaning and function alongside prefixes proper we include here components with a controversial status like *vice-*, *makro-* 'macro-', *mini-*, *ultra-*, *hiper-* 'hyper-', in the Slavic literature also referred to as prefixoids (see Avramova 2003: 38–43 and references there).

All prefixes and prefixoids combine with both native and borrowed nominal bases. The majority of formants can be added to both personal and non-personal nouns, introducing additional features to the semantics of the derived noun, e.g., high ~ low degree of sth. (*mega-skandal* 'mega scandal', *svrăh-dobiv* 'overproduction'), hierarchy (*pod-predsedatel* 'deputy president; lit. under-president'), temporal modification (*post-komunizăm* 'post-communism', *neo-konservator* 'neoconservative'); contradiction, counteraction, negation, deprivation (*kontra-dejstvie* 'counteraction', *ne-istina* 'non-truth'), apparent similarity (*kvazi-kultura* 'quasi culture', *psevdo-demokrat* 'pseudo-democrat'), repetition (*re-kvalifikacija* 'requalification'), reversal (*de-kriminalizacija* 'decriminalization'), etc. (see Avramova 2003, Georgieva 2007 and the literature quoted there; Krumova-Cvetkova 2007; Čoroleeva 2007).

4.1.2 Suffixation

Bulgarian nouns can be derived with the help of a number of native suffixes as well as by suffixes borrowed from Greek, Latin, West European languages, and Turkish. The most common suffixes are: *-(a)džij-/-čij-, -ak-/-jak-, -an-, -ank-, -janin-, -ant-, -ar-, -arnik-, -arnic-, -(a)cij-, -džijnic-/-čijnic-, -e-, -enc-, -er-, -(e)c-, -ier-, -izacij-, -iz(ă)m-, -in-, -in'-, -ist, -ic, -ičk-, -išt-, -k-, -kin'-, -l-, -l'-, -lij-, -lăk-, -nik-, -nic-, -ovec-, -ovnik-, -or-, -stv-, -uvane-, -ušk-, -c-, -č-, -(č)anin-, -čik-, -čic-, -štin-, -'or-*, etc. They are involved in the production of the following word-formation categories:

Personal nouns, e.g., names of professions or sportsmen: *ključar* 'locksmith' (← *ključ* 'key'), *vădičar* 'angler' (← *vădica* 'fishing rod'), *magaziner* 'shop assistant' (← *magazin* 'shop'), *restorantor* 'restaurateur' (← *restorant* 'restaurant'), *štangist* 'heavyweight lifter' (← *štangi* pl. 'weight') (see Dimitrova 1962); names of followers/supporters of doctrines or ideas, often derived from proper names, e.g., *hegelianec* 'Hegelian' (← *Hegel*); names of inhabitants, e.g., *plevenčanin* 'inhabitant of the town of Pleven' (← *Pleven*); names of persons according to special attributes or predilections: *gărbuško* 'hunchback' (← *gărbica* 'hump'), *domovnik* 'homebody' (← *dom* 'home'), and personal nouns expressing similarity: *rambovec* 'Rambo man' (← *Rambo*). Some borrowed agent nouns can be interpreted as the result of paradigmatic derivation (i.e. the result of paradigm change), although they have their origin in the source languages: *filolog* 'philologist' (← *filologija* 'philology'), *matematik* 'mathematician' (← *matematika* 'mathematics'), *hirurg* 'surgeon' (← *hirurgija* 'surgery'). The term backformation is not common in Bulgarian word-formation.

Abstract nouns: *majstorstvo, majstorlăk* 'mastery, skill' (← *majstor* 'master'), *dănovizăm* 'Danovism' (← *Dănov*, a Bulgarian philosopher and religious leader). With some nouns the semantic opposition "quality vs. activity" is not clear-cut (e.g., *varvarstvo, varvarština* 'barbarism' ← *varvari* 'barbarians');

Action nouns: *dăžduvane* 'sprinkle irrigation, rain-like irrigation' (← *dăžd* 'rain', there is no verb **dăžduvam* 'to irrigate, sprinkle') and activity nouns *gradinarstvo* 'gardening' (← *gradinar* 'gardener');

Place nouns: *drešnik* 'closet' (← *drehi* 'clothes'), *hlebarnica* 'baker's' (← *hljab* 'bread');

Collective nouns: *studentstvo* 'studentry' (← *student* 'student'), *vărbalak* 'willow-grove' (← *vărba* 'willow');

Diminutives: *hlebec* 'little bread' (← *hljab* 'bread'), *pilence* 'small chicken' (← *pile* 'chicken'). Diminutives usually have emotional connotations (e.g., *majčica* 'dear mother' ← *majka* 'mother'), whose significance is fully revealed in the context of communication. Most often this is endearment, but the respective words can also be ironic and pejorative, cf. *prijatelče* 'little friend' (← *prijatel* 'friend'), addressed to a child (diminutive ± endearment) and to a grown-up (irony or endearment);

Augmentatives: *răčište* 'huge hand' (← *răka* 'hand'), *junačaga* 'hero' (← *junak* 'hero');

Female personal and animal nouns: *direktorka* '(woman) director' (← *direktor* 'director'), *lăvica* 'lioness' (← *lăv* 'lion').

4.1.3 Circumfixation

The role of circumfixation in nominal derivation is less significant in Bulgarian. Circumfixes can be found mostly in abstract nouns, e.g., *bez-izhod-ica* 'impasse' (← *bez izhod* 'without exit'), *bez-sram-ie* 'shamelessness' (← *bez sram* 'without shame') – in these cases the derivatives are based on a prepositional phrase – and in formations denoting persons (*să-kilij-nik* 'prison-cell-mate; lit. with-cell-PERS' ← *kilija* '(prison) cell').

4.2 Deadjectival nouns

Suffixes form nominal derivatives in the following categories:

Abstract nouns: -*ost*-/-*est*-, -*štin*-, -*ot*-, -*otij*-, -*ic*-, -*stv*-, -*ij*-, e.g., *smelost* 'bravery' (← *smel* 'brave'), *krasota* 'beauty' (← *krasiv* 'beautiful');

Personal and non-personal nouns: -*ak*-/-*jak*-, -*ec*-, -*ik*-, -*nik*-, -*an*-, -*č*-, -*ar*-, -*ušk*-, -*uš*-, etc., e.g.: *hitrec* 'clever guy' (← *hităr* 'clever'), *slabak, slabuško* 'weakling' (← *slab* 'weak'); *krivak* '(shepherd's) crook' (← *kriv* 'crooked'), *južnjak* 'south wind' (← *južen* 'southern'), *gluhar* 'wood grouse' (← *gluh* 'deaf').

A specific place among the various means of deadjectival word-formation is held by "univerbation" (Murdarov 1983: 115), in Slavic word-formation defined as a combination of ellipsis and suffixation, which most often results in the formation of a single word from a phrase or multi-word expression. Formally, the word is derived from an adjective, e.g., *kabel-ark-a* coll. 'cable TV channel' (← *kabel-na televizija* 'id.'); see also Martincová (2015) on multi-word expressions and univerbation in Slavic.

4.3 Deverbal nouns

Deverbal nouns are derived with the suffixes *-až-, -(a)lk-/-(i)lk-, -(a)ln'-/-(i)ln'-, -an-, -ank-, -ant-, -anč-, -ar-, -arn-, -arnic-, -(a)tor-, -ač-, -ačk-, -ačnic-, -b-, -džijk-, -ež-, -enij-, -ec-, -(i)v-, -izacij-, -istk-, -itb-, -ic-, -išt-, -(j)arnik-, -k-, -kin'-, -l-, -l'-, -n-, -n'-, -ne-, -nij-, -nik-, -nic-, -ovač-, -ovk-, -ot-, -tv-, -tel-, -telk-, -tor-, -cij-, -ăk-, -jor-,* etc.

A c t i o n   n o u n s: *pisane* 'writing' (← *pisa-*, aorist stem of *piše* 'to write'), *borba* 'struggle' (← *bori se* 'to struggle') (see Kaldieva 1977). Paradigmatic derivation of abstract nouns consists in: a) zero suffixation (*lov* 'hunt' ← *lovi* 'to hunt'); b) zero-suffixation + historically conditioned alternations (*boj* 'beating; fight' ← *bie* 'to beat') (Radeva 2007: 134); c) addition of an inflection, sometimes accompanied by morphophonemic alternation: *uteh-a* 'comfort' (← *uteši* 'to comfort');

A g e n t   n o u n s: *pisatel* 'writer' (← *pisa-*, aorist stem of *piše* 'to write'), *čistač* 'cleaner' (← *čisti* 'to clean') and names of persons according to a special attribute or predilection: *ljubitel* 'lover (of)' (← *ljubi* 'to love, like'), *zabravan, zabravanko, zabravančo* 'forgetful person' (← *zabravja* 'to forget');

F e m a l e   a g e n t   n o u n s: *pluvkinja* 'female swimmer' (← *pluva* 'to swim'), *čistačka* 'cleaning lady' (← *čisti* 'to clean');

P a t i e n t   n o u n s: *pratenik* 'envoy' (← *praten* 'sent');

O b j e c t   n o u n s   a n d   r e s u l t   n o u n s: *četivo* 'reading matter' (← *čete* 'to read'), *čertež* 'drawing' (← *čertae* 'to draw'), *tvorba* 'creation' (← *tvori* 'to create'), and nouns going back to paradigmatic derivation such as *nagrada* 'prize, award' (← *nagradi* 'to reward');

I n s t r u m e n t   n o u n s: *brăsnač* 'razor' (← *brăsne* 'to shave'), *otvaračka* 'opener' (← *otvarja* 'to open'), *sečivo* 'tool' (← *seče* 'to cut');

P l a c e   n o u n s: *igrište* 'playing ground' (← *igrae* 'to play'), *pečatnica* 'printing house' (← *pečata* 'to print').

4.4 Denominal adjectives

4.4.1 Suffixation

Denominal adjectives are formed primarily by suffixation and, less often, by circumfixation and paradigmatic derivation.

The suffixes forming r e l a t i o n a l adjectives include *-(e)n-*, *-ov-/-ev-*, *-in-*, *-sk-*, *-ičesk-*, *-ič(e)n-*, *-ovsk-*, *-ensk-*, *-ešk-*, *-o(v)en-/-ev(e)n-*, etc. Relational adjectives denote individual relatedness as, for instance, in *djadov* 'granddad's' (← *djado*) or general relatedness to persons (*momčeški* 'boy's', but also 'boyish' ← *momče*), place (*gorski* 'forest' (adj.) ← *gora*), time (*leten* 'summer' (adj.) ← *ljato*), material (with further differentiations like purpose, presence of sth., etc.), e.g., *jagodov* '(made of) strawberry' (← *jagoda*), *čaen* '(for) tea' (← *čaj*), *glicerinov* 'containing glycerin' (← *glicerin*), *benzinov* 'petrol' (← *benzin*), etc. (Maslov 1982: 102–108; Stojanov 1983: 153–156). Relational adjectives like *vălči* 'wolf(ish)' (← *vălk* 'wolf'), *goveždi* 'bovine' (← *govedo* 'ox') are formed by paradigmatic derivation ("with historical alternation of the final consonant of the base and the ending *-i* in the common form for masc. sg."; Maslov 1982: 110), mostly from nominal bases denoting animals.

Q u a l i t a t i v e adjectives are formed with the suffixes: *-av-/-jav-*, *-iv-*, *-(e)liv-*, *-at-*, *-est-*, *-(e)n*, *-it-*, *-ovit-*, *-ovat-*, *-ov(e)n/-ev(e)n-*, etc. Adjectives with a p o s s e s s i v e meaning are, for instance, *răždiv* 'rusty' (← *răžda* 'rust'), *treskav* 'feverish' (← *treska* 'fever'), *blatist* 'swampy' (← *blato* 'swamp'), in connection with a quantitative modification (larger/more than average), e.g., *mustakat* 'moustached' (← *mustak* 'moustache') or *dăždoven* 'rainy' (← *dăžd* 'rain'). S i m i l a r i t y is expressed in adjectives like *kestenjav* 'chestnut-coloured, auburn' (← *kesten* 'chestnut'), *djavolit* 'devilish' (← *djavol* 'devil') (Stojanov 1983: 151–153).

4.4.2 Circumfixation

Another productive way of forming denominal adjectives is c i r c u m f i x a t i o n, e.g., *meždu-grad-ski* 'inter-city', *pred-izbor-en* 'pre-electional', *bez-motor-en* 'motorless', *svrăh-zvuk-ov* 'supersonic', etc. The mixed type of prefixation + paradigmatic derivation has a more limited role, e.g., *bezbrad* 'beardless' (← *bez brada* 'without a beard').

4.5 Deadjectival adjectives

Deadjectival adjectives are formed by prefixes and suffixes.

Both native (*văz-, do-, lăže-, ne-, pre-, pred-, polu-, pro-, protivo-, svrăh-*, etc.), and borrowed, mostly from Greek and Latin, formants (*a-, anti-, kvazi-, kontra-, makro-, maksi-, mega-, mono-, multi-, super-, ultra-, hiper-*, etc.) participate in prefixation, expressing various qualitative-quantitative, temporal and other meanings. The high intensity of the property is signaled by prefixes like *svrăh-, super-, ultra-, mega-, pre-*, e.g., *svrăhmošten* 'super powerful', *preskăp* 'overexpensive'.

Low intensity of the property is expressed by the suffixes *-av-, -kav-, -ikav-, -enikav-, -eznikav-, -ič(ă)k-, -ovat-*, etc. (e.g., *bolnav* 'sickly' ← *bolen* 'sick', *červenikav* 'reddish' ← *červen* 'red'), rarely by prefixes like *văz-: văzkisel* 'sourish' (Stojanov 1983: 151–153; Radeva 2007: 167–169; Čoroleeva 2007: 80–81; Georgieva 2007). In addition to the meaning 'low intensity of a property' some adjectives with the suffix *-ič(ă)k-* contain the connotation of diminutiveness and endearment, e.g., *miličăk* 'dearest' (← *mil* 'dear').

4.6 Deverbal adjectives

There is no specific category of deverbal active adjectives in Bulgarian. Their function is taken over by the present active participles in *-št-*. In the course of time some participles have turned into adjectives but this has no relevance to present-day synchronic word-formation. However, some adjectives in *-tel(e)n-* can express active meaning, e.g., *napoitelen dăžd* 'rain which irrigates', *napoitelen kanal* 'canal which serves for irrigation' (← *napoi* 'to irrigate'). Adjectives with active or passive meaning can also be formed with the suffix *-liv-*, cf. *pesteliv* 'thrifty; who likes to save' (← *pesti* 'to save (money)', but *čupliv* 'fragile, which can be easily broken' (← *čupi* 'to break').

Deverbal adjectives are formed with the suffixes *-il(e)n-, -al(e)n-, -tel(e)n-, -itel(e)n-, -atel(e)n-* (Stojanov 1983: 153), *-im-, -em-, -aem-, -uem-* (Maslov 1982: 108) and signify the purpose/function of an action (*spalen* '(for) sleeping' ← *spi* 'to sleep') or the ability to perform an action (*sgăvaem* 'folding, collapsible' ← *sgăva se* 'to fold'). Adjectives containing the suffixes *-av-, -kav-, -iv-, -liv-, -tel(e)n-* express a modal/potential meaning, including inclination (*čupliv* 'fragile, easily broken' ← *čupi se* 'to break', *razgovorliv* and *razgovorčiv* 'talkative' ← *razgovorja* 'to talk'), purpose/intention (*jadliv* 'edible' ← *jade se* 'is eaten'), etc.

4.7 Verbal derivation

In Bulgarian, new verbs are derived by means of prefixation, suffixation, postfixation, and several mixed types. There is a close connection between verb formation and the categories of aspect and aktionsart. Unlike authors who assume that aspect is a purely grammatical category, hence the perfective and imperfective verbs are treated as aspectual pairs (forms of the same verb), we regard aspect as a lexico-grammatical category (see Kucarov 1999: 482 and the bibliography there), and the perfective and imperfective as two separate verbs whose word-formation is to be treated separately. The aktionsarten, expressed derivationally, influence the semantics of the derived verb (see section 4.7.3).

About 30 suffixes are involved in verbal derivation, on their own or in combination with a prefix or a postfix. Verbs of the 1st conjugation type (irrespective of the part of speech of the motivating base) are formed with the suffixes: *-n-*, *-ae-*, *-ee*, verbs of the 2nd conjugation with the suffixes *-i-*, *-(n)iči-*, *-ol-/-oli-*, *-oti-*, *-ori-*, *-ti-*, *-č-*. The greatest variety is observed in the formants appearing in verbs of the 3rd conjugation (Stojanov 1983: 227–228): *-a-*, *-ae-*, *-ja-*, *-va-*, *-ova-*, *-uva-*, *-stvuva-*, *-ava-*, *-ka-*, *-ira-*, *-izira-*, *-asa-/-jasa-*, *-isa-*, *-osa-*.

4.7.1 Denominal verbs

Denominal verbs are formed by means of suffixation, circumfixation, suffixation + postfixation, prefixation + postfixation, and express a variety of meanings (Radeva 2007: 232–269):
a) Agentive: *kmetuva* 'to serve as mayor' (← *kmet* 'mayor'); in the meaning 'to behave like': *gărčee se* 'to adopt Greek manners' (← *grăk* 'Greek');
b) Inchoative: *vampirjasa* 'to become a vampire' (← *vampir* 'vampire');
c) Inchoative and factitive: *varvarizira* 'to barbarize' (← *varvari* 'barbarians'), *ponemči* 'to Germanize' (← *nemci* 'Germans');
d) Inchoative-ingressive: *svečeri se* 'evening sets in' (← *večer* 'evening');
e) Stative: *gladuva* 'to go hungry' (← *glad* 'hunger'), *sramuva se* 'to be ashamed' (← *sram* 'shame');
f) Ornative: *bojadisa* 'to paint' (← *boja* 'paint'), *zatrevi* 'to plant with grass' (← *treva* 'grass'), *bradjasa* 'to grow a beard, have a 5 o'clock shadow' (← *brada* 'beard');
g) Causative/Factitive: *filmira* 'to film, turn into a film' (← *film* 'film'), *agni se* 'to lamb' (← *agne* 'lamb');
h) Instrumental: *rendosa* 'to plane away, down' (← *rende* 'plane'), *zaključi* 'to lock' (← *ključ* 'key');

i) Locative: *lageruva* 'to camp' (← *lager* 'camp'), *oblakăti se* 'to lean, prop oneself on one's elbows' (← *lakăt* 'elbow');
j) Temporal: *denuva* 'to spend the day' (← *den* 'day');
k) Privative: *obezglavi* 'to behead' (← *glava* 'head'), etc.

4.7.2 Deadjectival verbs

There are four ways of forming deadjectival verbs in Bulgarian: 1. Suffixation (with the formants *-ee-, -i-, -ira-, -izira-, -uva-,* etc.); 2. Circumfixation (with the circumfixes *do-...-ee-, za-...-ee-, na-...-ee-, -iz-...-ee-, o-...-ee-, po-...-ee-, u-...-ee-, za-...-n-, o-...-n-, pri-...-n-, s-...-n-, u-...-n-, v-...-i-, za-...-i-, iz-...-i-, o-...-i-, pod-...-i-, pri-...-i-, raz-...-i-, s-...-i-, u-...-i-,* etc.); 3. Suffixation + postfix *se*; 4. Circumfixation + postfixation.

In terms of their semantics the derived verbs can be a) s t a t i v e: *sinee* 'to show, appear blue' (← *sin* 'blue'), *gordee se* 'to be proud' (← *gord* 'proud'); b) i n c h o a t i v e: *belee* 'to turn white' (← *bjal* 'white'), *ožadnee* 'to become thirsty' (← *žaden* 'thirsty'), c) f a c t i t i v e: *mokri* 'to make wet' (← *mokăr* 'wet'), *vludi* 'to madden' (← *lud* 'mad'), *zazdravi* 'to strengthen' (← *(po-)zdrav* 'strong(er)'), etc.

4.7.3 Deverbal verbs

Deverbal verbs are the product of prefixation, suffixation, mixed types, and paradigmatic derivation.

Nineteen native prefixes are used to form new verbs: *v- (vă-), văz-, do-, za-, zad-, iz-, na-, nad-, o- (ob-), ot-, po-, pod-, pre-, pred-, pri-, pro-, raz-, s- (să-), u-*. In addition to their semantic and word-formation function they have the lexico-grammatical function of perfectivization; much less often the basic verb is perfective or bi-aspectual (Stojanov 1983: 216). From an imperfective verb, perfective verbs are derived with the help of prefixes introducing various meanings (see Stojanov 1983: 217–226; Radeva 2007: 171–175), thus the verb *piše* 'to write' has 14 prefixal derivatives.

Verbal prefixes express spatial meanings such as movement 'inwards' (*v-leti* 'to fly in(to)'), 'outwards' (*iz-leti* 'to fly out'), 'away from' (*ot-ide* 'to go (away)'), 'closer towards sth.' (*do-jde* 'to come'), 'closer together' (*s-mete* 'to sweep together'), 'underneath' (*pod-kopae* 'to undermine'), 'above' (*văzsedne* 'to mount'); separation (*raz-vie* 'to unfold'), etc. or non-spatial meanings (aktionsart, etc.):

a) Inchoative: *pro-hodi* 'to learn how to walk', *văz-gordee se* 'to become haughty'; in impersonal verbs, e.g.: *pri-spi mi se* '(I) get sleepy; lit. verb-3PERS.SG. PERS.PRONOUN-DAT REFLEXIVE PARTICLE', *pri-ljuti mi* '(I) begin to feel hot taste';
b) Cessation of the activity: *pre-žali* 'to cease grieving for', *ot-sărdi se* 'to stop being angry'; various resultative meanings: *iz-lekuva* 'to cure';
c) Completive: *do-sipe* 'to add some more liquid, to top up';
d) Limited duration: *po-mălči* 'to keep silent for a while';
e) Summative-distributive: *na-rodi* 'to give birth to a number of children'; some prefixal-postfixal verbs have the same categorial meaning, e.g., *zasedi se* 'to stay for quite a while' (← *sedi* 'to stay');
f) Attenuative: *pro-săchne* 'to get somewhat drier'; such is the meaning of some circumfixal verbs, e.g., *pobodva* 'to prick slightly' (← *bode* 'to prick');
g) Semelfactive: *pro-šumoli* 'to give a single rustling noise';
h) Anticipatory: *pred-plati* 'to pre-pay';
i) Reverse activity: *de-mobilizira* 'to demobilize';
j) Repeated activity: *re-investira* 'to reinvest', etc. (cf. Maslov 1982: 118–119; Stojanov 1983: 284–287; Radeva 2007: 171–176).

Several suffixes with different functions and meanings participate in the formation of deverbal verbs: *-n-* derives semelfactive verbs from imperfective verbs: *zvănne* 'to give a ring' (← *zvăni* 'to ring') and inchoative verbs: *revne* 'to start roaring' (← *reve* 'to roar'); *-ka-* derives imperfective verbs from perfective verbs, e.g., *ahka* 'to gasp repeatedly' (← *ahne* 'to give a gasp'); *-va-* and *-vava-* express iterative-delimitative meaning together with the imperfectivization of the verb, e.g., *prohărkva* 'to snore every now and then' (← *prohărka* 'to give a snore'); *-a-*, *-va-*, *-ava-/-java-*, *-uva-* have an imperfectivizing function; morphophonemic alternation is common, cf. *izlita* 'to take off (ipf.)' (← *izleti* 'to take off (pf.)'), *dovežda* 'to bring (ipf.)' (← *dovede* 'to bring (pf.)').

Some suffixes as, e.g., *-ka-*, *-inka-* derive "verbs with the meaning of diminutiveness and endearment, characteristic of popular speech and especially of child and caretaker language" (Maslov 1982: 116), cf. *spinka* 'to go to bye-byes' (← *spi* 'to sleep').

Formants like *-oti-* and *-ori-* derive imperfective verbs with a pejorative connotation from imperfective verbs: *draskoti* 'to scribble' (← *draska* 'to scribble'), *skitori* 'to gad about' (← *skita* 'to wander').

P o s t f i x a t i o n is an analytical way of forming two types of verbs with the help of the movable reflexive particles (postfixes) *se*, *si* added to the basic verb: a) direct (accusative) reflexives with *se*, e.g., *mija se* 'to wash oneself' (← *mija* 'to wash'), and b) indirect (dative) reflexives with *si*, cf. *kupuvam si* 'to buy for oneself' (← *kupuvam* 'to buy'). For more on the meaning of the two types of reflexive verbs see Maslov (1982: 123).

4.7.4 Deadverbial and deinterjectional verbs

Deadverbial circumfixal verbs like the impersonal verbs *do-măčn-ee mi* '(I) start feeling sad, sorry' (← *măčno* 'sad, sorry'), *pri-loš-ee mi* '(I) start feeling sick' (← *lošo* 'bad'), etc. have inchoative meaning.

A small number of Bulgarian suffixal verbs are based on interjections, e.g., *tupne* 'to thump' (← *tup* 'thump'), *kuka* 'to cuckoo' (← *ku-ku* 'cuckoo'), *ohka* '(to say) ouch' (← *oh* 'ouch'), *muči* 'to moo' (← *mu* 'moo'), etc. (Szymański 1977; Radeva 1991: 207).

4.8 Adverbial derivation

Adverbs can be derived from adjectives, verbs and adverbs.
   Deadjectival adverbs are formed by means of the following suffixes:
a) *-o*, e.g., *dălgo* 'long', coincides with the adjectival neuter singular inflection, cf. the singular of the adjective 'long': *dălăg* masc., *dălga* fem., *dălgo* neut. (see also Maslov 1982: 128);
b) *-i* is added to bases of relational-qualitative adjectives in *-sk-*, *-šk-*, *-ičesk-*, *-k:* *bratski* 'fraternally', *čoveški* 'humanely'. These adverbs are homonymous with the masculine singular and common plural form of the adjectives, cf. *bratski* (adj.) *pozdrav* 'fraternal greeting', *bratski* (adj.) *otnošenija* 'fraternal relations', and *pregărnaha se bratski* (adv.) 'they embraced fraternally, like brothers';
c) *-ata*, *-eškata* (characteristic of colloquial style), *-eškom*: *slepeškom*, *slepeškata* 'blindly' (← *sljap* 'blind'), *zdravata* 'hard' (← *zdrav* 'strong'). Some of these adverbs are homonymous with the definite-articled singular feminine form of the adjective, cf. *zdravata* (adj.) *osnova* 'the strong base' and *zagazil si zdravata* (adv.) 'you are in deep trouble' (Maslov 1982: 129).

Deverbal adverbs are derived with the suffixes *-eškata* and *-eškom*, e.g., *tičeškom*, *tičeškata* 'at a run' (← *tiča* 'to run') (Maslov 1982: 129).
   Deadverbial adverbs are formed
a) with the suffixes *-ičko*, *-ko*, *-inko*, *-anka*, *-inka*: The resulting adverbs have the meaning of intensification or attenuation of the property, combined with endearment, e.g.: *ranko*, *raničko* 'somewhat early + endearment' (←*rano* 'early'), *seginka* 'now + endearment; coll.' (← *sega* 'now');

b) by prefixation of pro-adverbs: *do-tam* 'up-to-there', *na-njakăde* 'to somewhere', *ot-sega* 'from now on' (Radeva 1991: 209);
c) with the formants *edi-, gode-, da e* from interrogative adverbs (*kăde* 'where', *koga* 'when', and *kak* 'how'): *edi-kăde* 'such-and-such place', *koga-gode* 'some time', *kak da e* 'somehow, so-so';
d) with the postfix *si* to express indefiniteness: *edi-koga si* 'such and such a time', *njakăde si* 'some place'.

5 Conversion

There is no unanimous interpretation of conversion in Slavic, including Bulgarian word-formation studies, so that various phenomena have been subsumed under this term. Some consider it a means of word-formation; others as transition from one part of speech into another; yet others, as both of these (Bednaříková 2009: 138–149; see also Manova 2011: 55–124). Radeva (1991: 51) considers paradigmatic derivation to be a kind of conversion where "the inflection is the formal marker of the derivative's belonging to a particular part of speech". (See section 4.1; cf. also article 8 in this volume on Polish.)

6 Minor processes of word-formation

Other means of word-formation (reduplication, clipping, and blending) have a limited role in standard Bulgarian.

Reduplication produces interjections like *ha-ha* 'ha-ha', *aj-aj* 'oh dear', *iha-ha* 'wow', etc. (Stojanov 1983: 470).

Clipping is more common in slang, e.g., *spoko* (← *spokojno* 'take it easy; lit. (be) calm'); some clippings occur in colloquial style: *spec* (← *specialist* 'specialist'), etc.

Blending as a manifestation of the ludic aspect of language is typical of spheres such as advertising, brand names, fiction, and it is difficult to formulate systematic rules for it (Stamenov 2007). Most of the blends are occasionalisms and have little chance of being established as permanent lexical units. However, in the past one or two decades due to a more relaxed attitude towards language use and an increasing influence of the English language, more and more blends are being formed, so that blending can be expected to gain greater popularity (cf. Stamenov 2007). Examples are *vlastitutka* lit. 'governmentute' (← *vlast* 'government' + *prostitutka* 'prostitute'), *demokratura* lit. 'democratorship' (← *demokracija* 'democracy' + *diktatura* 'dictatorship'), etc.

7 Conclusion

Derivation and composition, i.e. the formation of single-word items, are the main means of forming lexical units in Bulgarian. Phrasal naming units are not so common and mostly limited to terminology. The word-formation means and patterns combine traditional Slavic-Bulgarian and modern European features. Internationalization in the sphere of word-formation has its effect on Bulgarian too, mainly by making available new foreign means of word-formation and models of composition. Word-formation in Bulgarian is not isolated from the integrative processes which are characteristic for the development of modern European languages.

8 References

Andrejčin, Ljubomir (1944): *Osnovna bălgarska gramatika*. Sofija: Hemus.
Avramova, Cvetanka (2003): *Slovoobrazuvatelni tendencii pri săštestvitelnite imena v bălgarskija i češkija ezik v kraja na XX vek*. Sofija: Heron Press.
Bagasheva, Alexandra (2017): On a subclass of nominal compounds in Bulgarian: The nature of phrasal compounds. In: Carola Trips and Jaklin Kornfilt (eds.), *Further investigations into the nature of phrasal compounding*, 81–117. Berlin: Language Science Press.
Bagasheva, Alexandra (2020): Derivational networks in Bulgarian. In: Lívia Körtvélyessi, Alexandra Bagasheva and Pavol Štekauer (eds.), *Derivational Networks Across Languages*, 33–41. Berlin/Boston: De Gruyter Mouton.
Baltova, Julija (1978): Složnite săštestvitelni imena v bălgarskija knižoven ezik prez epohata na Văzraždaneto. (Slovoobrazovatelno-semantičen i funkcionalen analiz). Ph.D. dissertation, Institut za bălgarski ezik Sofia.
Baltova, Julija (1985): Dvusăstavni substantivni konstrukcii v săvremennija bălgarski knižoven ezik. *Izvestija na Instituta za bălgarski ezik* 26: 81–133.
Bednaříková, Božena (2009): *Slovo a jeho konverze*. Olomouc: Univerzita Palackého.
Belentschikow, Renate (2015): Dictionaries. In: Peter O. Müller, Ingeborg Ohnheiser, Susan Olsen and Franz Rainer (eds.), *Word-Formation. An International Handbook of the Languages of Europe*. Vol. 3, 2333–2354. Berlin/Boston: De Gruyter Mouton.
Beron, Petăr (1824): *Bukvar s različni poučenija*. [Brašov.]
Cejtlin, Ralja Michajlovna (1986): *Leksika drevnebolgarskih rukopisej X–XI vv*. Sofija: Izdatel'stvo Bolgarskoj akademii nauk.
Conev, Ben'o (1934): *Istorija na bălgarskija ezik*. Vol. 2. Sofija: Izdanie na Sofijskija universitet.
Čoroleeva, Marija (2007): *Semantičnata kategorija stepen i nejnoto izrazjavane v bălgarskija ezik*. Sofija: Akademično izdatelstvo "Prof. Marin Drinov".

Dejanova, Marija, Lili Laškova, Emilija Perniška and Dina Staniševa (1980): Slovoobrazuvane na slavjanskite složni prilagatelni. *Slavjansko ezikoznanie* 2: 13–105.

Dimitrova, Milka (1962): Nomina agentis v knižovnija bǎlgarski ezik. *Izvestija na Instituta za bǎlgarski ezik* 9: 141–210.

Georgieva, Elena (1967): Složni sǎštestvitelni v sǎvremennija bǎlgarski knižoven ezik (s ogled predimno kǎm po-novi obrazci). *Izvestija na Instituta za bǎlgarski ezik* 13: 157–202.

Georgieva, Cvetelina (2007): Inovacionni procesi pri imennata prefiksacija v bǎlgarskija knižoven ezik ot kraja na 20 i načaloto na 21 vek. Ph.D. dissertation, Institut za bǎlgarski ezik Sofija.

Harizanov, Boris (2018): Word Formation at the Syntax-Morphology Interface: Denominal Adjectives in Bulgarian. *Linguistic Inquiry* 49(2): 283–333.

Herej-Szymańska, Krystyna (1978): *Derywacja czasowników denominalnych we współczesnym bułgarskim języku literackim*. Wrocław: Ossolineum.

Holiolčev, Hristo (1965): Dialektni nastavki za obrazuvane na sǎštestvitelni imena ot mǎžki rod v bǎlgarskite govori. *Izvestija na Instituta za bǎlgarski ezik* 12: 157–198.

Igov, Angel (1967): *Struktura na složnite dumi v južnoslavjanskite ezici*. Sofija: Nauka i izkustvo.

Ilieva, Kornelija, Snežina Karag'ozova, Gergana Mihajlova, Jordan Penčev and Elena Todorova (1999): *Slovoobrazuvatelen rečnik na sǎvremennija bǎlgarski knižoven ezik*. Sofija: Akademično izdatelstvo "Prof. Marin Drinov".

Ivančev, Svetomir (1978): Edin neopisan semantiko-slovoobrazovatelen glagolen model v sǎvremennija bǎlgarski knižoven ezik. In: Svetomir Ivančev, *Prinosi v bǎlgarskoto i slavjanskoto ezikoznanie*, 250–270. Sofija: Nauka i izkustvo.

Kaldieva, Stefana (1977): Otvlečeni sǎštestvitelni ot glagolni osnovi v sǎvremennija bǎlgarski knižoven ezik. Ph.D. dissertation, Institut za bǎlgarski ezik Sofija.

Kaltz, Barbara and Odile Leclercq (2025): Word-formation research from its beginnings to the 19th century. In: Peter O. Müller, Susan Olsen and Franz Rainer (eds.), *Word-Formation – History, Theories, Units and Processes*, 25–42. Berlin/Boston: De Gruyter Mouton.

Kočev, Ivan (1971): Dialektni kategorii i tipove pri slovoobrazuvaneto na sǎštestvitelnoto ime. *Izvestija na Instituta za bǎlgarski ezik* 20: 107–185.

Kolarova, Maria (2010): Models of verb-centred compound nouns in English and Bulgarian. Ph.D. dissertation, University of Sofia.

Krumova-Cvetkova, Lilija (2007): *Semantičnata kategorija količestvo i nejnoto izrazjavane v bǎlgarskija ezik*. Sofija: Akademično izdatelstvo "Prof. Marin Drinov".

Kucarov, Ivan (1999): Morfologija. In: Todor Bojadžiev (ed.), *Sǎvremenen bǎlgarski ezik. Fonetika, leksikologija, slovoobrazuvane, morfologija, sintaksis*, 277–497. Sofija: "Petǎr Beron".

Lekov, Ivan (1958): *Slovoobrazovatelni sklonnosti na slavjanskite ezici*. Sofija: Izdatelstvo na Bǎlgarskata akademija na naukite.

Maldjieva, Viara (2009): *Gramatyka konfrontatywna bułgarsko-polska*. Vol. 9: *Słowotwórstwo*. Warszawa: SOW.

Manova, Stela (2011): *Understanding Morphological Rules. With Special Emphasis on Conversion and Subtraction in Bulgarian, Russian and Serbo-Croatian*. Dordrecht: Springer.

Martincová, Olga (2015): Multi-word expressions and univerbation in Slavic. In: Peter O. Müller, Ingeborg Ohnheiser, Susan Olsen and Franz Rainer (eds.), *Word-Formation. An International Handbook of the Languages of Europe*. Vol. 1, 742–757. Berlin/Boston: De Gruyter Mouton.

Maslov, Jurij Sergeevič (1982): *Gramatika na bǎlgarskija ezik*. Sofija: Nauka i izkustvo.

Mengel, Swetlana (2025): Historical word-formation in Slavic. In: Peter O. Müller, Susan Olsen and Franz Rainer (eds.), *Word-Formation – Language Contact and Diachrony*, 483–506. Berlin/Boston: De Gruyter Mouton.

Mladenov, Stefan (1929): *Geschichte der bulgarischen Sprache*. Berlin/Leipzig: de Gruyter.
Molhova, Jana (1986): *The Noun. A Contrastive English-Bulgarian Study*. Sofia: Naouka i Izkoustvo.
Mostrova, Tatjana (2005): Săštestvitelni ot glagolna osnova v pametnici ot XIV vek. Ph.D. dissertation, Kirilo-Metodievski naučen centăr pri Bălgarskata akademija na naukite Sofija.
Murdarov, Vladko (1983): *Săvremenni slovoobrazovatelni procesi*. Sofija: Nauka i izkustvo.
Neef, Martin (2025): Synthetic compounds in German. In: Peter O. Müller, Susan Olsen and Franz Rainer (eds.), *Word-Formation – Special Patterns and Restrictions*, 71–84. Berlin/Boston: De Gruyter Mouton.
Ohnheiser, Ingeborg (2025): Compounds and multi-word-expressions in Slavic. In: Peter O. Müller, Susan Olsen and Franz Rainer (eds.), *Word-Formation – Special Patterns and Restrictions*, 171–197. Berlin/Boston: De Gruyter Mouton.
Perniška, Emilija (1980): *Semantika na složnite prilagatelni v săvremennija bălgarski ezik*. Sofija: Izdatelstvo na Bălgarskata akademija na naukite.
Radewa, Sabina (1955): Budowa i znaczenie wyrazów złożonych w języku bułgarskim. *Studia z filologii polskiej i słowiańskiej* 1: 384–417.
Radeva, Vasilka (1991): *Slovoobrazuvaneto v bălgarskija knižoven ezik*. Sofija: Universitetsko izdatelstvo "Sv. Kliment Ochridski".
Radeva, Vasilka (2007): *V sveta na dumite. Struktura i značenie na proizvodnite dumi*. Sofija: Universitetsko izdatelstvo "Sv. Kliment Ochridski".
Scatton, Ernest A. (1984): Derivational morphology. In: Ernest A. Scatton, *A Reference Grammar of Modern Bulgarian*, 245–310. Columbus, OH: Slavica Publishers.
Selimski, Ljudvig (1983): Iz istorijata na nastavkata -'sk- v bălgarskija ezik: Prilagatelni na -ьск- /-'sk-/ v tekstove ot XVII–XVIII vek. Part 1: Uvod. Formalen analiz. *Trudove na VTU "Kiril i Metodij"* 18(2): 159–186.
Selimski, Ljudvig (1984): Iz istorijata na nastavkata -'sk- v bălgarskija ezik. Prilagatelni na -ьск- /-'sk-/ v tekstove ot XVII–XVIII vek. Part 2: Semantičen analiz. Zaključenie. *Trudove na VTU "Kiril i Metodij"* 19(2): 105–127.
Selimski, Ljudvig (2003): Projavi na tendencijata kăm internacionalizacija v južnoslavjanskite ezici. In: Ingeborg Ohnheiser (ed.), *Komparacja systemów i funkcjonowania współczesnych języków słowiańskich. 1. Słowotwórstwo/Nominacja*, 103–126. Opole: Uniwersytet Opolski.
Sgall, Petr (ed.) (1986): *Mluvnice češtiny. Vol. 1: Fonetika. Fonologie. Morfonologie a morfemika. Tvoření slov*. Praha: Academia.
Stamenov, Hristo (2007): Teleskopija v bălgarskoto slovoobrazuvane. In: Aleksandra Bagaševa (ed.), *Za čoveka i ezika. Sb. naučni statii, posveteni na 60-godišninata na prof. d.f.n. M. Penčeva*, 225–231. Sofija: Universitetsko izdatelstvo "Sv. Kliment Ochridski".
Stamenov, Christo (2015): Borrowing word-formation: *-ing* suffixation and blending in Bulgarian. *Contrastive Linguistics* 40(3): 163–197.
Stojanov, Stojan (1964): *Gramatika na bălgarskija knižoven ezik*. Sofija: Nauka i izkustvo.
Stojanov, Stojan (ed.) (1983): *Gramatika na săvremennija bălgarski knižoven ezik. Vol. 2: Morfologija*. Sofija: Izdatelstvo na Bălgarskata akademija na naukite.
Szymański, Tadeusz (1968): *Słowotwórstwo rzeczownika w bułgarskich tekstach XVII–XVIII wieka*. Wrocław: Ossolineum.
Szymański, Tadeusz (1977): *Derywacja czasowników onomatopeicznych i ekspresywnych w języku bułgarskim*. Wrocław: Ossolineum.
Teodorov-Balan, Aleksandăr (1940): *Nova bălgarska gramatika*. Sofija: Čipev.
Tetovska-Troeva, Margarita (1988): *Otglagolni imena za lica v bălgarskite govori. Nomina agentis*. Sofija: Izdatelstvo na Bălgarskata akademija na naukite.

Bonifacas Stundžia
11 Lithuanian

1 Introduction
2 General overview
3 Composition
4 Derivation
5 Conversion
6 Backformation
7 Reduplication
8 Clipping
9 References

Abstract: This article presents a survey of the word-formation system of standard Lithuanian, which is notable for its highly morphological character and for the predominant role of derivation and "paradigmatization", a word-formation process that consists in the mere change of the inflectional paradigm, although a change in part of speech is not obligatory (in contrast to conversion). Suffixal derivation is the most productive method of forming words. A two-stem structure and the absence of verbal instances are characteristic features of composition. Backformation, reduplication and clipping play no noticeable role, and blending and word-creation are not characteristic of standard Lithuanian.

1 Introduction

The description of Lithuanian word-formation started with the first grammars by Klein (1653) and Sappuhn and Schultz (1673). Although fragmentary, both grammars described the main word-formation processes of Lithuanian, including conversion, mostly from a synchronic point of view (see Urbutis 2008 [1999]: 630). Later the description of word-formation followed the principles of historical-comparative linguistics. Important chapters on word-formation were included in Lithuanian grammars by Schleicher (2008 [1856]: 252–335) and Kurschat (1876: 71–131). The first fundamental research on Lithuanian word-formation belongs to Aleksandrow (1888) and Leskien (1891). Aleksandrow analyzed nominal composition, while Leskien devoted a monograph to nominal suffixation, focussing on

Bonifacas Stundžia, Vilnius, Lithuania

https://doi.org/10.1515/9783111420523-011

the origin of suffixes and on correspondences of Lithuanian derivatives in Latvian and Old Prussian. A substantial contribution to both historical and synchronic descriptions of Lithuanian word-formation was made by Skardžius whose monograph (Skardžius 1996 [1943]) covered the whole system of word-formation except for adverbial formation. A similar methodology was characteristic of Otrębski's research (Otrębski 1965). Both scholars based their analyses on dialectal and Old Lithuanian data; however, Otrębski's description was slightly more oriented towards modern usage (cf. Keinys 1999: 32–33; Urbutis 2008 [1999] 630). The most comprehensive synchronic description of the Modern Lithuanian word-formation system, especially the nominal one, was carried out in two volumes of the grammar edited by Ulvydas (1965–71, Vol. 1: 251–473 (Formation of nouns, author V. Urbutis), 550–603 (Formation of adjectives, author A. Valeckienė), 635–636 (Formation of numerals, author V. Mažiulis), 718–721 (Formation of pronouns, author A. Valeckienė); 1965–71, Vol. 2: 218–297 (Formation of verbs, authors I. Jašinskaitė and J. Paulauskas), 508–533, 538–542 (Suffixal derivation of adverbs, author K. Ulvydas)). As far as verb formation is concerned, the best synchronic description was given in the grammar edited by V. Ambrazas (2005 [1994]: 385–410, author E. Jakaitienė). The development of the nominal word-formation system has been analyzed exhaustively by S. Ambrazas (1993, 2000, 2011). Short descriptions of the word-formation system of standard Lithuanian were presented by Keinys (1999) and Urbutis (2008 [1999]). Urbutis's monograph (2009 [1978]) was a major contribution to word-formation theory in Lithuanian.

2 General overview

In Lithuanian the majority of complex words are formed by means of two word-formation processes, viz. derivation and composition, the first process being much more productive than the second.

In the case of derivation, suffixal derivatives are most typical of Lithuanian, while prefixal derivatives are much rarer in the word-formation system.

Hundreds of derivational suffixes, in particular the nominal ones, are characteristic of standard Lithuanian, but only a small number of them are productive. Pure prefixal derivatives are characteristic of verbal derivation (e.g., *su-láuk-ti* 'to wait (till)' ← *láuk-ti* 'to wait'), while prefixation in the nominal system as a rule is followed by a change in the inflectional paradigm (IP) of the base word and by a generalization of the inflectional paradigms *-is* (unstressed) / *-ys* (stressed, both masculine) or *-ė* (feminine) in derivatives, e.g., *pa-jū́r-is* (IP *-is*) 'seashore' ← *jū́r-a* (IP *-a*) 'sea', *pa-tvor-ỹs* (IP *-ys*) '(a place) by the fence' ← *tvor-à* (IP *-a*) 'fence', *pa-vard-ė̃* (IP *-ė*) 'surname' ← *var̃d-as* (IP *-as*) 'name'.

The change in inflectional paradigm and the generalization of said inflectional paradigms are characteristic of the second component of compounds as well, e.g., *skaĩt-vard-is* (IP *-is*) 'numeral; lit. number-name' (cf. *var̃d-as* (IP *-as*) 'name'), *mės-gal-ỹs* (IP *-ys*) 'a piece of meat' (cf. *gãl-as* (IP *-as*) 'piece, bit'), *jūr-lìg-ė* (IP *-ė*) 'seasickness' (cf. *lig-à* (IP *-a*) 'illness'). The inflectional paradigms *-is* and *-ė* both of the second component of compounds and of the base word of prefixal derivatives remain, as a rule, unchanged, e.g., *pùs-brol-is* (IP *-is*) 'cousin', *į̃-brol-is* (IP *-is*) 'stepbrother' (cf. *bról-is* (IP *-is*) 'brother'), *žvỹr-duob-ė* (IP *-ė*) 'gravel pit' (cf. *duob-ė̃* (IP *-ė*) 'pit'), *pó-veržl-ė* (IP *-ė*) 'spacer' (← *veržl-ė̃* 'screwnut').

Neoclassical formations are to be treated separately because of the preservation of original inflectional paradigms and different accentual behaviour, cf. *kilo-mètr-as* 'kilometer' (← *kilo-* 'kilo-', *mètr-as* 'meter'), but *kíet-metr-is* 'solid cubic meter' (← *kíetas, -à* 'solid', *mètr-as* 'meter'), *makro-program-à* 'macroprogramme' (← *makro-* 'macro-', *program-à* 'programme'), but *pã-program-ė* 'subprogramme' (← *pa-* 'sub-', *program-à* 'programme').

Conversion, which is as important as (or even more important than) prefixal derivation, is labelled as a third type of derivation, so-called paradigmatic derivation (for more see section 5).

Only affixes play the part of word-formation formants, while alternations of segmental and/or suprasegmental elements play a supplementary role in the word-formation processes. Circumfixation is rare in Lithuanian. Backformation, reduplication, blending and clipping are not common in standard language.

3 Composition

Characteristic features of composition in Lithuanian are the two-stem structure (mostly simplex stems), and the absence of verbal compounds. The majority of compounds are assigned to the following inflectional paradigms (IP) which are productive in derivatives as well: masculine nom.sg. *-is* (unstressed) / *-ys* (stressed), and feminine nom.sg. *-ė*.

There are compound nouns (including nominalized adjectives) and nouns in general that constitute pairs of different gender marked by said inflectional paradigms, e.g., *žem-dirb-ỹs* m., *žem-dirb-ė̃* f. 'farmer' (← *žẽm-ė* 'soil', *dìrb-ti* 'to work', IPs *-ys* and *-ė*); *ilg-a-pir̃št-is* m., *ilg-a-pir̃št-ė* f. 'filferer, filcher' (← *ìlg-as, -à* 'long', interfix *-a-*, *pir̃št-as* 'finger', IPs *-is* and *-ė*). The inflectional paradigms *-a* (feminine and the so-called common gender nouns) and *-as, -a* (masculine/feminine adjectives) sometimes attach to compounds as well, e.g., *šlãp-drib-a* f. 'sleet, snowy rain' (← *šlãp-ias, -ià* 'wet, moist', *drìb-ti* 'to fall down', IP *-a*), *ak-i-plėš-a* (common gender) 'impudent, insolent person' (← *ak-ìs* 'eye', interfix *-i-*, *pléš-ti* 'to tear', IP *-a*), *ketùr-link-as, -a* 'fourfold' (← *ketur-ì* m. 'four', *leñk-ti* 'to bend, bow'), including qualitative apophony <en/in>, IPs *-as, -a*.

About half of the compounds have interfixes: *-(i)a-, -i-, -(i)o-, -ė-, -(i)u-, -y-, -(i)ū-*, e.g., *krauj-ã-gysl-ė* 'blood-vessel' (← *kraũj-as* 'blood', interfix *-a-*, *gýsl-a* 'vein', IP *-ė*), *gryn-a-kraũj-is, -ė* 'pure-blood' (← *grýn-as, -à* 'pure', interfix *-a-*, *kraũj-as* 'blood', IPs *-is, -ė*), *duj-ó-kauk-ė* 'gas-mask' (← *dùj-os* pl. 'gas', interfix *-o-*, *káuk-ė* 'mask', IP *-ė*), *virš-ù-galv-is* 'vertex' (← *virš-ùs* 'top', interfix *-u-*, *galv-à* 'head', IP *-is*).

The majority of both nominal and adjectival compounds are determinative compounds whose first component, as a rule, determines the second, i.e. the head component. Endocentric compounds prevail in nominal composition (e.g., *šón-kaul-is* 'rib' ← *šón-as* 'side', *kául-as* 'bone', IP *-is*), while adjectival compounds, as a rule, belong to the exocentric type (e.g., *silpn-a-prõt-is, -ė* 'weak-minded' ← *sil̃pn-as, -à* 'weak', interfix *-a-*, *prõt-as* 'mind', IPs *-is, -ė*). There are exocentric compound nouns (mostly *bahuvrīhi* type) as well, e.g., *juod-a-darb̃-is* m., *juod-a-darb̃-ė* f. 'unskilled worker' (← *júod-as, -à* 'black, dirty', interfix *-a-*, *dárb-as* 'work', IPs *-is, -ė*), *kupr-a-nugãr-is* 'camel' (← *kupr-à* 'hump', interfix *-a-*, *nùgar-a* 'back', IP *-is*). The formal difference between compound nouns and adjectives in some cases is expressed not only by the inflectional paradigm but also by accentuation, cf. the noun *ketùr-kamp-is* 'quadrangle' and the adjective *ketur-kam̃p-is, -ė* 'quadrangular' (← *ketur-ì* m. 'four', *kam̃p-as* 'angle', IPs *-is* (noun) and *-is, -ė* (adj.)).

Copulative compounds occur very rarely in Lithuanian, e.g., *kurč̃-nebyl-is, -ė* 'deaf-mute' (← *kurč̃-ias, -ià* 'deaf', *nebyl-ùs, -ì* 'dumb, mute', IPs *-is, -ė*).

A nominal first member is characteristic of the majority of nominal and some adjectival compounds, e.g., *líet-palt-is* 'raincoat' (← *liet-ùs* 'rain', *pált-as* '(over)coat', IP *-is*), *vaĩs-med-is* 'fruit tree' (← *vaĩs-ius* 'fruit', *mẽd-is* 'tree', IP *-is*), *šeiv-a-kõj-is, -ė* 'spindle-legged' (← *šeiv-à* 'bobbin', interfix *-a-*, *kój-a* 'leg', IPs *-is, -ė*), including circumflex metatony. Adjectives (more frequent in adjectival compounds), numerals, verbs, adverbs and, in rare cases, prepositions and pronouns also occur as the first member, e.g., *bendr-ã-but-is* 'hostel' (← *beñdr-as, -à* 'common', interfix *-a-*, *bùt-as* 'flat', IP *-is*), *aukšt-a-ū̃g-is, -ė* 'tall, of large stature' (← *áukšt-as, -à* 'tall', interfix *-a-*, *ū̃g-is* 'height', IPs *-is, -ė*), *pirm-ã-dien-is* 'Monday' (← *pìrm-as, -à* 'first', interfix *-a-*, *dien-à* 'day', IP *-is*), *gyvén-viet-ė* 'settlement' (← *gyvén-ti* 'to live', *viet-à* 'place', IP *-ė*), *daũg-tašk-is* 'three dots, ellipsis' (← *daũg* 'many', *tãšk-as* 'dot', IP *-is*), *tarp-ù-kar-is* 'interwar period' (← *tar̃p* 'between', interfix *-u-*, *kãr-as* 'war', IP *-is*), *sav-a-nõr-is, -ė* 'volunteer' (← *sãv-as, -à* 'one's own', interfix *-a-*, *nór-as* 'wish', IPs *-is, -ė*), including circumflex metatony.

Synthetic compounds with a verbal second component – in some works also referred to as "verb-centered" compounds – comprise about one quarter of both noun and adjective compounds, with the latter group being less frequent. The verbal element as a rule coincides with the past- or present-tense stem as is shown by the 3rd person (formally identical in singular and plural), which in the following description for brevity's sake is referred to as PRESENT or PAST (the second verbal component of a compound can be based on the infinitive stem as well). The formation of a compound is also completed with the generalization of the inflectional paradigms -is/-ys or -ė (e.g., šien-pjov-ỹs m., šien-pjov-ė̃ f. 'haymaker' ← šiẽn-as 'hay', pjóv-ė PAST of pjáu-ti 'to cut', IPs -ys, -ė), and there is no suffix involved except in isolated instances as, e.g., žuv-ėd-r-a 'tern' ← žuv-ìs 'fish', ėd-a/ėd-ė PRESENT/PAST of ės-ti 'to eat', suffix -r-, IP -a (in the latter case the word-formation process is to be interpreted as circumfixation).

As a rule, the first member of synthetic (verb-centered) nominal compounds is a noun (with adjectives, numerals, pronouns and adverbs also occurring in this position). The meanings of said compounds are similar to the meanings of a) agent nouns – m./f., b) instrument nouns, and c) action nouns, e.g.,

a) darb-dav-ỹs, -ė̃ 'employer' (← dárb-as 'work, job', dãv-ė PAST of dúo-ti 'to give', IPs -ys, -ė), ūk-ved-ỹs, -ė̃ 'manager' (← ū̃k-is 'economy, household', vẽd-ė PAST of vès-ti 'to manage', IPs -ys, -ė); jaun-a-ved-ỹs, -ė̃ 'bridegroom, bride' (← jáun-as, -à 'young', interfix -a-, vẽd-ė PAST of vès-ti 'to marry, wed', IPs -ys, -ė); pirm-ã-gim-is, -ė 'firstborn child' m./f. (← pìrm-as, -à 'first', interfix -a-, gìm-ti 'to be born', IPs -is, -ė); sav-i-myl-a (common gender) 'self lover, egoist' (← sav-è 'oneself', interfix -i-, mýl-i PRESENT of myl-ė́-ti 'to love', IP -a); čiã-buv-is, -ė 'native, indigenous' (← čià 'here', bùv-o PAST of bū́-ti 'to be', IPs -is, -ė);

b) laĩk-rod-is 'clock' (← laĩk-as 'time', ród-o/ród-ė PRESENT/PAST of ród-y-ti 'to show', IP -is), véid-rod-is 'mirror' (← véid-as 'face', ród-o/ród-ė, IP -is), bùlv-ia-kas-ė 'potato-digging machine' (← bùlv-ė 'potato', interfix -ia-, kàs-ti 'to dig', IP -ė);

c) sav-i-gyn-a 'self-defence' (← sav-è 'himself, herself', interfix -i-, gýn-ė PAST of gìn-ti 'to defend', IP -a), lãp-krit-is 'November' (← lãp-as 'leaf', krìt-o PAST of krìs-ti 'to fall', IP -is), vien-ã-skait-a 'singular' (← víen-as, -à 'one', interfix -a-, skaĩt-o/ skaĩt-ė PRESENT/PAST of skait-ý-ti 'to count', IP -a).

The first member of synthetic adjectival compounds with a verbal second member is based on a noun (e.g., mės-ė̃d-is, -ė 'carnivorous' ← mės-à 'meat', ėd-a/ėd-ė PRESENT/PAST of ės-ti 'to eat', IPs -is, -ė), numerals (e.g., pirm-ã-gim-is, -ė 'firstborn' ← pìrm-as, -à 'first', interfix -a-, gìm-ti 'to be born', IPs -is, -ė), adverbs (e.g., tol-ia-rẽg-is, -ė 'long-sighted, far-sighted' ← tol-ì 'far', interfix -ia-, rẽg-i PRESENT of reg-ė́-ti 'to see', IPs -is, -ė), adjectives (e.g., gyv-ã-ved-is, -ė 'viviparous' ← gýv-as, -à 'live, alive', vẽd-a/vẽd-ė PRESENT/PAST of vès-ti 'to give birth to', IPs -is, -ė), and pronouns, e.g., *vis-a-žìn-is, -ė* 'omniscient' (← *vìs-as, -à* 'all', interfix *-a-*, *žìn-o* PRESENT of *žin-ó-ti* 'to know', IPs *-is, -ė*).

Composition is a rare phenomenon among numerals, pronouns and adverbs. Numerals from 11 to 19 and from 20 to 90 can be mentioned (e.g., *penk-ió-lik-a* '15' ← *penk-ì* '5', interfix *-io-*, *lìk-ti* 'to remain, be left', IP *-a*, *dvì-dešimt* '20' ← *dvì* f. 'two', *dẽšimt* 'ten'), pronouns (e.g., *kel-ió-lik-a* 'some (between 11 and 19)' ← *kel-ì* 'some', interfix *-io-*, *lìk-ti* 'to remain, be left', IP *-a*, *vìs-k-as* 'everything' ← *vìs-as, -à* 'all, whole', *k-às* 'who, what', IP *-as*), and adverbs (e.g., *an-à-pus* 'on that side, on the other side' ← *an-às, -à* 'that, that one', interfix *-a-*, *pùs-ė* 'side').

(For more on composition see Urbutis 1961b; 2008: 98, 115–116; Ulvydas 1965–71, Vol. 1: 437–473, 591–603; Keinys 1999: 69–74, 80–82, 84–85, 98; V. Ambrazas 2005 [1994]: 150–167, 228–238.)

4 Derivation

In the nominal, adjectival and adverbial word-formation system, suffixal derivatives are much more widespread than prefixal ones, however, in verbal derivation the latter type prevails. (See also section 5 on conversion and "paradigmatic derivatives".)

In inflectable derived words, suffixes as the main derivational formants are accompanied by inflectional paradigms (IP) which, as a rule, differ from the inflectional paradigms of the base words and serve as a secondary means of derivation (hence, suffixes are usually listed with endings of the nominative case or 3rd person). Cf., e.g., the denominal suffixal noun *egl-ýn-as* 'fir grove' (suffix *-yn-*, IP *-as*) and the base word *ẽgl-ė* 'fir tree' (IP *-ė*); the denominal suffixal adjective *lauk-ìn-is, -ė* 'field, wild' (suffix *-in-*, IPs *-is, -ė*) and the base noun *laũk-as* 'field' (IP *-as*); the deverbal suffixal verb *var-inė́-ja/var-inė́-jo* (PRESENT/PAST of *var-inė́-ti* 'to drive there and back', suffix *-inė-*, IPs *-ja/-jo*) and the base verb *vãr-o/vãr-ė* (PRESENT/PAST of *var-ý-ti* 'to drive', IPs *-o/-ė*).

The same phenomenon is characteristic of many prefixal derivatives as well, cf. the denominal prefixed noun *pa-láng-ė* 'windowsill' (prefix *pa-*, IP *-ė*) and the base word *láng-as* 'window' (IP *-as*); the deadjectival prefixed adjective *apý-jaun-is, -ė* 'rather young' (prefix *apy-*, IPs *-is, -ė*) and the base word *jáun-as, -à* 'young' (IPs *-as, -a*), but – without a difference in the inflectional paradigms between all prefixal derivatives and their base words – *àt-neš-a, -ė* (PRESENT/PAST of *at-nèš-ti* 'to bring') ← *nẽš-a, -ė* (PRESENT/PAST of the base verb *nèš-ti* 'to carry'), *ne-gražùs, -ì* 'not beautiful, not nice' ← *gražùs, -ì* 'beautiful, nice'.

In addition to the derivational processes just mentioned, circumfixation is also attested to in Lithuanian, cf. the following prefixal-suffixal denominal derivatives: the adjective *prieš-laik-ìn-is, -ė* 'premature, untimely' (prefix *prieš-* 'before', suffix *-in-*, IPs *-is, -ė*) ← *laĩk-as* 'time', the adverb *pa-kel-iuĩ* 'on the way' (prefix *pa-* 'on', suffix *-iui*) ← *kẽl-ias* 'road, way', and the verb *į̃-žẽm-in-ti* 'to ground' (prefix *į̃-* 'in, into', suffix *-in-*, infinitive suffix *-ti*) ← *žẽm-ė* 'ground'.

As far as derivational affixes are concerned, attention should be paid to some suffixes beginning in back vowels which can have both "hard" and "soft" variants. The "hard" variant is, as a rule, attached to a base stem which ends in a hard consonant, while the "soft" variant is mostly attached to a stem ending in a palatalized consonant, cf. the derivatives with the suffixes *-(i)uot-as, -a* and *-(i)au-ti: auks-úot-as, -a* 'gilded' (← *áuks-as* 'gold') and *sluoksn-iúot-as, -a* 'flaky' (← *slúoksn-is* 'layer'), *piet-áu-ti* 'to have dinner' (← *piẽt-ūs* pl. 'dinner') and *vakarien-iáu-ti* 'to have supper' (← *vakariẽn-ė* 'supper').

4.1 Nominal derivation

Suffixal derivatives comprising hundreds of word-formation types of unequal productivity predominate in nominal derivation in Lithuanian. Prefixal and converted ("paradigmatic") derivatives are much less frequent and cover fewer word-formation types. The most productive prefix *pa-* is characteristic of ca. one third of prefixal nouns.

Three groups of nominal derivatives, i.e. denominal, deadjectival and deverbal nouns, are characterized, as a rule, by typical derivational affixes. Nevertheless, in some cases the same derivational affix occurs in two or even three groups, e.g., the suffixes *-inink-as, -ė* (cf. *krẽpš-inink-as, -ė* m./f. 'basketballer' ← *krepš-ỹs* 'basket', *bendr-iniñk-as, -ė* m./f. 'participator' ← *beñdr-as, -à* 'common', and *liùd-inink-as, -ė* m./f. 'witness' ← *liùd-y-ti* 'to witness') and *-(i)uomen-ė* (cf. *jaun-úomen-ė* 'youth' ← *jáun-as, -à* 'young', and *kar-iúomen-ė* 'army' ← *kar-ỹs* 'soldier').

4.1.1 Denominal nouns

Denominal **personal nouns** with the exception of some prefixed instances (e.g., *be-dařb-is, -ė* m./f. '(the) unemployed; lit. without a job' ← *dárb-as* 'job', *pa-tév-is* 'stepfather' ← *tév-as* 'father', *į̃-vaik-is* 'adopted child' ← *vaĩk-as* 'child') are derived by means of more than 50 suffixes. The most productive of them are as follows: *-iet-is, -ė* m./f. (e.g., *miest-iẽt-is, -ė* 'town-dweller' ← *miẽst-as* 'town, city', *europ-iẽt-is, -ė* 'European' ← *Europ-à* 'Europe'), *-inink-as, -ė* m./f. (e.g., *daĩl-inink-as, -ė* 'painter' ← *dail-ė̃* 'art', *darb-iniñk-as, -ė* 'worker' ← *dárb-as* 'work'), *-ist-as, -ė* m./f. (e.g., *karjer-ìst-as, -ė* 'careerist' ← *karjer-à* 'career', *taks-ìst-as, -ė* 'taxi-driver'

← *taksì* 'taxi'), *-ik-as*, *-ė* m./f. (e.g., *elèktr-ik-as*, *-ė* 'electrician' ← *elektr-à* 'electricity', *satỹr-ik-as*, *-ė* 'satirist' ← *satyr-à* 'satire'), *-ant-as*, *-ė* m./f. (e.g., *diplom-ánt-as*, *-ė* 'diploma holder, undergraduate' ← *diplòm-as* 'diploma, degree', *muzik-ánt-as*, *-ė* 'musician' ← *mùzik-a* 'music') (the latter three are Latinate suffixes and prefer, as a rule, Latinate bases).

Lithuanian has special suffixes which characterize the **matrimonial status** of women and are attached, as a rule, to the husband's surname: *-ien-ė* is the suffix denoting a married woman (e.g., *Jakáit-ien-ė* ← *Jakáit-is*) while for unmarried women the suffixes are *-ait-ė*, *-yt-ė*, *-ut-ė*, and *-(i)ūt-ė* depending on the inflectional paradigm of the father's surname, e.g., *Ambraz-áit-ė* ← *Ambrãz-as*, *Kein-ýt-ė* ← *Kein-ỹs*, *Butk-ùt-ė* ← *Bùtk-us*, *Skardž-iū̃t-ė* ← *Skařdž-ius*. Rare appellatives derived by adding said suffixes also exist, e.g., *ból-ien-ė* 'brother's wife' ← *ból-is* 'brother', *karal-íen-ė* 'king's wife, queen', *karal-áit-ė* 'king's daughter, princess' ← *karãl-ius* 'king', *kunigaikšt-ýt-ė* 'duke's daughter, princess' ← *kunigáikšt-is* 'duke, prince'.

Denominal **status nouns** are derived by adding several suffixes, the most productive of which is *-yst-ė* (e.g., *gimin-ỹst-ė* 'relationship, kinship' ← *gimin-ė̃* 'family, kin', *žemdirb-ỹst-ė* 'agriculture' ← *žemdirb-ỹs*, *-ė̃* m./f. 'farmer'). Productive suffixes also include *-yb-ė* (e.g., *brol-ýb-ė* 'brotherhood' ← *ból-is* 'brother', *šun-ýb-ė* 'dirty, mean trick' ← *šuõ* 'dog' (acc.sg. *šùn-į*)), the Latinate suffix *-izm-as* (e.g., *idiot-ìzm-as* 'idiocy' ← *idiòt-as* 'idiot', *popier-ìzm-as* 'red tape' ← *põpier-ius* 'paper').

Denominal **place nouns** are derived by means of ca. 17 prefixes and 17 suffixes. The most productive prefixes are *pa-* 'along', *už-* 'over, beyond, outside, the other side of', and *prie-* 'at, by' (e.g., *pa-jū́r-is* 'seashore', *ùž-jūr-is* 'overseas country' ← *jū́r-a* 'sea', *ùž-miest-is* 'outskirts', *príe-miest-is* 'suburb' ← *miẽst-as* 'town, city'), whereas the most productive suffixes are *-yn-as* (e.g., *puš-ýn-as* 'pine forest' ← *puš-ìs* 'pine') and *-in-ė* (e.g., *kav-ìn-ė* 'café' ← *kav-à* 'coffee'). Because of the change in the inflectional paradigms prefixal derivation is similar to circumfixation.

Denominal **collective nouns** are derived by adding several suffixes, the most productive of which is *-ij-a* (e.g., *draug-ij-à* 'company' ← *draũg-as*, *-ė* m./f. 'friend', *žmon-ij-à* 'mankind' ← *žmón-ės* pl. 'people', *gyvūn-ij-à* 'fauna' ← *gyvū́n-as* 'animal'). The suffixes *-yn-as* (e.g., *žvaigžd-ýn-as* 'constellation' ← *žvaigžd-ė̃* 'star', *laiv-ýn-as* 'fleet' ← *laĩv-as* 'ship') and *-ūr-a* (*aparat-ūr-à* 'apparatus' ← *aparãt-as* 'apparatus', *profes-ūr-à* 'professorate' ← *profèsor-ius*, *-ė* m./f. 'professor') can also be included (the latter suffix is a Latinate one).

Lithuanian is known as a language with a host of **diminutives** and **melioratives**, which are derived by ca. 15 suffixes. The most productive suffixes *-ėl-is*, *-ėl-ė* and *-ė̃l-is*, *-ė̃l-ė* are in complementary distribution: the first suffix-pair is attached to disyllabic nouns, while the second is combined with polysyllabic nouns, e.g., *vaik-ėl-is* 'small child' ← *vaĩk-as* 'child', *dukr-ėl-ė* 'little daughter' ← *dukr-à* 'daughter', *katin-ėl-is* 'little cat' ← *kãtin-as* 'cat', *vasar-ėl-ė* (meliorative) ← *vãsar-a* 'summer'. A few more suffixes that could be mentioned are the following: *-(i)uk-as* (e.g., *rat-ùk-as* 'small wheel' ← *rãt-as* 'wheel', *žąs-iùk-as* 'gosling' ← *žąs-ìs* 'goose'), *-ut-is, -ut-ė* (e.g., *niek-ùtis* 'knick-knack' ← *niẽk-as* 'nothing', *kėd-ùt-ė* 'small chair' ← *kėd-ė̃* 'chair'), *-ait-is, -ait-ė* (e.g., *pyrag-áit-ė* 'pastry' ← *pyrãg-as* 'cake', *kepur-áit-ė* 'little cap' ← *kepùr-ė* 'cap'), *-yt-is, -yt-ė* (e.g., *brol-ýt-is* (meliorative) ← *bról-is* 'brother', *kat-ýt-ė* 'little cat' ← *kat-ė̃* 'cat'), *-užis, -už-ė* (e.g., *draug-ùž-is, -ė* m./f. (meliorative) ← *draũg-as, -ė* 'friend'), *-ul-is, -ul-ė* (e.g., *Diev-ùl-is* (meliorative) ← *Diẽv-as* 'God', *tet-ùl-ė* 'auntie' ← *tet-à* 'aunt'). The suffixes *-ėl-is, -ėl-ė* and *-(i)ukas, -(i)uk-ė* can also be attached to diminutive bases, e.g., *broluž-ėl-is* (meliorative) ← *brolùž-is* (meliorative) ← *bról-is* 'brother'; *merguž-ėl-ė* (meliorative) ← *merg-ùž-ė* (meliorative) ← *merg-à* 'girl'; *senel-iùk-as, -ė* (meliorative) ← *sen-ėl-is, -ė* '(little) old man, woman' ← *sẽn-is, -ė* 'old man, woman'.

4.1.2 Deadjectival nouns

The majority of deadjectival derivatives comprise q u a l i t y n o u n s formed by adding ca. 15 suffixes, of which the more productive ones are *-um-as* (e.g., *aukšt-ùm-as* 'height' ← *áukšt-as, -à* 'high, tall', *ger-ùm-as* 'kindness, goodness' ← *gẽr-as, -à* 'good, kind') and *-yb-ė* (e.g., *lyg-ýb-ė* 'equality' ← *lýg-us, -ì* 'equal', *puik-ýb-ė* 'splendour, pride' ← *puik-ùs, -ì* 'splendid'). A few more suffixes can be mentioned, e.g., *-ov-ė* (*sen-óv-ė* 'old times, antiquity' ← *sẽn-as, -à* 'old, ancient') and *-yst-ė* (*Jaun-ỹst-ė* 'youth' ← *jáun-as, -à* 'young').

Only a few deadjectival suffixal derivatives are attested to in the following word-formation categories which are more typical for denominal formations (see section 4.1.1): p e r s o n a l n o u n s (e.g., *šaun-uõl-is, -ė* m./f. 'fine, decent person' ← *šaun-ùs, -ì* 'valiant', *gyv-ū̃n-as* 'animal, living being' ← *gýv-as, -à* 'live, living, alive', *blaiv-iniñk-as, -ė* m./f. 'teetotaller' ← *blaiv-ùs, -ì* 'sober'), c o l l e c t i v e n o u n s (e.g., *bendr-úomen-ė* 'community' ← *beñdr-as, -à* 'common'; *jaun-ìm-as* 'youth, young people' ← *jáun-as, -à* 'young') and p l a c e n o u n s (e.g., *aukšt-um-à* 'hill' ← *áukšt-as, -à* 'lofty').

4.1.3 Deverbal nouns

A c t i o n n o u n s, one of the most plentiful word-formation categories in respect to the number of derivatives it has, are formed by means of ca. 50 suffixes, the most productive and regular of which is *-im-as/-ym-as* attached to the past-tense stem of the base verb (the allomorph *-ym-as* only attaches to *-yti, -o, -ė* verbs), e.g., *ėj-ìm-as* 'going, walking' ← *ėj-o* (PAST of *eĩ-ti* 'to go, walk'), *važiãv-im-as* 'drive, driving' ← *važiãv-o* (PAST of *važiúo-ti* 'to go, drive, ride'), *rãš-ym-as* 'writing' ← *rãš-ė* (PAST of *raš-ý-ti* 'to write'). Other suffixes attach not only to the past-tense stem but also to the infinitive and sometimes to the present-tense stem of the base verb. Below are a number of productive derivational suffixes of action nouns: *-t-is* (e.g., *bū-t-ìs* 'being' ← *bū́-ti* 'to be', *užduo-t-ìs* 'task, job, target' ← *užduó-ti* 'to give, set'), *-es-ys* (e.g., *liūd-es-ỹs* 'sadness' ← *liūd-i* PRESENT of *liūdė́-ti* 'to be sad'), *-ul-ys* (e.g., *spind-ul-ỹs* 'ray, beam' ← *spiñd-i* PRESENT of *spindė́-ti* 'to shine, beam'), *-yb-a*, pl. *-yb-os* (e.g., *kūr-ýb-a* 'creative work, creation' ← *kū́r-ė* PAST of *kùr-ti* 'to create', *rad-ýb-os* '(finder's) reward' ← *rãd-o* PAST of *ràs-ti* 'to find'), *-sm-as* (e.g., *eĩ-sm-as* 'traffic' ← *eĩ-ti* 'to go, walk, run'), Latinate *-(i)acij-a* (e.g., *privatiz-ãcij-a* 'privatization' ← *privatiz-úo-ti* 'to privatize', *izol-iãcij-a* 'isolation' ← *izol-iúo-ti* 'to isolate').

About 40 suffixes are employed to derive deverbal r e s u l t n o u n s, but only few of them are productive: *-in-ys* (e.g., *krov-in-ỹs* 'load' ← *króv-ė* PAST of *kráu-ti* 'to load, lade'), *-al-as* (e.g., *gėr-al-as* 'drink' ← *gė́r-ė* PAST of *gér-ti* 'to drink'). Deverbal result nouns are also formed by means of conversion or "paradigmatic derivation" (see section 5.3), and some of them go back to metonymic shifts of action nouns.

A g e n t n o u n s also comprise a sizeable class of derivatives. They can be formed by means of ca. 50 suffixes, the majority of which attach to the past-tense or to the infinitive stem of the base verb. The suffixes *-toj-as, -a, -ėj-as, -a* and *-ėl-is, -ė* (all m./f.) are the most productive in this class, e.g., *móky-toj-as, -a* 'teacher' ← *móky-ti* 'to teach', *kūr-ė́j-as, -a* 'creator, author' ← *kū́r-ė* (PAST of *kùr-ti* 'to create'), *pasilėid-ė̃l-is, -ė* 'dissolute person' ← *pasilė́id-o* (PAST of *pasilė́is-ti* 'to become dissolute'). Other productive suffixes are as follows: *-ik-as, -ė* m./f. (e.g., *ėj-ìk-as, -ė* 'walker' ← *ė̃j-o* PAST of *eĩ-ti* 'to walk'), *-l-ys, -ė̃* m./f. (e.g., *bėg-l-ỹs, -ė̃* 'fugitive' ← *bė́g-ti* 'to run'), *-ūn-as, -ė* m./f. (*keik-ū̃n-as, -ė* 'one who swears' ← *kéik-ti-s* (reflexive verb) 'to swear'), *-tin-is, -ė* m./f. (e.g., *áuklė-tin-is, -ė* 'pupil' ← *áuklė-ti* 'to educate, train').

I n s t r u m e n t n o u n s are derived by means of more than 30 suffixes, which attach to the infinitive or past-tense stem of the base verb, and are not very productive. The more common of these are: *-tuv-as* (e.g., *šaldy-tùv-as* 'refrigerator' ← *šáldy-ti* 'to freeze'), *-ikl-is* (e.g., *krov-ìkl-is* 'charger' ← *króv-ė* PAST of *kráu-ti* 'to charge'), *-t-as* (*kél-t-as* 'ferry' ← *kél-ti* 'to ferry'), *-tuk-as* (e.g., *trin-tùk-as* 'eraser' ← *trìn-ti* 'to erase'), *-al-as* (e.g., *rãš-al-as* 'ink' ← *rãš-ė* PAST of *rašý-ti* 'to write').

Deverbal p l a c e n o u n s are much rarer than denominal or deadjectival ones, and mostly take the productive suffix *-ykl-a* (e.g., *leid-yklà* 'publishing house' ← *lė́id-o* PAST of *lė́is-ti* 'to publish').

Deverbal nouns denoting celebrations and feasts mostly take the suffix *-tuv-és* pl. (e.g., *ves-tùv-és* 'wedding' ← *vès-ti* 'to marry, wed', *išleis-tùv-és* 'seeing-off party' ← *išléis-ti* 'to let out').

(For more on nominal derivation see Ulvydas 1965–71, Vol. 1: 251–436; Keinys 1999: 36–69; V. Ambrazas 2005 [1994]: 86–150; Urbutis 2008 [1999]: 112–115.)

4.2 Adjectival derivation

Suffixal derivatives with ca. 130 suffixes (most with low productivity) play a central role in adjectival (mostly denominal) derivation. Prefixal and "paradigmatic derivatives" are also frequent (the latter type only occurs in deverbal derivation, see section 5). Circumfixation is attested to in rare cases, but is slightly more frequent than in nominal derivation.

4.2.1 Denominal adjectives

Suffixation is common, while prefixation is limited in denominal adjectives.

The majority of prefixal instances consist of privative adjectives taking the productive prefix *be-* 'un-, in-, -less, without', which triggers regular circumflex metatony or shift of stress to the penultimate syllable (e.g., *be-darb-is, -ė* 'unemployed, workless, without work' ← *dárb-as* 'work, job', *be-laĩsv-is, -ė* 'slave' ← *láisv-ė* 'freedom', *be-stubùr-is, -ė* 'invertebrate' ← *stùbur-as* 'vertebral column').

The majority of suffixal relational adjectives take the highly productive suffix *-in-is, -ė* (e.g., *jū́r-in-is, -ė* 'maritime' ← *jū́r-a* 'sea', *ryt-ìn-is, -ė* 'morning (adj.), eastern' ← *rýt-as* 'morning', *ry-taĩ* pl. 'the east', *darb-ìn-is, -ė* 'work-related' ← *dárb-as* 'work'). Other suffixes are unproductive, e.g., *-utin-is, -ė* (*virš-utìn-is, -ė* 'upper' ← *virš-ùs* 'top, upper part').

Qualitative denominal adjectives are derived by means of several dozen suffixes, the most productive of which are *-išk-as, -a* (e.g., *draũg-išk-as, -a* 'friendly' ← *draũg-as, -ė* 'friend') and *-(i)uot-as, -a* (e.g., *muil-úot-as, -a* 'soapy' ← *muĩl-as* 'soap') to derive similative adjectives, and *-ing-as, -a* (e.g., *laim-ìng-as, -a* 'happy' ← *láim-ė* 'happiness'), *eil-iúot-as, -a* 'rhymed' ← *eĩl-ės* pl. 'verse'), *-ėt-as, -a* (e.g., *saul-ėt-as, -a* 'sunny' ← *sául-ė* 'sun'), *-ot-as, -a* (e.g., *lig-ót-as, -a* 'ailing, sickly' ← *lig-à* 'illness'), and *-in-as, -a* (e.g., *ámž-in-as, -à* 'eternal, everlasting' ← *ámž-ius* 'century, age') to derive possessive adjectives.

4.2.2 Deadjectival adjectives

Deadjectival adjectives are formed by adding both prefixes and suffixes and usually express a t t e n u a t i o n, cf. derivatives with the productive prefixes *apy-* and *po-* (e.g., *apý-balt-is, -ė, pó-balt-is, -ė* 'partly, rather, pretty white' ← *bált-as, -à* 'white') as well as with the suffix *-ok-as, -a* (e.g., *balt-ók-as, -a* 'whitish, somewhat white' ← *bált-as, -à* 'white'). Other derivational affixes are not productive.

Deadjectival e v a l u a t i v e adjectives are derived by means of a group of endearment suffixes with intensifying meaning. The only productive suffixes among them are *-ut-is, -ė* and *-utėl-is, -ė* differing in the degree of intensification (e.g., *balt-ùt-is, -ė* 'very white', *balt-utė̃l-is, -ė* 'very very white' ← *báltas, -à* 'white').

The opposite (n e g a t i v e) meaning of deadjectival adjectives is expressed by adding the highly productive prefix *ne-* (e.g., *ne-graž-ùs, -ì* 'not beautiful, not nice' ← *graž-ùs, -ì* 'beautiful, nice', *ne-laimìng-as, -a* 'unhappy' ← *laimìng-as, -a* 'happy', *ne-dìdel-is, -ė* 'not big, not large' ← *dìdel-is, -ė* 'big, large').

4.2.3 Deverbal adjectives

Deverbal adjectives are rarer than denominal or deadjectival adjectives. They are derived by adding the semiproductive suffixes *-l-us, -i; -r-us, -i*, etc., and express both active and passive meanings, cf. *taik-l-ùs, -ì* 'well-aimed, accurate' ← *táik-ė* (PAST of *táik-y-ti* 'to aim') and *sek-l-ùs, -ì* 'shallow' ← *sèk-ti* 'to become lower, sink', *plėš-r-ùs, -ì* 'predatory, raptorial' ← *plė́š-ti* 'to rob, plunder' and *tamp-r-ùs, -ì* 'elastic' ← *tem̃p-ti* 'to stretch' (frequent apophony and metatony are characteristic of said derivatives).

(For more on adjectival derivation see Ulvydas 1965–71, Vol. 1: 550–591; Keinys 1999: 75–80; V. Ambrazas 2005 [1994]: 191–227; Urbutis 2008 [1999]: 97–98.)

4.3 Verbal derivation

Both prefixal and suffixal derivation is characteristic of verbs, the first process being more active but attested only in deverbal verbs. Circumfixation is rather limited. Reflexivization can also be understood as a derivational process (cf. V. Ambrazas 2008 [1997]: 226–234). Deverbal verbs are much more frequent than denominal verbs, and especially deadjectival verbs. Deverbal derivation can be accompanied by apophony as well as by a relatively regular acute metatony, which are extremely rare in denominal and deadjectival derivation.

The verbs are derived by adding 14 highly productive prefixes and nine basic suffixes which have ca. 80 variants, cf. *-(i)o-ti* and *-čio-ti, -no-ti, -sno-ti; -y-ti* and *-dy-ti, -sty-ti*.

4.3.1 Denominal verbs

Denominal verbs are derived by adding seven basic suffixes, i.e. *-(i)uo-ti, -(i)au-ti, -(i)o-ti, -ė-ti, -in-ti, -y-ti, -inė-ti*. They belong to the following derivational categories (a–d) or have the following derivational meanings (e–g) (the derivational categories a–c are also characteristic of deadjectival verbs, see section 4.3.2):

a) Factitive verbs, e.g., *-(i)uo-ti* (*por-úo-ti* 'to couple, pair' ← *por-à* 'couple, pair', *eil-iúo-ti* 'to form up, draw up' ← *eil-ė̃* 'row, line', *konspekt-úo-ti* 'to take notes' ← *konspèkt-as* 'notes'), *-in-ti* (*lietùv-in-ti* 'to Lithuanize' ← *lietùv-is* 'Lithuanian'), *-(i)o-ti* (*auk-ó-ti* 'to give sacrifice, offer' ← *auk-à* 'sacrifice, offering', *vag-ó-ti* 'to furrow, plough' ← *vag-à* 'furrow');

b) Verbs of performance, e.g., *-(i)au-ti* (*gydytoj-áu-ti* 'to practice medicine' ← *gýdytoj-as* 'doctor', *karal-iáu-ti* 'to reign' ← *karãl-ius* 'king'), *-inė-ti* (*šnip-inė́-ti* 'to spy' ← *šnìp-as* 'spy');

c) Inchoative verbs, e.g., *-ė-ti* (*angl-ė́-ti* 'to become charred' ← *angl-ìs* 'coal', *žvėr-ė́-ti* 'to become brutal' ← *žvėr-ìs* 'beast'), *-(i)uo-ti* (*gar-úo-ti* 'to evaporate' ← *gãr-as* 'steam, vapour'), *-y-ti* (*vanden-ý-ti* 'to grow, become watery' ← *vanduõ* (acc.sg. *vánden-į*) 'water');

d) Instrumental verbs, e.g., *-(i)uo-ti* (*irkl-úo-ti* 'to row, pull' ← *ìrkl-as* 'oar', *bur-iúo-ti* 'to sail' ← *bùr-ė* 'sail'), *-(i)o-ti* (*mešker-ió-ti* 'to fish' ← *mešker-ė̃* 'fishing rod');

e) Verbs with the meaning 'to look for, collect what is indicated by the base word', e.g., *-(i)au-ti* (*gryb-áu-ti* 'to gather mushrooms' ← *grỹb-as* 'mushroom', *vyšn-iáu-ti* 'to pick cherries' ← *vyšn-ià* 'cherry');

f) Verbs with the meaning 'to participate in the activities indicated by the base word', e.g., *-(i)au-ti* (*puot-áu-ti* 'to feast, banquet' ← *puot-à* 'feast, banquet', *lenktyn-iáu-ti* 'to compete, race' ← *lenktỹn-ės* 'competition'), *-(i)úo-ti* (*sport-úo-ti* 'to go in for sports' ← *spòrt-as* 'sport', *gastrol-iúo-ti* 'to tour' ← *gastròl-ės* 'tour');

g) Verbs with the meaning 'to be consumed (gripped, seized) by what is indicated by the base word', e.g., *-(i)o-ti* (*liepsn-ó-ti* 'to flame' ← *liepsn-à* 'flame'), *-(i)uo-ti* (*slog-úo-ti* 'to have a cold' ← *slog-à* 'cold', *pūl-iúo-ti* 'to fester' ← *pū́l-iai* 'pus').

4.3.2 Deadjectival verbs

Deadjectival verbs are derived by adding seven basic suffixes, i.e. *-in-ti, -au-ti, -inė-ti, -ė-ti, -en-ti, -(i)uo-ti, -(i)oti*, and belong to the following derivational categories:
a) Factitive verbs, e.g., *-in-ti* (*gẽr-in-ti* 'to improve, make better' ← *gẽr-as, -à* 'good', *žẽm-in-ti* 'to lower, debase' ← *žẽm-as, -à* 'low'), *-(i)o-ti* (*bjaur-ó-ti* 'to make foul, dirty' ← *bjaur-ùs, -ì* 'ugly, hideous, disgraceful');
b) Verbs of performance, e.g., *-(i)au-ti* (*gudr-áu-ti* 'to contrive, do cleverly' ← *gudr-ùs, -ì* 'clever, cunning', *nuolaidž-iáu-ti* 'to compromise, connive' ← *nuolaid-ùs, -ì* 'yielding, compliant'), *-inė-ti* (*dyk-inė-ti* 'to idle, loaf' ← *dỹk-as, -à* 'idle, free'), *-ė-ti* (*gars-ė́-ti* 'to sound, be/become famous' ← *gars-ùs, -ì* 'loud; famous'), *-en-ti* (*švepl-én-ti* 'to lisp' ← *švẽpl-as, -à* 'lisping'), *-(i)o-ti* (*kvail-ió-ti* 'to fool (about), play the fool' ← *kvaĩl-as, -à* 'foolish, stupid');
c) Inchoative verbs, e.g., *-ė-ti* (*pìlk-ė́-ti* 'to turn grey' ← *pìlk-as, -à* 'grey', *tams-ė́-ti* 'to become dark(er)' ← *tams-ùs, -ì* 'dark'), *-uoti* (*rud-úo-ti* 'to grow/be brown, turn reddish' ← *rùd-as, -à* 'brown, red'), *-y-ti* (*gelton-ý-ti* 'to turn yellow' ← *geltón-as, -a* 'yellow').

4.3.3 Deverbal verbs

Deverbal verbs can be derived by adding both prefixes and suffixes.

Prefixes express that the action, process or state denoted by the base verb is, was or will be started (e.g., *už-dainúoti* 'to begin to sing' ← *dainúoti* 'to sing') or finished (e.g., *iš-mèsti* 'to throw out' ← *mèsti* 'to throw'). Prefixal derivatives, as a rule, pick out different characteristics of the action expressed by the base verb, e.g.,
a) Direction: *iš-eĩti* 'to go out', *į-eĩti* 'to enter, go in', *pra-eĩti* 'to pass, go by/past', *ap-eĩti* 'to go, pass (to go around, evade)' ← *eĩti* 'to go';
b) Duration: *pér-gyventi* 'to outlive', *pa-gyvénti* 'to live, stay', *nu-gyvénti* 'to have lived one's life; to ruin' ← *gyvénti* 'to live';
c) Intensity: *į-gérti* 'to take some drink', *pér-gerti* 'to drink too much' ← *gérti* 'to drink', *ap-ramìnti* 'to calm, quieten, console for a while' ← *ramìnti* 'to calm, quieten, console', *pra-vérti* 'to open slightly' ← *vérti* 'to open';
d) Repetition of an action: *pér-dažyti* 'to recolour, repaint' ← *dažýti* 'to colour, paint', *at-kùrti* 'to recreate' ← *kùrti* 'to create'.

Suffixal deverbal verbs take nine basic suffixes, and can be attributed to the following word-formation categories:

a) Iteratives: *-(i)o-/-(s)no-ti* (e.g., *bėg-ió-ti* 'to run (about), fuss' ← *bėg-ti* 'to run', *kil-ó-ti, kil-nó-ti* 'to lift time and again' ← *kél-ti* 'to lift, raise' – including qualitative apophony <el/il>, *keik-snó-ti* 'to swear a little' ← *kéik-ti* 'to swear'), *-(d)inė-ti* (e.g., *bėg-inė-ti* 'to run about, run to and fro' ← *bėg-ti* 'to run', *pul-dinė-ti* 'to attack from time to time' ← *pùl-ti* 'to attack'), *-(d)/-(st)y-ti* (e.g., *dauž-ý-ti* 'to break, crush' ← *daũž-ti* 'to strike, hit', *stùm-dy-ti* 'to push, shove time and again' ← *stùm-ti* 'to push, shove', *pìl-sty-ti* 'to pour out, bottle' ← *pìl-ti* 'to pour'), *-au-ti* (e.g., *švilp-au-ti* 'to whistle time and again' ← *švil̃p-ti* 'to whistle' – including acute metatony), *-(s)ė-ti* (e.g., *čiršk-ė́-ti* 'to chirp time and again' ← *čiřšk-ė* PAST of *čiřkš-ti* 'to chirp'), *link-sė́-ti* 'to nod, bow time and again' ← *liñk-ti* 'to bend');
b) Causatives: *-(d)in-ti* (e.g., *lės-in-ti* 'to feed birds and poultry' ← *lès-ti* 'to peck', *sprog-dìn-ti* 'to blow up, explode' ← *spróg-ti* 'to burst'), *-(d)y-ti* (e.g., *mók-y-ti* 'to teach' ← *mók-a* PRESENT of *mok-ė́-ti* 'to know how', *gìr-dy-ti* 'to give to drink, make drunk' ← *gér-ti* 'to drink' – including qualitative apophony <er/ir>);
c) Diminutives: *-(s)telė-ti* (e.g., *plik-telė-ti* 'to get, go a little bald' ← *plìk-ti* 'to grow, go bald', *žil-stelė-ti* 'to grey, go somewhat grey' ← *žìl-ti* 'to grey, go grey'), *-ė-ti* (*palūk-ė́-ti* 'to wait for a short time' ← *paláuk-ti* 'to wait'). On the possibility of circumfixation see below;
d) Duratives: *-(d)ė-ti* (e.g., *klūp-ė́-ti* 'to be on one's knees' ← *klaũp-ti-s* 'to kneel down', *mér-dė-ti* 'to be dying' ← *miř-ti* 'to die' – including qualitative apophony <ir/er> and acute metatony), *-(s)o-ti* (*klū̃p-o-ti* 'to be on one's knees' ← *klaũp-ti-s* 'to kneel down' – including qualitative apophony <au/ū> and acute metatony, *vėp-só-ti* 'to gawk' ← *vėp-ti* 'to lower');
e) Semelfactives: *-(s)telė-ti* (e.g., *šūk-telė-ti* 'to give a cry' ← *šaũk-ti* 'to cry' – including qualitative apophony <au/ū> and acute metatony, *trink-telė-ti* 'to bang, slam (once)' ← *treñk-ti* 'to crash, bang, strike' – including qualitative apophony <en/in> and acute metatony, *mó-stelė-ti* 'to wave once quickly' ← *mó-ti* 'to wave').

Among the many deverbatives that exist, there are instances that, as a rule, are treated as circumfixal diminutives derived by simultaneously adding the prefix *pa-* and the suffix *-ė-ti* (e.g., *pa-bėg-ė́-ti* 'to run a little' ← *bėg-ti* 'to run', *pa-lyp-ė́-ti* 'to climb a little' ← *lìp-ti* 'to climb' – including quantitative apophony <i/i:>). Nevertheless, many verbs of said type could be interpreted as formations derived by adding the suffix *-ė-ti* to the prefixed base verbs, e.g., *panėš-ė́-ti* 'to carry for a while, a little' ← *panėš-ti* 'to carry' – including apophony <e/ė> (Keinys 1999: 97; Urbutis 2009 [1978]: 340).

There are also suffixal verbs (ca. 15 %), which are mostly iteratives and semelfactives that may be interpreted as interjectional derivatives, e.g., *pliùmp-čio-ti, pliump-sė́-ti* 'to plop (rather frequently)', *pliùmp-telė-ti* 'to plop once' ← *pliùmpt* 'plop', *val-iúo-ti* 'to shout hurrah' ← *valiõ* 'hurrah, hurray!'). It is occasionally difficult to establish whether a suffixal verb is based on an interjection or verb because of the fact that some interjections are derived from verbs.

(For more on verbal derivation see Ulvydas 1965–71, Vol. 2: 218–298; Jakaitienė 1973: 8–59; Keinys 1999: 86–97; V. Ambrazas 2005 [1994]: 385–406.)

4.4 Adverbial derivation

Suffixal and deadjectival derivatives dominate in the word-formation subsystem of adverbs. In addition, there is a group of circumfixal derivatives. Prefixation is not characteristic of adverbial derivation, except in rare cases, e.g., *ùž-vakar* 'the day before yesterday' ← *vãkar* 'yesterday'.

The majority of adverbs are derived by means of several dozen suffixes, the most productive of which is *-(i)ai* (deadjectival and departicipial derivatives), e.g., *ger-aĩ* 'well' ← *gẽr-as, -à* 'good', *graž-iaĩ* 'beautifully, nicely' ← *graž-ùs, -ì* 'beautiful, nice', *vỹkus-iai* 'successfully' ← *vỹkęs* m., *vỹkus-i* f. 'successful' (active past participle of *vỹk-ti* 'to be a success'), *neĩgiam-ai* 'negatively' ← *neĩgiam-as, -à* 'negative' (passive present participle of *neĩg-ti* 'to deny, negate'), *nelaukt-aĩ* 'unexpectedly' ← *neláukt-as, -à* 'unexpected' (passive past participle of *neláuk-ti* 'to not expect').

Other productive or partly productive suffixes are the following: *-yn* (mostly deadjectival derivatives), e.g., *žem-ỹn* 'down, downwards' ← *žẽm-as, -à* 'low', *maž-ỹn* 'decreasingly' ← *mãž-as, -à* 'small, little'; *-omis/-om* (mostly deverbal, but also deadjectival and sometimes denominal derivatives), e.g., *sėd-omìs/sėd-õm* 'in sitting position' ← *sėd-i* (PRESENT of *sėd-ė́-ti* 'to sit'), *greit-omìs/greit-õm* 'hastily, hurriedly' ← *greĩt-as, -à* 'quick, prompt, speedy', *juok-omìs/juok-õm* 'jokingly, for fun' ← *juok-aĩ* pl. 'jokes'; *-te, -tinai* (deverbal derivatives "used with verbs of the same root to intensify or emphasize their meaning", V. Ambrazas 2008 [1997]: 384), e.g., *neš-tè, neš-tinaĩ* ← *nèš-ti* 'to carry', *žiūrė́-te, žiūrė́-tinai* ← *žiūrė́-ti* 'to look'. Sometimes *-tinai* derivatives can have special meanings, e.g., *im-tinaĩ* 'inclusive' ← *im̃-ti* 'to take'; *-(i)aip* (depronominal, denumeral and sometimes deadjectival derivatives), e.g., *kit-aĩp* 'in another way' ← *kìt-as, -à* 'other', *antr-aĩp* 'otherwise, differently' ← *añtr-as, -à* 'second', *nauj-aĩp* 'in a new way' ← *naũj-as, -à* 'new'.

Circumfixation is realized mostly by simultaneously adding the prefix *pa-* and the suffix *-iui*, e.g., *pa-dien-iuĩ* 'by the day, every other day' ← *dien-à* 'day', *pa-kel-iuĩ* 'on the way' ← *kẽl-ias* 'road'. Other prefixes and suffixes also occur, e.g., *pra-dien-iuĩ* 'every other/second day' ← *dien-à*, *pró-tarp-iais* 'at intervals' ← *tárp-as* 'interval'. Circumfixal adverbs are, as a rule, denominal formations.

(For more on adverbial derivation see Ulvydas 1965–71, Vol. 2: 500–542; Keinys 1999: 98–102; V. Ambrazas 2005 [1994]: 429–431; Urbutis 2008 [1999]: 432–433.)

5 Conversion

Lithuanian linguists understand conversion as a real (and not presumed) derivational process which seems to be as, or even more, productive than prefixation. The result of conversion is a new word which differs from the base word in the inflectional paradigm and frequently, but not necessarily, also in the word class, including, as a rule, a metatony/shift of stress and/or apophony in the root of the base word. Cf. *knỹg-ius* 'bibliophile' ← *knyg-à* (acc.sg. *knỹg-ą*) 'book', *puõdž-ius* 'potter' ← *púod-as* 'pot', *vasãr-is* 'February' ← *vãsar-a* 'summer' (all given instances are nouns; derivatives differ from the base words in their inflectional paradigms, including circumflex metatony in the second and shift of stress to the penultimate syllable in the third example); *šū̃k-is* 'slogan' ← *šaũk-ti* 'cry, shout' (deverbal noun with qualitative apophony <au/ū>). The process of conversion frequently also includes morphophonemic changes in the prefix of the base word, e.g., the prefixes *pri-*, *nu-* of the base verb take the allomorphs *prie-*, *nuo-* in derivatives (*príe-raš-as* 'addition, postscript' ← *pri-rãš-ė* PAST of *priraš-ý-ti* 'to add', *núo-raš-as* 'copy' ← *nu-rãš-ė* PAST of *nuraš-ý-ti* 'to copy').

The derivatives in question are labelled as paradigmatic, or inflectional, derivatives according to the Lithuanian word-formation tradition (Lith. *galūnių vediniai*, see Urbutis 1961a; 2009 [1978]: 333–340). In this case, inflections of derivatives perform a double function: they are affixes both of inflectional and derivational morphology. Thus *knỹg-ius* and *vasãr-is* are interpreted as denominal paradigmatic *-ius* and *-is* derivatives, while *šū̃k-is* as a paradigmatic deverbal *-is* derivative (with the nominative singular endings serving as markers both of derivational status and inflectional paradigms).

Conversion is widespread in Lithuanian nominal and adjectival derivation. It seems that it plays a certain role in verbal derivation as well but this aspect has not yet been studied.

5.1 Nominal conversion

Deverbal conversion predominates, while deadjectival conversion is relatively rare and denominal conversion is quite rare.

Denominal converted nouns, as a rule, consist of personal/profession nouns characterized by the inflectional paradigms *-ius* m., *-ė* f. and *-is/-ys* m., e.g., *daĩnius, -ė* 'singer, poet, bard' ← *dainà* 'song', *ragãnius, -ė* 'sorcerer, magician' ← *rãgana* 'witch' (including a shift of stress to the penultimate syllable), *šiaur-ỹs* (acc.sg. *šiaũr-į*) 'north wind' ← *šiáur-ė* 'north'), including circumflex metatony. There is also a small group of female nouns characterized by the inflectional paradigm *-ė*, e.g., *kalakùt-ė* 'turkey hen' ← *kalakùt-as* 'turkey-cock'.

Deadjectival converted nouns represent quality and personal nouns characterized as a rule by the inflection classes *-is/-ys* (*-ė*), e.g., *greĩt-is* 'speed' ← *greĩt-as, -à* 'quick, speedy', *skõn-is* 'taste' ← *skan-ùs, -ì* 'delicious, tasty', *márg-is, -ė* m./f. 'a speckled/piebald/spotted animal' ← *márg-as, -à* 'motley, variegated, of many colours', *kvail-ỹs, -ė̃* m./f. 'fool' ← *kvaĩl-as, -à* 'foolish'. Some place nouns ending in *-ė* are also attested to, e.g., *núošal-ė* 'offside' ← *nuošal-ùs, -ì* 'secluded, solitary, retired'.

Deverbal converted nouns represent a) result nouns, b) action nouns, and c) agent nouns characterized by the inflectional paradigms *-a, -as, -is/-ys* (*-ė*), *-ė, -ius* (the most copious is the first class, and the most productive is the IP *-a*), e.g.,

a) *išmald-a* 'alms' ← *išmeld-ė* (PAST of *išmels-ti* 'to beg successfully'), with qualitative apophony <el/al>, *skald-à* 'broken stone' ← *skáld-ė* (PAST of *skáld-y-ti* 'to split'), *užraš-as* 'note' ← *užrãš-ė* (PAST of *užraš-ý-ti* 'to note (down)'), *plyš-ỹs* 'cleft, crack' ← *plýš-ti* 'to split, crack', *riek-ė̃* 'slice' ← *riẽk-ti* 'to slice', *skýr-ius* 'chapter, section' ← *skýr-ė* (PAST of *skìr-ti* 'to separate, detach, divide'), with circumflex metatony;

b) *apklaus-à* 'interrogatory' ← *apkláus-ti* 'to interrogate', *slaug-à* 'nursing' ← *slaũg-ė* (PAST of *slaug-ý-ti* 'to nurse'), *skrỹd-is* 'flight' ← *skrìd-o* (PAST of *skrìs-ti* 'to fly'), with quantitative apophony <i/i:>, *juõk-as* 'laugh' ← *juõk-ti-s* 'to laugh';

c) *drim̃b-a* 'lout, bumpkin' ← *drim̃b-a* (PRESENT of *drìb-ti* 'to fall down'), including acute metatony, *užúomarš-a* 'forgetful person' ← *užmir̃š-ti* 'to forget'), including allomorphs of the prefix <už-/užuo-> and qualitative apophony <ir/ar>, *plep-ỹs, -ė̃* 'chatterer' ← *plẽp-a* (PRESENT of *plep-ė́-ti* 'to chatter'), *sárg-as, -ė* m./f. 'watchman' ← *sérg-i* (PRESENT of *sérg-ė-ti* 'to watch'), with qualitative apophony <er/ar> (mostly pejorative derivatives).

There are also deverbal converted nouns characterized by the inflection classes *-as* (plural *-ai*), *-a, -ė* and *-is/-ys* which denote d) instruments, sometimes e) places, and f) celebrations/feasts, e.g.,

d) *spaũd-as* 'stamp' ← *spáud-ė* (PAST of *spáus-ti* 'to press'), with circumflex metatony; *ãpav-as* 'footwear' ← *àpav-ė* (PAST of *apaũ-ti* 'to put on shoes'), *sag-à* 'button' ← *sèg-ti* 'to button' (including qualitative apophony <e/a>), *dìld-ė* 'file'

← dìld-ė (PAST of dìldy-ti 'to file'), stabd-ỹs 'brake' ← stãbd-ė (PAST of stabd-ý-ti 'to brake');
e) pérėj-a 'pass, passage' ← pérėj-o (PAST of pérei-ti 'to cross'), guõl-is 'bed, couch' ← gùl-ė (PAST of gul̃-ti 'to lie down'), including apophony <u/uo>;
f) atlaid-aĩ pl. 'church festival' ← atléid-o (PAST of atléis-ti 'to absolve, remit sins'), including qualitative apophony <ei/ai>.

(For more on nominal conversion see Urbutis 1961a; 2008 [1999]: 112–115; Ulvydas 1965–71, Vol. 1: 251–423; Keinys 1999: 55–62; V. Ambrazas 2005 [1994]: 86–145.)

5.2 Adjectival conversion

Adjectival conversion is not as developed as nominal conversion in Lithuanian. Denominal adjectives of this type are very rare (e.g., šiaur-ùs, -ì 'northern, cold' ← šiáur-ė 'north'). The majority of widely used converted adjectives are deverbal, which are characterized by the productive inflectional paradigms -us m., -i f. They occur with both active and passive meanings, cf. gab-ùs, -ì 'gifted' ← gẽb-a (PRESENT of geb-ė́-ti 'to know how, be able to'), including qualitative apophony <e/a>, valg-ùs, -ì 'having an appetite' ← válgo (PRESENT of válg-y-ti 'to eat') and talp-ùs, -ì 'capacious, spacious' ← tel̃p-a (PRESENT of til̃p-ti 'to go in, fit in, find room'), including qualitative apophony <el/al>, deg-ùs, -ì 'inflammable' ← dèg-ti 'to burn', pažang-ùs, -ì 'progressive' ← pažeñg-ti 'to make progress', including qualitative apophony <en/an>. Deverbal converted adjectives characterized by the inflectional paradigms -as m., -a f. are rarer, e.g., paláid-as, -à 'loose, untied, dissolve' ← paléid-o (PAST of paléis-ti 'to let go, loosen'), including qualitative apophony <ei/ai>.

(For more see Ulvydas 1965–71, Vol. 1: 550–586; Keinys 1999: 78; V. Ambrazas 2005 [1994]: 191–223; Urbutis 2008 [1999]: 98.)

5.3 Verbal conversion

The following rare deadjectival and denominal formations could be treated as instances of verbal conversion, e.g., bráng-o (PAST of bráng-ti 'to rise in price') ← brang-ùs, -ì 'expensive', bùk-o (PAST of bùk-ti 'to grow, get blunt') ← bùk-as, -à 'blunt', šãš-o (PAST of šàš-ti 'to scab, grow scabby') ← šãš-as 'scab'.

5.4 Adverbial conversion

Many adverbs are adverbialized case forms of nouns, especially the following:
a) nominative, e.g., *val-ià* '(it) is allowed, one may' ← *val-ià* 'will';
b) accusative, e.g., *trupùt-į* 'slightly, little' ← *trupùt-is* 'a little, a bit, some';
c) instrumental, e.g., *gret-à* 'side by side' ← *gret-à* 'file, rank', *kart-ù* 'together' ← *kar̃t-as* 'time'.

There are adverbialized case forms of adjectives and pronouns as well, in particular the following:
a) dative, e.g., *ilg-ám* 'for long' ← *ìlg-as* m. 'long', *trump-ám* 'for a short while' ← *trum̃p-as* m. 'short', *k-ám* 'why, what for' ← *k-às* 'what';
b) instrumental, e.g., *slapt-à* 'secretly' ← *slapt-à* f. 'secret', *ger-úoju* 'voluntarily, of one's own free will' ← *ger-àsis* m. 'the good (abstr. noun)';
c) genitive, e.g., *k-õ* 'why' ← *k-às* 'what'.

(For more see V. Ambrazas 2008 [1997]: 382.)
Deverbal adverbial conversion is not characteristic of Lithuanian.

6 Backformation

Backformation is not characteristic of standard Lithuanian. Only isolated instances of supposed desuffixation (a) and deprefixation (b) are attested to, e.g.,
a) *ãras* 'eagle' (a poetic word) ← *erẽlis* 'eagle' (a borrowing from Slavic, interpreted as a diminutive with the suffix *-el-is*);
b) *mẽnė* 'hall' ← *priemenė̃* 'entry, entrance room' (interpreted as a derivative with the prefix *prie-*).

7 Reduplication

Reduplication, except for onomatopoeic words, is not characteristic of Lithuanian word-formation. Only isolated instances of reduplicated nouns, adjectives and adverbs are attested to, e.g., *mãž-mož-is* 'trifle, small point' ← *mãž-as, -à* 'small', *niẽk-niek-is* 'trifle, nothing' ← *niẽk-as* 'nothing'; dialectal *sén-sen-is, -ė* 'very old' ← *sén-as, -à* 'old', *kar̃t-kart-ėmis* 'at times, from time to time' ← *kar̃t-as* 'time'.

A great many onomatopoeic words are distinguished by a reduplicated structure, e.g., *bra-bràkšt* ← *bràkšt* 'crack!', *či-čìnkt* ← *čìnkt* 'chink!', *du-dùn* ← *dùn* 'crash!' (see V. Ambrazas 2008 [1997]: 444–445).

8 Clipping

Clipping is a phenomenon of informal language, especially jargon, e.g., kòmpas ← kompiùteris 'computer', mãgas ← magnetofònas 'tape recorder'. Standard Lithuanian possesses some borrowed clippings (e.g., metrò 'metro' ← metropolitėnas 'metropolitan') and clipped compound calques, e.g., kol-ū́kis 'collective farm' (cf. Russian kol-choz) ← kolektỹvas 'collective', ū́kis 'farm'; spec-drabùžiai 'overalls, protective outer garments' (cf. Russian spec-odežda) ← speciãlūs 'special', drabùžiai 'garments' (regular compounds could have been kolektyv-ū́kis and special-drabužiaĩ).

Acknowledgements

I would like to thank Dr. Jurgis Pakerys (Vilnius University) for useful comments and suggestions which led to some improvements and corrections. Thanks are also due to Dr. Birutė Ryvitytė and Jayde Will (Vilnius University) for the correction of my English. All shortcomings and misinterpretations are, of course, mine.

9 References

Aleksandrow, Aleksander (1888): *Litauische Studien.* 1: *Nominalzusammensetzungen.* Dorpat: Hermann.
Ambrazas, Saulius (1993): *Daiktavardžių darybos raida.* Vol. 1: *Lietuvių kalbos veiksmažodiniai vediniai.* Vilnius: Mokslo ir enciklopedijų leidykla.
Ambrazas, Saulius (2000): *Daiktavardžių darybos raida.* Vol. 2: *Lietuvių kalbos vardažodiniai vediniai.* Vilnius: Mokslo ir enciklopedijų leidybos institutas.
Ambrazas, Saulius (2011): *Būdvardžių darybos raida.* Vilnius: Lietuvių kalbos institutas.
Ambrazas, Vytautas (ed.) (2005 [1994]): *Dabartinės lietuvių kalbos gramatika.* 4th ed. Vilnius: Mokslo ir enciklopedijų leidybos institutas.
Ambrazas, Vytautas (ed.) (2008 [1997]): *Lithuanian Grammar.* 2nd ed. Vilnius: Baltos lankos.
Jakaitienė, Evalda (1973): *Veiksmažodžių daryba (priesagų vediniai).* Vilnius: Vilniaus V. Kapsuko universiteto leidybinis skyrius.
Keinys, Stasys (1999): *Bendrinės lietuvių kalbos žodžių daryba.* Šiauliai: Šiaulių universiteto leidykla.
Kurschat, Friedrich (1876): *Grammatik der littauischen Sprache.* Halle/S.: Verlag der Buchhandlung des Waisenhauses.
Leskien, August (1891): *Die Bildung der Nomina im Litauischen.* Leipzig: Hirzel.
Otrębski, Jan (1965): *Gramatyka języka litewskiego.* Vol. 2: *Nauka o budowie wyrazów.* Warszawa: Państwowe Wydawnictwo Naukowe.
Pakerys, Jurgis (2020): Derivational networks in Lithuanian. In: Lívia Körtvélyessi, Alexandra Bagasheva and Pavol Štekauer (eds.), *Derivational Networks Across Languages,* 333–345. Berlin/Boston: De Gruyter Mouton.

Schleicher, August (2008 [1856]): Litauische Grammatik. In: Ilja Lemeškin and Jolanta Zabarskaitė (eds.), *Lituanistinis Augusto Schleicherio palikimas – Das lituanistische Erbe August Schleichers*. Vol. 1: 150–508. Vilnius: Lietuvių kalbos institutas [1st ed. of the *Litauische Grammatik*. Prag: Calve].

Skardžius, Pranas (1996 [1943]): *Rinktiniai raštai*. Vol. 1: *Lietuvių kalbos žodžių daryba*. Vilnius: Mokslo ir enciklopedijų leidykla.

Stundžia, Bonifacas and Dalius Jarmalavičius (2019): *Daiktavardžių dūryba vokiškuose XVII–XVIII a. baltų kalbų žodynuose*. Vilnius: Vilniaus universiteto leidykla.

Ulvydas, Kazys (ed.) (1965–71): *Lietuvių kalbos gramatika*. 2 Vol. Vilnius: Mintis.

Urbutis, Vincas (1961a): Dabartinės lietuvių kalbos galūnių darybos daiktavardžiai. *Kalbotyra* 3: 27–60.

Urbutis, Vincas (1961b): Sudurtinių daiktavardžių daryba. In: Jonas Kazlauskas, Adelė Laigonaitė and Vincas Urbutis (eds.): *Dabartinė lietuvių kalba*, 65–121. Vilnius: Valstybinė politinės ir mokslinės literatūros leidykla.

U[rbutis], V[incas] (2008 [1999]): Būdvardžių daryba, Daiktavardžių daryba, Prieveiksmių daryba, Veiksmažodžių daryba, Žodžių daryba. In: Vytautas Ambrazas and Kazys Morkūnas (eds.), *Lietuvių kalbos enciklopedija*, 97–98, 112–116, 432–433, 593–594, 629–631. 2nd ed. Vilnius: Mokslo ir enciklopedijų leidybos institutas.

Urbutis, Vincas (2009 [1978]): *Žodžių darybos teorija*. 2nd ed. Vilnius: Mokslo ir enciklopedijų leidybos institutas.

Vaskelienė, Jolanta (2024): Žodžių daryba. In: Asta Balčiūnienė, Albinas Drukteinis, Rūta Kazlauskaitė and Jolanta Vaskelienė (eds.), *Praktinė bendrinės lietuvių kalbos gramatika*, 311–488. Vilnius: Vilniaus universiteto leidykla.

Monica Genesin and Joachim Matzinger
12 Albanian

1 Introduction
2 General overview
3 Composition
4 Derivation
5 Conversion
6 Backformation
7 Reduplication
8 Blending
9 Clipping
10 References

Abstract: This article provides an overview of the available and productive word-formation patterns of modern Albanian. Affixation and compounding are the prevalent processes of word-formation in Albanian. As the Albanian language is very open to foreign lexical influences, many foreign word-formation patterns have been adopted. A very fruitful period of coining new words was the time of the national awakening in the 19th century when the core base of the modern Albanian lexicon was created.

1 Introduction

Albanian is first attested in written literary texts in the second half of the 16th century. The texts of the 16th to the beginning of the 18th century belong exclusively to the genre of theological literature and represent the Old Albanian language period. From the first attestations on, two major Albanian dialect areas are clearly discernible, the Gheg dialect in the north of Albania and in Kosova and the Tosk dialect in the south. As Albania had been under Ottoman rule since the second half of the 14th century, all these Old Albanian texts were written and published in Italy by Catholic clergymen. Inside Albania, it wasn't until the beginning of the 19th century that an independent literary production came into being as a consequence of the national awakening (*Rilindja kombëtare*) which led to the

Monica Genesin, Lecce, Italy
Joachim Matzinger, Vienna, Austria

https://doi.org/10.1515/9783111420523-012

creation of the independent Albanian state in 1912. In the field of word-formation this was a very fruitful period witnessing the process of the abundant coinage of new words with inherited patterns but also with patterns of the neo-classical word-formation which entered the Albanian language at this time (see Buchholz and Fiedler 1979). The neoclassical patterns in association with word-formation patterns which Albanian adopted in preliterate times from Latin, Greek, the Slavic languages, Italian, and Turkish give the Albanian language the characteristic of being very open to foreign lexical influences (for a short sketch of the language history of Albanian, see Matzinger 2006: 16–26).

The lack of a comprehensive codification of the Albanian lexicon from the first attestations up to the present day often causes difficulties in researching Albanian lexicological matters under diachronic perspectives. The word-formation processes of the Old Albanian period in particular have not yet been treated satisfactorily. At least for Modern Albanian word-formation some useful descriptions are at hand. Major works of reference are Xhuvani and Çabej (1962, 1975), Newmark, Hubbard and Prifti (1982), Domi (2002), Hysa (2004), and Buxheli (2008) on verbal derivation.

2 General overview

As Albanian belongs to the Indo-European language family, its word-formation principles are typically those of the Indo-European language type. For this reason overt processes with affixes and composition are the prevalent rules of word-formation in the nominal as well as in the verbal system (Emil Lafe in Domi 2002: 58–79). With regard to affixation, the patterns with suffixes predominate, nevertheless in adjectival as well as in verbal derivation prefixation is well represented. As is the case in many other languages, a variety of word-formation patterns in the area of nominal derivation undergo conversion, creating both nouns as well as adjectives (e.g., the suffixes -ár, -ës, -ník, see section 4.2). As regards nominal compounding, all types of Indo-European compounds (determinative, possessive, and coordinative compounds) can be found in Albanian. In contrast to many other languages, suprasegmental phenomena are not used (with the sole exception of the accent shift of some cases in the number distinction).

3 Composition

While composition is nowadays a productive process of word-formation (see Fatmir Agalliu in Domi 2002: 147–151), in the oldest stages of Albanian it seemed to be less used, as evidenced by the attestations of the Old Albanian texts (Genesin and Matzinger 2005). With respect to the compositional elements, the following types of nominal compounds can be found in Albanian:

Noun + noun: coordinative compounds, e.g., *deledash* 'hermaphrodite' ← *dele* 'sheep' + *dash* 'ram', *juglindje* 'southeast' ← *jug* 'south' + *lindje* 'east'; determinative compounds: in the original Albanian type the second element modifies the first element, e.g., *ditëlindje* 'birthday' ← *ditë* 'day' + *lindje* 'birth', *bregdet* 'seashore' ← *breg* 'shore' + *det* 'sea'. A second type displays the first element as modifier of the second element. This type has obviously been created after the model of compounds in other European languages, e.g., *dorëshkrim* 'handwriting' ← *dorë* 'hand' + *shkrim* 'writing' (cf. Italian *manoscritto* 'id.'), *kryeqytet* 'capital (city)' ← *krye* 'head' + *qytet* 'city' (cf. German *Hauptstadt* 'id.'). In another subtype the second element bears the ending of the ablative case *-i* or *-e* thus clearly showing the fusion of two formerly autonomous elements, e.g., *vajguri* 'petroleum' ← *vaj* 'oil' + *gur* 'stone', *punëdore* 'handwork' ← *punë* 'work' + *dorë* 'hand'; possessive compounds, e.g., *zemërgur* 'stony-hearted' ← *zemër* 'heart' + *gur* 'stone', *syshqiponjë* 'eagle-eyed' ← *sy* 'eye' + *shqiponjë* 'eagle'; synthetic compounds: the verbal element appears as an agentive noun or as a verbal abstract noun, e.g., *bukëpjekës* 'baker' ← *bukë* 'bread' + *pjekës* 'baker', *letërkëmbim* 'correspondence' ← *letër* 'letter' + *këmbim* 'exchange'. Very limited is the type with a true verbal element, e.g., *vëmendje* 'attention' ← *vë* 'to put' + *mendje* 'mind' (Newmark, Hubbard and Prifti 1982: 177).

Noun + adjective: determinative compounds, e.g., *lulekuqe* 'poppy' ← *lule* 'flower' + (*i*) *kuq* (fem. (*e*) *kuqe*) 'red', *tatëmadh* 'grandpa' ← *tatë* 'papa' + (*i*) *madh* 'big'; possessive compounds, e.g., *fatbardhë* 'lucky, fortunate' ← *fat* 'fate, destiny' + (*i*) *bardhë* 'white', *zemërgjerë* 'generous' ← *zemër* 'heart' + (*i*) *gjerë* 'broad'.

Adverb + noun: determinative compounds, e.g., *bukurshkrim* 'nice handwriting, calligraphy' ← *bukur* 'beautifully, nicely' + *shkrim* 'writing', *keqkuptim* 'misunderstanding' ← *keq* 'badly' + *kuptim* 'comprehension'; synthetic compounds (with agentive nouns in *-ës*; the derivations function as nouns and adjectives), e.g., *keqbërës* 'evildoer; harmful' ← *keq* 'badly' + *bërës* 'doer', *mirëdashës* 'benevolent (person)' ← *mirë* 'well' + *dashës* 'lover'.

Pronoun/number + noun: determinative compounds, e.g., *vetëbesim* 'self confidence' ← *vetë* 'self' + *besim* 'belief', *dyluftim* 'duel' ← *dy* 'two' + *luftim* 'combat'; possessive compounds (the second member shows the ending *-sh* of the ablative plural case), e.g., *tringjyrësh* 'tricolored' ← *tre* (fem. *tri*) 'three' + *ngjyrë* 'color', *disajavësh* 'of several weeks duration' ← *disa* 'several' + *javë* 'week'; synthetic compounds (with agentive nouns in *-ës*; the derivations function as nouns and adjectives), e.g., *vetëdashës* 'volunteer, voluntary; egoist, selfish' ← *vetë* 'self'

+ *dashës* 'lover', *vetëvrasës* 'suicidal, one who has committed suicide' ← *vetë* 'self' + *vrasës* 'killer'.

Adjective + adjective: coordinative compounds (the two elements are connected with the vowel *-o-*), e.g., *materialoteknik* 'material and technical' ← *material* 'material' + *teknik* 'technical', *teknikoshkencor* 'technical and scientific' ← *teknik* 'technical' + *shkencor* 'scientific'.

Number/quantifier + adjective: possessive compounds, e.g., *dyvjeçar* 'biannual' ← *dy* 'two' + *vjeçar* 'annual', (*i*) *shumanshëm* 'many-sided' ← *shumë* 'much, many' + (*i*) *anshëm* 'lateral'.

4 Derivation

4.1 Nominal derivation

In the following sections on nominal and adjectival derivation, the affixes responsible for the productive patterns will be presented, minor patterns will be mentioned only briefly unless they are of some special interest.

4.1.1 Denominal nouns

In Albanian denominal nouns are typically derived by suffixation and only to a lesser extent by prefixation.

Prefixation is seen with the following derivations:
bashkë- 'co-, joint', e.g., *bashk-autor* 'co-author' ← *autor* 'author', *bashkë-pronar* 'co-owner' ← *pronar* 'owner', *bashkë-sundim* 'joint rule' ← *sundim* 'rule';
kundër- 'counter-', e.g., *kundër-forcë* 'counterforce' ← *forcë* 'force', *kundër-zjarr* 'counterfire' ← *zjarr* 'fire';
mos- 'non-, dis-', e.g., *mos-besim* 'mistrust, distrust' ← *besim* 'belief, trust', *mos-kënaqësi* 'dissatisfaction' ← *kënaqësi* 'satisfaction', *mos-qenie* 'non-existence' ← *qenie* 'existence';
pa- 'un-, in-', e.g., *pa-durim* 'impatience' ← *durim* 'patience', *pa-pastërti* 'impurity' ← *pastërti* 'purity', *pa-qartësi* 'unclarity' ← *qartësi* 'clarity'.

Other prefixes are listed in Fatmir Agalliu in Domi (2002: 145–146) and in the exhaustive treatment of Hysa (2004: 63–106). Albanian has adopted several neoclassical prefixes mostly with borrowed nouns:
anti-, e.g., *anti-fashist* 'anti-fascist' ← *fashist* 'fascist', *anti-grimcë* 'anti-particle' ← *grimcë* 'particle';

super-, e.g., *super-fuqi* 'superpower' ← *fuqi* 'power', *super-prodhim* 'overproduction' ← *prodhim* 'production'.

The following nominal types are derived with suffixes:

a) Personal nouns (persons with a particular relation to the base):
   -ár, e.g., *argjend-ar* 'silversmith' ← *argjend* 'silver', *derr-ar* 'swineherd' ← *derr* 'pig', *pron-ar* 'owner' ← *pronë* 'property';
   -(ë)s (*-ës* after bases ending in consonant, *-s* after bases ending in vowel), e.g., *gjak-ës* 'person who takes blood vengeance, killer' ← *gjak* 'blood', *derë-s* 'doorman' ← *derë* 'door';
   -tár, e.g., *anë-tar* 'member' ← *anë* 'side', *pyll-tar* 'forester' ← *pyll* 'forest', *shkrim-tar* 'writer' ← *shkrim* 'piece of writing, writing';
   -ór, e.g., *dasm-or* 'wedding celebrant' ← *dasmë* 'wedding', *malës-or* 'mountaineer' ← *malësi* 'mountainous region'.

   Suffixes to derive inhabitants or to denote ethnic origin are:
   -ák, e.g., *austri-ak* 'Austrian' ← *Austri* 'Austria', *durrs-ak* 'inhabitant of Durrës, of/from Durrës' ← *Durrës*;
   -as, e.g., *qytet-as* 'city dweller' ← *qytet* 'city', *tiran-as* 'inhabitant of Tirana, of/from Tirana' ← *Tiranë*.

   As a result of almost 500 years of Ottoman domination of Albania, the lexicon of Albanian has been heavily influenced by the (Ottoman-)Turkish language. Thus, as a result of language contact, not only many lexemes but also some word-formation patterns have entered Albanian. One of them is the suffix *-xhí/-çí* (*-xhi* after voiced consonants and vowels, *-çi* after voiceless consonants) from Turkish *-cI/-çI* (the suffix vowel follows the "great vowel harmony", the distribution of *-cI/-çI* in Turkish is quite the same as given for Albanian) to denote professions, e.g., *bakër-xhi* 'coppersmith' (modern Albanian *bakërpunues*) < Turkish *bakırcı*. The suffix gained a certain productivity in the older varieties of the language and was used with Albanian bases as well, e.g., *vorra-xhi* 'gravedigger' ← (Gheg) *vorrë* 'grave' (in modern Albanian replaced by *varrmihës*). A certain productivity is seen with some neoclassical suffixes:
   -íst, e.g., *futboll-ist* 'football player' ← *futboll* 'football', *tank-ist* 'tank driver' ← *tank* 'tank';
   -iér, e.g., *banak-ier* 'bartender' ← *banak* 'service counter, bar', *post-ier* 'postman' ← *postë* 'post, post office'.

b) Status nouns (abstract nouns and collective nouns):
   -í, e.g., *gjakës-i* 'blood vengeance, bloodshed' ← *gjakës* 'person who takes blood vengeance, killer', *drejtor-i* 'directorate, directorship' ← *drejtor* 'direc-

tor', *dhelpër-i* 'action performed with wiliness, trick' ← *dhelpër* 'vixen, fox', *zejtar-i* 'craft, craftsmanship, the crafts' ← *zejtar* 'craftsman'. In some cases the base of the derivation resembles the plural stem, e.g., *mbretër-i* 'kingdom' ← *mbret* (plural *mbret-ër*) 'king', *njerëz-i* 'people' ← *njeri* (plural *njerëz*) 'human being'. Besides the regular suffix *-i*, the two variants *-ërí* and *-ësí* are used with some derivatives, e.g., *rob-ëri* 'slavery' ← *rob* 'serf, captive', *mal-ësi* 'mountainous region' ← *mal* 'mountain'. Among some neoclassical suffixes *-ízëm* has gained a certain productivity, e.g., *fanat-izëm* 'fanaticism' ← *fanatik* 'fanatic', *terror-izëm* 'terrorism' ← *terror* 'terror'. It is interesting to note that the neoclassical suffix *-(a)cion*, though found in a number of Albanian nouns, is a constituent part of whole borrowed nouns but has not led to an independent word-formation pattern (Hysa 2004: 117 and 127).

c) Place nouns:

-íshtë/-íshte, e.g., *ah-ishtë* 'beech forest' ← *ah* 'beech', *balt-ishtë* 'ground that gets muddy quickly' ← *baltë* 'mud', *lul-ishte* 'flower garden' ← *lule* 'flower', *misër-ishte* 'field of corn' ← *misër* 'corn';

-íně, e.g., *balt-inë* 'muddy ground' ← *baltë* 'mud', *kodr-inë* 'hilly land' ← *kodër* 'hill, low mountain';

-ájë (in most cases the derivatives are restricted to the Gheg dialectal area), e.g., *kren-ajë* 'peak of a hill or mountain' ← *krye* 'head', *lug-ajë* 'deep, wide and long valley' ← *lug* 'dale';

-tóre, e.g., *qebap-tore* 'shop that makes and sells kebab' ← *qebap* 'kebab', *barna-tore* 'drugstore' ← (plural) *barna* 'medicinal plants'.

d) Feminine nouns:

-e (the regular feminine motion suffix), e.g., *fshatar-e* 'female peasant' ← *fshatar* 'peasant', *mësues-e* 'female teacher' ← *mësues* 'teacher';

-éshë, e.g., *luan-eshë* 'lioness' ← *luan* 'lion', *mik-eshë* 'female friend' ← *mik* 'friend'. In a few instances the base resembles the plural stem, e.g., *mbretër-eshë* 'queen' ← *mbret* (plural *mbret-ër*) 'king', *priftër-eshë* 'priestess' ← *prift* (plural *prift-ër*) 'priest'.

A very small number of feminine nouns are derived with the suffix *-úshë*, e.g., *ar-ushë* 'she-bear' ← *ari* 'bear', *dren-ushë* 'doe, hind' ← *dre* 'stag, deer'.

e) Masculine nouns (all patterns for masculine motion are highly restricted displaying only a few derivatives):

-án, e.g., *quk-an* 'tom turkey' ← *qukë* 'turkey hen', *vej-an* 'widower' ← *ve* 'widow';

-ók, e.g., *pat-ok* 'male goose' ← *patë* 'goose'.

f) Diminutives:
-*th*, e.g., *fjalor-th* 'pocket dictionary' ← *fjalor* 'dictionary', *gur-th* (medicine) 'calculus in a body organ' ← *gur* 'stone';
-*(ë)z* (-*ëz* after bases ending in consonant, -*z* after bases ending in vowel), e.g., *dritë-z* 'hole in the top of the chimney' ← *dritë* 'light', *zog-ëz* 'little birdie' ← *zog* 'bird';
-*icë*, e.g., *petk-icë* 'small-sized garment' ← *petk* 'outer garment', *rrug-icë* 'small street, alley' ← *rrugë* 'street';
-*ák* (in some instances with a pejorative meaning), e.g., *dor-ak* 'handle/grip of a tool/instrument' ← *dorë* 'hand', *burr-ak* 'short ugly man' ← *burrë* 'male person, man'.

g) Instrument nouns:
-*óre*, e.g., *fishek-ore* 'cartridge belt, cartridge case' ← *fishek* 'cartridge, bullet', *grosh-ore* 'wide-bellied clay pot for boiling beans' ← *groshë* 'white bean'.

4.1.2 Deadjectival nouns

Most deadjectival nouns are quality nouns, few are concrete nouns:
-*ërí* (the suffix is linked almost exclusively with secondary adjectives ending in -*shëm*), e.g., *gjall-ëri* 'liveliness' ← (*i*) *gjallë* 'alive', *domosdoshm-ëri* 'indispensability' ← (*i*) *domosdoshëm* 'indispensable', *qëndrueshm-ëri* 'stability' ← (*i*) *qëndrueshëm* 'stable';
-*(ë)sí*, e.g., *aft-ësi* 'capability' ← (*i*) *aftë* 'capable', *ëmbël-si* 'sweetness' ← (*i*) *ëmbël* 'sweet', *gjat-ësi* 'length' ← (*i*) *gjatë* 'long';
-*í*, e.g., *bukur-i* 'beauty' ← (*i*) *bukur* 'beautiful', *pasur-i* 'wealth, property' ← (*i*) *pasur* 'wealthy, rich';
-*icë*, e.g., *pak-icë* 'small amount/number' ← *pak* 'not much, little', *shum-icë* 'multitude, large quantity' ← *shumë* 'much, many, a lot of'. The neoclassical suffix -*izëm* is found here too, e.g., *majt-izëm* 'leftism' ← (*i*) *majtë* 'left', *geg-izëm* 'language feature belonging to the Gheg dialect' ← *gegë* 'Albanian from Ghegëria, Gheg';
-*(ë)sírë* with the Gheg variant -*(ë)sínë* (the overwhelming majority of its derivatives has a concrete meaning), e.g., *verdh-ësirë* 'yellow-tan color' ← (*i*) *verdhë* 'yellow', *ëmbël-sirë* 'cake, cookie' ← (*i*) *ëmbël* 'sweet', *thell-ësirë* 'deep place, abyss' ← (*i*) *thellë* 'deep'.

4.1.3 Deverbal nouns

Deverbal nouns fall into four semantic categories (verbal bases are cited in the 3rd person singular):

a) Action nouns:
    -ím, e.g., *kërk-im* 'search, research' ← *kërkon* 'to seek, search for', *vepr-im* 'action, activity' ← *vepron* 'to be active, act', *këmb-im* 'change, exchange' ← *këmben* 'to change, exchange';
    -je (the suffix is attached to the stem of the participle), e.g., *ardh-je* 'arrival' ← *vjen* (suppletive participle (*i*) *ardh-ur*) 'to come, arrive', *hyr-je* 'entry, introduction' ← *hyn* (participle (*i*) *hyr-ë*) 'to enter', *armatos-je* 'armament' ← *armatos* (participle (*i*) *armatos-ur*) 'to provide with arms', *shpif-je* 'slander' ← *shpif* (participle (*i*) *shpif-ur*) 'to slander';
    -ésë, e.g., *ban-esë* 'residence' ← *banon* 'to reside', *von-esë* 'delay' ← *vonon* 'to arrive late', *kth-esë* 'bend in the road, turn, change' ← *kthen* 'to turn, bend', *pag-esë* 'payment' ← *paguan* 'to pay';
    -i (only with a few examples), e.g., *dëshm-i* 'testimony' ← *dëshmon* 'testify', *lakm-i* 'voracious desire, greed' ← *lakmon* 'to have a voracious desire';
    -ímë (the bases are for the most part verbs which denote weather conditions or different kinds of sounds), e.g., *bu(m)bull-imë* 'thunder' ← *bu(m)bullin* 'to thunder', *vetët-imë* 'lightning, lightning bolt' ← *vetëtin* 'to shine bright, flash', *xixëll-imë* 'twinkling light' ← *xixëllon* 'to twinkle, sparkle';
    -më, e.g., *fry-më* 'breath, breathing' ← *fryn* 'to blow', *gri-më* 'crumb, particle' ← *grin* 'to cut into small fragments', *pështy-më* 'spittle' ← *pështyn* 'to spit out';
    -átë, e.g., *dhur-atë* 'gift, present' ← *dhuron* 'to offer as gift', *gjyk-atë* 'law court, tribunal' ← *gjykon* 'to judge', *ur-atë* 'prayer' ← *uron* 'to wish well';
    -ë, e.g., *lyp-ë* 'begging for alms' ← *lyp* 'to beg for', *rrjedh-ë* 'flow, stream' ← *rrjedh* 'to flow'.

b) Agent nouns:
    -ës (-*ës* after bases ending in consonant, with verbs in -*ón* the outcome is -*úes* as a consequence of the contraction of -*ó+ës*; a variant -*yes* appears with a few verbs in -*én*), e.g., *krij-ues* 'creator' ← *krijon* 'to create', *mës-ues* 'teacher' ← *mëson* 'to teach', *rrëf-yes* 'storyteller' ← *rrëfen* 'to narrate', *ndjek-ës* 'pursuer, follower' ← *ndjek* 'to chase, pursue, follow';
    -ës, e.g., *kënd-es* 'rooster, cock' ← *këndon* 'to sing', *rrëmb-es* 'robber' ← *rrëmben* 'to take with force'.

c) Instrument nouns:
   -ésë, e.g., *fsh-esë* 'broom' ← *fshin* 'to clean off', *kull-esë* 'colander, filter' ← *kullon* 'to cleanse of unwanted matter', *mbul-esë* 'protective covering, envelope' ← *mbulon* 'to cover';
   -ës, e.g., *çel-ës* 'key' ← *çel* 'to open', *mat-ës* 'measuring device' ← *mat* 'to measure', *tund-ës* 'milk churn' ← *tund* 'to shake, churn'.

d) Place nouns:
   -inë, e.g., *çmend-inë* 'loony bin' ← *çmend* 'to drive crazy', *grem-inë* 'ravine, chasm' ← *gremiset* 'to fall from a high place', *rrafsh-inë* 'level ground, plain' ← *rrafshon* 'to make flat with the ground, to level'.

4.2 Adjectival derivation

Albanian has a rich variety of suffixes with which to generate different kinds of adjectives, however most of them show only a few derivatives. Prefixation is seen with deadjectival adjectives only. An important morphological feature divides Albanian adjectives into two major classes, one class with an obligatorily preposed definite article (articulated adjectives) and one without such an element (unarticulated adjectives). It is characteristic of most unarticulated adjectives that they are used as nouns by conversion (Newmark, Hubbard and Prifti 1982: 200; Buchholz and Fiedler 1987: 346–348; see here section 5.1). In the following section only the productive patterns of both classes will be presented.

4.2.1 Denominal adjectives

Denominal adjectives are qualitative adjectives and relational adjectives:
-ák, e.g., *dimër-ak* 'wintry' ← *dimër* 'winter', *vez-ak* 'oval' ← *vezë* 'egg';
-ár, e.g., *gënjesht-ar* 'lying, deceitful' ← *gënjeshtër* 'lie', *vjesht-ar* 'ripening in autumn' ← *vjeshtë* 'autumn';
-ník, e.g., *bes-nik* 'true to one's word, faithful' ← *besë* 'pledge, word of honor', *fis-nik* 'noble' ← *fis* 'clan, tribe';
-ór, e.g., *dimër-or* 'wintry' ← *dimër* 'winter', *mal-or* 'mountainous' ← *mal* 'mountain';
-ósh, e.g., *mjekr-osh* 'wearing a beard' ← *mjekër* 'beard', *vjetull-osh* 'with thick eyebrowes' ← *vjetull* 'eyebrow';

(*i*) *-shëm* (the most productive suffix for adjectives), e.g., (*i*) *frik-shëm* 'frightening, scary' ← *frikë* 'fear, fright', (*i*) *zakon-shëm* 'ordinary' ← *zakon* 'habit, common practice';
-tár, e.g., *guxim-tar* 'brave' ← *guxim* 'daring, courage', *kombë-tar* 'national' ← *komb* 'nation';
(*i*) *-(ë)të*, e.g., (*i*) *ar-të* 'golden' ← *ar* 'gold', (*i*) *gur-të* 'of stone' ← *gur* 'stone'.

4.2.2 Deadjectival adjectives

Prefixes serve in most cases to express negation, in some cases intensification. Adjectives derived with suffixes are either referential adjectives or approximative-attenuative adjectives:

Derivation with prefixes:
jo- 'non-' (with unarticulated adjectives), e.g., *jo-alkoolik* 'non-alcoholic' ← *alkoolik* 'alcoholic', *jo-fetar* 'non-religious' ← *fetar* 'religious';
pa- 'un-, in-' (with articulated adjectives), e.g., (*i*) *pa-aftë* 'unable, inept' ← (*i*) *aftë* 'capable, able', (*i*) *pa-diskutueshëm* 'non subject to further discussion' ← (*i*) *diskutueshëm* 'disputable';
ndër- 'inter-', e.g., *ndër-kombëtar* 'international' ← *kombëtar* 'national', (*i*) *ndër-gjegjshëm* 'conscious' ← (*i*) *gjegjshëm* 'obedient, receptive';
stër- (augmentative), e.g., (*i*) *stër-lashtë* 'very old, ancient' ← (*i*) *lashtë* 'ancient', (*i*) *stër-madh* 'enormous' ← (*i*) *madh* 'big, large, tall'.

Several neoclassical prefixes are seen in Albanian:
anti-, e.g., *anti-alkoolik* 'anti-alcoholic' ← *alkoolik* 'alcoholic', *anti-njerëzor* 'inhumane' ← *njerëzor* 'humane';
super-, e.g., *super-automatik* 'completely automatic' ← *automatik* 'automatic'.

Derivation with suffixes:
(*i*) *-shëm* (bases are adverbs), e.g., (*i*) *atje-shëm* 'of that place' ← *atje* 'at that place, over there', (*i*) *sivjet-shëm* 'of this year' ← *sivjet* 'this year';
-ósh, e.g., *bardh-osh* 'pale' ← (*i*) *bardhë* 'white', *madh-osh* 'bulky, massive' ← (*i*) *madh* 'big, large, tall'.

4.2.3 Deverbal adjectives

Deverbal adjectives are for the most part qualitative adjectives:
-ës (in most cases the suffix is attached to the stem of the participle), e.g., *djeg-ës* 'burning, inflammable' ← *djeg* (participle (*i*) *djeg-ur*) 'to burn', *ngjit-ës* 'adhesive' ← *ngjit* (participle (*i*) *ngjit-ur*) 'to attach';
(*i*) -*shëm* (the suffix is attached to the stem of the participle), e.g., (*i*) *ardh-shëm* 'future, coming' ← *vjen* (suppletive participle (*i*) *ardh-ur*) 'to come, arrive', (*i*) *djeg-shëm* 'combustible' ← *djeg* (participle (*i*) *djeg-ur*) 'to burn', (*i*) *pi-shëm* 'potable' ← *pi* (participle (*i*) *pi-rë*) 'to drink'.

4.3 Verbal derivation

Verbs are derived chiefly from nouns, from other verbs, from adjectives and adverbs, only a few verbs are derived from other parts of speech like numbers, pronouns, particles and onomatopoeic bases. Derived verbs follow the conjugations 1 and 2, both comprising verbs ending respectively in a vowel or diphthong plus the ending -*n* or any consonant (on the Albanian conjugational classes see Newmark, Hubbard and Prifti 1982: 39–44), e.g., *pun-o-n* 'to work' ← *punë* 'work', *holl-o-n* 'to make thin' ← (*i*) *hollë* 'thin', *ndal-o-n* 'to stop' ← *ndal* 'to stop', *po-h-on* 'to admit' ← *po* 'yes' (with a hiatus-filling -*h*-), *ajr-o-s* 'to ventilate' ← *ajër* 'air', *ngul-it* 'to insert, drive in' ← *ngul* 'to implant', *zvarr-it* 'to drag' ← *zvarrë* 'dragging'. The majority of derived verbs follow conjugation 1. Regarding the formal aspects of verbal derivation, derived verbs are constructed predominantly by affixation (prefixation, suffixation, circumfixation), while only a limited number of verbs are derived by conversion (see section 5.3). There are approximately 30 prefixes used to generate verbs, and among them the most productive ones are: *për-*, *sh-* (with the phonological variants *ç-* and *zh-*), followed by *s-/z-*, *n-/m-*, *mbi-*, *nën-*, *stër-*, *shpër-*, *ri-*, *ndër-* (Shaban Demiraj in Domi 2002: 348–353), e.g., *për-forc-on* 'to reinforce' ← *forc-on* 'to strengthen' (← *forcë* 'force, power'), *për-bluan* 'to brood over' ← *bluan* 'to mill', *s-kuq* 'to make red' ← (*i*) *kuq* 'red', *m-plak* 'to make old' ← *plak* 'old', *zh-vesh* 'to take off, strip' ← *vesh* 'to put on clothes', *mbi-shkruaj* 'to inscribe' ← *shkruaj* 'to write', *nën-shtroj* 'to submit' ← *shtroj* 'to lay down', *stër-nxeh* 'to overheat' ← *nxeh* 'to make hot', *shpër-dredh* 'to untwist' ← *dredh* 'to twist', *ri-botoj* 'to republish' ← *botoj* 'to publish', *ndër-lidh* 'to bring into contact' ← *lidh* 'to tie, bind'. As can be deduced from some of the examples given above the prefixes *për-*, *sh-*, *s-* sometimes induce an intensifying meaning or lead to a new semantic nuance of the verb. Other prefixes generate antonyms with partially identical stems, e.g., *shkarkon* 'to unload' vs. *ngarkon* 'to load', *ngul* 'to thrust in, implant' vs. *shkul* 'to uproot'. Though there are no derivational bases to be found with these verbs in the synchronic lexicon they may be considered as derived (Newmark, Hubbard and Prifti 1982: 110; Shaban Demiraj in Domi 2002: 351).

Suffixation is the most common derivational process for deriving verbs from nouns and adjectives. The most productive suffix is *-ó-* (with its extensions *-lló-*, *-ró-*, *-só-*, *-tó-*, *-zó-*; Newmark, Hubbard and Prifti 1982: 111) following the conjugational class 1: *dark-o-n* 'to dine' ← *darkë* 'dinner', *afr-o-n* 'to bring close' ← *afër* 'near', *mish-ë-ro-n* 'to embody' (with an anaptyctic vowel *-ë-*) ← *mish* 'meat, flesh', *ëmbël-so-n* 'to sweeten' ← (*i*) *ëmbël* 'sweet', *asgjë-so-n* 'to annihilate' ← *asgjë* 'nothing', *copë-to-n* 'to break up into pieces' ← *copë* 'bit', *dorë-zo-n* 'to surrender' ← *dorë* 'hand', *një-zo-n* 'to unite, join' ← *një* 'one'. The extended variant *-llo-* (with its allomorphs *-lli-/-lle-*) is for the most part seen with onomatopoeic verbs, e.g., *fërfë-llo-n* 'to beat the wings, fly', *gurgu-llo-n* 'to gurgle', *bu(m)bu-lli-n* 'to thunder', *hinge-lli-n* 'to neigh' (of a horse). Derived verbs with the suffixes *-s/-ís* and *-ós* (with their extensions *-atís* and *-atós*) follow the conjugational class 2, e.g., *balt-os* 'to spatter with mud' ← *baltë* 'mud', *arrat-is* 'to go into exile' ← *arrati* 'exile', *boj-atis* 'to paint' ← *bojë* 'paint', *helm-atis* 'to poison' ← *helm* 'poison'.

Verbs formed by circumfixation are usually derived from nouns or adjectives and are as a rule inflected according to the conjugational class 1 (Newmark, Hubbard and Prifti 1982: 117), e.g., *për-pun-on* 'to refine, revise' ← *punë* 'work', *z-bardh-on* 'to whiten' ← (*i*) *bardhë* 'white', *z-bukur-on* 'to beautify' ← (*i*) *bukur* 'beautiful, pretty', *n-gur-os* 'to petrify' ← *gur* 'stone'.

Compounding is a rather minor pattern in the production of verbs (Newmark, Hubbard and Prifti 1982: 118; Buxheli 2008: 335–345). The first compositional element is either an adverb or a noun: adverb+verb, e.g., *bashkë-banon* 'to cohabit' ← *bashkë* 'together' + *banon* 'to reside', *bashkë-bisedon* 'to converse' ← *bashkë* 'together' + *bisedon* 'to discuss', *mirë-pret* 'to welcome' ← *mirë* 'well' + *pret* 'to receive', *kundër-vë* 'to put into opposition' ← *kundër* 'against' + *vë* 'to put, place'; noun+verb, e.g., *duar-trokit* 'to clap hands' ← *duar* 'hands' (plural of *dorë*) + *troket* 'to knock, beat', *dëm-shpërblen* 'to indemnify' ← *dëm* 'damage' + *shpërblen* 'to repay, recompense', *këmbë-ngul* 'to put one's foot down' ← *këmbë* 'foot' + *ngul* 'to insert'.

Verbs formed by univerbation are not numerous. They originate from verbal or prepositional phrases (Newmark, Hubbard and Prifti 1982: 119; Buxheli 2008: 347–348), e.g., *vëren* 'to observe, notice' ← *vëre* 'to pay attention', *falënderon* 'to thank' ← *falem(i)nderit* 'thank you; lit. to pray to the honour'.

4.3.1 Denominal verbs

Denominal verbs are typically generated with the suffix *-ó-* (and its extensions *-lló-, -ró-, -só-, -tó-, -zó-*) and follow thus conjugational class 1 (see section 4.3), e.g., *bes-o-n* 'to believe' ← *besë* 'belief', *xixë-llo-n* 'to sparkle' ← *xixë* 'spark', *nusë-ro-n* 'to act as a proper bride' ← *nuse* 'bride', *frikë-so-n* 'to frighten' ← *frikë* 'fear, fright', *dëm-to-n* 'to damage' ← *dëm* 'damage', *valë-zo-n* 'to undulate' ← *valë* 'wave'. Other denominal verbs are derived with the suffixes *-s/-ís* and *-ós* (and its extensions *-atís* and *-atós*) and follow conjugational class 2 (see section 4.3), e.g., *bezd-is* 'to bother' ← *bezdi* 'bother', *kallaj-is* 'to coat with tin, solder' ← *kallaj* 'solder, tin', *helm-atis* 'to poison' ← *helm* 'poison', *fund-os* 'to sink' ← *fund* 'bottom', *arm-atos* 'to arm' ← *armë* 'munitions, arm(s)'.

4.3.2 Deadjectival verbs

Deadjectival verbs are generated with the suffixes and their extensions presented in section 4.3.1, e.g., *çal-o-n* 'to limp' ← *çalë* 'lame', *holl-o-n* 'to make thin' ← (*i*) *hollë* 'thin', *kuq-ëlo-n* 'to become reddish' ← (*i*) *kuq* 'red', *fisnikë-ro-n* 'to ennoble' ← *fisnik* 'noble', *ëmbël-so-n* 'to sweeten' ← (*i*) *ëmbël* 'sweet', *shpesh-ëto-n* 'to increase the frequency of something' ← (*i*) *shpeshtë* 'frequent'.

4.3.3 Deverbal verbs

Deverbal verbs are generated with the suffixes and their extensions presented in section 4.3.1, e.g., *ndal-o-n* 'to stop' ← *ndal* 'id.', *shtjell-o-n* 'to explain, unfold' ← *shtjell* 'to throw, unfold', *njof-to-n* 'to announce' ← *njeh* 'to come to know', *shkund-ullo-n* 'to shake' ← *shkund* 'id.', *ngulit* 'to insert, drive in' ← *ngul* 'to implant'.

4.4 Adverbial derivation

As there are articulated adjectives and unarticulated adjectives in Albanian (see section 4.2), the derivation of adverbs depends on which class an adjective follows. As a rule adverbs of the unarticulated class are derived with suffixes, whereas adverbs of the articulated class by conversion. A third type of adverb is generated by univerbation whereby one element consists of a pro-form. A fourth type of adverb is formed by reduplication as will be shown in section 7.

Adverbs with suffixes:

-(i)sht (*-isht* after a base ending in consonant, *-sht* after a base ending in an oxytone vowel; the suffix is attached to nouns too), e.g., *gjerman-isht* 'in German (language)' ← *gjerman* 'German', *politik-isht* 'politically' ← *politik* 'political', from nouns, e.g., *gabim-isht* 'by mistake' ← *gabim* 'mistake', *natyr-isht* 'naturally' ← *natyrë* 'nature';

-as or *-azi* (attached to nominal, adjectival, and verbal bases), e.g., *krah-as* 'arm in arm' ← *krah* 'arm', *radh-as/radh-azi* 'each in turn, in a row' ← *radhë* 'serial order, row', *majt-as* 'to the left' ← (*i*) *majtë* 'left', *fsheht-as/fsheht-azi* 'secretly' ← (*i*) *fshehtë* 'hidden, secret', *fal-as* 'free of charge' ← *fal* 'to offer, give';

-çe (adverbs from nouns in colloquial speech), e.g., *derr-çe* 'stubbornly' ← *derr* 'pig', *qen-çe* 'like a dog' ← *qen* 'dog'.

Adverbs by conversion: adverbs of articulated adjectives are generated from the masculine form by deletion of the article (adjectives derived with the suffix *-të* additionally lose the final *-ë*), e.g., *mirë* 'well' ← (*i*) *mirë* 'good', *keq* 'badly' ← (*i*) *keq* 'bad', *natyrshëm* 'naturally' ← (*i*) *natyrshëm* 'natural', *lart* 'above' ← (*i*) *lartë* 'high'.

Adverbs by univerbation: pro-form+verb, e.g., *kudo* 'everywhere' ← *ku* 'where' + *do* '(it) wants', verb+pro-form, e.g., *diku* 'somewhere' ← *di* 'knows' + *ku* 'where'.

5 Conversion

5.1 Nominal conversion

Nominal conversion occurs predominantly in the formation of nouns from an adjectival base, and to a much lesser extent from verbs.

Nouns from adjectives/participles: a) Personal nouns, e.g., *bes-nik* 'man of his word' ← adj. 'true to one's word, faithful', *gënjesht-ar* 'liar' ← adj. 'lying, deceitful', *malës-or* 'mountaineer' ← adj. 'from the mountains', *i ri* 'young boy' ← adj. 'young', *i vdekur* 'dead person' ← participle 'dead'; b) Abstract nouns: in this class two types occur set apart by their grammatical gender, a feminine type in the singular or in a few cases in the plural, and a neuter type, e.g., *e drejta* (*a* is the postposed definite article) 'right, law; justice' ← (*i*) *drejtë* 'straight, true, right', *e vërteta* 'truth' ← (*i*) *vërtetë* 'true', *e shkuara* 'the past' ← (*i*) *shkuar* (participle/adjective) 'gone; past', (plural) *të ardhurat* 'income' ← (*i*) *ardhur* (participle/adjective) 'that which has come', (neuter plural with the postposed definite article) *të folurit* 'speech ability, speech' ← (*i*) *folur* (participle/adjective) 'spoken', *të zitë* 'blackness' ← (*i*) *zi* 'black'. As a consequence of the continuous reduction of the neuter gender in Albanian, the last type is not productive any longer. However, in older varieties of Albanian the conversion of adjectives into neuter nouns was the unmarked and thus most productive way to generate abstract nouns. Only with the reduction of the neuter gender have the derivational types with suffixes as seen in sections 4.1.1 and 4.1.3 experienced a steady increase (Matzinger 2007: 69–71).

Nouns from verbs: (masculine nouns), e.g., *mund* 'effort' ← *mund* 'to overcome, be able', *tjerr* 'spun yarn' ← *tjerr* 'to spin'.

5.2 Adjectival conversion

Adjectives from nouns: As can been seen in the sections 4.1 and 4.2, a number of derivational suffixes are ambiguous with respect to their interpretation as nouns or adjectives depending on the given syntactic context. Beside these derivations, there are many non-derived nouns which are open to undergo conversion to adjectives, e.g., *plak* 'old, aged' ← *plak* 'old man', *trim* 'brave, courageous' ← *trim* 'heroic man'.

5.3 Verbal conversion

Only a few verbs are generated by conversion from nouns or adjectives, e.g., *ndryshk* 'to make rusty, rust' ← *ndryshk* 'rust', *kuq* 'to make red' ← (*i*) *kuq* 'red'.

5.4 Adverbial conversion

Adverbs from nouns are derived either from the indefinite or definite accusative case, or from the ablative case, e.g., *mot* 'next year' ← *mot* 'year; weather', *vjet* 'last year' ← *vjet* 'year', *natën* 'at night' ← *natë* (definite accusative *natën*) 'night'. Adverbs from the ablative case are derived from a substantivized neuter adjective as their base, e.g., *së afërmi* 'close up' ← (*i*) *afërm* 'close', *së shpejti* 'very soon' ← (*i*) *shpejtë* 'fast'.

6 Backformation

In some historical instances a noun was added to the vocabulary alongside an Albanian verb ending in *-it* (< Slavic verbs with infinitive in *-iti*), which was assumed to be a verbal suffix. The noun was derived from this secondarily generated verbal stem with the suffix *-i* (see section 4.1.3), e.g., *çud-i* 'surprise; wonder' ← *çudit* 'to amaze, surprise', *mërz-i* 'boredom, annoyance' ← *mërzit* 'to bore, annoy'. Other backformations can be seen in words like *punësi* 'employment' ← *papunësi* 'unemployment'.

7 Reduplication

Reduplication is a typical feature of adverbial locutions. Two types of reduplication are discernible, one type formed by direct reduplication and an other type with the interposed conjunction *e* 'and' or the interposed prepositions *për* 'for' and *më* 'to, at'.

Noun + noun: *pjesëpjesë* 'in parts' ← *pjesë* 'part', *vendevende* 'here and there' ← *vend* (plural *vende*) 'place', *çift e çift* 'in couples' ← *çift* 'couple', *ditë për ditë* 'daily' ← *ditë* 'day', *gojë më gojë* 'from mouth to mouth, privately' ← *gojë* 'mouth'.

Adverb + adverb: *avashavash* 'very slowly' ← *avash* 'slowly', *hollëhollë* 'in great detail' ← *hollë* 'thinly', with the conjunction *e* 'and', *shpejt e shpejt* 'within a very short time' ← *shpejt* 'quickly'.

Reduplication in the verbal system is found with onomatopoeic verbs, e.g., *çuçurit* 'to whisper', *bu(m)bullin* 'to thunder'.

8 Blending

Blending does not occur very often, only a few examples can be given, e.g., *kaposh* 'rooster, cock' ← *kapua* 'capon' + *kokosh* 'rooster, cock', *rrëmon* 'to dig, excavate' ← *rrëmih* 'id.' + *gërmon* 'to dig, dig out' (both examples cited after Emil Lafe, personal communication).

9 Clipping

Clipping is barely detectable in Albanian, the very few examples show that they belong to colloquial speech, e.g., *pafshim* 'goodbye, so long' ← *mirupafshim* 'id.', *begs* 'student at the Skanderbeg military school in Tirana' ← *skënderbegas* 'id.' (both examples cited after Emil Lafe, personal communication; for a few other examples see Lloshi 1994: 189).

10 References

Boretzky, Norbert (1975): *Der türkische Einfluß auf das Albanische*. Vol. 1: *Phonologie und Morphologie der albanischen Turzismen*. Wiesbaden: Harrassowitz.

Buchholz, Oda and Wilfried Fiedler (1979): Zur Herausbildung des modernen gesellschaftlichen Wortschatzes im Albanischen. In: *Zur Herausbildung des modernen gesellschaftlichen Wortschatzes in Südosteuropa. Beiträge zur Balkanlinguistik 4*, 102–178. Berlin: Akademie der Wissenschaften der DDR, Zentralinstitut für Sprachwissenschaft.

Buchholz, Oda and Wilfried Fiedler (1987): *Albanische Grammatik*. Leipzig: Verlag Enzyklopädie.

Buxheli, Ludmila (2008): *Formimi i foljeve në gjuhën e sotme shqipe*. Tiranë: Kristalina-KH.

Çabej, Maklena (2021): Agglutinative words and locutions in the Albanian language: Morphological processes in word-formation. *European Journal of Economics, Law and Social Sciences* 5(2): 307–312.

Dançetoviq, Vojisllav (1960): *Sufiksi diminutiv i emnave të gjuhës shqipe*. Prishtinë: Rilindja.

Domi, Mahir (ed.) (2002): *Gramatika e gjuhës shqipe*. Vol. 1: *Morfologjia*. Tiranë: Maluka.

Genesin, Monica and Joachim Matzinger (2005): Nominalkomposition im Missale des Gjon Buzuku: Zu Form, Semantik und Anwendung des Wortbildungstyps in einer Balkansprache. In: Günter Schweiger (ed.), *Indogermanica. Festschrift Gert Klingenschmitt. Indische, iranische und indogermanische Studien dem verehrten Jubilar dargebracht zu seinem fünfundsechzigsten Geburtstag*, 413–434. Taimering: Schweiger VWT-Verlag.

Hysa, Enver (2004): *Formimi i emrave me ndajshtesa në gjuhën shqipe*. Tiranë: Mësonjëtorja.

Lloshi, Xhevat (1994). Substandard Albanian and its relation to Standard Albanian. In: Norbert Reiter, Uwe Hinrichs and Jiřina van Leeuwen-Turnovcová (eds.), *Sprachlicher Standard und Substandard in Südosteuropa und Osteuropa. Beiträge zum Symposion vom 12.–16. Oktober 1992 in Berlin*, 184–194. Wiesbaden: Harrassowitz.

Matzinger, Joachim (2006): *Der altalbanische Text [E] Mbsuame e Krështerë (Dottrina cristiana) des Lekë Matrënga von 1592. Eine Einführung in die albanische Sprachwissenschaft*. Dettelbach: Röll.

Matzinger, Joachim (2007): Prinzipien der altalbanischen nominalen Wortbildung und die deverbalen nomina actionis im Korpus des Gjon Buzuku. *Studime* 14: 63–73.

Newmark, Leonard, Philip Hubbard and Peter Prifti (1982): *Standard Albanian. A reference grammar for students*. Stanford: Stanford University Press.

Paçarizi, Rrahman (2019): Conversion in Albanian. *Posznan Studies in Contemporary Linguistics* 55(3): 579–600.

Paçarizi, Rrahman (2024): The Definition and Typologies of Conversion and Compounding in Albanian Word Formation in a Crosslinguistic Approach. *Forum for Linguistic Studies* 6(3): 529–542.

Sherko, Esmeralda (2015): Compound Pronouns in English and Albanian. *European Journal of Language and Literature Studies* 1(2): 36–41.

Thomaj, Jani (1999): *Leksikologjia e gjuhës shqipe*. Tiranë: shblu.

Xhuvani, Aleksandër and Eqrem Çabej (1962): *Prapashtesat e gjuhës shqipe*. Tiranë: Mihal Duri.

Xhuvani, Aleksandër and Eqrem Çabej (1975): Parashtesat e gjuhës shqipe. In: Mahir Domi (ed.), *Çështje të gramatikës së shqipes së sotme*. Vol. 2, 5–55. Tiranë: Mihal Duri.

Angela Ralli
13 Greek

1 Introduction
2 General overview
3 Composition
4 Derivation
5 Blending
6 References

Abstract: This article deals with word-formation in Modern Greek. It provides a basic description of the structure and properties of compounding, derivation and blending, which is followed by explanations drawn from various theoretical analyses that have been proposed in the literature. All issues and claims are illustrated with a number of examples, which, for clarity reasons, are given in a broad phonological transcription.

1 Introduction

Since the early sixties, word-formation in Modern Greek (hereafter Greek) has triggered increasing interest within linguistic research (see, among others, Koutsoudas 1962) and a variety of morphological phenomena have been analyzed within the framework of various linguistic schools, resulting in a number of studies, both descriptive and explanatory (see Ralli 2003 for the state-of-the-art of Greek morphology). Basic questions, such as "what is the structure of words", "what are the basic units and rules/patterns responsible for the analysis and generation of morphologically-complex items", "what is the relation between the various word-formation processes" and "where is the locus of word-formation in grammar" have received a variety of answers, depending on the theoretical approach one deals with.

This article should be seen as a synthesis of the major points that can be found in the existing literature on Greek word-formation of the last forty years, but when needed, reference is made to older works as well. Issues that have attracted attention, such as constituency, headedness, selection, etc. are dealt with

Angela Ralli, Patras, Greece

in the following sections, and certain major works regarding Greek morphology are cited. Although Greek has a wide variety of intriguing phenomena affecting word-formation, there are areas that are relatively well studied, e.g., compounding, and areas that still call for a thorough exploration (e.g., prefixation).

The main sections of this article are dedicated to derivation and compounding, but hints to inflection are also made. The reason for this choice relies on the fact that Greek nouns, adjectives, verbs and certain pronouns are overtly inflected and their endings are part of the word structure, most of the time intermingling with the other constituents of the word. For clarity reasons, I list the word bases (stems) and the derivational suffixes with the appropriate inflectional endings. The latter are included in parentheses, together with other material which is irrelevant for the argumentation. Parentheses are absent only when the entire base is used for compounding or derivational purposes, i.e. when a base coincides with a free word. Conventionally, nominal words are given in the nominative singular forms; the first person singular of the present tense is provided for verbs, since Modern Greek has lost its overt infinitival forms. Moreover, all Greek examples are listed in a broad phonological transcription, and stress is assigned properly.

It is worth pointing out that word-formation via conversion or stem-internal vocalic change (ablaut) is also possible, but in Greek, these operations are of limited productivity and usually affect stems, since the presence of overtly realized inflection renders difficult the change of category of the word as a whole. On the one hand, conversion is restricted to a small production of denominal verbal stems (e.g., $ɣlosoloɣ_V(ó)$ 'to talk about language, behave like a linguist' ← $ɣlosolóɣ_N(os)$ 'linguist'). On the other hand, ablaut applies only to learned stems of Ancient Greek origin (e.g., $lóɣ_N(os)$ 'speech, oration' ← $léɣ_V(o)$ 'to talk, say', $apox_N(í)$ 'abstention' ← $apéx_V(o)$ 'to be off').

2 General overview

Morphology is a particularly developed component in the grammar of Greek, since it displays productive word-formation patterns for both derivation and compounding. Greek morphology is mainly stem-based in that most words are formed by adding an affix – prefix or suffix – to a stem (derivation), or a stem to another stem or word (compounding). Stems can be either morphologically simple (i.e. stems without any affixal or other material), or morphologically complex. On synchronic grounds, morphologically-simple stems coincide with roots. In Ancient (Classical) Greek (5th and 4th c. BC), however, a distinction between the two notions was necessary since roots gave rise to stems with the addition of thematic vowels. For instance, the Ancient Greek word *ánthrōpos* 'man, human being' contained the root *anthrōp-*, the thematic vowel *-o-* and the inflectional ending *-s*, i.e. the case (nominative) and number (singular) exponent. Nowadays, thematic vowels have lost their original stem-forming role and the border between stems and roots is blurred. Since the distinction between the two notions is not structurally relevant, most of the time thematic vowels are considered to be parts of the inflectional endings (Ralli 2005). Thus, *ánθropos*, today's form for 'man, human being', is analyzed as containing the root/stem *anθrop-* and the inflectional ending *-os*. Note that in this article, the term *stem* is used to refer to both roots and stems.

Greek belongs to the fusional type of languages, in that the words of its major grammatical categories bear inflection, and inflectional endings are portmanteau morphemes, combining more than one morpho-syntactic feature. Nouns, adjectives, and certain pronouns inflect for gender, case, and number, while they are distributed into several inflection classes (ten according to Ralli 2005). Articles express the same morpho-syntactic features of nouns and adjectives, but they do not display a transparent and thus, analyzable structure, into stem and inflectional ending. Verbs are morphologically marked for voice, aspect, tense, person and inflection class (mood has lost its overt marking in Modern Greek), and are divided into two basic inflection classes. Generally, inflected words are formed on the basis of combining a stem and an inflectional ending, as in the pattern [Stem-INFL]$_{Word}$ (e.g., *δróm-os* 'road-MASC.NOM.SG.', *oré-os* 'nice-MASC.NOM.SG', *péz-o* 'play-IMPERF.PRES.1SG'). The structure is slightly more complex in the perfective form of verbs, where the ending contains an aspectual marker *-s-* (+perfective) and the portmanteau morpheme combining the features of past, person and number: [[Stem-INFL]$_{Stem}$-INFL]$_{Word}$, as in *δó-s-ame* 'give-PERF-PAST.1PL' 'we gave' (Ralli 2005). Inflection is generally realized as suffixation. The augment *e-* in the past tense of verbs is the only case where inflection could be considered to appear as a prefix, and in fact, it indicated the past tense in Ancient Greek. Nowadays, the use of *e-* is connected with the presence of stress, since it is absent in unstressed position (compare *é-δo-s-a* 'I gave' with *δó-s-ame* 'we gave'). Since its occurrence is not compulsory in the past tense, its inflectional status is doubtful. In fact, in the literature, it has been often considered as a morpho-phonologically inserted element (Babiniotis 1972; Ralli 2005).

Derivation appears as suffixation, or prefixation. It forms stems out of stems and affixes. As already mentioned, a derived stem needs an inflectional ending in order to become a word, and be used for syntactic purposes. The general patterns of Greek derived words are the following:

(1) a. [[Stem DSUF]$_{Stem}$-INFL]$_{Word}$ b. [[PREF Stem]$_{Stem}$-INFL]$_{Word}$
[[xor$_N$-év$_V$]$_V$-o]$_V$ [[á-ɣnost$_A$]$_A$-os]$_A$
dance-DSUF-IMPERF.PRES.1P.SG   PREF-known-NOM.SG
'I dance'   'unknown'
c. [PREF Word]$_{Word}$
[para-ɣeló$_V$]$_V$
PREF-laugh.IMPERF.PRES.1P.SG
'I laugh a lot'

(1b) and (1c) differ with respect to the morphological status of the base, i.e. whether the prefix is added to a stem or to a word. As proposed by Ralli (2004), the criteria for selecting a stem or a word are mainly phonological (change of stress), and semantic (change of meaning). For instance, while the prefix *a-* triggers a change of stress of the adjective it is attached to (cf. *áɣnostos* 'unknown' and *ɣnostós* 'known'), there is no such change in a verb like *ɣeló* 'to laugh', when it accepts *para-* 'a lot'. It should be noticed that more than one affix can be added to a base, the exact number of which is restricted by the various constraints and selectional restrictions which operate on derivational structures (see section 4 for more information).

Contrary to inflection, the form of which has become poorer in Modern Greek as compared to Ancient Greek, the language has experienced a significant growth of compounding since the Hellenistic period (ca. 3rd c. BC–3rd c. AD). It is important to note that in the late medieval period (after the 13th c. AD), a considerable number of verb-verb coordinative compounds is introduced (Manolessou and Tsolakidis 2009; Ralli 2009b), which make Greek diverge from all the other Indo-European languages, where coordination usually affects nominals. Compounding is based on the combination of two lexemes (see Bauer 2001: 695 for a proper definition of the process). In Greek, the first constituent is usually a stem, while the second can be a stem or a word. There are few exceptions as far as the first constituent is concerned, namely, cases where an invariant adverbial word is used, such as in the example *ksanaɣráfo* 'to rewrite' (*ksaná* 'again' + *ɣráfo* 'to write'). A linking element *-o-* appears between the two lexemes (e.g., *sime-o-stolizmós* 'flag decoration' ← *simé(a)* 'flag' + *stolizmós* 'decoration'); it is a semantically empty element originating from an ancient thematic vowel (Ralli and Raftopoulou 1999), the presence of which indicates the process itself. As such, it has been called "compound marker" (Ralli 2008a). Crucially, the marker is not realized if the first constituent is an uninflected word, or if the second constituent begins with a vowel which is stronger than /o/ on the sonority hierarchy (á > a > é > e > ó > o > í > i > ú > u) proposed by Hatzidakis (1905–07) and subsequently elaborated by Kaisse (1982). For instance, there is no compound-internal *-o-* in *ksanaɣráfo* 'rewrite' (← *ksaná* 'again' + *γráfo* 'write') and in *laðémboros* 'oil merchant' (← *láð(i)* 'oil' + *émboros* 'merchant'). However, when the two constituents are in a loose structural relation, the -*o*- is present, even if the second constituent begins with a strong vowel. This is the case for compounds which bear a coordinative relation between their two members (e.g., *piγenoérxome* 'to come (and) go' ← *piγén(o)* 'to go' + *érxome* 'to come'). It should be noticed that the Greek -*o*- appears in a wide range of non-native (also called "neoclassical") compounds of other European languages, that is, in compounds whose constituent parts have been borrowed from Ancient Greek or Latin (e.g., *ge-o-graphy*, *soci-o-linguist*, etc.).

Compounds show inflection on their right-hand constituents. If the second constituent is a word, the compound bears the inflectional ending of the word (e.g., *eleokaliérγia* 'olive culture' ← *elé(a)* 'olive' + *kaliérγia* 'culture'). However, a different inflectional ending may be used from that of the second constituent – when taken in isolation – if this constituent is a stem (e.g., *laðolémono* 'oil (and) lemon (sauce)' ← *láð(i)* 'oil' + *lemón(i)* 'lemon').

Although compounding differs from derivation, the order of application between the two processes, the use of certain units of an unclear status, the so-called "affixoids", as well as the existence of specific constraints affecting both processes prove that compounding and derivation intermingle in such a way that only the same grammatical domain can handle compounds and derived words properly. In previous work, I have suggested that this domain should be morphology (Ralli 2010). In fact, as shown below, Greek compounds are one-word units, morphologically and phonologically, exhibiting all the morphological properties of words. However, under the influence of English, the emergence of certain recent formations of phrasal structure, displaying semi-visibility to syntactic operations, suggests that another type of phrasal compounding is under development in Greek. Most of these formations constitute terms, are restricted in the domain of specific sublanguages (science, football, etc., e.g., *ðeltío kerú* 'weather report'), and their formation argues in favour of morphology-syntax interaction (see section 3.5, as well as Ralli and Stavrou 1998 and Ralli 2013a).

Finally, it should be noted that the well-known neoclassical formations of most European languages (e.g., *ánθropoloγía* ~ anthropology, *imisferio* ~ hemisphere, etc.) are compounds, since they obey the laws of Greek compounding. Many of them are calques, which are fully integrated into the Greek morphological system in that they combine stems, and bear Greek affixes and inflection. For instance, the English term *neology* has been reformulated in Greek as *neoloγía*, where the stems *ne*- 'young' and -*loγ*- 'doctrine about language' are linked to each other by the compound marker -*o*-, and the combination as a whole accepts the derivational affix -*ia* (there is no overtly realized inflectional suffix in this example). Crucially, as observed by Ralli (2008b), the neoclassical type of formations is formed productively in Greek, as proven by the large number of neologisms appearing each day in the media. A considerable number of them belong to synthetic compounds, which contain deverbal bound stems, i.e. stems that cannot be free with the presence of inflectional affixes (see section 3.4).

3 Composition

Compounding as a very productive word-formation process of the Greek has been attested since Homeric Greek (Tserepis 1902). It produces compounds belonging to the major grammatical categories of nouns, adjectives and verbs. Nouns display combinations of two nouns (e.g., *kreatayorá* 'meat market' ← *kréa(s)* 'meat' + *ayorá* 'market') and adjective and noun (e.g., *asximópapo* 'ugly duckling' ← *ásxim(o)* 'ugly' + *pap(í)* 'duck'). Adjectives combine two adjectives (e.g., *ikonomikopolitikós* 'economic-political' ← *ikonomik(ós)* 'economic' + *politikós* 'political'), a noun and an adjective (e.g., *laomísitos* 'hated (by the) people' ← *la(ós)* 'people' + *misitós* 'hated'), or an adverb with an adjective (e.g., *aðikoxaménos* 'lost in vain' ← *áðik(a)* 'in vain' + *xaménos* 'lost'). Verbs may contain either a noun and a verb (e.g., *xaropalévo* 'to fight (with) death' ← *xár(os)* 'death' + *palévo* 'to fight'), two verbs (e.g., *aniyoklíno* 'to open (and) close' ← *aníy(o)* 'to open' + *klíno* 'to close') or an adverb and a verb (e.g., *kakopernó* 'to badly live' ← *kak(á)* 'badly' + *pernó* 'to pass, live'). As claimed in previous work (Ralli 2009a), adverbial compounds, in their vast majority, are secondary formations resulting from a suffixation process, which adds the most common adverbial suffix *-a* to primary compounds, usually adjectives (e.g., *vorioanatoliká* '[north-east]$_{ADV}$' ← *vorioanatolik(ós)$_A$* 'north-east' + *-a$_{ADV}$* ← *vóri(os)$_A$* 'north' + *anatolikós$_A$* 'east').

It is worth noticing that the nominal stems participating in compounds do not always coincide with those that appear in the citation form, that is, in the nominative singular: they often display an allomorphic variation which is usually found in other cases and/or in the plural (e.g., *ematokílizma* 'wallowing in blood' ← *émat-os* 'blood-GEN' (*éma* 'blood.SG') + *kílizma* 'wallowing', *papaðopéði* 'altar boy' ← *papáð-es* 'priest-PL' (*papá-s* 'priest-SG') + *peðí* 'boy'). See Ralli (2103a) for more details.

3.1 Stress and morphological structure

Greek compounds bear only one stress (they are phonological words), but do not have a uniform stress pattern. In many cases, stress is located on the antepenultimate syllable, independently of the position of stress of the compound members, when taken in isolation (e.g., *kuklóspito* 'doll's house' ← *kúkl(a)* 'doll' + *spít(i)* 'house'). In other cases, stress falls on the same syllable as that of the second constituent of the compound (e.g., *xartopetséta* 'paper napkin' ← *xart(i)* 'paper' + *petséta* 'napkin'). As suggested by Nespor and Ralli (1996), the position of stress in Greek compounds depends on their structure. Compounds containing stems, such as *kuklóspito*, do not have fixed stress properties, and as such, are submitted to a compound-specific phonological law placing stress on the antepenultimate syllable. On the other hand, compounds combining a stem and a word, like *xartopetséta*, keep the stress of the right-hand word, *petséta* and, as such, have fixed stress properties. As proposed by Ralli (2007, 2009a, 2013a), stress properties and the form of the inflectional ending are the basic criteria for classifying Greek compounds into four structural patterns: a) stem + stem (e.g., *rizógalo* 'milk (and) rice (pudding)' ← *ríz(i)* 'rice' + *yál(a)* 'milk'); b) stem + word (e.g., *xrisavyí* 'golden dawn' ← *xris(í)* 'golden' + *avyí* 'dawn'); c) word + stem (e.g., *eksóδikos* 'extrajudicial' ← *ékso* 'out' + *δík(i)* 'trial'); d) word + word (e.g., *ksanavrísko* 'to find again' ← *ksaná* 'again' + *vrísko* 'to find'). In fact, compounds whose second constituent is a stem are stressed on the antepenultimate syllable and may bear a different inflectional ending from that of the second member, when taken in isolation. This is not the case for the other two categories which keep the stress and the ending of their right-hand word. It should be noticed that the most widespread and productively formed types are a) and b), while c) and d) account for only a few examples.

Inflection appears on the right-hand side of a Greek compound. It is worth noting, though, that a very limited number of Ancient Greek compounds with word-internal inflection is still in use, such as *niktilambís* (Ancient Greek *nyktilampēs*) 'shining at night' ← *niktí* 'night.DAT' + *-lambis* 'who shines' and *nunexís* (Ancient Greek *nounekhēs*) 'well minded' ← *nun* 'mind.ACC' + *-ex-is* 'who has'. These compounds contain the ancient inflected forms *niktí* (there is no dative case in Modern Greek) and *nun* (nowadays, *-n* has been lost from accusative forms) on their left-hand constituent, and should be analyzed as fossilized cases.

3.2 Headedness in compounding

Many Greek compounds are endocentric obeying Williams' (1981) right-hand head rule, according to which the head occupies the second position of the structure and is responsible for transmitting to the compound its grammatical category and basic meaning (e.g., *kokinóxoma*$_N$ 'clay earth' ← *kókin(o)*$_A$ 'red' + *xóma*$_N$ 'earth', *kozmoksákustos*$_A$ 'world known' ← *kózm(os)*$_N$ 'world' + *ksakustós*$_A$ 'known', *siyovrázo*$_V$ 'to simmer' ← *siy(á)*$_{ADV}$ 'low' + *vrázo*$_V$ 'to boil'). Greek also contains a considerable number of so-called "exocentric" compounds (Ralli and Andreou 2012). Typical examples of these cases are *kalótixos*_A 'who has good luck' ← *kal(ós)*_A 'good' + *tíx(i)*_N 'luck' and *misoyínis*_N 'misogynist' ← *mis(ó)*_V 'to hate' + *yin(i)*_N 'woman'. Exocentric compounds show a unique behavior with respect to a number of points: a) the grammatical category and other morpho-syntactic features are not inherited from any of the stems. For instance, *kalótixos* may be used as an adjective of masculine gender, while the right-hand member is a feminine noun (*tíx(i)* 'luck') and the left-hand member (*kal(í)* 'good') is an adjective agreeing with the noun in the feminine gender; b) their inflectional endings are usually different from those of the second member, when taken separately (cf. *kalótixos* and *tíxi*); c) semantically, the meaning of the compound does not denote a subset of the entities expressed by the second member of the formation, as opposed to what happens with the meaning of endocentric compounds. For example, *misoyínis* does not designate a kind of woman but rather someone who hates women.

Finally, a category of compounds which is also problematic for headedness involves the coordinative compounds (also called "dvandva", see section 3.3), such as *alatopípero* 'salt (and) pepper' ← *alát(i)* 'salt' + *pipér(i)* 'pepper', or *aniyoklíno* 'to open (and) close' ← *aníy(o)* 'to open' + *klíno* 'to close', since both constituents are of an equal status and neither of them prevails over the other. Formations like these could be treated as headless, but in the literature, they have also been treated as double-headed (see Kageyama 2009 for Japanese coordinative compounds) or even headed (see Ralli 2013a for the Greek ones) because it may be the case that certain morphosyntactic features of the second constituent are inherited by the compound as a whole (e.g., *yinekópeða* 'women-(and)-children.NEU' ← *yinék(es)*.FEM 'women' + *peð(iá)*.NEU 'children').

3.3 Compound-internal relations and order of constituents

The basic constituents of a compound formation, that is, the two stems or the stem and the word that participate in the structure of a compound, may be in a subordinative, attributive, or coordinative relation (Scalise and Bisetto 2009). In the first two cases, the left-hand member acts like a modifier of the right-hand member, as in the examples *ayrióyata* 'wild cat' ← *áyri(a)* 'wild' + *yáta* 'cat' (attributive relation) and *ðraxmofoniás* drachma-killer 'miserable' ← *ðraxm(í)* 'drachma (Greek coin)' + *foniás* 'killer' (subordinative relation). Among the productively formed compounds, we also find cases showing a coordinative relation, i.e. compounds the constituents of which are of the same category. For example, two verbs (e.g., *anavozvíno* 'to switch on (and) off' ← *anáv(o)* 'to switch on' + *zvíno* 'to switch off'), two nouns (e.g., *psomotíri* 'bread (and) cheese' ← *psom(í)* 'bread' + *tirí* 'cheese'), or two adjectives (e.g., *pikróylikos* 'bitter-sweet' ← *pikr(ós)* 'bitter'

+ *ylikós* 'sweet') are concatenated without the overt use of a conjunction, and neither constituent modifies the other.

In compounds with a subordinative or an attributive relation the constituent order is strict: the modifier precedes the head. There are a few examples, though, which seem to contradict this order, since their constituents combine in a more or less flexible order:

(2) a. *karδioxtípi*   vs.   b. *xtipokárδi*
      'heartbeat'   lit. 'beat-heart'
      kefalóponos   vs.   *ponokéfalos*
      'headache'   lit. 'ache-head'

As argued by Ralli (2007, 2008b), these occurrences do not constitute real counter-examples to the property of fixed order. An explanation is found in the long history of the Greek language: examples like (2a) display the typical structure of Modern Greek compounds, where the modifier (*karδiá* 'heart' and *kefál(i)* 'head') precedes the head (*xtíp(os)* 'beat' and *pónos* 'pain', respectively), whereas, examples like (2b) belong to an Ancient Greek exocentric pattern, where a verb (e.g., *xtip(ó)* 'to beat', *pon(ó)* 'to be in pain') precedes its complement (*karδiá* 'heart' and *kefál(i)* 'head', respectively). Similar compound structures are formations like *filómusos* 'who loves (Ancient Greek *phileō*) art' and *misoyínis* 'who hates (Ancient Greek *miséō*) women'.

In coordinative compound structures, the constituent parts should, in principle, be placed in a free order, since neither constituent modifies the other. In fact, such cases are common among adjectives (cf., for example, *makróstenos* 'long (and) narrow' with *stenómakros* 'narrow (and) long'). As opposed to adjectives though, the constituent order is rather fixed in nouns and verbs, as shown by the examples *laδolémono* 'oil (and) lemon' (*lemonólaδo* 'lemon (and) oil') or *aniyoklíno* 'to open (and) close' (*klinaníyo* 'to close (and) open'). One can assume that this fixed constituent-order may be imposed by independent pragmatic reasons: for example, the order may follow temporal iconicity, or the constituents appearing first express more basic concepts than constituents occupying the second position (see also Andriotis 1957). However, as shown in Ralli (2013a), pragmatic reasons are not sufficient for explaining the fixed order of constituents bearing a coordinative relation.

3.4 Compounds with a verbal/deverbal element

Verbal and deverbal (synthetic) compounds are abundant in Greek, and new formations are frequently coined. It has been suggested by Ralli (2007, 2008b, 2009a) that most of verbal compounds, especially those containing a noun as their left constituent (e.g., *xartopézo* 'to play cards' ← *xart(í)* 'paper' + *pézo* 'to play', *afisokoló* 'to stick posters' ← *afís(a)* 'poster' + *koló* 'to stick'), are innovative formations, since they did not exist in Ancient Greek. On the other hand, deverbal compounds, that is, compounds whose second constituent is a deverbal noun or adjective (see section 4.2 (7d, 9b)), were common in Ancient Greek, and are still productively created today.

It is important to stress that, in both verbal and deverbal compounds, the complement/argument of the verbal head, or of the deverbal head, can be saturated by the non-head (the left-hand member), and saturation occurs within the limits of the compound structure. For instance, in a compound like *katsikokléftis* 'goat-thief', the first constituent *katsík(a)* 'goat' is the "theme" of the base *klétfi(s)* who steals 'thief'. Generally, there is a range of semantic roles that are usually expressed by the first constituent of a Greek verbal or deverbal compound (see Di Sciullo and Ralli 1999, and Ralli 2013a for details). For an illustration, consider the following examples:

(3) a. *pontikofáγoma* 'rat eating'   Agent: *pontík(i)* 'rat, mouse'
    b. *karδiokataktitís* 'heart-conqueror'   Theme: *karδi(á)* 'heart'
    c. *oksiγonokólisi* 'welding'   Instrument: *oksiγón(o)* 'oxygen'
    d. *liθóstrotos* 'stone paved'   Material: *líθ(os)* 'stone'
    e. *ematokílizma* 'wallowing in blood'   Location: *éma* 'blood'
    f. *aγrotoδanioδótisi* 'farmer-loan-giving'   Goal: *aγrót(is)* 'farmer'
    g. *poltopíisi* 'pulp-making'   Result: *polt(ós)* 'pulp'

It is worth noticing that a particular class of deverbal compounds contains stems which remain bound, even under the presence of an inflectional ending, and for certain linguists (cf. Anastasiadi-Symeonidi 1996), they could be assigned the status of affixoids. For instance, in (4), the second constituent is not a free unit and cannot become one, even with the appropriate inflectional ending:

(4)   Compound   Deverbal stem
    a. *ktinotrófos* 'cattle-breeder'   -*trof*- (← *tréf(o)*)   'to feed')
    b. *anθropofáγos* man eater 'cannibal'   -*faγ*- (← *tró(o)*,   'to eat', aorist *éfaγ(a)*)
    c. *rasofóros* cassock carrier 'clergyman' -*for*- (← *fér(o)*)   'to carry')
    d. *γlosolóγos* tongue talker 'linguist' -*loγ*- (← *léγ(o)*)   'to talk')

As shown by Ralli (2008b), bound stems belong to nominals, and derive from a verbal base of an Ancient Greek origin, often with a simple change of the stem-internal vowel (ablaut, e.g., 4a, c, d), and rarely through a conversion of the stem allomorph of the aorist tense (4b). It should be noticed that some autonomous inflected words share the same form with certain bound stems, but bear a different meaning. For instance, the bound stems *-loy(os)* 'who talks about, specialist of a discipline' and *-for(os)* 'who carries/bears' exist side-by-side with the free words *lóyos* 'speech, oration' and *fóros* 'tax', respectively. The latter originate from the same verbal stem as the corresponding bound stems, but on synchronic grounds, they constitute distinct derivatives.

Constructions containing a bound item have always been in use in Greek, throughout its long history (Chantraine 1933). Many of them originate from Ancient Greek, such as *θeolóyos* 'who talks about the divine, theologian' (← Ancient Greek *theós* 'God' + *-loy-* (← Ancient Greek *lég(ō)* 'to talk')) and have undergone the most striking diachronic changes which affected Greek during the Hellenistic period. Other constructions are recent creations for the specific purposes of scientific terminology, due to scientific and technological development, particularly in the nineteenth century. In today's language, many of these constructions have become part of the every-day vocabulary, and bound stems currently combine with stems of common words for the creation of neologisms, as illustrated by the examples *burδolóyos* 'who talks trash' (← *búrδ(a)* 'trash' + *-loy-*) and *katsariδoktóno* 'cockroach-repellent' (← *katsaríδ(a)* 'cockroach' + *-kton-* 'killer'). In addition, they can serve as a base to further word-formation, since they may accept a derivational suffix (e.g., *-ia*) for the production of derivative nouns. For instance, *kerδoskopía* 'speculation' (← *kérδ(os)* 'profit' + *-skop-* (← Ancient Greek *skopéō* 'to target, observe')) is formed on the basis of *kerδoskóp(os)* 'speculator', *efθinofovía* 'fear of responsibilities' on *efθinófov(os)* 'who fears responsibilities' (← *efθin(i)* 'responsibility' + *-fov-* (← *fov(áme)* 'to fear')), etc.

Similar constructions appear in the vocabulary of other languages, and are listed under the class of neoclassical formations, which are complex words consisting of stems of Ancient Greek and/or Latin origin (e.g., English *sociologist*, French *sociologue*, Italian *sociologo*, etc.). Interestingly, several of these words belong to a vocabulary of internationalisms, because they have the same meaning, and a quasi identical form in various languages. Consider, for instance, the Greek word *astronómos*, which appears as *astronomer* in English, *astronome* in French, *astronomo* in Italian, etc.

3.5 Phrasal compounds

In recent years, there has been a tendency to form terms which display characteristics of noun phrases, but also certain properties of compounds (for details, see Anastasiadi-Symeonidi 1986, 1996; Ralli and Stavrou 1998; Ralli 2013a, b). Structurally, these constructions contain an adjective and a noun (e.g., *psixrós pólemos* 'Cold War') or two nouns (e.g., *praktorío idíseon* agency news 'news agency', *pedí θávma* child wonder 'wonder boy'). In the first case, the adjective agrees with the noun head in gender, number and case, while in the second case, the non-head (second constituent) is assigned genitive case by the head (*praktorío idíseon*), or it displays an invariant form in the nominative singular (*pedí θávma*). The salient properties which make these constructions resemble compounds imply a certain degree of structural opacity. For instance, it is impossible to reverse the order of their constituents, as is usually the case with common noun phrases in Greek, their non-head cannot be independently modified, and no item, or parenthetical expression, can be inserted between the constituents. Moreover, in the case of adjective-noun formations, the definite article cannot be doubled, unlike what is the case for the corresponding phrases (cf. *o meyálos o pólemos* the big the war 'the big war' with **o psixrós o pólemos* the cold the war 'the Cold War'). Also, adjective-noun constructions may be subject to derivational suffixation on the condition that the inflectional ending of the adjective is truncated and a compound marker is introduced between the adjective and the noun (e.g., *psixr-o-polem-ik(ós)* 'Cold-War like' ← *psixrós pólemos* 'Cold War'). Nevertheless, both types of formations share with noun phrases the property of containing two independent inflected words, corresponding to two phonological words, and their constituents are placed in the same order as that of noun phrases with a similar structure. Moreover, they differ from compounds in that there is no compound marker between their members.

Following recent work, I have claimed (Ralli 2013a, b) that these formations constitute phrasal compounds. Assuming that compounding is a word-formation process which cuts across morphology and syntax, depending on the language one deals with, I have proposed that Greek one-word compounds are morphological objects since they are subject to morphological rules and principles and are formed from proper morphological units (stems and compound marker). On the contrary, phrasal compounds showing semi-visibility to syntactic operations, are created in syntax. Their phrasal nature is also proven by the fact that there is no clear borderline between them and the noun phrases, since their syntactic visibility is scalar, depending on the particular example one deals with. For instance, while *léksi klidí* word key 'key word' is strongly opaque, *ánθropos ktínos* man beast 'human beast' is rather transparent.

Finally, it is worth adding that formations of a compound-internal appositive relation, like *metafrastís δierminéas* 'translator interpreter', fall under the same category of phrasal compounds, since they share with them the same semi-syntactic/semi-word properties.

4 Derivation

Greek derivation is realized either as prefixation or suffixation. Compared to prefixation, suffixation displays more variability. While prefixes are usually transparent to the properties of the base, most suffixes can be category-changing, and transmit their features to derivative formations. As such, they are heads of their structures.

With respect to their origin, affixes may be divided into three categories: a) affixes which originate from Ancient Greek and are still in use (e.g., *-osini* in a deadjectival noun like *kalosíni* 'goodness' ← *kal(ós)* 'good' + *-osini*); b) affixes which are the product of grammaticalization, i.e. those deriving from other affixes or words (e.g., the prefix *kse-* which results from the combination of the Ancient Greek preposition *ek-* with the verbal syllabic augment *e-* (e.g., *kseperno* 'to surmount, overcome' ← *kse-* + *pernó* 'to pass', Ralli 2004); c) affixes which are borrowed from other languages. Among those of the third category, one finds examples originating from Italian (e.g., the verbal suffix *-ar(o)* ← Italian *-are*, as in *voltáro* 'to stroll' ← *vólt(a)* 'stroll' + *-ar(o)*), Turkish (e.g., the nominal suffix *-dzi(s)* ← Turkish *-cI*, in nouns denoting profession, as in *xalvadzís* 'halva seller' ← *xalvá(s)* 'halva' + *-dzi(s)*), and Slavic (e.g., the diminutive suffix *-itsa* which forms feminine nouns from feminine bases, as in *δaskalítsa* 'little female teacher' ← *δaskál(a)* 'female teacher' + *-itsa*).

Finally, as is usually the case for all word-formation processes, there are different degrees of productivity, depending on the process and on the type of the affix involved (Bauer 2001). For example, diminution (e.g., *kukláki* 'little doll' ← *kúkl(a)* 'doll' + *-aki*) is subject to fewer constraints, and thus more productive, than the formation of deverbal nouns (see section 4.2). Furthermore, within the same process, certain derivational affixes are more productively used than others of the same type. Consider the suffix *-iz(o)*, which creates verbs out of nominal bases (e.g., *alatízo* 'to salt' ← *alát(i)* 'salt' + *-iz(o)*): its productivity prevails over that of the also denominal suffix *-en(o)* (e.g., *anaséno* 'to breathe' ← *anás(a)* 'breath' + *-en(o)*).

4.1 Prefixation

As proposed in earlier work (Ralli 2005), there are two kinds of prefixes: (a) bound prefixes and (b) prefixes which have an autonomous form, but do not bear a clear-cut lexical meaning, since the latter is determined in relation with the meaning of the base which combines with the prefix. Prefixes of the second type originate from certain Ancient Greek prepositions, which, already in Classical Greek, were used as preverbs. Some of these preverbs keep the old prepositional function in certain fixed expressions (e.g., *aná xíras* ← Ancient Greek *aná kheíras* 'at hand'), while others (*antí, apó, katá, metá*) appear as prepositions or adverbs, in restricted contexts, and with a specific meaning. For instance, *apó* denotes the provenance in a sentence like *íme apó tin Eláda* 'I am from Greece', and *metá* has an adverbial function, expressing the future, as in the sentence *θa se ðo metá* 'I will see you later'.

(5) a. Bound prefixes: *a-* (*á-ɣnostos* 'unknown'), *ðis-* (*ðis-prófertos* 'unpronouncable'), *ef-* (*ef-parusíastos* 'presentable'), *kse-* (*kse-xorízo* 'to distinguish');
b. Preverbs: *aná* (*anaféro* 'to report'), *antí* (*antiɣráfo* 'to copy'), *apó* (*apoxoró* 'to leave'), *ðiá* (*ðiaɣráfo* 'to erase'), *is* (*ispnéo* 'to breathe in'), *ek* (*ekpnéo* 'to breathe out'), *en* (*entíno* 'to tighten'), *epí* (*epivlépo* 'to supervise'), *katá* (*kataɣráfo* 'to register'), *metá* (*metaθéto* 'to transpose'), *pará* (*parakáno* 'to overdo'), *perí* (*periɣráfo* 'to describe'), *pro* (*protíno* 'to propose'), *pros* (*prostréxo* 'to hasten'), *sin* (*sintonízo* 'to coordinate'), *ipér* (*ipertonízo* 'to overstress'), *ipó* (*ipoɣráfo* 'to sign').

Prefixes attach to stems or to words, depending on the case (Ralli 2004). In the first case, an inflectional ending follows prefixation ([[Prefix Stem]-INFL]), while in the second case, the prefix combines with an already inflected base ([Prefix [Stem-INFL]]). When prefixes are added to stems there may be changes to the base, formal and semantic, while in formations combining prefixes and inflected words, the latter remain invariable. For instance, verbs prefixed with *apó* may undergo vowel deletion and change of meaning (e.g., *apéxo* 'to be off' ← *apó* + *éxo* 'to have'). In contrast, a structure with the prefix *pará*, denoting an excessive realization of the event, like the verb *paraéxo* 'to over-have' (← *pará* + *éxo* 'to have'), is fully transparent, formally and semantically.

Prefixes have certain properties which make them behave similarly to the left-hand components of compounds. These properties have probably led grammarians (e.g., Triantaphylidis 1991) to assign to prefixation the status of compounding. One such property is that many preverbs do not change the category of the base they attach to. For instance, the preverb *ipér* can be combined with a verb (*ipertonízo* 'to overstress' ← *ipér* + *tonízo* 'to stress'), a noun (*iperánθropos* 'superhuman' ← *ipér* + *ánθropos* 'man, human being') or an adjective (*ipersínxronos* 'super-modern' ← *ipér* + *sínxronos* 'contemporary, modern'). Moreover, as observed in Ralli (2013a), there are cases of prefixation and compounding which share the property of exocentricity, as opposed to suffixation where exocentricity is absent. Consider the adjective *ámiros* 'unlucky' containing the prefix *a-*, the stem *mir-* of the noun *míra* 'luck' and the inflectional ending *-os*. Since neither of the constituents justifies the adjectival category and properties of *ámiros*, formations of this type could be treated as exocentric.

4.2 Suffixation

As already mentioned, most suffixes are category-changing and impose categorial and selectional requirements on the type of the base they combine with. For instance, the verbal suffix *-ar(o)* (6b) selects nominal bases of foreign origin (Ralli 2012) and the deverbal *-ma* selects verbal bases of more than one syllable, in contrast with *-simo*, which requires verbal bases of one syllable (see Drachman and Malikouti-Drachman 1994 for more details):

(6) a. *aníy-ma*   ←   *aníy(o)*   + *-ma*   vs.   *lí-simo*   ←   *lín(o)* + *-simo*
       'opening'   'to open'   'unfastening'   'to unfasten'
    b. *sulats-áro* ← *suláts(o)* + *-ar(o)*
       'to stroll'   'stroll'

It has been proposed by Melissaropoulou and Ralli (2010) that selectional properties are not derivable by rule but are lexical specifications of the particular suffixes. Among the lexically-specified morpho-syntactic properties characterizing both stems and derivational suffixes, it is worth mentioning the feature of inflection class which indicates the type of inflection of the derived noun, adjective or verb. Moreover, suffixes are also lexically marked for stress properties, which determine the place of stress of the derived items (e.g., *vark-áδa* 'boating' ← *várk(a)* 'boat'). See Revithiadou (1999) for details about stress assignment on morphological structure.

A derived word has only one inflectional marker, but it may involve more than one derivational suffix. The cumulative order of derivational suffixes follows from their categorial and selectional properties. For instance, a derived word like *ekpeδeftikós* 'educational' contains the prefix *ek*, the stem *peδ-* of the word *peδí* 'child', the verbal suffix *-ev-*, the nominal suffix *-ti-*, the adjectival suffix *-ik-* and the closing inflectional suffix *-os* ([[[[ek[peδ-ev]]-t]-ik]-ós]).

The following list displays the most frequent derivational suffixes in Greek. They are classified according to their category and the category of the base they select. Suffixes and examples are taken from Ralli (2005: 147–154).

(7) Noun suffixes
    a. Denominal suffixes
    a1. Various denominal suffixes

-izm(os)	elinizmós	'Hellenism'	←	élin(as)	'Greek'
-isti(s)	elinistís	'Hellenist'	←	élin(as)	'Greek'
-ia	lemoniá	'lemon tree'	←	lemón(i)	'lemon'
-iliki	proeðrilíki	'presidency'	←	próeðr(os)	'president'
-ona(s)	eleónas	'olive field'	←	elé(a)	'olive'

       NB. -iliki is of Turkish origin (-lIk).
    a2. Suffixes of ethnic nouns

-[i/o]ti(s)	Meɣarítis	'inhabitant of Mégara'	
	Pireótis	'~ Pireás	(Piraeus)'
-[i/a]n(os)	Zakinθinós	'~ Zákinθos	(Zante)'
	Afrikanós	'~ Afrikí	(Africa)'
-i/e(os)	Lézvios	'~ Lézvos	(Lesbos)'
	Kerkiréos	'~ Kérkira	(Corfu)'
-ez(os)	Verolinézos	'~ Verolíno	(Berlin)'

       NB. -ez(os) originates from the Italian -ese.
    a3. Suffixes of professional nouns

-a(s)	ɣalatás	'milk man'	←	ɣála	'milk'
-dzi(s)	taksidzís	'taxi driver'	←	taksí	'taxi'
-ari(s)	varkáris	'boatman'	←	várk(a)	'boat'
-ieri(s)	portiéris	'doorman'	←	pórt(a)	'door'
-aðor(os)	tornaðóros	'turner'	←	tórn(os)	'lathe'
-isti(s)	poðosferistís	'soccer player'	←	poðósfer(o)	'soccer'
-ia(s)	isoðimatías	'rentier'	←	isóðima	'income'

       NB. As already stated, -dzi(s) is of Turkish provenance (-cI) and is the most frequent of all suffixes creating professional nouns. -aðor(os) and -ieri(s) originate from the Italian -atore and -iere, respectively, while -ari(s) comes from the Latin -arius.
    a4. Diminutive suffixes

-aki	anθropáki	'little man'	←	ánθrop(os)	'man/human being'
-itsa	kuklítsa	'little doll'	←	kúkl(a)	'doll'
-uli(s) /ula/uli	ɣatúlis.MASC/ ɣatúla.FEM/ ɣatúli.NEU	'little cat'	←	ɣát(a)	'cat'

NB. *-aki* is the most frequent diminutive suffix in Standard Modern Greek. It combines with nouns of all gender values, and creates neuter diminutives (Melissaropoulou and Ralli 2008). The suffix *-itsa* is feminine, selects feminine bases and, as already mentioned, originates from Slavic. As for *-uli(s)/-ula/-uli*, they form masculine (*-uli(s)*), feminine (*-ula*) and neuter (*-uli*) diminutives, respectively. It should be noticed that the diminutive suffixes *-aki* and *-uli(s)/ula/uli* can also be added to adjectival bases in order to form diminutive nouns (see c. below). In other words, they can be category-changing.

a5. Augmentative suffixes

-ar(os)/-ara	*póδaros*.MASC/ *poδára*.FEM	'big foot'	←	*póδ(i)*.NEU	'foot'
-akla(s)/-akla	*ádraklas*.MASC/ *adrákla*.FEM	'big man'	←	*ádr(as)*.MASC	'man'

NB. Greek augmentatives are exclusively masculine and feminine. Diminutives belong to all three gender values, although neuters are more frequent (Melissaropoulou 2009).

a6. Suffixes forming female nouns (see also Pavlakou and Koutsoukos 2009)

-isa	*taverniárisa*	'female tavern owner'	←	*taverniár(is)*	'male tavern owner'
-ina	*δikiyorína*	'female lawyer'	←	*δikiyór(os)*	'male lawyer'
-u	*taksidzú*	'female taxi driver'	←	*taksidz(ís)*	'male taxi driver'

b. Deverbal suffixes

-ti(s)	*xoreftís*	'dancer'	←	*xorév(o)*	'to dance'
-tira(s)	*kinitíras*	'engine'	←	*kin(ó)*	'to move'
-ea(s)	*singraféas*	'writer'	←	*sinɣráf(o)*	'to write'
-si	*lísi*	'solution'	←	*lín(o)*	'to solve'
-m(os)	*skotomós*	'killing'	←	*skotón(o)*	'to kill'
-simo	*δésimo*	'fastening'	←	*δén(o)*	'to fasten'
-ma	*δiávazma*	'reading'	←	*δiaváz(o)*	'to read'
-ia	*kaliérɣia*	'culture'	←	*kalierɣ(ó)*	'to cultivate'
-i(o)	*ɣrafío*	'office, desk'	←	*ɣráf(o)*	'to write'
-tria	*xoréftria*	'female dancer'	←	*xorév(o)*	'to dance'

NB. *-ti(s)* and *-tira(s)* form both agent and instrumental nouns.

c. Denominal and deadjectival suffixes

-otita	*anθropótita*	'humanity'	←	*ánθrop(os)*	'human being'
	aɣaθótita	'goodness'	←	*aɣaθ(ós)*	'good'
-osini	*nikokirosíni*	'tidiness'	←	*nikokir(á)*	'housekeeper'
	kalosíni	'goodness'	←	*kal(ós)*	'good'

-ila	kapníla	'smoky smell'	←	kapn(ós)	'smoke'
	kokiníla	'redness'	←	kókin(os)	'red'
-aδa	varkáδa	'boating'	←	várk(a)	'boat'
	aspráδa	'whiteness'	←	áspr(os)	'white'
-aki	mikráki	'little person'	←	mikr(ós)	'little'
-uli	omorfúli	'little beautiful person'	←	ómorf(os)	'beautiful'

NB. *-osini* does not generally combine with bases of popular origin. *-aδa* originates from the Venetian *-ada*.

(8) Adjectival suffixes
    a. Denominal

-im(os)	nómimos	'legal, legitimate'	←	nóm(os)	'law'
-er(os)	laδerós	'oily'	←	láδ(i)	'oil'
-eni(os)	asiménios	'silver made'	←	asím(i)	'silver'
-isi(os)	vunísios	'mountainous'	←	vun(ó)	'mountain'
-ik(os)	nomikós	'legal'	←	nóm(os)	'law'
-in(os)	ksílinos	'wooden'	←	ksíl(o)	'wood'
-ios	uránios	'celestial'	←	uran(ós)	'sky'

NB. Adjectival suffixes are listed in their masculine form. Their feminine and neuter counterparts end in *-i/-a* and *-o*, respectively.

    b. Deverbal

-t(os)	skepastós	'covered'	←	skepáz(o)	'to cover'
-sim(os)	katikísimos	'inhabitable'	←	katik(ó)	'to inhabit'
-tiri(os)	kinitírios	'motive, driving'	←	kin(ó)	'to move'
-te(os)	plirotéos	'payable'	←	pliro(no)	'to pay'
-men(os)	ayapiménos	'beloved'	←	ayap(ó)	'to love'

NB. *-tiri(os)* and *-te(os)* are of learned origin and do not combine with popular bases. *-men(os)* forms past participles; it is listed together with the adjectival suffixes, since participles in *-men(os)* are inflected like adjectives and have adjectival properties.

    c. Deadjectival (diminutives)

-uli(s)/-ula/	asprúlis.MASC/	'whitish'	←	áspr(os).MASC	'white'
-ulik(o)	asprúla.FEM/				
	asprúliko.NEU				
-utsik(os)/	meyalútsikos.MASC/	'biggish'	←	meyál(os).MASC	'big'
-utsiki/	meyalútsiki.FEM/				
-utsik(o)	meyalútsiko.NEU				

NB. *-utsik(os)* resulted from a combination of the Italian diminutive suffix *-uccio* and the Greek adjectival suffix *-ik(os)*. *-ulik(o)* contains a combination of the noun suffix *-uli* and the adjectival *-ik(o)*.

(9) Verbal suffixes
   a. Denominal
      -ar(o)   filmáro   'to film'   ←   film   'film'
      NB. As mentioned above, -ar(o) originates from the Italian infinitival marker -are (Ralli 2012).
   b. Denominal and deadjectival
      -iz(o)   zoɣrafízo   'to paint'   ←   zoɣráf(os)   'painter'
               kaθarízo   'to clean'   ←   kaθar(ós)   'clean'
      -ev(o)   psarévo   'to fish'   ←   psár(i)   'fish'
               aɣriévo   'to become wild'   ←   áɣri(os)   'wild'
      -on(o)   kliδóno   'to lock'   ←   kliδí   'key'
               areóno   'to thin out'   ←   are(ós)   'loose, thin'
      -en(o)   θerméno   'to heat'   ←   θerm(ós)   'hot'
               anaséno   'to breathe'   ←   anás(a)   'breath'

(10) Adverbial suffixes
     -a   kalá   'well'   ←   kal(ós)   'good'
     -os   akrivós   'exactly'   ←   akriv(ís)   'exact'
     NB. Both suffixes form adverbs out of adjectival stems. -os is the Ancient Greek suffix -ōs; nowadays, it combines with bases of learned origin.

5 Blending

In Greek, blending is a rather novel but fast developing word-formation process, which is mostly found in the vocabulary of slang, used by young people and other well-defined social groups. According to Ronneberger-Sibold (2006) blends are deliberate creations resulting from the structural fusion of two words, the by-product of which is the truncation of segmental material from the inner edges of the two constituents, or from only one of them. With respect to Greek, it has been proposed by Ralli and Xydopoulos (2012) that blends resemble compounds, since they involve the combination of at least two lexemes, are phonological words, and their structure follows the structure of (stem + word) compounds (see section 3). In fact, Greek blends and compounds combine the same grammatical categories: there are noun-noun (e.g., aɣapúδi 'love song' ← aɣáp(i) 'love' + (traɣ)úδi 'song') or adjective-noun instances (e.g., vlaksitzís 'stupid taxi driver' ← vlaks 'stupid' + (taks)itzís 'taxi driver'), noun-verb (e.g., siδirázo 'to buy a newspaper in order to get the CD' ← siδí 'CD' + (aɣo)rázo 'to buy'), adverb-verb (e.g., ipuleɣízo 'to approach in an insidious manner' ← ípul(a) 'insidiously' + (pros)eɣízo 'to approach') and verb-verb ones (e.g., *vrexalízi* 'it rains in small drops' ← *vréx(i)* 'it rains' + *(psi)xalízi* 'to drizzle'), as well as adjective-adjective combinations (e.g., *psidrós* 'tall and fat' ← *psi(lós)* 'tall' + *(xo)drós* 'fat'). Moreover, the constituent members of both categories bear the same functional relations, that is, subordinative, attributive and coordinative. Subordinative and attributive blends are subject to rightward headedness, exactly like endocentric compounds, where the head transmits its category and specific meaning to the new formation. Crucially though, and as opposed to compounding, where exocentric constructions are productively built, Greek blending does not show any exocentric structures. Furthermore, blends are subject to a form reduction affecting both constituents, while the marker -o-, which is obligatory in compounds, never surfaces in blends.

Blends bear a prosodic structure, as put forward in the relevant literature (Arvaniti 1998): while the first constituent can be reduced to the point of keeping only the onset of the first syllable and the second constituent, i.e. the head, is reduced but keeps the maximum of material. Since blends, like compounds, are subject to right-headedness, Ralli and Xydopoulos (2012) have suggested that maximization of the size of the head makes the structure easier to identify, and facilitates the semantic recoverability of the formation. Generally, the following instances of segment reduction can be identified: a) the syllabic length of the second constituent is maintained, while the first constituent contributes two syllables to the blend (e.g., *si.di.rá.zo* 'to buy a newspaper in order to get the free CD' ← *si.dí* 'CD' + *a.yo.rá.zo* 'to buy'); b) the first syllable of the second constituent is replaced in its entirety by that of the first constituent (e.g., *vlá.ma* 'extremely stupid' ← *vlá.kas* 'stupid' + *vlí.ma* 'thick'); c) the syllabic structure of the first constituent is almost entirely reduced except for the onset of its first syllable, which replaces the onset of the first syllable of the second constituent (cases termed "acroblends" by Koutita-Kaimaki and Fliatouras 2001) (e.g., *kró.po.li* 'wax and propolis' ← *ke.rí* 'wax' + *pró.po.li* 'propolis'); d) the entire form of the second constituent is kept, and only the onset of the first one is added to it, producing voicing, where applicable (e.g., *kré.vo.me* 'to burp while having a haircut' ← *ku.ré.vo.me* 'to have a haircut' + *ré.vo.me* 'to burp'). As generally noticed by Ronneberger-Sibold (2006), the extent of form reduction varies, depending on the speaker's willingness to communicate a small or bigger part of the meaning of the combination.

Since blends are created intentionally, it is worth mentioning Ralli and Xydopoulos' (2012) suggestion that blending is situated at the boundary of linguistic competence and creativity. On the one hand, blends share structural properties with compounds, thus, blending could be considered as part of the native speaker's linguistic competence. On the other hand, blends differ from compounds in that speakers always create them intentionally, for specific communicative purposes.

6 References

Anastasiadi-Symeonidi, Anna (1986): *I neologia stin koini neoelliniki*. Thessaloniki: Epistimoniki Epetirida Filosofikis Scholis.
Anastasiadi-Symeonidi, Anna (1996): I neoelliniki sinthesi. In: Georgia Katsimali and Fotis Kavoukopoulos (eds.), *Zitimata neoellinikis glossas*, 97–120. Rethymno: University of Crete.
Andreou, Marios and Angela Ralli (2015): Form and meaning of bahuvrihi compounds: evidence from Modern Greek and its dialects. In: Laurie Bauer, Lívia Körtvelyessy and Pavol Štekauer (eds.), *Semantics of Complex Words*, 163–186. Dordrecht: Springer.
Andriotis, Nikolaos (1957): Ta parataktika rimatika sintheta stin elliniki glossa. In: *Afieroma sti mnimi tou man. Triantafillidi*, 43–61. Thessaloniki: University of Thessaloniki.
Arvaniti, Amalia (1998): Endiksis prosodiakis domis se prosfata leksika migmata tis ellinikis. *Studies in Greek Linguistics* 18: 68–82.
Babiniotis, Gergios (1972): *To rima tis ellinikis*. Athens: Idryma Sofias Saripolou.
Bauer, Laurie (2001): *Morphological Productivity*. Cambridge: Cambridge University Press.
Chantraine, Paul (1933): *La formation des noms en grec ancien*. Paris: Klincksieck.
Di Sciullo, Anna Maria and Angela Ralli (1999): Theta-role saturation in Greek deverbal compounds. In: Artemis Alexiadou, Geoffrey Horrocks and Melita Stavrou (eds.), *Issues of Greek Generative Syntax*, 175–189. Dordrecht: Kluwer.
Drachman, Gaberell and Angeliki Malikouti-Drachman (1994): Stress and Greek compounding. *Phonologica* 1992: 55–64.
Efthymiou, Angeliki (2024): Unveiling Prefix systems: Exploring semantic and lexical categories in Modern Greek through onomasiological and semasiological perspectives. *SKASE Journal of Theoretical Linguistics* 21(2): 2–17.
Hatzidakis, Georgios (1905–07): *Meseonika ke nea ellinika*. Athens: Sakellariou.
Kageyama, Taro (2009): Isolate: Japanese. In: Rochelle Lieber and Pavol Štekauer (eds.), *The Oxford Handbook of Compounding*, 512–526. Oxford: Oxford University Press.
Kaisse, Ellen (1982): On the preservation of stress in Modern Greek. *Linguistics* 20: 59–82.
Koutita-Kaimaki, Myrto and Asimakis Fliatouras (2001): Blends in Greek dialects: A morphosemantic analysis. In: Angela Ralli, Brian Joseph and Mark Janse (eds.), *Proceedings of the First International Conference of Modern Greek Dialects and Linguistic Theory*, 117–130. Patras: University of Patras.
Koutsoudas, Andreas (1962): *Verb Morphology of Modern Greek*. The Hague: Mouton.
Koutsoukos, Nikos and Angeliki Efthymiou (2023): Derivational morphology in Modern Greek. The state-of-the art. *Journal of Greek Linguistics* 23: 215–286.
Koutsoukos, Nikos and Maria Pavlakou (2009): A construction-morphology account of agent nouns in Modern Greek. *Patras Working Papers in Linguistics* 1: 107–126.
Manolessou, Io and Angela Ralli (2025): From Ancient Greek to Modern Greek. In: Peter O. Müller, Susan Olsen and Franz Rainer (eds.), *Word-Formation – Language Contact and Diachrony*, 507–530. Berlin/Boston: De Gruyter Mouton.
Manolessou, Ionna and Symeon Tsolakidis (2009): Greek coordinated compounds: Synchrony and diachrony. *Patras Working Papers in Linguistics* 1: 23–39.
Melissaropoulou, Dimitra (2009): Augmentation vs. diminution in Greek dialectal variation: An optimal system. In: Fabio Montermini, Gilles Boyé and Jesse Tseng (eds.), *Selected Proceedings of the 6th Décembrettes. Morphology in Bordeaux*, 125–137. Somerville, MA: Cascadilla Press.

Melissaropoulou, Dimitra (2015): Evaluative morphology in Greek. In: Nicola Grandi and Livia Körtvelyessy (eds.), *Handbook of Evaluative Morphology*, 269–277. Edinburgh: Edinburgh University Press.

Melissaropoulou, Dimitra and Angela Ralli (2008): Headedness in diminutive formation: Evidence from Modern Greek and its dialectal variation. *Acta Linguistica Hungarica* 55: 183–204.

Melissaropoulou, Dimitra and Angela Ralli (2010): Greek derivational structures: Restrictions and constraints. *Morphology* 20: 343–357.

Melissaropoulou, Dimitra and Angela Ralli (2020): Derivational networks in Greek. In: Lívia Körtvélyessi, Alexandra Bagasheva and Pavol Štekauer (eds.), Derivational Networks Across Languages, 347–359. Berlin/Boston: De Gruyter Mouton.

Nespor, Marina and Angela Ralli (1996): Morphology-phonology interface: Phonological domains in Greek compounds. *The Linguistic Review* 13: 357–382.

Ralli, Angela (2003): Morphology in Greek linguistics: The state-of-the-art. *Journal of Greek Linguistics* 4: 77–130.

Ralli, Angela (2004): Stem-based versus word-based morphological configurations: The case of Modern Greek preverbs. *Lingue e Linguaggio* 2(2): 241–275.

Ralli, Angela (2005): *Morfologia*. Athens: Patakis.

Ralli, Angela (2007): *I sinthesi lekseon. Diaglossiki morfologiki prosengisi*. Athens: Patakis.

Ralli, Angela (2008a): Compound markers and parametric variation. *STUF – Language Typology and Universals* 61: 19–38.

Ralli, Angela (2008b): Composés déverbaux grecs à radicaux liés. In: Dany Amiot (ed.), *La Composition dans une perspective typologique*, 189–210. Arras: Artois Presses Université.

Ralli, Angela (2009a): I.E. Hellenic. In: Rochelle Lieber and Pavol Štekauer (eds.), *The Oxford Handbook of Compounding*, 453–464. Oxford: Oxford University Press.

Ralli, Angela (2009b): Modern Greek V V dvandva compounds: A linguistic innovation in the history of the Indo-European languages. *Word Structure* 2(1): 49–68.

Ralli, Angela (2010): Compounding versus derivation. In: Sergio Scalise and Irene Vogel (eds.), *Cross-disciplinary Issues in Compounding*, 57–76. Amsterdam/Philadelphia: Benjamins.

Ralli, Angela (2012): Contact-induced morphology: Loan-verb formation in Griko and Heptanesian. *Italia Dialettale* 73: 111–132.

Ralli, Angela (2013a): *Compounds in Modern Greek*. Berlin: Springer.

Ralli, Angela (2013b): Compounding and its locus of realization: Evidence from Greek and Turkish. *Word Structure* 6(2): 181–200.

Ralli, Angela (2020a): Matter versus pattern replication in compounding: evidence from the Asia Minor Greek dialectal variety. *Morphology* 30(4): 423–446.

Ralli, Angela (2020b): Affixoids: an intriguing intermediate morphological category. In: Livia Körtvelyessy and Pavol Štekauer (eds.), *Complex Words, A Festschrift to Laurie Bauer*, 217–240. Cambridge: Cambridge University Press.

Ralli, Angela (2022): Morfologia. Athens: Patakis. Updated and augmented version of Ralli (2005).

Ralli, Angela (2023): Left headedness in compounds of a right-headed language. *Roczniki Humanistyczne* 1(6): 203–225.

Ralli, Angela and Marios Andreou (2012): Revisiting exocentricity in compounding: Evidence from Greek and Cypriot. In: Ferenc Kiefer, Maria Ladani and Peter Siptar (eds.), *Current Issue in Morphological Theory*, 65–82. Amsterdam/Philadelphia: Benjamins.

Ralli, Angela and Maria Raftopoulou (1999): I sinthesi os diachroniko fenomeno schimatismou lekseon. *Studies in Greek Linguistics* 1998: 389–403.

Ralli, Angela and Melita Stavrou (1998): Morphology-syntax interface: A-N compounds versus A-N constructs in Modern Greek. In: Geert Booij and Jaap van Marle (eds.), *Yearbook of Morphology 1997*, 243–264. Dordrecht: Kluwer.

Ralli, Angela and George Xydopoulos (2012): Blend formation in Modern Greek. In: Vincent Renner, François Maniez and Pierre Arnaud (eds.), *Cross-disciplinary Perspectives on Lexical Blending*, 35–50. Berlin: Mouton de Gruyter.

Revithiadou, Anthi (1999): *Headmost Accent Wins*. The Hague: Holland Institute of Generative Linguistics.

Ronneberger-Sibold, Elke (2006): Lexical blends: Functionally tuning the transparency of complex words. *Folia Linguistica* 40(1–2): 155–181.

Scalise, Sergio and Antonietta Bisetto (2009): The classification of compounds. In: Rochelle Lieber and Pavol Štekauer (eds.), *The Oxford Handbook of Compounding*, 34–53. Oxford: Oxford University Press.

Triantaphyllidis, Manolis (1991): *Neoelliniki grammatiki*. 3rd ed. Thessaloniki: Idryma Manoli Triantaphyllidi.

Tribulato, Olga and Angela Ralli (2024): Compounding. In: Georgios K. Giannakis (ed.), *Encyclopedia of Greek Language and Linguistics Online*. Brill [Online available at: https://doi.org/10.1163/2666-6421_GLLO_COM_059742].

Tserepis, Georgios (1902): *Ta sintheta tis ellinikis glossis*. Athens: Sakellariou.

Williams, Edwin (1981): On the notions of 'lexically related' and 'head of the word'. *Linguistic Inquiry* 12: 245–274.

David Erschler
14 Ossetic

1 Introduction
2 General overview
3 Composition
4 Derivation
5 Conversion
6 Reduplication
7 Clipping
8 References

Abstract: In Iron and Digor Ossetic (Eastern Iranian, The Central Caucasus) word-formation patterns are different for nouns and verbs. For nouns, the dominant strategies are compounding and suffixation. The boundary between compounds and noun phrases is not very clear. Denominal verbs are formed by compounding with light verbs, most frequently 'to do' and 'to be', whereas deverbal verbs are mostly formed by prefixation. Given that virtually all Ossetians are bilingual, borrowing from Russian has largely replaced the formation of new words on an Ossetic basis.

1 Introduction

Ossetic is a cover term for two closely related Eastern Iranian languages spoken in the Central Caucasus, Iron and Digor. Digor is only spoken in North Ossetia, an autonomous republic within Russia, whereas dialects of Iron are spoken both in North and South Ossetia. As far as word-formation is concerned, the two languages are fairly similar, although not all affixes are shared between them. In this article, when Iron and Digor forms are presented simultaneously, the Iron form will precede the Digor form: *gədə/tikis* 'cat'. When only one form is shown without indicating its provenance, it means that it is shared by both languages: *leg* 'man, husband'.

Nowadays Ossetic is being rapidly replaced by Russian, a circumstance not without (unfortunate) consequences for the productivity of word-formation pro-

David Erschler, Beer Scheva, Israel

cesses. Virtually any Russian word can be occasionally used in spoken Ossetic and borrowing has largely replaced word-formation in natural discourse. In the written language, some processes are still productive.

Grammars of Ossetic (Axvlediani 1963; Abaev 1964; Bagaev 1965; Isaev 1966; Medojty 2003; Takazov 2009) all have sections dealing with word-formation. Gabaraev's (1977) monograph deals with word-formation in Iron Ossetic and contains references to papers of native researchers. The most prominent dictionaries are Miller (1972 [1927–34]), Abaev (1958–89), Takazov (2003), and Guriev (2004). Takazov (2003, 2015) are the only dictionaries specifically dealing with Digor.

2 General overview

2.1 Word classes in Ossetic

Ossetic has only two open word classes: nouns and verbs. Adjectives and non-clitic adverbs are not morphologically distinct from nouns in Ossetic, whereas clitic adverbs form a closed class. Potential adjectives do not overtly agree with nouns within noun phrases, nor show any special morphology when used separately as nouns (for non-trivial abbreviations, see the list at the end of the article): cf. Iron *rənčən šabi-jə sur* sick child-OBL near 'near a sick child' and *rənčən-ə sur* sick-OBL near 'near a sick (person)'. Accordingly, I will not distinguish denominal, deadjectival, and deadverbial formations in the rest of this article.

That said, the maximal structure of a noun is prefix-stem-suffixes: *ɐ-gom-əg/ɐ-gom-ug* NEG-mouth-SUFF 'helpless' (← *kom* 'mouth'); Digor *ɐm-χuz-on-ʒijnadɐ* COM-kind-SUFF-SUFF 'similarity', see section 4.1.1 on the semantics of the suffixes *-on* and *-ʒijnadɐ*.

Verbs are simplex or complex. Complex verbs consist of a nominal and a light verb (usually 'to do' or 'to be'), see examples in section 4.2.1. Simplex verbs form a closed class. They have two stems, present and past. The present and the past stem are similar to each other, but the relationship is not regular, and both stems need to be cited: *kɐn-*, *kod-* 'to do'. Slightly abusing the notation, I will only cite the present stem of the very frequent verb 'to do'. The copula 'to be' is highly irregular, it shows pervasive suppletion in the present and uses different stems to form the infinitive, the past, and, in Digor, also the future. The maximal structure of a simplex verb is preverb-conative.affix-stem-tense.mood.agreement. For a complex verb, the pattern is preverb-conative.affix-nominal.part light.verb.stem-tense.mood.agreement. The conative affix does not have very clear aspectual semantics. Example (1) illustrates these patterns:

(1) a. simplex verb
    ra-cəj-cud-an   Digor
    PRV-CON-go.PST-PST.1PL
    'we finally went out'
  b. complex verb
    ra-səj-gepp   *kod-toj*   Iron
    PRV-CON-jump do.PST-PST.3PL
    'they almost jumped out (but did not do so)'

2.2 Main characteristics of word-formation

Non-concatenative morphology is fairly uncommon, and few non-trivial morphophonological processes are attested. One general requirement is that hiatus be avoided. The glottal stop *ʔ*, and the glides *j* and *w* are inserted as regular epenthetics. The distribution of *ʔ* and *j* is unclear, *w* is inserted before *u* and *o*. Long consonant clusters tend to be avoided as well. Admittedly, Ossetic morphophonology is understudied and many details are yet unknown.

Non-trivial morphophonological phenomena are: consonant gemination (triggered by certain preverbs, see section 4.2.1), insertion of an idiosyncratic epenthetic consonant (also triggered by some preverbs), metathesis (triggered by a nominal suffix *-jag*, see section 4.1.1), and voicing of a voiceless consonant (it occurs in compounds, see section 3, and after certain nominal prefixes, see section 4.1.1). For nouns, suffixes are much more numerous than prefixes. For finite verbs, only prefixes are used for the purposes of word-formation. On the other hand, non-finite verb forms are all derived by suffixation. Circumfixes and infixes do not exist. Neoclassical word-formation is unattested in modern Ossetic. In general, loaned suffixes are only used in forming personal names, see section 4.1.1.

I am aware of only one example of a "bracketing paradox" in Ossetic. It occurs with the suffix *-(j)ag* both in Iron and Digor: Digor *ači gorettag* has a reading 'someone from this city', suggesting the bracketing [*ači goret*]-*jag* [this city]-SUFF. The reading 'this person from a city' is available as well.

2.3 Compounding vs. syntax

2.3.1 Nominal compounds

Noun phrases and compounds are hard to tell apart, because the word order in the noun phrase is fairly rigid and no overt agreement exists between words within a noun phrase. On the other hand, no special linking morphemes are used in compounds. Furthermore, clitics may not intervene in the noun phrase.

In favorable cases, certain tests may be used to distinguish noun phrases and compounds. Some roots, when they serve as the second part of a compound, have their initial consonant become voiced: for instance, -*gond* (← *kond*, the past participle of 'to do'): *pajda-gond* usefulness-do.PST.PRT 'used'; *lɐg-gond* 'tomboy' (*lɐg* 'man'). An alternative analysis would be to posit that roots with voiced initial consonants have been reanalyzed as suffixes.

Certain roots appearing in a collocation do not function as separate words. Collocations with such roots should, of course, also be treated as compounds: *ɐrš-geš/ɐrs-gɐs* bear-look 'a person who owns a tame bear and shows it at fairs, etc.' (← *arš/ars* 'bear' + *keš/kɐs* 'look.PRS'). The stem *keš/kɐs* does not occur separately.

An additional test is only applicable in Digor. Quite a few Digor nouns preserve a vestige of the old nominative marker, the suffix -*ɐ*, see section 4.1.1. If a noun requires this suffix in its citation form, then the bare stem of such a noun cannot function as a free form. In some collocations, the first noun occurs without this suffix: *zɐnχ(*ɐ)-kos-ɐg* earth-work-PRS.PRT 'crop farmer' (but *zɐnχ-ɐ* 'earth'). Therefore, such collocations should probably be treated as compounds.

When all these tests are inapplicable, the collocation is ambiguous between a compound and a noun phrase: Digor *aχsen-nez* 'stomach ache' (← *aχsen* 'stomach' + *nez* 'illness'). However, whatever their interpretation, such collocations carry a considerable functional load in the language.

Furthermore, some possessive noun phrases function as single nouns: *məd-ə bənz/mud-i bindzɐ* honey-OBL fly 'bee'. To argue that such entities are indeed single words, one can use the fact that any modifiers must precede the whole collocation:

(2) a. štər məd-ə bənz   b. *məd-ə štər bənz   Iron
    big honey-OBL fly   honey-OBL big bee
    'big bee'

In "real" possessive noun phrases the possessor precedes modifiers:

(3) lɐppu-j-ə štər kʷəz   Iron
    boy-EP-OBL big dog
    'a boy's big dog'

Many kin terms are formed after this pattern: *fəd-ə fəd/fid-i fidɐ* father-OBL father 'paternal grandfather' *mad-ə χo/mad-i χʷɐrɐ* mother-OBL sister 'maternal aunt', etc.

2.3.2 Verbal compounds

Wordhood of simplex verbs is not an issue, as no morpheme within a simplex verb may occur as a separate word. It should be noted, however, that enclitics may end up inside a verb. In Digor, they may be inserted between the preverb and the stem (4a) of a simplex verb, or between the conative affix and the stem. In Iron, enclitics may only be inserted between the conative affix and the stem (4b).

(4) a. *ra=j serf-ta* Digor
    PRV=ACC.3SG wipe.PST-PST.3SG
    '(S/he) wiped it.'
  b. *fe-sej=nə bərš-toj* Iron
    PRV-CON=ACC.1PL overcome.PST-PST.3PL
    '(They) have almost overcome us.'

The status of complex verbs is more delicate, because the majority of nominal parts and all light verbs do function as separate words. However, the order of the nominal part and the verb cannot be changed, and they have to be immediately adjacent, although there are some qualifications. These qualifications militate against an analysis which assumes that light-verb stems are verbalizing suffixes. The first qualification concerns the placement of clitics. When a preverb is affixed to the nominal part, then it is only clitics that may intervene between the nominal part and the verb, see (5). Clitics may also intervene in the nominal part, exactly in the same manner as in the case of simplex verbs.

(5) a. *fe-gon=ej kod-ta* Digor
    PRV-open=ACC.3SG do.PST-PST.3SG
    'S/he opened it.'
  b. *ba-jgom=ej kod-toj* Iron
    PRV-open=ACC.3SG do.PST-PST.3PL
    'S/he opened it.'

The second qualification concerns the placement of wh-phrases, negation markers, and negative indefinites. When a preverb is present, all these items must precede the preverb. However, in the absence of a preverb, these items may be placed either before the nominal part (6a), or between the nominal part and the light verb (6b), with a subtle difference in interpretation. In this example, the complex verb is *nəχeš-tə kən-* talk-PL do- 'to talk'. When the parts of a complex verb are thus split, the word status of the complex verb is unclear.

(6) a. *kej-imɐ   nəχeš-tɐ   ken-əš?*   Iron
    who-COM talk-PL do-PRS.2SG
    'Who are you talking to?'
    (Ajlarty 2002: 142)

   b. *nəχeš-tɐ kej-imɐ   ken-əš?*   Iron
    talk-PL who-COM do-PRS.2SG
    'Who are you TALKING to?'

Another borderline case is the formation of the causative. It is formed analytically, as the infinitive of the verb (see section 4.1.2) plus an appropriate form of the verb 'to do'. When a preverb is present, the resulting complex behaves in the same manner as a complex verb, (7a–b). However, in the absence of a preverb, the infinitive of the lexical verb may even be placed after the light verb, (7c–d).

(7) a. *fəd=ej   alan-en š-araž-ən   kod-ta*   Iron
    father=ACC.3SG A.-DAT PRV-build-INF do.PST-PST.3SG
    'The father made Alan build it. / The father made someone build it for Alan.'

   b. **fəd=ej   alan-en kodta   š-araž-ən*
    father=ACC.3SG A.-DAT do.PST-PST.3SG PRV-build-INF
    Idem (intended reading)

   c. *alan medine-jə žar-ən   kod-ta*   Iron
    A. M.-OBL sing-INF do.PST-PST.3SG
    'Alan made Madina sing.'

   d. *alan medine-jə təχ-ej   kod-ta   žar-ən*   Iron
    A. M.-OBL force-ABL do.PST-PST.3SG sing-INF
    'Alan forced Madina to sing.'

Finally, it is worth noting that periphrastic verbs, formed as the combination of a converb (section 4.1.2) and the light verb 'to do' definitely do not constitute single words, cf. (8). Periphrastic forms are used when it is the predicate itself that has to be focused. Finite verbs cannot be focused in Ossetic, so, when it is necessary to focus the predicate, the periphrastic form is used, and it is the converb that gets focused. The preverb (if necessary) and tense-mood-agreement exponents are then carried by the light verb, cf. (8). This process is fully productive.

(8) *cewu-ge=der dew   fed-bel   ra-kod-tan*   Digor
    go-CVB=EMP you.OBL trace-SUP PRV-DO.PST-PST.1PL
    'And it is because of you (lit. after you) that we did go.'
    (Tobojti 2004: 93)

2.3.3 Demarcating compounding and derivation

The only reasonable way to demarcate compounding and derivation is to check whether the (potential) affix has a cognate independent lexeme. However, the semantics of such stems in compounds may differ significantly from that of free forms (see examples in section 3). It is not very clear how to classify the formation of complex verbs and of the causative.

3 Composition

Although, as it has already been mentioned, Ossetic compounds are very close to syntactic constructions, native speakers perceive some of them as single words (even when tests do not yield unambiguous results), and therefore it is probably justified to discuss the properties of compounds in Ossetic. Coordination of compound constituents (like in the German *Schul- und Universität-s-streik* school- and university-LINK-strike 'school and university strike') is usually impossible.

Many personal nouns are created as compounds with the present participle of the verb 'to do', whose first consonant is voiced in such compounds: *dzol-gɐn-ɐg/zul-gɐn-ɐg* bread-do-PRS.PRT 'baker'.

Appositive compounds are fairly uncommon. One example is *wad-təməʁ/wad-tumuʁ* wind-snow.storm 'snow storm'. Words like the Iron *sɐgat-nəgʷəlɐn* northwest 'Northwest' are probably calques from Russian. Exocentric compounds are rather uncommon as well. From a formal point of view, there is no morphological difference between endo- and exocentric compounds: compare *fəd rən/fud run* bad sickness 'epidemic', an endocentric compound, with *šaw nɐməg/saw nɐmug* black seed 'bilberry', an exocentric compound.

A number of nominal stems function similarly to affixes and it is difficult to distinguish them from such. For a very small number of nouns/adjectives, compounding with *šaw-/saw-* 'black' expresses intensification: *šaw-rešuʁd/saw-resuʁd* black-beautiful 'very beautiful', *šaw-rašəg/saw-rasug* black-drunk 'very drunk', *šaw-žɐrond/saw-zɐrond* black-old 'very old'. This model is not productive. Another, equally non-productive type of non-compositional compound is only present in Iron: *ɐrvəl < arv-əl* sky-SUP, when prefixed to a temporal stem, means 'every': *ɐrvəl-bon* 'every day' (← *bon* 'day'); *ɐrvəl-až* 'every year' (← *až* 'year'). Furthermore, there are a small number of non-productive spatial prefixes: *raž-/raz-* 'in front of', e.g., *raž-amon-ɐg/raz-amon-ɐg* front-indicate-PRS.PRT 'manager, leader', *faštɐ-/feštɐ-* 'behind', e.g., *feštɐ-žad/feštɐ-zad* 'left behind, backward'. Such formations may be listed among compounds, because these prefixes all have cognate noun stems.

The noun *bən/bun* 'bottom, root' gives rise to several series of compounds. Suffixed to basic color terms, it yields an attenuative meaning: *šərχ-bən/surχ-bun* 'reddish' (← *šərχ/surχ* 'red'), *bur-bən/bor-bun* 'yellowish, brownish' (← *bur/bor* 'yellow, brown'), etc. With names of trees, it yields the meaning 'forest of Ns': *berž-bən/bɐrz-bun* 'birch forest' (← *berž/bɐrze* 'birch-tree'), *tulz-bən/toldz-bun* 'oak forest' (← *tulz/toldze* 'oak'), etc.

The root *garž/garz* in compounds means 'tool for': *kʷəš-en-garž/kos-en-garz* work-MOD.INF-tool 'working tool', Iron *χʷəšš-en-garž* lie-MOD.INF-tool 'bedding', etc. As an independent word it survives, for instance, in the Iron plurale tantum *geržte* 'weapons'.

The combinations of a converb with an infinitive (see section 4.1.2) that are based on the same stem V, are single words with the (non-compositional) meaning 'while doing V': *zur-ge zur-ən/dzor-ge dzor-un* talk-CNV talk-INF 'while talking', *sewge-sewən/caw-ge cew-un* go-CNV go-INF 'while walking, on the way'.

4 Derivation

4.1 Nominal derivation

As adjectives and adverbs are morphologically indistinct from nouns, it hardly makes sense to consider deadjectival and deadverbial nouns separately.

4.1.1 Denominal nouns

Denominal nouns are formed by prefixation and suffixation. Furthermore, some case-marked nouns have been reanalyzed into new lexemes.

Most **prefixes** enjoy very limited productivity, if any. Prefixes cannot attach to conjoined nouns: i.e. PREF-noun₁ and noun₂ cannot mean PREF-noun₁ and PREF-noun₂. The meanings of prefixes can be classified in the following manner: a) privative ('negation/lack of N'): *e-*, *ene-*; b) 'sharing N': *em-*; c) comitative ('with N'): *ed-*; d) intensive ('intense N'): *fər-/fur-*; e) 'self-': *χed-/χʷed-*; f) a number of temporal/locative prefixes. In addition, verb nominalizations may occur with verb prefixes, see sections 4.1.2 and 4.2.2:

a) **privative** *e-* 'negation of N': *kad/kade* 'glory, honor' → *e-gad/e-gade* 'dishonor'. If the root begins with a voiceless consonant, the consonant becomes voiced when preceded by this prefix. A relatively large number of words occur with this prefix; however, it does not seem to be productive anymore.

The fully productive prefix ɐnɐ- also expresses negation or lack of N. The test distinguishing it from the preposition ɐnɐ 'without', is their interaction with deictics and/or possession markers: the preposition must precede such items, while the prefixal ɐnɐ- must follow them: Digor ači ɐnɐzongɐ adɐjmag this NEG-known person 'this unknown person' vs. ɐnɐ ači zongɐ adɐjmag without this known person 'without this known person'.

b) The meaning 'together with N, sharing N' can be expressed by the prefix ɐm-, e.g., ɐm-nom 'namesake' (← nom 'name'); ɐm-ɐχšt/ɐm-ɐχst 'simultaneous shooting' (← ɐχšt/ɐχst 'shot'), etc. This prefix also causes voicedness in the first consonant of the root: Digor ɐm-garɐ 'peer, age-mate' (← karɐ 'age'). The prefix is productive to a certain extent.

c) The comitative prefix ɐd- is compatible with common nouns and noun phrases (Digor ɐd=ustur bel with=big spade 'with a big spade'), but not with personal names, pronouns or noun phrases modified by deictics: Digor *ɐd= ɐ=ustur bel with=POSS.3SG=big spade, intended reading: 'with his/her big spade'. This motivates treating it as a prefix and not as a preposition. When marked with this prefix, the noun phrase may not receive any overt case marker, except the already mentioned vestigial nominative marker -ɐ. Native speakers vary as to whether this prefix may be adjoined to animates and specific or definite noun phrases. (Definiteness need not be overtly marked in Ossetic, so the latter effect is not a result of incompatibility of this prefix with any lexical material.) For possessive phrases, the grammaticality depends on the position of the possessor on the animacy/referentiality scale:

(9) a. *ɐd Soslan-i kuj   Digor
       with Soslan-OBL dog
    b. ?ɐd biččew-i kuj   Digor
       with boy-OBL dog
    c. ɐd bandon-i k'aχ   Digor
       with chair-OBL leg

d) The intensive prefix fər-/fur- is not productive. Some examples are fər-sin/fur-čijnɐ 'intense joy' (← sin/čijnɐ 'joy'), fər-mašt/fur-mast 'intense wrath' (← mašt/mast 'wrath').

e) χed-/χʷed- 'self-'. The suffix mostly occurs in artificially created words: χed-teχ-ɐg/χʷed-teχ-ɐg self-fly-PRS.PRT 'plane'. Normally, the Russian loanword samal'ot is used for 'plane'.

f) Additionally, there exist a number of spatial/temporal nominal prefixes. Their productivity is extremely limited, but in Digor it is somewhat higher than in Iron. These prefixes are feš-/fes- 'after' (productive only in the temporal sense): *faš-kʷəšt/fes-kust* after-work.NMZ.PST 'time after work'; *mid-/med-* 'within': Iron *mid-χoχ* within-mountain 'within mountains', Digor *med-χedzare* within-house 'indoors'; Digor *ende-* 'outside': *ende-dwar* outside-door 'outdoors'; *del-* 'below': *del-arm* below-arm 'armpit'; *wel-* 'above' *wel-χezar/wel-χedzare* above-house 'the flat roof of a traditional mountain house'. Of these, only *feš-/fes-* seems to be truly productive, in particular in Digor; for instance, it can attach to loaned roots: Digor *fes-urok-te* after-class-PL 'the time after classes', with the Russian loan *urok* 'class'. The spatial prefixes are not productive even in Digor: **del-st'ol* below-table, intended reading 'space below a table'.

The number of **suffixes** is much larger than that of prefixes. Some suffixes allow suspended suffixation, i.e. *noun₁ and noun₂-SUFF* can mean *noun₁-SUFF and noun₂-SUFF*. Admittedly, not all suffixes have clear semantics. Dedicated suffixes that form **personal nouns** are: the associative plural marker *-i-/-e-* (cf. (e) below), and suffixes *-i* (f) and *-oj* (g), mostly used to form nicknames. Besides that, personal nouns are formed with wide-purpose suffixes *-eg* (b), *-on* (c), *-(j)ag* (d), and *ʤan/-gun, -gin* (l). There are no dedicated suffixes for **status nouns**, wide-purpose abstract noun suffixes *-ad/-ade* and *-zinad/-ʤijnade* (h) are used to this end. Place nouns are formed with the suffixes *-ʤan/-gun* (l) and *-don/-done* (m). Diminutives in the proper sense do not exist, hypocoristics are only formed from personal names with loaned suffixes (r). Augmentative suffixes do not exist. Below, I list all derivational nominal suffixes I have been able to find in Ossetic.

a) A suffix on the border between inflection and derivation is the vestigial nominative *-e*, which appears with the plural marker in both languages and, in Digor, with a considerable number of singular nouns. Its function in the modern language is not very clear: For instance, it is compatible with some case markers, a kind of behavior hardly expected for a case marker: Digor *zenχ-e̱-bel* earth-NOM?-sup 'on the ground'. In the plural, it is deleted: Digor *belas̱e* 'tree', but *beles-te* 'trees'. The suffix is productive in Digor in the sense that Russian feminine nominative ending *-a* is reinterpreted as this suffix in loanwords: *brička* britzka.NOM 'a kind of kart', *brick-i* britzka.OBL (from the Russian *brička*).

b) A considerable number of nouns feature the suffix *-eg* (it is homonymous with a nominalizing suffix, see section 4.1.2), e.g., *šteg/esteg* 'bone'. Roots of such nouns often do not function as independent words. However, this suffix can attach to some extant words as well: Digor *gun-gun* 'nasality (of voice)' → *gun-gun-eg* 'a person with nasal voice'. In the plural, the suffix takes the form *-ʤə-/-gu-:* *didineg/dedeneg* 'flower', *didin-ʤə-te/deden-gu-te* 'flowers'.

c) The suffix -*on* (productively) forms nouns meaning 'bearer of the feature X, expressed by the root': *kɐšg-on/kɐsg-on* 'Kabardian' (← *kɐšɐg/kɐsɐg* 'Kabardia'). It is widely used for calquing Russian adjectives: *kommuniston* 'communist'. In the plural, this suffix takes the form *-ɐ-/-ɐn-* and triggers consonant gemination in the plural marker: *kɐšg-ɐ-ttɐ/kɐsg-ɐn-ttɐ* 'Kabardians'.

d) In **personal nouns** the suffix *-(j)ag* means 'person from X': *mɐškʷə-jag/ mɐsku-jag* 'a person from Moscow'). The suffix *-gojmag* only forms the words *šəlgojmag/šilgojmag* 'woman' and *nɐlgojmag* 'man' (← *šəl-/šil-* 'female', *nɐl* 'male'). In the plural, the *-ag* in *-(j)ag* and *-gojmag* becomes *-ɐg-*. Diachronically, *-gojmag* is *-gom-jag*. Another function of the suffix *-jɐg*, is to form words with the meaning 'intended for N': Digor *χodɐ* 'hat' → *χoddag* 'material to make a hat of'. This suffix has the following morphophonological properties: if the root it attaches to ends with a vowel, then the suffix appears in its original form: *pajda* + *-jag* → *pajdajag* 'something useful' (← *pajda* 'usefulness'). If the root ends in *l*, *n*, *m*, or *r*, metathesis occurs: *šɐr/sɐr* 'head' → *šɐjrag/sɐjrag* 'main'. If the root ends in a cluster or *χ*, then the suffix surfaces as *-ag*: *χoχ/χʷɐnχ* 'mountain' → *χoχ-ag/χʷɐnχ-ag* 'alpine'. For all other final consonants, the *-j-* of the suffix gets assimilated yielding a geminated consonant: Digor *χodɐ* → *χoddag*; *taš/tas* 'fear' → *teššag/tessag* 'dangerous'; Digor *bɐllec* 'wish' → *bɐlleccag* 'desirable object'. I have not been able to find any ʁ-final stems that would be compatible with this suffix.

e) The **associative plural suffix** *-i-/-e-*, attaches to personal names to form nouns meaning 'group of people including N'. It has to be followed by the plural marker: *šošlan-i-tɐ/soslan-e-tɐ* S.-ASS-PL 'Soslan and others'. When the name ends in *-ɐ*, in Digor the *-ɐ-* disappears: *mɐdin-e-tɐ* M.-ASS-PL 'Madina and others' (← *Mɐdinɐ*). In Iron, the epenthetic *-j-* is inserted in this case: *mɐdinɐ-j-i-tɐ*. With other final vowels, the hiatus is treated in the same way in both languages. Normally, this suffix only attaches to Ossetic names, but some examples of it attaching to foreign names are attested in published fiction: *korotkov-i-tɐ* K.-ASS-PL 'Korotkov (a Russian surname) and his group'.

f) The suffix *-oj* creates the meaning 'person with abnormal X': Iron *quš-oj* 'person with big ears' (← *quš* 'ear'), Digor *bil-oj* 'person with very thick or very thin lips' (← *bilɐ* 'lip'). This suffix is not productive: Iron **šɐr-oj* (← *šɐr* 'head'), intended meaning 'a person with a very large/small head'.

g) In Iron, nicknames and animal names can be formed by the suffix *-i*: *fənz-i* '(a nickname for a) person with a big nose' (← *fənz* 'nose'); *wurš-i* '(a nickname for a) white animal' (← *wurš* 'white'). This suffix is not productive: **šɐr-i* (← *šɐr* 'head'), **bəl-i* (← *bəl* 'lip'). Insofar as I was able to check, Digor lacks a cognate for this suffix.

h) Abstract nouns, including s t a t u s n o u n s, are formed with the suffixes -ad/-adɐ and -zinad/-dʒijnadɐ: Digor ɐnsuvɐr-dʒijnadɐ 'brotherhood' (← ɐnsuvɐr 'brother'), Iron χisaw-ad 'administration' (← χisaw 'boss'); Iron šabər-zinad 'peace' (← šabər 'quiet'). The suffix -zinad/-dʒijnadɐ allows suspended affixation: Digor ɐnsuvɐr ɐma suʁdɐg-dʒijnadɐ 'brotherhood and sanctity' (← ɐnsuvɐr 'brother', suʁdɐg 'clean'). Words formed in this manner are often perceived by native speakers as artificial, but the two suffixes are fairly productive in written texts. In the plural, the *a* in the last syllable of these suffixes becomes ɐ: Digor χʷarž-dʒijnɐd-tɐ good-ABSTR-PL 'different manifestation of the good', Iron χisaw-ɐd-tɐ boss-ABSTR-PL 'governments').

i) An additional suffix forming abstract nouns is -ɐχ/-ɐnχɐ. Respective nouns are singularia tantum. In Digor, this suffix very marginally allows suspended affixation: ?*fud ɐma χʷɐrzɐnχɐ in the meaning fud-ɐnχɐ ɐma χʷɐrz-ɐnχɐ 'bad and good (nouns)' (← fud 'bad', χʷɐrz 'good'). This suffix is non-productive.

j) The non-productive -əkkon/-ikkon and -əgon/-igon combine with certain temporal and locative nouns: nər/nur 'now' → nər-əkkon/nur-ikkon 'modern', bon 'day' → bon-əgon/bon-igon 'in the daytime'; wɐlɐrd- 'from the upper side' → wɐlɐrd-əgon/wɐlɐrd-igon 'living above the speaker'. In the plural, it takes the form -əkkɐ/-ikkɐn and triggers the gemination of the consonant in the plural marker.

k) The suffix -ən/-in is used to express the meaning 'made of': qɐd-ən/ʁɐd-in 'wooden' (← qɐd/ʁɐdɐ 'wood'); dur-ən/dor-in 'made of stone or clay, clay jar' (← dur/dor 'stone'); Digor ɐrʁ-in 'made of clay' (← ɐrʁ 'clay'). The suffix still enjoys some productivity: the Iron words žmiš-ən 'made of sand' (← žmiš 'sand') and žɐχχ-ən 'made of earth' (← žɐχχ 'earth') were judged possible by consultants.

l) The productive suffixes -dʒən/-gun and -dʒən/-gin mean 'with X': moj-dʒən/mojnɐ-gin 'married (about a woman)' (← moj/mojnɐ 'husband'); k'abuška-dʒən/k'abuska-gun 'pie with cabbage' (← k'abuška/k'abuska 'cabbage'). The same suffix is present in (no longer transparent) šaw-dʒən/saw-gin 'Christian priest' (← šaw/saw 'black'). The distribution of -gun and -gin in Digor is unknown, and, for some stems, both suffixes are possible: ɐrʁ-gin/ɐrʁ-gun 'area with clay-rich soil'.

m) To form names of containers or spaces intended for a specific use, the suffix -don/-donɐ is used: χor-don/χʷar-donɐ 'granary' (← χor/χʷar 'grain'); šɐkɐr-don/sɐkɐr-donɐ 'sugar bowl'. In the plural, an alternation occurs: šɐkɐr-dɐ-ttɐ/sɐkɐr-dɐn-ttɐ. The suffix -šton/-ston is only present in the words Irašton/Iriston 'Ossetia' and Gʷərzəšton/Gurdʒiston 'Georgia'.

n) In a number of words, the suffix -əg/-ug is present: fad-əg/fad-ug 'trouser leg' (← fad 'foot'). It is productive insofar as it is used for creating some artificial words, e.g., *bonəg/bon-ug* 'diary' (← *bon* 'day'); Iron *χajəg* 'particle (a grammar term)' (← *χaj* 'part').

o) The distributive suffix *-gaj* can be fairly accurately translated by the English *-wise*: *čəšəl-gaj/mink'ij-gaj* 'gradually' (← *čəšəl/mink'ij* 'small'), Digor *rɐnʙɐ-gaj* 'linewise, line by line' (← *rɐnʙɐ* 'line'). Normally, for Digor stems ending in -ɐ, the -ɐ is dropped before *-gaj*: *χedzar-gaj* 'house by house' (← *χedzarɐ̱* 'house'), *bɐlas-gaj* 'tree by tree' (← *bɐlasɐ̱* 'tree'). However, even these formations are nouns, and not adverbs, insofar as they can carry number and case marking: Iron *adɐm-ə k'ord-gɐj-tt-ɐj* people-OBL group-wise-PL-ABL 'people by groups' (the change *gaj* → *gɐj* is triggered by the plural marker).

p) Besides that, some non-productive suffixes with unclear or hard-to-define meanings are present in a very small number of words each: *-əndz/-indzɐ* in *qed-əndz/ʙed-indzɐ* 'onion' (← *qed/ʙedɐ* 'wood'); *-əkk/-ikkɐ* in *wɐr-əkk/wɐr-ikkɐ* 'lamb' and Iron *šɐn-əkk* 'kid' (← *wɐr* 'lamb', Indo-European *sken 'baby animal', Abaev 1979: 71); *-c/-cɐ* in *rajgʷər-c/igur-cɐ* 'birth' (← *rajgur-/igur-* 'to give birth'); *-oj/-ojnɐ* in *kʷəroj/kurojnɐ* 'mill', *wiš-oj/wes-ojnɐ* 'besom' (← *wiš/wes* 'osier'); *-in/-ijnɐ* in *feš-sew-in/fes-cɐw-ijnɐ* behind-go.PRS-SUFF 'servant'; *-dan* in *saj-dan/caj-dan* 'teapot' (← *saj/caj* 'tea'), *-ɐn* in *šɐr-ɐn/sɐr-ɐn* 'smart' (← *šɐr/sɐr* 'head'). This list is probably non-exhaustive.

q) The attenuative suffix *-gomaw* productively attaches to words denoting a gradable quality, it may mean either 'a weak manifestation of the quality X' or 'a slightly excessive manifestation of the quality X with respect to a certain salient scale'; 'the speaker is not sure whether the quality X is sufficiently present': *šərχ-gomaw/surχ-gomaw* red-SUFF 'reddish'; *štər-gomaw/us-tur-gomaw* big-SUFF 'a bit too large (about clothes)'; *žerond-gomaw/zerond-gomaw* old-SUFF 'oldish, a bit too old'; *beržond-gomaw/bɐrzond-gomaw* high-SUFF 'a bit too high/tall', etc. It is incompatible with non-gradable qualities: Iron **durən-gomaw* made.of.stone-SUFF.

r) There are no diminutives properly speaking. Hypocoristic suffixes only exist for proper names. The loaned Russian suffix *-ik* may attach to clipped proper nouns: *As-ik* (a male name), *Fat-ik* (a female name). With some male proper names, *-əqo/-iqo* serves as a hypocoristic (rare): *šɐrmɐt/sɐrmɐt* → *šɐrmɐt-əqo/sɐrmɐt-iqo*. This suffix is obviously similar to the Georgian hypocoristic *-ik'o*, but the reasons why *q* appears in Ossetic instead of *k'* are unclear. Augmentatives (or, rather, intensifiers) exist only for basic color terms and very few other nouns (see section 3 on compounding with *šaw-/saw-* and section 6 on reduplication and suffixation of *-id*).

Some frozen case forms have been reanalyzed as nouns: *fən-ɐj/fun-ɐj* 'sleep' (← *fən/fun*, which means 'dream' in the modern language, with the ablative *-ɐj*), ɐreʤə/ɐregi 'late, of late' (← ɐreg 'late', in the modern language only a bound stem, with the oblique -ə/-i). These nouns can be marked with case suffixes and the plural suffix -tɐ:

(10) tarf funɐj-tɐ bacan   Digor
    deep sleep-PL happened.to.us
    'We fell fast asleep.'
    (Xidirti 2007: 42)

Normally, the plural marker precedes a case marker, and double case marking is impossible, and therefore this test indeed shows that such case-marked forms have been reanalyzed as nouns.

4.1.2 Deverbal nouns

For simplex verbs, nominalizations are formed on the basis of the stem: aχod-ən/ aχod-un stem-INF 'to ritually taste a sacrificial pie'. For complex verbs, nominalizations are formed on the basis of the nominal part and the appropriate nominalization of the light verb: Digor ʁigɐ dar-un annoyance hold-INF (← ʁigɐ dar-) 'to disturb, annoy'. Except for the past participle, all nominalizations are formed on the basis of the present stem. Nominalizations may be modified by preverbs (or, on an alternative analysis, they may be formed on the basis of verbs with preverbs).

    The infinitive is formed by the suffix -ən/-un. It serves as action noun: Iron ɐrba-sɐw-ən PRV-go-INF 'arrival'. The modal infinitive is formed by the suffix -ɐn. Modal infinitives are used in certain constructions expressing necessity, but also mean 'instrument or place for Ving': bad-ɐn sit-MOD.INF 'bench, stool', χʷəšš-ɐn/χuss-ɐn lie-MOD.INF 'bed', Digor χʷar-ɐn paint-MOD.INF 'paint'.

    The past participle is usually identical to the past stem of the verb, but the relationship is sometimes irregular: for the verb 'to do', the past stem is kod-, whereas the past participle is kond. The past participle may also serve as action noun, Iron ɐrba-səd PRV-go.PRT.PST 'arrival'. The past participle serves as a basis for the stem of the (finite) impersonal, see section 4.2.2.

    Agent nouns are identical to the present participle, formed by the suffix -ɐg, and the habitual participle, formed by the suffix -ag/-agɐ. Examples are Digor χuj-ɐg sew-PRS.PRT and χuj-agɐ sew-HAB 'one who regularly sews'.

    A patientive noun is formed by the suffix -inag/-ujnag, Digor χuj-ujnag 'thing to be sewn'. The suffix can be actually analyzed as -ən/-un + -jag > -inag/-

ujnag. However, the semantics is not quite compositional, nor can *-jag* attach to other nominalizations.

The converb is formed by the suffix *-gɐ*. In its basic function, it denotes an action simultaneous with, or preceding to, the one expressed by the finite verb, cf. (11).

(11) *fezzɐg-i ɐmbeš-i   met   ɐr-war-gɐ   ɐz nɐma fɐ-wwidton*   Digor
     fall-OBL middle-OBL snow PRV-rain-CNV I not.yet PRV-see.PST.1SG
     'I have never seen it snowing (lit. snow raining) in mid-fall.'
     (Sabajti 2010: 34)

In this function, converbs are often marked with the ablative. For intransitive verbs, the converb also serves as an active participle: *teχ-gɐ* fly-CNV 'flying'. For transitive verbs, it serves as a passive participle (with the meaning 'that can be Ved'): *χer-gɐ/χʷer-gɐ* eat-CNV 'edible'; *dus-gɐ qug/doc-gɐ ʁog* milk-CNV cow 'dairy (lit. milkable) cow'.

Finally, Digor has a modal deverbal formation meaning 'the subject is likely to do X/going to do X (but maybe will not do so)'. It is formed on the basis of the infinitive by suffixing *-ijaw* to it:

(12) *fɐstagmɐ politikɐ-mɐ=der   ra-χez-un-ijaw   adtɐncɐ*
     at.last   politics-ALL=EMP PRV-climb-INF-MOD be.PST.3PL
     'Finally, they were going to switch to (discussing) politics.'
     (Sk'odtati 2008: 112)

4.2 Verbal derivation

By default, most preverbless verbs are imperfective, and adding a preverb perfectivizes them. However, this generalization has quite a few exceptions. In what follows, I explicitly indicate the cases when a form carrying a preverb will nevertheless be imperfective.

4.2.1 Denominal verbs

As it has already been mentioned, complex verbs consist of a nominal part and a light verb. The test distinguishing complex verbs and idiomatic expressions is whether a preverb can attach to the nominal part:

(13) a. Complex verb
 ba-ʁigɐ=ɐj   dard-ta   Digor
 PRV-grief=ACC.3SG   hold.PST-PST.3SG
 'S/he annoyed (or disturbed) him/her.'
 b. Idiomatic expression
 *ba-zɐrdɐ-bɐl=ɐj   dard-ta   Digor
 PRV-heart-SUP=ACC.3SG   hold.PST-PST.3SG
 c. ᵒᵏzɐrdɐ-bɐl=ɐj   ba-dard-ta   Digor
 heart-SUP=ACC.3SG   PRV-hold.PST-PST.3SG
 'S/he memorized it (lit. held it on the heart).'

Light verbs are 'to do', 'to be' (highly productive); laš-, laš-/las-, las- 'to pull', which has limited productivity; and completely unproductive keš-, kašt-/kɐs-, kast- 'to look', dar-, dard- 'to hold', mar-, mard- 'to kill', and mɐl-/mard- 'to die'. The choice of 'to do' vs. 'to be' is a rather subtle issue, and for the lack of space it cannot be taken up here. The difference between light verbs and suffixes is discussed in section 2.3.2.

The use of the light verb 'to pull' indicates the suddenness of the action: Digor ni-ggɐpp lasta jump pull.PST.3SG 's/he suddenly jumped off' vs. ni-ggɐpp kodta jump do.PST.3SG 's/he jumped'. Examples of complex verbs with non-productive light verbs are: ɐnqɐl-mɐ keš-/ɐnʁɐl-mɐ kɐs- 'to wait, hope' (← ɐnqɐl-mɐ/ ɐnʁɐl-mɐ hope-ALL); qag dar-/ʁigɐ dar- 'to disturb, annoy' (← qag/ʁigɐ 'grief, disturbance'); mešt-ɐj mar-/mɐst-ɐj mar- 'to tease' (← mašt-ɐj/mast-ɐj wrath-ABL); Iron tuχɐn-ɐj mɐl- 'to suffer' (← tuχɐn-ɐj suffering-ABL).

Usually, the nominal part of a complex verb carries no case marking. In very rare instances, case-marked nouns do occur: Iron ɐr-žonag-əl kɐn- PRV-knee-SUP do 'to kneel'. The presence of the plural marker on the nominal part normally indicates verbal plurality. For some "adjectives", the verb A-PL kɐn- means 'to frequently be in the state A': Iron rənčan-tɐ kɐn- 'to frequently fall sick' (← rənčan 'sick'). For deverbal verbs of this type, see section 4.2.2.

4.2.2 Deverbal verbs

Deverbal verbs can be formed in the following ways: by prefixing a preverb, by inserting the conative affix between the preverb and the stem, and by forming a complex verb on the basis of an appropriate nominalization. Furthermore, complex verbs can be formed on the basis of the reduplicated stem of a simplex verb or the reduplicated nominal part of the complex verb. Additionally, the impersonal form can be formed (at least for some simplex verbs) on the basis of the dedicated impersonal stem.

Preverbs have spatial meanings, similar to the ones described in the next paragraph. Besides that, all preverbs except *fa-* always have a telicizing function. Furthermore, each preverb has a host of non-spatial (and often elusive) meanings. They cannot be discussed here for reasons of space. The semantics of a verb with a preverb can be non-compositional: *ba-kɐn-* lit. 'do inwards, with the deictic center outside' may mean 'to close (a door)'.

The following preverbs are productive in modern Ossetic: *ɐr-*, *ba-*, *ɐrba-*, *ra-*, *š-/is-*, *nə-/ni-*, *fɐ-*, and, in Iron, *a-*. Besides that, Iron has an unproductive preverb *sɐ-*. Although historically *ɐrba-* is a combination of *ɐr-* and *ba-*, synchronically this segmentation does not make sense: *ɐr-* means movement downwards, when the deictic center is below; *ba-* means movement inwards, when the deictic center is outside, whereas *ɐrba-* means movement inwards, when the deictic center is inside. In modern Ossetic, multiple prefixation is impossible.

Preverbs cannot take scope over conjoined verbs: Digor *ba-warzta ɐma zarta* PRV-love.PST.3SG and sing.PST.3SG has only the interpretation 'fell in love and sang', i.e. the preverb can only scope over the first conjunct. If both conjoined verbs carry a copy of the preverb, the interpretation is different: Digor *ba-warzta ɐma ba-zarta* means 'fell in love and started singing'.

Many preverbs show irregular morphophonological behavior. For instance, the preverb *nə-/ni-* triggers gemination of the initial consonant of the verb stem, if the latter begins with a single consonant: Iron *nə-liz-* → *nə-lliz-* 'to run downwards (with the deictic center above)'. If the verb stem begins with a vowel other than *ɐ* an epenthetic consonant is inserted (and geminated): Iron *ažɐl-* 'to sound (about the echo)' → *nɐ-jj-ažɐl*. In Iron, if the stem begins with *ɐ* and a single consonant, the stem-initial vowel gets deleted: *ɐvɐr-* 'to put (ipf.)' → *nəvɐr-* 'to put (pf.)'. In Digor, *ni+ɐCV* yields *nijCV*: *ɐguppɐg kɐn-* 'to suffocate (ipf.)' → *nijguppag kan-* 'to suffocate (pf.)'. In the case of cluster-initial stems, the preverb attaches directly to the cluster: Iron *nə-star kɐn-* 'to exaggerate' (← *štər* 'big'); Digor *ni-st'alu-gin un* 'to become full of stars' (← *st'alugin* 'with stars'). Furthermore, some verbs show exceptional behavior. For instance, in Digor, the verb *ɐvɐr-* 'to put' yields *nivvɐr-* instead of the expected **nivɐr-*. In Digor, the preverb *fɐ-* shows similar behavior, whereas in Iron it only causes vowel assimilation under certain circumstances: Iron *fɐ-ɐvdiš-* → *fe-vdiš-* 'to show'. For lack of space, I do not describe its properties here in any detail.

Furthermore, in Iron, the preverbs *a-*, *ra-*, *ba-*, *ɐr-*, *ɐrba-*, *nə-*, and *fɐ-* interact in a peculiar manner with *a-*initial simplex verbs. If such a verb is compatible with the respective preverb, an epenthetic *-s-* is inserted. In the case of *nə-*, the epenthetic is *-cc-*. Remarkably, in the case of *ɐr-*, an insertion of any epenthetic consonant is not phonologically motivated at all. This rule is non-productive, for most complex verbs the hiatus is resolved in a regular manner: *a-ʔ-aftid kɐn-* PRV-EP-empty do 'to quickly empty', but **ʔa-s-aftid kɐn-*. For some speakers, a regular epenthetic *-j-* is also acceptable in some cases: both *nə-cc-agur-* and *nə-jj-agur-* 'to start intensively looking for' were judged acceptable (← *agur-*, *agʷərd-* 'to look for'). I have been able to find only one complex verb that requires *-s-* insertion. It is *aχʷər kɐn-* 'to learn, teach'. Thus, the rule concerns only about a dozen stems.

One of the main functions of the conative affix *-sɐj-/-cɐj-* is to indicate that the action was unfinished or prematurely stopped. However, that does not exhaust all its functions, the matter needs further study. This affix is inserted between the preverb and the verb stem, cf. (1). It is more productive in Iron than in Digor.

Several derivational means can be used to express v e r b a l p l u r a l i t y (i.e. the plurality of the respective event: the action is either repeated, or frequent, or performed by a number of agents.) The extent to which these processes are productive is, unfortunately, unknown. Such verbs can be formed from the plural of the past participle (if the original verb is simplex) or of the nominal part (if the original verb is complex): Digor *ra-kɐšt-itɐ kɐn-* PRV-look.PST.NMZ-PL do 'to look out in different directions' (← *kast* look.PST.NMZ); Digor *fɐ-ggepp-ittɐ kɐn-* PRV-jump-PL do '(for many people) to jump' (← *gepp kɐn-* 'jump'). This form is imperfective.

For some verbs with preverbs, the reduplicated 2nd person imperative form may be used to form a complex verb with the meaning 'to frequently do X'. In Iron, the 2nd person imperative form coincides with the present stem, whereas in Digor it carries the suffix *-ɐ*, cf. Digor *fɐ-kkɐsɐ-fɐ-kkɐsɐ kɐn-* 'to frequently look at' (← *kɐs-* look.PRS), Iron *a-bad-a-bad kɐn* 'to frequently sit down' (← *bad-* sit.PRS). Clitics may not be inserted between the two copies of the reduplicand. This type of verb is imperfective. The reduplicated nominal part may not carry the plural marking. Preverbs cannot attach on top of the one already present: *PRV-*a-bad-a-bad kɐn*.

From the second person of the imperative of a simplex verb, or from the nominal part of a complex verb, a new complex verb can be productively formed with the meaning 'X in opposite directions'. It is a complex verb of the form *ra-stem ba-stem do*: Digor *ra-dzorɐ ba-dzorɐ kɐn-* 'to negotiate, converse' (← *dzor-ɐ* talk-IMP.2SG); *ra-gepp ba-gepp kɐn-* 'to jump back and forth' (← *gepp kɐn-* 'to jump'). The preverbs *fɐ-* and, in Iron, *a-*, may be affixed to such verbs: Iron *fɐ-ra-wən ba-wən=ɐj kodta* PRV=RA-see BA-see=ACC.3SG did 'she viewed it for a while' (← *wən* see.PRS, in Iron the 2nd person of the imperative coincides with the present stem). Both *ra-ba-*complex verbs and *ra-ba-*verbs modified by preverbs are imperfective. The nominal part of such a complex verb is a noun denoting the corresponding action. Clitics may not be inserted between the *ra*-stem and *ba*-stem. The *ra-ba*-part may not carry the plural marking.

The i m p e r s o n a l form lies at the boundary between derivation and inflection. For many speakers, especially younger ones, this form is available only for a handful of verbs. The subject cannot be overtly expressed with this form, which motivates the choice of the term. The impersonal is formed on the basis of a special stem. Normally, it is the past stem with suffix *-ɐ*: for instance, *fəštɐ/finstɐ* write.IPS (← *fəšt/finst* write.PST). The verb 'to do' is exceptional: instead of the expected *kondɐ an irregular form *čəndɐ/kindɐ* is used. The finite morphology is expressed by the 3sg future subjunctive or the 3sg imperative of the copula suffixed to the stem. Certain tests show, however, that the verb stem and the copula have amalgamated into a single word. The form is used in rhetorical questions. It is most frequently used in two expressions:

(14) a. *sə   (ba)-čəndɐ-wa?*   b. *sə   žaʁdɐ-wa?*   Iron
        what PRV-do.IPS-SUB.FUT.3SG   what say.IPS-SUB.FUT.3SG
        'What is there to say?'   'What is there to do?'

4.3 Derivation of numerals

Many small morphophonological irregularities exist in the formation of numerals. Moreover, the languages have several counting systems: a vigesimal and a decimal one in both languages; and an additional decimal system, the so-called "shepherd count", in Digor. The decimal system in Iron was artificially calqued from Digor in the 1920s, according to Bagaev (1965: 212).

4.3.1 Cardinal numerals

Cardinal numerals differ from nouns in several aspects. First, both in Iron and Digor, in the numeral phrase they assign the oblique case to the noun, when the whole phrase is in the nominative, cf. (15). Second, Digor numerals and numeral phrases have a separate series of case suffixes.

(15) *ɐrtɐ   bɐχ-ə   χiž-ənc*   Iron
     three horse-OBL graze-PRS.3PL
     'Three horses are grazing.'

Low cardinal numerals are non-derived. I list them here for the irregularities in the formation of derived numerals to become visible: *ju/jew* '1'; *dəwwɐ/duwwɐ* '2';

ɐrtɐ '3'; səppar/cuppar '4'; fonz/fondz '5'; ɐχšɐž/ɐχsɐz '6'; ɑvd '7';ašt/ast '8'; farašt/farast '9'; dɐš/dɐs '10'.

Numbers between 11 and 19 are formed by compounding the appropriate unit with dɐš/dɐs '10'. Unexpected linking morphemes or root changes may occur: juwɐndɐš/jewɐndɐs '11'; dəww̱adɐš/duw̱adɐs '12'; ɐrtəndɐš/ɐrtindɐs '13' səppɐrdɐš/cuppɐrdɐs '14'; fənddɐš/finddɐs '15'; ɐχsɐrdɐš/ɐχsɐrdɐs '16'; ɐvddɐš/ɐvddɐs '17'; ɐštdɐš/ɐstdɐs '18'; nudɐš/nɐwudɐs '19'.

Decimal numerals are fairly irregular: dəw-ən/duw-in '20'; ɐrt-ən/ɐrt-in '30'; səppor/cuppor '40'; fɐnzaj/fɐndzaj '50'; ɐχšaj/ɐχsaj '60'; ɐvdaj '70'; ɐštaj/ɐstaj '80'; nɐwɐz/nawɐdzɐ '90'; šɐdɐ/sɐdɐ '100'; ɑvd šɐdə/ɑvd sɐdi '700'. The oblique marker -ə/-i appears on 'hundred' only if no other numerals follow. A Turkic loanword mijn/min is used for 'thousand'. Complex numerals in the decimal count are formed after the pattern thousands-hundreds-tens-ones, e.g., Digor duwɐ mijnduwɐ sɐdɐɐrtin farast two thousand two hundred thirty nine '2,239'.

In the vigesimal count: ššɐz/insɐj '20'; dɐš ɐmɐ ššɐz/dɐs ɐma insɐj 10 and 20 '30'; dəwiššɐzə/duwinsɐj two-twenty '40'; dɐš ɐmɐ dəwiššɐzə/dɐs ɐma duwinsɐj '50'; ɐrt-i-ššɐzə/ɐrt-insɐj three-twenty '60'; dɐš ɐmɐ ɐrt-i-ššɐzə/dɐs ɐma ɐrt-insɐj '70'; səppar-ə-ššɐzə/cuppar-insɐj four-twenty '80'; dɐš ɐmɐ səppar-ə-ššɐzə/dɐs ɐma cuppar-insɐj ten and four-twenty '90'; fonz-ə-ššɐzə/fondz-insɐj '100'.

Digor has another series, based on the root -sɐdʒi: duwin-sɐdʒi '40', ɐrtin-sɐdʒi '60'; cuppar-insɐdʒi '80', fondz-insɐdʒi '100', etc.

To form numerals up to 380, multiples of twenty are used: Digor duwadɐs-insɐdʒi twelve-twenty '240', nɐwudɐs-insɐdʒi nineteen-twenty '380'. For numerals starting from 400, multiples of fonz-ə-ššɐzə/fondz-insɐj '100' are used: Iron ɑvd fonzəššɐzə '700'. Actually, the numerals 200 and 300 can be expressed as multiples of 100 as well.

In the vigesimal count, the pattern is 'thousands hundreds numeral.below.twenty and multiple.of.twenty': Iron farašt fonzəššɐzə ɐštdɐš ɐmɐ dəwiššɐz mina səppar fonzəššɐzənudɐš ɐmɐ ɐrtiššɐzə '958,479' (Bagaev 1965: 211). However, nowadays in the spoken language Russian loanwords are often used for higher cardinals.

In the Digor shepherd count (Takazov 2009: 51), the unit of count is two, because sheep were counted pairwise. Some numerals have forms different from that in the standard decimal count: artin '30', čippor '40', fɐndzaj '50', aχšej '60', avdej '70', aštej '80'. Complex numerals are formed as ones-and-tens: cuppar ɐma nawɐ '94'. An exception are numbers that are equal to eight modulo 10, a special form of the word eight is used there without the conjunction: aštin nawɐ '98'.

4.3.2 Ordinal numerals

Ordinal numerals are derived from the cardinal ones by the suffixes -*ɐm* and -*ɐjmag* in Iron and only -*ɐjmag* in Digor. The three exceptions are the lower ordinals: *fæccag*/*ficcag* 'first' and *də-kkag*/*du-kkag* 'second', *ɐrt-əkkag*/*ɐrt-ikkag* 'third'. All higher simplex ordinals are formed regularly, by affixing -*ɐm* or -*ɐjmag* to the right edge of the numeral: *səppɐr-ɐjmag*, *səppɐr-ɐm*/*cuppɐr-ɐjmag* 'fourth', *ɐrtiššɐzɐjmag*, *ɐrtiššɐzɐm*/*ɐrtinsɐjɐjmag* '60ᵗʰ (vigesimal)'; *šɐd-ɐjmag*/*sɐd-ɐjmag* '100ᵗʰ (decimal)'. In the case of a complex numeral, the ordinal suffix is attached to the right edge of the cardinal numeral. The choice of the suffix is conditioned by the rightmost word in the cardinal: Digor *ɐvddɐs ɐma duwinsɐj-ɐjmag* '57ᵗʰ (vigesimal)', Iron *min fonz šɐdɐ səppor ɐrtə-kkag* '1,543ʳᵈ (decimal)'. Morphosyntactically, ordinal numerals are identical to nouns: Digor *sɐd-ɐjmag-ɐn* hundred-ORD-DAT 'to the hundredth'.

4.3.3 Distributive numerals

Distributive numerals are formed by suffixing -*gaj* to the cardinal ones. Some minor changes happen to the stem (only irregular forms are listed): *də-gaj*/*du-gaj* 'by twos'; *ɐrtə-gaj*/*ɐrti-gaj* 'by threes'; *səppɐr-gaj*/*cuppɐr-gaj* four-DISTR 'by fours'; *fɐnz-gaj*/*fɐndz-gaj* 'by fives'; *ɐvd-gaj* 'by sevens'; *ɐšt-gaj*/*ɐst-gaj* 'by eights'; *farɐšt-gaj*/*farɐst-gaj* 'by nines'. Some speakers adjoin the suffix directly to cardinal nouns without causing any alterations for numerals larger than three. Even such speakers require the respective alternations to occur in the plural: *səppɐr-gɐj-ttɐ*/*cuppɐr-gɐj-ttɐ*.

The numeral -*gaj* is obviously similar to the homonymous nominal suffix (see section 4.1.1) but the latter does not trigger any changes in the noun it attaches to, therefore, the nominal and the numeral suffixes are synchronically distinct. Morphosyntactically, distributive numerals are identical to nouns: they can receive plural and case marking, cf. Digor *ɐrtigɐj-tt-ɐj* three.DISTR-PL-ABL 'by threes', and behave as regular modifiers in a noun phrase: Iron *dəgaj χɐdɐ-ttɐ* two-DISTR shirt-PL 'two shirts each'.

4.4 Derivation of pronouns

Personal and reciprocal pronouns are non-derived. Oblique forms of personal pronouns serve as stems for substantivized pronouns: *mɐn* I.OBL → *mɐn-on* 'mine', *maχ* → *maχ-on* 'ours'.

Reflexives are formed as possessive proclitic + reflexive stem χi/χe: mɐ-χi/ mɐ-χe myself.OBL. Reflexive pronouns can be substantivized as well: mɐ-χi/mɐ-χe → mɐ-χi-won/mɐ-χe-won 'my own one'. Intensifiers (i.e. functional analogs of 'himself' in *John did it himself*) are formed as possessive proclitic + stem -χɐdɐg/ χʷɐdɐg: mɐ-χɐdɐg/mɐ-χʷɐdɐg 'I myself'.

There exist derived demonstratives: *a-sə/a-či* PROX-what, and *wu-sə/je-či* DIST-what. In Digor, the proximal *a* and the distal *je* function as independent words as well, e.g., *je* is used as the 3ʳᵈ person singular personal pronoun. Digor has an additional distal demonstrative *wo-či*, whose stem *wo-*, not an independent word, also appears in non-nominative forms of the distal deictic *je*, e.g., wo-j he/ she/it-OBL. What historically were the inessive forms of the distal and proximal pronouns, have been reanalyzed into the words *am/ami* 'here' and *wəm/womi* 'there'. The meanings 'in this/that one' are expressed by combinations of the oblique forms with appropriate postpositions, e.g., Iron *wəj χʷərf-ə* she/he/it.OBL in-OBL 'in her/him/it'.

Non-negative indefinites are formed on the basis of wh-words by affixes *is-/jes-*, *-dɐr*, and *-dɐrittɐr*. Negative indefinites are formed by the prefix *ni-/ne-*: *nisə/ne-či* NEG-what 'nothing'. In certain non-interrogative contexts, wh-words themselves may function as indefinites (with the meaning 'some elements of a specific salient set'):

(16) ka štukaturkɐ kodta <u>ka</u> pec dasta　　　　　　　　　　　Digor
　　 who plaster[Rus] do.PST.3SG who stove build.PST.3SG
　　 'Some were doing the plaster and some were constructing the stove.'
　　 (Legkojti 2009: 48)

Certain case forms of wh-words may undergo conversion. First, what historically was the inessive of 'who', the wh-word *kɐm/kɐmi*, now only means 'where'. The meaning 'in whom' is expressed by appropriate postpositions. Second, the superessive plural form of 'who', *kɐ-wəl-t-ə/kɐ-bɐl-t-i* who.IDR-SUP-PL-OBL undergoes conversion to mean 'where, by which trajectory': Iron *kɐ-wəl-t-ə a-səd* who.IDR-SUP-PL-OBL PRV-go.PST 'Which road did s/he take?'. The respective form of the *-dɐr* series indefinite means 'somewhere, by some trajectory': Digor *kɐ-bɐl-dɐr-t-ife-ndɐj* who.IDR-SUP-IDF-PL-OBL PRV-away-PST.3SG 'S/he got away somewhere.' Third, the oblique form of 'who', *kɐj/ke*, serves as a wide-purpose complementizer (Erschler 2012). Fourth, the Digor *kumɐ* 'where to' is the allative of *ku*, which synchronically only serves as the complementizer 'where, if'. The same stem is present in the Iron *nikʷə* 'never'.

4.5 Oaths

Oaths are formed from nouns and pronouns by the means of the suffix -*stɐn*: Digor *aboni stɐn* today OATH 'I swear by today' *χucaw-i stɐn* God-OBL OATH 'I swear by God', *mɐ=χe stɐn* POSS.1SG=REFL OATH 'I swear by myself' (consultants judge the latter oath possible, although fairly impertinent). Alternatively, this suffix can be treated as a stem, but it never appears on its own.

5 Conversion

Given that nouns and adjectives are not distinct, it hardly makes sense to speak about deadjectival conversion.

Two negated verbs in the 3rd person of the future subjunctive have been reanalyzed as nouns: *maguša/magosa* < *ma kuš-a/ma kos-a* NEG.IMP work-SUB.FUT.3SG 'idler'; *mazura/madzora* < *ma zur-a/ma dzor-a* NEG.IMP talk-SUB.FUT.3SG 'taciturn person'. Alternatively, these examples may be interpreted as instances of reanalysis.

Arguably, there is one case of conversion of pronouns into nouns: the allative of the reflexive pronoun is reanalyzed as a noun 'at home' and as adjectives meaning 'my/our/their kind of, local, indigenous', cf. (17). It is not clear whether this is possible for all numbers and persons.

(17) a. 'at home'
 cuma sɐ=χe-mɐ   divan-bel ɐvduld-ɐj   Digor
 as.if POSS.3PL=self-ALL couch-SUP slouch.PST-PST.3PL
 'As if he was sprawling on a couch at home.'
 (Maliti 2008: 15)
 b. 'local'
 duwɐ nɐχe-mɐ   χwɐnχag sɐw furk'a-j   Digor
 two POSS.1PL=self-ALL alpine   black ram-OBL
 'two local alpine black young rams'
 (Sabajti 2010: 6)

When quoted, any word is converted into a noun, and may be marked with an appropriate case suffix as required by the context. In example (18), the verb receives the dative marking, i.e. is treated as a noun. (The use of the dative marking in the possessive construction shows that the infinitive is considered as a verb's inalienable possession.)

(18) mivdišeg <u>fendə-jen</u>   nej   infinitivon forme   Iron
     verb   want.PRS.3SG-DAT NEG.exists infinitive form
     'The verb <u>fendə</u> ('wants') lacks the infinitive form.'
     (Medojty 2003: 173)

6 Reduplication

Reduplication is fairly marginal in Ossetic. For verbs, reduplication serves to form the verb with the meaning 'to frequently do X', see section 4.2.2, whereas for nouns, reduplication expresses a wider variety of meanings. Clitics may not intervene between reduplicands, and therefore reduplicated entities form single noun phrases (or even words, but I am not aware of any tests that would distinguish between words and noun phrases in this case).

Names of some geographic entities can be reduplicated yielding the meaning 'along the edge of the object': *don-don* 'along the river' (← *don* 'water, river'), *qəd-qəd/ʁede-ʁede* 'along the edge of the forest' (← *qəd/ʁede* 'forest'). This reduplication is judged impossible, when the object either lacks an edge (e.g., for *kom* 'gorge'), or when it is abnormal to walk along its edge (e.g., for *fendag* 'road'). Reduplicated nouns of this type do not allow case marking. In this sense, they are "true" adverbs.

Some allative-marked nouns may be reduplicated, with the meaning 'gradually in the direction X': *deleme-deleme* 'gradually downwards' (← *deleme* 'downwards'), *asərdem-asərdem* 'gradually hither'. In Iron, some nouns can be reduplicated to be used as depictives, cf. (19a), i.e. functional analogs of 'drunk' in *Bill studied morphology <u>drunk</u>*; e.g., *kʷʼələχ-kʷʼələχ* 'limping', *gʷəbər-gʷəbər* 'slightly bending down (in order to hide oneself)'. The normal way to form a depictive is to obligatorily mark the noun with the ablative, cf. (19b):

(19) a. *kʷʼələχ-kʷʼələχ-(*ej) sədiš*   Iron
        limping-*ABL   go.PST.3SG
        'S/he walked limping.'
     b. *rašag-*(ej) sədiš*   Iron
        drunk-ABL go.PST.3SG
        'S/he walked drunk.'

In Iron, the nouns *χezar* 'house' and *qew* 'village' serve as the basis for reduplication-like formations *χezar-i-χezar* 'among homes, from home to home' and *qew-i-qew* 'among villages, from village to village'. The pattern does not seem to be productive. Apparently, the marker of one of the indefinite series, -dɐritter (see section 4.4) is formed on the basis of -dɐr following to a similar pattern.

Converbs (see section 4.1.2) may undergo reduplication as well, although in Iron this phenomenon is fairly marginal, and converb-infinitive compounds are normally used in that language for this purpose. Examples (from Digor) are χodgɐ-χodgɐ 'laughing' (← χod-gɐ laugh-CNV), dzorgɐ-dzorgɐ 'talking' (← dzor-gɐ talk-CNV), nɐmgɐ-nɐmgɐ 'beating' (← nɐm-gɐ beat-CNV). The semantic difference between reduplicated and non-reduplicated converbs is unknown. Like non-reduplicated converbs, reduplicated ones may be marked by the ablative: Digor dzorgɐ-dzorgɐ-j 'talking-ABL'. The case marking may not appear on both copies of a converb.

In a limited manner, m- and w-reduplication is attested, for instance, c'ɐndɐg-mɐndɐg/c'undɐg-mundɐg 'having shut one's eyes tight' (the word c'ɐndɐg/c'undag does not exist); Digor cɐlqe-wɐlqe 'lumbering'. The process is not productive.

A considerable number of onomatopoetic words are reduplicated. In this case, the respective non-reduplicated words often do not exist: c'ip-c'ip/č'ip-č'ip 'sound produced by young chickens', χart-χart/χirt-χirt 'sound of scratching, squeaking, or riffle', etc.

For a number of basic color terms, an intensified form is obtained by reduplication and suffixing of -id: šarχ-šarχ-id/surχ-surχ-id 'bright red' (← šarχ/surχ 'red'), wurš-wurš-id/wors-worš-id 'bright white' (← wurš/wors 'white'), etc.

7 Clipping

Productively, clipping is used to form hypocoristics from personal names, e.g., Aslan → As, Zɐline → Zɐli, Fatimɐ → Fati. Clipped forms can attach the suffix -ik, see section 4.1.1. Arguably, clipping is also responsible for situations when the first syllable of a wh-word, or a preverb, are repeated after the verb. The former phenomenon is relatively common in colloquial speech, whereas the latter seems to be fairly rare. Using the truncated forms kɐ or sɐ/cɐ in isolation, is impossible.

(20) a. <u>kɐ</u>dɐm sɐw-əš=<u>kɐ</u> Iron
     where.to go-PRS.2SG=WH

   b. <u>sɐ</u>mɐn liz-əš=<u>sɐ</u> Iron
     why run-PRS.2SG=WH

   c. <u>ra</u>-kɐš ra Iron
     PRV-look.IMP.2SG PRV
     'Look!/Watch out!'
     (Bagaev 1965: 315)

Besides that, in Iron, the 2sg imperative of the verb *kæn*- 'to do' can be formed by clipping: *kæ*. The non-clipped form, *kæn*, is used as well. Any other instances of clipping have not been attested.

Acknowledgements

Much of the data used in this article have been collected in the course of my field work in North Ossetia in 2007–2012. I thank all my consultants for their patience and readiness to help. I am particularly grateful to Aslan Guriev and Elizaveta Kochieva, whose help was crucial in organizing the trips (and who also provided some of the judgments for this article), and to Fedar Takazov for numerous discussions. I thank Lisa Bylinina, Ekaterina Lyutikova, and Dmitri Sitchinava for comments to earlier versions of this article.

Abbreviations

ALL	allative	HAB	habitual
ASS	associative plural	IDF	indefinite
CNV	converb	IDR	indirect (stem)
COM	comitative	LINK	linking morpheme
CON	conative	MOD	modal
DIST	distal deictic	PROX	proximal deictic
DISTR	distributive	PRV	preverb
EMP	emphatic	SUB	subjunctive
EP	epenthetic	SUP	superessive

8 References

Abaev, Vasilij (1958–89): *Istoriko-ėtimologičeskij slovar' osetinskogo jazyka*. 4 Vol. Leningrad: Nauka.
Abaev, Vasilij (1964): *A Grammatical Sketch of Ossetic*. The Hague: Mouton.
Ajlarty, Asæxmæt (2002): *Fæzzygon didindžytæ*. Dzæudžyqæu: Ir.
Axvlediani, Georgij (ed.) (1963): *Grammatika osetinskogo jazyka*. Vol. 1. Ordžonikidze: SOIGSI.
Bagaev, Nikolaj (1965): *Sovremennyj osetinskij jazyk*. Vol. 1. Ordžonikidze: Severo-Osetinskoe knižnoe izdatel'stvo.
Erschler, David (2018): Ossetic. In: Geoffrey Haig and Geoffrey Khan (eds.), *The Languages and Linguistics of Western Asia. An Areal Perspective*, 859–891. Berlin/Boston: De Gruyter Mouton.
Erschler, David (2020): Iron Ossetic. In: Maria Polinsky (ed.), *Handbook of the Languages of the Caucasus*, 641–685. Oxford: Oxford University Press.

Erschler, David (2022): A dedicated nominal singular morpheme without singulative semantics. *Morphology* 32(2): 249–276.
Gabaraev, Nikolaj (1977): *Morfologičeskaja struktura slova i slovoobrazovanie v sovremennom osetinskom jazyke*. Tbilissi: Mecniereba.
Isaev, Magomed (1966): *Digorskij dialekt osetinskogo jazyka*. Moskva: Nauka.
Legkojti, Giuærgi (2009): Næ karnæ. *Iræf* 2: 10–65.
Maliti, Vaso (2008): *Uadzimistæ*. Dzæugighæw: Ir.
Medojty, Bobolka (2003): *Nyrykkon iron ævzag. Morfologi*. Tsxinval: s.e.
Miller, Wsewolod (1972 [1927–34]): *Ossetisch-Russisch-Deutsches Wörterbuch*. Ed. by Alexander Freiman. The Hague/Paris: Mouton.
Sabajti, Sulejman (2010): *Radzurdtæ*. Dzæugighæw: Gassiti Viktori nombæl rauaghdon-poligrafion kustuat.
Sk'odtati, Elbrus (2008): Radzurdtæ. *Iræf* 1: 88–117.
Takazov, Fedar (2003): *Digoron-urussag dzurduat*. Dzæugighæw: Alaniston.
Takazov, Fedar (2009): *Grammatičeskij očerk osetinskogo (digorskogo) jazyka*. Vladikavkaz: SOGU.
Takazov, Fedar (2015): *Digoron-Urussag dzurduat; Urussag-Digoron Dzurduat*. Dzæugighæw: Ul'yanovskiy dom pečati.
Tobojti, Cæræg (2004): K'axnad cæuj Særisæfænmæ. *Iræf* 4: 79–139.
Xidirti, Ramzan (2007): Mæ cardi ænk'ard turæq. *Iræf* 3: 12–82.

Kaarina Pitkänen-Heikkilä
15 Finnish

1 Introduction
2 General overview
3 Composition
4 Derivation
5 Conversion
6 Backformation, blending and clipping
7 References

Abstract: Even though Finnish has a very rich derivational morphology and many productive suffixes, the most productive word-formation method in Finnish is compounding. However, Finnish word-formation has mainly been described through derivation and as a consequence, compounding has been studied less. Finnish has ample material to serve as the basis for the description of the structure of complex words: the dictionaries contain only 10–15 percent simplexes, while the rest are compounds and derivatives that are based on them. Perhaps for this reason, Finnish word-formation has often been described in terms of the established vocabulary.

1 Introduction

During the 19th century, linguists specialising in Finnish focussed on its versatility and the freedom of its word-formation. For example, Elias Lönnrot, professor of Finnish in Helsinki in 1854–1862, taught word-formation in his lectures. His retained notes contain extensive collections and formulas of derivation as well as some descriptions regarding compounding and onomatopoetic words. He considered derivation "the richness and the loveliest feature of Finnish" and referred to potential vocabulary already at that time, long before it became a topic in linguistics (Pitkänen 2005). Some years later, in 1877, August Ahlqvist examined the derivation of nouns and adjectives, classifying the derivatives into semantic categories and into "blurry" and "clear" derivational types.

However, to date, a comprehensive monograph or textbook that concentrates on word-formation and covers both derivation and compounding has not yet

Kaarina Pitkänen-Heikkilä, Helsinki, Finland

been written. Grammars have instead naturally presented word-formation (e.g., Setälä 1898; Penttilä 1957), the most comprehensive being the descriptive *Iso suomen kielioppi* (Hakulinen et al. 2004). Furthermore, Finnish word-formation has been examined typically in terms of language history, not actually from the perspective of vocabulary growth. For example, L. Hakulinen's (1979 [1941]) handbook on the structure and development of Finnish includes a description of word-formation using old derivatives and compounds. Itkonen (1966) examines the means of word-formation in a monograph that concerns the study and structure of Finno-Ugric. A later monograph by Häkkinen (1990) discusses derivatives and compounds and concerns the origin of Finnish words. In addition, Karlsson examines derivation in his book on Finnish phonology and morphology (1983) and the textbook by Lepäsmaa, Lieko and Silfverberg (1996) also introduces Finnish derivation particularly to students learning Finnish as a foreign language. In his textbook on the structure of Finnish words, Koivisto (2013) also examines word-formation.

The distinguishing features of Finnish word-formation have been described in many articles and studies. Concerning derivation, many articles and extensive studies have been written, for instance, on the productivity of suffixes, the relationship between base and suffix, the derivation by correlations, the particular derivational types and historical derivation, and these include the works by Lehtinen (1976, 1979, 1993), Kangasmaa-Minn (1977, 1982, 1983, 1984), Koski (1978, 1979, 1981, 1982), Rintala (1978, 1985), Räisänen (1978, 1979, 1985, 1986, 1988), Kulonen (Kulonen-Korhonen 1985, 2010), Länsimäki (1987, 1988), Kytömäki (1989, 1990, 1992, 1993) and Laakso (1990, 2000, 2005), Koivisto (1991, 1995, 2006, 2008, 2013). As the editor of the *Iso suomen kielioppi* [The large grammar of Finnish], Koivisto has also been responsible for a description of a vast part of it. Pitkänen (2005, 2008, Pitkänen-Heikkilä 2013, 2015) has also examined derivation and compounding, particularly term-formation in the languages for special purposes.

Compared to derivation, fewer studies in general have explored the mechanisms of compounding. However, research has begun to focus more on the structure of compounds, for example, on the various compound types. Also many articles concerned with language planning discuss compounds (e.g., Laaksonen 1984). Furthermore, the semantics of compounds has been analysed by Seppänen (1981) and Räisänen (1986, 1988), and the structure of compounds or of particular compound types have been explored among others by Saukkonen (1973), Rahtu (1984), Häkkinen (1987), Vesikansa (1989), Heinonen (2001) and Malmivaara (2004). In addition, the history of compounds has been analysed by Häkkinen and Björqvist (1991) and Vaittinen (2003, 2007). In his doctoral thesis, Mäkisalo (2000) examined the position of Finnish compounds between the lexicon and the grammar.

It is important to note that in the descriptions of Finnish word-formation far less space is devoted to compounding in comparison to derivation. This has been explained by noting the simplicity of compounding: the familiar elements are compounded without morphological modifications. This lack of attention, however, does not represent the whole picture of the significance of composition: some of the compounds appeared frequently in the vocabulary of what is referred to as Old Literary Finnish (from the 16th to the beginning of the 19th century), and a great number of compounds are found in modern Finnish (Häkkinen 1991: 33, 37).

This article is based primarily on the sources mentioned above (especially Karlsson 1983, Vesikansa 1989, Lepäsmaa, Lieko and Silfverberg 1996 and Hakulinen et al. 2004) and most of the examples cited here have also been gathered from these authors' works, but due to space restrictions, this article offers a very limited description of Finnish word-formation.

2 General overview

Finnish is a member of the Finno-Ugrian language family; it belongs to the Baltic Finnic languages that are spoken around the Gulf of Finland by about 7 million people. It is one of the two official languages of Finland and an official minority language in Sweden. Finnish is spoken by about five million people who reside mainly in Finland. There are also notable Finnish-speaking minorities in Sweden, Norway, Russia, Estonia, Brazil, Canada, and the United States.

Finnish word-formation consists mainly of compounding and suffixal derivation.

Compounding is the most productive method of word-formation in present-day Finnish. The most important restrictive factor is semantics: all material can be combined that yields an understandable concept. New compounds are typically formed by combining two or more independent words but new compounds can also be derived from earlier compounds (e.g., *viikonloppu* 'weekend' → *viikonloppu-isin* 'in the weekends') or phrases (*pitkätukka* 'long hair' → *pitkätukka-inen* 'a person who has long hair') (Vesikansa 1989: 213; Häkkinen 1990: 144–145).

A compound is an entity that consists of two or more words, but as a unit of language it behaves like one word. An important semantic characteristic of a compound is that it names a concept (cf. Itkonen 1966: 234, 237). Contrary to many other languages, compounds in Finnish are always complex words, never phrases. Practically, however, the border between compound and fixed phrase is unstable: the more fixed the connection is, the more probable it is that the structure is a compound. The clearest marker of a compound can be stress. The primary stress is placed on the first element of a compound, while in a fixed phrase both elements can have primary stress. Problems of demarcation concern the cases in which the first element appears in some other case than the nominative (e.g., the genitive) – if the first element is in the nominative, the interpretation as a compound is the only possibility (Häkkinen 1990: 146–147).

Moreover, words that include a prefix, such as *epä+rehellinen* 'dishonest', *epä+miellyttävä* 'unpleasant' and *ei-toivottu* 'unwanted' are considered to be compounds (Finnish has only two native prefixes, *epä-* and *ei-*, and these both express negation). In addition, certain prefix-like compound parts are used among others in the vocabularies of special fields (many of them have been adopted as calques from foreign languages). Finnish words can have also foreign prefixes (e.g., *anti-*, *mono-*, *ultra-*) that are also considered as compound parts. Compounding and neoclassical word-formation are discussed in section 3.

The derivational methods of Finnish are derivation by suffixes and derivation by correlations, and they include backformation too (see, for example, Lepäsmaa, Lieko and Silfverberg 1996: 17–18). Derivation by correlations means that the formation is based on correlative patterns: words in the same word group do not necessarily have a clear base but have close root elements and a connection in their meaning and a new member of the group is motivated by a parallel word series (e.g., *jyräjää* 'to rumble' : *jyrisee* : *jyristää* : *jyrinä* : *jyry* 'rumble' ~ *humajaa* 'to hum' : *humisee* : *humistaa* : *humina* : *humu* 'hum'; *ime-ä* 'to suck, absorb' : *ime-yty-ä* 'to be absorbed' : *ime-yt-tä-ä* 'to get sth. to be absorbed, be saturated' ~ *sito-a* 'to bind' : *sito-utu-a* 'to commit, bind oneself' : *sito-ut-ta-a* 'to get sb. to bind oneself', cf. Räisänen 1978: 329; Koivisto 2013: 314–318; cf. also Kerge 2016 on Estonian). A further method can be derivation by particular morphological patterns or formulas (Hakulinen et al. 2004: 172–173). Sometimes the phonological variation found in the onomatopoetic and descriptive vocabularies is thought to belong to derivation, as are conversion and clipping (e.g., Häkkinen 1990: 109–110; Lepäsmaa, Lieko and Silfverberg 1996: 18–19). Section 4 examines mainly suffixal derivation, but also discusses the phonological variation found in the onomatopoetic and descriptive vocabulary. Conversion will be considered in section 5, backformation, blending and clipping in section 6.

When examining Finnish word-formation, it is difficult or even impossible to isolate the phenomenon of "word-creation", because the new concepts have been traditionally named in terms of word-formation. This means that novel words are native coinings – new simplexes, derivatives and compounds. Particularly in the 19th century, when the usage of Finnish expanded into the several domains of usage, many new words were consciously formed on the basis of native material while loans were intentionally avoided. For example, the collection of derivative words by Lönnrot includes 3,700 simplexes classified according to the final elements of the words. Based on this collection, he composed specific derivation formulas that were used when forming new words for his Finnish-Swedish dictionary (1867–1880) (Pitkänen 2005). In the 19th century, many new derivatives were coined, even analogically by means of unproductive suffixes; today new phenomena are usually named by compounding. Consciously formed neologisms are, however, often loan translations that are formed word-to-word by relying on foreign models. In this overview the creative methods in section 6 include more unexpected formations, such as clippings, acronyms and blends. Clipping also includes the formation of slang words with certain suffixes.

3 Composition

Many of the compounds' structures will be introduced next with nominal compounds, although adjectival and verbal compounds possibly contain them also.

3.1 Nominal compounds

Most Finnish compounds are nominal compounds, and the largest structural group consists of d e t e r m i n a t i v e c o m p o u n d s whose first element is in the nominative case (*sade+takki* 'raincoat', *silmä+lasi+kotelo* 'eyeglass box'). In addition, new compounds mainly belong to this group. Finnish has a few c o o r d i n a t i v e c o m p o u n d s; according to Saukkonen's (1973) estimate, only approximately 200 lexemes occur in dictionaries (such as *parturi-kampaaja* 'barber-hairdresser', and *jääkaappi-pakastin* 'fridge-freezer'). Historically, the dvandva compounds are the oldest type of compound in the Baltic Finnic languages. One example of this type of old compound is *maailma* 'world' (*maa* 'earth' + *ilma* 'air') (Itkonen 1966: 235).

The first element occurring in the n o m i n a t i v e c a s e of the determinative compounds expresses an essential feature of the entity that is named in the second element. Furthermore, the semantic relationship between the parts of the compound is free; it only indicates that things are somehow associated with each other (Seppänen 1981). However, compounds with the nominative in the first position often have an established meaning, although other readings are also possible in principle. Lexicalised compounds can also be used in some contexts in the meaning that elements allow by the grammar, e.g., *katu+kauppias* 'street vendor' could according to the grammar, refer to both a 'vendor who works in the street' and a 'vendor who sells streets', similarly *kala+kauppias* 'fishmonger' can refer to both a 'vendor who sells fishes' and a 'fish who works as vendor' (Räisänen 1988: 3–5).

There are some semantic groups that have the nominative in the first position of the compound: they can express, e.g., material (*timantti+sormus* 'diamond ring'), place or location (*häkki+lintu* 'cage bird', *etelä+raja* 'southern border'), time (*joulu+yö* 'Christmas night', *tiistai+konsertti* 'Tuesday concert'), an instrument (*kirje+ystävä* letter-friend 'pen friend', *verkkokauppa* net-store 'online store') or a quality (*kylmä+kaappi* 'cold cupboard', *kuiva+kukka* dry-flower 'dried flower') (Vesikansa 1989: 222–223; Hakulinen et al. 2004: 396–397).

The second typical case for the first element of a nominal compound is the g e n i t i v e. The functions are predominately the same as those of the nominative, but the semantic relationship between the elements is not equally open and free (Hakulinen et al. 2004: 398). The genitive on the first element of nominal compounds indicates which domain the referent of the second element belongs to (e.g., *tuoli-n+jalka* chair's leg 'leg of a chair', *kuuse-n+oksa* 'branch of a spruce', *velje-n+poika* brother's-son 'fraternal nephew', *mere-n+ranta* 'seashore'). Moreover, the first element in the nominative can express the same relationship (e.g., *jalka+pohja* leg-bottom 'track', *pöytä+laatikko* table-box 'drawer'); in languages for special purposes, the part-whole relations of the concepts are also expressed by nominal compounds in which the first element is in the nominative (Laine 2007: 327–328; Pitkänen 2008: 271–272). The genitive can also occur in the plural (*äiti-en+päivä* 'Mothers' Day'). When the second element is deverbal, the genitive on the first element often expresses the subject or the object of the corresponding verb phrase (e.g., *talo-n+rakenn-us* 'house building' – *rakentaa talo* 'to build a house', *auringo-n+nous-u* 'sunrise' – *aurinko nousee* 'the sun rises').

The first part of the compound can also be in some other case (e.g., *maasta+muutt-o*, country-from-migration 'emigration', *käde-stä+ennusta-ja* hand-from-soothsayer 'palmist'), especially if the second element of the compound is an action or agent noun.

The first member of a compound can also be a stem that does not occur as an independent word. These types of "casus componens"-forms are roots (e.g., *suur+kaupunki* ← *suuri* 'big', *kaupunki* 'city') or have an extra element (e.g., *jalk-o+pää* 'foot of the bed' ← *jalka* 'foot, leg', *pää* 'head'). The first element can also be prefix-like material that expresses location or other relationships or negation (e.g., *lähi+kauppa* local-store 'convenience store', *pika+ruoka* 'fast food'). Furthermore, the foreign elements of the neoclassical compounds belong to this group (e.g., *geo+kätkö* 'geocache', *ultra+ääni* 'ultrasound').

Subtypes of determinative compounds are iterative and *bahuvrīhi* compounds. I t e r a t i v e compounds emphasise the prototypic meaning of a noun (e.g., *ruoka+ruoka* food-food 'antonym of fast food'). In the b a h u v r ī h i compounds (e.g., *kalju+pää* bald-head 'baldie', *kiero+silmä* crooked-eye 'person who has crooked eyes', *tyhjä+tasku* empty-pocket 'person who has empty pockets'), the referent is not the same nor does it belong to the same category as the referent of the second element; the literal meaning is a characteristic of a person that is named by the compound. In addition, the referent typically is a human being or another living creature. *Bahuvrīhi* compounds are predominantly affect words and in Finnish dictionaries, they constitute a few hundred entries (Vesikansa 1989: 250–253; Hakulinen et al. 2004: 407–410). A p p o s i t i v e compounds (e.g., *lapsi+näyttelijä* 'child-actor', *poika+viikari* 'boy-urchin') are a subtype of coordinate compounds, their first element does not clearly define the second element but the second element can also be interpreted as defining, and with the first element, as representing the whole (e.g., *lapsi+näyttelijä* is at the same time a child and an actor).

3.2 Adjectival compounds

Finnish has considerably fewer adjectival compounds than nominal compounds. The first element of an adjectival compound can be another adjective (e.g., *paha-n+hajuinen* 'foul-smelling', *tumma-n+vihreä* 'dark green'), a noun (*kivi+kova* 'rock hard', *tuli+kuuma* fire-hot 'boiling'), a pronoun (*joka+päivä-inen* every-day-ADJ 'everyday') or a numeral (*kaksi+vuot-ias* two-year-ADJ 'two-year old', *kolmi+osa-inen* three-part-ADJ 'consisting of three parts'). The most common adjectival compounds are those that have an *inen*-derivative as a second element; they can also be analysed as derivatives from a phrasal base. The case of the first element of an adjectival compound is typically the nominative or genitive.

A noun in the genitive in the first position can express comparison (e.g., *kuva-n+kaunis* picture's-beautiful 'beautiful like a picture', *langa-n+laiha* thread's-thin 'thread thin, thin as a thread', *yö-n+musta* night's-black 'black as the night'), an adjective in the genitive in the first position modifies the second element in some other way (e.g., *helaka-n+punainen* 'bright red', *puhta-an+valkoinen* 'clean white').

The methods used in languages for special purposes to form adjectival compounds are characteristic of this category. For example, the compounds of plant names reflect the conceptual system by the method in which the name of a subordinate concept is formed using the first part of the name of a superordinate concept as the second part of the subordinate concept, such as terms describing the leaf like *pari+leht-inen* pair-leaf- ADJ 'feathered, pinnated' → *tasa+par-inen* 'paripinnate', *tois+par-inen* 'bipinnate'; *saha+laita-inen* saw-margin-ADJ 'serrated'

→ *tois+saha-inen* 'biserrate', *vasto+saha-inen* 'reversed serrate'. They are free loan translations from Latin or Greek terms; therefore, for instance, terms with *pari-* 'bi-' or *vasto-* 'retro-' are basically referred to as neoclassical compounds (Pitkänen 2008: 267; Pitkänen-Heikkilä 2013).

In addition, compounds that have a participle form as the second part can be used as adjectives. They typically have a first element that could be an object or a subject in the corresponding verb phrase (e.g., *asian+tunte-va* fact-know-PARTICIPLE 'expert, well-informed', *madon+syö-mä* 'worm-eaten'). Adjectival compounds can also be coordinative (*sini+valkoinen* 'blue and white'); *bahuvrīhi* compounds have an adjectival usage as well (e.g., *keltanokka matkalainen*, composed of *kelta+nokka* yellow-beak 'newcomer, tenderfoot' and *matkalainen* 'wayfarer').

3.3 Verbal compounds

Verbal compounds contain a verb as the second element and they make use of the complete inflectional paradigm of verbs. In comparison to nominal and adjectival compounds, verbal compounds are a small minority, constituting approximately 250 lexemes in dictionaries, even though that number has increased in the last decades. The first element of verbal compounds is a noun or adjective, a nominal stem, an adverb or a particle (Rahtu 1984; Hakulinen et al. 2004: 414).

Verbal compounds have been formed typically by compacting phrases (e.g., *irtisanoa* ← *sanoairti* 'to dismiss', composed of *sanoa* 'to say' and *irti* 'aweigh, loose') or by adding a prefix-like first element to the verb (*ali+arvioida* 'to underestimate', *yli+velkaantua* 'to get into debt over'). Verbs can also be derived from compounds (e.g., *valokuva-ta* 'to take photos' ← *valo+kuva* light-picture 'photo', *huutokaupa-ta* 'to auction' ← *huuto+kauppa* shout-trade 'auction', *yksinkertais-ta-a* 'to simplify' ← *yksin+kerta-inen* 'simple'), or arise as backformations (*aivopes-tä* 'to brainwash' ← *aivo+pes-u* 'brainwash', *palovakuut-ta-a* 'to take out a fire insurance' ← *palo+vakuut-us* 'fire insurance', *ilotulit-ta-a* 'to use fireworks' ← *ilo+tulit-us* 'fireworks', composed of *ilo* 'delight, pleasure' and *tulit-ta-a* 'to fire').

4 Derivation

Typical cases of derivation in Finnish involve a suffix being added to the end of a stem. Sometimes this suffix causes modifications in the stem, and moreover, the boundary between the stem and derivative is not always clear. In addition, to distinguishing derivative words from simplexes is not always easy, and analytically it is sometimes best to place the words on a continuum of derivative-like words (cf. Räisänen 1978; Hakulinen et al. 2004: 173–175). It is important to note that occasionally the end of a word can resemble a Finnish suffix even though the word is borrowed.

Descriptions of Finnish derivation have often used old derivatives that the Finns themselves do not automatically recognise to be derivatives because those words have become established as lexemes. The objective of this description is to provide examples that people can currently recognise as derivatives, in other words, derivatives that can be identified as having been formed from a certain stem.

Finnish has nearly 200 derivational types – over one hundred nominal and adjectival suffixes and about fifty verbal suffixes (Vesikansa 1977: 11). This overview can only introduce some of them. It is important to note that, due to vowel harmony, the suffixes often have two allomorphs; this is expressed in the examples by capital letters (e.g., *U* = *u* and *y*). In addition, due to morphophonological changes, the suffixes show allomorphic variation (e.g., *-inen* : *-ise-*, *-in* : *-ime-*, *-itse* : *-it-*).

A suffix can change the lexical category of a stem word (e.g., *laula-a* 'to sing' → *laul-u* 'song') or can modify the meaning of the stem within a lexical category (*laula-a* → *laul-el-la* 'to sing continually'). Finnish derivation can be described through various derivational types that are classified according to their typical word classes and stem words. It is, however, common, for the same suffixes to also be added to stems of various word classes (e.g., *-iO: kasv-io* 'flora' ← *kasvi* 'plant', *kylm-iö* 'cold room' ← *kylmä* 'cold', *ol-io* 'creature' ← *olla* 'to be') or to form new derivatives in several word classes (e.g., *-kAs: asia-kas* 'customer' ← *asia* 'thing', *viikse-käs* 'moustached' ← *viikset* 'moustache'). The same stem can also be followed by many different suffixes (e.g., *syö-jä-tär* 'man-eater' ← *syö-jä* 'eater' ← *syö-dä* 'to eat'; *asu-nto-la* 'dorm' ← *asu-nto* 'apartment' ← *asu-a* 'to live'; *tutu-stu-tta-a* 'to familiarise' ← *tutu-stu-a* 'to familiarise oneself with' ← *tuttu* 'familiar').

4.1 Nominal derivation

4.1.1 Denominal nouns

Denominal nouns in Finnish have many derivational types for p e r s o n a l n o u n s, such as the derivatives with the suffixes *-lAinen*, *-skA*, *-tAr* or *-(U)ri*. The very productive suffix *-lAinen* expresses that someone belongs to a group (e.g., *suku-lainen* 'relative' ← *suku* 'family', *kansa-lainen* 'citizen' ← *kansa* 'people'), a place (*kaupunki-lainen* 'townsman, town resident' ← *kaupunki* 'town, city', *helsinki-läinen* 'person from Helsinki'), a nation (*suoma-lainen* 'Finn') or is the adherent of an ideology (*marxi-lainen* 'Marxist'). In addition, the suffix *-(U)ri*, which takes bases of all major lexical categories, can also form denominal agent nouns (e.g., *part-uri* 'barber' ← *parta* 'beard', *mets-uri* 'lumberman' ← *metsä* 'forest').

The suffix *-skA* borrowed from Swedish and the indigenous *-tAr* form both feminine counterparts to masculine nouns (e.g., *professor-ska* 'wife of professor', *Virta-ska* 'wife of Virtanen'; *laulaja-tar* 'songstress' ← *laulaja* 'singer', *ystävä-tär* 'female friend' ← *ystävä* 'friend'); however, both of these are currently rare.

Another major group of derivational types is constituted by place nouns, for instance, the nouns with suffix *-iO, -lA, -Us(tA)* (: *Ukse*), *-nkO* or *-nne*. Place nouns with the suffix *-iO* are, e.g., *kahv-io* 'cafeteria' (← *kahvi* 'coffee') and *minister-iö* 'ministry'; this suffix can also be added to an adjectival or verbal stem (e.g., *tyhj-iö* 'vacuum' ← *tyhjä* 'empty'; *keitt-iö* 'kitchen' ← *keittää* 'to cook', *luk-io* 'upper secondary school' ← *lukea* 'to read'). The *lA*-derivatives typically indicate a building where people or animals live (e.g., *mummo-la* 'grandmother's place' ← *mummo* 'grandmother', *pappi-la* 'manse' ← *pappi* 'priest'; *kana-la* 'henhouse' ← *kana* 'hen', *sika-la* 'piggery' ← *sika* 'pig'); this derivative type also includes surnames (*Heikki-lä* ← *Heikki*). In addition, the suffixes *-Us* or *-UstA* express "relative" places such as *jal-usta* 'base, podium, a part on which foot rests' (← *jalka* 'foot') and *sein-us* (or *sein-usta*) 'region near the wall' (← *seinä* 'wall'). The suffixes *-nkO* and *-nne* are more uncommon, e.g., *ala-nko* 'lowland' (← *ala-* 'under, lower'), *jyrkä-nne* 'bank, cliff' (← *jyrkkä* 'abrupt').

The third group of denominal nouns consists of collective nouns such as those with the suffix *-(i)kkO, -(i)stO* or *-Ue* (e.g., *hylly-kkö* 'shelves' ← *hylly* 'shelf', *linnu-sto* 'birdlife' ← *lintu* 'bird', *pesue* 'brood' ← *pesä* 'nest'). Many of these derivatives can at the same time refer to a collective and a natural location (e.g., *kiv-ikko* 'rocky ground' ← *kivi* 'boulder, stone', *pensa-ikko* 'shrubbery' ← *pensas* 'shrub', *koiv-ikko* 'birch forest' ← *koivu* 'birch', *kuus-isto* 'spruce copse' ← *kuusi* 'spruce', *saar-isto* 'archipelago' ← *saari* 'island').

The most productive diminutive suffix in Finnish is *-nen* (e.g., *kirja-nen* 'booklet', *lintu-nen* 'little bird', *tyttö-nen* 'little girl'); this is also the second element of many affective suffix combinations (e.g., *-Onen, -kAinen, -kkOnen, -rAinen*: *lapso-nen* ← *lapsi* 'child', *lapsu-kainen* ← *lapsi* 'child', *miekko-nen* ← *mies* 'man', *pappa-rainen* ← *pappa* 'old man, grandfather'). Furthermore, the diminutive suffix *-kkA* often occurs in combined suffixes (e.g., *-UkkA*: *lehdykkä* 'leaflet' ← *lehti* 'leaf').

4.1.2 Deadjectival nouns

Deadjectival nouns can be formed, for example, with the suffixes -e^x, -(U)ri and -(U)Us. (The ^{x} after the -e means that the suffix produces gemination or lengthening of the first phoneme of the next word for historical reasons.) -e^x is not productive but it has typically been used when consciously forming novel words, e.g., *kuume* 'fever' (← *kuuma* 'hot'), *hyve* 'virtue' (← *hyvä* 'good'), *muste* 'toner, ink' (← *musta* 'black'). It was especially popular in the 19th century and also with verbal stems. Personal nouns with *-Uri* are typically denominal; deadjectival formations are rare and often have a pejorative meaning (e.g., *julm-uri* 'brute' ← *julma* 'cruel', *laisk-uri* 'idler' ← *laiska* 'lazy', *tyhm-yri* 'fool' ← *tyhmä* 'dull'); similar to these are the nouns formed with the suffix *-Us*, such as *kömpel-ys* 'clumsy lout' (← *kömpelö* 'clumsy') or *typer-ys* 'idiot' (← *typerä* 'silly'), however cf. *vanhus* 'senior' ← *vanha* 'old'). The highly productive suffix *-(U)Us* creates quality nouns, for example, *rikka-us* 'richness' (← *rikas* 'rich'), *vaike-us* 'arduousness, difficulty' (← *vaikea* 'difficult'), *nuor-uus* 'youngness, youth' (← *nuori* 'young') and *suomalais-uus* 'Finnishness' (← *suomalainen* 'Finnish, Finn'). It is a suffix that can, in principle, produce quality nouns from any adjective, and even from some nouns (e.g., *äiti-ys* 'motherhood' ← *äiti* 'mother'). In certain special languages, however, it seems to be impossible for semantic reasons to derive quality nouns from absolute adjectives (Pitkänen-Heikkilä 2015).

4.1.3 Deverbal nouns

The semantic types of deverbal nouns include nouns denoting action, result of action, actor, instrument and place. Action and result nouns can be formed using the suffixes -e^x, -mA, -minen, -mUs, -nA, -ntA, -nti, -ntO, -O, -Os, -U, -Us and -UU.

Action nouns can be formed by adding the highly productive suffixes *-minen* (e.g., *luke-minen* 'reading', *teke-minen* 'doing', *ajattele-minen* 'thinking') and *-nti* (e.g., *tupakoi-nti* 'smoking', *pysäköi-nti* 'parking'). In addition, the descriptive verbs with *-istA* can become action nouns with *-nA* (e.g., *heli-nä* ← *hel-istä* 'to jingle', *suhi-na* ← *suh-ista* 'to whiz').

Action nouns and sometimes result nouns can also be created by adding the following suffixes: *-O* (e.g., *tul-o* 'coming, arrival' ← *tulla* 'to come', *läht-ö* 'leaving, departure' ← *lähteä* 'to leave', *lep-o* 'rest' ← *levätä* 'to sleep, rest', *luettel-o* 'list, directory' ← *luetella* 'to enumerate', *kielt-o* 'proscription' ← *kieltää* 'to forbid, deny') and *-U* (e.g., *ajattelu* 'thinking' ← *ajatella* 'to think', *kättel-y* 'shaking hands' ← *kätellä* 'to shake hands', *juoksu* 'run, running' ← *juosta* 'to run'). The suffix *-O* has also been used to form the lexicalised names of the senses: *kuul-o* 'hearing' (← *kuulla* 'to hear') and *tunt-o* 'sense of touch' (← *tuntea* 'to touch, feel').

Both action and result nouns are formed by the suffixes *-mA* (e.g., *elä-mä* 'life' ← *elää* 'to live', *muistel-ma* 'memoir' ← *muist-el-la* 'to look back, commemorate' ← *muista-a* 'to remember'), *-mUs* (*aiko-mus* 'intention, plan' ← *aiko-a* 'to be going to', *kysy-mys* 'question' ← *kysy-ä* 'to ask'), *-Us* (*metsäst-ys* 'hunting' ← *metsä-stä-ä* 'to hunt' ← *metsä* 'forest', *rakenn-us* 'building, house' ← *rakenta-a* 'to build'), *-ntA* (*uusi-nta* 'replay' ← *uusi-a* 'to replay', *kosi-nta* 'proposal of marriage' ← *kosi-a* 'to propose marriage to'), *-ntO* (*opi-nto* 'study' ← *oppi-a* 'to learn', *keksi-ntö* 'innovation' ← *keksi-ä* 'to coin, contrive, fabricate') and *-Os* (*piirr-os* 'drawing' ← *piirtä-ä* 'to draw', *te-os* 'work, opus, writing' ← *tehdä* 'to do'). In addition, result nouns are created by the suffix $-e^x$ as in *raaste* 'grated food' ← *raastaa* 'to grate') and *vihj-e* 'clue, tip' (← *vihjata* 'to suggest, allude to').

The suffix *-jAinen* (: *jAise-*) creates plural words that are names of ceremonies (for example, *ava-jaise-t* 'opening ceremony' ← *avata* 'to open', *hauta-jaise-t* 'funeral' ← *haudata* 'to bury', *myy-jäise-t* 'rummage sale' ← *myydä* 'to sell').

Deverbal agent nouns are formed by adding the suffixes *-jA* and *-(U)ri*. The suffix *-jA* names a person or an animal that acts (e.g., *kertoja* 'narrator' ← *kertoa* 'to tell', *lukija* 'reader' ← *lukea* 'to read'; *kahlaaja* 'shorebird, wading bird' ← *kahlata* 'to wade, ford'). In addition, *-jA* is typically used to form the names of professions (*opetta-ja* 'teacher', *kalasta-ja* 'fisherman'). Derivatives with the suffix *-(U)ri* are also mainly agent nouns and names of professions (e.g., *huija-ri* 'swindler' ← *huijata* 'to swindle', *leip-uri* 'baker' ← *leipoa* 'to bake').

Both agentive suffixes can also form instrument nouns (e.g., *pullonavaa-ja* 'bottle opener' ← *avata* 'to open', *mitta-ri* 'indicator, measure' ← *mitata* 'to measure'). The common suffix for instrument nouns, however, is *-in* (: *-ime-*) (e.g., *lask-in* 'calculator' ← *laskea* 'to calculate', *ava-in* 'key' ← *avata* 'to open', *soit-in* 'musical instrument' ← *soittaa* 'to play'). The stem is often a verbal phrase (*kahvin+keit-in* 'coffee machine' ← *keittää* 'to cook', *hiusten+kuiva-in* 'hairdryer' ← *kuivata* 'to dry').

The suffix *-mO* expresses the place where the action occurs (e.g., *kampaa-mo* 'hairdresser's' ← *kammata* 'to comb', *leipo-mo* 'bakery' ← *leipoa* 'to bake').

4.2 Adjectival derivation

Because Finnish adjectival suffixes can follow stems from various lexical categories they are not typically classified on the basis of stem words but by the suffix types. Adjectival derivatives can be categorised as possessive (the largest group), privative (or caritive, as it is called in Finno-Ugric studies) and approximative (or moderative) adjectives. Adjectival derivatives are typically denominal and the most common suffix is -(i)nen, which is often also an element of complex suffixes (-llinen, -mAinen).

The (i)nen-derivatives are typically p o s s e s s i v e, sometimes with an additional nuance of abundance (e.g., *arpi-nen* 'scarred' ← *arpi* 'scar', *lika-inen* 'dirty' ← *lika* 'dirt, smutch'). Complex suffixes are used to form possessive adjectives (*pilku-llinen* 'dotted' ← *pilkku* 'dot') but also adjectives of r e s e m b l a n c e (*äidi-llinen* 'motherly' ← *äiti* 'mother', *poika-mainen* 'boyish' ← *poika* 'boy'). Other possessive suffixes are, for example, *-liAs* and *-vA* (e.g., *avu-lias* 'caring' ← *apu* 'aid, help', *une-lias* 'sleepy' ← *uni* 'dream, sleep', *järke-vä* 'sensible' ← *järki* 'sense, sanity'), in addition *-isA*, *-kAs* and *-kkA*, that also expresses abundance (e.g., *kala-isa* 'rich in fish' ← *kala* 'fish', *ääne-käs* 'noisy' ← *ääni* 'voice', *nuore-kas* 'youthful' ← *nuori* 'young', *puna-kka* 'reddish' ← *puna* 'red color').

P r i v a t i v e adjectives are formed by adding the suffix *-tOn* to noun or adjective stems (e.g., *sana-ton* 'wordless', *pilve-tön* 'cloudless', *virhee-tön* 'flawless'; *kesy-tön* 'wild, untamed' ← *kesy* 'tame').

A p p r o x i m a t i v e adjectives can be formed by the suffixes *-hkO* and *-htAvA*. The derivatives with *-hkO* express low intensity (e.g., *suure-hko* 'fairly big', *lämpimä-hkö* 'quite warm'). Adjectives with *-htAvA* express the concept of approximation (e.g., *vanha-htava* 'archaid, dated' ← *vanha* 'old', *harma-htava* 'greyish' ← *harmaa* 'grey').

Deverbal adjectives are typically participles. The suffix *-mA* is used to form the agent participles (*rakasta-ma* ← *rakasta-a* 'to love', *laula-ma* ← *laula-a* 'to sing', for instance, *kaikki-en rakasta-ma lapsI* everybody-ACCUSATIVE love-PARTICIPLE child 'a child whom everybody loves', *minu-nlaula-ma-ni laulu* I-ACCUSATIVE sing-PARTICIPLE-POSS.S.1. song 'a song that I sing'). The suffix *-mAtOn* is used to form negative participles (*rakasta-maton* 'unloved', *kirjoitta-maton* 'unwritten', *kutsu-maton* 'uninvited', *oppi-maton* 'uneducated', *teke-mätön* 'undone'). The other suffixes used for participles are *-nUt* and *-vA* (in the active) and *-ttU* and *-ttAvA* (in the passive), for example, *onnistu-nut* 'successful' (← *onnistua* 'to manage, succeed'), *kiiltä-vä* 'shiny' (← *kiiltää* 'to shine'), *tunne-ttu* 'famous, well-known' (← *tuntea* 'to know'), and *makse-ttava* 'payable, due' (← *maksaa* 'to pay'). It is important to note that the meanings of the participles are often lexicalised as, for example, in the deverbal nouns *etsivä* 'detective' (← *etsiä* 'to look for') and *tehtävä* 'job, commission' (← *tehdä* 'to do').

Deverbal adjectives can also be created with *-einen* (*kielt-einen* 'adverse, negative' ← *kieltää* 'to forbid, deny'), *-(e)liAs* (*antelias* 'munificent, open handed' ← *antaa* 'to give', *puhelias* 'talkative' ← *puhua* 'to speak') and *-vAinen* that expresses also a p r o p e n s i t y to do something (*naura-vainen* 'laughing, ridibund' ← *nauraa* 'to laugh', *ymmärtä-väinen* 'understanding' ← *ymmärtää* 'to understand').

-vAinen-derivatives are close to *VA*-participles but express permanent or repeated features. In Finnish studies all three adjective types are also called possessive because they express a feature that somebody has – even when they have a verbal stem.

4.3 Verbal derivation

In the verbal derivation of Finnish, a certain suffix can be added to a verb stem, a noun or an adjective stem; a stem can be followed by more than one suffix. Typically, many new verb derivatives can be formed from a stem (e.g., *kuva* 'picture' → *kuvata* 'to picture', *kuvastaa* 'to mirror, reflect', *kuvittaa* 'to illustrate', *kuvailla* 'to describe', *kuvitella* 'to imagine'; *laulaa* 'to sing' → *laulella* 'to sing continually', *lauleskella* 'to sing casually', *laulahtaa* 'to utter a singing'; *ääni* 'voice' → *ääntää* 'to pronounce', *äänestää* 'to vote', *äänittää* 'to record').

The semantic groups of verb derivatives include causative (e.g., *-(i)stA-*, *-Oi-*, *-ntA-*, *-tA*, *-ttA-*), factitive (*-A-*, *-itse-*, *-OittA-*, *-ttA-*), reflexive (*-(i)stU-*, *-ittU-*, *-OitU-*, *-ntU-*, *-VntU-*, *-tU-*, *-U-*, *-UtU-*), frequentative (*-ele-*, *ile-*, *-skele-*) and momentative (*-AhtA-*, *-Aise-*) verbs. Furthermore, descriptive and onomatopoetic verbs (typically *-ise-*) constitute a unique verb type.

In the following, the typical semantic roles of certain verb types are described. While good translations of these are difficult to find, a description of the semantic roles may help in understanding them better.

4.3.1 Denominal and deadjectival verbs

Various types of denominal and deadjectival verbs are called "causatives" in the studies of verbal derivation of Finnish, for example, verbs with suffixes *-(i)stA-* and *-ntA-* that are also called factitive. The verbs with *-(i)stA-* express 'to make (like) A' (e.g., *jalo-sta-a* 'to refine, sophisticate' ← *jalo* 'fine, august, high-minded', *om-ista-a* 'to have' ← *oma* 'own') and 'to take N into possession' (e.g., *marja-sta-a* 'to collect berries' ← *marja* 'berry'). The deadjectival *ntA*-derivatives mean 'to render', 'to result in' or 'to make (more) A' (e.g., *vanhe-nta-a* 'to age, make older' ← *vanha* 'old'), denominal derivatives mean 'to result in some state or situation' (*vaara-nta-a* 'to risk' ← *vaara* 'danger, risk').

In addition, adding the suffix *-tA* to nouns and particularly to adjectives creates causative verbs. Typical stems are the nouns or adjectives that end in *-s* or the adjectival derivatives with *-inen* (e.g., instrumentative *keihäs-tä-ä* 'to spear' ← *keihäs* 'spear'; "instructive" (i.e. ornative) *panos-ta-a* 'to load' ← *panos* 'pellet, load'; factitive *kaunis-ta-a* 'to embellish' ← *kaunis* 'beautiful', *suomalais-ta-a* 'to make something or someone more Finnish' ← *suomalainen* 'Finnish' and *inhimillis-tä-ä* 'to humanise' ← *inhimillinen* 'human').

The derivatives with *-(O)ittA-* are also causative verbs such as factitive *elävöittä-ä* 'to enliven, invigorate' (← *elävä* 'alive, living') and instructive *kuki-tta-a* 'to give flowers, strew with flowers' (← *kukka* 'flower'). The suffix *-Oi-* serves to form causative verbs such as *paket-oi-da* 'to packet' (← *paketti* 'package, packet'), *numer-oi-da* 'to number' (← *numero* 'number') and *radi-oi-da* 'to broadcast, radio' (← *radio*).

The highly polysemic suffix *-A-* can be added to many types of nominal stems, as well as to loanwords and slang words. This suffix does not have a clear specific meaning; it creates verbs like instructive *aida-ta* (: *aita-a-*) 'to fence in' (← *aita* 'rail, barrier'), instrumentative *grilla-ta* (← *grilli* 'grill') and *googla-ta* (← *Google*), privative *ilma-ta* 'to release contained air' (← *ilma* 'air'), causative *kasa-ta* 'to pile, mass' (← *kasa* 'pile, mass') and directional *kuopa-ta* 'to put to hole, bury oneself' (← *kuoppa* 'hole, pit').

The verbs with *-itse-* mean 'operating with something' (e.g., instrumentative *luk-it-a* (: *luk-itse-*) 'to lock' ← *lukko* 'lock' and *lääk-it-ä* 'to medicate' ← *lääke* 'medicine') or 'making similar as N/making for A' (e.g., factitive *vang-it-a* 'to imprison' ← *vanki* 'prisoner', *vill-it-ä* 'to agitate, drive wild' ← *villi* 'wild').

Denominal and deadjectival reflexive verbs can be formed by adding the suffixes *-OitU-*, *-ne-* and *-(i)stU-*. They express the notions of beginning or change. Such i n c h o a t i v e verbs are called "translative" in Finnish linguistics, borrowing the name of the translative case that marks 'becoming something' on the noun. The *-OitU-* derivatives express a process of beginning or becoming (*aavikoitu-a* 'to desertify' ← *aavikko* 'desert, wasteland', *vakav-oitu-a* 'to become serious' ← *vakava* 'serious'), similar to the derivatives with *-ne-* (*vanhe-ta* (: *vanhe-ne-*) 'to grow old' ← *vanha* 'old', *rohje-ta* 'to dare, venture' ← *rohkea* 'courageous'). The suffix *-(i)stU-* also creates inchoative verbs (e.g., *hoik-istu-a* 'to become thinner' ← *hoikka* 'thin', *ilo-stu-a* 'to become delighted' ← *ilo* 'joy, delight'). The suffixes *-ittU*, *-VntU-* and *-UtU-* can be called reflexive verbs that create so-called "receptive" (e.g., *mets-itty-ä* 'to become covered with forest' ← *metsä* 'forest', *velka-antu-a* 'to run into debt' ← *velka* 'debt') and directional (*ranta-utu-a* 'to come/go ashore' ← *ranta* 'strand, shore') verbs.

Denominal and deadjecival frequentative verbs can be formed, for example, with the suffix *-ile-* and unproductive *-O* (e.g., *kynä-il-lä* (: *kynä-ile-*) 'to compose, write' ← *kynä* 'pen', *pyörä-il-lä* 'to cycle' ← *pyörä* 'wheel, bicycle', *ilke-il-lä* 'to be malicious again and again' ← *ilkeä* 'malicious, wicked'; *mel-o-a* 'to paddle, use a paddle' ← *mela* 'paddle', *sauv-o-a* 'to ski, use skiing sticks' ← *sauva* 'stick'; also privative *latv-o-a* 'to pollard' ← *latva* 'top', *ves-o-a* 'to prune' ← *vesa* 'shoot'). Their meanings are all close to deverbal frequentative verbs; they name repeated and continuous actions and are also called frequentative in Finnish studies (e.g., Hakulinen et al. 2004).

4.3.2 Deverbal verbs

Frequentative verbs with the suffixes *-ele-*, *-ile-* and *-skele-* denote an action that happens often and repeatedly (e.g., *huud-el-la* ← *huutaa* 'to shout', *itke-skel-lä* ← *itkeä* 'to cry', *pyörty-il-lä* ← *pyörtyä* 'to pass out'). The verbs with *-Aise-* and *-AhtA-* express momentary and punctual action, called momentative in Finno-Ugric languages (e.g., *pes-ais-ta* 'to wash quickly' ← *pestä* 'to wash', *potk-ais-ta* 'to kick one time' ← *potkia* 'to kick continuously'; *huud-ahta-a* 'to shout momentarily' ← *huutaa* 'to shout', *tork-ahta-a* 'to doze off for a while' ← *torkkua* 'to doze').

The suffixes *-ttA-* and *-UttA-* are used to form causative verbs (e.g., *herät-tä-ä* 'to awake (tr.)' ← *herätä* 'to awake (itr.)', *kasva-tta-a* 'to grow (tr.)' ← *kasvaa* 'to grow (itr.)', *lakka-utta-a* 'to stop, discontinue (tr.)' ← *lakata* 'to stop, discontinue (itr.)') or the "curative" verbs that express 'to have somebody do something' (e.g., *pese-ttä-ä* 'to have washed' ← *pestä* 'to wash', *rakenn-utta-a* 'to have sb. build sth.' ← *rakenta-a* 'to build', *syö-ttä-ä* 'to feed' ← *syödä* 'to eat', *tee-ttä-ä* 'to let sb. do sth.' ← *tehdä* 'to do').

The suffixes *-UtU-* and *-ntU-* create reflexive derivatives (e.g., *puke-utu-a* ← *pukea* 'to dress, clothe', *pese-yty-ä* ← *pestä* 'to wash', *jakaa-ntu-a* 'to divide' ← *jakaa* 'to share'). Some of these have passive (e.g., *aja-utu-a* 'to be driven' ← *ajaa* 'to drive') or anticausative meanings (*ava-utu-a* 'to open by itself' ← *avata* 'to open'; *lisää-nty-ä* 'to increase (itr.)' ← *lisätä* 'to increase (tr.)'), in the same way as derivatives with *-U-* and *-tU-* (e.g., *kaat-u-a* 'to fall down' ← *kaata-a* 'to turn over, fell', *parant-u-a* 'to heal spontaneously, get better' ← *paranta-a* 'to heal, make better', *inspiroi-tu-a* 'to be inspired' ← *inspiroi-da* 'to inspire').

4.3.3 Onomatopoetic and descriptive verbs

Words that are termed "onomatopoetic and descriptive" in Finnish linguistics (or simply "expressive", according Jarva 2003; Kulonen 2010 and Koivisto 2013: 189–198) have some kind of phonological motivation – voice imitations or other descriptions with phonemic form. They do not have a lexemic base as a root, but rather some phonological material. It is constantly possible to form more of them; the only limitations are the number of phonemes and their possibilities of combination (phonotactics). The new expressive words have often been formed by changing vowels or consonants of the stem of some existing expressive word. In Finnish this kind of word-formation is called *stem derivation* (e.g., Koivisto 2013: 322).

This kind of phonological modification not only concerns verbs, but occurs frequently with expressive verbs. When examining descriptive and onomatopoetic words, it is often difficult to determine which words are related etymologically as well as the exact nature of the derivational relationship and, as a consequence, which is the original word (Häkkinen 1990: 113). According to Hakulinen (1979: 260), this type of vocabulary in Finnish is "so rich and productive that it can be considered one of the most characteristic features of Finnish vocabulary".

Expressive words typically imitate some phenomenon that can be heard, seen or perceived by another mode of perception; often the phenomenon is a sound, a movement or an appearance. These kinds of words are a part of more comprehensive affected vocabulary that is used to indicate attitudes toward the issue in question (Itkonen 1966: 204; Koivisto 2013: 192–193).

Because the expressive words do not have a lexemic base, their origin and formation differ from the typical derivatives. The formation depends on analogy, certain morphological formulas and correlation. Typical are the word sets or series in which the endings of the words are identical but the beginnings show phonemic variation; this variation pertains particularly to the first syllables (Koivisto 2013: 193).

Based on phonological modification, we may distinguish the series mentioned below, all of which have very similar meanings, although the descriptive hue and typical contexts can also be very different. The examples often contain a derivative type with the suffix *-ise-* (or momentative *-AhtA-*) and they can be nominalised by the suffix *-nA* (e.g., *liristä* (: *lirise-*) 'to purl' → *liri-nä*, *kahista* (: *kahise-*) 'to rustle' → *kahi-na*). Since translating this kind of verb can be difficult, the examples below have only very general translations:

a) Verbs describing 'smudging': *tahri-a – tuhri-a – töhri-ä*;
b) Verbs describing the sound of water (e.g., 'to purl', 'to gurgle'): *liri-stä – lori-sta – loti-sta – läti-stä – liti-stä*;
c) Verbs describing other types of voices, e.g., 'to hum', 'to drone' or 'to whoosh': *humi-sta – hymi-stä – hyri-stä – huri-sta*; *kahista – kohi-sta* 'to rush' – *kopi-sta – kori-sta – koli-sta* 'to clack' – *kilistä – kalista*; *piri-stä* (e.g., like a telephone) – *päri-stä* (e.g., like an alarm clock) – *pöri-stä* (e.g., like an insect).

4.4 Adverbial derivation

Finnish does not have as many adverbial suffixes as verbal, nominal or adjectival ones. There are only about ten derivational types, and most of them are unproductive. The most productive suffixes are *-sti* and *-(i)ttAin*. Finnish adverbial derivatives usually express manner, but they also often express amount, time or position.

The suffix *-sti* forms adverbs expressing manner, amount and intensity. The most common use of this suffix is its addition to the adjective stem, e.g., *kaunii-sti* 'beautifully', *selvä-sti* 'clearly'. The derivatives with *-sti* can be formed basically from all adjectives, the derivation is limited only because not all adjectives express manner or amount (e.g., adjectives that express color, age, shape or size). The derivatives are primarily formed from adjectives that are descriptive and categorising (e.g., *tyylikkää-sti* 'stylishly', *epätoivoise-sti* 'desperately'). Somewhat similar are also denominal derivatives with *-sti* (e.g., *kiiree-sti* 'hastily' ← *kiire* 'haste', *leiki-sti* 'not seriously' ← *leikki* 'play, children's activity') and derivatives with numeral stems (*kolme-sti* 'three times', *tuhanne-sti* 'thousand times').

The derivatives with *-isin* express a point in time (e.g., *päiv-isin* 'in the daytime' ← *päivä* 'day', *perjanta-isin* 'on Fridays' ← *perjantai* 'Friday'), origin (e.g., *synty-isin* 'by birth' ← *syntyä* 'to be born', *koto-isin* 'coming from, originating from' ← *koti* 'home') or manner (e.g., *kolm-isin* 'between three' ← *kolme* 'three', *väk-isin* 'by force' ← *väki* 'force, power', *jalka-isin* 'by foot' ← *jalka* 'foot'). This suffix is typically added to nouns.

The derivatives with the suffixes *-(i)kkAin*, *-(i)tUsten* and *-(i)tUksin* express the symmetrical location, position or state of an object. The nominal stem expresses the part of the body that is symmetric with the location or position of the object. These suffixes are not different in meaning and the derivatives are also synonymous with the *-ttAin*-derivatives: *selä-kkäin* = *selä-tysten* = *selä-tyksin* = *seli-ttäin* 'back to back' ← *selkä* 'back'; *rinna-kkain* = *rinna-tusten* = *rinna-tuksin* 'abreast' ← *rinta* 'breast'; *syli-kkäin* = *syli-tysten* = *syli-tyksin* ← *syli* 'lap'.

The suffix *-lti* can be added to adjectives, forming adverbials expressing manner and amount (e.g., *ohue-lti* 'thinly' ← *ohut* 'thin', *pitkä-lti* 'mainly' ← *pitkä* 'long') that are very similar to the derivatives with *-sti*.

Derivatives with *-itse-* express the way, route, instrument, method or manner of an action (e.g., *maante-itse* 'by road', *post-itse* 'by mail', *mer-itse* 'by sea', *puhelim-itse* 'by phone').

The suffix *-ttAin* can be added to the nominal stem with a distributive meaning (e.g., *aluei-ttain* 'from region to region' ← *alue* 'region', *päivi-ttäin* 'daily' ← *päivä* 'day'). This derivational type can also express a large amount if the stem is a numeral or a word that refers to a measure or a group (e.g., *kymmeni-ttäin* 'dozens' ← *kymmenen* 'ten', *sadoi-ttain* 'hundreds' ← *sata* 'hundred', *joukoi-ttain* 'en masse' ← *joukko* 'group, crowd', *metrei-ttäin* ← *metri* 'meter').

5 Conversion

Conversion is a very marginal phenomenon in Finnish and it typically occurs between nouns (or adjectives) and verbs, when the verb is primary and the noun motivated by it. Some stems occur both as nouns (or adjectives) and as verbs (e.g., *sula* adj. 'molten', *sula* noun 'smelt', *sula-a* 'to melt', *tahto* 'will, volition', *tahto-a* 'to will'). However, this type of phenomenon is a historical relic and no longer a productive process.

6 Backformation, blending and clipping

Backformation is based on the analogy with existing derivational relations. For example, the verbs *liimata* 'to glue' (← *liima* 'glue') and *naulata* 'to nail' (← *naula* 'nail') have been formed as a result of normal suffixation but through their influence, other nouns have been backformed, such as *tarra* 'decal, sticker' (← *tarrata* 'to grab') as well as *rieha* 'happening' (← *riehua* 'to rage') and *jytä* (colloquial 'rock music' ← *jytistä* 'to rumble'). Today, new backformations are formed on the basis of deverbal noun compounds, yielding new verbs such as *pakkolunastaa* 'to expropriate' (← *pakko+lunastus* 'expropriation', from *pakko* 'necessity, compulsory' and *lunastus* 'reclaim') and *suruliputtaa* (← *suru+liputus* 'flag at half-mast', from *suru* 'sorrow' and *liputus* 'flagging').

The source words of blends are typically synonymous or have close meanings (e.g., *viinakset* 'alcohol' + *juomat* 'drink' → *juomakset*). Other old Finnish blends are possibly *hempeä* (*hellä* 'tender' + *lempeä* 'lenient') and *vaisto* 'intuition' (*vainu* 'scent' + *aisti* 'sense'), whereas the new blends are typically playful and can be used consciously, for example, in literature (Häkkinen 1990: 121; Hakulinen et al. 2004: 191). According to Häkkinen (2003: 41), blends have also currently been used as a normal word-formation process, for instance, for creating new animal names; for example, the earlier bird name *maanärhi* (*maa* 'earth', *närhi* 'jaybird') has been changed to *marhi* because the bird is not actually a jaybird but belongs to another bird family.

Clippings can be created, for instance, by removing a part from an original word (e.g., *ale* ← *alennus* 'discount', *ope* ← *opettaja* 'teacher'; likewise names: *Kata* ← *Katariina*), by forming acronyms with the first letters of the compound or phrases (*oy* ← *osake+yhtiö* 'joint-stock company', *tv* ← *tele+visio*) and by combining parts of compounds or phrases (e.g., *mopo* 'moped' ← *moottori+polkupyörä* ← *moottori* 'motor' + *polkupyörä* 'bicycle', *polku* 'pedaling, treading', *pyörä* 'wheel').

Finnish slang words are often formed by clipping plus suffixation. The typical suffixes are *-Ari* and *-is* (: *-ikse-*). These suffixes typically shorten the stem and cause only a stylistic modification. The *Ari*-derivatives have three syllables and the source word is typically a compound (e.g., *ost-ari* ← *ostoskeskus* 'shopping center', *tekst-ari* ← *tekstiviesti* 'text message', *syd-äri* ← *sydänkohtaus* 'heart attack'). The suffix *-is* has been borrowed from Swedish (e.g., *godis*) and it forms derivatives that have two syllables. The source words in these formations are also typically compounds (e.g., *kor-is* ← *koripallo* 'basketball', *huolt-is* ← *huoltoasema* 'service station') but they can also be simplexes and even loanwords (e.g., *mah-is* ← *mahdollisuus* 'chance', *fut-is* ← *football*).

Acknowledgements

I am very grateful to Vesa Koivisto for his comments on the manuscript.

7 References

Ahlqvist, August (1877): *Suomen kielen rakennus. Vertaavia kieliopillisia tutkimuksia.* Vol. 1: *Nominien Synty ja Taivutus. Suomalainen Runo-oppi.* Helsinki: SKS.

Bikupska, Anna Maija (2018): *Verbi verbistä: Puolan ja suomen johdetun verbileksikon merkitysrakenteen vertailua.* Helsinki: Helsingin yliopisto.

Hakulinen, Lauri (1979 [1941]): *Suomen kielen rakenne ja kehitys. Neljäs, korjattu ja lisätty painos.* 4th ed. Helsinki: Otava.

Hakulinen, Auli, Maria Vilkuna, Riitta Korhonen, Vesa Koivisto and Tarja Riitta Heinonen (2004): *Iso suomen kielioppi.* Helsinki: SKS.

Häkkinen, Kaisa (1987): Suomen kielen vanhoista ja uusista yhdysverbeistä. *Sananjalka* 29: 7–27.

Häkkinen, Kaisa (1990): *Mistä sanat tulevat. Suomalaista etymologiaa.* Helsinki: SKS.

Häkkinen, Kaisa (2003): *Linnun nimi.* Helsinki: Teos.

Häkkinen, Kaisa and Pia Björqvist (1991): Varhaisnykysuomen yhdyssanat. *Sananjalka* 33: 31–53.

Heinonen, Tarja (2001): Harmaaturkit herkkusuut – bahuvriihit sanakirjassa ja kieliopissa. *Virittäjä* 105: 625–634.

Itkonen, Erkki (1966): *Kieli ja sen tutkimus.* Porvoo: WSOY.

Jarva, Vesa (2003): *Venäläisperäisyys ja ekspressiivisyys suomen murteiden sanastossa.* Jyväskylä: Jyväskylän yliopisto.

Kangasmaa-Minn, Eeva (1977): Verbien piiloderivaatiosta. *Sananjalka* 19: 5–25.

Kangasmaa-Minn, Eeva (1982): Derivaatiokielioppia I: Verbijohdokset. *Sananjalka* 24: 43–63.

Kangasmaa-Minn, Eeva (1983): Derivaatiokielioppia II: Verbikantaiset nominijohdokset. *Sananjalka* 25: 23–42.

Kangasmaa-Minn, Eeva (1984): Derivaatiokielioppia III: Nominikantaiset nominijohdokset. *Sananjalka* 26: 81–96.

Karlsson, Fred (1983): *Suomen kielen äänne- ja muotorakenne.* Porvoo: WSOY.

Kerge, Krista (2016): Estonian. In: Peter O. Müller, Ingeborg Ohnheiser, Susan Olsen and Franz Rainer (eds.), *Word-Formation. An International Handbook of the Languages of Europe.* Vol. 5, 3228–3259. Berlin/Boston: De Gruyter Mouton.
Kim, Jaegno (2020): *Hulisemisesta hulinaksi. Onomatopoieettisuuden haalistuminen suomen fonesteemisten substantiivien valossa.* Helsinki: Helsingin yliopisto.
Koivisto, Vesa (1991): *Suomen verbikantaisten UtU-verbijohdosten semantiikkaa.* Helsinki: SKS.
Koivisto, Vesa (1995): *Itämerensuomen refleksiivit.* Helsinki: SKS.
Koivisto, Vesa (2006): Suomen sananjohdon morfofonologiaa. *Virittäjä* 110: 539–567.
Koivisto, Vesa (2008): Sananmuodostuksen elämää. In: Tiina Onikki-Rantajääskö and Mari Siiroinen (eds.), *Kieltä kohti,* 190–217. Helsinki: Otava.
Koivisto, Vesa (2013): *Suomen sanojen rakenne.* Helsinki: SKS.
Koski, Mauno (1978): Suomen sananjohdon perustyypit. In: *Papers from the Conference on General Linguistics,* 103–117. Turku: SKY.
Koski, Mauno (1979): Nykysuomen *(i)kkO-*johdosten semantiikkaa. In: Jussi Kallio (ed.), *Sanomia. Juhlakirja Eeva Kangasmaa-Minnin 60-vuotispäiväksi 14. 4. 1979,* 214–247. Turku: Turun yliopisto.
Koski, Mauno (1981): Mitä leksikaalistuminen on? In: *Sananmuodostuksen ongelmia,* 5–27. Turku: SKY.
Koski, Mauno (1982): *Suomen johto-opin morfologiaa.* Turku: Åbo Akademi, suomen kielen laitos.
Kulonen, Ulla-Maija (2010): *Fonesteemit ja sananmuodostus. Suomen kontinuatiivisten U-verbijohdosten historiaa.* Helsinki: SKS.
Kulonen-Korhonen, Ulla-Maija (1985): Deverbaalisten *U-*verbijohdosten semantiikkaa. *Virittäjä* 89: 290–309.
Kytömäki, Leena (1989): Teettoverbit: Johdon ja taivutuksen välimaastoa. *Sananjalka* 31: 61–79.
Kytömäki, Leena (1990): Nominikantaisten verbijohdosten rakennemalleja. *Sananjalka* 32: 49–73.
Kytömäki, Leena (1992): *Suomen verbiderivaation kuvaaminen 1600-luvulta nykypäiviin.* Turku: Turun yliopisto.
Kytömäki, Leena (1993): Verbijohdosten typologia, sanakirjamerkitys ja käyttö. In: Sirkka Saarinen, Jorma Luutonen and Eeva Herrala (eds.), *Systeemi ja poikkeama. Juhlakirja Alho Alhoniemen 60-vuotispäiväksi 14. 5. 1993,* 259–271. Turku: Turun yliopisto.
Laakso, Johanna (1990): *Transitiivinen verbinjohdin NE itämerensuomalaisissa kielissä.* Helsinki: SUS.
Laakso, Johanna (2000): Development tendencies in Finnic derivation systems. In: M. M. Jocelyne Fernandez-Vest (ed.), *Grammaticalisation aréale et sémantique cognitive. Les langues fenniques et sames. Actes du Colloque International du C.N.R.S. tenu les 9 et 10 avril 1999 en Sorbonne,* 105–118. Eesti Keele Sihtasutus = Fondation de la Langue Estonienne.
Laakso, Johanna (2005): Johdon ja taivutuksen diakronisista suhteista. In: Johanna Vaattovaara, Toni Suutari, Hanna Lappalainen and Riho Grünthal (eds.), *Muuttuva muoto. Kirjoituksia Tapani Lehtisen 60-vuotispäivän kunniaksi,* 93–109. Helsinki: Helsingin yliopiston suomen kielen laitos.
Laaksonen, Kaino (1984): Yhdyssanavirheet kuriin! *Virittäjä* 88: 509–517.
Laine, Päivi (2007): *Suomi tiellä sivistyskieleksi. Suomenkielisen maantieteen sanaston kehittyminen ja kehittäminen 1800-luvulla.* Turku: Turun yliopisto.
Länsimäki, Maija (1987): *Suomen verbikantaiset in:ime -johdokset.* Helsinki: SKS.
Länsimäki, Maija (1988): Mallien osuudesta sanojen johtamisessa. *Virittäjä* 92: 230–237.
Lehtinen, Tapani (1976): Synkronisia ja diakronisia näkökohtia johto-opillisesta produktiiviudesta. In: Raija Lehtinen, Tapani Lehtinen, Pirkko Nuolijärvi and Heikki Paunonen (eds.), *Kielitieteellisiä lehtiä: Kotikielen Seuran sadannen toimintavuoden täyttyessä,* 88–97. Helsinki: SKS.
Lehtinen, Tapani (1979): *Itämerensuomen verbien historiallista johto-oppia. Suomen avajaa, karkajaa -tyyppiset verbit ja niiden vastineet lähisukukielissä.* Helsinki: SUS.

Lehtinen, Tapani (1993): Korrelaatio sananmuodostustekijänä: Suomen *aise-, äise*-loppuisten verbien derivaatio- ja merkityshistoriaa. *Virittäjä* 97: 171–186.
Lepäsmaa, Anna-Liisa, Anneli Lieko and Leena Silfverberg (1996): *Miten sanoja johdetaan. Suomen kielen johto-oppia*. Helsinki: Finn Lectura.
Malmivaara, Terhi (2004): Luupää, puupää, puusilmä: Näkymiä sananmuodostuksen analogisuuteen ja bahuvriihiyhdyssanojen olemukseen. *Virittäjä* 108: 347–363.
Mäkisalo, Jukka (2000): *Grammar and Experimental Evidence in Finnish Compounds*. Joensuu: University of Joensuu.
Nummila, Kirsi-Maria (2019): Lainasanojen vaikutus suomen kirjakielen johtomorfologiaan. Diakroninen tutkimus johdinten lainautumisesta kirjallisilla vuosisadoilla. *Virittäjä* 123: 165–193.
Pahikkala, Jussi (2020): Lounaismurteiden translatiivisia verbityyppejä. *Virittäjä* 124: 103–110.
Penttilä, Aarni (1957): *Suomen kielioppi*. Porvoo: WSOY.
Pitkänen, Kaarina (2005): "Suomen kielen suurin rikkaus ja ihanin ominaisuus". Elias Lönnrotin johto-oppia. *Virittäjä* 109: 52–82.
Pitkänen, Kaarina (2008): *Suomi kasvitieteen kieleksi. Elias Lönnrot termistön kehittäjänä*. Helsinki: SKS.
Pitkänen-Heikkilä, Kaarina (2013): Term formation in a special language: How do words specify the concepts? In: Pius ten Hacken and Claire Hopkin (eds.), *The Semantics of Word Formation and Lexicalization*, 66–82. Edinburgh: Edinburgh University Press.
Pitkänen-Heikkilä, Kaarina (2015): Adjectives as terms. *Terminology* 21(1): 76–101.
Pitkänen-Heikkilä, Kaarina (2018): Tiedesanaston suomentamista koskevat normit: Eläintaksonomisen sanaston kehittämisestä 1800-luvulla ja 2000-luvulla. *Virittäjä* 122: 523–560.
Pitkänen-Heikkilä, Kaarina (2020): Derivational networks in Finnish. In: Lívia Körtvélyessi, Alexandra Bagasheva and Pavol Štekauer (eds.), *Derivational Networks Across Languages*, 373–384. Berlin/Boston: De Gruyter Mouton.
Rahtu, Toini (1984): Suomen nominialkuiset yhdysverbit. *Virittäjä* 88: 409–430.
Rintala, Päivi (1978): Sananjohdon produktiivisuudesta ja sen rajoituksista. In: Alho Alhoniemi, Jussi Kallio, Mauno Koski, Päiva Rintala and Kalevi Wiik (eds.), *Rakenteita. Juhlakirja Osmo Ikolan 60-vuotispäiväksi 6.2.1978*, 151–164. Turku: Turun yliopisto.
Rintala, Päivi (1985): Eräät deverbaaliset substantiivityypit suomessa ja virossa. In: Hannu Remes (ed.), *Lähivertailuja*, 52–82. Turku: Turun yliopisto.
Räisänen, Alpo (1978): Kantasanan ja johdoksen suhteesta. *Virittäjä* 82: 321–344.
Räisänen, Alpo (1979): Segmentaation ongelmasta suomen kielen johto-opissa. *Virittäjä* 83: 167–178.
Räisänen, Alpo (1985): Suomen kielen *ne-* ja *ntu-, nty*-johtimiset translatiiviverbit. *Virittäjä* 89: 1–32.
Räisänen, Alpo (1986): Sananmuodostus ja konteksti. *Virittäjä* 90: 155–163.
Räisänen, Alpo (1988): *Suomen kielen u-johtimiset verbit*. Helsinki: SKS.
Saukkonen, Pauli (1973): Suomen kielen yhdyssanojen rakenne. In: *Commentationes Fenno-Ugricae in honorem Erkki Itkonen sexagenarii die XXVI mensis aprilis anno MCMLXXIII. Erkki Itkonen 60v*, 332–339. Helsinki: SUS.
Seppänen, Lauri (1981): Nominaalikompositumien semantiikkaa. In: *Sananmuodostuksen ongelmia*, 69–82. Turku: Turun yliopisto.
Setälä, E. N. (1898): *Suomen kielen oppikirja. Äänne- ja sanaoppi. Oppikouluja ja omin päin opiskelua varten*. Helsinki: Otava.
Toropainen, Tanja (2017): *Yhdyssanat ja yhdyssanamaiset rakenteet Mikael Agricolan teoksissa*. Turku: Turun yliopisto.
Tyysteri, Laura (2015): *Aamiaskahvilasta ötökkätarjontaan. Suomen kirjoitetun yleiskielen morfosyntaktisten yhdyssanarakenteiden produktiivisuus*. Turku: Turun yliopisto.
Vaittinen, Tanja (2003): Vanhan kirjasuomen yhdysverbit. *Sananjalka* 45: 45–66.

Vaittinen, Tanja (2007): Mikael Agricolan teosten yhdysadjektiivit. *Virittäjä* 111: 523–542.
Vesikansa, Jouko (1989): Yhdyssanat. In: Jouko Vesikansa (ed.), *Nykysuomen sanavarat*, 213–258. Porvoo: WSOY.
Viimaranta, Johanna (2020): Suomen veden ääniin liittyvien imitatiivien vakiintuneisuus erityyppisten aineistojen pohjalta. *Sananjalka* 62: 125–155.
Ylikoski, Jussi (2018): Prolatiivi ja instrumentaali: suomen *-(i)tse* ja *-teitse* kieliopin ja leksikon rajamailla. *Sananjalka* 60: 7–27.

Ferenc Kiefer
16 Hungarian

1 Introduction
2 General overview
3 Composition
4 Derivation
5 Conversion
6 References

Abstract: This article gives an overview of Hungarian word-formation. Hungarian has a rich inventory of word-formation devices, including compounding, suffixation, and conversion. Nominal and adjectival compounding are productive processes. Derivaton is performed by suffixation. Hungarian has a considerable number of productive derivational suffixes. Conversion of adjectives to nouns is productive. The formal and semantic characteristics of these devices will be discussed.

1 Introduction

Hungarian is an agglutinating language, which has both a rich inflectional and a rich derivational morphology. A general overview of Hungarian morphology can be found in the descriptive grammar of Kenesei, Vago and Fenyvesi (1998). Up to the eighties theoretical papers have concentrated more on individual phenomena of inflectional morphology rather than on word-formation. This is partly due to the fact that in derivational morphology – in contrast to inflectional morphology – the syntax-morphology or phonology-morphology interface does not raise particular problems. There is no comprehensive study of Hungarian word-formation in English, however, an important number of articles deal with particular problems of word-formation such as noun incorporation (Kiefer 1990–91), prefix reduplication (Kiefer 1995), or irregular morphology (Ladányi 2000). Ladányi (2000) discusses the productivity of certain derivational suffixes in considerable detail. An overview of compounding can be found in Kiefer (2009). A comprehensive and theoretically oriented grammar (Kiefer 1992–2008), written in Hungarian, was published in four volumes; the final volume is dedicated to the structure of the lexicon.

Ferenc Kiefer, Budapest, Hungary

Throughout this article the following phonological notation will be used in affixes: *A* stands for the vowels *a* and *e*, *Ó* for the vowels *ó* and *ő*, *Ú* for the vowels *ú* and *ű*, finally *V* stands for the vowels *a, o, ö, e*, where the choice is determined by vowel harmony.

2 General overview

The first comprehensive descriptive studies of word-formation in Hungarian were published in 1960 as chapters of the grammar of Hungarian (see Tompa 1961). Following tradition, this grammar did not make a clear distinction between productive and unproductive processes. Recent advances in theoretical linguistics have been incorporated into the grammar of Hungarian edited by Borbála Keszler (Keszler 2000). For the diachronic aspects of Hungarian word-formation see Forgács (2025).

The major word-formation processes in Hungarian are composition and derivation. Derivation is performed exclusively by suffixation. The language does not distinguish between particle and prefixed verbs, all complex verbs are particle verbs. The prefix *leg-* marks the superlative, but comparison does not belong to word-formation.

New words may also be productively created by means of conversion (see section 5). Productive conversion is restricted to adjectives, verbs do not participate in conversion.

Foreign words are easily accommodated to the Hungarian system. Nouns such as *internet* and *email* (or with Hungarian spelling *ímél*) have become current nouns in Hungarian, foreign verbs, however, can only be turned into Hungarian words if they are supplied with a verbal derivational suffix: e.g., *save – szév-el, format – format-t-ál, edit – edit-ál, install – install-ál*. Note that *save, format, edit, install* are not words in Hungarian, they are considered abstract nominal stems from which verbs can be derived. This is a very productive process in Hungarian.

Backformations are gaining ground in Hungarian and can be considered to be a semi-productive process in contemporary Hungarian. Some examples are given in (1):

(1) *tényfeltár* 'to disclose facts' (*tény* 'fact' + *feltár* 'to disclose')
 ← *tényfeltárás* 'disclosure of facts'
 házkutat 'to house search' (*ház* 'house' + *kutat* 'to search')
 ← *házkutatás* 'house search'
 agymos 'to brainwash' (*agy* 'brain' + *mos* 'to wash')
 ← *agymosás* 'brainwash'

Semantically, backformations come from various domains, their spread can be explained by frequency of use and salience.

Clipping, too, occurs in Hungarian but normally the reduced stem receives a diminutive suffix: *doktor* → *dok+i*, *paradicsom* 'tomato' → *par+i*. Occasionally we may also encounter blending: *film* + *internet* → *filmternet* 'internet café in a movie theatre' but such formations are rare and do not get lexicalized.

3 Composition

3.1 Productive patterns

Compounding is a very productive process in Hungarian (cf. Kiefer 2009). The vast majority of productive compounds are endocentric and right-headed. The head belongs to one of the categories N, V, A, the non-head is either N or A. V occurs as head in backformations only. This reduces the number of genuine compounds to four patterns. Words are concatenated without any morphological marking. Nominal compounds are recursive and all compounds have a binary structure. Adverbs, pronouns and postpositions occur in unproductive, lexicalized compounds only. Examples for productive compounds are given in (2).

(2) a. N+N
    ház+tető 'housetop, roof'
    tök+mag 'pumpkin seed'
    mondat+fajta 'sentence type'
   b. A+N
    hideg+front 'cold front'
    kis+agy 'little/hinder brain'
    orgona+karzat 'organ-loft'
   c. N+A
    kő+kemény 'stone-hard'
    méreg+drága poison expensive 'terribly expensive'
    euro+kompatibilis euro compatible 'compatible with the Euro'
   d. A+A
    sötét+zöld 'dark green'
    bal+liberális 'left liberal'
    rövid+látó 'shortsighted'

The vast majority of compounds belong to the N+N type, A+A compounds with a non-derived head are rather rare. The binary structure (indicated by hyphens) and the recursivity of N+N compounds is exemplified in (3).

(3) *vér+nyomás* 'blood-pressure'
vér+nyomás+mérő 'blood-pressure measure'
vér+nyomás+mérő+készülék 'blood-pressure measuring-apparatus'
vér+nyomás+mérő+készülék+gyártó 'blood-pressure measuring-apparatus producer'
vér+nyomás+mérő+készülék+gyártó+cég 'blood-pressure measuring-apparatus producing firm'

Compounding in Hungarian has been influenced by German to a considerable extent. During the language reform at the beginning of the 19th century thousands of German compounds were translated word-by-word into Hungarian. The great number of loan translations enhanced considerably the productivity of already existing compounding patterns.

3.2 Synthetic compounds

Synthetic compounds contain a deverbal head which is either an action noun derived from the verbal base by means of the suffix *-Ás*, or an agent noun derived from the verbal base by means of the suffix *-Ó* (cf. Laczkó 2015). Both derivations are productive.

3.2.1 Action nouns in head position

Some examples are given in (4).

(4) *ebéd+főzés* 'dinner cooking', *könyv+írás* 'book writing', *ház+építés* 'house building', *zene+hallgatás* 'music listening', *utca+söprés* 'street cleaning', *fa+vágás* 'wood cutting'

The deverbal head in (4) is derived from transitive verbs, the deverbal noun inherits the theme argument of its base. However, as pointed out by several authors, the relationship between the head and the non-head is different from the predicate-argument structure known from syntax. Therefore, it is more adequate to call the arguments semantic arguments in the case of compounds. The following relationship holds between the head and the non-head:

(5) The non-head of a synthetic compound in which the head is derived from a transitive verb may satisfy the theme argument of the base.

Much less frequently, the head may also be derived from an intransitive verb:

(6) a. *liba+gágogás* goose gaggling 'gaggling of a goose/geese', *kutya+ugatás* dog barking 'barking of a dog/dogs', *légy+zümmögés* fly buzzling 'buzzling of a fly/flies'
b. *rózsa+nyílás* rose opening 'opening of a rose/roses', *orgona+virágzás* lilac blooming 'blooming of a lilac/lilacs', *gyümölcs+érés* fruit ripening 'ripening of fruit'

In (6a) the head is derived from verbs denoting sound emission of an animal, and in (6b) from verbs denoting phenomena of nature. The non-head in (6a) is certainly not a typical agent: a goose does not act intentionally. If we call the non-typical agent actor, the following generalization can be formulated. The non-head of a deverbal compound in which the head is derived from an intransitive verb of "emission of sounds" may be interpreted as the actor argument of the base. In the case of (6b) the non-head undergoes a certain change, it can thus be interpreted as the patient argument of the base. Note that the examples in (6b) involve unaccusative verbs, which in English do not seem to allow synthetic compounds (cf. Grimshaw 1990: 69). The examples in (6a, b) thus permit the formulation of the following generalizations.

(7) The non-head of a deverbal compound in which the head is derived from an intransitive verb may satisfy either the actor or the patient argument of the base. The choice depends on the semantics of the base: verbs denoting phenomena of nature require a patient argument, emission-of-sound verbs an actor argument.

The same non-head may be interpreted either as a patient or as a theme argument depending on whether the base is intransitive or transitive. For example, the noun *csökken+és* 'decline' is derived from the intransitive verb *csökken*; the noun *csökkent+és*, on the other hand, comes from the transitive (causative) verb *csökkent*. Hence *csökkenés* may take a patient and *csökkentés* a theme argument:

(8) a. *ár+csökkenés* price decline 'decline in prices'
b. *ár+csökkentés* price reduction 'reduction of prices'

Deverbal nouns derived from particle verbs are relatively rare in head position but there are some examples.

(9) a. *ér+el-meszesedés* artery calcification 'arteriosclerosis'
    b. *csont+át-ültetés* bone transplantation 'bone grafting'

The head in (9a) is derived from an intransitive verb, hence the non-head is interpreted as a patient argument. On the other hand, the head in (9b) is derived from a transitive verb, consequently the non-head can only be interpreted as theme argument.

3.2.2 Agent nouns in head position

The head in the compounds (see examples under (10)) is an agent noun derived from a transitive verb and the non-head may be interpreted as the theme argument of the base:

(10) *regény+író* 'novel-writer', *újság+olvasó* 'newspaper reader', *zene+kedvelő* 'music-lover'

Agent nouns derived from particle verbs can also occur in head position. We may thus get (11):

(11) *csont+át-ültető* bone transplanter 'transplanter of bones'

Many of these compounds are lexicalized entities whose head denote an occupation or an institutionalized activity. In such cases the head does not seem to have any argument structure, yet these compounds are interpreted on the basis of what constituted the input to lexicalization.

3.3 Phrasal constructs

The phrasal constructs "bare noun + verb" exhibit some features which make them similar to compounds (Kiefer 1990–91):

(12) a. *Péter levelet   ír.*
        Peter letter-ACC writes
        'Peter is writing a letter.'
     b. *Anna újságot   olvas.*
        Anna newspaper-ACC reads
        'Anna is reading a newspaper.'

The bare nouns in (12a, b) are not referential and have a generic reading exactly like the non-head in the corresponding compounds *levél-írás* 'letter writing'/ *levél+író* 'letter writer' and *újság-olvasás* 'newspaper reading'/*újság+olvasó* 'newspaper reader'. The bare noun in these constructions cannot be pluralized, nor can it be modified. The phrasal constructs in (13a, b) can no longer denote a "complex activity", i.e. 'letter-writing' or 'newspaper-reading':

(13) a. *Péter hosszú levelet   ír.*
       Peter long   letter-ACC writes
       'Peter is writing a long letter.'
   b. *Anna német   újságot   olvas.*
       Anna German newspaper-ACC read
       'Anna is reading a German newspaper.'

In addition, the complex verb must express an institutionalized activity: the phrasal constructs in (14a, b) are unacceptable:

(14) a. *Péter cédulát ír.*
       Peter slip-ACC writes
       'Peter writes a slip.'
   b. *Anna hirdetést   olvas.*
       Anna poster-ACC reads
       'Anna is reading a poster.'

However, by constructing an appropriate context which turns the activities in (14a, b) into something institutionalized, (14a, b) may become acceptable.

In sum, then, the only difference between compounds and phrasal constructs is that the former are morphological constructs and the latter are not.

3.4 Exocentric compounds

Bahuvrīhi compounds can be formed with some regularity to denote types of people just as in English and other Germanic languages: *kopasz+fej* 'bald-head', *nagy+orr* 'big-nose', *hosszú+láb* 'long-leg'. Their underlying structure is (15).

(15) [Det [Adj N-Suffix] HUMAN]$_{NP}$

The suffix *-Ú* is an argument-taking suffix: the derivatives **fej+ű* 'headed', **orr+ú* 'nosed', **láb-ú* 'legged' are ungrammatical. By adding an appropriate adjective to these derivatives we receive the grammatical expressions *kopasz+fejű* 'bald-headed', *nagy+orrú* 'big-nosed', *hosszú lábú* 'long-legged'. The exocentric compounds are arrived at by deleting the adjectival suffix.

3.5 Derivation outside composition

Compounds may undergo various derivational processes. In fact, the derivations whose input is a noun do not take into consideration the internal structure of the noun if the noun satisfies the input condition of the derivation. Thus, for example, N+N compounds can undergo diminutive formation as shown in (16). The diminutive suffix is *-(cs)kA*, the base compounds are taken from (2a).

(16) [*ház+tető*]+*cske* house roof DIM 'small house roof'
[*tök+mag*]+*ocska* pumpkin seed DIM 'small pumpkin seed'

Compounds can be the input to further derivational processes, exactly like simple words. For example, from the compound *tök+mag* 'pumpkin seed' it is possible to derive the noun *tök+mag+os* pumpkin seed NOMINAL SUFFIX 'person who sells pumpkin seeds', the adjective *tök+mag+nyi* pumpkin seed ADJECTIVAL SUFFIX 'quantity corresponding to a pumkin seed' and the verb *tök+mag+oz* pumpkin seed VERBAL SUFFIX 'to eat pumpkin seeds'. Since any verb can be nominalized by the suffix *-Ás*, we also get (17):

(17) [[[*tök+mag*]$_N$+*oz*]$_V$+*ás*]$_N$ 'eating of pumpkin seeds'

From the derived verb *tökmagoz* 'to eat pumpkin seeds', the diminutive form (18) can be derived:

(18) [[[*tök+mag*]$_N$+*oz*]$_V$ +*gat*]$_V$ 'to eat pumpkin seeds leisurly'

And again (18) can be the input to the nominalization rule which yields (19).

(19) [[[[*tök+mag*]$_N$+*oz*]$_V$+*gat*]$_V$+*ás*]$_N$]]]]

This shows already that the particular features of Hungarian word-formation show up in derivational morphology rather than in compounding.

4 Derivation

Derivation of complex words in Hungarian is possible by suffixation only. Suffixation determines the category of the output word, which can be captured by assuming a right-hand head rule for both suffixation and compounding.

4.1 Nominal derivation

Table 16.1 summarizes the productive nominal suffixes, obsolete derivational suffixes will not be discussed.

Tab. 16.1: Nominal derivation.

suffix	base category	meaning	example
-kA	noun	diminutive	tál+ka 'little bowl'
-(V)cskA	noun	diminutive	kert+ecske 'small garden'
-I	noun	hypocoristic	Fer+i (← Ferenc)
-sÁg	noun	profession/function	asztalos+ság 'joiner's trade' menedzser+ség 'manager's profession'
	adjective	abstract property	lusta+ság 'laziness'
-(V)s	noun	profession	postá+s 'postman'
-Ás	verb	action noun	tanul+ás 'learning'
-Ó	verb	agent noun	tanul+ó 'pupil'
-(s)di	noun	action noun	katoná+sdi 'playing soldiers' (← katona 'soldier', see (h) below)

a) Diminutive formation

The suffix -kA or -(V)cskA is used to derive diminutives:

(20) a. ember+ke 'little man', tányér+ka 'small plate'
   b. tej+ecske 'little milk', láb+acska 'small foot'

Diminutives can only be derived productively from nominal bases. Of the two diminutive suffixes -(V)cskA is the more productive: while (21a) are possible though unusual derivatives, the derivatives in (21b) are (apparently for phonological reasons) unacceptable.

(21) a. *ember-ecske* 'little man', *tányér-ocska* 'small plate'
    b. **tej+ke* 'little milk', **láb+ka* 'little foot'

It would seem that all monosyllabic nouns as well as all bisyllabic nouns ending in the vowel *a* or *e* (which are lengthened before suffixes and become *á* and *é*, respectively) take the suffix *-(V)cskA*. It should be noted that the number of lexicalized nouns ending in *-ka* or *-ke* is considerable: *tálka* 'small bowl', *zárka* 'cell', *padka* 'small bench', which also means that the suffix *-kA* does occur with monosyllabic nouns but the derivatives become lexicalized easily (Dressler 1989; Ladányi 2007: 160–161). This is explained by the fact that bisyllabic words are optimal morphological units because they represent a single prosodic foot.

(22) **almá+ka* 'small apple', **körté+ke* 'small pear', **kefé+ke* 'small brush'

The impossibility of (22) may be due to the fact that words ending in long *á* or *é* occur only exceptionally in Hungarian (Ladányi 2007: 161).

If no morphophonological constraints intervene doublets may occur:

(23) *asztal+ka/asztal-ocska* 'small table', *bárány+ka/bárány+ocska* 'small lamb', *gödör+ke/gödr+öcske* 'little hole', *levél+ke/level+ecske* 'small leaf'

As in many other languages, the diminutive suffix often carries a pragmatic meaning.

b) Hypocoristic formation

The suffix *-i* is the most common suffix used to derive hypocoristics:

(24) *Ferenc* → *Fer+i*, *Antal* → *Ant+i*, *Krisztina* → *Kriszt+i*, *Erzsébet* → *Erzs+i*

As can be seen, the suffix *-i* is attached to the truncated stem which is identical to the maximal first syllable of the full name: *Fer, Ant, Krisz, Erzs*.

Since Hungarian morphology is basically word-based, the formation of hypocoristics belongs to irregular morphology.

c) The derivation of abstract nouns from adjectives

Monomorphemic adjectives can take the suffix *-sÁg* to derive abstract nouns: *fekete+ség* 'blackness' from *fekete* 'black', *magas+ság* 'height' from *magas* 'high', *lusta+ság* 'laziness' from *lusta* 'lazy', *szép+ség* 'beauty' from *szép* 'beautiful'. The suffix *-sÁg* combines often with abstract adjectives derived from nouns (*figyelem* 'attention' → *figyelm+es* 'attentive' → *figyelmes+ség* 'attentiveness', *akarat* 'will' → *akaratos* 'wilful' → *akaratos+ság* 'wilfulness') and with adjectives containing the privative suffix (*pénz* 'money' → *pénz+telen* 'penniless' → *pénztelen+ség* 'impecuniosity') to yield abstract nouns. It also occurs with names of profession of foreign origin: *bróker+ség* 'brokerage'.

d) The derivation of abstract nouns denoting trades
The suffix *-sÁg* is also used to derive abstract nouns from nouns denoting an occupation or professions: *asztalos* 'joiner' → *asztalo+ság* 'joiner's trade', *menedzser* 'manager' → *menedzser+ség* 'manager's profession'.

e) The derivation of nouns of profession
The suffix *-(V)s* is primarily used to derive names of profession from concrete nouns: *asztal* 'table' → *asztal+os* 'joiner', *kárpit* 'upholstery' → *kárpit+os* 'upholsterer'. In fact, it can also be argued that the suffix *-(V)s* is used to derive adjectives in the first place, and the nouns are the result of conversion. This can be seen clearly in the case of neologisms: *szoftver+es cég* 'software firm', *hardver+es cég* 'hardware firm'. From these adjectives we can derive the names of profession *szoftver+es* 'person who specializes in software' and analogously *hardver+es* 'person specializing in hardware' (cf. section 5 on conversion).

f) The derivation of action nouns
Actions nouns are derived by means of the suffix *-Ás*: *tanul* 'to learn, study' → *tanul+ás* 'learning, studying', *főz* 'to cook' → *főz+és* 'cooking' (cf. Laczkó 2000). Action nouns may denote a simple event, a complex event or the result of the activity. Nouns derived from particle verbs have normally a complex event reading but – depending on the semantics of the verb – they may also have a simple event and a result reading. Cf. *alá+ír* 'to sign' (German *unter+schreiben*) → *alá+ír+ás* 'signing, signature'.

(25) a. *Péter aláírása olvashatatlan volt.*
      Peter signing illegible was
      'Peter's signature was illegible.'
   b. *Aláírás közben ne zavarj!*
      signing during NEG disturb
      'Don't disturb me during signing!'

c. *A   levélnek   Péter által történő   aláírása nagy esemény volt.*
   DET letter-DAT Peter by   happening signing great event   was
   'The signing of the letter by Peter was a great event.'

Examples (25a, b, c) demonstrate that the same form, i.e. *aláírás* 'signing' may be used to denote a result, a simple event and a complex event.

At the same time such action nouns as *megérkez+és* 'arrival', *megír+ás* 'writing up', *elérés* 'reaching' have only a complex event reading.

g) The derivation of agent and instrument nouns as well as nouns denoting a typical location or a simple event

The suffix *-ó* is used to derive nouns from verbs with the following meanings: a) agent nouns such as *tanít+ó* 'teacher', *szerel+ő* 'fitter, mounter'; b) instrument nouns such as *ás+ó* 'spade' from *ás* 'to dig', *vés+ő* 'chisel'; c) typical location of an activity such as *olvas+ó* 'reading room', *vár+ó* 'waiting room'; d) simple events such as *esküv+ő* 'wedding' from *esküszik* 'to wed, marry', *válogat+ó* 'selection match' from *válogat* 'to select'. The derivation of simple event nouns is not productive and the nouns in c) are the shortened forms of the compounds *olvasó+terem, váró+terem*, where *terem* stands for 'room'.

The primary meaning of agent nouns is 'occasional performer of the activity' and we get a name of profession if this activity gets institutionalized: an occasional teacher becomes then 'teacher as profession, an occupation'.

Since the suffix *-ó* is identical to the present participle suffix it is also possible to interpret the agent nouns as a result of adjective-to-noun conversion.

h) The suffix *-(s)di*

The suffix *-(s)di* is an old derivational suffix which has been reactivated recently and gives rise to a number of derivatives (Ladányi 2007: 142–153). This derivational suffix occurs with certain nominal and verbal bases. For example,

(26) *képviselő+sdi* deputy + *-sdi* 'being a deputy'

The suffix *-(s)di* adds a playful touch to the activity at hand, in (26) it concerns the activity of being a deputy.

The base may also be a verb:

(27) a. *aláír+ós+di* 'playing the signing of papers'
     b. *befektet+ős+di* 'playing investing things'

The meaning of the derivatives in (27) can be derived compositionally, though the segmentation is not without problems. The suffix *-(V)s* means that the activity denoted by the verbal base (which in itself, too, may be morphologically complex) is typical of someone, e.g., *aláír+ós* 'to sign' + typical property can be said of someone who signs things without any reflection. The suffix *-di* adds a playful touch to that meaning. The situation is similar in the case of (27b): the verb *befektet* means 'to invest' and *befektet+ős* is someone whose typical property is investing, and again the suffix *-di* adds to that a playful character.

In addition to the suffixes enumerated in Table 16.1, Hungarian has some derivational suffixes of foreign origin which are summarized in Table 16.2:

Tab. 16.2: Nominal derivational suffixes of foreign origin.

suffix	base category	meaning	example
-itás	A	abstract noun	*intim+itás* 'intimacy'
-ista	N	follower of N	*peresztrojk+ista* 'adherent to perestroyka'
		practitioner of N	*novell+ista* 'writer of short stories'
		member of N	*kollég+ista* 'member of a college'
-izmus	N/A	ideology	*kádár+izmus* 'kadarism', *modern+izmus* 'modernism'

The suffix *-itás* occurs only with foreign bases, which is a reliable sign of its restricted productivity. The other two foreign suffixes are productive in Hungarian. The suffix *-ista* can be attached to proper names that represent a political, philosophical trend (*hitler+ista* 'adherent to the nazi ideology'), to nouns denoting a community, a school (*frad+ista* 'fan of the soccer club FRADI'), field of expertise (*algebr+ista* 'specialist of algebra'), etc. The base can also be an adjective: *modern → modernista* 'adherent to modernism'. The suffix *-izmus* can be attached to proper names or nouns with which some kind of trend can be associated such as in the case of *kádár+izmus* 'kadarism'.

4.2 Adjectival derivation

The productive adjectival derivational suffixes are summarized in Table 16.3.

Tab. 16.3: Adjectival derivation.

suffix	base category	meaning	example
-i	N	pertaining to N	művészet+i 'pertaining to art'
-beli	N	pertaining to N	intézet+beli 'of the institute'
-(V)s	N	covered with N	kavics+os 'covered with gravel'
-tAlAn	N/V	lacking N	felhő+tlen 'cloudless'
		unVed	mos+atlan 'unwashed'
-nyi	N	amount of N	tenyér+nyi 'handful'
-(j)Ú	N	having N	(hosszú) haj+ú '(long-)haired'
-Ós	V	sensitive to V	fáz+ós 'susceptible to cold'
-Ó	V	be Ving	megdöbbent+ő 'shocking'
-hAtÓ	V	be Vable	olvas+ható 'readable'

a) The adjectival suffixes -i and -beli

The suffix -i can be attached to a wide variety of nouns, which can be, among other things, names of professions (*orvos* 'medical doctor' → *orvos+i* 'medical'), names of functions (*elnök* 'president' → *elnök+i* 'presidential'), institutions (*akadémia* 'academy' → *akadémia+i* 'academic'), place name (*Budapest* → *budapest+i* 'of/from Budapest'), an artistic or scientific field (*nyelvészet* 'linguistics' → *nyelvészet+i* 'linguistic', *festészet* 'painting' → *festészet+i* 'painting (adj.)'), proper names (*Roosevelt* → *Roosevelt+i* (*politika*) 'Roosevelt's (politics)'). Excluded as bases are mass nouns (**arany+i* 'golden'), names of animals and plants (**macska+i* 'feline', **rózsa+i* 'of roses'). The suffix -beli has a related meaning and can be attached to nouns which have similar meanings to the ones enumerated in connection with the suffix -i. In the case of names of institutions both suffixes can be used: *intézet+i* and *intézet+beli* (e.g., a problem which came up in an institut or institution can be referred to as either *intézet+i probléma* or *intézet+beli probléma*).

b) The adjectival suffix -(V)s

Similarly to the suffix -*i* the suffix -*(V)s*, too, has a wide variety of uses. The base noun may denote names of objects, plants or animals. In that case the derivative means: 'supplied/equipped with N', e.g., *cukor* 'sugar' → *cukr+os* 'containing sugar, supplied with sugar'. But the base noun can also denote an institution or an organisation such as *iskola* 'school' → *iskolá+s* 'of school'.

c) The privative suffix -(V)tAlAn

The privative suffix corresponds to English -*less* in the case of nominal bases and to the English prefix *un-* in the case of verbal bases. The derivative *felhő+tlen* 'cloudless' is the antonym of *felhő+s* 'cloudy'. In the case of verbal bases the following particular feature of Hungarian should be noted. The base for the derivation is the verbal stem, semantically, however, the derivative makes reference to the corresponding participle. E.g., the derivative *mos+atlan* 'unwashed' is not the antonym of *mos* 'to wash', which is the base of the derivative, but of the participial form *mos+ott* 'washed'. The derivation of privatives is largely determined by their part-whole relation whereas negative derivatives can be formed from any transitive verbal base.

d) The suffix -nyi

The suffix -*nyi* can be attached to any noun whose denotatum can be used as a measure, e.g., *ujj+nyi* 'inch long/thick/broad', *láb+nyi* 'one foot long', *öklöm+nyi* 'as big as my fist', *ház+nyi* 'as big as a house', etc.

e) The suffix -Ós

The base of the suffix -*Ós* can be a transitive or intransitive verb. In the former case the verb must contain a frequentative suffix: **néz+ős* vs. *néze+eget+ős* 'having the habit of looking around' (from *néz* 'to look'), in the latter case the verb must denote a psychological or physical property: *mosolyg+ós* 'smiling' (from *mosolyog* 'to smile'), *reszket+ős* 'trembling' (from *reszket* 'to tremble').

f) The participial suffix -Ó

Adjectives can be derived from present participles if the verb has a source subject argument and an experiencer argument. We thus get adjectives such as *dühít+ő* 'enraging', *fáraszt+ó* 'tiring', *szórakoztat+ó* 'amusing'. If the arguments of the base verb do not satisfy the above conditions, no adjective can be derived. Compare the derivatives *olvas+ó* 'reading', *játsz+ó* 'playing', *fut+ó* 'running', which are not adjectives.

g) The composite suffix *-hAtÓ*

The suffix *-hAtÓ* is a composite suffix composed of the verbal root *-hat* 'may, can' and the participial suffix *-Ó*. However, *-hAtÓ* can by no means be considered to be the participial form of *VhAt* since – in contrast to *VhAt* where the external argument is always the subject argument of the verbal base – the external argument of the derivatives *VhAtÓ* is always the object argument of the base verb. This also means that though any verb can take the possibility suffix *-hAt* the suffix *-hAtÓ* can only be attached to transitive base verbs: **ugrál+ható fiú* 'jump+able boy', but *olvas+ható könyv* 'read+able book'.

Before concluding the discussion of adjectival suffixes, two remarks are in place. The first remark concerns the derivational suffix *-i*, whose status is not quite clear (see Kenesei 2014 for a more detailed discussion). The derivatives can be classified as prenominal modifiers (the suffix *-i* can be said to be an attributivizer) on the one hand, and as parts of compounds, on the other. When N+N compounding is not available, *-i* affixation saves the day as in *asztal+i lámpa* vs. **asztal+lámpa* 'table lamp', *kert+i bútor* vs. **kert+bútor* 'garden furniture', *udvar+i lakás* vs. **udvar+lakás* 'apartment overlooking the courtyard'.

On the other hand, however, in many cases *-i* derivatives behave like genuine adjectives: *barát+i* 'friendly', *nagyon baráti* 'very friendly', *baráti+bb* 'friendlier'; *költő+i* 'poetic', *nagyon költői* 'very poetic', *költői+bb* 'more poetic'; *elmélet+i* 'theoretic', *nagyon elmélet+i* 'very poetic', *elméleti+bb* 'more theoretical'; *dráma+i* 'dramatic', *nagyon dráma+i* 'very dramatic', *drámai+bb* 'more dramatic'. Consequently, we will keep the suffix *-i* in our list.

Another property of the suffix is that it can take syntactic phrases as its base, especially when reference is made to place or time. In this case it can be considered to be an attributivizer. Consider

(28) [[[*az elmúlt 3 év*] +*i*] *jelentés*]
 the past 3 year +i report
 'the report of the past 3 years'

The function of the suffix *-i* to turn syntactic phrases into prenominal modifiers, however, has nothing to to do with word-formation.

The second comment concerns the suffix *-(j)Ú*, which must have two words in its base: The form **haj+ú* 'haired' is in itself unacceptable, the base can only be something like *hosszú haj* 'long hair' from which *hosszú haj+ú* 'long-haired' can be derived. This means that the suffix *-(j)Ú* is attached to phrases rather than to words and it is used to derive prenominal attributes (cf. also Kenesei 1995).

The situation is quite parallel to the corresponding Germanic suffixes, compare English *long-haired*, German *langhaarig*.

4.3 Verbal derivation

The productive verbal derivational suffixes are summarized in Table 16.4.

Tab. 16.4: Verbal derivation.

suffix	base category	meaning	example
-(V)z	N	to do N	*motor+ozik* 'to ride a motorcycle'
-(V)l	N	to do N	*print+el* 'to print'
-ál	V	to V	*install+ál* 'to install'
(s)kVd(ik)	A/N	to be A to be an N	*ideges+kedik* 'to be nervous' *bíró+skodik* 'to be judge'
-(V)gAt	V	to V a little bit	*olvas+gat* 'to read leisurely'
-(t)At	V	to let V	*olvas+tat* 'to let read'
-At	V	to cause to V	*mozg+at* 'to move (tr.)' (← *mozog* 'to move (itr.)')
-(t)Atik	V	to be Ved	*olvas+tatik* 'to be read'
-An	any onomatopoetic root		*zizz+en* 'to give a rustling sound'
-(V)g	any onomatopoetic root		*ziz+eg* 'to rustle'
-Ul	A	to become A	*zöld+ül* 'to become green'
-Vdik	A	to become A	*sötét+edik* 'to become dark'
-ít	A	to make more A	*mély+ít* 'to make deeper'
-(V)sít	A	to make A	*német+esít* 'to Germanize'
-(V)sVdik	A	to become A	*német+esedik* 'to become German'
-izál	A	to make A	*modern+izál* 'to modernize'

a) The verbal suffixes *-(V)z*, *-(V)l* and *-ál*

The suffixes *-(V)z* and *-(V)l* are both used to derive verbs from nouns but the former is more productive. The latter can only be used under specific conditions; for example, monosyllabic stems ending in a vowel get the suffix *-(V)l* as in *park+ol* 'to park', *voks+ol* 'to vote', *print+el* 'to print'. Note that foreign stems are considered nominal stems whatever their status is in the source language, i.e. *print* is considered a nominal stem by the Hungarian system from which the verb *print+el* is derived. In the case of new loanwords the two derivational suffixes are in complementary distribution: *ímél (email)+ezik* 'to send an email message' vs. **ímél+el* and *szkenn+el* 'to scan' vs. **szkenn+ez(ik)*. In some cases doublets may occur, however. This is the case when the phonological and the lexico-semantic conditions are in conflict. Polysyllabic stems should receive the suffix *-(V)z(ik)*, but if the stem is a polysyllabic English word denoting sport or gymnastics, we often get doublets: *jogging+ol* 'to jog', *jogging+oz(ik)*.

The suffix *-ál* is used to accommodate foreign polysyllabic verbs into the Hungarian verbal system: *install+ál* 'to instal', *format(t)+ál* 'to format', *edit+ál* 'to edit', *invit+ál* 'to invite'. The suffix, which is not related to the suffix *-(V)l*, has to obey a phonological condition: the polysyllabic stem must not contain front vowels only (they must either all be back vowels or the stem must contain mixed vowels). Polysyllabic stems containing only front vowels take the suffix *-(V)l* as in *menedzs+el* 'to manage'.

b) The suffix -(s)kVd(ik)

Verbs can be derived by means of the suffix *-(s)kVd(ik)* either from adjectival or from nominal bases. The adjectival bases denote a human property and are morphologically complex: they contain either the negative suffix *-(V)tlAn*, as in *nyug+talan* 'restless' (from *nyugszik* 'to rest'), or the adjectival suffix *-(V)s*, as in *alázat+os* 'humble' (from *alázat* 'humbleness'). By adding the verbal suffix we get *nyugtalan+kodik* 'to be worried' and *alázatos+kodik* 'to humble oneself'.

In the cases of nominal bases the resulting meaning is 'to be/profess N', as in *tanár+kodik* 'to be teacher', *színész+kedik* 'to be actor', *mérnök+ösködik* 'to be engineer'.

c) The attenuative suffix -(V)gAt

Verbs with an attenuative meaning are derived by means of the suffix *-(V)gAt*, as in *olvas+gat* 'to read leisurely', *rajzol+gat* 'to draw pictures now and then', *énekel+get* 'to sing now and then', etc. In case the base verb is not durative but punctual, the derived verb expresses repetition: *nyit+ogat* 'to open repeatedly', *csuk+ogat* 'to close repeatedly', *ad+ogat* 'to give repeatedly, keep giving', *nyom+ogat* 'to push repeatedly'. We find quite a few lexicalized forms among the attenuative derivatives, e.g., *lát+ogat* 'to visit' from *lát* 'to see' + *gAt*, *hall+gat* 'to listen, keep silent' from *hall* 'to hear' + *gAt*, *emle+get* 'to speak often of sb./sth.'

from the fictive root *emle* + *gAt*, *u+gat* 'to bark' from the onomatopoetic root *u* + *gAt* 'to bark', *óbé+gat* 'to lament' from the onomatopoetic root *óbé* + *gAt*, etc.

d) The factitive and the causative
The factitive is derived by means of the suffix *-(t)At*: *olvas+tat* 'to let/make read', *rajzol+tat* 'to let/make draw pictures', *énekel+tet* 'to let/make sing'. The factitive must be distinguished from the causative, though the two suffixes may be formally identical. Both require a causer but the factitive presupposes an executor. A derivative may contain both a causative and a factitive suffix, as in *forg+at* (causative)+*tat* (factitive) 'to make sb. turn sth.'. The derivative *forg+at* just means 'to cause sth. to turn', there is no third participant involved.

The causative suffix can only be attached to non-agentive verbs, the factitive only to agentive verbs. (For details, see Kiefer and Komlósy 2011.) Note that both the factitive and the causative can be followed by the attenuative suffix *-(V)gAt*: *forg+at*(causative)+*tat*(factitive)+*gat*(attenuative) 'to make sb. turn sth. from time to time'. The attenuative suffix can be followed by the possibility suffix, which, however, cannot be used to derive new words.

e) The passive
The passive suffix *-(t)Atik* can be attached to any transitive verb though it is hardly used. The passive disappeared almost completely from the language by the end of the 19th century. Some actually existing but rarely used derivatives are *ad+atik* 'to be given', *megnéz+etik* 'to be seen', *enged+tetik* 'to be permitted'. Passive forms such as *olvas+tatik* 'to be read', *bizonyít+tatik* 'to be proven', *rendel+tetik* 'to be ordered' are obsolete.

f) The onomatopoetic verbs
Derivatives containing the suffix *-(V)g* or *-An* are onomatopoetic verbs. Verbs with the suffix *-(V)g* denote a continuous sound, verbs with the suffix *-An* a sudden sound. Any sound-imitating sequence can serve as a root, provided that it ends in a consonant. Such sequences may be termed onomatopoetic roots. The onomatopoetic verbs often come in pairs: *kop+og* 'to patter' vs. *kopp+an* 'to clap', *rez+eg* 'to rustle' vs. *rezz+en* 'to give a (sudden) rustling sound', *dör-ög* 'to thunder' vs. *dörr-en* 'to give a thundering sound'. The first members of these pairs are durative, the second ones punctual verbs.

g) Deadjectival verbs
Deadjectival verbs are derived from monosyllabic stems by means of the suffix *-Ul* and from polysyllabic stems by means of the suffix *-Vdik*. Compare *sárg+ul* 'to

turn yellow', *szép+ül* 'to get prettier', *vak+ul* 'to go blind' and *vörös+ödik* 'to redden', *okos+odik* 'to become sensible', *magas+odik* 'to grow higher', which are all change-of-state verbs. In case the stem ends in a vowel, this vowel is deleted before the derivational suffix: *sárga* 'yellow' → *sárg+ul* 'to turn yellow', *barna* 'brown' → *barn+ul* 'to turn brown'.

The suffix *-ít* is the causative equivalent of the two suffixes mentioned in the previous paragraph: *szép+ít* 'to make prettier', *magas+ít* 'to make higher'. In this case, too, the last vowel of the stem gets deleted before the derivational suffix: *barna* 'brown' → *barn+ít* 'to make brown', *fekete* 'black' → *feket+ít* 'to blacken'.

The causative suffix *-(V)sít* is similar to the previous suffix and it could also be analyzed as consisting of the suffix *-Vs*, as in *német+es* 'German-like', and the causative suffix *-ít*; there is, however, a serious semantic argument against this analysis: *német+esít* means 'to Germanize' and not 'to make more German-like'. Consequently, *-(V)sít* must be treated as a separate suffix.

The suffix *-(V)sVdik* is the non-causative equivalent of the previous suffix: *német+esedik* 'to become German'. In both cases the base adjective is an ethnic name.

h) Foreign roots

In the case of foreign adjectives verbs are derived by means of the suffix *-izál*, as in *szinkron+izál, digital+izál, immun+izál, modern+izál*. This suffix corresponds to German *-isieren*.

i) Prefix reduplication

In connection with verbal derivations the case of reduplicated particles should not be left unmentioned. Hungarian particle verbs are phrasal predicates rather than words (Booij 2010: 118). Hungarian does not distinguish between prefix and particle verbs, however, the reduplication of the verbal particle results in genuine prefixed verbs. Compare:

(29) a. *el+olvas egy könyvet* 'He/she reads a book.'
  b. *el-el+olvas egy könyvet* 'He/she reads a book from time to time.'

Note that – in contrast to (30a) – (30b) cannot be negated (by descriptive negation), and it cannot contain any focus constituent. The reason is that the position immediately preceding the verb is the position of the negative particle as well as that of the focused constituent. But reduplicated particles cannot be moved from their preverbal position:

(30) a. *El-el nem olvas egy könyve.
   REDUPL.PART NEG read DET book-ACC
   'He/she does not read a book from time to time.'
   b. El-el egy újságot olvas.
   REDPL.PART DET newspaper-ACC read
   'He/she reads a newspaper.'

The reduplicated particle and the verb form an inseparable unity which cannot be interrupted and no part of it can be moved into another position.

Reduplication is not without limitation: (i) the particle of stative verbs cannot be reduplicated (*el-el+áll 'to stick out (from time to time)'), (ii) particles longer than two syllables cannot be reduplicated (*keresztül-keresztül+fut 'to run across'). A semantic restriction concerns particle verbs denoting irreversible events such as fel+robban 'to explode'. However, the particle can be reduplicated even in such cases if the change concerns (sub)sets rather than individuals: *Egy-egy bomba fel-felrobbant* 'A bomb exploded now and then'.

4.4 Adverbial derivation

Adverbs can productively be derived from adjectives and from nouns, cf. Table 16.5.

Tab. 16.5: Adverbial derivation.

suffix	base category	meaning	example
-(A)n	A	adverbial meaning	meleg+en 'warm'
-Ul	A		lengyel+ül 'Polish'
-lAg	A		elméleti+leg 'theoretically'
-kor	N/Num	temporal	érkezés+kor 'at arrival', öt+kor 'at five'
-(V)stUl	N	comitative	család+ostul 'together with the family'

The distribution of the deadjectival suffixes is fully predictable. The suffix -(A)n is attached to base adjectives as well as to derived adjectives; in the case of derived adjectives; however, the suffix must not be one of the suffixes -i, -beli, -nyi or -tAlAn. Adverbs and adjectives are systematically kept apart morphologically. Compare *Szeretem a meleg* (Adj) *levest* 'I like warm soups' – *A levest melegen*

(Adv) *szeretem* 'I like soups warm'. Note also the formal difference between *lengyel lány* 'Polish girl' and *lengyel+ül beszélek* 'I speak Polish'. The adjectives with the suffix *-i* or *-beli* take the adverbial suffix *-lAg* and adjectives with the negative suffix *-tAlAn* as well as ethnic adjectives take the adverbial suffix *-Ul*. The temporal *-kor* is only possible with event nouns and numerals, the comitative can be attached to any concrete noun.

5 Conversion

Conversion is not a typical derivational device in Hungarian. It occurs productively only in the case of certain types of adjectives.

As we saw above the suffix *-i* can productively be used to derive adjectives with a number of different meanings. Substantivization, however, is possible in the case of the meaning 'person stemming/coming from N' only: *vidék+i* Adj 'coming/stemming from the countryside' → *vidék+i* N 'country (wo)man'; *város+i* Adj 'stemming/coming from a town' → *város+i* N 'townsman, townswoman'; *budapest+i* Adj 'stemming/coming from Budapest' → *budapest+i* N 'person coming from or living in Budapest'; *kálócfapuszta+i* Adj 'coming/stemming from Kálócfapuszta' → *kálócfapuszta+i* N 'person coming from or living in Kálócfapuszta'. Sometimes the substantivized adjectives can also refer to a product coming from a certain place, and the "product meaning" may get lexicalized: *Tokaj* → *tokaj+i* '(sweet) wine from Tokaj'.

The adjectival suffix *-(V)s* can be used to derive adjectives from nouns denoting objects, animals, plants, institutions, mass nouns, proper names, temporal intervals (Kiefer and Ladányi 2000: 183–185). Some of these adjectives can be substantivized to yield names of professions with the meaning 'practice N or work with N'. Such a conversion is possible (i) in the case of persons doing a certain sport, e.g., *bob* 'bob-sled' → *bob+os* 'practicing bob-sled (Adj)' → *bob+os* 'person practicing bob-sled'; *gördeszka* 'skateboard' → *gördeszká+s* 'practicing skateboard (Adj)' → *gördeszká+s* 'person practicing skateboard'; the base noun can denote any sports equipment; (ii) persons selling some merchandise, e.g., *zöldség* 'vegetables' → *zöldség+es* 'of vegetables (Adj)' → *zöldség+es* N 'greengrocer'; *öv* 'belt' → *öv+es* 'belted (Adj)' → *öv+es* 'merchant selling belts'; (iii) names of musicians, e.g., *klarinét* → *klarinét+os* 'having to do with the clarinet (Adj)' → *klarinét+os* 'clarinetist'; *cseleszta* 'celesta' → *cseleszta+s* 'having to do with the celesta (Adj)' → *cselesztás* 'musician playing the celesta'.

6 References

Benczes, Réka and Erzsébet Tóth-Czifra (2015): Language Play and Linguistic Hybridity as Current Trends in Hungarian Word-Formation. *Hungarian Cultural Studies* 8 [Online available at: https://doi.org/10.5195/ahea.2015.212].
Booij, Geert (2010): *Construction Morphology*. Oxford: Oxford University Press.
Dressler, Wolfgang U. (1989): Prototypical differences between inflection and derivation. *Zeitschrift für Phonetik, Sprachwissenschaft und Kommunikationsforschung* 42: 3–10.
Forgács, Tamás (2025): From Old Hungarian to Modern Hungarian. In: Peter O. Müller, Susan Olsen and Franz Rainer (eds.), *Word-Formation – Language Contact and Diachrony*, 553–574. Berlin/Boston: De Gruyter Mouton.
Grimshaw, Jane (1990): *Argument Structure*. Cambridge, MA: MIT Press.
Kenesei, István (1995): On bracketing paradoxes in Hungarian. *Acta Linguistica Hungarica* 43: 153–173.
Kenesei, István (2014): On a multifunctional derivational affix: Its use in relational adjectives or nominal modification, and phrasal affixation in Hungarian. *Word Structure* 7(2): 214–239.
Kenesei, István, Robert M. Vago and Anna Fenyvesi (1998): *Hungarian*. London/New York: Routledge.
Keszler, Borbála (ed.) (2000): *Magyar grammatica*. Budapest: Nemzeti Tankönyvk.
Kiefer, Ferenc (1990–91): Noun incorporation in Hungarian. *Acta Linguistica Hungarica* 40 (1–2): 149–177.
Kiefer, Ferenc (1992–2008): *Strukturális magyar nyelvtan*. 4 Vol. Budapest: Akadémiai Kadió.
Kiefer, Ferenc (1995): Prefix reduplication in Hungarian. *Acta Linguistica Hungarica* 43: 175–194.
Kiefer, Ferenc (2003): Alaktan. In: Katalin É. Kiss, Ferenc Kiefer and Péter Siptár, *Új magyar nyelvtan*, 189–284. Budapest: Osiris Kiadó.
Kiefer, Ferenc (2009): Uralic, Finno-Ugric: Hungarian. In: Rochelle Lieber and Pavol Štekauer (eds.), *The Oxford Handbook of Compounding*, 527–541. Oxford: Oxford University Press.
Kiefer, Ferenc and András Komlósy (2011): On the order of word-class preserving derivational suffixes in the Hungarian verb. *Word Structure* 4(2): 171–184.
Kiefer, Ferenc and Mária Ladányi (2000): Morfoszintaktikailag semleges képzések. In: Ferenc Kiefer (ed.), *Strukturális magyar nyelvtan*. Vol. 3: *Morfológia*, 165–214. Budapest: Akadémiai Kiadó.
Laczkó, Tibor (2000): Az ige argumentumszerkezetét megőrző főnévképzés. In: Ferenc Kiefer (ed.), *Strukturális magyar nyelvtan*. Vol. 3: *Morfológia*, 293–407. Budapest: Akadémiai Kiadó.
Laczkó, Tibor (2015): Nominalization in Hungarian. In: Peter O. Müller, Ingeborg Ohnheiser, Susan Olsen and Franz Rainer (eds.), *Word-Formation. An International Handbook of the Languages of Europe*. Vol. 2, 1241–1253. Berlin/Boston: De Gruyter Mouton.
Ladányi, Mária (2007): *Produktivitás és analógia a szóképzésben. Elvek és esetek*. Budapest: Tinta Könyvkiadó.
Palágyi, László, Erzsébet Tóth-Czifra and Réka Benczes (2020): Derivational networks in Hungarian. In: Lívia Körtvélyessi, Alexandra Bagasheva and Pavol Štekauer (eds.), *Derivational Networks Across Languages*, 385–398. Berlin/Boston: De Gruyter Mouton.
Tompa, József (ed.) (1961): *A mai magyar nyelv rendszere. Leíró nyelvtan*. Vol. 1: *Bevezetés, hangtan, szótan*. Budapest: Akadémiai Kiadó.
Tóth-Czifra, Erzsébet (2015): Suffixation and what else? A cognitive linguistic analysis of the Hungarian deverbal suffix -Ó. *Studia Linguistica Hungarica* 30: 4–29.

Xabier Artiagoitia, José Ignacio Hualde and Jon Ortiz de Urbina
17 Basque

1   Introduction
2   General overview
3   Composition
4   Derivation
5   Conversion
6   Backformation
7   Reduplication
8   Blending
9   Clipping
10 Word-creation
11 References

Abstract: This article offers an overview of the main processes of word-formation in Basque. Basque possesses a relatively large number of derivational suffixes. Several types of compounds also enjoy productivity. Some compounds and derived words show the application of complex morphophonological rules. Other types of word-formation are also discussed.

1 Introduction

Basque is a language isolate and the only surviving pre-Indo-European language of Western Europe. A well-known feature of Basque is that it displays ergative-absolutive morphology. Most Basque-speakers are found in northern Spain, in the Autonomous Community of the Basque Country (ACBC, comprising the provinces of Bizkaia, Gipuzkoa and Araba/Álava), where it is an official language together with Spanish. There are smaller numbers of speakers in the region of Navarre, where it has a more limited official status, and, across the Spanish-French political border, in the western half of the Départment des Pyrénées Atlantiques, where it is not official. Although the historical Basque-speaking territory has contracted significantly, the trend towards the disappearance of the language has been re-

---

Xabier Artiagoitia, Vitoria-Gasteiz, Spain
José Ignacio Hualde, Urbana-Champaign, USA
Jon Ortiz de Urbina, Bilbao, Spain

https://doi.org/10.1515/9783111420523-017

versed in the last few decades and the number of speakers is now growing, at least in the ACBC, thanks to officialization and the introduction of the language in the school system. Nowadays there are about 700,000 native speakers. Nevertheless, there are virtually no adult monolingual speakers left. Standard Basque (*euskara batua*), was developed by the Basque Academy starting at the end of the 1960s and has been very successful. Although local dialects often have prestige for their speakers, there is a trend towards convergence.

The detailed study of word-formation in Basque began with the work of Azkue (1923–25). Two monographs studies on compounding, written in Basque, are Euskaltzaindia (1987–92) and Azkarate (1990). The volume edited by Pérez Gaztelu, Zabala and Gràcia (2004) focuses on the boundaries between composition, on the one hand, and derivation and/or syntax, on the other.

On derivation, from a diachronic perspective, Múgica (1978) is worth mentioning. Villasante (1976) is another useful work on Basque derivation and composition, with extensive exemplification from Pedro de Axular's *Gero* (1643), a classical work that is widely considered a model of written expression in Basque. Trask's (1997) treatment of the Basque lexicon and its historical development is relatively brief, but contains a number of interesting observations.

Two recent grammars written in English, Hualde and Ortiz de Urbina (2003) and de Rijk (2008) include relatively extensive sections on compounding and derivation. De Rijk (2008) is especially rich in exemplification of words created with different affixes.

2 General overview

2.1 Preliminaries

In its inflectional morphology, Basque comes close to the agglutinative ideal of allowing clear segmentation of roots and affixes (although there are some portmanteau affixes and a few other deviations from the ideal). Nominal inflection is all done by means of suffixes, e.g., *mendi-tik* 'from the mountain', *mendi-eta-tik* 'from the mountains'. In verbal inflection, on the other hand, we find both prefixes and suffixes, e.g., *i-bil-i* 'walk, participle', *n-a-bil* 'I walk', *d-a-bil* 's/he walks', *d-a-bil-tza* 'they walk'.

Both derivation and compounding are common processes of word-formation. Derived words are almost exclusively formed by suffixation. There are only a couple of prefixes and these are either borrowed from Romance languages (*des-egin* 'to undo', *des-lotu* 'to untie', *des-oreka* 'lack of balance') or calqued on their model (*ez-ezagun* 'unknown' ← *ez* 'not'). However, in verbal morphology we can identify a fossilized derivational causative prefix *e-ra-* in a handful of verbs. This process is not productive and there have often been shifts in meaning, so that the original causative function of the prefix is for the most part opaque to speakers, e.g., *entzun* 'to hear', *e-ra-ntzun* 'to answer'; *i-kas-i* 'to learn', *i-rakats-i* 'to teach'.

The basic distinction between derivation and compounding is that in compounds the last member also exists as an independent word. Problems of analysis arise because a suffix may gain status as an independent word and, conversely, a formerly independent word may be lost outside of compounds. An example of the first type is the suffix *-(t)asun* '-ness', which has been promoted to independent word as *tasun* with the meaning of 'quality, feature' (see section 4.1.1). De Rijk (2008), following Múgica (1978), uses the term *parasuffix* to refer to "a free morpheme occurring as the final member in a large number of useful compounds" (de Rijk 2008: 229). In this class, he includes *zale* 'fond', *bide* 'way', *gabe* 'without, lacking' and *gai* 'matter', among others. The Basque Academy, Euskaltzaindia, uses the term *erdi-atzizki* 'semisuffix' to refer to this group of items. Pérez Gaztelu (2004) concludes that, since these "parasuffixes" or "semisuffixes" are, in fact, independent nominal or adjectival roots, the words in which they occur as last member are compounds.

Regarding the distinction between compounding and syntactic concatenation, in N+Adj exocentric compounds, such as *belarri-luze* 'long-eared, donkey' (← *belarri* 'ear' + *luze* 'long'), the two members occur in their normal syntactic order, cf. *belarri luze* 'long ear'. In some dialects, there is an accentual difference, but this does not happen in the standard language. The same sort of ambiguity may arise in compounds with *gabe* 'without', e.g., *gupida-gabe* 'pitiless, cruel' vs. *gupida(rik) gabe* 'without pity', if used without optional partitive marking (*-rik*) on the noun (see Odriozola 2004). In N+N compounds the absence of genitive inflection on the first noun indicates morphological fusion, cf. *bake-zale* 'peace-loving' vs. *bakearen zale* 'fond of peace'. With location nouns there is fluctuation regarding the use of the genitive and, thus, morphological or syntactic structure: *mahai(aren) azpitik* 'from under the table, from the bottom of the table' (← *mahai* 'table' + *-aren* 'genitive singular' + *azpi* 'bottom' + *-tik* 'from').

Phrasal verbs are considered in section 3.3.

There are a few cases of lexicalized sentences or phrases, which can take further derivational and inflectional affixes, as in *nahi-ta-ez* 'necessarily' (← *nahi* 'want' + *ta* 'and' + *ez* 'not'), *nahitaezko* 'obligatory'; *ba-da-ez-pa-da* 'just in case' (← *ba* 'if' + *da* 'is' + *ez* 'not' + *ba* 'if' + *da* 'is'), *badaezpadako* 'uncertain').

2.2 Morphophonological alternations

There are some morphophonological transformations that affect the ending of nouns when they occur in non-final (non-head) position in compounds and in derived forms. Thus, for instance, *begi* 'eye' appears as *bet-* in compounds such as *bet-ile* 'eyelash' and *bekain* 'eyebrow' (← *bet-* 'eye' + *gain* 'top'). Although these transformations have some complexity, the nouns that participate in these alternations form a closed class.

With trisyllabic or longer nouns, as well as with some bisyllabic nouns ending in a high vowel, the last vowel is deleted: *itsas-gizon* 'seaman' (← *itsaso* 'sea' + *gizon* 'man'), *itsas-bazter* 'coast'. If, after deletion of the final vowel, the last consonant is a rhotic tap, it is replaced by *-l*: *gal-eper* 'quail' (← *gari* 'wheat' + *eper* 'partridge'); *afal-ordu* 'supper time' (← *afari* 'supper' + *ordu* 'hour'). In the same context, *-d*, *-g* are replaced by *-t*, which can, in its turn, be deleted before another consonant: *errepide* 'highway' (< *erret-bide* ← *errege* 'king' + *bide* 'road, trail'). With bisyllabic nouns ending in a non-high vowel, we find neutralization of the mid vowels with *-a*: *erla-tegi* 'beehive' (← *erle* 'bee' + *tegi* 'place'); *usa-tegi* 'dovecote' (← *uso* 'dove' + *tegi* 'place'). There are also a few other irregularities affecting nouns ending in *-n*: *egur-aldi* 'weather' (← *egun* 'day' + *aldi* 'time') or that historically had an intervocalic *-n-*, which was preserved in the compositional form of the noun: *ardo* 'wine' (< *ardano), *ardan-tza* 'vineyard'. The compositional form of *gizon* 'man' is *giza-*, which is found in compounds like *giza-seme* 'man; lit. man-son'. A few other exceptional changes are also found.

These alternations may be analogically extended. So, from *merkatari* 'merchant' a form *merkatal* 'commercial' has been created, as in *merkatalgo* 'commerce'. The neologistic school of the turn of the 20th century led by Sabino Arana promoted the creation of new forms following these patterns, mostly to avoid loanwords (see Pagola 2005). One example is *gotzain* 'bishop; lit. soul-keeper' (← *got-* 'soul' + *zain* 'keeper'), where *got-* is a previously inexistent compositional form of *gogo* 'intention, memory' (with its meaning broadened to 'soul', to avoid the borrowing *arima* 'soul' < Lat. *anima*), created by analogy with *begi/bet-* 'eye', *ogi/ot-* 'bread', etc. Although most of these neologisms have not prospered, some remain in the language (see section 4.1.1).

There are also alternations affecting the initial segment of the second member of the compound and derivational suffixes. One alternation, already illustrated in some examples above, is due to the devoicing of stops after a voiceless segment; for instance, for *bide* 'way, path, road', cf. *adi-bide* 'example' (← *adi-tu* 'to listen, understand'), *adi-eraz-pide* 'way of expressing' (← *eraz-i* 'causative').

Morpheme-final affricates become fricatives before another stop in compounds and derived words, *ikaztun* 'coal seller' (← *ikatz* 'coal' + *-dun*), cf. *esne-*

dun 'milkman'. In the same context, the first stop systematically deletes, making the reason for the devoicing opaque, as in *arkazte* 'lamb' (< *art-gazte* ← *ardi* 'sheep' + *gazte* 'young'), *okin* 'baker' (< *ot-gin* ← *ogi* 'bread' + *-gin* 'to make'). In a few cases, devoicing is found without any obvious phonetic reason, so the initial consonant of *gabe* 'without' is devoiced in *uste-kabe* 'accident' (← *uste* 'opinion, belief').

Another alternation in morpheme-initial position is produced by the voicing of stops after /n/ and /l/, cf. *txerri-tegi* 'pig sty' vs. *ardan-degi* 'tavern'.

There are exceptions to both the devoicing after voiceless obstruents and the voicing after nasals and liquids, e.g., *ikas-bide* 'learning method' (*ikas* 'to learn'), *euskal-tegi* 'Basque-teaching institution' (*euskal-* < *euskara* 'Basque language').

A few morphemes have a vowel-initial allomorph and another allomorph starting with /t/ or /k/, e.g., *eri-tasun* 'illness', *osa-sun* 'health' (*osa-asun* ← *oso* 'complete, healthy' + *-asun*); *jarr-era* 'position', *hiz-kera* 'way of speaking', *ibil-era* ~ *ibil-kera* 'way of walking'; *haurr-ide* 'sibling' (← *haur* 'child'), *lan-kide* 'co-worker' (← *lan* 'work'). This alternation is synchronically unmotivated. Some derivational suffixes thus have up to three forms (e.g., *-tar, -dar, -ar* 'originating from', *-tegi, -degi, -egi* 'place'), as we can see, for instance, comparing *Bizkai-tar* 'Bizkaian', *Usurbil-dar* 'person from Usurbil', *Burgi-ar* 'person from Burgi'. In a couple of cases, a consonant-initial form that arose in compounds has become an independent form with a different meaning. This is clearly the case with *kume* 'offspring of an animal' vs. *ume* 'child', where the former must have arisen in compounds like *kata-kume* 'kitten', with an originally epenthetic consonant. Likely, *talde* 'group' (vs. *alde* 'side') has resulted from reanalysis in compounds like *art-alde* 'flock of sheep'.

Finally, suffix-initial affricates become /t/ after a fricative, cf. *antola-tzaile* 'organizer', *nahas-taile* 'embroiler'.

This covers the most regular alternations. There are, nevertheless, a few, less common, additional idiosyncrasies that we leave aside.

2.3 Neoclassical formations

In present-day Basque, neoclassical formations usually have essentially the same shape as in Spanish (replacing <c> with <k> or <z> depending on its phonetic value and without accent marks): *telefono, mikrobiologia, filologia, elektromagnetismo*, with a few exceptions such as *telebista* 'television' and except that the ending *-lari* is optionally used to derive names of professions, as in *fonologilari* 'phonologist', *sintaxilari* 'syntactician'. An earlier proposal made in the 1970s to use classical spelling in technical words (*telephono, photographia*, etc.) did not prosper. Earlier proposals (from the beginning of the 20th century) to replace all technical vocabulary, including neoclassical formations, with native compounds have also been mostly abandoned. Nevertheless, some of these calques, like *urrutizkin* 'telephone' (← *urruti* 'far' + *hitz* 'word' + *kin* 'tool'), are still in the passive vocabulary of some speakers and are listed in dictionaries. Some such coined terms employed only in specialized fields, especially in linguistics, have become established (e.g., *aurr-izki* 'prefix', *atz-izki* 'suffix', where *(h)izki* ← *hitz* 'word', is a neologism for 'letter, grapheme, affix').

Classical prefixes are usually replaced with native equivalents such as locative nouns; e.g., *azpi-* 'sub-, infra-' (*azpi-multzo* 'subset', *azpi-egitura* 'infrastructure'), but not always, e.g., *infra-gorri* 'infrared', *ultra-more* 'ultraviolet'. In some cases, classical prefixes have been translated by means of suffixes, more in accordance with the morphological structure of the language, where prefixation is rare. Thus, for 'pre-history', *histori-aurre* is preferred to *aurre-historia* (*prehistoria* is also found) and for 'semivowel' (Sp. *semivocal*) both *semibokal* and *bokalerdi* have been coined. An interesting example of reordering of morphemes in calques, avoiding prefixes, is the word *hil-ez-kor* 'immortal, eternal' (← *hil* 'to die' + *ez* 'no' + *-kor*), due to the 18th century lexicographer Manuel Larramendi and formed on older *hil-kor* 'mortal'.

3 Composition

Several types of compounds are frequent and productive in Basque.

3.1 Nominal compounds

3.1.1 Determinative compounds

In determinative N+N compounds, very common and productively formed in Basque, the head is final. Thus from *behi* 'cow' and *esne* 'milk' we can obtain *behiesne* 'cow's milk' and *esnebehi* 'dairy cow'. A couple more examples, illustrating the allomorphy rules mentioned in section 2.2, are *usakume* 'young pigeon' (← *uso* 'dove' + *kume* 'offspring') and *itsasgizon* 'seaman' (← *itsaso* 'sea' + *gizon* 'man').

With a V+N structure, we find examples like *pasa-leku* 'passage way', *irakurgai* 'reading matter', *ikas-bide* 'learning method', *abia-puntu* 'starting point', *senda-belar* 'medicinal herb' (← *senda-tu* 'to cure' + *belar* 'grass, herb') and many others. These compounds are formed with the verb radical.

In contrast, there is only a relatively small number of determinative nominal compounds with a N+Adj structure; that is, formed with a noun and adjective in the same order in which they appear in a noun phrase. The meaning of the compound is relatively transparent from that of its formatives in some examples and much less so in others. In some of these compounds the morphophonological rules described in section 2.2 apply and therefore they are different from the corresponding syntactic phrases of noun and adjective. Others do not differ, except that in some western dialects they may receive a different accentual pattern. Examples are: *arkazte* 'lamb' (← *art*- 'sheep' + *gazte* 'young' vs. *ardi gazte* 'young sheep'), *gaztanbera* 'cottage cheese' (← *gaztan*- 'cheese' + *bera* 'soft' vs. *gazta bera* 'soft cheese'), *saguzar* 'bat' (← *sagu* 'mouse' + *zahar* 'old'), *neskazahar* 'spinster' (← *neska* 'girl' + *zahar* 'old'), *udaberri* 'spring' (← *uda* 'summer' + *berri* 'new'), *zori-on* 'good luck, happiness' (← *zori* 'luck' + *on* 'good'). The same structure is much more productive in the creation of exocentric nominal and adjectival compounds, see section 3.1.3.

3.1.2 Copulative compounds

Co-compounding is a common process in Basque. N+N co-compounds (dvandvas) are almost always plural: *anai-arrebak* 'brothers and sisters', *neska-mutilak* 'girls and boys', *Bizkai-Gipuzkoetan* 'in Bizkaia and Gipuzkoa' (examples are given with inflection, to show their plural character, but inflection is phrase-level in Basque, cf. *anai-arreba gazte-ak* 'young siblings'). Notice that nominal co-compounds have the same structure as N+N determinative compounds. Generally the semantics (or knowledge of the world) makes the interpretation unambiguous. Thus *ardi-zakurrak* (← *ardi* 'sheep' + *zakur* 'dog') will be interpreted as a determinative compound 'sheep dogs', but the compound *ardi-bildotsak* (← *bildots* 'lamb') receives the co-compound interpretation 'sheep and (their) lambs'.

The only exceptionally singular co-compounds are those referring to a substance with two components, such as *kafesne* (← *kafe* 'coffee' + *esne* 'milk'), more readily interpretable as a co-compound 'coffee and milk' than as determinative compound 'coffee-ish milk'.

The members of a co-compound may be any two nouns that refer to entities that tend to occur together or can be associated semantically or contextually; e.g., *ikasle-irakasleak* 'students and teachers', *hanka-besoak* 'legs and arms'. In lexicalized co-compounds the order of the two members is fixed and one can discern both phonological (shorter member precedes longer) and semantic criteria (e.g., older generation before younger generation, *aita-semeak* 'father and son(s)', male before female, *seme-alabak* 'sons and daughters', etc.) in the positioning of the two members (Jacobson 1982).

Occasionally, co-compounds may have more than two members. Thus, on the basis of the common *zeru-lurr-ak* 'heaven and earth', the three-member compound *zeru-lur-itsaso-ak* 'heaven, earth and sea' was coined.

Nominal co-compounds may be formed by combining two participles or verbal radicals, as in *har(tu)-eman* 'give and take, relationship' (← *har-tu* 'to take' + *eman* 'to give'), *joan-etorri* 'coming and going, round trip' (← *joan* 'to go' + *etorri* 'to come'), *sal-erosi* 'trade, buying and selling operations' (← *sal-du* 'to sell' + *eros-i* 'to buy'). With an Adj+Adj structure we find a handful of nominal compounds like *luze-labur* 'length' (← *luze* 'long' + *labur* 'short'), *on-gaitzak* 'pros and cons' (← *on* 'good' + *gaitz* 'bad'). Some of these compounds can be used as singular nouns.

3.1.3 Exocentric compounds

Compounds with the structure N+A and the meaning 'having a N that is A' are more or less freely formed: *praka-gorri* 'someone with red pants', *buru-handi* 'big-headed', *sudur-luze* 'having a long nose', *bihotz-bera* 'soft-hearted', *mihi-luze* 'with a long tongue, talkative'. Some exocentric N+A compounds have acquired unpredictable, lexicalized meanings: *belarri-luze* 'long-eared, donkey', *belarri-motz* 'short-eared, non-Basque, Spaniard', *hega-luze* 'long-fin, type of tuna'. Many of these compounds may be used either as nouns or as adjectives.

On the other hand, N+N exocentric compounds are very rare. An example would be *txori-buru* 'simpleton; having the head of a bird' (← *txori* 'bird' + *buru* 'head'). With a numeral as first member we find examples like *lau-buru* 'type of cross' (← *lau* 'four' + *buru* 'head').

3.2 Adjectival compounds

Compounds with the structure A+A may combine two opposing adjectives, such as *gazi-geza* 'sweet and sour' (← *gazi* 'salty' + *geza* 'insipid'), *busti-lehor* 'wet-dry' or two quasi-synonyms, *alfer-nagi* 'lazy', *eder-galant* 'beautiful and gallant'. A+A adjectives are also freely formed with colors, *zuri-urdin* 'white and blue', *gorri-beltz* 'red and black'.

As mentioned in section 3.1.3, compounds with the structure N+A, which are very productive, may be adjectives or nouns. With an essentially adjectival function we find, for instance, *eskuzabal* 'generous' (← *esku* 'hand' + *zabal* 'wide, open'), *bihozbera* 'soft-hearted, tender' (← *bihotz* 'heart' + *bera* 'soft'), *begi-urdin* 'blue-eyed' (← *begi* 'eye' + *urdin* 'blue'), *ile-gorri* 'red-haired'.

Some adjectives that combine with verbs to form V+A compound adjectives are *berri* 'new', *gaitz* 'difficult', *bera* 'soft', *erraz* 'easy' and *ezin* 'impossible'; e.g., *ezkonberri* 'just married', *argitaraberri* 'just published', *jaioberri* 'just born', *asegaitz* 'hard to satisfy', *ulergaitz* 'difficult to understand', *sentibera* 'sensitive', *ulerterraz* 'easy to understand', *konponerraz* 'easy to fix', *kontaezin* 'innumerable, uncountable', *gaindiezin* 'unsurmountable'.

For reduplicated adjectives, see section 7.

3.3 Verbal compounds

Causative verbs are productively formed with *-arazi* 'to cause', e.g., *galarazi* 'to cause to lose', *janarazi* 'to force to eat', *jakinarazi* 'to let know'. This is so even for the few verbs that have historically derivational causatives with *e-ra-* (see section 2), since these have acquired special meanings; e.g., *e-torr-i* 'to come', *e-torr-arazi* 'to cause to come', *e-ra-torr-i* 'to derive'.

Leaving causatives apart, strictly speaking, there are only a handful of verbal compounds in Basque, if by this we mean structures that always behave as a single morphological unit. With a N+V structure, examples include *buruberotu* 'to drive crazy' (← *buru* 'head' + *berotu* 'heat' ← *bero* 'hot'), *indarberritu* 'to recover strength' (← *indar* 'strength' + *berritu* 'to renew' ← *berri* 'new'), *itxuraldatu* 'to transform' (← *itxura* 'aspect' + *aldatu* 'to change'), *odolustu* 'to bleed' (← *odol* 'blood' + *hustu* 'to empty' ← *huts* 'empty'). With an A+V structure we find *oniritzi* 'to consider good', formerly 'to love' (← *on* 'good' + *iritzi* 'to consider, opine'), *onartu* 'to accept' (← *on* 'good' + *hartu* 'to take').

On the other hand, some very frequent "phrasal verbs" consist of an uninflected noun (the object) and the light verb *egin* 'to do, make', e.g., *lo egin* 'to sleep' (← *lo* 'sleep'), *hitz egin* 'to talk' (← *hitz* 'word'). Two other verbs that show a certain amount of productivity in these constructions are *eman* 'to give' and *hartu* 'to take'; e.g., *amore eman* 'to give up, desist', *musu eman* 'to kiss', *hitz eman* 'to promise', *arnasa hartu* 'to breathe', *parte hartu* 'to take part', *hitzartu* 'to agree' (← *hitz* + *hartu*). With other verbs, there are just a handful of expressions. Generally these can be considered to be phrasal verbs rather than true compounds because a) it is possible to use partitive inflection on the noun; e.g., *ez duzu lorik egin* 'you have not slept at all' (*lo-rik* 'sleep-partitive'), *ez dugu parterik hartu* 'we have not taken any part', and b) the uninflected noun maintains syntactic freedom and, for instance, can be postponed in interrogatives: *non egin duzu lo?* 'where have you slept?', *noiz egiten duzu lan?* 'where do you work?'. Nevertheless, one finds different degrees of lexicalization (see Oyharçabal 2006). Phrasal verbs differ from free syntax in that the noun is uninflected (if not taking the partitive), cf. *sagarra jan* 'to eat the apple' (*sagar* 'apple') but not **sagar jan*; cf. also *lan egin* 'to work' (phrasal verb) vs. *lana egin* 'to do the work' (free syntax). Using this criterion, phrasal verbs can also be distinguished from verbal idioms like *botoa eman* 'to vote' (← *boto-a* 'vote-DET') or *adarra jo* 'to make fun' (lit. 'to play the horn'; *adarr-a* 'horn-DET', *jo* 'to hit, play'), where the direct object bears singular inflection, and from other idiomatic phrases with complements in specific cases; e.g., *kontuan hartu* 'to take into account' (← *kontu-an* 'account-LOC'), *buruz ikasi* 'to learn by heart, memorize' (lit. *buru-z* 'head-INSTR' + *ikasi* 'to learn').

In a couple of compounds with *hartu* 'to take' an original ergative inflection has been fossilized, e.g., *lokartu* 'to fall asleep' < *loak hartu* (← *lo-a-k* 'sleep-DET-ERG').

In *pipijan* 'sawdust created by moths' (← *pipi* 'moth' + *jan* 'to eat'), *harjo* 'worm eaten' (← *har* 'worm' + *jo* 'to hit'), a verb is compounded with what would be its subject. But these are essentially participles, used as adjectives or nouns, as the glosses indicate.

Verbs like *onetsi* 'to consider good, accept' (*on* 'good'), *gaitzetsi* 'to reject', *ederretsi* 'to consider beautiful', are formed on the same A+V pattern of *oniritzi* 'to consider good, love', *onartu* 'accept'. The difficulty in the analysis is that the verb *etsi* nowadays has the meaning of 'to despair, lose all hope, accept with resignation', which is considerably more restricted than the meaning we must give it in structures with *-etsi*.

3.4 Adverbial compounds

Place adverbs enter into the compounds *han-hemen* 'here and there' (← *han* 'yonder' + *hemen* 'here') and *han-hor-hemen* 'here and there' (*hor* 'there'). The common phrase *honahemen* 'here it is' (← *hona* 'here-ALLAT' + *hemen* 'here-LOC') is probably not to be analyzed as a compound, given its inflection.

Time adverbials also enter into compounds such as *gaur-biharretan* 'today and tomorrow' (← *gaur* 'today' + *bihar* 'tomorrow' + *-etan* 'LOC-PL'). Nevertheless, the result in these cases is a nominal compound, given the fact that it takes nominal inflection.

Nominal compounds with locative or instrumental inflection may have an essentially adverbial function. More interestingly, there are examples where an uninflected N+N co-compound has an adverbial meaning; e.g., *buru-belarri* 'eagerly' (← *buru* 'head' + *belarri* 'ear'). With a determinative structure we find, e.g., *musu truk* 'in exchange for a kiss, gratis' (← *musu* 'kiss' + *truke* 'exchange').

A nominal compound forms the base of adverbial derivation in examples like *arnasestuka* 'panting' (← *arnasestu* 'pant, difficult breathing' ← *arnasa* 'breath' + *estu* 'narrow' + *-ka* 'adverbial suffix').

4 Derivation

4.1 Nominal derivation

Nominal derivation is very productive in Basque, at least as far as the number of suffixes involved is concerned. A few suffixes can have both N and A categories.

4.1.1 Denominal nouns

We first discuss agentive denominal suffixes, next suffixes denoting a great amount or having a collective meaning. The remaining suffixes are discussed in strict alphabetical order.

The suffix *-ari* (< Latin *-arius*) with its variants *-lari*, *-dari* and less frequently *-kari*, is generally described as a denominal suffix that creates p e r s o n a l n o u n s paraphrasable as 'someone who performs a profession or an activity related to the base': *aizkolari* 'woodcutter' (← *aizkora* 'axe'), *bertsolari* 'verse-maker' (← *bertso* 'poem'). This suffix is fully productive with nominal bases, e.g., *blogari* 'blogger'. It is generally in complementary distribution with *-le* and *-t(z)aile*, which have a similar meaning but take verbal bases. This situation, however, is relatively new in the language (Oyharçabal 1996; Saizar 2004); deverbal agent nouns with *-ari* were once not rare in the language: *gidari* 'guide, driver' (← *gida-tu* 'to guide'), *ibiltari* 'walker' (← *ibil-i* 'to walk').

With the variant *-kari*, originally an adverbial suffix, we find denominal nouns to name types of periodicals: *egunkari* 'daily newspaper' (← *egun* 'day'), *astekari* 'weekly magazine' (← *aste* 'week').

Two further denominal agentive suffixes are *-gin* and *-gile*, both related to the verb *egin* 'to do, make'. They follow the pattern [N-*gin*/*gile*]$_N$ = 'someone who produces, processes or makes N'. The suffix *-gin* is no longer productive and is found in nouns referring to old professions like *okin* 'baker' (← *ogi* 'bread' + *gin*). The suffix *-gile* is productive and can be found in both old and new professions: *bizargile* 'barber' (← *bizar* 'beard'), *zinemagile* 'film-maker'.

The p o s s e s s i v e s u f f i x *-dun*, usually paraphrased as 'possessor of', is denominal and gives rise to both nouns and adjectives (cf. section 4.2.1 for the adjectival value and the apparently non-derivational use of -*dun*). The adjectival use of this suffix is fully productive, but there are also many nouns formed with -*dun*: *eledun* 'spokesperson' (← *ele* 'word, speech'), *euskaldun* 'Basque speaker' (← *euskal* ← *euskara* 'Basque language'), *hiztun* 'speaker' (← *hitz* 'word'), *txapeldun* 'beret-holder, winner' (← *txapel* 'beret'). There are also a few deverbal -*dun* nouns, e.g., *jostun* 'sewer' (← *jos-i* 'to sew').

Several suffixes produce collective nouns, place nouns, or nouns denoting 'a great amount of'. The suffix -*di* was originally added to tree and plant nouns to denote a natural grouping of that tree or plant: *haritz* 'oak' → *hariz-ti* 'forest of oak trees', *mahats* 'grape' → *mahas-ti* 'vineyard'. S. Arana promoted this suffix to create neologisms, the best known of which is *Euskadi* 'Basque Country' (formerly *Euzkadi* ← *euzko-di* 'grouping of Basques', where *euzko* is a stem invented by Arana for 'Basque person'). This has led to the revival of the suffix -*di* with bases other than tree or plant names: *legedi* 'legislation' (← *lege* 'law'). The suffix -*(t)eria*, of Romance origin, serves the same purpose in the creation of collective nouns, e.g., *gazteria* 'youth, young people' (← *gazte* 'young'), *ontziteria* 'tableware' (← *ontzi* 'receptacle'). Finally, -*tza* also conveys the idea of abundance or great amount in words like *jendetza* 'large group of people' (← *jende* 'people'), *dirutza* 'great amount of money' (← *diru* 'money'). When denominal, this suffix may also form profession, position or status nouns: *alkatetza* 'mayorship' (← *alkate* 'mayor'), *zuzendaritza* 'management' (← *zuzendari* 'director'). For the deverbal use of -*tza*, see section 4.1.3. The eastern suffix -*go* is the exact equivalent of this use of -*tza*: *ikaslego* 'studentship' (← *ikasle* 'student'). In many cases, Standard Basque has favored one choice over the other, but often the two words exist: *irakaslego*/*irakasletza* 'teaching profession, professorship'.

The suffix -*kada*, etymologically related to a similar Romance suffix, is usually denominal. It may denote a blow or movement such that the base is the instrument: *bihozkada* 'heartbeat' (← *bihotz* 'heart'), *burukada* 'head-blow' (← *buru* 'head'); as in Romance, it also yields measurements: *ahokada* 'mouthful', *katilukada* 'cupful'. Finally, with NP-*egin* verbs, it gives rise to action nouns that denote one instance of the action: *zurrut egin* 'to swig' → *zurrutada* 'a swig'.

The suffix -*keta* (variant -*eta*) is an action noun suffix, productive with verbal bases (see section 4.1.3), yet it is found in several examples with a nominal base: *berriketa* 'talk, gossip' (← *berri* 'news'), *gogoeta* 'thought, reflexion' (← *gogo* 'mind'), *zezenketa* 'bullfight' (← *zezen* 'bull'). In eastern dialects, the denominal use may also convey the idea of abundance or action: *diruketa* 'great amount of money' (← *diru* 'money'), *arrainketa* 'fishing' (← *arrain* 'fish').

The suffix -*keria*, of Romance origin, takes both noun and adjective bases. It denotes an abstract negative quality or a pejorative action. Examples from noun bases include *astakeria* 'donkey-nonsense' (← *asto* 'donkey'), *nahikeria* 'caprice, base desire' (← *nahi* 'desire'), *umekeria* 'childish action' (← *ume* 'child'); it is true, however, that many of these noun bases often display a qualifying, adjective-like, behavior.

The suffix *-ki*, when denominal (see also section 4.1.3 for its deverbal use), usually indicates 'i t e m, piece'. Thus, when applied to edible animals, the corresponding derived noun with *-ki* means meat of the relevant animal: *txerriki* 'pork' (← *txerri* 'pig'), *idiki* 'ox-meat' (← *idi* 'ox'). A similar idea is present in *odolki* 'blood sausage' (← *odol* 'blood'), *esneki* 'milky product' (← *esne* 'milk') or even the neologism *euskalki* 'Basque dialect' (← *euskara* 'Basque language').

Little attention is paid to *-ko* as a derivational suffix in traditional grammar (e.g., Villasante 1976 and de Rijk 2008 ignore it completely). This is so because *-ko* is mostly a functional adposition that forms locative genitives or qualifying genitives inside noun phrases (e.g., *Bilbo-ko gizona* 'a man from Bilbao', *hiru urte-ko ardoa* 'a wine of three years'); sometimes it is simply an adposition required for PPs and other phrases NP-internally (*eskolara-kobidea* 'the path to the school' ← *eskolara* 'to the school') or part of a complex adposition (cf. *zu-re-ki-ko dudan zorra* 'the debt I have towards you'). Be it as it may, *-ko* gives rise to many nouns and this derivational use is often tied to a locative interpretation: *lekuko* 'witness' (← *leku* 'place') would literally be '(someone) at the place'. Nouns of this flavor include *belarritako* 'earring' (← *belarri* 'ear'), *buruko* 'pillow' (← *buru* 'head'), *gerriko* 'belt' (← *gerri* 'waist'), *milurteko* 'millenium' (← *mila urte* 'one thousand years'). In other cases, *-ko* derived nouns indicate a blow into the corresponding body part: *muturreko* 'punch in the face' (← *mutur* 'mouth'), *masaileko* 'blow to the cheek' (← *masail* 'cheek').

When applied to geographic names and proper nouns, the suffix *-tar* is totally productive in the creation of nouns denoting o r i g i n and clan or family names: *britaniar* 'British', *bilbotar* 'Bilbaoan, native of Bilbao', *johnsondar* 'someone of the Johnson family' (for the use of this suffix with adjectives derived from nouns, see section 4.2.1). The suffix *-tar* can also attach to common nouns that may be identified as a location (de Rijk 2008: 130): *baserritar* 'farmer' (← *baserri* 'farm'), *herritar* 'inhabitant, citizen' (← *herri* 'village, country'), *estralurtar* 'extraterrestrian' (← *lur* 'earth').

The suffix *-tasun* roughly means 'q u a l i t y', as its promotion to an independent word meaning 'feature' in the fields of theology and linguistics shows (e.g., *Jesusen tasunak* 'Jesus's qualities', *tasun bereizgarriak* 'distinctive features'). Its base is generally an adjective (see section 4.1.2), but it may also be a noun: *aitatasun* 'fatherhood' (← *aita* 'father'), *adiskidetasun* 'friendship, friendliness' (← *adiskide* 'friend'). Several quantifiers also take *-tasun*: *batasun* 'unity, union' (← *bat* 'one'), *aniztasun* 'variety, diversity' (← *anitz* 'many').

Finally, the suffixes -*tegi* and -*te* roughly mean 'p l a c e' (originally 'shed') and 't i m e /period', respectively: *hiztegi* 'dictionary' (← *hitz* 'word'), *liburutegi* 'library' (← *liburu* 'book'); *eurite* 'rain period' (← *euri* 'rain'), *gerrate* 'war-time' (← *gerra* 'war').

4.1.2 Deadjectival nouns

As explained in the previous section, both -*tasun* and -*keria* may take a nominal base as well as an adjectival base. It is, however, with the latter that they are fully productive: *askatasun* 'freedom' (← *aske* 'free'), *edertasun* 'beauty' (← *eder* 'beautiful'), *hurbiltasun* 'proximity' (← *hurbil* 'near'). Some minimal pairs illustrate the difference in meaning between the two suffixes: *handitasun* 'greatness, enormity' vs. *handikeria* 'arrogance, excessive grandeur' (← *handi* 'big'), *txikitasun* 'smallness' vs. *txikikeria* 'small triviality' (← *txiki* 'small'), *zorotasun* 'craziness, the illness/situation of being crazy' vs. *zorakeria* 'despicable act of craziness' (← *zoro* 'crazy').

The suffix -*era*, more common with verbal bases (cf. section 4.1.3), is also attached to adjectives of dimension: *lodiera* 'thickness' (← *lodi* 'thick'), *zabalera* 'width' (← *zabal* 'wide').

4.1.3 Deverbal nouns

Deverbal noun suffixation is also highly productive. First, we discuss deverbal a g e n t n o u n s. Afterwards, we consider action and result nouns. Then, we turn to the productive suffix -*gailu* 'machine'. The rest of the discussion goes by strict alphabetical order.

Both -*le* and -*t(z)aile* form deverbal a g e n t n o u n s, which usually take agentive (either regular transitive or unergative) verbs as their base. The division of labor between the two is morphophonologically conditioned: verbs whose participle (i.e. the citation form) ends in an older participial ending (viz. in -*n* or in a sibilant, -*r* or -*l* followed by -*i*) tend to take the suffix -*le*: *edan* 'to drink' → *edale* 'drinker', *entzun* 'to hear' → *entzule* 'hearer', *ikus-i* 'to see' → *ikusle* 'viewer', *idatz-i* 'to write' → *idazle* 'writer', *irakurr-i* 'to read' → *irakurle* 'reader'; on the other hand, verbs whose participle ends in a vowel, in any other consonant or in the productive participial ending -*tu* usually take -*t(z)aile*: *garbi-tu* 'to clean' → *garbitzaile* 'cleaner', *hil* 'to kill' → *hiltzaile* 'killer', *jaso* 'to receive, raise' → *jasotzaile* 'receiver, raiser'; the allomorph -*taile* is reserved to verbal stems with a secondary ending in a sibilant (after removing the participial ending): *bikoiz-tu* 'to double, subtitle' → *bikoiztaile* 'voice-dubber'. This division of labor, in turn, suggests that presently only *-t(z)aile* is productive in Standard Basque.

Most unaccusative verbs do not participate in this kind of suffixation, with a couple of unexpected exceptions: e.g., *egoile* 'resident' (← *egon* 'to stay'). In general, if a verb participates in the inchoative/causative alternation, the suffix *-le* or *-t(z)aile* will be possible only with the transitive value: thus, for the alternation *sortu* 'to emerge, be born, create', we get *sortzaile* 'creator/*emerger', necessarily tied to the transitive meaning; likewise, from *hil* 'to die, kill', we get *hiltzaile* 'killer/*dier'. Regular unergative verbs which do not participate in the NP-*egin* construction can take the relevant suffix: *jazarle* 'attacker, aggressor' (← *jazarr-i* 'to attack'), *mintzatzaile* 'talker' (← *mintza-tu* 'to talk'), *kolaboratzaile* 'collaborator' (← *kolabora-tu* 'to collaborate'), *mendekatzaile* 'avenger' (← *mendeka-tu* 'to take revenge'); for unergative verbs of the NP-*egin* type, either a compound with *egile* 'doer' (reducible to the suffix *-gile*) exists or *-ari* can be directly attached to the noun: *barre egile* 'laughing person' (← *barre egin* 'to laugh'), *langile* 'worker' (← *lan egin* 'to work'), *dantzari* 'dancer' (← *dantza egin* 'to dance'), *iheslari* 'fleer' (← *ihes egin* 'to flee, get away'), *korrikalari* or *lasterkari* 'runner' (← *korrika egin*, *lasterka egin* 'to run').

Event and result nouns are typically expressed by the suffixes *-keta* (already mentioned in its denominal use in section 4.1.1), *-kuntza* and *-pen*, which usually take regular transitive verbs, provided these are activity, non-stative, verbs (cf. *jakin* 'to know' → **jakiketa*, **jakipen*, **jakikuntza*). According to de Rijk (2008: 693), in principle both *-keta* and *-kuntza* would be action nouns (the first one presenting the action in process and the other as already completed), whereas *-pen* would refer more to the result or outcome of an action. Although de Rijk's observation may be true for some *-pen* words (e.g., *itxaron* 'to wait' → *itxaropen* 'expectation, hope' never has an eventive interpretation) or for a few examples where two suffixes alternate (e.g., *irakats-i* 'to teach' → *irakaskuntza* 'action of teaching, teaching business, teaching profession' vs. *irakaspen* 'lesson, amount of things learned'), the fact is, however, that the three suffixes can form true action nouns and, likewise, denote the result or outcome of an action. Moreover, for verbs that take both *-keta* and *-kuntza*, the two nominals are often synonyms (cf. *zapal-du* 'to step on, oppress' → *zapalketa* = *zapalkuntza* 'repression'). Here are some examples of each suffix: *azterketa* 'examination' (← *azter-tu* 'to examine'), *banaketa* 'separation, distribution' (← *bana-tu* 'to separate, distribute'), *erosketa* 'purchase' (← *eros-i* 'to buy'), *konponketa* 'repair' (← *konpon-du* 'to repair'); *hobekuntza* 'improvement' (← *hobe-tu* 'to improve'), *ikerkuntza* 'investigation, research' (← *iker-tu* 'to research, investigate'); *askapen* 'liberation' (← *aska-tu* 'to liberate'), *azalpen* 'explanation' (← *azal-du* 'to explain'), *ukapen* 'negation' (← *uka-tu* 'to negate'). The suffix *-pen* has a *-men* variant (not to be confused with the also deverbal suffix -*men* 'capacity' below) for idiosyncratic phonological reasons: *aipamen* 'mention' (← *aipa-tu* 'to mention'), *hondamen* 'destruction' (← *honda-tu* 'to destroy'). This -*men* variant is usually connected with -*mendu*, itself derived from Latin -*mentum*; Basque has a few words with -*mendu*, applied to native or loaned verbs, some of which do have an action interpretation: *luzamendu* 'lengthening, delay, moratorium' (← *luza-tu* 'to lengthen') (cf. also *luzamen, luzapen*). Regarding the division of labor among -*keta*/-*kuntza*/-*pen*, in general one does not find a single verb that takes all three suffixes in Standard Basque: some -*kuntza* and -*keta* alternations exist, some -*keta* and -*pen* alternations exist (*erakuts-i* 'to show' → *erakusketa* 'exhibition', *erakuspen* 'exhibition, amount of things exhibited'), but fewer -*kuntza* and -*pen* alternations are found. As a corollary, it is worth pointing out that the word for language is *hizkuntza* 'language' (← *hitz* 'word'), one of the few exceptions where -*kuntza* takes a noun base, perhaps because the corresponding verb is of the NP-*egin* form (*hitz egin* 'to speak; lit. word make') and these verbs hardly ever participate in their entire form in derivational processes. There is also a fourth, non-productive, action noun suffix linked to -*kuntza*, namely -*kunde*. Some of the few words that have this suffix are, however, pretty common in Standard Basque: *erakunde* '(body of) organization' (← *era-tu* 'to organize'; cf. also *eraketa* 'organization'), *hauteskunde* 'election' (← *hautets-i* 'to elect'), *zabalkunde* 'diffusion' (← *zabal-du* 'to spread').

Other action nouns include -*era*, -*tza* and -*t(z)e*. The suffix -*era* (with the variant -*kera* after radicals ending in a sibilant or affricate) is clearly related to the word *era* 'manner', which suggests that these are compounds: *ibilera* '(manner of) walking' (← *ibil-i* 'to walk'), *idazkera* '(manner of) writing' (← *idatz-i* 'to write'). However, it is often the case that the derived noun means, not the manner of carrying out an action, but the action itself, or even the result of the action. Interestingly, both transitive and intransitive (including unaccusative) verbs may take -*era*: *egoera* 'situation' (← *egon* 'to stay'), *eskaera* 'petition' (← *eska-tu* 'to ask for'), *gertaera* 'happening, event' (← *gerta-tu* 'to happen'), *igoera* 'ascension' (← *igo* 'to climb'), *sorrera* 'birth, emergence' (← *sor-tu* 'to emerge'); the word *sarrera* (← *sar-tu* 'to enter') is particularly telling since it offers the entire range of possibilities: it can be an eventive nominal (cf. *ikusgarria izan zen zure Donostiako sarrera* 'Your entering Donostia was spectacular'), but it also means 'the result of entering, entry', 'entrance', 'way of entering' or 'introduction', and even the physical object 'ticket' (cf. Sp. *entrada*). The no longer productive deverbal -*tza* (an allomorph of -*kuntza* according to de Rijk 2008: 693) is found in a few cases: *emaitza* 'gift' (← *eman* 'to give'), *laguntza* 'assistance' (← *lagun-du* 'to help'). Finally, -*t(z)e* is simply a syntactic suffix that can nominalize virtually any verb and give rise to nominalized clauses; however, some words with this suffix have been lexicalized as true nouns. Common examples include: *adiskidetze* 'reconciliation'

(← *adiskide-tu* 'to reconciliate'), *baketze* 'pacification' (← *baketu* 'to pacify, make peace'), *euskalduntze* 'Basquization, teaching of the Basque language' (← *euskaldun-du* 'to Basquize, teach Basque').

The instrumental suffix *-gailu* is in today's Basque the most popular one to name new machines or technological devices. It originated in the eastern dialects and has become very frequent in the last decades: *berogailu* 'heater' (← *bero-tu* 'to heat'), *garbigailu* 'washing machine' (← *garbi-tu* 'to wash'), *igogailu* 'elevator' (← *igo* 'to climb, elevate'), *ordenagailu* 'computer' (← *ordena-tu* 'to order', cf. Sp. *ordenador*).

As for the rest of deverbal suffixes, the non-agentive *-ari* is one of the best studied (Saizar 2004): this suffix is no longer productive and it usually creates object nouns. According to Saizar (2004), most of these derived nouns come from transitive verbs, so that the *-ari* object would refer to the internal argument of the verb: *edari* 'beverage' (← *edan* 'to drink'), *eskari* 'petition' (← *eskatu* 'to ask for'), *ikuskari* 'spectacle' (← *ikusi* 'to see'), *janari* 'food' (← *jan* 'to eat'); *gerta-kari* 'happening' (← *gerta-tu* 'to happen'; cf. also *gertaera* 'event') would be one of the few exceptions of a non-transitive verb base. The deverbal suffix *-dura* refers to the resulting object or consequence of a mental process or action: *egitura* 'structure' (← *egin* 'to do'), *elikadura* 'nutrition' (← *elika-tu* 'to nourish'), *harridura* 'astonishment, surprise' (← *harri-tu* 'to get surprised'). The deverbal suffix *-ki* can also give rise to instruments whereby an action takes place or, in the case of creation and destruction verbs, the outcome of that action. It is no longer productive: *aldaki* 'copy, variant' (← *alda-tu* 'to change'), *idazki* 'document, written matter' (← *idatz-i* 'to write'), *iragarki* 'announcement' (← *iragarr-i* 'to announce'). A phonologically similar suffix *-kin* is generally related to the notions 'remainder' or 'resulting product': *hondakin* 'residue' (← *honda-tu* 'to get spoiled, spoil'), *eranskin* 'annex, supplement' (← *erants-i* 'to add'); again, most of the verbs taking *-kin* are regular transitive and the noun refers to their object argument; but we find one well-known exception: *etorkin* 'immigrant' (← *etorr-i* 'to come'). The suffix *-kizun* is generally possible with regular transitive verbs; the relationship with the base verb is paraphrasable as 'susceptible to be V-ed'. Thus, *eginkizun* means 'work to do' (← *egin* 'to do'), *igarkizun* 'riddle' (← *igarr-i* 'to guess'). Finally, we will briefly mention the suffix *-men*, roughly paraphrasable as 'capability': *dastamen* 'sense of taste' (← *dasta-tu* 'to taste'), *entzumen* 'sense of hearing' (← *entzun* 'to hear'), *irudimen* 'imagination' (← *irudi-tu* 'to imagine, consider'). Some deverbal nouns with *-men* denote action, but these would in principle be allomorphs of *-pen* (cf. *zoramen* 'thrill, ecstasy' ← *zora-tu* 'to become/make someone crazy').

4.2 Adjectival derivation

4.2.1 Denominal adjectives

Basque only has one productive suffix for the creation of r e l a t i o n a l adjectives from nouns, namely the afore-mentioned *-tar* (cf. section 4.1.1), which, when attached to place names, creates both origin nouns and adjectives: *italiar bat eta hiru bilbotar* 'one Italian and three Bilbao-citizens' but also *andre italiar bateta hiru mutil bilbotar* 'one Italian woman and three Bilbaoan boys'. Although unusual, these adjectives may have an argumental interpretation: *inbasio germaniarrak* 'Germanic invasions' (i.e. invasion by the Germanics). The suffix *-tar* can also apply to proper names and give rise to classificatory adjectives: *ikuspegi chomskyar berria* 'the new Chomskyan point of view', *teoria darwindarrak* 'Darwinian theories'. There are also relational (classificatory) *-tar* adjectives derived from common nouns: *atzerritar* 'foreign' (← *atzerri* 'foreign country'), *basotar* 'barbarian' (← *baso* 'wood'), *eskuindar* 'rightist' (← *eskuin* 'right-hand'). All these may be used as qualifying adjectives. It is worth noting that the eastern and similar suffix *-tiar* is sometimes mixed up with *-tar* in its adjectival use giving rise to two versions of a similar word; thus, the variant *ezkertiar* 'leftist' (← *ezker* 'left-hand') is the only one accepted in Standard Basque to the detriment of *ezkertar*.

The suffix *-tar* can also attach to the numeral *bi* 'two' and create the corresponding classificatory adjective: *sistema bitar bat* 'a binary system' (← *bi* 'two'). In general, however, numerals and quantifiers resort to the suffixes *-kun* and *-koitz* to form classificatory adjectives: *bakoitz, bakun* 'single, consisting of a single piece' (← *bat* 'one'); *bikun, bikoitz* 'double, consisting of two pieces' (← *bi* 'two'); *anizkoitz, anizkun* 'multiple, consisting of many pieces' (← *anitz* 'many').

As anticipated in section 4.1.1, the p o s s e s s i v e s u f f i x *-dun* is certainly denominal and gives rise to both nouns and adjectives, but its status as purely derivational is problematic given that its base seems to be a [N-Adj] constituent (bare NP from the point of view of the DP hypothesis) or even a QP ([N-(Adj)-Q]): *begi berde-dun neska* 'a green-eyed girl', *hiru hanka-dun aulkia* 'a chair with three legs'. In the latter two cases, *-dun* looks more like a functional adposition that introduces some sort of predication structure. That aside, many *-dun* nouns can be used as adjectives: *euskaldun* 'Basque speaker' (← *euskara* 'Basque language') but also *andre euskaldun bat* 'a Basque-speaking woman'. There are, however, some *-dun* words that are typically only adjectives, especially those that describe personal qualities (physical or not): *bizardun* 'bearded' (← *bizar* 'beard'), *bizidun* 'animate' (← *bizi* 'life'), *dirudun* 'rich' (← *diru* 'money'). Most of the exceptions with a verbal base are adjectives: *edatun* 'heavy drinking' (← *edan* 'to drink'), *ikastun* 'studious' (← *ikas-i* 'to study').

The suffix *-tsu* is both denominal and deadjectival (cf. section 4.2.2). When denominal, it usually conveys the idea of abundance: *diru* 'money' → *dirutsu* 'rich', *ile* 'hair' → *iletsu* 'hairy', *indar* 'force, strength' → *indartsu* 'strong', *pozoin* 'poison' → *pozointsu* 'poisonous'. There are a few cases where denominal *-dun* and *-tsu* adjectives compete for the same meaning: *dirutsu* and *dirudun* are true synomyms.

Both *-koi* and *-ti* are typically only denominal adjective suffixes. The former indicates tendency or propensity and is found in a few words like *barnekoi* 'spiritual, intimist' (← *barne* 'interior, inside'), *etxekoi* 'home-loving' (← *etxe* 'home'), *elizkoi* 'devout' (← *eliza* 'church'). The exception to a nominal base is found in examples with possessive pronouns + *-koi*: *berekoi* 'egocentric' (← *bere* 'his, her'), *neurekoi* 'as of me, egocentric' (← *neure* 'my own'). The suffix *-ti*, on the other hand, is far more productive; it also conveys the idea of propensity or tendency but often with a pejorative value: *basati* 'savage' (← *baso* 'forest, jungle'), *gezurti* 'liar' (← *gezur* 'lie'), *negarti* 'easy cryer, crybaby' (← *negar* 'cry').

4.2.2 Deadjectival adjectives

Basque has a very limited set of deadjectival adjective suffixes; one salient suffix is *-tsu* (cf. section 4.2.1), which roughly means 'almost', 'more or less' when applied to adjectives: *berdin* 'similar' → *berdintsu* 'more or less similar', *ber* 'identical' → *bertsu* 'almost identical'. We find this use of *-tsu* with some adverbs too: *oraintsu* 'more or less now' (← *orain* 'now'), *honelatsu* 'almost this way' (← *honela* 'this way').

The rest of deadjectival adjective suffixes are mostly diminutives and, as such, are not restricted to adjectives, but shared by other categories. Color adjectives usually take the diminutive *-xka*: *gorrixka* 'reddish' (← *gorri* 'red'), *zurixka* 'whitish' (← *zuri* 'white'), whereas other adjectives would take *-xko*, originally a noun diminutive (de Rijk 2008: 156): *handixko* 'rather big' (← *handi* 'big'), *harroxko* 'rather arrogant' (← *harro* 'arrogant'). The suffix *-txo*, productive with nouns, is also possible in the examples given: *gorritxo, zuritxo, handitxo, harrotxo*.

4.2.3 Deverbal adjectives

The most productive deverbal adjective suffixes are *-garri* and *-kor*, which have been extensively studied by Artiagoitia (2003) and Oyharçabal (2003) respectively. The suffix *-garri* is restricted to verbs that have two arguments and has a twofold value: first, it creates modal-passive adjectives out of regular transitive verbs such that the adjective is predicated of the object argument of the verb with the meaning 'that can/should be V-ed': *barkagarri* 'forgivable' (← *barka-tu* 'to forgive'), *ulergarri* 'comprehensible' (← *uler-tu* 'to understand'), *ikusgarri* 'worth seeing' (← *ikus-i* 'to see'), *gorrotagarri* 'detestable' (← *gorrota-tu* 'to detest, hate'), *zenbakarri* 'countable' (← *zenba-tu* 'to count'). Besides, *-garri* also forms a c t i v e adjectives out of psychological verbs of the *preoccupare* type (with experiencer objects): *aspergarri* 'boring' (← *asper-tu* 'to bore'), *erakargarri* 'attractive' (← *erakarr-i* 'to attract'), *hunkigarri* 'touching, impressive' (← *hunki-tu* 'to impress'). This pattern also extends to verbs whose subject is some sort of instrumental, non-agentive, argument: *aringarri* 'palliative' (← *arin-du* 'to palliate, lessen'), *babesgarri* 'protecting' (← *babes-tu* 'to protect'), *kutsagarri* 'contagious' (← *kutsa-tu* 'to infect, contaminate'), *lagungarri* 'helping' (← *lagun-du* 'to help').

This suffix is productive only in its adjectival value, but there are also nouns (tied to the active value) coined with *-garri*: *euskarri* 'holder' (← *euts-i* 'to hold' + *-garri*), *txikigarri* 'diminutive' (← *txiki-tu* 'to diminish'). In many cases, the noun coexists with the adjectival use: *freskagarri* 'refreshment' (N), 'refreshing' (A) (← *freska-tu* 'to refresh'); *gehigarri* 'additive, addendum' (N), 'additional, supplementary' (A) (← *gehi-tu* 'to add'); *lasaigarri* 'tranquilizer' (N), 'relaxing' (A) (← *lasai-tu* 'to calm, relax').

The suffix *-kor* is another productive deverbal adjectival suffix that generally takes intransitive (mostly unaccusative) verbs as its base: *erorkor* 'that falls easily' (← *eror-i* 'to fall'), *hauskor* 'that breaks easily' (← *hauts-i* 'to break'), *sarkor* 'easily penetrating' (← *sar-tu* 'to enter'). Some non-unaccusative intransitives may take *-kor*, but these never have an agent argument: *distirakor* 'that shines easily' (← *distira-tu* 'to shine'), *iraunkor* 'durable' (← *iraun* 'to last'). In the case of the few transitive verbs that may take *-kor* (e.g., *emankor* 'fruitful, productive' ← *eman* 'to give, produce'), Oyharçabal (2003) argues that these satisfy the theme/object argument lexicon-internally, in which case they assimilate to the previous pattern; this is shown by the fact that *-kor* adjectives cannot form compounds with the original theme argument of the verb: *arbola honek limoi asko ematen ditu* 'this tree produces many lemons; lit. tree this-ERG lemon many give AUX' → *arbola hau emankorra da* 'this tree is productive', but **arbola hau limoi-emankorra da* 'this tree is lemon-productive'. In cases like this the *-kor* adjective is necessarily predicated of a non-agentive subject: *gizonak odola eman du* 'the man donated/gave blood' → **gizona emankorra da* 'the man is productive'.

Other potential deverbal adjective suffixes are *-gaitz* and *-ezin*, in examples like *ulergaitz* 'hard to understand' (← *uler-tu* 'to understand'), *aldakaitz* 'hard to change' (← *alda-tu* 'to change'), *ulertezin* 'incomprehensible', *aldaezin* 'unchangeable'; but given the independent word status of *gaitz* and *ezin*, these words are generally regarded as compounds in the Basque grammatical tradition (cf. Euskaltzaindia 1992, also section 3.2). The noun suffixes *-t(z)aile* and *-le* also form adjectives occasionally: *izar distiratzailea* 'the shining star' (← *distira-tu* 'to shine'), *hatz erakusle-a* 'index finger; lit. signaling finger' (← *erakuts-i* 'to show'). The same is true of *-ari*: *zezenadarkaria* 'a goring bull' (← *adar* 'horn'), *andreibiltaria* 'good-walking woman' (← *ibil-i* 'to walk').

4.3 Verbal derivation

Verbal derivation in Basque is accomplished through conversion (see section 5.3; also Odriozola 2003). Strictly speaking, the only deverbal form in Basque is *-arazi* 'to cause', generally taken to be a verb itself, giving rise to compound verbs (cf. section 3.3): *eman* 'to give' → *emanarazi* 'to cause to give'. Nonetheless, this verb doesn't exist as independent word in present-day Basque, so it could be taken as a purely suffixal form (de Rijk 2008: 377 calls it a "causative auxiliary").

4.4 Adverbial derivation

In present-day Basque, manner adverbs are generally derived by the productive suffixes *-ki* and *-ka*. The former can form both denominal, e.g., *gizonki* 'manly' (← *gizon* 'man'), *maisuki* 'masterly' (← *maisu* 'master') and, above all, deadjectival adverbs such as *trebeki* 'skillfully' (← *trebe* 'skillful'), *ongi* 'well' (← *on* 'good'), *sutsuki* 'ardently' (← *sutsu* 'ardent'). Loaned adjectives can form the corresponding adverb following the same pattern: *sozial* 'social' → *sozialki* 'socially', *ekonomiko* 'economical' → *ekonomikoki* 'economically'. The suffix *-ka* generally conveys the idea of manner by iteration or repetition. Its base can be a noun, e.g., *eztul* 'cough' → *eztulka* 'coughing; lit. cough after cough', *kolpe* 'blow, knock' → *kolpeka* 'by means of repeated blows', *talde* 'group' → *taldeka* 'in groups'; a quantifier, e.g., *ehun* 'hundred' → *ehunka* 'by hundreds', *bina* 'two each' → *binaka* 'two by two'; and also a verb, provided it admits an iterative interpretation: *bultzatu* 'to press' → *bultzaka* 'by means of repeatedly pressing', *jo* 'to play, hit' → *joka* 'repeatedly hitting/playing', *esan* 'to say' → *esaka* 'repeatedly saying'.

The so-called stative partitive (de Rijk 1972, 1995) can also be regarded as a derivational suffix that produces predicative adverbs (usually from adjectives). Examples of this sort include *bakar* 'only, single' → *bakarrik* 'alone', *gazte* 'young' → *gazterik* 'young, at young age', *gaixo* 'sick' → *gaixorik* '(state of being) sick'.

The suffix *-ero*, historically derived from *oro* 'every', also forms time adverbs; its base is always a noun that constitutes some time unit: *egun* 'day' → *egunero* 'every day', *urte* 'year' → *urtero* 'every year', *maiatza* 'May' → *maiatzero* 'every May'.

There exist other suffixes to derive (mainly manner) adverbs, but most of them are no longer productive and give rise to lexicalized adverbs. These include *-ro: argi* 'clear' → *argiro* 'clearly', *berri* 'new' → *berriro* 'again'; *-to* as in *txar* 'bad' → *txarto* 'badly', *on* 'good' → *ondo* 'well'; *-kiro* (basically a combination of *-ki* and *-ro*), e.g., in *maitekiro* 'lovingly' (← *maite* 'dear'); and the reverse combination *-roki*, as in *argiroki* 'clearly' (← *argi* 'clear'; cf. the also existing adverbs *argiro* and *argiki* 'clearly').

5 Conversion

Conversion is particularly productive to derive nouns (section 5.1) and verbs (section 5.3).

5.1 Nominal conversion

Deadjectival nouns can be freely formed in Basque: *handia* 'the big (one)', *handiak* 'the big (ones)', *aberatsa(k)* 'that rich one(s)', *frantsesa* 'the French (one), the French (language)', *berria* '(piece of) news', *politikoak* 'politicians, political (persons)', etc. A syntactic analysis with an empty noun provides an alternative to conversion.

Construction-bound deadjectival conversion is found in expressions like *zeruaren ederra* 'what a beautiful sky, the beauty of the sky; lit. of the sky beautiful' (← *eder* 'beautiful'), *gauaren iluna* 'what a dark night, the dark(ness) of the night' (← *ilun* 'dark'). Genitive in *-ren* and the meaning indicates the adjective is behaving as a noun.

Participles (also infinitives, see section 4.1.3) are often converted into nouns: *erratuak* 'flaws' (← *erratu* 'to fail, err'), *gatzatua* 'curd' (← *gatzatu* 'to curdle'), *esana* 'proverb, saying' (← *esan* 'to say'), even dvandva nouns like *joan-etorriak* 'affairs' (← *joan* 'to go', *etorri* 'to come').

There are few converted deadverbial nouns: *oraina* 'the present, now', *lehena* 'the past, before', *eza* 'rejection, lack' (← *ez* 'not').

5.2 Adjectival conversion

Participles can be freely used as adjectives: *oso emana* 'very much given (to)' (← *eman* 'given'), *gauza nahiko jakina* 'fairly (well-) known thing' (← *jakin* 'known'). Apart from this, adjectival conversion is uncommon in Basque. A few nouns and adjectives share the same form, as in *argi* 'light, clear', *bero* 'hot, heat', *gose* 'hunger, hungry', *zorrotz* 'sharp, cutting edge'.

5.3 Verbal conversion

Open class elements, even phrases, can become verbal roots and display verbal inflection; we will exemplify with the perfective form (*-tu*). See section 4.3 and de Rijk (2008, ch. 7.4 and 12.3).

Denominal and deadjectival verbs are particularly common: *harritu* 'to astonish' (← *harri* 'stone'), *poztu* 'to rejoice' (← *poz* 'joy'), *kezkatu* 'to worry' (← *kezka* 'worry'). Sandhi phenomena (cf. section 2.2) may occur, such as mid vowel lowering in *osatu* 'to recover, complete' (← *oso* 'whole'), *askatu* 'to free' (← *aske* 'free') or l/r alternation, e.g., *ugaldu* 'to increase' (← *ugari* 'plenti(ful)'; *ugaritu* also exists).

Adverb(ial)s may also become verbs: *berandutu* 'to become late' (← *berandu* 'late'); *musukatu* 'to kiss repeatedly' (← *musu* 'kiss', *musuka* 'with many kisses'; section 4.4), *sailkatu* 'to classify' (← *sail* 'class', *sailka* 'by class'). However, adverbial bases with adverbializing suffixes like *-ik* or *-ki* do not convert into verbs. Interrogative pronouns can also be converted: *zenbatu* 'to count' (← *zenbat* 'how much/many').

Nouns in the allative case (*-ra* 'to') can easily be converted: *lurreratu* 'to land' (← *lurrera* 'to the land'), *bururatu* 'to occur, come to mind' (← *burura* 'to the head'), *niganatu* 'to come, bring, assimilate to me' (← *nigana* 'to me'). Nouns with other postpositions do not follow this conversion pattern. Thus, we find *etxeratu* 'to go home' but not *etxetik(a)tu* 'leave from home'. A few forms with the adnominal marker *-ko* exist: *etxekotu* 'to become part of the house, familiarize with the house' (← *etxeko* 'of the house'), *gaurkotu* 'to modernize' (← *gaurko* 'of today'). Sometimes a full phrase converts: *bere herriratu* 'to go/take to his village' (← *bere herrira* 'to his village'), and even *andere-hantu* 'to turn into a great lady' (de Rijk 2008: 274).

5.4 Adverbial conversion

Some adjectives can be used as adverbs, often alternating with them: *zintzo(ki) jokatu* 'to play fair', *gogor(ki) eutsi* 'to hold on firm(ly)', *garbi(??ki) ikusi* 'to see clear(ly)', *azkar(??ki) ibili* 'to walk fast'. Which adjectives can be converted into adverbs depends on the adjective but also on the verb it modifies: *zuhur jokatu* 'to act judiciously, wisely' is normal, but *zuhur elkartu, jantzi, esan* 'to combine, dress, say wisely' much less so.

6 Backformation

Backformation is scarce in Basque. An old derived nominal (see section 4.1.3) *er(h)aile* 'killer' has given rise to the new verb *er(h)ail* 'to assassinate'. Similarly, from *euskara* 'Basque language' *eusko* 'ethnically Basque' was formed (traditional *euskalduna* 'Basque' actually means 'Basque speaker').

7 Reduplication

Full intensificational reduplication is common with adjectives and adverbs: *handi-handia* 'very big', *gorri-gorria* 'very red', *astiro-astiro* 'very slowly'. Full reduplication with nouns is found in isolated cases like *egi-egia* 'the real truth' or completely lexicalized forms like *amama* 'grandmother' (← *ama* 'mother'), *ait(e)ite* (< *aitaita*) 'grandfather' (← *aita* 'father'). Many temporal and locative phrases can be reduplicated to indicate exact time or location: *aurre-aurrean* 'right in front', *zuzen-zuzenean* 'straight ahead'. Emphatic manner can also be conveyed by reduplicating a noun with a case ending: *bihotz-bihotzez* 'with the heart, best wishes', *argi-argitan* 'in full light'. Other reduplicated bases include modifiers (*ia-ia* 'almost, barely', *oso-oso* 'very, very'), a pronoun (*berbera* 's/he him/herself, the very same one') and copulative verbal forms in headless relatives (*garen-garena* 'exactly what we are', *den-dena* 'absolutely everything, exactly what it is'). Bizkaian displays "distributed duplication" (de Rijk 2007: 881): repeated temporal and locative nominals receive an 'every/each' interpretation: *goizean goizean* 'each morning'.

Expressive reduplication often alters the shape of the base, so *m-* (very seldom *b-*) occurs as onset: *duda-mudak* 'doubts' (← *duda* 'doubt'), *hasi-masiak* 'rudiments' (← *hasi* 'begin'), *zirimiri* 'drizzle'.

Reduplication is common in expressive formations and in sound symbolism (Ibarretxe 2006): *barra-barra* 'in abundance', *mara-mara* 'falling softly and abundantly (snow, tears, rain)'. Many of these also show the *m*-alternation: *isil-misilka* 'whispering' (← *isil* 'silent' + -*ka*), *totel-motelka* 'stuttering' (← *totel* 'stutterer'). Onomatopoeic reduplication often displays /a/ to /i/ vowel shifts (as in *zig-zag*), seldom /i/ to /o/: *dinbili-danbala* 'repeatedly hitting', *tiki-taka, tipi-tapa* 'walking with small paces', *bilin-balan* 'tumbling down', *kili-kolo* 'wobbling (mostly of weak, sick people)', etc. Vowel and onset shift co-occur in *zirri-parra* 'mess, tangle', *kikili-makala/kikili-mokolo* 'wobbling'.

8 Blending

There is little blending in the traditional vocabulary, although it plays a major role in the creation of new words for products, institutions, etc. This type of blending often hinges on shared sounds in the contact area of the two items (which may be subject to clipping): *Tekniker* (*Tekniko* + *iker* 'research'), *euskalabel* 'Basque (quality) label' (*euskal* 'Basque' + *label*). Haplology is also found in more traditional words, e.g., *sagardo* 'cider' (← *sagar* 'apple' + *ardo* 'wine').

9 Clipping

Clipping is very seldom found in Basque (but see section 2.2). Informally, names are occasionally right-clipped if long (*Ganeko(gorta)ra* 'to Ganeko(gorta)'), or, like in Spanish, to create hypochoristic forms (*Bego(ña)*, *Esti(baliz)*, *Itzi(ar)*, etc.). Clipping can co-occur with more important strategies such as expressive palatalization (*Domingo* → *Txomin*, *Antonio* → *Antton*; see also Hualde 2015 on affective palatalization in Basque) or the addition of diminutive suffixes (*Estibaliz* → *Estitxu*). Masculine names in *-io* clip the *-o* to form feminine names: *Anttoni(o)*, *Emili(o)*, *Iñaxi(o)*. Clipping to *-i*, however, also occurs in exclusively masculine names: *Xabier* → *Xabi*, *Txabi*, *Santiago* → *Xanti* (Salaberri 2009). Clipping in nouns is fairly uncommon, colloquial, and found mostly in borrowed Spanish clipped nouns: *telean* 'on TV'.

10 Word-creation

Early 20th century neologisms exploited derivation and compounding. When based on bound morphemes extracted by philological analysis, the resulting words were totally or partially opaque. From the reconstructed formative **aba* 'relative, ancestor', compounds like *aberri* 'fatherland' (← *herri* 'country') or *abizen* 'surname' (← *izen* 'name') were formed. Similarly, backformation on *irakurri* 'to read', interpreting *-ra-* as an old causative prefix, produced *ikur* 'sign', and from it, *ikurriña* '(Basque) flag'. These examples have become naturalized, although initially opaque. The development of a Basque bilingual administration since the 1980s and the "normalization" process of Basque, including its use as a university language in all fields, have spawned specialized terminologies on the basis of borrowings as well as productive derivation and compounding processes.

11 References

Artiagoitia, Xabier (2003): The case of an enlightening, provoking and admirable Basque derivational suffix with implications for the theory of argument structure. In: Bernard Oyharçabal (ed.), *Inquiries into the Lexicon-Syntax Relations in Basque*, 147–183. Bilbao/San Sebastián: Supplements of ASJU.

Artiagoitia, Xabier (2020): Derivational networks in Basque. In: Lívia Körtvélyessi, Alexandra Bagasheva and Pavol Štekauer (eds.), *Derivational Networks Across Languages*, 455–464. Berlin/Boston: De Gruyter Mouton.

Azkarate, Miren (1990): *Hitz elkartuak euskara*. San Sebastián: Universidad de Deusto-EUTG.

Azkarate, Miren and Patxi Altuna (2001): *Euskal morfologiaren historia*. Donostia: Elkarlanean.

Azkue, Resurrección María de (1923–25): *Morfología vasca*. Published in fascicles in *Euskera*. [Repr. in 3 Vol., 1969, Bilbao: La Gran Enciclopedia Vasca].

Euskaltzaindia [Basque Academy] (1987–92): *Hitz-elkarketa*. 4 Vol. Bilbao: Euskaltzaindia.

Hualde, José Ignacio (2015): Affective palatalization in Basque. In: Peter O. Müller, Ingeborg Ohnheiser, Susan Olsen and Franz Rainer (eds.), *Word-Formation. An International Handbook of the Languages of Europe*. Vol. 1, 517–524. Berlin/Boston: De Gruyter Mouton.

Hualde, José I. and Jon Ortiz de Urbina (eds.) (2003): *A Grammar of Basque*. Berlin: Mouton de Gruyter.

Ibarretxe, Iraide (2006): *Ttipi-ttapa ttipi-ttapa … Korrika!!!* Motion and sound symbolism in Basque. In: Joseba Lakarra and José Ignacio Hualde (eds.), *Studies in Basque and Historical Linguistics in Memory of R. L. Trask*, 499–518. Bilbao: Servicio Editorial de la Universidad del País Vasco.

Jacobsen, William (1982): Basque copulative compounds: A problem in irreversible binomials. In: Monica Macaulay (ed.), *Proceedings of the 8th Annual Meeting of the Berkeley Linguistic Society*, 384–397. Berkeley, CA: Berkeley Linguistic Society.

Lakarra, Joseba A. (1995): Reconstructing the pre-Proto-Basque root. In: José I. Hualde, Joseba A. Lakarra and R[obert] L. Trask (eds.), *Towards a History of the Basque Language*, 189–206. Amsterdam/Philadelphia: Benjamins.

Lakarra, Joseba A. (2003): Temas para un prólogo: Forma canónica, tipología holística diacrónica y reconstrucción del protovasco. *Oihenart* 23: 277–347.

Múgica, Luis María (1978): *Origen y desarrollo de la sufijación euskérica*. San Sebastián: Ediciones Vascas.

Odriozola, Juan Carlos (2003): Verb-deriving processes in Basque. In: Bernard Oyharçabal (ed.), *Inquiries into the Lexicon-Syntax Relations in Basque*, 185–222. Bilbao/San Sebastián: Supplements of ASJU.

Odriozola, Juan Carlos (2004): Estructuras con *gabe* 'sin' en vasco. In: Elixabete Pérez Gaztelu, Igone Zabala and Lluïsa Gràcia (eds.), *Las fronteras de la composición en lenguas románicas y en vasco*, 355–391. San Sebastián: Universidad de Deusto.

Oyharçabal, Beñat [Bernard] (1996): Hitz eratorriak Materreren *Dotrina Christiana* delakoan. *Lapurdum* 1: 37–72.

Oyharçabal, Beñat (2003): *-kor* atzizkiaz. In: Jesús M. Makatzaga and Bernard Oyharçabal (eds.), *Euskal Gramatikari eta literaturi buruzko ikerketak XXI. Mendearen atarian Iker* 14(1), 357–383. Bilbao: Euskaltzaindia.
Oyharçabal, Beñat (2006): Basque light verb constructions. *Anuario del Seminario de Filología Vasca "Julio de Urquijo"* 40(1–2): 787–806.
Pagola Hernández, Inés (2005): *Neologismos en la obra de Sabino Arana Goiri*. Bilbao: Euskaltzaindia.
Pérez Gaztelu, Elixabete (2004): Fronteras entre la sufijación y la composición: Algunos casos del vasco (*alde, aldi, bide, kide, zain, zale*). In: Elixabete Pérez Gaztelu, Igone Zabala and Lluïsa Gràcia (eds.), *Las fronteras de la composición en lenguas románicas y en vasco*, 165–238. San Sebastián: Universidad de Deusto.
Pérez Gaztelu, Elixabete, Igone Zabala and Lluïsa Gràcia (eds.) (2004): *Las fronteras de la composición en lenguas románicas y en vasco*. San Sebastián: Universidad de Deusto.
de Rijk, Rudolf P. G. (1972): Studies in Basque Syntax. Relative Clauses. Ph.D. dissertation, MIT, Cambridge, MA.
de Rijk, Rudolf P. G. (1995): Basque manner adverbs and their genesis. *Anuario del Seminario de Filología Vasca "Julio de Urquijo"* 29(1): 53–82.
de Rijk, Rudolf P. G. (2008): *Standard Basque. A progressive grammar*. Cambridge, MA: MIT Press.
Saizar, Mirari. (2004): *Ari* euskal atzizkiaren azterketa morfologikoa. *Sancho el Sabio* 20: 101–124.
Salaberri, Patxi (2009): *Izen ttipiak euskaraz*. Bilbo: Euskaltzaindia.
Trask, Robert L. (1997): *The History of Basque*. London: Routledge.
Villasante, Luis (1976): *Palabras vascas compuestas y derivadas*. Oñati: Editorial Franciscana Aranzazu.

Joseph Brincat and Manwel Mifsud

18 Maltese

1 Introduction
2 General overview
3 The Semitic stratum
4 The Romance stratum
5 The English influence
6 References

Abstract: New words in Maltese can be formed on Semitic roots or on Romance and English bases, but the latter, being mainly Anglo-Latinisms, tend to reinforce or adapt the Romance element of the vocabulary. Romance and English words are inflected according to Semitic patterns, whereas derivations and compounds add Romance prefixes and suffixes to words of both Semitic and Romance origin. Some English words of Germanic origin are also subjected to such adaptations.

1 Introduction

Arabic was introduced in Malta with the Muslim conquest of 870, and around the year 1000 the spoken variety was of the Maghreb type with characteristics similar to those of Sicilian and Andalusian Arabic. Latin as a high language was introduced by the Normans in 1127 and contact with Arabic stopped with Frederick II's deportation of Muslims in 1246. Diglossia with Chancery Sicilian (1127–1530), Italian (1530–1936) and English (since 1800) as high languages, together with the large-scale immigration of Romance speakers at the lower social levels, increased the Maltese vocabulary by a slow but progressive adoption of Romance terms in all domains (Brincat 2008, 2011). The growth of the Maltese lexicon can be gauged by comparing the number of entries in the first known dictionary compiled apparently by a Provençal knight, Thezan, between 1600 and 1647 (Cassola 1992), 3,110 words, with the more systematic *Ktyb yl klym Malti/Lexicon* published by Michelantonio Vassalli in 1796, about 18,000 entries (Sammut 2002), and with the scientific *Maltese-English Dictionary* published by Joseph Aquilina in 1987–90. Out

Joseph Brincat, Msida, Malta
Manwel Mifsud, Msida, Malta

of the latter's 41,016 lexemes 13,293 are of Arabic origin, 21,519 are of Sicilian and Italian origin, and 2,511 are from English (Brincat 2011: 406–409). There are also 406 words from Latin and French which bring up the number of non-Semitic words to 60.23 % of the total. Even more interesting for our present purposes are the 1,491 local formations, mainly consisting of an Arabic base with Romance affixes or a Romance stem with Semitic suffixes. As a result the Maltese lexicon reveals a flexible structure that, while keeping and simplifying the fundamentally Arabic morphological rules and core vocabulary, over a thousand years has adapted and still adapts well to the communicative needs of a dynamic population which has grown from 5,000 to 415,000 inhabitants living in 316 sq km, 90 km from Sicily and 290 from the Tunisian coast.

2 General overview

As can be deduced from the introduction, the most striking feature of the Maltese language is perhaps its mixed nature at all linguistic levels. In this small habitat, languages with very different lexical repertoires and morphological structures have been in close contact for centuries and have gradually developed into a fairly homogeneous system. However, the basic structural differences are still present and radically separate the two elements both conceptually, i.e. in their way of conceiving and expressing reality, and technically, i.e. in their different word-formation processes, that is at their very base. In the Semitic stratum, the basic concept is typically expressed through a sequence (or *root*) of three or four consonants which are then interdigitated into a number of morphological templates, called *forms* (or *binyanim*), to define the lexeme. Following that, the lexeme can be inflected either internally or externally. Subsequent accretions (mainly of Sicilian, Italian or English origin) introduced a different configuration in which a continuous *stem* conveys the basic concept and affixes are added to develop it both in the derivative and the inflectional directions.

Due to the protracted timespan during which the two morphologies have interacted, there must have been a sustained effort to create a common interface between them. This is evinced by several hybrid formations of different types. In one type a Romance suffix is added to a Semitic element which is treated like a stem: *fenk-ata* 'rabbit stew' ← Semitic Maltese (SM) *fenek* 'rabbit' + Romance Maltese (RM) *-ata*; *dar-un* 'large house' ← SM *dar* 'house' + RM *-un* (augmentative suffix); *lagħq-iżmu* 'servilism' ← SM *lagħaq* 'to lick, be servile to' + RM *-iżmu* '-ism'; *tell-ár* 'auto panel beater' ← SM *tella* 'to beat out' + RM *-ar* (agentive suffix). In a second group, words are formed on the Semitic Maltese patterns following the abstraction of a sequence of root consonants from what used to be a Romance or English stem: *mpitter* 'painted' (root: *p-t-r*) ← Rom. *pittore* 'painter'; *tipjip* 'smoking' (root: *p-j-p*) ← Rom. *pipa* 'pipe'; *fajjar* 'hurl' (root: *f-j-r*) ← Eng. *fire*. It will be seen that, at the word-formation level, such hybridization can give rise also to compounds in which the two elements hark back to two different origins.

However, these limited points of contact, intriguing as they may be, should not be taken as indicative of the mainstream development of Maltese word-formation. On the contrary, during the last century especially, one has witnessed the gradual but steady impoverishment of the Semitic Maltese lexical stock (due both to social change and to sociolinguistic factors) and the stagnation of most of its traditional derivative devices, in favour of the less exacting formations of Romance and English. Word-formation in Maltese is thus gradually shifting from the Semitic root-based morphology to the European stem-based morphology, and the latter is probably responsible for some choices even within the Arabic stratum itself. It has been noted (Mifsud 1995a), for example, that Arabic inflectional features expressed through affixation stand a better chance to survive and remain productive than others involving internal changes. Such is the case, for example, of the SM sound plural *-ijiet* (*omm-ijiet* 'mothers', *aħbar-ijiet* 'news'), which has not only survived but is often applied to words of Romance and English origin (e.g., *prinċp-ijiet* 'princes', *kowt-ijiet* 'coats').

This background will probably suffice to explain why each of the two main strata in Maltese (Semitic and European) is of its own nature prone to certain types of word-formation discussed here and less inclined towards others, and why they are not equally responsive to each of the word-formation tools.

Before we turn to a more detailed description of word-formation in Maltese, a short observation is in order concerning terminology. A distinction is made here between r o o t (Semitic, consonantal *k-t-b*) and s t e m (Romance and English, *żvilupp-* → *żviluppatùr* 'developer', *bricks* → *briksa* 'one brick'). "Semitic" refers mainly to Arabic but the definition is often used to avoid misunderstandings since the Maltese variety has distanced itself considerably from Classical Arabic (Kaye and Rosenhouse 1997) owing to the islands' history (it lost contact with Classical Arabic in 1246), culture (the way of life was mainly southern Italian up to World War II and increasingly Anglo-American nowadays) and religion (the Maltese are Catholic). On the other hand the term "Romance" is used when reference is made to Sicilian, Italian and Anglo-Latin terms collectively. The orthography of Maltese uses the Latin system with diacritics as follows (for a basic phonetic description, see Mifsud 1995b: 14–17) (see Table 18.1).

Accents are only shown on the final vowel of Romance words like *kwalità*, *kafè*, *virtù*. In this article the acute accent is used to facilitate the reader's pronun-

Tab. 18.1: Grapheme-phoneme correspondences in Maltese.

ċ = [tʃ]	*ċena* 'dinner'	k = [k]	*karta* 'paper'	ħ = [ħ]	*ħajt* 'wall'		
ġ = [dʒ]	*ġdid* 'new'	g = [g]	*gidba* 'a lie'	h = mute;	*hena* 'joy'		
ż = [z]	*żejt* 'oil'	z = [ts]	*ziju* 'uncle'	gh = mute;	*għajn* 'eye'		
x = [ʃ]	*xena* 'scene'	j = [j]	*jum* 'day'				
q = [ʔ] glottal stop *qalb* 'heart'				ie = [iː]	*kien* '(he/it) was'		

ciation by showing stress in Romance words that lose the final syllable: *kuntrást, kampnár, kattív.*

3 The Semitic stratum

3.1 Composition

Due to their root-based morphology, Semitic languages are generally averse to those word-formation tools in which words are juxtaposed or develop laterally. Writing about composition in Modern Arabic, Vincent Monteil (1960: 132) admits: "L'arabe ne peut pas réunir deux mots par une voyelle thématique comme font le latin et le grec, ni les joindre selon les composés de l'anglais ou de l'allemand. *La composition n'est pas dans son génie.*" [Arabic cannot unite two words with a thematic vowel as Latin and Greek do, nor can it join them together in the manner of English or German compounds. *Composition is not in its nature.*] In fact, compounds proper are not too frequent in either modern Arabic or Maltese, and most of them are the historical result of formations that have lost their syntactic significance to varying degrees. The following classes of historical compounds are noteworthy.

3.1.1 Phrases in the construct state

The construct state is a typically Semitic syntactic construction involving two members (normally nouns) in a genitive relation, the first member being the headword and the second indicating a relation with the head. The nature of the relation could range from the possessive to a more loosely relational one. The first component is automatically definite and does not take an article. Hence the typical construction noun + (article + noun): *dar il-kaptan* '(the) house (of) the captain', *tmiem il-ġimgħa* '(the) end (of) the week'.

Some construct-state phrases, however, tend to move away from the realm of syntax to become compounds, and could eventually fuse into a single word. One could think of different reasons for this, among which: a) the tendency of construct-state phrases to prosodically behave as a word (cf. Benmamoun 2006), and b) the loss of transparency or the metaphorical content of one of the components (*qamħirrun* 'maize, Indian corn' ← *qamħ* 'corn' + *ir-Rum* 'the Greeks'; *qawsalla* 'rainbow' ← *qaws* 'arch' + *Alla* 'God'). The weaker the syntactic relation becomes, the easier it will be for the phrase to assume the status of a single noun and be treated as such, e.g., in pluralization. But one can observe a continuum of examples exhibiting greater or lesser integration: a) *il-kelb il-baħar* 'shark; lit. the-dog [of] the-sea', where *kelb* takes the article, but pluralization still splits the construct state: *klieb il-baħar* lit. 'dogs the-sea'; b) *il-ħmar-il-lejl* 'nightmare; lit. the donkey (of) the night', where *ħmar* takes the article, but pluralization is a suffix added at the end of the construct state: *ħmar-il-lejlijiet* lit. 'donkey-the-nights'; c) *bniedem* 'man' (← *bin Adam* lit. 'son (of) Adam'), a construct-state phrase treated as one word both prosodically and morphologically and forming the plural via suffixation (*bnedmin*); d) *qamħirrun* 'maize' (← *qamħ ir-Rum* lit. 'corn (of) the Greeks'), treated as a type noun, i.e. *qamħirrun*, to which -*a* is added to develop a singulative; e) *qawsalla* 'rainbow', pl. *qawsalel* (< *qaws Alla* lit. 'God's bow or arch') with an internal plural.

Maltese *bu-*, now considered as a prefix, harks back to Ar. *'abu* 'father of, possessor of, person particularly conspicuous for sth.' which once stood as the first noun of a construct-state formation: *bumunqar* 'weevil' ← *bu-* + *munqar* 'beak', *butwila* 'tall fellow' ← *bu-* + *twila* 'tall', *budebbus* 'broomrape' ← *bu-* + *debbus* 'mace, club'.

3.1.2 Further cases of univerbation based on Semitic elements

A number of words, mostly adverbs and prepositions, are compounds consisting of a preposition followed by a noun or adverb, just as in English *afternoon, forever*. Not infrequently they are hybrid formations made up of Semitic and Romance elements: *madwar* 'around' (← *ma'* 'with' + *dwar* 'surroundings'), *maġenb* 'beside' (← *ma'* 'with' + *ġenb* 'side'), *xi mindaqqiet* 'at times' (← *xi* 'some' + *minn* 'from' + *daqqiet* 'times'), *bħal* 'such as' (← *bi* 'with, in' + *ħal* 'situation, condition'), *minkejja* 'in spite of' (← *minn* 'from' + *nkejja* 'spite'), *minfuq* 'in spite of it all' (← *minn* 'from' + *fuq* 'up'), *bħalkieku* 'as if' (← *bħal* 'like' + *kieku* 'if'), *bħalissa* 'currently' (← *bħal* 'like' + *issa* 'now'), *għalkemm* 'although' (← *għal* 'for' + *kemm* 'so much'), *għalhekk* 'for this reason' (← *għal* 'for' + *hekk* 'so'), *daqshekk* 'that much, enough' (← *daqs* 'as much as' + *hekk* 'so'), *għarkupptejh* 'kneeling' (← obsolete *għala* 'on' + *rkupptejh* 'his knees'), *flimkien* 'together' (← *fi* 'in' + *l-imkien* 'the (= one) place'), *kultant* 'sometimes' (← *kull* 'every' + *tant* 'so much'), *kulħadd* 'everyone' (← *kull* 'every' + *ħadd* 'one'), *mingħajr* 'without' (← *minn* 'from' + *għajr* 'other than'), *tassew* 'truly' (← *ta'* 'of' + *sew(wa)* 'truth'), *flok* 'instead of' (← *fi* 'in' + *lok* 'place'), *tadam* 'tomatoes' (← (*tuffieħ*) *ta' Adam* 'Adam's (apple)').

A few compounds are the result of the fusion of three different elements: *minflok* 'instead of' (← *minn* 'from' + *fi* 'in' + *lok* 'place'), *għaldaqstant* 'however' (← *għal* 'for' + *daqs* 'as much as' + *tant* 'that much'), *tabilħaqq* 'truly' (← *ta'* 'of' + *bi* 'with' + *ħaqq* 'truth'), *madankollu* 'however' (← *ma'* 'with' + *dan* 'this' + *kollu* 'all').

A number of pronouns exhibit the ending *-iex* ('what, that which'), originally an independent pronoun standing as the object of the preceding preposition. Another set ends with the relative pronoun suffix *-lli*, but here the pronominal sense has often been lost: *biex* 'with what, so that' (← *bi* 'with' + *-iex* 'what'), *fiex* 'in what' (← *fi* 'in' + *-iex* 'what'), *fuqiex* 'on what' (← *fuq* 'on' + *-iex* 'what'), *għaliex* 'for what, why' (← *għal* 'for' + *-iex* 'what'), *mniex* 'from what' (← *minn* 'from' + *-iex* 'what'); *billi* 'since' (← *bi* 'with' + *-lli* 'that which'), *filli* 'no sooner ...' (← *fi* 'in' + *-lli* 'that which'), *talli* 'because of' (← *ta'* 'of' + *-lli* 'that which'), *malli* 'as soon as' (← *ma'* 'with' + *-lli* 'that which').

Some phrases consisting of head + descriptive also ended up as compounds: *qarabagħli* 'marrows' (← type-noun *qara* 'marrows' + *bagħli* 'unirrigated'), *qarabocċa* 'a millet grain' (← *qara* 'marrows' + *bocċa* 'spherical').

A handful of verbal phrases, especially prepositional verbs, are the historical fusion of highly-used expressions, and possibly were already present in one of the Arabic varieties which reached the islands: *ġieb* 'to bring' (← *ġie* 'to come' + *bi* 'with'), *amba* 'to need, have some use for' (probably ← *għamel* 'to do' + *bi* 'with'), *kellu* 'to have' (← *kien* + suffix *-lu* lit. 'to belong + to').

3.1.3 Compounds after Romance models

Some nouns hark back to Romance compounds imported bodily into the language or phrases which could not be analyzed into the component parts and were taken up by the monolingual speakers as a whole: *parafangu* 'mudguard; lit. keep-out-mud', *reġipettu* 'bra; lit. support-bust', *taljakarti* 'paper-knife; lit. cut-paper', *salvavita* 'circuit-breaker; save-life', *salvawomu* 'life-jacket; lit. save-man', *ġiggifogu* 'fireworks; lit. game of fire', cf. It. *gioco di fuoco*, *firdiferru* 'metal wire; lit. wire of iron', cf. It. *fil di ferro*. The first of these examples, made up of verb + noun, are noteworthy for having served as models to some of the writer Manwel Dimech's fanciful creations in the past (Dimech 1901), such as *aħlilinka* 'scribbler, poor writer; lit. waste-ink' or *bażżasnajja*' 'dabbler, bad craftsman; lit. frighten-crafts'.

3.1.4 Compounding in modern Maltese

All the above, however, are in the realm of diachrony. Compounding in modern Maltese is largely limited to calques on parallel formations of Italian or English origin which are current in the media. Some locally formed compounds, however, occur: *mara-raġel* 'virago' (← *mara* 'woman' + *raġel* 'man'), *mara-ħuta* 'siren' (← *mara* 'woman' + *ħuta* 'fish'), *rabta ċoff* 'unbinding commitment' (← *rabta* 'tie' + *ċoff* 'bow, slip-knot'), *riegla ċomb* 'plumb-line' (← *riegla* 'ruler' + *ċomb* 'lead, plumb-'), *(l-)hekk imsejjaħ* 'so-called' (← *hekk* 'so' + *imsejjaħ* 'called').

It is interesting to note that Maltese writers with a sharply functional view of language seem to be more prone to mould it to suit their needs and more ready to let foreign syntax suggest novel formations: *tablagħadd* 'uncountable' (M. A. Vassalli; ← *ta'* 'of' + *bla* 'without' + *għadd* 'count'); *(it-)tagħmelxijiet* 'the don'ts, things not to do' (Juann Mamo; ← *tagħmelx* 'don't do' + plural suffix *-ijiet*). Manwel Dimech coined words for most of the grammatical terminology in his *Il Chelliem Inglis* (1901) replacing learned technical nouns with more mnemonic local compounds: *misem* 'adjective; lit. with-noun', *megħmil* 'adverb; lit. with-action', *flokisem* 'pronoun; lit. for-noun', *maleħni* 'consonant; lit. non-vocalic', *lillej* 'dative; lit. to + adj. suffix', etc. These words remained hapax legomena.

In the sixties and seventies of the last century, compounding (as well as blending and clipping) became fashionable again as a means of developing the local linguistic resources to meet the pressing lexical needs of a changing society. Culturally they also represented a daring effort to force the strict limitations of traditional word-formation based mainly on Semitic derivation and to experiment with Maltese in a more creative and flexible way. Only a few of these compounds, however, managed to find favour with the media and the speaking community: *ittra-bomba* 'letter-bomb', *storjaritratti* 'picture-story; lit. story pictures', *linji-gwida* 'guidelines; lit. lines-guide', *teletara* 'television', *vapurarja* 'hydrofoil' (← *vapur* 'ship' + *arja* 'air'), *student-ħaddiem* 'working student; lit. student-worker', *is-snin sittin* 'the sixties; lit. the years (the) sixties'. Rather than being local creations, these words are calques, except for *teletara* and *vapurarja* which were soon rejected.

More recent attempts at launching new compounds hardly meet with a more favourable welcome: *ġabradati* 'database' (← *ġabra* 'collection' + *dati* 'data'), *taqsi-*

ma-studju 'study unit' (← *taqsima* 'section' + *studju* 'study'), *ittre* 'email' (← *ittr-* the stem of *ittra* 'letter' + *e-*, the first letter of *elettronika* 'electronic'; on the English model *email*, but following Maltese syntax, in which adjectives follow the noun they qualify).

For a stimulating discussion on what could be considered as compounds in Maltese, cf. Fabri (2009).

3.2 Derivation

As indicated in the introduction to this article, derivation is genetically the stronghold of Maltese word-formation. The lexeme (or root) in the form of a sequence of three or four consonants is inserted into a number of templatic forms (or binyanim) giving rise to different but related nominal or verbal lexemes. While on one hand this system tends to be very egocentric and impervious, on the other hand – given the infinite possibilities of consonantal sequences and the considerable number of forms – one cannot say that it is a completely closed system, since a) the possibility of developing new lexemes from old material is far from exhausted (cf. new creations like *tisliba* 'crossword puzzle' ← *s-l-b* 'cross', *tisbiħ* 'embellishment' ← *s-b-ħ* 'beauty') and b) in the case of Maltese, new root bases of Romance extraction have sometimes joined the old stock of Arabic roots (cf. *fannad* 'to dig deep' ← *f-n-d* ← RM *fond* 'deep', *pejjep* 'to smoke' ← *p-j-p* ← RM *pipa* 'pipe').

3.2.1 Verbal derivation

Since some of the nominal templates are derived from corresponding verbal templates, it would be best here to treat verbal derivation first.

Semitic Maltese has nine canonical verbal templates for triconsonantal roots and two for roots with four consonants, listed in Table 18.2. Although traditional grammar associates a host of different meanings with these forms, current expert opinion (cf. Borg 1988) tends to redimension this view and to hold that most of these forms fall squarely into the active-passive distinction. Other meanings tend to be relegated to the status of fringe phenomena and more refined nuances end up as lexical qualities of the individual verbs rather than general semantic tendencies. Table 18.2 presents a list of the verbal templates into which Maltese interdigitates the consonantal sequence (here represented as 1–4) to form new verbs, together with their canonical meaning/s. (Superscript [a] indicates the long vowel *a* [ɐ] or its Imāla reflex [ɪː], which is orthographically represented by *ie*.)

Tab. 18.2: Verbal templates in Maltese word-formation.

	Form	Main meaning	Examples
1	'1v2v3	the basic meaning:	
		transitive	kiteb 'to write', rifes 'to tread on'
		intransitive	daħal 'to enter', niżel 'to go down'
2	'1v22v3	transitive of 1 (itr.)	daħħal 'to introduce'
		intensive of 1 (tr.)	qalla 'to fry repeatedly'
		relative (denominative)	serrep 'to meander' (← serp 'snake')
3	'1ª2v3	transitive of 1 (itr.)	biegħed 'to place far away'
4	–	–	–
5	't1v22v3	passive/reflexive of 2	tqassam 'to be distributed'
6	't1ª2v3	passive/reflexive of 3	tbierek 'to be blessed'
7		passive/reflexive of 1	
a	'n1v2v3		ngabar 'to be gathered' ← gabar
b	'nt1v2v3		ntrifes 'to be trod upon' ← rifes
c	'n1tv2v3		nstema' 'to be heard' ← sema'
8	'1tv2v3	passive/reflexive of 1	ntefaq 'to be spent' ← nefaq
9	12ª3	inchoative	twāl 'to become taller'
10		(originally inchoative)	
a	'stv12v3		stenbaħ 'to wake up'
b	'st1v22v3		stkerrah 'to loathe'
Q1	'1v23v4	the basic meaning	ħarbat 'to destroy'
Q2	't1v23v4	passive/reflex. of Q1	tħarbat 'to be destroyed'

3.2.2 Nominal derivation

With the exception of a handful of forms which are formed externally (e.g., singulative nouns and relational adjectives), nominal forms are obtained through the insertion of the 3 or 4 consonants of a root-base into one or more of the nominal or adjectival forms in Table 18.3. The list is not exhaustive, but it should suffice to give an idea of the more important formations.

This is an impressive array of morphological tools which could have been of great help to the budding language in meeting the lexical needs along its history, and especially in the periods of major social activity and upheaval. Things, how-

Table 18.3: Nominal templates in Maltese word-formation.

Noun	Form	Template	Examples
Noun: verbal	1	1v23	talb 'praying', serq 'stealing'
	1	12v̄3	dfin 'burying', ħsad 'reaping', ħruġ 'going out'
	1	1v2'3ᵃn	serħan 'resting'
	2/5	tv1'2ī3	taħbit 'knocking/being knocked'
	3/6	t1v'2ī3	tberik 'blessing/being blessed'
	7	n12ī3	ndħil 'interfering'
	10	stv1'2ī3	stenbiħ 'rising up'
	Q1/Q2	t1v2'3ī4	tqarbin 'giving/receiving Communion'
Noun: verbal – singulative		-a	talba 'a prayer', taħbita 'a knock'
Participle: active		'1ᵃ2v3	ħiereġ 'going out'
Participle: passive	1	mv1'2ū3	miksur 'broken'
	2	'm1v22v3	mfaddal 'collected'
	3	'm1ᵃ2v3	mwieled 'born'
	5	mvt'1v22v3	mitkellem 'spoken'
	10	mvs'tv23v4	mistagħġeb 'dumbfounded'
	Q1	'm1v23v4	mħarbat 'destroyed'
Noun: agentive		1v2'2ᵃ3	kittieb 'writer'
Noun: of place		mv1'2v3	maħżen 'store'
Noun: of instrument		mv1'2ᵃ3	moqdief 'oar'
Noun: of type – singulative		-a	ħadida 'iron bar'
Noun: of quality		12v'3ija	kburija 'pride'
Noun: diminutive		'12vjjv3	tfajjel 'small boy'
Adjective: relational		-ī	Malti 'Maltese'

ever, worked out in quite a different way since many of these tools became gradually less productive and their members were often reduced to closed lists without any clear connection between them in the mind of the speakers. Some forms, however, have been put to good use at least by language-conscious individuals from the linguistic or mediatic spheres in their search for a "Maltese" alternative to sheer imports. However, some of these creations, ingenious as they might be, never actually got off the ground or were eventually replaced by imported words. The contrary, one must observe, practically never happens. Here are some examples:

a) Verbal nouns: *tisbiħ* 'embellishment' (← *s-b-ħ* 'beauty'), *tisliba* 'crossword puzzle' (← *s-l-b* 'cross'), *ċempila* 'phone-call' (← *ċ-m-p-l* 'to ring (a bell)'), *titqiba* 'an inoculation' (← *t-q-b* 'to bore, pierce'), *sahra* 'overtime' (← *s-h-r* 'to stay up late');

b) Place nouns: *mitjar* 'airport' (← *t-j-r* 'to fly'), *miksaħ* 'refrigerator' (← *k-s-ħ* 'cold'), *mafkar* 'monument' (← *f-k-r* 'to remember'), *mirmed* 'ash-tray' (← *r-m-d* 'ash');

c) Agent nouns: *kelliem* 'spokesman' (← *k-l-m* 'to talk');

d) Passive participles: *mleħħen* '(phonetics) voiced' (← *l-ħ-n* 'voice'), *mniffes* '(phonetics) voiceless' (← *n-f-s* 'breath').

3.3 Conversion

In a highly inflected language such as Maltese one can hardly expect to come across any cases of conversion, since all word classes would be strongly marked. In fact, the transfer of the qualities of one word class to another occurs only occasionally, and even then it is merely a stylistic device and not a morphological development, as the following examples can show: *Il-Jien u lil hinn minnu* 'The Ego (lit. Myself) and beyond it'; *irid jaf il-kif u l għala* 'he would like to know the reason and the modality (lit. the why and the how)'; *Forsi raġel ħażin* 'Suspicion (*forsi* 'perhaps' used as a personification) is a wicked man'.

An interesting case of development bordering on conversion is the verb *daka/idaki* 'to do or mention "that" thing' used to describe the action of someone who, at a loss for the proper name, refers to things merely by the demonstrative *dak* 'that'. Such a person may even ask one to fetch him/her *il-x'jismu* 'the what's-its-name' or *il-x'jgħidulu* 'the what's-it-called'. One may occasionally come across sporadic creations of this type in literature, such as Juann Mamo's ingenious *jinestasi* 'he becomes ecstatic, spellbound' in *Ulied in-Nanna Venut fl-Amerka*, 1930, p. 10, an effective verbalization of the phrase *in estasi* 'ecstatic, absent-minded'.

Perhaps nearer to true conversions is the canonical possibility in Semitic Maltese to derive verbs of the second or the quadriliteral forms from nouns or adjectives, but here again the word is remodelled on the template of the second form, so that one can hardly speak of true conversions: *xemx* 'sun' → *xémmex* 'to put in the sun', *serp* 'snake' → *sérrep* 'to meander', *serdúq* 'cock' → *ssérdaq* 'to behave arrogantly'.

3.4 Backformation

As in other languages, backformation in Maltese is a sporadic phenomenon rather than a regular word-formation process. Noteworthy examples seem to be the result of friction between the two morphologies in contact, such as singulative nouns which give rise to (rather than derive from) type nouns of Romance origin, e.g., *palma* 'a palm tree', *sardina* 'a sardine', *gawwija* 'a gull' and *qaraboċċa* 'a millet grain' (cf. It. *sardina*, It. *palma*, Latin *gavia*, Sic. *boccia*) from which type nouns *palm, sardín, gawwi, qarabóċċ* are backformed.

Metanalysis may also occasionally give rise to backformation: The 8th form *mtela* 'to be filled' (root *m-l-j* with infix *-t-*) is pronounced **ntela* due to its assimilated pronunciation, and hence reinterpreted as the 7th form (with prefix *n-*) of a supposed **tela* (root *t-l-j*) from which a novel verbal noun *tilja* is formed, besides the more orthodox *milja* (for similar cases of metanalysis resulting in reformed root sequences, cf. Mifsud 1995b: 315–317).

3.5 Reduplication

Although Maltese, like other Semitic languages, does not particularly favour reduplication, it shares with other Arabic dialects the tendency to develop quadriliteral root bases with an iterative meaning and an onomatopoeic effect by the reduplication of biradical roots: *mess* (root *m-s-s*) 'to touch' → *mesmes* (root *m-s-m-s*) 'to finger, tamper with', *bass* 'to break wind' → *basbas* 'to break wind frequently', *saff* 'to suck' → *sefsef* 'to suck greedily with a smacking sound'.

At the level of the phrase, modern Maltese makes use of a number of patterns displaying reduplication, mainly with an adverbial meaning and presumably due to the influence of Romance, even though the lexical material may be of Semitic origin: *ħelu ħelu* 'nicely', *fuq fuq* 'superficially', *baxx baxx* 'stealthily', *kutu kutu* 'underhandedly', *bil-mod il-mod* 'slowly, gradually'. In other cases, reduplication conveys a "distributive" meaning: *bieb bieb* 'door-to-door', *wieħed wieħed* 'one by one' (for a detailed review of reduplication in Maltese against a comparative background, cf. Stolz 2003–04).

3.6 Blending

Foreign though they may seem, one can find sporadic formations involving blending in modern Maltese which, however, are hardly ever spontaneous developments. Rather, they tend to be the products of very literate persons in search of an idiosyncratic or catchy name for an innovation: *sinktíb* 'shorthand', made up of *sin(g)* 'line' or *sin(jal)* 'sign' and *ktib* 'writing', coined by G. Ransley in 1937; *Maltraljàn* 'Australian Maltese', made up of *Malt(i)* 'Maltese' and *(Aws)traljan* 'Australian', coined by R. Bovingdon.

Some more recent examples are the product of mediatic influence: *Indifest*, from *Indi(pendenza)* 'Independence' + *fest(a)* or *fest(ival)*, an annual festival celebrating Independence; *Festubru*, from *fest(ival)* 'festival' + *(Ot)tubru* 'October', the name of a festival organized in the Gozitan village of Kerċem in October; *Żinnternet*, made up of colloquial *żinn* 'lie' + *(i)nternet*, for 'internet fibs', the name of a popular newspaper column.

3.7 Clipping

Clipping is rare in Maltese, but it may be resorted to mainly for a euphemistic purpose, namely to decrease the immediate impact of an offensive word by making its stem less apparent, e.g., *(v)irġni* 'Virgin (Mary)', *(S)antamarija* 'Saint Mary'. The innocent word *ħaxix* 'grass, vegetables' is often used instead of vulgar *ħaxi* (lit. 'sexual intercourse' but used in the sense of 'illegal dealings, cheating').

A similar euphemistic effect is sometimes obtained in exactly the opposite way, that is by shrouding the offensive word in a longer and innocent one; thus *kazz|ola* 'kitchen pan' is used in place of vulgar *kazz* 'penis' in expressions like: *x'il-kazzola trid?* 'What the hell do you want?'. It is also used to avoid disrespectful exclamations, like *Madoffi* instead of *Madonna*.

4 The Romance stratum

4.1 Words of Sicilian and Italian origin

4.1.1 Adaptation

Maltese has adopted a very large number of words from Sicilian and Italian, the majority of which are nouns, 13,420, but there are also 3,898 adjectives, 2,290 verbs and 597 adverbs. One must point out that they are all subject to Semitic inflection. Italian and Anglo-Latin words are also adapted to the Sicilian vocalic system and to some of its consonantal patterns. In Sicilian the Latin vowels A, I, U never change but E and O become [i] and [u] only when they are long: short E and O remain [e] and [o]. In Maltese this pattern was adopted with all the Sicilian words and by analogy it is also applied to words adopted from Italian as well as to English words of Latin origin: It. *corona* ~ Sic. *curuna* > M. *kuruna*, It. *catena* ~ Sic. *catina* > M. *katina*, *velo* ~ *velu* > *velu*, *tela* ~ *tila* > *tila*, *voce* ~ *vuci* > *vuċi*. As to consonants, the main changes concern /s/ > /ʃ/ preceding /k/, /m/, /p/ and /t/ in some of the earlier loans, and gemination. Initial gemination is most common in verbs: *ibbenéfika* ← *benefica(re)* 'to benefit', *iffirma* ← *firma(re)* 'to sign' (cf. Mifsud 1995b: 142–168), final gemination marks nouns whose last consonant is *ġ*, *n*, or *l*: *kulléġġ* ← *collegio* 'college'; the voiced palatal nasal [ñ] and the voiced palatal lateral [ʎ] lose their palatal character when the following unstressed vowel is dropped, and so they become long *n* or *l* (*-nn*, *-ll*): *disínn* ← *disegno* 'design', *portafóll* ← *portafoglio* 'wallet'. Internal gemination characterizes *b*, *ġ*, *t*, and *z*: *formidabbli* ← *formidabile*, *inkredibbli* ← *incredibile*, *kulleġġjata* ← *collegiata* 'collegiate (church)', *indikattív* ← *indicativo*, *prestazzjoni* ← *prestazione* 'performance'. Besides, Maltese often drops the final unstressed vowel in singular forms: *fil* 'wire' ← *filo* ~ *filu*, *kulúr* 'colour' ← *colore* ~ *culuri*, but stress remains as in the original Italian (Brincat 2011: xi, 119, 457–459).

Productive Sicilian vowel patterns are applied to all new words from Italian, including learned terms, when they show suffixes as in: *perċentwali* ← *percentuale* 'percentage', *penetranti* ← *penetrante* 'penetrating', *similitudni* ← *similitudine* 'similitude', *televiżjoni* ← *televisione* 'television', *globaliżmu* ← *globalismo* 'globalism'. Of course there are exceptions, like the Sicilian feminine suffix *-issa* which is retained in words adopted a long time ago, like *barunissa* 'baroness', but does not figure in the more recent ones, *dottoressa*, *studentessa* which keep the Italian *-essa* (however, *studentessa* is receding owing to the local analogical adaptation *studenta* 'female student'). The closing of the Italian diphthong *-eo* to *-ew* in the singular and *-ei* to *-ej* in the plural, is consistent: *mużéw* ← *museo*, *mużéj*/*mużewijiet* ← *musei* 'museum/s'; *Ewropéw* ← *europeo*, *Ewropéj* ← *europei* 'European'. Another interesting case concerns the passive participle when the Sicilian suffix *-utu* > *-ut* substitutes the passive participles (and adjectives) which in Italian end in *-ito*: *ferito*, *tradito*, *rifinito* become *ferút*, *ittradút*, *irfinút*, and by analogy create forms that are unknown in Sicilian and Italian, like *ikkoreġút* 'corrected, chided', *sparixxút* 'disappeared', *splodùt* 'exploded'. These are based respectively on the stem of the Italian third person singular form of the present tense: *corregge* + *-uto*, *sparisce* + *-uto* and *esplode* + *-uto*. However, strong exposure to modern Italian has reduced the productivity of these creative suffixes: *stabbilít* ← *stabilito* 'established', *definít* ← *definito* 'defined', *suġġerít* ← *suggerito* 'suggested'. Some derivatives forming adjectives from passive participles are based on nouns instead of the verbal forms: *pitturati* 'painted' ← *pittura* 'painting, a painting', *skulturati* 'sculpted' ← *scultura* 'sculpture, a sculpture', *ġuramentati* 'sworn' ← *giuramento* 'oath' (cf. It. *dipinti*, *scolpiti*, *giurati*).

The large number of words integrated from Sicilian and Italian obviously implies that most derivatives and compounds have been absorbed ready-made. Derivatives adopted from Italian when the Sicilian base was already in use in Maltese are readily recognizable, thus creating phonetic contrasts: *baxx – bassezzi* ('low' ~ 'lowness'), *falz – iffalsifika* ('false' ~ 'falsify'), *polz – pulsazzjoni* ('pulse' ~ 'pulsation'), *penzjoni – pensjonánt* ('pension' ~ 'pensioner'), *ċatt – pjattaforma* ('flat' ~ 'platform'), *ċanga – pjanċa* ('block for cutting meat', later 'beef' ~ 'plank'), *ċar – ikkjarifika* ('clear' ~ 'clarify'), *gaġġa – gabbjetta* ('cage' ~ 'small birdcage'), *Franza – Franċiż* ('France' ~ 'French'), *qanpiena – kampnár* ('bell' ~ 'belfry'). The contrast can be quite marked when it implies different lexemes with the same basic meaning, as in *flixkún* (← Old Sic. *flascuni* 'flask, bottle') and *ibbottiljắt* 'bottled', which may have been slightly adapted from Italian *imbottigliato* or derived from English *bottle* + -*at* (← It. -*ato*, translating English -*ed*).

The most common Romance suffixes are: -*abbli*, -*aġni*, -*ál*, -*ali*, -*anti*, -*ár*, -*át*, -*attív*, -*ázz*, -*azzjoni*, -*ibbli*, -*iċi*, -*ier*, -*issa*, -*ist*/-*ista*, -*ittív*, -*iż*, -*iżmu*, -*izzju*, -*joni*, -*udni*, -*ún*, -*úr*, -*út*, -*úż*, as shown in the following examples: *probabbli* 'probable', *vojtaġni* 'nonsense', *abitwali* 'habitual', *penetranti* 'piercing', *nutár* 'notary', *żbaljất* 'mistaken', *kumbattív* 'combative', *katnázz* 'padlock', *dikjarazzjoni* 'declaration', *possibbli* 'possible', *pittriċi* 'paintress', *arġentier* 'silversmith', *barunissa* 'baroness', *dentíst* 'dentist', *pożittív* 'positive', *Ingliż* 'English', *realiżmu* 'realism', *preġudizzju* 'prejudice', *deċiżjoni* 'decision', *karettún* 'cart', *kaċċatúr* 'hunter', *ferút* 'wounded', *kurjúż* 'curious', derived from Sicilian or Italian *probabile*, *vuotaggine*, *abituale*, *penetrante*, *notaro*, *sbagliato*, *combattivo*, *catenaccio*, *dichiarazione*, *possibile*, *pittrice*, *argentiere*, *baronessa*, *positivo*, *inglese*, *realismo*, *pregiudizio*, *decisione*, *carretto*, *cacciatore*, *ferito*, *curioso*.

As a consequence, the need for forming new words doesn't seem to be pressing because a base like *familja* 'family' has been followed by most of its Italian derivatives: *familista, familjari, familjarità, iffamiljarizza, familjarizzazzjoni, familjarmént*. The same is true of common prefixes like *in-*, *pre-*, and *ri-* which have numerous derivatives recorded in Aquilina (1987–90). Recent and learned ones are well represented too: *tele-* has 42 derivatives, *tri-* has 29, and *viċi-* has 15. An interesting example is the more specialized *semi-*, present in 19 derivatives, all of which are in Sabatini-Coletti (2006), which has 143 such entries, except two, *semikadenza* and *semitrill* which have been adopted from English. However, Sicilian and Italian affixes have been assimilated to such an extent that they have become models for the creation of new terms by analogy. As a result some of them have become productive and therefore a proper discussion of word-formation in Maltese will focus on idiosyncratic processes that are applied automatically to Semitic bases, to newly-adopted Italian terms, as well as to English words of Latin and occasionally of Germanic origin.

4.1.2 Hybrid formations on Semitic bases

Derivations like *fenkata* 'rabbit stew', *xemxata* 'sunstroke', *ħmarún* 'a big donkey' (metaphorical for 'a very stupid person'), *sakranázz* 'drunkard', *tellár* 'panel-beater', and *alabibiżmu* 'carelessness', are based on the Semitic lexemes *fének* 'rabbit', *xemx* 'sun', *ħmar* 'donkey', *tella'* 'to raise', and the expression *ala biebu* 'he does not care' with the addition of *-ata* (← -*ata*), *-un* (← Sic. -*uni*, It. -*one*), -*ar* (← -*aro*), and -*iżmu* (← -*ismo*). The suffixes -*ut* (← -*uto*) and -*at* (← -*ato*) are often applied to verbs of Arabic origin to form the passive participle: *emmnút* ← *émmen* 'to believe', *ittamát* ← *ittáma* 'to hope'. Lexical formations with a Semitic stem and a Romance prefix are less frequent; the commonest example is *Arċisqof* 'archbishop' ← It. *arċi-* + Sem. *isqof* 'bishop'.

Although function words are almost all of Arabic origin, there have been hybrid compounds to fill in semantic gaps: *intánt* 'in the meantime', *sadanittánt/sadattánt* 'in the meantime, until then', *peress li* 'on account of', *appík (li)* 'about to', *disentu* 'continually, without interruption'. They are almost all adverbs.

4.1.3 Maltese derivations with Romance bases and suffixes

Romance terms can go through various changes in Maltese, but one must not stop at a comparison with Italian. Lexemes which seemed to have been formed locally can be found in Sicilian: in this way *ajkla* 'eagle', *delizzju* 'hobby', *travu* 'beam' and *vojt* 'empty' turn up in the *Vocabolario Siciliano* (VS) as *aicula*, *ddilizziu*, *travu* and *voitu* with the same meanings. However, the derived form *vojtagni* 'nonsense' can be considered a local formation because the suffix -*agni* ← -*aggine* has been modified and added to the Sicilian base *vojt-* and the term **voitaggini* is not recorded in the VS. The same goes for *tostàgni*, which adds the same suffix to the base *tost-* (← It. *tosto* or Sic. *tostu*), but it can also be a syncopated form of *tustitàggini/tustutàggini* which has the same meaning in VS, 'cheekiness'.

Italian nouns ending in -*e*, which becomes -*i* in Maltese, create difficulties because their gender is not easily defined, contrary to endings in -*a* (sg.f.) and -*u* (sg.m.), and so they could be seen as plural forms (m. and f.). In such cases nouns can be assigned analogous forms for each gender, and adjectives can be modified to agree with the nouns they qualify. Therefore It. *studente* and *cantante* drop the final vowel in the masculine form and change it to -*a* in the feminine: *studént*, *studenta*, *kantánt*, *kantanta*, as do the It. adjectives *ignorante* and *lugubre*: *injoránt*, *injoranta*, *lugubra*, *lugubru*. Consequently the forms with final -*i* mark the plural of both m. and f., e.g., *studenti*, *kantanti*, *injoranti*, *lugubri*. Analogy is also applied to Italian masculine words of Greek origin ending in -*a*, such as *problema* and *sistema*, which become feminine. On the other hand, personal nouns ending in *-ista* drop final *-a* to produce the masculine form when denoting a profession (*dentist* ← It. *dentista, xjentist, xjentista* f. ← It. *scient-* + *ist* of Eng. *scientist*) or an ideology (*nazzjonalist* ← It. *nazionalista, laburist* ← It. *laburista* or Eng. *labourist*, though *Labourite* is more common in English) but retains final *-a* in adjectives (*Gvern Nazzjonalista, Partit Laburista*).

The most common changes are semantic. Three examples are *paxxùt* (← It. *pasciuto*/Sic. *pasciutu* 'well fed and shows it'), which means 'sitting or lying down comfortably' in Maltese, *armatura* ('suit of armour' in Italian and Sicilian), which has extended its meaning to 'shop window', and *entratura* ('entrance' in It. and Sic.), which also means 'entrance fee'. Some words modify their meaning by changing grammatical category, like *partitarju* sg.m. 'supporter of political party or other clubs', which is an adjective in Italian ('partisan'), and *veru, vera* (← It. *vero, vera* 'true', an adjective which in Maltese is more often used as an adverb). Occasionally, an expression can be lexicalized, like the concessive conjunction *avolja* ← *hai voglia* 'although, in spite of', and its local synonymous derivative *allavolja* ← **hai la voglia*.

Some words are coined by taking Romance stems and adding suffixes that are absent in the original. For instance, *ċuċ* 'ass, stupid person' ← Sic. *ciucciu* produces *ċuċún* 'a very stupid person' and *ċuċésk* 'silly'; *paprata* 'blunder' ← It. *papera* + *-ata, preparamenti* ← *prepara* + *-menti* 'preparations' (cf. It. *preparativi*), *dispramènt* ← *dispera* + *-mento* 'despair' (cf. It. *disperazione*), *allegruż* ← *allegro* + *-oso* 'happy' (cf. It. *allegro* 'cheerful'), *argumentúż* ← *argomento* + *-oso* 'quarrelsome' (cf. It. *litigioso*), (*triq*) *traffikuża* (← *traffiku* + *-uż*; It. (*via*) **trafficosa*, cf. It. *viatrafficata*). The highly productive suffix *-un* ← *-one* which, as we have seen above, is applied to Semitic bases (*ħmarún* ← *ħmar*), also creates augmentatives on Romance bases: *kontún* ← *conto* 'bill' + *-one*, as in the expression *kont kontún* 'a hefty bill'. In Italian **preparamenti*, **disperamento*, **allegroso*, **argomentoso* and **contone* do not exist, and neither do **pubblicatore* and **sviluppatore*. In Maltese *pubblikatúr* 'publisher' and *żviluppatúr* 'developer' have been formed under the semantic pressure of English on the bases of *ippubblika* 'he publishes' and *żviluppa* 'he develops' + the agentive *-tur* (← It. *tore*, Sic. *-turi*) for Eng. *-er* (cf. It. *editore* and *imprenditore edile*).

Clipping is not very common, apart from abbreviated vocative forms, such as first names *Ġużé, Marì* for the full names, and titles *Pa, Ma', Zi', Sur*, which follow the southern Italian pattern with truncation after the stressed syllable for *Ġużeppi, Marija, Papà, Mamà, Ziju/Zija* 'uncle/aunt', *Sinjúr* 'Sir'. Forms like *Ġuż, Pawl, Karm, Sa', Dott, Profs, Mons* for *Pawlu, Karmenu, Karmena, Sinjura, Dottór, Professúr, Monsinjúr* are local, the latter two being phonetic renderings of the English written abbreviated forms *Profs.* and *Mons.* for *Professor* and *Monsignor*.

A few lexical examples are: *abbli* ← *probabbli* 'probable', *arriv* ← *arrivederċi* 'goodbye, until we meet again' and *parenza* ← *apparenza*.

5 The English influence

English was introduced under British rule in 1800 and became an official language in 1814, together with Italian up to 1934, and then with Maltese from 1934 to the present (Italian was dropped in 1936). Anglicization was resisted throughout the nineteenth century but increased rapidly in the twentieth. Although penetration of English words into the standard language has been slow (only 2,511 were recorded by Aquilina 1987–90, just 6 % of the total, in 1990), nowadays code-switching with English is widely resorted to in everyday speech.

A simple modification to commonly-used English words adds the ending *-a* to consonant-final terms and marks them as singular and feminine: a kettle becomes *kitla* and a pudding is *pudina*. Some terms are derived from the plural form, where the morpheme *-s* is seen as part of the base, thus producing *briksa* 'a brick' ← *briks* 'bricks', *ċipsa* 'one chip' ← *ċips* 'chips'. In rare cases, like *bans* ← *buns* 'bun', although *-a* is not added, the *-s* is considered part of the base, so that when the Semitic plural morpheme is added it forms *bansijiet* 'buns'. Final *-a* can also be added to non-count mass nouns to form singulatives, as in *simenta* ← *cement* 'a patch of land covered with cement'. *Pedala* (sg.f.) could also be considered a similar modification from English *pedal* because Italian *pedale* is masculine and the Sicilian word is *pidali* (the bicycle was introduced in the British period).

Strong modifications took place when knowledge of English was scarce (primary school became compulsory as late as 1946), especially when the term entered common usage. Examples from low domains are: *pajpli* ← *pipeclay* 'fine white clay used for cleaning white canvas shoes', *spákxin* ← *inspection* 'gutter or drain box' and *sajbórt* ← *sideboard*. However, nowadays, since English is not only taught in the primary and secondary schools but is actually a medium of instruction for at least half the subjects in both, the influence of English has become considerable, pronunciation is usually more faithful to the original and it can also affect words that had been adopted from Italian. *Alkoħol* ← *alcohol* (vs. It. *alcool*), *emfasizza* ← *emphasize* (vs. It. *enfatizza*), *iħħarmonizza* ← *harmonize* (cf. *armonizza*, from It. *armonizzare*), *olternattiva* ← *alternative* (vs. It. *alternativa*), *réstorant* ← *restaurant* (vs. *restorànt* ← It. *ristorante*) and *riċenti* ← *recent* (vs. It. *recente*) may not all be accepted as standard forms, but they certainly reveal the new tendency.

Due to the strong exposure to and frequent use of English, the need has been felt to greatly increase the vocabulary of Maltese to fill in certain gaps in the finer nuances of learned and specialized terminology, especially since, on joining the European Union, Maltese was recognized as an official language and specialized documents had to be translated into Maltese in domains which were previously served only or mainly by English. However, the adoption and adaptation of English words had already been increasing since the 1950s. The main processes of derivation concerned verbal bases. English verbs are subjected to Semitic morphological patterns which have been described by Mifsud (1995b: 213–251), but here only the forms of the infinitive, which is used to create nouns, of the passive participle, which creates adjectives, and of the verbal noun of unity are considered. These receive Romance suffixes. The passive participle is formed by adding -*at*, -*ata*, -*ati* (respectively sg.m., sg.f. and pl.m. and f.), and occasionally -*ut* (← It. -*uto*) to produce *ipparkját* 'parked', *ibbukkját* 'booked', *ipprintját* 'printed' and *spellút* 'spelt'. The verbal nouns are formed by adding -*ar* (← It. -*are*) to the English base as in *l-ipparkjár* '(act of) parking', *l-iffilmjár* 'filming', *l-ibbukkjár* 'booking', *l-ipprintjár* 'printing', but *spelling* retains its English pronunciation. The verbal noun of unity adds -*atura* to the base and produces *ċekkjatura* 'one act of checking', *settjatura* 'one act of setting' and *weldjatura* 'one act of welding' (Mifsud 1995b: 248–250), by analogy with Romance-based terms like *sparatura* (cf. It. and Sic. *sparata*).

Doublets are sometimes formed when the adaptation of an English term is introduced next to an Italian term, such as *bilingwi* ~ *bilingwali* (← It. *bilingue* ~ Eng. *bilingual*), *bilingwiżmu* ~ *bilingwaliżmu* (← *bilinguismo* ~ *bilingualism*). Examples of the sort are increasing: *sinjifikanti* ← Eng. *significant* (vs. *sinjifikattiv* ← It. *significativo*), *xjentíst* ← *scientist* (vs. *xjenzját* ← It. *scienziato*), *maġġorità* ← *majority* (vs. *maġġoranza* ← It. *maggioranza*), *persentaġġ* ← *percentage* (vs. *perċentwali* ← It. *percentuale*), *diżappuntamént* ← *disappointment* (vs. *diżappúnt* ← It. *disappunto*). However, sometimes the two forms may take on different semantic nuances in line with the lexical stratigraphy, e.g., *ikkarga* (← *caricare*) vs. *iċċarġja* (← *to charge*): the old-established Italian term means 'to charge a gun', whereas the English term is used for 'charging a price' or charging the battery of electronic devices. Anglo-French *chauffeur* changes the suffix to create *xufier* 'driver', by analogy with *kuċċier* ← Sic. *cucchieri* 'coachman' and *infermier* ← It. *infermiere* 'nurse'. The ending of adverbs in -*ly* is automatically substituted by -*ment* (← It. -*mente*): *allegatamént* (← *allegedly*). Words without a suffix can have one added to them as in the case of the ethnic adjective *Ġermaniż* ← German + -*ese*, by analogy with *Ingliż* and *Franċiż* (← It. *inglese, francese*), a kind of pleonastic word-formation. The English influence on certain ethnic nouns and adjectives is recognizable by the suffix: *Palestinján* and *Libján* carry the English suffix (← *Palestini-*

an, Libyan), which is different from the Italian one: *palestinese, libico*. The same productive suffixes have been added to *Iżraeljàn* (← Eng. *Israeli* + *-jàn*, vs. It. *israelita*) and also to local Semitic place-names: the inhabitants of Msida, Sliema and Birkirkara are called *Misidjani, Slimiżi* and *Karkariżi* (← *(Bir)kirkara* + *-esi*).

Anglo-Latinisms generally retain their meaning when adapted to a Sicilianate form. In most cases the meanings in Sicilian and Italian coincide with the English but in some cases they differ. Therefore words like *suġġétt, appuntát, kummentarju, direttorju, prosekutúr* (← It. *soggetto, appuntato, commentario, direttorio, prosecutore*) assume the English meanings of 'subject', 'appointed', 'commentary', 'directory', 'prosecutor', the Italian equivalents being: *materia* 'school subject' or *argomento* 'topic', *nominato, radiocronaca* or *telecronaca, elenco telefonico, pubblico ministero*). In these examples the change is semantic. Some English words which are of Latin origin, but have been usually adopted through French, are given an Italianate or Sicilianate form even if they do not exist in Italian: words like *awditúr* 'auditor', *kostitwenza* 'constituency', *platitudni* 'platitude', *evalwazzjoni* 'evaluation', *okkupanza* 'occupancy' do not have phonetic equivalents in Italian (*auditore, *costituenza, *platitudine, *evaluazione, *occupanza) because the terms are *revisore dei conti, distretto elettorale, luogo comune* or *banalità, valutazione, presenze negli alberghi*.

Certain words adopted from Italian keep the original meaning but can add new ones. *Indirízz* 'a place' with its verbal derivative *indirizza* 'to address' has taken on English meanings which Italian does not share, so that nowadays newscasters often speak about *Il-Gvern indirizza l-problema tat-traffiku* 'the Government addressed the traffic problem' or *il-Ministru indirizza l-ħaddiema* 'the Minister addressed the workers'. Likewise, *strumentali* has come to be used for 'decisive', translating English (*to be*) *instrumental*, and *effettív* is not only 'real, actual' as in Italian *effettivo*, but also 'effective' (in It. *efficace*). In some cases it has been necessary to adapt an Italian word, already in use, as a substitute for an English word which could be ambiguous. Occasionally, adding a new meaning to a term whose cognate is already used in Maltese, like *forma* ← It. *forma* 'form', is considered undesirable, and so a different but approximately similar word is used to render the new meaning. This happened in the case of Eng. *form* 'a printed document with blank spaces for information to be inserted', whose Italian equivalent, *modulo*, never entered Maltese: it has been substituted by *formula* (more commonly *formola* to distinguish it from *formula* 'formula'), because *forma* is widely used for 'shape'. In certain cases phonetic similarity is enough to create new words: *allegát* ← *alleged*, *relatát* ← *related*, *attentát* ← *attempt* (for a more detailed discussion on English words in Maltese see Brincat 2006 and 2012).

The most serious problem resulting from bilingualism in Malta is code-switching. It is not easy at all to define where code-switching stops and where standard Maltese begins. At present code-switching is being resorted to in speech at all social levels and in all domains (except the literary one), albeit in varying degrees. This, however, mainly depends on an individual basis. And yet, besides English words for new inventions like *washing-machine, dishwasher, fridge, mixer, cooker*, and so on, one can notice creeping relexification even in the home: *shower, bathroom, toilet, bedroom, sitting-room, dining-room* are replacing the traditional *doċċa, kamra tal-banju, loki, kamra tas-sodda, kamra tal-ikel*. Spelling English words according to the Maltese alphabet seems to be the easiest solution in the short term, but the compromise does not satisfy everybody. The process of modernisation is, of course, unstoppable but one wonders whether its magnitude (every English word of the 650,000 in the OED is available for code-switching) and the unprecedented speed at which it is happening will have serious repercussions on the language.

6 References

Aquilina, Joseph (1987–90): *Maltese-English Dictionary*. 2 Vol. Malta: Midsea Books.
Benmamoun, Elabbas (2008): Construct state. In: Cornelis H. M. Versteegh (ed.), *Encyclopedia of Arabic Language and Linguistics*. Vol. 1, 477–482. Leiden: Brill.
Borg, Albert (1988): *Ilsienna. Studju grammatikali*. Malta: Ħas-Sajjied.
Borg, Albert and Marie Azzopardi-Alexander (1997): *Maltese*. London: Routledge.
Brincat, Joseph M. (2006): Anglicismi a confronto: l'uso di parole inglesi a Malta e in Italia come viene riflesso nei dizionari. In: Raffaella Bombi (ed.), *Studi linguistici in onore di Roberto Gusmani*. Vol. 1, 293–301. Alessandria: Edizioni dell'Orso.
Brincat, Joseph M. (2008): Malta. In: Cornelis H. M. Versteegh (ed.), *Encyclopedia of Arabic Language and Linguistics*. Vol. 3, 141–145. Leiden: Brill.
Brincat, Joseph M. (2011): *Maltese and Other Languages. A Linguistic History of Malta*. Malta: Midsea Books.
Brincat, Joseph (2012): La produttività del superstrato sull'adstrato nell'integrazione di elementi esogeni. In: Vincenzo Orioles and Giampaolo Borghello (eds.), *Per Roberto Gusmani. Studi di ricordo*. Vol. 2, 61–72. Udine: Forum.
Brincat, Joseph M. (2018): Maltese: blending Semitic, Romance and Germanic lexemes. *Lexicographica* 33 (2017): 207–223.
Brincat, Joseph M. (2021): *Maltese and Other Languages. A Linguistic History of Malta. 2nd revised edition*. Malta: Midsea Books.
Cassola, Arnold (1992): *The Biblioteca Vallicelliana 'Regole per la Lingua Maltese'*. Malta: Said International.
Dimech, Emmanuel (2001): *Il Chelliem Inglis*. Malta: Stamperia tal Gazzetta di Malta.
Fabri, Ray (2009): Compounding and adjective-noun compounds in Maltese. In: Bernard Comrie, Ray Fabri, Elizabeth Hume, Manwel Mifsud, Thomas Stolz and Martine Vanhove (eds.), *Introducing Maltese Linguistics*, 207–231. Amsterdam/Philadelphia: Benjamins.

Gatt, Albert and Ray Fabri (2018): Borrowed affixes and morphological productivity: A case study of two Maltese nominalisations. In: Patrizia Paggio and Albert Gatt (eds.), *The languages of Malta*, 143–169. Berlin: Language Science Press.

Kaye, Alan S. and Judith Rosenhouse (1997): Arabic dialects and Maltese. In: Robert Hetzron (ed.), *The Semitic Languages*, 263–311. London: Routledge.

Kontzi, Reinhold (1981): L'elemento maltese nel maltese. *Journal of Maltese Studies* 14: 32–47.

Mifsud, Manwel (1995a): The productivity of Arabic in Maltese. In: Joseph Cremona, Clive Holes and Geoffrey Khan (eds.), *Proceedings of the 2nd International Conference of L'Association Internationale Pour la Dialectologie Arabe, Cambridge, 10–14 September 1995*, 151–160. University of Cambridge: Faculty of Oriental Studies.

Mifsud, Manwel (1995b): *Loan Verbs in Maltese. A Descriptive and Comparative Study*. Leiden: Brill.

Mifsud, Manwel (2008): Maltese. In: Cornelis H. M. Versteegh (ed.), *Encyclopedia of Arabic Language and Linguistics*. Vol. 3, 146–159. Leiden: Brill.

Monteil, Vincent (1960): *L'arabe moderne*. Paris: Klincksieck.

OED = *Oxford English Dictionary* http://www.oed.com [last access 9 Mar 2015].

Saade, Benjamin (2016): Adverbial derivation in Maltese and Italian: A starting point for studies in cross-linguistic productivity. *STUF – Language Typology and Universals* 69(4): 547–563.

Saade, Benjamin (2019): Assessing productivity in contact: Italian derivation in Maltese. *Linguistics* 57(1): 59–86.

Saade, Benjamin (2020a): Derivational networks in Maltese. In: Lívia Körtvélyessy, Alexandra Bagasheva and Pavol Štekauer (eds.), *Derivational Networks Across Languages*, 475–483. Berlin/Boston: De Gruyter Mouton.

Saade, Benjamin (2020b): Quantitative approaches to productivity and borrowing in Maltese derivation. *Morphology* 30(1): 447–467.

Sabatini-Coletti (2006): *Il Sabatini Coletti. Dizionario della lingua italiana*. Milano: Rizzoli and Larousse.

Sammut, Frans (ed.) (2002): *Mikiel Anton Vassalli. Lexicon*. Malta: SKS.

Stolz, Thomas (2003–04): A new Mediterraneanism: Word iteration in an areal perspective: A pilot-study. *Mediterranean Language Review* 15: 1–47.

VS = Piccitto, Giorgio, Giovanni Tropea and Salvatore Trovato (1977–2002): *Vocabolario Siciliano*. 5 Vol. Palermo: Centro Studi Filologici e Linguistici Siciliani.

Jens Wilkens
19 Turkish

1 Introduction
2 General overview
3 Composition
4 Derivation
5 Conversion
6 References

Abstract: The article is a short overview of word-formation in Modern Turkish. As derivation is the most important method employed in the creation of new lexical items, the article focuses mainly on derivational suffixes. The lexicon of Turkish has been substantially reshaped since the early 1930s by state language planning, the aim of which was to sort out Arabic and Persian loans and to replace them by Turkish equivalents. Because inherited words – mainly from the dialects or from old written sources – were not always at hand, new words and terms had to be formed from inherited base words by suffixation. Sometimes obsolete suffixes were revived or even pseudo-suffixes were created.

1 Introduction

Modern Turkish evolved from Ottoman Turkish and belongs to the Southwestern or Oghuz branch of the Turkic languages. Turkish is the official language of the Republic of Turkey. Furthermore, sizeable groups of Turkish speakers live in several countries of Southeastern Europe (Bulgaria, Romania, Greece, Macedonia, Serbia), in Northern Cyprus, in the Commonwealth of Independent States as well as in migrant communities of Western Europe (especially Germany) and North America. There are approximately 70 million native speakers of Turkish.

Word-formation in Modern Turkish is relatively unexplored. Studies of word-formation in late Ottoman and early modern Turkish are rare and usually only found in short chapters in reference grammars. General reflections were provided by Atalay (1946), Mansuroğlu (1960), Dizdaroğlu (1962), Göksu (1966), and Cüceloğlu (1973). Overviews of inflectional and derivational morphology are found in

Jens Wilkens, Göttingen, Germany

https://doi.org/10.1515/9783111420523-019

Hatiboğlu (1974) and Özel (1977). Demircan (1977) is a general morphological description of how suffixes are attached to their bases. Some of these works are actually guidebooks with the aim to facilitate the creation of neologisms. Frankle's study (1948) is a comparative approach dealing with the formation of denominal nouns in Turkic languages. Some deverbal nouns are studied by Römer (1991). Mungan (2002) investigates deverbal nouns from a morphological and syntactical perspective. Particular suffixes active in nominal word-formation are investigated by Ercilasun (1975), Erdal (1998, 2000) and others. Diminutives are dealt with in Kononov (1969) and Tosun (1978). Tosun investigates similatives as well. Schakir (1933) explores denominal verb formation in Turkic languages in general with a special focus on the suffixes *-lA-* and *-A-*. Verbs derived by the suffix *-lA-* are studied by İleri (2007) as well. Frequentative verbs are treated in the article by Banguoğlu (1956). Bassarak's (1985) demarcation between verbal inflection and derivation was taken up again by Knobloch (1987), who made a distinction between syntactical and lexical derivation. Nominal composition is explored in Dede (1982), König (1987) and Röhrborn (1990). But the most comprehensive and detailed study in this field is van Schaaik (2002) providing a new theoretical framework. Higher order compounds, complements of which can be complex phrases or even whole sentences, are dealt with in a separate article by van Schaaik (2000). A contrastive approach (German/Turkish) investigating fixed word combinations in the language of economy and finance with a special focus on phraseological units is Aktaş (2008), who deals with nominal compounds as well. A contrastive study of word-formation in Turkish and English is provided by Tosun (1977), whereas Ülkü (1980) is a contrastive investigation of German and Turkish word-formation. Kahramantürk (1999) provides a contrastive analysis of nominal word-formation in Turkish and German. A profound treatment of the neologistic vocabulary can be found in Röhrborn (2003), which provides in the appendix a lexicon of deverbal nouns. The main aim of the study is to elucidate language contact phenomena between European languages and Turkish in the field of word-formation. Other important works on neologisms are Scharlipp (1978) and several articles by Röhrborn (1996, 1998, 2000, 2002). Zülfikar (1991) deals with problems of forming terms in Turkish, discusses general rules of word-formation and gives a long list of derivational and inflectional morphemes with examples. In his work on the relationship of Turkish with western languages, Sarı (2008) discusses among other things the impact of European languages on the formation of Turkish terms. Neologisms are treated in detail.

Siemieniec-Gołaś (1997) investigates the formation of nouns in 17th-century Ottoman transcription texts. Another important book in the field of historical linguistics is Stachowski (1996), a historical dictionary of nouns derived from verbs by means of the suffix *-cX/-(y)XcX*. Anyone who wants to study diachronic aspects of word-formation in Turkic languages would have to consult the magnum opus by Erdal (1991) on Old Turkic.

Hereafter suffixes are presented in morphophonemic transcription. Preharmonic archphonemes are given in capital letters (A = a ~ e, I = ı ~ i, U = u ~ ü, X = ı ~ i ~ u ~ ü, C = c ~ ç, G = g ~ ğ, K = g ~ k, T = d ~ t). Contrary to common usage in Turkic studies, nominal juncture is not expressed by the sign + but with a hyphen.

2 General overview

Modern Turkish represents a language of the agglutinating and synthetic type of morphology. In general, one morphological marker represents one specific grammatical category, but in derivational morphology polysemy can be observed. Word-formation in Turkish has a clear and systematic character. Derivation from base words (primary lexical units) by suffixation is dominant. Infixes and circumfixes are absent. The existence of prefixes in Turkish is a matter of dispute (Johanson 1990: 167–170). Some authors have reckoned formations such as *başparmak* 'thumb' (← *baş* 'first' + *parmak* 'finger') as compounds, others as prefixations. Already Frankle (1948: 2–3) declared herself against Deny's (1938) view that we are dealing with prefixes. As formations with *ana, alt, baş, dış, iç, ön, öz* and *üst* are formed by juxtaposition with a following noun they should be treated as compounds. Indo-European prefixation was obviously imitated when in the 1930s short-lived formations arose in which the first syllable of *yardım* 'help' was attached to words such as *başkan* 'president' to form *yarbaşkan* 'vice-president' (Lewis 1999: 94). Now 'vice-president' is expressed by the compound *başkan yardımcısı*. Reduplication (e.g., *sapsarı* 'bright yellow' ← *sarı* 'yellow') is occasionally discussed as belonging to prefixation.

When a suffix is attached to a base the latter usually remains unchanged except for some phonotactic operations which occur in certain environments: a) stem allomorphy, i.e. voicing of unvoiced stem finals if a suffix beginning with a vowel is attached, b) syncopation of unstressed vowels in words with more than one syllable, c) simplification through haplology, and d) truncation (elision of final consonants of the base words when combined with suffixes). Vowel mutation and apophony are unknown in Turkish (an exception being the pronominal paradigm). Phenomena such as clipping (*kondu* 'unauthorized building set up in one night' ← *gecekondu*; Balcı 2006: 87–88) or blending (*Türkilizce* 'Turkish highly influenced by English' ← *Türkçe* 'Turkish' + *İngilizce* 'English'; Lewis 1999: 133) are sometimes met with. Backformation is rarely encountered. The verb *iletiş-* 'to communicate' is a rather recent backformation of the noun *iletişim* 'communication' (Balcı 2006: 88). By backformation *eksi* 'minus' is derived from *eksik* 'deficient' (Lewis 1999: 66).

To create new lexical items Turkish disposes of an abundance of suffixes. Allomorphs are conditioned by phonotactic operations, one of which is synharmonism, better known as vowel harmony. The oppositions in the vowel system are: front vs. back, high vs. low and unrounded vs. rounded. The main opposition, i.e. front vs. back, determines the shape of suffixes although this rule is not universally applied. In words with front/back harmony the last vowel determines the suffix required, e.g., *elma* 'apple' (base word) and *elma-lık* 'apple garden'. The opposition front vs. back determines the phonotactics of bases and suffixes. Suffixes beginning with consonants alternate depending on the stem final of the base, i.e. voiced suffixes after stem finals ending in vowels or voiced consonants and unvoiced suffixes after stem finals ending in unvoiced consonants.

In Turkish long suffix strings are common and certain rules determine the order of suffixes. Generally, derivational precede inflectional suffixes in the suffix string. When case suffixes are used in derivation they can be followed by derivational suffixes (*iç-ten-lik* 'sincerity' ← *iç-ten* 'sincere' ← *iç* 'inside, core' with ablative suffix). Sometimes it is difficult to distinguish between derivational and inflectional suffixes, especially in the verbal domain (reflexive, causative, passive, reciprocal-cooperative suffixes). These suffixes have inflectional *and* derivational properties (Bassarak 1985). The suffixes where the derivational character is most highly pronounced are those deriving reflexive (*-(X)n-*) and reciprocal (*-(X)ş-*) verbs. They follow the verbal root directly (Bassarak 1998: 8). In this article voice suffixes are treated as derivational suffixes because with some restrictions they can be further expanded with other voice suffixes or with suffixes from the nominal domain forming deverbal nouns.

In neologisms a revival of unproductive derivational suffixes is quite common. In the ongoing process of language planning in Turkey, archaisms and loans play only a minor role whereas neologisms are coined to adapt the language to the exigencies of modern times and to the changes of social structure, technology, science, etc. After Persian and Arabic lost prestige in the early years of the Republic of Turkey, an unprecedented effort of language reform took place after the year 1930, leading to the formation of a large number of new words (see also Schönig 2025 on historical word-formation in Turkish). Sometimes the rules of word-formation in Turkic languages were violated by adding deverbal suffixes to nouns or denominal suffixes to verbs. Numerous neologisms were quite short-lived because they were not accepted by the speakers. The arena of language planning was the nominal domain whereas newly formed verbs are rare. But analytical formations of verbs with a neologistic nominal first element are quite common.

In Turkish the distinction between derivation and composition is at times not easy to determine. The same holds true for nominal inflection and derivation because certain words with case suffixes can become fossilized. Moreover, some base words are no longer extant in Turkish whereas their derivates are still widely used.

We can distinguish several word classes: nouns, pronouns, adjectives, adverbs, postpositions, interjections, conjunctions and verbs. Turkish does not always provide a clear morphological distinction between word classes. In these cases a judgment to which word class a word belongs can only be inferred from context and syntax. Words bearing plural, possessive and usually also case suffixes are nouns. But petrified forms can function as adverbs or postpositions, etc. as well. Except for these cases particles, interjections, adverbs and adjectives in attributive position do not take inflectional suffixes.

Widespread in Turkish are onomatopoetics, the term *mimetic word-formation* covering more phenomena than onomatopoetics (Ido 1999). Simple reduplication of a sound is common (e.g., *pıt pıt atmak* 'to pound (of the heart)'). One device for forming mimetic words is vowel alternation in reduplication. By exchanging the vowel, semantic differences can be communicated, e.g., by changing the vowel *a* to *ı* the connotation of lightness, smallness and quickness is conveyed: *patır-patır* 'sound of footsteps' vs. *pıtır-pıtır* 'sound of rapid footsteps' (Ido 1999: 69).

3 Composition

Composition is a common type of word-formation in Turkish, especially important are nominal compounds of the type *ev kapısı* 'front-door' (← *ev* 'house' + *kapı* 'door' + compound marker). This example displays one basic feature of Turkish composition with the compound marker *-(s)I* (3rd person singular possessive suffix). In Turkish grammar the type *evin kapısı* 'the door of the house' cannot be assigned to composition proper but is a genitive construction. Most Turkish compounds are right-headed. Left-headed compounds of the Persian *iżāfet*-type such as *hüküm-i hümayun* 'imperial edict' (← *hüküm* 'edict' + the Persian *iżāfet* element *-i* + *hümayun* 'imperial, royal') were gradually discarded during the Turkish language reform.

In the combination noun + noun with a compound marker, the latter is deleted if followed by a genuine possessive suffix, e.g., *para çanta-m* 'my purse' (not **para çanta-sı-m*). If such a combination is expanded by an adjective suffix the compound marker is missing too: e.g., *güneş gözlük-lü* 'with sun glasses' vs. *güneş gözlüğ-ü* 'sun glasses' (in this case *-ü* is the compound marker) (van Schaaik 2002: 69). Compounds are not restricted to the boundaries of a word in the traditional sense of the term. In spelling a particularly tight combination of words without a compound marker is reflected in *dilbilim* 'linguistics' (← *dil* 'language' + *bilim* 'science'); with a compound marker: *demiryolu* 'railway' (← *demir* 'iron' + *yol* 'way' + compound marker). Determinative compounds without a compound marker are usually restricted to attributive relationship (*altın bilezik* 'gold bracelet' ← *altın* 'gold, golden' + *bilezik* 'bracelet'). The first constituent can, e.g., denote the material or sex of the second constituent. A noteworthy exception of a first constituent which denotes the material of the second bearing the ablative suffix is *kar-dan adam* 'snowman' (← *kar* 'snow' + ablative suffix *-TAn* + *adam* 'man'). Synthetic compounds are also to be found in Turkish such as *ağaç-kakan* 'woodpecker' (← *ağaç* 'tree, wood' + *kak-* 'to strike'). Here the second element is originally a participle which is not a lexical item in its own right. Another example is the neologism *bilgi-sayar* 'computer' (← *bilgi* 'information' + *say-* 'to count'). Determinative compounds without an inflectional element are *anne-anne* 'maternal grandmother' (← *anne* 'mother' + *anne* 'id.') or *baba-anne* 'paternal grandmother' (← *baba* 'father' + *anne* 'mother').

Except for exocentric compounds such as *el-i açık* 'generous; lit. his hand open', where a head is missing, the last element (the head) can either be a basic noun (in root compounds) or a noun derived from a verbal base (in synthetic compounds) (van Schaaik 2002: 13–17). The head in root compounds can be either an adjective or a noun. Head nouns can be compounded with adjectives (*karadeniz* 'Black Sea' ← *kara* 'black' + *deniz* 'sea'), participles (*yanardağ* 'volcano', aorist participle of *yan-* 'to burn' + *dağ* 'mountain'), numerals (*yüzyıl* 'century' ← *yüz* '100' + *yıl* 'year') or nouns as complement. A negative aorist as complement is *tüken-mez-kalem* 'ballpen; lit. inexhaustible pen'. In complex terms composition and suffixation can be combined, e.g., *çok-karı-lı-lık* 'polygyny' (← *çok* 'many' + *karı* 'wife' + adjective marker *-lı* + abstract noun suffix *-lık*). Argument inheritance can be observed in deverbal nouns such as *dış-a-vurum* 'expression' and deverbal adjectives such as *iç-e-kapanık* 'autistic' (both with dative suffix). Adjectives as heads can take nouns (*sütbeyaz* 'milkwhite' ← *süt* 'milk' + *beyaz* 'white') or adjectives as complements.

A co-compound is, e.g., *karı koca* 'wife and husband, married couple'. This type of a co-compound in which the two constituents are co-hyponyms of the superordinate term is common in Turkish (cf. *alış-veriş* 'trade' ← *alış* 'buying' + *veriş* 'selling'), and is found even with verbal roots such as *gel-git* 'tide' (← *gel-* 'to come' + *git-* 'to go'). Unlike determinative compounds which often consist of more than two constituents co-compounds are generally restricted to two constituents (see also Wälchli 2025 on co-compounds).

To form verbs from nouns, compounding by means of an auxiliary verb (*yap-, et-*) is wide-spread already in Ottoman Turkish. Often both elements are written as one word, e.g., *akdetmek* 'to contract (marriage)' (*akit* 'contract' with syncopation of the vowel *i* and sonorization of the final consonant). Some verbal phrases are formed by a converb element and a base element, e.g., *alıp ver-* 'to quarrel, be excited'. Johanson (1995: 315) emphasized the "strong semantic fusion" and the "tendency towards lexicalization". To denote aspect-temporal relations, modality, actionality, etc., constructions with a lexical verb followed by an auxiliary are used in Turkish. Some auxiliaries appear as bound suffixes such as *-(y)Abil-* (*bil-* 'to know') after the stem of the lexical verb (*yaz-abil-ir* 'he is able to write').

4 Derivation

As there is no strict distinction between nouns and adjectives in Turkish, we have to mention some suffixes under "nominal derivation" *and* under "adjectival derivation" (cross-references are not given). Numerals are traditionally treated as adjectives. One has to bear in mind that a single derivational suffix may have different etymologies (Berta 1991). Foreign suffixes are mentioned only occasionally as they are – with very few exceptions – no longer productive.

Due to the polysemy of many suffixes an arrangement according to the suffixes involved in word-formation would be preferable. To ensure consistency within the volume such an arrangement is impossible. A single suffix is thus treated under several categories or word-formation meanings.

4.1 Nominal derivation

4.1.1 Denominal nouns

Personal nouns are formed with the following suffixes:
-CX: a productive suffix deriving agent nouns; subgroups can be distinguished: a) names of persons by profession: *diş-çi* 'dentist' (← *diş* 'tooth'); b) agent nouns – persons who carry out an action sometimes or at the moment: *yol-cu* 'traveler' (← *yol* 'way'); c) names of adherents of a particular world view: *Atatürk-çü* 'kemalist'; d) names of consumers of food or drink: *içki-ci* 'drunkard' (← *içki* 'liquor, drink'); *-lX*: inhabitant nouns, e.g., *İstanbul-lu* 'a person from İstanbul'; *-TAş*: socia-

tive nouns, cf. *vatan-daş* 'fellow countryman' (← *vatan* 'native country'), sometimes with pejorative meaning, e.g., *omuz-daş* 'companion, crony' (← *omuz* 'shoulder'); *-(X)l*: agent nouns, e.g., *ard-ıl* 'successor' (← *art* 'back').

In some studies a suffix *-msAr* is assumed but the example *kötümser* 'pessimist(ic)' is an aorist participle of the neologistic verb *kötümse-* 'to be pessimistic' which itself is derived from the neologism *kötüm* 'disapproval' (← *kötü* 'bad') (cf. Lewis 1999: 77).

Instrument nouns are derived with *-CAk*: *oyun-cak* 'toy' (← *oyun* 'play').

Place nouns are formed with the suffixes *-(A)rI*: *dış-arı* 'outside; foreign country; province' (← *dış* 'outside'); *-(A)y*: *yüz-ey* 'surface' (← *yüz* 'face, surface'); *-lXk*: indicates a place abundant in that which is denoted by the base, e.g., *yemiş-lik* 'orchard' (← *yemiş* 'fruit'); *-(X)l*: *kum-ul* 'dune' (← *kum* 'sand').

Abstract nouns contain the suffix *-lXk*: *asker-lik* 'military service' (← *asker* 'soldier'); the suffix is often combined with the preceding suffix *-CX*. Especially common is the combination in the denotation of a certain mental, political or religious attitude such as *atatürk-çü-lük* 'Kemalism', rarely professions such as *banka-cı-lık* 'banking' and branches of science such as *sözlük-çü-lük* 'lexicography' (← *sözlük* 'dictionary').

Collective nouns are formed with *-(A)n*: originally a plural suffix (e.g., *er-en* 'men'), now a neologistic suffix: *kök-en* 'root (ling.), origin' (← *kök* 'root'); *-gil(ler)*: a composite suffix (*-gil* + plural suffix *-ler*): *turunç-giller* 'citrus fruits' (← *turunç* 'bitter orange'); also with terms of kinship: *amcam-gil(ler)* 'the family of my uncle' (← *amca-m* 'my uncle'); *-lXk*: *komşu-luk* 'neighbourhood' (← *komşu* 'neighbour').

Evaluative categories are represented by nouns with the suffixes *-Ak*: metaphorical designations and diminutives, e.g., *baş-ak* 'ear (of grain), (archaic) arrow-head' (← *baş* 'head'); *-cAğIz*: *çocuk-cağız* 'poor child' (← *çocuk* 'child'); *-CAk*: *yavru-cak* 'poor child' (← *yavru* 'young, small child'); *-CXk*: *ağ-cık* 'retina' (← *ağ* 'net'); *-mAn*: originally mostly augmentatives, e.g., *türk-men* 'Turkmen, a real Turk' (← *türk* 'Turk'); *-çe* (a copy from Persian): *il-çe* 'district' (← *il* 'land').

Varia comprise formations with the suffixes

-(A)mIk/-(A)mUk: derives designations for diseases and plants, e.g., *kız-amık* 'measles' (*kız is the base of *kızıl* 'red'); further expanded: *kız-amık-çık* 'rubella' (the suffix *-CXk* derives names for diseases as well, cf. *pamuk-çuk* 'thrush' ← *pamuk* 'cotton'); *kara-muk* (← *kara* 'black') has two different meanings 1. 'rash on the body'; 2. 'corn cockle';

-(A)rIk: a rare composite suffix attached to place nouns, e.g., *iç-erik* 'content; implicit' (← *iç* 'interior');

-CA: derives 1. designations of languages, e.g., *Türk-çe* 'Turkish' (← *Türk* 'Turk'); 2. female nouns, e.g., *tanrı-ça* 'pagan goddess' (← *tanrı* 'god'), a neologism based on old Serbo-Croatian loans such as *çariçe* 'tsarina';

-*laç*: dishes such as *süt-laç* 'rice-pudding' (← *süt* 'milk'); the suffix does not follow synharmonism;
-*lAmA*: dishes, e.g., *şeker-leme* 'candy' (← *şeker* 'sugar');
-*lXk*: similatives (in kinship terms), e.g., *ana-lık* 'stepmother' (← *ana* 'mother');
-*mer*: *kat-mer* 'complexity; flaky pastry' (← *kat* 'floor, layer'); the suffix does not follow synharmonism;
-*(X)l*: results of action, e.g., *taş-ıl* 'petrifaction' (← *taş* 'stone').

Nouns denoting purpose/suitability/inclination/concrete relationship are formed with -*CXl*: personal nouns, indicating mainly an inclination or affinity to what is designated by the base word, e.g., *kadın-cıl* 'Casanova' (← *kadın* 'woman'), and animal names such as birds of prey indicating their favourite prey, e.g., *tavşan-cıl* 'golden eagle' (← *tavşan* 'hare'). Suitability/purpose is expressed by -*lXk*: *pabuç-luk* 'shoe rack' (← *pabuç* 'shoe'). The following suffixes express a concrete relationship with the base, usually the designation of a body part, cf. -*CXn*: *kulak-çın* 'earflap' (← *kulak* 'ear'); birds' names, e.g., *kaşık-çın* 'spoonbill' (← *kaşık* 'spoon'; similarity of the bird's beak with the base is denoted), *çamur-cun* 'a small kind of duck' (← *çamur* 'mud'; the base denotes the natural habitat); -*dXrXk*: *eğin-dirik* 'poncho' (← *eğin* 'upper part of the back'); -*sAk*: *burun-sak* 'muzzle (for young lambs)' (← *burun* 'nose').

Neologistic suffixes were created during the Turkish language reform, cf.
-*(A)t*: *söz-et* 'libretto' (← *söz* 'word');
-*nA* (a pseudo-suffix): *öz-ne* 'grammatical subject' (← *öz* 'self') is in fact derived by analogy according to *nesne* 'object' (← *ne ise* 'whatever' + *ne* 'what');
-*TAm*: *gün-dem* 'agenda' (← *gün* 'day');
-*tay*: extracted from *kurultay* 'congress' (metanalyzed as *kurul-tay*, but originally going back to Mongol *qurilta ~ quriltai* 'assembly'); first attached to verbal stems it was used to derive denominal nouns such as *yargı-tay* 'Supreme Court of Appeal' (← *yargı* 'decision') as well;
-*Xt*: *boy-ut* 'dimension' (← *boy* 'height, length').

4.1.2 Deadjectival nouns

Deadjectival nouns (including denumeral formations, see section 4, introduction) are derived with the suffixes -*(A)ç*, an unproductive suffix, e.g., *düz-eç* 'spirit level' (← *düz* 'flat'), and -*lXk*. The latter derives a) mainly **abstract nouns**, e.g., *doğru-luk* 'correctness' (← *doğru* 'straight, correct'); *güvenilir-lik* 'reliability' is derived from a complex base (aorist participle of a passive verb from the base *güven-* 'to trust in'); b) nouns with numeral bases denoting the **age or value**: *kırk-lık* 'forty years old'; other nouns derived from numerals are *bir-lik* 'unity'

(← *bir* 'one') and *bir-inci-lik* 'first rank' (← *birinci* 'first'); c) denumeral nouns denoting the value of a banknote: *bin-lik* 'thousand pound note' (← *bin* 'thousand').

Deadverbial is *aşağı-lık* 'inferiority' (← *aşağı* 'below'), depronominal is, e.g., *ben-lik* 'ego' (← *ben* 'I').

The suffix *-(X)z* forms collectives or groups of siblings from numerals, e.g., *iki-z* 'twin(s)' (← *iki* 'two').

Suffixes deriving neologisms are, e.g., *-(A)n*: *düz-en* 'system, organization' (← *düz* 'flat'); *-(A)y*: *bir-ey* 'individual' (← *bir* 'one'); *-lAm*: *denk-lem* 'equation' (← *denk* 'equal'); *-mAn*: *uz-man* 'specialist' (← *uz* 'capable'); *-Xl*: *çoğ-ul* 'plural' (← *çok* 'many'); *-gen*: this suffix which is attached to numerals deriving names of geometric figures, is not affected by synharmonism, cf. *altı-gen* 'hexagon' (← *altı* 'six').

4.1.3 Deverbal nouns

Action nouns (most terms are neologisms) are formed with the suffixes
-(A)v: *sına-v* 'examination' (← *sına-* 'to test');
-(A)y: *ol-ay* 'event' (← *ol-* 'to become');
-KX: *uy-ku* 'sleep' (← *uyu-* 'to sleep', with syncopation);
-KXn: denoting calamities, e.g., *bas-kın* 'sudden attack, raid' (← *bas-* 'to assault');
-mA: *oku-ma* 'reading' (← *oku-* 'to read'); with an extension of meaning: *danış-ma* 'the act of making enquiries, information (office)' (← *danış-* 'to consult');
-(X)m/-yXm: action nouns originally denoting a single action, e.g., *biç-im* 'act of cutting' (← *biç-* 'to cut'), now often referring to general actions;
-(X)ntX/-tX (the latter with stems ending in *-n*): nouns denoting a continous, intermittent or incomplete action, e.g., *gez-inti* 'short walk' (← *gez-* 'to go for a walk'), often derived from verbs denoting unpleasant feelings, e.g., *tiksin-ti* 'disgust' (← *tiksin-* 'to be disgusted with');
-(y)Xş: mostly from simple bases, e.g., *dön-üş* 'return' (*dön-* 'to return'); reciprocal bases are shortened by haplology, e.g., *uğra-ş* 'fight' (← *uğraş-ış). Often the manner of an action is denoted: *otur-uş* 'manner of sitting' (← *otur-* 'to sit').

Some suffixes derive action nouns and result nouns, e.g., *-bAç*: from intransitive or reflexive base words, e.g., *dolam-baç* 'winding, turn' (← *dolan-* 'to wind round'), *saklan-baç/saklam-baç* (in combination with the verb *oyna-* 'to play') 'hide-and-seek (game)' (← *saklan-* 'to hide oneself'); *-mAcA*: *boğ-maca* 'whooping-cough' (← *boğ-* 'to strangle'); often referring to playful activities: *bilmece* 'riddle, puzzle' (← *bil-* 'to know').

Abstract nouns (including designations of mental faculties) are formed with the suffixes
-A: doğ-a 'nature' (← doğ- 'to be born');
-(A)k: belle-k 'memory' (← belle- 'to learn by heart');
-cA: düşün-ce 'thought' (← düşün- 'to think');
-(X)m/-yXm: bil-im 'science' (← bil- 'to know');
-(y)AcAk, originally a future participle: gel-ecek 'future (noun and adjective)' (← gel- 'to come');
-(Xn)ç (with stems ending in -n- the suffix is only -ç): bas-ınç 'pressure' (← bas- 'to press').

Agent nouns comprise formations with the following suffixes:
-(A)k: kaç-ak 'refugee' (← kaç- 'to flee');
-cX (with verbs ending in -n) such as öğren-ci 'student' (← öğren- 'to learn') or
-(y)XcX: oku-yucu 'reader' (← oku- 'to read');
-gXç: bil-giç 'know-all' (← bil- 'to know');
-KAn: saldır-gan 'aggressor' (← saldır- 'to attack'); as a designation of a class of animals: sürün-gen 'reptile' (← sürün- 'to creep, crawl');
-KXn: in neologisms, e.g., gez-gin 'traveler' (← gez- 'to travel');
-mA: dön-me 'renegade, transsexual' (← dön- 'to turn');
-mAn: neologisms, analogies to Germanic designations for professions and persons (Engl. postman, Germ. Milchmann), e.g., okut-man 'lecturer' (← okut- 'to teach'), öğret-men 'teacher' (← öğret- 'to teach');
-(X)k: tanı-k 'witness' (← tanı- 'to recognize');
-(X)mcAk: a metaphorical agent noun is ör-ümcek 'spider' (← ör- 'to twist, braid');
-(X)r, originally an aorist participle: okur 'reader' (← oku- 'to read');
-(y)An, originally a participle: çevir-en 'translator' (← çevir- 'to translate'); some agent nouns are metaphorical, cf. sıç-an 'mouse, rat' (← sıç- 'to defecate'); common are terms of mathematics: böl-en 'divisor' (← böl- 'to divide').

Non-personal nouns (characterized by or having a relation to what is designated by the base) are formed with
-(A)GAn: gez-egen 'planet' (← gez- 'to go for a walk');
-mAz, originally a negative aorist participle: tüken-mez 'ballpen' (← tüken- 'to be exhausted');
-mXş, originally a past participle from intransitive stems: geç-miş 'past (n.)' (← geç- 'to pass');
-tay, a neologistic suffix (see section 4.1.1) deriving designations for administrative bodies and councils: sayış-tay 'Superior Audit Office' (← sayış- 'to settle accounts');
-X: öl-ü 'corpse' (← öl- 'to die');
-(X)m/-yXm: ak-ım 'current (n.)' (← ak- 'to flow');
-(X)n: ak-ın 'stream' (← ak- 'to flow');

-(X)r, originally an aorist participle: *gel-ir* 'income' (← *gel-* 'to come');
-(X)t: sark-ıt 'stalactite' (← *sark-* 'to hang down').

Result nouns (most terms are neologisms) are derived with the suffixes
-(A)k: öden-ek 'compensation' (← *öden-* 'to be paid');
-(A)l: a) *çök-el* 'residue' (← *çök-* 'to sink down') (≈ subject of the base verb) or b) *kur-al* 'rule' (← *kur-* 'to found, set up') (≈ object of the base verb);
-(A)m: a) *dön-em* 'period' (← *dön-* 'to turn around') (≈ subject of the base verb) or b) *kur-am* 'theory' (← *kur-* 'to establish') (≈ object of the base verb);
-(A)mAk: kaç-amak 'evasion, pretext' (← *kaç-* 'to flee');
-(A)nAk: sağ-anak 'shower, downpour' (← *sağ-* 'to pour out rain');
-(A)v, a suffix borrowed from Bashkurt and Kazakh (Lewis 1999: 95): *türe-v* 'derivation' (← *türe-* 'to be derived');
-KA: bildir-ge 'declaration' (← *bildir-* 'to communicate', a causative stem);
-KX: in the inherited vocabulary only with monosyllabic base verbs, e.g., *er-gi* 'attainment, success' (← *er-* 'to attain'), in neologisms also with disyllabic base verbs;
-mA: zehir-len-me 'intoxication' (← *zehir-len-* 'to be intoxicated'), some derivatives denote dishes, cf. *kavur-ma* 'broiled or fried meat' (← *kavur-* 'to roast');
-mAç: de-meç 'statement' (← *de-* 'to say');
-mXk: il-mik 'sling, loop' (← *il-* 'to knot');
-TX: çık-tı 'product' (← *çık-* 'to come out'); often from inchoative, denominal verbs referring to colour designations, cf. *morar-tı* 'bruise' (← *morar-* 'to turn violet');
-X: göster-i 'demonstration' (← *göster-* 'to show');
-(X)k: düş-ük 'miscarriage' (← *düş-* 'to fall, miscarry');
-(X)m/-yXm: çöz-üm 'solution' (← *çöz-* 'to solve'); the shape of the suffix is different in *dene-yim* 'experience' (← *dene-* 'to try') with an intercalated glide;
-(X)mcAk: bürü-mcek 'bundle, silk worm's cocoon' (← *bürü-* 'to wrap up');
-(X)n: yay-ın 'publication' (← *yay-* 'to spread, publish');
-(Xn)ç (often from intransitive or reflexive bases): *iğren-ç* 'disgust' (← *iğren-* 'to feel disgust');
-(X)ntX/-tX (the latter with stems ending in *-n*): *oy-untu* 'excavation, section' (← *oy-* 'to hollow out'); collective nouns designating a rest or the result of entropy, e.g., *yık-ıntı* 'ruins' (← *yık-* 'to destroy');
-(X)t: yaz-ıt 'inscription' (← *yaz-* 'to write');
-yIk: eri-yik '(chem.) solution, lye' (← *eri-* 'to dissolve, melt').

Object nouns are formed with *-mAk: ye-mek* 'food' (← *ye-* 'to eat'); *-sAk: tut-sak* 'prisoner' (← *tut-* 'to grasp, hold'); *-(y)ACAk: yi-yecek* 'food' (← *ye-* 'to eat').

Instrument nouns can be derived by means of the following suffixes:
-(A)ç: bağla-ç 'conjunction' (← *bağla-* 'to bind, join');
-(A)k: tara-k 'comb' (← *tara-* 'to comb');

-(A)sI: giy-si 'clothes' (← *giy-* 'to put on, wear'; older forms are *giy-esi ~ gey-esi*);
-cAk: salın-cak 'swing' (← *salın-* 'to sway');
-cX (with verbs ending in *-n*) or *-(y)XcX: al-ıcı* 'receiver' (← *al-* 'to receive').

Some words may function either as agent nouns or as instrument nouns, such as *kes-ici* 'butcher' and 'butcher's knife' (← *kes-* 'to cut');
-KA: süpür-ge 'broom' (← *süpür-* 'to sweep');
-KAç: süz-geç 'filter' (← *süz-* 'to filter'), *yüz-geç* 'fin'; colloquially 'good swimmer' (← *yüz-* 'to swim');
-KX: bıç-kı 'saw' (← *bıç-* 'to cut');
-KXç: soy-guç 'potato peeler' (← *soy-* 'to peel');
-mAç: em-meç 'suction pump' (← *em-* 'to suck');
-mAk: çak-mak 'lighter' (← *çak-* 'to light, kindle');
-X: dürt-ü 'goad' (← *dürt-* 'to prod');
-(X)m/-yXm: donat-ım 'equipment, (stage) properties' (← *donat-* 'to equip');
-(X)n: ölç-ün 'standard, norm' (← *ölç-* 'to measure');
-(X)r, originally an aorist participle: *aç-ar* 'key; aperitif' (← *aç-* 'to open');
-(X)t: taşı-t 'means of transportation' (← *taşı-* 'to transport');
-(y)AcAk, originally a future participle: *sil-ecek* 'windscreen wiper' (← *sil-* 'to wipe').

Place nouns (most words are neologisms) comprise formations with the suffixes
-(A)k: dur-ak 'stop, halt' (← *dur-* 'to stop'); a neologistic term is *çık-ak* 'place of articulation (phon.)' (← *çık-* 'to come out');
-(A)mAk: bas-amak 'step, rung' (← *bas-* 'to step');
-cAk: korun-cak 'depot' (← *korun-* 'to be kept');
-KAn: koru-ğan 'bunker, shelter' (← *koru-* 'to shelter');
-X: bat-ı 'west' (← *bat-* 'to set (of the sun)');
-(X)t: geç-it 'passage' (← *geç-* 'to pass');
-(y)Xş: gir-iş 'entrance' (← *gir-* 'to enter').

4.2 Adjectival derivation

4.2.1 Denominal adjectives

The following categories can be distinguished.

Relational adjectives are derived with *-lXk*, a productive suffix occurring in derivatives referring to periods of time, e.g., *gün-lük* 'daily' (← *gün* 'day') and in complex formations with numerals as a complement denoting duration, weight, extension, value, etc., e.g., *yüz kilo-luk* 'weighing a hundred kilos'.

Adjectives designating the affinity to, participation in or characterization by what is denoted by the base are formed with: *-CXl*: *ot-çul* 'graminivorous' (← *ot* 'grass'); *-(I)t*: *yaş-ıt* 'contemporary' (← *yaş* 'age'); *-TAş*: *öz-deş* 'identical' (← *öz* 'self').

Further categories are constituted by similative adjectives with the suffixes *-CA*: *çocuk-ça* 'childish' (← *çocuk* 'child'); *-sX*: *çocuk-su* 'childish' (← *çocuk* 'child'); *-sXl*: *ağaç-sıl* 'arboreal' (← *ağaç* 'tree'); *-(X)msX*: *kadın-ımsı* 'effeminate' (← *kadın* 'woman'); possessive adjectives, e.g., *-lX*: *akıl-lı* 'intelligent' (← *akıl* 'intelligence'); privative adjectives, e.g., *-sXz*: *ses-siz* 'mute' (← *ses* 'sound') (sometimes nouns arise in this pattern by conversion as well: *tel-siz* 'wireless, walkie-talkie'), and collective adjectives, cf. *-lX*: only when derived from numerals, e.g., *üç-lü* 'threesome, trio' (← *üç* 'three'). Other adjectives are formed with the suffixes *-(A)ç*: *kır-aç* 'infertile' (← *kır* 'barren land'); *-(A)k*: *orta-k* 'common' (← *orta* 'centre, the public'); *-TAn*: *sıra-dan* 'ordinary' (← *sıra* 'series').

Neologistic adjectives comprise formations with the suffixes *-(A)t*: *baş-at* 'dominant' (← *baş* 'head'); *-(A)l* (*yer-el* 'local' ← *yer* 'place') and *-sAl* (*duygu-sal* 'affective, sensitive' ← *duygu* 'feeling'). The latter were copied from French (cf. *culturel*) to replace the Arabic adjective suffix *-î*. From the neologism *kutsal* 'holy' (← *kut* 'good fortune') which was invented to replace the Arabic loan *kudsî* 'holy' the suffix *-sAl* was extracted to become a new and productive suffix (Lewis 1999: 102).

4.2.2 Deadjectival adjectives

Adjectives expressing intensification are formed with the suffixes *-mAn*: *koca-man* 'enormous' (← *koca* 'big'); *-(X)CXk*: *az-ıcık* 'very little' (← *az* 'few'); with truncation of the final *-k* of the base: *küçü-cük* 'tiny, minute' (← *küçük* 'small').

Resemblance and attenuation are expressed by
-CA: *küçük-çe* 'smallish' (← *küçük* 'small');
-cAk: *büyü-cek* 'rather big' (← *büyük* 'big'), with truncation of the final consonant of the stem;
-CXl: modification and gradation, e.g., *ak-çıl* 'whitish' (← *ak* 'white');
-(I)msI: *ekşi-msi* 'sourish' (← *ekşi* 'sour');
-rAk, originally an augmentative suffix, now an unproductive suffix indicating a low degree of a property (maybe influenced by *-(X)mt(ı)rak*): *boz-rak* 'grayish' (← *boz* 'gray'); the neologism *dış-rak* 'exoteric' (← *dış* '(on the) outside') shows no gradation;
-sI (quite rare): *kızıl-sı* 'reddish' (← *kızıl* 'red');

-(X)mt(ı)rak (the suffix does not follow synharmonism): *ekşi-mtrak* 'sourish' (← *ekşi* 'sour'), *mor-umtırak* 'slightly purple' (← *mor* 'purple');
-(X)mtUl (also *-(X)mtIl*), an archaic suffix: *göğ-ümtül* 'bluish' (← *gök* 'blue').

Other suffixes are *-(A)k: sol-ak* 'left-handed' (← *sol* 'left'); *-(I)t: karşı-t* 'opposite' (← *karşı* 'contrary, opposite'); *-(X)ncX* forms mainly ordinals from cardinals, e.g., *bir-inci* 'first' (← *bir* 'one').

4.2.3 Deverbal adjectives

Deverbal adjectives express active or passive meaning.

Lexicalized participles comprise formations with the following formants: *-KAn: atıl-gan* 'enterprising' (← *atıl-* 'to throw oneself into'); *dövül-gen* 'forgeable' is a "projection participle" (Erdal) from the passive *dövül-* 'to be forged'; *-mXş* (past participles from intransitive stems): *geç-miş* 'past' (← *geç-* 'to pass'); *-TIK: tanı-dık* 'known, familiar' (← *tanı-* 'to know, recognize'); *-(y)AcAk* (originally a future participle): *ol-acak* 'feasible' (← *ol-* 'to be, become'); *-(y)An: andır-an* 'analogue' (← *andır-* 'to remind'); *-(y)AsI* (archaic): *görül-esi* 'worth seeing' (← *görül-* 'to be seen').

Negated participles are formed with *-mAdIk: görül-medik* 'unseen, unprecedented' (← *görül-* 'to be seen') and *-mAz: geçir-mez* 'impermeable' (← *geçir-* 'to let through').

Adjectives denoting personal traits are formed with the suffixes *-(A)cAn*, a rare suffix: *sev-ecen* 'loving, tender' (← *sev-* 'to love'); *-(A)k: ürk-ek* 'timid' (← *ürk-* 'to be frightened'); *-KAç: utan-gaç* 'shy' (← *utan-* 'to be shy'); *-(X)ntX/-tX: uyu-ntu* 'indolent, lazy' (← *uyu-* 'to sleep').

Resultative adjectives are formed with
-KXn: çök-kün 'sunken, collapsed, depressive' (← *çök-* 'to sink');
-mA: dök-me 'cast (of metals), piece-meal, loose' (← *dök-* 'to cast');
-vAn: yay-van 'broad' (← *yay-* 'to spread out');
-X: dur-u 'crystal clear' (← *dur-* 'to stand still');
-(X)k (mainly from monosyllabic verbs): *kes-ik* 'cut off' (← *kes-* 'to cut');
-(X)lX: as-ılı 'suspended' (← *as-* 'to hang up').

Further categories are represented by formations with the suffixes
-(A)GAn: dur-ağan 'still' (← *dur-* 'to stand still');
-(A)l: dur-al 'static' (← *dur-* 'to stand');
-(A)y: yap-ay 'artificial' (← *yap-* 'to make');
-mAl: sağ-mal 'milk-giving' (← *sağ-* 'to milk');
-sAl: gör-sel 'visual' (← *gör-* 'to see');

-(Xn)ç (with stems ending in *-n-* the suffix is only *-ç*): *kork-unç* 'dreadful, what ought to be feared' (← *kork-* 'to fear');
-(y)XcX or *-cX* (with verbs ending in *-n*) formed from transitive bases: *yap-ıcı* 'constructive' (← *yap-* 'to make').

4.3 Verbal derivation

4.3.1 Deverbal verbs

The following categories of deverbal verbs can be distinguished:

a) Actionality
-AlA-: iterative action, e.g., *it-ele-* 'to push repeatedly, thump' (← *it-* 'to push');
-(I)ştIr-, a composite suffix (reciprocal + causative), marks intensified or repetitive action: *ara-ştır-* 'to investigate' (← *ara-* 'to search');
-(X)klA-: repetitive or intermittent action, e.g., *uyu-kla-* 'to doze' (← *uyu-* 'to sleep'), *dürt-ükle-* 'to prod repeatedly or continually' (← *dürt-* 'to prod');
-(X)msA-: similatives or verbs denoting extenuation of the semantics of the base, e.g., *ağla-msa-* 'to whine' (← *ağla-* 'to weep'), *gül-ümse-* 'to smile' (← *gül-* 'to laugh').

b) Diathesis and voice
In Turkish there are four verbal categories marked by diathesis and voice (valency-changing) suffixes: reflexive, passive, causative and reciprocal-cooperative verbs. After suffixation, these stems may serve as base verbs which can be further expanded with other voice suffixes or with suffixes forming deverbal nouns. Verbs with voice suffixes behave like basic verbal stems and modal and tense suffixes attach to them.

c) Passive verbs
The morphological marker of passive verbs is *-(X)l-* except for stems ending in *-l-* to which the suffix *-Xn-* is added: *sev-il-* 'to be loved' (← *sev-* 'to love') but *böl-ün-* 'to be divided' (← *böl-* 'to divide'). Stems ending in vowels, take the suffix *-n*: *de-n-* 'to be said' (← *de-* 'to say'). There is an intransitivizing use of the suffix *-(X)l-* which should be distinguished from its passivizing function. The difference is especially important when a causative suffix follows, because genuine passives combine with causatives to create new lexical meanings, whereas intransitives

with causatives would convey the same meaning as the simple underived base (Erdal 1996: 80–81).

d) Reflexive and medial verbs
Only a limited number of verbal stems can be turned into reflexive verbs by means of *-(X)n-*. Some of these verbs can be passives as well: *yıka-n-* 'to wash oneself, be washed' (← *yıka-* 'to wash'). Passivity can be marked by an additional passive suffix, e.g., *yıka-n-ıl-* 'to be washed'. Sometimes new meanings are created by adding the reflexive suffix, cf. *çek-in-* 'to feel embarrassed, have scruples' (← *çek-* 'to draw, pull') or *düş-ün-* 'to think (about)' (← *düş-* 'to fall'). Reflexive verbs can be expanded by the causative suffixes.

e) Reciprocal and cooperative verbs
These verbs are formed with the suffix *-(X)ş-*, denoting genuine reciprocals with transitive base verbs: *öp-üş-* 'to kiss each other' (← *öp-* 'to kiss') and cooperative verbs with intransitive base verbs: *gül-üş-* 'to laugh together' (← *gül-* 'to laugh'). This suffix can be attached to only a few base verbs. In some cases stems expanded with *-(X)ş-* take on a new meaning, e.g., *al-ış-* 'to get used to' (← *al-* 'to take') or *gel-iş-* 'to develop (itr.)' (← *gel-* 'to come'). Some verbs denote an action which lacks direction or course: *uç-uş-* 'to fly about' (← *uç-* 'to fly') or they intensify the action: *kok-uş-* 'to stink' (← *kok-* 'to smell'). Some reciprocals are formed from base verbs with a reciprocal pronoun, e.g., *birbirini gör-* 'to see each other' (← *bir* 'one' + *bir* 'one' with accusative suffix ı *gör-* 'to see'). The causative suffix may be attached to *-(X)ş-*.

f) Causative verbs
Causatives are formed from transitive and intransitive base verbs with different suffixes depending on the verbal stem, cf.
-Ar-: This suffix attaches only to a few base verbs, e.g., *çık-ar-* 'to extract' (← *çık-* 'to go out');
-t-: The suffix attaches to polysyllabic and some monosyllabic stems ending in vowels: *büyü-t-* 'to enlarge' (← *büyü-* 'to grow'). Stems ending in *-l-* or *-r-* take this suffix as well: *getir-t-* 'to let bring' (← *getir-* 'to bring');
-TXr-: The most common suffix is realized with a voiceless consonant after stems ending in voiceless consonants, e.g., *yap-tır-* 'to let make, let build' (← *yap-* 'to make'), and with a voiced consonant after stems ending in voiced consonants and monosyllabic stems ending in vowels, e.g., *öl-dür-* 'to kill' (← *öl-* 'to die'). *-TXr-* attaches to most verbal stems ending in consonants and to some monosyllabic stems ending in vowels;

-Xr-: Monosyllabic stems ending in consonants take on this suffix, e.g., *bit-ir-* 'to bring to an end' (← *bit-* 'to come to an end');
-Xt-: Some monosyllabic stems ending in consonants (especially in *-k-*) are expanded by this suffix, e.g., *kork-ut-* 'to frighten' (← *kork-* 'to fear').

Some exceptions are, e.g., *kaldır-* 'to raise, pick up' vs. *kalk-* 'to stand up, rise' or *göster-* 'to show' vs. *gör-* 'to see'. Composite causative suffixes are not uncommon, e.g., *bil-dir-t-* 'to cause to inform' (← *bil-* 'to know').

4.3.2 Denominal verbs

The word-formation meaning of some suffixes varies according to the part of speech of their respective base words (see especially *-lA-*), e.g.,
-A- forms transitive verbs, e.g., *kan-a-* 'to bleed' (← *kan* 'blood') and intransitive verbs, e.g., *yaş-a-* 'to live' (← *yaş* 'age');
-(A)ş-: *yan-aş-* 'to approach' (← *yan* 'side');
*-(A)t-: from a synchronic point of view we should reckon with this suffix in *göz-et-* 'to look after' (← *göz* 'eye'), but in Old Turkic the verb was most likely pronounced *küzäd-*, and this verb is not related to *köz* 'eye';
-lA-: one of the most productive suffixes, e.g., *baş-la-* 'to begin' (← *baş* 'head, beginning');
-lAn-: a composite suffix (*-lA-* + *-n-*) forming intransitive or medial denominal and deadjectival verbs with the meaning 'to acquire that which is denoted by the base' or 'to come in contact with that which is denoted by the base', e.g., *aydın-lan-* 'to brighten' (← *aydın* 'bright'); *güneş-len-* 'to sunbathe' (← *güneş* 'sun');
-(X)k-: forms intransitive verbs derived from adjectives, e.g., *ac-ık-* 'to be hungry' (← *aç* 'hungry'), nouns: *göz-ük-* 'to seem' (← *göz* 'eye') or numerals: *bir-ik-* 'to gather' (← *bir* 'one').

Causative verbs can be derived by means of *-lAndIr-*, a composite suffix (*-lAn-* + causative *-TXr-*): *at-landır-* 'to let mount (a horse)' (← *at* 'horse'); *-lAştIr-*, a composite suffix (*-lAş-* + causative *-TXr-*): *sık-laştır-* 'to move together closely' (← *sık* 'dense, thick'); *-lAt-*, a composite suffix (*-lA-* + causative *-t-*), deriving causative verbs from nouns: *kir-let-* 'to make dirty, rape' (← *kir* 'dirt') and adjectives: *geniş-let-* 'to expand' (← *geniş* 'wide').

Inchoative verbs are formed with the following suffixes: *-(A)l-* attaches to adjectives denoting a change of quality, quantity, shape, direction, e.g., *ince-l-* 'to become thin' (← *ince* 'thin'); some bases ending in *-k* drop this consonant, e.g., *yükse-l-* 'to rise' (← *yüksek* 'high'); *-(A)r-* derives verbs denoting chiefly a change of color, e.g., *mor-ar-* 'to turn violet' (← *mor* 'violet'); *-lA-* derives inchoative verbs from adjectives, e.g., *geniş-le-* 'to widen' (← *geniş* 'wide'); *-lAş-*, originally a composite suffix (-lA- + -ş-), forms inchoative verbs only from adjectives: *kalın-laş-* 'to become thick' (← *kalın* 'thick, dense').

Reciprocal verbs are formed with *-lAş-*, a composite suffix (-lA- + -ş-); when the base is a noun the verbs usually denote reciprocal voice: *haber-leş-* 'to exchange news, communicate' (← *haber* 'news'). An exception is *yer-leş-* 'to settle' (← *yer* 'place, abode').

Mental action verbs are derived by *-sA-*: when added to nouns, the verbs are transitive, e.g., *önem-se-* 'to consider important' (← *önem* 'importance'), or intransitive, e.g., *su-sa-* 'to become thirsty' (← *su* 'water'); when added to adjectives, the verbs are transitive: *küçük-se-* 'to despise' (← *küçük* 'small'); *-(X)msA-* derives verbs from adjectives or pronouns: *ben-imse-* 'to regard (something) one's own' (← *ben* 'I'); see also *-(X)rgAn-: acı-rgan-* 'to feel sorry for sb.' (← *acı* 'worry').

The following suffixes attach to onomatopoetics and interjections, cf. *-KXr-: fış-kır-* 'to bubble, fizz' (← *fışfış* 'splashing noise'); *-lA-: hav-la-* 'to bark' (← *hav hav* 'bow-wow'), *ah-la-* 'to sigh' (← *ah* 'ah!'); *-TA(n)-: gümbür-de-* 'to rumble' (← *gümbür gümbür* 'rumbling'); *-n* has to be added when the agent is a human being.

4.4 Adverbials

In Turkish, adverbials are adverbs, postpositions and adverbial noun phrases. Some adverbs are old loans, e.g., *daima* 'always', *hataen* 'mistakenly' or *tamamen* 'completely' (all from Arabic). Petrified nouns with case suffixes can be adverbs: *gerçek-ten* 'really' (ablative), *söz-de* 'supposedly' (locative). The composite converbial suffix *-TXkçA* can be used adverbially: *git-tikçe* 'gradually' (← *git-* 'to go'). The infinitive marker (-mAk) combined with the privative suffix *-sXz* and the (now obsolete) instrumental suffix *-In* is used adverbially, e.g., *dur-mak-sız-ın* 'continually' (← *dur-* 'to stand, remain'). Some postpositions are originally converbs such as *gör-e* 'according to' (← *gör-* 'to see' + *-A* converb) or *ol-arak* 'as, being' (← *ol-* 'to be' + *-(y)ArAk* converb). The postposition *gibi* 'like' goes back to the noun *kip* 'pattern' (with possessive suffix). An example derived from the noun *boy* 'height, length' with possessive suffix, pronominal *-n-* and the equative suffix *-CA* is *boy-u-n-ca* 'lengthwise, along'. From nominal (*çocuk-ça* 'childishly' ← *çocuk* 'child') or adjectival bases (*yavaş-ça* 'gently' ← *yavaş* 'gentle') adverbs can be derived by means of the suffix *-ÇA*. With *-rA* adverbs of place, locative pronouns, interrogatives or nouns are expanded; this suffix has to be combined with *-lX* or case suffixes (e.g., *bu-ra-da* 'here', *ne-re-de* 'where', *ne-re-li* 'whence'). Through conversion some adjectives shifted in preverbal position may function as adverbs.

Denominal adverbs are derived with the following suffixes:
-CAsI, e.g., *hak-çası* 'really, frankly' (← *hak* 'truth');

-In, the now obsolete instrumental, e.g., *yaz-ın* 'in summer' (← *yaz* 'summer');
-lArCA, e.g., *hafta-larca* 'for weeks' (← *hafta* 'week' the plural suffix *-lAr* + the nearly obsolete equative suffix *-CA*); also with numerals, cf. *bin-lerce* 'thousands of' (← *bin* 'thousand');
-lArI, a composite suffix (plural + possessive suffix) forming adverbs denoting a certain time: *sabah-ları* 'in the morning' (← *sabah* 'morning');
-leyin usually derives adverbs from nouns denoting a time of the day; the suffix does not follow synharmonism: *akşam-leyin* 'in the evening' (← *akşam* 'evening'); a few adverbials are derived from pronouns with an extra suffix *-ci*: *ben-ci-leyin* 'just as me' (← *ben* 'I');
-TAn, e.g., *top-tan* 'wholesale' (← *top* 'total(ity)'); from an interrogative pronoun: *ne-den* 'why' (← *ne* 'what').

Deadjectival adverbs are formed with the suffixes *-CA*: *yavaş-ça* 'gently' (some formations are adjectives), to be further expanded by adding the intensifying suffix *-CIk*: *usul-ca-cık* 'gently', the base *usul* 'gently' is an adverb; *-CAk*: *çabucak* 'very quickly' (← *çabuk* 'quick(ly)'), with truncation of the final *-k*; *-CAnA*: *güzel-cene* 'nicely' (← *güzel* 'nice, beautiful'); *-CAsInA*: *aptal-casına* 'stupidly' (← *aptal* 'stupid').

Deverbal adverbs are, e.g., formed by *-(y)AsI-yA*, an expanded form of *-(y)AsI*, cf. *öl-esi-ye* 'exceedingly' (← *öl-* 'to die').

5 Conversion

Conversion is a common feature of Turkish because the boundary between nouns and adjectives is not as clear-cut as in other languages. Infinitives and participles in *-AcAk*, *-dXk*, *-mAz*, *-(X)r* and *-(y)An* can be used as nouns. When inflectional suffixes are missing, context is the only means to determine whether a word is an adjective or a noun or an adverb or an adjective. Conversion of the verbal stem is quite rare, words such as *güreş* 'wrestling' or *yarış* 'competition' are not simple products of conversion (← *güreş-* 'to wrestle'; ← *yarış-* 'to compete'). They are likely to be derived by haplology (← **güreşiş*; ← **yarışış*) (Röhrborn 2003: 71, and already Erdal 1991: 264 for Old Turkic). But neologistic terms such as *ayra* 'exception' and the verb *ayra-* 'to except' may be examples of conversion of the verbal stem (Röhrborn 2003: 71). One may add *kayşa* 'landslip, landslide' and *kayşa-* 'to slip, slide'. Some nouns which from a synchronic point of view are converted verbal stems, e.g., *acı* 'pain(full)' vs. *acı-* 'to hurt' (itr.), are due to loss of final *-G* (cf. Old Turkic *ačıg* 'grief; bitter') which is dropped already in Old Anatolian.

Even declarative sentences can be converted to nouns, e.g., *imambayıldı* 'a dish (of aubergines); lit. the Imam fainted', *gecekondu* 'a house erected overnight; lit. it took up residence overnight'.

6 References

Aktaş, Ayfer (2008): *Usuelle Wortverbindungen in der Wirtschaftssprache im Deutschen und ihre Entsprechungen im Türkischen*. Frankfurt/M.: Lang.
Atalay, Besim (1946): *Türkçe'de Kelime Yapma Yolları*. İstanbul: İbrahim Horoz Basımevi.
Balcı, Ayla (2006): Unit 6: Word-formation processes. In: Zülal Balpınar (ed.), *Turkish Phonology, Morphology and Syntax*, 77–94. 3rd ed. Eskişehir: Anadolu Üniversitesi.
Banguoğlu, Tahsin (1956): Türkçede tekerrür fiilleri. *Türk Dili Araştırmaları Yıllığı Belleten*: 111–123.
Bassarak, Armin (1985): Zur Abgrenzung zwischen Flexion und Derivation (anhand türkischer Verbformen). In: Wolfgang Ullrich Wurzel (ed.), *Studien zur Morphologie und Phonologie*. Vol. 1, 1–50. Berlin: Akademie der Wissenschaften der DDR, Zentralinstitut für Sprachwissenschaft.
Bassarak, Armin (1998): Suffixpositionen nach türkischen Verbwurzeln und Substantiven. In: Nurettin Demir and Erika Taube (eds.), *Turkologie heute – Tradition und Perspektive. Materialien der dritten Deutschen Turkologen-Konferenz Leipzig, 4.–7. Oktober 1994*, 7–16. Wiesbaden: Harrassowitz.
Berta, Árpád (1991): Gedanken zur Erforschung der Wortbildungselemente im Türkischen. *Acta Orientalia Academiae Scientiarum Hungaricae* 45(2–3): 205–217.
Cüceloğlu, Doğan (1973): Türkçe türetme ekleri üzerine bir çalışma. *Hacettepe Üniversitesi Sosyal ve Beşerî Bilimler Dergisi* 5(1): 47–56.
Dede, Müşerref Ağan (1982): A semantic analysis of Turkish nominal compounds. *İnsan Bilimler Dergisi / Journal of Human Sciences* 1: 87–102.
Demircan, Ömer (1977): *Türkiye Türkçesinde Kök-Ek Bileşmeleri*. Ankara: Ankara Üniversitesi Basımevi.
Deny, Jean (1938): Existe-t-il des préfixes en turc? *Bulletin de la Société de Linguistique de Paris* 39: 51–65.
Dizdaroğlu, Hikmet (1962): *Türkçede Sözcük Yapma Yolları*. Ankara: Ankara Üniversitesi Basımevi.
Ercilasun, Ahmet Bican (1975): -maç/-meç eki üzerine. *Türk Dili ve Edebiyatı Dergisi* 21: 83–88.
Erdal, Marcel (1991): *Old Turkic Word Formation. A Functional Approach to the Lexicon*. 2 Vol. Wiesbaden: Harrassowitz.
Erdal, Marcel (1998): On the verbal noun -(y)Iş. In: Kâmile İmer and Leyla Subaşı Uzun (eds.), *Doğan Aksan Armağanı*, 53–68. Ankara: Ankara Üniversitesi Dil ve Tarih-Coğrafya Fakültesi.
Erdal, Marcel (2000): *Açık* and *kapalı*: The Turkish resultative deverbal adjective. *Turkic Languages* 4(1): 22–30.
Frankle, Eleanor (1948): *Word Formation in the Turkic Languages*. New York: Columbia University Press.
Göksel, Aslı and Aysel Kapan (2020): Derivational networks in Turkish. In: Lívia Körtvélyessi, Alexandra Bagasheva and Pavol Štekauer (eds.), *Derivational Networks Across Languages*, 423–433. Berlin/Boston: De Gruyter Mouton.
Göksu, Sadık (1966): *Türkçenin Üreme Yolları ve "Dil Devrimciliğimiz"*. İstanbul: Son Telgraf Matbaası.
Hatiboğlu, Vecihe (1974): *Türkçenin Ekleri*. Ankara: Ankara Üniversitesi Basımevi.
Ido, Shinji (1999): Mimetic word formation in Turkish. *Asian and African Studies* 8(1): 67–73.

İleri, Esin (2007): Überlegungen zur Untersuchung der Verben auf +lA-mAk. In: Hendrik Boeschoten and Heidi Stein (eds.), *Einheit und Vielfalt in der türkischen Welt. Materialien der 5. Deutschen Turkologenkonferenz Universität Mainz, 4.-7. Oktober 2002*, 116-130. Wiesbaden: Harrassowitz.

Johanson, Lars (1990): Studien zur türkeitürkischen Grammatik. In: György Hazai (ed.), *Handbuch der türkischen Sprachwissenschaft*. Part 1, 146-278. Budapest: Akadémiai Kiadó.

Johanson, Lars (1995): On Turkic converb clauses. In: Martin Haspelmath and Ekkehard König (eds.), *Converbs in Cross-Linguistic Perspective*, 313-347. Berlin/New York: Mouton de Gruyter.

Kahramantürk, Kuthan (1999): *Nominale Wortbildungen und Nominalisierungen im Deutschen und im Türkischen. Ein Beitrag zur deutsch-türkischen kontrastiven Linguistik.* Heidelberg: Groos.

Knobloch, Clemens (1987): Syntaktische und lexikalische Derivation beim türkischen Verb: Ein Beitrag zur Diskussion um den Unterschied zwischen Wortbildung und Flexion. In: Werner Abraham and Ritva Århammar (eds.), *Linguistik in Deutschland. Akten des 21. Linguistischen Kolloquiums, Groningen 1986*, 155-167. Tübingen: Niemeyer.

König, Wolf Dietrich (1987): Nominalkomposita im Türkischen. *Zeitschrift für Sprachwissenschaft* 6(2): 165-185.

Kononov, A[ndrej] N[ikolaevič] (1969): Isimlerin ve sıfatların küçültme şekilleri ve söz yapımı. *Türk Dili Araştırmaları Yıllığı Belleten* 1968: 81-88.

Lewis, Geoffrey (1999): *The Turkish Language Reform. A Catastrophic Success.* Oxford: Oxford University Press.

Mansuroğlu, Mecdud (1960): Türkiye Türkçesinde söz yapımı üzerinde bazı notlar. *Türk Dili ve Edebiyatı Dergisi* 10: 5-24.

Mungan, Güler (2002): *Türkçede Fiillerden Türetilmiş Isimlerin Morfolojik ve Semantik Yönden İncelenmesi.* İstanbul: Simurg.

Özel, Sevgi (1977): *Türkiye Türkçesinde Sözcük Türetme ve Bileştirme.* Ankara: Ankara Üniversitesi Basımevi.

Röhrborn, Klaus (1990): Der Begriff des Nominalkompositums in der türkeitürkischen Sprachwissenschaft. *Zeitschrift der Deutschen Morgenländischen Gesellschaft* 140: 51-67.

Röhrborn, Klaus (1996): Studien zum neologistischen Wortschatz des Türkischen: Bildung von Verbalabstrakta durch Konversion und subtraktive Wortbildung. In: Lars Johanson, Árpád Berta, Bernt Brendemoen and Claus Schönig (eds.), *Symbolae Turcologicae. Studies in Honour of Lars Johanson on his Sixtieth Birthday, 8 March 1996*, 175-180. Stockholm: Almqvist & Wiksell.

Röhrborn, Klaus (1998): Restrukturierte Lexeme in der türkischen Sprachreform. *Turkic Languages* 2: 270-283.

Röhrborn, Klaus (2000): Neologistische Archaismen im Türkeitürkischen. In: Çiğdem Balım-Harding and Colin Imber (eds.), *The Balance of Truth. Essays in Honour of Professor Geoffrey Lewis*, 301-307. İstanbul: Isis Press.

Röhrborn, Klaus (2002): Verbalpräfigierung in der neologistischen Wortbildung des Türkeitürkischen. *Nairiku ajia gengo no kenkyū / Studies on the Inner Asian Languages* 17: 189-202.

Röhrborn, Klaus (2003): *Interlinguale Angleichung der Lexik. Aspekte der Europäisierung des türkeitürkischen Wortschatzes.* Göttingen: Vandenhoeck & Ruprecht.

Römer, Claudia (1991): „Verbalnomen" oder „Partizip"? Bemerkungen zu einigen türkischen deverbalen Nomina. *Der Islam* 68(2): 304-319.

Sarı, Mustafa (2008): *Türkçenin Batı Dilleriyle İlişkisi.* Ankara: Türk Dil Kurumu.

van Schaaik, Gerjan (2000): Higher order compounds in Turkish: Some observations. In: Aslı Göksel and Celia Kerslake (eds.), *Studies on Turkish and Turkic Languages*, 113-120. Wiesbaden: Harrassowitz.

van Schaaik, Gerjan (2002): *The Noun in Turkish. Its Argument Structure and the Compounding Straitjacket.* Wiesbaden: Harrassowitz.

Schakir, Saadet (1933): *Denominale Verbbildungen in den Türksprachen.* Roma: Scuola Tipografica Pio X.
Scharlipp, Wolfgang-Ekkehard (1978): *Untersuchungen zur Morphologie und Substitution türkeitürkischer Neologismen.* Hamburg: Buske.
Schönig, Claus (2025): Historical word-formation in Turkish. In: Peter O. Müller, Susan Olsen and Franz Rainer (eds.), *Word-Formation – Language Contact and Diachrony,* 575–599. Berlin/Boston: De Gruyter Mouton.
Siemieniec-Gołaś, Ewa (1997): *The Formation of Substantives in XVIIth Century Ottoman-Turkish.* Kraków: Księgarnia Akademicka Wydawnictwo Naukowe.
Stachowski, Stanisław (1996): *Historisches Wörterbuch der Bildungen auf -CI/-ICI im Osmanisch-Türkischen.* Kraków: Księgarnia Akademicka Wydawnictwo Naukowe.
Tosun, Cengiz (1977): A contrastive study of word-formation by affixation in Turkish and English. Ph.D. dissertation, Department of English Language and Literature Hacettepe University Ankara.
Tosun, Cengiz (1978): Türkçede küçültme ve benzetme ekleri. *Genel Dilbilim Dergisi* 1(1): 48–54.
Ülkü, Vural (1980): *Affixale Wortbildung im Deutschen und im Türkischen. Ein Beitrag zur deutsch-türkischen kontrastiven Grammatik.* Ankara: Ankara Üniversitesi Basımevi.
Wälchli, Bernhard (2025): Co-compounds. In: Peter O. Müller, Susan Olsen and Franz Rainer (eds.), *Word-Formation – Special Patterns and Restrictions,* 145–169. Berlin/Boston: De Gruyter Mouton.
Zülfikar, Hamza (1991): *Terim Sorunları ve Terim Yapma Yolları.* Ankara: Atatürk Kültür, Dil ve Tarih Yüksek Kurumu.

Gulnara Iskandarova
20 Bashkir

1 Introduction
2 General overview
3 Composition
4 Derivation
5 Conversion
6 Reduplication
7 Clipping
8 Conclusion
9 References

Abstract: Bashkir is one of the Turkic languages spoken in the Russian Federation. The typological features of an agglutinative language are also reflected in Bashkir word-formation. In this article, the most productive word-formation processes, i.e. composition, derivation, conversion, and reduplication are investigated from a structural, semantic and comparative point of view.

1 Introduction

Bashkir belongs to the Kipchak group of the Turkic languages and is closest to Tatar. It is the official language of the Republic of Bashkortostan, also common in the Republic of Tatarstan, and in some other regions of Russia. The number of Bashkir native speakers in Russia is about 1,4 million people, most of them are Bashkir-Russian bilinguals. The Bashkir script was originally based on the Arabic alphabet, which was spread among the Bashkirs after the adoption of Islam in the 10th century. First details about Bashkir can be found in Mahmud al-Kashgari's "Compendium of the Languages of the Turks" (1072–1074), cf. Auèzova (2005). The earliest written monuments date back to the 14th century. In 1930 a Latin-based alphabet had been introduced, which was in turn replaced by an adapted Cyrillic variant in 1938.

Bashkir became a subject of linguistic research in the second half of the 19th century. The author of the first scholarly grammar of Bashkir (1948) was Nikolaj K. Dmitriev. Nicholas Poppe with the *Bashkir Manual* (1962) and other

Gulnara Iskandarova, Baku, Azerbaijan

publications, Ahnaf A. Ûldašev, Zinnur G. Uraksin, and others have much contributed to the study of Bashkir. Bashkir word-formation, however, is still insufficiently investigated, the apparent lack of modern theoretical and empirical studies confirms this fact. The "Grammar of the modern Bashkir literary language" (Ûldašev 1981) and the monograph "Bashkir nominal word-formation" (Garipov 1959) can be regarded as standard reference works. As auxiliary texts we consulted works on word-formation of other Turkic languages, for example, Tatar (Ganiev 1974) and Turkish (Kononov 1956), as well as studies of Russian turcologists (Sevortân 1966; Tenišev 1988; Šerbak 1994). In addition, we refer to studies on word-formation of other languages, unrelated to Bashkir, for example, Russian (Ermakova 1984), as well as to comparative descriptions of other European languages (Revzina 1969; Gak 1985).

The examples in this article are rendered using the transliteration ISO 9 1995.

2 General overview

Bashkir is an agglutinating language and shows the following essential features in the field of word-formation:
a) A word/stem can be followed by several affixes, cf. *balyǩ* 'fish' → *balyǩ-sy* 'fisherman' → *balyǩsy-lyǩ* 'fishing, fishery';
b) An affix can have several variants which are caused by vowel harmony: the vowel of the affix is assimilated to the vowel of the stem;
c) Another distinguishing characteristic is the absence of the grammatical category of gender. The value 'female' is expressed by adding *ǩatyn* 'woman, wife' or *ǩyẓ* 'girl' (both in the general meaning 'female being') + possessive suffix -*y* (-*y*, -*e*, -*o*, -*ô* after consonants; -*hy*, -*he*, -*ho*, -*hô* after vowels), e.g., *hind ǩatyny/ǩyẓy* 'Indian woman', *francuz ǩatyny/ǩyẓy* 'Frenchwoman';
d) The boundaries between the parts of speech are blurred, a fact that promotes the efficiency of conversion (cf. section 5), although this term is not generally accepted in the Turkologic literature. Depending on its position in a syntactic construction, a lexical unit can act either as a noun or as an adjective or a verb (cf. Johanson 1998: 38: "Verbals may also be nominal stems."; see also Ülkü 1980: 191 on the nominal use of Turkic adjectives and participles without morphological marking);
e) Derivation is a productive word-formation process in Bashkir, but the means of word-formation and inflection are not clearly separated from each other. For example, in connection with nouns the affix -*ly* can derive new words with the meaning of personal/agent nouns, e.g., *at-ly* 'horseman', qualitative

adjectives, e.g., *taš-ly* 'stony', but it is also used in comitative forms with the value of possession, e.g., *at-ly* 'with a horse, having a horse', *taš-ly* 'with stones, having stones'.

Prefixation is not typical of Bashkir word-formation. Some prefixes of mainly Latin and Greek origin occur in Russian loanwords only, but they are not distinguished as prefixes in Bashkir, e.g., *antifašist* 'antifascist', *telereporter* 'TV reporter', etc. Similar prefixal formations with native Bashkir stems are sporadic, e.g., *antidon"â* 'antiworld', *superjondoẓ* 'superstar'. This fact reminds us of the following statement about Turkish: "Äußerst interessant und völlig neu ist die Voranstellung von europäischen Präfixen vor türkische Wörter (*süper-*, *de-/des-*, *tele-*)" [The attachment of European prefixes in front of Turkish words (*süper-*, *de-/des-*, *tele-*) is extremely interesting and absolutely new] (König 1992: 16).

Diachronically, a case of semi-suffixation can be observed in the word-formation model N + *-man/-men*, denoting personal nouns. The origin of the second element has not yet been determined unequivocally: some scholars assume an (early) influence of Western European (Germanic) languages (*man*, *Mann*) (cf. also article 19 on Turkish, section 4.1.3), others regard *-man/-men* as a possible loan from Arabic or Persian. The element *-man/-män* occurs also in some Tatar words (Ganiev 1974: 127); in Turkish, its rate is somewhat higher (cf. Kahramantürk 1999: 63). In Bashkir, *-man/-men* can only be found in some primordial agent/personal nouns, as, e.g., *eẓärmän* 'pursuer' (cf. the verb *eẓärläu* 'to persue'), *tärzeman* 'translator' (cf. the corresponding stem in the verbal compound *tärzemä iteu* 'to translate', see section 3.3), *hônärmän* 'good master' (cf. *hônäre* 'skill, mastery'). New Bashkir words with *-man/-män* are not created. Russian loanwords of the type *kongressmen* 'congressman', *šoumen* 'showman, entertainer', *barmen* 'barkeeper', *ombudsmen* 'ombudsman', etc., act in Bashkir as simplexes and cannot be decomposed as "base + *-men*".

3 Composition

3.1 Nominal compounds

3.1.1 Determinative compounds

In Bashkir, it is difficult to differentiate between determinative compounds and syntactic word combinations. Therefore composition as a means of word-formation in Turkic languages is not generally acknowledged (cf. Tenišev 1988: 138). In

Gabain's *Alttürkische Grammatik* [Old Turkish Grammar] (1950) compounds are examined in the section "Syntactic word combinations".

Diachronically, compounds have developed from various types of word combinations and are based upon various kinds of syntactic/syntagmatic relations (Garipov 1959: 154). Also from the synchronic perspective, the formation of compounds in Bashkir as well as in other Turkic languages is more likely to be a syntactic problem than an issue of word-formation. Nevertheless in linguistic turcology there are various classifications of complex nouns which put in the forefront either semantic, or morphological, or phonetic criteria.

As shown in Braun (2000), the basic way of forming determinative compounds is by means of what she calls "suffixation in compounding". The compounds in question consist of two nominal components and the possessive suffix of the 3rd person singular (-*hy*, -*he*, -*ho*, -*hô* after vowels, -*y*, -*e*, -*o*, -*ô* after consonants), which is mainly attached to the second component, i.e. the head of a compound. In Turkologic literature such compounds are called izafet constructions. They express a possessive connection between the determining and the determined word in a syntactic structure. The second constituent is mostly a deverbal or denominal derivative, e.g., Bashkir *kitap hatyu-sy-hy* 'bookseller; lit. book-sell-AGENT-POSS'. Sometimes the second constituent is a non-derived (or loan) word, e.g., *radio diktor-y* 'radiospeaker; lit. radio speaker-POSS'.

Besides determinative compounds there is another type of compounding in Bashkir: Verbal derivatives with the suffix -*sy*/-*se* which do not exist as autonomous words often occur as second elements, e.g., *zakon syġaryu-sy* 'lawgiver; lit. law-give-AGENT', *kitap tôpláu-se* 'bookbinder; lit. book-bind-AGENT'. Often the first constituent of a compound occurs in an oblique case as can be seen in the corresponding case suffixes, e.g.,

(1) a. *fortep'âna-la ujnau-sy*
    piano-LOC   play-AGENT
    'pianist'
   b. *ukyu-zy tamamlau-sy*
    school-ACC leave-AGENT
    'school-leaver'

3.1.2 Copulative compounds

In the formation of Bashkir copulative compounds there are special models, explicitly expressing a copulative meaning. Two models are productive: S_1-*ly* + S_2-*ly* and S_1 + S_2. Formations with the affix -*ly*/-*le* are of particular interest. The suffix combines with both components which are connected by a hyphen, e.g., *ataly-kyzly* 'the father with the daughter', *k̆äjnäle-kilenle* 'the mother-in-law with the daughter-in-law', but cf. also co-compounds like *irle-k̆atynly* 'married couple' (← *ir* 'husband, man', *k̆atyn* 'wife, woman'). In such formations, the suffix *-ly/-le* has a double function: it serves as word-formation affix and as grammatical affix expressing a copulative connection (similar to the conjunction 'and'), cf. Garipov (1959: 120). In Old Turkish the word-formation structure S_1-*li/-lı* + S_2-*li/-lü* was also common, it expressed 'both ... and ...', e.g., *ädgüli ayïyli* 'both good and bad' (cf. Gabain 1950: 159).

The productive model $S_1 + S_2$ is characteristic of a rather great number of "sociative compounds", some of which can be regarded as co-compounds (cf. Wälchli 2025). The components are either antonymous, or synonymous, or otherwise paradigmatically related, and form designations of relationship (synchronically often with an ironic nuance), e.g., *tuġan-yryu* 'relatives; lit. brother-tribe', *ata-baba* 'forefathers; lit. father-grandfather', *ata-ásá* 'parents; lit. father-mother'. These compounds are limited to kinship terms.

3.2 Adjectival compounds

Coordinative adjectival compounds (in the Bashkir literature on word-formation also called "paired adjectives"), determinative adjectival compounds, and juxtapositions are formed either syntactically or morphologically and syntactically in order to express the coordinative or subordinative relations of the components.

C o o r d i n a t i v e adjectival compounds can be regarded as a semantic combination of the meanings of their (simple or derived) components. These components can be either antonyms (*ak̆ly-k̆araly* 'black and white; lit. white-black'), or synonyms (*tămlă-tatly* 'very tasty; lit. tasty-sweet'), or otherwise semantically related elements. In derived components the most common affix is *-ly/-le*, e.g., *ak̆ly-kükle* 'white-blue', *k̆arly-âmġyrly* 'snowy-rainy'.

In d e t e r m i n a t i v e adjectival compounds, the head can be non-derived or derived. As modifying components one finds either simple adjectives (*k̆ara kük* 'dark blue'), approximative adjectives (*ak̆hyl ješel* 'whitish green'), or derived adjectives in *-taj* (*taštaj k̆aty* 'firm as a stone; lit. stone-ADJ firm'). If the head is a suffixal adjective, the modifying component can be a non-derived adjective (*ak̆ jok̆-lo* 'in white stockings'), a derived adjective (*asyk̆ kùṇel-le* 'good-natured'), a noun in the nominative case (*aġas ḣap-ly* 'with a wooden handle; lit. wood-handle-SUFF'), a simple numeral (*biš jyl-lyk̆* 'five years (old), quinquennial'), or an adjectival reduplication (*matur-matur kuldăk-lă* 'beautifully dressed').

There are also juxtapositions of an adjective and a specifying component which can be expressed by the pronoun *ùẕ* 'one's (own)' (e.g., *ùẕ ally* 'independent; lit. one's (own) front side-ADJ'), a noun in the nominative case (e.g., *ès-kerle* 'rancorous, full of rancour; lit. soul-dirty'), or an adjective (*aǩ-buẕ* 'grey; lit. white-light grey').

3.3 Verbal compounds

In the "Bashkir Grammar" (Ûldašev 1981: 213), verbal compounds are termed "compounding forms of affixal character". These verbs are the result of so-called analytical word-formation (noun + auxiliary verb *iteù* 'to do'; cf. also the term *light verb* in other articles of this series), e.g., *bajram iteù* 'to celebrate; lit. holiday do', *âl iteù* 'to have a rest; lit. rest do'. Other verbs, such as *kil-* 'to come', *bir-* 'to give', *ḥal-* 'to put', etc., are used as auxiliary verbs in single cases only, e.g., *joǩo kileù* 'to want to sleep; lit. (the) dream come', *komanda bireù* 'to order, command; lit. (the) order allow', *ǩarmaǩ ḥalyu* 'to fish; lit. fishing tackle put'.

There are also some verbs formed on the model "Russian infinitive + Bashkir auxiliary verb". As auxiliary verb one usually finds *iteù* 'to do', e.g., *strahovat' iteù* 'to insure', *konfiskovat' iteu* 'to confiscate', *mobilizovat' iteù* 'to mobilize', etc. In these cases the auxiliary verb serves adaptation purposes.

Some polysemous verbs, as, for instance, *torou*, *bireù*, and *ǩarau* can also function as auxiliary verbs in verbal compounds of the type "Gerund in *-(a)j* or *-p* + auxiliary verb". The auxiliary verb, deprived of its original lexical meaning, expresses various kinds of verbal aktionsart, such as inchoativity, iterativity, intensity, and other meanings. The auxiliary verb *torou*, for instance, occurs in verbal compounds which denote the continuation of an action, e.g., *uǩyj torou* 'to continue to read (reading); lit. reading stand', *ašaj torou* 'to continue to eat (eating); lit. eating stand'. In verbal compounds like *âḥap bireù* 'to make sth. for sb.; lit. (after) having made (sth.) give (it) to sb.', *alyp bireù* 'to give (sth.) to sb.; lit. (after) having taken (sth.) give (it) to sb.' the auxiliary verb *bireù* denotes that the action is done for somebody (the addressee or beneficiary). Verbal compounds consisting of the gerund of the autosemantic verb and the auxiliary verb *ǩarau* designate the attempt to perform an action, e.g., *ḥorašyp ǩarau* 'to try to find out; lit. asking look', *ḥejlášepkarau* 'to try to talk; lit. talking look', etc. (Ûldašev 1981: 216–223). The formation of aktionsart in Turkic languages is interpreted ambiguously: as a phenomenon of inflection (Kononov 1956; Sevortân 1966), as word-formation (Dmitriev 1948), or both (Ûldašev 1981).

4 Derivation

4.1 Nominal derivation

Affixes in Turkic languages are, as a rule, highly polysemous. Moreover, most of them can be combined with stems of different parts of speech. Due to these facts they are usually presented in a semasiological description, not according to word-formation categories. The suffix -*sy*/-*se* (the variants -*so*/-*sô* occur extremely seldom), for instance, can be attached to verbal and nominal bases, and covers a wide range of meanings, e.g., deverbal **agent nouns** (*aġartyusy* 'house painter' ← *aġartyu* 'to whitewash'), denominal **personal nouns**, denoting persons according to their habits or occasional activities (*âlġansy* 'liar' ← *âlġan* 'lie (n.)', *tămăkese* 'smoker' ← *tămăke* 'tobacco', *eṇeùse* 'winner' ← *eṇeù* 'victory'), followers of an ideological orientation (*leninsy* 'Leninist'). There is a relatively large group of personal nouns in -*sy*, motivated by designations of body parts (or their metonymic meanings), e.g., *aâǩsy* 'carrier' (← *aâǩ* 'foot'), *baššy* 'leader' (← *baš* 'head'), *ǩolaǩtaš* 'confidant' (← *ǩolaǩ* 'ear'), *telse* 'linguist' (← *tel* 'tongue, language'), and others. Besides, the suffix -*sy*/-*se* can derive designations of tools, objects, etc., e.g., *ǩamsy* 'small whip' (← *ǩam* 'shaman'), *hôjônsô* 'a gift to somebody who brought a joyful message' (← *hôjônôs* 'joy'). The basic function of the suffix -*sy*/-*se* is the formation of denominal agent nouns. In dictionaries they are attested much more frequently than deverbal agent nouns in -*sy*/-*se*, as denominal word-formation is especially productive in Bashkir (cf. Garipov 1959; on similar cases in Turkish, cf. Tekinay 1981: 29).

There are also a number of agent nouns derived from nouns denoting a material or substance. These derivatives are rather ancient and denote old professions, e.g., *taššy* 'mason' (← *taš* 'stone'), *altynsy* 'jeweler' (← *altyn* 'gold'), *kômôššô* 'jeweler, seller of jewels' (← *kômôš* 'silver'), *timerse* 'smith' (← *timer* 'iron'). Historically 'handicraftsman-manufacturer' and 'producer-dealer' were often combined in one person, cf. Turkish derivatives such as *aynacı* 'producer and seller of mirrors' (← *ayna* 'mirror'), *baltacı* 'producer and seller of axes; woodcutter' (← *balta* 'axe') (Kononov 1956: 103).

The suffix -*daš*/-*dăš*/-*taš*/-*tăš*/-*ẓaš*/-*ẓăš* derives denominal personal nouns with a sociative meaning ('with, together'). There are different semantic groups, such as neighbourship, alliance, community, contemporaneity, kinship, cf. *yẓandaš* 'neighbour of the strip of land between two fields' (← *yẓan* 'strip of land between two fields'), *auyldaš* 'inhabitant of the same village' (← *auyl* 'village'), *kvartirẓăš* 'next-door neighbour' (← *kvartir* 'flat'); *soûzdaš* 'ally' (← *soûz* (a Russian loanword) 'union'), *kurstaš* 'fellow student' (← *kurs* 'course'); *jăštăš* 'person of the same age' (← *ĵǟš* 'age'), *zamandaš* 'contemporary' (← *zaman* 'epoch'); *isemdǟš* 'namesake' (← *isem* 'name'), *ǩaryndaš* 'uterine children, younger sister, sister' (← *ǩaryn* 'stomach'). Cf. also deverbal *ultyrẓaš* 'interlocutor' (← *ultyryu* 'to sit').

More than 15% of all nouns are formed with the suffix *-lyǩ/-lek/-loǩ/-lôk*. The semantics of the words formed by means of this suffix is wide and diverse:

a) Denominal a c t i o n n o u n s, denoting professional actions, various kinds of activities or duties, e.g., *hunarsylyǩ* 'hunting' (← *hunarsy* 'hunter'), *malsylyǩ* 'cattle breeding' (← *malsy* 'cattle-breeder'), *baǩsasylyǩ* 'gardening' (← *baǩsasy* 'garden');

b) Denominal and deadjectival a b s t r a c t n o u n s, e.g., *kešelek* 'humanity' (← *keše* 'human (being)'), *ǩolloǩ* 'slavery' (← *ǩol* 'slave'), *ǩatylyǩ* 'hardness' (← *katy* 'hard, iron'), *sibǟrlek* 'beauty' (← *sibǟr* 'beautiful');

c) Denominal p l a c e n o u n s, denoting natural or cultivated areas, e.g., *aġaslyǩ* 'grove' (← *aġas* 'tree'), *bolonloǩ* 'meadows' (← *bolon* 'meadow'), *urmanlyǩ* 'wooded, woody place' (← *urman* 'wood, forest'), *besǟnlek* 'mow' (← *besǟn* 'hay'), or workshops, e.g., *timerlek* 'smithy' (← *timer* 'iron'), *utynlyǩ* 'timber merchant's' (← *utyn* 'timber').

The suffix *-kys/-kes* with the variants *-ġys/-ges, -ġos/-ġôs, -kos/-kôs* is specialized in the formation of i n s t r u m e n t n o u n s from transitive verbs, e.g., *jyuġys* 'bast' (← *jyuyu* 'to wash'), *ôẓġôs* 'breaker' (← *ôẓôy* 'to break'), *ǩyrynġys* 'razor' (← *ǩyrynyu* 'to shave'). This instrumental suffix can also express the meaning of a g e n t n o u n s, e.g., *belges* 'expert' (← *beleu* 'to know'), *ǩorotǩos* 'wrecker' (← *ǩorotou* 'to do harm to sb.') (cf. Ischtuganowa 2003: 196).

4.2 Adjectival derivation

More than 80% of adjectives in modern Bashkir are derivatives. About 15 suffixes can be attached to verbal bases (e.g., *-an, -ar, -ger, -ges, -ġaj, -ġyn, -dyǩ, eẓ, -eš, -keù, -ma, -naǩ, -sek* with their variants, and a few others), and about ten to nominal bases (e.g., *-a, -daš, -sa, -sel, -tyǩ, -hel, -šel,* etc.). The overwhelming majority of affixes, including the most productive in the derivation of adjectives (*-ly/ -le, -heẓ, -san, -ge, -lek, -heù, -aǩ, -ġas, -kel, -dǟm* and their variants), combine with both nominal and verbal stems or with stems whose meaning and grammatical status are ambiguous. The most productive suffixes are *-ly* and *-heẓ*.

The general semantics of all adjectives in *-ly* is p o s s e s s i v e. The adjectives can be derived from abstract nouns in *-lyǩ/-lek*, e.g., *izgelekle* 'benevolent' (← *izgelek* 'good' (n.)), *kešelekle* 'human' (← *kešelek* 'mankind'), *tuǩlyǩly* 'nutritious' (← *tuǩlyǩ* 'nutritiousness'). Much less often *-ly* connects with verbs in *-(y)u/-(e)ù*.

The respective derivatives retain a nuance of actional or modal meaning and thus show a certain similarity to participles, e.g., *egeùle* 'harnessed' (← *egeù* 'to harness'), *maǩtauly* 'honourable' (← *maǩtau* 'to praise'). Adjectives in *-ly*, derived from names of colours, belong to the most ancient adjectives in Bashkir and other Turkic languages. Their number is rather insignificant, e.g., *aǩly* 'with white spots' (← *aǩ* 'white'), *ǩaraly* 'with a black background, prevalence of black color' (← *ǩara* 'black'). Adjectives in *-ly* can also be derived from numeral bases, e.g., *ikele* 'double' (← *ike* 'two'), *etele* 'seventh' (← *ete* 'seven'). Finally, it is worth mentioning that adjectives in *-ly* show a large inventory of non-native bases, e.g., Arab (*vaǩytly* 'temporary' ← *vaǩyt* 'time', *serle* 'secret' ← *ser* 'secret' (n.), *šartly* 'conditional' ← *šart* 'condition'), and – most widespread – from Russian, e.g., *parly* 'paired' (← *par* 'pair'), *rătle* 'decent' (← *răt* 'number, order'), cf. Russ. *para*, *râd*.

Adjectives in *-ḥeẓ* can usually be regarded as antonyms of words derived from the same bases by means of the suffix *-ly*. The suffix *-ḥeẓ* expresses a p r i v - a t i v e meaning (rarely: incompleteness), e.g., *kerḥeẓ* 'pure, faultless, innocent' (← *ker* 'dirt'), *ûnḥeẓ* 'confused' (← *ûn* 'sense'), *sikḥeẓ* 'boundless' (← *sik* 'border'). Adjectives with this suffix can also be derived from some verbs (*ârašhyẓ* 'unsuitable' ← *ârašyu* 'to correspond'), or pronouns (*ḥeẓḥeẓ* 'without you' ← *ḥeẓ* 'you (pl.)').

Adjectives with the suffix *-san/-săn* express a d i s p o s i t i o n and are mainly derived from verbal or deverbal stems (e.g., *oâlsan* 'timid' ← *oâl-* 'to be ashamed', *yšanmausan* 'mistrustful' ← *yšanmau* 'mistrust'). Some adjectives in *-san* are derived from nominal stems: *ujsan* 'thoughtful' (← *uj* 'thought'), *èššăn* 'hardworking' (← *èš* 'work').

4.3 Verbal derivation

Prefixation of Bashkir verbs is uncommon, and suffixation is not productive in verbal word-formation. Basically, one can specify two groups:
a) Verbs, derived from nominal and partially from verbal bases by means of suffixes which today are neither productive nor active, e.g., *-laš, -lan, -lat, -aj, -ar, -al*. Many of these suffixes have merged with the verbal roots and are no longer perceived as suffixes (Ûldašev 1958: 48).
b) There are verbal suffixes, which are incorporated into a verbal root, namely, the negation suffix *-ma/-mă* and numerous suffixes of grammatical voice (*-l, -š, -t, -n*, etc.), cf. *jyuyu* 'to wash' – passive: *jyuylyu* 'to be washed'; reflexive: *jyuynyu* 'to wash oneself'; causative: *jyuẓyrtyu* and *jyuẓyryu* 'to force to wash'; reciprocal: *jyuyšyu* 'to wash each other'. As we are dealing here with the formation of grammatical forms, it seems to be justified to refer to this kind

of word-formation as to "intraverbal grammatical word-formation" (Ûldašev 1958: 64). Wunderlich, in contrast, claims that these categories must be regarded as derivational if they can be followed by another derivational suffix (cf. Wunderlich 2015). In the examples above this would be the case, e.g., in *jyuynyu* 'to wash oneself' + instrument suffix *-ġys* → *jyuynġys* 'washbasin'.

4.4 Adverbial derivation

The most productive suffix for deriving adverbs is *-sa/-sǎ*, which combines mostly with the plural of nouns in *-ar* (e.g., *balalarsa* 'childly', *aẓnalarsa* 'for weeks', *jyldarsa* 'for years'), or with the genitive of personal pronouns, e.g., *miṇeṇsǎ* 'in my opinion' (← *miṇeṇ* 'mine'), *beẓẓensǎ* 'in our way' (← *beẓẓen* 'ours'). This is a rare case of inflection inside derivation.

The suffix *-laj/-lǎj* is one of the most specific adverbial suffixes. In Bashkir, there are about 50 adverbs in *-laj/-lǎj*, e.g., temporal adverbs derived from some verbal nouns in *-(y)š/-(e)š* (*baryšlaj* 'in passing, on the way' ← *baryš* 'development, process', *kajtyšlaj* 'on the way back' ← colloquial *kajtyš* 'returning'), and from names of the seasons or times of the day (*ǩyšlaj* 'in the winter' ← *ǩyš* 'winter', *âǩtylaj* 'before dark, twilight' ← *âǩty* 'light').

Adverbs with the suffix *-lata/-lǎtǎ* are derived from concrete nouns, some cardinal numerals and few qualitative adjectives, e.g., *aǩsalata* 'with money' (← *aǩsa* 'money'), *sejlǎtǎ* 'in a crude way' (← *sej* 'crude'), *ikelǎtǎ* 'doubly' (← *ike* 'two'), *ôslǎtǎ* 'three times as much' (← *ôs* 'three').

5 Conversion

Conversion (also referred to as "zero derivation" or "zero suffixation") is a specific phenomenon of agglutinative languages. All parts of speech can pass into each other without any formal change. Peculiar for Bashkir are not only such types of conversion as "V → N" (*âẓyu* 'to write' → *âẓyu* 'letter') or "Participle → N" (*uǩyusy* 'reading' → *uǩyusy* 'reader'), but also "V (infinitive) → A" (*ireù* 'to thaw' → *ireù* (*it*) 'defrosted (meat)'), or "Participle → Adv", e.g., *siratlašyp* (present participle of *siratlašyu* 'to alternate') → *siratlašyp* 'serially, by turns'. These are cases of the so-called contextual or occasional conversion (Kurbatov et al. 1969: 158), in contrast to the lexicalized or "pure conversion". To the latter belong words (going back to plural forms of adjectives) which have completely passed into the category of nouns, e.g., *jǎšler* 'youth' (cf. *jǎš* 'young'), *ǩyzyldar* 'Red Army men' (cf. *ǩyzyl* 'red'), *jǎšeldǎr* 'members of the Green Party' (cf. *jǎšel* 'green').

The possibility of converting some verbal forms into nouns, pronouns, adverbs, particles or interjections might lead us to question the presence of parts of speech. Nevertheless, we speak about traditional parts of speech, as we cannot deny them due to the multifunctional character of some words. This means, for example, that words which are in a relation of conversion to each other can be considered as lexical and grammatical homonyms. If we did not distinguish parts of speech it would be senseless to speak about conversion. Conversion in the Turkic languages remains a controversial issue whose description also depends on the linguistic tradition and possible influences of the description of non-Turkic languages. In fact, the term *conversion* is avoided or not accepted by some turkologists (see also Menz 2016 on Gagauz and Csató 2016 on Karaim) in contrast to, e.g., Kurbatov et al. (1969) who regard conversion along with derivation and composition as the most important means of nominal word-formation in Tatar (see also Károly 2016 on Tatar and article 21 on Chuvash).

In Bashkir, adjectives, infinitives, and participles can be converted into nouns:

A → N: This is the most productive type of conversion. Both simple (*tintăk* 'silly' → *tintăk* 'silly person') and derived adjectives (*ujsan* 'thoughtful' (from *uj* 'thought') → *ujsan* 'thoughtful person') can be converted to personal nouns.

Participle → N: From the historical point of view, Bashkir derivatives in -*sy* represent converted present participles, e.g., *âzyusy* 'writing' → *âzyusy* 'writer, sb. who writes', *kôtôùse* 'waiting for, expecting' → *kôtôùse* 'shepherd' (Ûldašev 1981: 315–316). The majority of Bashkir participles have become nouns and are no longer perceived as participles. Also some future participles in -*(y)r* have passed into the class of nouns and become lexicalized, e.g., *aldar* 'liar' (← *aldau* 'to lie'), *ûlbaşar* 'robber' (← *ûl* 'way' + *başar* 'coming').

V (infinitive) → N: The initial form of a verb is mostly converted without any formal change into an action noun, e.g., *aldau* 'to lie' → *aldau* 'lie', *ašau* 'to eat' → *ašau* 'meal', *ujnau* 'to play' → *ujnau* 'game'. In some cases the infinitive root is converted into personal nouns/agent nouns and action nouns, e.g., *auyryu* 'to be ill' → *auyryu* 'sick person, patient' and 'illness, disease', *armaj* 'to birch' → *armaj* 'executioner' and 'birching, corporal punishment with a birch rod'.

6 Reduplication

Reduplication belongs to the most ancient word-formation means in Bashkir (and Turkic languages in general), its perpetuation is evidence of the archaic character of the language.

In his book *Einführung in die altaische Sprachwissenschaft* [Introduction to Altaic Linguistics] the turkologist Gustaf Ramstedt specified the phenomenon of reduplication as follows: "Sowohl die mongolische als die türkische Volksliteratur hat [...] einen grossen Vorrat von Synonyma, Wortdoubletten und an sich sinnlosen Reimwörtern, die alle nur für den beabsichtigten Wortklang und nur als stilistisches Mittel beliebt und gebraucht werden" [The Mongolian as well as the Turkish popular literature [...] has a considerable stock of synonyms, word doublets and actually senseless rhyme words which are popular with everybody only for the deliberate word-sound and are used only as stylistic means.] (Ramstedt 1952: 253–254).

The following adverbs and adjectives can be seen as f u l l r e d u p l i c a t i o n s: *vaḵyt-vaḵyt* 'from time to time; lit. time-time, *ḵat-ḵat* 'repeatedly; lit. times-times' (*ḵat* is a multiplication adverb), *byš-byš* (onomatopoeic) 'in a whisper', *aṡyġys-aṡyġys* 'very urgent; lit. urgent-urgent', *tôrlô-tôrlô* 'very different; lit. different-different', *ùtker-ùtker* 'very sharp; lit. sharp-sharp'.

I n c o m p l e t e r e d u p l i c a t i o n is observed, if a) the second component represents only a slightly phonetically changed variant of the first component, e.g., *malaj-šalaj* (ironically) 'boys' (← *malaj* 'boy'), *timer-tomor* 'iron objects' (← *timer* 'iron'), *ybyr-sybyr* (*balalar*) 'small (children)'; b) the second component differs phonetically from the first one, e.g., *eget-elän* 'guys, young men' (← *eget* 'young man'), *etem-eşer* 'orphans' (← *etem* 'orphan'), *kurše-kulän* 'neighbours' (← *kurše* 'neighbour'). The second component of such formations cannot be used independently.

Some authors (cf. Ûldašev 1981) also regard formations like *năşel-năsăp* 'relatives; lit. tribe-tribe', *ḵatyn-ḵyz* 'women; lit. woman-girl' as reduplications. We have treated similar designations, which are based on synonymous or other paradigmatic relations between their constituents as copulative compounds (cf. section 3.1.2); see also Wälchli (2025) on co-compounds.

7 Clipping

In Bashkir, the most common types of clipping are the following:
a) The clipped word consists of the initial letters of each word of a multi-word expression, e.g., *BDPI* 'Baškir State Pedagogical Institute' (← *Baškort däuält pedagogiâ instituty*), *BDU* 'Bashkir State University' (← *Baškort däuält universitete*);
b) The clipped unit consists of the initial parts (syllables) of the elements of a multi-word expression (the following examples are calques of the corre-

sponding Russian designations), e.g., *zavkom* 'factory committee' (← *zavod komitete*), *rajkom* 'district committee' (← *rajon komitete*);
c) A part of the first word of a multi-word expression is clipped and joins with the second word, e.g., *dramtuŋăräk* 'theatrical circle' (← *dramatik tuŋăräk*), cf. Russ. *dramkružok* 'id.';
d) The word consists of the initial part of the first and the base of the second word of a multi-word expression, e.g., *partojošma* '(Communist) Party organization' (← *partija ojošmaḩy*), cf. Russ. *partorganizaciâ* 'id.'.

8 Conclusion

We have presented the basic word-formation processes in modern Bashkir. Various examples show that the word-formation categories of Bashkir do not differ considerably from those of, e.g., German or English. However, they display some specific features connected with language typology.

In nominal word-formation we distinguish composition (determinative and copulative compounds), derivation (suffixation), reduplication, and clipping. Moreover, conversion of adjectives, adverbs, pronouns, verbs (infinitives) and verbal forms is highly developed in Bashkir word-formation. The formation of determinative compounds has a close connection to syntax, and in some cases it is difficult to differentiate between compound words and syntactic constructions. In the field of derivation, denominal suffixation is very productive. Special attention has to be paid to the great number of reduplications which reflect the archaic character of Bashkir. In certain cases, however, the borderline between reduplication and copulative composition is blurred so that some turkologists regard reduplication as part of composition.

Suffixal derivation, composition and reduplication equally participate in the formation of nouns, adjectives, and adverbs. In verbal word-formation analytical composition is productive, while prefixation is absent; suffixation is poorly developed and has mainly a grammatical function (e.g., in grammatical voice formations).

9 References

Auèzova, Zifa-Alua M. (ed.) (2005): Mahmud al-Kašgari, *Diwan lugat at-Turk*. Perevod, predislovie i kommentarii Z.-A. M. Auèzovoj; indeksy sostavil R[obert] Ermers. Almaty: Dajk-Press.
Braun, Friederike (2000): Gender in the Turkish language system. *Turkic Languages* 4(1): 3–21.

Csató, Éva Á. (2016): Karaim. In: Peter O. Müller, Ingeborg Ohnheiser, Susan Olsen and Franz Rainer (eds.), *Word-Formation. An International Handbook of the Languages of Europe*. Vol. 5, 3442–3451. Berlin/Boston: De Gruyter Mouton.
Gabain, Annemarie von (1950): *Alttürkische Grammatik (mit Bibliographie, Lesestücken und Wörterverzeichnis, auch Neutürkisch)*. 2nd ed. Leipzig: Harrassowitz.
Gak, Vladimir G. (1985): *Sravniteľnaâ tipologiâ francuzskogo i russkogo âzykov*. Moskva: Prosvešenie.
Ganiev, Fuat A. (1974): *Suffiksaľnoe slovoobrazovanie v sovremennom tatarskom literaturnom âzyke*. Kazan': Tatarskoe knižnoe izdateľstvo.
Garipov, Talmas M. (1959): *Baškirskoe imennoe slovoobrazovanie*. Ufa: Akademiâ nauk SSSR, Baškirskij filial.
Dmitriev, Nikolaj K. (1948): *Grammatika baškirsogo âzyka*. Moskva/Leningrad: Izdateľstvo Akademii nauk SSSR.
Ermakova, Oľga P. (1984): *Leksičeskoe značenie proizvodnyh slov v russkom âzyke*. Moskva: Nauka.
Ischtuganowa, Gulnara (2003): *Die semantische Wortbildungskategorie Nomen Agentis in der deutschen und baschkirischen Sprache*. Stuttgart: ibidem.
Johanson, Lars (1998): The structure of Turkic. In: Lars Johanson and Éva Ágnes Csató (eds.), *The Turkic Languages*, 30–66. London/New York: Routledge.
Kahramantürk, Kuthan (1999): *Nominale Wortbildungen und Nominalisierungen im Deutschen und im Türkischen. Ein Beitrag zur deutsch-türkischen kontrastiven Linguistik*. Heidelberg: Groos.
Károly, László (2016): Tatar. In: Peter O. Müller, Ingeborg Ohnheiser, Susan Olsen and Franz Rainer (eds.), *Word-Formation. An International Handbook of the Languages of Europe*. Vol. 5, 3398–3413. Berlin/Boston: De Gruyter Mouton.
König, Wolf (1992): Entwicklungen im Türkischen seit 1980. *Arbeiten zur Mehrsprachigkeit* 47: 1–25.
Kononov, Andrej N. (1956): *Grammatika sovremennyh tûrkskih âzykov*. Moskva/Leningrad: Izdateľstvo Akademii nauk SSSR.
Kurbatov, Hèlef R., Lejla T. Mahmutova, Lidiâ P. Smolâkova and Èdhâm R. Tenišev (1969): *Sovremennyj tatarskij literaturnyj âzyk*. Moskva: Nauka.
Menz, Astrid (2016): Gagauz. In: Peter O. Müller, Ingeborg Ohnheiser, Susan Olsen and Franz Rainer (eds.), *Word-Formation. An International Handbook of the Languages of Europe*. Vol. 5, 3433–3442. Berlin/Boston: De Gruyter Mouton.
Poppe, Nicholas (1962): *Bashkir Manual. Descriptive grammar and texts with a Bashkir-English glossary*. Bloomington: Indiana University; The Hague: Mouton.
Ramstedt, G[ustaf] (1952): *Einführung in die altaische Sprachwissenschaft*. Vol. 2: *Formenlehre*. Helsinki: Suomalais-Ugrilainen Seura.
Revzina, Oľga G. (1969): *Struktura slovoobrazovateľnyh polej v slavânskih âzykah*. Moskva: Izdateľstvo MGU.
Sevortân, Èrvand V. (1966): *Affiksy imennogo slovoobrazovaniâ v azerbajdžanskom âzyke. Opyt sravniteľnogo issledovaniâ*. Moskva: Nauka.
Šerbak, Aleksandr M. (1994): *Vvedenie v sravniteľnoe izučenie tûrkskih âzykov*. Sankt-Peterburg: Nauka.
Tekinay, Alev (1981): Personenbezeichnende Suffixe in der deutschen und türkischen Wortbildung: Eine kontrastive Analyse. *Zielsprache Deutsch* 3: 29–34.
Tenišev, Èdhâm R. (1988): *Sravniteľno-istoričeskaâ grammatika tûrkskih âzykov. Morfologiâ*. Moskva: Nauka.
Ûldašev, Ahnaf A. (1958): *Sistema slovoobrazovaniâ i sprâženiâ glagolov v baškirskom âzyke*. Moskva: Izdateľstvo Akademii nauk.
Ûldašev, Ahnaf A. (1981): *Grammatika sovremennogo baškirskogo literaturnogo âzyka*. Moskva: Nauka.

Ülkü, Vural (1980): *Affixale Wortbildung im Deutschen und im Türkischen. Ein Beitrag zur deutsch-türkischen kontrastiven Grammatik*. Ankara: Ankara University Basimevi.

Wälchli, Bernhard (2025): Co-compounds. In: Peter O. Müller, Susan Olsen and Franz Rainer (eds.), *Word-Formation – Special Patterns and Restrictions*, 145–169. Berlin/Boston: De Gruyter Mouton.

Wunderlich, Dieter (2015): Valency-changing word-formation. In: Peter O. Müller, Ingeborg Ohnheiser, Susan Olsen and Franz Rainer (eds.), *Word-Formation. An International Handbook of the Languages of Europe*. Vol. 2, 1424–1466. Berlin/Boston: De Gruyter Mouton.

Galina N. Semenova and Alena M. Ivanova
21 Chuvash

1 Introduction
2 General overview
3 Composition
4 Derivation
5 Conversion
6 Reduplication
7 Clipping
8 References

Abstract: This article describes the main word-formation procedures of Chuvash. Composition based on izafet-constructions of determinative compounds, and co-ordinative compounds, including co-compounds, as well as reduplication belong to the most ancient and still productive models. Active processes can be seen in the field of compounding combined with affixation, and in derivation. Numerous formations are characterized by morphophonemic alternations. Prefixation is not typical of Chuvash. The status of conversion is regarded controversially. Backformation, blending, and word-creation are not attested.

1 Introduction

In early studies of Chuvash, questions of word-formation have been comparatively poorly studied. Investigations into derivational affixes and compounding can be found in Ašmarin's works (Ašmarin 1898) in which the author describes word-formation models and the most common formants of nouns, adjectives, and verbs.

A more detailed analysis of the word-formation of different parts of speech is provided by *Materialy po grammatike sovremennogo čuvašskogo âzyka* [Materials for a Grammar of Modern Chuvash] (1957) and *Morfologiâ sovremennogo čuvašskogo âzyka* [Morphology of Modern Chuvash] (Pavlov 1965).

It is worth mentioning that the appendix to the academic Chuvash-Russian Dictionary contains an article on word-formation affixes in Chuvash comprising

Galina N. Semenova, Cheboksary, Russia
Alena M. Ivanova, Cheboksary, Russia

https://doi.org/10.1515/9783111420523-021

an indexation of 93 Chuvash derivative affixes – some archaic which are no longer productive as well as the highly productive affixes (Skvorcov 1982). This index can be regarded as the basis for an affix dictionary.

The word-formational and the derivational system of Chuvash is examined in detail by Andreeva (1995) and Andreev (2008, 2009). The system of compound nouns, their formation and functioning, is described in Semenova's monograph (2005). As an example of one of the more recent studies *Čuvašskaâ affiksologiâ* [Chuvash Affixology] by Sergeev (2009) is to be mentioned.

The examples in this article are rendered using the transliteration ISO 9 1995.

2 General overview

Chuvash is a Turkic language – the only surviving member of the Oghur branch – spoken west of the Urals in central Russia. It is the native language of the Chuvash people (that number approximately two million) and one of the official languages of Chuvashia. Chuvash has been greatly influenced by the Finnic languages and Russian. In the modern lexicon of Chuvash one finds also Tatar, Mari, and Mongolic loanwords, besides ancient Arab, Mongol and Persian loans.

The Chuvash word has a typically agglutinative structure: the root morpheme is followed on the right by the derivative affix(es) and – after them – by the inflectional affixes. According to the rules of synharmony most morphemes have two variants, e.g., *ŭkermerĕ* 'didn't paint' ← *ŭk* 'to fall' (root) + *-er-* (verb forming affix) + *-me-* (negation affix) + *-r-* (past tense affix) + *-ĕ* (3rd person affix); *tašlamarĕ* 'didn't dance' ← *tašă* 'dance' (root) + *-la-* (verbal derivational affix) + *-ma-* (negation affix) + *-r-* (past tense affix) + *-ĕ* (3rd person affix). In Chuvash linguistics all derivational and grammatical suffixes are subsumed under the term *affix*.

The main (and also the most productive) word-formation models in Chuvash are composition and affixation.

In composition numerous phonetic changes at the boundary of the respective components can be observed, e.g.,

a) Omission of one or more sounds at the end of one of the components (apocope): *asanne* 'grandmother on the father's side' (← *aslă* 'main, head' + *anne* 'mother'); *ankarti* 'threshing-floor' (← *avăn* 'drying-house' + *karta* 'fence');

b) Elision of the initial vowel of the second component caused by the final sound of the preceding component: *pahčalăk* 'wicket-gate' (← *pahča* 'garden' + *alăk* 'door'), *hulaš* 'big city' (← *hula* 'city' + *ăš* 'inward, inside'), *uraj* 'floor' (← *ura* 'foot' + *aj* 'underside');

c) Omission of one or more sounds within one of the components (syncope): *alšălli* 'towel' (← *ală* 'hand' + *šăl* 'to towel off'), *čaršav* 'curtain' (← *čatăr* 'tent' + *šav* 'noise');
d) Metathesis: *hušamat* 'surname' (← *hušma* 'additional' + *ât* 'name'), *tĕkĕltura* 'bumble-bee' (← *tĕklĕ* 'plumy' + *tura* 'comb');
e) Articulatory accommodation (assimilation): *kĕšĕr* 'this night' (← *ku* 'this' + *şĕr* 'night'), *kăşal* 'this year' (← *ku* 'this' + *çul* 'year'), *şăvarni* 'shrovetide' (← *şu* 'summer' + *èrne* 'week').

A complex system of affixation as well as reduplication and abbreviation are also actively used. Prefixation is not typical of Chuvash; it can be observed, e.g., in some pronouns and numerals formed with the prefixes *ta-/te-*, *ni-*. The status of conversion is discussed controversially.

3 Composition

Like other Turkic languages, Chuvash is rich in different types of compounds with several characteristic subtypes, such as izafet-compounds in the categories of determinative compounds, and co-compounds of two or more components within the category of coordinative compounds.

3.1 Determinative compounds

Nominal compounds with a subordinative relation between the components have a nominal – noun or adjective – modifier and a nominal head or, rarely, a verbal head (non-finite forms).

A specific feature of Chuvash as a Turkic language is the occurrence of *izafet* in combination with compounding. Izafet denotes a determinative combination of two nouns. Traditionally, three types of izafet are distinguished:

Izafet I is characterized by the lack of morphological markers signalling the connection between the components, i.e. the designation is based on juxtaposition, e.g., *timĕr kĕreşe* 'iron shovel' (← *timĕr* 'iron' + *kĕreşe* 'shovel'), see section 3.1.1.

Izafet II is characterized by a possessive affix of the 3rd person (*-ĕ* or *-i*) attached to the determined word (head), e.g., *šyvtumlamĕ* 'water drop' (← *šyv* 'water' + *tumlam* 'drop' + *-ĕ* (possessive affix)), *ûltaš parni* 'friend's present' (← *ûltaš* 'friend' + *parne* 'present' + *-i* (possessive affix), see section 3.1.2.

Izafet III is a combination of two nouns the first of which is followed by the affix of the possessive case (genitive) -ăn/-ĕn/-n, the second by the possessive affix: *annen tutără* 'mother's scarf' (← *anne* 'mother' + -*n* (affix of the possessive case) + *tutăr* 'scarf' + -*ĕ* (possessive affix)), see section 3.1.2.

Other categories are constituted by compounds with a qualitative adjective as the first component (see section 3.1.3), and compounds with a nominal modifier and a verbal (infinitive, gerund or participial) head, see section 3.1.4.

3.1.1 Compounds formed on the pattern of izafet I

Words of this pattern are deeply rooted in the Chuvash lexicon. The many complex nouns belong to different semantic groups:
- Animals: *šĕkĕ pulă* 'sterlet' (← *šĕkĕ* 'bug' + *pulă* 'fish'), *jĕke hűre* 'rat' (← *jĕke* 'spindle' + *hűre* 'tail');
- Plants: *šyv suhan* 'water plant' (← *šyv* 'water' + *suhan* 'onion'), *asav hăâr* 'cucumber for seeds' (← *asav* 'canine' + *hăâr* 'cucumber');
- Months and days of the week: *aka ujăh* 'April' (← *aka* 'sowing' + *ujăh* 'month'), *şu ujăh* 'May' (← *şu* 'summer' + *ujăh* 'month');
- Household devices and appliances: *jĕs ala* 'sieve made of copper wire' (← *jĕs* 'copper' + *ala* 'sieve'), *şavra kurka* 'round bowl, scoop (for refreshing)' (← *şavra* 'circle' + *kurka* 'bowl, scoop');
- Meals: *kĕl pašalu* 'cake made of unleavened dough' (← *kĕl* 'cinder' + *pašalu* 'cake'), *kašăk şămah* 'dumplings' (← *kašăk* 'spoon' + *şămah* 'dumplings'), *şatma şimĕş* 'cake of leavened dough' (← *şatma* 'pan' + *şimĕş* 'meal');
- Different notions of Chuvash ethnography and history: *vutăš hĕr* 'mermaid' (← *vutăš* 'water sprite' + *hĕr* 'girl'), *vupăr karčăk* 'witch' (← *vupăr* 'eclipse, darkness' + *karčăk* 'grandma'), *ûr pike* 'Snow White' (← *ûr* 'snow' + *pike* 'lady').

Numerous compounds consist of first or second serial elements, cf. compounds with the first element *ama* 'female', or *aşa* 'male': *ama vylăh* 'female animal', *ama jytă* 'female dog', *ama jyvăş* 'female tree, plant (of dioecious plants)'; *aşa kušak* 'male cat', and compounds with the following second elements:

puş 'head': *vĕlle puş* 'main hive' (← *vĕlle* 'hive' + *puş*), *âl puş* 'head of the village, rural chief' (← *âl* 'village' + *puş*), *čălha puş* 'socks' (← *čălha* 'stocking' + *puş*);

kuş 'eye': *şălkuş* 'water spring' (← *şăl* 'spring' + *kuş*), *čĕpkuş* 'splinter' (← *čĕp* 'chicken' + *kuş*), *jĕpkuş* 'eye of a needle' (← *jĕp* 'needle' + *kuş*);

aj 'under, bottom': *haphaj* 'space between the gate and the ground' (← *hapha* 'gate' + *aj*), *armanaj* 'bran' (← *arman* 'mill' + *aj*);

um 'in front of, front side': *alkum* 'porch' (← *alăk* 'door' + *um*), *kămakum* 'space in front of the stove' (← *kămaka* 'stove' + *um*), *kăkărum* 'front of a woman's robe embroidered with coloured stripes' (← *kăkăr* 'breast' + *um*);

şi 'up, upper side': *utşi* 'hay time' (← *ut* 'hay' + *şi*), *âlşi* 'village community' (← *âl* 'village' + *şi*).

3.1.2 Compounds formed on the pattern of izafet II

This type comprises nouns whose second components contain possessive affixes of the 3rd person singular (*-e* and *-i*). On the second izafet pattern, Common Turk nominal units are formed.

The most ancient nouns in the group of izafet II compounds with the affix *-ĕ* are names of gods, feasts and rites. In order to understand the structure of the following examples it should be pointed out that the words *atte* 'father' and *anne* 'mother' undergo phonetic changes in the expression of possessive meaning, e.g., *atte* 'father' – *aşu* 'your father' – *aššĕ* 'his/her father'; *anne* 'mother' – *annŭ* 'your mother' – *amăšĕ* 'his/her mother', e.g., *hĕvel aššĕ* 'Sun's father', *hĕvel amăšĕ* 'Sun's mother', *şĕr aššĕ* 'Soil's father'. Moreover, this type of compounds is largely represented by the following lexico-semantic groups:

- Plants: *pileš kurăkĕ* 'tansy' (← *pileš* 'ashberry' + *kurăk* 'grass'), *kĕşĕ kurăkĕ* 'celandine' (← *kĕşĕ* 'itch' + *kurăk*), *vir kurăkĕ* 'timothy grass' (← *vir* 'millet' + *kurăk*);
- Animals: *pyl hurčĕ* 'bee' (← *pyl* 'honey' + *hurt* 'bee'), *kupăsta lĕpĕšĕ* 'cabbage white butterfly' (← *kupăsta* 'cabbage' + *lĕpĕš* 'butterfly');
- Parts of the human body, diseases: *šămă săsălĕ* 'marrow' (← *šămă* 'bone' + *săsăl* 'marrow'), *ura hyrămĕ* 'calf' (anat.) (← *ura* 'leg' + *hyrăm* 'abdomen');
- Miscellaneous: *tu hušăkĕ* 'gorge in the mountains' (← *tu* 'mount' + *hušăk* 'slit'), *čeček tusanĕ* 'pollen' (← *čeček* 'flower' + *tusan* 'dust'), *tűšek pičĕ* 'pillowcase' (← *tűšek* 'feather-bed' + *pit* 'tick').

(In many complex words the second component is spelled with the cyrillic "soft sign" (ь, transliterated as ') instead of the possessive affix (*-ĕ*): *vutčulĕ* (← *vut* 'fire' + *čul* 'stone') > *vutčul'* 'flint', *ĕškunĕ* (← *ĕş* 'work' + *kun* 'day') > *ĕşkun'* 'workday'.)

The izafet II compounds with the affix *-i* will be again presented in lexico-semantic groups:

- Names of ancient gods, rites: *karta syhči* 'court or yard guard' (← *karta* 'yard' + *syhčă* 'guard'), *uj turri* 'god of the livestock, field god' (← *uj* 'field' + *tură* 'god');

- Parts of the human body: *aâk pĕrči* 'rib' (← *aâk* 'flank' + *pĕrčĕ* 'small part'), *pit şămarti* 'cheek' (← *pit* 'face' + *şămarta* 'egg'), *kuş harši* 'eyebrow' (← *kuş* 'eye' + *harša* 'frame');
- Plants: *upa sarri* 'fern' (← *upa* 'bear' + *sară* 'yellow colour'), *văkăr hűri* 'plantain' (← *văkăr* 'ox' + *hűre* 'tail');
- Animals: *jyt pulli* 'tadpole' (← *jyt* 'dog' + *pulă* 'fish'), *ĕne nărri* 'shard beetle' (← *ĕne* 'cow' + *nără* 'beetle');
- Material culture: *şăraşşi* 'lock' (← *şăra* 'key' + *uşă* 'lock'), *čĕrşitti* 'apron' (← *čĕr* 'knees' + *şitti* 'cover');
- Meals: *űt šűrpi* 'meat soup' (← *űt* 'body' + *šűrpe* 'pottage'), *şatma ikerči* 'pancakes' (← *şatma* 'pan' + *ikerčĕ* 'cake').

3.1.3 The pattern "Qualitative adjective + noun"

Colour adjectives as first component (modifier) are the most numerous in this group, especially: *sară* 'yellow', *šură* 'white', *hĕrlĕ* 'red'. The respective compounds denote animals and plants, diseases, natural phenomena, etc., cf. *šură tulă* 'rice; lit. white wheat', *šură kăšman* 'sugar beet; lit. white beetroot', *hura părşa* 'beans; lit. black peas', *hura şil* 'tornado; lit. black wind', *sară kăšman* 'fodder beet; lit. yellow beetroot', *hĕrlĕ šatra* 'measles; lit. red rush', *hĕrlĕ kukamaj* 'ladybird; lit. red grandma'.

3.1.4 The pattern "Non-finite verb form + noun"

Words, formed on the following patterns are most abundant:
a) Infinitive in *-ma/-me* + N: *larma hĕr* 'girl staying at/visiting her relatives and doing some (needle)work' (← *lar* (dictionary entry form of the verb) 'to sit' + *hĕr* 'girl'), *şĕrme puân* 'very rich man' (← *şĕr* 'to rot' + *puân* 'rich man');
b) Gerund ending in *-a/-e* + N: *kara şăvar* 'loudmouth' (← *kar* 'to open' + *şăvar* 'mouth', *jĕre ača* 'crybaby' (← *jĕr* 'to cry' + *ača* 'kid');
c) Past participle with the affix *-nă/-nĕ* + N: *ăşalană şămarta* 'fried eggs' (← *ăşala* 'to fry' + *şămarta* 'egg'), *kasnă salma* 'home-made noodles' (← *kas* 'to cut' + *salma* 'dumplings').

The most productive pattern is "N + Past participle with the affix *-i*" denoting:
- Rites and feasts: *hĕve hupni* 'wedding rite' (← *hĕv* 'bosom' + *hup* 'to close'), *salam ăsatni* 'commemoration rite' (← *salam* 'greeting, bow' + *ăsat* 'to see off');

- Objects, meals, persons: *al tytti* 'smart women garment worn on the shoulders' (← *al* 'hand' + *tyt* 'to take'), *şămarta hăpartni* 'omelet' (← *şămarta* 'egg' + *hăpart* 'to lift'), *âl păhi* 'inspector' (← *âl* 'village' + *păh* 'to look'), *tur şyrni* 'one's promised husband or wife' (← *tură* 'God' + *şyr* 'to write'), *čun savni* '(the) beloved' (← *čun* 'soul, heart' + *sav* 'to love');
- Diseases: *šănăr turtni* 'spasms' (← *šănăr* 'tendon' + *turt* 'to pull'), *ûn kajni* 'bleeding' (← *ûn* 'blood' + *kaj* 'to go away'), *yjhă věşni* 'insomnia' (← *yjhă* 'sleep' + *věş* 'to flee'), *šatra kasni* 'smallpox vaccination' (← *šatra* 'pox' + *kas* 'to cut');
- Expressive and emotional designations: *čun illi* 'monster, brute' (← *čun* 'soul' + *il* 'to take'), *sehre hăppi* 'something awful' (← *sehre* 'horror' + *hăp* 'to detach');
- State of mind and nature: *kămăl věşni* 'excitement' (← *kămăl* 'cheer' + *věş* 'to flee'); *pilěk kasni* 'labour pains' (← *pilěk* 'loins' + *kas* 'to cut'), *kaş pulni* 'dusk' (← *kaş* 'night' + *pul* 'to be'), *ujăh těttěmlenni* 'lunar eclipse' (← *ujăh* 'moon' + *těttěmlen* 'to get dark').

3.2 Coordinative compounds

3.2.1 Nominal coordinative compounds

Compounds with coordinative relations between the components (in Chuvash word-formation also called "pair nouns" or "couple nouns") are ancient forms of this word-formation model. They consist of two (or more) simple words belonging to the same part of speech. Each of them (in general, the second component) can have the corresponding grammatical forms (number, case, etc.), and the compound as a whole can function as any phrase in the sentence. They can be parts of word combinations and become the basis for the derivation of new words. Besides lexico-grammatical and phonetic features, these words also show semantic regularities: not any word can be united with another to form a copulative compound, but only those which are connected paradigmatically, by closeness in meaning, as, e.g., synonymic, antonymic, and associative correlations.

Coordinative compounds with s y n o n y m o u s components are formed by combining two full synonyms or words similar in meaning. The characteristic feature of these nouns is their integrative collective meaning that is based on the connection of names of objects or abstract nouns: *aš-kakaj* 'meat; lit. meat-meat', *ěmět-šuhăš* 'dreams; lit. dream-thought', *văj-hal* 'power; lit. power-energy', *ûmah-halap* 'fairy tales; lit. fairy tale-tale'.

Antonymic coordinative compounds denote states and abstract qualities. The components of these nouns have contrasting meanings of time, space, age, sex, etc.: *laru-tăru* 'situation; lit. sitting-staying', *vată-vĕtĕ* 'old and young; lit. old-small', *nuša-yrlăh* 'sadness and joy; lit. misfortune-bliss', *ir-kaş* 'day and night; lit. morning-night'.

The group of coordinative compounds with associative relations between the components is the most abundant in comparison to the two preceding groups. The components of these words are related conceptually, e.g., *tuta-şăvar* 'mouth area; lit. lip-mouth', *şĕtĕk-şurăk* 'rags; lit. rag-scrap', *sĕt-turăh* 'dairy products; lit. milk-sour milk'. The meaning of associative compounds is often more complex than the sum of the meanings of their components, i.e. the compound has the meaning of a general concept, or a hyperonym of the hyponymous components. Many of them can be regarded as co-compounds, e.g., *kurka-şăpala* 'kitchen utensils', whereas the meaning of the components are 'round scoop' and 'ladle'. The word *şĕr-šyv* lit. 'soil-water' has the meaning 'one's own people, motherland, where the ancestors remain'. In some cases, such words have a triple or quadruple structure: *laši-ĕni-surăh* 'cattle, livestock; lit. horse-cow-sheep', *èreh-săra-kărčama* 'alcoholic beverages; lit. vodka-beer-home brew', *vărămtuna-šăna-ŭpre* 'mosquitos; lit. mosquito-fly-midge', *şippi-jĕppi-čĕntĕrĕ* 'sewing things; lit. needless-threads-laces'. (See also Wälchli 2025 on co-compounds.)

There are numerous lexicalized formations, but also compounds whose first or mostly second component has lost its meaning in contemporary Chuvash. These words bear traces of Turkic-wide lexical interaction that had place in the past. It is also possible that the "dead components" of these words are primordial Chuvash words which are no longer used nowadays. In the following examples the meaning of the whole word is equal to the first component, cf. *kŭršĕ-aršă* 'neighbours', *namăs-simĕs* 'shame', *hypar-hănar* 'rumours', *čun-čĕm* 'soul', *âškĕrĕm* 'adults', *ûmăş-tĕrĕš* 'fortuneteller', *hăna-vĕrle* 'guests'.

3.2.2 Coordinative compounds in other parts of speech

Other parts of speech – adjectives, pronouns, adverbs, numerals and verbs – can also serve as productive base for the formation of compounds.

Compared to nominal coordinative compounds, adjectives are less numerous, e.g., *hura-šură* 'black and white', *usal-haâr* 'wicked and angry'. There are also some coordinative compounds with non-finite verb forms: *kĕrekentuhakan* 'visitor, visiting (person)' (← *kĕreken* present participle of *kĕr* 'to come in' + *tuhakan* present participle of *tuh* 'to exit'), *kilen-kaân* 'visitor, visiting (person)' (← *kilen* iterative participle of *kil* 'to come' + *kaân* iterative participle of *kaj* 'to go away'), *pulnă-irtně* 'it was and went off' (← *pulnă* past participle of *pul* 'to be' + *irtně* past participle of *irt* 'to go off'); *iltes-tăvas* (*pulsan*) '(if) you happen to hear about' (← *iltes* future participle of *ilt* 'to hear' + *tăvas* future participle of *tu* 'to do').

The following may serve as examples of a d v e r b s: *ělěk-aval* 'long ago; lit. before now-anciently', *paân-yran* 'one of these days; lit. today-tomorrow', *unta-kunta* 'somewhere; lit. there-here'. P r o n o m i n a l compounds are, e.g., *văl-ku* 'something or other; lit. he/she/it-this', *hăšě-pěri* 'some; lit. which-one among many'. N u m e r a l compounds express approximation, e.g., *şiččě-sakkăr* 'seven or eight; lit. seven-eight', *pěr-ik* 'one or two; lit. one-two'.

3.2.3 Conclusion

The characteristic feature of Chuvash coordinative compounds is their closed structure and their ability to function morphologically and syntactically exclusively as one lexical unit like a simple word. The components of the majority of these compounds consist of elements also known from other Turkic languages (cf. *ûltaš-tantăš* 'peer; lit. friend-coeval', *hěr-tantăš* 'girlfriends; lit. girl-coeval', *ěş-puş* 'affairs; lit. work-head', *sim-pyl* 'honey beverage; lit. syrup-honey'. As cocompound can be regarded *hěr-yvăl* 'heirs; lit. girl-son'). Moreover, primordial Chuvash words and borrowings from Russian, Arab and Persian play an important role in the formation of coordinative compounds with one or two components borrowed from

– Arab (A., underlined) or Persian (P., underlined): *šăpa-ăraskal* (A.) 'fate; lit. fate-happiness', *hěn-asap* (A.) 'continuous illness; lit. pain-suffering', *kěměl-merčen* (P.) 'jewellery; lit. silver-coral, pearl', etc. In the following nouns only the origin of the first component can be attested, whereas the second element is no longer semantically transparent in Chuvash, e.g., *hypar-hănar* (A.) 'news', *muhmăr-suhmăr* (A.) 'drunkenness, hangover', *asar-piser* (P.) 'evil spirit(s)';
– Russian (R., underlined): *jěrke-norma* 'order; lit. order-norm', *pulăştuh-èreh* 'drinking session; lit. bottle-alcohol' (R. *poluštof*), *pustav-kavir* (R. *kovër*) 'broadcloths and carpets', *katka-pičke* (R. *bočka*) 'cooper's products; lit. vat-barrels', *hěş-păşal* (R. *piščal'*) 'arms, weapons; lit. sword, sabre-gun, arcebus';
– the neighbouring Uralic languages Mari (M., underlined) or Udmurt (U., underlined): *şyrma-şatra* (M.) 'ravines; lit. ravine-small ravine', *părşa-âsmăk* (M.) 'pulses, legumes; lit. pea-lentil', *kěvě-şemě* (U.) 'music, melody'; both lit. 'tune, melody, song', *sětel-pukan* (U.) 'furniture; lit. desk-chair'.

The above-mentioned examples attest to the mixture of different people and tribes. The elements of Persian, Arab, Russian, Mari, Tatar, Bashkir and other languages are interlaced in Chuvash as Chuvash people have always been close to these nations in the course of their history.

3.3 Combination of composition and affixation

Complex words of this structural type consist of two stems and one affix, where neither the combination of the first two nor of the last two elements exists as free word. In Chuvash this model is used to form words of different parts of speech.

3.3.1 Nouns

The following models serve as an active source of neologisms (and terms) in different fields of science.

N+N+AFF: *alăstalăh* 'domestic craft' (← *ală* 'hand' + *ăsta* 'master craftsman' + *-lăh*), *kămăl-sipetlĕh* 'morality, morals' (← *kămăl* 'soul, mood' + *sipet* 'decency, honesty' + *-lĕh*);

A+N+AFF: *tŭrkămăllăh* 'frankness' (← *tŭrĕ* 'straight' + *kămăl* 'soul, mood' + *-lăh*), *tŭrkĕteslĕh* 'rectangle' (← *tŭrĕ* 'straight' + *kĕtes* 'angle' + *-lĕh*);

Num+N+AFF: *pĕršuhăšlăh* 'unanimity' (← *pĕr* 'one' + *šuhăš* 'idea' + *-lăh*), *ikĕpitlĕh* 'duplicity' (← *ikĕ* 'two' + *pit* 'face' + *-lĕh*), *ikčĕlhelĕh* 'bilingualism' (← *ikĕ* 'two' + *čĕlhe* 'language' + *-lĕh*);

N+V+AFF: *alşyru* 'manuscript' (← *ală* 'hand' + *şyr* 'to write' + *-u*), *âtparu* 'denomination' (← *ât* 'name' + *par* 'to give' + *-u*), *şulşŭrev* 'journey' (← *şul* 'way' + *şŭre* 'to go' + *-v*), *tĕnčekurăm* 'world-view' (← *tĕnče* 'world' + *kur* 'to see' + *-ăm*), *hĕveltuhăş* 'east' (← *hĕvel* 'sun' + *tuh* 'to go out' + *-ăş*), in contrast to *tuhăş* 'sunrise'.

3.3.2 Adjectives

Two models should be mentioned here:

A+N+AFF: *mănkămăllă* 'arrogant' (← *măn* 'big' + *kămăl* 'soul, mood' + *-lă*); as an independent adjective *kămăllăh* has the meanings 'tender, gentle, cordial; pleasant, nice; satisfied, content';

Num+N+AFF: *pĕrenlĕ* 'unambiguous, unequivocal' (← *pĕr* 'one' + *en* 'side' + *-lĕ*).

3.3.3 Verbs

A+N+AFF: *mănkămăllan* 'to pride oneself on sth.' (← *măn* 'big' + *kămăl* 'soul, mood' + *-lan*);

A+Particle *mar*+AFF: *tasamarlan* 'to become unscrupulous, dishonarable' (← *tasa* 'clean' + *mar* 'not' + *-lan*), *tikĕsmarlan* 'to become uneven' (← *tikĕs* 'even, flat' + *mar* 'not' + *-lan*).

4 Derivation

Prefixation is not productive in Chuvash word-formation. There are only two elements: *ta-/te-* and *ni-*. They can form:
a) Indefinite and negative pronouns: *takam* 'somebody' (← *kam* 'who'), *tahăš* 'someone' (← *hăš* 'which'), *temĕn* 'something' (← *mĕn* 'what'); *nikam* 'nobody' (← *kam* 'who'), *nihăš* 'no one' (← *hăš* 'which'), *nimĕn* 'nothing' (← *mĕn* 'what');
b) Adverbs of place and time: *tahşan* 'sometime' (← *hăşan* 'when'), *taşta* 'somewhere' (← *ăşta* 'where'); *nihşan* 'never' (← *hăşan* 'when'), *nişta* 'nowhere' (← *ăşta* 'where').

4.1 Nominal derivation

There are numerous affixes in Chuvash to form nouns. The most productive are *-şă/-şĕ*, *-lăh/-lĕh*, *-čăk/-čĕk* and some others.

4.1.1 Denominal nouns

Denominal nouns belong to the following categories:
    A b s t r a c t n o u n s: *-lăh/-lĕh*, e.g., *ačalăh* 'childhood' (← *ača* 'child'), *ètemlĕh* 'mankind' (← *ètem* 'man'); *-tăk: măškăltăk* 'rubbish' (← *măškăl* 'mockery');
    P e r s o n a l n o u n s: *-şă/-şĕ*, e.g., *asamşă* 'magician' (← *asam* 'magic'), *kĕvĕşĕ* 'musician' (← *kĕvĕ* 'music'); *-čah: ăččah* 'scientist' (← *ăs* 'intellect'); *-kĕč: tĕpkĕč* 'heir' (← *tĕp* 'ground'); *-taš/-teš: enteš* 'fellow-countryman' (← *en* 'side, place'); *-tah: puştah* 'madcap' (← *puş* 'head').
    N o n-p e r s o n a l n o u n s: *-lăh/-lĕh*, e.g., *kuşlăh* 'eyeglasses' (← *kuş* 'eye'); *-kăč/-kĕč: măjkăč* 'collar' (← *măj* 'neck');

Place nouns: *-el/-al*, e.g., *těpel* 'living-room' (← *těp* 'basis, fundament'), *hyşal* 'backside' (← *hyş* 'back'); *-sar*: *ûmansar* 'oak forest' (← *ûman* 'oak'), *şăkasar* 'lime-tree forest' (← *şăka* 'lime-tree');

Collective nouns (some semantically overlapping with place nouns): *-lăh/-lĕh*, e.g., *hurănlăh* 'birch grove' (← *hurăn* 'birch'), *šurlăh* 'swamps' (← *šur* 'swamp');

-lak: *părlak* 'black ice' (← *păr* 'ice');

Diminutives: *-ška/-ške*, e.g., *şunaška* 'little sledge' (← *şuna* 'sledge'), *tynaška* 'little calf' (← *tyna* 'calf'), *hűreške* 'little tail' (← *hűre* 'tail'); *-kka/-kke*: *cămărkka* 'little fist' (← *cămăr* 'fist'), *Petěrkke* 'little Peter' (← *Petěr*); *-ske*: *těmeske* 'little hill' (← *těme* 'hill').

4.1.2 Deadjectival nouns

Abstract nouns are derived with the affix *-lăh/-lĕh*, e.g., *tasalăh* 'cleanness' (← *tasa* 'clean'), *şepěşlěh* 'tenderness' (← *şepěş* 'tender'). (For more abstract nouns and concrete nouns as possible result of conversion see section 5.)

4.1.3 Deverbal nouns

Deverbal nouns belong to the following categories:

Action nouns: *-u/-ű*, e.g., *větelenű* 'haste' (← *větelen* 'to haste, hurry'), *ănlantaru* 'explanation' (← *ănlantar* 'to explain'); *-ăm/-ĕm*: *űsěm* 'height' (← *űs* 'to grow'), *kuşăm* 'movement' (← *kuş* 'to move'); *-ma/-mè*: *vyrma* 'reaping' (← *vyr* 'to harvest'), *larma* 'get-together' (← *lar* 'to sit').

Abstract nouns: *-u/-ű*, e.g., *ûratu* 'love' (← *ûrat* 'to love'), *věrenű* 'study' (← *věren* 'to study'); *-ăm/-ĕm*: *ûhăm* 'current' (← *ûh* 'to flow'), *vilěm* 'death' (← *vil* 'to die'); *-ă/-ě*: *sută* 'sale' (← *sut* 'to sell'); *-av/-èv*: *čuhlav* 'guess' (← *čuhla* 'to guess'), *šellev* 'pity, compassion' (← *šelle* 'to take pity on sb.');

Result nouns: *-čăk/-čěk*, e.g., *űkerčěk* 'picture' (← *űker* 'to draw'), *surčăk* 'saliva' (← *sur* 'to spit'); *-ă/-ě*: *kasă* 'furrow' (← *kas* 'to cut'), *čělě* 'piece' (← *čěl* 'to chip'); *-ăk/-ěk*: *tatăk* 'piece, part' (← *tat* 'to cut'), *şěrěk* 'rottenness' (← *şěr* 'to rot'); *-ăm/-ěm*: *půlěm* 'room' (← *půl* 'to enclose'), *kălarăm* 'edition' (← *kălar* 'to edit'); *-măš/-měš*: *hăratmăš* 'scarecrow' (← *hărat* 'to scare'), *ilěrtměš* 'seduction' (← *ilěrt* 'to seduce');

Agent nouns: *-čăk/-čěk*, e.g., *askănčăk* 'depraved man' (← *askăn* 'to deprave'), *ěšelenčěk* 'bustler' (← *ěšelen* 'to haste, hurry');

Instrument nouns: -kăč/-kĕč, e.g., larkăč 'seat, saddle' (← lar 'to sit'), hĕskĕč 'pincers' (← hĕs 'to press'); -kă: čyškă 'fist' (← čyš 'to beat'); -mak/-mek: čikmek 'stairs, ladder' (← čik 'to stick into'); -lăh/-lĕh: vitlĕh 'cover' (← vit 'to cover'); -ăš/-ĕš: syrăš 'feeding-rack' (← syr 'to circle'); -a/-e: păra 'gimlet' (← păr 'to turn round'), vişe 'measure' (← viş 'to measure'), -ă/-ĕ: uşă 'key' (← uş 'to open').

Place nouns: -ăm/-ĕm, e.g., lakăm 'pit' (← lak 'to get stuck'); -ăş/-ĕş: tuhăş 'east, sunrise' (← tuh 'to come out'), anăş 'west, sunset' (← an 'to descend').

4.2 Adjectival derivation

4.2.1 Denominal adjectives

The most productive affixes are -lă/-lĕ (possessive meaning), e.g., văjlă 'strong' (← văj 'strength'), sisĕmlĕ 'sensitive' (← sisĕm 'sense'), and the privative affix -săr/-sĕr: ilemsĕr 'ugly' (← ilem 'beauty'), kămălsăr 'unkind' (← kămăl '(good) mood').

4.2.2 Deadjectival adjectives

Deadjectival adjectives express modification, sometimes specialization of the semantics of the base adjective, partly as a result of comparison, e.g., -mas/-mes: şămlamas 'shaggy-haired' (← şămlă 'wool-covered'), hĕrlemes 'crimson' (← hĕrlĕ 'red'); -ška/-ške: kătraška 'curly-headed' (← kătra 'curly'), şinşeške 'slender' (← şinşe 'thin'); -ttaj/-ttej: şămălttaj 'light-minded' (← şămăl 'light'), mănttaj 'awkward' (← măn 'big'); -anka/-enke: šuranka 'pale' (← šură 'white').

Another very productive way to modify adjectives is the combination with intensifying particles as, e.g., vĕr (vĕrşĕnĕ 'completely new'), šar (šar pylak 'very sweet'), jam and tĕm (jam hura, tĕm hura 'absolutely, completely black'), and others. (Such particles may also be combined with nouns, e.g., hăr tălăh 'complete orphan'.) This kind of modifying is, however, not regarded as a word-formation procedure.

4.2.3 Deverbal adjectives

Deverbal adjectives denote a quality according to the result of an action or to the process, e.g., -ăk/-ĕk: şĕmrĕk: 'broken' (← şĕmĕr 'to break'), sŭnĕk 'extinct' (← sŭn 'to extinguish'), -čăk/-čěk: věčěrhenčěk 'angry' (← věčěrhen 'to get angry'), jătănčăk 'collapsing' (← jătăn 'to tumble down').

4.3 Verbal derivation

4.3.1 Denominal verbs

Productive affixes are -la/-le, -lan/-len, -lat/-let, -laš/-leš, less productive are -at/-et/-t, -ăn/-ĕn, -ar/-er and others, for instance, verbs with the meaning 'to perform the action denoted by the base word': puşla and puşăn 'to begin' (← puş 'beginning'), ĕmĕtlen 'to dream' (← ĕmĕt 'dream'), sienlet 'to damage' (← sien 'damage'); inchoative verbs: ăslan 'to become clever' (← ăs 'intellect'); factitive/causative verbs: tăvanlat 'to make related' (← tăvan 'relatives'); tuslaš 'to make friends' (← tus 'friend'), şurat 'to give birth' (← şura 'baby animal'), and instrumental verbs: kĕşĕt 'to itch' (← kĕşĕ 'scab'), šăvar 'to irrigate, water' (← šyv 'water').

4.3.2 Deadjectival verbs

Productive affixes are -lan/-len, -lat/-let, -laš/-leš, -ar/-er), cf. inchoative verbs such as ajvanlan 'to grow stupid' (← ajvan 'stupid'), lŭpperlen 'to become sluggish' (← lŭpper 'slow'), kăvakar 'to turn blue' (← kăvak 'blue'), and factitive verbs, e.g., şivĕčlet 'to sharpen' (← şivĕč 'sharp'), ăšăhlat 'to make shallow' (← ăšăh 'shallow'), and others like tanlaš 'to compete with' (← tan 'equal').

4.3.3 Deverbal verbs

Deverbal verbs are derived with the following productive affixes: -tar/-ter, -ăl/-ĕl, -ar/-er, -at/-et, -ăş/-ĕş, -aš/-eš, -ăn/-ĕn, -ăš/-ĕš, and others. The corresponding verbs constitute the following categories:
a) Reflexive verbs: parăn 'to surrender' (← par 'to give'), saltăn 'to take off one's clothes, undress' (← salt 'to untie'), puştarăn 'to gather (together)' (← puştar 'to gather, put together');
b) Passive verbs: sujlan 'to be elected, chosen' (← sujla 'to elect, choose'), tytăn 'to be caught, kept' (← tyt 'to hold, keep');
c) Reciprocal verbs: kalaş 'to talk' (← kala 'to speak, say'), savăš 'to love each other' (← sav 'to love');

d) Causative verbs: şiter 'to feed' (← şi 'to eat'), şyvărttar 'to make sleep' (← şyvăr 'to sleep'), űker 'to drop, let fall' (← űk 'to fall'), ěrčet 'to grow sth.' (← ěrče 'to breed').

4.3.4 Verbs derived from other parts of speech

There are some smaller groups of denumeral verbs, e.g., ikkělen 'to doubt' (← ikkě 'two'), depronominal verbs, e.g., urăhlan 'to change' (← urăh 'another'), pětěmlet 'to summarize' (← pětěm 'whole').

Verbs derived from onomatopoeic interjections, or from interjections referring to gestures, are an active model of Chuvash word-formation. The affixes are the same as in the formation of denominal verbs, e.g., măšlat 'to breathe through the nose' (← măš 'sound of puffing'), kěrle 'to make noise' (← kěr 'sound of noise'), lăplan 'to calm' (← lăp 'sound of a slight slap'), čaškăr 'to rustle' (← čaš 'imitation of the noise'), vělkěš 'to unfasten' (← věl 'sound of slight vibration').

5 Conversion

In Chuvash linguistics conversion has not yet been studied in detail. Some Turkologists do not acknowledge conversion as a word-formation procedure because numerous stems/words cannot be clearly determined according to their part of speech, e.g., as nominal or adjectival stem (see also articles on other Turkic languages, e.g., Menz 2016 on Gagauz and Csató 2016 on Karaim). Other linguists, for instance, Pavlov (1964), consider conversion as a productive means of Chuvash word-formation.

Most numerous are examples of nominal conversion (N ← A):
a) Designations of persons according to a specific feature: şamrăk 'young man' (← şamrăk 'young'), sukkăr 'blind person' (← sukkăr 'blind'), ût 'stranger' (← ût 'strange, foreign'), věşkěn 'boaster' (← věşkěn 'boastful'), ěşčen 'workaholic, workman' (← ěşčen 'industrious, hard working');
b) Designations of objects according to specific features: pěrkelenşěk 'small wrinkle' (← pěrkelenşěk 'wrinkled'), jănăš 'error, mistake' (← jănăš 'uncorrect'), şěrěk 'mould' (← şěrěk 'rotten');
c) Abstract qualities: ăšă 'heat, warmth' (← ăšă 'hot, warm'), sivě 'cold, coldness' (← sivě 'cold'), tűlek 'silence' (← tűlek 'silent');
d) Designations of places, areas: ajlăm 'low place' (← ajlăm 'low'), tűrem 'plain (n.)' (← tűrem 'plain');

e) The base of nominal conversions in the meaning of collective nouns can also be coordinative adjectival compounds, e.g., *vĕtĕr-šakăr* 'a clutch of children, kids' (← *vĕtĕr-šakăr* 'small'), *şĕtĕk-şurăk* 'rags, old clothes, things', in non-collective meaning 'ragamuffin, ragged fellow' (← *şĕtĕk-şurăk* 'torn, lacerated').

There are also some cases of nominal conversion from verbs, e.g., *kĕvĕş* 'jealousy, envy' (*kĕvĕş* 'to be jealous, envy'), or verb forms (participles), e.g., *vĕreneken* 'pupil' (← *vĕreneken* 'learning'), *vulakan* 'reader' (← *vulakan* 'reading'), *pulăşakan* 'helper, assistant' (← *pulăşakan* 'helping').

Other nominal conversions go back to onomatopoeic words (e.g., *nărik-nărik* 'pig, piglet', *šăj-šaj* 'noise', *kikkirik* 'crown of the cock'), or to numerals (e.g., *pillĕk* 'number five, school grade' ← *pillĕk* 'five').

6 Reduplication

In Chuvash the following models of reduplication of words or parts of words can be observed: a) reduplication of words of an identical sound structure (absolute repeating); b) reduplication of words of a different sound structure (partial or divergent repeating); c) reduplication in combination with affixation.

6.1 Nouns

Reduplicated nouns, based on sound imitation (onomatopoeia), deserve to be mentioned first: *kukkuk* 'cuckoo', *tŭntŭn* 'blind man's buff', *čučču* 'swing', *tŭttŭt* 'pipe', *mărmăr* 'cat'. These examples are very old. The repetition of syllables was first used in Chuvash for naming birds or denoting children's games. Later the onomatopoeic word became lexicalized. Words originating in children's speech are very close to the examples cited above: *tette* 'toy', *tutu* 'car', *tŭttŭ* 'milk', *pipi* 'boo-boo, hurt (place)', *memme* 'bread', *hamham* 'dog', *mumu* 'cow'.

Some nouns are formed as a result of phonetically divergent reduplication. The first component in these words is the bearer of the lexical meaning, the second serves reduplication purposes, e.g., *kăltăk-kaltăk* 'defaults, lacks', *parne-sarne* 'gifts', *karčăk-kĕrčĕk* 'old women'.

Sometimes reduplication is accompanied by case affixes: *mihhi-mihhipe* 'with whole sacks; lit. sack-sack.COM', *şultan şul* 'year after year, year in, year out; lit. year.ABL-year', *alran al* (*tytsa*) '(to go) hand in hand; lit. hand.ABL-hand', *sămahran sămah* 'word by word; lit. word.ABL-word'.

6.2 Adjectives

The components of the reduplicated adjectives can be identical, e.g., *şăt-şăt* 'well matching (about clothes)' (← *şăt* 'tight, close-fitting'), *vĕtĕ-vĕtĕ* 'small-small', or show modifications in spelling/pronunciation, e.g., *akăš-makăš* 'extraordinary, splendid' (the meaning of the reduplication is lexicalized), *kăjttă-kajttă* 'torn, ragged' (← *kăjttă* 'bad, unfit'). Reduplicated adjectives can also be based on sound imitations, e.g., *vărt-vart* 'hardworking' (← *vărt* onomatopoeic about a fast movement).

There are also examples of incomplete reduplication, as a rule, in the first component, e.g., *puš-pušă* 'completely empty' (← *pušă* 'empty'), *čip-čiper* 'very beautiful' (← *čiper* 'beautiful').

Reduplication accompanied by affixation can be observed in the following examples: *tŭrĕren tŭrĕ* 'very straight', *hĕrlĕren hĕrlĕ* 'very red', *matturtan mattur* 'very good guy' (originally, *-ren* and *-tan* are ablative inflections, here they express additional intensification).

6.3 Other parts of speech

Reduplication is also attested in other parts of speech, e.g.,

Adverbs: *haľ-haľ* 'just about', *ăşta-ăşta* 'wherever; lit. where-where', *kăšt-kašt* 'just a bit; lit. little-little', *ilĕm-tilĕm* 'at the crack of dawn' (the meaning of the reduplication is lexicalized);

Numerals: *şĕr-şĕr* 'hundreds' (← *şĕr* 'hundred'), *pin-pin* 'thousands' (← *pin* 'thousand'), *pinĕn-pinĕn* 'by the thousands', *pĕr-pĕrinpe* 'together; lit. one with one' (← *per* 'one');

Verbs: *čupaťčupať* 'runs and runs', *sisĕni-sisĕnmi* 'barely noticeable' (← *sisĕni* obsolete participle of *sis* 'to notice, feel' + negated participle; the negation is expressed by the affix *-mi*);

Onomatopoeic words: *čănkăr-čănkăr* 'ringing'; onomat. 'ding dong', *păšăl-păšăl* 'whisper', *păt-pat* 'rarely, somewhere'; onomat. 'drip-drop' (sound of water (rain) drops), *kăšăr-kašăr* 'quickly'; onomat. 'rustle-rustle' (sound of a rustle), *kăn-kan* 'imitation/designation of a dull, stupid look'.

7 Clipping

The appearance of clipped words and abbreviations in the modern languages is caused by the need for information encoding and compression. Chuvash multi-word expressions are the base of numerous abbreviations and mixed forms. Clipping of single words is not common unless they are constituents of underlying multi-word expressions (see below). Abbreviations and (partial) clippings are regarded as a special word-formation procedure showing features of motivation and morphonological characteristics. In the literature on Chuvash word-formation two basic types of abbreviations are distinguished:

a) Abbreviations that are exclusively used in written form:
initial abbreviations consisting of the first letters of complex words and word combinations, e.g., *h.-t.* 'sunrise' (← *hĕveltuhăş*), *č. h. s.* 'Chuvash folk-art' (← *čăvaš halăh sămahlăhĕ*), *u. k.* 'in other words' (← *urăhla kalasan*);
abbreviations consisting of the first and the final letter or a part of a word: *r-n* 'region' (← *rajon*), *min-vo* 'ministry' (← *ministerstvo*);
syllabic abbreviations: *ûlt.* 'comrade' (← *ûltaš*), *tĕsl.* 'for example' (← *tĕslĕhren*), *ĕm.* 'century' (← *ĕmĕr*);

b) Abbreviations that are also used in oral speech, i.e. results of abbreviation and clipping (of parts) of complex denominations and recurrent word combinations:

Due to language economy, some recurrent word combinations are subject to abbreviation and clipping. The results (letters, syllables, parts of a word) function as lexical units. In modern Chuvash they are basically nouns. According to their structure, several types can be distinguished:
combination of the initial letters (phonemes) of the underlying words, e.g., *ČNK* 'Chuvash National Congress' (← *Čăvaš naci kongresĕ*), *ČR* 'The Chuvash Republic' (← *Čăvaš respubliki*), *ČPU* 'Chuvash State University' (← *Čăvaš patšalăh universitečĕ*);
combination of the initial parts of the underlying words, e.g., *ham. kor.* 'own correspondent' (← *hamăr korrespondent*), *čăv. kal.* 'Chuvash calendar' (← *čăvaš kalendarĕ*), *rajĕştăvkom* 'district executive board' (← *rajonti ĕş tăvakan komitet*);
combination of the initial part (syllable) of the first word and the entire second word: This variety of abbreviation is also represented by borrowings from Russian. In the calque of the underlying designation (word combination) the head word is adapted to the Chuvash form of izafet II – in the following examples, -*ĕ* is the 3rd person possessive affix, cf. section 3.1.2): *medpunkt* 'first-aid post' (← *medicina punkčĕ*; with alternation *t* > *č* before -*ĕ*), *telecentr* 'television centre' (← *televideni centrĕ*). There are also loan translations with domestic Chuvash words: *informkălarăm* 'information broadcast' (← *informaci kălarămĕ*), *telehupah* 'TV club' (← *televideni hupahĕ*), *avtoşul* 'highway' (← *avtomobiľ şulĕ*).

8 References

Ašmarin, Nikolaj I. (1898): *Materialy dlâ issledovaniâ čuvašskogo âzyka*. Kazan': Tipo-litografiâ Imperatorskogo universiteta.
Ašmarin, Nikolaj I. (1976): Zametki po grammatike čuvašskogo âzyka. In: Nikolaj I. Ašmarin, *Čuvašskij âzyk*, 3–86. Čeboksary: Čuvašskoe knižnoe izdateľstvo.
Andreev, Valerij V. (2007): *Teoretičeskie i prikladnye aspekty čuvašskogo slovoobrazovaniâ*. Čeboksary: Čuvašskij universitet.
Andreev, Valerij V. (2008): *Sposoby i modeli slovoobrazovaniâ v čuvašskom âzyke*. Čeboksary: Čuvašskij universitet.
Andreev, Valerij V. (2009): *Teoriâ i praktika čuvašskogo slovoobrazovaniâ*. Čeboksary: Čuvašskij universitet.
Andreeva, Evdokiâ A. (1995): *Affiksaľnoe glagoľnoe slovoobrazovanie v čuvašskom âzyke*. Čeboksary: Čuvašskij pedagogičeskij universitet.
Csató, Éva Á. (2016): Karaim. In: Peter O. Müller, Ingeborg Ohnheiser, Susan Olsen and Franz Rainer (eds.), *Word-Formation. An International Handbook of the Languages of Europe*. Vol. 5, 3442–3451. Berlin/Boston: De Gruyter Mouton.
Materialy po grammatike sovremennogo čuvašskogo âzyka. Part 1: *Morfologiâ*. (1957): Čeboksary: Čuvašskoe gosudarstvennoe izdateľstvo.
Menz, Astrid (2016): Gagauz. In: Peter O. Müller, Ingeborg Ohnheiser, Susan Olsen and Franz Rainer (eds.), *Word-Formation. An International Handbook of the Languages of Europe*. Vol. 5, 3433–3442. Berlin/Boston: De Gruyter Mouton.
Pavlov, Ivan P. (1965): *Morfologiâ sovremennogo čuvašskogo âzyka*. Čeboksary: Čuvašskoe knižnoe izdateľstvo.
Semenova, Galina N. (2005): *Kompozitoobrazovanie v čuvašskom âzyke i ego nacionaľnaâ specifika*. Moskva: Prometej.
Sergeev, Leonid P. (2009): *Čuvašskuû affiksologiâ*. Čeboksary: Čuvašskij pedagogičeskij universitet.
Skvorcov, Mihail I. (1982): Slovoobrazovateľnye affiksy čuvašskogo âzyka. In: Mihail I. Skvorcov, *Čuvašsko-russkij slovar'*, 661–664. Moskva: Russkij âzyk.
Wälchli, Bernhard (2025): Co-compounds. In: Peter O. Müller, Susan Olsen and Franz Rainer (eds.), *Word-Formation – Special Patterns and Restrictions*, 145–169. Berlin/Boston: De Gruyter Mouton.

Danara Suseeva
22 Kalmyk

1 Introduction
2 General overview
3 Composition and adjacent processes (juxtaposition)
4 Derivation
5 Conversion
6 Reduplication
7 References

Abstract: Kalmyk is an agglutinative language with the following word-formation procedures: composition (and, close to composition, active/productive juxtaposition based on lexicalized word combinations), derivation, conversion, and reduplication. Other procedures, such as backformation and clipping, have not been registered so far. Under the influence of Russian, calquing – especially in composition and derivation – plays a significant role in the enlargement of the vocabulary.

1 Introduction

By its origin, Kalmyk belongs to the Western (Oirat) branch of the Mongolic language family, its grammatical structure is agglutinating. Going back to a combination of the related Torgut, Derbet and Khoshut dialects, the language of the Kalmyks in Russia is the result of its development during the recent centuries. Avoiding the hostilities of feudal strife, the speakers of these dialects left their homeland in Central Asia (Dzungaria) to finally join the Russian empire of their own free will. The long-standing peaceful coexistence of Russians and Kalmyks had a beneficial influence on their languages. Thus the impact of the Russian language can be felt not only in the Kalmyk vocabulary but also in its word-formation. Kalmyk is spoken by about 174,000 native speakers in the Autonomous Republic of Kalmykia where it is the official language. Kalmykia, a federal subject of the Russian Federation, is situated in the south of the European part of Russia.

The earliest records of Kalmyk can be found in glossaries of the 17th and 18th centuries. Thus after his visit to Russia, N. Witsen (1641–1717) published a

Danara Suseeva, Èlista, Russia

treatise where he described his experiences and encounters with people, and among other things he included a glossary of 335 Kalmyk words into his work. Witsen's list contained a number of derivatives, such as *Zargyczy* 'Richter' [judge], *Chulchaiczy* 'Schelm' [prankster], *Gegetiay* 'Helder' [clear, bright], *Bajartay* 'Zy zijn vrolyk' [they are cheerful, merry], etc. (Witsen 1705 [1692]: 297–304). Another work by P. J. von Stralenberg (1730) dealt with different nationalities of Russia, their languages and histories. It also contained a Kalmyk dictionary which included over a thousand lexical items and dozens of derivatives among them, for instance, *Burchatzchi* 'ein Mahler' [painter], *Bitziatzchi* 'der Schreiber' [scribe], *Beletzchi* 'ein Handschuhmacher' [glovemaker], etc. (Stralenberg 1730: 137–156; Krueger 1975: 32–42).

In the 19th century some issues of Kalmyk word-formation were discussed in the grammars by Bobrovnikov (1849) and Popov (1847). Bobrovnikov paid special attention to such nominal suffixes as *-či* (*dalabči* 'cloak, coat' ← *dala* 'shoulder blade'), *-l* (*mèdèl* 'knowledge' ← *mèdè-* 'to know'), and *-ur/-ùr* (*ôlgùr* 'hanger' ← *ôlgô-* 'to hang') (Bobrovnikov 1848: 52–60). Other types of Kalmyk word-formation had not been discussed by these scholars. Kotvič (1929) focused in his grammar on the suffixation processes found in natural Kalmyk speech in the first quarter of the 20th century. In his comparative study of the Kalmyk language and related Oirat dialects of Mongolia and China, Ramstedt (1935) showed that despite the time and distance separating them, they still had preserved a certain number of common word-formation resources up to the turn of the 19th and 20th centuries. While studying identical affixes in related Mongolian languages, Vladimircov paid special attention to the phenomena accompanying affixation (sound change patterns, clipping, infixing, etc.) (Vladimircov 1929: 331–344).

The second half of the 20th century saw an active discussion of Kalmyk word-formation issues in the works by Badmaev (1959), Pûrbeev (1971), Nominhanov (1976), Todaeva (1976), Suseeva (1978, 1995, 1997), Pavlov (2000), and others.

The examples in this article are rendered using the transliteration ISO 9 1995.

2 General overview

The most productive procedures of Kalmyk word-formation are composition (and different types of juxtaposition), suffixation, conversion and reduplication. Kalmyk may differ in morphotactics and morphonology from other languages of the Mongolic family. Furthermore, identical root words and derivational suffixes may be exploited in the various related languages in different ways. Whereas the Kalmyk root *diil(h)* 'to overcome, defeat', for instance, serves as the base for derivatives such as *diil-n̥ḥù* 'superior', *diil-lt* and *diil-vr* 'victory', *diil-ắč* 'victor, winner', corresponding derivatives of the Mongolian verb *dijlè(h)* are not attested inspite of the same inventory of suffixes; the Mongolian equivalents are not connected by derivation. Other differences may be explained by different naming needs of the speech communities (due to the natural environment, the Mongolian word *modon* 'wood, timber, forest, log', for instance, has more derivatives than Kalymk *modn* 'id.') or the influence of different language contacts (the Mongolian derivative *dèlg-ùùr* 'shop' ← *dèlgèh* 'to display, spread, lay' + *-ùùr* has no formal equivalent in Kalmyk (← *delgh* + *ul/-ùl*) because in the 17th–18th century Russian *lavka* '(small) shop' was borrowed and in the 19th century was followed – as also in Russian – by the loanword *magazin* 'shop'.

Composition is always based on two words with coordinative or determinative relations, e.g., a) *ôdr* 'day' + *sô* 'night' → *ôdr-sô* '24 hours, day (and night)'. Several coordinative compounds can be regarded as co-compounds (*èk* 'mother' + *èck* 'father' → *èk-èck* 'parents'); b) *ḥar* 'hand' + *kôrắ* 'saw' → *ḥar kôrắ* 'handsaw', *nùr* 'face' + *ùzdg* 'seeing' → *nùrzdg* 'mirror', *dara* 'goddess' + *èk* 'mother' → *dắrk!* (interjection) 'O God!', etc. (see section 3).

Affixation is almost completely represented by suffixation, cf. some derivatives from the verb *med-h* 'to know': *med-mž̦* 'reputation, publicity', *med-rgh* 'arrogant, presumptuous', *med-mắr* 'intelligibly, clearly', etc. (see section 4).

Nouns and adjectives can also go back to conversion (see section 5), e.g., *nomt* 'scholar' (← *nom-t* comitative case 'with knowledge'), *tatdg* 'box, case' (← *tat-dg* participle of the verb *tat-h* 'to pull, draw').

Reduplication comprises the iteration of identical or phonetically slightly varying words or stems, e.g., *ắrắ-ắrắ* 'barely, faintly', *cevr-cer* 'very clean', *šulun-dulun* 'very quick' (see section 6).

Another means of designation is calquing, i.e. literal translation of foreign lexical items, e.g., Russ. *černozem* 'black soil' > Kalm. *ḥar ḥazr* (← *ḥar* 'black' + *ḥazr* 'land, soil'), Russ. *zeml-e-trâs-enie* 'earth quake' > Kalm. *ḥazr čičrlḥn* (← *ḥazr* 'earth' + *čičr-* verbal stem 'tremble' + suffix *-lḥn*). There are also cases of phraseological calquing, cf. Russ. *smena vremeni goda* 'change of seasons' > Kalm. *žilin cag sollḥn* lit. 'year-time-change'. Complete calquing takes place when all parts of a lexical item (stems and morphemes) are translated into Kalmyk, e.g., linguistic terms such as Russ. *pad-ež* 'case' > Kalm. *kiisk-vr*, Russ. *sklon-enie* 'declension' > Kalm. *kiisk-lḥn* (the Russian terms are, in turn, loan translations from Latin). Examples of incomplete calquing are semi-calques like *telezắng* 'TV news' < Russ. *telenovosti*, *tehdôn̥* 'technological assistance' < Russ. *tehpomošč̦*. Both complete and partial calquing are quite productive in the field of Kalmyk terminology. Calquing should be kept apart from semantic loans as in the case of Russ. *tovarišč̦* 'comrade' > Kalm. *ùr*, one of whose original meanings 'peer' was extended.

Cases of so-called lexical-semantic word-formation (metaphorization and metonymic transfers) such as *tolḫa* 'head' > *tolḫa* '(burial) mound', *haalḫa* 'gate' > *haalḫa* 'road, way', or *bagš* 'prior, superior (of a monastery)' > *bagš* 'teacher' are not included into our survey.

The present article aims at describing the synchronic level of the Kalmyk word-formation system, in the field of derivation proceeding from the methodology and terminology of Russian linguistics (cf. Švedova 1970; Ârceva 1990). Its basic unit is the word-formation type, i.e. "a derivation model which is a generalization based on particular lexical items characterized by i) a common formal element serving to differentiate motivated words from their bases, ii) a common word class of their bases, and iii) a common semantic relationship of motivated words and their bases" (Švedova 1970: 39). For instance, some Kalmyk verbs, such as *ilrh* 'to become clear', *kôkrh* 'to become blue', *sǎǎhrh* 'to become better, improve', etc. belong to the same word-formation type since i) they possess a common derivational formant (suffix) -*r*-; ii) they are motivated by items of one and the same word class – adjectives (*il* 'clear, obvious', *kôk* 'blue', *sǎǎhn* 'pretty'); iii) they have a similar meaning: 'to yield a quality (characteristic of the motivating adjectives)'.

The structure of a derived stem resulting from affixation is always binary as it consists of a base and a derivational formant. The base may be a) a root (*gemšǎ(h)* 'to blame' ← *gem* 'blame'); b) a derived stem (*gemn-lḫn* 'accusation, blaming' ← *gemnh* 'to accuse', blame' ← *gem*); c) a compound (*kùč-kôlsč* 'worker' ← *kùč-kôlsn* 'work, labor'), or d) a multi-word expression/phrase (*balḫs toshlḫn* 'urban construction' ← *balḫs tosh(h)* 'to build towns and cities').

The derivational semantics of a derivative may or may not coincide with its lexical meaning. Thus, for example, the word *ùldl* has three lexical meanings: 1. 'remaining part, remnant' (*Vasilij tatčasn tǎmkin' ùldl ḫulmt tal hajv* 'Vassily threw the remnants of his tobacco into the fire'); 2. 'vestige' (*davsn cagin ùldl* 'the vestige of the old days'); 3. 'descendant' (*Tǎk Zula haan' ùldl, Taṇsg Bumb haan' ač* 'Tyak Zula Khan's descendant he was, Tanggsak Bumba Khan's grandson he was'). Here the second and third lexical meanings cannot be understood on the basis of the constituent parts of the given word (*ùld-* + -*l*). These are extended, figurative meanings while the first meaning is derived from the meaning of the base and can in fact be presented in a formulaic way: that which is the result of an action named by the base verb *ùldh* 'to remain, stay'.

To illustrate the relationship between the derivational and lexical meanings in terms of a particular derivative, let us give another example: thus in the case of *bičǎč* 'writer, someone who (professionally) writes books, stories, etc.' the derivational and lexical meanings do not coincide while in the case of *umšač* 'reader' they do.

Derivational meanings may be accompanied by various specifications depending on the meaning of the base, e.g., 'to yield sth.' > 'to yield offspring': *kičglh* 'to produce puppies' (← *kičg* 'puppy'), *hurḥlh* 'to lamb' (← *hurḥn* 'lamb'), or 'object related to another object' > 'object serving as cover for another object': *dal-vč* 'adornment on the shoulders of clothes' (*kiilgindal-vč* 'adornment on the shoulders of a shirt') and 'cover for shoulders, cape, cloak, tippet' (← *dala* 'shoulder'), *èlk-vč* 'apron' (← *èlkn* 'liver'), etc.

The derivational meaning is characteristic of a group of derivatives united by the common word class of their bases, as well as by the structural and semantic similarities of their suffixes, e.g., *tùšg* 'support' (← *tùšg(h)* 'to hold something up, support'), *zurg* 'picture' (← *zur(h)* 'to draw'), *bičg* 'letter' (← *bič(h)* 'to write'), *hurg* 'meeting' (← *hur(h)* 'to gather, meet'). These derivatives have the common derivational meaning 'result of an action named by the base' and are formed from verbs with the help of one and the same suffix *-g*.

Word-formation processes may be accompanied by morphonological phenomena, i.e. *sandhi* (Marouzeau 1960: 259). Thus the following processes often take place at the boundary of base and suffix:

a) Truncation of the base (*arsč* 'tanner' ← *ars(n)* 'leather, skin', *hurḥlh* 'to lamb' ← *hurḥ(n)* 'lamb');
b) Superposition of morphemes/phonemes (*áádgo* 'fearless' ← *ááadg* 'fearful' + *-go* (*uga*) 'less, without', *meddgo* 'ignorant' ← *meddg* 'having knowledge, learned' + *-go*);
c) Interfixation (*keḥáč* 'doer' ← *ke(h)* 'to do' + *ḥ* + *-áč*, *zùùḥáč* 'wearer' ← *zùù(h)* 'to wear' + *ḥ* + *áč*); here the interfix *ḥ* helps to avoid the irregular combinations of sounds [e-á] and [ùù-á];
d) Regular sound changes (*acan* 'load, weight' ← *ačh* 'to load'; *mordh* 'to mount a horse' ← *môrn* 'horse').

3 Composition and adjacent processes (juxtaposition)

Composition, as well as affixation, is a productive procedure of Kalmyk word-formation. Compounds consist of two components (e.g., *kùč-kôlsn* 'work, labour' ← *kùčn* 'power' + *kôlsn* 'sweat, fig. pursuit') which distinguishes them from derivatives formed from compounds with the help of a suffix (*kùč-kôlsč* 'worker, labourer' ← *kùč-kôlsn* 'work, labour'). Besides, compounds (e.g., *har modn* 'oak tree') have a more specialized meaning as compared with their occurrence in phrases (*degd har modn* 'too dark tree').

Compounding can be accompanied by phonetic modifications and changes in stress patterns. The compound *naḥc ah* 'uncle on the maternal side' (← *naḥc* 'uncle' + *ah* 'elder, senior') may serve as an illustration of a morphonological process taking place at the boundary between the two stems: the initial vowel of the second component *ah* is shortened as a result of the transformation into the intonation pattern of the compound. Instead of the two stresses on its components it preserves only the stress of its first component, which leads to the reduction of the vowel of the second component and, in accordance with current norms, *naḥc ah* is pronounced as [naḥch].

The order of the components of a compound is as a rule fixed while it is free in a phrase (cf. *môrn âlmn* 'jerboa of a big size; lit. horse jerboa' and *Teegt môrn boln âlmn ùzgdnắ* 'You can see horses and jerboas in the steppe'). However, there are exceptions to the rule, cf. *ger-mal/mal-ger* 'household, farmstead' (see below).

The components of compounds may be combined by coordinating or subordinating types of connection.

Components with a coordinating connection form binary compounds, such as *ger-mal* 'household, farmstead' (← *ger* 'house' + *mal* 'cattle', which can be regarded as co-compound, see Wälchli 2025), and dvandvas (cf. Bauer 2004: 41) as, e.g., *ắắh-ič̌h* 'to be scared and shy' (← *ắắh* 'to be scared' + *ič̌h* 'to be shy'), *adḥn-šidḥn* 'in a great hurry' (← *adḥn* 'in a hurry' + *šidḥn* 'very fast'). They are usually written with a hyphen, e.g., *ôrk-bùl* 'family' (← *ôrk* 'family' + *bùl* 'group').

Compounds formed from components with a subordinating type of connection can be grouped into endocentric and exocentric (cf. Bloomfield 1968: 255–257). The semantics of endocentric compounds is motivated by the meanings of their components, e.g., *ulan šavr* 'red soil; lit. red clay', *caḥan ḥujr* 'flour, semolina; lit. white flour'. Unlike endocentric compounds, the semantics of exocentric compounds is not motivated by the meanings of their components, e.g., *ùkr har* 'sedge; lit. cow tongue', *ùkr nùdn* 'currant; lit. cow eye'.

3.1 Nominal compounds

The components of dvandvas can be non-derived or derived (marked by an underline), e.g., *ùg-kùr* 'dialogue; lit. word-conversation', *ôdr-sô* 'day and night; lit. day-night', *ô-ḥundl* 'sadness, sorrow; lit. grievance-rueful feelings', *surḥuľ-èrdm* 'education; lit. study/teaching-specialization/qualification'. In Kalmyk word-formation, combinations of the negative particle *ès* as first component and a verbal noun as second are also considered as a type of copulative compound, e.g., *ès medlḥn* 'ignorance; lit. NEG knowledge', *ès ắdlclḥn* 'inequality, disparity; lit. NEG equality'.

Productive determinative (endocentric) N+N compounds consist of a noun in the nominative or in an oblique case as first component and a deverbal noun as second component, e.g.:

N.NOM+N: *ḥazr kôdllḥn* 'earthquake' (← *ḥazr* 'earth' + *kôdllḥn* 'movement');

N.ACC+N: *ḥazr usllḥn* 'irrigation' (← *ḥazr* 'earth, soil' + *usllḥn* 'watering');

N.INSTR+N: *usartetklḥn* 'water supply' (← *usar* (nom. *usn*) 'water' + *tetklḥn* 'supply').

Besides, there are compounds of the type N.GEN+N, where the head can also be a non-derived noun, e.g., *ùkrǎ maḥn* 'beef; lit. cow's meat'.

The head of compounds is grammatically dominant as it carries case and number inflections, for example, nominative: *bǎǎdl-žirḥl* 'life, lifestyle; lit. state/condition-life', genitive: *bǎǎdl-žirḥl-in*, instrumental case: *bǎǎdl-žirḥl-ǎr*, etc. In *ah-dùùnr* 'siblings', *èk-ècknr* 'parents', the plural suffix *-nr* is attached to the second component. Case endings always follow the plural suffix, e.g., pl. nom. *ah-dùùnr* 'siblings', pl. dat. *ah-dùùnr-t*, pl. instr. *ah-dùùnr-ǎr*.

Determinative compounds may be characterized by a morphonological phenomenon called condensation, i.e. the formation of a long vowel when the final vowel of the first stem coincides with the initial one of the second stem. For example: *sanaldlḥn* 'rueful feelings, worry' (← *sana* + *aldlḥn* ← *sana(n)* 'thought' + *aldh* 'to lack, lose'). This case illustrates internal sandhi at the boundary of stems. The number of such examples in Kalmyk is limited, though they appear from time to time.

Nominal compounds of the structure N+N denote:

Females: *èm ḥalun* 'she-goose; lit. woman/female goose', *èm taka* 'hen; lit. woman/female chicken';

Males: *èr kùn* 'man, male; lit. male human', *èr taka* 'cock; lit. man/male chicken';

Diminutives of nouns denoting objects, animals and plants: *ôôkn čolun* 'pebbles; lit. fat stone' (the first component can be explained by the similarity of the stones' form and size with the body fat of sheep), *hôn âlmn* 'jerboa; lit. sheep jerboa';

Augmentatives: *ùkr čolun* 'boulder; lit. cow stone', *ùkr bôôlžrḥn* 'blackberry, gooseberry; lit. cow raspberry' (the first component *ùkr* 'cow' is used in the metaphorical meaning 'big');

Collective nouns (here: co-compounds): *aaḥ-šaṇḥ* 'tableware; lit. bowl-ladle', *èd tavr* 'goods; lit. cloth good';

Abstract nouns (some of them can be regarded as hyperonyms of the hyponymic components; see also Wälchli 2025 on co-compounds), e.g., *hur-čig* 'moisture; lit. rain-wetness', *učr-uth* 'sense, essence; lit. reason-content'; cf. also the above-mentioned compounds with a deverbal head;

Concrete nouns (expressing relations of origin or instrumental relations), e.g., *ùkrắ maḥn* 'beef; lit. cow's meat', *môrnă maḥn* 'horse meat', *kermn devl* 'fur coat; lit. squirrel coat', *ḥal kerm* 'steam boat; lit. fire boat', etc.

Nominal compounds of the type A+N are less characteristic of Kalmyk: *har ḥujr* 'rye flour; lit. black flour', *caḥan ḥujr* 'wheat flour; lit. white flour'.

3.2 Adjectival compounds

Adjectival compounds can have the following structures:

N+A: *cusn ulan* 'purple, crimson; lit. blood red';

A+A: *kôk buurl* 'blue-gray, dove-coloured'. One or both constituents can also be derived adjectives, e.g., *ắmtắ-kiitắ* 'alive, animate; lit. alive-breathing', *ke-sắắhn* 'beautiful; lit. smart-pretty'.

Depending on the semantics of the components adjectival compounds denote:

Qualities resulting from the combination of two characteristics, mostly colors (when simple adjectives are combined), e.g., *har ulan* 'brown, dark; lit. black red', *šar ulan* 'orange; lit. yellow red', *al ulan* 'red; lit. pink red';

Intensification can be motivated by a comparison (when nouns and adjectives are combined), e.g., *oošk ulan* 'pink, rosy; lit. lungs red, i.e. red (pink) as the color of lungs', or based on the combination of synonymous adjectives, e.g., *bajrta-bahta* 'vivacious, exuberant' (← *bajrta* 'happy, merry' + *bahta* 'high-spirited'), *sag sergg* 'vigilant, watchful; lit. careful alert', *digtắ-tagta* 'neat, fit; lit. exact-accurate'; *amr-taavr* 'calm; lit. relaxed-complacent';

Generalization of qualities (the components of the corresponding compounds can be regarded as synonyms): *èèmtắ-dalta* 'strong' (← *èèmtắ* 'with strong shoulders' + *dalta* 'broad-shouldered'), *aḥu ik* 'colossal; lit. spacious big', *amtta-šimttắ* 'tasty, delicious; lit. tasty-juicy', *atata-marḥata* 'controversial, disputable; lit. envious-contentious'.

3.3 Verbal compounds

Verbal compounds usually denote the intensity of an action, e.g., *èlvžh-dèlvžh* 'to be in abundance, rich in; lit. abound-overflow'. Both components can be synonymous or at least closely related verbs, e.g., *ắắh-ič̆h* 'to be scared, shy; lit. be scared-be ashamed', *môškh-môlžh* 'to investigate; lit. inquire-interrogate' (fig.), or the second element, lacking a clear meaning of its own, merely adds a shade of intensity to the meaning of the first one, e.g., *èvlh-dovlh* 'to persuade'.

3.4 Adverbial compounds

Adverbial compounds can consist of non-derived or derived adverbs, e.g., *dav-zuur* 'temporarily (← *dav* 'at once' + *zuur* 'on the way'); *bajrtaḥar-bahtaḥar* 'gladly; lit. gladly-gladly'. They may denote:
a) Manner: *digtăgăr-tagtaḥar* 'neatly; lit. correctly-accurately';
b) Time: *nevčkn-zuur* 'for a short time; lit. a bit-on the way';
c) Place: *iigắn-tiigắn* 'back and forth; lit. here-there';
d) Degree: *neg-kiiḥắr* 'at a gulp, at one draught; lit. one-with air'.

3.5 Adjacent processes (juxtaposition)

Juxtaposition shows several similarities with composition. In numerous cases, it is difficult to draw a clear-cut borderline between the two types of designation. For this reason, regular juxtaposition of words (word-forms) with a subordinating relationship between their components are traditionally included into studies on Kalmyk word-formation and summarized under a term coined in analogy to Russ. *sraščenie* 'fusion, adhesion (of words)'.

3.5.1 Adjectives based on juxtaposition

The formations may have the following structures:

A+N.COMIT in *-ta/-tă*: *baḥ nasta* 'young' (← *baḥ* 'young' + *nasta* comit. of *nasn* 'age'), *ut kùzùtắ* 'long-necked' (← *ut* 'long' + *kùzùtắ* comit. of *kùzùn* 'neck');

N+A: *kôl nùckn* 'barefoot' (← *kôl* 'foot' + *nùckn* 'bare'), *sanamr* 'calm, relaxed' (← *sana(n)* [n subtracted] 'thought' + *amr* 'calm');

A+nominalized present participle in *-dg*: *amr hắắldg* 'low-melting, fusible' (← *amr* 'calm, easy' + *hắắldg* 'melting');

Adv+nominalized past particple in *-sn*: *deer kelgdsn* 'above mentioned';

Adv+A: *ôrgn delgrngù* 'widespread; lit. widely spread'.

The general meaning of the corresponding adjectives is 'having X, characterized by X', e.g., inherent characteristics of persons, such as *caḥan sedkltă* 'kind-hearted' (← *caḥan* 'white' + *sedkltă* comit. 'thought, heart'), *sắn uhata* 'decent, good' (← *sắn* 'good' + *uhata* 'thought'), *hurc keldg* 'eloquent' (← *hurc* 'sharp' + *keldg* 'speaking'), *sanan zùùsn* 'haughty' (← *sanan* 'thought' + *zùùsn* 'wearing'); physical characteristics of persons or animals, e.g., *ik nùdtă* 'large-eyed' (← *ik* 'large, big' + *nùdtă* comit. 'eyes'), *ik hamrta* 'with a big nose'; or physical properties of objects, e.g., *ădl bôôrtă* 'isosceles' (← *ădl* 'equal' + *bôôrtă* comit. 'side, thigh'), *săn činrtă* 'solid, of good quality' (← *săn* 'good' + *činrtă* comit. 'quality').

3.5.2 Verbs based on juxtaposition

Verbal mergers are lexical items consisting of two words with a lexically dominant first component and a verb as second component. They are a productive means in the formation of verbs:

Adverbial participle (gerund) in *-ž/-č* + V: *olž avh* 'to find out' (← *olž* '(when) finding' + *avh* 'to take'), *avč ḥarh* 'to take out' (← *avč* 'taking' + *ḥarh* 'to leave');

Adverbial participle (gerund) in *-ad/-ăd* + V: *dahulad avh* 'to accompany' (← *dahulad* 'accompanying' + *avh* 'to take'), *hagsaḥad avh* 'to dry out' (← *hagsaḥad* 'after drying' + *avh* 'to take');

N.ACC+V: *tămk tath* 'to smoke' (← *tămk* 'tobacco' + *tath* 'to pull, inhale'), *tără tărh* 'to sow' (← *tără* 'corn' + *tărh* 'to sow');

Adv+V: *ažg avh* 'to become aware, feel' (← *ažg* 'carefully, closely' + *avh* 'to take'), *hooran cuhrh* 'to back, retreat' (← *hooran* 'back, backwards' + *cuhrh* 'to back, retreat');

Onomatopoeic word + *gih* 'to speak': *hab-hab gih* 'to grumble', *havčg-havčg gih* 'to feel ill at ease'.

The above-mentioned types denote, for instance,
a) Verbs of motion: *nisž jovh* 'to fly' (← *nisž* 'flying' + *jovh* 'to go'), *gùùž irh* 'to run into' (← *gùùž* 'running' + *irh* 'to come');
b) Action verbs: *kež avh* 'to carry out, perform' (← *kež* 'doing' + *avh* 'to take'), *maltž avh* 'to dig out' (← *maltž* 'digging' + *avh* 'to take');
c) Speech verbs: *kelž ôgh* 'to say, answer' (← *kelž* 'having said' + *ôgh* 'to give'), *căălḥž ôgh* 'to explain' (← *căălḥž* 'having explained' + *ôgh* 'to give');
d) Verbs of perception: *sonž avh* 'to hear' (← *sonž* 'hearing' + *avh* 'to take'), *ùzž avh* 'to see' (← *ùzž* 'seeing' + *avh* 'to take');
e) Verbs of thought: *sana sanh* 'to think, reflect' (← *sana* 'thought' + *sanh* 'to think'), *sedkl zovh* 'to worry' (← *sedkl* 'thought' + *zovh* 'to suffer');
f) Onomatopoeic verbs: *bur-bur gih* 'to bobble', *ḥoš-ḥoš gih* 'to make loud noise', etc.

4 Derivation

Derivation is one of the most productive procedures of Kalmyk word-formation. Each word class has its own set of suffixes. Nouns, adjectives, verbs and adverbs can be derived by suffixation from simple stems, e.g., *zuruľ* 'drawing, sketch' (← *zur-(h)* 'to draw' + *-uľ*), from derived stems, e.g., *aṇḥučllḥn* 'hunting' (← *aṇḥučl-(h)* 'to hunt' + *-lḥn* (← *aṇḥuč-* 'hunter' + *-l* ← *aṇḥ-* 'animal' + *-uč*)), or from p h r a s e s, e.g., *tằrằ tằrằč* 'sowman; lit. seed sow-AGENT' (← *tằrằ tằr(h)* 'to sow seeds').

Derivation can be accompanied by morphonological phenomena at the boundary of the base and the derivational suffix. In particular, these are:
a) Clipping of the final consonants of the base word, e.g., *ars-č* 'tanner, skinner' (← *arsn̩* 'skin'), *altlh* 'to gild' (← *altn̩-* 'gold'), *giiglh* 'to lighten, relieve' (← *giign̩* 'light'), *giigrh* 'to lighten, relieve' (← *giign̩* 'light');
b) Infixation, e.g., *zùùḥằč* 'wearer' (← *zùù(h)* 'to wear'); in this case *ḥ* is inserted between the base and the suffix in order to avoid a combination of three vowels *ùùằ*, which is not typical of Kalmyk;
c) Superposition of phonemes, e.g., *ằằdgo* 'fearless, courageous' (← *ằằdg* 'fearful, cowardly' + *-go* (← particle *uga* 'no, without');
d) Alternation of phonemes which can be explained diachronically or by synchronic phonetic phenomena such as vowel harmony, cf., for instance, the use of the suffix variants *-ta*/*-tằ* in *amtta* 'tasty, delicious' (← *amt-n̩* 'taste, flavor' + *-ta*) and *ằvrtằ* 'angry, bad' (← *ằvr* 'behavior, nature' + *-tằ*).

One and the same suffix can derive words of different categorial meanings. For example, the verb-forming suffix *-l* is used to form both transitive and intransitive verbs from nominal stems, cf. *zarlh* 'to announce' (← *zar* 'announcement'), *davslh* 'to salt' (← *davsn* 'salt'), *uhalh* 'to think, ponder, reflect' (← *uhan* 'thought') and *uurlh* 'to be, get angry' ← *ur* 'anger'), *zôrglh* 'to dare, venture' (← *zôrg* 'courage'), *šarlh* 'to become yellow' (← *šar* 'yellow').

4.1 Nominal derivation

Nouns are mostly derived from nouns, adjectives and verbs by numerous suffixes, for instance, *-lḥn, -lt, -an/ằn-, -vr, -ač/-ằč, -c, -mž, -g, -m, -dl, -lh, -l, -uľ/-ùľ, -r, -ha/-hằ, -ul/-ùl, -š*, etc. A small group of denumeral nouns denote female and male animals according to their age, e.g., *ḥunžn* 'a three-year-old cow' and *ḥunn* 'a three-year-old bull' (both derived from *ḥun* 'three'), *dônžn* 'a four-year-old cow' and *dônn* 'a four-year-old bull' (both ← *dôn* 'four').

4.1.1 Denominal nouns

Denominal nouns are formed with the help of productive suffixes, such as -č, -da/-dǎ, -la/-lǎ, -vč and non-productive suffixes, such as -t, -tn, -g, etc. They belong to the following categories:

Personal nouns, designating professions and occupations, e.g., malč 'shepherd' (← mal 'cattle'), selvgč 'adviser' (← selvg 'advice'), nomt 'scholar, scientist' (← nom 'scholarship, science'), and persons according to specific traits or characteristics, e.g., sahlt 'bearded man' (← sahl 'beard');

Non-personal nouns, e.g., hancvč 'armlet, muff' (← hanc(n) 'sleeve'), čeežvč 'breastplate' (← čeež 'breast'), and names of animals, motivated by designations which are connected to time or place, e.g., noḥala 'leveret born in spring' (← noḥan 'spring green grass'), devǎlǎ 'leveret born in summer' (← devǎ 'alpine meadow');

Collective nouns: živrtn 'birds, bird life' (← živr 'wing'), aratn 'carnivore' (← ara(n) 'fang');

Singulatives: tôlg 'lamb' (← tôl 'offspring'), humg 'speck of dust' (← hum 'dust').

4.1.2 Deadjectival nouns

Nouns are derived from adjectives with the help of suffixes such as -č, -da/-dǎ, -la/-lǎ, -žṇ, -gčn, -c, etc. Some of them are productive and are used in the formation of both nouns and adjectives: -č, -da/-dǎ, -la/-lǎ. Non-productive are, e.g., -žṇ and -c. Attributive nouns comprise the categories of personal nouns, e.g., sǎǎhlǎ 'a beauty' (← sǎǎh(n) 'pretty'), baruč 'right-hander' (← baru(n) 'right'), solḥač 'left-hander' (← solḥa 'left'), hatuč 'miser' (← hatu 'hard, callous'), and non-personal nouns. The latter are mostly derived from color adjectives, e.g., harada 'swallow' (← hara 'black'), boržṇ 'wild duck' (← bor 'grey'), šarc 'sienna' (← šar 'yellow').

4.1.3 Deverbal nouns

The formation of nouns from verbs is one of the most productive word-formation procedures. Thus the Kalmyk verb is a dominant word class not only in grammar but also in word-formation. Deverbal nouns are formed with the help of the productive suffixes -ač/-ǎč, -lḥn, -lt, -an/-ǎn, -ul/-ùl/-ur/-ùl, -mž, -c, etc. Non-productive are, for instance, -lṇ, -a/-ǎ, -dl, -l, -r. Deverbal nouns comprise the following word-formation categories:

Abstract nouns: *gùùlhn* 'run, race' (← *gùù(h)* 'to run'), *umšlhn* 'reading' (← *umš(h)* 'to read'), *aglhllhn* 'isolation' (← *aglhl(h)* 'to seclude'), *adhm* 'haste' (← *adh(h)* 'to be in a hurry');

Result nouns: *kôkrǎn* 'blueness' (← *kôkr(h)* 'to become blue'), *cuglran* 'meeting' (← *cuglr(h)* 'to gather, meet'), *toolvr* 'reflection' (← *tool(h)* 'to reflect, consider'), *soṇshvr* 'message, information' (← *soṇsh(h)* 'to inform');

Agent nouns: *asrač* 'guardian' (← *asr(h)* 'to look after, take care'), *ahlač* 'head' (← *ahl(h)* 'to run, head');

Instrument nouns: *dusahul* 'pipette' (← *dusa(h)* 'to drop'), *èèrùl* 'spindle' (← *èèr(h)* 'to spin'), *tata* 'harness' (← *tat(h)* 'to pull, drag'), *bôglǎ* 'cork' (← *bôgl(h)* 'to shut, close');

Place nouns: *cuthlṇ* 'estuary' (← *cuth(h)* 'to flow'), *ùvlzṇ* 'wintering ground' (← *uvlz(h)* 'to spend winter, stay in winter').

4.2 Adjectival derivation

The results of adjectival derivation are actively completed by adjectival juxtapositions (cf. section 3.5.1) and converted adjectives, e.g., adjectives with relational meaning converted from nouns in the genitive case and with qualitative-possessive meaning converted from nouns in the comitative case (cf. section 5.2).

4.2.1 Denominal adjectives

Adjectives are derived from nouns with the help of the productive suffixes *-rhg*, *-ta/-tǎ*, *-vr/-vtr/-vcr* and the non-productive suffixes *-č*, *-t*, *-lg*, *-vṇ*, *-ul*. Relational adjectives are mainly formed with *-a/-ǎ*, *-ta/-tǎ*, *-č*, *-lg*, and *-vṇ*. The suffixes *-rhg*, *-vr/-vtr/-vcr* and others are used to derive qualitative adjectives. Each of the suffixes has a general meaning which may obtain a specific meaning when combining with certain bases. Some adjectives may have both a relational and a qualitative meaning, cf., e.g., *surhmẓta* 'referring to education, educational' and 'well-bred' (← *surhmẓ* 'education'). Some examples:

Relational denominal adjectives: *čiknǎ* 'related to the ear' (← *čikn* 'ear'), *ùkrǎ* 'related to the cow' (← *ùkr* 'cow'), *zùrkni* 'cardiac, heart (adj.)' (← *zùrkn* 'heart'), *nùdni* 'ocular' (← *nùdn* 'eye'), cf. also section 5.2;

Qualitative adjectives mostly convey possessive meaning, e.g., *uhata* 'clever, wise' and *uharlg* 'clever' (← *uhan* 'mind, intellect'), *čiigtǎ* 'moist, wet' (← *čig* 'moisture'), *ùùltǎ* 'cloudy' (← *ùùl* 'cloud'), *čidltǎ* 'strong' (← *čidl* 'strength'), *cecglg* 'blooming, flowering' (← *cecg* 'flower'). The meaning of some possessive adjectives is connected to a quantitative modification ('characterized by the abundance of that which is denoted by the base word'), e.g., *mahlg* 'stout, corpulent' (← *mahn* 'flesh, meat'), *uulrhg* 'mountainous' (← *uul* 'mountain'), *usrhg* 'water-rich, abounding in water' (← *usn* 'water'). A predilection/inclination towards the object denoted by the base is expressed by adjectives like *mahsg* 'loving meat' (← *mahn* 'meat'), similarity by adjectives such as *usvku* 'watery' (← *usn* 'water'), *čolunšṇ* 'stonelike' (← *čolun* 'stone').

4.2.2 Deadjectival adjectives

Deadjectival adjectives are formed with the productive suffixes -*vr*/-*vtr*/-*vcr*/-*cr*, -*hn*/-*kn* and the non-productive suffix -*gčn*. They express different kinds of modification, for instance, approximation or diminutive meaning: *borvtr* 'greyish' (← *bor* 'grey'), *haluvtr* 'rather hot' (← *halun* 'hot'), or endearment, a positive attitude towards the bearer of the property, e.g., *sắăhn* 'pretty' (← *să(n)* 'good'), *bičkắn* 'tiny' (← *bičk(n)* 'little'). A special group of modificational adjectives is used to denote the color of a female animal, e.g., *hoogčn* 'cream' (← *ho* 'light-yellow'), *borgčn* 'grey' (← *bor* 'grey').

4.2.3 Deverbal adjectives

Deverbal adjectives are formed with the productive suffixes -*ḥr*/-*gr*/-*hr*, -*vr*, -*ṇḥu*/ -*ṇḥù*, -*ha*/-*hắ*, -*mha*/*mḥắ*, -*mtha*/-*mthắ*, -*mg*, -*u*/-*ù*, -*g*; non-productive suffixes are -*ṇ*, -*ml*/-*mr*. They belong to the following categories:

Active adjectives (sometimes including the meaning of inclination), e.g., *inắmthắ* 'laughsome' (← *inắ(h)* 'to laugh'), *ažglmtha* 'observant' (← *ažgl(h)* 'to observe'), *čadmg* 'dexterous, clever, nimble' (← *čad(h)* 'to be able'), *doḥlṇ* 'lame, limping' (← *doḥl(h)* 'to limp'), *sergg* 'brisk, lively' (← *serg(h)* 'to brighten, get lively'), *omgrhg* 'haughty' (← *omgr(h)* 'to be proud (of), haughty');

Resultative adjectives: *budml* 'painted' (← *bud(h)* 'to paint'), *hatml* 'dried' (← *hat(h)* 'to dry'), *hagsu* 'dry' (← *hags(h)* 'to dry'), *ôlgmr* 'knitted' (← *ôlg(h)* 'to knit'), etc. (In Kalmyk, these adjectives are not identical with participles as might be suggested from the English equivalents.)

4.2.4 Deadverbial adjectives

Deadverbial adjectives are derived by means of the productive suffix -*k* and refer to qualities associated with the meaning of the bases, such as temporal characteristics, e.g., *nôkắdùrk* 'tomorrow's' (adj.) (← *nôkắdùr* 'the day after tomorrow' (adv.)), *ôckôldùrk* 'yesterday's' (← *ôckôldùr* 'yesterday'), and l o c a l characteristics as, e.g., *ôôrk* 'near, close-by' (adj.) (← *ôôr* 'near, close-by'), *ardk* 'back, backward' (← *ard* 'behind, in the back').

4.3 Verbal derivation

Verbs can be derived from nominal, adjectival, adverbial and verbal stems, and from onomatopoeic words. A few verbs are derived from numerals, e.g., *hojrdh* 'to do sth. twice' and *hojrlh* 'to double' (both from *hojr* 'two').

Some suffixes (e.g., *-l* and *-d*) are highly productive, deriving verbs from stems of different word classes; some are of low productivity such as *-žṇn* deriving verbs only from onomatopoeic words, e.g., *šaržṇnh* 'to thunder, clatter, bellow' (← *šar-šar gih* 'to make loud, noisy sounds'). Depending on the meaning of the bases, the general processual meaning of the suffixes *-l* and *-d* becomes specified in the derivatives.

Verbal suffixes may indicate lexical-grammatical categories, such as transitivity/intransitivity. Intransitive verbs are often derived with the suffix *-d*, while transitive verbs are formed by means of the suffix *-l*.

4.3.1 Denominal verbs

Denominal verbs are derived with the productive suffixes *-l*, *-d*, *-n*, *-rh*, *ž*, *-š*, *-čl*, *-ld*. Unproductive suffixes are *-n'*, *-z*, *-tr*, *-ms*, *-č*. Denominal verb formation can be accompanied by morphonological phenomena, occurring at the boundary of the base and the suffix, e.g.,
a) Clipping of the base, in particular, its final consonant *n*, e.g., *èlgsh* 'to show family feelings' (← *èlgn* 'relative, member of family');
b) Alternation of short and long vowels in the root (stem), e.g., *uurlh* 'to be angry' (← *ur* 'anger, wrath');
c) Insertion of a sound between the base and the suffix, e.g., *anḥah* 'to open' (← *an* 'crack, hole' + *ḥ* + suffix *-a*).

Denominal verbs denote an action or a state related to the base, with the following meanings:
a) 'to be (like) N': *bermsh* 'to behave like a daughter-in-law, in a modest way' (← *ber* 'daughter-in-law'), *solṇtrh* 'to be iridescent' (← *solṇḥ* 'rainbow'), *salkdh* 'to be windy' (← *salkn* 'wind');

b) 'to become N': *ônčrh* 'to become an orphan' (← *ônčn* 'orphan'), *hatučrh* 'to become a miser, avaricious, stingy' (← *hatuč* 'miser');
c) 'to make N': *zuralh* 'to plan' (← *zura* 'plan'), *kôôsth* 'to foam' (← *kôôsn* 'foam'), *duudh* 'to call' (← *dun* 'voice'), *tosdh* 'to butter' (← *tosn* 'butter'), *šatrch* 'to play chess' (← *šatr* 'chess' + -*c*);
d) 'to provide with N': *altlh* 'to cover with gold' (← *alt(n)* 'gold'), *davslh* 'to salt' (← *davsn* 'salt' + -*l*);
e) 'to act with the help of N': *tovčlh* 'to button' (← *tovč* 'button'), *arḥmẓlh* 'to rope' (← *arḥmẓ* 'lasso');
f) 'to act where/when N': *kôvắlh* 'to go along the bank of a river, lake, etc.' (← *kôvắ* 'bank'), *usčh* 'to swim' (← *usn* 'water'), *ùvlzh* 'to spend winter somewhere' (← *ùvl* 'winter').

Cf. also other examples of denominal verbs like *nasrhh* 'to be proud of one's age' (← *nasn* 'age').

4.3.2 Deadjectival verbs

Deadjectival verbs are formed with the productive suffixes -*d*, -*t*, -*l*, -*rh*, -*r*, and non-productive suffixes, such as -*c*, -*š*, etc. Kalmyk deadjectival verbs can be inchoative or factitive:
a) 'to become A': *hatudh* 'to become too hard, firm' (← *hatu* 'hard, firm'), *harlh* 'to blacken' (← *har* 'black'), *kùrṇth* 'to brown' (← *kùrṇ* 'greyish brown'), *tenglh* 'to become stupid' (← *teng* 'stupid'), *dogšrhh* 'to become furious' (← *dogšn* 'fierce, furious'), *kôkrh* 'to turn blue' (← *kôk* 'blue'), *ắdlch* 'to become identical' (← *ắdl* 'identical'), *zerlgšh* 'to become wild' (← *zerlg* 'wild');
b) 'to make A': *zuzalh* 'to thicken' (← *zuzan* 'thick'), *batlh* 'to strengthen, fasten' (← *bat* 'strong, reliable'), *giigrh* 'to lighten' (← *giigṇ* 'light');
c) verbs with both meanings: *haludh* 'to heat' and 'to become hot' (← *halun* 'hot'), *batrh* 'to strengthen' and 'to become stronger' (← *bat* 'strong, reliable').

4.3.3 Deadverbial verbs

They are formed by means of the productive suffixes -*l* and -*d*, e.g., *ḥazalh* 'to regard sb. as a stranger' and *ḥazadh* 'to stay outside' (both derived from *ḥaza* 'outside, outdoors'), and non-productive suffixes such as -*r*, -*š*, e.g., *dimirh* 'to worsen' (← *dimi* 'in vain'), *deeršh* 'to climb up, be superior' (← *deer* 'above'). Deadverbial verbs can also denote actions in respect to their temporal modifications, e.g., èrtlh 'to be ready very early (at dawn)' and èrtdh 'to be too early' (both derived from èrt 'early'), and local or directional modifications, e.g., ômărlh 'to go on, forward' (← ômắrắ(n) 'forward'), ôôrdh 'to approach' (← ôôr 'near, close by').

4.3.4 Deverbal verbs

Deverbal verbs are formed with the help of the productive suffixes -a/-ắ, -r, -rh, -ž, -ḥ. They express s e m e l f a c t i v i t y, e.g., honžh 'to spend a night' (← hon(h) 'to spend nights'), or express c a u s a t i o n / t r a n s i t i v i t y when derived from an intransivite verb, e.g., bajsah 'to make sb. happy' (← bajs(h) 'to be happy'), zovah 'to torture, torment' (← zov(h) 'to suffer, worry, be anxious'), bajžrhh 'to show off one's richness' (← bajž(h) 'to get rich'), cf. also surḥh 'to teach' (← sur(h) 'to ask'), or i n t r a n s i t i v i t y, e.g., cuglrh 'to get together' (← cugl(h) 'to collect'). Non-productive suffixes such as -č- are also found in deverbal verb formation, e.g., akč-h 'to dry up, wither sth.' (← ak-h (itr.) 'to get dry, dry up, wither').

4.3.5 Verbs derived from onomatopoeics

These verbs are mostly formed with the suffix -žṇ- and denote actions associated with the reproduction of sounds of animate or inanimate objects, e.g., žiržṇh 'to murmur, babble' (← žir-žir), torlh 'to chirp, twitter' (← tor-tor).

In the following groups of verbs, gih signalizes the meaning of action ('to do', 'to make', 'to utter', etc.) in accordance with the meaning of the onomatopoeic bases: reproduction/imitation of visual perceptions, e.g., ders-ders gih 'to slip by, glimpse', gilṇ-gilṇ gih 'to glisten, shimmer', or of tactile perceptions, e.g., dag-dig gih 'to tremble, shake'.

4.4 Adverbial derivation

Adverbs are formed from nominal, adjectival and adverbial stems with the help of the productive suffixes -aḥa/-ắḥắ, -a/-ắ, -d, -dan/-dắn, -gšan/-gšắn, -aran/-ắrắn, -ar/-ắr, -asn'/-ắsn'. Most suffixes are represented by allomorphs induced by sound harmony. Non-productive suffixes such as -kan/-kắn and -hn are also used, e.g., šinkắn 'just' (← šin 'new'), odahn 'recently' (← oda 'now, at the moment').

D e n o m i n a l adverbs are derived by means of the productive suffixes -d, -a/-ắ, -as/-ắs, -ar/-ắr and denote
a) Time: ùvld 'in winter' (← ùvl 'winter'), namra 'in autumn' (← namr 'autumn');

b) Place (and direction): *èrgnd* 'around' (← *èrgn* 'outskirts'), *èknắs* 'from the starting point' (← *èkn* 'the very beginning');
c) Manner: *tavarn* 'in comfort, comfortably' (← *tav* 'convenience, comfort'), *èndùḥắr* 'by mistake' (← *èndù* 'mistake').

Deadjectival adverbs with the productive suffixes *-d, -dan/-dắn, -ar/-ắr* also express time: *môṇkind* 'for ever, perennially' (← *môṇkin* 'perennial'); place: *delgùdắn* 'everywhere' (← *delgù* 'continuous'); manner: *cevrắr* 'cleanly' (← *cevr* 'clean'), *ôtkắr* 'thickly, densely' (← *ôtkn* 'dense, thick').

Deadverbial adverbs with the productive suffixes *-gšan/gšắn, -aḥa/-ắḥắ, -as/-ắs, -asnʹ/-ắsnʹ, -d* denote time: *kezắd* 'always' (← *kezắ* 'always'), *èrtắr* 'early' (← *èrt* 'early'), *èrtinắḥắ* 'earlier' (← *èrtinắ* 'earlier'), and place: *doras* 'from below' (← *dor* 'below'), *ḥazaḥac* 'outside' (← *ḥaza* 'outside'), *ḥazagšan* 'outside' (← *ḥaza* 'outside, outdoors'), *tendắḥắ* 'there, over there' (← *tend* 'there'), etc.

5 Conversion

Conversion is an affixless type of word-formation which involves the transformation of the word class, e.g., *tatdg* (noun) 'drawer' (← *tatdg* (participle) 'drawing' ← *tat(h)* 'to draw'). Another example: the participle *ahlgč* 'being in charge' is converted into the noun *ahlgč* 'elder' with a new meaning, nominal grammatical categories (case and number), the syntactic functions of a noun and thus another combinability, etc.

There are two types of conversion: a) incomplete (occasional), and b) complete (morphological) conversion. In the proverb *Èdgắsnd – èmč kergo, ḥatlsnd – oṇḥc kergo* 'The one who has recovered needs no doctor, the one who has crossed the river needs no boat' the two conversions *èdgắsnd* and *ḥatlsnd* are incomplete, i.e. non-lexicalized past participles of the verbs *èdgắh* 'to cure' and *ḥatlh* 'to cross a river, sea, etc'. Occasional conversions are often used in formulaic expressions (proverbs and sayings), in fiction and oral speech. Unlike complete conversions, which are regularly recorded in dictionaries as full-fledged lexical items of a certain word class with its inherent characteristics, incomplete conversions are seldom registered by dictionaries. This section focusses on complete conversions.

Depending on the word class, it is usual to distinguish nominal, adjectival and adverbial conversion. Cases of verbalization and pronominalization have not been registered in modern Kalmyk so far.

5.1 Nominal conversion

Most converted nouns go back to present participles with the suffixes *-gč* and *-dg*, e.g., *hajgč* 'addresser, sender' (← *hajgč* 'addressing, throwing (a letter, etc.)' ← *haj(h)*). Others go back to past participles of the *-sn*-type, e.g., *šùùsn* 'juice' (← *šùùsn* 'sifted, filtered' ← *šùù(h)*). The semantics of nouns converted from participles can be described in the framework of deverbal nominal categories such as:

Agent nouns, e.g., *surḫgč* 'somebody who teaches, instructor' (← *surḫgč* 'teaching, instructing' ← *surḫ(h)*), *tatgč* 'defender' (← *tatgč* 'defending' ← *tat(h)*).

Instrument nouns, e.g., *kôrgắgč* 'freezer' (← *kôrgắgč* 'freezing, cooling' ← *kôrgắ(h)*), *teegč* 'device for carrying, transporting load' (← *teegč* 'carrying, transporting' ← *tee(h)*);

Result nouns, e.g., *aldg* 'something left out, overlooked' (← *aldg* 'left out, overlooked' ← *ald(h)*), *kelgč* 'predicate' (← *kelgč* 'speaking' ← *kel(h)*), *boodg* 'sheaf, bundle' (← *boodg* 'tying' ← *boo(h)*). (As can be seen by the last example, the specific temporal meaning of the participle may be lost in the converted noun.)

5.2 Adjectival conversion

5.2.1 Adjectives converted from participles

The corresponding adjectives can have active or passive (resultative) meaning, e.g., *bičdg* '(for) writing' (← *bičdg* 'writing'), *bùrdg* 'loose, dry' (← *bùrdg* 'free-running, free-flowing'), *bùlùdsn* 'sharp' (← *bùlùdsn* 'sharpened'). The following participles can serve as base of conversion: present participles of the *-dg*-type, e.g., *tevčdg* 'patient, tolerant' (← *tevčdg* 'bearing, tolerating' ← *tevč(h)*), *tasldg* 'detachable' (← *tasldg* 'being torn off, detached' ← *tasl(h)*); present participles of the *-gč*-type, e.g., *devšgč* 'progressive, advanced' (← *devšgč* 'advancing' ← *devš(h)*); past participles of the *-sn*-type, e.g., *tasrsn* 'torn off, detached' (← *tasrsn* 'torn off, detached' ← *tasr(h)*); *salsn* 'separated' (← *salsn* 'separated' ← *sal(h)*).

5.2.2 Adjectives converted from nouns (comitative or genitive case forms)

It should be noted that abstract and concrete nouns in the comitative ('with, together') with the ending *-ta/-tä* are most readily adjectivized (they usually correspond to qualitative adjectives with a possessive meaning, cf. section 4.2.1), e.g., *arḫta* 'able, capable' (← *arḫta* 'abilities-COM'), *ḫaruta* 'unprofitable, unsuccessfull' (← ḥaruta 'losses-COM'), gerltǎ 'alight, lit' (← gerltǎ 'light, illumination-COM'), ḥašuta 'bitter' (← ḥašuta 'bitterness-COM'); amtta 'tasteful, delicious', bôktǎ 'hump-backed', buuta 'armed' (← buuta 'rifle-COM'). Occasionally, adjectives with a qualitative-possessive meaning can be converted from nouns in the genitive (-in): balč-gin 'muddy, dirty' or -i, e.g., zùrkni 'heartful'.

Adjectives converted from the genitive usually express possessive-relational meaning (genitive ending: -in), e.g., arslŋgin 'lion's', aṇḥučin 'hunter's, hunting'. The relational meaning of converted adjectives goes also back to genitives in -i, e.g., nasni 'related to age' or -in, e.g., buuḥin 'related to a rifle', bulgin in bulgin usn 'spring water', aratin in aratin-sùl 'fox tail'. Conversion of the genitive is also found in adjectives, denoting a temporal relation according to the meaning of their base, e.g., agčmin 'minute-long' (← agčmin 'moment, minute-GEN'), ashni 'related to the evening'. Some adjectives are converted from nominal genitive forms in -a/-ǎ, e.g., cergǎ 'related to army, military'.

When comparing the results of conversion and derivation, we can observe a parallelism of two processes: a) conversion (transition of participles and oblique case forms into other parts of speech), and b) suffixal formation of new words in analogy to the "products" of conversion. The noun uhan 'mind, intellect' in the instrumental case uhata 'with intellect', for instance, has become adjectivized in the meaning 'clever'. In analogy to this form, new adjectives are derived with the suffix -ta/-tǎ.

Despite the possibility of adjectivization, the comitative form with the inflectional ending -ta/-tǎ and the denominal word-formation type with the suffix -ta/-tǎ are sometimes regarded as homonyms, cf. also medǎtǎ (N.COMIT) 'with knowledge' and medǎtǎ (A) 'knowledgable, experienced'. Their difference is obvious in semantics, morphology, word-formation, syntax, and syntagmatics: The noun denotes an object and is characterized by the grammatical categories of number and case, e.g., medǎt-nr (nom. pl.) 'people with knowledge; experienced, senior people', while the adjective medǎtǎ refers to a quality and is grammatically characterized by its non-declensional character. The former can be the subject of a sentence while the latter is an attribute; the noun cannot be combined with the suffix -vr whereas the adjective combines with it to form the qualitative adjective medǎtǎ-vr 'very advanced in years'.

5.3 Adverbial conversion

Adverbialization is a way of forming adverbs by converting nouns, nominalized adjectives in oblique cases, and adverbial participles (gerunds).

Adverbs can be converted, for instance, from nouns in the instrumental case: *durarn* 'voluntarily, freely' (← *durarn* (instr.) 'of one's own free will' ← *durn* (nom.) 'will, wish'), *zôrgắr* 'of one's own will' (← *zôrgắr* 'with will, wish' ← *zôrg* (nom.) 'will, wish'), or elative case: *dundas* 'from inside' (← *dundas* 'from middle position' ← *dund* (nom.) 'middle position'), *dotras* 'from within' (← *dotras* 'from the inside' ← *dotr* (nom.) 'the inside').

According to their semantics, converted adverbs are grouped into
a) Qualitative adverbs: *tùrùḥắr* 'from hand to mouth' (← *tùrùḥắr* 'poverty' (instr.)), *ùlùḥắr* 'in abundance' (← *ùlùḥắr* (instr.) 'abundance');
b) Adverbs of manner: *hulhaḥắr* 'secretly' (← *hulhaḥắr* 'theft' (instr.)), *aṇginắr* 'in a beastly way' (← *aṇginắr* 'beast' (instr.));
c) Adverbs of degree: *zôvắr* 'rightfully' (← *zôvắr* 'right' (instr.));
d) Adverbs of time: *zunar* 'in summer' (← *èn zunar* 'this summer'), *ôdrắr* 'at daytime' (← *èn ôdrắr* 'this day');
e) Adverbs of place: *zahas* 'from the end, at the end' (← *èn zahas* 'from this end' (elat.)), *dotras* 'from inside' (← *èn dotras* 'from this internal part' (elat.)), etc.

Adverbs can also be converted from adverbial participles (gerunds) ending in *-ad/-ád*: *šamdad* 'quickly' (← *šamdad* 'hurrying' ← *šamd(h)*), *ḥắrglắd* 'in a silly, stupid way' (← *ḥắrglắd* 'being silly, becoming stupid' ← *ḥắrgl(h)*), *hurniḥắd* 'sadly' (← *hurniḥắd* 'being sad, in grief' ← *hurni(h)* 'to grieve, lament, sorrow'); or *-ž̧/-č̇*: *dắkž̧* 'again, again and again' (← *dắkž̧* 'repeating' ← *dắk(h)*).

6 Reduplication

Kalmyk nouns, adjectives and adverbs can be formed by reduplication. In some cases there is a correlation between the formation type of reduplicatives and their semantics.

Reduplicatives are based on the core vocabulary of Kalmyk, including a special group of descriptive and onomatopoeic units which refer to natural phenomena. A phonosemantic analysis of reduplicatives has shown that some of the phonetic changes in this lexis are associated with conveying sound images, e.g., *ivr-šivr* 'rustle' (← *ivr-ivr* 'swarm, e.g., of worms' + *šivr*, i.e. *ivr* is repeated with an additional sibilant [š]). However, most reduplicatives convey the meaning of collectives, singulatives, and intensity of a quality.

Reduplication involves sound interchanges, clipping and addition of sounds, e.g.,
a) Interchanges of the initial sound of the base with [m]: *šikr-mikr* 'sweets' (← *šikr* 'sugar'), *zaḥsn-maḥsn* 'all fish products' (← *zaḥsn* 'fish'); with [s]:

mahn-sahn 'meats' (← *mahn* 'meat'), *bah-sah* 'odds and ends' (← *bah* 'bit'); with [t]: *naku-taku* 'effort' (← *naku* 'effort'); with [d]: *šulun-dulun* 'fast and quick' (← *šulun* 'fast');
b) Vowel interchanges in the roots, e.g., *a-ù*: *barṇ-bùrṇ* 'darkness, dusk' (← *bùrṇ* 'darkness'); *a-u*: *taltṇ-tultṇ* 'wide' (← *taltṇ* 'wide'); *ắ-ù*: *zắrm-zùrm* 'some, few' (← *zắrm* 'some');
c) Clipping of sounds and sound combinations, e.g., *ildr-bildr* 'dishonest' (← *bildr* 'false'), *ilmn-žilmn* 'deserted, empty' (← *žilmn* 'open'), *cevr-cer* 'clean' (← *cevr* 'clean'), *zắŋg-zắ* 'news, rumors' (← *zăŋg* 'news, message');
d) Addition of sounds, e.g., *orm-morm* 'place, room' (← *orm* 'place'), *eṇ-hoṇ* 'whim' (← *eṇ* 'folly'), *ilv-žilv* 'trick, treachery' (← *ilv* 'magic'). Units such as *morm*, *hon*, *žilv* do not exist as free forms.

6.1 Nominal reduplication

Reduplicated nouns may be of the following types:
a) The first component is a non-derived noun, and the second repeats it with the initial sound changed, e.g., *mahn-sahn* 'meat and other meat products', *ŝikr-mikr* 'sugar and other sweet products';
b) The first component is a noun, and the second repeats it with an additional initial sound, e.g., *orm-morm* 'place', *ôṇ-hoṇ* 'complaint, whim';
c) The first component repeats the second one with a change of its root vowel, e.g., *barṇ-bùrṇ* 'darkness, dusk';
d) The second component is a clipped form of the first one, e.g., *zắŋg-zắ* 'news' (← *zăŋg* 'piece of news').

The reduplicated nouns express u n i t y, c o l l e c t i v i t y, p l u r a l i t y, e.g., *bah-sah* 'trifles', *mahn-sahn* 'meats', *ivr-šivr* 'rumors', *tasrha-tasarha* 'odds and ends', and others, e.g., *ilv-žilv* 'deception'.

6.2 Adjectival reduplication

According to their structure, reduplicated adjectives fall into the following types:
a) The second component repeats the first one with a change of its root vowel, e.g., *zắrm-zùrm* 'some, few' (← *zắrm* 'some'), *taltṇ-tultṇ* 'wide' (← *taltṇ* 'wide');
b) The second component repeats the first one with a change of its initial consonant, e.g., *šulun-dulun* 'fast, quick' (← *šulun* 'fast');

c) The first component repeats the second one with its initial consonant subtracted, e.g., *ildr-bildr* 'dishonest' (← *bildr* 'false'), *ilmn-žilmn* 'desolate' (← *žilmn* 'open');
d) The second component is derived from the first one, e.g., *săn-sǎǎhn* 'wonderful' (← *săn* 'good' + *sǎǎhn* 'pretty');
e) The first component is a clipped form of the second one, e.g., *ca-caḥan* 'whitest' (← *ca-* + *caḥan* 'white');
f) The second component is a clipped form of the first one, e.g., *cevr-cer* 'very clean' (← *cevr* 'clean' + *cer*).

Reduplicative adjectives denote a high degree of a quality (similar to the meaning of the superlative). The intensity of a quality is expressed if the base is repeated without phonetic changes or if it is partly shortened, e.g., *ut-ut* 'longest' (← *ut* 'long'), *hatu-hatu* 'hardest' (← *hatu* 'hard'), *cevr-cer* 'very clean' (← *cevr* 'clean'), etc. The meaning of intensification can be accompanied by a certain generalization of features which sums up semantically related qualities, cf. *šulun-dulun* '(very) lively, agile' (← *šulun* 'fast, quick' + *dulun*), *ildr-bildr* 'dishonest' (← *ildr* + *bildr* 'false'), *ilmn-žilmn* 'desolate' (← *ilmn* 'open' + *žilmn*), where *dulun, ildr, žilmn* and other similar repetitions are formal indicators of the above mentioned generalization.

6.3 Adverbial reduplication

In terms of their structure reduplicated adverbs may be of the following types:
a) The first component is a non-derived adverb, the second one repeats it, e.g., *salu-salu* 'separately' (← *salu* 'individually, separaely'), *onc-onc* 'separately, one by one' (← *onc* 'single, specific');
b) The second component repeats the first one with its initial sound subtracted and the root vowel changed, e.g., *buzr-azr* 'dirty' (← *buzr* 'dirty');
c) The first component is a clipped form of the second, e.g., *gev-gentkn* 'suddenly' (← *gentkn* 'suddenly');
d) The second component is derived from the first one, e.g., *daru-darun'* 'after, one after another' (← *daru* 'after' + *darun'* 'then, after'), *dara-daraḥar* 'in order, steadily' (← *dara* 'order' + *daraḥar* 'steadily').

The meaning of reduplicative adverbs can differ from their bases insofar as it tends to be of a more particular character, e.g., *salu-salu* 'separately from each other' (← *salu* 'separately (in a general sense)', *onc-onc* 'each in its (separate) place' (← *onc* 'separately' (without specification)).

Reduplicative adverbs denote a high degree of the quality (manner) in which an action is performed: *cevr-cer* 'very neatly, tidily, cleanly' (← *cevr* 'cleanly, tidily'); indefinite expressions of time, e.g., *kezǎ-âza* 'once' (← *kezǎ* 'when'); unspecified expressions of place + intensification, e.g., *ca-caaran* 'farther and farther' (← *caaran* 'farther'), and frequency, intensification: *haâ-haâ* 'seldom-seldom', *dǎkn-dǎkn* 'many times' (← *dǎkn* 'another time, again'), *baahn-baahn* 'just a bit, very little' (← *baahn* 'a little'), etc.

7 References

Ârceva, Viktoriâ N. (ed.) (1990): *Lingvističeskij ènciklopedičeskij slovar'*. Moskva: Sovetskaâ Ènciklopediâ.
Badmin Bata (1959): *Xaľmg kelnǎ učebnik*. Part 1: *Xùv. Fonetik boln morfolog*. Èlst: Chaľmg degtr ḥar ḥač.
Bauer, Laurie (2004): *A Glossary of Morphology*. Edinburgh: Edinburgh University Press.
Bloomfield, Leonard (1968): *Language*. Moscow: Progress.
Bobrovnikov, Aleksej A. (1849): *Grammatika mongoľsko-kalmyckogo âzyka*. Kazan': Universitetskaâ tipografiâ.
Kotvič, Vladislav L. (1929): *Opyt grammatiki kalmyckogo razgovornogo âzyka*. Rževnice u Pragi: Izdanie Komissii Kuľturnyh rabotnikov v Čehoslovenskoj Respublike.
Krueger, John R. (1975): *The Kalmyk-Mongolian Vocabulary in Stralenberg's Geography of 1730*. Stockholm: Almqvist & Wiksell.
Marouzeau, Jules [Maruzo, Ž.] (1960): *Slovar' lingvističeskih terminov*. Perevod s francuzskogo N. D. Andreeva pod red. A. A Reformatskogo. Moskva: Izdateľstvo inostrannoj literatury.
Nominhanov, Ceren-Dordži (1976): *Očerk istorii kalmyckoj pis'mennosti*. Moskva: Nauka.
Pavlov, Dorij A. (2000): *Voprosy istorii i strojâ kalmyckogo literaturnogo âzyka*. Èlista: Kalmyckij gosudarstvennyj universitet.
Popov, Aleksandr V. (1847): *Grammatika kalmyckogo âzyka*. Kazan': Universitetskaâ tipografiâ.
Pûrbeev, Georgij C. (1971): Funkcionaľnoe čeredovanie zvukov v mongoľskih âzykah. *Voprosy âzykoznaniâ* 3: 89–93.
Ramstaedt, Gustav J. (1935): *Kalmückisches Wörterbuch*. Helsinki: Suomalais-Ugrilainen Seura.
Sanžeev, Garma D. (ed.) (1983): *Grammatika kalmyckogo âzyka. Fonetika i morfologiâ*. Èlista: Kalmyckoe knižnoe izdateľstvo.
Stralenberg, Philipp J. von (1730): *Das Nord- Und Ostliche Theil Von Europa Und Asia: In So Weit Solches Das Ganze Rußische Reich Mit Siberien Und Der Grossen Tatarey in Sich Begreiffet, in Einer Historisch-Geographischen Beschreibung*. Stockholm: In Verlegung des Autoris.
Suseeva, Danara A. (1978): *Zakonomernosti razvitiâ kalmyckogo âzyka v sovetskuû èpochu. Razvitie slovoobrazovaniâ*. Èlista: Kalmizdat.
Suseeva, Danara A. (1994): *Slovoobrazovanie častej reči v russkom i kalmyckom âzykah*. Èlista: Kalmyckij gosudarstvennyj universitet.
Suseeva, Danara A. (1995): *Školʹnyj slovar' morfem kalmyckogo âzyka*. Èlista: Kalmyckij gosudarstvennyj universitet.
Suseeva, Danara A. (1997): *Slovoobrazovateľnyj slovar' kalmyckogo âzyka*. Èlista: Kalmyckoe knižnoe izdateľstvo.

Suseeva, Danara A. (1998): *Kontrastivnaâ grammatika kalmyckogo i mongol'skogo âzykov. Morfologiâ. Morfonologiâ.* Èlista: Kalmyckij gosudarstvennyj universitet.
Švedova, Natal'â Û. (ed.) (1970): *Grammatika sovremennogo russkogo literaturnogo âzyka.* Moskva: Nauka.
Todaeva, Bulâš H. (1976): *Opyt lingvističeskogo izučeniâ èposa "Džangar".* Èlista: Kalmyckoe knižnoe izdatel'stvo.
Vladimircov, Boris Â. (1929): *Sravnitel'naâ grammatika mongol'skogo pis'mennogo âzyka i chalchasskogo narečiâ.* Leningrad: Izdatel'stvo Leningradskogo Vostočnogo Instituta.
Wälchli, Bernhard (2025): Co-compounds. In: Peter O. Müller, Susan Olsen and Franz Rainer (eds.), *Word-Formation – Special Patterns and Restrictions*, 145–169. Berlin/Boston: De Gruyter Mouton.
Witsen, Nicolaes (1705 [1692]): *Noord en Oost Tartarye.* Amsterdam: Halma.

Viacheslav A. Chirikba
23 Abkhaz

1 Introduction
2 General overview
3 Composition
4 Derivation
5 Conversion
6 Reduplication
7 Neoclassical word-formation
8 Other types of word-formation
9 References

Abstract: To create new words, Abkhaz uses practically limitless resources of both compounding and affixation, as well as of their combination. Compounding is a dominant means of word-formation across the parts of speech. In verb formation prefixation is prevalent, while suffixation plays a modest role. In the derivation of other word classes suffixation is more prominent. Reduplication is a common mechanism in verb and adverb formation, but it is only modestly represented in noun formation. Another usual means to form new words is conversion. Neoclassical word-formation in Abkhaz is prefixal.

1 Introduction

Abkhaz, together with its sister languages Abaza, Circassian (i.e. Adyghe and Kabardian, regarded as separate languages, see Lander 2016 and Matasović 2016) and extinct Ubykh form the Western branch of the North-Caucasian language family, its Eastern branch being represented by such languages as Chechen, Ingush, Avar, Lezgi, Tabasaran, Lak, Dargwa, Udi, etc. Abkhaz is spoken mainly in Abkhazia and in Turkey. Smaller Abkhaz communities are scattered over some Middle East countries and Western Europe.

Abkhaz has three dialects: Abzhywa, Bzyp and Sadz; Ahchypsy and Tsabal represent two additional (sub)dialects; of all these, only Abzhywa and Bzyp are preserved in Abkhazia, the rest are spoken now only in Turkey. Sadz is the most divergent of all the dialects. The number of Abkhaz speakers in Abkhazia is

Viacheslav A. Chirikba, Moscow, Russia

122,069, according to the 2011 population census. The number of speakers in the diaspora (mainly in Turkey) is estimated as being between 200,000 and 500,000.

Abkhaz acquired its written form around the middle of the 19th century, and has since managed to create a rich literature, having developed various genres and styles. The creation of a literary language and the need to invent masses of new terms catering to the ever increasing cultural needs of the Abkhaz society has given rise to extensive coining of new words and the exploitation of the available means of word-formation. The main chronological stages of this new tendency can be subdivided in three periods: 1. the second part of the 19th century and the beginning of the 20th century saw the publication of the first ABC textbooks (starting from 1865), containing both original and translated texts, numerous translations of Christian texts from Russian (starting from 1866), the publication of first literary works (starting from 1912 with pieces by Dyrmit Gulia), the working out of orthographic norms, as well as the choice of a dialectal base; 2. from 1921 until approximately 1940, the modernization of the early Soviet period resulted in a wealth of newly-coined words expressing new notions and realities; 3. the post-Soviet period (from 1992 on), which has been marked by the need to create new terminology and stylistic norms necessary for the official language of the Republic of Abkhazia in various domains such as education, science, government and politics.

2 General overview

Word-formation in Abkhaz has been the subject of studies by Kvarčelija (1953), Šinkuba (1956, 2008 [written in 1945]), Šakryl (1961), Gabunija (1971, 1985), Kaslandzia (1976, 1998), Xecija (1988), Čkadua (2005), Klyčeva (2009), Amičba (2010); it is also discussed in the relevant chapters of grammatical descriptions of Abkhaz, such as in *Grammatika abxazskogo jazyka* (1968: 45–48, 51–52, 160, 185–188), Hewitt (1979: 242–255), Chirikba (2003: 26–29, 31–32, 54–55, 56), among others.

As other languages of the North-Western branch of the North-Caucasian language family, Abkhaz is an agglutinative polysynthetic language characterized by extensive prefixation and moderate suffixation. The verbal system is extremely complex, occupying the central part of the grammar, in sharp contrast with the modestly developed nominal morphology. The verb can contain a dozen or so prefixes (expressing agreement, aspect, location and directionality), each occupying a rigidly fixed slot in the verbal template. Verbs formally distinguish between finite and non-finite forms. Being an ergative language and lacking overt nominal cases, Abkhaz, unlike its sister languages, realizes its ergative vs. absolutive strategy solely by means of the order of prefixed agreement markers. Another idiosyncratic feature of Abkhaz that sets it apart from Circassian and Ubykh is the presence of gender and/or class distinctions on verbal agreement markers, possessive prefixes, numerals and some pronouns.

The process of word-coinage is still active in connection with the expanding functions of Standard Abkhaz as a state language. To produce new words, Abkhaz uses practically limitless resources of both compounding and affixation, also in combination. Neoclassical word-formation in Abkhaz is based exclusively on prefixation.

Another derivational means is conversion. A specific feature of Abkhaz is the weak categorial distinction between verbs and nouns, nouns and adjectives, adjectives and adverbs, which allows for their easy incorporation into a paradigm belonging to another word class.

Abkhaz has many monosyllabic roots, so that the compounds are relatively short. On the other hand, the language abounds in words produced by long strings of morphemes, e.g., the noun *a-gʷ.a.bzəja.ra.čʲapá.r.ta* 'sanatorium' (7 morphemes) and the deverbal adjective *j.áj.c.rə.də.r.kʼə.la.xʲa.w* '(one which is) generally accepted' (10 morphemes). New morphemes are added at the edge of the base: *a-tʼʷə́* 'possession' → *a-tʼʷə́.la* 'country' → *a-tʼʷə́.la.wajʷ* 'citizen' → *a-tʼʷə́.la.wajʷ.ra* 'citizenship' → *a-tʼʷə́.la.wajʷ.ra.da (jə́.qʼa.w)* '(being) stateless' → *a-tʼʷə́.la.wajʷ.ra.da.ra* 'statelessness' → *a-tʼʷə́.la.wajʷ.ra.da.ra.tʼʷ* 'pertaining to statelessness' → *a-tʼʷə́.la.wajʷ.ra.da.ra.tʼʷ-kʷa* 'those pertaining to statelessness' → *a-tʼʷə́.la.wajʷ.ra.da.ra.tʼʷ-kʷa-gʲə* 'and those pertaining to statelessness'.

In compounds the stress can fall either on one of the constituent parts (e.g., *a-lakʼ=jʷák'-ra* 'to hesitate; lit. taking down-taking up'), or on both, especially when the compound represents a somewhat looser unit (e.g., *ájšʷa=čʲára* 'feast; lit. table-eating'). A common phonological process involved in compounding is the elision of the final unstressed vowel before the onset of the second constituent, e.g., *a-x=a-čʼə́* 'face' (← *a-xə́* 'head', *a-čʼə́* 'mouth'), *a-gʷar=bžʲára* 'side street' (← *a-gʷára* 'yard', *a-bžʲára* 'between'), etc.

For the sake of economy I shall not gloss in this article the definite-generic article *a-*. Furthermore, in cases when the root contains the initial vowel (*a-*), I do not mark the presence of the definite-generic article (i.e. [*a-*]*a*...). I use the hyphen (-) to mark the article (*a-*), the masdar suffix (*-ra*), or the plural marker, the equal sign (=) to divide the constituents of a compound, and a period (.) to mark a morpheme boundary. Non-self-explanatory abbreviations are explained at the end of the article.

3 Composition

Compounding is a productive means of word-formation across the parts of speech. Stems which create a compound can be simplex or complex. Complex stems can be compound, derived, or a combination of both compounding and derivation. Binary compounds are formed by the combination of two stems, e.g., *á-wrəs=šʷa* 'the Russian language; lit. Russian-speech'. Multi-stem compounds are formed by three or more stems, e.g., *a-bəz.šʷa=də́r.ra* 'linguistics; lit. language [tongue-speech]-know-ABSTR'. In writing the compounds can appear as a single word (e.g., *a-sáxʲa=təxjʷə* 'artist', from *a-sáxʲa* 'picture' and *təxjʷə* 'one who takes off'), as a hyphenated binary unit (e.g., *áwra=á-tbaara* 'body-build, figure', from *áwra* 'height' and *á-tbaara* 'breadth'), or as a combination of two or more words (e.g., *latʾʷarádatʾʷəj a-rc'ará* 'distance learning', *a-tʾʷə́lawajʷratʾʷ tagə́lazaašʲa a-nc'árta* 'registry office').

Compounds can be endocentric, i.e. contain the head within the compound itself, or exocentric. Examples of endocentric compounds are: *a-mšə́n=ʒ(ə)* 'sea-water', *a-msə́r=kʲaad* 'parchment; lit. Egypt-paper', *á-ga=pša* 'sea wind; lit. shore-wind'. Examples of exocentric compounds: *a-dərgan=c'ə́xʷa* 'wagtail (a kind of bird); lit. griddle-tail', *a-cgʷə́=xš* 'spurge, euphorbia (a kind of plant); lit. cat-milk', *a-dʷə́=yba* 'train; lit. field-ship', *á-žʷ=ləmha* 'hound's-tongue, Cynoglossum (a kind of plant); lit. cow-ear', etc.

3.1 Nominal compounds

There are various ways of describing nominal compounds. I take here as the point of departure the classification proposed by Bisetto and Scalise (2009), who classify compounds according to the nature of the semantic relation obtaining between their components as subordinate, attributive or coordinate.

3.1.1 Subordinate compounds

The relationship within subordinate compounds can be formulated as 'the X of the Y', e.g., *a-žʷ=xš* 'cow-milk = the milk of the cow', *a-kəta=nxámjʷa* 'agriculture = the economy of the village', etc.

Subordinate N+N compounds are right-headed. Structurally they are of the following sub-types:

a) simplex noun + simplex noun: *a-wasá=xʲčʲa* 'shepherd; lit. sheep-shepherd', *á-mca=bz* 'flame; lit. fire-tongue', *a-ʒʲa=psá* 'salary; lit. labour-price', *a-sə́s=cʷa* 'lamb skin', *ajxá=mjʷa* 'railway; lit. iron-road', *á-žʷ=k'ambašʲ* 'cow-buffalo'. Incidentally, in the latter case a variant exists with the reverse order of constituents: *a-k'ambášʲ=a-žʷ*, lit. 'buffalo-cow'. The presence of the definite-generic article in the second part of this compound suggests that the latter, unlike *á-žʷ=k'ambašʲ*, should be analyzed as a coordinate/dvandva compound, rather than a subordinate one.

b) simplex noun + compound noun: *a-kəta=nxámjʷa* 'agriculture; lit. village=household', *a-bzá=lapš* 'evil eye of a live person; lit. alive-evil eye', *a-x=apôc* 'tooth; lit. head-front tooth';

c) simplex noun + derived noun: *a-q'arma=c'ə̂.s* 'nightingale; lit. hop-bird [bird-DIM.SUF]', *a-k'aléj=t.šʲ.jʷə* 'tinsmith; lit. tin-who tins', *a-mšə́n=kʷə.lajʷ* 'pirate; lit. sea-attacker', *á-xaa=čʲə.s* 'pastry; lit. sweet-food'; for the last example, cf. *a-čʲə̂.s=xaa* 'sweet food', where *xaa* is adjective;

d) compound noun + simplex noun: *a-čə̂.bya=q'aza* 'master of horse-riding; lit. horse back=master', *a-x.a.čˈ=sáxʲa* 'face, image; lit. face-picture', *á-la.pš=tʷhʷa* 'spell/charm against the evil eye; lit. evil eye=spell';

e) compound noun + compound noun: *a-fə̂.mca=dʷə.yba* 'electric train; lit. electricity [lightning-fire]=train [field-ship]);

f) compound noun + derived noun: *a-taʒ.šʷá=q'a.c'a.jʷ* 'quarrel-maker; lit. home-speech= PREV+do-AGENT.SUF', *áb.ayʲ=ʒə.s* 'male goatling; lit. goat-semen=goatling-DIM';

g) derived noun + simplex noun: *á-hasab.ra=šʷq'ʷə* 'maths textbook; lit. count-ABSTR=book', *a-k'ʲə́pxʲ.ga=mašʲəna* 'type-writer; lit. instrument of typing=machine';

h) derived noun + compound noun: *á-ž.ra=xə.kʷ* 'ditchbank; lit. ditch=edge above sth.';

i) derived noun + derived noun: *a-gʷə̂.m.bəl=ǯʲbara.ra* 'cruelty; lit. heart-NEG-burn=hard-ABSTR', *a-bəz.šʷa=də̂r.ra* 'linguistics; lit. language [tongue-speech]= knowledge [know-ABSTR]', *a-wə̂.s=wə.ra* 'work, labour; lit. work=do-ABSTR'.

[N+V]ₙ compounds are exocentric and represent the combination of a noun with the pure stem of the verb. They have the following structures:

a) simplex noun + simplex verb: *á-la=pš* 'view; lit. eye-look', *a-čˈ=k'ə̂* 'catching disease; lit. mouth-catch';

b) simplex noun + derived verb: *a-c'la=r.k'ʷə̂kʷ* 'woodpecker; lit. tree=CAUS-split', *ážʷa=p.q'a* 'proverb; lit. word-cut', *a-šʷq'ʷə=n.c'á* 'certificate; lit. document=write down';

c) compound noun + simplex verb: *a-fə̂.mca=nəq'ʷa* 'electric locomotive; lit. electricity [lightning-fire]=walk';

d) derived noun + simplex verb: *a-gʷ.ta=kʼə́* 'wish, venture; lit. heart-inside=catch';
e) derived noun + derived verb: *a-cʷ.kʷə=r̥.pá* 'wave; lit. top [skin-top]=CAUS-jump', *a-wə.t.ra=tə́.x* 'vegetables; lit. kitchen-garden=take off'.

[V+N]_N compounds are not numerous: *a-psšʲá=xa* 'time for rest; lit. to rest=time for', *á-mdər=págʲara* 'haughty ignoramus; lit. not know=haughtiness', etc.

Though asyndetic N+N subordinate compounding is more usual, there are also **possessive compounds**, i.e. compounds containing possessive person and (if in the singular) gender prefixes which function as infixes. Such compounds are left-headed, e.g., *a-pa=j-pá* 'grandson; lit. son=his-son', *a-pha=l-pá* 'grandson; lit. daughter=her-son', *áb=j-ašʲa* 'paternal uncle; lit. father=his-brother', *án=l-ahʷšʲa* 'maternal aunt; lit. mother=her-sister', *án=l-ašʲa-j-pha* 'maternal niece; lit. mother=her-brother-his-daughter', *a-nap'=á-xʷda* 'wrist; lit. hand=its-neck', *šʲəbžʲ=a-gʷə* 'noon; lit. noon=its-heart', *a-šʲxa=r-án* 'queen bee; lit. bee=their-mother', *á-šʲxa=rə-wa* 'mountaineer; lit. mountain=their-people', *a-ləmha=rə́-jʷ* 'earring; lit. ear=their-*metal', *a-t'ʷə=jə-t'ʷə́.x* 'slave of the slave; lit. slave=his-slave'. In the case of *án=šʲa* 'maternal uncle', the nature of the compound can still be regarded as being in a possessive relation ('mother-[*her]-brother'), even though possession is not explicitly expressed.

3.1.2 Attributive compounds

Attributive compounds contain a modifier and an explicit (in endocentric compounds) or implicit (in exocentric compounds) head. The [N+A]_N, [Adv+V]_N and [N+Quant]_N compounds are left-headed, the other structural types – [A+N]_N, [Pro+N]_N and [Quant+N]_N – are right-headed.

In [N+A]_N compounds A is usually represented by a primary, i.e. non-derived adjective, though derived ones also occur. Structurally these compounds can be of the following types:
a) simplex noun + simplex adjective: *á-mza=čʼa* 'young moon; lit. moon-young', *á-mat=apšʲ* 'red snake; lit. snake-red', *a-mjʷa=də́w* 'main road; lit. road-big', *a-tʷ=áʒa* 'forage; lit. hay-raw', *a-nášʷ=apšʲ* 'clay; lit. earth-red', *án=xʷa* 'mother-in-law; lit. mother-crooked';
b) simplex noun + derived adjective (negated deverbal adjective): *a-wál=m.šʷa* 'defaulter; debt=NEG-pay', *a-ps=tá.m* 'nitrogen; lit. soul=inside-NEG';
c) compound noun + simplex adjective: *á-la.pš=xaa* 'tender look; lit. look [eye-look]=sweet', *a-gʷə́.c'=ápšʲ* 'surmullet (a kind of fish); lit. heart-under=red';

d) derived noun + compound adjective: *a-čʲɘmaza.ra=č'.k'ɘ* 'catching desease; lit. desease=mouth catching';
e) derived noun + derived adjective: *a-ra.šɘ́=m.c'aa* 'unsalted walnut butter; lit. walnut butter=NEG-salty', *a-sɘ́.s=m.q'aa* 'silent lamb; lit. lamb=NEG-cry'.

In [A+N]ₙ compounds the attribute is represented by a primary or derived adjective. Those containing a non-derived adjective are not numerous: *a-baa=psɘ́* 'bad; lit. rotten-soul', *a-baa=fjʷɘ́* 'bad smell; lit. rotten-smell', *a-bzá=k'ap'an* 'live weight', *á-xaa=čʲɘ.s* 'pastry; lit. sweet-food', etc. Compounds containing a derived adjective are much more common and can be written either a) as one word, or b) as two words. Examples of a): *a-t'ʷɘ́.m=wajʷɘ* 'foreigner; lit. not belonging=man', *a-t'ʷɘ́.m=dgʲɘl* 'foreign country', *a-xa.t'ʷ=psá* 'net cost; lit. own-price', *a-xa.t'ʷ=k'rít'ik'a* 'self-criticism'. Examples of b): *ajxa.t'ʷɘ́ cha* 'iron bridge', *a-xʲ.t'ʷɘ́ macʷáz* 'golden ring', *a-ok'eánnɘrcʷ.t'ʷɘj*, *a-t'ʷɘ́la* 'oversea(s)', *lat'ʷaráda.t'ʷɘj a-st'udént* 'correspondence student', etc.

[Adv+V]ₙ compounds: *(a-)mala=k'ráfa* 'parasite, sponger; lit. gratis-eat', *a-mala=náq'ʷa* 'bicycle; lit. by itself-walk', *znɘk'=xʲara* 'one milk yield; lit. once-milking', *á-šʲtaxʲ=ažʷa* 'afterword', *apxʲa=gɘ́la* 'leader; lit. at front=stand'.

[Pro+N]ₙ compounds: *a-xála=rc'aga* 'teach-yourself book; lit. self=teaching instrument', *a-xata=psá* 'cost price; lit. own=cost'.

[Quant+N]ₙ compounds: *a-jʷɘ́=maa* 'a kind of harp; lit. two-handle', *a-pšʲá=ša* 'Thursday; lit. the fourth-day', *a-x=šʲap'ɘ́* 'tripod; lit. three-leg', *á-jʷ=bɘzšʷara* 'bilingualism; lit. two=language-ness'.

[N+Quant]ₙ compounds: *a-mš-jʷɘnjʷažʷa* 'funeral repast on the fortieth day; lit. day=forty', *á-rmʒaa=zejžʷ* 'innumerable number of soldiers; lit. army-not disappearing=nineteen', *a- gʷɘ́=jʷbara* 'suspicion, doubt, duplicity; lit. heart=doubleness'.

3.2 Coordinate (dvandva) compounds

In this type of compound both members are hierarchically equal and represent two semantic heads. Coordinate compounds can be formed asyndetically by simple juxtaposition of roots, or be linked by one or more coordinating particles.

3.2.1 Coordinate N+N compounds

Asyndetic examples: *a-šʷága=zága* 'measure, criterion; lit. size measurer=measurer', *a-xaára=bzaára* 'benefit, good; lit. sweetness=aliveness', *ájmak'=ájč'ak'* 'dispute; lit. quarrel=kindling', *á-jʷada=mratašʷára* 'north-west; lit. upwards=sunset'.

Coordinate N+N compounds can also be formed with the help of coordinating conjunctions -j(ə), -j(ə)-j(ə), -gʲə-gʲə: Examples: a-čʲe-j=ǯak'a 'hospitality feast; lit. bread-and=salt', a-cʷá-j=žʲ 'body; lit. skin-and=flesh', gá-j=šʲxá-j 'everywhere; lit. coast-and=mountain-and', ánə-j=abə-j 'parents; lit. mother-and=father-and', wax-gʲə́=čən-gʲə 'twenty-four hours; lit. night-time-and=day-time-and'.

Less closely-knit coordinate compounds have both parts stressed and marked for definiteness: a-gʷə́la=á-zla 'close neighbour; lit. neighbour-close', a-x[ə]=a-čʲə́ 'face; lit. head-mouth', á-fat'ʷ=á-žʷt'ʷ 'food, supply; lit. food-drink', á-wa=a-tənxá 'close relative; lit. relative-relative'. In cases like á-ʒra=a-psrá 'death, destruction; lit. disapperance-death', á-fara=á-žʷra 'feast; lit. eat-drink', a-jʷrá=á-pxʲara 'literacy; lit. writing-reading' there is a typical lack of clear differentiation between the verbal noun (suffix -ra) and abstract noun (also suffix -ra), which means that the compound can be equally interpreted as V+V. In the dictionaries the entries with masdars are often followed by their homonymic nominal counterparts (e.g., a-də́r-ra 'to know; lit. knowing'; a-də́r.ra 'knowledge').

Some such compounds can fluctuate between a looser (when both parts are marked for definiteness) or a tighter form, cf. a-šʷq'ʷə=a-bəyʲšʷə́//a-šʷq'ʷə́=bəyʲšʷə́ 'documents and papers', á-hatər=á-p'at'əw̌//á-hatər=p'at'əw 'honour, respect', a-cʷá=a-žʲə́//a-cʷá-j=žʲ 'body', á-fara=á-žʷrá//á-fara=žʷra 'feast; lit. eating-drinking', etc. A subset of these less closely-bound copulative compounds represent alliterative words with the replacement of the initial consonant in the second constituent (see section 6 on echo-reduplication): á-raxʷ=a-šʷaxʷ 'various cattle' (← á-raxʷ 'cattle'), a-mál=a-šʲál 'wealth, possessions' (← a-mál 'wealth'), etc.

3.2.2 Coordinate [V+V]_N compounds

Examples: a-náj=aaj 'visitors; lit. go-come', wə-najšʲ=w-aajšʲ (zərhʷawá) 'respected person; lit. (about whom they say) you.MASC-please go=you.MASC-please come', wə-hʷan=s-hʷán 'rumour; lit. you.MASC-say-PIDF=I-say-PIDF', á-q'am=janə́m 'tall tale; lit. be-NEG=it-be on-NEG', a-naga=jʷága 'transportation; lit. thither-carry=upwards-carry'. Here the underlying verbal forms represent imperatives (wə-najšʲ=w-aajšʲ), past indefinite forms (wə-hʷan=s-hʷán), negative present tense forms (jə́q'am=janə́m), or a combination of pure stems (a-naga=jʷága).

3.2.3 Appositive nominal coordinate compounds

The constituent parts of these compounds contain different descriptions of the same referent or event. They are of various structural types:

a) [N+N]ₙ: *á-byamq'ʷ=xač'sakʷ* 'lazy fop; lit. not bending back=face with powder on', *á-mca=šawra* 'fever; lit. fire-heat', *á-ʒra=a-psrá* 'death, destruction; lit. disappearance-death';
b) [A+A]ₙ: *má.m.gʷ.dəw=čə.r.bá.q'ʲant'az* 'one who tries to look rich, but is in fact very poor; lit. have-NEG-heart-big=REFL-CAUS-see-naked';
c) [V+A]ₙ: *á-c'a.šʲəc=c'a.baa* 'envious person; lit. below-envy=below-rotten';
d) [V+V]ₙ: *a-zə́mha=zə́mc'a* 'tubby person; lit. not growing=who is not learning'.

3.3 Adjectival compounds

The following types of adjectival compounds occur: [N+A]ₐ, [N+V]ₐ, [A+A]ₐ, [V+V]ₐ.

a) [N+A]ₐ compounds: *žʷa=žʷálat'ʷəj (ájtaga)* 'literal (translation)', *ájlərk'aaga=də́rratarat'ʷ (wə́sšʷq'ʷəjʷəra)* 'reference-information (document)', *a-lada=mragálarat'ʷəj (a-pšá)* 'south-eastern (wind)';
b) [N+V]ₐ compounds: *a-gʷə́=mbəl* 'heartless, cruel; lit. heart=NEG.burn', *á-ma=rja* 'easy; lit. hand=CAUS.lie', *a-gʷ=k'ə́* 'nice; lit. heart-catch', *a-č'=k'ə́* 'nice; lit. mouth-catch';
c) [A+A]ₐ compounds: *(a-byʲə́) q'ʲáq'ʲa=xʷxʷa-kʷá* 'prolonged (leaves); lit. (leaf) flat=prolonged-PL', *a-psə́.m=bza.m* 'more dead than alive; lit. dead-NEG=alive-NEG', *ápswa=á-wrəs (žʷar)* 'Abkhaz-Russian (dictionary)'; unlike the former examples, the last one represents a less tightly-knit unit with both parts independently marked for definiteness and stress. There are also appositive adjectival echo compounds, with a meaningless second part, e.g., *a-bža.m=čá.m* 'unfinished, half-made' (← *bža* 'half', *ča*?, *-m* NEG);
d) [V+V]ₐ compounds: *á-na.ʒa=[a]a.ʒa* 'tall, full-grown; lit. grown up=brought up'.

3.4 Verbal compounds

Verbal stem structure is represented by the following models: simplex root (*ca* 'to go'), compound root (*bzəja.ba* 'to love; lit. well-see'), derived root (*z.wə* 'for-do'), complex root (*q'a.c'a* 'to do, make', with preverb *q'a-* and root *c'a*), simplex root + extension (*pš.aa* 'to search', root *pš* 'to look' and extension *-aa*), complex root + extension (*tə.ž.aa* 'to undig', with preverb *tə-*, the root *ža* and extension *-aa*). The root/stem is usually represented by one phoneme or by a biphonemic combination (*a* 'to be', *k'(ə)* 'to catch', *šʲ(ə)* 'to kill', *ba* 'to see', *ga* 'to carry'), though more complex structures also occur. Sometimes a directional infix can be inserted into a complex stem structure, cf. $g^w.a.ta$ 'to notice; lit. PREV(heart)-DIRECT-give'.

Compounding in verb formation is somewhat less common than in noun formation. The following structures obtain: $[N+V]_V$ (nominal root + verbal root), $[Adv+V]_V$ (adverbial root + verbal root), $[V+V]_V$ (verbal root + verbal root). Besides, there are analytical verbal compounds containing a lexical verb and an auxiliary or light verb.

3.4.1 $[N+V]_V$ compounds

Examples: $a\text{-}t^wa\text{=}r.x\text{-}rá$ 'to mow; lit. hay-mowing', $a\text{-}k'onflík't'\text{=}q'a.c'a\text{-}ra$ 'to make conflict; lit. conflict-making', $á\text{-}q'ac'aš^ja\text{=}q'a.c'a\text{-}ra$ 'to copy, mimic; lit. manner of doing=do', $ač^já\text{=}š^wa\text{-}ra$ 'to hunt quails; lit. quail-hunting'. This model can be regarded as representing incorporation.

Analytical $[N+V]_V$ compounds usually make use of such auxiliaries as $a\text{-}w\text{-}rá$ 'to do, prepare', $a\text{-}z.wə\text{-}rá$ 'to make for sb.', $a\text{-}ga\text{-}rá$ 'to produce sound', $á\text{-}ta\text{-}ra$ 'to give'; e.g., $a\text{-}bə́sta\ a\text{-}w\text{-}rá$ 'to prepare maize pap; lit. maize pap-preparing', $a\text{-}cənx^wrá\ a\text{-}z.wə\text{-}rá$ 'to compensate; lit. compensation doing-for', $a\text{-}zzəbž^jə́\ a\text{-}ga\text{-}rá$ 'to buzz; lit. buzz-voice sounding', $a\text{-}hámta\ á\text{-}ta\text{-}ra$ 'to give a present'. Examples of other auxiliary verbs: $a\text{-}bibliot'ék'a\ áj.k^wə.r.š^wa\text{-}ra$ 'to make up a library; lit. library-compiling', $a\text{-}xbaj^wlašá\ á\text{-}c'əs\text{-}ra$ 'to contuse; lit. brain shaking', $á\text{-}lj^wak'\ a\text{-}xə́.l.c'\text{-}ra$ 'to smoke; lit. sooth getting off', etc.

3.4.2 V+V compounds

Examples: $a\text{-}na.j\text{=}áa.j\text{-}ra$ 'to walk; lit. thither-go=hither-coming', $a\text{-}na.ga\text{=}áa.ga\text{-}ra$ 'to carry thither and hither'.

3.4.3 Appositive $[V+V]_V$ compounds

Examples: $áj.k^w.pa\text{-}ra\text{=}áj.s\text{-}ra$ 'to make a violent uproar' (both parts meaning 'to fight'), $a\text{-}š^wa\text{-}rá\text{=}a\text{-}za\text{-}rá$ 'to measure carefully' (both meaning 'to measure').

3.4.4 Analytical $[Adv+V]_V$ compounds

Examples: $jəbaapsnə́\ a\text{-}x.c^wá.ž^wa\text{-}ra$ 'to compromise; lit. badly talk over'), $a\text{-}k'ooperácijala\ a\text{-}č.áj.d.k'ə.la\text{-}ra$ 'to co-operate; lit. by cooperation assembling', etc.

3.5 Adverbial compounds

Most adverbs consisting of two lexical units are cases of reduplication (see section 6.3). Examples of true compounding are less numerous, cf. *jaxʲa=n.t'ʷá.ra.k'* 'the whole day; lit. today=LOC-sit-ABSTR-IDF', *wac'ʷ[ə]=á-šʲtaxʲ* 'day after tomorrow; lit. tomorrow=its-after', *arma=yʲərma* 'topsy-turvy, otherwise, contrariwise; lit. left-rightish', *nada=aadá* 'crosswise', *baša=malá* 'uselessly; lit. in vain=for nothing', *xara=byʲára* 'dispersedly' (← *xara* 'far'), *waxá=wac'ʷə́* 'these days, soon; lit. tonight-tomorrow', etc. Examples of appositive compounding: *gʷə́.k'=psə.k'.a.la* 'cordially; lit. heart-IDF=soul-IDF-its-by', *xə.la=gʷə́.la* 'in disorder, higgledy-piggledy; lit. by head, by heart'. The next pair of examples are based on the juxtaposition of words belonging to semantically opposite lexical units: *waxán.la=čán.la* 'twenty-four hours; lit. by night, by day', *xácʷa.la=hʷsa.la* 'all; lit. by men-by women'.

4 Derivation

4.1 Nominal derivation

4.1.1 Prefixation

Prefixation is rarely used in nominal derivation; among the few examples, cf. *á-z(ə).bža* 'half, one of the halves' (← *zə* 'one', *ábža* 'half'), *a-z.q'áza* 'master' (← *z-* BENF, *q'áza* 'master'), *a-cʷ.máčʲ.ra* 'deficiency; lit. DETR-small-ABSTR', etc.

4.1.2 Suffixation

Suffixation is quite a common means for deriving nouns from other nouns, verbs and adjectives. The most productive derivational suffixes are:
a) *-ar*, forming abstract nouns: *a-matʷ[a].ár* 'subject' (← *á-matʷa* 'clothes, things'), *ažʷ[a].ár* 'dictionary' (← *ážʷa* 'word'), *a-mz[a].ár* 'calendar' (← *á-mza* 'month');
b) *-ga*, forming deverbal nouns with instrumental meaning: *a-žə́.ga* 'shovel' (← *a-ž-rá* 'to dig'), *a-jʷə́.ga* 'pen' (← *a-jʷ-rá* 'to write');
c) *-jʷə*, mostly deverbal agent nouns: *a-ʒərjʷ.jʷə* 'listener' (← *á-ʒə.rjʷ-ra* 'to listen'), *a-bzə́jaba.jʷ* 'amateur' (← *a-bzə́ja.ba-ra* 'to love'), *a-yʲə́čʲ.jʷə* 'thief' (← *a-yʲə́čʲ-ra* 'to steal');

d) *-lə.x*, meaning '(product) made of': *a-lasa.lə́x* 'made of wool', *a-nap'.lə́x* 'needlework; lit. made by hand';
e) *-m.ta*, forming result nouns: *á-laga.mta* 'beginning' (← *á-la.ga-ra* 'to begin'), *a-nc'á.mta* 'note' (← *a-n.c'a-rá* 'to write down');
f) *-ra*, forming abstract nouns: *á-pšʒa.ra* 'beauty' (← *á-pšʒa* 'beautiful'), *a-nc'ə́.ra* 'lifetime' (← *a-n.c'-rá* 'to live a life'); the suffix is etymologically the same as the masdar suffix;
g) *-ra.x*, with the meaning 'result of': *a-maʒa.rá́x* 'something stolen' (← *á-maʒara* 'secrecy'), *a-pšaa.rá́x* 'something excellent, perfect' (← *á-pšaa.ra* 'to find');
h) *-r.ta*, forming place nouns: *a-tə́žʲə.rta* 'publishing house' (← *a-tə́.žʲ-ra* 'to publish'), *a-pssʲá.rta* 'place of rest' (← *a-ps.šʲá-ra* 'to have rest');
i) *-šʲa*, indicating 'manner of': *a-wajʷə́.šʲa* 'human quality' (← *a-wajʷə́* 'man, human'), *a-pstázaa.šʲa* 'way of life' (← *a-pstázaa.ra* 'life');
j) *-ta*, expressing 'location': *a-gʷ.tá* 'centre' (← *a-gʷə́* 'heart'), *á-šʲ.ta* 'trace' (← *šʲ-* 'foot');
k) *-t'ʷ(ə)*, an attributive suffix: *a-zc'aa.t'ʷə́* 'question, problem' (← *a-z.c'.aa-rá* 'to ask about'), *a-psaá.t'ʷ* 'bird' (cf. Abaza *pss.ɦa-ra* 'to fly');
l) *-wa*, an ethnic suffix: *áps.wa* 'Abkhazian', *ágər.wa* 'Megrelian';
m) *-xʷ*, denoting an object somehow related to the base (probably from *a-xʷə́* 'share, part'): *ážʷa.xʷ* 'speech' (← *ážʷa* 'word').

The following derivational suffixes are less productive:
a) *-c* 'single': *a-byʲə́.c* '(single) leaf' (← *a-byʲə́* 'leaf'), *a-dá.c* 'root' (← *a-dá* 'root');
b) *-nə.za* 'attached to': *a-mjʷa.nə́za* 'provisions' (← *á-mjʷa* 'road'), *a-ma.nə́za* 'shield' (< **ma* 'hand');
c) *-s* 'young N': *a-sə́.s* 'lamb', *a-hʷə́.s* 'calf', *árpə.s* 'young man';
d) *-s.pá//-z.ba* 'young, small N': *a-phʷə́.spá//a-phʷə́.zba* 'young woman' (cf. *a-phá* 'daughter'), *áhʷa.spá//áhʷa.zba* 'knife' (cf. *áhʷa* 'sword');
e) *-za*: *apə́.za* 'leader' (← *apə-* 'in front of'), *a-jʷə́.za* 'friend' (cf. *jʷ(ə)-* 'two'?), *a-xə́.za* 'blanket' (← *a-xə́* 'head').

4.1.3 Infixation

A rare example of infixation is the insertion of the negative particle *m(ə)*, according to the following models: a) N-NEG-N, b) N-NEG-V, e.g., a) *a-xac'a.m.phʷə́s* 'heroic woman; lit. man-NEG-woman', *a-šʲá.m.ašʷə.ga* 'garget, *Phytolacca americana*; lit. blood-NEG-paint-AGENT'; b) *čʲá.n.m.čʲa* 'late for dinner because of laziness; lit. time of eating-NEG-eat', etc.

4.2 Adjectival derivation

4.2.1 Prefixation

The few adjectival prefixes are the detrimental (malefactive) prefix *cʷə-* and the benefactive prefix *zə-* 'for', both expressing approximation of a quality: *a-cʷə́.š* 'grey, pale; lit. DETR-white', *a-cʷə́.q'apšʲ* 'reddish; lit. DETR-red', *a-zə́.q'apšʲ* 'reddish; lit. BENF-red', etc.

4.2.2 Suffixation

Suffixation is a usual means of deriving adjectives:
a) *-ʒa*: *á-pš.ʒa* 'beautiful' (← *a-pš-rá* 'to look'), *aajgʷa.ʒá* 'the nearest' (← *aajgʷá* 'close, nearby');
b) *-ʒʒa*: *a-dǝ́w.ʒʒa* 'great' (← *a-dǝ́w* 'big');
c) *-da*, a privative suffix: *a-ncʷá.da* 'godless', *a-zjʷə́.da* 'healthy' (← *a-zjʷá* 'plague, contagion');
d) *-t'ʷ(ə)*, a very productive adjectivizing suffix (from *a-t'ʷə́* 'possession'): *a-psabá-ra.t'ʷ* 'natural' (← *a-psabára* 'nature'), *a-bjʷá.t'ʷ* '(of) copper' (← *a-bjʷá* 'copper'), *a-xʲ.t'ʷə́* 'golden';
e) *-t'ʷə.j*, another productive adjectivizing suffix, derived from the former: *a-tǝ́pan.t'ʷəj* 'local' (← *a-tǝ́p* 'place'), *jaxʲa.t'ʷə́j* 'contemporary' (← *jaxʲá* 'today'), *c'aq'a.t'ʷə́j* 'which is below' (← *á-c'aq'a* 'below');
f) *-xʷ(ə)*, expressing 'possession of a feature or quality' (probably from *a-xʷə́* 'share, part'), e.g., *a-rə́cha.xʷ* 'miserable' (← *a-rə́cha* 'poor'), *a-cʷəršʷá.xʷ* 'wretched' (← *a-cʷə.ršʷá-ra* 'to frighten sb.').

4.3 Verbal derivation

4.3.1 Prefixation

Verbal derivation by means of preverbs which express directional or orientational parameters ('up', 'down', 'thither', 'hither', 'on top', 'inside', 'outside', and many others) is very common. So from the verb *gəla* 'to stand, stand up' we have *á-d.gəla-ra* 'to stand close to X', *á-va.gəla-ra* 'to stand beside, next to X', *á-c'a.gəla-ra* 'to stand under', *á-kʷ.gəla-ra* 'to stand on top', *a-xa.gəla-ra* 'to stand above', etc. Some verbs cannot function without preverbs, for instance the verb *la* 'to enter': *á-la.la-ra* 'to enter into the mass', *a-tá.la-ra* 'to enter inside', *á-c'a.la-ra* 'to enter underneath', *a-jʷn.á.la-ra* 'to enter inside the house', etc. The combination of two or more preverbs to form new verbs is not uncommon: *a-n.aá.la-ra* 'to pass, fit' (←*na* 'thither', *aa* 'hither', *la* 'to go'), *áj.d.č'a.hʷa.la-ra* 'to tie up to each other' (← *aj-* 'reciprocal', *d(ə)-* 'close to', *č'a* 'mouth, face', *hʷa* 'to tie', plus the extension *-la*).

A very large group of verbs is formed by means of preverbs based on terms for such body-parts as *a-gʷə́* 'heart' and *a-xə́* 'head'; the first preverb a) forms verbs expressing mental or spiritual activities, the other one b) is responsible for actions occurring above the object, cf. a) *a-gʷ.bəl-rá* 'to worry about' (← *a-bəl-rá* 'to burn'), *a-gʷə.r.jʷa-rá* 'to worry' (← *a-r.jʷa-rá* 'to make dry'), *a-gʷ.á.la.šʷa-ra* 'to remember' (← *á-la.šʷa-ra* 'to fall in the mass (of small objects)'), b) *a-xə́.r.pa-ra* 'to make jump over sth.' (← *á-r.pa-ra* 'to make jump'), *a-xə́.s-ra* 'to cross over sth.' (← *s-* 'to pass'), etc.

Some other verbal **prefixes** are:
a) *cʷ(ə)-*, detrimental (malefactive): *a-cʷ.ca-rá* 'to escape, flee sb.', *a-cʷ.ga-rá* 'to take from sb. against his/her will';
b) *z(ə)-*, benefactive: *a-z.gʷ.á.ta-ra* 'to remark, reproach', *a-z.q'áza-ra* 'to be a master in something';
c) *z(ə)-*, potential (etymologically connected with the former prefix): *a-zə́.m.čʲha-ra* 'to have no patience';
d) *r(ə)-*, causative: *a-r.ba-rá* 'to show' (cf. *a-ba-rá* 'to see'), *a-r.jáša-ra* 'to correct' (cf. *a-jáša* 'straight');
e) *aj-*, reciprocal (with intransitive verbs): *áj.pš-ra* 'to look like, be similar' (*a-pš-rá* 'to look'), *áj.sa-ra* 'to argue, compete with each other';
f) *aj.ba-*, reciprocal (with transitive verbs): *áj.ba.šʲ-ra* 'to fight, be at war' (← *a-šʲ-rá* 'to kill'), *áj.ba.ga-ra* 'to marry each other' (cf. *a-ga-rá* 'to take, carry');
g) *aj.c(ə)-*, comitative: *áj.c.dər-ra* 'to be well-known' (← *a-də́r-ra* 'to know'), *áj.c.wə-ra* 'to collaborate, work together' (cf. *a-w-rá* 'to do, work');
h) *aj.z(ə)-* 'together for': *áj.z.ga-ra* 'to collect, bring together', *áj.z.hʷa-ra* 'propose sb. to sb. as a wife or husband' (cf. *á-hʷa-ra* 'to ask');
i) *aj.ma-* 'together, mutually': *áj.ma.k'-ra* 'to argue, quarrel with each other' (cf. *a-k'-rá* 'to catch'), *áj.ma.da-ra* 'to connect' (← *da-* 'to lead');
j) *amxa-* 'involuntarily': *ámxa.ps-ra* 'to kill accidentally' (← *a-ps-rá* 'to die'), *ámxa.ba-ra* 'to see involuntarily'.

4.3.2 Suffixation

The derivational verbal suffixes are as follows:
a) *-šʲa* 'to regard as': *á-xʷəmga.šʲa-ra* 'to regard as loathsome' (← *á-xʷəmga* 'loathsome'), *á-pxa.šʲa-ra* 'to feel shy' (← *a-pxá* 'loss, deprivation');

b) -r̆k' 'to turn to' (from the causative verb a-r̆k'-rá 'to make hold'): a-pstám.r̆k'-ra 'nitriding' (← a-pstám 'nitrogen'), a-rə́cxʷ.r̆k-ra 'to date' (← a-rə́cxʷ 'numeral');
c) -t'ʷ 'to turn to' (from the verb a-t'ʷ-rá 'to possess, relate to, pertain to'): abžʲár.da.t'ʷ-ra 'to demilitarize' (← abžʲar.da 'weapon-without'), á-kʷəjt.t'ʷ-ra 'to allow' (← kʷəjt 'free');
d) -xa 'to become': ájpš.xa-ra 'to assimilate, become alike' (← ájpš 'alike'), á-mgʷadəw.xa-ra 'to become pregnant; lit. big belly-become'.

Of the two verbal root-extension suffixes, -aa- and -la-, the first expresses centrifugal movement (a-t.pr.aa-rá 'to fly (hither) from inside'), while the second one is centripetal (á-la.ga.la-ra 'to bring into the mass'). These suffixes are quite productive in the derivation of new verbs.

4.4 Adverbial derivation

There is a repertory of affixes which are used to form adverbs from nouns, adjectives, quantifiers or verbal forms. Some of these are given below:
a) -ʒa, superlative: ak'ə́r.ʒa 'very' (← ak'ə́r 'many'), naʒá.ʒa 'forever' (cf. a-naʒá.ra 'edge, end of X', á-na.ʒa-ra 'to reach, get to');
b) -hʷa, a "quotative" suffix (etymologically related to a-hʷa-rá 'to tell'), often used to produce adverbs out of sound-descriptive words: á-fər.hʷa 'instantaneously', a-šʲšʲə́.hʷa 'noicelessly', xʲarčʲ=xʲárčʲ.hʷa 'producing noice, splash'; some words with this suffix, however, are probably not sound-descriptive, e.g., aárla.hʷa 'hardly, scarcely';
c) -k'ʷa, expressing 'manner' (in negative formations): č'ə́.m.t.k'ʷa 'silently' (← a-č'.t-rá 'to shout'), -xʷartá.m.k'ʷa 'badly, improperly' (← a-xʷartá 'benefit, good');
d) instrumental -la: bzə́ja.la 'well' (← a-bzə́ja 'good'), maʒa.lá 'secretly' (← á-maʒa 'secret');
e) privative -da: xʷə́.da=psá.da 'gratis' (← a-xʷ, a-psá 'price'), xə́.m.pa.da 'undoubtedly' (← a-xə́.pa-ra 'to jump over');
f) -na: z.nə 'once' (← z < *za 'one'), tə́nčʲ.na 'quietly' (← a-tə́nčʲ 'quiet');
g) -šakʷ: xʷmár.šakʷ 'jokingly' (← á-xʷmar-ra 'to play'), cʷgʲá.šakʷ 'to spite of sb.' (← á-cʷgʲa 'bad');
h) -šʷa 'as if, like': wama.šʷá 'surprisingly' (← á-wama 'sth. terrible'), záa.šʷa 'somewhat earlier' (← záa 'early, beforehand');
i) -xa 'becoming': -aapsa.xá 'tired' (← áa.psa-ra 'to be tired'), -rə́chaxʷ.xa 'miserably' (←a-rə́chaxʷ 'miserable').

5 Conversion

Conversion, a word-formation device creating words out of other classes of words without a formal change, is common in Abkhaz. I shall give here examples of the following types of conversion: verb to noun, verb to adjective, adjective to noun, noun to adjective, adjective to adverb, and postposition to adverb.

5.1 Verb to noun

5.1.1 Masdar form → noun

The masdar form of the verb can be converted into a noun. Cf. such examples as *áj.ba.šʲ-ra* 'to fight, be at war' → *ájbašʲra* 'war', *áj.ma.da-ra* 'to connect' → *ájmadara* 'link, communication', *áj.lə.m.ga-ra* 'not to understand' → *ájləmgara* 'absurdity', *áj.n.aa.la-ra* 'to reconcile' → *ájnaalara* 'reconciliation'. A deverbal noun derived through conversion often has a stress position different from the base verb, e.g., *a-jʷ-rá* 'to write' vs. *a-jʷə́ra* 'writing', *a-pxa-rá* 'to warm' vs. *a-pxára* 'warmth', *a-z.ha-rá* 'to grow' vs. *a-zhára* 'success, flourishing'.

5.1.2 Pure stem form → noun

The pure stem form of the verb (i.e. without the masdar suffix) can also be used to form a deverbal noun, cf. *a-pə́.šʷa-ra* 'to try' → *a-pə́šʷa* 'experience', *á-l.x-ra* 'to choose' → *a-lə́x* 'ingredient', *á-d.c'a-ra* 'to give order' → *a-dc'á* 'task', *á-c'ʷax-ra* 'to hide' → *a-c'ʷaxə́* 'store', *a-zə́.m.ha-ra* 'not to grow', *a-zə́.m.c'a-ra* 'not to be able to learn' → *(a-)zə́mha=zə́mc'a* 'tubby person'.

It seems that the difference between the derivation with or without masdar suffix lies not in the semantic output, but rather in a somewhat lower productivity of conversion by using a pure stem form, though, admittedly, there are cases when both masdar and pure stem forms can be used to form a noun without any change in the meaning, cf. *a-pə́šʷará*//*a-pə́šʷa* 'experiment' (← *a-pə́.šʷa-ra* 'to try'); note that the same word in the meaning 'experience' (see above) is used only without the suffix -*ra*.

5.2 Verb to adjective

From verbal stems: *a-gʷ.ra.ga-rá* 'to trust' → *a-gʷragá* 'reliable', *a-č'ə́.xa-ra* 'to wake up' → *a-č'ə́xa* 'vivid, energetic'. From verbal adjectives (participles): *ak'rə.z.-*

c'á.z.k'.wa 'important; lit. much-REL-PREV-REL-hold-PRES.PART', *z.cʷa.z.t'ʷə̂.m* 'pregnant; lit. REL-skin-REL-belong-NEG'. Analytical participial constructions are also quite common, for example according to such models such as name + participle *jə.z.má.w* 'having' (e.g., *á-int'eres Ø.z.má.w* 'interesting'), name + *jə.z.lá.w* 'containing' (e.g., *á-mčʲ Ø.z.lá.w* 'powerful'), adverb + *jə̂.q'a.w* 'being' (e.g., *aajgʷá jə̂.q'a.w* 'nearby'). Cf. also *ak'ə́r j.a.psá.w* 'dear, respected; lit. who has much value', *zə́.la.xʲ ajkʷə̂.w* 'sad; lit. whose forehead is dark', *hʷaá z.má.m* 'endless; lit. border which-not-having', *a-cént'r Ø-axʲ jə.ca.wá* 'centripetal; lit. the one who is going to the centre'.

5.3 Adjective to noun

Examples: *á-q'apšʲ* 'red' → 'a red one', *a-bzája* 'good' → 'a good one', *áp.xʲa.t'ʷə.j* 'first' → 'the first one', etc.

5.4 Noun to adjective

Examples: *áps.wa* 'Abkhaz' → *áps.wa žʷlar* 'the Abkhaz people', *a-mšə́n* 'sea' → *a-mšə́nʒə* 'sea water'.

5.5 Adjective to adverb

Adverbs formed from adjectives by conversion usually differ from the former by the absence of the definite-generic article, e.g., *a-tə́nčʲ* 'calm' → *tənčʲ* 'calmly', *á-ckʲa* 'clean' → *ckʲa* 'clearly'; sometimes this is accompanied by the shift in stress position: *áajgʷa* 'near' → *aajgʷá* 'nearby, recently', *á-las* 'quick' → *lassə̂* 'quickly'.

5.6 Postposition to adverb

Example: *á-c'aq'a* 'under' → *c'aq'á* 'below, downwards'.

6 Reduplication

6.1 Nominal reduplication

In noun formation, reduplication does not play such a prominent role as it does in verb and adverb formation. The following types of reduplication can be mentioned: a) deverbal nouns based on reduplicated verbal stems; b) nouns formed by reduplication of sound-descriptive or movement-descriptive elements; c) full reduplication of the nominal root:

a) *a-hʷa.n=hʷá.x* 'rumour; lit. tell-PIDF=tell-again', *a-naj=áaj.ra* 'walk; lit. go=come.ABSTR';
b) *a-q'ap=q'áp* 'wooden shoes', *a-k'ʷə́=k'ʷəw* 'cuckoo', *á-də=d(ə)* 'thunder', *á-k'ʲat'=k'ʲat'ra* 'top of the tree';
c) *a-š=šá* 'fat' (< *šə=šá < *ša=šá), *a-kʲa=kʲá* 'hoop made of thread or vine', *á-gʲa=gʲa* 'circle'.

A specific type of reduplication, very common in Abkhaz, is e c h o - r e d u p l i c a - t i o n, whereby the onset of the second part of the compound is replaced by another consonant. The most popular initial increment in the second part of the reduplications is the resonant *m-*, which represents a very wide areal feature (cf. Chirikba 2008: 55–56). The resonant *m-* can either replace the initial sound on the second constituent, as in *ažʷ=mážʷ* 'rags' (← *ážʷ* 'old'), *a-xʷač'ʲa=máč'ʲa* 'worms, caterpillars, etc.' (← *a-xʷáč'ʲa* 'larva, caterpillar'), or be placed before the initial sound of the second member of the reduplicated complex: *aʒa=máʒa* 'raw things' (← *áʒa* 'raw'), *a-baá=mbaá* 'rot, decay' (← *a-baá* 'rot'), *a-xʷ=mə́xʷ* 'leftovers' (← *a-xʷə́* 'food'), etc. If a word with an initial *m-* is to be "echoed", another consonant is used to replace it, cf. *a-matʷa=jʷə́tʷa* 'all kinds of clothes' (← *á-matʷa* 'clothes'), *á-makar=č'ʲakárra* 'all kinds of threats' (← *á-makarra* 'threat'), *a-mál=a-š'ʲál* 'wealth, possessions' (← *a-mál* 'wealth'). Besides *m*, other consonants can also be used, cf. *a-gʷam=sám* 'all rubbish/rubbish and such' (← *a-gʷám* 'rubbish'), *á-raxʷ=á-šʷaxʷ* 'all kinds of cattle/cattle and such' (← *á-raxʷ* 'cattle'). In most cases such formations function as collective nouns, though in cases like *a-xaga=ʒága* 'oaf, softhead' (← *a-xága* 'idiot') the semantics of collectiveness is not present.

6.2 Adjectival reduplication

There are quite a number of reduplicated adjectives, e.g., *á-gʲa=gʲa* 'round', *a-k'ʲá=k'ʲa* 'hard, rough', *a-k'az=k'áz* 'transparent and shining', *á-cər=cər* 'shining', *a-*

šam=šám 'clear (of a sight or glance)'. Examples of echo-reduplication with the typical m-replacement: *a-gaza=mazá* 'foolish' (← *a-gazá* 'foolish'), *a-p'áš^w=maš^w* 'well cared-for' (← *a-p'áš^w* 'clean, tender'), etc.

6.3 Adverbial reduplication

Adverbial reduplication comes in two varieties, one without an affix and one in which it is combined with a suffix:
a) *važ^wə́=važ^wə* 'often', *xaz=xazə́* 'separately', *ak'=ák'a* 'one by one', *x^wǎč'^j(ə)=x^wǎč'^jə́* 'little by little', *mač'^j=máč'^j* 'little by little', *xrǎž^j=xrǎž^j* 'occasionally', *lassə́=lassə* 'often', *xama-xáma* 'in all directions';
b) *znə́=zən.la* 'from time to time', *aár.la=aár.la* 'with difficulty'.

Examples of echo-reduplication: *á-k'^wša=mək'^wša* 'all around' (← *á-k'^w.ša-ra* 'to go around'), *aajg^wá=səjg^wa* 'nearby' (← *áajg^wa* 'near').

6.4 Verbal reduplication

Reduplication is quite common in verb formation, cf. *á-bar=bar-ra* 'to clack, blab', *á-k'^jər=k'^jər-ra* 'to neigh', *á-cər=cər-ra* 'to shine', *a-pažj=pážj-ra* 'to prance', etc. Echo-reduplication is also popular, especially with the m-replacement, cf. *a-k'aləšj=maləšj-ra* 'to walk carelessly', *a-yəzə=məz-ra* 'to moan', *a-x^jat'əj=mat'əj-ra* 'to bend (of resilient objects)', *a-k^wac=maca-rá* 'to move'. Other kinds of replacement: *a-makar=čjakár-ra* 'to threaten', *á-š^wəj=pšjəj-ra* 'to curse', *a-h^wəlǝ́=səl-ra* (beside *a-h^wəlǝ́=h^wəl-ra*) 'to splash (of big quantity of fish)', etc.

Some verbs can be regarded as derived according to the sound symbolic connotations attributed to certain consonants. As examples of such formations, a number of verbal roots with the general meaning 'to hang swinging or dangling from side to side' can be cited, their semantic nuances, depending on the form and mass of the object, being expressed by different consonants, cf. *á-k'al=k'ala-ra* (of small and thin objects), *á-k'^wal=k'^wala-ra* (of somewhat heavier objects)', *á-q'al=q'ala-ra* (of bigger objects). Another verb with a similar semantics and phonetic shape (*á-gjal=gjala-ra*) could be a part of this set, but it refers to objects of any mass and shape, though tending to denote somewhat heavier ones.

7 Neoclassical word-formation

In case of the borrowed Russian words with classical affixes, the latter can stay within the borrowed item, or be replaced by native elements: R. *avantjurizm* 'adventurism' > Abkhaz *avant'iurízm̀//avant'iúra.ra* (with the abstract suffix *-ra*), R. *alogizm* 'alogism' > *alogízm̀//a-lógik'a.da.ra* (with the suffix *-da.ra* 'without'), R. *antidemokratičeskij* 'anti-democratic' > *ant'i.demok'rát'ia.t'ʷ//a-demok'rát'ia= č'a.gəla.ra.t'ʷ* (with *a-č'a.gə́la.ra.t'ʷ* 'oppositional'). Cf. also R. *akademizm* 'academicism' > *ak'ademízm*, beside pleonastic *ak'ademízm.ra*.

There are many neoclassical formations construed on the model of borrowed Russian compounds where the borrowed classical element remains intact, while the Russian part of the borrowed item is translated. Neoclassical word-formation in Abkhaz is prefixal, i.e. the classical (Greek or Latin) elements exclusively occupy the first part of the word. Examples: *agro-* 'agricultural': *agropq'ára* 'agricultural rule', *agroaaglə́xrat'ʷ* 'agro-industrial'; *ant'i-* 'against': *ant'imatʷaš́ʲár* 'antimatter', *ant'idəwnéj* 'antiworld'; *avia-* 'aviatic': *avianə́q'ʷgaga* 'aircraft carrier', *aviapšə́xʷra* 'air reconnaissance'; *avt'o-* 'auto-': *avt'omjʷá* 'highway', *avt'omjʷakʷc'ajʷə́* 'traffic controller'; *bio-* 'biological': *a-biofə́mca* 'biocurrent', *a-bioxačʲhara* 'biostability'; *evro-* 'European': *a-evroxʷapšrá* 'Eurovision'; *fot'o-* 'photographic': *a-fot'otə́xra* 'photographing', *a-fot'osáxʲa* 'photo, picture'; *k'ino-* 'cinematographic': *a-k'inoq'ázara* 'film art', *a-k'inosáxʲa* 'motion picture'; *k'ont'r-* 'against': *a-k'ont'ržʷə́lara* 'counterattack', *a-k'ónt'rdgalara* 'counter-offer'; *mega-* 'mega-': *a-megadəwnéj* 'mega-world'; *met'a-* 'meta-': *a-met'abəzšʷá* 'metalanguage'; *mik'ro-* 'micro-': *a-mik'rodəwnéj* 'microcosm', *a-mik'roxʷtáč'ʲ* 'microparticle'; *p'ara-* 'para-': *a-p'aramxəldə́zt'ʷ* 'paramagnetic'; *t'ele-* 'tele-': *a-t'elexʷapšrá* 'television', *a-t'elešʷága* 'telemetering'; *t'ermo-* 'thermo-': *a-t'ermogʷə́cʷt'ʷ* 'thermonuclear', *a-t'ermomxəldə́zt'ʷ* 'thermomagnetic'; *video-* 'video-': *a-vídeonc'amta* 'video recording'.

8 Other types of word-formation

8.1 Clipping

Clipping is occasionally observed in word-formation: *a-mazán.k'ʷadər* 'a type of female saddle', from *amazánk'ʷa k'ʷadər* 'Amazonian saddle'; *wə.s.t!* 'you.MASC take it!', an interjection-like clipped verbal form, derived from *jə.wə́.s.t.wa.jt'* 'it-to you.MASC-I-give-PRES-FIN'; *wə.hʷa.n=s.hʷá.n* 'rumour', from *jə.wə.hʷá.n=*

jə.s.hʷá.n 'it-you.MASC-say-PIDF=it-I-say-PIDF'; *a-hʷa.n=hʷá.x* 'rumour', from *jə.PERSON.hʷá.n=jə.PERSON.hʷá.x-t'* 'it-X-say-PIDF=it-X-say-again-PAST'.

Unlike the form *wə.s.t!* 'you.MASC take it!', where the verbal agreement partially remains, despite the dropping of the object marker (cf. *bə.s.t!* 'you.FEM take it!', *šʷə.s.t!* 'you.PL take it!', etc.), the form *(a-)wə.hʷa.n=s.hʷá.n* 'rumour, gossip' is fully lexicalized, since, apart from dropping the object marker, it can take the definite-generic article, and keeps the personal markers (*wə-* 'you.MASC', *s-* 'I') in fossilized form.

8.2 Acronyms

During the Soviet era, Abkhaz borrowed from Russian quite a number of acronyms: R. *part.kom* > *a-p'art'k'óm* 'party committee', *rab.kor* > *a-rabk'ór* 'worker-correspondent', *rab.fak* > *a-rabfák* 'workers' courses', etc. Many of these are now out of use. In other cases only one part of the Russian acronymic compounds was borrowed, while the other part was translated, to produce hybrid Russian-Abkhaz compounds. Despite the fact that some of the Russian originals were combinations of two or more clipped words (like *polit.ruk*, *kom.so.mol*), while other complex acronyms preserved one part of the compound intact (like *polit.učeba*), the general practice was to render both types by borrowing the first clipped part, while translating the second part (either clipped or intact).

Examples of both parts of the complex acronym clipped in the source language: R. *kol.xoz* > Abkhaz *a-k'ol=n.xá.ra* 'collective farm' (*a-n.xa.rá* 'farming'), R. *sov.xoz* > *a-sov=n.xá.ra* 'Soviet farm', R. *kom.so.mol* > *a-k'om=č'ár* 'Young Communist League' (*a-č'ár* 'youth'), R. *polit.ruk* > *a-p'olit'=nap'xgajʷə* 'political superviser'.

Cases when the second part of the Russian original represents the whole word: R. *polit.otdel* > *a-p'olit'=qʷšá* 'political department', R. *polit.učeba* > *a-p'olít'=c'ara* 'political education', R. *agit.punkt* > *agit'=tə́p* 'propaganda centre', R. *tex.nadzor* > *a-t'éx=xəlapšra* 'engineering supervision', R. *tex.osmotr* > *a-t'éx=gʷátara* 'equipment check-up'.

Acronyms in the form of individual letters are rare in Abkhaz, cf. such examples as *ATA*, which stands for *At'ʷə́lawajʷrat'ʷ tagə́lazaašʲa atájʷərta* 'registry office', *EME* for *Éjdgəlo Amilátkʷa r-Éjč'k'aara* 'United Nations Organization', *MHc* for *megaherc* 'megahertz', etc.

8.3 Blending

Among the instances of blending one can mention such examples as *án=šʲa* 'maternal uncle', from a fuller but unattested form **án=l.jašʲa* lit. 'mother-her-brother', with an attested variant form *án=l.aš/a*; *sẹ́jdrəw* 'I wouldn't know' (in the Abzhywa dialect), from *sa jə.z.dər.wa.j* ? lit. 'I it-I-know-QU', colloquial *xʷəmčxán* 'in the evening', from **xʷə.l[a].apə.č.xá.n* (from an older form **qʷə.l[a].apə.mš.qá.n*), with an intermediate form *xʷəlbəčxán*, etc.

8.4 Gemination

Gemination of the root consonant, apart from its spontaneous usage for emphatic purposes, is also employed in word-formation to create verbs with an intensifying semantics, cf. *a-hʷa-rá* 'to speak' vs. *á-hʷhʷa-ra* 'to shout, cry', *a-p.žʷa-rá* 'to tear' vs. *a-pə.žʷžʷa-rá* 'to tear in small pieces', *a-p.č-rá* 'to break' vs. *a-p.čč-rá* 'to break in many pieces'.

Abbreviations

ABSTR	abstract suffix	NEG	negative
BENF	benefactive	NFIN	non-finite
CAUS	causative	PIDF	past indefinite
DETR	detrimental	POT	potential
DIM	diminutive	PRES	present
DIRECT	directional affix	QU	question
IDF	indefinite article	SUF	suffix
FIN	finite		

9 References

Amičba, Valentina (2010): *Acəngəla apsua bazšʷač'ə (apsua-abaza dialek't'kʷa zeg/ə reič'arpšrala)*. Aq'ʷa [Suxum]: Apsnət'ʷəi ahʷəntkarrat'ʷ universitet'.

Aristava, Šota K., Xuxut S. Bgažba, M. M. Cikolia, Lidija P. Čkadua, Konstantin S. Šakryl (eds.) (1968): *Grammatika abxazskogo jazyka. Fonetika i morfologija*. Suxumi: Alašara.

Bisetto, Antonietta and Sergio Scalise (2009): Classification of compounds. In: Rochelle Lieber and Pavol Štekauer (eds.), *The Oxford Handbook of Compounding*, 49–82. Oxford: Oxford University Press.

Chirikba, Viacheslav (2003): *Abkhaz*. München: LINCOM Europa.

Chirikba, Viacheslav (2008): The problem of the Caucasian Sprachbund. In: Pieter Muysken (ed.), *From Linguistic Areas to Areal Linguistics*, 25–93. Amsterdam/Philadelphia: Benjamins.

Čkadua, Lidija (2005): *Glagol'noe slovoobrazovanie v abxazskom jazyke*. Suxum: Abxazskij institut gumanitarnyx issledovanij im D. I. Gulia.

Gabunija, Zinaida (1971): Slovoobrazovanie imen suščestvitel'nyx v abxazskom jazyke. Ph.D. dissertation, Kabardino-Balkarskij gosudarstvennyj universitet, Nal'čik.

Gabunija, Zinaida (1985): K voprosu o kompozitnom slovoobrazovanii v abxazskom i russkom jazykax. In: *Rol' russkogo jazyka v žizni narodov Severnogo Kavkaza i razvitie ix literaturnyx jazykov*, 75–81. Groznyj: s.n.

Hewitt, Bernard George (in collaboration with Z. K. Khiba) (1979): *Abkhaz*. Amsterdam: North-Holland Publishing Company.

Kaslandzija, Vladimir (1976): Tipy i sposoby obrazovanija složnyx slov v abxazskom jazyke. Ph.D. dissertation, Institut jazykoznanija Akademii nauk SSSR, Moskva.

Kaslandzija, Vladimir (1998): *Složnye slova v abxazskom jazyke*. Suxum: Alašara.

Klyčeva, Larisa (2009): Imennoe slovosočetanie v abxazskom i abazinskom jazykax. Ph.D. dissertation, Abxazskij institut gumanitarnyx issledovanij im. D. I. Gulia, Suxum.

Kvarčelija, Aleksej (1953): Gagol'noe slovoobrazovanie v abxazskom jazyke. Ph.D. dissertation, Institut jazykoznanija Akademii nauk SSSR, Moskva.

Lander, Yury (2016): Adyghe. In: Peter O. Müller, Ingeborg Ohnheiser, Susan Olsen and Franz Rainer (eds.), *Word-Formation. An International Handbook of the Languages of Europe*. Vol. 5, 3508–3527. Berlin/Boston: De Gruyter Mouton.

Matasović, Ranko (2016): Kabardian. In: Peter O. Müller, Ingeborg Ohnheiser, Susan Olsen and Franz Rainer (eds.), *Word-Formation. An International Handbook of the Languages of Europe*. Vol. 5, 3527–3535. Berlin/Boston: De Gruyter Mouton.

O'Herin, Brian (2020): Abaza and Abkhaz. In: Maria Polinsky (ed.), *Handbook of the Languages of the Caucasus*, 447–488. Oxford: Oxford University Press.

Šakryl, Konstantin (1961): *Affiksacija v abxazskom jazyke*. Suxumi: Abgosizdat.

Šinkuba, Bagrat (1956): Udvoenie v abxazskom jazyke. *Trudy abxazskogo instituta jazyka, literatury i istorii* 27: 193–212.

Šinkuba, Bagrat (2008): Imennoe slovosloženie v abxazskom jazyke. In: Bagrat Šinkuba, *Sobranie sočinenij*. Vol. 6: *Stat'i, issledovanija, vystuplenija*, 221–247. Suxum: s.n.

Xecija, Anatolij (1988): *Neologizmy v abxazskom jazyke*. Tbilisi: Mecniereba.

Timur Maisak and Dmitry Ganenkov
24 Aghul

1 Introduction
2 General overview
3 Composition
4 Derivation
5 Reduplication
6 References

Abstract: Word-formation processes in Aghul (a Northeast Caucasian language spoken in Daghestan, Russia) include both compounding and derivation. Verbal compounding is very productive and is the primary way of enriching the verbal lexicon in the modern language, using borrowed Russian verbs. In contrast, although there are quite a large number of nominal compounds, they seem to be fixed expressions and no new compounds are created. Derivation is mainly suffixal with the exception of verbal locative and repetitive derivation achieved by prefixes. Various types of full reduplication, as well as echo-reduplication and partial reduplication are fairly productive.

1 Introduction

Aghul (also spelled Agul) is a language from the Lezgic branch of the Northeast Caucasian (Nakh-Daghestanian) family. Within the branch, the closest relatives of the language are Tabassaran and Lezgian, which share many of its word-formation strategies. There are more than 30,000 first-language speakers of Aghul in Russia, mainly in mountainous areas of South Daghestan (the Aghul district and the Kurah district). The language divides into seven dialects which display more or less significant differences with respect to all aspects of grammar. This work is based on the Huppuq' dialect spoken in the village of Huppuq'. Data for this article come from field work of both authors and from consultations with the native speaker linguist Solmaz Merdanova (Moscow).

Aghul is an ergative language with predominantly agglutinative morphology, having a rich case system (about thirty case forms, including numerous locatives)

Timur Maisak, Moscow, Russia
Dmitry Ganenkov, Leipzig, Germany

https://doi.org/10.1515/9783111420523-024

and a huge verbal paradigm (several dozens forms, both synthetic and periphrastic). The basic clause-level word order is SOV, dependents typically precede heads in other phrase types as well. In contrast to most languages of the family, Aghul does not have either gender or person agreement.

Previous work on Aghul includes a number of grammatical sketches (Dirr 1907; Šaumjan 1941; Magometov 1970; Sulejmanov 1993; Tarlanov 1994; Merdanova 2004) covering most of phonology and inflectional morphology and to a lesser degree syntax. However, the previous work on the language gives very few details about word-formation and, generally, derivational morphology of the language has not been dealt with specifically in any other source.

2 General overview

Word-formation in Aghul includes compounding, derivational prefixation and suffixation, and reduplication. No examples of conversion, backformation, blending, or clipping have been identified in Aghul.

3 Composition

3.1 Nominal compounds

There are no productive types of nominal compound formation. However, a number of fixed compound expressions (dvandvas) are attested, cf. *dadar-bawar* 'parents' (← *dad-ar* 'father-PL' + *baw-ar* 'mother-PL'), *kunar-lakar* 'garments' (← *kun-ar* 'clothes-PL' + *lak-ar* 'shoe-PL'), *aχun-jurʁan* 'bed' (← *aχun* 'sleeping place' + *jurʁan* 'blanket'). Morphologically such expressions often consist of two plural marked nouns which either form a complex stem with respect to case markers or take inflectional morphology independently of one another: *dadar-bawaris* 'to parents' (← *dad-ar* 'father-PL' + *baw-ar-is* 'mother-PL-DAT') or *dadaris-bawaris* 'to parents' (*dad-ar-is* 'father-PL-DAT' + *baw-ar-is* 'mother-PL-DAT'). Semantically, such expressions typically include two conceptually close words that together denote a cover term for both. Some of them have become conventionalized with a completely non-compositional meaning, though, as in *jaʁar-ʔüšer* 'misfortunes' (← *jaʁ-ar* 'day-PL' + *ʔüš-er* 'night-PL').

3.2 Verbal compounds

Like in other Lezgic languages, simplex (synchronically unanalyzable) verb stems constitute the minor part of the verbal lexicon. There are many derived prefixal verbs (see section 4.3.1), but most verbs are complex and consist of two parts – a coverb (or "nominal part") and a light verb, cf. *ʔüsse xas* 'to get old' (← *ʔüsse* 'old' + *xas* 'to become'), *un aq'as* 'to call' (← *un* 'sound' + *aq'as* 'to do'), *masa ic'as* 'to sell' (← *masa* 'for pay' + *ic'as* 'to give').

Light verbs, that host all tense and aspect marking, include such high-frequency verbal lexemes with generalized meaning as *xas* 'to become', *(a)q'as* 'to do, make', *ic'as* 'to give', *jarнas* 'to beat', *ʕ̩as* 'to go, come' and some others, as well as the stative verb *a* 'to be (inside)'. Coverbs include nouns, adjectives, adverbs, and also bound stems which are not used outside complex verbs. The most common types of coverbs are:

a) Nouns in the absolutive case, cf. *haraj aq'as* 'to shout' (← 'shout' + 'to do'), *kar aq'as* 'work' (← 'job' + 'to do'), *paj aq'as* 'to divide' (← 'part' + 'to do'), *p:adark:a aq'as* 'to give as a present' (← 'gift' + 'to do'), *mez ic'as* 'to lick' (← 'tongue' + 'to give'), *ubur ic'as* 'to obey, listen to' (← 'ear' + 'to give'), *niʔ duas* 'to smell' (← 'smell' + 'to pull'), *gulla jarнas* 'to shoot, fire' (← 'bullet' + 'to beat'), *murs jarнas* 'to get mouldy' (← 'mould' + 'to beat'), *p'ac ik'as* 'to kiss' (← 'kiss' + 'to put into'), *t'ink'~t'ink' ʕ̩as* 'to drip' (← 'drop-drop' + 'to go, come'). The nominal part of such compounds can take plural marking when expressing iterative or multiplicative meaning;

b) Ideophones, which mainly co-occur with the verb 'to do', cf. *č'aq'raq' aq'as* 'to creak', *č'emp' aq'as* 'to champ', *ʕamf aq'as* 'to bark', *mew aq'as* 'to meow'. Ideophones as coverbs are close to nouns in that they can take plural marking, cf. *č'emp'-er aq'as* 'to champ constantly'. A further characteristic of ideophones is that they occur in reduplicated form (see section 5.1.2);

c) Adjectives, that form regular inchoative/causative pairs of complex verbs with light verbs *xas* 'to become' vs. *aq'as* 'to do' respectively, cf. *buš xas* 'to weaken (itr.)' / *buš q'as* 'to weaken (tr.)' (← *buš* 'weak'), *нüt:e xas* 'to get sharp (itr.)' / *нüt:e q'as* 'to sharpen (tr.)' (← *нüt:e* 'sharp'), *нazur xas* 'to get ready, prepare (itr.)' / *нazur q'as* 'to get ready, prepare (tr.)' (← *нazur* 'ready');

d) Adverbs, cf. *wart: xas* 'to win' (← *wart:* 'up' + *xas* 'to become'), *č'uq' xas* 'to diminish, get smaller (itr.)' (← *č'uq'* 'a bit, a little' + *xas* 'to become'). A productive group of complex statives is based on deadjectival adverbs in -*di* and a stative verb *a* 'to be (inside)', cf. *širindi a* 'to be tasty, feel taste' (← *širin* 'tasty'), *pašmandi a* 'to feel sad' (← *pašman* 'sad'), *šat:t:i a* 'to be glad, feel joyful' (< *šad-di a* ← *šad* 'glad');

e) Deverbal components, borrowed from Azeri (one of the main contact languages of South Daghestan in the past) and Russian. Azeri verbs were borrowed in the form of participles in -*miš*, cf. *aldatmiš aq'as* 'to divert, distract; to befool' (← Az. *aldat-* 'to deceive, befool' + 'to do'), *bašlamiš aq'as* 'to begin' (← Az. *bašla-* 'to begin' + 'to do'), *begemiš xas* 'to like' (← Az. *bəjən-* < *bəgən-* 'to like' + 'to become'), *išlemiš aq'as* 'to use' (← Az. *išlən-* 'to use' + 'to do'), *jašamiš xas* 'to live' (← Az. *jaša-* 'to live' + 'to become'). Russian verbs are borrowed in the infinitive form, cf. *arganizawat: aq'as* 'to organize' (← Rus. *organizovat'* 'to organize' + 'to do'), *služit: aq'as* 'to serve' (← Rus. *služit'* 'to serve' + 'to do'), *sazdawat: xas* 'to be created' (← Rus. *sozdavat'* 'to create' + 'to become'), *starac:a xas* 'to try hard, do one's best' (← Rus. *staratsja* 'to try, seek' + 'to become'). In modern language, the formation of complex verbs based on Russian infinitives is the most productive way of introducing new verbal lexemes. Many such combinations are occasional and occur in situations of code-mixing;

f) Verbal stems in -*r*, derived from the imperfective stem of dynamic verbs or the only stem of statives. This group is lexically restricted, as an *r*-stem is attested in less than twenty verbs. Dynamic *r*-stems only form causative compounds with *(a)q'as* 'to do', cf. *ag̟ar-q'as* 'to show' (← *ag̟as* 'to see'), *ruq:ar-q'as* 'to dry (tr.)' (← *ruq:as* 'to get dry (itr.)'), *ruʁar-q'as* 'to cool' (← *ruʁas* 'to get cold'), *ʁuzar-q'as* 'to stop (tr.)' (← *ʁuzas* 'to stop (itr.)'), *uq'ar-q'as* 'to seat' (← *uq'as* 'to sit down'). Two statives form inchoative/causative pairs similar to those that are formed from adjectives, cf. *ʜar-xas* 'to learn, get to know' / *ʜar-aq'as* 'to teach, make known' (← *ʜaa* 'knows'), *it:ar-xas* 'to fall ill, begin to ache' / *it:ar-q'as* 'to feel pain, make feel pain' (← *it:aa* 'is ill, aches'). On the place of this class of verbs among other means of expressing causative contrasts, cf. Daniel, Maisak and Merdanova (2012);

g) Apart from *r*-stems and borrowed deverbal components, many other coverbs represent bound stems that are not used outside complex verbs. Some of such stems go back to nouns, e.g., *gunt'* (→ *gunt' xas* 'to collect, gather (itr.)' and *gunt' aq'as* 'to collect, gather (tr.)') is probably related to *k'unt'* 'heap', and *masa* (→ *masa ic'as* 'to sell') seems to be an ergative form of an obsolete noun *mas* 'payment'. Some components are etymologically related to adjectives and probably represent obsolete nouns (see section 4.2), e.g., *ʔat:* (→ *ʔat: aq'as* 'to limp', cf. *ʔat:e* 'lame'), *mert:* (→ *mert: xas* 'to clear (itr.)' and *mert: aq'as* 'to clear (tr.)', cf. *mert:e* 'clear'), *č'ir* (→ *č'ir xas* 'to go bad' and *č'ir aq'as* 'to spoil', cf. *č'ire* 'barren'). The component *huk:* occurring in *huk: ic'as* 'to run' might be of verbal origin, as it resembles the root found in *q-uk:as* 'to run down, pursue', a verb with a locative POST prefix (see section 4.3.1).

Morphosyntactically, complex verbs do not represent a uniform class: some of them are close to free syntactic combinations of verbs and object noun phrases, while others are lexicalized to a considerable degree and approach simplex verb stems. In a standard case, the two parts of complex verbs are always adjacent (the coverb precedes the light verb). They can be separated when the lexical meaning of the verb is topicalized, and the coverb – which mainly expresses the lexical meaning – occurs on the left periphery, while the light verb occupies its usual position; cf. (1) with ʜar-aq'as 'to teach, make known' containing a bound component (enclosed in angle brackets in the glossing line). On the other hand, a finite verb can be put on the left periphery in the context of enumeration of successive events, cf. (2) with gunt' aq'as 'to collect, gather (tr.)' – in this case the two parts of a complex verb are also not adjacent.

(1) ʜar   zun   gi-s   aq'-a-s-e ...
    \<know\> I(ERG) that-DAT do-IPF-INF-COP
    'As for teaching, I will teach him ...' (but I do not know when this will happen)

(2) aq'-u-ne   aʜa-t:-i   wuri   gunt' ...
    do-PF-PFT big-SUBST-ERG all(ABS) \<gather\>
    '(And so,) the chief gathered everyone together ...'
    (then he spoke and asked everyone to make a decision)

In the majority of complex verbs containing a transitive light verb (aq'as 'to do', ic'as 'to give') the coverb occupies the position of patientive noun phrase in the absolutive case; cf. such verbs as huk: ic'as 'to run', č'emp' aq'as 'to champ', ʕamf aq'as 'to bark', ʔat: aq'as 'to limp', un aq'as 'to call' which only subcategorize for an ergative agent (3). In another group of verbs like p:adark:a aq'as 'to give as a present', paj aq'as 'to divide', q'at' aq'as 'to cut, detach' (← 'piece' + 'to do'), the coverb is rather an "incorporated" component which is different from the patientive noun phrase (4):

(3) dad-a   gada-jis   un   aq'-a-a.
    father-ERG son-DAT   sound(ABS) do-IPF-PRS
    'The father calls his son.'

(4) ruš-a   uč-in   jerχe č'ar-ar   q'at'   q'-u-ne.
    girl-ERG self-GEN   long   hair-PL(ABS)   piece(ABS) do-PF-PFT
    'The girl cut off her long hair.'

Though still retaining the ability to occur separately, the components of some complex verbs tend to morphologize (this is especially true of combinations with bound parts). This can be seen from the position of regular prefixal markers – negative *da-* and repetitive *qa-* (on the latter, see section 4.3.2). As a rule, only the light verb can bear these prefixes, as it is the locus of all verbal marking (cf. *ʜazur da-xas* 'not to get ready' or *ʜazur qa-xas* 'to get ready again' ← *ʜazur xas* 'to get ready'). However, some verbs prefer the position of prefixes before the whole complex, cf. *qa-gunt'-aq'as* 'to gather again' (← *gunt' aq'as*), *qa-un-aq'as* 'to call again' (← *un aq'as*), which shows that *gunt'aq'-* and *unaq'-* have been almost reanalysed as non-segmentable verb stems.

Another manifestation of univerbation is the change of the inflection type of a complex verb vis-à-vis the corresponding light verb. Thus, while the verb *aq'as* 'to do' has the imperative form with a vocalic affix, cf. *aq'-e* 'do!', many complex verbs display a variation of the imperative form which can have either vocalic suffix or zero marking (cf. *gunt'-aq'e ‖ gunt'-aq'* 'gather!', *ʜar-aq'-e ‖ ʜar-aq'* 'teach!', *mert:-aq'-e ‖ mert:-aq'* 'clean!'). Some lexemes even have the zero marked imperative as the only possible variant, cf. *ag̮ar-aq'* 'show!', *č'ir-aq'* 'spoil!', *žin-aq'* 'hide!'.

As an example of a completely morphologized complex verb, cf. *žinuxas* 'to hide (itr.)', that is historically based on a combination of the light verb *xas* 'to become' and the bound component *žin-*. Apart from the correlation with the transitive counterpart *žin-aq'as* 'to hide (tr.)', nothing in the synchronic behaviour of this verb points to its compound nature.

4 Derivation

4.1 Nominal derivation

4.1.1 Denominal nouns

The suffix *-ʕ̮el* is the only productive means for creating denominal derivations of nouns. Used with nouns denoting status or occupation, it produces **abstract nouns** denoting activities performed by people of the profession: *p:ač:ahʕ̮el* (← *p:ač:ah* 'king'), *pirsidat:elʕ̮el* (← *pirsidat:el* 'head of local administration'), *dijark:aʕ̮el* (← *dijark:a* 'milkmaid'), *uʙriʕ̮el* (← *uʙri* 'thief'), *ʜulašuwʕ̮el* (← *ʜulašuw* 'guest'), etc. Complex verbs consisting of such nouns and the verb *aq'as* 'to do' yield the meaning 'to serve, work as X', cf. *dijark:aʕ̮el aq'as* 'to work as a milkmaid'.

Another widespread derivational suffix is *-či*, which is of Turkic origin and derives a g e n t n o u n s: *deweči* 'cameleer' (← *dewe* 'camel'), *zürneči* 'zurna player' (← *zürne* 'zurna, a musical wind-instrument'), *ʜaramči* 'sinner' (← *ʜaram* 'sin'). Although this suffix is restricted to Turkic and Arabic loanwords and is not added to native nouns, Aghul speakers recognize it as a derivational suffix and generally understand the internal structure of such derivations.

Besides these, there are a number of unproductive suffixes used to form a noun from another noun. All of them are of very restricted use and are identified only in a handful of nouns each. The suffix *-kar* is found in Persian loanwords, and also forms agent nouns: *zijankar* 'saboteur' (← *zijan* 'harm, damage'), *fitnakar* 'person who spreads discord' (← *fitna* 'discord, contention'). The suffixes *-aqan* and *-qban* are found in several nouns denoting agents engaged in traditional activities: *ʜupːaqan* 'shepherd' (← *ʜub* 'sheep'), *ʕurčaqan* 'hunter' (← *ʕurč* 'game, animal hunted'), *ʜünirqban* 'herdsman' (← *ʜüni* 'cow'), *raʜuqban* 'miller' (← *raʜ* 'mill'). The suffixes *-ač* and *-ač'* form pejorative personal nouns: *funač* 'fat person' (← *fun* 'belly'), *χukač* 'glutton' (← *χuk* 'animal's stomach'), *q'at'ač'* 'person who picks up and smokes cigarette butts' (← *q'at* 'piece, incl. cigarette butt').

4.1.2 Deadjectival nouns

The abstract suffix *-ʕ̣el* discussed in the previous section is also used as a productive means of forming q u a l i t y n o u n s from adjectives: *reʜetʕ̣el* 'easiness' (← *reʜet* 'easy'), *ǯag̣arʕ̣el* 'whiteness' (← *ǯag̣ar* 'white'), *saʁʕ̣el* 'health' (← *saʁ* 'healthy'). In rare cases, this suffix occurs with participles, cf. *ajeʕ̣el* 'being in a place' (← *a-je* + *ʕ̣el* '{IN}be-PART' + 'ABSTR').

4.1.3 Deverbal nouns

The regular way to turn verbs into nouns is to derive an a c t i o n n o m i n a l (traditionally called "masdar"), by adding the suffix *-b* to the perfective stem of the verb: *aq'ub* 'doing' (← *aq'-u* 'do-PF' + *-b* 'NMLZ'), *ruχub* 'reading' (← *ruχ-u* 'read-PF' + *-b* 'NMLZ'), *k'ib* 'dying, killing' (← *k'-i* 'die, kill-PF' + *-b* 'NMLZ'). An action nominal can be derived from all verbs except for the statives, which do not have a perfective stem. Morphologically, the action nominal is a regular noun taking all nominal inflection including plural and case markers, cf. Table 24.1. Syntactically, however, the action nominal typically behaves as a verbal head, since a) it preserves the verbal argument structure and does not

Tab. 24.1: Partial paradigm of the action nominal *ruχub* 'reading' (← *ruχas* 'to read').

	SG	PL
ABS	*ruχ-u-b* read-PF-NMLZ(ABS)	*ruχ-u-b-ar* read-PF-NMLZ-PL(ABS)
ERG	*ruχ-u-b-a* read-PF-NMLZ-ERG	*ruχ-u-b-ar-i* read-PF-NMLZ-PL-ERG
DAT	*ruχ-u-b-as* read-PF-NMLZ-DAT	*ruχ-u-b-ar-is* read-PF-NMLZ-PL-DAT

allow genitive marking of either the subject or the object, and b) it allows adverbial modification, as in (5).

(5) gi   (naq'   gada-ji   pe?   qat:k'-i-b-ak-as)
    that(ERG) yesterday boy-ERG chicken(ABS) steal-PF-NMLZ-SUB/CONT-ELAT
    qat:q'-u-ne.
    tell-PF-PFT
    'He told (us) about the boy's stealing of the chicken yesterday.'

There are also a handful of historical deverbal nouns in *-al*, though this suffix is not used productively in the modern language: *uʁal* 'rain' (← *uʁas* 'to rain'), *it:al* 'disease' (← *it:aa* 'is ill, aches'), *ugal* 'rash, itch' (← *ugas* 'to itch').

4.2 Adjectival derivation

There is no productive and regular way to derive adjectives in Aghul. Diachronically, many adjectives are derived from either nouns or verbs. Noun-based adjectives have a final vowel of an unknown origin: *mič'e* 'dark' (← *mič'* 'darkness'), *k'are* 'black' (← *k'ar* 'blackness, black yarn'), *mize* 'small, fine' (← *miz* 'small amount'). Most verb-based adjectives formally represent participles, which are the only way to express certain notions: for example, *ruʁu* 'cold' (← *ruʁas* 'to get cold'), *q:uq:u* 'firm' (← *q:uq:as* 'to get firm'), *c'üre* 'old, not new' (← *c'uras* 'to fray (of clothes)'), but some others are generally no longer perceived as participles.

Aghul possesses a large number of adjectives with the suffixes *-lu* and *-suz*, borrowed from Azeri. Like with the suffix *-či*, Aghul speakers clearly recognize the two adjectival markers as derivational. Derived adjectives with the suffix *-lu* denote presence of a quality, while adjectives with the suffix *-suz* express absence of a quality, cf. *baχt:lu* 'happy' vs. *baχt:suz* 'unhappy' (← *baχt:* 'happiness').

4.3 Verbal derivation

The only way to derive a verb from a noun or adjective is by forming a complex verb (see section 3.2). Deverbal derivation of verbs, apart from forming inchoative/causative pairs from certain *-r*-stems, involves purely morphological means and is represented by locative and repetitive prefixation.

4.3.1 Locative prefixation

Locative prefixation is not fully productive: the combinability of prefixes with verbal roots is restricted, and many derived prefixed verbs have idiomatic meaning. About a half of the 120 dynamic verbal roots has prefixed derivatives, but only about 30 roots have more than one prefixed derivative. On the whole, about 350 dynamic prefixed verbs have been found. There are also 14 stative prefixed verbs derived from two roots, 'to be, be located' and 'to still be, remain'.

There are two sets of locative prefixes and two slots for them. The first set includes seven prefixes that mark l o c a l i z a t i o n and specify a particular spatial domain of a ground where a figure is located (below we give an abbreviation for the localization and then specify its basic meaning): *ʔ-* IN 'inside a container', *ʕ-* INTER 'inside liquid or substance', *h-* ANTE 'in front of a ground', *q-* POST 'behind a ground', *f-* APUD 'near a ground', *al-* SUPER 'on the horizontal surface' and *k-* SUB/CONT 'below'/'attached to a ground'. The realization of the IN marker is always zero, according to a general rule that glottal stop is not pronounced before vowels. The first vowel of the SUPER prefix can be dropped when it is not the nucleus of a closed syllable. The SUB/CONT marker is palatalized and triggers fronting of the next vowel (/a/ > /e/, /u/ > /ü/). All prefixes have allomorphs with a subsequent vowel when they occur before a consonant (cf. *a-* IN, *ʕa-* INTER, *ha-* ‖ *hi-* ANTE, *qa-* ‖ *qi-* ‖ *qu-* POST, *fa-* APUD, *ala-* SUPER, *ke-* ‖ *ki-* ‖ *kü-* SUB/CONT); the distribution of allomorphs partly depends on the phonological context, and partly is morphologically or lexically conditioned.

The second set includes prefixes that mark o r i e n t a t i o n and indicate whether a figure moves in a particular direction, or rests at a spatial domain defined by the localization marker. The markers are: *-č-* ‖ *-ča-* LAT (lative) 'motion towards', *-at:-* ELAT (elative) 'motion from', *-ʁ-* ‖ *ʁa-* UP 'motion up' and *-a-* ‖ *-da-* DOWN 'motion down'. The orientation slot is optional, so there may be verbs with

Tab. 24.2: Verbs with localization prefixes.

Localization prefix	Stative verb, root 'to be'		Dynamic verbs, root 'to put' (no orientation prefix)	
IN	áa	'is inside (a container)'	íxas	'to put inside (a container)'
INTER	ʕáa	'is inside (a substance)'	ʕ-íxas	'to put inside (a substance)'
SUPER	áldea	'is on'	al-íxas	'to put on; to build; to appoint'
SUB/CONT	kéa	'is under'/'is in contact'	k-íxas	'to put under; to hang; to light (fire)'
ANTE	háa	'is in front'	h-íxas	'to put in front'
POST	qáa	'is behind'	q-íxas	'to put close to; to turn on (the light)'
APUD	fáa	'is near'	f-íxas	'to put near'

a localization prefix only, but no verbs with an orientation prefix only (on a few exceptions with the UP marker, see below). The absence of the orientation slot usually triggers lative reading in dynamic verbs. In statives, which never have the orientation slot filled, the meaning is always essive ('no motion').

There are no verb roots for which all of the 35 logically possible combinations with locative prefixes exist. The root *-ix-* 'to put' has as many as 32 derivatives; other roots having more than ten include: *-at-* 'to let, leave', *-arx-* 'to get into, find oneself in', *-uč'-* 'to get into (with effort), climb', *du-* ‖ *d̥-* 'to pull, drag', *-aq-* 'to pour, scatter', *ʕ̥-* 'to go/come', *-ik'-* 'to put (with effort), thrust', *-ik-* 'to drive, turn out', *-iš-* 'to jump, twitch', *-dark-* 'to turn, spin'; note that the roots starting with a hyphen are bound, i.e. they do not occur outside prefixal derivatives. Examples of verbs with locative prefixes are given in Tables 24.2 and 24.3.

In dynamic verbs, the localization slot precedes the orientation slot: [LOCALI-ZATION [ORIENTATION [V$_{ROOT}$]]]. The structure of locative prefixation in verbs is parallel to the structure of locative case forms, which also consist of two (suffixal) slots, one for localization and one for orientation: [[[N$_{STEM}$] LOCALIZATION] ORIEN-TATION]. Localization markers in the nominal paradigm are historically identical to localization prefixes in verbs; nominal orientation markers, on the contrary, have a different form and a different set of values (only LAT and ELAT, the absence of orientation marker has an essive or lative interpretation). It is typical for a verb with a localization prefix to subcategorize for a noun phrase in a corresponding locative form, cf.:

(6) *ruš-a   gardan-iq šarf   q-ix-i-ne.*
    girl-ERG neck-POST scarf(ABS) POST-put-PF-PFT
    'The girl put a scarf on her neck.'

Tab. 24.3: Verbs with localization and orientation prefixes (root 'to put').

Localization prefix	Dynamic verbs (LAT orientation)	Dynamic verbs (ELAT orientation)	Dynamic verbs (UP orientation)	Dynamic verbs (DOWN orientation)
IN	a-č-íxas 'to bring inside; to hit, slap'	át:-ixas 'to take from inside'	a-ʁ-íxas 'to put up and inside'	a-dá-jxas 'to throw down from inside'
INTER	ʕa-č-íxas 'to put in (a substance); to hit, slap'	ʕ-át:-ixas 'to take from (a substance)'	ʕa-ʁ-íxas 'to rise in the throat, choke'	ʕ-á-jxas 'to pull down (the pants)'
SUPER	al-č-íxas 'to put on (the upper surface)'	al-át:-ixas 'to take from (the upper surface)'	al-ʁ-íxas 'to put above oneself'	al-á-jxas 'to throw down from (the upper surface)'
SUB/CONT	ki-č-íxas 'to put under'	k-ét:-ixas 'to take from under/from a surface'	ke-ʁ-íxas 'to raise (along a surface)', 'to raise (a person)'	k-é-jxas 'to throw down from under/from a surface'
ANTE	hi-č-íxas 'to put in front'	h-át:-ixas 'to take from the front'	–	h-á-jxas 'to throw down from the front'
POST	qi-č-íxas 'to put behind'	q-át:-ixas 'to take from behind; to betroth'	–	q-á-jxas 'to throw down from behind'
APUD	fa-č-íxas 'to slap (in face)'	f-át:-ixas 'to throw away; to lie down flat'	–	f-á-jxas 'to put down; to humiliate'

(7) šünük:̥-il jurʁan al-č-aq!
 child-SUPER shawl(ABS) SUPER-LAT-pour(IMP)
 'Cover the child with a shawl!'

(8) gada-ji lak ke-t:-ik'-i-naa jurʁan-ik-as.
 boy-ERG leg(ABS) SUB/CONT-ELAT-thrust-PF-RES.PRS blanket-SUB/CONT-ELAT
 'The boy stuck his leg out from under the blanket.'

Many prefixal verbs have idiomatic meanings, although in most cases the underlying locative metaphor is more or less clear, cf. *uq:as* 'to fight' (← IN-'to stick to'), *ačaqas* 'to button' (← IN-LAT-'to pour') / *at:aqas* 'to unbutton' (← IN-ELAT-'to pour'), аʁatas 'to curse, swear' (← IN-UP-'to let'), ʕačixas 'to slap, hit' (← INTER-LAT-'to put'), qikʼas 'to lock' (← POST-'to put with effort'), qučʼas 'to copulate' (← POST-'to get into'), qučučʼas 'to start' (← POST-LAT-'to get into'), qat:ikʼas 'to steal' (← POST-ELAT-'to put with effort'), ališas 'to entreat, beg' (← SUPER-'to jump'), alaʕ̥as 'to boil over' (← SUPER-DOWN-'to go'), alajkas 'to clear up (of weather)' (← SUPER-DOWN-'to drive'), küčʼas 'to confess' (← SUB/CONT-'to get into'). Such verbs often retain the locative subcategorization of one of the arguments, cf. ʕačixas 'to smash in' (who: ergative; in what: inter-essive) or küčʼas 'to confess' (who: absolutive; to what: sub/cont-essive).

Though in most cases the identification of locative prefixes in a verb stem is straightforward, there are about three dozen verbs for which it is not immediately clear whether they contain a prefix or not. Such verbs can have isolated roots (which do not occur elsewhere) and lack locative semantic components. What allows one to suspect a historical prefix in these lexemes is their stress pattern (simplex verbs have a stress on the ultimate syllable of a stem, while in prefixal verbs the stress moves to the penultimate syllable) and often their subcategorization frame. Thus, it is probable that there is the ANTE prefix in híšas 'to run away' and húrχas 'to ask', the INTER prefix in ʕarák:as 'to beg, tramp', the SUB/CONT prefix in kiχít:as 'to give a start', the POST prefix in qúχas 'to trust, believe' and the IN-ELAT prefix combination in át:uzas 'to pour out'. Though, for example, the root in qúχas 'to trust, believe' seems to be isolated, the fact that the object of trust is encoded by the post-essive case points to the non-arbitrary link between the first stem consonant of this verb and the POST marker. A completely lexicalized prefixal verb is χut:úrfas 'to look' (who: absolutive; at what: dative), for which only comparative dialectal data can reveal an etymological POST prefix, cf. Central Aghul qu-t:urfanas or Burkikhan qa-durfas 'to look' (who: absolutive; at what: post-essive). There are also several verbs denoting vertical body posture, which may contain the orientation UP marker without any localization marker, cf. ʁájšas 'to get up, rise', ʁútʼas 'to stand upright', ʁúzas 'to stand still', ʁahád̥as 'to lift, raise (from ground)'.

For further details on locative prefixation in the Huppuqʼ dialect, see Maisak and Merdanova (2002). In other dialects, there is some variation in the number of affixes and their form, as well as in the number of slots. First, most Aghul dialects distinguish between k:- SUB vs. k- CONT localizations (both in verbal prefixes and in the nominal paradigm); the merger of these two localizations is characteristic only of southern varieties of Aghul. Second, the number of oppositions in the orientation slot and the form of corresponding affixes may vary. Finally, in some dialects three locative prefixal slots can be filled, as the LAT/ELAT and UP/DOWN markers are not mutually exclusive, cf. fa-t:a-ʁ-učʼas APUD-ELAT-UP-climb.INF 'to rise (of sun, moon)' (Magometov 1970: 166).

4.3.2 Repetitive prefixation

Unlike locative prefixation, repetitive prefixation is unrestrictedly productive with non-stative verbs: the repetitive marker can co-occur with any verb stem, including those that already have locative prefixes (cf. examples in Table 24.4). Most stative verbs do not co-occur with the repetitive prefix, although there are a couple of exceptions, cf. *qa-k:andea* 'wants again' (← *k:andea* 'wants'), *qa-it:aa* 'is ill again' (← *it:aa* 'is ill').

Tab. 24.4: Verbs with repetitive prefixes.

q-aʁás 'to say again, tell more'	← *aʁás* 'to say'
q-ag̊ás 'to see again'	← *ag̊ás* 'to see'
qa-uχás 'to drink again'	← *uχás* 'to drink'
qa-facás 'to seize again'	← *facás* 'to seize'
qa-ʕutás 'to eat again'	← *ʕutás* 'to eat'
qu-hátas 'to send back'	← *hátas* 'to send'
qa-áqas 'to pour inside again'	← *áqas* 'to pour inside' (IN-'to pour')
qa-íxas 'to put inside again'	← *íxas* 'to put inside a container' (IN-'to put')
qa-ʕíxas 'to put into a mass again'	← *ʕ-íxas* 'to put into a mass, liquid' (INTER-'to put')
q-alíxas 'to put above again'	← *al-íxas* 'to put on an upper surface' (SUPER-'to put')
q-alčárxas 'to meet again'	← *al-č-árxas* 'to meet' (SUPER-LAT-'to get.to')

Variants of the repetitive are partly phonetically, partly lexically conditioned: *q-* appears before stems in /a/ (sometimes in other vowels as well); *qa-* appears before stems in /i/, /u/, /e/ and in consonants (including the unpronounced glottal stop of the localization prefix); *qu-* is used with the imperfective stems of motion verbs *ʕ̊as* 'to go, come' and *χas* 'to bring, take', the suppletive imperative *qujaχ* 'go away again!' (← *quʕ̊as* 'to go, come') and with the verb *hatas* 'to send'; and *qi-* is used with the suppletive imperative *qišaw* 'come again!' (← *quʕ̊as* 'to go/come'). As a rule, repetitive prefixes are atonic and do not cause stress shift; the exceptions are *q-áq'as* 'to do again; to repair' (← *aq'ás* 'to do, make') and *qá-jc'as* 'to give back' (← *ic'ás* 'to give').

The repetitive prefix precedes locative prefixes: [REPETITION [LOCALIZATION [ORIENTATION [V$_{ROOT}$]]]. In the Keren dialect, the repetitive marker normally follows the locative prefixes, cf. *k:et:a-q-arxas* 'to be destroyed again' (← *k:et:arxas* 'to be destroyed, fall apart') which corresponds to *qa-k:et:arxas* in the Huppuq' dialect. This probably means that the position of the repetitive before the locative prefixes in Huppuq' should be regarded as a comparatively recent "externalization" of this prefix.

Though being close in form, the repetitive and the POST localization prefix clearly represent two distinct morphemes. First, the POST prefix attaches to roots, including bound roots while the repetitive prefix attaches to stems already containing locative prefixes, but not to bound roots. Second, POST and repetitive derivatives differ in stress position, cf. *qá-ʁut'as* 'to stand leaning one's back on sth.' vs. *qa-ʁút'as* 'to stand up again' (← *ʁút'as* 'to stand upright'). Finally, POST and repetitive markers can co-occur in one and the same derivative verb, cf. *qa-q-árxas* 'to fall behind again' (← *q-árxas* 'to fall behind'). On the whole, the distinction between locative and repetitive prefixes is similar to the distinction between lexical vs. superlexical (or internal vs. external) prefixes which is often made for the Slavic languages: internal/lexical prefixes are tightly connected to the lexical semantics of the root, can induce argument structure changes and many combinations with them are idiomatic, while external/superlexical prefixes contribute more predictable aspect-like meanings, repetition being one of them.

The default meaning of the repetitive prefix, available to all derivatives, is r e p e t i t i v e proper 'again' (one-time repetition of an event involving same participants). With 'to give' and motion verbs, which are among the most frequent lexemes occurring with the repetitive, it usually conveys the r e d i t i v e meaning 'backwards'. Among other meanings associated with the repetitive prefix are: a d d i t i v e 'an event of the same type is repeated with different participants' (9); c o n s e c u t i v e 'an event is added to the series of events' (10); r e s p o n s i v e 'an action is produced in response to some previous action' (11); r e s t i t u t i v e 'an earlier state is restituted as the result of a reversion of an earlier event' (12). The repetitive derivatives of the two frequent verbs *xas* 'to become' and *aq'as* 'to do', apart from the default meaning 'again', also display idiomatic meanings, cf. *qa-xas* 'to get better, recover', *q-aq'as* 'to heal, cure, repair'.

(9) *aχp:a če   dad=ra   qa-k'-i-ne,   it:ar-x-u-na.*
    then our:EXCL father(ABS)=ADD RE-die-PF-PFT be.ill-become-PF-CONV
    (Soon after telling about her mother's death.) 'Then our father fell ill and also died.'

(10) *χab x-u-či   šuw=ra   q-alčarx-u-ne*
     back become-PF-COND husband(ABS)=ADD RE-(SUPER-LAT)get.to-PF-PFT
     it:a-jde.
     be.ill-PART
     (Telling about troubles in her life.) 'Besides, I got a husband who was ill.'

(11) *ti   qa-ix-a-a   za-s   pul   req:-ü?.*
     that(ERG) RE-(IN)put-IPF-PRS я-DAT money(ABS) road-IN
     (I sent that woman some sheep wool.) 'She sends me (back) the money.'

(12) wa?, suwar,   me q:enfet-ar   qa-gunt'-q'-a-s ...
    no   Suwar(ABS) this candy-PL(ABS) RE-<gather>-do-IPF-INF
    (After the candies fell and scattered all over the ground.) 'No, Suwar, let us gather all these candies again ...'

Repetitive prefixation is attested only in two southern dialects of Aghul – the Huppuq' dialect and the Keren dialect. A prefix with similar form (q-/χ-) and function exists in Lezgian, where repetitive is "so regular that it could even be considered an inflectional category of the verb" (Haspelmath 1993: 174). Given that southern Aghul dialects have for ages been in tight contact with neighboring Lezgian-speaking villages (Lezgian being the dominant language of the Kurah district of Daghestan), it is most plausible to assume that the repetitive marker was borrowed in these dialects from Lezgian.

4.4 Adverbial derivation

Adverbs are regularly formed from adjectives by means of the suffix -di/-t:i and denote a state: četindi 'being in difficulty' (← četin 'difficult'), ǯagˢardi 'being white' (← ǯagˢar 'white'), suq:urdi 'being blind' (← suq:ur 'blind'); on complex verbs based on such derivatives see section 3.2. When used with nouns denoting time spans, the same affix yields adverbs with the meaning 'the whole time span': jaʁdi 'the whole day' (← jaʁ 'day'), ist:i 'the whole year' (← is 'year').

Most nouns denoting time spans have a temporal form which in many, though not all, cases coincides with the ergative case of the noun: isa 'in (such a) year' (← is 'year'), wazala 'in (such a) month' (← waz 'month'). A few other unproductive suffixes that form temporal adverbs from nouns are also attested: cul-ana 'in fall' (← cul 'fall'), ʔurd-ana 'in winter' (← ʔurd 'winter'), ʕul-ana 'in summer' (← ʕul 'summer'), xid-ana 'in spring' (← xid 'spring'), jaʁ-uji 'in daytime' (← jaʁ 'day').

Tab. 24.5: Manner and locative adverbs from simplex demonstrative stems.

	stem	manner adverb	allative adverb	locative adverb
'near the speaker'	me	mi-št:i	mi-č	mi-sa
'near the hearer' / 'above the speaker'	le	li-št:i	li-č	li-sa
'below the speaker'	ge	gi-št:i	gi-č	gi-sa
'away from both speaker and hearer'	te	ti-št:i	ti-č	ti-sa

Demonstrative pronouns form three series of adverbs: manner adverbs ('in this/ that way') are formed by means of the suffix *-št:i*, the allative adverbs ('in this/ that direction') include the suffix *-č*, and the locative adverbs ('here/there') are formed with the help of the suffix *-sa*, cf. Table 24.5. The origin of the latter marker is the noun *us* ‖ *is*, attested in most other dialects but obsolete in Huppuq', e.g., *mi-sa* 'here' < **mi us.a-ʔ* 'in this place' ('this' + 'place-IN').

5 Reduplication

5.1 Reduplication of nouns

5.1.1 Echo-reduplication

Echo-reduplication is used to introduce a generalized set of objects or situations. It involves the repetition of a word or phrase with phonological modification of its second occurrence. The most productive and frequent type is *m*-reduplication, which represents an areal phenomenon. In words starting with a consonant this consonant is replaced by /m/, cf. *šeʔ~meʔ* 'all sorts of things' (← *šeʔ* 'thing'), *kar~mar* 'all sorts of jobs' (← *kar* 'job'), *peʔ~meʔ* 'hen and/or something else like that' (← *peʔ* 'hen'), *guni~muni* 'bread and/or something else like that' (← *guni* 'bread'). In words starting with a vowel, /m/ is prefixed, cf. *aš~maš* 'pilaw and/or something else like that' (← *aš* 'pilaw'). As an example of *m*-reduplication of the nominal part of a complex verb, cf. (13): here, *žarit'* in *žarit' aq'as* 'to fry, roast' is a borrowed Russian infinitive.

(13) sa   bic'i   *žarit'-ar* – *marit'-ar*   aq'-u-na ... faqaj-na
one little \<fry\>-PL RDP:\<fry\>-PL do-PF-CONV RE:bring:PF-CONV
i-naa   žahut'-il-di.
give:PF-RES.PRS Jew-SUPER-LAT
'Having a bit roasted it and all that ... he brought and gave it to the Jew.'

Aghul also possesses a few irregular nominal compounds with echo-reduplication, requiring the change of vowels to /ü/: *šeʔ-šüʔ* (← *šeʔ* 'thing'), *kasib-küsüb* (← *kasib* 'poor'), *gada-güdü* (← *gada* 'boy'). In one case, the first consonant changes to /q:/, cf. *ʔazab-ar-q:azab-ar* (← *ʔazab-ar* 'torture-PL'). Such compounds are borrowed from Azeri or Persian and are not productive in Aghul.

5.1.2 Reduplication of the nominal part in complex verbs

The nominal parts of certain complex verbs normally occur in reduplicated form. This is true of some verbs denoting decomposition and destruction (cf. *rug~rug xas* 'to get torn to tatters', *tika~tika aq'as* 'to divide, break into pieces', *miz~miz aq'as* 'to cut small, crumble') and verbs based on ideophones (cf. *нar~нar aq'as* 'to laugh loudly', *lurp~lurp aq'as* 'to flap', *t'ink'~t'ink'ʕ̣as* 'to drip'). In the latter verb class, ideophones can be duplicated more than once, especially when persistent reproduction of sound is implied, cf. *ʔü~ʔü~ʔü aq'as* 'to crow', *на~на~на aq'as* 'to laugh loudly'.

5.2 Reduplication in adjectives and adverbs

Full reduplication of adjective stems is used for intensification, cf. *bic'i~bic'i* 'very small' (← *bic'i* 'small'), *baha~baha* 'very expensive' (← *baha* 'expensive'). The same is true of adverbs derived from adjectives (see section 4.4), cf. *deχi~deχi-di* 'very quickly' (← *deχi* 'quick'), *jawaš~jawaš-t:i* 'very slowly, quietly' (← *jawaš* 'slow, quiet'), the latter adverb is also attested in contracted forms *jawajawašt:i, jawawašt:i*.

Full reduplication of adjective stems is also used to express universal quantification, often with distributive interpretation ('one by one'), cf. *baba~baba ʁ̣anar* 'all the big stones' (← *baba* 'big'), *ire~ire jemišar* 'all the red fruits' (← *ire* 'red').

5.3 Reduplication in verbs

Like adjective stems, participle stems can be reduplicated to express universal quantification. This is mostly characteristic of the perfective participle, cf. *užu~užu q'ut'ur* 'every baken cake one by one' (← *užas* 'to bake'), *lik'i~lik'i gaf* 'every word s/he wrote' (← *lik'as* 'to write'), *agu~agu-f* 'everything that has been seen' (← *ag̣as* 'to see', substantivized participle). For details on the types of reduplication in the verbal domain, cf. Maisak and Merdanova (2014).

5.4 Distributive reduplication of numerals

Partial or full reduplication is used to derive distributive numerals:

(14) awala ča-s   i~ic'u   manat-ar   c'-a-f-ij ...
     before we:EXCL-DAT RDP:ten   rouble-PL(ABS) give-IPF-SUBST-COP:PST
     'In older times, we were given ten roubles each ...'

Tab. 24.6: Distributive numerals from underived stems.

Distributive	Stem	
sása	← sa	'1'
ʔúʔu	← ʔu	'2'
xíxibu	← xibú	'3'
jéjeq'u	← jaq'ú	'4'
ʕáʕafu	← ʕafú	'5'
jéjerxi	← jerxí	'6'
jéjeri	← jerí	'7'
múmuja	← mujá	'8'
jéjerč'˳a	← jarč'˳á	'9'
íic'u	← ic'ú	'10'
q:áq:a	← q:a	'20'

Tab. 24.7: Distributive numerals from derived stems.

Distributive	Stem	
c'ác'asa	← c'ása	'11'
c'ác'aʔu	← c'áʔu	'12'
c'éc'exibu	← c'éxibu	'13'
c'éc'ejaq'u	← c'éjaq'u || c'éjeq'u	'14'
c'ác'aʕfu	← c'áʕafu	'15'
c'éc'ejerxi	← c'éjerxi	'16'
c'éc'ejeri	← c'éjeri	'17'
c'ác'amuja	← c'ámuja	'18'
c'éc'ejarč'˳a	← c'éjarč'˳a || c'éjerč'˳a	'19'
jéjaχc'ur || jéjeχc'ur	← jaχc'úr	'40'
xíxibuq:a	← xibuq:á	'60'
jéjeq'uq:a	← jaq'uq:á	'80'

In underived numeral stems ('one' to 'ten' and 'twenty'), the first syllable is reduplicated, and attracts the stress position: cf. *xí~xibu* 'by three; three each' (← *xibú* 'three'); see Table 24.6. As the stems of 'one', 'two' and 'twenty' all have monosyllabic CV structure, partial reduplication of these numerals is identical to the full one, cf. *sá~sa* 'by one; one each' (← *sa* 'one'). Reduplication of the syllable /ja/ in numerals 'four' and 'nine' is accompanied by vowel change /a/ > /e/, cf. *jéjeq'u* 'by four; four each' (← *jaq'ú* 'four'). Underived numerals 'hundred' and 'thousand' which morphologically fall into the class of nouns, are fully reduplicated to derive distributive counterparts, cf. *ʕ˳erš~ʕ˳erš* 'by hundred; hundred each' (← *ʕ˳erš* 'hundred'), *aʙzúr~aʙzúr* 'by thousand; thousand each' (← *aʙzúr* 'thousand').

Derived numeral stems ('eleven' to 'nineteen' and 'forty' which are all based on 'ten', and 'sixty' and 'eighty' based on 'twenty') use either partial reduplication of the first syllable or full reduplication, cf. *c'ác'asa or c'ása~c'ása* 'by eleven; eleven each' (← *c'ása* 'eleven'), *jéjaχc'ur* ‖ *jéjeχc'ur* or *jaχc'ur~jaχc'ur* 'by forty; forty each' (← *jaχc'úr* 'forty'); see Table 24.7.

In complex numerals, only the head (which occupies the final position) is reduplicated, cf. *jaχc'úr=na íic'ukitab* forty-and by ten books 'fifty books each'.

6 References

Daniel, Mikhail A., Timur A. Maisak and Solmaz R. Merdanova (2012): Causatives in Agul. In: Pirkko Suihkonen, Bernard Comrie and Valery Solovyev (eds.), *Argument Structure and Grammatical Relations. A Crosslinguistic Typology*, 76–136. Amsterdam/Philadelphia: Benjamins.

Dirr, Adolf (1907): Aguľskij jazyk. *Sbornik materialov dlja opisanija mestnostej i plemën Kavkaza* 37: I–XV, 1–188.

Haspelmath, Martin (1993): *A Grammar of Lezgian*. Berlin/New York: Mouton de Gruyter.

Magometov, Aleksandr A. (1970): *Aguľskij jazyk. Issledovanija i teksty*. Tbilisi: Mecniereba.

Maisak, Timur A. and Solmaz R. Merdanova (2002): Sistema prostranstvennyx preverbov v aguľskom jazyke. In: Vladimir A. Plungjan (ed.), *Issledovanija po teorii grammatiki*. Vol. 2: *Grammatikalizacija prostranstvennyx značenij v jazykax mira*, 251–294. Moskva: Russkie slovari.

Maisak, Timur A. and Solmaz R. Merdanova (2014): Konstrukcii s povtorom glagola v aguľskom jazyke. In: *Acta Linguistica Petropolitana*. Vol. 10, Part 3: *Studia typologica octogenario Victori Khrakovskij Samuelis filio dedicata*, 396–422. Sankt-Peterburg: Nauka.

Merdanova, Solmaz R. (2004): *Morfologija i grammatičeskaja semantika aguľskogo jazyka (Na materiale xpjukskogo govora)*. Moskva: Sovetskij pisateľ.

Sulejmanov, Nadir D. (1993): *Sravniteľno-istoričeskoe issledovanie dialektov aguľskogo jazyka*. Maxačkala: DNC RAN.

Šaumjan, Rafaeľ M. (1941): *Grammatičeskij očerk aguľskogo jazyka s tekstami i slovarëm*. Moskva/Leningrad: Izdateľstvo AN SSSR.

Tarlanov, Zamir K. (1994): *Aguly. Ix jazyk i istorija*. Petrozavodsk: Izdateľstvo Petrozavodskogo gosudarstvennogo universiteta.

Wolfgang Schulze
25 Lak

1 Introduction
2 General overview
3 Composition
4 Derivation
5 Conversion
6 Reduplication
7 References

Abstract: Word-formation in Lak (most likely the sole member of an independent branch of East Caucasian) is dominated by both compounding and derivation. Verbal compounding is strongly related to incorporation strategies. Lak is marked for a highly elaborated system of nominal derivation, whereas adjectival and adverbial derivation is rather restricted. Derivation is in principle absent in the formation of verbs. Reduplication techniques are relevant to all open word classes. Contrary to other East Caucasian languages, the import of foreign lexical units (mainly from Kumyk Turkic, Persian, and Arabic) has not restricted the productivity of native word-formation patterns.

1 Introduction

Lak is an East Caucasian language spoken by some 90,000 to 100,000 people in the central regions of the Republic of Daghestan (Russia). Lak speakers live quite compactly along the Lak Koysu river from Arakul and Katrul in the south up to Kuba and Chukna in the north (see Schulze 2011 for details). The municipal center is the administrative center of the Lak District, Kumux, inhabited by some 3,000 people. Lak has been a written language since the early 20th century. Its first writing system was based on Arabic that had been used in an informal way since 1750. In 1928, a Latinized version became the official standard. This system, however, was again replaced by a Cyrillic-based orthography in 1938. The Kumux dialect served as the basis for the establishment of a normative version of Lak. Today, Lak is present not only in local discourse, but also in printed media and

Wolfgang Schulze, Munich, Germany

radio. Most Lak speakers are bilingual, having acquired Russian as a second language during schooling. In the rural parts of Lakistan (the informal name for the Lak region), bilingualism mainly concerns varieties of Dargi (a distant relative of Lak), Avar (an East Caucasian language of the Avar-Andian branch), and (toward the east) Kumyk (Kipchak Turkic).

The position of Lak within the East Caucasian language family is still a matter of discussion. The language shows important structural and lexical isoglosses with both the northern Nakh languages (such as Chechen) and the southern (Lezgian) branch of the language family. Nevertheless, it is marked for a high degree of innovative features that set it apart from these languages. Certain aspects of both grammar and lexicon seem to relate it more directly to the neighboring Dargi varieties. However, it still is unclear whether we are dealing with an immediate genetic relationship or with secondary convergence.

The documentation of the Lak lexicon started with Uslar (1890) and culminated in the excellent dictionary by Xajdakov (1962), supplemented by Murkelinskij (1971) and Džidalaev (1987). Unfortunately, these younger dictionaries rarely include dialectal material. Lak word-formation patterns were first addressed by Uslar (1890). The Lak grammar by Žirkov (1955) includes valuable hints, although it lacks a specialized section on this topic. The same is true for the brief treatment in Bouda (1971). Word-formation as such is discussed in more detail by Xajdakov (1961) and by Abdullaev and Ėľdarova (2003). Šaxmanova (2003) summarizes the patterns of noun formation, whereas Šamsudinova (2009) discusses verb formation in more details.

2 General overview

Although historical language contact (especially with Kumyk, Persian, and Arabic) has played a crucial role in the formation of the Lak lexicon, borrowing strategies have not weakened the native means of word-formation to the extent found especially in some of the southern East Caucasian languages. This holds for both compounding and derivation. Compounding is not only present in lexical forms whose components are still transparent today, but also in many nouns and adjectives that are marked for a pronounced polysyllabic structure. However, it still is an unachieved task in historical comparative research to analyze the underlying complex structure of these forms (e.g., *baʕwaq'ulu* 'low wall used as a bench', *ganʒaʦ'alaʁaj* 'woman's headscarf', or *meχ:it'ulliw* 'dances'). Compounding is present especially in the formation of nouns, adjectives, and verbs. Quite in accordance with the typology of other East Caucasian languages, verbal compounding is dominated by incorporation strategies that serve to produce a wide array of verbal lexical concepts. Disregarding idiomatic expressions, we can describe at least seven light verbs that are involved in the formation of such compounds.

Exempting certain verbal categories that are located at the borderline between grammar and lexicon (such as aspect-stem formation), derivation is confined to nouns, adjectives, and adverbs. The nominal domain is marked for a large set of derivational morphemes, whereas adjectives are derived with the help of a single strategy that turns both nouns and verbs into adjectives. Adverbs are derived in just the same way as adjectives, taking, however, a different morpheme.

Technically speaking, all derivational means are suffixes in present-day Lak. From a historical point of view, Lak verbs could be marked for locative preverbs as is still true for neighboring Dargi. However, in most cases, these preverbs have fused with the lexical stem and no longer form a separate pattern.

Reduplication is a very common word-formation technique in Lak. It shows up in nearly all word classes except for basic verbs.

The Lak data do not give evidence of processes related to backformation, blending, and clipping. In addition, the available data do not give evidence for word-creation processes.

The Lak data given in this article include a number of derived forms components of which are no longer used independently in present-day Lak. Due to the lack of historical sources it is sometimes difficult to ascertain the meaning of these elements without a lengthy discussion of possible cognates in related languages. These components are indicated by a question mark throughout this article. The corresponding terms are referred to in order to illustrate that word-formation processes must have been typical for earlier stages of Lak, too.

3 Composition

3.1 Nominal compounds

3.1.1 Determinative compounds

Lak has at least eight types of determinative compounds, all of which are endocentric:

Simple N+N compounds

These compounds are difficult to distinguish from copulative compounds. Examples are *varani-tf'elmu* 'ostrich; lit. camel sparrow', *χ:aʕʦara-tf'elmu* 'bat; lit.

skin sparrow', ʁal-barts' 'lion; lit. pelt wolf', ini-q'ali 'flour; lit. oat flour + gallon', buʕrχ-t:uk:u 'squirrel; lit. hare donkey', q:ultʃ:a-k'ulu 'mouse, rat; lit. ? + mouse', murts'u-q:at:a 'cookhouse; lit. corner house', ʃ:aχ:a-naj 'wasp; lit. ? + bee', ʁat:ara-urt:u 'pasture; lit. sheep meadow', q:up:a-χ:alaχ: 'pin; lit. cupola needle', ʒeʁil-χ:ullu 'path; lit. ? + way', patʃ:aħ-ʃ:ar 'queen; lit. king woman', q:aħwa-ʃ:ars:a 'prostitute; lit. prostitute woman', ʃ:arʃ:u-yanna 'cloth; lit. ? + cloth', maq'ara-ærwat'i 'turtle; lit. hard shell (of a nut) + frog', tʃart-tarak'i 'barrier; lit. 'chimney + ?'. This type frequently occurs with toponyms such as t:arts'-murlu 'name of a group of rocks; lit. post rock' or p:a-bak'u 'name of a hill; lit. awl hill'. Very rarely, the two terms tʃu 'man' and ʃ:ar 'woman' are used as a second part of compounds for sex differentiation, cf. qamali-tʃu 'male guest' vs. qamali-ʃ:ar 'female guest'.

To this group we can add the names of the days. They all have q'ini 'day' as their second segment preceded by noun-like elements frequently used for their own distinction: itni-q'ini 'Monday', cf. Kumyk itni-gün (Arabic 'iṯnayn 'two'), t:alat-q'ini 'Tuesday', cf. Kumyk talat-gün (Arabic ṯalāṯ 'three'), arwaħ-q'ini 'Wednesday', cf. Kumyk arbah-gün (Arabic 'arbaʕ 'four'), χamis-q'ini 'Thursday', cf. Kumyk xamis-gün (Arabic ḥams 'five'), nuʕʒmar-q'ini 'Friday, week', perhaps a distorted version of Kumyk cuma-gün (Arabic jumʕa), χ:ullun-q'ini 'Saturday', cf. χ:ullu 'way'(?), alħat-q'ini 'Sunday' (Arabic al-aḥad 'first').

N.OBL+N compounds

In such compounds, the first noun is marked for an oblique stem that, however, lacks a case suffix. The oblique stem forms cannot be used independently. Obviously, these compounds reflect an older use of the oblique stem to encode a relational junction between the two nouns. Examples include nit:i-us:u 'uncle; lit. mother.OBL brother', but:a-us:u 'uncle; lit. father.OBL brother', ʃ:ina-χ:ullu 'canal; lit. water.OBL way', neχ:a-matʃ 'river bed; lit. river.OBL meadow', jat:i-k:atʃ:i 'sheepdog; lit. sheep.OBL dog', χ:alla-bak'u 'hey meadow; lit. hey.OBL meadow', ærtʃ'a-q:at:a 'womb; lit. child.OBL house', qaralu-k:urt:a 'collarbone; lit. below arm + wheel', baʒana-t:uk:u 'snail; lit. brother-in-law.OBL donkey' (?).

N.GEN+N compounds

This compositional type is extremely frequent and productive. Often, it is difficult to decide whether we are dealing with a standard genitive construction, such as but:al huqa 'father's shirt', t:uk:ul burtʃu 'skin of donkey; lit. donkey.GEN skin', or whether the resulting structures represent single concepts. N.GEN+N compounds are typical with kinship terms, such as us:il-ʃ:ar 'daughter-in-law (of a woman); lit. brother.GEN woman', duʃnil-ars 'grandson; lit. daughter.GEN son', arsnal-ars 'grandson; lit. son.GEN son', duʃnil-duʃ 'granddaughter; lit. daughter.GEN daughter', (u)s:il-duʃ 'niece; lit. brother.GEN daughter', arsnal-duʃ 'granddaughter; lit. son.GEN daughter', *lasnal-ninu* 'mother-in-law (of a man); lit. husband.GEN mother', *ʃ:arnil-ninu* 'mother-in-law (of a woman); lit. wife.GEN mother', *but:al-ninu* 'grandmother; lit. father.GEN mother', *nit:ul ninu* 'grandmother; lit. mother-GEN mother', *(u)s:il-œrtʃ* 'nephew; lit. brother.GEN child', *lasnal-p:u* 'father-in-law (of a man); lit. husband.GEN father', *but:al-p:u* 'grandfather; lit. father.GEN father, *nit:ul p:u* 'grandfather; lit. mother-GEN father', *but:al-s:u* 'father's sister', *nit:ul-s:u* 'mother's sister', *arsnal-ʃ:ar* 'daughter-in-law (of a man); lit. son.GEN wife'.

The following examples also suggest the presence of compounds: *t:uk:ul tsʷu* 'thymus; lit. donkey.GEN salt', *t:uk:ul nis* 'mushroom; lit. donkey.GEN cheese', *t:uk:ul nak'* 'spurge; lit. donkey.GEN milk', *witʃ'il us* 'earring; lit. ear.GEN shoe', *naˤk'un-naˤ < naˤk'ul naˤ* 'bird cherry; lit. dragonfly.GEN brain', *laˤlulul-tʃaru* 'jewel; lit. belt.GEN stone', *paˤlutral-hiwx* 'acorn; lit. soothsayer.GEN nut', *pirmalulzallu* 'farmer; lit. farm.GEN lord', *ʃinᵃ/ᵤl-zamana* 'season; lit. year.GEN time', *ʃahnal-latʃ'a* 'maize, corn; lit. Shah.GEN wheat', *inʒiral-murx* 'banyan; lit. fig.GEN tree', *t:arlil-murx*; 'conifer; lit. needle.GEN tree', *œnak'ul-œrtʃ* 'chicken; lit. hen.GEN child', *burħal-t:ark'* 'spine; lit. ? + bone', *murxiral-t:arts* 'tree trunk; lit. tree.GEN post', *t'annul-ust:ar* 'carpenter; lit. wood.GEN master', *tʃaril-ust:ar* 'mason; lit. stone.GEN master', *mux:al-ust:ar* 'smith, blacksmith; lit. iron.GEN master', *k:unukral-qaqimur* 'egg yolk; lit. egg.GEN yellow.DEF', *majlul-tʃiraq* 'candle; lit. tallow.GEN light', *x:aˤltsul-tʃuqa* 'spider web; lit. spider.GEN cloth', *duniaˤl suk:uʃawu* 'earthquake; lit. earth.GEN shaking', *kiraʒral-ʃ:in* 'mortar; lit. chalk.GEN water', *x:aˤx:aˤl-ʃ:in* 'sap; lit. plant.GEN water', *zunzul-tʃani* 'dawn; lit. ?.GEN light'. The two terms *qurs:ul-ʒa* 'furrow' and *qurs:ul-dak'i* 'titmouse' (both without a sure analysis) illustrate that the segments of some of these compounds are no longer used as independent terms.

N.LOC+N

Some N+N compounds link the two segments with the help of a locative case, for instance *nisiraj-tʃ:at'* 'pierogi with cheese; lit. cheese.SUPERESSIVE1 bread', *buruws:annujx-k:urtʃ* 'grout with dried apricots; lit. apricot.SUPERESSIVE2 grout', *witʃ'iluwun-dux:u* 'centipede; lit. ear.ILLATIVE going into', *ʒipluwu-karʃ:i* 'handkerchief, rag; lit. pocket.INESSIVE cloth'.

A+N compounds

These compounds belong to one of two subtypes:
a) unmarked adjectives, that is adjectives that lack the attributive marker *-s:a* or one of its definite variants (*-ma* (human males, singular), *-mur* (other singulars), *-mi* (plural)). This type is especially frequent with concepts related to the categories of inner body parts, plants, and animals, e.g., *k'uˤla-x:uˤt:u*

'small intestine; lit. narrow intestine', *ganz-χ:uʕt:u* 'colon; lit. thick intestine', *mutʃʼi-χ:uʕt:u* 'blind gut; lit. blind intestine', *ganz-litʃ:a* 'large cnemis; lit. thick bone', *buχ-litʃ:a* 'pelvic bone; lit. used bone', *duχ-laʕqʼa* 'iliac region; lit. used stomach', *qʼa-bak* 'vertex; lit. even head', *kʼaʕla-maʃaku* 'clary sage; lit. white clary', *kʼaʕla-t:ullan* 'white henbane', *luħi-tʼutʼi* 'vine grape; lit. black fruit', *muʕrʃ-quʕru* 'garden pea; lit. small pea', *luħi-quʕru* 'field bean; lit. black pea', *natsʼu-metʃ* 'sorrel (*rumex confertus*); lit. sweet nettle', *natsʼu-marχ:a* 'liquorice; lit. sweet root' (cf. Greek *glukurrhiza* 'liquorice' ← γλυκύς (*glukus* 'sweet') + ρίζα (*rhiza* 'root'), *murtʃʼi-kʼulu* 'mole; lit. blind mouse', *luħi-qatsʼ* 'whim; lit. black grasshopper', *luħi-tʃʼelmu* 'starling; lit. black sparrow'. Other examples are *duqʼra-ħan* 'alcoholic beverage; lit. thick drink', *quʕmu-musi* 'quicksilver; lit. wild gold', *ʁarʁ-artsu* 'silver; lit. broken silver', *sina-œrʃ:i* 'clay; lit. clammy earth', *ganz-ʒira* 'buttocks; lit. thick rib', *kʼaʕla-maχ* 'tin, tinplate; lit. white iron', *tʃʼiri-neχ* 'rivulet; brook, lit. little river', *daʕrq:un-ninu* 'stepmother; lit. false (class II) mother', *œwq:un-p:u* 'stepfather; lit. false (class I) father'.

b) The compounds of this group include adjectives that add one of the attributive markers mentioned above. With most of these compounds, the degree of cohesion is not very high. Examples are: *kʼaʕχs:a-tʃul* 'left (side)', *urtʃʼaχs:a-tʃul* 'right (side)', *dirzs:a-œʃ* 'intention, purpose; lit. rising line', *dirzs:a-dars* 'ghost, phantom; lit. rising lesson', *qʼuʕltʼs:a-za* 'secret; lit. secret thing', *tʼœns:a-qʼanq* 'fragrant, good smelling; lit. nice smell', *qunmur-s:u* 'older sister; lit. old sister', *tʃʼiwimur-s:u* 'younger sister; lit. young sister', *qunama-us:u* 'older brother; lit. old brother', *tʃʼiwima-us:u* 'younger brother; lit. young brother', *ʁajkus:a-qu* 'furrow; lit. plowing field', *laqs:a-tʃʼu* 'sound, noise; lit. high sound'.

Adv+N

This type is rather restricted because of the underlying incompatibility of nouns and adverbs, as long as the nouns are not deverbal units (masdars). Nevertheless, Lak occasionally uses mainly locational adverbs to specify nominal concepts. Examples include *jalt:u-huqa* 'shirt; lit. up shirt', *jalt:u-ħaʒak* 'trousers; lit. up trouser', *jalt:u-janna* 'outer garment; lit. up cloth', *lurt:u-huqa* 'singlet; lit. low shirt', *lurt:u-janna* 'lingerie; lit. low cloth', *tʃʼaraw-duʃ* 'relatives of bride; lit. near girl', *arħal-ʃ:ar* 'best woman; lit. together woman', *luw-ars* 'stepson; lit. below son', *luw-duʃ* 'stepdaughter; lit. below daughter'. With deverbal nouns (-*u*, see the next paragraph), we get, for instance, *jalt:u-uk:u* 'supervisor; lit. from up coming', *jalt:u-turu* 'cover; lit. up throwing', *x:itʃʼuχ-daħu* 'apron; lit. to the front binding'. The reverse type (N+Adv) is documented in at least one compound, namely *aχt:aj-*

maq 'afternoon; lit. noon after' (cf. the N+N form *aχt:ajn-tʃ'un* 'noon, midday; lit. noon time').

N + N

The second segment of these compounds is a verb nominalized with the help of the suffix *-u* (see section 4.1). This suffix produces a g e n t n o u n s in the broadest sense, identical in form to participles. This compounding technique is based on an underlying incorporation strategy. Usually, the first nominal functions as the agent of the verb, if intransitive, or as the patient of the verb, if transitive. In Lak, the general alignment pattern is ergative-driven, using class markers as agreement elements on the verb. Accordingly, class markers that "ergatively" agree with the intransitive agent or with the transitive patient show up in the corresponding compounds, too, as long as there are no phonetic constraints. Examples are (Roman numbers refer to class markers): *tsʷu-bitʃu* 'bin for salt; lit. salt III.sprinkling', *kaʁar-bitʃu* 'bin for sugar; lit. sugar III.sprinkling', *ʃ:a-buk:u* 'pressing iron; lit. line III.accompanying', *maq-laqu* 'orator; lit. word expressing', *surat-riʃ:i* 'photographer; lit. image producing', *latʃ:i-butu* 'instrument used to crush garlic; lit. garlic III.crushing', *tʃ'enpi-ruʕq'u* 'cigarette paper; lit. spittle absorbing', *guʒ-bawu* 'rape; lit. strength III.doing', *t'aħunt:iw-dawu* 'potter; lit. creamware.PL IV.doing', *daχ:ana-dawu* 'trade, barter; lit. exchange IV.doing', *daʕrq:u-ʃ:awu* 'cold (catarrh); lit. cold becoming'.

N U M + N

Numerals may constitute the first segment of nominal compounds, too. Examples are: *ʃan-tʃ'ap'i* 'clover; lit. three leaf', *ʃan-batʃ'u* 'road junction; lit. three divisor', *k'inni-tʃu* 'twins; lit. two.OBL man'.

3.1.2 Copulative compounds

True copulative compounds usually are dvandvas. Examples are *buʕq'u-œj* 'blame, rebuke; lit. blame rebuke', *t'aħni-k'itʃ'u* 'dishes; lit. mug bowl', *ʃanu-k'aralu* 'bed; lit. mattress pillow', *bak'-ʃ:ik'* 'intestines of animals; lit. head hoof', *puʕrun-tʃ'il* 'dishes; lit. glass shard', *k:ulla-jansaw* 'ammunition; lit. bullet + (gun) powder', *maχ:a-χ:atin* 'condiment; lit. 'root + ?', *urt:u-ʃ:in* 'vegetation; lit. grass water', *aʒari-œnak'i* 'fowl; lit. cock chicken', *ninu-p:u* 'parents; lit. mother father'.

3.2 Adjectival compounds

Lak has two types of adjectival compounding, A+A and N+A.

The A+A type is rare. Normally, these compounds are copulative in nature. In some instances, they are difficult to distinguish from reduplicated structures that show a heavy distortion of the second element. Note that the adjectival/attributive marker -s:a (see section 3.1.1, A+N compounds) is added only to the second element. Examples are ut:a-k'uʕla-s:a 'narrow; lit. broad narrow', s:uma-laqu-s:a 'long and narrow', luħi-ts'an-s:a 'very dark; lit. dark dark', naʕk'-talati-s:a 'blue-like; lit. blue + ?', ærʧ'i-k'uri-s:a 'colored; lit. colored + ?', luħi-purʃ:i-s:a 'dark-skinned; lit. dark skinny', qaqi-matʃ'a-s:a 'pale; lit. yellow + ?'. Reduplication-like structures are for instance ʧ'iwi-q'iwi-s:a 'small + ?' and butʃ-q'utʃ-s:a 'corpulent; lit. fat + ?'. In some cases, the cohesion between the two adjectives is not as strong as in the examples given so far. This type of "adjectival aggregation" is illustrated, for instance, by qunmas:a-ħallajs:a 'having existed since long, long-time; lit. old living'.

In N+A compounds, the second segment usually is a verb-like element, turned into a verbal adjective (participle). This type includes negated forms based on the negative copula -aq:a- 'not being', cf. taχsir-baq:a-s:a 'innocent; lit. guilt III.not-being', æq'lu-baq:asa 'insane, crazy; lit. mind III.not-being', k:ak:an χ:uj-baq:a-s:a 'ugly; lit. looking good III.not-being'. Frequently, the nominal element of adjectival compounds based on verbal adjectives represents the incorporated element of underlying complex verbs, as in maz-q:ak'ul-s:a 'mute; lit. language not knowing', ærmu-laqi-s:a 'durable; lit. life extending', ʃ:ar-durtsu-s:a 'married man; lit. woman filled', kutak-du-s:a 'strong, mighty, powerful; lit. power being', ʃ:ar-xus:a 'married woman; lit. woman becoming'. In many cases, the incorporated element cannot be safely characterized as "nominal", due to the fact that the corresponding element is no longer used independently. Examples are maħat:al-xu-s:a 'surprised, astonished; lit. astonishment being' and laʕq'luwu-xu-s:a 'pregnant; lit. in birth being'. The fact that Lak allows the unmarked conversion especially of verbal adjectives into nouns conditions that such N+A compounds are semantically difficult to distinguish from nominal compounds. For instance, the above-mentioned term ʃ:ar-xu-s:a can be used both as an attribute, e.g., t:ul ʃ:ar-xu-mur s:u 'my married sister', or as a noun, e.g., ta: ʃ:ar-xu-s:a dur 'she is a married woman'.

Only few compounds have a simple adjective as their second element, e.g., ærmu-k'ul-s:a 'wise; lit. life knowing', dak'-t'ajla-s:a 'faithful; lit. heart direct'. Some of these compounds may be liable to a nominal, exocentric interpretation. Nevertheless, the data available do not allow a conclusive picture yet.

3.3 Verbal compounds

Lak verb formation is dominated by incorporating techniques based on a greater number of light verbs, some of which form productive paradigms. The incorporated element can be again a verb (in its masdar form), a noun, an adjective/adverb, or a deictic element. A nominal that is incorporated into the verbal structure may trigger a corresponding class marker on the verb (class I (human males) Ø-, class II (elder women) *d-*, class III (other women, some animates, other objects) *b-*, class IV (other animates, objects, etc.) *d-*; note that this list refers only to the singular). In some complex verbs, the incorporated element cannot be safely identified from a synchronic point of view.

The light verbs used to derive complex verbs usually classify the underlying concept with respect to the dimension of transitivity (intransitive, transitive, causative, anticausative), although secondary semantic processes may obscure this overall strategy. Note that, in addition, the light verbs may show up in different (some suppletive) stem forms that reflect aspectual features (perfective/imperfective/iterative). The semantics of the incorporated element as well as the resulting verbal concept may favor one of these stem variants, cf. *haz-xun* (perfective) 'to rise; lit. high become' vs. *quna-qanan* 'to grow; lit. big become' (imperfective). The following light verbs represent productive classes (CM = class marker):

The light verb CM-*an* 'to make, do' (factitives, causatives):

N+V: *taxsirlu an* 'to convict' ← *taxsir* (Arabic *taqṣīr*) 'guilt', *amru b-an* 'to command, order' ← *amru* (Arabic *'amr*) 'order', *baʁiʃla b-an* 'to forgive' ← Kumyk *bağišlamaq* 'id.', *bajan b-an* 'to announce' ← *bayan* 'declaration', *huʒum b-an* 'to attack' ← Kumyk *hužum* 'attack', *zaral b-an* 'to harm, injure, damage' ← Kumyk *zaral* 'wound', *ikram b-an* 'to worship' ← Arabic *'ikrām* 'worshipping', *k'uʃ:in b-an* 'to urinate' ← *k'uʃ:in* 'urine', *lurk'an d-an* 'to ambush' ← *lurk'an* 'ambush', *naʦena d-an* 'to curse' ← *naʦena* 'spell', *qu ærʁa d-an* 'to cultivate, till; lit. make a field clean' (← 'field' + 'cultivated'), *ts'a d-an* 'to praise' ← *ts'a* 'name', *ʃ:urʃ:u b-an* 'to whisper' ← *ʃ:urʃ:u* 'susurration'.

V+V: *baʦ'an b-an* 'to cease, stop' ← *b-aʦ'an* 'to stop (itr.)', *buwtʃ'in b-an* 'to explain' ← *-uwtʃ'in* 'to understand', *bujur b-an* 'to command, order' ← Kumyk *bujurmaq* 'to order', *han b-an* 'to send' ← *han* 'to go', *daq:a d-an* 'to lose' ← *-aq:a* 'to be not', *duʦin d-an* 'to measure' ← *-uʦin* 'to weigh', *k:ak:an b-an* 'to show' ← *k:ak:an* 'to see', *laħan b-an* 'to bend' ← *laħan* 'to bend (itr.)', *leq'an d-an* 'to destroy' ← *leq'an* 'to get broken', *tapʃir b-an* 'to betray' ← Turkic *tapšur-* 'to hand over'.

A+V: *harta d-an* 'to spread out' ← *harta* 'broad', *duzal d-an* 'to build' ← *duzal* 'prosperous', *haz d-an* 'to pick up' ← *haz* 'high', *kut'a b-an* 'to cut down' ← *kut'a* 'short', *q:urtal d-an* 'to end (temporal)' ← *q:urtal* 'finished', *litʃ'i b-an* 'to divide, separate, share' ← *litʃ'i* 'separate', *marts' b-an* 'to peel' ← *marts'* 'pure', *ħurħa b-an* 'to retard, delay' ← *ħurħa* 'slow', *χ:as:al b-an* 'to save, rescue' ← *χ:as:al* 'saved', *qun b-an* 'to raise, plant' ← *qun* 'big, old', *tsatʃ'un b-an* 'to collect, gather' ← *tsatʃ'u* 'together' (cf. *tsatʃ'un d-an* 'to have sexual intercourse').

First element being unclear: *qaʕwrin an* 'to deceit' ← ?, *k'unk'u b-an* 'to pull' ← ?, *k'ura d-an* 'to twist' ← ?, *k:utʃ:u d-an* 'to squeeze, wring' ← ?, *q:ala b-an* 'to pile up' ← ?.

The light verb CM-*ulun*/CM-*ull-an* 'to give':

This light verb usually produces factitives and causatives (some exceptions apply). Many verbs include a nominal segment, but V+V and A+N also occur.

N+V: *baχtʃu b-ulla* 'to hinder, prevent' ← *aχtʃu* 'obstacle', *daru b-ullan* 'to cure, heal' ← Persian *dārū* 'medicine', *iχtilat b-ullan* 'to speak, talk' ← Arabic *iħtilāt* 'talk', *zurzu b-ullan* 'to fever' ← 'shiver', *lax:in b-ullan* 'to teach' ← *lax:in* 'to learn', *artsu d-ullan* 'to pay' ← *artsu* 'silver', *burʒiraj b-ulun* 'to lend' ← Arabic *burj* 'debt', *daħawu d-ullan* 'to tie, bind' ← *daħawu* 'connection', *duɕæ d-ullan* 'to pray, bless' ← Arabic *duʕa* 'prayer, bless', *kajaluwʃiwu* 'to rule, govern' ← *kajaluwʃiwu* 'rulership', *minnat b-ullan* 'to ask, request' ← Arabic *minna* 'favor', *paχru b-ullan* 'to boast' ← *paχru* 'pride', *pikri b-ullan* 'to think' ← Arabic *fikr* 'thought', *ruχsat b-ulun* 'to let, permit' ← Arabic *ruħsa* 'allowance', *s:ugru d-ullan* 'to rebuke, scold' ← *s:ugru* 'scolding (plural)', *sual b-ulun* 'to ask (question, inquire)' ← Arabic *su'āl* 'question', *χijallu b-ullan* 'to dream' ← Arabic *ħayāl* 'vision, chimera' (plural in Lak), *χ:allu d-ullan* 'to spin' ← *χ:al-lu* 'thread, yarn (plural)', *qʷardu* 'to swear' ← *qʷar-du* 'oath (plural)', *quʕltʃu b-ullan* 'to shake' ← *quʕltʃu* 'shaking', *ts'a d-ullan* 'to bless' ← *ts'a* 'name', *tsurk b-ullan* 'to steal' ← *tsurk* 'theft', *tʃak b-ullan* 'to pray' ← *tʃak* 'prayer', *tʃani b-ullan* 'to shine' ← *tʃani* 'light', *tʃ:ar d-ullan* 'to thresh' ← *tʃ:ar* 'threshing'.

A+V: *baχ:ana b-ullan* 'to change' ← *baχ:ana* 'different', *hanaʁi b-ullan* 'to roll' ← *hanaʁi* 'rotating', *maʃhur b-ullan* 'to preach' ← Arabic *mašhūr* 'important', *maq b-ulun* 'to promise' ← *maq* 'related to hand', *muʕrʃb-ullan* 'to crush, grind' ← *muʕrʃ* 'small, little', *sakin b-ullan* 'to mold (clay)' ← *sakin* 'gathered', *ħala b-ullan* 'to stir, mix' ← *ħala* 'mixed', *qin b-ullan* 'to cure, heal' ← *qin* 'good'.

V+V: *bas b-ullan* 'to crush, grind' ← Kumyk *basmaq*, *lajan d-ullan* 'to pinch' ← 'to be aslant', *χ:aʕχ:an b-ullan* 'to ride' ← *χ:aʕχan* 'to throw oneself onto (a horse)'.

First element being unclear: *buʁ b-ullan* 'to choke' ← ?, *s:uku b-ullan* 'to scrape' ← ?, *ts'araјχ d-ullan* 'to roast, fry' ← ?.

The light verb *t'un/utʃin* (< *uki-*) 'to say':

This light verb is normally used with concepts related to the production of sounds, especially by humans. The verb has not been grammaticalized to the extent present in other, especially southern East Caucasian languages. Nevertheless, it is also used with some verbal concepts that do not belong to the group just mentioned. Sound-related terms are, for instance, *aw-aw- t'un* 'to howl' (onomatopoetic), *balaj t'un* 'to sing' ← *balaj* 'song', *baʕ-baʕ t'un* 'to stutter, stammer' (onomatopoetic), *ʁalʁa t'un* 'to say, speak' ← *ʁalʁa* 'talking', *k'artʃ'a t'un* 'to vomit' ← *k'artʃ'a* 'emesis', *k'unt'a t'un* 'to drop' ← *k'unt'a* 'drop', *q'ats'a t'un* 'to bite' ← *q'ats'(a)* 'mouth', *mur-mur t'un* 'to mumble' (onomatopoetic), *piʃ t'un* 'to smile' ← *piʃ* 'smile', *p:aj t'un* 'to kiss' ← *p:aj* 'kiss', *puw t'un* 'to spit' ← *puw* 'spittle', *uh-q:ak t'un* 'to groan' (onomatopoetic), *χ:uʕmχ:u t'un* 'to snore' ← *χ:uʕnχ:u* 'snoring', *ts'ir-ts'ir t'un* 'to shriek, screech' (onomatopoetic), *tʃawx t'un* 'to splash' ← ?, *ʃuʕt' t'un* 'to whistle' ← *ʃuʕt'* 'whistle', *œntʃ utʃin* 'to sneeze' ← *œntʃ* 'sneeze', *wew utʃin* 'to shout, cry out' ← *wew* (interjection), *pus utʃin* 'to break wind' (onomatopoetic), *ɦunq utʃin* 'to hiccough' (onomatopoetic), *ts'up' utʃin* 'to suck' (onomatopoetic), *tʃ'eq' utʃin* 'to break wind' ← ?.

The following compounds suggest a stronger grammaticalization of the light verb: *œrtʃ:a t'un* 'to lame' ← *œrtʃ:a* 'lame', *s:unt'a t'un* 'to smell at' ← *s:unt'(a)* 'sniffing', *t'urk'u t'un* 'to play' ← *t'urk'u* 'play', *qapa t'un* 'to seize, grasp' ← *qap(a)* 'snap, bite', *lants' utʃin* 'to lick' ← **lants'* 'licking', *χ:aʕrk utʃin* 'to creep, crawl' ← *χ:aʕrk* 'creeping', *tʃant'a utʃin* 'to wake up' (cf. *tʃani* 'light', old adessive?).

The light verb *xun/qanan* 'to become':

This light verb serves to form intransitive expressions or anticausatives. Some of these lexical forms are calques from Kumyk. Examples are: *aʕlapar qanan* 'to dwell, live' ← ?, *harta xun* 'to spread out' ← *harta* 'broad, plane', *xyltʃu-k'ut'u xun* 'to cringe, flinch' ← ?, cf. *k'ut'u xun* 'to agitate', *ʁan xun* 'to approach' ← *ʁan* 'close, near', *suk:u xun* 'to move' ← ?, *quna qanan* 'to grow' ← *quna* 'big, old', *haz xun* 'to climb, rise' ← *haz* 'high', *laway xun* 'to climb, go up' ← 'up', *χ:as:al xun* 'to flee' ← *χ:as:al* 'saving from danger', *zana xun* 'to come back' ← ?, *k'ul xun* 'to learn' ← *k'ul* 'knowing', *maqunmaj xun* 'to retreat' ← *maqunmaj* 'down, back (class III)', *ʃ:ar xun* 'to marry' ← *ʃ:ar-* 'wife', a calque from Kumyk *egre barmaq*, *muʕt'i(y) xun* 'to obey' ← *muʕt'iy* 'obedient', a calque from Kumyk *tabi bolmaq*, *muk'ru xun* 'to admit, confess' ← Kumyk *mükür* 'confession', cf. Kumyk *mükür bolmaq* 'to be confessing', *dindir xun* 'to surrender' ← *din-* 'quiet' (?), a calque from Kumyk *qolğa barmaq*, *bat xun* 'to disappear' ← ?, a calque from Kumyk *yoq bolmaq*, *œrtʃ'an xun* 'to conceive' ← *œrtʃ'* 'child, son (dative)', a calque from Kumyk *aylı bolmaq*.

The light verb *-ik'an* 'to be':

This light verb is frequently added to adverbial forms marked for the suffix *-nu*, cf. *anawarnu -ik'an* 'to hasten, hurry' ← *anawar* 'quick', *wiχnu -ik'an* 'to believe' ← *wix* 'believing', *-unu -ik'an* 'to own, possess' ← *-u* 'to be', *ɦajpnu -ik'an* 'to regret, be sorry' ← ħajp 'pity' (Arabic), k'ulnu -ik'an 'to know' ← k'ul 'knowing', χ:iranu b-ik'an 'to love' ← χ:ira 'beloved', bursawnu -ik'an 'to be respectful' ← bursaw 'respect'. The following terms illustrate non-adverbial lexical bases. The meaning of these lexical stems is etymologically unclear: f:ajwk'un -ik'an 'to sit' ← ?, q:is b-ik'an 'to crouch' ←?, park -ik'an 'to fly off, flush' ← park ?, la b-ik'an 'to hide' ← ?.

The light verb -uk:an 'to get out':
Apart from its function to indicate 'motion', this light verb often denotes a change of state. Examples are: tajla -uk:an 'to direct towards' ← tajla 'direct', œʧuχ -uk:an 'to correct oneself' ← œʧuχ 'correct, right, open', badal -uk:an 'to take revenge' ← ?, baralun -uk:an 'to become a witness, testify' ← bar(a) 'witness', bat'i b-uk:an 'to prepare oneself' ← bat'i ?, weχs:a d-uk:an 'to disembowel' ← weχs:a 'intestines', ʒuʃ d-uk:an 'to hasten' ← ?, ʧ'uq:a d-uk:an 'to be exhausted' ← ʧ'uq:a 'exhausted', imam d-uk:an 'to be put out, in a spiritual state' ← imam 'belief', q:yʃ b-uk:an 'to dress up' ← ?, k'yla b-uk:an 'to impoverish' ← k'yla 'slim', lœqi -uk:an 'to grow' ← lœqi 'long, tall' (often shortened to lœ -uk:an), manʁal d-uk:an 'to brace, flatten' ← manʁal 'pressing iron', marʦ' b-uk:an 'to end' ← marʦ' 'perfect, clean, absolute', taza -uk:an 'to be hale, lusty, spry' ← taza 'hale, lusty, spry', t'ar b-uk:an 'to show up, become apparent' ← t'ar 'hearing'.

The light verb k:ak:an 'to see':
This is the least grammaticalized light verb. When used with the causative light verb b-an, it denotes concepts of 'showing'. Examples are: lajq'nu k:ak:an 'to esteem' ← lajq'nu 'worthy', maʁ k:ak:an ban 'to run away; lit. make see the tail (maʁ)', norma k:ak:an ban 'to set up a norm; lit. make see the norm', qin k:ak:an 'to regard with favor' ← qin 'good', mak' k:ak:an 'to dream' ← mak' 'sleep'.

4 Derivation

Quite in accordance with the typology of many other East Caucasian languages, derivational morphology is especially relevant in the formation of nominal and adjectival concepts, whereas verb formation mainly relies on compounding.

4.1 Nominal derivation

Although some derivational suffixes have become specialized with respect to the word class to which they are added, it is difficult to delimit the corresponding derivational morphemes with respect to this criterion. Some of the suffixes may occur with more than one major word class (nouns, adjectives, verbs). In addition some lexical stems cannot be assigned to a distinct word class because they show up in their independent form only as parts of an incorporated structure (compound). Quite in accordance with other East Caucasian languages, the semantic domains covered by the individual derivational morphemes are rather general, matching standard classification to a certain extent only. Accordingly, reference to this classification is tentative rather than biunique.

4.1.1 Denominal nouns

The suffix -ʧi borrowed from Turkic is the most productive element for forming denominal nouns. Usually it denotes a profession or a person typically related to a given issue (a g e n t n o u n s in the widest sense). It is present not only with borrowed nouns, but also with native nouns. Examples include ħilla-ʧi (~ ħilla-kar) 'sly, artful person' ← ħilla 'sly, artful' (cf. Kumyk hillaçı 'sly person'), ts'uʃinna-ʧi 'innovator' ← ts'u 'new' (second part unclear), ʧakmak-ʧi 'bootmaker' ← ʧakmak 'boot', ʧarχi-ʧi 'fellow believer' ← ?, zijarat-ʧi 'pilgrim' ← zijarat 'grave of a holy person' (Arabic ziyārat 'visit'), zijan-ʧi 'vermin' ← zijan 'damage', kumag-ʧi 'helper' ← kumag 'help' (Kumyk kömek), q:alaj-ʧi 'tin coater', q:aral-ʧi 'guardian' ← Kumyk qaravul 'guard', iʃbaʒaran-ʧi 'businessman', bak'-ʧi 'guide' ← bak' 'head'. The suffix -ʧi competes with the element -kar that has been borrowed from an Iranian language, most likely Persian.

Contrary to -ʧi, the suffix -kar is no longer productive. Examples are: piʃa-kar 'craftsman' ← piʃa 'craft', s:aʕt-kar 'clockmaker' ← s:aʕt 'time, hour' (Arabic saʕat 'hour'), tamaħ-kar 'pretentious person' ← tamaħ 'appetite, pretension' (Arabic ṭamaʕ 'greed, desire'), zulmu-kar 'oppressor' ← zulmu 'pressure' (Arabic ẓulm 'oppression'), sænat-kar 'craftsman' ← sænat 'profession', æq'lu-kar 'wise person' ← æq'lu 'wise' (Arabic ʕaqil 'wise'), dæʔwi-kar 'claiman' ← dæʔwi 'complaint, charge' (Arabic daʕwa 'call, appeal').

The denominal suffix -un mainly derives pejorative terms to denote the human character, cf. ʃ:yrt'un 'liar' ← ʃ:yrt' 'lying', warxun 'coward' ← ?, xyrtun 'litter lout' ← xyrt 'pear' (?), karʃ:un 'effeminate man' ← karʃ: 'cloth', ʧ'urtun 'effeminate man' ← ?.

The denominal suffix -χana (< Persian 'house') produces nouns denoting the p l a c e where something typically happens or is typically present: basma-χana 'printing house' ← Kumyk basma 'printed', ilʧi-χana 'embassy' (Kumyk ilçi 'ambassador'), q'as:ab-χana 'slaughterhouse' ← q'as:ab 'slaughtering' (Arabic qassāb 'butcher'), puʧ-χana 'post office' ← puʧ (Russian počta) 'post', t:upt:up-χana 'artillery position' ← *t:up* 'bullet' (reduplicated), *diwan-χana* 'courthouse' ← *diwan* 'court' (Persian *diwān* 'court'). *-alu* derives place nouns from nouns and adjectives that are sometimes marked for a locative case. Examples are *ej-alu* 'ruins' ← *ej* ?, *q:at'-alu* 'place inside the house' ← *q:ata* 'house', *wiw-alu* 'interior' ← *wiw* 'inside', *k'i-tf'iraw-alu* 'street; lit. region between two walls'. Another way of deriving such nouns is the use of the suffix *-zannu* (perhaps ← *zanan* 'to go (durative)) that refers to places where something is typically stored, such as *χ:ala-zannu* '(hey) meadow' ← **χ:ala* 'hey' (cf. *χ:ala-bak'u* 'hey stack; lit. hey-hill'), *para-zannu* 'dung pile' ← *para* 'dung', *ʁat:ara-zannu* 'gathering place for livestock' ← *ʁat:ara* 'livestock'.

Contrary to other, especially southern East Caucasian languages, the Turkic suffix *-luğ* has not been adopted as a productive suffix in Lak. It only shows up with some loans, such as *q:atʃaʁ-luʁ* 'robbery' ← *q:atʃaʁ* 'bandit' (Kumyk *qaçaq* 'bandit'), *patʃ:aħ-luʁ* 'kingdom' ← *patʃ:aħ* 'king' (Persian *pādišāh* 'king'), *saw-luʁ* 'greeting toast', *sal-luʁ* 'salute' ← *sal(am)* 'hallo' (Arabic *salām*), *χan-luʁ* 'regime of a Khan' (Kumyk *xan* 'khan'), *χarӡ-luʁ* 'expenses' ← *χarӡ* 'expense' (Arabic *ḥarj* 'expense'), and *q:ul-luʁ* 'service' (Kumyk *qulluğ* 'service' ← *qul* 'slave, servant').

4.1.2 Deadjectival nouns

The suffix *-u* turns adjectives into p e r s o n a l n o u n s denoting 'someone who is X'. The resulting concepts are typically related to body feature. Adjectives ending in a vowel substitute this vowel by *-u*, cf. *murtʃ'u* 'a blind one' ← *martʃ'i* 'blind', *æk:u* 'beautiful person' ← *æk:i* 'beautiful', *ærk:u* 'lame person' ← *ærtʃ:a* 'lame', *q:yk'u* 'deaf person' ← *q:yk'i* 'deaf'.

The extremely productive suffix *-ʃiwu* (often reduced to *-ʃiw*) forms mainly q u a l i t y n o u n s derived from adjectives and sometimes nouns. Secondarily, some nouns may have developed a more concrete meaning. Historically, *-ʃiwu* is derived from the light verb *xun* 'to become' in its iterative stem form *ʃawan*, just as it is true for *ʃawu*, see below. In this sense, it is rather deverbal in nature than deadjectival or denominal. From a synchronic point of view, however, it should be regarded mainly as a deadjectival and denominal morpheme, because some of the nouns marked for *-ʃiwu* no longer possess the corresponding verb form. Examples are: *qin-śiwu* 'goodness' ← *qin* 'good', *zirak-ʃiwu* 'quickness' ← *zirak* 'quick', *zija-ʃiwu* 'uselessness' ← *ziya* 'useless, used', *zunχ:i-ʃiwu* 'steep slope' ← *zunχ:i* 'steep', *insap-ʃiwu* 'action in according with clear conscience' ← *insap* 'clear conscience, justice', *it:i-ʃiwu* 'wetness' ← *it:i* 'wet', *iʃla-ʃiwu* 'activity, energy' ← *iʃla* 'active, alive', *ħalliχ-ʃiwu* 'slowness' ← *ħalliχ* 'slow', *x:itʃ'unaj-ʃiwu* 'success' ← *x:itʃ'unaj* 'towards, onword, ahead', *ts'aq'-ʃiwu* 'strength, power' ← *ts'aq'* 'power', *murdal-ʃiwu* 'perfidy' ← *murdal* 'unclean person', *naʒas-ʃiwu* 'nefariousness' ← *naʒas* 'heinous person', *s:inχral-ʃiwu* 'excitation' ← *s:inχral* 'stirred up, excited', *tunt-ʃiwu* 'strength of drink, especially tea' ← *tunt* 'strong (of tea)', *ħaran-ʃiwu* 'ungodliness' ← *ħaran* 'ungodly'.

Another suffix derived from *ʃawan* 'to become' (iterative) is *-ʃin* occurring in some abstract concepts such as *ut:ara-ʃin* 'life, animate world' ← *ut:a-* 'alive' (class marked), *qamalu-ʃin* 'hospitableness' ← *qamali* 'guest', *jalur-ʃin* 'length' ← *jalur* 'up', *t'alaw-ʃin* 'claim, demand' ← *t'alaw-dan* 'to make a claim (borrowed from Arabic *ṭalab* 'claim')', *ħadur-ʃin* 'readiness' ← *ħadur* 'ready' (Arabic *ḥāḍir* 'ready').

The suffix *-ʃaw(u)* (again derived from *ʃawan* 'to become' (iterative)) forms abstract nouns just as *-ʃiw(u)*. However, it focuses on processual rather than on resultative aspects, cf. the pair *miskin-ʃawu* 'pauperization', but *miskin-ʃiwu* 'poverty' (both derived from *miskin* 'poor', itself borrowed from Arabic *miskīn* 'poor'). Other examples are *muraχas-ʃawu* 'liberation' ← *muraχas* 'free', *itʃ'allil-ʃawu* 'taming' ← *itʃ'allil* 'tame', *χ:œlt'a-ʃawu* 'thinning' ← *χ:œlt'a* 'thin, clear', *kajp-ʃawu* 'drunkenness' ← *kaip* 'drunk', *kuklu-ʃawu* 'release' ← 'light (weigh)', *kutʃ-ʃawu* 'relocation' ← ? (cf. *kutʃ ban* 'to move, relocate'), *q:aʃ:i-ʃawu* 'anger' ← *q:aʃ:i* 'angry', *lagal-ʃawu* 'change' ← *lagal 'changing', *ħala-ʃawu* 'mixture, mixing' ← *ħala* 'intermingled'.

4.1.3 Deverbal nouns

The deverbal morpheme *-ála* (accentuated on the first syllable) denotes a g e n t n o u n s in the broadest sense: *quzala* 'farmer' ← *qu* 'field' (the element *-z-* reflects an older verbal stem, perhaps *zanan* 'to go'), *balajt'ala* 'singer' ← *balaj* 'song' + *t'-un* 'to say', *ʃanaʃala* 'someone who is dozy' ← *ʃanan* 'to sleep' + *ʃawan* 'to become', *zumat'ala* 'mourner' ← *zuma t'un* 'to mourn', *q:awt'ala* 'dancer' ← *q:aw t'un* 'to dance', *q'urq'ut'ala* 'rodent' ← *q'urq'u t'un* 'to gnaw', *q'yq'ala* 'blemish' ← ?, *lœwzala* 'bawd' ← ?, *χ:ynχ:ut'ala* 'snorer' ← *χ:ynχu t'un* 'to snore'. More rarely, it derives nouns different from this basic concept, cf. *qinbala* 'profit, benefit' ← *qin* 'good', *utʃala* 'saying' ← *utʃin* 'to say'. There is a variant of *-ala* accentuated on the second syllable (*-alá*). This suffix is present especially in nouns denoting agricultural terms, derived both from nouns and verbs. Examples are: *χ:ilaχ:ala* 'carter (of grain, bread)' ← *χ:ilan* (reduplicated) 'to conduct a cart', *tʃ'utʃ'ala* 'somone who weeds professionally' ← *tʃ'un* (reduplicated) 'the weed', *tsultsala* 'mower' ← *tsulan* (reduplicated) 'to mow', *ʁazala* 'thresher' ← ?, *quzala* 'farmer' ← *qu* 'field' + *zun* 'to work', *zuzala* '(agricultural) worker' ← *zun* (reduplicated) 'to work'.

Deverbal nouns denoting 'someone (regularly) doing something' are marked with the suffix *-u* that is normally added to the verbal stem, cf. *ħatʃ'u* 'drunkard'

← ḣatʃʼan 'to drink', duruχ:u 'tailoress' ← duruχlan 'to sew', ʃyʃu 'laundress' ← ʃyʃin 'to wash', lasu 'buyer' ← lasun 'to take in hands', busu 'story teller' ← busan 'to tell', latʃʼin uk:u 'fighter' ← latʃʼin uk:an 'to fight', leχ:u 'pilot' ← leχ:an 'to fly', din daq:u 'unbeliever' ← din 'belief' + negative copula daq:a-. Secondarily, deverbal nouns marked with -u may refer to various semantic domains, cf. lis:u 'narrow strip' ← lis:an 'to cut into strips', bazu 'fissure' ← bazin 'to tie', baχtʃu 'baffle, bar, hurdle' ← baχtʃin 'to hinder', biχ:u 'sheep going to be slaughtered' ← biχ:an 'to slaughter, cut'.

The suffix -awu derives deverbal a b s t r a c t n o u n s. It represents a masdar form of the verb -an 'to make, do'. Examples are dawu 'work' ← -an 'to do, make' (petrified class marker -d), tʃ:awu 'love' ← *tʃ:an 'to love' (reconstructed), batʃʼawu 'distribution' ← batʃʼin 'to divide', batʃ:awu 'deviation' ← batʃ:in 'to be awry', q:awtʼawu 'dance' ← q:aw tʼun 'to dance'.

Another deverbal suffix is -ija used mainly to derive concepts denoting the object or result of an action. Examples include dukija 'food' ← dukan 'to eat', ḣatʃʼija 'drink' ← ḣatʃʼan 'to drink', laχ:ija 'clothing' ← laχ:an 'to dress', tʃ:utʃija 'combustible' ← tʃ:utʃ:in 'to burn', χ:aˤχija 'plant' ← χ:aˤχaˤn 'to grow'.

The derivational paradigm of Lak makes use of other suffixes that are, however, less productive than those mentioned so far. For instance, the suffix -in shows up with certain nouns denoting the manner of an action or instruments used in this action, such as zananzin 'way of walking' ← zanan (reduplicated) 'to go', kanakin 'means to eat' ← kanan (reduplicated) 'to eat'. The suffix -i may show up with terms denoting instruments, for instance, χ:arti 'grater' ← χ:art dan 'to grate', tsʼartsʼi 'scale of wood' ← tsʼartsʼan 'to scratch'; but note qʼusi 'hump, knob' ← qʼus ikʼan 'to be bent'.

4.2 Adjectival derivation

Contrary to many other East Caucasian languages, Lak does not use the genitive (marked by -l) systematically to derive relational adjectives. Nevertheless, the corresponding derivational strategy is documented for some adjectives, such as k:artʃ:ul ~ k:artʃ:al 'related to teeth' ← k:artʃ:i 'tooth', musil 'golden' ← musi 'gold', minanul 'original' ← mina 'home town', maχmurdanul 'velvet (adjective)' ← maχmur 'velvet', œralunnal 'related to war' ← œral 'army', χ:yltʼukural 'related to pancake' ← χ:yltʼuku 'pancake', tʃʼirt:ataʃ:al 'bearded' ← tʃʼiri 'beard' (the segment -taʃ: is unclear), lampalul 'related to lamp' ← lampa 'lamp', ʃatlul 'snake-like' ← ʃat 'snake', ḣaltʼuqannal ~ ḣaltʼilul 'related to cottage industry' ← ḣaltʼi 'home work', konstitutsijalul 'constitutional' ← konstitutsija 'constitution', q:atul 'related to house/room' ← q:at:a 'house/room', nitsʼajquwaral 'related to hemp' ← nitsʼajquwa 'hemp'. In some instances, the genitive form is also used with negated adjectives, such as *insantal baq:a-s:a* 'uninhabited; lit. related to human(s) not being' (see below).

Unless used in incorporated form, all other adjectives take the marker *-s:a*. When used with definite/specific referents, this marker is substituted by *-ma* (reference to a human male in the singular), *-mur* (reference to other referents in the singular), or *-mi* (plural referents). In addition, these morphemes can be added to any noun or verbal participle turning it into an a t t r i b u t i v e adjective. Most importantly, *-s:a* may follow case marked nouns, too, cf. *q:at-l-uwu-s:a* 'being inside the house' ← *q:ata* (inessive) 'house', *zuma-n-uj* 'being on the bench' ← *zuma* (superessive) 'bench', *q:aʃaw-aj-s:a* 'ill; lit. being in illness' ← **q:aʃaw* (essive) 'illness', *iʃ-ir-aj-s:a* 'occupied, busy; lit. being at work' ← *iʃ* (essive) 'work', *mazq'az-r-aj-s:a* 'caressing; lit. being at caress' ← *mazq'az* (essive) 'caress', *ʃ:œlmaq-r-aj-s:a* 'wrong, false; lit. being at lie' ← *ʃ:œlmaq* 'lie' (*ʃ:œlmaq* is again derived from the adjective *ʃœ:lu* 'false'), *nervnaj-s:a* 'nervous; lit. being on nerve' ← *nerv* (essive) 'nerve', *itʃ'al-l-il-s:a* 'related to home' ← *itʃ'alu* (genitive) 'fireplace at home, home', *k:aʃi-l-s:a* 'hungry' ← *k:aʃi* (genitive) 'hunger', *manʁaw-s:a* 'twanging' ← *manʁaw* (absolutive) 'a person that twangs'. Examples for the use of *-s:a* with adverbs are *patʃ'u-s:a* 'general' ← *patʃ'u* 'together' and *lawaj-s:a* 'high, important' ← *lawaj* 'up, above'. Note that an underlying noun can again be derived from an adverb by adding the corresponding referential class marker ('the X one'), cf. *maqun-m-aj-s:a* 'being behind, rear; lit. being on the rear one', *lax:u-wa-s:a* 'of yesterday' ← *lax:u* 'yesterday'.

Depending on their concrete semantics, all adjectives can form secondary generic variants that denote the permanent presence of the quality expressed by the adjective. These adjectives are derived from the corresponding generic adverb (see section 4.3) by adding the adjectival marker *-s:a*: *guʒ-s:a* 'strong' → *guʒ-nu* 'strongly' → *guʒ-n-Ø-a* 'strongly' ('by nature/permanent', here class I) → *guʒ-n-Ø-a-s:a* 'strong' (by nature/permanent), *ʃ:yllin* 'green' → *ʃ:yllin(-n)u* 'verdantly' → *ʃ:yllin-(n)-m-a* 'always verdantly' → *ʃ:yllin-(n)-m-a-s:a* 'always green, evergreen' (here class III). Accordingly, *ʃ:yllins:a murx* denotes a 'green tree' (being green at the moment of reference), whereas *ʃ:yllin(n)mas:a murx* refers to an 'evergreen tree'.

4.3 Adverbial derivation

Contrary to other especially southern East Caucasian languages, Lak clearly distinguishes between adjectives and adverbs. Lak adverbs are frequently derived with the help of the suffix *-nu*. This element replaces the suffix *-s:a* present with corresponding adjectives, cf. *marts'-nu* 'purely' vs. *marts'-s:a* 'clean, pure', *qan-nu* 'nearly' vs. *qan-s:a* 'near', *tʃan-nu* 'rarely' vs. *tʃan-s:a* 'few', *tʃ'œwu-nu* 'often' vs. *tʃ'œwu-s:a* 'many' (*-w-* is a class marker). Parallel to adjectives that are derived from nouns with the help of *-s:a*, *-nu* can be added to nouns, too. Examples are *guʒ-nu* 'strongly' ← *guʒ* 'strength', *zaħmat-nu* 'difficultly' ← *zaħmat* 'work, labor', *natʃ-nu* 'scrupulously' ← *natʃ* 'shame'.

All adverbs can be marked for the feature 'permanent/generic'. In this case, the adverb adds a class marker plus the element *-a*. The vowel *-u* of the adverbial suffix is deleted. A phrasal example (cf. Žirkov 1955: 125) is:

(1) ga-y   murx-ru daiman k'int:ul-gu   ʁint:ul-gu
     DOWN.THERE-PL   tree-PL always winter.GEN-and   summer.GEN-and
     ʃ:yllin(-n)-<u>m-a</u>   b-ik'-ay-s:a-r
     green-ADV-III.PL-DUR   III-be-PRES-ASS-3
     'Those trees down there are always green in winter time as well as in summer time.'

For instance, the above-mentioned adverb *marts'-nu* 'purely' forms its generic version as follows: *marts'-n-Ø-a* (class I), *marts'-n-n-a* < **marts'-n-r-a* (class II), *marts'-n-ma* < *marts'-n-b-a* (class III), *marts'-n-na* < **marts'-n-d-a* (class IV) 'purely (by nature/always)'.

A special set of modal adverbs is formed with the help of the suffix *-kun* (< *kunu*, past gerund of *utʃin* 'to say') that is added to corresponding deictic stems: *ukun* < *wukun 'in this way' (proximal *wa:*), *mukun* 'in that way, thus' (medial *ma:*), *tukun* 'in that way, thus' (distal *ta:*), *k'ukun* 'in that way, thus' (distal (above) *k'a:*), *gukun* 'in that way, thus' (distal (below) *ga:*). The same suffix occurs in *cukun* 'how' ← *ci* 'what'. Most other adverbs are derived from nouns with the help of corresponding case forms, cf. *k'int:ul* 'in winter' (genitive), *ʁint:ul* 'in summer' (genitive), *k'yrχ:il* 'in the morning' (genitive), *wa-s:aˤtraj* 'now; lit. in this hour' (inessive), *x:uway* 'at night' (inessive).

5 Conversion

In Lak, conversion mainly concerns the following domains:
a) conversion of verbal masdars into referential nouns. Examples are *lurk'an-dan* 'ambush' ← 'to prepare an ambush', *dukra-dukan* 'meal' ← 'to eat a meal', *mak'-k:ak:an* 'dream' ← 'to dream, see a phantom', *burtʃu-lik:an* 'flaying, skinning; lit. skin take off';

b) conversion of adjectives into nouns. Examples include *k'yrχ:il-s:a* 'breakfast' ← 'morning-', *axt:ajns:a* 'dinner' ← 'noon-', *hant:ajns:a* 'supper' ← 'evening-', *ʃ:ars:a* 'woman' ← 'female', *ʃ:irtans:a* 'a remedy for roundworms' (no adjectival form attested), *ts'ukuls:a* 'goat skin' ← 'related to goat' (← *ts'uk(u)* ← 'goat');
c) conversion of locative-marked nouns into adverbs. Examples for this type are given in section 4.3.

6 Reduplication

Reduplication is a rather common technique in Lak to mark specific connotations or semantic nuances of a given lexeme. According to Lak informants, reduplication is productive especially in spontaneous speech. Nevertheless, quite a number of such forms have been conventionalized and are thus included in the Lak lexicon. In some cases, reduplication has an intensifying function. With many lexical forms, however, the function underlying reduplication remains unclear. This is also due to the fact that the simplex variant frequently remains unattested. From a technical point of view, reduplication usually applies to the full lexical stem. Syllable reduplication is not attested except for certain verbal stems that use this technique to derive an aspectual (progressive) stem (morpheme *-la-*), cf. (CL is short for "class morpheme") CL-*it-* 'to let' → CL-*it-la-t-* (progressive), *las-* 'to take' → *las-la-s-* (progressive), *bus-* 'to say' → *bus-la-s-* (progressive). Basically, Lak distinguishes four types of reduplication:

a) Full reduplication. Examples are *biza-biza ban* 'to gather speed for a jump', *warz-warz t'un* 'to pull oneself out', *wat-wat t'un* 'to shiver out of pain', *wez-wez t'un* 'to dripple', *ʒiri-ʒiri bahan* 'to burst', *zew-zew* 'whistle', *zig-zig t'un* 'to cling', *q'aj-q'aj* 'stuff', *lah-lah-s:a* 'low, below', *maqa-maqs:a* 'rear, backmost', *par-par* 'brightness', *p'aʕr-p'aʕr t'un* 'to chat, gabble continuously', *p'ur-p'ur t'un* 'to buzz, growl'. An instance of doubled reduplication is present with *lawlawʃawʃaw dan* 'to take into possession';
b) Many reduplicated forms follow the model of Turkic (here: Kumyk) reduplication that is characterized by stem initial consonantal variation, cf. *œlaw-tʃœ-law* 'panic', *baʙri-saʙri* 'mesentery', *œpur-tʃapur* 'rummage', *hawur-zawur* 'threat', *hawu-tawu-s:a* 'soft boiled', *daxa-maxa* 'a little bit' ← *daxa* 'id.', *diri-q'iris:a* 'quick' ← *diri* 'id.', *kajp-ʃajp* 'joy, happiness', *q:uk'-muk's:a* 'stuttering', *natsʕu-q'atsʕu* 'sweet taste', *parχ-ʃarχ* 'disturbance, breach of the peace', *p'aʕq'-ʃaʕq'* 'explosion', *bitu-χ:itu* 'uncontrolled shooting';
c) More rarely, the consonant alternation concerns the second syllable of a stem, as in *harza-hartas:a* 'wide, broad' ← *harza* 'sufficient', *liχ:a litʃ:a ban* 'to dismember' ← *liχ:an* 'to fade';

d) Vowel alternation shows up in some entries, such as *buza-bazar* 'staff (at home)' ← *buza* 'thing' and *hajt-hujt* 'cry of joy during feasts and marriage ceremonies' (expressive base).

7 References

Abdullaev, Isa X. and Roza G. Ėľdarova (2003): *Voprosy leksiki i slovoobrazovanija lakskogo jazyka.* Maxačkala: Institut jazyka, literatury i iskusstva im. Gamzata Cadasy, Dagestanskij naučnyj centr RAN.
Bouda, Karl (1971): *Lakkische Studien.* Heidelberg: Winter.
Džidalaev, Nursilan S. (1987): *Russko-lakskij slovar'.* Maxačkala: Dagučpedgiz.
Friedman, Victor A. (2020): Lak. In: Maria Polinsky (ed.), *Handbook of the Languages of the Caucasus,* 201–241. Oxford: Oxford University Press.
Murkelinskij, Gadži B. (1971): *Grammatika lakskogo jazyka.* Maxačkala: Institut jazyka, literatury i iskusstva im. Gamzata Cadasy, Dagestanskij naučnyj centr RAN.
Schulze, Wolfgang (2011): The Lak Language. *Nová filologická revue* 1: 11–36.
Šamsudinova, Seľminaz Ė. (2009): Slovoobrazonavie glagolov v lakskom jazyke. Ph.D. dissertation, Dagestanskij Gosudarstvennyj Universitet, Maxačkala.
Šaxmanova, Zagidat Ė. (2005): Slovoobrazonavie suščestviteľnyx v lakskom jazyke. Ph.D. dissertation, Dagestanskij Gosudarstvennyj Universitet, Maxačkala.
Uslar, Petr K. (1890): *Lakskij jazyk.* Tiflis: Izdanie Upravlenija Kavkazskago Učebnago Okruga.
Xajdakov, Said M. (1961): *Očerki po leksike lakskogo jazyka.* Moskva: Izdateľstvo Akademii nauk SSSR.
Xajdakov, Said M. (1962): *Laksko-russkij slovar'.* Moskva: Gosudarstvennoe izdateľstvo inostrannyx i nacionaľnyx slovarej.
Žirkov, Lev I. (1955): *Lakskij jazyk. Fonetika i morfologija.* Moskva: Izdateľstvo Akademii nauk SSSR.

Madzhid Khalilov and Zaira Khalilova

26 Avar

1 Introduction
2 General overview
3 Composition
4 Derivation
5 Conversion
6 Reduplication
7 References

Abstract: This article describes various means of word-formation in Avar. Among them are compounding, derivation, conversion, reduplication, and the formation of complex nominals based on two processes, compounding and derivation. Avar, as a language with a rich history of language contacts, has borrowed derivational suffixes from Turkic and Persian languages.

1 Introduction

Avar belongs to the Avar-Andic-Tsezic branch of the Nakh-Daghestanian language family. It is a written language and is one of the most widely spoken languages of Daghestan. Avar, spoken by about 900,000 speakers, plays a crucial role in Daghestan, as it is a lingua franca for the speakers of many minor languages of the Andic and Tsezic branches. Being a lingua franca, Avar still has a great influence on its neighboring languages.

Avar is an absolutive/ergative language. It is a verb-final language with a basic SOV word order, though with no rigid order of the major clause constituents. Agreement is always triggered by the absolutive argument. Avar has a rich nominal morphology with three genders in singular and two genders in plural. It also has an extensive system of grammatical and locative cases. All cases other than absolutive are based on an oblique stem.

Madzhid Khalilov, Makhachkala, Russia
Zaira Khalilova, Moscow, Russia

https://doi.org/10.1515/9783111420523-026

2 General overview

Avar is rich in derivational morphology; in particular nominal derivation shows many derivational suffixes. Derivation in Avar is very productive and sometimes quite complex, including the stacking of two or more derivational suffixes: *w-eke-ru-qan-ɬi* I-run-MASDAR-AGENTIVE-ABSTRACT 'runner'. In most languages, one of the key distinguishing features of compounds is the absence of inflectional morphology between the constituents of a compound. In Avar, by contrast, the first constituent of a compound may retain inflectional suffixes and the resultant compound may then be inflected further as a whole word:

(1) ħarc'iƛ'ɬel ← ħarc'i-ƛ' ɬe -l
    'saucer' dish.OBL-SUB.ESSIVE put.MASDAR NZ

3 Composition

Compound words in Avar are numerous and are found as different parts of speech, particularly as nouns. Compounding is the most productive process of forming new words in Avar. Compounds are defined as words that consist of two or more compounding elements or bases. Compound words can be determinative or copulative. Determinative compounds are compounds that have a head noun and a modifying element. Copulative compounds are compounds, also known as dvandva, that have two separate semantic heads.

3.1 Nominal compounds

Noun-noun compounds are the most common and the most productive type among other nominal compounds in Avar. The majority of nominal compounds are endocentric, though exocentric ones are also found.

    Determinative noun-noun compounds are very numerous and can have different patterns of formation. Most often, determinative compounds are based on mere juxtaposition of a head noun and a modifying element, as in *c'araʕ* 'dish' (← *c'a* 'fire' + *raʕ* 'vessel'), *ččuʕiʕin* 'seashell' (← *ččuʕi* 'fish.OBL' + *ʕin* 'ear'), *ħamiračʼ* 'horse ephedra' (← *ħami* 'donkey.OBL' + *račʼ* 'tail'). Often the meaning of a compound is not predictable from its constituents, as in *boƛ'onac'* 'furuncle' (← *boƛ'o* 'cowhouse.OBL' + *nac'* 'louse') and *ʕodokaru* 'blackberry' (← *ʕodo* 'ground.OBL' + *karu* 'mulberry'). Determinative compounds are always right-headed.

Avar co-compounds can be divided into the following groups: (i) synonymic compounds, e.g., *ray-ƛ'al* 'war; lit. war-quarrel', *nič-namus* 'conscience; lit. shame-conscience'; (ii) co-hyponymic compounds, e.g., *šaq'i-q'alam* 'pen and ink, writing materials; lit. ink-pen', *gulla-xer* 'ammunition; lit. bullet-gunpowder'; (iii) antonymic co-compounds, e.g., *awal-axir* 'beginning and end; lit. beginning-end', *roƛ'i-ƛ'al* 'love and hate; lit. love-hate'.

Adjective-noun compounds are right-headed with a modifier preceding a head. Such compounds usually contain a stem-form adjective, i.e. adjectives are presented with a truncated gender/number suffix, as in *beccabaƛ'* 'caecum' (← *beccab* 'blind' + *baƛ'* 'gut') and *t'ok'c'ar* 'nickname' (← *t'ok'ab* 'spare' + *c'ar* 'name').

Avar has possessive noun-adjective compounds (*bahuvrīhi*), which are exocentric. In such compounds, the first constituent is a noun combined with truncated forms of adjectives (i.e. with no gender/number suffix), e.g., *anisxalat* 'dreamer' (← *aniŝ* 'dream' + *xalataw* 'long'), *bok'onbit'* 'rectangle' (← *bok'on* 'corner' + *bit'arab* 'straight'), *mahk^weš* 'camomile' (← *mah* 'smell' + *k^wešab* 'bad'). Note that such noun-adjective compounds are left-headed, whereas the determinative compounds are always right-headed.

Adverb-noun compounds are based on adverbs and nouns in the absolutive form, as in *t'adhobo* 'upper grindstone' (← *t'ad* 'above' + *hobo* 'mill') and *q'asik^wen* 'dinner' (← *q'asi* 'in the evening' + *k^wen* 'food'). Nominal compounds can also be based on adverbs combined with verbal nouns (masdars), e.g., *k'ibiƛ'i* 'bifurcation' (← *k'iyide* 'by two' + *biƛ'i* 'division'), *k'iborłi* 'drilling (so that the object breaks in two pieces)' (← *k'iyide* 'by two' + *borłi* 'drilling').

Nominal compounds can be based on adverbs and truncated past participles. Such adverb-participle compounds are exocentric as they lack a head. They are used to name animals and objects, cf. *cebebux̌* 'apron' (← *cebe* 'in front' + *bux̌uneb* 'tie.PTCP') and *reładakunč'* 'firefly' (← *rełeda* 'at night' + *kunč'uleb* 'shine.PTCP').

Converb-noun compounds are not very numerous in Avar. Here converb is defined as a non-finite verbal form used to form adverbial clauses. In such compounds the modifying converb precedes the head, as in *quqančed* 'pancake' (← *quqan* 'saw.CVB' + *čed* 'bread') and *swerunžo* 'wooden stick' (← *swerun* 'roll.CVB' + *žo* 'thing').

Noun-participle compounds are based on nouns combined with a truncated participle, as in *ʕuč'alt'am* 'supplier' (← *ʕuč'al* 'fork.PL' + *t'amuleb* 'putting') and *k^werbač'* 'handkerchief' (← *k^wer* 'hand' + *bač'uneb* 'cleaning').

All converb-participle compounds are exocentric as they lack both a grammatical and a semantic head. Such nominal compounds are formed by combining the converbal verbal form with the truncated form of the participle. Converb-participle compounds are used to name animals or objects, as in *buħun-xut'* 'cigarette butt' (← *buħun* 'burn.CVB' + *xut'arab* 'leave.PTCP'), *buħunč'ik'* 'pottage, soup' (← *buħun* 'burn.CVB' + *č'ik'uleb* 'lick.PTCP'), *łutunbay* 'a fearful dog that fights while running away' (← *łutun* 'run.CVB' + *bayuleb* 'fight.PTCP').

3.2 Adjectival compounds

Compound adjectives can be determinative or copulative.

Copulative adjective-adjective compounds are based on adjectives which have different sets of meaning, as in *č'eʕeral-qaħal* 'black and white; lit. black-white', and *baħaral-xeral* 'old and young; lit. old-young'.

Most noun-adjective compounds have a second element taken from a limited set of adjectives. Some noun-adjective compounds are based on the adjective *λ'erab* 'colorful' designating different shades of color. Such compounding is very productive, e.g., *hac'uλ'erab* 'having the color of honey' ← *hac'u* 'honey.OBL', *raqdaλ'erab* 'having the color of ashes' ← *raqda* 'ashes.OBL'. Other noun-adjective compounds are based on the adjective *maħaw*, which is derived from the noun *maħ* 'smell'. However, when the adjective *maħaw* 'smelly' is combined with nouns it does not have its direct meaning but rather a comparative connotation, as in *cimaħaw* 'bear-like, awkward' ← *ci* 'bear', and *cermaħaw* 'fox-like, sly' ← *cer* 'fox'. Still other noun-adjective compounds are based on the adjective *ħalab* 'abundant'. Such compound adjectives have the meaning 'abundant of, full of', as in *c'amħalab* 'salty' ← *c'am* 'salt', and *łimħalab* 'watery, liquid' ← *łim* 'water'.

Avar has a very productive way of forming numeral-adjective compounds by combining truncated numerals with denominal adjectives, e.g., *k'it'alayab* 'two-storied' (← *k'igo* 'two' + *t'alayab* 'storied'), *łaboxilab* 'three-legged' (← *łabgo* 'three' + *boxilab* 'legged'), *anλ'yatab* 'with seven layers' (← *anλ'go* 'seven' + *yatab* 'layered').

Adverb-participle compounds are based on adverbs combined with the participle *kkarab* 'happen.PTCP', as in *c'aħilkkarab* 'greyish' ← *c'aħil* 'dimly', *t'erenkkarab* 'thinnish' ← *t'eren* 'thinly', *qaħkkarab* 'whitish' ← *qaħ* 'whitely', which designate color terms.

Adverb-adjective compounds are based on adverbs plus adjectives. Such adjectives often denote different shades of color, e.g., *kanč'baʕarab* 'bright red' (← *kanč'* 'brightly' + *baʕarab* 'red') and *bec'ʕurčč'inab* 'dark green' (← *bec'* 'dark' + *ʕurčč'inab* 'green').

3.3 Verbal compounds

Compounding in verbs is very productive.

Noun-verb compounds are based on nouns combined with specific verbs, e.g., the verb *yine* 'to crumble', as in *mac'ayine* 'to gossip' ← *mac'a* 'gossip.OBL', *ʕarzayine* 'to complain' ← *ʕarza* 'complain.OBL.PL', or the verb *ine* 'to go', as in *sasine* 'to calm down' ← *sas* 'noise', *bodine* 'to be dishonored' ← *bod* 'people.army.LOC', *ɬadaqine* 'to go somewhere without purpose' ← *ɬadaq* 'water.LOC'. (Note that Avar verbs are cited in the infinitival form in *-ne* and *-ze*.) The examples above seem to be cases of grammaticalization, where the meaning of one of the verbs is thoroughly bleached.

Causative verbs in Avar are verb-verb compounds based on combining a lexical verb with the truncated form of the verb *habize* 'to do'. Such causative formation is productive, and it can be found in all verbal classes. Examples are *xʷezabize* 'to make die' (← *xʷeze* 'to die' + *habize* 'to do') and *λ'urizabize* 'to make roll' (← *λ'urize* 'to roll' + *habize* 'to do').

Numeral-verb compounds are very productive. They are based on truncated numerals plus verbs, e.g., *k'ič'ʷaze* 'to combine, stack by two' (← *k'igo* 'two' + *č'ʷaze* 'to kill'), *k'ibekize* 'to break in two (pieces)' (← *k'igo* 'two' + *bekize* 'to break'), *k'iborɬize* 'to break through' (← *k'igo* 'two' + *borɬize* 'to make a hole, drill').

3.4 Adverbial compounds

Compounding in adverbs is very productive.

Noun-adverb compounds are based on nouns in the oblique form combined with adverbs, as in *čexat'ade* 'flat on one's back' (← *čexa* 'stomach.OBL' + *t'ade* 'upwards') and *k'alayorλ'e* 'prone, face downwards' (← *k'ala* 'mouth.OBL' + *yorλ'e* 'down').

Adverb-adverb compounds are based on two adverbs, as in *cere-q'ad* 'the day before yesterday' (← *cere* 'earlier, before' + *q'ad* 'in the day time') and *son-q'asi* 'yesterday evening' (← *son* 'yesterday' + *q'asi* 'in the evening'). Coordinate compound adverbs combine adverbs with different meanings, e.g., *kisa-kibego* 'everywhere' (← *kisa* 'from where' + *kibego* 'everywhere'). Some compound adverbs are based on adverbs which are antonyms, e.g., *q'asi-q'ad* 'all day long' (← *q'asi* 'in the evening' + *q'ad* 'in the day time') and *roq'o-q'ʷat'iw* 'everywhere' (← *roq'o-w* 'at home' + *q'ʷat'iw* 'outside'). In some adverbs one of the parts of the compound adverb means the same as the whole word, as in *baɬgo-ʕat'go* 'secretly'

(← *bałgo* 'secretly' + *ʕat'go* 'damply') and *č'ago-ʕat'go* 'vividly' (← *č'ago* 'vividly' + *ʕat'go* 'damply').

3.5 Synthetic compounds

Avar not only has compounding and derivation but also complex means of word-formation such as compounding together with derivation. Such compounds can be described as "synthetic compounds", of the type *churchgoer* where neither *church go* nor *goer* are independent words. We call such word-formation "complex word-formation". Such word-formation processes are used to derive nouns and not other parts of speech. Very often such complex compounds are based on a noun/adverb plus a verb (usually the truncated form of an infinitive *łeze* 'to put') plus the suffix *-l*.

Complex nominals based on full or truncated adverbs combined with a truncated form of an infinitive plus the suffix *-l* are *t'ałel* 'lid' (← *t'ad* 'above' + *łeze* 'to put' + *-l*), *γorλ'č'el* 'ambush' (← *γorλ'* 'under' + *č'eze* 'to stand' + *-l*) and *cadaqłel* 'supplement' (← *cadaq* 'together' + *łeze* 'to put' + *-l*).

Complex nominals can be based on nouns in the full or truncated forms, in absolutive and oblique forms combined with the truncated form of an infinitive plus the suffix *-l*, e.g., *čiraqłel* 'stick for a lamp' (← *čiraq* 'lamp' + *łeze* 'to put' + *-l*), *kʷełel* 'glove' (← *kʷer* 'hand' + *łeze* 'to put' + *-l*), *ħarčiλ'łel* 'saucer' (← *ħarčiλ'* 'under the plate' + *łeze* 'to put' + *-l*), *mergiλ'łel* 'support for spindle' (← *mergiλ'* 'under the spindle' + *łeze* 'to put' + *-l*).

4 Derivation

Another process of forming new words in Avar is derivation, which includes native and non-native derivation.

4.1 Nominal derivation

Nominal derivation is the most productive. Derivational suffixes are usually attached to absolutive or oblique forms of nouns.

4.1.1 Denominal nouns

The suffix -*ti*, which is one of the most productive suffixes, derives a b s t r a c t
n o u n s and concrete nouns from nouns in the absolutive and oblique cases, e.g.,
baq'-ti 'sunny side' ← *baq'* 'sun', *emen-ti* 'fatherhood' ← *emen* 'father', *insuq-ti*
'fatherland' ← *insuq* 'father.LOC'. -*ti* derives abstract nouns from verbal nouns
(masdars), as in *boži-ti* 'trust' ← *boži* 'believing' and *berhen-ti* 'victory' ← *berhin*
'winning'. The suffix -*ti* derives abstract nouns from nouns that already have
a derivative suffix, as in *axiqan-ti* 'gardening' ← *axi-qan* (*axi* 'garden' + -*qan*)
'gardener'.

Another derivational suffix -*ro*, which is productive, derives a g e n t, p l a c e
and i n s t r u m e n t n o u n s from verbal nouns, as in *borxa-ro* 'hoist' ← *borxi*
'lifting' and *ččuk'a-ro* 'tool for excoriation (of animal skin)' ← *ččuk'i* 'stripping the
skin off'. The suffix -*ro* can be used to derive nouns that denote negative traits
of character, e.g., *hanč'e-ro* 'person who bites' ← *hanč'ey* 'biting' and *sent'ero* 'person who puts his nose into other people's business' ← *sent'ey* 'sniffing.DUR'. The
suffix -*ro* forms nouns that denote natural phenomena, as in *sʷerdi-ro* 'whirlpool'
← *sʷerdi* 'rotating' and *čʷaxde-ro* 'waterfall' ← *čʷaxdey* 'current.DUR'.

The suffix -*han*, which is presumably a borrowed suffix from Persian, is not
very productive. It is attached to nouns in the absolutive and to oblique forms to
derive agent nouns, e.g., *habi-han* 'miller' ← *habi* 'mill.OBL', *bogo-han* 'cook' ←
bogo 'breakfast.OBL', *koro-han* 'stoker, boiler man' ← *koro* 'oven'.

The suffix -*qan* is very productive. This suffix can attach to the absolutive
and to the oblique forms of nouns. Very often it derives nouns denoting professions, e.g., *halt'u-qan* 'worker' ← *halt'i* 'work', *hanč'i-qan* 'fowler, poultry breeder'
← *hanči* 'bird.PL', *raɫda-qan* 'sailor' ← *raɫda* 'sea.OBL'. It can also derive agent
nouns with negative traits of character, e.g., *mac'i-qan* 'squealer' ← *mac'i*
'tongue.OBL' and *čuhu-qan* 'arrogant man' ← *čuhu* 'pride.OBL'. The suffix -*qan* can
derive agent nouns from nouns not only in their base or oblique stem but also
from nouns in the locative cases, as in *čot'a-qan* 'horseman, rider' ← *čot'a*
'horse.LOC' and *ɫet'a-qan* 'raftsman' ← *ɫet'a* 'water.LOC'. The suffix -*qan* can also
derive agent nouns from truncated forms of verbal nouns (masdars) with some
modification of the stem, as in *wekeru-qan* 'male racer' ← *wekeri* 'running (of
male gender)', *yekeru-qan* 'female racer' ← *yekeri* 'running (of female gender)'
and *bekeru-qan* 'fast horse' ← *bekeri* 'running (of non-human gender)'. Note that
the meaning of the last three examples is conditioned by the prefixal gender/
number markers *w-* (for male), *y-* (for female), and *b-* (for animal).

The suffix -*č*, which is productive, derives nouns from other nouns and adverbs. It forms nouns that express evaluative/descriptive names of people. It derives agent nouns from nouns either in the absolutive or in the oblique form, as in *k'ala-č* 'talker, chatterer' ← *k'ala* 'mouth.OBL', *ħoxo-č* 'dimwit' ← *ħoxo* 'stub.OBL' and *miqi-č* 'man with a big moustache' ← *miqi* 'moustache.OBL'.

The suffix *-či* is very productive. It is presumably a borrowed suffix from a Turkic language. Cf. examples with borrowed Turkic nouns plus the suffix *-či*: *tuken-či* 'seller' ← *tuken* 'shop' and *quluq-či* 'employee' ← *quluq* 'work'. Borrowed nouns from Arabic (e.g., *zaħmat-či* 'toiler' ← *zaħmat* 'difficulty') and Russian can also be used with the suffix *-či*, e.g., *traktor-či* 'tractor driver' ← *traktor* 'tractor', *kolxoz-či* 'collective farmer' ← *kolxoz* 'farm', *pulemet-či* 'machine gunner' ← *pulemet* 'machine gun'. They mostly denote professions. However, the status of the suffix *-či* is debatable, mainly because Avar already has a lexeme *či* with the meaning 'man, person' which can also be used for derivation, as in *hoko-či* 'driver of a bullock cart' ← *hoko* 'bullock cart', *heresi-či* 'liar' ← *heresi* 'lie' or *yalmayir-či* 'brawler' ← *yalmayir* 'scandal'. The suffix *-či* derives nouns from nouns either from the absolutive or genitive cases, as in *q'ali-či* 'drummer' ← *q'ali* 'drum', *kopol-či* 'merry person' ← *kopol* 'joy.GEN' and *q'ʷat'ul-či* 'idler, reveller' ← *q'ʷat'ul* 'street.GEN'.

Another suffix used in nominal derivation is *-k*, which is productive. It derives agent nouns from nouns in the absolutive and oblique forms. It expresses descriptive names of people and animals, e.g., *heresi-k* 'liar' ← *heresi* 'lie', *t'oħo-k* 'lousy person' ← *t'oħo* 'tetter.OBL', *nodo-k* 'animal with a spot on its forehead' ← *nodo* 'forehead'. This suffix also derives nouns from verbal nouns (masdars), as in *beč'a-k* 'weakling' ← *beč'ay* 'fading.DUR' or *barŝu-k* 'touchy person' ← *barŝi* 'offending'.

The suffix *-lo* is productive. It derives nouns from nouns which stand in the oblique form, as in *maxxa-lo* 'hip' ← *maxx* 'iron.OBL' and *t'eha-lo* 'lentil' ← *t'eha* 'flower.OBL'. The suffix *-lo* also derives agent and instrument nouns from verbal nouns and the truncated forms of verbal nouns in the durative forms, as in *qama-lo* 'robber' ← *qama-* 'stealing.OBL', *k'ʷere-lo* 'winnower' ← *k'ʷerey* 'winnowing.DUR' and *gere-lo* 'roller, rolling pin' ← *gerey* 'rolling.DUR'.

4.1.2 Deadjectival nouns

The suffix *-či* derives p e r s o n a l n o u n s from the truncated forms of adjectives, as in *bixin-či* 'good man' ← *bixin* 'masculine', *baħar-či* 'brave man' ← *baħar* 'young' and *kapur-či* 'atheist, infidel' ← *kapur* 'unbelieving'. The derived forms are evaluative personal nouns.

4.1.3 Deverbal nouns

The suffix *-či* derives evaluative p e r s o n a l n o u n s from non-finite verbal forms (converbs), as in *waq'un-či* 'hungry person' ← *waq'un* 'get.up.CVB' and *ʕorc'un-či* 'full person' ← *ʕorc'un* 'get.full.CVB'.

The suffix *-ɬi* can derive a b s t r a c t n o u n s from the affirmative copula *bugo* 'be.PRS' and the negative copula *heč'o* 'be.PRS.NEG', e.g., *bugo-ɬi* 'richness, property' ← *bugo* 'be.PRS' and *heč'o-ɬi* 'poverty' ← *heč'o* 'be.PRS.NEG'.

4.1.4 Deadverbial nouns

The suffix *-č* derives evaluative p e r s o n a l n o u n s from manner adverbs, as in *k'odo-č* 'giant' ← *k'odo* 'greatly', *λ'ara-č* 'fat, obese person' ← *λ'ara* 'fatly' and *ɬama-č* 'gentle, soft person' ← *ɬama* 'fluidly'. Some adverbs, when used with the suffix *-č*, require the epenthetic vowel *-u-*, as in *ʕinq'u-č* 'deaf person' ← *ʕinq* 'deafly' + *-u* and *gʷanzu-č* 'rude person' ← *gʷanz* 'rudely' + *-u*. Presumably the suffix *-č* originated from the noun *či* 'man, person'. In Avar *či* 'man, person' as a normal noun can be used with modifiers, as in *ħinq'ulew či* 'fearful person' and *q'oq'aw či* 'short person'. Additionally such noun phrases with *či* can have short forms, as in *ħinq'ulew či* 'fearful person' – *ħinq'uč* 'coward' and *hit'inaw či* 'small person' – *hit'ič* 'baby'.

The suffix *-qan* derives agent nouns from place adverbs, as in *cebe-qan* 'leader (in herd) (e.g., he-goat)' ← *cebe* 'ahead' and *cewe-qan* 'leader, guide' ← *cewe* 'ahead'. Note that the interpretation of these examples is based on the adverb *cewe/cebe* 'ahead', which has a gender/number infix *-w-* designating human male and *-b-* referring to animal.

The suffix *-ɬi* derives abstract and concrete nouns from adverbs, e.g., *sʷeruq-ɬi* 'surroundings' ← *sʷeruq* 'around' and *ʕodob-ɬi* 'low place' ← *ʕodob* 'down'.

The suffix *-k/-uk* forms personal nouns from manner adverbs, e.g., *becc-uk* 'blind man' ← *becc* 'blindly', *pasa-k* 'libertine' ← *pasat* 'depravedly'.

4.2 Adjectival derivation

Adjective derivation is very productive.

4.2.1 Denominal adjectives

The suffix -(y)a combined with a gender number marker -b, -w, -y, or -l, is used to derive adjectives from nouns. As a rule, the -yab (-yaw, -yay, -yal) is attached to vowel-final nouns, e.g., *daru-yab* 'medical' ← *daru* 'medicine' and *zahru-yab* 'poisonous' ← *zahru* 'poison'. The suffix -ab (-aw, -ay, -al) is attached to consonant-final nouns, e.g., *bet'er-ab* 'main' ← *bet'er* 'head' and *kep-ab* 'merry, joyful' ← *kep* 'joy'. This kind of derivation is quite productive, especially in modern written forms of the language (e.g., in poems and proverbs). Borrowed nouns can also be used for derivation with the suffix -yab (-yaw, -yay, -yal), e.g., nouns borrowed from Russian, as in *ekonomiki-yab* 'economical' ← *ekonomika* 'economics' and *literaturi-yab* 'literary' ← *literatura* 'literature'.

The suffix -se combined with a gender number suffix -b, -w, -y, or -l derives adjectives from nouns with the meaning 'suitable for'. The base for derivation is often a noun in the dative case. This suffix is very productive with proper nouns, as in *Aḥmadiye-seb* 'suitable for Ahmed' ← *Aḥmadiye* 'Ahmed.DAT', but also with common nouns, as in *rat'liye-seb* 'suitable for clothes' ← *rat'liye* 'clothes.DAT'.

4.2.2 Deadjectival adjectives

The suffix -siya(b) is mostly used to derive approximative adjectives from truncated forms of color adjectives, as in *baʕar-siyab* 'reddish' ← *baʕarab* 'red', *č'eʕer-siyab* 'blackish' ← *č'eʕerab* 'black' and *t'ohil-siyab* 'yellowish' ← *t'ohilab* 'yellow'.

Another suffix which derives adjectives from other adjectives is the suffix -ab, which is productive. The derived adjectives express comparative degree as well as intensification, as in *k'udiyab-ab* 'bigger, really big' ← *k'udiyab* 'big' and *č'eʕerab-ab* 'more black, really black' ← *č'eʕerab* 'black'.

4.2.3 Deadverbial adjectives

The suffix -(y)a combined with a gender number suffix -b, -w, -y, or -l derives adjectives from adverbs, as in *kʷeš-ab* 'bad' ← *kʷeš* 'badly', *łik'-ab* 'good' ← *łik'* 'well', *šuli-yab* 'strong' ← *šula* 'strongly, firmly'.

The suffix -se plus a gender number marker -b, -w, -y, or -l, is used to derive adjectives from adverbs. Such derivation is very productive, e.g., *kidago-seb* 'constant, regular' ← *kidago* 'constantly', *t'ocebe-seb* 'first' ← *t'ocebe* 'in the first place'.

4.3 Verbal derivation

4.3.1 Denominal verbs

The suffix -*xxin* is very productive. It derives verbs from nouns that stand in the absolutive or in the oblique singular or oblique plural forms. The suffix -*xxin* derives verbs with the meaning 'to be in the state of', as in *bečexxine* 'to be attached to a calf' ← *beče* 'calf', *maλ'ixxine* 'to be sleepy' ← *maλ'i* 'sleep.OBL' and *kart'axxine* 'to wear through, be well-worn' ← *kart'a* 'hole.OBL.PL'. The suffix -*xxin* also derives verbs from verbal nouns (masdars). Here the derived verbs have the meaning 'to become', as in *betaxxine* 'to curl, become curly' ← *beta* 'curling.OBL' and *bosaxxine* 'to become unstable, be tense' ← *bosa* 'taking.OBL'.

The suffix -*čin* is productive. It derives verbs from nouns that stand in the oblique or locative forms. The derived verbs express change of state as well as the meaning 'to be in the state of', e.g., *roxdočine* 'to be in heat (of animal)' ← *roxdo* 'herd.OBL', *qalačine* 'to be covered with crust, ice' ← *qala* 'crust.OBL.PL', *ħurt'ačine* 'to become dusty' ← *ħur-t'a* 'dust.LOC'.

The suffixes -*d*- and -*and*-, which are productive, are used to derive durative verbs from nouns, as in *zigardize* 'to groan' ← *zigar* 'complaint', *c'ohodize* 'to be busy stealing' ← *c'oho* 'theft.OBL' and *basandize* 'to play (of animal)' ← *bas* 'calf'.

The suffixes -*i* and -*in* are the most productive verbal suffixes in Avar. These suffixes are verbal noun (masdar) suffixes, and they are used to derive verbs from nouns that stand in the absolutive form, as in *ʕet'ize* 'to sweat' ← *ʕet'* 'sweat' and *yizine* 'to become dirty' ← *yiz* 'dirt'.

Avar has a number of less productive suffixes present in a few verbs. The suffix -*ʕay* derives verbs from nouns and expresses a change of state, e.g., *t'ilʕaze* 'to become numb' ← *t'il* 'stick', *c'ulʕaze* 'to grow stiff' ← *c'ul* 'wood'. The suffix -*kkin* derives verbs from nouns, e.g., *ħekkine* 'to become soft' ← *ħe* 'wax' and *c'akkine* 'to smoulder' ← *c'a* 'fire'. The suffix -*hi*/-*hin* is used to derive verbs from nouns and verbal nouns, e.g., *talahize* 'to rob' ← *tala* 'grabbing' and *balahize* 'to watch' ← *bala* 'watching.DUR.OBL'.

4.3.2 Deverbal verbs

The suffixes -*old*- and -*dar*- are used to derive durative-frequentative verbs from other verbs, as in *heq'oldize* 'to drink hard' ← *heq'eze* 'to drink', *qʷadarize* 'to write often (also of a writer)' ← *qʷaze* 'to write', *λ'urdize* 'to dance' ← *λ'urize* 'to roll'.

4.3.3 Deadverbial verbs

Avar has a distinct class of inchoative verbs which are derived with the productive suffix *-ɬi* from adverbs, as in *kʷešɬize* 'to become bad' ← *kʷeš* 'badly', and *ƛ'eruq'ɬize* 'to become pale' ← *ƛ'eruq'* 'wanly'. In the inchoative/causative pairs, the causative is productively formed with the verb *habize* 'to do', e.g., *kʷešɬizabize* 'to make bad' ← *kʷešɬize* 'to become bad', *bercinɬizabize* 'to make beautiful' ← *bercinɬize* 'to become beautiful' (cf. section 3.3).

The suffixes *-d-*, *-dar-* and *-qaqd-* are used to derive durative verbs from adverbs, as in *cebeqaqdize* 'to hover about' ← *cebe* 'in front', *xaduqaqdize* 'to start searching' ← *xadub* 'after', *req'dize* 'to limp' ← *req'* 'limpingly'.

The suffix *-i* is used to derive verbs from adverbs, as in *hadurize* 'to get ready, prepare' ← *hadur* 'ready' and *beʕerize* 'to sharpen' ← *beʕer* 'sharply'.

4.3.4 Denumeral verbs

Verbal derivation from numerals is not very productive. This suffix *-ɬi* is used to form inchoative verbs with the meaning 'to become', as in *coɬize* 'to join, become one' ← *co* 'one' and *k'iɬize* 'to divide (in two), become two' ← *k'igo* 'two'.

4.3.5 Onomatopoetic verbs

Avar has a small class of onomatopoetic verbs that all have stem-final *-d* and refer to the sounds that animals make, e.g., *hihidize* 'to neigh', *mimidize* 'to meow', *c'ic'idize* 'to chirp', *ʕeʕedize* 'to crow', *baʕdize* 'to bleat', *čik'dize* 'to squeak', *zuzudize* 'to hum'.

4.4 Adverbial derivation

4.4.1 Denominal adverbs

The suffix *-gi*, which is quite productive, is used to derive manner adverbs from nouns, e.g., *ras-gi* 'not a bit; lit. not even a hair' ← *ras* 'hair' and *axir-gi* 'at last' ← *axir* 'end'.

The suffix *-go* is productive. It derives adverbs from nouns in the absolutive and oblique cases and from personal pronouns. The derived adverbs with *-go* have the meaning 'in the manner of', as in *ḥamiqe-go* 'donkey-like' ← *ḥamiqe* 'donkey.LOC' and *ccidal-go* 'angrily' ← *ccidal* 'anger.GEN'.

Another derivative suffix is *-sa*. It derives manner adverbs from nouns, e.g., *deʕen-sa* 'with one head down' ← *deʕen* 'he-goat' and *xibil-sa* 'on one side' ← *xibil* 'side'.

The suffix *-dal* derives time adverbs from nouns that denote different seasons, e.g., *ix-dal* 'in spring' ← *ix* 'spring', *λ'in-dal* 'in winter' ← *λ'in* 'winter', *riʔi-dal* 'in summer' ← *riʔi* 'summer'.

The suffix *-q'*, which is productive, derives manner adverbs from nouns in the oblique stem. The suffix *-q'* denotes absence or shortage of some quality of a noun, e.g., *koco-q'* 'ugly, without face' ← *koco* 'face.OBL', *resu-q'* 'poorly' ← *resu* 'possibility.OBL'.

4.4.2 Deverbal adverbs

The suffix *-go* is productive. It derives adverbs from non-finite verbal forms (converbs), as in *uryun-go* 'intentionally' ← *uryun* 'think.CVB' and *tuban-go* 'finally, fully' ← *t'uban* 'fulfil.CVB', but also from verbs that stand in the optative form, as in *baqʷad-go* 'dryly' ← *baqʷad* 'be.dry.OPT' and *biččad-go* 'wetly' ← *biččad* 'become.wet.OPT'.

The suffix *-ʕan*, which is productive, derives adverbs from verbs, as in *ʕeze-ʕan* 'many, much' ← *ʕeze* 'to suffice' and *xʷeze-ʕan* 'till death' ← *xʷeze* 'to die'.

The suffix *-isa* derives manner adverbs from non-finite verbal forms (participles), e.g., *begun-isa* 'inside out' ← *begun* 'turn.PTCP' and *bit'un-isa* 'correctly, right' ← *bit'un* 'straighten.PTCP'.

4.4.3 Deadverbial adverbs

The suffix *-sa* derives manner adverbs from other adverbs, e.g., *ʕeb-sa* 'across' ← *ʕeb* 'widely', *beʕer-sa* 'with blade end in front' ← *beʕer* 'sharply', *xala-sa* 'along' ← *xalat* 'long'.

5 Conversion

Another type of word-formation in Avar is conversion. Nominal conversion from adjectives is very productive. When adjectives are substantivized, they denote people and objects rather than abstract nouns.

There are some nouns that, diachronically, have undergone conversion from adjectives. But synchronically such nouns are real substantives and not modifiers, though formally they have adjective features, i.e. the gender/number suffixes *-w* and *-y*, which differentiate male and female persons. Such nouns are *ʕolilaw* 'young man', *ƛ'erilaw* 'peer', *maʕarulaw* 'highlander, Avar man', *maʕarulay* 'highlander, Avar woman'.

In partial conversion adjectives can be used both as substantives and modifiers. Nominal conversion from adjectives and participles is very productive, e.g., from adjectives: *baharaw* 'young' → *baharaw* 'fiancé' and *ccidalaw* 'angry' → *ccidalaw* 'angry man', or from participles: *untaraw* 'sick' → *untaraw* 'patient'.

Avar has nominal conversion from adverbs, e.g., *beʕuq'* 'uglily' → *beʕuq'* 'ugly person', *c'odor* 'carefully' → *c'odor* 'clever man'.

6 Reduplication

Reduplication is very productive in Avar.

6.1 Nominal reduplication

Reduplication in Avar can be full and partial. Full reduplication is found in onomatopoetic words, as in *q'irŝ-q'irŝi* 'squeak, crunch'. Nouns can be presented as fully reduplicated forms with no base for reduplication, as in *kʷalkʷal* 'hindrance, obstacle' (← *kʷal* + *kʷal*), *laq'laq'* 'stork' (← *laq'* + *laq'*) and *ɣarɣar* 'fever' (← *ɣar* + *ɣar*).

The most common reduplication in Avar is a kind of partial reduplication: reduplicated nouns can be formed by copying the whole stem and changing the initial consonant to /m/. This reduplication indicates either diversity (plurality) or resemblance among the entities, i.e. 'different things like this', e.g., *rak'-mak'* 'heart and things like it' ← *rak'* 'heart', *ʕašt'i-mašt'i* 'axe and things like it' ← *ʕašt'i* 'axe', *oc-moc* 'bull and things like it' ← *oc* 'bull'. Nouns having a vowel in the onset just add /m/ to the reduplicant, as in *asar-masar* 'impression and things like it' ← *asar* 'impression' and *axir-maxir* 'end and things like it' ← *axir* 'end'. Nouns with initial /m/ do not undergo this kind of reduplication.

6.2 Adjectival reduplication

Reduplication in adjectives is productive. In the reduplicated forms, the CVCV copy precedes the base. Such reduplication in adjectives implies emphasis, e.g., *ƚik'a-ƚik'ab* 'really good' ← *ƚik'ab* 'good' and *qaha-qahal* 'really white' ← *qahab* 'white'.

Avar has partial reduplication with /m/ in adjectives, i.e. the onset consonant in the root word is changed to /m/ in the reduplicant. In such reduplication the copy precedes the base. In such reduplication the general meaning is diversity (plurality) and resemblance among the qualities, i.e. 'different things like this', e.g., *č'eʕe-meʕeral* 'black and suchlike' ← *č'eʕeral* 'black' and *č'aħi-maħiyal* 'big and suchlike' ← *č'aħiyal* 'big'.

6.3 Verbal reduplication

Verbal reduplication is quite productive. The most common reduplication is partial reduplication, when the copy precedes the base. The reduplicated verbal forms have intensifying meaning, as in *bah-bahize* 'to wear till holes' ← *bahize* 'to wear out', *bek-bekize* 'to break in pieces' ← *bekize* 'to break', and *c'a-c'aze* 'to stretch' ← *c'aze* 'to pull'.

Some reduplicated verbs are formed by changing the original consonant into -*d*- in the reduplicated word, e.g., *šur-šudize* 'to rustle' ← *šurize* 'to move' and *qʷa-qʷadize* 'to touch upon' ← *qʷaze* 'to touch'.

6.4 Adverbial reduplication

Full reduplication of adverbs, which is very productive, serves to tone down the meaning of an adverb, as in *cebe-cebe* 'a bit ahead' ← *cebe* 'ahead', *naqa-nuqu* 'a bit from behind' ← *naqa* 'from behind', or it can have distributive meaning, as in *bat'a-bat'a* 'individually' ← *bat'a* 'separately', *dah-dah* 'a little each time' ← *dah* 'few', *q'asi-q'asi* 'each evening' ← *q'asi* 'in the evening'.

In partial reduplication of adverbs, which is productive and serves a variety of functions, the copy precedes the base. Partial reduplication can express distributive meaning, e.g., *rada-radal* 'each morning' ← *radal* 'in the morning', *riʔi-riʔidal* 'every summer' ← *riʔidal* 'in summer', *baŝa-baŝad* 'in two, half-and-half' ← *baŝad* 'equally'. It can also intensify the meaning of an adverb, e.g., *ask'o-ask'ob* 'a bit closer' ← *ask'ob* 'close', *žani-žanib* 'further inside' ← *žanib* 'inside', *xadu-xadub* 'a bit later' ← *xadub* 'afterwards, later'. Additionally, the reduplicated adverb can require the adverbial suffix -*go*, as in *razi-rakigo* 'in good mood/spirits' ← *razi* 'contentedly' and *ʕaga-ŝagargo* 'approximately' ← *ʕaga(r)* 'near'. Partial reduplication is also found in adverbs presented as locative noun phrases, e.g., *zama-zamanał* 'usually' ← *zamanał* 'for a short time', *raq-raqalde* 'from side to side' ← *raqalde* 'to one's side', *bak'-bak'alda* 'in different places' ← *bak'alda* 'on one's place'. Finally, partial reduplication is used to derive manner adverbs from converbs, as in *q'ał-q'ałun* 'brightly' ← *q'ałun* 'become.light.CVB' and *t'ir-t'irun* 'stubbornly' ← *t'irun* 'be.stubborn.CVB'.

Abbreviations

ABS	absolutive	NEG	negation
CVB	converb	NZ	nominalizer
DUR	durative	OBL	oblique
GEN	genitive	PTCP	participle
LOC	locative		

7 References

Abdullaev, Magomed and Jakub Sulejmanov (1965): *Avarskij jazyk*. Maxačkala: Dagučpedgiz.

Alekseev, Mixail E. and Boris M. Ataev (1998): *Avarskij jazyk*. Moskva: Academia.

Alekseev, Mixail E., Boris M. Ataev, Magomed A. Magomedov, Magomed I. Magomedov, Gulžanat I. Madieva, Patimat A. Saidova and Džalil S. Samedov (2012): *Sovremennyj avarskij jazyk*. Maxačkala: Aleph.

Alixanov, Said Z. (1986): Suffiksaĺnoe obrazovanie glagolov v avarskom jazyke. In: Zapir Abdullaev (ed.), *Voprosy slovoobrazovanija dagestanskix jazykov*, 47–56. Maxačkala: Tipografija Dagestanskogo naučnogo centra Rossijskoj akademii nauk.

Bokarev, Aleksandr A. (1949): *Sintaksis avarskogo jazyka*. Moscow: Izdatelstvo Akademii nauk SSSR.

Džidalaev, Nurislam S. and Said Z. Alixanov (1985): *Genezis avarskogo slovoobrazovateĺnogo élementa -či*. Maxačkala: Tipografija Dagestanskogo naučnogo centra Rossijskoj akademii nauk.

Forker, Diana (2018): The semantics of evidentiality and epistemic modality in Avar. In: Diana Forker and Timur Maisak (eds.), *The semantics of verbal categories in Nakh-Daghestanian languages*, 188–214. Leiden: Brill.

Forker, Diana (2020): Avar. In: Maria Polinsky (ed.), *The Oxford Handbook of Languages of the Caucasus*, 242–279. Oxford: Oxford University Press.

Gimbatov, Magomed M. (2006): *Avarsko-russkij slovar'*. Maxačkala: DNC RAN.

Madieva, Gulžanat I. (1980): *Morfologija avarskogo literaturnogo jazyka*. Maxačkala: Izd. Dagestanskogo gosudarstvennogo universiteta.

Magomedov, Magomed I. and Said Z. Alixanov (2008): *Slovoobrazovanie v avarskom jazyke*. Maxačkala: Tipografija Dagestanskogo naučnogo centra Rossijskoj Akademii nauk.

Mallaeva, Zajnab M. (2007): *Glagol avarskogo jazyka: Struktura, semantika, funkcii*. Maxačkala: IJaLI.

Osmanov, Jusup U. (2000): *Struktura složnyx slov v avarskom literaturnom jazyke*. Maxačkala: Izd. Dagestanskogo gosudarstvennogo universiteta.

Saidova, Patimat A. (2007): *Zakatalskij dialekt avarskogo jazyka*. Maxačkala: IJaLI.

Saidova, Patimat A. (2008): *Dialektologičeskij slovaŕ avarskogo jazyka*. Saint-Petersburg: Nauka.

Žirkov, Lev I. (1948): *Slovoobrazovanie v avarskom jazyke*. Maxačkala: Izd. Akademii nauk SSSR, Dagestan.

Map of languages

634 — Map of languages

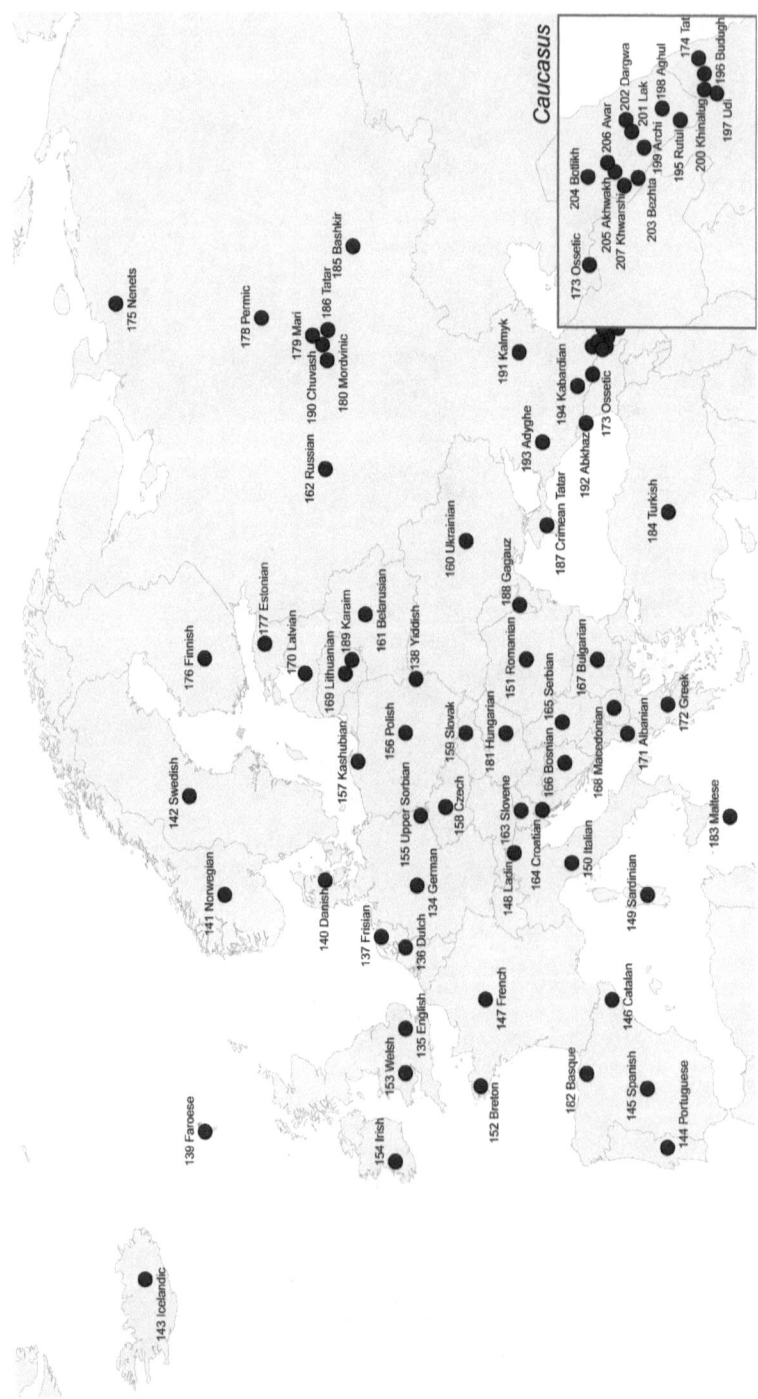

Map of languages: The map plots the geographic locations of the 74 languages treated in Müller et al. (2015–2016). In that handbook series the article number is placed in front of the language name. The articles 134–168 are found in volume 4, the articles 169–207 in volume 5.

The current volume contains 26 of these language portraits of word-formation phenomena in the Indo-European and Non-Indo-European languages of Europe. Each language family as well as the isolated language Basque is taken into consideration. The order of the word-formation portraits has the following macrostructure: 1. Indo-European: Germanic (articles 1–4), Romance (5–6), Celtic (7), Slavic (8–10), Baltic (11), Albanian (12), Greek (13), Indo-Iranian (14). 2. Uralic (15–16). 3. Basque (17). 4. Semitic (18). 5. Turkic (19–21). 6. Mongolic (22). 7. North Caucasian (23–26).

Index

Abaza 553, 564
Abkhaz 553–574, 634
Abzhywa 553, 574
acronym 75, 126, 139, 149, 153–154, 187, 203, 373, 387, 573
adjective 87, 101, 170, 244, 516, 523, 535–536, 545, 569
– active adjective 15, 235, 267
– approximative adjective 495, 626
– dispositional adjective 15, 121, 209
– evaluative adjective 38, 115, 123, 141–142, 147, 150, 177, 624–625
– negative adjective 115
– non-dispositional adjective 209
– passive adjective 235
– passive-potential adjective 121
– possessive adjective 200, 381, 539
– privative adjective 14
– qualitative adjective 40, 118–119, 207, 233, 307, 309, 500, 510, 512, 539, 545–546
– relational adjective 39, 109–110, 117–120, 123–124, 136, 145, 147, 152, 196, 207, 224, 234, 261, 266, 307, 453–454, 539, 612
– resemblance adjective 146
– resultative adjective 40, 144, 545
– similative adjective 118
adverb 1–2, 9–11, 20, 22–23, 36, 40–41, 52, 56–59, 69–71, 80, 84–86, 94, 97–98, 106, 110, 123–125, 135, 137, 139, 141, 148–153, 167, 182–185, 195, 198, 212–213, 215–216, 227–228, 240–241, 244–246, 257, 271–272, 278, 280–283, 292–293, 296, 301, 308–314, 322, 330, 335, 342, 348, 353, 364, 376, 386, 395, 413, 426, 435, 437–440, 449, 451, 457, 460–461, 463, 471, 485–486, 500–503, 515, 517, 523, 535, 537, 543–544, 546–547, 549, 553, 555, 567–570, 579, 591–593, 602, 605, 613–615, 619–622, 625–626, 628–631
adverbial 9–10, 17, 19–20, 22, 30, 40–41, 49, 57–58, 69–71, 86, 97–98, 123, 125, 148, 150, 152–153, 176, 178, 181–182, 184–185, 200, 215, 227–228, 271–272, 278, 282, 292–293, 296, 311–314, 320, 322, 330, 335, 385–386, 413–414, 426–427, 437, 439–440, 456,
485–486, 500, 535–536, 541, 543–544, 546–547, 549–550, 563, 567, 571, 584, 591–592, 597, 607, 613–614, 619, 621–622, 628–629, 631–632
Adyghe 553, 634
affix 2, 4, 8, 10–18, 36, 40, 43, 49, 50–51, 59, 72–73, 81, 87, 111, 119–120, 125, 132, 159–160, 195–196, 201, 204, 206, 221, 224–225, 242, 246, 252, 254, 279, 283, 288, 293, 300, 302, 318–322, 329, 341–342, 345, 347, 356, 358, 362, 394, 418–419, 446, 459, 492, 494–495, 497–498, 507–512, 516–524, 528, 567, 571–572, 582, 591
– conative affix 342, 345, 356, 358
– intensive affix 125
affixoid 2, 51, 58–59, 65, 81, 87–88, 255, 262, 321, 326
agglutinating language 393, 492
Aghul 577–595, 634
Ahchypsy 553
Akhwakh 634
Aktionsart 69, 211, 224, 268–269, 496
Albanian 299–315, 634
– Old Albanian 299–301
allomorph 35–37, 39, 115, 132, 142, 144, 169, 176–177, 286, 293–294, 310, 322, 327, 377, 421–422, 432–433, 469–470, 543, 585
alternation 35–36, 39, 132, 195, 217, 243, 265–266, 270, 279, 352, 361, 420–421, 431–432, 439–440, 507, 524, 537, 541, 615
– vowel alternation 169, 471, 616
analogy 6, 30, 118, 147, 186, 385, 387, 420, 458–460, 463, 475, 535, 546
– local analogy 42–43
analytic nominal structure 254
Andalusian 445
Anglo-Latinism 445, 464
antonymic 513, 619
approximation 99, 119, 147, 381, 515, 565
Arabic 445–448, 450, 452, 456, 460, 467, 470, 480, 485, 491, 493, 583, 597, 600, 605–606, 608–611, 624
Archi 119, 634
attenuation 271

https://doi.org/10.1515/9783111420523-028

augmentative 114, 119, 140–141, 147, 196, 216, 308, 333, 350, 446, 461, 474, 480
Avar 553, 598, 617–632, 634
Avar-Andic-Tsezic branch 617

backformation 23, 30, 33–34, 43–44, 107, 110, 125, 140, 153, 186–187, 212, 215–216, 245, 247, 263, 277, 279, 296, 314, 372, 376, 387–388, 394–395, 440–441, 456, 469–470, 507, 527, 578, 599
Baltic Finnic 371, 373
base 3–4, 8, 17, 19, 21–22, 31, 36–45, 51, 58–73, 81, 87–88, 90–100, 109, 114, 116, 119–123, 126, 139, 141–143, 145–149, 152, 154, 160, 162, 166–170, 172, 175–177, 197–198, 200, 204, 206, 208–211, 222, 231, 233–234, 238–241, 266, 278–279, 282–283, 286, 289–291, 293, 299, 303–304, 312–313, 318, 320, 326–327, 329–332, 370, 372, 375, 384–385, 396–398, 400–401, 404–410, 412–414, 427–430, 432–437, 440, 446, 459–460, 462–463, 467, 469–476, 478, 480, 482–486, 503, 514, 519, 522, 524, 528, 530–531, 537, 540–541, 545–547, 549, 554–555, 564, 568, 623, 626, 630–631
– non-native base 2, 99–100, 499
Bashkir 491–503, 516, 634
Bashkir-Russian bilingual 491
Basque 417–442, 634
Belarusian 634
Bezhta 634
binary structure 31–32, 136, 194, 395
blend 23–24, 44–45, 75, 117, 153, 187, 216, 246–247, 272, 335–336, 373, 387
blending 23–24, 30, 43–44, 49, 51, 74–75, 100–101, 107, 125–126, 153, 157, 186–187, 216–217, 246, 272, 277, 279, 314, 317, 335–336, 372, 387–388, 395, 441, 451, 456–457, 469, 507, 574–575, 578, 599
– mixed blending 247
borrowed formant 254–255
borrowed word-formation 72–74, 99–100
Bosnian 634
Botlikh 634
Breton 157, 634
Budugh 634
Bulgarian 251–273, 634
– Contemporary Bulgarian 251

– Middle Bulgarian 251
– Modern Bulgarian 254, 256, 261–262
– Old Bulgarian 251, 253–256
Bzyp 553

Catalan 117, 634
Celtic 157, 162, 634
Chechen 553, 598
Chuvash 501, 507–524, 634
Circassian 553, 555
circumfixation 205–206, 208, 210–213, 230–232, 234–237, 239–241, 262, 264, 266, 268–269, 279, 281–282, 284, 287–288, 291–292, 309–310
clipping 24–25, 30, 43–44, 49, 51, 74–75, 100–101, 107, 126, 154, 157, 187, 217, 245, 247, 272, 277, 279, 297, 314–315, 365–366, 372–373, 387–388, 395, 441, 451, 457, 461, 469, 502–503, 523–524, 527–528, 537, 541, 547–548, 572–573, 578, 599
co-compound 423–424, 426, 472–473, 495, 502, 507, 509, 514, 529, 532–533, 619
– antonymic co-compound 619
– appositional co-compound 32
– co-hyponymic co-compound 619
– synonymic co-compound 513, 619
collocation 182–183, 227, 344
combining form 35, 73, 106, 111, 114, 132–133, 135–138, 160, 197
compound 2–10, 23, 25, 30–35, 43–44, 51–59, 65, 75, 80–87, 92–94, 100, 106–111, 125, 132–138, 146, 158–159, 164–165, 168–170, 174, 186–188, 196–199, 222–223, 225–228, 243–246, 252, 255–262, 279, 297, 300–302, 320–330, 341, 343–348, 365, 369–376, 387–388, 395–400, 404, 408, 417, 419–427, 431–432, 436–437, 441, 445, 447–452, 459–460, 468–469, 471–472, 493–496, 502–503, 507–516, 529–535, 555–563, 570, 572–573, 577–582, 592, 599–609, 618–622
– adjectival compound 7–9, 34, 49, 52, 55–56, 84–85, 93, 108–110, 133, 136–137, 200–201, 226–227, 244, 259–260, 280–281, 375–376, 393, 423–425, 495–496, 522, 534, 561, 604, 620
– adverbial compound 9–10, 49, 57, 86, 98, 227–228, 322, 426–427, 535, 563, 621–622

Index — **639**

- appositive compound 134, 259, 347, 563
- argument-head compound 34
- attributive compound 558–559
- *bahuvrīhi* compound 374–376, 399
- coordinative compound 6, 9, 31–32, 34, 51–52, 54, 255, 259, 300–302, 320, 324–325, 507, 509, 513–516, 529
- copulative compound 107, 168, 199–201, 280, 423–424, 494–495, 502–503, 513, 532, 560, 600, 603, 618
- determinative compound 6, 9, 31, 34, 51–52, 54, 107, 197–200, 255, 257–259, 280, 301, 373–374, 422–423, 472, 493–494, 503, 507, 509–510, 533, 599–603, 618–619
- *dvandva* compound 187, 373, 557, 559–561
- endocentric compound 280, 324, 336, 347, 532, 556, 558
- exocentric compound 137, 199, 225, 243, 257, 280, 323–324, 347, 399–400, 419, 424, 472, 532, 556, 558
- genitive compound 12, 81–84, 89, 94
- government compound 3
- iterative compound 374, 579
- multi-stem compound 556
- neoclassical compound 111, 261, 321, 374, 376
- nominal compound 4–8, 10, 23, 33–35, 51–55, 75, 84, 93, 107–108, 133–135, 137, 186, 197–200, 226–227, 261, 281, 300–301, 343–344, 373–375, 395, 422–424, 426–427, 468, 471, 493–495, 509, 523–534, 556–559, 577–578, 592, 599–604, 618–620
- occasional compound 7
- phrasal compound 5, 82–84, 321, 328–329
- possessive compound 301–302
- prepositional compound 57–58, 86–87
- quasi compound 197, 261–262
- right-headed compound 9, 52, 134
- root compound 258, 472
- subordinate compound 556–558
- syntagmatic compound 106–107, 110, 118
- synthetic compound 33, 227, 255, 257–260, 280, 301, 322, 325, 396–398, 472, 622
compounding 598, 603–604, 608, 617–618, 620–622
compound marker 320–321, 328, 471–472
compound stress rule 32
confix 5, 7, 10

consonant gemination 343, 351
consonantal variation 615
construct 3, 13, 106, 125, 133–134, 184, 201, 206, 213, 363, 431, 438, 448–449, 471, 492, 530, 600
construct state 448–449
construct-state phrase 449
container 112, 140, 352, 585–586, 589
conversion 1, 20, 25, 29–30, 33–34, 37, 40, 49, 71–72, 81, 96, 98–99, 107, 121–123, 132, 142–144, 149–153, 157, 181–185, 193, 195–196, 198, 200, 209–210, 212, 242–245, 272, 277, 279, 282, 286, 300, 307, 309, 311–312, 318, 327, 362–364, 372, 387, 393–394, 403–404, 414, 437–440, 455, 480, 485–487, 491–492, 500–501, 503, 507, 509, 518, 527–529, 553, 555, 568–569, 578, 604, 614–615, 617
- adjectival conversion 21–22, 42, 124, 151–152, 184, 214, 295, 313, 438–439, 545–546
- adverbial conversion 22, 125, 152–153, 185, 215, 296, 313, 439–440, 544, 546–547
- nominal conversion 2, 21, 41–42, 124, 147, 151, 182–184, 213–214, 293–295, 312–313, 438, 521–522, 545, 629–630
- syntactic conversion 21
- verbal conversion 22, 42, 124, 152, 185, 215, 293, 295–296, 313, 439
Crimean Tatar 634
Croatian 634
cumulative meaning 238
Czech 634

Daghestan 577, 580, 591, 597, 617
Danish 49, 52, 79, 99, 634
Dargwa 553, 634
derivation 1–3, 10–20, 22, 36–41, 49–52, 59–71, 74, 79–80, 90–98, 105, 111–123, 131, 138–150, 158, 161, 165, 168–182, 186, 193–195, 201–213, 217, 225, 228–241, 251, 262–273, 277–279, 282–293, 302–312, 317–319, 321, 329–335, 347–363, 369–373, 376–386, 394, 400–414, 418–419, 427–438, 441–442, 451–455, 463, 467–471, 473–486, 492, 497–501, 503, 513, 517–521, 527, 529–530, 537–544, 546, 553, 556, 563–568, 577, 582–592, 597–599, 608–614, 618, 622–629
- adjectival derivation 13–15, 39–40, 63–66, 94–95, 117–121, 145–148, 180–181, 287–

288, 293, 302, 307–309, 380–382, 406–409, 434–437, 473, 479–482, 498–499, 519–520, 539–541, 565, 584–585, 612–613, 625–626
- adverbial derivation 20, 30, 40–41, 69–71, 97–98, 123, 150, 181–182, 271–272, 292–293, 311–312, 385–387, 413–414, 427, 437–438, 500, 543–544, 567, 591–592, 597, 613–614, 628–629
- nominal derivation 11–13, 37–39, 60–63, 72, 91–93, 112–117, 138–145, 170–180, 202, 264, 283–287, 300, 302–307, 348–355, 377–380, 401–405, 427–433, 453–455, 473–479, 497–498, 517–519, 537–539, 563–564, 582–584, 597, 608–612, 618, 622–625
- verbal derivation 15–20, 40, 60, 66–69, 72, 95–96, 122–123, 131, 145, 148–150, 181, 254, 268–271, 278, 282, 287–289, 292–293, 300, 309–312, 355–359, 382–385, 394, 409–413, 437, 452–453, 482–484, 499–500, 508, 520–521, 541–543, 565–567, 585–591, 627–628
derivative 4, 8, 13, 15–16, 23, 25, 36–39, 41–44, 67, 113–114, 139–153, 159, 169–170, 194–195, 202–204, 206–207, 209, 211–213, 215, 217, 222, 224, 228–230, 245, 252, 262, 264, 269, 272, 278–279, 282–283, 285–288, 290, 292–293, 296, 304–305, 307, 327, 329, 369–370, 372–373, 375–378, 380–386, 388, 399–402, 404–405, 407–408, 410–411, 446–447, 458–459, 461, 464, 478–479, 494, 497–499, 501, 508, 531, 541, 585–586, 590–591, 623, 629
- phrase-based derivative 3
devoicing 420–421
dialect 79, 157–159, 164, 166–167, 172, 174, 187, 253–254, 258, 299, 305, 341, 418–419, 423, 428–429, 433, 456, 467, 527–528, 553, 574, 577, 588–589, 591–592, 597
diathesis 482
Digor 341–346, 349–363, 365
diminution 7, 12, 123, 329
diminutive 39, 62, 65, 81, 93, 114–115, 119, 140–141, 157–158, 169, 171–172, 174, 176–177, 196, 201, 204, 212, 216, 230, 246, 264, 285, 291, 296, 305, 329, 332–334, 350, 378, 395, 400–402, 435–436, 441, 454, 468, 474
- circumfixal diminutive 291
Dutch 52, 82, 245, 634

East Caucasian 597–598, 607–610, 612–613
eclipsis 162
electronic corpora 29
endearment 264, 267, 270–271, 288
English 20, 29–46, 50, 75, 82, 100, 114, 117, 132–133, 150, 154, 158–161, 164–165, 169, 171–175, 177, 180–181, 184, 186–187, 196–197, 213, 217, 222, 226, 255–258, 262, 272, 297, 321, 327, 353, 393, 397, 399, 407, 409–410, 418, 445–449, 451–452, 458–459, 461–465, 468–469, 503, 540, 634
- English influence 462–465
ergative 143, 151, 417, 426, 430–431, 554, 577, 580–581, 588, 591, 603, 617
Estonian 634
ethnic noun 146, 332, 463
event nominalization 37
expletive 43, 45–46

Faroese 49, 52, 57, 79–80, 82, 634
feminization 36, 124
- female animal 140, 205, 510, 540
- female person 230, 242, 630
Finnish 369–388, 634
Finno-Ugrian language family 371
foreign 4, 31, 80, 83, 97, 106–107, 109, 147, 180, 196–198, 202, 207, 224, 254–255, 262, 273, 299–300, 331, 351, 370, 372–374, 394, 403, 405, 410, 412, 434, 451, 456, 473–474, 521, 529, 559, 597
- foreign formant 255
- foreign root 412
French 20, 49, 60, 62, 66, 106–107, 111, 113, 117, 132–133, 135, 140, 145, 151–152, 154, 159, 171, 187, 203, 213, 327, 438, 446, 459, 464, 480, 634
Frisian 634
fusional language 319

Gagauz 501, 521, 634
gemination 343, 351–352, 357, 379, 458, 574
gender 53, 84, 86, 110, 134–135, 140, 142, 146, 174–175, 182, 214, 222, 242, 312–313, 319, 324, 328, 333, 460, 492, 555, 558, 578, 617, 619, 623, 625–626, 630
- common gender 54, 56, 71, 279–281
- gender-assignment 108

Index — **641**

generalization 41, 278–279, 281, 355, 397, 530, 549
genitive 79–84, 89, 94, 161, 165, 167–169, 172–174, 181, 183–184, 296, 372, 374–375, 419, 429, 438, 448, 500, 510, 533, 546, 584, 612–614, 624, 632
- genitive case 51, 55, 159, 328, 539, 545
- genitive construction 471, 600
geographical variation 106
German 1–25, 29–30, 50, 52, 57, 62, 82, 99, 105, 110, 151, 159, 171, 201, 208, 227, 255, 257–258, 301, 312, 347, 396, 399, 403, 409, 412, 448, 468, 503, 634
- Low German 49, 60, 66, 69, 72
Germanic 6, 30, 50, 52, 107, 111, 159, 242, 399, 409, 434, 445, 459, 477, 493, 634
- East North Germanic 49
Greek 35, 49, 60, 62, 65, 73, 106, 115, 132, 137–138, 146, 193, 197, 201, 224, 251, 255–256, 261–263, 267–268, 300, 317–336, 376, 448, 460, 493, 572, 602, 634
- Ancient Greek 137, 318–321, 323, 325–327, 329–330, 335
- Homeric Greek 322
- Modern Greek 317–320, 323, 325, 333

head 31, 34, 52–53, 56, 71, 82, 84–86, 97, 110, 134–137, 151, 162–164, 167–168, 180, 197, 200, 207, 225–228, 243, 259, 280, 325–326, 328, 336, 351, 395–398, 401, 422, 424, 448, 450, 472, 494–495, 509–510, 524, 533–534, 556, 558, 563, 583, 595, 602–603, 618–620, 629
- left-headed 133–137, 198, 471, 558, 619
- right-headed 5, 8–9, 31–32, 49, 51–52, 58, 107, 109, 134–137, 198, 323, 336, 395, 471, 556, 558, 619
homonymous particle 15
homonymous stem 2
Hungarian 146, 393–414, 634
hybrid formation 446, 449, 460
hypocorism 62–63, 196
hypocoristic 44, 62, 101, 114, 230, 234, 246, 350, 353, 365, 401–402

Icelandic 49, 52, 57, 79–101, 634
ideophone 579, 593

idiomatic meaning 587, 590
impersonal form 7, 270–271, 354, 357, 359
incorporation 19, 82, 393, 555, 597, 599, 603
Indo-Iranian 634
infixation 12, 30, 36, 43–46, 209, 537, 564
Ingush 553
initial mutation 162–163
intensification 7, 14, 138, 146, 148–149, 240, 246, 254, 271, 288, 308, 347, 440, 523, 549–550, 593, 626
intensifying function 147, 153, 615
interfix 179, 199–200, 226, 257–259, 262, 279, 281–282, 531
- interfix -o- 197, 201, 225, 280
internationalisation 196
internationalism 111, 138, 154, 327
Iranian 609, 634
- Eastern Iranian 341
Irish 157–188, 634
- literary Irish 160
Iron 341–354, 356–362, 364–366
Italian 123, 132, 145, 300–301, 327, 329, 332, 334–335, 434, 445–447, 451, 457–464, 634
iteration 109, 123, 244, 246, 437, 529
iterative action 482
izafet I 509–510
izafet II 509, 511–512, 524

juxtaposition 228, 469, 509, 527–528, 531–536, 559, 563, 618

Kabardian 351, 553, 634
Kalmyk 527–550, 634
Karaim 501, 521, 634
Kashubian 634
Kazan School 222
Khinalug 634
Khwarshi 634
Kipchak 491, 598

Ladin 634
Lak 263, 518–519, 587, 597–616, 634
language contact 303, 468, 598
language name 634
Latin 35, 49, 60, 62, 65–67, 73, 106, 111–112, 117, 119–120, 126, 132, 137–138, 161, 163, 193, 197, 201, 224, 261–263, 267, 300, 321,

327, 332, 376, 427, 432, 445–448, 456–459, 464, 491, 493, 529, 572
Latvian 278, 634
learned word-formation 80–81
lenition 162–163
lexicalization 30–32, 110, 133, 398, 426, 473
Lezgi 553
Lezgic 577, 579
linking element 6, 8, 51–52, 54–55, 82, 89, 133, 136, 138, 225, 320
linking vowel 107, 114, 162, 197, 225, 255, 257–260
Lithuanian 277–297, 634
localization 138, 147, 149, 585–590

Macedonian 254, 634
Maltese 445–465, 634
- Romance Maltese 446
- Semitic Maltese 446–447, 452, 455
Mari 461, 508, 515–516, 634
meliorative 114, 285
mental action 433
merger 196, 217, 588
modification 4, 11–12, 14, 40, 42, 180, 263, 266, 385, 388, 462, 480, 519, 540, 584, 592, 623
- premodification 160, 167
- stylistic modification 388
Mongolian 502, 528–529
Mongolic 508, 527–528, 634
Mordvinic 634
morpheme-final affricate 420
morphophonological alternation 36, 39, 132, 420–421
multi-word expression 30, 258, 265, 502–503, 524, 530
mutation 4, 469
- initial mutation 162–163

Nakh-Daghestanian 577, 617
name 62–63, 75, 87, 93, 101, 107, 110, 124, 126, 136, 146, 184, 198, 213, 216–217, 222, 230, 260, 278, 351, 353, 375, 383–384, 387, 402, 404, 406, 412, 427, 433, 455, 457, 569, 598, 600, 619–620, 634
- name of trees 428
- name of sciences 213
- nickname 87, 101, 350–351, 619

native 2, 4, 36, 63, 65–66, 69–70, 73, 99–111, 115, 133–134, 158–160, 163, 173, 180–181, 184, 187, 196, 262–263, 336, 342, 347, 372, 418, 422, 429, 432, 467, 491, 493, 527, 572, 577, 583, 597–598, 609, 622
- native formant 254
- native stem 60
negation 12, 14, 70, 121, 139, 234–235, 240, 308, 345, 348–349, 372, 374, 412, 431, 499, 508, 523, 632
Nenets 634
neoclassical word-formation 49, 63, 72–74, 79, 99–100, 343, 372, 553, 555, 572
- neoclassical base 35
- neoclassical element 35, 73, 137, 163, 225
- neoclassical formation 31, 35, 160, 279, 321, 327, 421–422, 572
- neoclassical prefix 65, 302, 308
Neo-Latin 109, 112, 117
neologism 37, 81, 160–161, 164, 194, 197, 223–224, 322, 327, 373, 403, 420, 422, 428–429, 441, 468, 470, 472, 474, 476–480, 516
non-head 326, 328, 396–398
Norse
- East Nordic 79, 95
- Old Norse 79, 95
North-Caucasian 553–554
Northeast Caucasian 577
Norwegian 49, 52, 56, 79–80, 159, 634
noun 1, 3, 8, 11, 14, 16, 31–34, 36–37, 39, 42, 44, 51–52, 55–59, 65, 71, 84, 92, 98, 108–109, 118, 151–152, 157–159, 161, 163, 165, 167–168, 175–179, 181–186, 197–198, 206–208, 282, 293, 301, 314, 322, 324, 326, 328, 335, 342–344, 400–401, 419–420, 423, 428–433, 449, 454, 471–472, 485, 496, 509, 532–533, 544–546, 548, 555–558, 568–570, 581, 583, 618–622, 625–626
- abstract noun 37, 51, 60, 72, 112, 114, 124, 139, 151, 157, 168, 176–179, 205, 214, 224, 232, 243–244, 258, 262, 264–265, 301, 303, 312–313, 350, 352, 402–403, 405, 472, 498, 513, 518, 560, 563–564, 611, 623, 629
- action noun 11, 13, 81, 91, 116, 124, 143, 145, 206, 257, 281, 286, 294, 306, 354, 379, 396, 401, 403–404, 428, 431–432, 476, 501

Index — **643**

- agent noun 11, 13, 51, 60, 81, 91–92, 116, 144–145, 198, 206, 257, 263, 281, 294, 306, 374, 378, 380, 396, 398, 401, 404, 427, 430, 455, 473–474, 477, 479, 492, 497, 501, 563, 583, 603, 623–625
- case-marked noun 348, 356, 613
- collective noun 38, 141, 243, 303, 428, 478, 522, 570
- concrete noun 305, 403, 414, 500, 518, 545, 623, 625
- ergative marked noun 591
- ethnic noun 146, 332, 463
- feminine noun 80, 89, 143, 151, 182, 195, 214, 304, 324, 329
- inanimate noun 229
- inhabitant noun 473
- instrument noun 11, 13, 91–92, 116, 140, 142, 145, 153, 206, 224, 257, 281, 305, 307, 380, 404, 479, 624
- masculine noun 304, 313, 378
- non-abstract noun 205
- non-personal noun 203, 205–206, 242, 258, 262, 264, 477, 517, 538
- object noun 581
- patient noun 13, 603
- personal noun 198
- place noun 310
- professional noun 332
- quality noun 12, 38, 114, 116, 140–142, 305, 379
- result noun 142, 144, 151, 286, 294, 379–380, 430, 564
- singulative noun 453, 456
- status noun 11, 115, 196, 303
numeral 86, 133, 149, 162–163, 198, 200, 227, 257, 279, 375, 386, 424, 434, 475, 495, 499, 595, 621
- cardinal numeral 244, 359, 361, 500
- decimal numeral 360
- distributive numeral 361, 593–594
- ordinal numeral 182, 361

oath 363
Oghuz 467
onomatopoetic 25, 365, 369, 372, 382, 384–385, 409, 411, 471, 485, 607, 628, 630
orientation 160, 497, 565, 585–589
Ossetic 341–366, 634

paradigmatic process 29–30, 42–43
passive 7, 15, 121, 147, 168, 206, 209, 226, 235, 239, 267, 288, 292, 295, 355, 381, 411, 422, 452–455, 458, 460, 463, 470, 475, 481–483, 499, 520, 545
pejorative 23, 58, 60, 112, 114–115, 123, 141, 177, 230, 258, 264, 270, 294, 305, 379, 428, 435, 474, 583, 609
Permic 634
phonetic change 508, 511, 547, 549
plural 21, 53, 56, 71, 81, 89, 107, 110, 134–135, 165, 169–170, 173, 176–177, 182–188, 200, 271, 281, 294, 301, 304, 310, 312, 322, 351–354, 356, 358–359, 361–362, 374, 380, 423, 447, 449, 451, 458, 460, 462, 471, 474, 486, 500, 533, 555, 578–579, 583, 613, 617, 627
- associative plural 350, 366
plural marking 134, 358–359, 579
Polish 193–217, 272, 413–414, 634
polysynthetic language 554
Portuguese 634
possession 51, 118, 213, 234, 349, 363, 382, 493, 555, 558, 560, 565, 570, 615
possessive 14, 40, 51–52, 109, 118, 178, 199–200, 208, 300–302, 344, 349, 362–363, 380–382, 435, 448, 471, 485–486, 492, 494, 509–511, 524, 539, 546, 555, 558, 619
postfixation 212, 224, 236, 239, 245, 261, 268–269
prefix 10, 13, 15–20, 22, 42, 51, 58, 63, 66, 68–69, 71, 81, 91, 94–97, 120, 123, 138, 147–149, 164, 166–168, 194–195, 202, 208, 210–213, 224, 231, 243, 268, 282–283, 287–288, 291–294, 296, 318–320, 329–331, 348–349, 362, 372, 374, 376, 393–394, 407, 419, 441, 449, 456, 460, 565–566, 580, 587, 591
- classical prefix 65, 302, 308, 422
- comitative prefix 113
- gender prefix 558
- intensive prefix 119
- locative prefix 348, 585–586, 588–590
- negative prefix 18, 41, 90, 113, 166, 412, 582
- numeral prefix 149
- oppositive prefix 95, 97, 149
- orientation prefix 586–587
prefixation 19, 21, 30, 41, 49, 51, 63, 65, 68, 70–71, 81, 90–91, 94–95, 97, 106, 131–132, 149,

157, 159–160, 164, 168, 202, 208, 211, 221, 224, 228, 230, 234, 236–238, 240, 243–244, 254–255, 262, 266–269, 272, 278, 287, 292–293, 300, 302, 307, 309, 319, 329–331, 341, 348, 357, 422, 469, 493, 499, 503, 507, 509, 517, 553–555, 563, 565, 578
- locative prefixation 585–586, 588–589
- repetitive prefixation 585, 589, 591
prefixoid 51, 58, 80–81, 87–88, 90, 202, 262
premodifier 174
- adjectival premodifier 166–167
- nominal premodifier 157, 166–167
privative 14, 16–17, 22, 122, 229, 269, 348, 380, 383, 403, 407, 485, 565, 567
prosodic morphology 29, 36, 43–46
- prosodic constraint 46
- prosodic restriction 40
- prosodic structure 35, 336
puristic word-formation 83

reduplication 1, 23, 105, 107, 119, 125, 131, 153, 157, 186, 193, 216, 221, 246, 277, 279, 296, 299, 311, 314, 353, 364–365, 393, 413, 417, 456, 469, 471, 491, 495, 501–503, 507, 509, 522, 527–529, 547–550, 553, 563, 570–571, 578, 592, 594–595, 597, 599, 604, 617
- adjectival reduplication 495, 548–549, 570–571, 630–631
- adverbial reduplication 549–550, 571, 631–632
- full reduplication 125, 440, 570, 577, 593, 595, 615, 630–631
- incomplete reduplication 523
- nominal reduplication 216, 548, 570, 630
- prefix reduplication 393, 412
re-Romanization 132
resemblance 14, 82, 118, 146, 630–631
Romance 105–108, 115–116, 123, 132–133, 135–138, 143, 151, 418, 428, 445–450, 452, 456–463, 634
- Romance compound 450
- Romance element 445, 449
- Romance model 450
- Romance stratum 445, 457–462
Romanian 131–154, 261, 634
Russian 154, 171, 203, 221–248, 252–253, 261, 297, 341–342, 347, 349–351, 353, 360, 491–493, 496–497, 499, 503, 508, 515, 524, 527, 529–530, 554, 556, 572–573, 577, 580, 592, 598, 609, 624, 626, 634
Rutul 634

Sadz 553
sandhi phenomena 162, 439
Sardinian 634
Scandinavian 50
- Insular Scandinavian 49
- Mainland Scandinavian 49
Scottish Gaelic 157, 165
semantic-functional perspective 4
Semitic 447, 451–452, 456–457, 459–464, 634
- Semitic element 446, 449
- Semitic stratum 445–446, 448–457
Serbian 634
series 8, 51, 58, 117–119, 121, 125, 147, 177, 194, 197, 210, 348, 359–360, 362, 365, 372, 385, 496, 590, 592, 634
set phrase 168
short form 5, 24–25, 625
Sicilian 445–447, 457–462, 464
similarity 217, 229, 234, 263, 342, 464, 475, 499, 533
singulative 449, 453–454, 456, 462, 547
Slavic 193, 195, 201, 204, 224, 239, 251–258, 261–262, 265, 272, 296, 314, 329, 333, 590, 634
Slovak 634
Slovene 634
Spanish 105–126, 417, 421, 441, 634
- Cuban Spanish 111
specialisation 161, 196
stem 5, 8, 21, 35–36, 39, 60, 62–63, 81, 83, 90, 94, 169, 185, 199–200, 211, 214–215, 222, 225, 227, 243, 245, 247, 257, 265, 281, 283, 286, 304, 306, 309, 314, 318–321, 323–324, 326–327, 330–331, 335, 342, 344–345, 347–348, 354, 356–359, 361–363, 374, 376–378, 380, 382, 385–386, 388, 395, 402, 407, 410, 412, 428, 446–447, 452, 457–458, 460, 469–470, 473, 480, 483, 486, 492–493, 521, 529–530, 533, 541, 557, 561–562, 568, 578, 580, 583, 588–589, 591, 594, 599–600, 605, 610–611, 615, 617, 619, 623, 629–630
- homonymous stem 2

stress 16, 30, 32–33, 35–37, 39, 44, 52, 60, 62, 68, 81, 126, 132–133, 158, 163–165, 167, 169, 187, 258, 287, 293–294, 318–320, 322–323, 326, 331, 372, 448, 458, 532, 555, 561, 568–569, 588–590, 594
- antepenultimate stress 35–36
- default stress 163
- main stress 35, 44, 258
- right-stressed 32
stress assignment 30, 32, 132–133, 331
stress variability 32
suffix 2, 10–11, 13, 16–18, 20, 23, 30, 37–43, 51, 58, 60, 62–72, 80–81, 88, 90–97, 99–101, 114, 116–122, 124, 126, 143–150, 157–158, 161, 169–170, 173–174, 177, 180–181, 184–186, 196–197, 199–201, 204–208, 210–211, 213–214, 224, 227, 238–239, 243–245, 247, 257–259, 267, 281–284, 286–288, 291–292, 296, 303–312, 314, 318, 321–322, 327, 329, 331, 333–335, 343–344, 349–359, 361, 363, 365, 370, 376–383, 385–386, 395–396, 399, 403–414, 419, 421–422, 427–437, 446, 449–451, 458, 460–461, 463, 468–486, 492, 494–495, 497–500, 529–531, 533, 537, 540–541, 543, 546, 555, 560, 564–565, 567–568, 571–572, 574, 582–585, 591–592, 600, 603, 607, 609–614, 619, 622–631
- approximative suffix 119
- attenuative suffix 410–411
- augmentative suffix 140, 147, 333, 350, 446, 480
- causative suffix 411–412, 482–484
- composite suffix 408, 474, 482, 484–486
- diminutive suffix 62, 93, 115, 119, 157, 201, 329, 332–334, 378, 395, 400–402, 441
- distributive suffix 361
- evaluative suffix 115, 141–142, 150
- homophonous suffix 62
- instrumental suffix 117, 485, 498
- neologistic suffix 474, 477
- non-productive suffix 93, 353, 538–540, 542
- participial suffix 407–408
- passive suffix 411, 483
- pejorative suffix 60, 112, 114–115, 123, 379, 435, 474, 583, 609
- possessive suffix 381, 471, 485–486, 492, 494
- privative suffix 403, 407, 485, 565

- Romance evaluative suffix 115
- stress-influencing suffix 35
suffixation 30–31, 39, 49, 51, 60–63, 66, 68–69, 81, 90–91, 94, 96–97, 106, 132, 139–140, 142–143, 145, 149, 151, 157, 164, 168–169, 176–177, 195, 202–205, 207–212, 224, 227–238, 241–244, 255, 262–263, 265–266, 268–269, 277, 287, 302, 309–310, 319, 322, 328–329, 331, 341, 343, 348, 350, 353, 387–388, 393–394, 401, 418, 430–431, 449, 467, 469, 472, 482, 499, 503, 528–529, 537, 553–554, 563, 565–566, 578
- zero suffixation 41, 242–244, 265, 500
suffixoid 51, 58, 81, 87–88, 92–93, 96, 98, 203, 255
superposition 531, 537
supine nominalization 132
Swedish 49–75, 79, 378, 388, 634
- Swedish family name 54
synonymous 58, 116, 147, 160–161, 167–168, 172, 174–176, 179, 184, 186, 225, 246, 386–387, 461, 495, 502, 513, 534
syntax-morphology divide 30

Tabasaran 553
Tat 12, 518, 634
Tatar 491–493, 501, 508, 516, 634
terminologisation 196
threatened language 158
transposition 4, 11–15, 136, 143, 168
Tsabal 553
Turkic 360, 467–470, 484, 491–494, 496–497, 499, 501, 508–509, 514–515, 521, 583, 597–598, 605, 609–610, 615, 617, 624, 634
Turkish 132, 263, 300, 303, 329, 332, 467–487, 492–495, 497, 502, 634
- Modern Turkish 467, 469
- Ottoman Turkish 467, 473

Ubykh 553, 555
Udi 553, 634
Ukrainian 634
univerbation 33, 52, 56, 84, 86, 133, 157, 165, 183–184, 188, 195, 203, 205, 213, 256, 265, 449–450, 582
Upper Sorbian 634

valency 3, 16, 19, 482
verb 1, 3, 7, 9, 15, 17, 19–21, 33, 36–37, 45, 52, 56, 65–69, 71, 82, 84–86, 90, 98–99, 108, 110, 122, 148–149, 168, 171–173, 175, 179, 182–183, 185, 197–198, 209, 211, 226–227, 239–240, 251, 258, 264, 268–270, 278, 282–283, 286, 290, 292–293, 310, 312, 314, 320, 322, 325, 330–331, 342–343, 345–348, 354–359, 363–366, 374, 376, 382, 385, 387, 396–400, 403–405, 407–408, 410–412, 422, 426–427, 431–433, 436–437, 439–440, 455, 468–469, 473, 475–476, 484, 486, 492, 496, 501, 508, 522, 536, 553–554, 557, 562, 565, 567–570, 579–582, 585–586, 588–593, 598, 603, 605, 608
– causative verb 397, 567
– converb 346, 348, 355, 365, 473, 485, 619–620, 625, 629
– co-verb 579–581
– descriptive verb 379, 384–385
– durative verb 627–628
– expressive verb 385
– factitive verb 289–290
– frequentative verb 383–384, 468, 627
– idiomatic verb 355, 585, 587
– inchoative verb 122, 152, 215, 270, 289–290, 383, 484–485, 628
– instrumental verb 122, 289
– iterative verb 437
– light verb 341–342, 345–346, 354–356, 425, 496, 562, 579, 581–582, 599, 605–608, 610
– particle verb 3, 15–20, 22–23, 52, 56, 394, 397–398, 403, 412–413
– performance verb 290
– phrasal verb 30, 52, 419, 425–426
– polysemous verb 496
– repetitive verb 577, 589, 591
– semelfactive verb 270
verbal plurality 356
voice 55, 182, 206, 239, 319, 350, 381–382, 384–385, 420, 470, 482, 485, 499, 503, 562

Welsh 157, 634
word-creation 25, 107, 126, 165, 187–188, 217, 248, 372, 441–442, 599

Yiddish 634

www.ingramcontent.com/pod-product-compliance
Lightning Source LLC
Chambersburg PA
CBHW031538300426
44111CB00006BA/92